BUSINESS

Its Legal, Ethical, and Global Environment

Seventh Edition

MARIANNE MOODY JENNINGS

Arizona State University

THOMSON

WEST

Australia · Canada · Mexico · Singapore · Spain · United Kingdom · United States

THOMSON

WEST

Business: Its Legal, Ethical, and Global Environment, Seventh Edition

Marianne M. Jennings

VP/Editorial Director:
Jack W. Calhoun

Publisher:
Rob Dewey

Acquisitions Editor:
Steve Silverstein, Esq.

Developmental Editor:
Bob Sandman

Executive Marketing Manager:
Lisa Lysne

Production Editor:
Tamborah Moore

Manager of Technology, Editorial:
Vicky True

Technology Project Editor
Christine Wittmer

Manufacturing Coordinator:
Charlene Taylor

Production House:
Stratford Publishing Services

Printer:
RR Donnelley/ Willard, OH

Art Director:
Michelle Kunkler

Cover and Internal Designer:
Lisa Albonetti, Cincinnati

Cover Image:
© Steve Allen/Brand X Pictures

Photography Manager:
John Hill

Photo Researcher:
Rose Alcorn

Library of Congress Control Number:
2004111930

For more information about our products,
contact us at:

Thomson Learning Academic Resource
Center 1-800-423-0563

Thomson Higher Education
5191 Natorp Boulevard
Mason, Ohio 45040
USA

Asia (including India)
Thomson Learning
5 Shenton Way
#01-01 UIC Building
Singapore 068808

Australia/New Zealand
Thomson Learning Australia
102 Dodds Street
Southbank, Victoria 3006
Australia

Canada
Thomson Nelson
1120 Birchmount Road
Toronto, Ontario
MIK 5G4
Canada

Latin America
Thomson Learning
Seneca, 53
Colonia Polanco
11560 Mexico
D.F.Mexico

UK/Europe/Middle East/Africa
Thomson Learning
High Holborn House
50/51 Bedford Row
London WCIR 4LR
United Kingdom

Spain (including Portugal)
Thomson Paraninfo
Calle Magallanes, 25
28015 Madrid, Spain

*To my roots, my mother and father, and
to my branches, sprouts, gardeners, and inspiration, my husband and children,
Terry, Sarah, Claire, Sam, and John*

Brief Contents

Contents

PART 2
BUSINESS: ITS REGULATORY ENVIRONMENT   151

PART 3
BUSINESS COMPETITION AND SALES

PART 4
BUSINESS AND ITS EMPLOYEES

699

CHAPTER 18
MANAGEMENT OF EMPLOYEE CONDUCT: AGENCY 700

CHAPTER 19
MANAGEMENT OF EMPLOYEE WELFARE 740

PART 5
BUSINESS FORMS AND CAPITALIZATION   839

APPENDICES

Preface

A DIFFERENT WORLD, BUT THE SAME ISSUES

Since the last edition of this book was published, the world has changed. The new economy that ended with the burst of the stock market bubble showed us that old tricks still abound. We have witnessed the collapses of what were once believed to be phenomena. Enron, WorldCom, Adelphia, HealthSouth, Parmalat, Arthur Andersen, Kmart, and others have been exposed for everything from questionable accounting practices to earnings management to embezzlement to obstruction of justice to fraud. Nortel, General Electric, Xerox, Royal Dutch, and Royal Ahold have had to issue earnings restatements. The Apollo Group, Halliburton, Qwest, and Marsh McLennan have all been under SEC scrutiny for their public disclosures regarding the states of their companies and/or finances. Since the past edition we have witnessed proof of the old adage, "The bigger they are, the harder they fall."

How these companies, their employees, and executives could have benefited from understanding and keeping at the forefront of their decision processes the basics of law and ethics. The legal and ethical environments of business are center stage. Congress made massive regulatory reform a reality with the passage of the Sarbanes-Oxley legislation on corporate governance, accounting regulation, and criminal penalties—as a result of the activities and problems of the companies noted and many others. Congress also passed new forms of government supervision and regulation through the USA Patriot Act as a result of political and world events, such as the attacks on the World Trade Center and the U.S. Pentagon in 2001. The world has changed, but law and ethics have retained their role and importance. In fact, now more than ever we need to understand the legal and ethical issues that affect our businesses and our lives. The knowledge base and even the questions in law and ethics remain the same but the underlying facts have changed. For example, we still debate the social responsibility role of business. Now we raise that issue in the context of Bayer's patent on Cipro (a drug that cures anthrax) and its cost for selling it. We delve into the pros and cons of sending production to other countries. We still have the question of when a contract is formed but now we face that question with "point and click" technology rather than faxes and letters. We continue to be concerned about our privacy as consumers but now we apply the law to our use of the Internet for our purchases and correspondence and wonder whether companies can use the information they find there. We still wonder about the extent of copyright law. Today we wonder if it applies when we use the Internet to download music, free of charge.

The world is different, but law and ethics remain a constant framework into which we fit the issues of the day. In the materials that follow, you have the chance to understand the marvelous stability of this framework and the ease with which you can apply it to this very different world. Be sure to look for descriptions of exciting new features such as Making Ethics Personal, the new Consider tutorials, and the changes to the Business Strategy Application exercises.

BUILDING THE BRIDGE: APPLYING LEGAL AND ETHICAL REASONING TO BUSINESS ANALYSIS

My students recently completed a project on the expansion of an Internet service provider (ISP) firm in South America. Because this project was their capstone experience for their degrees, their discussion of the strategic issues was phenomenal. The students offered classic SWOT analysis: Strengths, Weaknesses, Opportunities, and Threats. Should the company try cyber cafes? What about merging with cellular companies? How about working with cable firms? In came the students' economic analysis, factoring in the nature and importance of economic swings and the vulnerability of dot-coms. There was the cash burn rate, capital expenses and the advertising dollars. Their work demonstrated that we had trained very capable *business* students.

But with each presentation I found myself raising the same unanswered questions: What about copyright issues? What happens if the users download music on the ISP? What happens if digital technology allows circumvention of protections? What if the ISP is used for defamation? And what laws apply to disputes? Is it the law of Bolivia or the law of the United States? Will the ISP have to go to Brazil to defend lawsuits? When does a subscriber agree to a contract for service? What happens if companies that advertise use the subscribers' names and information and sell them to others? Is this a breach of privacy? And what about the ethical and social responsibility issues when pornography sites seek subscribers via this company's ISP? Our capable business students, adept at complex business analysis, stumbled over basic legal and ethical issues.

Why couldn't these students competently discuss legal issues? It was not for lack of exposure to the law. I taught my course "by the book," so to speak. Students could recite the components of a valid contract, rattle off the requirements for bankruptcy, recall from memory the antitrust statutes. Yet, I was coming to realize, this rote knowledge was not enough. One of my best former students, who had gone on to medical school, came to me perplexed about her office lease. She said that the complex in which she wanted to open her practice had a "no advertising" policy. In fact, she said that when she toured the premises with a leasing agent, the leasing agent turned to her and said, "You're not one of those doctors who advertises, are you? Because if you are, we can't lease to you. We have a policy against it." One of my best students, who knew the antitrust statutes well, could not apply them to her everyday business. Worse, perhaps, she could not *recognize* when to apply these statutes: She did not see the antitrust implications of the agent's statements nor the problems with the physicians in the complex taking such an approach to screening tenants.

I reached the conclusion that there were shortcomings in the standard approach to teaching business students law and ethics. Students were not ignorant of the law; rather, they simply lacked the necessary skills to recognize legal and ethical issues and to apply their knowledge of law and ethics to business decision making. As instructors, we were not integrating legal and ethical reasoning with business analysis. My conclusion led me to develop my own materials for classroom use and eventually led to the publication of the first edition of this book. Now in its seventh edition, *Business: Its Legal, Ethical, and Global Environment* brings to the classroom the most integrated approach to learning law and ethics available in the market today. Throughout every chapter and in every feature, students and instructors are continually reminded of how various legal and ethical principles apply in business contexts. For all areas of law and ethics, this book answers the question: How does this concept affect a business? This book builds a bridge for the student between knowledge of law and ethics and application of both in business. In fact, new to this edition is the Making Ethics Personal feature. My 28 years of teaching law and ethics finally brought this realization: business ethics is not easily grasped nor practiced in business because we depersonalize ethical issues. If we just allow the company or organization to make the decision, our ethics are not in question; the company's are. This new feature requires students to bring the ethical issue into their lives, their circumstances, their world. This feature also forces them to answer this question in a wide variety of contexts, "If it were you, and you were faced with the dilemma and required to make a decision, what would you do?"

STRENGTHENING THE BRIDGE: NEW CONTENT, BUSINESS APPLICATIONS, AND LEARNING AIDS

For the seventh edition, *Business: Its Legal, Ethical, and Global Environment* has undergone further refinement. New content has been added, new business applications integrated into every chapter, and the learning aids have been modified and refocused to help students understand and apply legal and ethical concepts.

New Content

The seventh edition of *Business: Its Legal, Ethical, and Global Environment* continues to meet its goal of helping students with their understanding of how law and ethics apply to the business world. The organizational structure continues from the sixth edition because the changes made then were well received. In general, each part begins with an overview that helps students see the importance of the various aspects of law in business management and operations. Part I offers the student an overview of the legal, ethical, and judicial environments of business. Part II covers the regulatory environments of business. The cyber law chapter, added last edition, has been revamped, updated, and reorganized to reflect the rapid changes in this area of business and law. Part III covers the law and ethics of competition and sales and has been reorganized to provide a more logical flow of material. Part IV covers the legal and ethical issues of business and employees. Part V covers the law and ethical dilemmas of business organization and capitalization. Sarbanes-Oxley crosses over all parts of the book because of its expansive reach. All aspects of this massive federal regulatory reform are covered in the book.

Ethics

Business Ethics and Social Responsibility (Chapter 2) offers new examples and insights on the application of ethics to business decision making. Chapter 2 has been restructured around the theme of "Making Ethics Personal." The new organization of the materials has the students exploring their personal values before delving into business ethics. Chapter 2 is chock full of the examples the last two years have netted—from Martha Stewart's difficulties to an entertaining and informative "Guess Who?" quiz on the companies that collapsed and the irony of their conduct and statements. Ethics coverage is also integrated throughout all chapters. Again, Making Ethics Personal is a new feature that helps students to personalize the decision-making process when faced with an ethical dilemma.

BUSINESS APPLICATIONS

Business Strategy

Each chapter contains a Business Strategy feature, which features an example and discussion of how the legal issues covered in the chapter must be integrated into or affect business strategic planning and decisions.

Biography

Each chapter contains at least one biography. Biographies (1- to 3-page features) provide students with business history through the study of individuals and companies involved with the area of law and ethics covered in the chapter. For example, Chapter 17, Antitrust Law, provides a look at the giant auction houses, Sotheby's and Christie's and how their chairmen and CEOs managed to violate the Sherman Act and end up with criminal trials, guilty pleas, and ended careers. Students can also read the story of the 15-year-old pump-and-dump king, Jonathan Lebed, as well as the life story and disastrous fall of Martha Stewart. Chapter 5 (Constitutional Law) includes a historical look at the U.S. Supreme Court.

For the Manager's Desk

Each chapter also contains at least one For the Manager's Desk. These readings provide students with excerpts from various business publications, including *Forbes, Wall Street Journal, Fortune,* and *Business Week,* as well as other publications, including *National Law Journal, California Management Review, American Business Law Journal,* and the *Real Estate Law Journal.* These readings, some short and others in-depth, offer students the opportunity to see how business interrelates with ethics and law.

LEARNING AIDS

Internet Margin Notes

For further student exploration, every chapter integrates World Wide Web addresses highlighting links to legal and business resources. At their option, students can review unedited cases and full statutes, visit governmental departments and international organizations, and examine relevant business materials. The text includes over 100 Web addresses.

Research Problems

Each chapter also contains a research problem for students to explore using both the Internet and other resources. The problems can be used in class or as assignments.

Case Headlines

Every court case has a case headline that summarizes what issues are involved in the case. In Managing Disputes: Alternative Dispute Resolution and Litigation Strategies (Chapter 4), students read *Wal-Mart Stores, Inc.* v. *Johnson,* a case that addresses the issue of our obligations regarding evidence for a potential civil suit. In the case, a customer is injured when a paper mache reindeer falls from an upper shelf and lands on his head and shoulders. The case title is memorable:

"'Reining' Deer at the Local Wal-Mart." The vivid one-line description and colorful facts of the case, a common thread throughout the case choices in the text, help students internalize the rules and lessons about not destroying evidence for a potential lawsuit.

Chapter Openers

Chapters begin with an opening problem, titled Consider . . . , which presents a legal dilemma relevant to the chapter's discussion and similar to those business managers need to handle. These are revisited and answered in the body of the chapter. For example, Chapter 1's opening Consider involves Shawn Fanning and his Napster company and its program for downloading music via peer-to-peer file sharing. Students will not only read about the *Napster* copyright infringement case in Chapter 1, they will read it after they have studied the *Sony* case in which the courts grappled with a similar infringement issue when the new technology was the VCR. This edition includes the final resolution of that case and the follow-up on subsequent technologies and programs for downloading music. Moreover, these answers are referenced in the text and clearly marked. Next, opening statements discuss the major topics of the chapter and present the general goals for the chapter in the form of questions to be answered. Finally, quotations, often humorous, pique students' interest and focus the chapter to the major issues.

Chapter Summary

Each chapter concludes with a summary that reinforces the major concepts of the chapter. Each summary is constructed around the key questions introduced at the start of the chapter and key terms presented throughout the chapter.

Business Strategy Applications

Each chapter has a business strategy exercise designed to teach the students how to use the materials they have learned in the chapter. The reference in the text directs students to the Web-based strategy application that uses tutorials, questions, research, exploration, writing, and analysis to help students grasp the legal and ethical principles, and, understand how they would use them in business. For example, for Chapter 1, the students have the chance to walk two new businesses through the laws that affect them. They read about two companies beginning businesses that will sell tickets to sporting and concert events over the Internet. They will see how these companies are affected by local laws, federal statutes, and even international law. For Chapter 5, they take a look at freedom of speech for corporations in the context of political donations and how those speech rights are balanced with regulations on contributions and how companies use the donations strategically. For Chapter 2, they do an integration exercise in which they compare codes of ethics for companies with the companies' financial performance. In Chapter 20, they will have the chance to study various approaches to diversity and develop a good diversity plan for their own companies.

These exercises have questions to help them review the chapter materials, questions to help them understand the application materials, and an assignment that they can do to bring knowledge, application, and strategy together. These exercises help students understand the material in the book, but they also provide an understanding of why the material is important and how it fits in the strategic plans and decisions of a business.

THINKING, APPLYING, AND REASONING: ORGANIZATION AND FEATURES

In addition to the new features added to this edition, the classic features have been updated and strengthened. The organization has been retained to continue to meet student needs in the classroom.

ORGANIZATION

As noted above, there are five parts in the book, which serve to organize the materials around business operations. Every chapter integrates international and ethical topics.

Part I

In four chapters, Part I offers an introduction to law, an introduction to business ethics and the judicial system, and a discussion of litigation and alternative dispute resolution. Part I provides students with a foundation in law and ethics, as well as legal and ethical reasoning, necessary for the areas of law in the chapters that follow. By being brief (four chapters), Part I offers instructors an early and logical break for exams.

Part II

In seven chapters, Part II covers the regulatory environment of business, including the following topics: constitutional law, administrative and international law, cyber law, business crimes and business torts, product advertising and liability, and environmental regulation. With the completion of Parts I and II, students have a grasp of the legal system, ethical boundaries, and the laws that affect business operational decisions, even those in cyberspace.

Part III

The five chapters in Part III present students with the legal and ethical issues surrounding competition and sales. Part III includes the following topics: real, tangible personal, and intellectual property; trade restraints and antitrust laws; contract and sales law; and financing of sales and leases, including credit disclosure and requirements. From the negotiation of price to the collection of accounts, this segment of the book covers all aspects of selling business products and services. This section has been reorganized so that contracts precede the complexities of property and competition.

Part IV

The three chapters in Part IV discuss the contractual and regulatory aspects of employer and employee relationships. Topics include agency law and employee conduct, management of employee welfare, and employment discrimination.

Part V

In Part V, students study the advantages and disadvantages of various business organizations and the regulation of the capital markets. The two chapters in Part V include the following topics: business organization, securities laws, and business combinations.

FEATURES

Court Cases

Edited court language cases provide in-depth points of law, and many cases include dissenting and concurring opinions. Case questions follow to help students understand the points of law in the case and think critically about the decision. The courts have been active since the last edition and there are many 2002–2004 case decisions throughout the book. Students will be able to study the suit brought against the Jenny Jones show by the parents of a young man who was killed by another young man after the two participated in a "secret crush" show for Ms. Jones. In studying agency law students will have the chance to read and discuss a case involving a suit against the Catholic church and a diocese for a priest's sexual abuse of a child who was serving as an altar boy. Scope of employment, master-servant relationships, and intentional conduct are all issues covered in the case. And what happens when employees work so many shifts and are so tired that they have accidents as they return home from work? Are their employers liable? What happens when a young man saves his Pepsi points to claim a Harrier Jet that he sees in a Pepsi spoof ad for "Pepsi stuff"? Does he get his jet?

Consider . . .

Consider problems, along with Ethical Issues boxes and Business Planning Tips, have been a part of every chapter since the first edition. Considers, often based on real court cases, ask students to evaluate and analyze the legal and ethical issues discussed in the preceding text. By being integrated into the text, students must address and think critically about these issues as they encounter them. Through interactive problems, students learn to judge case facts and determine the consequences. The Considers bring the most current topics into the book and the classroom. Students will be able to determine whether *Weekly Standard* editor Fred Barnes was defamed by Michael Moore. They can determine the relationship between the First Amendment and the Section 527 political organizations and their relationships to corporations.

Consider Tutorials

Each chapter now has a Consider Tutorial. These are application exercises that are simply in the usual Consider format, but with a twist. The tutorial walks the students through the problem. The Consider Tutorials include the following elements: THINK, APPLY, and ANSWER. The students are reminded of what they have just learned in the reading or the case via THINK. In the APPLY section, they are walked through how the case or principles just covered would apply in the circumstances presented in this Consider. After they have walked through this system of reasoning, ANSWER gives them the solution. However, immediately following the Consider Tutorial in the chapter is another Consider (often more) without the answer that now asks them to THINK, APPLY, and ANSWER on their own. The addition of this new tool should help students to develop the legal and ethical reasoning skills that will give them a strong foundation for applying legal and ethical principles for the course and eventually in business.

Ethical Issues

Ethical Issues boxes appear in every chapter and present students with real-world ethical problems to grapple with. Ethical Issues help integrate coverage of ethics into every chapter. Also, Making Ethics Personal brings a personal and real-life touch to these important issues.

Business Planning Tips

Students are given sound business and legal advice through Business Planning Tips. With these tips, students not only know the law, they know how to anticipate issues and ensure compliance.

E-Commerce and the Law

Most chapters also include a segment on the law as it relates to e-commerce. While the cyber law chapter offers a good overview, these chapter-by-chapter materials give students the chance to see how the new technology fits into the existing legal framework.

Exhibits

Exhibits include charts, figures, and business and legal documents that help highlight or summarize legal and ethical issues from the chapter. With the UCC revisions and the changes in criminal penalties under Sarbanes-Oxley, many of the charts are either new or updated.

End of Chapter Problems

The end of the chapter problems have been updated and focus more on actual cases. There are new chapter problems throughout the book with varied length for different instructor needs.

THE INFORMED MANAGER: WHO SHOULD USE THIS BOOK?

With its comprehensive treatment of the law, integrated business applications, and full-color design, *Business: Its Legal, Ethical, and Global Environment* is well suited for both undergraduate and MBA students. The book is used extensively in undergraduate education programs around the country. In addition, this edition has been class-tested with MBA students, and it is appropriate for MBA and executive education programs.

A NOTE ON AACSB STANDARDS

The strong presence of ethics, social responsibility, international law and issues, and the integration of other business disciplines make the book an ideal fit for meeting AACSB standards and curriculum requirements. The AACSB standards emphasize the need for students to have an understanding of ethical and global issues. The seventh edition continues with its separate chapter on ethics as well as ethical issues and dilemmas for student discussion and resolution in every chapter. The separate chapter on international law appears in expanded version in this edition, and each chapter has a segment devoted to international law issues. The seventh edition includes readings on language issues in contracts, women as executives in other cultures, the role of lawyers in other countries, and attitudes outside the United States on insider trading and antitrust laws.

This edition presents students with the legal foundation necessary for business operations and sales, but also affords the students the opportunities to analyze critically the social and political environments in which the laws are made and in which businesses must operate. Just an examination of the lists of the companies and individuals covered in the biographies and of the publications from which the For the Manager's Desk readings are taken demonstrates the depth of background the seventh edition offers in those areas noted as critical by the AACSB. The materials provide a balanced look at regulation, free enterprise, and the new global economy.

This edition continues margin notes that direct the student to various tools and topics available on the Internet. These margin notes offer students the opportunity to browse for more information or undertake projects for additional research and class work.

SUPPLEMENTS

Business: Its Legal, Ethical, and Global Environment offers a comprehensive and well-crafted supplements package for both students and instructors. Contact your Thomson Learning/West Legal Studies in Business Sales Representative for more details, or visit the Jennings Business Web site at http://jennings.westbuslaw.com.

Weekly Law Updates. Available to instructors and students is the weekly update on the law at http://jennings.westbuslaw.com. The weekly updated contributed by the author offers current events for discussion and analysis. The update features new decisions, new statutes, new regulations, and cites to current periodicals. The seventh edition includes references to these updates in the text. These notations appear next to topics in the book that are widely covered and updated in the Weekly Law Updates.

Student Study Guide. (ISBN: 0-324-30373-4) Written under the guidance of the author, the Study Guide provides the following for each chapter: an outline; chapter outlines, key terms; and matching, fill-in-the-blank, and short answer questions.

Instructor's Manual. (ISBN: 0-324-30375-0) The Instructor's Manual, written by the author, provides the following for each chapter: a detailed outline; answers to Considers, Ethical Issues, and case problems; briefs of all cases; supplemental readings; and interactive/cooperative learning exercises.

Test Bank. (ISBN: 0-324-30376-9) Written by the author, the Test Bank includes more than 1,500 questions in true-false, multiple-choice, and essay format. Answers to questions provide a subject word for easy identification and a classification indicating if they are intended for review of concepts or for analysis and application of concepts.

ExamView Testing Software—Computerized Testing Software. (ISBN: 0-324-30377-7) This testing software contains all of the questions in the printed test bank. This program is an easy-to-use test creation software compatible with Microsoft Windows. Instructors can add or edit questions, instructions, and answers; and select questions by previewing them on the screen, selecting them randomly, or selecting them by number. Instructors can also create and administer quizzes online, whether over the Internet, a local area network (LAN), or a wide area network (WAN).

Microsoft PowerPoint Lecture Review Slides. PowerPoint slides are available for use by students as an aid to note-taking, and by instructors for enhancing their lectures. Download these slides at http://jennings.westbuslaw.com.

Lesson Plans and Lectures. Lesson Plans and Lectures, available to download at http://jennings.westbuslaw.com, provides detailed lectures for each semester class period (32 lectures in all) plus sample syllabi, teaching tips, and content and reading quizzes.

West's Digital Video Library. Featuring 60+ segments on the most important topics in Business Law, West's Digital Video Library helps students make the connection between their textbook and the business world. Access to West's Digital Video Library is free when bundled with a new text, and students with a used book can purchase access to the video clips online. New to this edition are LawFlix, 12 scenes from Hollywood movies with instructor materials for each film clip. The author chose the clips and the IM materials were written by the author and include elements such as goals for the clips, questions for students (with answers for the instructor), background on the film and the scene, and fascinating trivia about the film, its actors, and its history. For more information about West's Digital Video Library, visit: *http://digitalvideolibrary.westbuslaw.com.*

West Legal Studies in Business Resource Center. This Web site offers a unique, rich, and robust online resource for instructors and students. *http://www.westbuslaw. com* provides customer service and product information, links to all text-supporting Web sites, and other cutting-edge resources such as *NewsEdge* and **Court Case Updates.**

LegalTrac. An excellent resource for research and writing assignments, *Legal-Trac*™ provides indexing for approximately 875 titles including major law reviews, legal newspapers, bar association journals and international legal journals, and also contains law-related articles from over 1,000 additional business and general interest titles. *LegalTrac*™ is available as an optional package with a new text.

The Business and Company Resource Center. *The Business & Company Resource Center (BCRC) is a premier online business research tool that allows you to seamlessly search thousands of periodicals, journals, references, financial information, industry reports, company histories, and much more. Visit *http://bcrc.swlearning.com* to learn more about this powerful tool. *BCRC* is available as an optional package with a new text.

The Wall Street Journal. For a nominal additional cost, any new West Legal Studies in Business text can be packaged with a card entitling students to a 15-week subscription to both the print and online versions of *The Wall Street Journal.* Instructors who have at least seven students activate their subscriptions will automatically receive their own free subscription.

A Handbook of Basic Law Terms, Black's Law Dictionary Series. This paperback dictionary, prepared by the editor of the popular *Black's Law Dictionary*, can be packaged for a small additional cost with any new West Legal Studies in Business text.

Student Guide to the Sarbanes-Oxley Act. This brief overview for undergraduate business students explains the Sarbanes Oxley Act, what is required of whom, and how it might affect students in their business life. This guide is available as an optional package with the text.

WestLaw®. Westlaw® West Group's vast online source of value-added legal and business information, contains over 15,000 databases of information spanning a variety of jurisdictions, practice areas, and disciplines. Qualified instructors who adopt West Legal Studies in Business textbooks may receive ten complimentary hours of Westlaw for their course (certain restrictions apply).

West Legal Studies in Business VHS Video Library. VHS videotapes on many business law issues are available (with some restrictions) to qualified adopters of West Legal Studies in Business texts. For more detailed information about the videos, please visit: *http://video.westbuslaw.com.*

About the Author

Professor Marianne Jennings is a member of the legal studies in business area of the Department of Supply Chain Management in the College of Business at Arizona State University and a professor of legal and ethical studies in business. She served as director of the Joan and David Lincoln Center for Applied Ethics from 1995–1999. Professor Jennings earned her undergraduate degree in finance and her J. D. from Brigham Young University. She has worked with the Federal Public Defender and U.S. Attorney in Nevada and has done consulting work for law firms, businesses, and professional groups, including AES, Boeing, Dial Corporation, Mattel, Motorola, the National Association of Credit Managers, Mesa Community College, Southern California Edison, the Arizona Auditor General, the Cities of Phoenix, Mesa, and Tucson, Midwest Energy Supply, Hy-Vee Foods, IBM, Bell Helicopter, Amgen, and VIAD.

She joined the faculty at ASU in 1977 as an assistant professor. She was promoted to associate professor in 1980 and to full professor in 1983. At ASU she teaches graduate courses in the MBA program in business ethics and the legal environment of business. She has authored more than 130 articles in academic, professional, and trade journals. Currently she has six textbooks and monographs in circulation. The fifth edition of her textbook, *Business Ethics: Case Studies and Selected Readings*, will be published in early 2005. The seventh edition of her textbook, *Real Estate Law*, was published in July 2004. She was added as a co-author to *Anderson's Business Law and the Legal Environment in* 1997 for the 17th Edition. The 19th Edition is now available. Her book, *Business Strategy for the Political Arena*, was selected in 1985 by *Library Journal* as one of its recommended books in business/government relations. In 2000, the *New York Times* MBA Pocket Series published her book on corporate governance. Her book on long-term success, *Building a Business Through Good Times and Bad: Lessons from Fifteen Companies, Each With a Century of Dividends*, was published in October 2002 and has been used by Booz, Allen, Hamilton for its work on business longevity. Her book, *A Business Tale: A Story of Ethics, Choices, Success, and a Very Large Rabbit*, a fable about business ethics, was chosen by Library Journal in 2004 as its business book of the year. *A Business Tale* was also a finalist for two other literary awards for 2004.

Her weekly columns are syndicated around the country, and her work has appeared in the *Wall Street Journal*, the *Chicago Tribune*, the *New York Times*, and the *Reader's Digest*. A collection of her essays, *Nobody Fixes Real Carrot Sticks Anymore*, was published in 1994. She was given an Arizona Press Club award in 1994 for her work as a feature columnist. She has been a commentator on business issues on *All Things Considered* for National Public Radio.

She has conducted more than 200 workshops and seminars in the areas of business, personal, and government, legal, academic and professional ethics. She has been named professor of the year in the College of Business in 1981, 1987, and 2000 and was the recipient of a Burlington Northern teaching excellence award. In 1999 she was given best article awards by the Academy of Legal Studies in Business and the Association for Government Accountants (AGA). AGA gave her a second best article award in 2004. She was named a Wakonse Fellow in 1994 and was named Distinguished Faculty Researcher for the College of Business that same year. She has been a Dean's Council of 100 Distinguished Scholars since 1995. In 2000 the Association of Government Accountants inducted her into its Speakers Hall of Fame.

She is a contributing editor for the *Real Estate Law Journal,* the *Corporate Finance Review,* and served as editor-in-chief for the *Journal of Legal Studies Education* from 2003–2004. She has received nine research grants. In 1984, she served as then Governor Bruce Babbitt's appointee to the Arizona Corporation Commission. In 1999 she was appointed by Governor Jane Dee Hull to the Arizona Commission on Character. During 1986–1988, she served as Associate Dean in the College of Business. From 1986–87, she served as ASU's faculty athletic representative to the NCAA and PAC-10. In 1999 she was elected president of the Arizona Association of Scholars.

She is a member of twelve professional organizations, including the State Bar of Arizona, and has served on four boards of directors, including that of Arizona Public Service from 1987–2000. She served as chair of the Bonneville International Advisory Board for KHTC/KIDR from 1994–1997 and was a weekly commentator on KGLE during 1998. She was appointed to the board of advisors for the Institute of Nuclear Power Operators in 2004 and serves on the board of trustees for Think Arizona, a public policy think tank. She has appeared on *CBS This Morning,* the *Today Show, CBS Evening News,* and *Dateline NBC.*

She is married to Terry H. Jennings of the Maricopa County Attorney's office, and has four children: Sarah, Claire, Sam, and John.

Acknowledgments

By its seventh edition, a book has evolved to a point of trademark characteristics. This book is known for its hands-on examples and readings for business managers. That trademark evolves because of the efforts of many. There are the reviewers and adopters of the text who provide ideas, cases, and suggestions for improvement and inclusion. For this edition, the following colleagues offered their seasoned advice:

Mitch Aglow, *Bucks County Community College*
Barbara Corvette, *Southwestern College*
Elizabeth Gingerich, *Valparaiso University*
Susan Martin, *Hofstra University*
Cynthia Mulliken, *Bellarmine University*
John Norwood, *University of Arkansas*
Daphyne Saunders-Thomas, *James Madison University*
John Wrieden, *Florida International University*
Mary-Kathryn Zachary, *State University of West Georgia*

Any edition of a book bears the mark of the editors who work to design, refine, market, and produce it. Four editions ago, Rob Dewey saw potential for the book and applied his enthusiasm and market insights to mold a somewhat ugly duckling into a four-color swan. This edition of the book has the imprimatur of Steve Silverstein who confronted me with a profound question, "Why can't those in business see these ethical dilemmas when they are in the midst of them?" His question forced me back to the drawing board and the new feature of Making Ethics Personal was born. Bob Sandman is destined to be a part of this book because he brings his soothing voice, calm attitude, and diligence about schedules, deadlines, and word counts to the often-overpowering left side of my brain. Tamborah Moore, the production editor, once again brought her eye for detail, her experience, and her insightful questions to the long haul of copyedit and page proofs. Kris Tabor has been with me since the first edition, helping with word processing, IMs, study guides, test banks, and venting. We mark 19 years of a terrific partnership with this edition.

This book also carries the unmistakable liveliness of an author who shares her life with four helpful children and one tolerant husband. Since the first edition of this book, I have added three children to our first, witnessed one graduate from college and the others grow up all too quickly in a household in which, "Mom, the UPS guy is here with page proofs," was their first spoken sentence. Their vibrancy is found in the color and charm of these pages. I am grateful for their unanimous and unwavering support for my work. I am finally grateful to my parents who taught me through their words and examples of the importance and rewards of ethics and hard work.

Marianne Moody Jennings

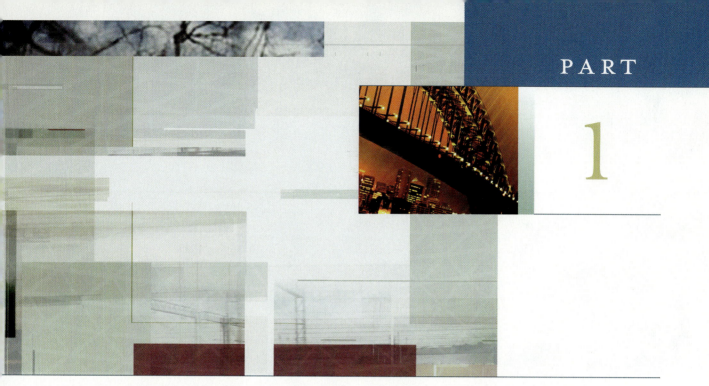

Business: Its Legal, Ethical, and Judicial Environment

Every business and businessperson need parameters for operation. What is legal? Where can I find the laws I need to know? How do I make decisions about legal conduct that, personally, is morally or ethically troublesome to me? What if I have a disagreement with a customer, employee, or shareholder? How can I resolve our differences? What forums are available for airing disputes?

This portion of the book explains what law is, where it can be found, how it is applied, and how legal disputes are resolved. Beyond the legal environment of a business, what is its ethical posture? Beyond operating a business within the bounds of the law, is the manager making ethical choices and behaving honorably in the conduct of business? Law and ethics are inextricably intertwined. A commitment to both is necessary and helpful in ensuring smooth operations and successful business performance.

1

Introduction to Law

Most people understand the law through their own experiences with it. More often than not, people are exposed to law through some personal problem. Some are exposed to law through traffic tickets. Others encounter the law when a problem arises with a landlord or lease. Many wonder about their rights when their e-mail is flooded with advertisements. Their understanding of the law may be limited by the anger they feel about the spam, their landlord, the traffic ticket. However, if there were no traffic laws, the roads would be a study in survival of the fittest; and, in the case of a troublesome landlord, the law provides a remedy when parties do not meet their agreed-upon obligations. We are just now grappling with the issue of spam and its related technological and privacy issues, and new laws are being developed and enforced to cover those who invade our electronic in-boxes.

Types of laws and penalties for violating them vary from state to state and from city to city; but, however much they vary, laws exist everywhere and at every level of government. Indeed, law is a universal, necessary foundation of an orderly society. It helps maintain order and ensures that members of a society meet minimum standards of conduct or risk penalties. Law is made up of rules that control people's conduct and their interrelationships. Traffic laws control not only our conduct when we are driving but also our relationships with other drivers using the roads. In some instances, we owe them a right-of-way and are liable to them for any injuries we cause by not following the traffic laws.

For up-to-date legal news and real-world business applications, click on **update** *at http://jennings.westbuslaw.com*

This chapter offers an introduction to law. How is law defined? What types of laws are there? What are the purposes and characteristics of law? Where are laws found, and who enacts them?

> This country's planted thick with laws from coast to coast— . . . —
> and if you cut them down— . . . d'you really think you could
> stand upright in the winds that would blow then?
> A MAN FOR ALL SEASONS, ACT I

CONSIDER...

Shawn Fanning, a young college student, moved the legal system to action when the relationship between copyright laws lagged behind the technology. His mainstream program that permitted the downloading of music from computer to computer over the Internet was a technological first, but was also a first for the Internet, copyrights, and the law. Using MP3 digital technology, Shawn founded Napster, a site where users could exchange their music. Napster was free, and its users called this downloading "peer-to-peer file sharing." Recording artists and record companies, however, referred to Napster as copyright infringement. "It's a technology no one anticipated and the law doesn't apply," was the observation of one legal expert. Don Henley, formerly of The Eagles, and Alanis Morrissette both testified before Congress that Napster deprived them of their royalty income and their rights in their intellectual property. The record companies filed suit against Napster and Fanning for copyright infringement. Mr. Fanning defended himself on the grounds that he made no money and only facilitated exchanges. Other programs soon developed, such as Aimster and Kazaa. The youthful developers had challenged the recording industry. The recording industry began to sue those using the programs for individual copyright infringement. The courts soon had active dockets on peer-to-peer file-sharing and infringement cases. How does the law determine the rights of the parties when there is a technological tidal wave like Napster and the second generation of peer-to-peer file sharing?

© RYAN MCVAY/PHOTODISC/GETTY IMAGES

DEFINITION OF LAW

Philosophers and scholars throughout history have offered definitions of law. Aristotle, the early Greek philosopher, wrote that "the law is reason unaffected by desire" and that "law is a form of order, and good law must necessarily mean good order." Oliver Wendell Holmes Jr., a U.S. Supreme Court justice of the early twentieth century, said that "law embodies the story of a nation's development through many centuries." Sir William Blackstone, the English philosopher and legal scholar, observed that law was "that rule of action which is prescribed by some superior and which the inferior is bound to obey." *Black's Law Dictionary* defines law as "a body of rules of action or conduct prescribed by the controlling authority, and having legal binding force." Law has been defined at least once by every philosopher, statesman, politician, and police officer.

Law is simply the body of rules governing individuals and their relationships. A society enacts most of those rules through a recognized governmental authority. It gives us basic freedoms, rights, and protections. Law offers a consistent model of conduct for members of society in their business and personal lives and gives them certainty of expectations. Plans, businesses, contracts, and property ownership are based on the expectation of the law's consistent protection of rights. Without such a consistent framework of legal boundaries, ours would be a society of chaos and confusion.

CLASSIFICATIONS OF LAW

Public versus Private Law

Public law includes laws that are enacted by some authorized governmental body. State and federal constitutions and statutes are all examples of public laws, as are the federal securities laws, state incorporation and partnership procedures, and zoning laws.

Private law, on the other hand, is developed between two individuals. For example, landlords usually have regulations for their tenants, and these regulations are private laws. Homeowners' associations have developed an important body of private law that regulates everything from the type of landscaping for homes in a subdivision to whether homeowners can erect basketball hoops in their driveways. The terms of a contract are a form of private law for the parties to that contract. Although the requirements for forming and the means for enforcing that contract may be a matter of public law, the terms for performance are the private law created by the parties to that rental contract. Employer rules in a corporation are also examples of private law; so long as those rules do not infringe any public rights or violate any statutory protections, those rules are a private law relationship between employer and employee and constitute part of the employee's performance standards.

Criminal versus Civil Law

A violation of a **criminal law** is a wrong against society. A violation of a **civil law** is a wrong against another person or persons. Criminal violations have penalties such as fines and imprisonment. Running a red light is an example of a criminal violation and generally carries a fine as punishment. Violations of civil laws require restitution: The party who violated the civil law must compensate the harmed party. If you do run a red light and strike and injure a pedestrian, you have committed a civil wrong and may be required to pay for that pedestrian's damages.

If you drive while intoxicated, you are breaking a criminal law and are subject to a fine, jail term, or license suspension. If you have an accident while driving intoxicated, you commit a civil wrong against anyone you injure. People who are injured as a result of your driving while intoxicated can file a civil suit against you to recover for injuries to their persons and property (cars).

There are other differences between civil and criminal laws and their enforcement. For example, there are different rights and procedures in the trials of criminal cases (see Chapter 9 for more details).

Substantive versus Procedural Law

Substantive laws are those that give rights and responsibilities. **Procedural laws** provide the means for enforcing substantive rights. For example, if Zeta Corporation has breached its contract to buy 3,000 microchips from Yerba Corporation, Yerba has the substantive right to expect performance and may be able to collect damages for breach of contract by bringing suit. The laws governing how Yerba's suit is brought and the trial process are procedural laws; the laws regarding subject matter and issues of the litigation are substantive laws.

Common versus Statutory Law

The term **common law** has been in existence since 1066, when the Normans conquered England and William the Conqueror sought one common set of laws governing a then very divided England. The various customs of each locality were compromised and conglomerated so that each locality would then operate under a "common" system of law. The judges in each locality developed this common law as they settled disputes. They consulted their fellow judges before making decisions so that their body of common law achieved consistency. This principle of following other decisions is referred to as *stare decisis*, meaning "let the decision stand" (see below and also Chapter 3). As a process of legal reasoning, it is still followed today. The courts use the judicial decisions of the past in making their judgments to provide for consistency or to serve as a basis for making a change in the law when circumstances are different.

As much of an improvement as it was, the common law was still just uncodified law. Because of increased trade, population, and complexities, the common law needed to be supplemented. As a result, **statutory law**, which is passed by some governmental body and written in some form, was created.

Today, in the United States, there is both common law and statutory law. Some of our common law still consists of principles from the original English common law. For example, how we own and pass title to real property area areas largely developed from English common law. There is, however, still a growing body of common law: The judicial system's decisions constitute a form of common law that is used in the process of *stare decisis*. Courts throughout the country look to other court decisions when confronted with similar cases. Statutory law exists at all levels of government—federal, state, county, city, and town.

Our statutory law varies throughout our nation because of the cultural heritages of various regions. For example, the southwestern states have marital property rights statutes—often referred to as community property laws—that were influenced by the Spanish legal system implemented in Mexico. The northeastern states have very different marital property laws that were influenced by English laws on property ownership. Louisiana's contract laws are based on French principles because of the early French settlements there.

Law versus Equity

Equity is a body of law that attempts to do justice when the law does not provide a remedy, or when the remedy is inadequate, or when the application of the law is terribly unfair. Equity originated in England because the technicalities of the common law often resulted in unresolved disputes or unfair resolutions. The monarchy allowed its chancellor to hear those cases that could not be resolved in the common law courts; eventually, a separate set of equity courts developed that were not bound by rigid common law rules. These courts could get more easily to the heart of a dispute. Over time, they developed remedies not available under common law. Common law, for example, usually permitted only the recovery of monetary damages. Courts of equity, on the other hand, could issue orders, known as **injunctions**, prohibiting certain conduct or ordering certain acts. The equitable remedies available in the **courts of chancery** were gradually combined with the legal remedies of the common law courts so that now parties can have both their legal and equitable remedies determined by the same court.

Today's courts award equitable remedies when the legal remedy of money damages would be inadequate. For example, in the copyright infringement cases that appear later in this chapter, the recording and motion picture industries brought suit seeking an injunction against the individuals and companies that provided the technological means for individual copies of movies and songs. The record companies, the movie producers, and the artists could never be adequately compensated with money for these forms of infringement because the continued use causes the loss of their exclusive copyrights. The remedy they sought and were given, with certain parameters, is an injunction that ordered the infringing programmers to halt the use of their programs for the downloading of copyrighted materials.

PURPOSES OF LAW

Keeping Order

Laws carry some form of penalty for their violation. Traffic violations carry a fine or imprisonment or both. Violations of civil laws also carry sanctions. If an employer discriminates against you for purposes of a pay raise or promotion, you can seek money damages. A driver who injures another while driving intoxicated must pay for the damages and the costs of the injuries the other person experiences. These penalties for violations of laws prevent feuds and other methods of settling disputes—for example, methods based on force.

In the past five years, Congress has been particularly active in passing legislation that targets terrorist activities as a means of keeping order and safety in the United States. The USA Patriot Act addresses a variety of legal issues from search warrants to reporting requirements for banks and others engaged in large-dollar transactions (see Chapters 9, 16, and 22). The purpose of these changes under the act was to keep the chaos terrorism creates in check.

Visit laws by subject matter:
http://www.law.indiana.edu/v-lib

Influencing Conduct

Laws also influence the conduct of society's members. For example, securities laws require certain disclosures to be made about securities before they can be sold to the public. The antitrust laws passed in the early twentieth century prohibited some methods of competition while they controlled others. In effect, these laws changed the way businesses operated.

Honoring Expectations

Businesses commit resources, people, and time with the expectation that the contracts for those commitments will be honored and enforced according to existing law. Investors buy stock with the knowledge that they will enjoy some protection in that investment through the laws that regulate both the securities themselves and the firms in which they have invested. Laws allow prior planning based on the protections inherent in the law.

Promoting Equality

Laws have been used to achieve equality in those aspects of life and portions of the country in which equality is not a reality. For example, the equal right to employment acts (see Chapter 20) were passed to bring equality to the job market. The social welfare programs of state and federal governments were created to further the cause of economic justice. The antitrust laws attempt to provide equal access to the free enterprise system.

Law as the Great Compromiser

A final and very important purpose of law is to act as the great compromiser. Few people, groups, or businesses agree philosophically on how society, business, or government should be run. Law serves to mesh different views into one united view so that all parties are at least partially satisfied. When disputes occur, the courts impose the law upon the parties in an attempt to compromise their two opposing views. The U.S. Supreme Court has provided compromises for business and labor through its interpretation of the statutes relating to union organizations, strikes, and other economic weapons (see Chapter 19). In the relationship between labor and management, the law serves as the mediator.

CHARACTERISTICS OF LAW

Flexibility

As society changes, the law must change with it. When the United States was an agricultural nation, the issues of antitrust, employment discrimination, and securities fraud rarely arose. However, as the United States became an industrialized nation, those areas of law expanded and continue to expand today. As the United States evolves toward a technological and information-based society, still more areas of law will be created and developed. The area of computer fraud, for example, was unknown thirty years ago; today, most states have criminal statutes to cover such theft (see Chapter 9). The introduction of the fax machine has required courts to reexamine how offers and acceptances of contracts are made and the Internet has resulted in legislation allowing electronic signatures to have the same force and effect as signatures on paper (see Chapter 13).

Changing circumstances require courts to review and interpret laws. Circumstances change through technology, sociology, and even biology. In the chapter's opening Consider, those who benefit and those who were affected struggled with the newfound technology of peer-to-peer file sharing. Downloading quality music via the Internet was now possible, and the issues of copyright protection and infringement became confusing because songs could be copied in a new way. Changing circumstances resulted in judicial review of a previously unaddressed issue.

Consistency

Although the law must be flexible, it still must be predictable. Law cannot change so suddenly that parties cannot rely on its existence or protection. Being able to predict the outcome of a course of conduct allows a party to rely on a contract or dissuades a party from the commission of a crime. For a contract, there is a judicial remedy for breach or nonperformance; for a crime, there is a prescribed punishment.

Pervasiveness

The law must be pervasive and cover all necessary areas; but, at the same time, it cannot infringe individual freedoms or become so complex that it is difficult to enforce. For example, laws cover the formation, operation, and dissolution of corporations. Laws govern corporate management decisions on expanding, developing, and changing the nature of the corporation. Laws also ensure that shareholders' rights are protected. The corporation has great flexibility in management, so long as it stays within these legal boundaries.

In the two following cases, the courts struggle as they try to honor law's purposes of keeping order and honoring expectations while also grappling with the unique issues modern technology and its applications and use raise in the context of balancing those purposes. The principle of *stare decisis* is at work in these two cases (see Chapter 3). Case 1.1, the *Sony* case, is briefed in Exhibit 1.1. A **brief** is a tool used by lawyers, law students, and judges to help them summarize a case and focus on its facts and the key points of the decision by the court. Case 1.2, the *Napster* case, provides the answer for the Consider problem posed at the beginning of the chapter.

CASE 1.1

Sony Corporation of America v. *Universal City Studios, Inc.*
464 U.S. 417 (1984)

Tape Delay: Contributory Infringement or Fair Use?

FACTS

Sony Corporation (petitioner) manufactures millions of Betamax video tape recorders (VTRs) and sells them through retail establishments (also included as petitioners in the case). The Betamax can record a broadcast off one station while the TV set is tuned to another channel. Tapes can be erased and reused. A timer in the Betamax can be used to activate and deactivate the equipment at predetermined times so the viewer/owner can record programs while not at home.

Universal City Studios, Inc. and Walt Disney Productions (respondents) produce and hold the copyrights on a substantial number of motion pictures and other audiovisual works. They can earn additional returns on these works by licensing limited showings on cable and network television, by selling syndicated rights for repeated airings on local TV, and by marketing programs on prerecorded videotapes or videodiscs.

Universal and Walt Disney brought a copyright infringement action against Sony and its retailers in Federal District Court. Universal and Walt Disney claimed that Betamax consumers were using their machines to record copyrighted works from commercially sponsored television. Evidence submitted by both parties indicated that most Betamax owners used their machines for "time-shifting," which is the practice of recording a program to view it at a later time and then erase it. Consumers used time-shifting to see programs they would otherwise miss because they were not at home, were otherwise occupied, or were viewing another station.

Universal and Walt Disney requested money damages, an accounting for profits, and an injunction against the manufacture and marketing of Betamax.

The District Court found there was no infringement and denied relief. The Court of Appeals held that Universal and Walt Disney were entitled to enjoin the sales of Betamax VTRs or to collect a royalty on each sale. Sony appealed.

JUDICIAL OPINION

STEVENS, Justice

From its beginning, the law of copyright has developed in response to significant changes in technology. Indeed, it was the invention of a new form of copying equipment—the printing press—that gave rise to the original need for copyright protection. Repeatedly, as new developments have occurred in this country, it has been the Congress that has fashioned the new rules that new technology made necessary.

In a case like this, in which Congress has not plainly marked our course, we must be circumspect in construing the scope of rights created by a legislative enactment which never contemplated such a calculus of interests. In doing so, we are guided by Justice Stewart's exposition of the correct approach to ambiguities in the law of copyright: "The limited scope of the copyright holder's statutory monopoly, like the limited copyright duration required by the Constitution, reflects a balance of competing claims upon the public interest: Creative work is to be encouraged and rewarded, but private motivation must ultimately serve the cause of promoting broad public availability of literature, music, and the other arts. The immediate effect of our copyright law is to secure a fair return for an 'author's' creative labor. But the ultimate aim is, by this incentive, to stimulate artistic creativity for the general public good. 'The sole interest of the United States and the primary object in conferring the monopoly,' this court has said, 'lie in the general benefits derived by the public from the labors of authors.' When technological change has rendered its literal terms ambiguous, the Copyright Act must be construed in light of this basic purpose."

The Copyright Act does not expressly render anyone liable for infringement committed by another. In contrast, the Patent Act expressly brands anyone who "actively induces infringement of a patent" as an infringer, 35 U.S.C. § 271(b), and further imposes liability on certain individuals labeled "contributory" infringers. . . . The absence of such express language in the copyright statute does not preclude the imposition of liability for copyright infringements on certain parties who have not themselves engaged in the infringing activity. For vicarious liability is imposed in virtually all areas of the law, and the concept of contributory infringement is merely a species of the broader problem of identifying the circumstances in which it is just to hold one individual accountable for the actions of another.

As the District Court correctly observed, however, "the lines between direct infringement, contributory infringement, and vicarious liability are not clearly drawn. . . ." The lack of clarity in this area may, in part, be attributable to the fact that an infringer is not merely one who uses a work without authorization by the copyright owner, but also one who authorizes the use of a copyrighted work without actual authority from the copyright owner.

Petitioners in the instant case do not supply Betamax consumers with respondents' works; respondents do. Petitioners supply a piece of equipment that is generally capable of copying the entire range of programs that may be televised: those that are uncopyrighted, those that are copyrighted but may be copied without objection from the copyright holder, and those that the copyright holder would prefer not to have copied. The Betamax can be used to make authorized or unauthorized uses of copyrighted works, but the range of its potential use is much broader.

The only contact between Sony and the users of the Betamax that is disclosed by this record occurred at the moment of sale. The District Court expressly found that "no employee of Sony had either direct involvement with the allegedly infringing activity or direct contact with purchasers of Betamax who recorded copyrighted works off-the-air."

If vicarious liability is to be imposed on petitioners in this case, it must rest on the fact that they have sold equipment with constructive knowledge of the fact that their customers may use that equipment to make unauthorized copies of copyrighted material. There is no precedent in the law of copyright for the imposition of vicarious liability on such a theory. The closest analogy is provided by the patent law cases to which it is appropriate to refer because of the historic kinship between patent law and copyright law. The two areas of the law, naturally, are not identical twins, and we exercise the caution which we have expressed in the past in applying doctrine formulated in one area to the other.

When a charge of contributory infringement is predicated entirely on the sale of an article of commerce that is used by the purchaser to infringe a patent, the public interest in access to that article of commerce is necessarily implicated. A finding of contributory infringement does not, of course, remove the article from the market altogether; it does, however, give the patentee effective control over the sale of that item. Indeed, a finding of contributory infringement is normally the functional equivalent of holding that the disputed article is within the monopoly granted to the patentee. For that reason, in contributory infringement cases arising under the patent laws the Court has always recognized the critical importance of not allowing the patentee to extend his monopoly beyond the limits of his specific grant.

continued

The staple article of commerce doctrine must strike a balance between a copyright holder's legitimate demand for effective—not merely symbolic—protection of the statutory monopoly, and the rights of others freely to engage in substantially unrelated areas of commerce. Accordingly, the sale of copying equipment, like the sale of other articles of commerce, does not constitute contributory infringement if the product is widely used for legitimate, unobjectionable purposes. Indeed, it need merely be capable of substantial noninfringing uses.

The question is thus whether the Betamax is capable of commercially significant noninfringing uses. In order to resolve that question, we need not explore all the different potential uses of the machine . . .

If there are millions of owners of VTR's who make copies of televised sports events, religious broadcasts, and educational programs such as Mister Rogers' Neighborhood, and if the proprietors of those programs welcome the practice, the business of supplying the equipment that makes such copying feasible should not be stifled simply because the equipment is used by some individuals to make unauthorized reproductions of respondents' works. The respondents do not represent a class composed of all copyright holders. Yet a finding of contributory infringement would inevitably frustrate the interests of broadcasters in reaching the portion of their audience that is available only through time-shifting.

Of course, the fact that other copyright holders may welcome the practice of time-shifting does not mean that respondents should be deemed to have granted a license to copy their programs. Third party conduct would be wholly irrelevant in an action for direct infringement of respondents' copyrights. But in an action for contributory infringement against the seller of copying equipment, the copyright holder may not prevail unless the relief that he seeks affects only his programs, or unless he speaks for virtually all copyright holders with an interest in the outcome. In this case, the record makes it perfectly clear that there are many important producers of national and local television programs who find nothing objectionable about the enlargement in the size of the television audience that results from the practice of time-shifting for private home use. The seller of the equipment that expands those producers' audiences cannot be a contributory infringer if, as is true in this case, it has had no direct involvement with any infringing activity.

Even unauthorized uses of a copyrighted work are not necessarily infringing. An unlicensed use of the copyright is not an infringement unless it conflicts with one of the specific exclusive rights conferred by the copyright statute.

If the Betamax were used to make copies for a commercial or profit-making purpose, such use would presumptively be unfair. The contrary presumption is appropriate here, however, because the District Court's findings plainly establish that time-shifting for private home use must be characterized as a noncommercial, nonprofit activity. Moreover, when one considers the nature of a televised copyrighted audiovisual work, and that timeshifting merely enables a viewer to see such a work which he had been invited to witness in its entirety free of charge, the fact that the entire work is reproduced does not have its ordinary effect of militating against a finding of fair use.

The timeshifter no more steals the program by watching it once than does the live viewer, and the live viewer is no more likely to buy pre-recorded videotapes than is the timeshifter. Indeed, no live viewer would buy a pre-recorded videotape if he did not have access to a VTR.

Today, the larger the audience for the original telecast, the higher the price plaintiffs can demand from broadcasters from rerun rights. There is no survey within the knowledge of this court to show that the rerun audience is comprised of persons who have not seen the program. In any event, if ratings can reflect Betamax recording, original audiences may increase and, given market practices, this should aid plaintiffs rather than harm them.

Of course, plaintiffs may fear that the Betamax will keep the tapes long enough to satisfy all their interest in the program and will, therefore, not patronize later theater exhibitions. It should also be noted that there is no evidence to suggest that the public interest in later theatrical exhibitions of motion pictures will be reduced any more by Betamax recording than it already is by the television broadcast of the film.

. . . [We] must conclude that this record amply supports the District Court's conclusion that home time-shifting is fair use. In light of the findings of the District Court regarding the state of the empirical data, it is clear that the Court of Appeals erred in holding that the statute as presently written bars such conduct.

Reversed.

CASE QUESTIONS

1. What is "time-shifting"?

2. What is the significance of the fair use doctrine in the court's decision?

3. What is the standard for imposing "vicarious liability for infringement"? What does the court examine in determining copyright vicarious infringement liability?

4. Has Sony infringed the rights of Universal and Walt Disney?

EXHIBIT 1.1	Sample Case Brief

Name of case:	*Sony Corporation of America* v. *Universal City Studios, Inc.*
Court:	U.S. Supreme Court
Citation:	464 U.S. 417 (1984)
Parties and their roles:	*Sony* Corporation (petitioner and defendant); Universal Studios, Inc. and Walt Disney Productions (plaintiffs and respondents)
Facts:	*Sony* manufactures video tape recorders (VTRs) that can record programs in homes. Universal and Walt Disney produce movies. They claimed that Sony's VTRs were being used to copy their protected and copyrighted films and that they were therefore entitled to some payment for this type of machine use.
Issues:	Does *Sony's* VTR and its use by its customers infringe on the filmmakers' copyright?
Lower court decision:	The District Court found no infringement. The Court of Appeals found for Universal and Walt Disney and held that they were entitled to either halt the sales of the VTRs or collect a royalty on each.
Decision:	No infringement by *Sony*.
Reasoning:	Congress did not give absolute control over all uses of copyright materials. Some uses (fair uses) are permitted. Consumer uses of the machines for time-shifting to watch shows at another time were not only noncommercial, they were beneficial to those who produced and advertised on the shows because they permitted greater audience exposure. Further, Sony could not be held vicariously liable for infringement using its equipment when it was not a party to such activity and the equipment had valuable uses apart from infringement.

CASE 1.2

A & M Records, Inc. v. *Napster, Inc.*
239 F.3d 1004 (9th Cir. 2001); affirmed 289 F.3d 1091 (9th Cir. 2002)

Downloading Music: Copyright Infringement or Peer-to-Peer File Sharing?

FACTS

Note: This case dealt with Napster as it originally existed for the peer-to-peer file sharing described in the opening Consider. To the extent Napster has changed its format, it is because of this decision and others following it.

A & M Records and others, including Geffen Records, Sony Music, MCA Records, Atlantic Recording, Motown Records, and Capital Records (plaintiffs), are in the business of the commercial recording, distribution, and sale of copyrighted musical compositions and sound recordings. They filed suit against Napster, Inc. (Napster) as a contributory and vicarious copyright infringer. Napster operates an online service for peer-to-peer file sharing (http://www.napster.com) so that users can, free of charge, download recordings via

the Internet through a process known as "ripping," which is the downloading of digital MP3 files. MP3 is the abbreviated term for audio recordings in a digital format known as MPEG-3. This compressed format allows for rapid transmission of digital audio files from one computer to another.

Napster's online service provides a search vehicle for files stored on others' computers and permits the downloading of the recordings from the hard drives of other Napster users. Napster provides technical support as well as a chat room for users to exchange information. The result is that users who register and have a password through Napster can download single songs

continued

and complete CDs or albums via the peer-to-peer file sharing.

The district court granted a preliminary injunction to the plaintiffs enjoining Napster from "engaging in, or facilitating others in copying, downloading, uploading, transmitting, or distributing plaintiffs' copyrighted musical compositions and sound recordings, protected by either federal or state law, without express permission of the rights owner."

The Ninth Circuit entered a temporary stay of the injunction in order to review the case.

JUDICIAL OPINION

BEEZER, Circuit Judge

Plaintiffs must satisfy two requirements to present a prima facie case of direct infringement: (1) they must show ownership of the allegedly infringed material and (2) they must demonstrate that the alleged infringers violate at least one exclusive right granted to copyright holders under 17 U.S.C. § 106. Plaintiffs have sufficiently demonstrated ownership. The record supports the district court's determination that "as much as eighty-seven percent of the files available on Napster may be copyrighted and more than seventy percent may be owned or administered by plaintiffs."

The district court also noted that "it is pretty much acknowledged . . . by Napster that this is infringement."

Napster contends that its users do not directly infringe plaintiffs' copyrights because the users are engaged in fair use of the material. Napster identifies three specific alleged fair uses: sampling, where users make temporary copies of a work before purchasing; space-shifting, where users access a sound recording through the Napster system that they already own in audio CD format; and permissive distribution of recordings by both new and established artists.

The district court considered factors listed in 17 U.S.C. § 107, which guide a court's fair use determination. These factors are: (1) the purpose and character of the use; (2) the nature of the copyrighted work; (3) the "amount and substantiality of the portion used" in relation to the work as a whole; and (4) the effect of the use upon the potential market for the work or the value of the work.

1. Purpose and Character of the Use

Courts have been reluctant to find fair use when an original work is merely retransmitted in a different medium.

A commercial use weighs against a finding of fair use but is not conclusive on the issue. The district court determined that Napster users engage in commercial use of the copyrighted materials largely because (1) "a host user sending a file cannot be said to engage in a personal use when distributing that file to an anony-

mous requester" and (2) "Napster users get for free something they would ordinarily have to buy."

Direct economic benefit is not required to demonstrate a commercial use. Rather, repeated and exploitative copying of copyrighted works, even if the copies are not offered for sale, may constitute a commercial use. In the record before us, commercial use is demonstrated by a showing that repeated and exploitative unauthorized copies of copyrighted works were made to save the expense of purchasing authorized copies.

2. The Nature of the Use

Works that are creative in nature are "closer to the core of intended copyright protection" than are more fact-based works. The district court determined that plaintiffs' "copyrighted musical compositions and sound recordings are creative in nature . . . which cuts against a finding of fair use under the second factor." We find no error in the district court's conclusion.

3. The Portion Used

"While 'wholesale copying does not preclude fair use per se,' copying an entire work 'militates against a finding of fair use.'" The district court determined that Napster users engage in "wholesale copying" of copyrighted work because file transfer necessarily "involves copying the entirety of the copyrighted work." We agree. See, e.g., *Sony Corp.* v. *Universal City Studios, Inc.*, 464 U.S. 417, 449–50, 104 S.Ct. 774, 78 L.Ed.2d 574 (1984) (acknowledging that fair use of time-shifting necessarily involved making a full copy of a protected work).

4. Effect of Use on Market

"Fair use, when properly applied, is limited to copying by others which does not materially impair the marketability of the work which is copied." A challenge to a noncommercial use of a copyrighted work requires proof either that the particular use is harmful, or that if it should become widespread, it would adversely affect the potential market for the copyrighted work. . . . If the intended use is for commercial gain, that likelihood [of market harm] may be presumed. But if it is for a noncommercial purpose, the likelihood must be demonstrated.

Addressing this factor, the district court concluded that Napster harms the market in "at least" two ways: it reduces audio CD sales among college students and it "raises barriers to plaintiffs' entry into the market for the digital downloading of music." The district court relied on evidence plaintiffs submitted to show that Napster use harms the market for their copyrighted musical compositions and sound recordings.

Here the record supports the district court's finding that the "record company plaintiffs have already expended considerable funds and effort to commence Internet sales and licensing for digital downloads." Having digital downloads available for free on the

Napster system necessarily harms the copyright holders' attempts to charge for the same downloads.

a. Sampling

Napster contends that its users download MP3 files to "sample" the music in order to decide whether to purchase the recording.

The district court determined that sampling remains a commercial use even if some users eventually purchase the music. The record supports a finding that free promotional downloads are highly regulated by the record company plaintiffs and that the companies collect royalties for song samples available on retail Internet sites. . . . [F]ree downloads provided by the record companies consist of thirty-to-sixty second samples or are full songs programmed to "time out," that is, exist only for a short time on the downloader's computer. In comparison, Napster users download a full, free and permanent copy of the recording.

b. Space-Shifting

Napster also maintains that space-shifting is a fair use. Space-shifting occurs when a Napster user downloads MP3 music files in order to listen to music he already owns on audio CD. Napster asserts that we have already held that space-shifting of musical compositions and sound recordings is a fair use. We conclude that the district court did not err when it refused to apply the "shifting" analyses of *Sony* . . . [w]here "the majority of VCR purchasers . . . did not distribute taped television broadcasts, but merely enjoyed them at home." Conversely, it is obvious that once a user lists a copy of music he already owns on the Napster system in order to access the music from another location, the song becomes "available to millions of other individuals," not just the original CD owner.

Traditionally, "one who, with knowledge of the infringing activity, induces, causes or materially contributes to the infringing conduct of another, may be held liable as a 'contributory'. Put differently, liability exists if the defendant engages in "personal conduct that encourages or assists the infringement."

Contributory liability requires that the secondary infringer "know or have reason to know" of direct infringement. The district court found that Napster had both actual and constructive knowledge that its users exchanged copyrighted music. The district court also concluded that the law does not require knowledge of "specific acts of infringement" and rejected Napster's contention that because the company cannot distinguish infringing from noninfringing files, it does not "know" of the direct infringement.

It is apparent from the record that Napster has knowledge, both actual and constructive, of direct infringement. Napster claims that it is nevertheless protected from contributory liability by the teaching of *Sony Corp.* v. *Universal City Studios, Inc.,* 464 U.S. 417,

104 S.Ct. 774, 78 L.Ed.2d 574 (1984). We disagree. We observe that Napster's actual, specific knowledge of direct infringement renders *Sony*'s holding of limited assistance to Napster.

The district court found actual knowledge because: (1) a document authored by Napster co-founder Sean Parker mentioned "the need to remain ignorant of users' real names and IP addresses 'since they are exchanging pirated music'"; and (2) the Recording Industry Association of America ("RIAA") informed Napster of more than 12,000 infringing files, some of which are still available. The district court found constructive knowledge because: (a) Napster executives have recording industry experience; (b) they have enforced intellectual property rights in other instances; (c) Napster executives have downloaded copyrighted songs from the system; and (d) they have promoted the site with "screen shots listing infringing files."

The *Sony* Court refused to hold the manufacturer and retailers of video tape recorders liable for contributory infringement despite evidence that such machines could be and were used to infringe plaintiffs' copyrighted television shows. The *Sony* Court declined to impute the requisite level of knowledge where the defendants made and sold equipment capable of both infringing and "substantial noninfringing uses."

We are bound to follow *Sony*, and will not impute the requisite level of knowledge to Napster merely because peer-to-peer file sharing technology may be used to infringe plaintiffs' copyrights. We depart from the reasoning of the district court that Napster failed to demonstrate that its system is capable of commercially significant noninfringing uses. . . . Regardless of the number of Napster's infringing versus noninfringing uses, the evidentiary record here supported the district court's finding that plaintiffs would likely prevail in establishing that Napster knew or had reason to know of its users' infringement of plaintiffs' copyrights.

To enjoin simply because a computer network allows for infringing use would, in our opinion, violate *Sony* and potentially restrict activity unrelated to infringing use. We nevertheless conclude that sufficient knowledge exists to impose contributory liability when linked to demonstrated infringing use of the Napster system.

We turn to the question whether Napster engages in vicarious copyright infringement. Vicarious copyright liability is an "outgrowth" of *respondeat superior.* In the context of copyright law, vicarious liability extends beyond an employer/employee relationship to cases in which a defendant "has the right and ability to supervise the infringing activity and also has a direct financial interest in such activities."

continued

Ample evidence supports the district court's finding that Napster's future revenue is directly dependent upon "increases in userbase." More users register with the Napster system as the "quality and quantity of available music increases." We conclude that the district court did not err in determining that Napster financially benefits from the availability of protected works on its system.

The district court determined that Napster has the right and ability to supervise its users' conduct. The ability to block infringers' access to a particular environment for any reason whatsoever is evidence of the right and ability to supervise. Here, plaintiffs have demonstrated that Napster retains the right to control access to its system. Napster has an express reservation of rights policy, stating on its website that it expressly reserves the "right to refuse service and terminate accounts in [its] discretion, including, but not limited to, if Napster believes that user conduct violates applicable law . . . or for any reason in Napster's sole discretion, with or without cause."

Turning a blind eye to detectable acts of infringement for the sake of profit gives rise to liability. The district court, however, failed to recognize that the boundaries of the premises that Napster "controls and patrols" are limited. Put differently, Napster's reserved "right and ability" to police is cabined by the system's current architecture. As shown by the record, the Napster system does not "read" the content of indexed files, other than to check that they are in the proper MP3 format.

Napster, however, has the ability to locate infringing material listed on its search indices, and the right to terminate users' access to the system. The file name indices, therefore, are within the "premises" that Napster has the ability to police. We recognize that the files are user-named and may not match copyrighted material exactly (for example, the artist or song could be spelled wrong). For Napster to function effectively, however, file names must reasonably or roughly correspond to the material contained in the files, otherwise no user could ever locate any desired music.

Napster's failure to police the system's "premises," combined with a showing that Napster financially benefits from the continuing availability of infringing files on its system, leads to the imposition of vicarious liability.

Napster may be vicariously liable when it fails to affirmatively use its ability to patrol its system and pre-clude access to potentially infringing files listed in its search index. Napster has both the ability to use its search function to identify infringing musical recordings and the right to bar participation of users who engage in the transmission of infringing files.

The preliminary injunction which we stayed is overbroad because it places on Napster the entire burden of ensuring that no "copying, downloading, uploading, transmitting, or distributing" of plaintiffs' works occur on the system.

As stated, we place the burden on plaintiffs to provide notice to Napster of copyrighted works and files containing such works available on the Napster system before Napster has the duty to disable access to the offending content. Napster, however, also bears the burden of policing the system within the limits of the system. Here, we recognize that this is not an exact science in that the files are user named. In crafting the injunction on remand, the district court should recognize that Napster's system does not currently appear to allow Napster access to users' MP3 files.

AFFIRMED IN PART, REVERSED IN PART AND REMANDED.

NOTE AND AFTERMATH: On remand, the district court refashioned the injunction and ordered Napster to remove from its files all songs provided by the plaintiffs for which they held a copyright. The task of blocking the songs proved arduous because the downloading of a song under an inexact name permitted downloading to continue. For example, a song provided as "Down to You" by the record company could still be downloaded if carried by the file users as "Down 2 You" or "Down 2 U."

CASE QUESTIONS

1. Describe what Napster is and how it works. Remember, you are describing Napster at the time of this case.

2. Did the court find that Napster had engaged in copyright infringement?

3. What factors does the court look at when examining fair use?

4. How does the court apply the *Sony* case?

5. Is Napster vicariously liable for the downloading of copyrighted songs by its users? What technological limitations exist in honoring the copyrights?

CONSIDER...   1.1

Write a brief for the *Napster* case in the same format as Exhibit 1.1 for the *Sony* case.

CONSIDER...   **1.2**

Suppose that a company developed a program for the peer-to-peer exchange of DVDs (movies) via the Internet. How would a challenge by the producers of the movies to the program developers be decided in federal court? *Metro-Goldwyn-Mayer Studios, Inc.* v. *Grokster, Ltd.*, 2004 WL 1853717 (9th Cir.2004).

THINK: Before answering this problem, review the decisions in the *Sony* and *Napster* cases. Recall the following.
1. We can record movies and songs for private, noncommercial use, or fair use.
2. Technology that permits copying of copyrighted materials is not an automatic violation of copyright law if:
    a. The technology has other uses.
    b. The developer would have no way to know who was using its product for infringement.
3. It is possible for a company and officers who develop technology that permits recording of copyrighted materials to be "vicariously liable" for infringement if they are aware that their technology or product is used for infringement, they benefit from the infringement uses, and they take no steps to halt the infringement despite the capability to do so.

APPLY: The use of the Sony Betamax for recording TV programs for individual use was fair use under the copyright laws. The mass sharing of copyrighted music via the Napster programs was found to be more than fair use. Further, the court determined that the executives of Napster were savvy enough to know the infringement was occurring.

ANSWER: You can answer this Consider by simply substituting the DVD technology for the Sony Betamax or for the peer-to-peer file sharing in Napster. Now, decide which one of the cases the DVD copying is more like. Does the company make the copying possible? Could the copying be done for more than personal use? Would consumers not buy DVDs as a result?

BUSINESS STRATEGY

The Dangers of Lawsuits as a Strategy

Another important lesson of both the *Sony* and *Napster* cases is the importance of business strategy. The VTR was the beginning of Blockbuster, video rentals, and a new revenue stream for Universal, Disney, and all other filmmakers. The possibilities still seem endless as the technology has evolved into DVD. DVD films include commentary from directors and additional scenes cut from the original film.

© SUSAN LEVAN/PHOTODISC/GETTY IMAGES

The same may be true for the capabilities of Napster. While the free downloading of songs is curbed by copyright laws, the music industry is just beginning its partnerships with Internet service providers to offer customers the ability to download music for a fee. America Online, Inc. (AOL) has already forged a partnership with Sony, one of the plaintiffs in the Napster case.

The law is one tool used to enforce rights and protect stability. However, sometimes the law is a stopgap measure or even something that interferes with the strategic planning for technological changes. Litigation and decisions are often not the best resolution to a problem. Here, both industries needed to look at the technology's possibilities and use it, not try to stop it.

CONSIDER...   1.3

What if the exchange service, the program developer for the exchange of the music files, developed an encryption device that shielded it from knowing who was using the program, for what, and how often? Could such a server claim immunity from copyright infringement for its development of the exchange program?

In re Aimster Copyright Litigation, 334 F.3d 643, (7th Cir. 2003), cert. denied, 124 S.Ct. 1069 (2004).

ETHICAL ISSUES

What do you think of the ethics of peer-to-peer file sharing? Is peer-to-peer file sharing the same as copyright infringement? Who is harmed by the activity? Who is helped? Do you think the users of Napster should have had permission to download the copyrighted music?

BUSINESS STRATEGY APPLICATION

The exercise on the Web site for Chapter 1 provides an opportunity to look at the legal issues two relatively new companies face as they begin operations in a new industry. You can see how many sources of law affect a business and how the law must be considered as part of a business's strategic plan.

CHECK THE WEB

This area of music and video downloading is an active one in the law. Be sure to check the Web site updates for your book to see what is new in this area of the law and what technologies have developed that require interpretation of the law.

MAKING ETHICS PERSONAL

How Lovely It Sounds! Peer-to-Peer File Sharing

You do not download music from the Internet unless you pay the fees for the songs. However, your roommate, child, or partner is not as committed as you are to avoiding copyright infringement. Their explanation? "It's just file sharing! A little P2P. It doesn't really hurt anyone, so could I use your computer? I know you don't do it, but there's nothing to stop me. I don't feel guilty about it."

You would really like to keep the peace between you, and it seems like a small thing. What would you do? How can you approach the issue? Do you believe your concerns about downloading and speaking up about it are different from the one faced by those executives and employees who were aware of the overstatements of company earnings or understatements of expenses? Why or why not?

THE THEORY OF LAW: JURISPRUDENCE

Law is the compromise of conflicting ideas. Not only do people differ in their thinking on the types of specific laws, they also differ on the theory behind the law or the values a legal system should try to advance or encourage. Many can agree on the definition of law and its purposes but still differ on how those purposes are best accomplished. The incorporation of theories or values into the legal process is, perhaps, what makes each society's laws different and causes law to change as society changes its values. These different theories or value bases for law are found in an area of legal study called **jurisprudence**, a Latin term meaning "wisdom of the law." The Manager's Desk called "A Primer on Jurisprudence" provides a brief overview on the philosophy of law.

Roscoe Pound, another legal philosopher and dean of Harvard Law School for twenty years, had a very different view of jurisprudence from Justice Holmes. His view was that law exists as the result of those who happen to be in power. In 1941, Pound wrote his famous credo, called "My Philosophy of Law."

There are many cases in which how the law should work is unclear. Conflicting philosophical views often come together in litigation. Judges and lawmakers must struggle to do the best good for the most members of society.

BUSINESS PLANNING TIP

In many contracts for copyrighted works or patented products, significant revenues are lost because technological changes are not anticipated. For example, many actors, writers, and others involved with television shows of the 1950s and 1960s do not enjoy the royalties from their shows running in what seems to be perpetual syndication as networks such as TV Land and Nick at Nite feature only television shows of other generations. Those involved in the production of these shows did not foresee what technology would permit. Walt Disney and Universal did not anticipate the VTR and its capability.

All parties need to put technology clauses in their agreements that cover any future means of distribution, whether by wire, sound satellite, or other means. In other words, the clauses must be written with an open end for evolving technology.

FOR THE MANAGER'S DESK

RE: A PRIMER ON JURISPRUDENCE (LEGAL PHILOSOPHY IN A NUTSHELL; FIVE MINUTES OF LEGAL PHILOSOPHY)

First Minute

"An order is an order," the soldier is told. "A law is a law," says the jurist. The soldier, however, is required neither by duty nor by law to obey an order that he knows to have been issued with a felony or misdemeanor in mind, while the jurists, since the last of the natural law theorists among them disappeared a hundred years ago, have recognized no such exceptions to the validity of a law or to the requirement of obedience by those subject to it. A law is valid because it is a law, and it is a law if in the general run of cases it has the power to prevail.

This view of the nature of a law and of its validity (we call it the positivistic theory) has rendered the jurist as well as the people defenseless against laws, however arbitrary, cruel, or criminal they may be. In the end the positivistic theory equates the law with power; there is law only where there is power.

Second Minute

There have been attempts to supplement or replace this tenet with another: Law is what benefits the people. That is, arbitrariness, breach of contract, and illegality, provided only that they benefit the people, are law. Practically speaking, that means that every whim and caprice of the despot, punishment without laws or judgment,

lawless killing of the sick—whatever the state authorities deem to benefit the people—is law. That *can* mean that the private benefit of those in power is regarded as a public benefit. The equating of the law with supposed or ostensible benefits to the people thus transformed a *Rechtsstaat* into a state of lawlessness.

No, this tenet should not be read as: Whatever benefits the people is law. Rather, it is the other way around: Only what is law benefits the people.

Third Minute

Law is the will to justice, and justice means: To judge without regard to person, to treat everyone according to the same standard.

If one applauds the assassination of political opponents and orders the murder of those of another race while meting out the most cruel, degrading punishments for the same acts committed against those of one's own persuasion, that is neither justice nor law.

If laws consciously deny the will to justice, if, for example, they grant and deny human rights arbitrarily, then these laws lack validity, the people owe to them no obedience, and even the jurists must find the courage to deny their legal character.

continued

Fourth Minute

Surely public benefit, along with justice, is an end of the law. Surely laws as such, even bad laws, have value nonetheless—the value of safety regarding the law against doubt. And surely, owing to human imperfection, the three values of law—public benefit, legal certainty, and justice—cannot always be united harmoniously in laws. It remains, then, only to consider whether validity is to be granted to bad, detrimental, or unjust laws for the sake of legal certainty or whether it is to be denied them because they are unjust or socially detrimental. One thing, however, must be indelibly impressed on the consciousness of the people and the jurists: There can be laws that are so unjust, so socially detrimental, that their validity, indeed their very character as laws, must be denied.

Fifth Minute

There are, therefore, principles of law that are stronger than any statute, so that a law conflicting with these principles is devoid of validity. One calls these principles the natural law or the law of reason. To be sure, their details remain somewhat doubtful, but the work of the centuries has established a solid core of them and they have come to enjoy such a far-reaching consensus in the declaration of human and civil rights that only the deliberate skeptic can still entertain doubts about some of them.

In religious language, the same thoughts have been recorded in Biblical passages. On the one hand it is written that you are to obey the authorities who have power over you. But then on the other, it is also written that you are to obey God before man—and this is not simply a pious wish, but a valid proposition of law. The tension between these two directives cannot, however, be relieved by appealing to a third—say, to the maxim: Render unto Caesar the things that are Caesar's and unto God the things that are God's. For this directive too, leaves the boundary in doubt. Rather, it leaves the solution to the voice of God, which speaks to the conscience of the individual only in the exceptional case.

Discussion Questions

1. What is the positivist's view of law? Does it matter to a positivist whether a law is just?

2. What type of law is stronger than any statute? What are its origins? Do you have an example of a principle today that would fit into this type of law?

3. If a law is unjust, is obedience to that law necessary? How should people respond or react to unjust laws? Is civil disobedience justified?

4. How does the author respond to the statement: Law is what benefits the people. Does he agree or disagree?

Source: "Funf Minuten Rechtsphilosophie," by Gustave Radbruch, translated by Stanley L. Paulson, in Rechtsphilosophie, and edited by Erik Wolf and Hans-Peter Schneider (Stuttgart: K. F. Koehler Verlag, 1973), pp. 327–29. Reprinted with permission of K. F. Koehler Verlag.

CONSIDER...   **1.4**

Maj. Gen. Antonio M. Taguba was the U.S. general who led an investigation of the conduct of U.S. soldiers in the Abu Ghraib prison in Iraq. The 54-page report documented brutal treatment of Iraqi prisoners, torture, and humiliation, all in violation of either the Geneva Convention for the treatment of prisoners of war or the standards of the Red Cross. Gen. Taguba referred to the treatment of the prisoners as consisting of "egregious acts and grave violations of international law."* One of the findings of the report is that the soldiers serving as prison guards had little training. Gen. Taguba recommended training for soldiers in when to disobey orders. A fellow officer said of Gen. Taguba, "If you want the truth; he's going to tell you the truth. He's a stand-up guy."†

Gen. Taguba's father was Staff Sgt. Tomas Taguba, a man who fought in the Battle of Bataan and was taken prisoner by the Japanese. He escaped from prison there and joined the fighters in Japan who opposed the government.

Based on these brief descriptions of these two men, what philosophy of law do you think they would follow?

* Douglas Jehl, "Head of Inquiry on Iraq Abuses Now in Spotlight," *New York Times*, May 11, 2004, A1, A12.
† Ibid.

Justice Oliver Wendell Holmes, in "The Common Law," had a different view of the theory of law than that expressed in "A Primer on Jurisprudence." In his famous essay written in 1918, at the height of World War I, Holmes rejected the notion of natural law. His essay began with the famous phrase, "The life of the law has not been logic; it has been experience." Holmes's opinion is that our interactions with each other constitute the foundation of law.

FOR THE MANAGER'S DESK

RE: THE COMMON LAW (IDEAS AND DOUBTS: OLIVER WENDELL HOLMES)

It is not enough for the knights of romance that you agree that his lady is a very nice girl—if you do not admit that she is the best that God ever made or will make, you must fight. There is in all men a demand for the superlative, so much so that the poor devil who has no other way of reaching it attains it by getting drunk. It seems to me that this demand is at the bottom of the philosopher's effort to prove that truth is absolute and of the jurist's search for criteria of the universal validity which he collects under the head of natural law.

The jurists who believe in natural law seem to be in that naive state of mind that accepts what has been familiar and accepted by them and their neighbors as something that must be accepted by all men everywhere. No doubt it is true that, so far as we can see ahead, some arrangements and the rudiments of familiar institutions seem to be necessary elements in any society that may spring from our own and that would seem to us to be civilized— some form of permanent association between the sexes— some residue of property individually owned—some mode of binding oneself to a specified future conduct— at the bottom of it all, some protection for the person.

It is true that beliefs and wishes have a transcendental basis in the sense that their foundation is arbitrary. You cannot help entertaining and feeling them, and there is an end of it. As an arbitrary fact people wish to live, and we say with various degrees of certainty that they can do so, only on certain conditions. To do it they must

eat and drink. That necessity is absolute. It is a necessity of a lesser degree but practically general that they should live in society. If they live in society, so far as we can see, there are further conditions. If I do live with others they tell me what I must do if I wish to remain alive. If I do live with others they tell me what I must do and abstain from doing various things or they will put the screws to me.

Discussion Questions

1. According to Justice Holmes, what makes people obey certain laws and subscribe to certain standards?
2. Why does he see natural law as evidence of man's desire to deal in superlatives?
3. Does Justice Holmes feel that everyone's view of natural law is the same?
4. Another legal philosopher, John Austin, stated, "The matter of jurisprudence is positive law: law, simply and strictly so called: or law set by political superiors to political inferiors." Does Justice Holmes's philosophy agree or disagree with this position? Is there a different theory advanced with this statement?

Source: Essay by Oliver Wendell Holmes; reprinted with permission from 32 *Harvard Law Review* 40 (1918). Copyright © 1918 by The Harvard Law Review Association.

FOR THE MANAGER'S DESK

RE: MY PHILOSOPHY OF LAW: ROSCOE POUND

I think of law as in one sense a highly specialized form of social control in a developed politically organized society—a social control through the systematic and orderly application of the force of such a society. In this sense it is a regime—the regime which we call the legal order. But that regime operates in a systematic and orderly fashion because of a body of authoritative grounds for or guides to determination which may serve as rules of decision, as rules of or guides to conduct, and as bases of prediction of official action, or may be regarded by the bad man, whose attitude is suggested by Mr. Justice Holmes as a test, as threats of official action which he must take into account before he acts or refrains from action. Moreover, it operates through a

judicial process and an administrative process, which also go by the name of law. . . .

Discussion Questions

1. Would it be fair to consider Dean Pound's view of the law as merely the rules of those in charge?
2. What is Dean Pound's view on how Holmes's "bad man" is controlled by law?
3. Does Dean Pound discount the theory of natural law?
4. Do you agree with Dean Pound's views?

Source: From *My Philosophy of Law* by Roscoe Pound. © 1941 West Publishing Corporation. Reprinted with permission of West Group.

CONSIDER...   1 . 5

Apply the theories of jurisprudence to the following situations.
 1. A supervisor has ordered an employee to inflate the company's earnings for the quarter so that their unit can meet their goals and attain their bonuses. Must the employee obey?
 2. Is a businessperson who believes the tax system to be unconstitutional justified in refusing to pay taxes? How will society react to such a position?
 3. Is there any example of a law that is accepted by everyone in society? What about the laws against speeding? What about the laws that restrict who can marry? What happens, according to the philosophers, when there is no common agreement on what the law should be?

SOURCES OF LAW

Laws exist in different forms at every level of government. As discussed earlier, law exists not only in statutory form but also in its common law form through judicial decisions. Statutory law exists at all levels of government. Statutes are written laws enacted by some governmental body with the proper authority—legislatures, city governments, and counties—and published and made available for public use and knowledge. These written statutes are sometimes referred to as codified law, and their sources, as well as constitutions, are covered in the following sections.

Constitutional Law

Explore the U.S. Constitution:
http://www.law.emory.edu/
FEDERAL/usconst.html

The U.S. Constitution and the constitutions of the various states are unique forms of law. **Constitutions** are not statutes because they cannot be added to, amended, or repealed with the same ease as can statutes. Constitutions are the law of the people and are changed only by lengthier and more demanding procedures than those used to repeal statutes.

Constitutions also tend to protect general rights, such as speech, religion, and property (see Chapter 5 for a more complete discussion). They also provide a framework for all other forms of laws. The basic rights and protections afforded in them cannot be abridged or denied by the other sources of law. In other words, a statute's boundaries are formed by constitutionally protected rights. Exhibit 1.2 is an illustration of the sources of law; constitutional law is at the base of the pyramid diagram because of its inviolate status.

Statutory Law at the Federal Level

Congressional Law

Explore the U.S. Code:
http://www.law.cornell.edu/
uscode

Congress is responsible for statutory law at the federal level. The laws passed by Congress become part of the **United States Code (U.S.C.)**. Examples of such laws are the 1933 and 1934 Securities Acts (see Chapter 22), the Sherman Act and other antitrust laws (see Chapter 17), the Equal Employment Opportunity Act (see Chapter 20), the National Labor Relations Act (see Chapter 19), the Truth-in-Lending Act (see Chapter 15), the USA Patriot Act (see Chapters 9 and 22), and the Internal Revenue Code (see Chapter 21).

Statutes from the U.S.C. are referenced or cited by a standard form of legal shorthand, often referred to as a **cite** or **citation**. The number of the title is put in front of "U.S.C." to tell which volume of the Code to go to. For example, "15 U.S.C." refers to Title 15 of the United States Code (Title 15 happens to cover securities).

EXHIBIT 1.2 Sources of Law

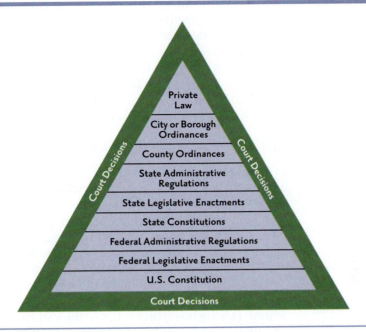

Private
Law

City or Borough
Ordinances

County Ordinances

State Administrative
Regulations

State Legislative Enactments

State Constitutions

Federal Administrative Regulations

Federal Legislative Enactments

U.S. Constitution

Court Decisions

There may be more than one volume that is numbered "15," however. To enable you to find the volume you need, the reference or cite has a section (§) number following it. This section number is the particular statute referenced, and you must look for the volume of Title 15 that contains that section. For example, the first volume of Title 15 contains §§ 1–11. A full reference or cite to a United States Code statute looks like this: 15 U.S.C. § 77. When a U.S.C. cite is given, the law cited will be a federal law passed by Congress.

Administrative Regulations

Another form of codified law exists at the federal level; it consists of regulations passed by administrative agencies. Called the **Code of Federal Regulations (C.F.R.)**, the administrative regulations at the federal level are extensive and affect virtually every business. The details of compliance with federal statutes (found in the U.S.C.) are found in the C.F.R. For example, sample forms for disclosure of credit information are found in the C.F.R., as are the Security and Exchange Commission's requirements for financial disclosures in the periodic reports of a public company. The specific requirements for product safety standards are administrative regulations of the Consumer Product Safety Commission. Chapter 6 provides a full discussion of regulation and administrative agencies.

Explore the Code of Federal Regulations:

http://www.access.gpo.gov/
nara/cfr/cfr-table-search.
html
or
http://www.gpoaccess.gov/
cfr/index.html

Executive Orders

Executive orders are laws of the executive branch of the federal government and deal with those matters under the direct control of that branch. For example, when Richard Nixon was president, he issued an executive order governing the classification and release of "top secret" documents. During his presidency, Jimmy Carter issued executive orders that required government contractors to employ a certain percentage of minority workers in their businesses in order to qualify for federal

Explore executive orders:
http://www.whitehouse.gov/
news/orders

projects (see Chapter 20). George Bush (43) issued one executive order requiring federal agencies to use alternative dispute resolution before going to court and another requiring them to implement recycling programs. On his second day as president, Bill Clinton issued an executive order reversing George H. W. Bush's (41) "gag rule" on abortion counseling. The same order also reversed a previous executive order banning the use of federal funds for research involving fetal tissue obtained from abortions. During his first 100 days in office, George W. Bush (43) issued an executive order banning the use of federal funds for abortion in other countries receiving U.S. financial assistance.

Statutory Law at the State Level

Legislative Law and State Codes

Explore the Uniform Commercial Code:
http://www.law.cornell.edu/ucc/ucc.table.html

Each state has its own code containing the laws passed by its legislature. **State codes** contain the states' criminal laws, laws for incorporation, laws governing partnerships, and contract laws. Much of the law that affects business is found in these state codes. Some of the laws passed by the states are **uniform laws**, which are drafted by groups of businesspeople, scholars, and lawyers in an effort to make interstate business less complicated. For example, the **Uniform Commercial Code** (UCC), which has been adopted in forty-nine states, governs contracts for the sale of goods, commercial paper, security interests, and other types of commercial transactions. Having this uniform law in the various states gives businesses the opportunity to deal across state lines with some certainty. Other uniform acts passed by many state legislatures include the Uniform Partnership Act (Revised), the Uniform Residential Landlord Tenant Act, the Model Business Corporation Act, and the Uniform Probate Code.

Explore the UCC and other uniform laws at the Commercial Law League of America:
http://www.clla.org *and* http://www.nccusl.org

State Administrative Law

Visit hyperlinks to state legislation:
http://www.washlaw.edu/uslaw/states/allstates/

Just as at the federal level, state governments have administrative agencies with the power to pass regulations dealing with the statutes and powers given by the state legislatures. For example, most states have an agency to handle incorporations and the status of corporations in the state. Most states also have a tax agency to handle income or sales taxes in the state.

Local Laws of Cities, Counties, and Townships

In addition to federal and state statutes, local governments can pass **ordinances** or statutes within their areas of power or control. For example, cities and counties have the authority to handle zoning issues, and the municipal code outlines the zoning system and whatever means of enforcement and specified penalties apply. These local laws govern lesser issues, such as dog licensing, curfews, and loitering.

Private Laws

Private laws are a final source of written law and are found in contracts and the landlord regulations agreed to, as discussed earlier in the chapter, under types of laws. These private laws are enforceable provided they are not inconsistent with rights and protections afforded under the other sources of laws (see Chapters 3 and 4).

Court Decisions

Looking at Exhibit 1.2, you can see that all of the sources of law just covered are surrounded in the pyramid by the term "court decisions." Often the language in the

BIOGRAPHY

ELIOT SPITZER: THE STATE ATTORNEY GENERAL WHO MOVED A NATION

Eliot Spitzer has been the attorney general of New York state since 1999. He is a 1981 Princeton graduate and a 1984 graduate of Harvard Law School, where he served as a law review editor. Following graduation from law school he served as a clerk to United States District Court Judge Robert W. Sweet. He then worked as an associate at Paul Weiss, Rifkind, Wharton, and Garrison, and then as an Assistant District Attorney in Manhattan from 1986–1992. He became Chief of the Labor Racketeering Unit, a unit that specializes in organized crime and political corruption cases.

His time as an assistant DA piqued his interest in setting policy through criminal prosecution and he established a goal of running for political office. He left the DA's office in 1992 to work in private practice and establish a financial base. From 1992–1998 he worked at the New York-based international law firm of Skadden, Arps, Slate, Meagher and Flom, and then at Constantine & Partners where he became a partner.

In 1994 he made his first bid for political office, running for attorney general of New York. He finished fourth out of a field of four candidates in the primary for the Democrat's slot on the ballot. In 1998 he ran again for attorney general of New York and ousted the Republican after a close race that required a recount that lasted six weeks.

While he has become a national figure over the past two years due to his pursuit of Wall Street analysts and their conflicts and contradictions in their private versus public reports on companies, he had long been an attorney general willing to use the law to establish public policy and force reforms in behaviors and in the laws. The following is a list of the areas he has tackled through litigation, along with the resulting reforms.

INDUSTRY	ISSUE	RESULTING REFORMS
Guns–Smith & Wesson	Safety	Company agreed to put safety locks on guns
Guns	Marketing	Self-restraint on distribution
Guns	Nuisance and costs of crime	Court found guns are societal problem best handled by legislation
Tobacco	Medicare costs	Tobacco settlement in which states are repaid for their costs from treating smokers
Predatory mortgage	High interest rates on home mortgage loans for subprime borrowers	Pending
Brokers and analysts	Analysts publicly said stocks were great in order to retain clients, even as they confessed in e-mails that they were junk	Settlements in the millions; Federal reforms
Mutual funds	Failure to disclose fees Conflicts on stock picks	Settlements in the millions; Federal reforms
NYSE–Dick Grasso	Excessive compensation	Suit is pending Federal reforms
Ticket scalping	Corruption at box offices; scalpers and ticket brokers' profits	Pending legislative reforms
Insurance industry	Fees; disclosures	Pending

Mr. Spitzer has been criticized for "government by lawsuit," but he has obtained reforms at the federal level through suits filed at the state level. Many have concluded he shamed the federal government into taking action. Others claim that his ambition is New York's governorship and the publicity on the cases is the means by which he will attain that goal. Others say that the resulting reforms have no relation to the

continued

wrongs. For example, in the mutual funds case, investors were profiting but Spitzer still demanded reforms through lower fees for mutual funds advisors. Professor Stephen Bainbridge of UCLA Law School, an expert in securities law, has noted of Spitzer's litigation and reforms, "It's as though you got busted for pot possession and the DA said you had to give up snowboarding."* Still others take issue with the state versus federal jurisdiction in these cases and the usurpation of federal laws by state authorities.

Nonetheless, Mr. Spitzer continues his active litigation agenda and his name is certain to continue to make national headlines. Mr. Spitzer says that since his arrival as the DA he has had his office assume a "take no prisoners" position on all cases.† His next area? Probably the price of gasoline.

* Ramesh Ponnuru, "Meet Eliot Spitzer," *National Review,* June 14, 2004, p. 26.
† Peter Elkind, "The Trials of Eliot Spitzer," *Fortune,* June 14, 2004, p. 33

statute is unclear, or perhaps whether the statute or ordinance applies in a particular situation is unclear. When there are these ambiguities or omissions in the statutory language, a decision rendered by a court in a dispute brought by one party against another serves to provide an interpretation or clarification of the law. These court decisions are then read along with the statutory language in order to give a complete analysis of the scope and intent of the statute.

FOR THE MANAGER'S DESK

RE: LAW AND MINUTIA

Two high school students, Jeff Koon and Andy Powell, did their homework in law and have written a book, *You May Not Tie an Alligator to a Fire Hydrant.* The book focuses on detailed sorts of laws around the United States, as well as outmoded ones that remain on the books, such as these examples.

- It is illegal in Illinois to hunt bullfrogs with a firearm.

- In Pacific Grove, California, it is illegal to molest butterflies.
- In Rhode Island, it is illegal to coast your car downhill in neutral.

For more information, you can go to the book or http://www.dumblaws.com.

CHECK THE WEB

Go to the book's Web site for regular updates and questions on sources of law. For example, what sources of law would govern the liability and legal issues in the nightclub fires that occurred in 2003? In one fire, the fire department said the pyrotechnics used by a performing rock group were done without a permit. In another, the club did not have the number of exits required under the code.

CONSIDER...   1.6

Often, businesspeople must read statutes, regulations, and ordinances to determine whether their business operations are legal, require licenses, or are otherwise regulated. Ticket brokers and scalpers would be affected by the following four New York statutes. Read them and then answer the questions that follow.

§25.13. Printing Price on Ticket

Every person, firm or corporation who owns, operates or controls a theatre, place of amusement or entertainment, or other place where public exhibitions, games, contests or performances are held shall, if a price be charged for admission thereto, print on the face of each such ticket or other evidence of the right of entry the price charged therefor by such person, firm or corporation. Such person, firm or corporation shall likewise be required to print or endorse thereon the maximum premium (not to exceed two dollars, plus lawful taxes), at which such ticket or other evidence of the right of entry may be resold or offered for resale. It shall be unlawful for any person, firm or corporation to resell or offer to resell such ticket or other evidence of the right of entry at any premium or price in excess of such maximum premium printed or endorsed thereon, plus lawful taxes, or so that the ultimate price to the purchaser of such ticket shall exceed a sum in excess of two dollars over and above the original price charged for admission as printed on the face of each such ticket or other evidence of the right of entry, plus lawful taxes.

§ 25.19. Posting of price lists; information to purchaser
In every principal office or branch office, bureau, agency or sub-agency of any licensee under this article, there shall be conspicuously posted and at all times displayed a price list showing the price charged by the person, firm or corporation owning, operating or controlling the theatre, place of amusement or entertainment, or the place where the public exhibition, game, contest or performance for which a ticket is being sold by such licensee, together with the price being charged by such licensee for the resale of such ticket, so that all persons visiting such place may readily see the same. The licensee shall also on request furnish each purchaser of a ticket with a receipt showing the same information.

§ 25.25. Violations; penalties
1. Every person, firm or corporation who resells any such ticket or other evidence of right of entry or engages in the business of reselling any such ticket or other evidence of the right of entry, without first having procured the license prescribed and filing of a bond required by this article shall be guilty of a misdemeanor. Every person, firm or corporation who violates any provision of this article shall be guilty of a misdemeanor. A conviction for any violation hereof shall be punishable by a fine not to exceed two hundred fifty dollars for the first violation, five hundred dollars for the second violation and one thousand dollars for any subsequent violation or by imprisonment for a period not to exceed one year, or both such fine and imprisonment as herein provided.
2. Notwithstanding the provisions of subdivision one of this section, any person who has not previously been convicted of violating this section and who sells less than six tickets shall be guilty of a violation, and upon conviction shall be punishable by a fine not to exceed one hundred dollars.

§ 25.27. Unlawful charges in connection with theatre tickets
1. Any owner, operating lessee, operator, manager, treasurer or assistant treasurer of any theatre wherein public performances are held, or of any stadium, arena, garden or other place of amusement showing sporting events, or his agent, representative, employee or licensee who, if a price be charged for admission thereto, exacts, demands, accepts or receives, directly or indirectly, any premium or price in excess of the regular or established price or charge, plus lawful taxes, as printed upon the face of each ticket or other evidence of the right of entry thereto, whether designated as price, gratuity or otherwise, shall be guilty of a misdemeanor. A conviction for each violation hereof shall be punishable by a fine not to exceed five hundred dollars or by imprisonment for a period not to exceed one year, or both.
2. The provisions of this section shall also apply to the sale of theatre tickets and tickets for sporting events to persons licensed to resell theatre tickets and tickets for sporting events, pursuant to the provisions of this article.

NOTE: These statutes remain in effect only until June 1, 2005. Previously, the New York legislature has used the pending expiration of these statutes to enact reforms related to ticket

continued

resales and ticket brokers. These provisions were enacted because the 2003 statutes were set to expire.

What is ticket speculation? Is it legal? Is it ethical? Are these statutes civil or criminal statutes? If you were a ticket broker, what would you need to do to comply with the law? Suppose that ticket brokers decided to sell options for events such as the NCAA's March Madness or the NFL's Super Bowl. A fan could purchase an option for a ticket to the Super Bowl just as the football season begins. If the fan's team makes it to the Super Bowl, the option is exercised for a ticket. If the fan's team does not make it to the Super Bowl, the fan could sell the option to someone else. In 2004, options for the NCAA Final Four basketball games were selling for about $600 each. Is this sale of futures in sports ticket markets a violation of any of these antiscalping laws? Can you think of some other sources of law that might apply here?

INTRODUCTION TO INTERNATIONAL LAW

Governmental changes in Germany and the former U.S.S.R., the evolution of the European Union, and the competitive skills of Japan and other nations have caused a dramatic change in the business marketplace. Businesses now operate in a global market. Companies headquartered in Japan have factories in the United States, and U.S. firms have manufacturing plants in South America. Trade and political barriers to economic development no longer exist. An international market requires businesses to understand laws beyond those of the United States.

Explore the Statute of the International Court of Justice:
http://www.icj-cij.org

International law is not a neat body of law like contract law or the UCC. Rather, it is a combination of the laws of various countries, international trade customs, and international agreements. Article 38(1) of the Statute of the International Court of Justice (a court of the United Nations that countries consent to have resolve disputes) is a widely recognized statement of the sources of international law:

> *The Court, whose function is to decide in accordance with international law such disputes as are submitted to it, shall apply:*
> *(a) international conventions, whether general or particular, establishing rules expressly recognized by the contesting states;*
> *(b) international custom as evidence of a general practice accepted as law;*

ETHICAL ISSUES

Does ticket scalping serve a purpose for some people? At the NCAA Final Four Basketball Tournament in 1992, midcourt seats were selling for $2,500. The late concert promoter Bill Graham once said, "If I wanted to, I could make more money scalping tickets than producing a show." Mr. Graham led a crusade for antiscalping legislation in California. Selling tickets at the event site is illegal in California, but ticket brokers are permitted to sell tickets at prices above the original cost so long as they operate away from the event.

Economist Steve Happel favors little or no regulation of scalping: "Look at the people on the Chicago Board of Trade. They buy wheat futures. Why are we so concerned about ticket scalpers?"

California state assemblyman Bill Lockyer, who has introduced antiscalping legislation, has stated, "The bro-

kering of tickets confers an advantage to the wealthy and the well connected that the fan of average means does not have. I still believe we need a law to stop the practice."

Does scalping encourage unethical behavior? For example, in exchange for alcohol, drugs, or money, homeless people in Texas are recruited to stand in ticket lines to buy tickets when there are limits on purchases. In California, a lawsuit was filed accusing a ticket broker of bribing ticket agency employees to obtain more and better seats to concert events that would later be sold for between ten and twenty times their face value. Would you participate in scalping, either as a buyer or a seller? Why or why not?

DO MORE RESEARCH AND STUDY ON TICKET SCALPING. Check the Web site for Chapter 1.

For a look at an economic analysis of ticket scalping, see http://www.cato.org/pubs/journal/cj15n1-4.html.

> (c) the general principles of law recognized by civilized nations;
>
> (d) judicial decisions and the teachings of the most highly qualified publicists of the various nations, as subsidiary means for the determination of rules of law.

Custom

Every country has its boundaries for allowable behavior, and these boundaries are unwritten but recognized laws. The standards of behavior are reflected in statements made by government officials. Among countries that have the same standards of acceptable behavior, there exists an international code of custom. Custom develops over time and through repeated conduct. For example, the continental shelf sea territorial standard came into existence in 1945 when President Harry S. Truman, in the Truman Declaration, established mileage boundary lines. Most countries accepted the declaration because it reflected their customary operations. By 1958, the standard became a part of the Geneva Convention.

Another example of international custom, though one not yet accepted by all nations, is the granting of diplomatic asylum. Some nations grant it, and others do not; it is an area of developing custom.

Explore foreign and international laws:
http://www.washlaw.edu/ forint/forintmain.html

Each individual country has its own customs peculiar to business trade. Businesses operating in various countries must understand those customs in negotiating contracts and conducting operations within those countries. For example, unlike the United States, most countries do not offer a warranty protection on goods and instead follow a philosophy of *caveat emptor,* "Let the buyer beware." Other countries also do not recognize the extensive rules of insurance and risk followed here with respect to the shipment of goods. Multinational firms must make provisions for protection of shipments in those countries with different standards.

Recently, the customs of China with respect to intellectual property, most particularly computer software, lagged behind those of Europe and the United States. Chinese custom was to separate infringement into two categories: ordinary and serious acts. Ordinary infringement is not regarded as a legal issue and requires only that the party apologize, destroy the software, and not engage in infringement again. Courts were rarely involved in ordinary infringement cases. However, the U.S. government demanded more protection for its copyright holders by imposing trade sanctions, and China eventually agreed to revise its customs and laws to afford protection. In this case, China's customs had to be changed to provide protection similar to that afforded in other countries.

Treaties

Examine various treaties:
http://untreaty.un.org/

A **treaty** is an agreement between or among nations on a subject of international law signed by the leaders of the nations and ratified by the nations' governing bodies. In the United States, treaties are ratified by the Senate and are included in the pyramid (Exhibit 1.2) as federal legislative enactments.

Treaties can be between two nations—**bilateral treaties**—or among several nations—**multilateral treaties**. There are also treaties recognized by almost all nations, which are called general or **universal treaties**. Universal treaties are a reflection of widely followed standards of behavior. For example, the Geneva Convention, a universal treaty covering the treatment of prisoners of war, has been the focus in the 2004 scandal related to the treatment of Iraqi prisoners of war. The Vienna Convention is a universal treaty covering diplomatic relations. The Warsaw Convention is a treaty that provides international law on the issues of liability for injuries to passengers and property during international air travel.

Private Law in International Transactions

Those businesses involved in multinational trade and production rely heavily on private law to assure performance of contractual obligations. Even though each country has a different set of laws, all of them recognize the autonomy of parties in an international trade transaction and allow the parties to negotiate contract terms that suit their needs, so long as none of the terms is illegal. **Party autonomy** allows firms to operate uniformly throughout the world if their contracts are recognized as valid in most countries. For example, most international trade contracts have a choice-of-law clause whereby the parties decide which country's law will apply to their disputes under the contract.

International Organizations

Some international organizations offer additions to international law. For example, the United Nations General Assembly has the authority to adopt resolutions to govern international relations and to censure companies that create difficulties in the international marketplace because of unfair dealings.

Act of State Doctrine

The **act of state doctrine** is a theory that protects governments from reviews of their actions by courts in other countries. In any action in which the government of a country has taken steps to condemn or confiscate property, the courts of other countries will not interfere. For example, in many cases, foreign countries engage in **expropriation** (also called **appropriation**), or the taking of private property. Also referred to as **confiscation** or **nationalization**, the process is really one of eminent domain, and courts of other countries will not interfere in this governmental process.

Trade Law and Policies

The importance of trade laws, tariffs, and policies has increased directly with increases in international business transactions. For example, the U.S. trade representative, once a dignitary position, has been upgraded to a cabinet-level position. Although Congress is responsible for enacting trade laws and various federal agencies are responsible for their administration, the U.S. trade representative assumes responsibility for negotiating trade agreements with foreign countries. The laws passed by Congress include import restrictions, tariffs, and enactments such as the Buy American Act (41 U.S.C. §§ 10a–10d [1987]), which requires federal agencies to give preference to U.S. suppliers in their procurement of goods and services. Chapter 7 provides additional details on trade laws, tariffs, restrictions, and trade agreements.

The United States and China used a trade agreement as the means for requiring the Chinese to afford greater intellectual property protections (patent, copyright, trademark) for U.S. businesses.

Explore GATT:
http://www.washlaw.edu/
forint/alpha/g/gatt.htm

Two important treaties to which the United States is a party have had a significant effect on our economy. The first is the Geneva-based General Agreement on Tariffs and Trade (GATT). GATT establishes uniform trade policies between the United States and the European Union nations. The goal of GATT has been called "borderless trade."

The second treaty is the North American Free Trade Agreement (NAFTA), which is a trade agreement among the United States, Canada, and Mexico. This lengthy agreement was signed by then-president George H. W. Bush in 1992 and

FOR THE MANAGER'S DESK

RE: HOW INTERNATIONAL ICE SKATING SCANDALS ARE RESOLVED

In an example of private law at work, the International Olympic Committee (IOC) dealt with issues of vote exchanges among judges for the pairs' figure skating competition. Canadian skaters David Pelletier and Jamie Sale were awarded a silver medal after what was called "the performance of a lifetime" in the competition. Their performance was flawless, although not as difficult as that of Elena Berezhnaya and Anton Sikharulidze, who were awarded the gold medal despite several errors in their performance.

The French judge on the panel, Marie Reine Le Gougne, said she was pressured by the Russians to rank the Russian team first. There may have been a *quid pro quo* arrangement with the French to assure the Russian

vote for the French competitors in ice dancing if the Russians could have the French vote in pairs.

Following public outcry and an investigation, the IOC awarded a second gold medal to the Canadian skaters. The decision was based on IOC rules, internal policies, and an internal fact-finding group. No criminal laws were broken, and it was up to the private body to take appropriate action for rules violations.

What ethical issues do you see in these events? Was the remedy appropriate? Would you have accepted the gold medal if you were the Canadian team?

Source: Selena Roberts, "Canadian Skaters Awarded Share of Olympic Gold; French Judge Suspended, Her Scoring Thrown Out," *New York Times,* February 16, 2002, A1, B21.

---

has been approved by the legislative bodies of all three countries. The agreement has permitted the free flow of goods, services, and capital among the three nations. Some have called the resulting trade from NAFTA a "borderless North America."

A new sort of treaty has arisen that requires those countries ratifying the treaty to change certain internal laws to achieve international uniformity. For example, the Kyoto Treaty requires the United States and other countries to substantially reduce their carbon dioxide emissions to address what some scientists believe is global warming. Not only do countries ratify the treaty, they also pass new laws within their countries for compliance. The Kyoto Treaty is at varying levels in different countries, from signing to ratification. The U.S. Senate did not ratify the Kyoto Treaty, by a 95 to 0 vote. More and more of these behavior- and law-changing treaties are being passed. In 2000, the U.S. Congress passed its E-sign law so that it could become one of many nations now subscribing to the requirement that electronic signatures be recognized as valid for purposes of contract formation.

Visit the NAFTA administration site:

http://www.mac.doc.gov/nafta/

Study the economic benefits of NAFTA:

http://www.naftaworks.org/

Uniform International Laws

Because trade barriers have been largely eliminated, contracts have been and are being formed between and among businesses from virtually all nations. However, not all nations have the same approach to contracts. Indeed, some nations have no contract laws or commercial codes. In an attempt to introduce uniformity in international contract law, the Vienna Convention adopted the UN convention on Contracts for the International Sale of Goods (CISG), which has been adopted widely. Similar to the UCC (see Chapter 13), the CISG has provisions on formation, performance, and damages. More information on the CISG can be found in Chapters 7, 13, and 14.

The European Union

Learn more about the European Union:

http://europa.eu.int/

Once referred to as the Common Market and the European Community (EC), the European Union (EU) is a tariff-free group of European countries that includes Austria, Belgium, Denmark, Finland, France, Germany, Greece, Ireland, Italy, Luxembourg, the Netherlands, Portugal, Spain, Sweden, and the United Kingdom. This group of twenty-five countries has joined together to enjoy the benefits

ETHICAL ISSUES

With NAFTA, 800,000 low-skill manufacturing jobs (such as those in the apparel, food-processing, and consumer-goods manufacturing industries) have been transferred to Mexico, where labor costs are lower. The effect of this transfer of labor is that U.S. blue-collar workers must retrain and retool. Economists maintain that the agreement now permits efficient use of resources and may reduce costs. Some labor representatives in the United States opposed NAFTA because of disparity in the wage levels in Mexico and the U.S.

minimum wage. Does NAFTA take advantage of a poorer economy and its workers? Should companies transfer their plants to Mexico to take advantage of the lower wages there? Who should pay the costs of retraining displaced U.S. workers? Recent economic studies have shown that there has been a net job gain in the United States, that is, there are more jobs here now than before NAFTA took effect. Apply your knowledge about economics to determine why there has been a net job gain.

of barrier-free trade. Formed in 1992, the single economic community requires member nations to subscribe to the same monetary standard, the elimination of immigration and customs controls, universal product and job safety standards, uniform licensing of professionals, and unified taxation schedules. The EU continues to evolve to trade as one country with the introduction of the euro, its single currency. More details on the governance of the EU and its laws can be found in Chapter 7.

SUMMARY

How is law defined?

- Law is a form of order. Law is the body of rules of society governing individuals and their relationships.

What types of laws are there?

- Public law—codified law; statutes; law by government body
- Private law—rules created by individuals for their contracts, tenancy, and employment
- Civil law—laws regulating harms and carrying damage remedies
- Criminal law—laws regulating wrongful conduct and carrying sentences and fines
- Statutory law—codified law
- Common law—law developed historically and by judicial precedent
- Substantive laws—laws giving rights and responsibilities
- Procedural laws—laws that provide enforcement rights

What are the purposes of law?

- Keep order; influence conduct; honor expectations; promote equality; offer compromises

What are the characteristics of law?

- Flexibility; consistency; pervasiveness
- Jurisprudence—theory of law

Where are laws found and who enacts them?

- Constitution—document that establishes structure and authority of a government
- Federal statutes—laws passed by Congress: the United States Code
- State statutes—laws passed by state legislatures, including uniform laws on contracts and business organizations
- Ordinances—local laws passed by cities, counties, and townships

What are the sources of international law?

- Treaties—agreements between and among nations regarding their political and commercial relationships
- Act of state doctrine—immunity of governmental action from discipline by other countries; sanctity of government's right to govern
- European Union—group of twenty-five nations working collectively for uniform laws and barrier-free trade
- Uniform laws—Contracts for the International Sale of Goods (CISG)

QUESTIONS AND PROBLEMS

1. Bryant Gunderson is a sole proprietor with a successful bungee-jumping business. He is considering incorporating his business. What levels and sources of law would affect and govern the process of incorporation?

2. Jeffrey Stalwart has just been arrested for ticket scalping outside the Great Western Forum in Los Angeles. Jeffrey sold a ticket to an Alanis Morrissette concert to an intense fan for $1,200; the face value of the ticket was $48. Ticket scalping in Los Angeles is a misdemeanor. Will Jeffrey's court proceedings be civil or criminal?

3. In 1933, Walt Disney Company entered into a contract with Irving Berlin, Inc., assigning musical copyrights in exchange for a share of Berlin revenues. The agreement exempted from copyright protection Disney's use of the assigned music in motion pictures. The music was used in several Disney feature-length cartoons (*Snow White* and *Pinocchio*) that were later made available for sale on videocassette. Mr. Berlin's heirs brought suit, alleging infringement. Was this new technology an infringement? Could videocassettes have been anticipated? (*Bourne* v. *Walt Disney Co.*, 68 F.3d 621 [2d Cir. 1995].)

4. Define and contrast the following:
 a. Civil law and criminal law
 b. Substantive law and procedural law
 c. Common law and statutory law
 d. Private law and public law

5. During the 2001 baseball season, Barry Bonds, a player with the San Francisco Giants, hit 73 home runs in one season, a new record that went beyond the 72 set by Mark McGwire in 2000. Mr. Bonds made his record-breaking home run in San Francisco. When he hit the home run, the ball went into the cheap seats. All agree that Alex Popov had his glove on the home-run ball. However, Patrick Hayashi ended up with the ball.

 Mr. Popov filed suit alleging that Mr. Hayashi assaulted Mr. Popov in order to get the ball. A substantial amount of videotape shows Mr. Popov's "gloving" of the ball. Mr. Popov says the ball belongs to him because he held that ball in a "Sno-cone position" and others wrested it from his control.

 Mark McGwire's ball from his record-breaking home run sold for $3 million. The battle for the Bonds home-run ball carries high financial stakes. What areas of law will be involved in the judge's determination of who gets the baseball? (Peter Page, "Ownership of historic baseball is in extra innings," *National Law Journal,* November 12, 2001.)

6. Jane Pregulman leases a one-bedroom apartment at Desert Cove Apartments. One of the regulations listed in her lease prohibits tenants from parking bicycles on their balconies or patios. What type of law is this?

7. Randy Redmond is an engineer with a city utility. The city has adopted an employment policy that creates a smoke-free work environment. Randy has smoked for fifteen years and now can no longer smoke at his desk. Is this a form of law? What is it? Is it enforceable? (For more discussion of this issue, see Chapters 19 and 20.)

8. Classify the following subject matters as substantive or procedural laws:
 a. Taxation
 b. Corporation law
 c. Evidence
 d. Labor law
 e. Securities

9. Mercury Corporation manufactures solar panels for residential use. Mercury is experiencing some sales resistance because homeowners fear that trees and buildings will block the sunlight from their solar panels. At this time there is no law in Mercury's state protecting light for solar panels. What governmental bodies could pass protective legislation?

10. Jose Camilo-Torres is a cacao farmer in Guyana. He has operated a large, successful business for twenty-two years and has sold his chocolate base product to U.S. companies such as M&M/Mars and Hershey's. After a change in government, Mr. Camilo-Torres's farm is taken over by the new government's agriculture department. Mr. Camilo-Torres will operate the farm and be paid a salary, but the profits will belong to the new government. Mr. Camilo-Torres has turned to his U.S. buyers for assistance. Can anything be done? Could the government's actions be set aside in a U.S. court? What if the government's takeover is unfair and does not provide Mr. Camilo-Torres with adequate compensation? What term applies to the government's takeover of the farm?

RESEARCH PROBLEM

The Cost of Corporate Wrongdoing

11. Read and analyze "Paying the Piper: An Empirical Examination of Longer-Term Financial Consequences of Illegal Corporate Behavior," 40 *Academy of Management Journal* 129 (1997), by Melissa S. Baucus and David A. Baucus. Then answer the following questions.
 a. What financial impact does illegal corporate behavior have on a company?
 b. How long does a company feel the impact of illegal behavior?
 c. How does the market react to illegal corporate behavior?

2

Business Ethics and Social Responsibility

update

For up-to-date legal news and real-world business applications, click on **update** *at http://jennings.westbuslaw.com.*

Since 2001, the business world has weathered scandal after scandal. A survey of high school students conducted by Junior Achievement and Deloitte Touche found that 45 percent of high school students believe business leaders are unethical. Another 38 percent are not sure if business leaders are ethical. Only 18 percent believe business leaders are ethical. In an honors thesis conducted by two seniors at Arizona State University, one student wrote in the comments on his survey, "If people can lie, and get away with it, good for them."

Is business ethical? Or is doing business just a matter of lying and getting away with it? Does anybody really care about ethics in business now? Do ethics matter? And what does it mean to be ethical in our lives and in business? This chapter discusses these questions and answers several others: What is ethics? How do they affect me? What is business ethics? Why is business ethics important? What ethical standards should a business adopt? How do employees recognize ethical dilemmas? How are ethical dilemmas resolved? How does a business create an ethical atmosphere?

There is no pillow as soft as a clear conscience.
KENNETH BLANCHARD AND NORMAN VINCENT PEALE
The Power of Ethical Management

Three people can keep a secret if two are dead.
HELL'S ANGELS
QUOTING BENJAMIN FRANKLIN

Goodness is the only investment that never fails.
HENRY D. THOREAU
Walden: "Higher Laws"

**A bad reputation is like a hangover. It takes a while
to get rid of, and it makes everything else hurt.**
JAMES PRESTON
Former CEO, Avon

**There is a big difference between what we have
the right to do and what is right.**
HON. JUSTICE POTTER STEWART
Associate Justice, U.S. Supreme Court, 1958–1981

CONSIDER...

1. What company's CEO was named *Business Week*'s CEO of the year for 2001?
2. What companies' CFOs were named CFO of the year for 1999, 2000, and 2001 by *CFO* magazine?
3. What company was ranked #44, #24, and #22 by *Fortune* for 1998, 1999, and 2000 among its 100 best companies to work for?
4. What company was described in 2001 as having a delivery and marketing model that would change its industry?
5. What CEO said in 2001, "We have no perks, not even parking spaces"?
6. What CEO said, "We are the good guys. We are on the side of angels"?

7. What company had a 64-page, award-winning code of ethics?*

*ANSWERS: 1. Dennis Kozlowski, Tyco, the $6,000-shower-curtain CEO. 2. WorldCom, Enron, and Tyco. 3. Enron. 4. HealthSouth (now emerging from bankruptcy after restating nearly $3 billion in revenues). 5. Dennis Kozlowski, Tyco, the man who used company funds to throw a birthday party for his wife, in Greece, complete with Jimmy Buffett entertainment. 6. Jeffrey Skilling, former CEO of Enron. 7. Enron.

© PHOTODISC/GETTY IMAGES

The chapter's opening Consider teaches us that often we look at what companies and business executives say and the fact that the companies are doing well and assume that they must be companies with high ethical standards. But all of the companies noted here, which were once recognized and given awards for their business ability and for their executives, have been indicted, are in financial difficulty, or both. The companies and their officers experienced legal and financial problems because they crossed ethical lines. They began with small misdeeds that grew larger until they had created a financial nightmare that ended with guilty pleas, trials, and tremendous losses for shareholders.

We look at their behavior and wonder why they thought they could get away with cooking the books, or why they believed they were entitled to loans from the company that they then forgave themselves so that they never had to repay them. We like to think of ourselves as so different from these so-called corporate criminals. But all of them were college graduates, nearly all with business degrees. All of them were respected by their friends and were active in community projects and institutions. These were once good people who lost sight of their ethics, business ethics, and the importance of ethics in success. Keeping ethics with us, in life and in business, can help us avoid the kinds of mistakes that so many bright and capable businesspeople have made. But, we wonder, what is ethics? How do we know when we have them? How do we keep them when we face pressures, whether on an important exam or for meeting the quarterly numbers or our sales quota at work? This chapter answers all of these questions.

WHAT IS ETHICS?

When we read about former Senator Bob Torricelli, an elected official and former senator from New Jersey who accepted a Rolex watch from a constituent who was courting the senator's vote on some important trade issues, stories about the situation label the former senator's conduct "unethical." When we read about Jason Blair, a young former reporter with the *New York Times* discovered to have fabricated his stories and lifted large segments from other reporters' work in other papers, the articles use the term "unethical." When we read about Dennis Kozlowski, the former CEO of Tyco, and his $6,000 shower curtain purchased with lavish bonuses and funds from officer loan programs perhaps not approved by Tyco's board of directors, we also read about the "lack of ethics."

We read about these types of situations in the newspaper each day. From politics to journalism to business, ethics crosses through the stories. But we also face ethical dilemmas ourselves. Two students purchase admission to see *The Day After Tomorrow,* and when they emerge from the theater they realize they are in an open area with access to other theaters. If they wanted to, they could slip into *Shrek 2* or *Harry Potter 3* and see it without paying for a ticket. "Who's to know?" they might think. "Hollywood makes too much money anyway." "It doesn't really hurt anyone." These are all thoughts similar to those running through the minds of the senator, the reporter, and the shower-curtain CEO. While we may believe we are different from business executives and others involved in scandals, we all face ethical dilemmas each day. Do I tell the clerk that he gave me too much change? Do I tell the shareholders about this loan I haven't repaid? Do I go back to pay for the laundry detergent that slipped through on the bottom of my cart? Do I give back the bonus I earned based on inflated numbers? Do I tell a potential buyer of my car that there is a hairline crack in the engine block? Do I tell buyers of my shares of stock in a pharmaceutical company that the FDA is about to hit the company with a large fine?

The fact pattern changes slightly. The parties' names and the subject matter vary, but the ethical issues are the same. Some conduct is more harmful, such as those situations in which there is a violation of a criminal statute. Still, regardless of the law, we look at the conduct of Mr. Torricelli, Mr. Blair, Mr. Kozlowski, the students in the theater, and the seller of the car, and we conclude, "It's just not right!"

We are probably unanimous in our conclusion that they all behaved unethically. We may not be able to zero in on what bothers us about their conduct, but we know an ethics violation, or an ethical breach, when we see one.

But what is ethics? What do we mean when we say that someone has acted unethically? Ethical standards are not the standards of the law. In fact, they are a higher standard. Sometimes referred to as normative standards in philosophy, ethical standards are the generally accepted rules of conduct that govern society. Ethical rules are both standards and expectations for behavior, and we have developed them for nearly all aspects of life. For example, there is no statute in any state that makes it a crime for someone to cut in line in order to save the waiting time involved by going to the end of the line. But we all view those who "take cuts in line" with disdain. We sneer at those cars that sneak along the side of the road to get around a line of traffic as we sit and wait our turn. We resent those who tromp up to the cash register in front of us, ignoring the fact that we were there first and that our time is valuable too.

If you have ever resented a line-cutter, you understand ethics and have applied ethical standards in life. Waiting your turn in line is a societal expectation. "Waiting your turn" is not an ordinance, a statute, or even a federal regulation. "Waiting your turn" is an age-old principle developed because it was fair to proceed with first in time, first to be served. "Waiting your turn" exists because when there are large groups waiting for the same road, theater tickets, or fast food at noon in a busy downtown area, we found that lines ensured order and that waiting your turn was a just way to allocate the limited space and time allotted for the traffic, the tickets, or the food. "Waiting your turn" is an expected but unwritten behavior that plays a critical role in an orderly society.

So it is with ethics. Ethics consists of those unwritten rules we have developed for our interactions with each other. These unwritten rules govern us when we are sharing resources or honoring contracts. "Waiting your turn" is a higher standard than the laws passed to maintain order. Those laws apply when physical force or threats are used to push to the front of the line. Assault, battery, and threats are forms of criminal conduct for which the offenders can be prosecuted. But the law does not apply to the stealthy line-cutter who simply sneaks to the front, perhaps using a friend and a conversation as a decoy. No laws are broken, but the notions of fairness and justice are offended by one individual putting him- or herself above others and taking advantage of others' time and position.

Because line-cutters violate the basic procedures and unwritten rules for line formation and order, they have committed an ethical breach. Ethics consist of standards and norms for behavior that are beyond laws and legal rights. We don't put line-cutters in jail, but we do refer to them as unethical. There are other examples of unethical behavior that carry no legal penalty. A married person who commits adultery does not commit a crime but does create a breach of trust with his or her spouse. We do not put adulterers in jail, but we do label their conduct with adjectives such as "unfaithful" and even use a lay term to describe adultery: "cheating."

Speaking of cheating, looking at someone else's paper during an exam is not a criminal violation. If you cheat on a test, your professor may sanction you and your college may impose penalties, but the county attorney will not prosecute you for cheating. But your conduct is unethical because you did not earn your standing and grade under the same set of rules applied to the other students. Just like the line-cutter, your conduct is not fair to those who spent their time studying. Your cheating is unjust because you are getting ahead using someone else's work.

FOR THE MANAGER'S DESK

RE: A STATE OF THE UNION ON ACADEMIC ETHICS

Because this is a chapter about ethics, lying would be out of the question. Ethics is not so difficult to understand, but it is difficult to practice. Data are available on the ethics of everyone from school-age children to graduate school students. In 1992, the Josephson Institute found that 61% of high school students reported that they had cheated at least once during a school year. By 2002, that number was 74%.* In 1997, a Rutgers University survey revealed that 26% of undergraduate students engaged in plagiarism in writing papers for their courses. In May 2001, that figure had increased to 54%, a doubling in four years.† According to Duke's Center for Academic Integrity, about 75% of college students confess that they have cheated in some way in college.‡ They describe taking notes and answers into exams, copying others' work, downloading and buying term papers from the Internet, and not contributing to team projects but still receiving credit for them. Certainly the Internet has made the task of plagiarism easier, but the rate of increase in that form of dishonesty as well as others indicates a troubling trend.

Both the Wharton School of Business at the University of Pennsylvania and Berkeley's Graduate School of Business have added new fees to their application processes. The fees, about $35, are used to do background checks on the students they admit to be sure that what the students put on their applications for graduate school is true information. For the fall 2003 class at Berkeley's MBA program at the Haas School of Business, there were 4,700 applicants; 100 students were accepted for the program. When the background checks were run on these 100 students, 5 lost their slots because their applications had false information, primarily related to number of years of job experience and their job titles. Student applicants, otherwise qualified with their GMAT scores and GPAs, will not be going to graduate school at Berkeley now or ever because they lied on their applications.

*See http://www.josephsoninstitute.org.
†Professor Donald McCabe of Rutgers University has conducted surveys on academic integrity for many years. His latest survey involved 4,500 student respondents nationwide. See http://www.academicintegrity.org, the Web site for the Center for Academic Integrity at Duke University, for more information.
‡Ibid.

These examples of cutting lines, committing adultery, and cheating on exams bring certain common adjectives to our minds: "That's not *fair!*" "That was *dishonest!*" "That was *unjust!*" You have just defined ethics for yourself. Ethics is more than common, or normative, standards of behavior. Ethics is honesty, fairness, and justice. The principles of ethics, when honored, ensure that the playing field is level, that we win using our own work and ideas, and that we are honest and fair in our interactions with each other, whether personally or in business.

ETHICAL ISSUES

In developing your personal standards, consider the following dilemmas, answers, and analyses.

1. If my boss asked me to lie to cover up his mistake, I would:
   a. Quit.
   b. Lie.
   c. Say it made me uncomfortable.
   d. Do it this time but refuse if it became a pattern.
2. If a vendor who was also a personal friend offered me a free laptop, I would:
   a. Turn it down and report the vendor to our purchasing officer.
   b. Accept the gift if it was personal rather than business-related.
   c. Ask my supervisor if I should accept it.
   d. Accept the gift but tell the vendor he will get no special consideration.

ANSWER a—the nonconformist who is difficult to get along with
ANSWER b—the negotiator who makes up the rules as he goes along
ANSWER c—the navigator who has the sound moral compass
ANSWER d—the wiggler who dodges ethical issues to protect his or her own interests

Courtesy of Mark Pastin, The Council of Ethical Organizations.

> update < **CHECK THE WEB**

Check the Web site for this chapter for regular updates on the state of ethics in the United States and the world.

 CONSIDER...   2.1

Why do we worry about ethics in school? What is the point of teaching young people to be honest? Why do we impose penalties for cheating? How does cheating affect those who do not cheat? What are some of the long-term consequences if those who cheat are permitted to pass courses, graduate with honors, and pursue careers in their fields?

MAKING ETHICS PERSONAL

The Oustanding Graduate Who Cheated, But for Others

Gerry Roscoe was the "Outstanding Graduating Senior" for the class of 2004 at State University. By tradition, the graduate chosen for this honor speaks at the commencement ceremonies for the university. Gerry was scheduled to give the student commencement address and had a job awaiting him on Wall Street in New York at one of the nation's largest investment banking firms.

Jill Swain and Eric Bourdeaux were also graduating seniors who knew Gerry. Jill and Eric knew that at least twice, Gerry had taken exams for others. One was a final exam during their sophomore year. The class was an economics course with 500 students. The exam was held in a large lecture hall and proctored by graduate students. ID was not required, and Gerry took the exam twice, once for his section and at another time for a friend who was having trouble with the course. Without a B on the mid-term, Gerry's friend's would have failed the course and lost his scholarship. The second instance was a final exam in finance. Finance 300 had been taught in sections of 50 students, but there was a common final with, again, 500 students in the room. The exam was proctored by one finance professor and graduate students. Gerry had taken Finance 300 one year before his girlfriend, Anissa Foulger, had, and she struggled through the course. She needed a B on the final exam in order to pass the course. If she did not pass, she jeopardized her transfer to a college in New York upon Gerry's graduation and employment there. Jill and Eric saw Gerry enter the common final for Finance 300, and he explained that he was taking the final for Anissa: "You understand. Everything is off if she doesn't make it through. She doesn't need this stuff. She is going into advertising. I can take it for her and she'll get her B."

If you were Jill or Eric, what would you have done at the time of the exams? What would you do now that Gerry has been given this "Outstanding Graduating Senior" honor? Does his dishonesty really hurt anyone? Wasn't Gerry just being noble by taking the exam for his friend? For his girlfriend? Is it any of your business? How is anyone harmed by what Gerry did?

WHAT IS BUSINESS ETHICS?

Now that we have an understanding of what ethics are and why we should care and also realize that we are involved in ethical dilemmas nearly every day, we can progress to a discussion of business ethics. What is business ethics?

Many have referred to "business ethics" as an oxymoron. The little jibe suggests that it is impossible to be in business and be ethical. Some see the pursuit of profit as being at odds with ethics. However, the term "business ethics" is actually a complex one with many layers of meaning. The first layer consists of basic values (covered in the following section) such as being honest, keeping promises, and not taking things that do not belong to you. Another layer consists of notions of fairness (also covered in the next section) such as how we treat others, including customers and employees who report to us. Still a third layer consists of issues related to how a business interacts with the community, the environment, and its neighbors.

The three layers of business ethics bring back into the purely quantitative models of business the elements of a fair playing field. Business ethics involve the study of fairness and moral standards amidst the pressure of earning a profit and providing returns to shareholders and others who have invested in the business.

A business faces the special problem of having to develop moral standards for a group of people who work together toward the common goal of profit for the firm. Individuals in the group have personal moral standards, but too often employees find that the moral standards imposed by managers at the top of a company result in possible harm to those at the bottom or to others outside the firm. An employee may feel compelled to resolve the conflict between loyalty to an employer and the performance of an illegal or immoral act ordered by that employer by simply following the employer's direction. In other words, in developing standards of business ethics, an employee has personal economic interests in continuing employment that may compromise personal moral standards. Businesses face the additional challenge of developing business standards that are consistent with individual standards and helping employees understand that their personal standards of honesty and fairness need not be different at work. To accomplish this meshing, business managers should understand the various sources of ethical standards.

Moral standards can be derived from different sources, and ethicists often debate about the origins of these standards. One theory is that our moral standards are simply the same as actual or **positive law**, that our ethical decisions are made simply upon the basis of whether an activity is legal. Positive law, or codified law, establishes the standard for ethical behavior. But compliance with positive law is not always ethical. For example, Enron created over 3,000 off-the-book entities in order to transfer its debt to them. If Enron owned less than 50 percent of these entities, it did not have to disclose on its financial statements that debt or its transfer. The result was that Enron's financial statements made the company look very healthy even while it was self-destructing. Most of the executives felt they were complying with not just the law but also the accounting standards that applied, a rule known as FASB 125 (Financial Accounting Standards Board). But when all of the off-the-book companies were found, and some 800 of them were located in the Cayman Islands, everyone referred to the conduct as "unethical." Professor Richard Leftwich has summed it all up: "It takes FASB two years to issue a ruling and the investment bankers two weeks to figure out a way around it." There is no violation of the letter of the law, but a violation of the spirit of the law presents an ethical dilemma.

Others believe that our moral standards are derived from a higher source and that they are universal. Often labeled **natural law**, this school of ethical thought supports the notion that some standards do not exist because of law (and, indeed, may exist in spite of laws). For example, at one time the United States permitted slavery. Even though the positive law allowed the activity and the standard of positive law considered slave ownership ethical, natural law dictated that the deprivation of others' rights was unethical.

Moral relativism (also called *situational ethics*) establishes moral standards according to the situation in which the dilemma is faced. Violation of the law, for example, is permitted if you are stealing to provide food for your starving family. Under moral relativism, adultery is justified when you are caught in an unhappy marriage, as is the business situation in which you engage in lying to avoid offending a coworker or a customer. Bribery is illegal in the United States, and most companies have firm policies against even accepting gifts as conflicts of interest; but some companies still use a relativist approach and argue that being competitive in international markets is different. They adhere to a philosophy of "When in Rome, do as the Romans do," following the standards and customs in a given country even though those same behaviors in the United States would be unacceptable and even illegal.

A final source of moral standards is religious beliefs or divine revelation. The source of standards can be the Bible, the Koran, or any inspired book or writing that is the cornerstone of a religion or faith and believed to have resulted from divine revelation.

WHAT ARE THE CATEGORIES OF ETHICAL DILEMMAS?

Regardless of the root or source of a company's or individual's ethical standards, certain categories of conduct involve ethical issues. The following twelve categories were developed and listed in *Exchange,* the magazine of the Brigham Young University School of Business.

Taking Things That Don't Belong to You

Everything from the unauthorized use of the Pitney-Bowes postage meter at your office for mailing personal letters to exaggerations on travel expenses to the downloading of music from the Internet without authorization belongs in this category of ethical violations. Using someone else's property without permission or taking property under false pretenses still means taking something that does not belong to you. A CFO (chief financial officer) of a large electric utility reported that, after taking a cab from LaGuardia International Airport to his midtown Manhattan hotel, he asked for a receipt. The cab driver handed him a full book of blank receipts and drove away. Apparently, the problem of accurately reporting travel expenses involves more than just employees.

Saying Things You Know Are Not True

A salesperson who tells a potential customer that a product carries a "money-back guarantee" when the salesperson knows that only an exchange is possible has said something that is not true, committed an ethical breach and possibly a violation of the law, and misled the customer. If a car dealer assures a customer that a car has not been in an accident and it has, an ethical breach has occurred. If a homeowner tells a buyer that a home has all copper plumbing in order to ensure a sale, and the home has plastic plumbing in some parts, that is an ethical breach too.

ETHICAL ISSUES

Actress Demi Moore starred in the 1995 movie entitled *The Scarlet Letter,* which was based on Nathaniel Hawthorne's book of the same name. Hollywood Pictures ran the following quote from a *Time* magazine review: " 'Scarlet Letter' Gets What It Always Needed: Demi Moore." The actual review by *Time* magazine read: "Stuffy old *Scarlet Letter* (1995) gets what it always needed: Demi Moore and a happier ending." A *Time* spokesman noted that the statement was clearly ironic. In the same review, the *Time* critic, Richard Corliss, referred to the movie as "revisionist slog" and gave it an F.

An ad for the 1995 movie *Seven* quoted *Entertainment Weekly* as calling it a "masterpiece." The actual review read, "The credits sequence . . . is a small masterpiece of dementia."

Ads for the movie *Thirteen Days* (2000), which is a depiction of the thirteen-day Cuban missile crisis during the Kennedy administration, included the descriptive phrases "by-the-numbers recreation" and "Close to perfect" in order to reflect what the producers saw as the strength of the film—its historical accuracy.

However, the ads included pictures of the Spruance-class destroyer and F-15 jet fighters. Neither of these defense systems was available in 1962, the time setting of the movie. These systems were not developed until the 1970s. Also, the movie ads showed the star, Kevin Costner, walking with the actors who played John and Robert Kennedy; that scene depicted in the ads is not part of the movie.

The movie studios pulled the ads after they had run for one weekend.

Ads by Sony studios had theater critic David Manning proclaim that *The Animal* (2001), starring Rob Scheider and ex-*Survivor* participant Colleen Haskell, was "another winner." Mr. Manning also gave a favorable review of Sony's *A Knight's Tale* (2001). However, David Manning is fictitious, a made-up critic created by marketing staff at Sony.

A movie industry observer stated in response to these examples, "The practice of fudging critics' quotes [in ads] is common."

Is the practice of fudging quotes ethical? Are some of these examples violations of any of the categories of ethical breaches?

Giving or Allowing False Impressions

An urban legend that has circulated among marketing departments around the country is the story of an infomercial ad that offered two CDs with all the hits of the 1980s on them. The infomercial emphasized over and over again, "All songs by original artists." Even the CDs carried the line, "All songs by original artists." When purchasers read the label with a closer eye and listened to the CDs, they discovered that all the songs were performed by one group, a group called "The Original Artists." While technically true, the advertising left a false impression with customers who assumed they would be buying songs as performed by the recording artists who made the songs popular.

Buying Influence or Engaging in Conflict of Interest

A company awards a construction contract to a firm owned by the father of the state attorney general while the state attorney general's office is investigating that company. A county administrator responsible for awarding the construction contract for a baseball stadium accepts from contractors interested in bidding on the project paid travel around the country to other stadiums that the contractors have built. The wife of a state attorney general accepts trading advice from the corporate attorney for a highly regulated company and subsequently earns, in her first foray into the market, over $100,000 in cattle futures.

All of these examples illustrate conflicts of interest. Those involved in situations such as these often protest, "But I would never allow that to influence me." That they have to insist they are not or would not be influenced is evidence of the conflict. Whether the conflict can or will influence those it touches is not the issue, for neither party can prove conclusively that a *quid pro quo* was not intended. The possibility exists, and it creates suspicion.

 CONSIDER . . .   **2 . 2**

Barbara Walters, as part of a Friday evening ABC television *20/20* news program broadcast, did a profile of Sir Andrew Lloyd Webber as a timely review of his career on the eve of the opening of his then-new Broadway play, *Sunset Boulevard.* The piece was very flattering to Mr. Webber and his work. On Monday morning, one of the New York papers revealed that Ms. Walters had a $100,000 investment in *Sunset Boulevard.* ABC issued an apology for not disclosing the information. Why should the information have been disclosed? Do you think disclosure is enough, or should Ms. Walters have removed herself from the story? Later, when *20/20* profiled Jerry Springer and *The Jerry Springer Show,* Ms. Walters announced that her daytime show, *The View,* competed with Mr. Springer's show but that she had no role in the production or content of the piece. Why did she make this disclosure?

Steps for Analyzing Ethical Dilemmas and Case Studies in Business
   1. Make sure you have a grasp of all the available facts.
   2. List any information you would like to have but don't and what assumptions you would have to make, if any, in resolving the dilemma.
   3. Take each person involved in the dilemma and list the concerns they face or might have. Be sure to consider the impact on those not specifically mentioned in the case. For example, product safety issues don't involve just engineers' careers and company profits; shareholders, customers, customers' families, and even communities supported by the business are affected by a business decision on what to do about a product and its safety issue.

continued

4. Develop a list of resolutions for the problem. Apply the various models for reaching this resolution. As you apply the various models to the dilemma, you may find additional insights for questions 1, 2, and 3. If the breach has already occurred, consider the possible remedies and develop systemic changes so that such breaches do not occur in the future.

5. Evaluate the resolutions for costs, legalities, and impact. Try to determine how each of the parties will react to and be affected by each of the resolutions you have proposed.

6. Make a recommendation on the actions that should be taken.*

Some Help for You on the Barbara Walters Case

THINK: To help in your analysis, consider the following list of the parties affected by this dilemma.

- Ms. Walters: Her credibility as a journalist is affected if there is an actual conflict or the appearance of a conflict.
- ABC News and *20/20:* While the producers and others associated with the show and the news division may not have known of Ms. Walters' investment, they are affected by the post-show disclosure of it in terms of their credibility.
- Viewers: Even unintentional conflicts cause viewers to lose trust.
- Mr. Webber and his investors in *Sunset Boulevard:* His credibility is affected by the undisclosed conflict and controversy.
- Ticket holders for *Sunset Boulevard:* Those who purchased tickets based on what they thought was news coverage may feel they were taken advantage of, and future ticket holders may not be willing to purchase until they feel there is a more objective evaluation.

APPLY: To further assist you in your analysis, consider the following categories.

- Conflict of interest: Ms. Walters had an economic interest in the show doing well and that interest was at odds with her journalistic role of objective reporting.
- Giving or allowing false impressions: Ms. Walters played the role of an objective journalist when she was really an investor in a critical project run by the subject of her interview.

ANSWER: Because the conduct has already occurred, your role becomes one of recommendation. You need to provide a recommendation that affords protection to all the parties listed as affected by the conduct. For example, to protect the credibility of the news organization, there will need to be a policy on journalists' disclosures of conflicts of interest, including any investments they hold with the companies or projects of the subjects of their interviews. That policy may require not only disclosure but also withdrawal from certain stories if the conflict seems too difficult to overcome. There are two ways to fix a conflict of interest: don't do it, or disclose the conflict to those affected. Sometimes disclosure is insufficient and one party must not engage in the conduct. It seems that Ms. Walters has begun adhering to such a policy as she made her disclosure on her other show and also declined to be part of the story.

*Adapted from Marianne M. Jennings, *Business Ethics: Case Studies and Selected Readings,* 5th ed. (2004).

Hiding or Divulging Information

Taking your firm's product development or trade secrets to a new place of employment constitutes an ethical violation: divulging proprietary information. Failing to disclose the results of medical studies that indicate that your firm's new drug has significant side effects is the ethical violation of hiding information that the product could be harmful to purchasers.

Taking Unfair Advantage

Many current consumer protection laws were passed because so many businesses took unfair advantage of customers who were not educated or were unable to discern the nuances of complex contracts. Credit disclosure requirements, truth-in-lending provisions, and regulations on auto leasing all resulted because businesses misled consumers who could not easily follow the jargon of long and complex agreements.

CONSIDER...   **2 . 3**

Kenneth Branch was an employee with Lockheed Martin in 1996. During that time Lockheed Martin was competing head-to-head with the Boeing Company for a government contract worth $5 billion. Mr. Branch interviewed for a job in Boeing's rocket division in 1996 and began employment at Boeing in January 1997.*

The government awarded the contract to Boeing. An internal investigation by Boeing revealed that Mr. Branch and his supervisor, William Erskine, had thousands of pages of proprietary documents from Lockheed Martin, including detailed information about Lockheed Martin's costs and specifications for the rocket contract. Boeing turned over 11 boxes of documents to Lockheed in 2003, some of which were marked "Proprietary."

Applying the model you learned in Consider 2.2, determine whether there were any ethical breaches in Boeing's conduct.

The author has performed consulting work for Boeing on changing its ethical culture. Why is this disclosure important in this text? Why is this disclosure important to you?

*Anne Marie Squeo and Andy Pasztor, "U.S. Probes Whether Boeing Misused a Rival's Document," *Wall Street Journal*, May 5, 2003, pp. A1, A7.

CONSIDER...   **2 . 4**

The Federal Trade Commission discovered that many credit card companies were using 10 A.M. as the cutoff time for posting that day's payments on credit cards, even though regular mail did not arrive at the credit card offices until afternoon. As a result, the companies charged $29.00 late fees to customers whose payments arrived by regular mail on the due date specified on their billing statements but after the 10 A.M. cutoff time. When this practice was implemented, there were no specific regulations on time-of-day postings or disclosure requirements for such creditor practices. Was the 10 A.M. cutoff time ethical? Was it ethical if credit card customers were not told? Was it ethical if they were told? What legal argument could be made that the posting time violated existing disclosure laws that addressed billing and notice requirements for credit cards?

CHECK THE WEB

Check the Web under this chapter as well as Chapter 15 for regular updates on ethical issues in credit contracts, credit card debt, and consumer financing and leasing issues.

Committing Acts of Personal Decadence

While many argue about the ethical notion of an employee's right to privacy, it has become increasingly clear that personal conduct outside the job can influence performance and company reputation. A company driver must abstain from substance abuse because of safety issues. Even the traditional company summer picnic has come under scrutiny as the behavior of employees at and following these events has brought harm to others in the form of alcohol-related accidents.

Perpetrating Interpersonal Abuse

A manager sexually harasses an employee. Another manager is verbally abusive to an employee. Still another manager subjects employees to humiliating correction in the presence of customers. In some cases, laws protect employees. However, many situations are simply ethical violations that constitute interpersonal abuse.

Permitting Organizational Abuse

Many U.S. firms with operations overseas, such as Unocal, Levi Strauss, The Gap, Nike, and Esprit, have faced issues of organizational abuse. The unfair treatment of workers in international operations appears in the form of child labor, demeaning wages, and too-long working hours. While a business cannot change the culture of another country, it can perpetuate—or alleviate—abuse through its operations there.

Violating Rules

Review Stanford University's "Code of Conduct for Business Activities":
http://adminguide.stanford. edu/1.pdf

Many rules, particularly those in large organizations that tend toward bureaucracy from a need to maintain internal controls or follow lines of authority, seem burdensome to employees trying to serve customers and other employees. Stanford University experienced difficulties in this area of ethics as it used funds from federal grants for miscellaneous university purposes. Questions arose about the propriety of the expenditures, which could have been approved through proper channels but were not. The rules for the administration of federal grant monies used for overhead were not followed. The result was not only an ethical violation but also damage to Stanford's reputation and a new president for the university.

Condoning Unethical Actions

Visit Lockheed Martin's Code of Ethics:
http://www.lockheedmartin. com

In this breach of ethics, the wrong results from the failure to report the wrong. What if you witnessed a fellow employee embezzling company funds by forging his signature on a check that was supposed to be voided? Would you report that violation? A winking tolerance of others' unethical behavior is in itself unethical. Suppose that as a product designer you were aware of a fundamental flaw in your company's new product—a product predicted to catapult your firm to record earnings. Would you pursue the problem to the point of halting the distribution of the product? Would you disclose what you know to the public if you could not get your company to act? In many companies such as Enron, WorldCom, and Tyco, the failure of employees to report the problems they saw permitted financial misconduct to go on so long that there was irreparable damage to many.

Balancing Ethical Dilemmas

Visit Levi Strauss & Company:
http://www.levi.com

In these types of situations, there are no right or wrong answers; rather, there are dilemmas to be resolved. For example, Levi Strauss struggled with its decision about whether to do business in the People's Republic of China because of known human rights violations by the government there. Other companies debated doing business in South Africa when that country's government followed a policy of apartheid. In some respects, the presence of these companies would help by advancing human rights and, certainly, by improving the standard of living for at least some international operations workers. On the other hand, their ability to recruit businesses could help such governments sustain themselves by enabling them to point to economic successes despite human rights violations.

RESOLUTION OF BUSINESS ETHICAL DILEMMAS

So far you know what business ethics is and you have a list of the areas that cover most ethical dilemmas. But if you were faced with an ethical dilemma, how would you resolve it? The resolution of ethical dilemmas in business is often difficult, even in firms with a code of ethics and a culture committed to compliance with ethical models for decision making. Managers need guidelines for making ethical choices. Several prominent scholars in the field of business ethics have developed models for use in difficult situations. This section covers those models.

Blanchard and Peale

The late Dr. Norman Vincent Peale and management expert Kenneth Blanchard offer three questions that managers should ponder in resolving ethical dilemmas: "Is it legal?" "Is it balanced?" "How does it make me feel?"

Browse antitrust cases at the U.S. Department of Justice: http://www.usdoj.gov

If the answer to the first question, "Is it legal?" is no, a manager should not proceed any further. An examination of the Justice Department's antitrust case against some of the country's best and largest universities demonstrates that managers still fail to ask the basic ethical question of whether they are in compliance with the law. In that case, twenty-two large private northeastern universities had agreed to offer the same financial aid packages to students, so that students' decisions on which institution to attend were based on factors other than the level of financial aid. This loan package arrangement was nothing more than an agreement on price; antitrust laws prohibit such agreements.

Answering the second question, "Is it balanced?" requires a manager to step back and view a problem from other perspectives—those of other parties, owners, shareholders, or the community. For example, an M&M/Mars cacao buyer was able to secure a very low price on cacao for his company because of pending government takeovers and political disruption. M&M/Mars officers decided to pay more for the cacao than the negotiated figure. Their reason was that some day their company would not have the upper hand, and then they would want to be treated fairly when the price became the seller's choice.

Answering "How does it make me feel?" requires a manager to do a self-examination of the comfort level of a decision. Some decisions, though they may be legal and may appear balanced, can still make a manager uncomfortable. For example, many managers feel uncomfortable about the "management" of earnings when inventory and shipments are controlled to maximize bonuses or to produce a particularly good result for a quarter. Although they have done nothing illegal, managers who engage in such practices often suffer such physical effects as insomnia and appetite problems. Known as the element of conscience, this test for ethics requires businesspeople to find the source of their discomfort in a particular decision.

The Front-Page-of-the-Newspaper Test

One very simple ethical model requires only that a decision maker envision how a reporter would describe a decision on the front page of a local or national newspaper. For example, with regard to the NBC News report on the sidesaddle gas tanks in GM pickup trucks, the *USA Today* headline read, "GM Suit Attacks NBC Report: Says show faked fiery truck crash." Would NBC have made the same decisions about its staging of the truck crash if that headline had been foreseen?

The validity of Martha Stewart's conviction for conspiracy and obstruction came into question when prosecutors charged their leading witness, Larry Stewart (no relation to Ms. Stewart), a forensics laboratory director and head of the U.S. Secret Service's forensics lab, with perjury. Mr. Stewart testified that he was directly involved in running the tests on ink used in documents prepared by Ms. Stewart's broker. In fact, he had not run the tests. Headlines read, "Witness in Martha Stewart Trial Charged with Perjury"[1] and "Could Martha Have a Get-out-of-Jail Card?"[2] Condensing conduct into a single phrase often gives a harsh dose of reality as well as an indication of consequences. In this case, the witness faced a criminal trial and a conviction was in jeopardy. This front-page-of-the-newspaper test helps with the analysis of ethical dilemmas by thinking through the consequences of a decision to act in a certain way.

When Salomon Brothers illegally cornered the U.S. government's bond market, the *Business Week* headline read, "How Bad Will It Get?"; nearly two years later, a follow-up story on Salomon's crisis strategy was headlined, "The Bomb Shelter That Salomon Built." During the aftermath of the bond market scandal, the interim chairman of Salomon, Warren Buffett, told employees, "Contemplating any business act, an employee should ask himself whether he would be willing to see it immediately described by an informed and critical reporter on the front page of his local paper, there to be read by his spouse, children, and friends. At Salomon we simply want no part of any activities that pass legal tests but that we, as citizens, would find offensive."[3]

Laura Nash and Perspective

Business ethicist Laura Nash has developed a series of questions that business managers should ask themselves as they evaluate their ethical dilemmas. One of the questions is, "How would I view the issue if I stood on the other side of the fence?" For example, in 1993, federal guidelines required meat to be cooked at 140 degrees Fahrenheit. At that time, however, Washington state proposed imposing a higher temperature requirement of 155 degrees. Burger King cooked its hamburgers at 160 degrees and Wendy's, Hardee's, and Taco Bell cooked their meat at 165 degrees.

Health and food industries experts supported a minimum cooking temperature of 155 degrees to be certain *E. coli* bacteria are eliminated. Jack-in-the-Box followed the legal minimum of 140 degrees. Would you want that information as a consumer? Given the trend toward higher temperatures and the pending regulation, would you want your meat cooked at a higher temperature? Although the cooking temperature was legal, there was an ethical issue of continuing to follow only the law when health experts felt there were concerns. Jack-in-the-Box did, in fact, experience an *E. coli* outbreak: one child died and three hundred other customers became ill.[4]

Other questions in the Nash model include: "Am I able to discuss my decision with my family, friends, and those closest to me?" "What am I trying to accomplish with my decision?" "Will I feel as comfortable about my decision over time as I do today?" The Nash model forces managers to seek additional perspectives as decisions are evaluated and implemented. For example, when William Aramony served as the CEO of United Way, he enjoyed such perks as an annual salary of close to $400,000, flights on the Concorde, and limousine service. Even though these benefits were about the same as those of other CEOs managing comparable assets, it would still be difficult to justify such benefits to a donor who earns $12,000 a year and has pledged 5 percent of it to United Way.

The *Wall Street Journal* Model

The *Wall Street Journal* model for resolution of ethical dilemmas consists of compliance, contribution, and consequences. Like the Blanchard–Peale model, any proposed conduct must first be in compliance with the law. The next step requires an evaluation of a decision's contributions to the shareholders, the employees, the community, and the customers. For example, furniture manufacturer Herman Miller decided both to invest in equipment that would exceed the requirements for compliance with the 1990 Clean Air Act and to refrain from using rainforest woods in producing its signature Eames chair. The decision was costly to the shareholders at first, but ultimately they, the community, and customers enjoyed the benefits.

Finally, managers are asked to envision the consequences of a decision, such as whether headlines that are unfavorable to the firm may result. The initial consequence for Miller's decisions was a reduction in profits because of the costs of the changes. However, the long-term consequences were the respect of environmental regulators, a responsive public committed to rainforest preservation, and Miller's recognition by *Business Ethics* as one of America's top twenty corporate citizens since 1992.

Explore the 1990 Clean Air Act:

http://www.law.cornell.edu/uscode/42/ch85.html

Other Models

Of course, there are much simpler models for making ethical business decisions. One stems from Immanuel Kant's categorical imperative, loosely similar to the Golden Rule, "Do unto others as you would have them do unto you." Treating others or others' money as we would want to be treated is a powerful evaluation technique in ethical dilemmas.

WHY WE FAIL TO REACH GOOD DECISIONS IN ETHICAL DILEMMAS

Very often, we look at the conduct of corporate executives, such as those in the opening Consider quiz, and wonder, "Where were their minds and what were they thinking when they decided to engage in such bad behavior?" Often those involved did not walk through the steps you have learned earlier in resolving ethical dilemmas. But, also, they slipped into rationalizations rather than analysis. The following sections provide a list and summary of each of the frequent statements of rationalization that we use to avoid facing ethical dilemmas (see Exhibit 2.1).

EXHIBIT 2.1 The Language of Rationalization

"Everybody else does it."

"If we don't do it, someone else will."

"That's the way it has always been done."

"We'll wait until the lawyers tell us it's wrong."

"It doesn't really hurt anyone."

"The system is unfair."

"I was just following orders."

"Everybody Else Does It"

When 15-year-old Jonathan Lebed was caught using many different screen names to post notices about the value of stocks he had purchased so that he could pump up their value and then sell them (pump and dump—see Chapters 8 and 22 for more details), he had made over $800,000 by taking advantage of others who believed the false notices posted. His father said that he was proud of his son because his son was doing what all the other analysts and investment firms on Wall Street were doing. "Everybody else does it" is a rationalization, but it is not an analysis of the ethical issues involved in conduct.

ETHICAL ISSUES

Since the time of his computer scam, Jonathan Lebed has finished high school, had a book written about him, appeared on *60 Minutes*, and is negotiating for the movie rights for the book. He also has his own Web site for his favorite stock picks, http://www.lebed.biz/. Mr. Lebed drives a $40,000 Mercedes. Does his experience tell you that adhering to ethics doesn't pay? Are there greater rewards for being unethical?

 CHECK THE WEB

When an example is used of an individual or company, always check the Web updates because there will be information about how the company is doing and what has happened to the individual since the time of the examples in the book.

"If We Don't Do It, Someone Else Will"

The rationalization of competition is that since someone will do it and make money, it might as well be us. For Halloween 1994, O. J. Simpson masks and plastic knives and Nicole Brown Simpson masks and costumes complete with slashes and bloodstains were offered for sale. When Nicole Simpson's family objected to this violation of the basic standard of decency, a costume-shop owner commented that if he didn't sell the items, someone down the street would. While nothing about the marketing of the costumes was illegal, ethical issues abound surrounding earning a profit from an event as heinous as the brutal murder of a young mother.

 CONSIDER...   **2 · 5**

Refer to the materials on companies on the Web site exercise for this chapter and read through their discussion of the issues, such as the environment, animal testing, and diversity. Do you see analysis of the ethical issues or do you see rationalization?

"That's the Way It Has Always Been Done"

Corporate or business history and business practices are not always sound. The fact that for years nothing has changed in a firm may indicate the need for change and an atmosphere that invites possible ethical violations. For example, until the Securities and Exchange Commission required corporate boards of directors compensation committees to make reports and to disclose the identities of their members, the sitting members of many of these committees had conflicts of interest. For example, a senior partner of a law firm who represented a given corporation often sat on that client's board and on its compensation committee. The result was that a lawyer whose firm was economically dependent on the corporation as a client was making salary determinations for the corporation's officers, who, of course, made the decisions about which law firm would represent their company. A conflict of interest existed, but everybody was doing it, and corporations had always been governed that way. Again, unquestioning adherence to a pattern of practice or behavior often indicates an underlying ethical dilemma.

Recently, with the failures of many dot-coms that did not follow time-tested guidelines for corporate structure, the issues of conflicts and sound practices have been raised. For example, Jeff Dachis, when questioned about why he had no outsiders on the board of Razorfish, the company he founded, responded, "I control 10 percent of the company. What's good for me is good for all shareholders. Management isn't screwing up. We've created enormous shareholder value." The company's stock premiered at $56 in June 1999 and by May 2001 was at $1.11 per share after revealing multimillion-dollar losses for 2000. Mr. Dachis was replaced as CEO in 2000, and the company added three outsiders to its board following the announcement of the losses. Razorfish and Mr. Dachis simply followed the patterns of the time, which included few or no outsiders on the board and a lack of independence on the board. While these practices may have followed what everyone was doing and the way they had always done things, they were not the best practices in keeping conflicts in check and in managing the company. For more discussion of board independence, see Chapter 21.

"We'll Wait until the Lawyers Tell Us It's Wrong"

Lawyers are trained to provide only the parameters of the law. In many situations, they offer an opinion that is correct in that it does not violate the law. Whether the conduct they have judged as legal is also ethical is a different question. Allowing law and lawyers to control a firm's destiny ignores the opportunity to make wise and ethical choices. For example, lawyers disagreed over whether the downloading of music over the Internet was a violation of copyright law. However, whether the downloading was legal does not answer the question of whether gaining access to and using someone else's intellectual property without permission or compensation were ethical.

"It Doesn't Really Hurt Anyone"

When we are the sole rubberneckers on the freeway, traffic remains unaffected. But if everyone rubbernecks, we have a traffic jam. If all of us made poor ethical choices, we would cause significant harm. A man interviewed after he was arrested for defrauding insurance companies through staged auto accidents remarked, "It didn't really hurt anyone. Insurance companies can afford it." The second part of his statement is accurate. The insurance companies can afford it—but not without cost to someone else. Such fraud harms all of us because we must pay higher premiums to allow insurers to absorb the costs of investigating and paying for fraudulent claims.

"The System Is Unfair"

Often touted by students as a justification for cheating on exams, this rationalization eases our consciences by telling us we are cheating only to make up for deficiencies in the system; yet just one person cheating can send ripples through an entire system. The credibility of grades and the institution come into question as students obtain grades through means beyond the system's standards. As we see events unfold in China, Italy, and Brazil, with government employees awarding contracts and rights to do business on the basis of payments rather than on the merits of a given company or its proposal, we understand how such bribery only results in greater unfairness within and greater costs to those countries. Many economists have noted that a country's businesses and economy will not progress without some fundamental assurance of trust.

"I Was Just Following Orders"

In many criminal trials and disputes over responsibility and liability, managers disclaim their responsibility by stating, "I was just following orders." There are times when individuals cannot follow the directions of supervisors, for they have been asked to do something illegal or immoral. Judges who preside over the criminal trials of war criminals often remind defendants that an order is not necessarily legal or moral. Values require us to question or depart from orders when others will be harmed or wronged. When the allegations of prisoner abuse in Iraq emerged, along with photos, one of the first defenses raised by lawyers for the soldiers being court-martialed for their role in the abuses was, "I was just following orders." Sometimes following orders is not the ethical thing to do.

SOCIAL RESPONSIBILITY: ANOTHER LAYER OF BUSINESS ETHICS

So far in this chapter we have covered two layers of business ethics, the basic categories as well as notions of fairness. But there is that third layer of ethics that focuses on relationships and conflicts among relationships.

In some ethical dilemmas in business, the interests of the shareholders might be different from the interests of the employees. Lower wages bring higher profits and returns, at least temporarily, to shareholders, but is shipping work overseas to countries where the wages are very low taking unfair advantage? In this third layer of business ethics, we look at the interests of those who are affected by business decisions, often called the stakeholders of the business. For example, suppose the business discovers that its air pollution control equipment is not state-of-the-art technology and that, although no laws are being violated, more pollution is being released than is necessary. To correct the problem, its factory must be shut down for a minimum of three months. The pollution will harm the air and the community, but the shutdown will harm the workers and the shareholders. The business must consider the needs and interests of all its stakeholders in resolving the ethical dilemma it faces. There has been much discussion and disagreement about this particular issue. In the following interview excerpt, economist Milton Friedman offers a different perspective on this ethical dilemma.

Q: Quite apart from emission standards and effluent taxes, shouldn't corporate officials take action to stop pollution out of a sense of social responsibility?

Milton Friedman: I wouldn't buy stock in a company that hired that kind of leadership. A corporate executive's responsibility is to make as much money for the shareholders as possible, as long as he operates within the rules of the game. When an executive decides to take action for reasons of social responsibility, he is taking money from someone else—from the stockholders, in the form of lower dividends; from the employees, in the form of lower wages; or from the consumer, in the form of higher prices. The responsibility of a corporate executive is to fulfill the terms of his contract. If he can't do that in good conscience, then he should quit his job and find another way to do good. He has the right to promote what he regards as desirable moral objectives only with his own money. If, on the other hand, the executives of U.S. Steel undertake to reduce pollution in Gary for the purpose of making the town attractive to employees and thus lowering labor costs, then they are doing the stockholders' bidding. And everyone benefits: The stockholders get higher dividends; the customer gets cheaper steel; the workers get more in return for their labor. That's the beauty of free enterprise. . . . To the extent that pollution caused by the U.S. Steel plant there is confined to that city and the people there are truly concerned about the problem, it's to the company's advantage to do something about it. Why? Because if it doesn't, workers will prefer to live where there is less pollution, and U.S. Steel will have to pay them more to live in Gary, Indiana.[5]

Ethical Postures for Social Responsibility

Often, decisions in dilemmas that involve stakeholders depend on the overall attitude of a company and its perspective on the role of business in society. The ethical perspective of a business often sets the tone for its operations and employees' choices. Historically, the philosophical debate over the role of business in society has evolved into four schools of thought on ethical behavior based on the responses to two questions: (1) Whose interest should a corporation serve? and (2) To whom should a corporation be responsive in order to best serve that interest? These questions have only two answers—"shareholders only" and "the larger society"—and the combination of those answers defines the school of thought. The following discussion is summarized in Exhibit 2.2.

Inherence
According to the inherence school of thought, managers answer only to shareholders and act only with shareholders' interests in mind. This type of manager would not become involved in any political or social issues unless it was in the shareholders' best interests to do so, provided the involvement did not backfire and cost the

---

EXHIBIT 2.2 Social Responsibility of Corporations

	MORAL QUESTION: WHOSE INTEREST SHOULD THE CORPORATION SERVE?	POLICY QUESTION: BEST WAY TO SERVE INTEREST IF THE CORPORATION IS RESPONSIVE TO:
Inherence	Shareholders only	Shareholders only
Enlightened self-interest	Shareholders only	Larger society
Invisible hand	Larger society	Shareholders only
Social responsibility	Larger society	Larger society

Source: Adapted with permission of *American Business Law Journal,* from Daryl Hatano, "Should Corporations Exercise Their Freedom of Speech Rights?" 22 A.B.L.J. 165 (1984).

firm sales. Milton Friedman's philosophy, as previously expressed, is an example of inherence. To understand how a business following the inherence school of thought would behave, consider the issue of a proposed increase in residential property taxes for school funding. A business that subscribes to the inherence school would support a school-tax increase only if the educational issue affected the company's performance and only if such a position did not offend those who opposed the tax increase.

Enlightened Self-Interest

According to this school of thought, the manager is responsible to the shareholders but serves them best by being responsive to the larger society. Enlightened self-interest is based on the view that, in the long run, business value is enhanced if business is responsive to the needs of society. In this school, managers are free to speak out on societal issues without the constraint of offending someone, as in inherence. Businesses would anticipate social changes and needs and be early advocates for change. For example, many corporations today have instituted job sharing, child-care facilities, and sick-child care in response to the changing structure of the American family and workforce. This responsiveness to the needs of the larger society should also be beneficial to shareholders because it enables the business to retain a quality workforce.

The Invisible Hand

The invisible hand school of thought is the opposite of enlightened self-interest. According to this philosophy, business ought to serve the larger society and it does this best when it serves the shareholders only. Such businesses allow government to set the standards and boundaries for appropriate behavior and simply adhere to these governmental constraints as a way of maximizing benefits to their shareholders. They become involved in issues of social responsibility or in political issues only when society lacks sufficient information on an issue to make a decision. Even then, their involvement is limited to presenting data and does not extend to advo-

---

CONSIDER...   2.6

Pepsico has an opportunity to expand into India. While Coca-Cola has had a presence in India, it has decided to pull out, and this billion-customer market remains untapped. Pepsico would work with the government to help farmers in India develop better techniques for producing crops and would provide jobs and job training in its bottling plants there so that it could help with the country's lagging economic development and poor nutrition. Nutrition among India's slum children in the urban areas and among most children in the rural areas is poor. Both income and food are limited.

Pepsico's market research shows that only a small percentage of the population in India, primarily in the cities, would have sufficient income to buy Pepsi soft drinks and Frito-Lay snacks. The vast majority of the population would have to spend about 20 percent of its weekly income to buy two Pepsi snacks.

Should Pepsico enter India and sell its products there? Wouldn't Pepsico play an important role in economic development? Which school of thought applies here? Would Pepsico be socially responsible by entering India with its products and programs or socially responsible by staying out of India?

cating a particular viewpoint or position. This school of thought holds that it is best for society to guide itself and that businesses work best when they serve shareholders within those constraints.

Social Responsibility

In the social responsibility school of thought, the role of business is to serve the larger society, which is best accomplished by being responsive to the larger society. This view is simply a reflection of the idea that businesses profit by being responsive to society and its needs. A business following this school of thought would advocate full disclosure of product information to consumers in its advertising and would encourage political activism on the part of its managers and employees on all issues, not just those that affect the corporation. These businesses adhere to the belief that their sense of social responsibility contributes to their long-term success.

WHY BUSINESS ETHICS?

Now that you have background on the types of ethical issues businesses face, background on social responsibility, and a framework for analysis of ethical issues, you may still be skeptical: "But why should a business worry about these things beyond just complying with the law? Why not just maximize under the system?" There are some compelling reasons for choosing ethical behavior, as discussed in the following sections.

Personal Accountability and Comfort: Business Ethics for Personal Reasons

Before looking at business data on the value of ethics, it is important to realize that the choices we make in our business lives must still feel personally comfortable. And it would be misleading to say that every ethical business is a profitable business. First, not all ethical people are good managers or possess the necessary skills for making a business a success; but there are many competent businesspeople who have suffered for being ethical and many others who seem to survive despite their lack of ethics. Columnist Dave Barry has noted that every time there is an oil spill, the oil companies ready themselves for the higher prices and profits that come because all that oil is lost at sea. Despite his conviction and jail term related to junk bond sales in the 1980s, Michael Milken recently earned a $50 million fee for helping Ted Turner negotiate a merger with Time Warner.[6] Many whistle-blowers, although highly respected, have been unable to find employment in their industries. If ethical behavior does not guarantee success, then why have ethics? The answer has to do with personal ethics applied in a business context. Ivan Boesky was once described as follows: "He beguiled everybody about his exhaustive research and canny stock analysis when he really made money the old-fashioned way. He stole it." Business ethics is really nothing more than a standard of personal behavior applied to a group of people working together to make a profit. Some people are ethical because it enables them to sleep better at night. Some people are ethical because of the fear of getting caught. But being personally ethical is a justification for business ethics—it is simply the correct thing to do. The parable of the Sadhu focuses on business ethics for personal reasons.

FOR THE MANAGER'S DESK

RE: THE PARABLE OF THE SADHU

[In 1982], as the first participant in the new six-month sabbatical program that Morgan Stanley has adopted, I enjoyed a rare opportunity to collect my thoughts as well as do some traveling. I spent the first three months in Nepal, walking 600 miles through 200 villages in the Himalayas and climbing some 120,000 vertical feet. On the trip my sole Western companion was an anthropologist who shed light on the cultural patterns of the villages we passed through.

During the Nepal hike, something occurred that has had a powerful impact on my thinking about corporate ethics. Although some might argue that the experience has no relevance to business, it was a situation in which a basic ethical dilemma suddenly intruded into the lives of a group of individuals. How the group responded I think holds a lesson for all organizations no matter how defined.

The Sadhu

The Nepal experience was more rugged and adventuresome than I had anticipated. Most commercial treks last two or three weeks and cover a quarter of the distance we traveled.

My friend Stephen, the anthropologist, and I were halfway through the 60-day Himalayan part of the trip when we reached the highpoint, an 18,000-foot pass over a crest that we'd have to traverse to reach the village of Muklinath, an ancient holy place for pilgrims.

Six years earlier I had suffered pulmonary edema, an acute form of altitude sickness, at 16,500 feet in the vicinity of Everest base camp, so we were understandably concerned about what would happen at 18,000 feet. Moreover, the Himalayas were having their wettest spring in 20 years; hip-deep powder and ice had already driven us off one ridge. If we failed to cross the pass, I feared that the last half of our "once in a lifetime" trip would be ruined.

The night before we would try the pass, we camped at a hut at 14,500 feet. In the photos taken at the camp, my face appears wan. The last village we'd passed through was a sturdy two-day walk below us, and I was tired.

During the late afternoon, four backpackers from New Zealand joined us, and we spent most of the night awake, anticipating the climb. Below we could see the fires of two other parties, which turned out to be two Swiss couples and a Japanese hiking club.

To get over the steep part of the climb before the sun melted the steps cut in the ice, we departed at 3:30 A.M. The New Zealanders left first, followed by Stephen and myself, our porters and Sherpas, and then the Swiss. The Japanese lingered in their camp. The sky was clear, and we were confident that no spring storm would erupt that day to close the pass.

At 15,500 feet, it looked to me as if Stephen were shuffling and staggering a bit, which are symptoms of altitude sickness. (The initial stage of altitude sickness brings a headache and nausea. As the condition worsens, a climber may encounter difficult breathing, disorientation, aphasia, and paralysis.) I felt strong, my adrenaline was flowing, but I was very concerned about my ultimate ability to get across. A couple of our porters were also suffering from the height, and Pasang, our Sherpa sirdar (leader), was worried.

Just after daybreak, while we rested at 15,500 feet, one of the New Zealanders, who had gone ahead, came staggering down toward us with a body slung across his shoulders. He dumped the almost naked, barefoot body of an Indian holy man—a sadhu—at my feet. He had found the pilgrim lying on the ice, shivering and suffering from hypothermia. I cradled the sadhu's head and laid him out on the rocks. The New Zealander was angry. He wanted to get across the pass before the bright sun melted the snow. He said, "Look, I've done what I can. You have porters and Sherpa guides. You care for him. We're going on!" He turned and went back up the mountain to join his friends.

I took a carotid pulse and found that the sadhu was still alive. We figured he had probably visited the holy shrines at Muklinath and was on his way home. It was fruitless to question why he had chosen this desperately high route instead of the safe, heavily traveled caravan route through the kali Gandaki gorge. Or why he was almost naked and with no shoes, or how long he had been lying in the pass. The answers were not going to solve our problem.

Stephen and the four Swiss began stripping off outer clothing and opening their packs. The sadhu was soon clothed from head to foot. He was not able to walk, but he was very much alive. I looked down the mountain and spotted below the Japanese climbers marching up with a horse.

Without a great deal of thought, I told Stephen and Pasang that I was concerned about withstanding the heights to come and wanted to get over the pass. I took off after several of our porters who had gone ahead.

On the steep part of the ascent where, if the ice steps had given way, I would have slid down about 3,000 feet, I felt vertigo. I stopped for a breather, allowing the Swiss to catch up with me. I inquired about the sadhu and Stephen. They said that the sadhu was fine and that Stephen was just behind. I set off again for the summit.

Stephen arrived at the summit an hour after I did. Still exhilarated by victory, I ran down the snow slope to congratulate him. He was suffering from altitude sickness, walking fifteen steps, then stopping, walking fifteen steps, then stopping. When I reached them,

Stephen glared at me and said: "How do you feel about contributing to the death of a fellow man?"

I did not fully comprehend what he meant.

"Is the sadhu dead?" I inquired.

"No," replied Stephen, "but he surely will be!"

After I had gone, and the Swiss had departed not long after, Stephen had remained with the sadhu. When the Japanese had arrived, Stephen had asked to use their horse to transport the sadhu down to the hut. They had refused. He had then asked Pasang to have a group of our porters carry the sadhu. Pasang had resisted the idea, saying that the porters would have to exert all their energy to get themselves over the pass. He had thought they could not carry a man down 1,000 feet to the hut, reclimb the slope, and get across safely before the snow melted. Pasang had pressed Stephen not to delay any longer.

The Sherpas had carried the sadhu down to a rock in the sun at about 15,000 feet and had pointed out the hut another 500 feet below. The Japanese had given him food and drink. When they had last seen him he was listlessly throwing rocks at the Japanese party's dog, which had frightened him.

We do not know if the sadhu lived or died.

For many of the following days and evenings Stephen and I discussed and debated our behavior toward the sadhu. Stephen is a committed Quaker with deep moral vision. He said, "I feel that what happened with the sadhu is a good example of the breakdown between the individual ethic and the corporate ethic. No one person was willing to assume ultimate responsibility for the sadhu. Each was willing to do his bit just so long as it was not too inconvenient. When it got to be a bother, everyone just passed the buck to someone else and took off. Jesus was relevant to a more individualist stage of society, and how do we interpret his teaching today in a world filled with large, impersonal organizations and groups?"

I defended the larger group, saying, "Look, we all cared. We all stopped and gave aid and comfort. Everyone did his bit. The New Zealander carried him down below the snow line. I took his pulse and suggested we treat him for hypothermia. You and the Swiss gave him clothing and got him warmed up. The Japanese gave him food and water. The Sherpas carried him down to the sun and pointed out the easy trail toward the hut. He was well enough to throw rocks at a dog. What more could we do?"

"You have just described the typical affluent Westerner's response to a problem. Throwing money—in this case food and sweaters—at it, but not solving the fundamentals!" Stephen retorted.

"What would satisfy you?" I said. "Here we are, a group of New Zealanders, Swiss, Americans, and Japanese who have never met before and who are at the apex of one of the most powerful experiences of our lives. Some years the pass is so bad no one gets over it. What right does an almost naked pilgrim who chooses the wrong trail have to disrupt our lives? Even the Sherpas had no interest in risking the trip to help him beyond a certain point."

Stephen calmly rebutted, "I wonder what the Sherpas would have done if the sadhu had been a well-dressed Nepali, or what the Japanese would have done if the sadhu had been a well-dressed Asian, or what you would of done, Buzz, if the sadhu had been a well-dressed Western woman?"

"Where, in your opinion," I asked instead, "is the limit of our responsibility in a situation like this? We had our own well-being to worry about. Our Sherpa guides were unwilling to jeopardize us or the porters for the sadhu. No one else on the mountain was willing to commit himself beyond certain self-imposed limits."

Stephen said, "As individual Christians or people with a Western ethical tradition, we can fulfill our obligations in such a situation only if (1) the sadhu dies in our care, (2) the sadhu demonstrates to us that he could undertake the two-day walk down to the village, or (3) we carry the sadhu for two days down to the village and convince someone there to care for him."

"Leaving the sadhu in the sun with food and clothing, while he demonstrated hand-eye coordination by throwing a rock at a dog, comes close to fulfilling items one and two," I answered. "And it wouldn't have made sense to take him to the village where the people appeared to be far less caring than the Sherpas, so the third condition is impractical. Are you really saying that, no matter what the implications, we should, at the drop of a hat, have changed our entire plan?"

The Individual versus the Group Ethic

Despite my arguments, I felt and continue to feel guilt about the sadhu. I had literally walked through a classic moral dilemma without fully thinking through the consequences. My excuses for my actions include a high adrenaline flow, a superordinate goal, and a once-in-a-lifetime opportunity—factors in the usual corporate situation, especially when one is under stress.

Real moral dilemmas are ambiguous, and many of us hike right through them, unaware that they exist. When, usually after the fact, someone makes an issue of them, we tend to resent his or her bringing it up. Often, when the full import of what we have done (or not done) falls on us, we dig into a defensive position from which it is very difficult to emerge. In rare circumstances we may contemplate what we have done from inside a prison.

Had we mountaineers been free of physical and mental stress caused by the effort and the high altitude, we might have treated the sadhu differently. Yet isn't stress the true test of personal and corporate values? The instant decisions executives make under pressure reveal the most about personal and corporate character.

continued

Among the many questions that occur to me when pondering my experience are: What are the practical limits of moral imagination and vision? Is there a collective or institutional ethic beyond the ethics of the individual? At what level of effort or commitment can one discharge one's ethical responsibilities?

Not every ethical dilemma has a right solution. Reasonable people often disagree; otherwise there would be no dilemma. In a business context, however, it is essential that managers agree on a process for dealing with dilemmas.

The sadhu experience offers an interesting parallel to business situations. An immediate response was mandatory. Failure to act was a decision in itself. Up on the mountain we could not resign and submit our résumé to a headhunter. In contrast to philosophy, business involves action and implementation—getting things done. Managers must come up with answers to problems based on what they see and what they allow to influence their decision-making processes. On the mountain, none of us but Stephen realized the true dimensions of the situation we were facing.

One of our problems was that as a group we had no process for developing a consensus. We had no sense of purpose or plan. The difficulties of dealing with the sadhu were so complex that no one person could handle it. Because it did not have a set of preconditions that could guide its action to an acceptable resolution, the group reacted instinctively as individuals. The cross-cultural nature of the group added a further layer of complexity. We had no leader with whom we could identify and in whose purpose we believed. Only Stephen was willing to take charge, but he could not gain adequate support to care for the sadhu.

Some organizations do have a value system that transcends the personal values of the managers. Such values, which go beyond profitability, are usually revealed when the organization is under stress. People throughout the organization generally accept its values, which, because they are not presented as a rigid list of commandments, may be somewhat ambiguous. The stories people tell, rather than printed materials, transmit these conceptions of what is proper behavior.

For twenty years I have been exposed at senior levels to a variety of corporations and organizations. It is amazing how quickly an outsider can sense the tone and style of an organization and the degree of tolerated openness and freedom to challenge management.

Organizations that do not have a heritage of mutually accepted, shared values tend to become unhinged during stress, with each individual bailing out for himself. In the great takeover battles we have witnessed during past years, companies that had strong cultures drew the wagons around them and fought it out, while other companies saw executives, supported by their golden parachutes, bail out of the struggles.

Because corporations and their members are interdependent, for the corporation to be strong the members need to share a preconceived notion of what is correct behavior, a "business ethic," and think of it as a positive force, not a constraint.

As an investment banker I am continually warned by well-meaning lawyers, clients, and associates to be wary of conflicts of interest. Yet if I were to run away from every difficult situation, I wouldn't be an effective investment banker. I have to feel my way through conflicts. An effective manager can't run from risk either; he or she has to confront and deal with risk. To feel "safe" in doing this, managers need the guidelines of an agreed-on process and set of values within the organization.

After my three months in Nepal, I spent three months as an executive-in-residence at both Stanford Business School and the Center for Ethics and Social Policy at the Graduate Theological Union at Berkeley. These six months away from my job gave me time to assimilate twenty years of business experience. My thoughts turned often to the meaning of the leadership role in any large organization. Students at the seminary thought of themselves as antibusiness. But when I questioned them they agreed they distrusted all large organizations, including the church. They perceived all large organizations as impersonal and opposed to individual values and needs. Yet we all know of organizations where people's values and beliefs are respected and their expressions encouraged. What makes the difference? Can we identify the difference and, as a result, manage more effectively?

The word "ethics" turns off many and confuses more. Yet the notions of shared values and an agreed-on process for dealing with adversity and change—what many people mean when they talk about corporate culture—seem to be at the heart of the ethical issue. People who are in touch with their own core beliefs and the beliefs of others and are sustained by them can be more comfortable living on the cutting edge.

At times, taking a tough line or a decisive stand in a muddle of ambiguity is the only ethical thing to do. If a manager is indecisive and spends time trying to figure out the "good" thing to do, the enterprise may be lost.

Business ethics, then, has to do with authenticity and integrity of the enterprise. To be ethical is to follow the business as well as the cultural goals of the corporation, its owners, its employees, and its customers. Those who cannot serve the corporate vision are not authentic business people and, therefore, are not ethical in the business sense.

At this stage of my own business experience I have a strong interest in organizational behavior. Sociologists are keenly studying what they call corporate stories, legends, and heroes as a way organizations have of transmitting the value system. Corporations such as Arco have even hired consultants to perform an audit of their corporate culture. In a company, the leader is the person who understands, interprets, and manages the corporate value system. Effective managers are then action-oriented people who resolve conflict, are tolerant of ambiguity, stress, and change, and have a strong sense of purpose for themselves and their organizations.

If all this is true, I wonder about the role of the professional manager who moves from company to company. How can he or she quickly absorb the values and culture of different organizations? Or is there, indeed, an art of management that is totally transportable? Assuming such fungible managers do exist, is it proper for them to manipulate the values of others?

What would have happened had Stephen and I carried the sadhu for two days back to the village and become involved with the villagers in his care? In four trips to Nepal my most interesting experiences occurred in 1975 when I lived in a Sherpa home in the Khumbu for five days recovering from altitude sickness. The high point of Stephen's trip was an invitation to participate in a family funeral ceremony in Manang. Neither experience had to do with climbing the high passes of the Himalayas. Why were we so reluctant to try the lower path, the ambiguous trail? Perhaps because we did not have a leader who could reveal the greater purpose of the trip to us.

Why didn't Stephen with his moral vision opt to take the sadhu under his personal care? The answer is because, in part, Stephen was hard-stressed physically himself, and because, in part, without some support system that involved our involuntary and episodic community on the mountain, it was beyond his individual capacity to do so.

I see the current interest in corporate culture and corporate value systems as a positive response to Stephen's pessimism about the decline of the role of the individual in large organizations. Individuals who operate from a thoughtful set of personal values provide the foundation of a corporate culture. A corporate tradition that encourages freedom of inquiry, supports personal values, and reinforces a focused sense of direction can fulfill the need for individuality along with the prosperity and success of the group. Without such corporate support, the individual is lost.

That is the lesson of the sadhu. In a complex corporate situation, the individual requires and deserves the support of the group. If people cannot find such support from their organization, they don't know how to act. If such support is forthcoming, a person has a stake in the success of the group, and can add much to the process of establishing and maintaining a corporate culture. It is the management's challenge to be sensitive to individual needs, to shape them, and to direct and focus them for the benefit of the group as a whole.

For each of us the sadhu lives. Should we stop what we are doing and comfort him; or should we keep trudging up toward the high pass? Should I pause to help the derelict I pass on the street each night as I walk by the Yale Club en route to Grand Central Station? Am I his brother? What is the nature of our responsibility if we consider ourselves to be ethical persons? Perhaps it is to change the values of the group so that it can, with all its resources, take the other road.

Discussion Question

Consider the closing questions Mr. McCoy poses. How do they apply to you personally and to businesses?

ETHICAL ISSUES

Consider the following statistics and evaluate where you stand on the conduct described.

A survey by O'Neill Associates reveals the following statistics.

- 75 percent of working adults overstate facts on their employment application.
- 70 percent of working adults have called in sick when they really were not sick.
- 6 percent of working adults have blamed a co-worker for a problem when it was truly their fault.
- 76 percent of working adults believe we do personal things during work time.
- 21 percent of working adults say that they have used company facilities or materials for personal tasks.

A study of résumé fraud includes these two findings.

- 22 percent of all résumés contain fraudulent information.
- That figure has doubled since 1998.

A study of workers' reactions to being asked to do something against their standards disclosed the following information.

- 25 percent of working adults were asked during the past year to do something that violated their personal ethical standards.
- 41 percent of those asked to do something that violated their personal ethical standards did it.
- 40 percent tried to resolve the situation without losing their jobs.
- 39 percent did talk to their bosses about it before doing anything.
- 5 percent quit.

Why do people falsify their résumés? Do the statistics on the workplace show employees are trying to solve problems as Bowen McCoy suggests?

IMPORTANCE OF VALUES IN BUSINESS SUCCESS

As you learn in other disciplines, from economics to management, business is driven by the bottom line. Profits control whether the firm can obtain loans or gain investors and serve as the sole indicator of the firm's success—and, in most cases, its employees' success, as well. Indeed, business firms can be defined as groups of people working together to obtain maximum profits. The pursuit of the bottom line, however, can occasionally distort the perspective of even the most conscientious among us. The fear of losing business and, consequently, losing profits and capital support can persuade people to engage in conduct that, although not illegal, is unethical. But those who pursue only the bottom line fail to recognize that a successful business is more like a marathon than a sprint, requiring that ethical dilemmas be resolved with a long-term perspective in mind. Indeed, those firms that adhere to ethical standards perform better financially over the long run.

Visit the Markkula Center for Applied Ethics at Santa Clara University:
http://www.scu.edu/ethics

A 1997 study on the relationship between corporate behavior and financial performance concluded that firms involved in regulatory or criminal violations or product liability litigation because of an unsafe product experience lower returns and slower sales growth even five years after their problems in these areas occur.[7]

The Tylenol tampering incident of 1982 offers one of the most telling examples of the rewards of being ethical. When Tylenol capsules were discovered to have been tainted with deadly poison, Tylenol's manufacturer, McNeil Consumer Products Company, a subsidiary of Johnson & Johnson, followed its code of ethics, which required it to put the interests of the consumer first. In what many financial analysts and economists considered to be a disastrous decision and a dreadful mistake, McNeil recalled all Tylenol capsules from the market—31 million bottles with a retail value of about $100 million. A new and safer form of a noncapsule Tylenol caplet was developed, and within a few months Tylenol regained its majority share of the market. The recall had turned out to be neither a poor decision nor a financial disaster. Rather, the company's actions enhanced its reputation and served to create a bond between Tylenol and its customers that was based largely on trust and respect for the integrity of the company and the product. (See "Leadership's Role in Ethical Choices" for further discussion of this issue.)

In contrast to the positive nature of ethical behavior is unethical behavior. For example, companies in the defense contracting business who were part of the spending and overcharging scandal several years ago are still reeling from the charges, struggling to regain credibility. Beech-Nut suffered tremendous earnings losses as a result of the discovery that its baby food "apple juice" did not in fact contain any real apple juice. Nestlé has endured many consumer boycotts since the early 1970s as a result of its intense—and what came to be perceived by the public as exploitative and unethical—marketing of infant formula in then–Third World nations, where the lack of sanitation, refrigeration, and education led to serious health problems in infants given the formula. In 1989, nearly twenty years after the infant formula crisis, Nestlé's new "Good Start" formula was slow in market infiltration and, because of continuing consumer resistance, did not perform as well as its quality and innovativeness would have predicted. Nestlé has never gained the market share or reputation its quality product deserves. As the Nestlé experience illustrates, a firm's reputation for ethical behavior is the same as an individual's reputation: It takes a long time to gain, but it can be lost instantly as the result of one bad choice.

Visit Beech-Nut:
http://www.beechnut.com

In 1992, Texaco was rocked by the disclosure of tape-recorded conversations among three executives about a racial discrimination suit pending against the company. The lawsuit involved 1,500 employees and alleged a pattern of discrimination by Texaco as well as a hostile environment. The tape-recorded conversations, although subsequently established as containing errors, quoted one executive as saying (accurately), "I'm still having trouble with Hanukkah. Now, we have Kwanza. (Laughter.)" (see Chapter 20). Several groups declared a boycott against Texaco, with a resulting $3 per share drop in the stock's value. Within days, Peter Bijur, Texaco's then-CEO, pledged to eliminate discrimination and settled the lawsuit for $176 million. Mr. Bijur's pledge ended the boycott and restored both earnings and stock value.

Visit Salomon Brothers, Inc.:
http://www.
salomonsmithbarney.com

Salomon Brothers, Inc., became the target of an eleven-month probe after it was discovered that Salomon bond traders were controlling the U.S. Treasury bond market through prearranged transactions using major customers' names. Almost immediately after the news of Salomon's cornering of the bond market appeared in national papers, there was a $29 million drop in earnings for one quarter. Further, Salomon paid $122 million in fines, was given a two-month suspension from bond trading, and was required to establish a $100 million fund to compensate other firms hurt by the cornering of the bond market. Bausch & Lomb and Enron executives and employees overstated company earnings, which were subsequently revealed in audits as accounting irregularities. Both companies experienced drops in share prices, sales, and earnings. Enron declared bankruptcy.

During the early 1990s, the financial returns on investments in derivative securities were enticing. Many firms, from Procter & Gamble through Gibson Greetings to Barings Bank, joined the bandwagon to invest in these risky ventures, which offered high returns, but which, if leveraged, could bring disaster if the high stakes turned against the firm. The risk and high exposure of these investment mechanisms were not disclosed to shareholders or the public. When the markets turned, the investments went bad and the firms experienced large financial write-offs or even, in the case of Barings Bank, bankruptcy. The firms now face lawsuits from shareholders and customers, and the Securities and Exchange Commission now strictly regulates derivatives through required, detailed disclosures (see Chapter 22 for more details).

*Visit the U.S. Securities and
Exchange Commission:*
http://sec.gov

Orange County, California, had invested heavily in derivatives and was heavily leveraged when the derivatives market turned the wrong way for its portfolio. The result was a reorganization in bankruptcy for the county. A financial newsletter commented, "It was the biggest orgy of bond speculation in world history." A professional surfer from Huntington Beach offered his views on the county's bankruptcy: "It all comes down to greed."

*Visit Orange County,
California:*
http://www.oc.ca.gov

The poor value choices of the aforementioned firms resulted in tremendous financial setbacks and, in some cases, destruction. The core values of a firm give it long-standing profitability. "The Tony Bennett Factor" offers some insight into longevity, profitability, and values.

In 1989, the Exxon oil tanker *Valdez* ran aground in Alaska's Prince William Sound, and 11 million gallons of crude oil leaked into Alaska's waters and onto its shores. Evidence of cutbacks in crews and maintenance levels for tankers dogged Exxon as the cleanup litigation continued through 1996. The Exxon name suffered because of its association with oil spills. Further, Congress permanently banned the *Valdez* from Prince William Sound.

Visit General Motors:
http://www.gm.com

As General Motors prepared to release its Chevrolet Malibu for production in 1976, an engineer drafted a memo about some issues with the placement of the car's gas tank and the likelihood of its explosion in the event of a rear-end collision. The memo discussed both the potential liability for such accidents and the costs of modifying the design. The Malibu went forward without production and design changes.

By 1981, there was some litigation related to rear-end collisions involving the Malibu and gas tank explosions. A lawyer working on the cases found the 1976 memo and explained the need to keep the engineer's thoughts and analysis from being disclosed. In December 1999, a jury awarded the victims of a Malibu rear-end collision and explosion over $107 million compensatory damages and $4.8 billion punitive damages (later reduced to $1.2 billion on appeal) and explained that its high damage verdict was directly attributable to the memo, the knowledge and the failure to disclose that information or take corrective action.

FOR THE MANAGER'S DESK

RE: THE TONY BENNETT FACTOR

I had blocked out the background noise offered courtesy of MTV and my teenager, but I glanced up and saw Tony Bennett. My parents raised me on Tony Bennett LPs back in the '50s. "I Left My Heart in San Francisco" enjoyed hours of play in Tyrone, Pa. And here he was back, "Tony Bennett Unplugged."

Mr. Bennett has not changed. Yet his success has spanned generations. Suddenly my work with a colleague, Prof. Louis Grossman, had new meaning. We had been studying business longevity, trying to determine what makes some businesses survive so successfully for so long.

Prof. Grossman and I began our study when we spotted a 1982 full-page ad in this newspaper placed by Diamond Match Co. The ad touted the company's 100 years of consistent dividend payments. Today's standards tell us that 100 quarters of dividend payments would be stellar. What kind of company was this? Were there others?

We discovered seven other industrial firms that could boast of making at least an annual dividend payment for a string of 100 years or more: Scovill, Inc.; Ludlow Corp.; Stanley Works; Singer Co.; Pennwalt, Inc.; Pullman, Inc.; and Corning Glass Works. Pullman, Ludlow and Stanley had unbroken chains of a century of quarterly dividend payments as well.

Mr. Bennett and our eight companies have survival in common. These survivors' tools make management theories of today seem trite. They had no shifting paradigms. No buzzwords.

Mr. Bennett recognized his strength as a balladeer and stuck with it, through everything from the Beatles to Hootie and the Blowfish. Although each of our companies recognized the importance of diversification, they all held fast to a WBAWI—or "what business are we in?"—philosophy. They knew their strengths, developed strong market presences based on those strengths and never forgot their roots. Mr. Bennett never performed without singing "I Wanna Be Around." Singer never left its sewing machines. Pullman never deserted its train cars. Diamond held on to its matches.

The firms diversified only when their strengths allowed. Scovill began as a brass button manufacturer and backed into brass manufacturing because it knew brass. Scovill bought Hamilton Beach because Hamilton Beach was a major brass purchaser. Scovill understood this customer's business.

Other companies have forgotten the WBAWI lesson and paid the price. Sears abandoned its catalog, insurance and real estate businesses and now struggles to find a retail presence. IBM has suffered for not understanding its business was the workplace, not mainframe computers. Its Lotus takeover shows it may recognize the PC as the workplace.

All Mr. Bennett needs are a microphone and a pianist to make music. All eight of our companies were low-cost producers. All eight were cost conscious. Scovill executive vice presidents with worldwide responsibilities shared a secretary. Spartan company headquarters were the rule for these firms. There were barely six-figure salaries for executives. By contrast, IBM's Louis Gerstner hired an executive chef at $120,000 just last month.

Mr. Bennett has used the same musical arranger for nearly 30 years. Our eight companies' management team histories are in direct contrast to the executive recruiting practices in vogue today. Scovill, founded during the Jefferson administration in 1803, had only 12 CEOs during its 100-year dividend run. Three of the companies (Singer, Stanley and Diamond) had CEOs who served for more than 40 years. Seven of the companies never had a CEO serve for fewer than 10 years. They were not afraid of home-grown management. Their officers and CEOs came up through the ranks. Management succession is found in all eight companies.

Perhaps this information demonstrates the importance of continuity and stability. The executives appreciated the tension between short-term results and long-term performance, but the short term did not control decision making. Donald Davis, chairman and CEO of Stanley Works, put it this way: "The tension is always there. One of the top management's toughest jobs really is to mediate between the two viewpoints—short-term profit results now versus investment for future development."

Mr. Bennett did and does spend time on the road in concert, in direct contact with audiences—no mega-tours, just constant gigs. And a full century before we heard of customer service, these firms sent their sales forces and vice presidents alike out on the road to talk directly with customers. They had interesting marketing studies: one-on-one feedback. Sales calls, follow-ups, replacements, and refunds allowed them to remain in the customers' minds and good graces.

One officer said it best: "Anyone can read the monthly financial reports: What we need to do is to interpret them so we can spot trends. We call on customers, on suppliers, we look at the bottom line of course, but we know how that line reached the bottom."

Mr. Bennett has never made a bad recording or disappointed during a live performance. Our eight firms had strong commitments to integrity. Their mantra was: "If there's integrity, there will be quality and profits." Their integrity manifested itself in more than just quality. Frederick T. Stanley, founder of Stanley Works, spoke of the intricate balance between automation and employ-ees: "Machines are no better than the skill, care, ingenuity and spirit of the men who operate them. We can achieve perfect harmony when shortening of an operation provides mutual advantages to the workman and the producers." Ethics before its time. Re-engineering done correctly in the 1800s. Nothing at the expense of the customer or the employee.

Our firms were no less remarkable than Mr. Bennett and his success with Generation X—his third generational conquest. The sad part of their stories is what happened following the takeover battles of the '80s. But that is a story for another time. For now, it is reassuring to realize that cost-consciousness, focus, customer service, home-grown management and integrity are keys to longevity. Today's management fads seem as shallow as Ice-T and Madonna. There is a simple Tony Bennett factor in success that makes today's fads much easier to debunk and infinitely easier to question.

BUSINESS STRATEGY APPLICATION

Be sure to look at this chapter's Web site exercise that allows you to research companies on the Internet and determine whether they have long-term qualities.

CONSIDER...   2.7

The companies mentioned in the chapter's opening Consider problem (Tyco, Enron, HealthSouth, and WorldCom) were relatively young companies. Enron had been in existence only since the 1990s, and WorldCom was not founded until the late 1980s. Tyco took over many older companies that were then gutted and no longer doing business. Now Enron is in bankruptcy. WorldCom and HealthSouth are trying to emerge from Chapter 11 bankruptcy. All the companies and/or their executives have been charged with financial improprieties. What conclusions can you reach about these companies, their financial misdeeds, and their survival?

Ethics as a Strategy

Ethical behavior not only increases long-term earnings; it also enables businesses to anticipate and plan for social needs and cultural changes that require the firm or its product to evolve. One of the benefits of a firm's ethical behavior and participation in community concerns is the goodwill that such involvement fosters. Conversely, the absence of that goodwill and consequent loss of trust can mean the destruction of the firm.

When methyl isocyanate gas leaked from the Union Carbide plant in Bhopal, India, in 1984, the deadly gas left over 2,500 dead and 200,000 injured. It was later discovered that there had been problems in the plant with some of the equipment designed to prevent such leaks. While actual liability issues were hotly debated in court, many ethical questions were raised regarding the plant and Union Carbide. Was it a wise decision to build the plant in a country with little expertise in the relevant technology? Did the people in the town know of the potential dangers of the plant? Why was a city of shacks allowed to be erected so close to the plant?

According to the Indian government, the plant had been operated well within legal and regulatory requirements, and Union Carbide's management had been cooperative in installing any additional equipment needed. Should Union Carbide have done more than was legally required? Did the plant operators need more training for such emergencies? Finally, the Bhopal incident raises many questions about the relationship between U.S. businesses and their operations in developing countries that may not be prepared to deal with the latest technologies and may not be fully informed about the associated risks.

The Value of a Good Reputation

A reputation, good or bad, stays with a business or an individual for a long time. Richard Teerlink, the former CEO of Harley-Davidson, has said, "A reputation, good or bad, is tough to shake." Another executive, lamenting his chances to try again, commented, "Would anybody let Roseanne sing the national anthem again?" Once a company makes poor ethical choices, it carries the baggage of those choices despite successful and sincere efforts to reform. Salt Lake City struggled to regain its credibility as the trials from the bribery allegations surrounding its winning the bid for the 2002 Winter Olympics progressed and companies withdrew sponsorships. Businesses were, at that time, unsure about the reputations and trustworthiness of those running the Salt Lake City Olympic operations. It took new leadership and a commitment to high ethical standards from Mitt Romney, now the governor of Massachusetts, to restore confidence in the Salt Lake City 2002 Winter Olympics.

Leadership's Role in Ethical Choices

George Fisher, the former CEO of Motorola and Kodak, has defined leadership as the ability to see around corners. In other words, a leader sees a problem before it becomes a legal issue or liability and fixes it, thus saving company time and money. All social, regulatory, and litigation issues progress along a timeline. As the issue is brought to the public's attention, either by stories or by the sheer magnitude of the problem, the momentum for remedies and reforms continues until behavior is changed and regulated. Ethical choices afford firms opportunities to take positions ahead of the curve. Firms can choose to go beyond the law and perhaps avoid regulation that might be costly or litigation that can be devastating. For example, the issues relating to the problems with asbestos dust in the lungs of asbestos workers and installers were clear in the 1930s. More studies needed to be done, but there was sufficient evidence to justify lung protection for workers and the development of alternative forms of insulation. However, the first litigation relating to asbestos and asbestos workers did not arise until 1968. For that thirty-year period, those in the business of producing and selling asbestos insulation products had the opportunity to take preventive actions. They chose to wait out the cycle. The result was a ban on asbestos and litigation at levels that forced the largest producer, Johns-Manville (now Manville), into bankruptcy. Leadership choices were available in the 1930s for offering warnings, providing masks, and developing alternative insulators. Johns-Manville chose to continue its posture of controlling information releases and studies. The liability issue progressed to a point of no choice other than bankruptcy and reorganization.

Every business regulation that exists today controls business conduct in an area where there was once no control but, rather, the opportunity for businesses to self-regulate by making good value choices. Before Congress and the Federal Trade Commission imposed requirements about credit disclosures (see Chapter 15), lenders and creditors had the option of designing their own disclosure forms and providing full information to buyers and debtors. That option was not chosen, and the result is a full scheme of regulation, including forms and advertising requirements. More recently, the problems resulting from a lack of candor in auto-leasing agreements have resulted in federal regulation of contracts in this consumer area. In spring 2001, all companies that issue credit cards began an expensive campaign to send all customers a right-to-privacy notice. Customers had to be given a choice as to when, how, and whether they wanted information about them and their spending habits used or disclosed. This expensive regulatory compliance effort resulted from too many companies using information about their customers without permission. That information was sold to other companies so that the customers could be specifically and successfully target-marketed based on their spending patterns. Consumer protests and litigation resulted in complex compliance and disclosure requirements that, in turn, led to substantial costs for doing business. Giving customers the right to protect their privacy from the outset would have eliminated the need for the substantial costs of compliance.

Ethical choices give businesses the freedom to make choices before regulators mandate them. Breaches of ethics bring about regulation and liability with few opportunities to choose and less flexibility. The notion of choices and leadership are diagrammed in Exhibit 2.3.

Every issue progresses along a cycle that begins with a *latency* phase, in which the industry is aware of a problem. The use of private information about consumers' buying patterns was well known in the marketing industry, but few

Visit the U.S. Federal Trade Commission:
http://www.ftc.gov

EXHIBIT 2.3 Leadership and Ethics: Making Choices before Liability

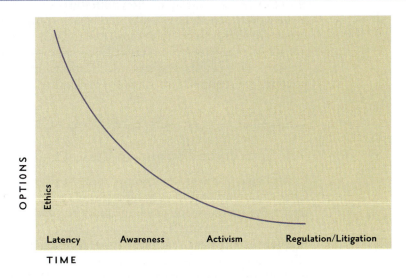

Source: Adapted from James Frierson's "Public Policy Forecasting: A New Approach," *SAM Advanced Management Journal,* Spring 1985, pp. 18–23.

consumers were aware of that use. The *awareness* stage begins when the popular press reports on an issue and raises questions. Once the public has knowledge of a problem, it responds by demanding assurance that the problem either is resolved or is not really an issue—or by calling for reform. The *activism* stage is one in which members of the public ask for either voluntary or regulatory reform. If voluntary reform is not forthcoming, those affected may sue or lobby for reform, or both. For example, a group of parents, police officers, and shareholders protested Time Warner's production of "Cop Killer," a song by the rap music artist Ice-T. The public outcry was strong both in the press and at Time Warner's shareholder meeting. Congress was considering holding hearings on record labels and record content. Time Warner eventually made a choice to voluntarily withdraw the song, later in the regulatory cycle when public outcry was strong but still in time to avert regulation. It is important to understand that Time Warner could have made the choice not to publish the Ice-T's song initially.

During 2004, the public again became active in demanding changes in the content of entertainment when Janet Jackson and Justin Timberlake's performance at the half-time show at the Super Bowl resulted in partial nudity on prime-time television. Entertainment and television executives undertook voluntary controls to prevent government controls. For example, the televised Academy Awards were on a five-second delay so that any mishaps could be edited out before broadcast. Some artists were not permitted to appear on awards shows because of their past behaviors on similar shows. Memos were sent to artists and actors asking them to show restraint in their behavior and comments. In another example, in 2004, Clear Channel Communications removed Howard Stern from its stations because of controversial content in Mr. Stern's syndicated radio show.

Few people realize one aspect of the Tylenol poisonings case (noted earlier in the chapter), which is that the issue of tamper-proof packaging had been a concern in the industry long before the poisonings involving Tylenol occurred. Those in the industry were concerned that packaging that did not signal unauthorized entry so that a buyer could spot tampering could open the door to the tragedy that eventually occurred. However, no one in the industry, despite knowledge of this issue, took steps to create tamper-proof packaging. The law did not require such a step; additional costs were associated with the packaging and retooling production; and some were worried that they would be at a competitive disadvantage if their products were harder to use than those that did not have the tamper-proof packages. By not solving the problem voluntarily, companies faced unpleasant results: First, the tragedy of the deaths, and second, additional regulations and costs imposed as the government required tamper-proof packaging.

CREATION OF AN ETHICAL CULTURE IN BUSINESS

The Tone at the Top and an Ethical Culture

Ethics begin at the top of a company. A business must have from its board and its CEO a commitment to earning a profit *within ethical boundaries*. Employees work under the pressures of meeting quarterly and annual goals and can make poor choices if the company's priority with respect to values and ethics is not made clear. Employees must see that those who evaluate and pay them really do care about ethics. Employees are convinced that ethics is important when they see officers comply with all of the provisions in the company code of ethics. They see the right tone at the top when ethical employees are rewarded and unethical conduct is punished. The tone at the top comes from actions by officers and executives that show they "walk the talk" about ethics.

Sarbanes–Oxley and an Ethical Culture

Following the collapses of Enron, WorldCom, and other companies noted in the chapter's opening Consider, Congress passed the most extensive reforms of corporate governance and financial reporting since the enactment of the 1933 and 1934 securities laws following the 1929 stock market crash.

While Sarbanes-Oxley has imposed many requirements on accountants, lawyers, directors, and officers (covered in Chapters 9 and 22), it also mandated the Federal Sentencing Commission to examine the types of things companies could do that would improve the ethical culture, thereby reducing the risk of misconduct and earning sentence reductions for companies that attempt to create an ethical culture but still have an ethical or legal lapse.

The Sentencing Commission determined that factors such as the following would be helpful in setting the tone of the company:

- A code of ethics
- Training for employees in the code and in ethics
- A means for employees to report misconduct anonymously
- Follow-up on reports employees make on misconduct
- Action by the board, including follow-up and monitoring, on complaints and reports made by employees
- Self-reporting and investigation of legal and ethical issues
- Sanctions and terminations for those within the company who violate the law and company rules, including officers
- A high-ranking officer, with the ability to communicate with the CEO and board, who is responsible for the code of ethics and ethics training in the company

> **BUSINESS PLANNING TIP**
>
> If you were to survey the best practices of companies on ethical cultures, you would find the following, according to a 2003 study by the Ethics Resource Center:
>
> The four key elements to a company with a good ethical culture are: (1) written standards of conduct, (2) ethics training, (3) ethics advice lines or offices, and (4) systems for anonymous reporting of misconduct.
>
> The study reported that 67 percent of large companies have all four components, but only 41 percent of smaller companies do.
>
> There is still much work to do. Only 56 percent of nonmanagement employees say that they would report an ethical or legal violation if they saw one.

The guidelines established do incorporate the factors most experts agreed were critical to setting an ethical culture in a company.

Reporting Lines: An Anonymous Ethics Line for an Ethical Culture

Most companies have either an ombudsperson or a hotline, or both, to which employees can anonymously report ethical violations. The anonymous reporting line is a minimum requirement for companies in this post-Sarbanes-Oxley era. In addition to encouraging employees to discuss issues with their supervisors, most companies now have some means by which employees can raise issues anonymously because there may still be fear and concern that their jobs are at stake. Under the sentencing guidelines, companies that can show they fostered an atmosphere in which employees were encouraged to come forward will fare much better in terms of fines and other punishments if there are any missteps. In order to encourage employees to report problems, companies have developed tools to heighten employee awareness of ethics and encourage them to raise concerns. Many companies have developed ethical news bulletins to offer employees examples of and guidelines on ethical dilemmas. Du Pont delivers an ethics bulletin to employees through its e-mail system. Blue Cross/Blue Shield has given employees Slinky toys for their desks with the hotline reporting number on them so that as employees think and perhaps use the Slinky to relieve pressure and stress, they will be reminded to report any problems.

BUSINESS STRATEGY

The Ethical Culture Executive: Ethics and Compliance Officers

More companies have ethics officers. Nearly one-third of these ethics officers are lawyers by training, and nearly 100 percent of them have been with their companies for fifteen years or more. Nearly all fellow employees describe their companies' ethics officers as "respected and trusted." All ethics officers report either to the board of directors, the CEO, or a senior vice president.

Of these ethics officers' investigations of complaints or allegations:

© PHOTODISC/GETTY IMAGES

- 44 percent result in positive changes in the organization's policies.
- 18 percent result in conveying information about company policies to employees.
- 38 percent required no changes in policies or further action.

Having an ethics officer is a positive factor in the federal corporate sentencing guidelines. Most companies report reduced fines when their own ethics officers' internal investigations result in self-reporting of conduct.

Developing an Ethics Stance

Both individuals and firms should decide up front what types of conduct they would never engage in and be certain that the rules are in writing, that everyone understands the rules, and that the rules will be enforced uniformly. Individuals can vary in their responses to various ethical dilemmas. For example, a woman who had taken $12,000 from her employer was terminated immediately upon the company's discovery of the embezzlement. At the company's next board meeting, the board members discussed the issue and had varying views. One director felt that taking something that does not belong to you is wrong and that termination was the appropriate action. Another director said that his remedy would be determined by whether the money was taken all at once or over a period of time. Another director said that his remedy would be determined according to why the employee took the money. Still another director noted that perhaps the employee did not understand that this type of action is wrong. The directors varied in their views on ethics. One is pragmatic—it is simply wrong. Another applies a relative approach—why did she take the money? Exhibit 2.4 diagrams the ethical stances of the directors.

Knowing where you stand as a company sends clear signals to employees. Knowing where you stand as an individual sends clear signals for the behavior of those around you. Taking a position on a set of values helps a company avoid the

EXHIBIT   2.4   Your Ethics Stance: The Embezzling Employee

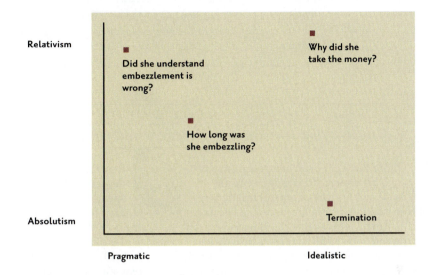

Source: Developed from Professor Patricia Pattison's presentation, "Teaching Ethics," Academy of Legal Studies in Business Annual Meeting, August 11–15, 1994, Dallas, Texas, and adapted from "Teaching Ethics" by D. R. Forsych, *Journal of Personality and Social Psychology.*

either/or conundrum in which tough situations are boiled down to something such as, "Either we release this product now with its flaws and meet the deadline and start getting earnings, or we don't and the company collapses." A value-based decision is one that says, "We as a company do not cheat our customers with poorly designed or manufactured products, and we don't hurt them with defective ones. Because of that value, we retool quickly to correct the problem and get the product out there as soon as possible." With this value-based decision, the company also makes a good business decision, for it has chosen to avoid the often destructive costs of releasing a defective product when there is knowledge of that defect. The GM Malibu case discussed earlier represents the destructive costs of deciding not to take action based on values but, rather, taking action based only on immediate returns.

ETHICAL ISSUES

A Condé Nast survey on ethics produced some interesting results:
- 64 percent of all women admitted they had cheated in some way in their lives.
- 75 percent of all men admitted they had cheated in some way in their lives.
- 25 percent of all the respondents in the survey believed men are "bigger cheaters."
- 16 percent said they had cheated with money matters or taxes.
- 59 percent said they had cheated with money matters or taxes because they believed they could get away with it.
- 24 percent said they had cheated with money matters or taxes because everyone else was doing it.

- For those who had not cheated, 98 percent of the women and 96 percent of the men said it was because of their individual sense of morals; 85 percent of the women and 72 percent of the men said it was because they did not want to hurt others; and 81 percent of the women and 72 percent of the men said cheating would cheapen the accomplishments they had achieved.
- Fear of getting caught was cited as the reason for not cheating among 19 percent of the women and 11 percent of the men.

Do you have any explanations for the data? Why do you think there are gender differences?

CHECK THE WEB

More surveys and studies are added on a regular basis. Check the Web site under Chapter 2 to see the latest in the new research on ethics and business and other types of ethics studies.

BIOGRAPHY

THE ENRON TRAGEDY FOR THE OFFICER WHO GOT OUT ON TIME: CLIFF BAXTER

Clifford Baxter, the son of a police officer, held his undergraduate degree from NYU and his MBA from Columbia. Mr. Baxter rose through the ranks of Enron to become its Vice Chairman. He was a model Houston citizen with a wife and two children and was heavily involved in community service. Ironically, his passion was Junior Achievement, a friend said, through which he hoped to help make sure that young people "understood the values of the free enterprise system."* Mr. Baxter left Enron in August 2001, shortly after Sherron Watkins, the famous whistle-blower, sent her memo on concerns about Enron's financial position, to Chairman Ken Lay. She had indicated in that memo that Mr. Lay should talk to Mr. Baxter if he wanted verification of the teetering financial condition of the company. Mr. Baxter sold most of his Enron stock at that time; thus, he avoided losing everything (as most Enron employees did) as the stock price dropped from $83 per share to just pennies per share. Mr. Baxter sold 577,000 shares of Enron stock between October 1998 and early 2001, for a total of $35.2 million. Enron released a statement upon Mr. Baxter's departure that he had taken early retirement to spend more time with his family. Enron began its long collapse in the fall of 2001 and by the end of the year, the company was in bankruptcy. Most of the senior officers in the company were indicted. However, Mr. Baxter was found dead in his 2001 Mercedes of a self-inflicted gunshot wound to the head at an area just a few miles from his suburban Houston home.†

What do you learn from this tragic story? What do you think caused Mr. Baxter to commit suicide? Wasn't it enough that he quit his job? Do you think the millions that he made by selling his stock affected him?

*Jim Yardley and Sheila K. Dewan, "*Despite His Qualms, Scandal Engulfed Executive,*" New York Times, January 27, 2002, p. 27.
†Jim Yardley, "*Critic Who Quit Top Enron Post Is Found Dead,*" New York Times, January 26, 2002, p. A1. Mary Babineck, "*Deceased Enron Executive Earned Respect in the Ranks,*" Houston Chronicle, January 26, 2002, at www.chron.com.

Being Careful about Pressure and Signals

There have been more earnings restatements filed with the Securities and Exchange Commission (SEC) from 2002 to 2004 than in the history of the SEC. Companies have examined their financial reports because of the collapse of Enron and World-Com (companies mentioned in the chapter's opening Consider) and concluded that perhaps they too have crossed some ethical lines in the way they have been reporting their revenues and profits. Following these corrections, the companies have done some introspection and determined that often they had company practices or sent signals to employees that led to their employees pushing the envelope in terms of financial reporting. Doing the right and ethical thing often got lost in the pressures employees felt with respect to goals and number quotas. These types of signals create a pressured environment in which employees fall into ethical lapses that often lead to illegal behavior. Here are a few signs of such an atmosphere of pressure that is ripe for unethical behavior.

1. Competition is so intense that business survival is threatened.

   Example: The Consider 2.3 example cited earlier in the chapter showed how Boeing got caught in this scenario.

2. Managers make poor judgments.

   Example: Chrysler executives had the odometers from their company cars disconnected so that the cars could later be sold as new.

3. Employees have few or no personal values.

   Example: Personal ethics are left at the company door because, as ethicist Albert Carr says, "Business is business," just as poker is poker.

4. Employees respond only to earnings demands. No constraints are placed on how the earnings are achieved.

   Example: At WorldCom, former CEO Bernard Ebbers described his business strategy as, "Our goal is not to capture market share or be global. Our goal is to be the No. 1 stock on Wall Street."[8] A special report commissioned by the bankruptcy court of WorldCom and created by former U.S. Attorney General Dick Thornburgh refers to WorldCom as a "culture of greed."[9]

   The following is an excerpt from 1997 that even reduces the numbers to a "per employee" basis for earnings:

   > *On a pro forma basis, total revenues increased over 30 percent on volume gains of 35 percent. WorldCom's efficiency in SG&A per revenue dollar is not at the expense of effectiveness, as the Company once again outstripped its major competitors with its ability to add incremental year-over-year internal revenue growth of $1.7 billion for the year. WorldCom continues to lead with the productivity of its employees. On average, each employee generates over $500,000 of revenue per year, based on 1997 results.[10]*

   In his 1998 report, Mr. Ebbers wrote that operating income rose 132 percent from 1997 to 1998, sales increased to $800 billion, and the price of WorldCom's stock rose 137 percent.[11] By 1999, Mr. Ebbers had little but numbers in his letter in the annual report: Internet business for WorldCom was up 57 percent, its data business was up 27 percent, its international business was up 53 percent, and its increase in net income was 217 percent.[12]

5. Managers and executives have been touting to analysts, investors, and the business media how well their company has been doing. In many cases, the reports by executives proclaim double-digit growth and make promises that

CONSIDER...   2 . 8

Top management must continue to emphasize that, above all, employees must perform within the ethical boundaries established by the company's code of ethics. When the state of California revealed that its undercover investigation of Sears Auto Centers found repeated patterns of unnecessary repairs, then-CEO Ed Brennan stated that employees had made mistakes by making poor choices. The pay incentive systems in the auto centers were tied to the receipts from repairs and sales of parts, and such an incentive system conflicted with the values established by Sears. Somehow the employees failed to grasp that the ethical standards were to take priority. Top management's continued emphasis on ethics can take the form of ongoing training and seminars in ethics for all employees. How does Sears change its ethical culture from the one that made the mistakes in the auto centers?

the company will continue the same pattern. Employees feel significant pressure to perform.

Example: Employees at HealthSouth (another company featured in the chapter's opening Consider) had tremendous pressure placed upon them to meet the numbers. In April 1998, CEO Richard Scrushy announced, with great fanfare, that HealthSouth had matched or beat earnings estimates for 47 quarters in a row.[13]

ETHICAL ISSUES IN INTERNATIONAL BUSINESS

The global market presents firms with more complex ethical issues than they would experience if operations were limited to one country and one culture. Moral standards vary across cultures. In some cases, cultures change and evolve to allow conduct that was not previously acceptable. For example, it is permissible in India for donors to sell body organs for transplantation. Residents of India have sold their kidneys to buy televisions or just to increase their standard of living. In the United States, the buying and selling of organs by donors is not permitted, but recently experts have called for such a system as a means of resolving the supply-and-demand dilemma that exists because of limited availability of donors and a relative excess of needy recipients.

In many executive training seminars for international business, executives are taught to honor customs in other countries and to "Do as the Romans do." Employees are often confused by this direction.

A manager for a U.S. title insurer provides a common example. He complained that if he tipped employees in the U.S. public-recording agencies for expediting property filings, the manager would not only be violating the company's code of ethics but could be charged with violations of the Real Estate Settlement Procedures Act and state and federal antibribery provisions. Yet that same type of practice is permitted, recognized, and encouraged in other countries as a cost of doing business. Paying a regulatory agency in the United States to expedite a licensing process would be bribery of a public official. Yet many businesses maintain that they cannot obtain such authorizations to do business in other countries unless such payments are made. So-called grease or facilitation payments are permitted under the Foreign Corrupt Practices Act (see Chapter 9), but legality does not necessarily make such payments ethical.

An inevitable question arises when custom and culture clash with ethical standards and moral values adopted by a firm. Should the national culture or the company code of ethics control?

Typical business responses to the question of whether cultural norms or company codes of ethics should control in international business operations are: Who am I to question the culture of another country? Who am I to impose U.S. standards on all the other nations of the world? Isn't legality the equivalent of ethical behavior? The attitude of businesses is one that permits ethical deviations in the name of cultural sensitivity. Many businesses fear that the risk of offending those in other countries is far too high to impose U.S. ethical standards on the conduct of business in other countries.

The successful operation of commerce depends on the ethical roots of business. A look at the three major parties in business explains this point. These parties are the risk-takers, the employees, and the customers. Risk-takers—those furnishing the capital necessary for production—are willing to take risks on the assumption that their products will be judged by customers' assessment of

CONSIDER...   2 . 9

Transparency International publishes an annual index of perceptions of corruption. Business executives are asked to rank countries on a scale from 1 to 10, with 10 being the least corrupt. The results for 2002 are as follows.

Corruption Perceptions Index (Transparency International, 2002)

Least Corrupt	Most Corrupt
Finland	Bangladesh
Denmark	Nigeria
New Zealand	Paraguay
Iceland	Madagascar
Singapore	Angola
Sweden	Kenya
Canada	Indonesia
Luxembourg	Azerbaijan
Netherlands	Uganda
United Kingdom	Moldova
Australia	Haiti
Norway	Ecuador
Switzerland	Cameroon
Hong Kong	Bolivia
Austria	Kazakhstan
United States	Vietnam

Why do you think the index appears as it does? Is there a correlation between economic development or its absence and corruption?

their value. Employees are willing to offer production input, skills, and ideas in exchange for wages, rewards, and other incentives. Consumers and customers are willing to purchase products and services so long as they receive value in exchange for their furnishing, through payment, costs and profits to the risk-takers and employees. To the extent that the interdependency of the parties in the system is affected by factors outside of their perceived roles and control, the intended business system does not function on its underlying assumptions.

The business system is, in short, an economic system endorsed by society that allows risk-takers, employees, and customers to allocate scarce resources to competing ends.

Although the roots of business have been described as primarily economic, this economic system cannot survive without recognition of some fundamental values. Some of the inherent—indeed, universal—values built into our capitalistic economic system, as described here, are as follows: (1) the consumer is given value in exchange for the funds expended; (2) employees are rewarded according to their contribution to production; and (3) the risk-takers are rewarded for their investment in the form of a return on that investment. Exhibit 2.5 depicts this relationship. Everyone in the system must be ethical. An economic system is like a four-legged stool. If corruption seeps into one leg, the economic system is off balance. In international business, very often the government slips into corruption with bribes controlling which businesses are permitted to enter the country and who is awarded contracts in that

BUSINESS PLANNING TIP

A new trend among international firms is to adopt international codes of ethics. For example, employees who are given gifts as part of cultural rituals must give them to the company. They are then donated to charity.

EXHIBIT   2.5   The Interdependence of Trust, Business, and Government

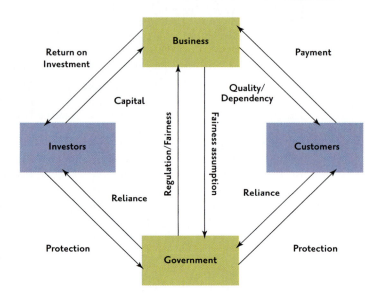

country. In the United States, the current wave of reforms at the federal level is the result of perceived corruption by businesses in their economic operations.

To a large extent, all business is based on trust. The tenets for doing business are dissolved as an economy moves toward a system in which one individual can control the market in order to maximize personal income.

Suppose, for example, that the sale of a firm's product is determined not by perceived consumer value but, rather, by access to consumers, which is controlled by government officials. That is, your company's product cannot be sold to consumers in a particular country unless and until you are licensed within that country. Suppose further that the licensing procedures are controlled by government officials and that those officials demand personal payment in exchange for your company's right to even apply for a business license. Payment size may be arbitrarily determined by officials who withhold portions for themselves. The basic values of the system have been changed. Consumers no longer directly determine the demand.

Beyond just the impact on the basic economic system, ethical breaches involving grease payments introduce an element beyond a now-recognized component in economic performance: consumer confidence in long-term economic performance. Economist Douglas Brown has described the differences between the United States and other countries in explaining why capitalism works here and not in all nations. His theory is that capitalism depends on an interdependent system of production. For economic growth to proceed, consumers, risk-takers, and employees must all feel confident about the future, about the concept of a level playing field, and about the absence of corruption. To the extent that consumers, risk-takers, and employees feel comfortable about a market driven by these basic assumptions, the investment and commitments necessary for economic growth via capitalism will be made. Significant monetary costs are incurred by business systems based on factors other than customer value, as discussed earlier.

In developing countries where there are "speed" or grease payments and resulting corruption by government officials, the actual money involved may not be significant in terms of the nation's culture. Such activities and payments introduce an element of demoralization and cynicism that thwarts entrepreneurial activity when these nations most need risk-takers to step forward.

Bribes and *guanxi* (gifts) in China given to establish connections with the Chinese government are estimated at 3 to 5 percent of operating costs for companies, totaling $3 billion to $5 billion of 1993's foreign investment. But China incurs costs from the choices government officials make in return for payments. For example, *guanxi* are often used to persuade government officials to transfer government assets to foreign investors for substantially less than their value. Chinese government assets have fallen over $50 billion in value during the same period of economic growth, primarily because of the large undervaluation by government officials in these transactions with foreign companies. China's economy was adrift because of this underlying corruption. Economic progress began with graft's elimination.

Perhaps Italy and Brazil provide the best examples of the long-term impact of foreign business corruption. While the United States, Japan, and Great Britain have scandals such as the savings and loan failures, political corruption, and insurance regulation, these forms of misconduct do not indicate corruption that pervades entire economic systems. The same cannot be said about Italy. Elaborate connections between government officials, the Mafia, and business executives were unearthed in the 1990s. As a result, half of Italy's cabinet resigned at one time, and hundreds of business executives were indicted. It has been estimated that the interconnections of these three groups cost the Italian government $200 billion, as well as compromising the completion of government projects.

In Brazil, the level of corruption has led to a climate of murder and espionage. Many foreign firms have elected not to do business in Brazil because of so much uncertainty and risk—beyond the normal financial risks of international investment. Why send an executive to a country where officials may use force when soliciting huge bribes?

The *Wall Street Journal* offered an example of how Brazil's corruption has damaged the country's economy despite growth and opportunity in surrounding nations. The governor of the northeastern state of Paraiba in Brazil, Ronaldo Cunha Lima, was angry because his predecessor, Tarcisio Burity, had accused Mr. Lima's son of corruption. Mr. Lima shot Mr. Burity twice in the chest while Mr. Burity was having lunch at a restaurant. The speaker of Brazil's Senate praised Mr. Lima for his courage in doing the shooting himself as opposed to sending someone else. Mr. Lima was given a medal by the local city council and granted immunity from prosecution by Paraiba's state legislature. No one spoke for the victim, and the lack of support reflected a culture controlled by self-interest that benefits those in control. Unfortunately, these self-interests preclude economic development.

Economists in Brazil document hyperinflation and systemic corruption. A Sao Paulo businessman observed, "The fundamental reason we can't get our act together is we're an amoral society." This businessperson probably understands capitalism. Privatization that has helped the economies of Chile, Argentina, and Mexico cannot take hold in Brazil because government officials enjoy the benefits of generous wages and returns from the businesses they control. The result is that workers are unable to earn enough even to clothe their families, 20 percent of the Brazilian population lives below the poverty line, and crime has reached levels of nightly firefights. Brazil's predicament has occurred over time, as graft, collusion, and fraud have become entrenched in the government-controlled economy.[14]

SUMMARY

What is ethics?

- Behavior beyond the law
- Day-to-day nature of ethics

What is business ethics?

- Moral standards—standards of behavior set by culture
- Moral obligations—standards of behavior set by natural law
- Moral relativism—moral standards by situation

What are the categories of ethical dilemmas in business?

- Taking things that don't belong to you
- Saying things you know are not true
- Giving or allowing false impressions
- Buying influence or engaging in conflict of interest
- Hiding or divulging information
- Taking unfair advantage
- Committing acts of personal decadence
- Perpetrating interpersonal abuse
- Permitting organizational abuse
- Violating rules
- Condoning unethical actions
- Balancing ethical dilemmas

How do employees resolve ethical dilemmas?

- Blanchard and Peale
- Front-page-of-the-newspaper test
- *Wall Street Journal* and stakeholders
- Laura Nash and perspective
- Categorical imperative

Why do we fail to reach good ethical decisions?

- "Everybody else does it."
- "If we don't do it, someone else will."

- "That's the way it has always been done."
- "We'll wait until the lawyers tell us it's wrong."
- "It doesn't really hurt anyone."
- "The system is unfair."
- "I was just following orders."

What is social responsibility and how does a business exercise it?

- Positive law—codified law
- Inherence—serves shareholders' interests
- Enlightened self-interest—serves shareholders' interest by serving larger society
- Invisible hand—serves larger society by serving shareholders' interests
- Social responsibility—serves larger society by serving larger society

Why is business ethics important?

- Profit
- Leadership
- Reputation
- Strategy

How does a business create an ethical atmosphere?

- Tone at the top
- Sarbanes-Oxley and corporate sentencing guidelines
- Code of ethics
- Reporting hotlines
- Ethical posture and developing an ethical stance

What are the ethical issues in international business?

- Corruption issues
- Economic systems and ethics

QUESTIONS AND PROBLEMS

1. E&J Gallo, the world's largest winery, has just announced that it will stop selling its Thunderbird and Night Train Express wines in the Tenderloin, the skid row of San Francisco, for six months. Gallo took the action after meeting with an activist group called Safe and Sober Streets, which has asked grocers to remove the high-alcohol wine from the district, where citizens say drunks create a menace. One retailer in the district said, "If I don't sell this, I will have to close my doors and go home."

Discuss the actions of Gallo and the dilemma of the retailers in the district. Be sure to discuss the type of philosophy each of them holds with respect to social responsibility and ethical dilemmas.

2. Paul Backman is the head of the purchasing department for L. A. East, one of the "Baby Bells" that came into existence after the divestiture of AT&T. Mr. Backman and his department purchase everything for the company, from napkins to wires for equipment lines.

S. C. Rydman is an electronics firm and a major supplier for L. A. East since 1984. Rydman is also the cosponsor of an exhibit at Wonder World, a theme park in Florida.

Rydman's vice president and CFO, Gunther Fromme, visited Mr. Backman in his office on April 3, 2004. Rydman had no bids pending at that time, and Mr. Fromme told Mr. Backman that he was there "for goodwill." Mr. Fromme explained that Rydman had a block of rooms at Wonder World because of its exhibit there and that Mr. Backman and his group could use the rooms at any time, free of charge.

Should Mr. Backman and his employees use the block of rooms? Why or why not?

3. The Association for Competitive Technology (ACT) is a trade group funded largely by Microsoft Corporation. During Microsoft's antitrust trial, ACT was active in public relations as it worked to convince everyone from the public to members of Congress that the antitrust case would thwart innovation in computers, software, and their uses.

Lawrence J. Ellison, chairman of Oracle Corporation, a software manufacturer and Microsoft competitor, was concerned that the public might not understand that ACT was funded by Microsoft and was not truly an independent group. Mr. Ellison and Bill Gates, the chairman of Microsoft, were known as fierce competitors and often referred to as each others' nemesis. Through Oracle, Mr. Ellison hired Group International, a private investigation firm headed by Terry Lenzner (who became famous for his work on the Watergate investigation during the Nixon administration and also for his work President Clinton's lawyers during the Paula Jones civil suit for sexual harassment). Group International was to find information tying Microsoft to ACT. Mr. Ellison described his hiring of Group International as his "civic duty."

Shortly after Group International was hired by Oracle, janitors working the night shift at the offices of ACT were offered $50–$60 each by Blanca Lopez, a woman who worked for Lenzner, if they would turn over ACT's trash to her rather than dumping it. The janitors refused, and Ms. Lopez returned the next evening and offered them $500 each for the trash plus $200 extra to the supervisor if he could convince the janitors to cooperate. All of the staff declined. Ms. Lopez left them her card, explained that she was working on a criminal case, and asked if they changed their minds.

When the janitors disclosed what had happened and the investigator was traced back to Mr. Ellison, he said, "All we did was to try to take information that was hidden and bring it into the light. I don't think that's arrogance. That's a public service."

Mr. Ellison also offered to box up all of Oracle's trash and send it to Mr. Gates in Redmond, Washington, noting, "We believe in full disclosure."

Do you think what Oracle did was legal? Do you think it was ethical? How do you evaluate Mr. Ellison's claim that he was performing a civic responsibility?

4. Old Joe Camel, originally a member of a circus that passed through Winston-Salem, North Carolina, each year, was adopted by R. J. Reynolds (RJR) marketers in 1913 as the symbol for a brand being changed from "Red Kamel" to "Camel." In the late 1980s, RJR revived Old Joe with a new look in the form of a cartoon. He became the camel with a "Top Gun" flier jacket, sunglasses, a smirk, and a lot of appeal to young people.

In December 1991, the *Journal of the American Medical Association (JAMA)* published three surveys that found the cartoon character Joe Camel reached children very effectively. Of children between the ages of 3 and 6 who were surveyed, 51.1 percent of them recognized old Joe Camel as being associated with Camel cigarettes.[15] The 6-year-olds were as familiar with Joe Camel as they were with the Mickey Mouse logo for the Disney Channel. The surveys also established that 97.7 percent of students between the ages of 12 and 19 had seen Old Joe and 58 percent thought the ads he was used in were cool. Camel was identified by 33 percent of the students who smoked as their favorite brand.[16]

Before the survey results appeared in *JAMA,* the American Cancer Society, the American Heart Association, and the American Lung Association had petitioned the FTC to ban the ads as "one of the most egregious examples in recent history of tobacco advertising that targets children."[17]

In 1990, Camel shipments rose 11.3 percent. Joe Camel helped RJR take its Camel cigarettes from 2.7 percent to 3.1 percent of the market.

Joe Tye, founder of Stop Teenage Addictions to Tobacco, has stated, "There is a growing body of evidence that teen smoking is increasing. And it's 100 percent related to Camel."[18]

Dr. John Richards summarized the study as follows: "The fact is that the ad is reaching kids, and it is changing their behavior."[19]

RJR spokesman David Fishel responded to the allegations with sales evidence: "We can track 98 percent of Camel sales; and they're not going to youngsters. It's simply not in our best interest for young people to smoke, because that opens the door for the government to interfere with our product."

Former U.S. Surgeon General Antonia Novello was very vocal in her desire to change alcohol and cigarette advertising. In March 1992, she called for the withdrawal of the Joe Camel ad campaign: "In years past R. J. Reynolds would have us walk a mile for a Camel. Today it's time we invite old Joe Camel himself to take a hike."[20]

The Centers for Disease Control reported in March 1992 that smokers between the ages of 12 and 18 prefer Marlboro, Newport, or Camel cigarettes, the three brands with the most extensive advertising.[21]

Teenagers throughout the country were wearing Joe Camel T-shirts. Brown & Williamson, the producer of Kool cigarettes, began testing a cartoon character for its ads, a penguin wearing sunglasses and Day-Glo sneakers. Company spokesman Joseph Helewicz stated that the ads are geared to smokers between 21 and 35 years old. Mr. Helewicz added that cartoon advertisements for adults are not new and cited the Pillsbury Doughboy and the Pink Panther as effective advertising images.

In mid-1992, then–Surgeon General Novella, along with the American Medical Association, began a campaign called "Dump the Hump" to pressure the tobacco industry to stop ad campaigns that teach kids to smoke. In 1993, the FTC staff recommended a ban on the Joe Camel ads. In 1994, then–Surgeon General Joycelyn Elders blamed the tobacco industry's $4 billion in ads for increased smoking rates among teens. RJR's tobacco division chief, James W. Johnston, responded, "I'll be damned if I'll pull the ads." RJR put together a team of lawyers and others it referred to as in-house censors to control Joe's influence. A campaign to have Joe wear a bandana was nixed, as was one for a punker Joe with pink hair.

Lawyers in a California suit against RJR discovered charts from a presentation at a September 30, 1974, Hilton Head, South Carolina, retreat of RJR top executives and board. The charts offered the following information:

Company	Brand	Share of 14- to 24-Year-Old Market
Philip Morris	Marlboro	33%
Brown & Williamson	Kool	17%
Reynolds	Winston	14%
Reynolds	Salem	9%

RJR's then–vice president of marketing, C. A. Tucker, said, "As this 14–24 age group matures, they will account for a key share of total cigarette volume for at least the next 25 years." The meeting then produced a plan for increasing RJR's presence among the under-35 age group, which included sponsoring NASCAR auto racing. Another memo described plans to study "the demographics and smoking behavior of 14-to-17 year olds." Internal documents about targeting young people were damaging. A 1981 RJR internal memo on marketing surveys cautioned research personnel to tally underage smokers as "age 18." A 1981 Philip Morris internal document indicated information about smoking habits in children as young as 15 was important because "today's

teen-ager is tomorrow's potential regular customer." Other Philip Morris documents from the 1980s expressed concerns that Marlboro sales would soon decline because teenage smoking rates were falling.

By late 1997, RJR began phasing out Joe Camel. New Camel ads featured men and women in their 20s, with a healthy look, in clubs and swimming pools, with just a dromedary logo somewhere in the ad. Joe continued as a youth icon. RJR also vowed not to feature the Joe Camel character on nontobacco items such as T-shirts. The cost of the abandonment was estimated at $250 million.

Philip Morris proposed its own plan to halt youth smoking in 1996, which includes no vending machine ads, no billboard ads, no tobacco ads in magazines with 15 percent or more of youth subscribers, and limits on sponsorships to events (rodeos, motor sports) where 75 percent or more of attendees are adults.

In 1998, combined pressure from Congress, the state attorneys general, and ongoing class action suits produced what came to be known as "the tobacco settlement." In addition to payment of $206 billion, the tobacco settlement in all of its various forms bars outdoor advertising, the use of human images (Marlboro man) and cartoon characters, and vending-machine sales.

Suppose you were the executive in charge of marketing for RJR. Would you have recommended an alternative to the Joe Camel character? What if RJR insisted on the Joe Camel ad?

Suppose you work with a pension fund that has a large investment in RJR. Would you consider selling your RJR holdings? Strategically, did RJR make a good business decision on Joe Camel ads?

Source: "Joe Camel Shills to Kids," *USA Today.* Copyright June, 1997. Reprinted with permission.

5. Chateau Giscours, a French winemaker, has been charged by the French government with adding cheap wine to its chateau wine. The allegations state that wines from two different vintages were mixed together and then sold as the more expensive vintage. In addition, the charges from the French government allege that the winemaker added excess sugar to increase the wine's alcohol content and that wood chips were used to give the wine the taste and smell of wine that had been aged in oak barrels.

The charges followed a two-year undercover investigation that included wine experts who were used to determine whether the practices were a one-time event or part of an ongoing pattern. The investigation began following a tip on the use of oak chips, but the investigation of the oak chips led to other issues.

Currently, the market of Bordeaux wines is at a pace and level that no one could have predicted. Competition among the sixty-one chateaus that produce wine is intense.

Why did the winemaker add the chips and sugar? What ethical issues do you see in the allegations? In the chateau wine industry?

6. Burns & McCallister, an international management consulting firm, is listed by *Working Mother* magazine as one of the top fifty firms in the United States for employment of working mothers and is listed as one of the top ten firms for women by *Working Woman* magazine. Burns & McCallister has earned this reputation for several reasons. First, nearly 50 percent of its partners are women. Second, the firm has a menu of employee benefits that include such things as flexible hours, sabbaticals, family leave, home-based work, and part-time partner-track positions.

However, Burns & McCallister has recently been the subject of a series of reports by both the *Los Angeles Times* and the *New York Times* because its policy on female executives in certain nations has become public. Burns & McCallister has learned, through its fifty years of consulting, that in certain countries in which they negotiate for contracts, women cannot be used in the negotiation process. The culture of many of these countries is such that women are not permitted to speak in a meeting of men. Burns & McCallister has thus implemented a policy prohibiting female partners from being assigned these potential account negotiations and later from the accounts themselves. Clerical help in the offices can be female, but any contact with the client must be through a male partner or account executive only.

For example, Japan still has a two-track hiring system, with only 3 percent of professional positions open to women. The remainder of the women in the workforce become office workers who file, wear uniforms, and serve tea. Dentsu, Inc., a large Japanese advertising firm, recently had a picture of the typical Dentsu "Working Girl" in its recruiting brochure. Surrounding the photo were comments primarily about her physical appearance: "Her breasts are 'pretty large'; her bottom is 'rather soft.'"[22]

Burns & McCallister is being criticized for its posture. The head of Burns & McCallister's New York office has explained:

Look, we're about as progressive a firm as you'll find. But the reality of international business is that if we try to use women, we don't get the job. It's not a policy on all foreign accounts. We've just identified certain cultures in which women will not be able to successfully land or work on accounts. This restriction does not interfere with their career track. It does not apply in all countries.

The National Organization for Women (NOW) would like Burns & McCallister to take the position that its standards in the United States apply to all its operations. NOW maintains that without such a posture,

change can never come about. Do you agree with Burns & McCallister's policy for certain cultures with regard to female partners? Given Burns & McCallister's record with regard to women, is the issue really relevant to women's advancement in the firm? If the cultures in which the prohibition of women traditionally applies bring in the accounts with the highest dollar values, would your opinion regarding the posture be different? Do you agree with the NOW position that change can never come about if Burns & McCallister does not take a stand?

Source: Case Studies in Business Ethics, 2nd ed., by Marianne M. Jennings, p. 118. Copyright © 1995. Reprinted with permission of South-Western College Publishing, a division of International Thomson Publishing. Fax 800-730-2215.

7. Coca-Cola has withdrawn its advertising from the World Wrestling Federation (WWF). Others that preceded Coca-Cola in withdrawing their advertising include the U.S. Army, AT&T, and Mars, Inc. WWF has promised to tone down its participants so that the sport can become more of a PG-rated program that parents can watch with their children.

The demographics of WWF show that its audience is primarily males between the ages of 12 and 24. This group is also a prime buying group, and ads on WWF will bring revenues. Do you think the corporations should have withdrawn their ads? Have they made a wise decision for their shareholders?

Source: Lionel Tiger, "Advertisers Finally Wrestle with Their Consciences," *Wall Street Journal,* December 8, 1999, p. A22.

8. Subway customers wrote to the executives of Subway and complained about Subway's sponsorship of the Howard Stern radio show, a nationally syndicated radio show. Mr. Stern, nicknamed the "Shock Jock," often has material of questionable taste on his program. Subway has a unique decision-making process for its ad placement. Because there are so many owners of Subway sandwich shops, a board of trustees elected by shop owners makes decisions on advertising policies for the entire chain of stores. The board met and recommended against advertising on Mr. Stern's show, but some owners object because they have no other radio advertising that is as effective at bringing in customers. Would you, as a Subway shop owner, keep or dump ads for Mr. Stern's show?

9. Heinz Ketchup holds 54 percent of the U.S. ketchup market, and nine of every ten restaurants feature Heinz ketchup. However, Heinz has learned that many restaurant owners simply refill Heinz bottles with cheaper ketchup, thereby capitalizing on the Heinz name without the cost. One restaurant owner explains, "It's just ketchup. The customers don't notice." There are no specific health regulations that apply, and owners are not breaking the law by refilling the bottles. Do you think this practice is ethical?

10. Several large manufacturers of infant and toddler products produced a product called an infant baby walker. An infant as young as four months can be placed in the walker and enjoy upright movements long before motor skills have developed sufficiently to permit such movements unaided. The result was that many infants injured themselves; nearly 30,000 injuries were reported in 1992. The American Medical Association (AMA) asked the federal Consumer Product Safety Commission to ban and recall the walkers because of the clear dangers they present; but, initially, the commission refused. The AMA has also expressed concern about possible long-term skeletal damage because infants who are not yet ready to stand unaided are standing in the walkers.

The industry continued to sell the walkers up to the time of the eventual ban in 1994, but what if you were a parent? Would you want to have the information about the walker's safety? Would you bring suit against the company if there were an injury to your child while using the walker? If the walkers are banned by the Consumer Product Safety Commission here in the United States, how would you feel about serving as an agent to export them for sale in other countries?

RESEARCH PROBLEM

Deadly Poison, Panic, and Patents

11. In fall 2001, following the deadly attacks on the World Trade Center, the United States experienced the first cases of anthrax it had seen since 1978. The sources of the anthrax spores were letters sent to the American Media, Inc. building in Florida, Tom Brokaw of NBC News, Dan Rather of CBS News, and Senators Edward Kennedy, Tom Daschle, and Patrick Leahy in the United States Senate. There were a series of deaths and cutaneous infections, and hundreds of employees at these organizations tested positive for exposure to the anthrax spores.

As a result of these exposures, the most effective antibiotic for treating anthrax, Cipro, was in high demand. Bayer A.G., a German company, owns the patent for this antibiotic and a significant ramp-up in production was needed to meet the increasing demand for those who had been exposed to anthrax. Bayer A.G.'s United States unit went into 24-hour shifts following the anthrax breakouts. Mr. Brokaw held up a bottle of Cipro on his program, "NBC Nightly News," and calmed a jittery public by saying, "In Cipro we trust." Workers at one of Bayer's U.S. plants cheered with the coverage.

However, executives at headquarters for the company remained silent for weeks about the company's ability to manufacture sufficient amounts of the patented antibiotic. Executives indicated that the company was concerned that if it appeared in the media it would seem to be taking advantage of the dire circumstances. Bayer's history made it wary of any involvement in international battles. Bayer A.G. had to pay reparations following World War II, and its patent for its world-famous aspirin, Bayer, was stripped from it and awarded to a U.S. company. It was not until 2000 that Bayer was once again permitted to use its name. The company's low profile during the anthrax scares was deliberate and explained by executives as a desire to avoid appearing "exploitive of the problem" of the infections and illnesses.

Frustrated with the lack of communication from Bayer, Canada suspended Bayer's patent in Canada and ordered other drug manufacturers to begin production of their pending generic formulas for Cipro. Other drug companies do have their own formulas developed and ready to go but could not produce these generics so long as Bayer held its patent protection. One company, Apotex, indicated its production method would not infringe on Bayer's patent, but Bayer threatened litigation and indicated it would deliver all the Cipro needed and/or ordered by both the United States and Canadian governments. Health officials were skeptical and one stated, "There's no way you can tell me getting it from six companies is going to be slower than getting it from one company."

Professor John W. Dienhart, a business ethics professor at Seattle University, stated that Bayer should be a "good corporate citizen." He added, "This is not breaking a patent but adjusting a patent to meet a particular need."

The U.S. Congress was considering suspension of the Cipro patent in the United States in order to increase production even more. The legislation would permit federal judges to suspend patents on the basis of public health issues.

In response to some panic in the United States, pharmacies in Mexico, permitted to sell Cipro without a doctor's prescription, as required in the United States, were ordering large amounts of Cipro, increasing their prices, and doing a great deal of profitable business from U.S. orders. For example, the Zipp Pharmacy, located in Ciudad Juarez, a border town, says its orders for Cipro increased fifteen times what they were before the 2001 anthrax infections. A nurse buying doses of Cipro for her entire family said, "What if there are mad runs on it? It's nice to have it around just in case."

Physicians at the Centers for Disease Control (CDC) were concerned about the Mexico purchases and use of the drug without physician prescription. They note the following problems: (1) Some people are allergic to Cipro and can become quite ill with just one dose; (2) Cipro has side effects for almost everyone including nausea, vomiting, and loss of appetite; (3) Cipro does have an effect on the brain including possible seizures and hallucinations or simple mood changes and insomnia; and (4) Cipro damages cartilage in the joints, especially when taken by children, and should be given to children only when there is the absolute need (i.e., there is an ongoing infection). The CDC has advised use of Cipro only upon determination of exposure or infection from anthrax.

Bayer continued to struggle with its position, promises, and public perception as the anthrax infections increased. Bayer's corporate policy is as follows:

We offer our customers a wide variety of products and services in areas ranging from health care and agriculture to plastics and specialty chemicals. Bayer is research-based and is aiming for technological leadership in its core activities.

Our goals are to steadily increase corporate value and generate a high value added for the benefit of our stockholders, *our employees and the community in every country in which we operate. We believe that our technical and commercial expertise involves responsibility to work for the common good and contribute to sustainable development.*

Bayer: Success through Expertise with Responsibility.

What decisions do you think Bayer should make in this situation? Should it suspend its patent voluntarily? What recommendations should it make on taking Cipro? Should it back the warning from the CDC? Is it wrong for Bayer to profit from this public health problem? Develop a memo that offers ethical guidelines for a Bayer executive.

For more information on anthrax, Cipro, and the ethical issues, visit the following Web sites:

- http://www.bayer.com
- http://www.cdc.gov
- http://www.cptech.org

The last Web site is one for Ralph Nader's Consumer Project on Technology and provides information on the patents and sale of Cipro.

NOTES

1. Greg Farrell, "Witness in Martha Stewart Trial Charged with Perjury," *USA Today*, May 24, 2004, p. 3B.

2. "Could Martha Have a Get-out-of-Jail Card?" *People*, June 7, 2004, p. 70.

3. Leah Nathan Spiro, "The Bomb Shelter Salomon Built," *Business Week*, Sept. 9, 1991, pp. 78–80.

4. Catherine Yang and Amy Barrett, "In a Stew Over Tainted Meat," *Business Week*, April 12, 1993, p. 36.

5. From "Interview: Milton Friedman," *Playboy*, February 1973. © 1973 *Playboy*.

6. Mr. Milken was required by the Securities and Exchange Commission to pay a fine for his involvement in the negotiations (see Chapter 22).

7. Melissa S. Baucus and David A. Baucus, "Paying the Piper: An Empirical Examination of Longer-Term Financial Consequences of Illegal Corporate Behavior," 40 *Academy of Management Journal* 129 (1997).

8. Barnaby J. Feder, "An Abrupt Departure Is Seen as a Harbinger," *New York Times*, May 1, 2002, pp. C1, C2.

9. Andrew Backover, "Report Slams Culture at WorldCom," *USA Today*, November 5, 2002, p. 1B.

10. Ibid.

11. Based on the annual report for 1998, posted at http://www.worldcom.com. (Note: because WorldCom no longer exists, the Web site is now http://www.mci.com.)

12. Based on Bernard Ebbers' letter to shareholders in the annual report for 1999, posted at http://www.worldcom.com. (Note: because WorldCom no longer exists, the Web site is now http://www.mci.com.)

13. Reed Abelson and Milt Freudenheim, "The Scrushy Mix: Strict and So Lenient," *New York Times*, April 20, 2003, pp. BU-1, 12.

14. This material was adapted from Larry Smeltzer and Marianne M. Jennings, "Why an International Code of Business Ethics Would Be Good for Business," 17 *Journal of Business Ethics* 57 (1998).

15. Kathleen Deveny, "Joe Camel Ads Reach Children, Research Finds," *Wall Street Journal*, December 11, 1991, p. B1.

16. Walecia Konrad, "I'd Toddle a Mile for a Camel," *Business Week*, December 23, 1991, p. 34. While the studies and their methodology have been questioned, their impact was made before the challenges and questions were raised.

17. Deveny, "Joe Camel Ads," p. B1.

18. Laura Bird, "Joe Smooth for President," *Adweek's Marketing Week*, May 20, 1991, p. 21.

19. "Camels for Kids," *Time*, December 23, 1991, p. 52.

20. William Chesire, "Don't Shoot: It's Only Joe Camel," *Arizona Republic*, March 15, 1992, p. C1.

21. "Selling Death," *Mesa Tribune*, March 16, 1992, p. A8.

22. Ted Holden and Jennifer Wiener, "Revenge of the 'Office Ladies,'" *Business Week*, July 13, 1992, pp. 42–43.

CHAPTER

3

The Judicial System

Our introduction to law included discussions of statutory law and common law. With so many statutes at so many levels, you perhaps might think that statutory law is a complete source of law. However, sometimes statutes need interpretation. Someone must determine when, how, and to whom statutes apply. Statutory law is not even half of all the law. The bulk of the law is found in judicial decisions. These decisions have both statutory interpretations and common law. This chapter covers the parties involved in these decisions as well as the courts that make them—what they decide, when they can decide, and how those decisions are made.

update

For up-to-date legal news and real-world business applications, click on **update** *at http://jennings.westbuslaw.com.*

For as thou urgest justice, be assured thou shalt have justice, more than thou desirest.
PORTIA
The Merchant of Venice, Act IV, Scene 1

CONSIDER...

Gail Lindgren is an entrepreneur who runs a small business called Moonbeams based in West Des Moines, Iowa. Ms. Lindgren designed and began selling JEANJANGLES, jewelry that hangs from the belt loops on jeans. Ms. Lindgren obtained a patent for the trinkets and, in addition to storming the Iowa jeans-wearer market, sold the JEANJANGLES on her Web site, http://www.jeanjangle.com (the company's original Web site). A California company, GDT, began selling "Jeans for the Hip," also called JEAN JEWEL. Ms. Lindgren became aware of GDT, its Web site, and product when *People* magazine did a feature story on the jean trinkets and friends called to congratulate her on her national success. There was further product confusion when singer Lance Bass of N'SYNC referred to the California products during a national radio interview that had listeners thinking again that Ms. Lindgren's product was enjoying newfound notoriety. Ms. Lindgren filed suit in federal district court in Iowa against GDT for infringement. GDT maintains that it has never been to Iowa, has no stores in Iowa, has no salespeople or other employees in Iowa, and cannot be required to come to Iowa to defend a lawsuit. Ms. Lindgren says that GDT has a Web site and is selling its jewels to residents in Iowa and must come to Iowa to defend a suit there because it is doing business there. Who is correct?

TYPES OF COURTS

In all U.S. court systems, there are two different types or levels of courts: trial courts and appellate courts.

Trial Courts

A **trial court** is the place in the judicial system where the facts of a case are presented. This court is where the jury sits if the case is a jury trial. Here the evidence and witnesses are presented and the first decision in the case is made, by either judge or jury. The procedures for trials and trial courts are covered in Chapter 4.

Appellate Courts

There is always at least one other court, an **appellate court**, that reviews a trial court decision to check the conduct of the judge, the trial, the lawyers, and the jury. This process of review helps assure that the lower court applied the law correctly and followed the rules of procedure. Further, this review system provides uniformity. In some appeals, the appellate court issues published opinions, which can then be referred to and used for resources in deciding future cases. However, there are many cases in which the appellate court issues unpublished opinions. Unpublished opinions have become a controversial issue; there have been proposals for change in how these opinions are treated and used. The Internet offers a means for making unpublished opinions available to lawyers and those who are litigating similar issues. While there is no prohibition against citing such opinions, the cite should always make clear that the opinion is an unpublished one.

CHECK THE WEB

Check the Web for updates on the use of unpublished opinions. For a look at some published versus unpublished opinions, go to http://www.courts.state.mn.us/.

HOW COURTS MAKE DECISIONS

The Process of Judicial Review

Appellate courts do not hold trials. Rather, they review what has been done by trial courts to determine whether the trial court, often referred to as the lower court or trial court, made an error in applying the substantive or procedural law in the case. This is the process of **judicial review**.

The appellate court atmosphere is very different from that of the trial court. There are no witnesses, no jury, and no testimony. No new evidence is considered; only the evidence presented at trial is reviewed. The court reviews a transcript of the trial along with all the evidence presented at trial to determine whether an error has been made.

In addition to the transcript and evidence, each of the parties to a case can present the appellate court with a **brief**, which is a summary of the case and the legal issues being challenged on appeal. The appellate brief is each side's summary of why the trial court decision or procedures were correct or incorrect. The parties make their arguments for their positions in the brief and support them with statutes and decisions from other cases. The brief serves as a summary of the major points of error the parties allege occurred during the trial. This type of brief, called an **appellate brief**, is very detailed. In fact, many refer to "briefs" as a misnomer because they are generally quite lengthy. Note that these briefs differ from the case brief presented in Exhibit 1.1.

Many appellate courts permit the attorneys for the opposing parties to make timed oral arguments in their cases. An **oral argument** is a summary of the points that have been made in each party's brief. The judge can also ask questions of the attorneys at that time. At the trial level, one judge makes all decisions. At the appellate level, more than one judge reviews the actions of the lower court in a case. The typical number is three, but, in the case of state supreme courts and the U.S.

Listen to oral arguments made before the Supreme Court:
http://www.oyez.org/oyez/frontpage

FOR THE MANAGER'S DESK

RE: A BRIEF SAMPLING

A number of Web sites provide sample case briefs you can read to see what companies and individuals argue in cases taken up on appeal. Explore the following sites.

- http://www.briefserve.com
- http://www.flcourts.org/sct/clerk/briefs
- http://www.nku.edu/~chase/library/kysctbriefs.htm
- http://www.ndcourts.com/Calendar
- http://www.supreme.courts.state.tx.us/
- http://www.ftc.gov/ogc/briefs.htm
- http://www.eeoc.gov/litigation/appbriefs.html
- http://www.osc.gov/library.htm#briefs
- http://www.sec.gov/litigation/briefs.shtml
- http://www.aipla.org
- http://www.adl.org/Civil_Rights/ab
- http://www.cato.org/pubs/legalbriefs/lbriefs.html
- http://childrensrights.org/Legal/cases.htm
- http://www.epic.org
- http://www.jlaw.com/Briefs
- http://www.legalmomentum.org
- http://www.citizen.org/litigation/briefs

Learn more about the Supreme Court justices:
http://www.law.cornell. edu/supct/justices/ fullcourt.html

Supreme Court, the full bench of judges on the court hears each case. For example, in U.S. Supreme Court decisions, all nine justices review the cases before the Court unless they have recused (disqualified) themselves because of some conflict.

The panel of appellate judges reviews the case and the briefs, hears the oral argument, and then renders a decision. The decision in the case could be unanimous or could be a split vote, such as 2 to 1. In the case of a split vote, the justice who is not in the majority will frequently draft a **dissenting opinion**, which is the judge's explanation for a vote different from that of the majority.

Checking for Error

A **reversible error** is one that might have affected the outcome of the case or would have influenced the decision made. Examples of reversible errors include the refusal to allow some evidence to be admitted that should have been admitted, the refusal to allow a particular witness to testify, and misapplication of the law.

When a reversible error is made, the appellate court **reverses** the lower court's decision. However, in some cases, the appellate court will also **remand** the case, which means the case is sent back to the trial court for further work. For example, if there is a reversal because some evidence should have been admitted that was not, the case is remanded for a new trial with that evidence admitted (i.e., allowed).

If there has not been an error, the appellate court simply **affirms** the decision of the lower court. An affirmed decision does not mean no mistakes were made; it means that none of the mistakes was a reversible error. The decision of the court is written by a member of the court who has voted with the majority. The decision explains the facts and the reasons for the court's reversal, remand, or affirmation.

In some appellate cases, the court will **modify** the decision of a lower court. The full case is neither reversed nor affirmed; instead, a portion or portions of the case are reversed or modified. For example, a trial court verdict finding a defendant negligent might be affirmed, but the appellate court could find that the damages awarded were excessive. In this type of decision, the case would be remanded for a redetermination of damages at the trial court level.

Statutory Interpretation

In addition to checking for error, appellate courts render interpretations of statutes. Often, statutes seem perfectly clear until a new factual situation not covered by the statute arises.

The Doctrine of *Stare Decisis*

Judicial review by appellate courts of lower court decisions provides the database for the doctrine of ***stare decisis***, a Latin term meaning "let the decision stand." The decisions of the appellate courts are written and often published so that they may be analyzed, reviewed, and perhaps applied in the future.

Setting Precedent

When a court reviews the decisions of lower courts, that court's previous decisions, along with decisions of other courts on the same topic, are consulted. This process of examining other decisions for help in a new case uses case **precedent**, which is the doctrine of *stare decisis*. Such judicial thinking requires an examination of all related cases to determine whether the issue has already been decided and whether the same decision should apply again. Following case precedent does not mean similar cases will be decided identically; several factors influence the weight given to precedent.

The Quality of Precedent

Where the case originated is one of the factors that influences the application of precedent in a case. In federal courts, precedent from other federal courts is strongest when the case involves federal statutes.

In state courts, prior decisions within a particular state's own court system are given greater weight than decisions from courts of other states. One state's courts are not obliged to follow the precedent of another state's courts; they are free to examine it and use it, but, as with all precedent, there is no mandatory requirement to follow another state's decisions.

The Purposes of Precedent

The purposes of precedent are the same as the purposes of law. Law offers some assurance of consistency and reliability. The judiciary recognizes these obligations in applying precedent. There must be stability and predictability in the way law functions. There is no exact formula for deciding a case, but consistency is a key element in applying precedent.

In addition to consistency, however, judges must incorporate into their legal thought the need for flexibility in the law. New twists in facts arise, and new technology develops; the judiciary must be receptive to the need for change. For example, in Chapter 1, the *Sony* and *Napster* cases illustrated the need for a reexamination of the scope of a law based on a newly evolved technology and its role in copyright law and protections.

The Interpretation of Precedent

There is more to using precedent than just finding similar cases. Every case decision has two parts. One is the actual rule of law, which technically is the precedential part. However, judges never offer just a rule of law in a case. The rule of law is given at the end of the case decision after a full discussion of their reasons and other

---

 CONSIDER...   3 . 1

The following rule appears in State University's current catalog:

> *A course in which a grade of C or better has been earned may not be repeated. The second entry will not be counted in earned hours or grade point index for graduation.*

Rod took his business math course and earned a C. Not satisfied with his grade but unaware of the catalog regulation, Rod took the math course again and this time earned a D. The registrar has entered the D grade in Rod's cumulative average. Rod objects based on the catalog rule, but the registrar says the rule applies only if a higher grade is earned. What should Rod do? Should the grade count?

Discussion

The purpose of the university regulation was to prevent students from retaking courses to earn a higher grade point average (GPA). In the factual situation, the student earned a lower grade. The registrar entered the lower grade hoping to create a deterrent for students retaking courses when they had a C or better. However, it is clear that a second grade, whether higher or lower, should not be entered.

Here's another follow-up question for you to solve on your own. Suppose that the registrar has always counted the lower grades in the cumulative GPA. Does Rod still have an effective argument? Is the registrar using a strained interpretation of the regulation?

precedent. This discussion is called the ***dicta*** of the case, in which case precedent may be cited to the benefit of each party. In some instances, the rule of law may benefit one party while the *dicta* benefits the other party.

A dissenting opinion is *dicta* and is often quoted in subsequent cases to urge a court to change existing precedent. Application of precedent is not a scientific process; there is much room for interpretation and variation.

When Precedent Is Not Followed

Precedent may not be followed for several reasons. Some of those reasons have already been given: The precedent is from another state, or the precedent is interpreted differently because of the *dicta* in that precedent. Precedent is also not followed when the facts of cases can be "distinguished," which means that the context of the facts in one case is different enough from those in other cases that the precedent cannot be applied. For example, suppose that a court decided that using roadblocks to stop motorists to check for drunk drivers is constitutional. Another court then decides that using roadblocks just to check for drivers' licenses is not constitutional. The first case can be distinguished because of the purpose of the roadblocks: to prevent a hazardous highway condition. The court may not see the same urgency or safety issue in roadblocks used for checking for drivers' licenses. The precedent can be distinguished.

The theories of law discussed in Chapter 1 may also control whether precedent is applied. For example, a court may not follow a precedent because of a moral reason or because of the need to change the law on the basis of what is moral or what is right. A precedent may also be abandoned on an economic theory, in which the court changes the law to do the most good for the most people. For example, a factory may be a nuisance because of the noise and pollution it creates. There is probably ample case law to support shutting down the factory as a nuisance. However, the factory may also be the town's only economic support, and its shutdown will mean unemployment for virtually the whole town. In balancing the economic factors, the nuisance precedent may not be followed or it may be followed in only a modified way.

Courts struggle with issues of fact and law and with changes in society as they apply precedent and consider modifications.

PARTIES IN THE JUDICIAL SYSTEM (CIVIL CASES)

Plaintiffs

Plaintiffs are the parties who initiate a lawsuit and are seeking some type of recovery. In some types of cases, they are called **petitioners** (such as in an action for divorce). The plaintiffs file their suit in the appropriate court, and this filing begins the process.

Defendants

Defendants are the ones from whom the plaintiffs want recovery. They are the ones charged with some violation of the civil rights of the plaintiff. In some cases, they are referred to as **respondents**.

BUSINESS PLANNING TIP

Business people should exercise caution in the protection of their lawyer-client privilege. Letters and memos to lawyers should be marked as privileged, and limitations should be placed on access to those letters and memos. Revealing to others your communications to your lawyer may cost you your privilege. Holding a conversation or meeting with your lawyer with others present may cost you your privilege, too. Privileged communications should be with your lawyer(s) only.

FOR THE MANAGER'S DESK

RE: THE PRIVILEGE OF LAWYERS

To whom does the attorney-client privilege belong? An attorney who is general counsel for a corporation or a lawyer who represents a corporation has but one client: the corporation. The privilege applies to her communication with that client. While officers and employees provide the attorney with the information about what the corporation did, the lawyer does not represent those officers and employees. In most situations, the interests of the officers and employees are the same as those of the corporations and a lawyer can work closely with the officers and employees to represent the corporation. However, there can be circumstances in which the corporation's interests are different from those of the employees. For example, suppose that a general counsel for a corporation learned that its officers had engaged in price-fixing. (See Chapter 9 for more discussion of criminal prosecutions of officers of a corporation and Chapter 17 for discussion of price-fixing and antitrust violations.) The general counsel would discuss the issue with the board (see Chapter 21) and perhaps conclude that it is best to disclose what has happened to the Justice Department. While the officers involved might object, they are not protected by any privilege with the corporation's attorney. The attorney is protecting her client, the company, by disclosing the misconduct and perhaps providing assurance that the board was unaware of the price-fixing, which would then reduce any penalties the company might be required to pay.

Lawyers

In most cases, each of the parties is represented by a **lawyer**. Lawyers have other functions besides representing clients in a lawsuit. Many lawyers offer "preventive" services. Lawyers draft contracts, wills, and other documents to prevent legal problems from arising. Clients are advised in advance so that they can minimize legal problems and costs.

The attorney-client relationship is a fiduciary one and one that carries privilege. The attorney is expected to act in the best interests of the client and can do so without the fear of having to disclose the client's thoughts and decisions. The **attorney-client privilege** keeps the relationship confidential and assures that others (even an adversary in a lawsuit) have limited access to lawyer-client conversations. One of the key areas of discussion, debate, and modified reforms under Sarbanes-Oxley has related to imposing upon corporate lawyers the duty to report fraud and other financial misdeeds of their client companies. Lawyers were concerned about the need for client confidentiality, and regulators and investors were concerned that lawyers have remained silent as financial frauds have been ongoing in companies. While the final version of the rules adopted pursuant to Sarbanes-Oxley (as of 2004) does not require lawyers to blow the whistle on their clients, they are required to take steps to notify the audit committee and board about misconduct and eventually resign if the conduct is not changed and rectified.

Under the American Bar Association's Model Rules for Professional Responsibility, attorneys are obligated to represent clients zealously. Once an attorney agrees to represent a client, that representation must be given to the best of the lawyer's ability. Because of the privilege, many lawyers know that their clients actually did commit a crime or breach a contract. However, the client's confession to an attorney is confidential. Even with that knowledge, it is the attorney's obligation to represent the client and make certain that the client is given all rights and protections under the law. A criminal defense attorney may know that her client has committed a crime. But committing a crime and the required proof for conviction of that crime are two different things. It is the lawyer's job to see that the other side meets its burdens and responsibilities in proving a case against the client. Lawyers do represent

Visit the American Bar Association Center for Professional Responsibility:
http://www.abanet.org/cpr/home.html

guilty people. Their role is to make sure that the system operates fairly with guilty and innocent people alike. Lawyers are not required to remain silent because of the confidentiality protections if a client is about to commit a crime. A lawyer representing a client accused of murder cannot disclose that the client confessed. However, a lawyer whose client vows to kill someone must make a disclosure in order to prevent a crime.

Lawyers and their titles and roles vary from country to country. Great Britain and most of Canada have *solicitors* and *barristers*. Solicitors prepare legal documents, give legal advice, and represent clients in some of the lesser courts. Barristers are the only "lawyers" who can practice before higher courts and administrative agencies. Quebec and France have three types of lawyers: the *avocat*, who can practice before the higher courts and give legal advice; the *notaire*, who can handle real property transactions and estates and can prepare some legal documents; and the *juriste* (legal counselor), who can give advice and prepare legal documents. In Germany, a lawyer who litigates is called *Rechtsanwalt* and a lawyer who advises clients but does not appear in court is called *Rechtsbeistand*. Japan has only one class of lawyers, called *Bengosh*, but does have the *Shiho-Soshi*, a type of advanced notary with the authority to incorporate companies, prepare documents, and create wills. In Italy, the two types of lawyers—whose roles are similar to the dual British system—are *avocati* and *procuratori*.

Judges

Judges control the proceedings in a case and, in some instances, the outcome. Trial judges control the trial of a case from presiding over the selection of a jury to ruling on evidence questions. (See Chapter 4 for more details on trial procedures.) Appellate judges review the work of trial court judges. They do not actually hear evidence but, rather, review transcripts. Their job is one of determining error but does not include conducting trials.

Judges are selected in various ways throughout the country. Some judges are elected to their offices. Some states have merit appointment systems, wherein judges are appointed on the basis of their qualifications. In some states, judges are appointed by elected officials subject to the approval of the legislature. In some states with appointed judges, the judges are put on the ballot every other year (or some other period) for retention; voters in these states do not decide whom they want as judges but do decide whether they want to keep them once they are in office. Federal judges are appointed by the president with Senate approval.

Name Changes on Appeal

The lawyers and the parties stay in the "game" even after a case is appealed. However, the names of the parties do change on appeal. The party appealing the case is called the **appellant**. Some courts also call the party appealing a case the **petitioner**. The other party (the one not appealing) is called the **appellee** or **respondent**.

Some states change the name of the case if the party appealing the case is the defendant. For example, suppose that Smith sues Jones for damages in a car accident. The name of the case at trial is *Smith* v. *Jones*. Smith is the plaintiff, and Jones is the defendant. If Smith wins the case at trial and Jones decides to appeal, Jones is the appellant and Smith is the appellee. In some courts, the name of the case on appeal becomes *Jones* v. *Smith*. Other courts leave the case name the same but still label Jones the appellant and Smith the appellee.

THE CONCEPT OF JURISDICTION

There are courts at every level of government, and every court handles a different type of case. In order for a court to decide or try a particular case, both parties to the case and the subject matter of the case must be within the established powers of the court. The established powers of a court make up the court's **jurisdiction**. *Juris* means law, and *diction* means to speak.

Jurisdiction is the authority or power of a court to speak the law. Some courts can handle bankruptcies, whereas others may be limited to traffic violations. Some courts handle violations of criminal laws, whereas others deal only with civil matters. The subject matter of a case controls which court has jurisdiction. For example, a case involving a federal statute belongs in a federal district court by its subject matter. However, there are federal district courts in every state, and jurisdiction also involves the issue of which court. ***In personam* jurisdiction**, or jurisdiction over the person, controls which of the federal district courts will decide the case. Determining which court can be used is a two-step process; subject matter and *in personam* jurisdiction must fit in the same court.

SUBJECT MATTER JURISDICTION OF COURTS: THE AUTHORITY OVER CONTENT

There are two general court systems in the United States: the federal court system (see Exhibit 3.1) and the state court system.

Learn more about the U.S. federal court system:
http://www.uscourts.gov/
or **http://www.fjc.gov**

The Federal Court System

The Trial Court of the Federal System

The **federal district court** is the general trial court of the federal system. However, federal district courts are limited in the types of cases they can hear; that is, their subject matter jurisdiction is limited. Federal district courts can hear three types of

EXHIBIT 3.1 The Federal Court System

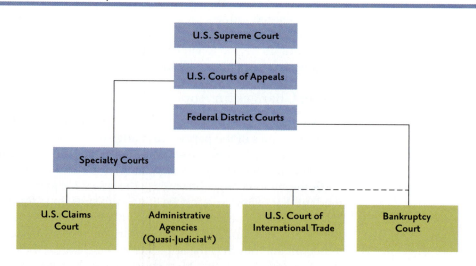

*For example, the Federal Trade Commission (FTC) or the National Labor Relations Bureau (NLRB).

cases: those in which the United States is a party, those that involve a federal question, and those that involve diversity of citizenship.

Jurisdiction When the United States Is a Party

Anytime the U.S. government is a party in a lawsuit, it will want to be tried in its own court system—the federal system. The United States is a party when it brings suit or when it is the defendant named in a suit. For example, if the Navy must bring an action to enforce a contract against a supplier, the United States is the plaintiff and the federal court system has subject matter jurisdiction. If a victim of a plane crash names the Federal Aviation Administration (FAA) in a suit, the United States is a defendant and the federal system again has jurisdiction.

Federal Jurisdiction for a Federal Question

The federal district court has jurisdiction over cases involving federal questions. For example, if a business is suing for treble damages (a remedy of three times the amount of damages experienced) under the federal antitrust laws (see Chapter 17), there is a federal question and the case may be brought in federal district court. A suit charging a violation of the Equal Protection Clause of the U.S. Constitution (see Chapter 5 for more details) also involves a federal question and can be brought in federal district court. Prosecutions for federal crimes also involve federal questions, and the United States will be a party as the prosecutor; these criminal cases are tried in federal district court. When the United States is a party in a case, the federal district court has exclusive jurisdiction.

Many federal questions can also be heard by a state court. For example, most state constitutions include the same Fifth Amendment protections included in the U.S. Constitution. A plaintiff often has a choice between federal and state court, and the decision to proceed in one forum as opposed to the other may be a strategic one based on the nature of the case, rules of procedure, and other factors related to differences between the two court systems.

Jurisdiction by Diversity

Most of the civil cases in federal district court are not there because they are federal questions or because the United States is a party. Most civil cases are in federal district court because the plaintiff and defendant are from different states and their case involves damage claims in excess of $75,000. Cases in which the parties are from different states qualify them for **diversity of citizenship** status, and federal district courts have the authority to hear these diversity cases. That authority is not exclusive; a state court can also hear diversity cases so long as neither party chooses to exercise the right to a federal district court trial. In diversity cases, state and federal courts have **concurrent jurisdiction**. Concurrent jurisdiction means that two courts have the authority to hear a case. By contrast, **exclusive jurisdiction** means that only one court has the authority to hear the case. For example, federal district courts have exclusive jurisdiction over cases in which the United States has charged an individual or corporation with a federal crime.

Federal courts decide controversies among citizens of different states for reasons that go back to fears about state court judges giving preferential or favorable treatment to citizens of their state, as opposed to nonresident parties. If the case is held in one side's state court, that side might have an unfair advantage or built-in prejudice because of the location of the court.

When corporations are parties to suits, the diversity issue is more complex. The citizenship of a corporation can be its state of incorporation or the state in which its principal office is located. This citizenship test is used for subject matter jurisdiction. The citizenship test for *in personam* jurisdiction has been greatly expanded.

It is important to understand that when a federal court tries a case on the basis of diversity, it is simply trying the case under the same state laws but without the local prejudice that might exist in a state court. In other words, federal courts do not rule under a different set of laws; they simply apply the state law in a different setting.

Limited Jurisdiction: The Special Trial Courts of the Federal System

Look for updates on federal courts:
http://www.federalcourts.com

Not all cases in which the United States is a party or in which there is a federal question are decided in federal district courts. The federal system also has specialized trial courts to handle limited matters. For example, there is a Tax Court in the federal system, the jurisdiction of which is limited to tax issues. If you should decide to challenge the Internal Revenue Service because it would not allow one of your deductions, your case would be heard in Tax Court. The bankruptcy courts make up a well-used limited court system within the federal system that have exclusive jurisdiction over all bankruptcies. No other court can handle a bankruptcy or bankruptcy issues. Bankruptcy courts are limited to handling bankruptcies and do not handle any other type of trial or suit.

The U.S. Claims Court is another specialized federal court: It handles the disputes on government contracts and other claims against the federal government such as eminent domain issues. (See Chapter 5 for more discussion of eminent domain and "takings.")

The U.S. Court of International Trade is a specialized court that focuses on international trade transactions regulated by federal agencies in various ways and also on customs issues.

Another court that is often discussed along with the federal system is the Indian Tribal Court. These courts of the Native American nations have exclusive jurisdiction over criminal and civil matters on the reservations. They are unique courts because of both their limited jurisdiction and their exclusivity, arising from their sovereign nature.

The Structure of the Federal District Court System

View a map and statistical reports of the federal districts:
http://www.uscourts.gov/districtcourts.html

There is at least one federal district per state. The number of federal districts in each state is determined by the state's population and caseload. States such as Arizona and Nevada have only one federal district each, whereas states such as Illinois and New York have many. The number of courts and judges in each federal district is also determined by the district's population and caseload. Even in those states in which there is just one district, there are several judges and multiple courtrooms for federal trials. There are ninety-four federal districts in the fifty states plus one each in the District of Columbia and Puerto Rico. Three territories of the United States (Guam, the Virgin Islands, and the Northern Mariana Islands) also have district courts, including a bankruptcy court.

The Importance of Federal District Court Decisions

The subject matter of cases qualifying for federal district court is important. Such cases involve the interpretation of federal statutes and often the resolution of constitutional issues. Because of the importance of these decisions, the opinions of federal district judges are published in a reporter series called the **Federal Supplement**, which reprints most opinions issued by federal district judges in every federal district. (Decisions of the Court of International Trade are also found in the *Federal Supplement*.) Cases in the *Federal Supplement* provide excellent precedent for

Review recent U.S. Courts of Appeals decisions:
http://www.law.emory.edu/FEDCTS

interpretation and application of federal statutes. Just as there is a system for citing statutes (see Chapter 1), there is a system for citing case opinions. Such a system is necessary so that precedent can be found easily for use in future cases.

All case cites consist of three elements: an abbreviation for the reporter, the volume number, and the page number. The abbreviation for the *Federal Supplement* is "F.Supp." or, for the second series, after volume 999, "F.Supp.2d." The volume number always appears in front of the abbreviation, and the page number appears after it. A formal cite includes in parentheses the federal district in which the case was decided and the year the case was decided. A sample federal district court cite of a case decided in the Eastern District of Michigan that dealt with the use of race as a criterion for undergraduate and law school admissions looks like this:

Gratz v. Bollinger
135 F.Supp.2d 790 (E.D. Mich. 2001)

This method of uniform citation not only helps ease the burden of research but also provides an automatic way to know where a case came from and how it can be used. A number of systems available on the Internet offer copies of court opinions for a fee.

The Appellate Level in the Federal System

Cases decided in federal district court and the specialized trial courts of the federal system can be appealed. These cases are appealed to the U.S. courts of appeals (formerly called the U.S. circuit courts of appeals).

> **update** ◁ | **CHECK THE WEB**

You can follow the *U.S.* v. *Microsoft* case all the way through the federal system in the Web site exercise for this chapter.

Structure   All of the federal district courts are grouped into **federal circuits** according to their geographic location. Exhibit 3.2 is a map that shows the thirteen federal circuits. Note that eleven of the circuits are geographic groupings of states; the twelfth is the District of Columbia, and the thirteenth is a nongeographic circuit created to handle special cases such as those involving patent disputes and issues, and appeals from the Court of Claims and Court of International Trade. Some scholars and members of Congress have proposed creating a fourteenth circuit by dividing the very large Ninth Circuit.

Each circuit has its own court of appeals. The office of the court's clerk is located in the city named in each of the federal circuits in Exhibit 3.2. The number of judges for each of the federal circuits varies according to caseload. However, most cases are heard by a panel of three of the circuit judges. It is rare for a case to be heard *en banc* (by the whole bench or all the judges in that circuit). One of the more famous cases to be heard *en banc* following a three-judge panel decision involved a father's challenge to his child being required to recite the Pledge of Allegiance because the phrase "under God" was in the pledge (*Elk Grove Unified School Dist.* v. *Newdow,* 292 F.3d 597 (CA9 2002) and 313 F.3d 500 (C.A. 9 2002) with *en banc* rehearing denied, 328 F.3d 466 (C.A. 9 2003).[1]

Procedures   The U.S. courts of appeals are appellate courts and operate by the same general procedures discussed earlier in the chapter. An appeal consists of a

EXHIBIT 3.2 The Thirteen Federal Judicial Circuits

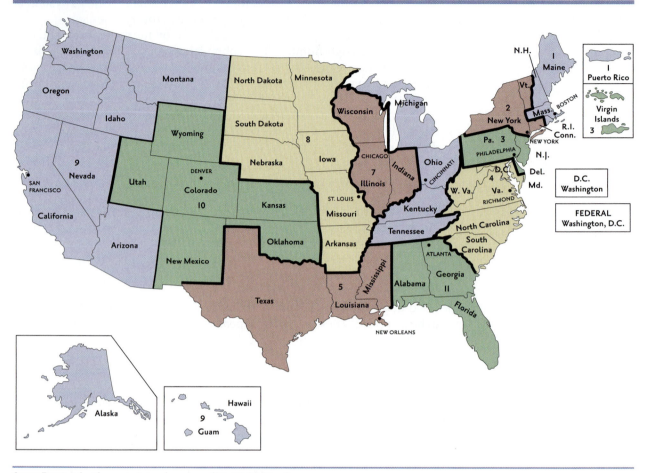

Source: Reprinted with permission and courtesy of West Publishing Company.

record of the trial in the court below (here, the federal district court), briefs, and possible oral argument. The standard for reversal is reversible error. Because the right of appeal is automatic, the appellate courts have tremendous caseloads. A full opinion is not given in every case. In the cases that are affirmed, the opinion may consist of that one word. Other decisions are issued as memorandum opinions for the benefit of the parties but not for publication.

Opinions   The opinions of the U.S. courts of appeals are published in the ***Federal Reporter***. The system of citation for these cases is the same as for the federal district court opinions. The abbreviation for the *Federal Reporter* is "F." (or sometimes "F.2d" or "F.3d"; the "2d" means the second series, which was started after the first "F." series reached volume 300, and now there is a third series—"3d"). A formal cite includes in parentheses the federal circuit and date of the decision. A sample U.S. court of appeals cite, the appeal of the *Gratz* case, would look like this:

Read about proposed changes in the federal court system:
http://app.com.uscourts.gov

Gratz v. Bollinger
188 F.3d 394 (6th Cir. 1999)

Review online Supreme Court cases:

http://law.cornell.edu/supct/index.html
and
http://www.supremecourtus.gov

The U.S. Supreme Court

A decision by a U.S. court of appeals is not necessarily the end of a case. There is one more appellate court in the federal system—the **U.S. Supreme Court**. However, the Supreme Court's procedures and jurisdiction are slightly different from those of other appellate courts.

Appellate Jurisdiction and Process   The Supreme Court handles appeals from the U.S. courts of appeals. This appeal process, however, is not an automatic right. The Supreme Court must first decide whether a particular case merits review. That decision is announced when the Court issues a **writ of certiorari** for those cases it will review in full. The Supreme Court, in its writ, actually makes a preliminary determination about the case and whether it should be decided. Only a small number of cases appealed to the Supreme Court are actually heard. In 1945, 1,460 cases were appealed to the court. By 1960, that number had grown to 2,313. Now the number averages about 7,000 each year, with 2002 (the latest year available from the court) having 8,255 cases. The court grants *certiorari* in about 120–140 cases and hears oral arguments and issues written opinions in about 70 to 80 cases. For example, in the 2002 term, the Supreme Court, of the 1,869 cases on its docket, heard oral arguments in 84 of those cases and issued 79 written opinions. All of the Supreme Court opinions issued in one year total 5,000 pages, including the majority, concurring, and dissenting opinions.

The court grants *writs of certiorari* in cases as a matter of discretion. *Certiorari* may be granted because there is a conflict among the circuits about the law or because the case presents a major constitutional issue. This *writ of certiorari* procedure also applies to other sources of appellate cases, such as those coming up through state supreme courts. Although the federal appellate workload of the U.S. Supreme Court is great, it is only part of the Court's jurisdictional burden. Decisions from

FOR THE MANAGER'S DESK

RE: A LOOK AT WHAT APPELLATE COURTS DO

The following chart, organized by federal circuits, shows the percentage of time the U.S. Supreme Court (2003) reverses the decisions of lower courts.

COURT	NUMBER OF CASES	PERCENT REVERSED OR VACATED
First Circuit	74	76%
Second Circuit	0	—
Third Circuit	4	75%
Fourth Circuit	4	25%
Fifth Circuit	6	100%
Sixth Circuit	7	71%
Seventh Circuit	4	50%
Eighth Circuit	5	80%
Ninth Circuit	22	77%
Tenth Circuit	3	100%
Eleventh Circuit	4	100%
D.C. Circuit	3	100%
Federal Circuit	1	100%
District Courts	2	50%
State appellate courts	7	71%

BIOGRAPHY

SANDRA DAY O'CONNOR: FIRST WOMAN ON THE U.S. SUPREME COURT BENCH

During his 1980 presidential campaign, Ronald Reagan said, "One of the first Supreme Court vacancies in my administration will be filled by the most qualified woman I can find, one who meets the high standards I demand for all my appointments." When Justice Potter Stewart stepped down in July 1981, Mr. Reagan had the responsibility of nominating a justice for the Supreme Court bench.

Sandra Day O'Connor, who earned her undergraduate and law degrees at Stanford University, was recommended by the late Senator Barry Goldwater and, ultimately, was nominated by Mr. Reagan and confirmed by the Senate on September 15, 1981. Confirmed by a vote of 99–0, she became the first woman to occupy the bench of the Supreme Court.

Justice O'Connor had served as a senator in the Arizona State Senate and was serving as an Arizona Court of Appeals judge at the time of her nomination.

Justice O'Connor was raised on her family's ranch in Eastern Arizona. When she graduated from high school at age 16, she went immediately to Stanford, where she earned both her bachelor's and J.D. degrees in five years total. Chief Justice William Rehnquist was in her law school class, and they graduated numbers 1 and 3, respectively, out of a class of 102. Despite her credentials, and having finished law school in only two years instead of the customary three, the best job offer she received from a law firm was one for the position of legal secretary. Ironically, William French Smith, who would later become her perhaps greatest proponent in advancing her nomination, was a partner in that law firm.

She worked as a deputy county attorney for two years in San Mateo, California, before she married. She traveled with her husband in his role as a member of the Army Judge Advocate General Corps but also worked as a civilian lawyer on Army cases.

She had three sons and worked in private practice until she became an assistant attorney general in Arizona. From 1969 to 1974, she served in the Arizona State Senate and was the first woman to serve as majority leader there. From 1974 to 1980, she was a trial judge for Maricopa County Superior Court. From 1980 to 1981, she served on Arizona's Court of Appeals.

When Mr. Reagan nominated Judge O'Connor, he described her as "truly a 'person for all seasons,' possessing those unique qualities of temperament, fairness, intellectual capacity and devotion to the public good which have characterized the 101 'brethren' who have preceded her."

The American Bar Association gave Judge O'Connor a qualified endorsement. The ABA noted her judicial temperament and integrity but felt that she did not have sufficient experience as a judge or attorney and that her experience was not "as extensive or challenging as that of some other persons." Many commented that a man with O'Connor's record would not have been nominated.

Two years later, Justice O'Connor, in a speech to the American Law Institute, spoke of how one gets to be a justice on the U.S. Supreme Court:

> *While there are many supposed criteria for the selection of a justice, when the eventual decision is made as to who the nominee will be, that decision from the nominee's viewpoint is probably a classic example of being the right person in the right spot at the right time. Stated simply, you must be lucky. That certainly is how I view my nomination.*

ISSUES

1. Do you think gender was the sole criterion?
2. Is Justice O'Connor right? Is it luck?

---

state supreme courts, for example, can be appealed to the U.S. Supreme Court. The Supreme Court also decides whether to review these cases. For example, in 2000, the U.S. Supreme Court granted *certiorari* on George W. Bush's appeal of a Florida Supreme Court decision on recounting the Florida ballots in the November 2000 presidential election. That case, because of its significance and its interpretation of statutory law and the role of judicial review, was granted *certiorari* and actually heard by the court with a resulting written opinion.

The U.S. Supreme Court also acts as a trial court or a court of **original jurisdiction** in certain cases. When one state is suing another state, the U.S. Supreme Court becomes the states' trial court. For example, the water dispute among California, Arizona, Colorado, and Nevada has been tried over a period of years by the U.S. Supreme Court. The Court also handles the trials (on espionage charges, for example) of ambassadors and foreign consuls.

Learn more about the state court system:
http://www.ncsconline.org

Structure   The U.S. Supreme Court consists of nine judges, who are nominated to the Court by the president and confirmed by the Senate. The appointment runs for a lifetime. A president who has the opportunity to appoint a Supreme Court justice is shaping the structure of the Court and the resulting decisions. For this reason, the U.S. Supreme Court is often labeled "conservative" or "liberal." The makeup of the bench controls the philosophy and decisions of the Court.

Opinions   Because the Court is the highest in the land, its opinions are precedent for every other court in the country. The importance of these opinions has resulted in three different volumes of reporters for U.S. Supreme Court opinions. The first is the ***United States Reports*** (abbreviated "U.S."). These reports are put out by the U.S. Government Printing Office and are the official reports of the Court. Because these reports are often slow to be published, two private companies publish opinions in the ***Supreme Court Reporter*** (abbreviated "S. Ct.") and the ***Lawyer's Edition*** (abbreviated "L. Ed." or "L. Ed.2d"). The three-part cite for *Gratz* v. *Bollinger* follows:

539 U.S. 244 (2003)
156 L. Ed.2d 257 (2003)
123 S.Ct. 2411 (2003)

Review state court decisions for selected states:
http://www.courts.wa.gov/
http://www.court.state.
nd.us/
http://www.in.gov/judiciary/
opinions/

The State Court Systems

Although each state court has a different structure for its court system and the courts may have different names, there is a basic structure in each state that is similar to the federal system. Exhibit 3.3 is a diagram of a sample state court system.

State Trial Courts

Each state has its own general trial court. This court is usually called a circuit, district, county, or superior court. It is the court in which nondiversity civil cases are heard and state criminal cases are tried.

EXHIBIT   3.3   Typical State Court System

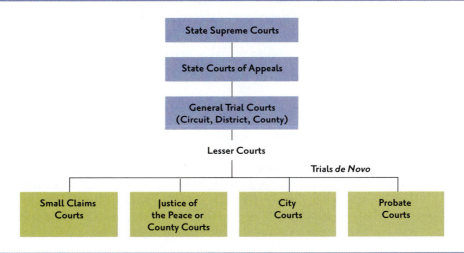

In addition to its general trial court, each state also has its own group of "lesser courts." These are courts with **limited jurisdiction**; they are comparable to the specialty courts of the federal system. For example, most states have a **small claims court** in which civil cases with minimal damage claims are tried. In a true small claims court, there are no attorneys. Parties represent themselves before a judge. Such a setting offers parties the chance to have a judge arrive at a solution without the expense of attorneys. The amount recoverable in small claims court is indeed very small: $200–$5,000 are the typical limits.

Most states also have a lesser court that allows the participation of lawyers but limits the amount that can be recovered. The idea is to take the burden of lesser cases away from the usually overburdened general trial courts. These courts are called **justice of the peace courts** or **county courts**.

Most cities also have their own trial courts, which are limited in their jurisdiction to the trial of lesser crimes, such as violations of city ordinances. Many states call these courts **traffic courts** because city ordinances involve so many traffic regulations.

In addition to these courts, some states have very specialized courts to handle matters that are narrow in their application of law but frequent in occurrence. For example, although probating (processing) a will and an estate involves narrow issues of law, there is a constant supply of this type of case. Many states have a special court to handle this and such related matters as guardianships for incompetent persons.

Many of the lesser courts allow appeals to a general state trial court for a new trial (**trial *de novo***) because not all judges in these lesser courts are lawyers and constitutional protections require a right of *de novo* appeal.

View the records of the Maricopa County Superior Court:
http://www.superiorcourt.maricopa.gov

State Appellate Courts

State appellate courts serve the same function as the U.S. courts of appeals. There is an automatic right of review in these courts. Some states have two appellate-level courts to handle the number of cases being appealed. The opinions of these courts are reported in the state's individual reporter, which contains the state's name and some indication that an appellate court decided the case. For example, state appellate decisions in Colorado are reported in *Colorado Appeals Reports* (abbreviated "Colo. App."). These opinions are also reported in a **regional reporter**. All of the states are grouped into regions, and opinions of state appellate courts are grouped into the reporter for that region. Exhibit 3.4 presents the various regions and state groupings. For example, Nevada is part of the Pacific region, and its appellate reports are found in the *Pacific Reporter* (abbreviated "P.," "P.2d," or "P.3d"). The following is a cite from a state court of appeals:

Felder v. State
579 S.E.2d 28 (Ga.App. 2003)

State Supreme Courts

Visit state courts online:
http://www.nccourts.org
http://www.courts.state.pa.us
http://www.courts.state.ny.us

State supreme courts are similar in their function and design to the U.S. Supreme Court. These courts do not hear every case because the right of appeal is not automatic. There is some discretion in what these supreme courts will hear. State supreme courts also act as trial courts in certain types of cases and are courts of original as well as appellate jurisdiction. For example, if two counties within a state have a dispute, the state supreme court would take the trial to ensure fairness. After a state supreme court decides an issue, it is important to remember that there is still a possibility of appeal to the U.S. Supreme Court if the case involves a federal question or an issue of constitutional rights.

EXHIBIT 3.4	National Reporter System Regions

Pacific (P. or P.2d)	Northwestern (N.W. or N.W.2d)	Northeastern (N.E. or N.E.2d)	Southeastern (S.E. or S.E.2d)
Alaska	Iowa	Illinois	Georgia
Arizona	Michigan	Indiana	North Carolina
(California)	Minnesota	Massachusetts	South Carolina
Colorado	Nebraska	(New York)	Virginia
Hawaii	North Dakota	Ohio	West Virginia
Idaho	South Dakota		
Kansas	Wisconsin	**Atlantic (A. or A.2d)**	**Southern (So. or So.2d)**
Montana		Connecticut	
Nevada	**Southwestern (S.W. or S.W.2d)**	Delaware	Alabama
New Mexico		District of Columbia	Florida
Oklahoma	Arkansas	Maine	Louisiana
Oregon	Kentucky	Maryland	Mississippi
Utah	Missouri	New Hampshire	
Washington	Tennessee	New Jersey	
Wyoming	Texas	Pennsylvania	
		Rhode Island	
		Vermont	

Note: California and New York each has its own reporter system.

Source: The national reporter system was developed by West Publishing Company. Reprinted with permission of West Publishing Company.

The opinions of state supreme courts are significant and are reported in the regional reporters discussed earlier. Many states also have their own reporters for state supreme court opinions. For example, California has the *California Reporter.* The state supreme court reporters are easily recognized because their abbreviations are the abbreviation of each state's name. The following cite is of a state supreme court decision:

Arizona v. Gonzalez-Perez
62 P.3d 126 (Ariz. 2003)

Judicial Opinions

Throughout the discussion of subject matter jurisdiction, published opinions of various courts have been mentioned. Although these opinions vary in their place of publication, the format is the same. Exhibit 3.5 is a sample page from a reporter, with each part of the excerpt identified. Opinions are reported consistently in this manner so that precedent can be found and used easily.

Venue

The concept of jurisdiction addresses the issue of which court system has the authority to try a case. The concept of **venue** addresses the issue of the location of the court in the system. For example, a criminal case in which a defendant is charged with a felony can be tried in any of a state's general trial courts. Heavy media coverage, however, may result in a judge's changing the venue of a case from the place where the crime was committed to another trial court where the publicity is less and it is easier to obtain an impartial jury.

EXHIBIT   3.5   Sample Page of a Case in a National Reporter

STATE v. REMY

Cite as 711 A.2d 665 (Vt. 1998)

case name —

STATE of Vermont

v.

Darlene A. REMY.

docket number — No. 97–152.

court — Supreme Court of Vermont.

April 17, 1998.

Defendant was convicted on a conditional guilty plea in the District Court, Unit No. 1, Bennington Circuit, Robert Grussing III, J., of driving under the influence (DUI). Defendant appealed. The Supreme Court, Morse, J., held that:

(1) police officer had probable cause to believe an assault against a household member had occurred, and therefore was authorized to make a warrantless arrest after stopping the vehicle; and (2) officer was entitled to stop the vehicle to issue a citation and then investigate further regarding probable cause to arrest for DUI.

decision of the court — Affirmed

decision issue research tool

1. Arrest   63.4(11)

Police officer, who had been informed of report that occupants of particular vehicle had been drinking and had committed assault against one occupant's former husband, had probable cause to believe an assault against a household member had occurred, and therefore was authorized to make a warrantless arrest after stopping vehicle. Rules Crim. Proc., Rule 3(a).

2. Automobiles   349(7)

Police officer with authority to make warrantless arrest of occupant of vehicle for assault of household member was entitled to stop the vehicle to issue a citation, and, having detected clear signs of intoxication, the officer was then authorized to investigate further in order to confirm or negate his suspicions regarding

probable cause to arrest for driving under the influence (DUI). Rules Crim.Proc., Rule 3(c).

———

William D. Wright, Bennington County State's Attorney, David R. Fenster, Deputy State's Attorney, and Mary Pat Murphy, Law Clerk (on the brief), Bennington, for Plaintiff–Appellee.

David A. Howard and Joyce Brennan, Law Clerk (on the brief), of Cormier & Howard, Bennington, for Defendant–Appellant.

attorneys for parties

Before AMESTOY, C.J., and GIBSON, DOOLEY, MORSE and JOHNSON, JJ.

MORSE, Justice. — judge deciding case

In these consolidated appeals defendant Darlene Remy challenges her conviction of driving under the influence of intoxicating liquor in violation of 23 V.S.A. § 1201(a)(2), and the related civil suspension of her license under 23 V.S.A. § 1205. She contends that the trial court erred in denying her motion to suppress all evidence relating to the DUI because the police: (1) lacked the statutory authority to stop and detain her under V.R.Cr.P. 3(c); and (2) lacked a reasonable suspicion of wrongdoing necessary to effectuate the stop. We affirm. — opinion

On February 1, 1997, at approximately 5:40 p.m., Officer Rowland of the Bennington Police Department responded to an assault complaint from Stephen Woodie. Woodie informed the officer that he had been on a service call for AAA in the parking lot of the Apple Valley Inn when a van driven by defendant approached. Woodie's former wife, Elaine Palmer, was a passenger in the van. Both women were yelling at Woodie. Palmer eventually got out of the van and punched Woodie in the mouth. At that point, Woodie left in his truck and returned to the service.

BUSINESS STRATEGY

Strategic Punitive Damages

In May 2001, Boeing Company announced that it was moving its corporate headquarters from Seattle, Washington, to Chicago, Illinois. When the announcement was made, many plaintiffs' lawyers for airline crash victims cheered. Cook County courts traditionally have juries drawn from blue-collar workers who tend to be very tough on business. One lawyer said, "Any case in Cook County is worth more than it would be in most places on earth." Cook County is home to a 1994 settlement for a US Air plane crash of $25.2 million for one family. The settlement remains the largest in aviation history.

Most airline crash suits are brought in federal district court because of the diversity of citizenship of the

© PHOTODISC/GETTY IMAGES

parties, the passengers, and the airlines. Which federal court remains a venue issue, and most courts will allow cases to be filed where the defendant is located; in the case of an airline, that venue is where it is headquartered. So, plaintiffs in airline crashes can now file in Cook County, Boeing's new residency for purposes of federal district court diversity.

In choosing a business location, the common strategic factors are often taxes, workforce, education resources, transportation, and climate. Businesses should add one more strategic factor: litigation climate.

Source: Blake Morrison, "Crash Lawyers Like Boeing Move," *USA Today,* May 16, 2001, p. 1A.

IN PERSONAM JURISDICTION OF COURTS: THE AUTHORITY OVER PERSONS

Once the proper court according to subject matter is determined, only half the job is done. For example, a case may involve a million-dollar claim between citizens of different states, in which case a federal district court has subject matter jurisdiction over the parties. But there are ninety-four federal districts, so how is it decided which federal court will hear the case? The case will be heard by the federal district court with *in personam* jurisdiction over the parties. Subject matter jurisdiction only partly determines which trial court has jurisdiction; the other jurisdictional issue is power over the parties involved in the case.

The various criteria for determining *in personam* jurisdiction are examined here and are outlined in Exhibit 3.6.

Ownership of Property within the State

A party who owns real property in a state is subject to the jurisdiction of that state's courts for litigation related to that property. Actually, this type of jurisdiction gives the court authority over the person because the person owns a thing in the state. Technically, this type of jurisdiction is called *in rem* **jurisdiction**.

Volunteer Jurisdiction

A court has jurisdiction over a person who agrees to be subject to that court. In some contracts, for example, the parties agree that any lawsuits will be brought in the seller's state. The seller's state courts then have jurisdiction over that volunteer buyer. Most Internet contracts have a venue clause.

EXHIBIT   3.6   Personal Jurisdiction

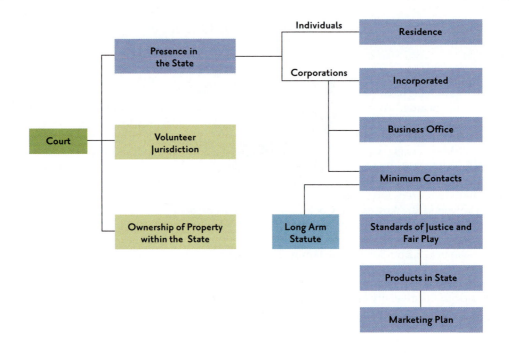

Presence in the State

The third and final way a state court can take jurisdiction is by the "presence" of a party in the state, which is determined by different factors.

Residence

Individuals are present in a state if they have a residence in that state. There are different definitions of residency for tax and election laws, but the requirement here is simply that the person live in the state some time during any given year.

Corporations are residents of the states in which they are incorporated. A corporation is also a resident of any state in which it has a business office with employees.

"Minimum Contacts"

Both corporations and residents can be subject to a state court's jurisdiction if they have "minimum contacts" in that state. The standard for **minimum contacts** is a fairness standard, which was established by the U.S. Supreme Court in *International Shoe* v. *Washington,* 326 U.S. 310 (1945). The Court basically required the states to notify out-of-state defendants of a suit and those defendants to have some contact with the state. Such contact can be simply the shipping of a product of the corporation into the state, or the contact can be advertising the firm's product or service in a magazine with national circulation. Fairness does not require an office or an employee in the state. A business is present if its products or ads make their way into the state. These standards for *in personam* jurisdiction are more liberal than the citizenship requirements for diversity actions.

Long–Arm Statutes: The Tools of Minimum Contracts

In order to follow the Supreme Court's ruling on fairness, all of the states have adopted **long arm statutes**. These statutes are appropriately named: They give courts the power to extend their arms of jurisdiction into other states. For example, suppose that Zeta Corporation is incorporated in Ohio and has its manufacturing plant there. Zeta ships its glass baking dishes to every state in the country, although it has no offices anywhere except in Ohio. Joan Berferd, who lives in Alabama, is injured when one of Zeta's baking dishes explodes. Can the Alabama courts allow Berferd to file suit there and require Zeta to come to Alabama to defend the suit? Yes, because a long arm statute is fair if it covers businesses shipping products to the state. Zeta entered the Alabama market voluntarily and must be subject to the Alabama courts. Long arm statutes generally cover businesses with offices in the state, businesses shipping products into the state, and businesses that cause a **tort** to be committed in that state.

Lindgren v. GDT, LLC (Case 3.1) provides an answer for the chapter's opening Consider.

For a look at long arm statutes and Internet securities transactions:
http://law.freeadvice.com/resources/articles/blueskylaws.htm

CASE 3.1

Lindgren v. *GDT, LLC*
312 F.Supp.2d 1125 (S.D. Iowa 2004)

Jangling Jewels on the Internet:
Can the Court Loop Them In?

FACTS

Gail Lindgren is an entrepreneur who runs a small business called Moonbeams based in West Des Moines, Iowa. In 1997, Ms. Lindgren designed and began selling JEANJANGLES, jewelry that hangs from the belt loops on jeans. Ms. Lindgren obtained a patent for the trinkets in 2000. JEANJANGLES are designed to hang from the belt loop and are made from sterling silver or gold-filled wire, with pieces incorporating such items as gold nuggets, glass, or abalone. Prices range from $18 to $58. JEANJANGLES may be purchased from Ms. Lindgren's Web site, http://www.jeanjangle.com, or from Teacups and Tiaras in West Des Moines, Iowa, and its online store.

A California company, GDT, began selling "Jeans for the Hip," also called JEAN JEWEL. GDT filed a trademark application for JEAN JEWEL on May 21, 2002. GDT's jewelry is made from sterling silver or gold and may contain semi-precious stones or glass. Prices range from $55 to $835. GDT maintains a Web site, http://www.jeanjewel.com, which began selling JEAN JEWEL merchandise in June 2003. From GDT's Web site, consumers can create a personal JEAN JEWEL account, browse product offerings, place orders, and have the product shipped to them anywhere in the world, including Iowa. An online order will be delivered by FedEx and "will arrive within 1–3 days after it is shipped anywhere in the continental U.S." JEAN JEWEL merchandise is also available at foreign and domestic retail outlets, although not in Iowa. GDT's principal place of business is Pacific Palisades, California.

Ms. Lindgren became aware of GDT, its Web site, and its product when *People* magazine did a feature story on the jean trinkets and friends called to congratulate her on her national success. There was further product confusion when singer Lance Bass of N'Sync referred to the California products during a national radio interview that had listeners thinking again that Ms. Lindgren's product was enjoying newfound notoriety. Ms. Lindgren filed suit in federal district court in Iowa against GDT for infringement. GDT maintains that it has never been to Iowa, has no stores in Iowa, has no salespeople or other employees in Iowa, no production facilities there, owns no real property there, and, therefore, cannot be required to come to Iowa to defend a lawsuit. Ms. Lindgren says that GDT has a Web site and is selling its jewels to residents in Iowa and must come to Iowa to defend a suit because it is doing business there. GDT filed a motion to dismiss the case for lack of *in personam* jurisdiction.

continued

JUDICIAL OPINION

LONGSTAFF, Chief Judge

In analyzing personal jurisdiction, the Court first examines whether the exercise of personal jurisdiction is proper under the forum state's long-arm statute; if so, the second question is whether the exercise of jurisdiction comports with due process.

(Iowa R. Civ. P. 1.306 permits jurisdiction to the extent allowed by the federal constitution.)

Due process requires that, in order to subject a nonresident to the jurisdiction of a state's courts, the nonresident must have "certain minimum contacts with it such that the maintenance of the suit does not offend 'traditional notions of fair play and substantial justice.'" *Int'l Shoe Co.* v. *Washington,* 326 U.S. 310, 316, 66 S.Ct. 154, 90 L.Ed. 95 (1945).

The application of [the minimum contacts] rule will vary with the quality and nature of the defendant's activity, but it is essential in each case that there be some act by which the defendant purposefully avails itself of the privilege of conducting activities within the forum State, thus invoking the benefits and protections of its laws. *Hanson* v. *Denckla,* 357 U.S. 235, 253, 78 S.Ct. 1228, 2 L.Ed.2d 1283 (1958). The Supreme Court repeatedly has applied the "purposefully avails" requirement of *Hanson.* The contacts with the forum state must be more than "'random,' 'fortuitous,' or 'attenuated.'" Minimum contacts must exist either at the time the cause of action arose, the time the suit is filed, or within a period of time immediately prior to the filing of the lawsuit.

The Eighth Circuit considers the following factors when evaluating the propriety of exercising jurisdiction under the due process clause: (1) the nature and quality of the contacts with the forum state; (2) the quantity of contacts with the forum state; (3) the relation of the cause of action to the contacts; (4) the interest of the forum state in providing a forum for its residents; and (5) the convenience of the parties.

The personal jurisdiction issue in this case is a close question. As the Supreme Court has noted, the determination of whether minimum contacts exist "is one in which few answers will be written 'in black or white. The greys are dominant and even among them the shades are innumerable.'"

The Eighth Circuit recently has indicated that when specific jurisdiction is premised on defendant's Web site contacts with the forum, the appropriate analytical framework is that of *Zippo Manufacturing Co.* v. *Zippo Dot Com. Inc.,* 952 F.Supp. 1119, 1124 (W.D.Pa.1997). The *Zippo* court observed that "the likelihood that personal jurisdiction can be constitutionally exercised is directly proportionate to the nature and quality of the commercial activity that an entity conducts over the Internet." The court employed a "sliding scale" to measure the nature and quality of the commercial activity central to its personal jurisdiction analysis. It noted:

At one end of the spectrum are situations where a defendant clearly does business over the Internet. If the defendant enters into contracts with residents of a foreign jurisdiction that involve the knowing and repeated transmission of computer files over the Internet, personal jurisdiction is proper. At the opposite end are situations where a defendant has simply posted information on an Internet Web site which is accessible to users in foreign jurisdictions. A passive Web site that does little more than make information available to those who are interested in it is not grounds for the exercise [of] personal jurisdiction. The middle ground is occupied by interactive Web sites where a user can exchange information with the host computer. In these cases, the exercise of jurisdiction is determined by examining the level of interactivity and commercial nature of the exchange of information that occurs on the Web site.

In the present case, GDT's site consists primarily of single point-of-sale transactions rather than . . . continuous, long-term contracts. While GDT's site allows visitors to establish an online account, the account is for convenience purposes only and entails no continuing obligations. Accordingly, GDT's less extensive site must also be evaluated in the middle *Zippo* category.

Prior to the filing of this action, GDT's only conduct directed at Iowa was the state's inclusion on a drop-down menu on the shipping page of GDT's Web site. The shipping page enabled shipment around the world—to Uzbekistan or Palau, if the customer so indicated. Shipments were contracted to FedEx as the third-party carrier, with the costs to be paid by the consumer. While GDT's Web site is both commercial and highly interactive, the site is arguably no more directed at Iowa than at Uzbekistan. "The fact that someone who accesses defendants' Web site can purchase a [JEAN JEWEL] does not render defendants' actions 'purposefully directed' at this forum." As GDT's Web site could be accessed anywhere, including Iowa, its existence does not demonstrate an intent to purposefully target Iowa.

There is no evidence that GDT took any purposeful action towards Iowa—it did not direct any paid advertising to Iowa or solicit Iowa residents to visit its Web site. It merely processed the orders from Iowa customers who visited its site. Furthermore, under both the California and Iowa versions of the U.C.C., the sales were made F.O.B. seller with the carrier acting as the buyer's agent. Title thus passed to the buyer in California when GDT delivered the items to FedEx for shipment. Consequently, the Internet sales were clearly made in California, and are an insufficient basis for personal jurisdiction over GDT in Iowa.

As an additional basis of personal jurisdiction, Lindgren seeks to invoke the "effects test" of *Calder* v.

Jones, 465 U.S. 783, 104 S.Ct. 1482, 79 L.Ed.2d 804 (1984). This test "allows the assertion of personal jurisdiction over non-resident defendants whose acts 'are performed for the very purpose of having their consequences felt in the forum state.'" The touchstones of the "effects test" are as follows:

A defendant's tortious acts can serve as a source of personal jurisdiction only where the plaintiff makes a *prima facie* showing that the defendant's acts (1) were intentional, (2) were "uniquely" or expressly aimed at the forum state, and (3) caused harm, the brunt of which was suffered—and which the defendant knew was likely to be suffered—there.

Here, Lindgren asserts that because the alleged confusion occurred in Iowa, and her principal place of business is in Iowa, the "brunt" of the injury is felt here. Additionally, she argues that her registration of the JEANJANGLES name put GDT on constructive notice that infringement of that name would harm her in Iowa. Lindgren claims that these factors support jurisdiction according to the *Calder* "effects test."

The Eighth Circuit has used the *Calder* test merely as an additional factor to consider when evaluating a defendant's relevant contacts with the forum, and circuit courts have declined to grant personal jurisdiction solely on the basis of forum state effects from an intentional tort. While *Calder* lends support to Lindgren's jurisdictional claims, it does not provide an independent basis for personal jurisdiction in the Eighth Circuit.

The facts of this case do not meet the "express aiming" requirement of *Calder.* GDT did not intentionally direct its activities at Iowa knowing that Lindgren could be harmed through its Web site. Lindgren contends that GDT had constructive notice, based on the presence of JEANJANGLES in the federal trademark database, that its JEAN JEWEL mark could infringe her trademark rights in Iowa. This contention, however, is undermined by the fact that the U.S. Patent and Trademark Office (USPTO) issued a Notice of Allowance for GDT's mark on September 16, 2003, signifying that the mark survived the trademark opposition period and has consequently been allowed for registration. Given that a USPTO examining attorney's search of the database failed to identify Lindgren's mark as confusingly similar to GDT's, this Court declines to find that such "constructive notice" evidences a purposeful intent on the part of GDT to target their activities at Iowa. Absent additional minimum contacts and evidence that defendant expressly aimed their conduct at Iowa, the *Calder* "effects test" does not support personal jurisdiction over GDT in Iowa.

Lindgren submits that GDT's use of the JEAN JEWEL mark to identify their Web site and products has caused actual confusion in the marketplace. Yet the only evidence of harm to Lindgren are the post-filing Internet sales. Even if the Court were to consider the post-filing sales to Iowa residents, those California purchases are not sufficient to subject GDT to personal jurisdiction in Iowa. They are, however, sufficient to confer personal jurisdiction over GDT in California. This Court recognizes that Iowa has a strong interest in providing a forum to protect its citizens from trademark infringement and unfair competition, and that Lindgren would no doubt be inconvenienced if forced to litigate her claim in California. These considerations do not, however, obviate the requirements of due process:

Even if the defendant would suffer minimal or no inconvenience from being forced to litigate before the tribunals of another State; even if the forum State has a strong interest in applying its law to the controversy; even if the forum State is the most convenient location for litigation, the Due Process Clause, acting as an instrument of interstate federalism, may sometimes act to divest the State of its power to render a valid judgment.

Viewing the circumstances of this case as a whole, Lindgren has failed to make a *prima facie* case of personal jurisdiction over GDT. GDT lacks minimum contacts with Iowa and considerations of fairness and justice do not warrant an exercise of personal jurisdiction by this Court. Although this Court lacks jurisdiction, it finds that Lindgren's claims may continue in the Central District of California, Western Division. Therefore, GDT's Motion to Dismiss is DENIED.

CASE QUESTIONS

1. Who developed the jeans jewelry first? Did either company cross the other in the federal records for patents and trademark registration?

2. What is the scope of Iowa's long arm statute?

3. What is the *Zippo* test and how is it applied here?

4. What is the *Calder* test and how is it applied here?

5. Can GDT be required to come to Iowa and defend the suit?

ETHICAL ISSUES

Evaluate the ethics of GDT in capitalizing on Lindgren's idea and market.

MAKING ETHICS PERSONAL

Guilt and Buying Knock-Offs

Now that you know the background of JEAN-JANGLES and JEAN JEWEL, would you purchase GDT's product? Why or why not? Suppose you were offered a counterfeit Burberry's purse for $25. The purse looks just like the store originals that cost $480. You could give it as a gift or resell it for as much as $75. Would you buy the purse? Why or why not? What difference does it make whether the purse is real or counterfeit? Is it your role to police trademark counterfeiters?

CONSIDER...   3.2

Since 1980, Richard B. King has run The Blue Note, a jazz club located in Columbia, Missouri. Bensusan Restaurant Corporation runs another jazz club, also called The Blue Note, in New York City. Bensusan applied for and obtained a federal trademark for its club name. In 1993, Bensusan's attorney wrote to Mr. King and asked that Mr. King refrain from using the name. Mr. King and Bensusan simply did not agree and parted ways until 1996, when Mr. King created a Blue Note Web site. The Web site had information about Mr. King's club, special dates of interest, a reference to it being "mid-Missouri's finest jazz club," and a note that it was not connected with The Blue Note of New York City. Bensusan filed suit in New York City for trademark infringement. The district court granted Mr. King's motion to dismiss the complaint for lack of jurisdiction, and Bensusan appealed. Can the New York federal court take jurisdiction over Mr. King and require him to come to New York City to defend the lawsuit? [*Bensusan Restaurant Corp.* v. *King*, 126 F.3d 25 (2d Cir. 1997).]

Steps for Analyzing This Case Study

THINK: 1. Determine how much of a presence Mr. King has in New York City.
   2. List contacts Mr. King has with residents of New York City.
   3. Determine whether Mr. King has tried to infiltrate the New York City jazz market.
   4. Determine the only way Mr. King could recruit New York Blue Note customers.

APPLY: Mr. King has no presence in New York City except for individuals who have access to his informational Web site. Mr. King has not targeted New York City customers and has no club in New York City, no office, no employees, and no property. By disclosing his geographic location, Mr. King makes certain that customers are not confused. Mr. King is not recruiting New York customers—only those who travel would be interested in his club.

ANSWER: There is no basis for granting jurisdiction. New York courts cannot require Mr. King to defend a lawsuit in New York.
   Apply the case law and this model for resolving Consider 3.3.

THE INTERNATIONAL COURTS

The decisions of international courts provide precedent for parties involved in international trade. However, one of the restrictions on international court decisions is that the decision binds only the immediate parties to the suit on the basis of their factual situation. International courts do not carry the enforcement power or authority of courts in the U.S. federal and state systems. They are consensual courts and are used only when the parties agree to use them.

There are several courts of international jurisdiction. The **International Court of Justice** (ICJ) is the most widely known court. It was first established as the Perma-

CONSIDER...   **3 · 3**

N-the-Water Publishing, Inc. dba Still N the Water Publishing produces hip-hop and rap music through sampling, the process of copying portions of prior master sound recordings directly onto new sound recordings and then rapping on top of the new sound recording. Bridgeport Music is the owner of the copyright for the music that Still N the Water has used for its rap and hip-hop song productions. Bridgeport is headquartered in Nashville, Tennessee, and Still N the Water is part of a series of record companies based in Florida and Texas. Bridgeport brought suit against Still N the Water in federal district court in Tennessee. Under Tennessee's long arm statute, jurisdiction may be asserted on "any basis not inconsistent with the constitution of this state or of the United States" [Tenn.Code Ann. § 20–2–214(a)(6)]. Still N the Water sells CDs in all 50 states with sales spread equally among the states and marketing plans for each of the states.

Can Still N the Water be required to come to Tennessee to defend the lawsuit? [*Bridgeport Music, Inc.* v. *Still N The Water Pub.* 327 F.3d 472 (6th Cir. 2003); *cert. denied* 124 S.Ct. 399, 157 L.Ed.2d 279 (2003).]

ETHICAL ISSUES

Evaluate the ethics of Still N the Water in using underlying copyrighted music for its rap and hip-hop songs without permission of the copyright holders.

Learn more about the International Court of Justice:
http://www.icj-cij.org

nent Court of International Justice (PCIJ) in 1920 by the League of Nations. In 1945, the United Nations (UN) changed the name and structure of the court. The ICJ is made up of fifteen judges, no more than two of whom can be from the same nation, who are elected by the General Assembly of the UN. The court has been described as having **contentious jurisdiction**, which is to say that the court's jurisdiction is consensual: When there is a dispute, the parties can agree to submit the dispute to the ICJ.

There are other international courts in addition to the ICJ. The European Union has its **Court of Justice of European Communities** and the **European Court of Human Rights**. Jurisdiction in these courts is also consensual. Finally, there is the **Inter-American Court of Human Rights**.

The decisions of these courts and decisions from individual countries' courts dealing with international law issues can be found in *International Law Reports*.

In recent years, London's Commercial Court, established over 100 years ago, has become a popular forum for the resolution of international commercial disputes. Over half the cases in this court involve foreign enterprises. Some companies choose London's Commercial Court as the forum for their disputes for several reasons, even though neither they nor their transactions have any connection with England. First, the court has the advantage of being a neutral forum. Second, for U.S. firms, the use of the English language in the court is important. Third, the court has a wide range of experience in international disputes, from shipping contracts to joint trading ventures. Fourth, the

BUSINESS PLANNING TIP

With national and international business transactions becoming so frequent, many contracts now include "forum selection" clauses. These portions of a contract to which the parties agree stipulate that if litigation is required, a particular court in a particular state or country will have jurisdiction over both parties. For example, a franchisor might have the forum selection clause provide that all litigation by franchisees would be in the state and city where the franchisor's principal office is located. Checking a contract carefully for these clauses will enable you to decide, before signing, whether you want to agree to travel to another state or country if litigation becomes necessary.

judges on the court were all once commercial litigators themselves and bring their depth of experience to the cases. Fifth, the court is known for its rapid calendar, moving cases along quickly. Major cases are heard within one year from the service of summons. Finally, the court has used a variety of creative remedies. The Commercial Court has issued pretrial injunctions to freeze assets, and its ties to the English government afford the injunctions international recognition. Perhaps the most famous of the Commercial Court's cases is its handling of the twenty class actions against Lloyd's of London.

Jurisdictional Issues in International Law

The jurisdiction of courts within a particular country over businesses from other countries is a critical issue in international law. A common subject in international disputes is whether courts in the United States, for example, can require foreign companies to defend lawsuits within the United States.

Conflicts of Law in International Disputes

The courts and judicial systems of countries around the globe vary, as do the procedural aspects of litigation. For example, in Japan there is no discovery process that permits the parties to examine each others' documents and witnesses prior to trial (see Chapter 4 for more details on discovery and the Japanese court system); and the United States permits lawyers to collect contingency fees and also permits broader tort recovery than would be available in most other countries.

Because of liberal discovery and recovery rules in the United States, many plaintiffs injured in other countries by products manufactured by U.S.-based firms want to bring suit in the United States to take advantage of our judicial system's processes and rules. However, the California Supreme Court has ruled in *Stangvik v. Shiley, Inc.,* 819 P.2d 858 (Cal. 1991), that if a plaintiff's home country provides an adequate forum for a dispute, the case cannot be brought in the United States. The suit involved family members of various patients who had died when their heart valves, manufactured by Shiley of Irvine, California, failed. The decision of the California Supreme Court required the plaintiffs to return to their home countries, where the recovery would be substantially less. However, states do differ on their conclusions about international product liability litigation; for a different result, see *Ison v. E.I. DuPont de Nemours and Co., Inc.,* 729 A.2d 832 (Del. 1999).

SUMMARY

What is the judicial process?

- Judicial review—review of a trial court's decisions and verdict to determine whether any reversible error was made

- Appellate court—court responsible for review of trial court's decisions and verdict

- Brief—written summary of basis for appeal of trial court's decisions and verdict

- Reversible error—mistake by trial court that requires a retrial or modification of a trial court's decision

- Options for appellate court:
  - Reverse—change trial court's decision
  - Remand—return case to trial court for retrial or reexamination of issues
  - Affirm—uphold trial court's decisions and verdict
  - Modify—overturn a portion of the trial court's verdict
  - *Stare decisis*—Latin for "let the decision stand"; doctrine of reviewing, applying, and/or distinguishing prior case decisions

- Case opinion—written court decision used as precedent; contains *dicta* or explanation of reasoning and, often, a minority view or dissenting opinion

Who are the parties in the judicial system?

- Plaintiffs/petitioners—initiators of litigation
- Defendants/respondents—parties named as those from whom plaintiff seeks relief
- Lawyers—officers of the court who speak for plaintiffs and defendants
- Attorney-client privilege—confidential protections for client conversations
- Appellant—party who appeals lower court's decision
- Appellee—party responding in an appeal

What courts can decide jurisdiction? The power of the court to hear cases

- Subject matter jurisdiction—authority of court over subject matter
- Jurisdiction over the parties: *in personam* jurisdiction
  - Voluntary
  - Through property
  - Presence in the state: minimum contacts
  - Residence
  - Business office

What are the courts and court systems?

Federal court system

- Federal district court—trial court in federal system; hears cases in which there is a federal question, the United States is a party, or the plaintiff and defendant are from different states (diversity of citizenship) and the case involves $75,000 or more; opinions reported in *Federal Supplement*
- Limited jurisdiction courts—bankruptcy courts, court of claims
- U.S. Courts of Appeals—federal appellate courts in each of the circuits; opinions reported in *Federal Reporter*
- U.S. Supreme Court—highest court in United States; requires *writ of certiorari* for review; acts as trial court (original jurisdiction) for suits involving states and diplomats

State court system

- Lesser courts—small claims, traffic courts, justice of the peace courts
- State trial courts—general jurisdiction courts in each state
- State appellate courts—courts that review trial court decisions
- State supreme courts—courts that review appellate court decisions

International courts

- Voluntary jurisdiction
- International Court of Justice—UN court; contentious (consensual) jurisdiction; reported in *International Law Reports*
- London Commercial Court—voluntary court of arbitration

QUESTIONS AND PROBLEMS

1. The brokerage firm of E.F. Hutton was charged with federal criminal violations of interstate funds transfers. In reviewing the case, the lawyers for the government discovered internal memorandums from and between branch managers in several states that outline a process for checking-kiting (a literal stringing together of checks and deposits) that enabled E.F. Hutton to earn interest on phantom deposits. Where will the case be tried? Which court system? Which court? Why?

What are the lawyer's obligations with respect to the document? What is the company's obligation? If you were a manager at E.F. Hutton, would you voluntarily disclose the document to the government?

2. Compare the procedures at the trial and appellate levels of the court system. Is additional evidence presented at the appellate level? Will a jury be present at both the trial and the appeal of the case? How many judges will hear the case at the trial and appellate levels?

3. Music Millennium is a business incorporated in Oregon ("Oregon MM") with its principal place of business located in Portland, Oregon. It opened its first retail outlet under the name "Music Millennium" in 1969 and now operates two retail music stores in Portland and also sells products through mail and telephone orders and its Internet Web site.

Millennium Music, Inc., is a South Carolina corporation and general partner of defendant Millennium Music, L.P., a South Carolina limited partnership ("LP"). It operates retail music stores in South Carolina under the name "Millennium Music" and sells products through its retail outlets and its Internet Web site, although the vast majority of sales occur at its retail stores. From March 1998 through September 1998, the LP sold fifteen compact discs to nine separate customers in six states and one foreign country. The sales totaled approximately $225. During the same period, its retail sales were $2,180,000. LP offers franchising circulars through the Internet and has two franchised stores in North Carolina.

LP has also purchased a small amount of compact discs from Allegro Corporation ("Allegro"), a distributor located in Portland, Oregon. Total purchases from Allegro in 1994–1997 totaled approximately one-half of one percent of inventory purchases for those years.

On or about July 7, 1998, Oregon MM received a credit document from Allegro. The credit was mailed to Oregon MM in error; the document apparently was intended for LP. On August 21, 1998, an Oregon resident, Linda Lufkin, purchased a compact disc from LP through its Web site. An attorney at the law firm for which Ms. Lufkin works requested that she purchase a compact disc from LP. Apparently, the attorney is an acquaintance of Oregon MM's counsel.

Oregon MM filed suit against LP on Oregon for its use of the name "Millennium Music" in connection with common law trademark rights. LP says it cannot be forced to come to Oregon to defend the suit. Is LP correct? [*Millenium Enterprises, Inc.* v. *Millennium Music, LP,* 33 F.Supp.2d 907 (D.Or. 1999).]

4. The domain name aol.org was registered by Korea DNS, a South Korean entity, on September 3, 2001, and subsequently transferred first to an individual, Sujin Jeon, and thereafter to an individual listed simply as "Will E." Here in the United States, the domain name AOL.COM is registered to its parent company and owner, Time Warner/AOL. That name has been held since 1996. On July 30, 2002, America Online, the holder of registered United States trademarks for AOL and AOL.COM, filed suit against the Korean company and individuals for infringement and violation of the Anticybersquatting Act. The Korean defendants filed a motion to dismiss on the grounds that the federal district court in Virginia, where AOL had filed suit and where its company headquarters are situated, did not have *in personam* jurisdiction over aol.org because it had no presence in the United States. Should the motion to dismiss be granted? [*America Online, Inc.* v. *Aol.Org,* 259 F.Supp.2d 449 (E.D. Va. 2003).]

5. Determine which court(s) would have jurisdiction over the following matters:
   a. The sale of securities without first registering them with the Securities and Exchange Commission, as required under 15 U.S.C. § 77 *et seq.*
   b. A suit between a Hawaiian purchaser of sunscreen lotion and its California manufacturer for severe sunburn that resulted in $65,000 in medical bills.

6. Jeffrey Dawes, the comptroller for Umbrellas, Inc., a New York Stock Exchange company, has been charged with two violations of the federal Foreign Corrupt Practices Act. In which court will he be tried?

7. A Delaware banking corporation was named as trustee for the large estate of a wealthy individual in that individual's will. The beneficiaries of the trust are the deceased's two children, one of whom lives in Pennsylvania and the other in Florida. The bank does business in Delaware only. Can the beneficiary in Florida successfully require the bank to submit to the jurisdiction of Florida courts? [*Hanson* v. *Denckla,* 357 U.S. 235 (1958).]

8. Eulala Shute lived in Arlington, Washington, and through a local travel agent purchased a seven-day Carnival cruise. The cruise began in Los Angeles, went to Puerto Vallarta, Mexico, and then returned to Los Angeles. Carnival Cruise Lines, Inc., the owner of the ship and the firm responsible for the cruise, is a corporation based in Miami, Florida. While the cruise ship was in international waters off of Mexico, Shute tripped and fell on a deck mat during a guided tour of the ship's galley.

Shute filed suit in federal district court in the state of Washington against Carnival to recover for her injuries. Could the Washington court take *in personam* jurisdiction over Carnival? [*Carnival Cruise Lines, Inc.* v. *Shute,* 499 U.S. 585 (1991).]

9. Hicklin Engineering, Inc., is a Minnesota corporation that manufactures transmission testing stands for worldwide sales. Hicklin's only place of business is Iowa. Aidco, Inc., is a Michigan corporation with its principal place of business in Michigan. Aidco also manufactures transmission testing stands for worldwide sales. Aidco sent letters to several of Hicklin's customers, raising questions about Hicklin's products and expertise and offering a promotion of its transmission stands. Aidco is not licensed to do business in Iowa and has no offices, employees, or agents there. Hicklin has filed suit in Iowa against Aidco for the tort of intentional interference with contractual relations. Can Aidco be required to come to Iowa to defend the suit? [*Hicklin Engineering, Inc.* v. *Aidco, Inc.,* 959 F.2d 738 (8th Cir. 1992).]

10. The words "I've fallen and I can't get up!" were part of a TV commercial for a device whose marketing was directed at the elderly and whose appeal was that the device was hooked to communication links with emergency care providers. In fact, the device provided a link, but not a direct link, to a "911" number; there would be some interlink delay in getting notification to emergency personnel. The devices, worn around the neck, were in fact a means of effecting communication when the wearer could not get to a phone. However, the device was not directly linked to a "911" number.

Officials in Arizona brought charges against the company for deceptive advertising. Standards in Arizona require proof only that someone could be misled by the commercials; actions against advertisers do not require proof that someone was actually misled. The devices have been a help to many people, bringing assistance to those who would otherwise, because of temporary or permanent mobility impairment, be unable to call for help. Officials in other states did not find the ads misleading. Does Arizona have jurisdiction?

If you were an official for the company, would you change all of your ads or modify only those in Arizona? Were the ads unethical?

RESEARCH PROBLEM

The Long Arm of the Law

11. Read the following additional cases and provide a summary of where the courts stand on Web sites and long-arm jurisdiction.

> *Inset Systems, Inc.* v. *Instruction Set, Inc.*, 937 F.Supp. 161 (D.Ct. 1996)
>
> *CompuServe, Inc.* v. *Patterson*, 89 F.3d 1257 (6th Cir. 1996)
>
> *Edias Software Int'l, L.L.C.* v. *Basis International Ltd., Ison* v. *E.I. DuPont de Nemours and Co., Inc.*, 729 A.2d 832 (Del. 1999); *Edias Software Int'l, L.L.C.* v. *Basis Int'l LTD.*, 947 F.Supp.413 (D.Ariz.1996)

Should there be a difference between a Web site with a toll-free number and a Web site from which goods can be ordered?

NOTE

1. The U.S. Supreme Court ruled that Mr. Newdow lacked standing to challenge the "under God" clause in the pledge of allegiance because he was not the custodial parent of his daughter. 542 U.S. ____ (2004), 124 S. Ct. 2301 2004 WL 1300159.

CHAPTER

4

Managing Disputes: Alternative Dispute Resolution and Litigation Strategies

The study of business regulation to this point has involved an overview of ethics, law, and the courts responsible for enforcing, interpreting, and applying the law. This chapter focuses on disputes and answers the following questions: How can businesses best resolve disputes? What strategies should a business follow if litigation is inevitable? How do courts proceed with litigation?

> **update**
>
> *For up-to-date legal news and real-world business applications, click on* **update** *at* *http://jennings.westbuslaw.com*

Everyone Makes Mistakes: Real Humor in the Court

The youngest son, the 20-year-old, how old is he?

How many times have you committed suicide?

Were you alone or by yourself?

—Q: You were shot in the fracas?
A: No, I was shot midway between the fracas and the navel.
LAWYERS' COURTROOM BLOOPERS FROM THE
COLLECTION OF WILLIAM LITANT, EDITOR
Massachusetts Bar Association Lawyers Journal

If I were asked where I place the American aristocracy, I should reply without hesitation that it occupies the judicial bench and bar.
ALEXIS DE TOCQUEVILLE (1805–1859)

Gateway computers included the following provision in its contract for sale of computers to consumers:

10. Dispute Resolution. Any dispute or controversy arising out of or relating to this Agreement or its interpretation shall be settled exclusively and finally by arbitration. The arbitration shall be conducted in accordance with the Rules of Conciliation and Arbitration of the International Chamber of Commerce. The arbitration shall be conducted in Chicago, Illinois, U.S.A., before a sole arbitrator. Any award referenced in any such arbitration proceeding shall be final and binding on each of the parties, and judgment may be entered thereon in a court of competent jurisdiction.

What type of arbitration is required? Is this clause valid and enforceable?

WHAT IS ALTERNATIVE DISPUTE RESOLUTION?

Alternative dispute resolution (ADR) offers parties alternative means of resolving their differences outside actual courtroom litigation and the costly aspects of preparation for it. ADR ranges from very informal options, such as a negotiated settlement between the CEOs of companies, to the formal, written processes of the American Arbitration Association. These processes may be used along with litigation or in lieu of litigation.

TYPES OF ALTERNATIVE DISPUTE RESOLUTION

Arbitration

Nature of Arbitration

Arbitration is the oldest form of ADR and is the resolution of disputes in a less formal setting than a trial. Many contracts today have mandatory arbitration clauses in them that require, in the event of a dispute, that the parties submit to arbitration. Other contracts, including many consumer auto insurance contracts, offer voluntary arbitration for consumers involved in disputes over their coverage.

Arbitration can be binding or nonbinding. **Binding arbitration** means that the decision of the arbitrators is final. The parties cannot appeal the decision to any court. **Nonbinding arbitration** is a preliminary step to litigation. If one of the parties is not satisfied with the result in the arbitration, the case may still be litigated.

Arbitration Procedures

Arbitration can be agreed upon well in advance. A contract may contain a future arbitration clause so that the parties agree at the time of contracting that any disputes will be submitted to arbitration. The parties may also agree to submit to arbitration after their dispute arises even though they do not have such a clause in their contract. The issue of mandatory arbitration, particularly when there are consumers involved or employees who have statutory rights, has been a focus of litigation. The Federal Arbitration Act (FAA) was passed to stop some of the judicial decisions that were holding arbitration clauses invalid, particularly in consumer contracts. In Case 4.1, the U.S. Supreme Court provided its interpretation of the binding nature of arbitration clauses in contracts under the FAA.

CASE 4.1

Green Tree Financial Corp. v. *Randolph*
531 U.S. 79 (2000)

A Mandatory Arbitration Clause? I Dispute That!

FACTS

Larketta Randolph (Respondent) purchased a mobile home from Better Cents Home Builders, Inc., in Opelika, Alabama. She financed this purchase through Green Tree Financial Corporation and its subsidiary (Petitioners). The contract that Ms. Randolph signed, the Manufactured Home Retail Installment Contract and Security Agreement, required that Ms. Randolph buy Vendor's Single Interest insurance, which protects the seller (vendor/Better Cents) or lienholder (Green Tree) against the costs of repossession in the event of default. The agreement also provided that all disputes arising from, or relating to, the contract, whether arising under case law or statutory law, would be resolved by binding arbitration. The arbitration clause provides:

All disputes, claims, or controversies arising from or relating to this Contract or the relationships which result from this Contract, or the validity of this arbitration clause or the entire contract, shall be resolved by binding arbitration by one arbitrator selected by Assignee with consent of Buyer(s). This arbitration Contract is made pursuant to a transaction in interstate commerce, and shall be governed by the Federal Arbitration Act at 9 U.S.C. Section 1. Judgment upon the award rendered may be entered in any court having jurisdiction. The parties agree and understand that they choose arbitration instead of litigation to resolve disputes. The parties understand that they have a right or opportunity to litigate disputes through a court, but that they prefer to re-solve their disputes through arbitration, except as provided herein. THE PARTIES VOLUNTARILY AND KNOWINGLY WAIVE ANY RIGHT THEY HAVE TO A JURY TRIAL EITHER PURSUANT TO ARBITRATION UNDER THIS CLAUSE OR PURSUANT TO A COURT ACTION BY ASSIGNEE (AS PROVIDED HEREIN). The parties agree and understand that all disputes arising under case law, statutory law, and all other laws, including, but not limited to, all contract, tort, and property disputes will be subject to binding arbitration in accord with this Contract. The parties agree and understand that the arbitrator shall have all powers provided by the law and the Contract.

Ms. Randolph sued Green Tree as part of a class action lawsuit, alleging that Green Tree violated the Truth in Lending Act (TILA), 15 U.S.C. § 1601 et seq. (see Chapter 15 for more information on this statute), by failing to disclose as a finance charge the $15 annual fee she was required to pay for the Vendor's Single Interest insurance requirement. She later amended her complaint to add a claim that petitioners violated the Equal Credit Opportunity Act, 15 U.S.C. §§ 1691–1691f (see Chapter 15), by requiring her to arbitrate her claims that arose under federal statutes. Green Tree filed a motion to compel arbitration, which the District Court granted. Ms. Randolph appealed, and the Court of Appeals held that the arbitration agreement failed to provide the minimum guarantees for protection of Ms. Randolph's statutory rights under the TILA. On that basis, the court held that the agreement to arbitrate posed a risk to Ms. Randolph's statutory rights and was therefore unenforceable. Green Tree appealed, and the U.S. Supreme court granted *certiorari*.

JUDICIAL OPINION

REHNQUIST, Chief Justice

We now turn to the question whether Randolph's agreement to arbitrate is unenforceable because it says nothing about the costs of arbitration, and thus fails to provide her protection from potentially substantial costs of pursuing her federal statutory claims in the arbitral forum. Section 2 of the FAA provides that "[a] written provision in any maritime transaction or a contract evidencing a transaction involving commerce to settle by arbitration a controversy thereafter arising out of such contract . . . shall be valid, irrevocable, and enforceable, save upon such grounds as exist at law or in equity for the revocation of any contract." In considering whether respondent's agreement to arbitrate is unenforceable, we are mindful of the FAA's purpose "to reverse the longstanding judicial hostility to arbitration agreements . . . and to place arbitration agreements upon the same footing as other contracts."

In light of that purpose, we have recognized that federal statutory claims can be appropriately resolved through arbitration, and we have enforced agreements to arbitrate that involve such claims. We have likewise rejected generalized attacks on arbitration that rest on "suspicion of arbitration as a method of weakening the protections afforded in the substantive law to would-be complainants." . . . [E]ven claims arising under a statute designed to further important social policies may be arbitrated because " 'so long as the prospective litigant effectively may vindicate [his or her] statutory cause of action in the arbitral forum,' " the statute serves its functions.

In determining whether statutory claims may be arbitrated, we first ask whether the parties agreed to submit their claims to arbitration, and then ask whether Congress has evinced an intention to preclude a waiver of judicial remedies for the statutory rights at issue. In this case, it is undisputed that the parties agreed to arbitrate all claims relating to their contract, including claims involving statutory rights. Nor does Randolph contend that the TILA evinces an intention to preclude a waiver of judicial remedies. She contends instead that the arbitration agreement's silence with respect to costs and fees creates a "risk" that she will be required to bear prohibitive arbitration costs if she pursues her claims in an arbitral forum, and thereby forces her to forgo any claims she may have against petitioners. Therefore, she argues, she is unable to vindicate her statutory rights in arbitration.

It may well be that the existence of large arbitration costs could preclude a litigant such as Randolph from effectively vindicating her federal statutory rights in the arbitral forum. But the record does not show that Randolph will bear such costs if she goes to arbitration. Indeed, it contains hardly any information on the matter. The record reveals only the arbitration agreement's silence on the subject, and that fact alone is plainly insufficient to render it unenforceable. The "risk" that Randolph will be saddled with prohibitive costs is too speculative to justify the invalidation of an arbitration agreement.

In Randolph's Motion for Reconsideration in the District Court, she asserted that "[a]rbitration costs are high" and that she did not have the resources to arbitrate. But she failed to support this assertion. She first acknowledged that petitioners had not designated a particular arbitration association or arbitrator to resolve their dispute. Her subsequent discussion of costs relied entirely on unfounded assumptions. She stated "[f]or the purposes of this discussion, we will assume filing with the [American Arbitration Association], the filing fee is $500 for claims under $10,000 and this does not include the cost of the arbitrator or administrative fees." Randolph relied on, and attached as an exhibit what appears to be informational material from the American Arbitration Association that does not discuss the amount of filing fees. She then noted "[The American Arbitration Association] further cites $700 per day as the average arbitrator's fee." For this proposition she cited a [*sic*] article in the Daily Labor Report, February 15, 1996, published by the Bureau of National Affairs, entitled Labor Lawyers at ABA Session Debate Role of American Arbitration Association. The article contains a stray statement by an association executive that the average arbitral fee is $700 per day. Randolph plainly failed to make any factual showing that the American Arbitration Association would conduct the arbitration, or that, if it did, she would be charged the filing fee or arbitrator's fee that she identified. These unsupported statements provide no basis on which to ascertain the actual costs and fees to which she would be subject in arbitration. In this Court, Randolph's brief lists fees incurred in cases involving other arbitrations as reflected in opinions of other Courts of Appeals, while petitioners' counsel states that arbitration fees are frequently waived by petitioners. None of this information affords a sufficient basis for concluding that Randolph would in fact have incurred substantial costs in the event her claim went to arbitration.

To invalidate the agreement on that basis would undermine the "liberal federal policy favoring arbitration

continued

agreements." It would also conflict with our prior holdings that the party resisting arbitration bears the burden of proving that the claims at issue are unsuitable for arbitration. We have held that the party seeking to avoid arbitration bears the burden of establishing that Congress intended to preclude arbitration of the statutory claims at issue. Similarly, we believe that where, as here, a party seeks to invalidate an arbitration agreement on the ground that arbitration would be prohibitively expensive, that party bears the burden of showing the likelihood of incurring such costs. Randolph did not meet that burden.

The judgment of the Court of Appeals is reversed on the issue of the validity of the arbitration clause.

CASE QUESTIONS

1. Describe the effect of the arbitration clause in the contract that Ms. Randolph signed.

2. What is the underlying dispute regarding her contract?

3. What is the relationship between the TILA and the FAA?

4. What problems did the court see with Ms. Randolph's arguments about costs of arbitration?

5. Is the arbitration clause valid and binding?

C O N S I D E R . . .   4 . 1

Review the arbitration clause in the chapter's opening Consider from the Gateway computers contract. Based on the *Randolph* case, do you think this clause is valid and enforceable against the consumers who buy Gateway computers? Does it make a difference that they must travel to Chicago for their arbitration? Incorporating what you learned in Chapter 3 about *in personam* jurisdiction, do you think that a Chicago court could force buyers to come to Chicago to defend a suit? Can the parties agree to submit to jurisdiction? What if the parties felt they had no choice but to submit to jurisdiction?

Visit the American Arbitration Association:

http://www.adr.org

Once the parties agree to arbitrate, they usually notify the American Arbitration Association (AAA), which for a fee will handle all the steps in the arbitration. The AAA is the largest ADR provider in the country, with an annual caseload of 230,000 for 2002, which is nearly a 100 percent increase from 1999. A 2003 study reports that 85 percent of Fortune 1000 companies use arbitration for their commercial contracts disputes. A tribunal administrator is appointed for each case, and this administrator communicates with the parties and helps move the arbitration along. The fee charged by the AAA depends on the amount and nature of the claim. For example, a claim between $75,000 and $150,000 has a fee of about $2,000 for filing, with the costs and expenses of the arbitrator not included. The arbitrator is generally paid by the hour. A multimillion-dollar arbitration case will have a $10,000–$15,000 fee plus arbitrator fees and expenses. Exhibit 4.1 is a sample AAA form of a demand for arbitration and the method for beginning arbitration. This document is the complaint form for arbitration.

Once a demand for arbitration is received, the tribunal administrator sends each of the parties a proposed list of arbitrators. Exhibit 4.2 is a sample of such a notice. The parties are given seven days to reject any of the proposed arbitrators and to rank the remaining named possibilities in the order of their preference. The tribunal tries to make a mutually agreeable choice but can submit a new list if necessary. If the parties cannot agree, the AAA appoints an arbitrator but will never appoint anyone rejected by one of the parties.

CHECK THE WEB

Check the Web for updates on arbitration cases, rules, and statistics.

EXHIBIT 4.1   Sample Demand for Arbitration

AMERICAN ARBITRATION ASSOCIATION
COMMERCIAL ARBITRATION RULES
DEMAND FOR ARBITRATION

MEDIATION is a nonbinding process. The mediator assists the parties in working out a solution that is acceptable to them. If you would like the AAA to contact the other parties to determine whether they wish to mediate this matter, please check this box. ☐ *There is no additional administrative fee for this service.*

TO: Name		Name of Representative (if known)		Name of Firm (if applicable)	
Address			Representative's Address		
City	State	Zip Code	City	State	Zip Code
Phone No.	Fax No.		Phone No.		Fax No.

The named claimant, a party to an arbitration agreement contained in a written contract, dated _____
providing for arbitration under the Commercial Arbitration Rules of the American Arbitration Association, hereby demands
arbitration thereunder.

IS THIS A DISPUTE BETWEEN A BUSINESS AND A CONSUMER?   Yes ☐   No ☐

THE NATURE OF THE DISPUTE

THE CLAIM OR RELIEF SOUGHT (the Amount, if Any)

DOES THIS DISPUTE ARISE OUT OF AN EMPLOYMENT RELATIONSHIP?   YES ☐   No ☐

IF THIS DISPUTE ARISES OUT OF AN EMPLOYMENT RELATIONSHIP, WHAT WAS/IS THE EMPLOYEE'S ANNUAL
WAGE RANGE? Note: this question is required by California law.
          ☐ Less Than $100,000   ☐ $100,000 - $250,000   ☐ Over $250,000

TYPES OF BUSINESS
Claimant _____   Respondent _____

HEARING LOCALE REQUESTED

You are hereby notified that copies of our arbitration agreement and this demand are being filed with the American Arbitration
Association at its_____ office, with a request that it commence administration of the arbitration. Under the
rules, you may file an answering statement within fifteen days after notice from the AAA.

Signature (may be signed by a representative)		Title		Date	
Name of Claimant		Name of Representative		Name of Firm (if Applicable)	
Address (to Be Used in Connection with This Case)			Representative's Address		
City	State	Zip Code	City	State	Zip Code
Phone No.	Fax No.		Phone No.		Fax No.

TO BEGIN PROCEEDINGS, PLEASE SEND TWO COPIES OF THIS DEMAND **AND THE ARBITRATION AGREEMENT**,
WITH THE FILING FEE AS PROVIDED FOR IN THE RULES, TO THE AAA. SEND THE ORIGINAL DEMAND TO THE
RESPONDENT.

Source: Form appears courtesy of the American Arbitration Association.

The hearing date is set at a mutually agreeable time. Between the time the date is set and the actual hearing, the parties have the responsibility of gathering together the evidence and witnesses necessary for their cases. The parties are, in effect, doing their preparation. The parties can also request that the other party bring certain documents to the hearing. Some arbitrators are given subpoena power in certain states; that is, they have the power to require the production of documents or to have a witness testify.

EXHIBIT   4.2   Sample List for Selection of Arbitrators

American Arbitration Association

Do not send this form to the other party.

CASE NUMBER: _____ DATE LIST SUBMITTED: _____

PARTIES: _____ AND _____

LIST FOR SELECTION OF ARBITRATOR(S)

After striking the name of any unacceptable arbitrator(s), please indicate your order of preference by number. We will try to appoint arbitrator(s) mutually acceptable who can hear your case promptly. Leave as many names as possible.

NOTE: Biographical information is attached. Unless your response is received by the Association by _____, all names submitted may be deemed acceptable.

REQUEST FOR DATES

To enable the arbitrator(s) to avoid fixing an inconvenient hearing date, please cross off the dates that are not acceptable for a hearing, but leave as many days as possible so that the first mutually agreeable date for hearing may be set. If a mutually agreeable date is not available for these two months, the arbitrator(s) is/are empowered under the rules to fix the time and place for each hearing. If this form is not returned by _____, it will be assumed that any open date is satisfactory to you. The hearing will then be scheduled for a date preferred by the other party.

NOTE: Saturdays, Sundays, and other unavailable days have been marked off.

Month of _____						
1	2	3	4	5	6	7
8	9	10	11	12	13	14
15	16	17	18	19	20	21
22	23	24	25	26	27	28
29	30	31				

Month of _____						
1	2	3	4	5	6	7
8	9	10	11	12	13	14
15	16	17	18	19	20	21
22	23	24	25	26	27	28
29	30	31				

Please note that hearings generally commence at _____ a.m./p.m.

I anticipate that my case will require _____ hours/days of hearing.

PARTY: _____

BY: _____ TITLE: _____

Your telephone or fax response to this inquiry will be appreciated and will expedite administration. Please refer to the telephone and fax numbers on the enclosed letterhead.   Form G4–4/88

Source: Form appears courtesy of the American Arbitration Association.

The parties need not have lawyers but have the right to use one under AAA rules. A rule requires that the AAA and other parties be notified if an attorney will be used and that the attorney be identified.

Although the atmosphere is more relaxed, an arbitration hearing parallels a trial. The parties are permitted brief opening statements, after which they discuss the remedy that is sought. Each of the parties then has the opportunity to present evidence and witnesses. There is a right of cross-examination, and closing statements are also given. Some of the emotion of a trial is missing because, although emotional appeal influences juries, an expert arbitrator is not likely to be influenced by it. After the close of the hearing, the arbitrator has thirty days to make a decision.

In binding arbitration, the arbitrator's award is final. The award and decision cannot be changed, modified, or reversed. Only the parties can agree to have the case reopened; the arbitrator cannot do so.

Many state courts, in order to encourage ADR, now impose mandatory arbitration in all cases involving amounts less than $25,000 or $50,000, for example. In Arizona, these mandatory arbitration proceedings are arbitrated by lawyers in the state, who are required to accept such assignments on a rotating basis either for a fee or as part of their *pro bono* activities. Such mandatory arbitration requirements have reduced the civil caseloads in many states by as much as 50 percent.

Mediation

Arbitration can be complex and expensive in spite of its self-imposed procedural limitations. However, other forms of ADR are readily available and relatively inexpensive. **Mediation** is one such alternative. In a 1999 survey by the *National Law Journal* and the AAA, 88 percent of lawyers indicated mediation as their preferred method of dispute resolution, with most noting that arbitration did not save much money or work over a full-blown trial.[1] However, a 2003 survey by the AAA indicates that lawyers in companies (85 percent) favor arbitration.[2] Mediation is a process in which both parties meet with a neutral mediator who listens to each side explain its position. The mediator is trained to get the parties to respond to each other and their concerns. The mediator

Visit a firm specializing in ADR, National Arbitration and Mediation (NAM):
http://www.namadr.com

BUSINESS PLANNING TIP

Many consumer sales agreements contain binding arbitration clauses, such as the following from Wells Fargo & Company.

Wells Fargo has adopted a Comprehensive Dispute Resolution Program, effective September 1, 1992, for certain disputes with account holders. The following amendment to your Consumer Disclosure Statement sets forth the terms of the Program. Your continued use of your account will constitute your agreement to this program. Please read this notice and keep it for future reference.

Always read and draft your agreements carefully.

FOR THE MANAGER'S DESK

RE: ARBITRATION AND EMPLOYMENT CASES

Some new statistics on employee arbitration have caused companies to question whether arbitration is the best approach to resolving employee disputes. The data, from the American Arbitration Association, indicate the following:

- Average length of employee arbitration: 246 days
- Average amount of employee award: $84,754
- Percentage of time employers were required to pay for employees' arbitration fees and costs: 70 percent
- Percentage of cases involving low-income workers: 43.5 percent
- Total number of employee arbitration cases filed last year: 2,159
- Percentage increase in employee arbitration cases since 1997: 60 percent

The U.S. Supreme Court has ruled that mandatory arbitration clauses in employee contracts are valid and enforceable, and employers continue to favor arbitration. Nearly 2,000 companies include mandatory arbitration as part of their employment contracts. At these compa-

nies, employees sign a waiver of their right to sue and agree to mandatory arbitration. However, corporate lawyers point to some negative aspects of employee arbitration.

- Lawyers for employees have free rein and can stretch out the proceedings, paperwork, and so on.
- There can be numerous hearings on issues, in addition to the arbitration hearing itself.
- Employees can win huge awards, such as one against a mutual fund company for $25 million in an arbitration brought by a former employee.
- Arbitrators are far less likely to dismiss a case. Thus even the most frivolous employee claims proceed to hearing and incur all the costs associated with a complete process.
- It is difficult to have an arbitration decision overturned by a court.
- The quality of the arbitrators can vary significantly.

For more information, see Joanne Gordon, "Here Come Da Judge," *Forbes*, December 9, 2002, p. 60.

For more information
about mediation in B2B
disputes, go to:
http://www.acrnet.org/
or
http://www.dr.bbb.org

For more information
about e-commerce dispute
resolution, also see:
http://www.adrworld.com

helps break down impasses and works to have the parties arrive at a mutually agreeable solution. Unlike an arbitrator, the mediator does not issue a decision; the role of the mediator is to try to get the parties to agree on a solution. Mediation is completely confidential. What is said to the mediator cannot be used later by the parties or their lawyers if litigation becomes necessary. Mediation is less expensive than arbitration and does not require that the parties bring lawyers. Mediation is not binding unless the parties have agreed to be bound by the decision.

Mediation has been a popular form of dispute resolution among business-to-business (B2B) e-commerce companies. Amazon.com and eBay have used mediation regularly in the resolution of disputes.

Medarb

Mediation arbitration (medarb) is a recent creation in which the arbitrator begins by attempting to negotiate between the two parties. If the arbitrator is unable to reach a settlement, the case proceeds to arbitration with the same party serving as arbitrator. One percent of the AAA's cases each year are decided by a medarb process.

The Minitrial

In a **minitrial**, the parties have their lawyers present the strongest aspects of their cases to senior officials from both companies in the presence of a neutral advisor or a judge with experience in the field. At the end of the presentations by both parties, the neutral advisor can provide several forms of input, which are controlled by the parties. The advisor may be asked to provide what his or her judgment would be in the case, or the advisor may be asked to prepare a settlement proposal based on the concerns and issues presented by the parties. Minitrials are more adversarial than mediation, but they are confidential; and the input from a neutral but respected advisor may help bring the parties together. A minitrial is not binding.

Rent-a-Judge

Many companies and individuals are discovering that the time that elapses between the filing of a lawsuit and its resolution is too great to afford much relief. As a result, a kind of private court system, known as **rent-a-judge**, is developing in which parties may have their case heard before someone with judicial experience without waiting for the slower process of public justice. These private courts are like *The People's Court* without the television cameras. The parties pay filing fees and pay for the judges and courtrooms. These private courts also offer less expensive settlement conferences to afford the parties a chance at mediation prior to their private hearing. This and the other methods of ADR previously discussed offer the opportunity to obtain final dispositions of cases more quickly and at less cost.

Summary Jury Trials

Under this relatively new method of ADR, the parties are given the opportunity to present summaries of their evidence to a judge and jurors. The jurors then give an advisory verdict to start the settlement process. If the parties are unable to agree on a settlement, a formal trial proceeds. This means of resolution gives the parties an idea of a jury's perception and assists in setting guide-

---

BUSINESS PLANNING TIP

Employers considering an arbitration clause in employment agreements should provide employees with both internal and external means for dispute resolution.

Internal means of employment dispute resolution:

a. Peer review

b. Ombudspersons

c. Mediation (with someone in the company but outside the employee's immediate area serving as mediator)

External means of employment dispute resolution:

a. Mediation (as done by an outsider)

b. Nonbinding arbitration

c. Final and binding arbitration

When developing an arbitration clause and policy for employees, follow these steps.

1. Decide the types of dispute included.

2. Decide who may serve as arbitrators.

3. Provide rules for fact-finding and discovery of evidence.

4. Give the same types of remedies employees would have under any statutory protections they have.

5. Give employees the same time frames for submitting claims that they have under a statute.

6. Do not preclude the right to file a complaint with an agency for violation of employment laws.

7. Notify all potential employees of the arbitration plan and its requirements and provisions.

8. Give disclosure on right of representation.

9. If you are implementing a new plan, give employees notice and adequate time to make decisions and adjustments.

lines for settlement. A **summary jury trial** occurs late in the litigation process, after the costs of **discovery** have been incurred. It can, however, save the expense of a trial.

Early Neutral Evaluation

Early neutral evaluation requires another attorney to meet with the parties, receive an assessment of the case by both sides, and then provide an evaluation of the merits of the case. The attorney, who is either a paid consultant or a volunteer through the state bar association, renders an opinion on the resolution of the case. The idea in this method of resolution is to encourage settlement. Because early neutral evaluation occurs before the discovery phase of the case, it can save time and money if the parties are able to settle.

Peer Review

A new form of dispute resolution called peer review has become popular particularly for disputes between employers and employees and is used by Darden Industries (Red Lobster, Olive Garden), TRW Inc., Rockwell International Corp., and Marriott International, Inc. Peer review, which is generally conducted within three weeks of demand, is a review by coworkers of the action taken against an employee (demotion, termination, discipline). These panels of fellow employees (one chosen by management, one chosen by the employee, and one chosen randomly) can take testimony, review documents, and make decisions that can include an award of damages.

Employers say that sometimes their decisions are reversed in peer review, but Darden Industries indicates that peer review has reduced employee litigation and legal fees. Of the 100 disputes handled each year in peer review, only 10 proceed to litigation.

Experiments in the use of peer review for customers, contractors, and physicians are ongoing around the country. The advantage many see in this new form of ADR is the perception by all involved of its fairness.

RESOLUTION OF INTERNATIONAL DISPUTES

Arbitration has been used in the international business arena since 1922. The **International Chamber of Commerce** (ICC) is a private organization that handles arbitration cases from parties in 123 countries. In 2003, the Arbitration Court of the ICC handled 583 requests for arbitration and issued 369 arbitration awards. Most requests for ICC arbitration come from Western countries, and the typical subject matters are trade transactions, contracts, intellectual property, agency, and corporate law. The following statistics were taken from the ICC's annual report for 2003.

- State or para-statal entities represented 11 percent of the parties.
- Places of arbitration were fixed in forty-seven different countries on five continents.
- Arbitrators of sixty-nine different nationalities were appointed or confirmed under the ICC Rules.
- The amount in dispute exceeded $1 million (U.S.) in 55.8 percent of new cases.

The ICC process is very similar to that discussed earlier for the American Arbitration Association. A request for arbitration is submitted to the ICC Secretariat in Paris; the parties can nominate arbitrators and choose the location for the

Visit the International Chamber of Commerce:
http://www.iccwbo.org

For a look at the types of awards made by the ICC, go to:
http://www.iccwbo.org/court/english/awards/awards.asp

You can find the standard ICC arbitration clause in over seventy-five languages at:
http://www.iccwbo.org/index_court.asp

Visit the ICC conciliation site and rules:
http://www.iccwbo.org
Click on the ICC International Court of Arbitration

Find full information on the ICC's work and process:
http://www.iccwbo.org/court/english/right_topics/stat_2003.asp

Visit the ICSID:
http://www.worldbank.org/icsid

Visit the UNCITRAL site:
http://www.uncitral.org/

arbitration hearing. The award of the ICC is final, and payment must be made at the location of the hearing.

The ICC also provides mediation, referred to as conciliation, services. In conciliation, the court assigns an expert to work with the parties to try to achieve a settlement of the case.

In addition to the ICC, the World Bank has established the International Center for Settlement of Investment Disputes (ICSID). The ICSID is an arbitral organization created specifically to hear disputes between investors and the nations in which they have made investments. This arbitration forum was created because of investors' fears that the courts of the nation in which they have invested may favor the government of that nation. Again, investment contracts can provide for the submission of disputes to the ICSID. Decisions of the ICSID are final and are enforceable as if they were court orders.

The United Nations Commission on International Trade Law (UNCITRAL) adopted a Model Law for Arbitration in 1985 that deals with where arbitration should be held (the parties can decide) and which country's laws should apply.

LITIGATION VERSUS ADR: THE ISSUES AND COSTS

Speed and Cost

Speed and cost are two compelling reasons businesses turn to ADR to resolve disputes. Costs of ADR are frequently one-tenth of the cost of litigating a dispute.

Protection of Privacy

There are other reasons parties may choose ADR. Whatever matter is in dispute can be kept private if referred directly to ADR; there are then no public court documents available for examination. Even when a suit is filed, the negotiated settlement achieved through alternative means can be kept private to protect the interests of the parties. When Dillard's, a national department store chain, and Joseph Horne Company, a department store based in Pittsburgh, were litigating over Dillard's conduct in a Horne's takeover, the parties' dispute centered on whether Dillard's was conducting due diligence in obtaining access to Horne's facilities and records, or whether Dillard's was actually running the stores in an attempt to drive down the acquisition price. The business press reported on the litigation and the underlying dispute. The information was not flattering to either party. Dillard's was portrayed as a large firm taking advantage of a small chain and engaging in unethical conduct with respect to verifying financial information prior to acquisition. Horne's was portrayed as naive and inept. Dillard's and Horne's settled the dispute, and both agreed to keep the terms of the settlement confidential. As a result, the very public litigation ended, and the focus on alleged misconduct changed because of the settlement and its private nature.

Creative Remedies

Often, without the constraints of court jurisdiction and the restraints of legal boundaries, a creative remedy can be crafted that helps both sides. For example, Intel, a computer chip manufacturer, experienced ongoing disputes with employees who left the company to begin their own businesses with products and

FOR THE MANAGER'S DESK

RE: SOUTHWEST AIRLINES AND CREATIVE DISPUTE RESOLUTION

In 1991, Dallas-based Southwest Airlines began a marketing campaign using the slogan, "Just Plane Smart." Greenville-based Stevens Aviation had been using the slogan "Plane Smart" to market its airline service business. Following posturing by lawyers, Kurt Herwald, the chairman of Stevens Aviation, called Herb Kelleher, the chairman of Southwest Airlines, and offered to arm wrestle for the rights to the slogan. Mr. Kelleher rented a wrestling auditorium, sold tickets to the event, and offered the proceeds to charity. Mr. Kelleher, then 61, lost to Mr. Herwald, then 38, who is also a weightlifter. Mr. Herwald said, "Just to show sympathy for the elderly and that there's no hard feelings, we've decided to allow Southwest Airlines to continue using our slogan." After the event, a commentator noted, "Not only did the companies save a court battle that would have taken years and cost several hundred thousand dollars, they gained loads of free publicity. They also made donations to charities."

Visit Intel Corporation:
http://www.intel.com

in areas that would compete with Intel. Intel's concern was whether the departing employees were taking with them technology that had been developed at and belonged to Intel. Using only the courts, Intel would find itself in lengthy, expensive, and complex litigation over engineering and developmental issues. Such litigation is costly not only in a monetary sense but also for the morale of employees charged with product development. Constant legal battles with former employees are not healthy for a corporate image within a company or from the outside.

After filing suit against one group of employees, Intel agreed, along with the former employees, to have an expert oversee the former employees' work in their business. The expert would have knowledge of Intel's product development that the employees had been involved with and would agree to notify all sides if the new company was infringing on any of Intel's patents. The expert agreed to oversee the new company's work for one year, at which point technology would make obsolete anything developed by the former employees while they were still at Intel. This creative solution permitted the former employees to operate their business, but it also provided Intel officials with the reassurance that their intellectual property was not being taken.

BUSINESS PLANNING TIP

Businesses such as Intel have now taken litigation strategy to a prevention stage. Intel and other firms, particularly those in high-tech and product development fields, now offer departing employees a partnership if they are leaving to start their own firms. The company provides a sort of incubator for the departing employee to get started in business. The company is an investor and will share in the returns the new product brings. The strategy here: Why try to beat them in litigation when you can join them with an investment?

Judge and Jury Unknowns

While a good case and preparation are often offered as explanations for victory in a lawsuit, many good cases, despite excellent preparation, are lost. There are unknowns in all forms of litigation. The unknowns are judges and juries and their perceptions and abilities. Research shows that 80 percent of all jurors have made up their minds about a case after only the opening statements in a trial have been made. Further research has shown that juries use their predetermined ideas in reaching a verdict. Finally, research shows that juries employ hindsight bias in their deliberation processes; that is, juries view the outcome of a set of facts and conclude that one party should have done more. Knowing that someone was injured often clouds our ability to determine whether that person should have been able to prevent the injury.

BIOGRAPHY

A PROFILE OF THE AMERICAN JUROR

Jurors' perceptions of corporations have not changed dramatically. While over three-fourths (76 percent) believe that "The strength of this country today is most based on the success of American business," one-half also doubt the honesty of corporations.

Jurors also have views of corporate priorities, as the following chart demonstrates.

HOW JURORS PERCEIVE CORPORATE PRIORITIES

Priority	What the Rank Is	What the Rank Should Be
Making a profit/protecting shareholders	1	4
Protecting executives	2	5
Protecting employees	4	1
Acting as good corporate citizens	5	3
Looking after customers	3	2

Jurors also have some other perceptions about corporations, including the following.

- Corporations know more about the issues, products, and concerns of the public than any other party, including government regulators.

- Corporations know about the facts of a lawsuit long before anyone else is aware of them.

- Jurors ascribe knowledge of one corporate employee to the entire corporation.

- Jurors believe that corporations know that they are using hazardous substances long before the EPA or any other agency finds them to be hazardous.

- Jurors believe that corporations do not tell all that they know.

- Most jurors are skeptical about the trustworthiness of corporations and don't expect them to be forthcoming with information, even during a trial.

- Failed memories, gaps in records, and missing or shredded documents are perceived to be intentional acts on the part of corporations and corporate executives.

- Jurors use gaps in records, failed memories, missing or shredded documents to fill in gaps if plaintiffs don't prove their cases. That is, jurors assume that the missing evidence a plaintiff needed to establish the elements for a case would be found in what is missing or has been destroyed.

- Jurors believe that corporations should set a higher standard and do more than the law allows them to do. They believe that corporations should prevent problems and anticipate issues.

- One-half of the jurors surveyed believe it is the responsibility of large corporations to help smaller companies succeed. Three-fourths agree that laws should protect smaller companies from their large competitors.

- Almost two-thirds (66 percent) of the jurors believe that "consumers benefit when strict rules prevent one company from getting too far ahead of its rivals."

- Jurors expect corporations to behave at a higher standard than they themselves would use. For example, most of them would be unwilling to spend an additional $1 for safety precautions that offer marginal benefits, but they expect the corporation to do so.*

For more information on jury service and the role of juries, view a handbook written by a state supreme court justice for use in his state: http://court.nol.org/community/jurorhandbook.htm.

*Charles Kauffman, "Jurors Carry Negative Presumptions," *National Law Journal*, January 19, 2004, pp. S1, S2.

Based on information about juries, such as that included in the Biography box, many businesses opt for a court trial in which a judge, not a jury, renders a decision. However, research with judges has demonstrated that even their case judgments are affected by predetermined ideas and hindsight bias, although to a lesser extent than jurors. "The Wild Card in Complex Business Litigation: The Jury" provides background information on the risks that juries pose for businesses in litigation.

FOR THE MANAGER'S DESK

RE: THE WILD CARD IN COMPLEX BUSINESS LITIGATION: THE JURY

Former Chief Justice Warren Burger was one of the most vocal critics on the issue of mandatory jury trials in complex civil cases with his feelings that juries waste time and are often incapable of understanding the issues presented to them and the application of the law to the case. England and a good part of the third-world nations have abandoned the jury system as an inadequate way of resolving civil disputes, but the United States seems to hang on as a holdout because of the constitutional aura surrounding the jury trial. This right is Jeffersonian in its origin and resulted from the complaints the colonists had against King George III for his trials without juries. Yet it is important to note that most criticisms regarding the use of juries in complex suits are focused on civil cases and not on criminal prosecutions.

In the 1978 IBM antitrust case, a jury heard five months of testimony on IBM's alleged monopolization of various market segments in the computer industry. Again, there was a deadlocked jury, and an interview with one of the jurors afterward gave some indication of the level of comprehension that resulted from the trial. The concept of "interface" was critical in the trial since the ability to interface would largely control whether there was ease of market entry and product compatibility.

Stephen J. Adler documents the following exchange in the case in *The Jury:*

Judge: "What is software?"

Juror: "That's the paper software."

Asked to define "interface," the juror said: "Well, if you take a blivet, turn it off one thing and drop it down, it's an interface change, right?"

The judge asked a second juror, "What about barriers to entry?"—to which she answered, "I would have to read about it."

A mistrial was declared.

In addition to the problems of complexity, there are additional difficulties with finding available jurors. Complex civil suits are quite lengthy, and this problem is only compounding. Trials are simply getting longer, as evidenced by the following statistics: in 1968, only 26 percent of the civil trials in federal district courts took one day; today that statistic is down to 14 percent; and in 1968, 75 cases lasted ten days or more and today that number is 359 cases. The question that arises about the jurors is, in cases like the five-month IBM trial, who were these people who were able to spend every day for five months sitting on a jury? Many critics noted that the result is an overabundance of retired individuals, housewives, and the unemployed. There is an absence of professionals and businesspeople who might have some experience with the issues. A cultural and financial gap is created when a jury has limited cross-sectional representation. The perceptions of individuals differ according to their circumstances. The late Peter Grace once noted that while he was working on the Grace Commission on government spending, he was dealing with billion-dollar deficits and it was difficult for him to return to his corporate life and get excited about million-dollar losses. He had adapted the standard of the federal government as a means of evaluating dollars. The same thing happens inversely with jurors. For example, the American Bar Association's study of juror deliberations indicated the verdict figures in a trade secret case ranged from $1 to $1.5 million, and one juror commented as follows:

"When you start talking millions, I can't relate to that. It doesn't mean anything to me. I have trouble paying $8 for parking every day."

Source: Adapted from Marianne Jennings and Chris P. Neck, "The Wild Card in Complex Business Litigation: The Jury." Reprinted with permission from the *Commercial Law Journal* 96, No. 1, p. 45. Copyright © 1991 by the Commercial Law League of America. All rights reserved.

Absence of Technicalities

Under ADR, the parties have the opportunity to tell their stories. The strict procedural rules and evidentiary exclusions do not apply in these forums, and many companies feel more comfortable because ADR seems to be more of a search for the truth than a battle of processes. A mediator can serve as a communication link between the parties and help them focus on issues and concerns. As one mediator expressed the benefit of ADR, "If you've done your job, . . . everyone goes home with big smiles."

Exhibit 4.3 provides a list of the benefits of ADR versus litigation.

EXHIBIT   4.3   Benefits of ADR versus Litigation

LITIGATION	ALTERNATIVE DISPUTE RESOLUTION
Technical discovery rules	Open lines of communication
Judicial constraints of precedent	Parties can agree to anything
Remedies limited (by law and precedent)	Creative remedies permitted
Backlog	Parties set timetable
Public proceeding	Privacy
Control by lawyers	Control by parties (or mediator/arbitrator)
Expensive	Cheaper
Strict procedures/timing	More flexibility
Judge/jury unknowns	Parties select mediator/arbitrator
Those who can afford to stay in win	Positions examined for validity
Judicial enforcement tools	Enforcement by good faith

FOR THE MANAGER'S DESK

RE: A CHECKLIST FOR WHEN TO LITIGATE

Costs

Every lawsuit costs time and money. Costs of litigation include but by no means end with attorneys' fees, and other significant costs are often not considered before a business decides to become embroiled in a legal battle.

Legal Costs

The total legal fee must be considered in every case of possible litigation. A lawyer should be required to give an estimate of fees for any suit before the suit begins. The estimate should always include discovery costs. . . .

Time Costs (Hidden Downtime)

Litigation costs time as well as money. Indeed, in many cases, the loss of time can be more devastating to a firm than the financial loss. If a firm takes part in major litigation, chances are that its officers and possibly its directors will be involved in depositions, other forms of pretrial discovery and paperwork, and eventually in the trial itself. This involvement inevitably diverts the attention of the officers from their normal duties. . . .

Image Costs

If a lawsuit attracts the attention of the media, a firm may incur money and time costs stemming from public relations. Someone must be available to explain the firm's position to reporters and perhaps initiate an affirmative campaign to minimize negative publicity about the suit.

Capital Costs

Many auditors require that pending litigation be listed in the financial reports of the company. Ongoing litigation that carries the potential for great financial loss to a business can have a negative effect on the firm's financial rating and the ability to raise capital.

Costs of Alternatives to Litigation

The costs of litigation should be compared with the costs of alternatives to litigation. For example, it may not add much to potential litigation costs to submit a case to arbitration before pursuing full litigation. Such arbitration may produce a settlement that makes the trip to court unnecessary.

Costs of Not Litigating

There are costs for litigating, but there are also costs for not litigating. If the stakes are high enough, litigation may be worth pursuing regardless of the expense. For example, if a suit challenges the land records and thus the title to the land on which the business is located, the cost of not responding to the suit may be the loss of the property and the expense of reestablishing the business at another site. In a trademark or trade name suit the cost may be a product or company name or label. In a patent infringement case, the failure to sue an infringer may undermine a company's sales and its exclusivity in the marketplace.

Sometimes the price of not litigating or of not responding vigorously to litigation can be a firm's very existence. For example, the product liability suits involving Johns-Manville and the other makers of asbestos threatened the lives of those firms because they involved the only product the firms made.

Public Relations Issues

Litigation is not a private matter. In every city, at least one reporter is assigned to the clerk's office in the state and federal courts for the purpose of checking on suits filed.

Many an electric bill goes unpaid simply because it is not good public relations for a utility company to appear in the newspapers and on television as the "bad guy" when a retired widow explains that the big power company has just filed suit because she has no money to pay her bill. . . .

Jury Appeal

When considering the effects of publicity on a case, a company should also consider the closely related matter of jury appeal. In some cases it will not matter how correct a business may be, how much of a remedy the law provides, or how wrong the other side is; the jury will simply side with the "little guy," and the business will have no chance of succeeding in the courtroom. For example, the Arthur Murray Dance Studios once fully litigated a case in which a man who had been severely injured in a car accident and was unable to complete the lessons in his contract with Arthur Murray (some 2,734 lessons, for which he had paid $24,812.40) sought to recover his payments on the grounds that performance had become impossible. It is really very difficult to build jury appeal into such a case.

Discussion Questions

1. List the factors you should consider as you make a decision to litigate.

2. At the awards show for the Academy of Motion Picture Arts and Sciences (Academy), a character dressed as Snow White appeared in the opening musical number and sang with actor Rob Lowe. Walt Disney, Inc., had not given the Academy permission to use the Snow White likeness, a trademarked Disney character. If you were the Walt Disney Corporation, would you sue the Academy?

3. List concerns you would have as an employer litigating a sexual harassment case.

Source: Frank Shipper and Marianne Jennings. *Avoiding and Surviving Lawsuits: The Executive Guide to Strategic Legal Planning for Business,* Jossey-Bass Publishing, Inc., pp. 59–73. Copyright © 1989. Excerpted and reprinted with permission of the authors.

WHEN YOU ARE IN LITIGATION . . .

There are times when a business must face litigation. In this portion of the chapter, the language, process, and strategies of civil litigation are explained.

How Does a Lawsuit Start?

For a look at what state and federal court systems are doing to improve the litigation process, visit the American Bar Association:
http://www.abanet.org/ justice

Lawsuits begin when people feel someone has violated their rights. Lawsuits are based on feelings. Whether rights have been violated and what damages were caused as a result of that violation are the issues that a trial determines. The only restriction on the filing of a suit is that the plaintiff's claim of right is based on some law, either statutory law or common law.

People begin lawsuits. The judicial system does not unilaterally begin the enforcement of civil rights. Individuals hold the responsibility of protecting their rights. The role of the judicial system is to determine whether those rights have been violated.

Although procedures vary from state to state, the following sections offer a general discussion of the procedures involved in a civil lawsuit. Exhibit 4.4 summarizes the trial process.

The Complaint (Petition)

The first step in a lawsuit is the filing of a document called a **complaint** or **petition**. The plaintiff must file the petition or complaint within certain time limits each state has for filing suit. These time limits are called **statutes of limitations**. They vary

EXHIBIT   4.4   The Trial Process

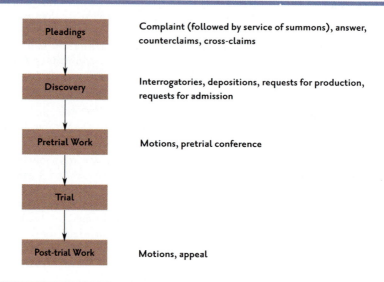

Pleadings	Complaint (followed by service of summons), answer, counterclaims, cross-claims
Discovery	Interrogatories, depositions, requests for production, requests for admission
Pretrial Work	Motions, pretrial conference
Trial	
Post-trial Work	Motions, appeal

depending on the type of rights involved in a suit. The typical statute of limitations for personal injuries is two years; the typical limitation for contracts is four years.

A complaint is a general statement of the plaintiff's claim of rights. For example, if a plaintiff is suing for a breach of contract, the complaint must describe the contract, when it began, and what the defendant did that the plaintiff says is a breach. Exhibit 4.5 shows a sample complaint in a suit over a car accident.

The complaint need not have every detail described in it. The standard for a valid complaint is that it must be definite enough in its description of what happened for the defendant to understand why the suit has been brought.

In addition to describing the violation of rights, the complaint must establish the subject matter jurisdiction of the court. For example, for a federal district court action, the complaint would have to show either that there was diversity and a damage claim of more than $75,000 or that a federal question was involved.

In some cases, the complaint is filed by a group of plaintiffs who have the same cause of action against one defendant. These types of suits, called **class action suits**, are typically filed in antitrust cases, shareholder actions against corporations, and employment discrimination cases. The class action suit enables a group of plaintiffs to share one lawyer and minimize litigation expenses while at the same time preserving their individual rights. Perhaps the most widely publicized type of class action lawsuit is the suit that results when a large jet airliner crashes and causes multiple deaths and injuries. All the plaintiffs were injured in the same event, and the defendant then litigates once with a group of plaintiffs. (See Chapter 11 for more information on product liability class action litigation.)

Another form of class action suit is the **derivative suit**, in which shareholders sue a corporation to recover damages for actions taken by the corporation. (See Chapter 21 for more information.)

The final paragraphs of a complaint list the damages or remedies the plaintiff wants. The damages may be a **legal remedy** such as money, in which case a dollar amount is specified. The plaintiff may seek an **equitable remedy**, such as specific performance in the case of an action for breach of contract. **Specific performance** is

Review current and concluded class action suits represented by Alexander, Hawes & Audet:
http://www.alexanderlaw.com/class.html

Visit a Web site with information on airline class action litigation:
http://www.AirSafe.com

Explore a Web site on silicone breast implant class actions:
http://www.pbs.org/wgbh/pages/frontline/implants

EXHIBIT 4.5 Sample Complaint

Reed C. Tolman, Esq. (006502)
TOLMAN & OSBORNE, P.C.
1400 E. Southern, Suite 625
Tempe, Arizona 85282
Attorneys for Plaintiffs

<table>
<tr><td colspan="2" align="center">SUPERIOR COURT OF ARIZONA
MARICOPA COUNTY</td></tr>
<tr>
<td>
CRAIG CONNER and KATHY CONNER,
husband and wife, individually
and on behalf of their minor
son, CASEY CONNER,

   Plaintiffs,

    v.

CARMEN A. CHENAL and THOMAS K.
CHENAL, wife and husband,

   Defendants,
</td>
<td valign="top">
CV92 - 91319

COMPLAINT
(Tort-Motor Vehicle)
</td>
</tr>
</table>

For their complaint, plaintiffs allege:

1. Plaintiffs and defendants are residents of Maricopa County, Arizona.
2. This Court has jurisdiction over the subject matter under the Arizona Constitution, Art. 6, § 14.
3. Casey Conner is the minor son of Craig and Kathy Conner.
4. Carmen A. Chenal and Thomas K. Chenal are wife and husband. At all times relevant hereto, Carmen A. Chenal was acting for and on behalf of the marital community of which she is a member.
5. On or about July 20, 1990, defendant Carmen A. Chenal was driving her motor vehicle in the vicinity of Primrose Path and Cave Creek Road in Carefree, Arizona. At the time, Casey Conner was a passenger in the back seat of defendants' vehicle, a 1976 Mercedes, ID No.11603312051326.
6. At all times relevant hereto, defendant Carmen A. Chenal had a duty to care properly for the safety of Casey Conner. That duty included the responsibility to place Casey in an appropriate and functioning seatbelt.
7. Prior to the accident that resulted in injuries to Casey Conner, Carmen A. Chenal knew that the right rear door of her vehicle was damaged and not functioning properly.
8. Despite the duty Carmen A. Chenal had to care properly for the safety of Casey Conner, and despite her knowledge of a malfunctioning right rear door, Carmen A. Chenal negligently failed to place Casey in an appropriate and functioning seatbelt and negligently and carelessly operated her vehicle in such a way that the right rear door opened and allowed Casey to be ejected from the vehicle while the vehicle was in operation.
9. Carmen A. Chenal's failure to exercise reasonable care for the safety of Casey and the failure to operate her vehicle in a careful and safe manner proximately caused Casey to suffer personal injuries.
10. As a result of Casey Conner's injuries, he has experienced physical and psychological suffering, and his parents have incurred medical and other expenses, as well as lost earnings.

WHEREFORE, plaintiffs request judgment against defendants for compensatory damages in an amount to be determined at trial.

DATED: this _____ day of July, 1992.
     TOLMAN & OSBORNE

By: _____
    Reed C. Tolman
    1400 E. Southern
    Suite 625
    Tempe, Arizona 85282

Source: Complaint appears courtesy of Tolman & Osborne, P.C., Tempe, AZ 85282.

an order of the court requiring a defendant to perform on a contract. In some cases, the plaintiffs just want the defendants to stop violating their rights. In those complaints, plaintiffs ask for **injunctions**, which are court orders requiring the defendant to stop doing the act complained of. In an action for nuisance, for example, an injunction orders the defendant to stop engaging in the conduct that causes the nuisance or orders the defendant to comply with a law or a previous decision. As another example, an injunction could order the construction of a fence to restrain animals that have become a nuisance.

The Summons

The complaint or petition of the plaintiffs is filed with the clerk of the appropriate court—that is, the court with subject matter jurisdiction, *in personam* jurisdiction, and venue. The defendant, however, will not know of the suit just because it is filed. Thus, the second step in a lawsuit is serving the defendant with a copy of the complaint and a **summons**, which is a legal document that tells the defendant of the suit and explains the defendant's rights under the law. Those rights include the opportunity to respond and the grant of a limited amount of time for responding. Exhibit 4.6 shows a sample summons.

A summons must be delivered to the defendant. Some states require that the defendant be given the papers personally. Other states allow the papers to be given to some member of the defendant's household or, in the case of a business, to an agent of that business. (See Chapter 18 for a discussion of an agent's authority to receive the papers notifying the business of a lawsuit.)

The summons is delivered by an officer of the court (such as a sheriff or magistrate) or by private firms licensed as **process servers**. Once the defendant is served, the server must file an affidavit with the court to indicate when and where the service was made. In rare circumstances, courts allow service of process by mail or by publishing the summons and complaint. These circumstances, however, are very limited and are carefully supervised by the courts.

The Answer

The parties' positions in a case are found in the **pleadings**. The complaint or petition is a pleading. The defendant's position is found in the **answer**, another pleading in a case. The defendant must file an answer within the time limits allowed by the court or risk default. The time limits are typically twenty days for in-state defendants and thirty days for out-of-state defendants. A failure to answer, or a **default**, is like a forfeit in sports: The plaintiff wins because the defendant failed to show up. The plaintiff can then proceed to a judgment to collect damages.

The defendant's answer can do any or all of several different things. The defendant may admit certain facts in the answer. While it is rare for a defendant to admit the wrong alleged by the plaintiff, the defendant might admit parts of the plaintiff's complaint, such as those that establish jurisdiction and venue. If the plaintiff already has correct venue, fighting that issue is costly, and admitting jurisdiction is a way to move on with the case. If, however, the court lacked *in personam* jurisdiction over the defendant, the defendant could deny the jurisdiction. (See Chapter 3 for more discussion of *in personam* jurisdiction.)

A denial is a simple statement in the answer whereby the defendant indicates that the allegation is denied. An answer might also include a statement that the defendant does not know enough to admit or deny the allegations in the complaint and might include a demand for proof of those allegations.

EXHIBIT   4.6   Sample Summons

Name:
Address:
City, State, Zip:
Telephone:
State Bar Code:
Client:

ARIZONA SUPERIOR COURT, County of

	ACTION NO:
	SUMMONS

THE STATE OF ARIZONA TO THE DEFENDANTS:

YOU ARE HEREBY SUMMONED and required to appear and defend, within the time applicable, in this action in this court. If served within Arizona, you appear and defend within 20 days after the service of the Summons and Complaint upon you, exclusive of the day of service. If served out of the State of Arizona—whether by direct service, by registered or certified mail, or by publication you shall appear and defend within 30 days after the service of the Summons and Complaint upon you is complete, exclusive of the day of service. Where process is served upon the Arizona Director of Insurance as an insurer's attorney to receive service of legal process against it in this state, the insurer shall not be required to appear, answer or plead until expiration of 40 days after date of such service upon the Director. Service by registered or certified mail without the State of Arizona is complete 30 days after the date of receipt by the party being served. Service by publication is complete 30 days after the date of first publication. Direct service is complete when made. Service upon the Arizona Motor Vehicle Superintendent is complete 30 days after filing the Affidavit of Compliance and return receipt or Officer's Return. RCP 4; ARS §§ 20-222, 28-502, 28-503.

Copies of the pleadings filed herein may be obtained by contacting the Clerk of Superior Court, _____ County, located at _____ , Arizona. RCF 4.1 (e).

SUMMONS
(Continued on Reverse Side)   1-1 ©LawForms 10-92 1-93

YOU ARE HEREBY NOTIFIED that in case of your failure to appear and defend within the time applicable, judgment by default may be rendered against you for the relief demanded in the Complaint.

YOU ARE CAUTIONED that in order to appear and defend, you must file an Answer or proper response in writing with the Clerk of this Court, accompanied by the necessary filing fee, within the time required, and you are required to serve a copy of any Answer or response upon the Plaintiffs' attorney. RCP 10(D); ARS 12-311; RCP5.

The name and address of plaintiffs' attorney is:

SIGNED AND SEALED this date :_____

· ..
Clerk

Method of Service: By   · ..
☐ Private Process Service   Deputy Clerk
☐ Sheriff or Marshall
☐ Personal Service
☐ Registered/Certified Mail (out of State)

SUMMONS   1-1 ©LawForms 11-67, 3-84, 1-93

Source: Form appears courtesy of National LawForms, Inc., Phoenix, AZ.

MAKING ETHICS PERSONAL

Keeping Peeking a Secret to Keep a Job

You work for a national retail chain that has stores in malls throughout the country. While using a dressing room, a customer discovered a peep hole into the dressing room that was located next to the manager's office. The customer stormed out of the store after complaining about the "invasion of privacy." Your manager asks you to go to Home Depot and buy the necessary supplies and tools to patch the peep hole. "We need to get this done before she shows up here again with a lawyer. And remember, this is just between you and me."

Realizing that you need the job, that you have bills to pay and tuition coming due, would you do as the manager asked? What harm, if any, do you see? What if the manager said, "I never really saw anything anyway." Would you keep the incident and your drywall work secret?

BUSINESS STRATEGY APPLICATION

On the book's Web site, go to the area for Chapter 4 and you can walk through the pleadings in the *U.S.* v. *Microsoft* case to see what a more complex complaint and answer look like and see how companies respond to complex charges such as those in an antitrust case.

An answer might also include a **counterclaim**, with which the defendant, in effect, countersued the plaintiff, alleging a violation of rights and damages against the plaintiff. The plaintiff must respond to the counterclaim using the same answer process of admitting and/or denying the alleged wrong. Exhibit 4.7 shows a sample answer.

The answer must be filed with the clerk of the court and a copy sent to the plaintiff. With the exception of amendments to these documents, the pleadings are now complete.

Seeking Timely Resolution of the Case

The fact that a suit has been filed does not mean that the case will go to trial. A great majority of suits are disposed of before trial because of successful motions to end them. **Motions** are requests to the court that it take certain action. They are usually made in writing and include citations to precedent that support granting the motion. Often the judge will have the attorneys present oral arguments for and against the motion, after which the court then issues a ruling on the motion.

Motion for Judgment on the Pleadings

Either in the answer or by separate motion, a defendant can move for judgment based just on the content of the pleadings. The theory behind a **motion for judgment on the pleadings** is that there is no cause of action even if everything the plaintiff alleges is true. For example, a plaintiff could file suit claiming the defendant is an annoying person; but unless the defendant is annoying to the extent of invading privacy or not honoring contracts, there is no right of recovery. The defendant in this case could win a motion for judgment on the pleadings because the law (perhaps unfortunately) does not provide a remedy for annoying people. A denial of a motion for judgment on the pleadings does not imply victory for the plaintiff. It simply means that the case will proceed with the next steps covered in this chapter.

EXHIBIT 4.7   Sample Answer

Grand, Canyon & Rafts
12222 W. Camelback
Phoenix, Arizona
555-5555
Attorneys for Defendant

SUPERIOR COURT OF ARIZONA

MARICOPA COUNTY

CRAIG CONNER and KATHY CONNER,)
 husband and wife, individually)
 and on behalf of their minor)
 son, CASEY CONNER,)
)
 Plaintiffs,)
)
 v.)
)
 CARMEN A. CHENAL and THOMAS K.)
 CHENAL, wife and husband,)
)
 Defendants,)
 _____)
	CV92-91319
	
	 ANSWER

For their answer, defendants respond to plaintiffs'
complaint as follows:

     1. Admit paragraph one.
     2. Admit paragraph two.
     3. Have no knowledge to admit or deny paragraph three.
     4. Have no knowledge to admit or deny paragraph four.
     5. Admit paragraph five.
     6. As for paragraphs 6 through 10, inclusive of plaintiffs'
complaint, defendants have no knowledge of the statements alleged and
deny all statements made therein.

Defendents deny any and all parts of plaintiffs' complaints
not specifically mentioned herein.
     DATED this _____ day of August, 1992.
       Grand, Canyon & Raft

By: _____
      Robert C. Canyon
      12222 W. Camelback
      Phoenix, Arizona

Motion to Dismiss

A **motion to dismiss** can be filed any time during the proceedings but usually is part of the defendant's answer. Such a motion can be based on the court's lack of subject matter or *in personam* jurisdiction. Again, if the case is not dismissed, it does not mean that the plaintiff wins; it just means that the case will proceed to the next steps and possibly trial.

BUSINESS STRATEGY

Wal-Mart: The Most Sued Company in America

As of June 2004, Wal-Mart was managing approximately 10,000 open lawsuits. The retail giant is sued, on average over the years, about 13 times per day for every day of the year. Most experts have concluded that Wal-Mart is sued more than any other entity except the U.S. government.

Wal-Mart is unique in that it has taken the position of fighting in many of the suits brought against it. Most corporations take a cost-benefit analysis and settle most lawsuits because it is cheaper for them to do so. Wal-Mart, however, is working to change the nature of litigation against corporations and fights most suits aggressively. The result of its stance is that the number of suits has leveled off despite Wal-Mart's increasing size and number of stores.

The types of lawsuits Wal-Mart has pending or has experienced include the following:

- Slip-and-fall cases where customers have been injured in a Wal-Mart store
- One case brought by the family of a woman shot by her husband, who had purchased the rifle at Wal-Mart
- Class action employment suits alleging discrimination
- Failure to report safety violations
- Wrongful termination of employment cases
- Unpaid overtime litigation by employees
- Shoppers injured in a "Furby" stampede when the toy was in demand at Christmas time

Wal-Mart also employs several different litigation strategies.

- It hires outside lawyers and pays them a flat fee.
- It has cases moved to federal district court, where judges are not elected.
- It settles those cases where the company or employees have done something wrong, but it fights ferociously when there is no fault.*

However, Wal-Mart has also experienced some litigation difficulties over the disclosure of evidence in the discovery process. (See Case 4.2, *Wal-Mart Stores, Inc.* v. *Johnson*, later in this chapter.) Once a company has evi-

© PHOTODISC/GETTY IMAGES

dence regarding a product, a contract, or conduct of employees, it is costly and illegal to try to hide that information before or during litigation.

Wal-Mart has experienced sanctions and bad publicity from a number of lawsuits in which it is a defendant for its alleged failure to be forthcoming with discovery requests and documents. The cases in which Wal-Mart has had issues of discovery abuse and sanctions include the following:

- *Bergeron* v. *Wal-Mart Stores*, No. 85405 (Dt. Ct. Laforche Par. La)
- *Christ* v. *Wal-Mart Stores*, No. 55747 (Dist. Ct. Liberty Co. Texas)
- *In re Visa Check/Mastermoney Antitrust Litigation*, No. 96–5283 (E.D.N.Y.)
- *Meissner* v. *Wal-Mart Stores*, No. A-159–432 (Dist. Ct. Jefferson Co.)

Wal-Mart released the following data on its litigation:

- 1998—20 sanctions for discovery abuse
- 1999—22 sanctions for discovery abuse
- 2000—10 sanctions for discovery abuse
- 2004—75 sanctions total for all years combined

In *McClung* v. *Delta Square Limited Partnership*, 937 S.W.2d 891 (Tenn. 1996), Wal-Mart's issues regarding discovery began. After the case was tried, the husband of the woman killed after being abducted from the parking lot at a Wal-Mart store learned that Wal-Mart had conducted a study and pilot program showing that store parking lots could be made safer with relatively little cost just by adding safety patrols. The study was not released to the husband during the litigation. When the report surfaced in other cases, plaintiffs' lawyers had the report in hand even as Wal-Mart denied in discovery requests that the report existed. Wal-Mart was sanctioned $18 million in one case for its failure to reveal the report.†

*Richard Willing, "Lawsuits Follow Growth Curve of Wal-Mart," *USA Today*, August 14, 2001, pp. A1, A2.
†Bob Van Voris, "Wal-Mart Mending Its Ways?" *National Law Journal*, January 22, 2001, pp. A1, A8.

Motion for Summary Judgment

A **motion for summary judgment** has two requirements. Summary judgment is appropriate only when the moving party is entitled to a judgment under the law and when there are no issues of fact. Actions brought on the basis of motor vehicle accidents, for example, always involve different witnesses' testimonies and variations in facts. These types of cases cannot be decided by summary judgment. There are cases, however, in which the parties do not dispute the facts but differ on the applications of law. Consider, for example, a dispute involving a contract for the repair of a computer, including service and parts. Different laws govern contractual provisions for services and provisions for goods. The parties do not dispute the facts: They agree goods and services are covered in the contract. At issue is the question about which law applies, and a summary judgment appropriately will resolve it. There may be other factual disputes about contract performance, but the partial summary judgment will determine which contract law will apply.

How a Lawsuit Progresses: Discovery

Trials in the United States are not conducted by ambush. Before the trial, the parties engage in a mandatory process of mutual disclosure of all relevant documents and other evidence. This court-supervised process of gathering evidence is called **discovery**. Under relatively recent changes to these procedural rules, the parties must offer to the other side lists of witnesses, all relevant documents, tangible evidence, and statements related to the case. Under the old discovery rules, the expense and difficulty of discovery techniques often meant the search for the truth was a cat-and-mouse game won by those with the most funds. Armed with the evidence in a case, the parties are more prepared, and perhaps more inclined, to negotiate a settlement. The new discovery rules provide for sanctions (penalties) for not turning over relevant documents at the start of a case. The following are the traditional tools of discovery.

Requests for Admissions

A **request for admissions** asks the other side to admit a certain fact. There is some incentive to admit the facts requested if they are true because if these facts are denied and then proved at trial, attorney fees can be recovered for the costs of proving the facts that were denied. Requests for admissions sometimes merely request the other party to admit that a document is authentic. For example, the parties might have a dispute about the amount due under a contract but should be willing to admit that they signed the contract and that it is authentic. These requests for admission reduce the length of trials because an admission establishes a fact as true.

Depositions

Depositions are the oral testimony of parties or witnesses that are taken under oath but outside the courtroom and before the trial. They can be taken long before a trial and help preserve a witness's or party's recollection. Depositions are also helpful in determining just how strong a case is. It is far better to discover damaging information in a deposition than it is to spend all the time and money to go to trial and discover the damaging testimony there.

Limitations on Discovery

Discovery has the general limitation of relevance. Only things that are evidence or could lead to the discovery of evidence are discoverable. However, discovery also has a specific limitation. Discovery cannot require the production of **work product**, which consists of the attorney's research, thoughts, analysis, and strategy. Discovery allows the other side the right to know all the evidence (if it asks for it), but it does not give the other side the right to know how that evidence will be used or what legal precedent supports a party's position. Discovery cannot request the production of legal research, trial strategy, or an attorney's comments or reactions to a witness.

Certain evidence in cases is not discoverable. Communications between lawyers and their clients is protected by a privilege and, except in certain limited circumstances, cannot be discovered or used by the opposition.

Requests for Production

A **request for production** requires the other side to produce requested documents that have not already been given under the new discovery rules. For example, if a business is suing to recover lost profits, the defendant will probably want to request the income statements and perhaps income tax returns of that business so that he or she can prepare for damages issues. A request for production can include medical records as well as tangible evidence. In *Wal-Mart Stores, Inc. v. Johnson* (Case 4.2), the failure to produce physical evidence that was part of an accident resulted in sanction for a store.

CASE 4.2

Wal-Mart Stores, Inc. v. *Johnson*
106 S.W.3d 718 (Tx. 2003)

"Reining" Deer at the Local Wal-Mart

FACTS

While stocking merchandise, a Wal-Mart employee accidentally knocked one or more decorative reindeer from a high shelf onto Monroe Johnson's head and arm. Mr. Johnson's fiancee, now his wife, was with him and heard but did not see the accident. When she went to investigate, she found her fiance dazed but still standing, with a cut on one arm and several reindeer lying at his feet. At the scene, Mr. Johnson told Phyllis McClane, a Wal-Mart supervisor who had come to investigate, that he was not hurt. After a Wal-Mart employee cleaned and bandaged his cut, Mr. Johnson and his fiancee left the store.

During her investigation, Ms. McClane took notes, photographed the reindeer, and obtained a written statement from the employee who caused the accident. She recorded the results of her investigation on a Wal-Mart form entitled "Report of Customer Incident." She attached the photo and the employee's statement, sending copies to the District Manager and claim management personnel. According to the incident report, Mr. Johnson neither threatened to sue nor indicated that Wal-Mart should pay any medical costs or other

damages. After completing the report, Ms. McClane discarded her notes.

That evening, Mr. Johnson's neck and arm began to hurt, and he could not sleep. The next day, his doctor prescribed muscle relaxers, pain killers, and physical therapy. Still in pain six months later, Mr. Johnson and his wife sued Wal-Mart. While suit was pending, Mr. Johnson consulted three more physicians and tried additional treatments without success. About seventeen months after the accident, a surgeon performed an anterior cervical discectomy and fusion on Mr. Johnson's neck.

During discovery, the Johnsons asked whether Wal-Mart still possessed the reindeer that fell on him. Wal-Mart did not, but the company offered to provide a "reasonable facsimile." The Johnsons did not want the facsimile, and the trial court prohibited Wal-Mart "from introducing into evidence a reasonable facsimile of the reindeer made the basis of this lawsuit."

At trial, the parties offered sharply divergent evidence about the composition and weight of the reindeer in question. Mr. Johnson testified that they were made of wood, each weighing as much as ten pounds. Ron Wheeler, the store manager, countered that the reindeer were made of papier mache and weighed only five to eight ounces each. Wal-Mart argued that such flimsy reindeer could not have proximately caused Mr. Johnson's neck problems, which it claimed resulted from an automobile accident years earlier. Mr. Wheeler also testified that Wal-Mart could not produce any of the reindeer because they had all been sold or, if broken, thrown away. Only the photograph of the reindeer was introduced in evidence, but its quality was too poor to substantiate or rebut either party's description.

Based on Wal-Mart's failure to keep the reindeer, the Johnsons requested and obtained the following jury instruction (see p. 145 for more information on jury instructions).

> *You are instructed that, when a party has possession of a piece of evidence at a time he knows or should have known it will be evidence in a controversy, and thereafter he disposes of it, makes it unavailable, or fails to produce it, there is a presumption in law that the piece of evidence, had it been produced, would have been unfavorable to the party who did not produce it. If you find by a preponderance of the evidence that Wal-Mart had possession of the reindeer at a time it knew or should have known they would be evidence in this controversy, then there is a presumption that the reindeer, if produced, would be unfavorable to Wal-Mart.*

The jury found for Mr. and Mrs. Johnson and awarded damages. Wal-Mart did not appeal the award or the damages. Rather, Wal-Mart appealed the jury instruction. The court of appeals affirmed, and Wal-Mart appealed again.

JUDICIAL OPINION

PHILLIPS, Chief Justice

Evidence may be unavailable for discovery and trial for a variety of reasons. Evidence may be lost, altered or destroyed willfully and in bad faith or it may be lost for reasons completely innocent. Sometimes, lost evidence may be easily replicated, or it may be so marginal that it has little or no effect on the outcome of the case. On other occasions, the loss or destruction of evidence may seriously impair a party's ability to present its case. A trial judge should have discretion to fashion an appropriate remedy to restore the parties to a rough approximation of their positions if all evidence were available.

In this case, the trial court decided to remedy what it perceived to be Wal-Mart's misconduct by giving a spoliation instruction. The instruction informed the jury that it must presume that the missing reindeer would have harmed Wal-Mart's case if the jury concluded that Wal-Mart disposed of the reindeer after it knew or should have known that they would be evi-

dence in the case. Such an instruction is a common remedy for spoliation, with roots going back to the English common law.

Our courts of appeals have generally limited the use of the spoliation instruction to two circumstances: [1] the deliberate destruction of relevant evidence and [2] the failure of a party to produce relevant evidence or to explain its non-production.

Although the parties argue their respective positions under this second circumstance at length, we need not decide whether a spoliation instruction is justified when evidence is unintentionally lost or destroyed, or if it is, what standard is proper. Rather we begin and end our analysis here with the issue of duty, the initial inquiry for any complaint of discovery abuse. Before any failure to produce material evidence may be viewed as discovery abuse, the opposing party must establish that the non-producing party had a duty to preserve the evidence in question.

Wal-Mart argues that it had no duty to preserve the reindeer as evidence because it had no notice that they would be relevant to a future claim. Specifically, Wal-Mart contends that it did not learn of the Johnsons' claim until all of the reindeer had been disposed of in the normal course of business. The Johnsons point out that Wal-Mart's extensive investigation on the day of the accident indicates its awareness of both the potential claim and the reindeer's importance to it. Wal-Mart responds that it routinely investigates all accidents on its premises, and this particular investigation revealed that Johnson had not been seriously injured and never indicated that he might seek legal relief. We agree that nothing about the investigation or the circumstances surrounding the accident would have put Wal-Mart on notice that there was a substantial chance that the Johnsons would pursue a claim.

Thus, as a foundation for the submission of the spoliation instruction in this case, the Johnsons had to show that Wal-Mart disposed of the reindeer after it knew, or should have known, that there was a substantial chance there would be litigation and that the reindeer would be material to it. We therefore agree with Wal-Mart that the trial court abused its discretion when it submitted the spoliation instruction to the jury because the Johnsons failed to establish that Wal-Mart had a duty to preserve the reindeer.

While we do not lightly reverse a judgment because of an erroneous instruction, we believe an unnecessary spoliation instruction is particularly likely to cause harm. Because the instruction itself is given to compensate for the absence of evidence that a party had a duty to preserve, its very purpose is to "nudge"

continued

or "tilt" the jury. Thus, if a spoliation instruction should not have been given, the likelihood of harm from the erroneous instruction is substantial, particularly when the case is closely contested.

We hold that the trial court erred in submitting the spoliation instruction in this case and that the spoliation instruction was harmful and probably caused the rendition of an improper judgment. Accordingly, we reverse the court of appeals' judgment and remand this case to the trial court for further proceedings.

CASE QUESTIONS

1. Describe the accident that led to the litigation.
2. What happened to the notes on the accident? The reindeer?
3. When does the duty to preserve evidence arise?
4. Why does the court worry about "tilting" or "nudging" the jury in the case?
5. What will happen to the case now?

 CONSIDER...   4 . 2

The obstruction of justice trial against the accounting firm of Arthur Andersen found the prosecution using the following types of evidence:
- Testimony from partners, employees, and consultants with Andersen
- E-mails between and among Andersen partners, employees, and consultants, both saved and deleted e-mails introduced into evidence
- A videotape of a partner making a presentation to employees on the pending SEC investigation in which he urged employees to get rid of excess files so that "nosy plaintiffs' lawyers" wouldn't be able to find damaging evidence
- The statistics on the e-mail deletions by Andersen employees, including the peak in e-mail deletions following the presentation that was shown on video and the instruction to get rid of unnecessary files
- The articles clipped and saved by Andersen employees relating to Enron and SEC investigations

What would the government need to show to establish that Andersen had engaged in spoliation?

THINK: In the *Wal-Mart* case, the court held that the reindeer would have needed to be destroyed by employees knowing that a suit was pending.

APPLY: What is different in this Andersen situation? What is the same?

ANSWER: The evidence shows that the Andersen employees had been briefed on at least the investigations, a likely source of litigation. With the investigations pending, the destruction of e-mails and other documents at that time meets the test for spoliation.

 CONSIDER...   4 . 3

Former investment banker Frank Quattrone, formerly with the investment banking firm of Credit Suisse First Boston (CSFB), was known as the financial wizard behind the dot-coms. He was the investment banker to turn to when a dot-com wanted to sell stock to the public for the first time through an initial primary offering (IPO). He was the underwriter for the IPOs for companies such as Cisco and Amazon.com.

The sales of shares in the dot-com companies was nearly a sure thing. The value of the shares could double, triple, and more during the first day of sales. Being able to buy the shares of the IPOs when they were first available was a critical part of making those returns. Investment banking firms were thus allocating the shares of these IPOs to influential executives in order to win their business. To lure more stock offerings to CSFB, the IPO allocations were given to the CEOs of companies such as Dell, WorldCom, and other rapidly rising stocks of the new economy.*

While the allocation systems have been the subject of consent decrees, and fines have been paid, the federal government could not find a criminal violation on the part of Mr.

Quattrone for the IPO allocations. What the federal government did find during its investigation was an e-mail from Mr. Quattrone to his employees in his unit on cleaning up their e-mail files.

While the IPO investigation was ongoing, Mr. Quattrone forwarded an e-mail from his colleague, a lawyer, Richard Char, to his staff on December 5, 2000, that included the following: "clean up those files."[†] Mr. Quattrone added those words to the forwarded e-mail that reminded the employees of CSFB's policy on record retention and destruction. As a result, Mr. Quattrone was charged with obstruction of justice.

What would be required to prove spoliation in this case?

[*]For example, the shares of VA Linux Systems, Inc. climbed 697.5 percent on their first day of public sales. Those who received the allocations were called "Friends of Frank." ("Inside Frank Quattrone's Money Machine," *Business Week*, October 13, 2003, pp. 104–11.)

[†]Andrew Ross Sorkin, "Ex-Banker Tells Court File Cleanup Was Policy," *New York Times*, October 10, 2003, pp. C1, C9.

ETHICAL ISSUES

Evaluate the ethics of the Andersen and CSFB employees. Why do you think they followed orders so willingly? Is "I was just following orders" a defense in criminal and civil cases? Is it a justification for conduct?

Resolution of a Lawsuit: The Trial

If a case is not settled (and many are settled literally on the courthouse steps), the trial begins.

The Type of Trial—Jury or Nonjury

Occasionally, the parties agree not to have a jury trial and instead have a trial to the court. In these cases, the judge acts as both judge and jury—both running the trial and determining its outcome. In highly technical cases it is sometimes better for both sides to have a knowledgeable judge involved than to try to explain the complexities of the case to a jury of laypersons.

If the parties do not agree on a nonjury trial, there are certain types of cases that carry a constitutional right to a trial by jury. The Seventh Amendment of the U.S. Constitution covers the jury requirement in civil trials:

> *In suits at common law, where the value in controversy shall exceed twenty dollars, the right of trial by jury shall be preserved, and no fact tried by a jury, shall be otherwise reexamined in any court of the United States other than according to the rules of common law.*

Although this right is limited to what existed at common law at the time the U.S. Constitution was adopted, many states have expanded the right under their state constitutions. The absolute right to a jury trial exists only in criminal cases as covered in Article III and the Fifth and Sixth Amendments of the U.S. Constitution.

The size of a jury varies; some states require only six jurors. A jury may have twelve to eighteen members, which includes alternates, particularly in long trials, to ensure that a panel of twelve participates fully in the trial.

BUSINESS PLANNING TIP

When in doubt, don't. That is, if there is any question about litigation or an investigation, do not destroy e-mails, documents, or tangible evidence.

Every company should have a document retention and file purging policy. Employees should follow the timelines on retention and destruction. And even when the designated time for destruction has arrived, if there is any doubt about pending litigation, investigations, or regulatory issues, the documents should be retained.

The pool of potential jurors and the selection of those jurors are resolved before trial. Usually, voting lists alone or combined with other lists (e.g., licensed drivers) are used as pools for potential jurors. People on these lists are randomly notified of a period of time during which they should report for jury duty. Many states excuse from jury duty certain individuals, like doctors and emergency workers, because of the needs they serve in society. Students are often excused if they are summoned for duty during the semester because of their peculiar obligations and time limitations on completing classes. Judges also usually have the power to excuse certain individuals who would experience hardship if they were required to serve. For example, a sole proprietor of a service business would have no income during the time of jury service and would probably be excused on a hardship basis.

Many more jurors than are needed are summoned to serve. These extra numbers are required because all the parties to a dispute participate in the selection of a jury. Once a pool is available, the court begins the process of *voir dire*, which determines whether a potential juror is qualified to serve. Most states have jurors complete a questionnaire on general topics so that the selection process can move quickly. The questionnaire covers personal information—age, occupation, and so on. The questionnaire might also ask whether the person has ever been a juror, a party to a lawsuit, or a witness. Exhibit 4.8 provides some sample *voir dire* questions.

EXHIBIT   4.8   Sample *Voir Dire* Questions

1. Do you know any of the parties or lawyers in this case? (Asked after the judge introduces all parties and lawyers.)
2. What is your occupation?
3. Are you married?
4. What is your spouse's occupation?
5. Have you ever served on a jury?
6. Are you in favor of compensation for emotional injuries?
7. Do you believe in compensation for victims of police misconduct?
8. Do you support capital punishment?
9. What is your educational background?
10. Did you attend private or public school?
11. What is your spouse's educational background?
12. What seminars, courses, and workshops have you taken since you left school?
13. How old are you?
14. Do you have children? What are their ages and sexes?
15. How would people describe you?
16. Do you believe that people bring about their own misfortunes?
17. Do you do volunteer work? What type?
18. Do you have any relatives who are police officers?
19. Do you belong to a political party?
20. Did you serve in the armed forces?
21. Have you read about this case or heard TV/radio reports about it?
22. Have you formed an opinion about this case?
23. Do you equate laziness with black people?
24. Do you think there is any difference between black and white people?
25. Do you believe black people commit more crimes than white people?

A juror can be removed from a jury panel for two reasons. First, a juror can be removed for cause, which means the juror is incapable of making an impartial decision in the case. If a juror is related to one of the attorneys in the case, for example, the juror would be excused for cause. Some jurors reveal their biases or prejudices, like racial prejudice, in the questionnaire they are required to complete. Others may express strong feelings of animosity toward the medical profession. Clearly, the removal of such jurors for cause in cases involving civil rights and malpractice suits, respectively, is an important part of trial strategy.

 C O N S I D E R . . .   **4 · 4**

Winona Ryder was arrested for shoplifting from Saks Fifth Avenue. The charges against her included theft and burglary for taking $5,600 in merchandise from Saks's Beverly Hills store.

The jury selection process in the trial uncovered the fact that Peter Guber, a Hollywood executive who was in charge of three films that starred Ms. Ryder (*Bram Stoker's Dracula, The Age of Innocence, Little Women*), was among the pool of jurors. When questioned by the judge, Mr. Guber assured him that he could be impartial in judging the evidence. Mr. Guber was allowed to remain on the jury.*

What argument could the prosecution have made against keeping Mr. Guber? What argument could the defense have made against Mr. Guber? What process could each side have used to have him removed from the jury?

*Rick Lyman, "For the Ryder Trial, a Hollywood Script," *New York Times,* November 3, 2002, p. SL-1.

 C O N S I D E R . . .   **4 · 5**

After she was found guilty of obstruction of justice and conspiracy (see Chapter 9) lawyers for Martha Stewart filed a motion for a new trial on the grounds that a juror on the case had possible undisclosed bias. The defense lawyers pointed out that juror Chappel Hartridge had checked "No" on the juror questionnaire when asked whether he had been accused of, charged with, or convicted of a crime. The lawyers for Ms. Stewart filed an affidavit from a former girlfriend of Mr. Hartridge's who indicated that he had been arrested and arraigned on charges of assaulting her. Mr. Hartridge's former girlfriend ultimately dropped the charges against him. What bias do you think Ms. Stewart's lawyers alleged? Are they right? Should the juror have been eliminated for cause?

U.S. v. Stewart
317 F.Supp.2d 432 (S.D.N.Y.2004)

Sometimes a juror cannot be excused for cause but an attorney feels uncomfortable about the juror or the juror's attitudes. In these circumstances, the lawyer issues a **peremptory challenge**, which excuses the juror. The peremptory challenge is the attorney's private tool. However, the use of peremptory challenges is limited. All states have a statute or court rule limiting the number of peremptory challenges an attorney may use in a trial. In recent years, the U.S. Supreme Court has ruled that there are some limitations on the use of peremptory challenges. The Court has indicated that such a challenge cannot be based on either race or gender. If the trial judge suspects that either of these factors may have induced one of the lawyers to seek a peremptory challenge, the lawyer will be required to produce a plausible explanation for the use of the peremptory challenge that is unrelated to race or gender.

CONSIDER... 4.6

Jimmy Elem was convicted of second-degree robbery in a Missouri trial court. During *voir dire*, the prosecutor struck (dismissed) two black men, offering the following explanation:

> *I struck [juror] number twenty-two because of his long hair. He had long curly hair. He had the longest hair of anybody on the panel by far. He appeared to not be a good juror for that fact, the fact that he had long hair hanging down shoulder length, curly, unkempt hair. Also, he had a mustache and a goatee-type beard. And juror number twenty-four also has a mustache and goatee-type beard. Those are the only two people on the jury . . . with facial hair. . . . And I don't like the way they looked, with the way the hair is cut, both of them. And the mustaches and the beards look suspicious to me.*

After his conviction, Mr. Elem challenged the prosecutor's use of the peremptory challenge on the two black men as racially motivated and demanded a new trial. Is the prosecutor's explanation race-neutral? [*Purkett* v. *Elem*, 514 U.S. 765 (1995).]

Jury selection is an art and a science. Jury consulting firms specialize in providing data to attorneys for jury selection. These firms do thorough checks of the potential jurors' backgrounds and offer statistics on the reactions of certain economic and social groups to trials and trial issues. Much about a case at trial is uncontrollable, but jury selection is a part of the process that, with thorough preparation, can increase the likelihood of desired results by ensuring an optimally favorable jury panel.

Jury or trial consultants perform jury profiles, find surrogate juries, and often conduct mock trials. The use of trial consultants has increased dramatically since the 1970s, and membership in the American Society of Trial Consultants has grown from 19 members in 1983 to 250 members today. Jury consultants were used to assist in defense victories in the Sean "Puffy" Combs shooting trial and the O. J. Simpson double homicide trial.[3]

Visit a jury consultant, Carolyn Robbins Jury Simulations, Inc.:
http://www.crjury.com

FOR THE MANAGER'S DESK

RE: JURY SELECTION IN HIGH-PROFILE CASES

Even though the criminal rape charges against him were dismissed, NBA basketball star Kobe Bryant's trial still had progressed to the point of jury selection. As part of the *voir dire* questions for the potential Bryant jurors, the 276 jury panelists were asked the following as part of their 82-question background sheet:

Have you ever studied or received training in medicine, psychology, psychiatry, social work, sociology, or counseling?

Have you received any training in law, law enforcement, or criminology?

What are your feelings about the sexual assault laws in Colorado?

Do you think that people who make a lot of money are treated better by our court system than other people?

Have you or anyone close to you ever felt in danger of being sexually assaulted by another person, including a stranger, acquaintance, or family member?

Do you have any bias for or against mental health care professionals?

Have you ever been afraid of or had any negative experience with an African-American individual?

In your opinion, in general do African Americans in our society experience (check one): a great deal of racial discrimination; some amount of racial discrimination; or no racial discrimination?

How do you feel about interracial relationships?

Do you have particularly strong feelings about, or have you or anyone close to you ever been affected by or involved in, a situation of marital infidelity? [At the time of the alleged rape, Mr. Bryant was married and had one child.]

Which of the following best describes your opinion of professional basketball players: very positive; positive; negative; very negative?

Trial Language

It is often difficult to piece together all the witnesses and evidence in a trial. A lengthy trial may leave the jurors confused. The attorney for each party, therefore, is permitted to make an **opening statement** that summarizes what that party hopes to prove and how it will be proved. Most attorneys also mention the issue of **burden of proof**, which controls who has the responsibility for proving what facts. Although the plaintiff has the burden of proving a case, the defendant has the burden of proving the existence of any valid defenses. There are various standards for meeting the burden of proof. In criminal cases, the standard is proof beyond a reasonable doubt. In civil cases, the standard is proof by a preponderance of the evidence.

Because the plaintiff has the burden of proof, the plaintiff presents his or her case and evidence first. The attorney for the plaintiff decides the order of the witnesses; questioning of these witnesses under oath is called **direct examination**. Although the defense cannot present witnesses during this part of the trial, it can question the plaintiff's witnesses after their direct examination is completed. The defense questioning of plaintiff witnesses is called **cross-examination**, after which the plaintiff may again pose questions to clarify under **redirect examination**.

Once the plaintiff has finished his case, there must be enough evidence to establish a **prima facie case**, one in which the plaintiff has offered some evidence on all the elements required to be established for recovery. Although the evidence may be subjected to credibility questions and challenged by defense evidence, there must be some proof for each part of the claim. If the plaintiff does not meet this standard, the defendant can and may make a motion for a **directed verdict**. This motion for a directed verdict is made outside the jury's hearing and argued to the judge. If it is not granted, the trial proceeds with the defendant's case.

If there is no directed verdict, the defendant has the same opportunity to present witnesses and evidence. Throughout the trial, the judge will apply the rules of evidence to determine what can and cannot be used as evidence. The typical evidence is a witness's testimony. However, there is also tangible evidence. In a contracts case, there is likely to be a great deal of paper evidence—letters, memos, and cost figures.

One of the evidentiary issues that has been debated and litigated over the past few years is the use of expert testimony in cases. The issue the courts face is determining whether the expert's testimony reflects scientific knowledge or whether the testimony is contrived for the trial (often called "junk science.") In *Daubert* v. *Merrell Dow Pharmaceuticals, Inc.* (see Case 4.3), the U.S. Supreme Court was faced with the issue of which experts and experiments should be allowed as evidence in a case.

CASE 4.3

Daubert v. *Merrell Dow Pharmaceuticals, Inc.*
509 U.S. 579 (1993)

Birth Defects from Pills: Junk or Truth?

FACTS

Jason Daubert and Eric Schuller (petitioners) were born with serious birth defects. Through their parents, they filed suit against Merrell Dow Pharmaceuticals, Inc. (respondent), the manufacturer of the antinausea drug Bendectin, which each mother had taken during the first trimester of her pregnancy.

One expert, Dr. Steven Lamm, filed an affidavit in the case stating that the use of Bendectin during the first trimester has not been shown to be a risk factor for birth defects. Eight experts for the Dauberts and Schullers concluded, based on animal and epidemiological studies, that Bendectin can cause birth defects.

continued

These experts had concluded that Bendectin can cause birth defects. Their conclusions were based upon *in vitro* (test tube) and *in vivo* (live) animal studies that found a link between Bendectin and malformations; pharmacological studies of the chemical structure of Bendectin that purported to show similarities between the structure of the drug and that of other substances known to cause birth defects; and the "reanalysis" of previously published epidemiological (human statistical) studies.

Merrell Dow moved for summary judgment, which the District Court granted, holding that the studies of the eight experts did not establish causation because the studies were recalculations of data previously published that established no causal link between the drug and birth defects. Further, the court ruled that the experts' work had not been published or subjected to peer review.

The court of appeals affirmed, and the Dauberts and Schullers appealed from that judgment.

JUDICIAL OPINION

Blackmun, Justice

The *Frye* (*Frye* v. *United States,* 293 F. 1013 [1923]) test has its origin in a short and citation-free 1923 decision concerning the admissibility of evidence derived from a systolic blood pressure deception test, a crude precursor to the polygraph machine. In what has become a famous (perhaps infamous) passage, the then Court of Appeals for the District of Columbia described the device and its operation and declared:

> Just when a scientific principle or discovery crosses the line between the experimental and demonstrable stages is difficult to define. Somewhere in this twilight zone the evidential force of the principle must be recognized, and while courts will go a long way in admitting expert testimony deduced from a well-recognized scientific principle or discovery, the thing from which the deduction is made must be sufficiently established to have gained general acceptance in the particular field in which it belongs. [emphasis added]

Because the deception test had "not yet gained such standing and scientific recognition among physiological and psychological authorities as would justify the courts in admitting expert testimony deduced from the discovery, development, and experiments thus far made," evidence of its results was ruled inadmissible.

The merits of the *Frye* test have been much debated, and scholarship on its proper scope and application is legion. Petitioners' primary attack, however, is not on the content but on the continuing authority of the rule. They contend that the *Frye* test was superseded by the adoption of the Federal Rules of Evidence. We agree.

"Relevant evidence" is defined as that which has "any tendency to make the existence of any fact that is of consequence to the determination of the action more probable or less probable than it would be without the evidence." Rule 401. The Rule's basic standard of relevance thus is a liberal one.

Here there is a specific Rule that speaks to the contested issue. Rule 702, governing expert testimony, provides:

> If scientific, technical, or other specialized knowledge will assist the trier of fact to understand the evidence or to determine a fact in issue, a witness qualified as an expert by knowledge, skill, experience, training, or education, may testify thereto in the form of an opinion or otherwise.

Nothing in the text of this Rule establishes "general acceptance" as an absolute prerequisite to admissibility. Nor does respondent present any clear indication that Rule 702 or the Rules as a whole were intended to incorporate a "general acceptance" standard. The drafting history makes no mention of *Frye,* and a rigid "general acceptance" requirement would be at odds with the "liberal thrust" of the Federal Rules and their "general approach of relaxing the traditional barriers to 'opinion' testimony."

The primary locus of this obligation is Rule 702, which clearly contemplates some degree of regulation of the subjects and theories about which an expert may testify. "*If scientific,* technical, or other specialized *knowledge will assist the trier of fact* to understand the evidence or to determine a fact in issue" an expert "may testify *thereto.*" The subject of an expert's testimony must be "scientific . . . knowledge." The adjective "scientific" implies a grounding in the methods and procedures of science. Similarly, the word "knowledge" connotes more than subjective belief or unsupported speculation. The term "applies to any body of known facts or to any body of ideas inferred from such facts or accepted as truths on good grounds."

Rule 702 further requires that the evidence or testimony "assist the trier of fact to understand the evidence or to determine a fact in issue." This condition goes primarily to relevance. "Expert testimony which does not relate to any issue in the case is not relevant and, ergo, non-helpful."

Ordinarily, a key question to be answered in determining whether a theory or technique is scientific knowledge that will assist the trier of fact will be whether it can be (and has been) tested. "Scientific methodology today is based on generating hypotheses and testing them to see if they can be falsified; indeed, this methodology is what distinguishes science from other fields of human inquiry."

Another pertinent consideration is whether the theory or technique has been subjected to peer review and publication. Publication (which is but one element of peer review) is not a *sine qua non* of admissibility; it does not necessarily correlate with reliability, see S. Jasanoff, The Fifth Branch: Science Advisors as Policymakers 61–76 (1990), and in some instances well-grounded but innovative theories will not have been published. Some propositions, moreover, are too particular, too new, or of too limited interest to be published. But submission to the scrutiny of the scientific community is a component of "good science," in part because it increases the likelihood that substantive flaws in methodology will be detected. The fact of publication (or lack thereof) in a peer-reviewed journal thus will be a relevant, though not dispositive, consideration in assessing the scientific validity of a particular technique or methodology on which an opinion is premised.

Finally, "general acceptance" can yet have a bearing on the inquiry. A "reliability assessment does not require, although it does permit, explicit identification of a relevant scientific community and an express determination of a particular degree of acceptance within that community." Widespread acceptance can be an important factor in ruling particular evidence admissible, and "a known technique that has been able to attract only minimal support within the community" may properly be viewed with skepticism.

The inquiry envisioned by Rule 702 is, we emphasize, a flexible one. Its overarching subject is the scientific validity—and thus the evidentiary relevance and reliability—of the principles that underlie a proposed submission. The focus, of course, must be solely on principles and methodology, not on the conclusions that they generate.

We conclude by briefly addressing what appear to be two underlying concerns of the parties and *amici* in this case. Respondent expresses apprehension that abandonment of "general acceptance" as the exclusive requirement for admission will result in a "free-for-all" in which befuddled juries are confounded by absurd and irrational pseudoscientific assertions. In this regard respondent seems to us to be overly pessimistic about the capabilities of the jury, and of the adversary system generally. Vigorous cross-examination, presentation of contrary evidence, and careful instruction on the burden of proof are the traditional and appropriate means of attacking shaky but admissible evidence. Additionally, in the event the trial court concludes that the scintilla of evidence presented supporting a position is insufficient to allow a reasonable juror to conclude that the position more likely than not is true, the court remains free to direct a judgment, Fed. Rule Civ. Proc. 50(a), and likewise to grant summary judgment. These conventional devices, rather than wholesale exclusion

under an uncompromising "general acceptance" test, are the appropriate safeguards where the basis of scientific testimony meets the standards of Rule 702.

Petitioners and, to a greater extent, their *amici*, exhibit a different concern. They suggest that recognition of a screening role for the judge that allows for the exclusion of "invalid" evidence will sanction a stifling and repressive scientific orthodoxy and will be inimical to the search for truth. It is true that open debate is an essential part of both legal and scientific analyses. Yet there are important differences between the quest for truth in the courtroom and the quest for truth in the laboratory. Scientific conclusions are subject to perpetual revision. Law, on the other hand, must resolve disputes finally and quickly. The scientific project is advanced by broad and wide-ranging consideration of a multitude of hypotheses, for those that are incorrect will eventually be shown to be so, and that in itself is an advance. Conjectures that are probably wrong are of little use, however, in the project of reaching a quick, final, and binding legal judgment—often of great consequence—about a particular set of events in the past. We recognize that in practice, a gatekeeping role for the judge, no matter how flexible, inevitably on occasion will prevent the jury from learning of authentic insights and innovations. That, nevertheless, is the balance that is struck by Rules of Evidence designed not for the exhaustive search for cosmic understanding but for the particularized resolution of legal disputes.

To summarize: "general acceptance" is not a necessary precondition to the admissibility of scientific evidence under the Federal Rules of Evidence, but the Rules of Evidence—especially Rule 702—do assign to the trial judge the task of ensuring that an expert's testimony both rests on a reliable foundation and is relevant to the task at hand. Pertinent evidence based on scientifically valid principles will satisfy those demands.

The inquiries of the District Court and the Court of Appeals focused almost exclusively on "general acceptance," as gauged by publication and the decisions of other courts.

Reversed and remanded.

CASE QUESTIONS

1. What is the difference between Merrell Dow's expert and the Daubert/Schuller experts?

2. Without their experts, do the Daubert and Schuller families have a case?

3. What is the standard for admission of scientific evidence?

4. How does this decision affect medical product liability suits?

CONSIDER...   4 · 7

Karsten Manufacturing Corporation filed suit against the Professional Golf Association (PGA) because the PGA had proposed a ban of Karsten's U-groove Ping brand clubs from professional play. Karsten hired Richard Smith, then an Arizona State University finance professor, to develop an economic model to correlate professional and consumer usage. Professor Smith's model showed that if pros play with Ping clubs, a proportionate number of duffers will play with them. If the pros cannot use Ping clubs, Karsten is out of business because amateur golfers will not purchase Karsten products. Professor Smith said he conducted valid regression analysis. The attorney for the PGA, Larry Hammond, called it "junk science" that interferes with the real issues in the case. Should the Smith model be admitted? Does it make a difference that the model was developed only for the case? Does it make a difference that Professor Smith's consulting firm was paid over $1 million for the model?

ETHICAL ISSUES

Thomas Talcott was a Dow Corning materials engineer in 1976, when Dow was developing its silicone breast implants. Mr. Talcott had questions about the safety of the implants and raised his concerns, but product development, production, and marketing went forward anyway. In 1991 and 1992, concerns about the safety of the breast implants increased, and a number of women filed lawsuits alleging that the implants had leaked and/or ruptured and caused cancer, lupus, and other autoimmune disorders. Lawyers for the women sought access to the company records from the time of product development. Are the lawyers entitled to those records?

If you had been Mr. Talcott and had strong feelings about the safety of a new product your employer was about to sell, what would you have done? Would it have done any good to bring it to the attention of all in the chain of command, from your supervisor up to the CEO? If you had been Mr. Talcott, would you have been able to continue to work for Dow Corning? Suppose that Mr. Talcott discussed his concerns about the safety of the implants with everyone in the chain of command, but still

the company planned to enter the market with this product. Would you notify a government agency or "leak" your information to the media? Why, or why not? Should Mr. Talcott say anything to the lawyers for the women?

Aftermath
Mr. Talcott left Dow Corning in 1976. He served as an expert witness for the women who brought implant suits and was paid $400 per hour. Since the time of the Dow Corning litigation, the government has considered allowing the use of the implants once again. The scientific debate over safety of the implants remains emotionally charged and scientifically confusing. In 2004, a scientific advisory panel to the FDA recommended that the 11-year ban on the implants be lifted with additional study and data required. However, in a rare step, the FDA rejected the advice of its own panel and refused to lift the ban.*

*Gina Kolata, "F.D.A. Panel Backs Breast Implants Made of Silicone," *New York Times,* October 16, 2003, A1. Steve Sternberg, "FDA rejects silicone implants," *USA Today,* January 9–11, 2004, 1A.

There are restrictions on the forms and types of evidence that can be used at trial. Most people are familiar with the hearsay rule of evidence. **Hearsay** is evidence offered by a witness who does not have personal knowledge of the information being given but just heard it from someone else. For example, suppose that Arkansas Sewing and Fit Fabric are involved in contract litigation. Fit Fabric says there was no contract. Arkansas Sewing has a witness who overheard the president of Fit Fabric talking to someone on a plane saying he had a contract with Arkansas Sewing but had no intention of performing on it. The witness's testimony of the airplane conversation is hearsay and cannot be used to prove the contract existed. The reason for the hearsay rule is to keep evidence as reliable as possible. The person testifying about the hearsay may not know of the circumstances or background of the conversation and is testifying only to what someone else said.

Once the evidence is presented and the parties are finished with their cases, there is one final "go" at the jury. The parties are permitted to make **closing arguments**, which review the presented evidence, highlight the important points for the jurors, and point out the defects in the other side's case. After the cases and closing arguments are presented, the jurors are given their **instructions**. These instructions tell the jurors what the law is and how to apply the law to the facts presented. The instructions are developed by the judge and all the attorneys in the case.

Jury deliberations are done privately; they cannot be recorded, and no one can attend the deliberations except the jurors. Jurors can but are not required to discuss what happened during the deliberations after they are ended and a decision is returned to the court.

The U.S. Supreme Court has ruled that jury verdicts need not be unanimous. A state can adopt a rule that requires only a simple majority or three-fourths of the jury to agree on a verdict. In those states requiring unanimous verdicts, it is not unusual for juries to be unable to agree on a verdict. The jurors have then reached a deadlock, which is called a **hung jury**. If a trial results in a hung jury, the case can be retried. There is, however, the additional expense of retrying the case.

The result of jury deliberations is the **verdict**. The verdict is given to the judge and is usually read by the judge's clerk.

Even after the verdict, the case is not over. The losing party can make several motions to get around the verdict. One such motion is for a new trial, wherein the attorney argues the need and reason for a new trial to the judge.

Another motion after the verdict, one that a judge is less likely to grant, is a motion for a **judgment NOV**. *NOV* stands for *non obstante veredicto,* which means "notwithstanding the verdict." In other words, the moving attorney is asking the trial judge to reverse the decision of the jury. The basis for granting a judgment NOV is that the jury's verdict is clearly against the weight of the evidence. Occasionally, juries are swayed by the emotion of a case and do not apply the law properly. It is, however, a strong show of judicial authority for a judge to issue a judgment NOV, and they are rare.

Even if no motions are granted, the case still may not be over; it can go to an appellate court for review. Such an appeal must be done within a specified time limit in each state. Here the trial has come full circle to the principle of judicial review and *stare decisis*. Exhibit 4.9 summarizes the steps in civil litigation.

ISSUES IN INTERNATIONAL LITIGATION

As noted earlier, international courts have no enforcement powers. They serve as avenues for voluntary mediation. However, courts in each nation in which a firm is doing business would have jurisdiction over that firm in the nation's court system. In a recent infringement dispute over Mattel's "Barbie" and the French doll "Sindy," the parties litigated in London, where both firms were doing business and the dolls were selling well.

Among the critical questions that arise in international litigation are: Which set of laws applies? What court is the appropriate forum for a lawsuit that involves citizens of different countries? For example, many non-U.S. citizens who are injured in their own countries by products made by U.S. firms will generally be able to recover more under the product liability and tort laws of the United States. In *Piper Aircraft Co.* v. *Reyno,* 454 U.S. 235 (1981), the pilot and five passengers were killed when a charter flight from Blackpool to Perth, Scotland, crashed in the Scottish highlands. The pilot and passengers were traveling in a twin-engine Piper Aztec, an

EXHIBIT 4.9 Steps in Civil Litigation

aircraft manufactured in Pennsylvania by Piper Aircraft Co. The British Department of Trade conducted an investigation of the crash and determined that its cause was mechanical failure. The relatives and estates of the passengers brought suit in the United States against Piper Aircraft. Scottish law does not recognize strict tort liability (see Chapter 11), and U.S. laws on liability and damages are far more favorable than those of Scotland. The U.S. Supreme Court held that the case was properly heard in Scotland because the accident was in Scotland and all the parties in the case were either English or Scottish.

A similar ruling was made with respect to the 2,500 victims of the Union Carbide gas leak in Bhopal, India. Some of the victims filed suit in the United States because the law and damages provisions here afforded them much greater relief. Their suit was dismissed to India, and the court added that Union Carbide would be required to submit to the jurisdiction of Indian courts and to follow discovery rules of the United States.

Some businesspeople feel the United States has too many lawyers and that too much legal activity leads to higher costs and a loss of our competitive edge in the international market.

Our legal system and its parties vary greatly from other countries' systems. "Following Japan in Reform" describes some of the limitations other countries use to control litigation.

FOR THE MANAGER'S DESK

RE: FOLLOWING JAPAN IN REFORM

Japan's Reforms for Controlling Litigation

Many businesspeople have argued that too many lawyers and lawsuits hurt the United States in the competitive international market. The following curbs instituted in Japan have been cited as ways of controlling litigation.

Limits on the Number of Lawyers

To become a *bengoshi* (lawyer) in Japan, an individual must win a slot at the Legal Training & Research Institute. This government-run school accepts only 2 percent of the 35,000 annual applicants. Only 400 new *bengoshi* are added each year to Japan's 14,336 lawyers.

Limits on Recovery

No class actions or contingent fees are permitted in Japan.

Costs to Plaintiffs

Plaintiffs are required to pay money to their lawyers up front. The amount required is 8 percent of the recovery sought plus the nonrefundable filing fee.

Discovery Limitations

There is no discovery from either side. Parties go to trial not knowing the evidence the other side will present. The theory here is that plaintiffs must be certain about their evidence before a case goes to trial.

Limits on Damage Awards

Judges, not juries, determine damages, and even in wrongful death cases the damages may not exceed $150,000.

Encouragement of Settlement and Cultural Disdain for Confrontation

In Japan, a cultural pride exists in being able to resolve disputes outside the courtroom; those who must litigate are looked down upon.

Discussion Questions

1. If the United States adopted the Japanese litigation system, would you feel that your rights would be affected?

2. Is the United States beginning to adopt a cultural attitude to eliminate confrontation by embracing ADR?

3. In the English court system, the loser pays court costs and the costs of the other party involved in the litigation. Should such a rule be adopted in the United States? In all cases? Would you be less willing to pursue a case for yourself or your company if you knew that you would be required to pay if you lost the case?

Sources: Michele Galen et al., "Guilty," *Business Week,* April 13, 1992, pp. 60–66; and *ABA Report on International Lawyers* (1990).

SUMMARY

How can businesses resolve disputes?

- Alternative dispute resolution (ADR)—means of resolving disputes apart from court litigation

Types of ADR:

- Arbitration—hearing with relaxed rules of evidence
- Mediation—third party acts as go-between
- Conciliation—international term for mediation
- Medarb—combination of mediation and arbitration
- Minitrial—private judge and courtroom; shortened trial
- Rent-a-judge—disputes resolved by hired judge
- Summary jury trial—advisory verdict by jurors in a mock trial
- Early neutral evaluation—third-party evaluation before litigation proceeds
- International Chamber of Commerce (ICC)— voluntary international court that offers arbitration in international disputes

What strategies should businesses follow if litigation is inevitable?

- *Voir dire*—jury selection method to screen bias
- Production—obtain and produce documents
- Deposition—questioning of witnesses under oath

How do courts proceed with litigation?

- Litigation—use of courts to resolve disputes
- Complaint—plaintiff's statement of a case
- Summons—document to serve defendant with lawsuit
- Answer—defendant's response in litigation
- Statute of limitations—time limit for filing suit
- Discovery—advance disclosure of evidence in case
- Deposition—testimony while under oath in advance of trial
- Reform—steps to limit suits and damage awards
- Trial—jury selection done through *voir dire*
- Opening statements
- Plaintiff's case
- Defendant's case
- Evidence can include testimony and tangible evidence; hearsay not admitted as evidence

QUESTIONS AND PROBLEMS

1. Anna's Dresses, Inc., was delinquent in its payment to one of its suppliers. Anna's intended to pay them, but it had a cash-flow problem and chose to pay rent to its landlord so as not to be evicted from its store rather than make a payment to the supplier. Anna's president is served with a complaint for breach of contract and a summons. The complaint lists the supplier as the plaintiff. What has happened? What must Anna's do now?

2. In the Johns-Manville asbestos litigation, Samuel Greenstone, an attorney for eleven asbestos workers, settled their claims for $30,000 and a promise that he would not "directly or indirectly participate in the bringing of new actions against the Corporation." The 1933 case settlement was documented in the minutes of Johns-Manville's board meeting. Could the information in the minutes be used in later litigation against Johns-Manville? How could a plaintiff's attorney obtain the information?

3. In question 2, do you feel Mr. Greenstone made an ethical decision in his agreement? Wasn't his loyalty to his eleven clients and his obligation to obtain compensation for them? Would you have agreed to the no-further-participation-in-a-lawsuit clause? Would you, if you had been an executive at Johns-Manville, have supported the clause?

4. Whaler Manufacturing entered into a contract to buy seven lathes from Hooper, Inc. Hooper delivered the machines, and Whaler was to pay for them over a period of one year. Detroit Second National Bank came to repossess the machines from Whaler because Hooper had failed to make payment. To stop the repossession, Whaler paid the bank the $5,000 due on Hooper's loan. Because Whaler had agreed to pay only $4,000 for the machines to Hooper, it stopped its payments. Hooper sued for breach of contract. In answering Hooper's lawsuit, what does Whaler need to include?

5. A discrimination suit by a former flight attendant against Atlantic East Airlines is going to trial. Jury selection has begun. An executive from Atlantic East notices that a member of the potential juror panel was a flight attendant responsible for pregnancy leave reforms among airline flight attendants during the early 1980s. This potential juror is no longer a flight attendant and is raising two small children at home. The executive informs Atlantic East's lawyer. Can the lawyer do anything to prevent the woman from sitting on the jury?

6. Applegate is in litigation with Magnifium over a contract breach. Applegate has been approached by a former janitor for Magnifium who can testify regarding conversations about the contract between Magnifium executives. The janitor heard them when the executives had stayed late at work and he was cleaning. Can Applegate use the statements at trial?

7. Robert Joiner began work as an electrician in the Water & Light Department of Thomasville, Georgia, in 1973. Mr. Joiner worked with and around electrical transformers that contained a fluid. In 1983, the city of Thomasville discovered that this fluid contained polychlorinated biphenyls (PCBs), a substance considered hazardous.

Mr. Joiner was diagnosed with lung cancer in 1991 and filed suit against General Electric, the manufacturer of the transformers, for negligence and product liability. Mr. Joiner had been a smoker, his parents were smokers, and there was a history of lung cancer in his family.

Mr. Joiner offered expert testimony on studies involving the injection of PCB into the stomachs of infant mice and resulting cancer. The experts had no epidemiological studies on PCB exposure. Should the expert testimony be admitted? [*General Electric Co.* v. *Joiner*, 522 U.S. 136 (1997).]

8. The ABC News program *Day One* ran two reports on February 28 and March 7, 1995, that left viewers with the impression that Philip Morris Company was spiking its cigarettes with nicotine to make them more addictive. Philip Morris filed a $10 billion defamation suit against Capital Cities/ABC, Inc., for defamation on March 24, 1995. The suit alleged that the "spiking" report was untrue. An ABC News spokesman said in response to the suit, "ABC News stands by its reporting on this issue."

Philip Morris is based in New York; the suit was filed in Richmond, Virginia; and a news conference to announce the suit was held in Washington, D.C., on the day hearings were to begin to determine whether the FDA should regulate nicotine as a drug. Philip Morris was not the primary target of the *Day One* report, but it was mentioned by name in the broadcasts. Philip Morris did not ask ABC for a retraction prior to filing suit.

J. D. Lee, a Knoxville, Tennessee, plaintiff's attorney who has had experience litigating against tobacco companies, noted that the prospect of getting his hands on Philip Morris's internal documents in such a suit made him gleeful: "I would have a field day with Philip Morris."

By September 1995, ABC and Philip Morris had settled the suit. ABC issued the following public apology and agreed to pay attorneys' fees for Philip Morris.

It is the policy of ABC News to make corrections where they are warranted. On February 28 and March 7, 1995, the ABC program, Day One, *aired segments dealing with the tobacco industry. Philip Morris filed a defamation lawsuit alleging that the segments wrongly reported that, through the introduction of significant amounts of nicotine from outside sources, Philip Morris "artificially spikes" and "fortifies" its cigarettes with nicotine, and "carefully controls" and "manipulates" nicotine for the purpose of "addicting" smokers.*

Philip Morris states that it does not add nicotine in any measurable amount from any outside source for any purpose in the course of its manufacturing process, and that its finished cigarettes contain less nicotine than is found in the natural tobacco from which they are made.

ABC does not take issue with those two statements. We now agree that we should not have reported that Philip Morris adds significant amounts of nicotine from outside sources. That was a mistake that was not deliberate on the part of ABC, but for which we accept responsibility and which requires correction. We apologize to our audience and Philip Morris.

ABC and Philip Morris continue to disagree about whether the principal focus of the reports was on the use of nicotine from outside sources. Philip Morris believes that this was the main thrust of the programs. ABC believes that the principal focus of the reports was whether cigarette companies use the reconstituted tobacco process to control the levels of nicotine in cigarettes in order to keep people smoking. Philip Morris categorically denies that it does so. ABC thinks the reports speak for themselves on this issue and is prepared to have the issue resolved elsewhere.

ABC and Philip Morris have agreed to discontinue the defamation action.

What do you think of Philip Morris's decision to litigate? Would you have made the same decision? Was it a public relations tactic as well as an enforcement of rights? What motivation did both sides have for settling the case? Evaluate the ethics of ABC News in running the story. Evaluate the ethics of Philip Morris in filing suit without first approaching ABC for a retraction.

9. The SEC investigation of Tyco International for possible securities law violations produced several e-mails.

The e-mails focus on two concerns about the company: accounting improprieties and the use of company funds by then-CEO Dennis Kozlowski. The e-mails were written by outside lawyers from the firm of Wilmer Cutler to former Tyco General Counsel, Mark Belnick. The e-mails are as follows.

March 23, 2000: E-mail from a Wilmer Cutler Partner, Lewis Liman, to Mark Belnick
There are payments to a woman whom the folks in finance describe to be Dennis's girlfriend. I do not know Dennis's situation, but this is an embarrassing fact.

(Note: The payments were later verified as being made from the Key Employee Loan Account to Karen Mayo, who subsequently became Karen Kozlowski.)

May 25, 2000: E-mail from a Wilmer Cutler Partner, William McLucas, to Mark Belnick
We have found issues that will likely interest the SEC, creativeness is employed in hitting the forecasts.

There is also a bad letter from the Sigma people just before the acquisition confirming that they were asked to hold product shipment just before closing. . . .

(This e-mail also went on to suggest that there was, in regard to Tyco's financial reports, "something funny which is likely apparent if any decent accountant looks at this.")

While Mr. McLucas and Mr. Liman cannot comment because of attorney-client privilege, others indicate that they followed up on the e-mails and asked officials at Tyco to correct the concerns and problems raised in the e-mails.

Are the e-mails privileged? How did the SEC gain access to them? Can they be used as evidence? Are they discoverable? (Laurie P. Coehn and Mark Maremont, "E-Mails Show Tyco's Lawyers Had Concerns," *Wall Street Journal,* December 27, 2002, pp. C1, C5.)

10. In October 1995, Saint Clair Adams applied for a job at Circuit City Stores, Inc., a national retailer of consumer electronics. Mr. Adams signed an employment application that included the following provision.

I agree that I will settle any and all previously unasserted claims, disputes or controversies arising out of or relating to my application or candidacy for employment, employment and/or cessation of employment with Circuit City, exclusively by final and binding arbitration before a neutral Arbitrator. By way of example only, such claims include claims under federal, state, and local statutory or common law, such as the Age Discrimination in Employment Act, Title VII of the Civil Rights Act of 1964, as amended, including the amendments of the Civil Rights Act of 1991, the Americans with Disabilities Act, the law of contract and the law of tort.

Mr. Adams was hired as a sales counselor in Circuit City's store in Santa Rosa, California.

Two years later, Mr. Adams filed an employment discrimination lawsuit against Circuit City in state court, asserting claims under California's Fair Employment Act. Circuit City filed suit in the U.S. District Court seeking to stop the state court action and to compel arbitration under the FAA. Mr. Adams says the arbitration clause violates his statutory rights for protection against employment discrimination and that he has the right to go to court, not arbitration. Who is correct? Can Mr. Adams be required to submit to arbitration? [*Circuit City Stores, Inc.* v. *Adams,* 532 U.S. 105 (2001).]

RESEARCH PROBLEM

Of Jurors, Stealth, and Grisham

11. Read John Grisham's novel *The Runaway Jury* or view the movie and determine how lawyers might have detected the presence of a stealth juror.

NOTES

1. Lisa Brennan, "What Lawyers Like: Mediation," *National Law Journal,* November 15, 1999, pp. A1, A10.

2. See http://www.adr.org.

3. Bob Van Voris, "Voir Dire Tip: Pick Former Juror," *National Law Journal,* November 1, 1999, pp. A1, A6.

Business: Its Regulatory Environment

A business is regulated by everything from the U.S. Constitution to the guidelines of the Consumer Product Safety Commission. Managers must know codified law as well as the law that develops as cases are litigated and new issues of liability arise. The regulatory environment of business includes penalties for criminal conduct and punitive damages for knowing injuries to customers. Part II describes the laws that regulate businesses and business operations, the sanctions that are imposed for violation of these laws, and the manner by which businesses can make compliance with the law a key part of their values.

Business and the Constitution

The U.S. Constitution is a remarkable document. It was drafted by a group of independent states two hundred years ago in an attempt to unify the states into one national government that could function smoothly and efficiently without depriving those independent states of their rights. The fact that it has survived so many years with so few changes indicates the flexibility and foresight built into the document.

This chapter covers the application of the U.S. Constitution to business. Several questions are answered: What are the constitutional limitations on business regulation? Who has more power to regulate business—the states or the federal government? What individual freedoms granted under the Constitution apply to businesses?

For up-to-date legal news and real-world business applications, click on **update** *at http://jennings.westbuslaw.com.*

> Some men look at constitutions with sanctimonious reverence, and deem them like the ark of the covenant, too sacred to be touched. . . . I am certainly not an advocate for frequent and untried changes in laws and constitutions. . . . But . . . laws and institutions must go hand in hand with the progress of the human mind.
>
> THOMAS JEFFERSON

> The history of the United States has been written not merely in the halls of Congress, in the Executive offices and on the battlefields, but to a great extent in the chambers of the Supreme Court of the United States.
>
> CHARLES WARREN

In 1996, Nike was inundated with allegations about its labor practices in shoe factories around the world. Nike responded to the negative reports and allegations with a series of press releases, ads, and op-ed pieces in newspapers around the country. In addition, Nike commissioned a report from former Atlanta mayor and U.S. ambassador, Andrew Young, on the condition of its factories around the world. Mr. Young issued a report in 1997 that reflected favorably on Nike and its labor practices. Nike cited the report in op-ed pieces, most particularly in a letter to the editor of the *New York Times* in response to a negative op-ed piece there on Nike's labor practices.

Marc Kasky filed suit against Nike in California alleging that the op-ed pieces and letters in response to negative op-ed pieces about Nike violated the False Advertising Law of California. The act permits state agencies to take action to fine corporate violators of the act as well as obtain remedies such as injunctions to halt the ads.

Nike challenged the suit on the grounds that such an interpretation and application of the advertising regulation violated its rights of free speech. The lower court agreed with Mr. Kasky and held that the advertising statute applied to Nike's defense of its labor practices, even on the op-ed pages of newspapers. Nike appealed to the U.S. Supreme Court. How should the court rule? Does the action under California law violate Nike's free speech rights?

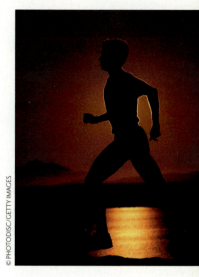

© PHOTODISC/GETTY IMAGES

THE U.S. CONSTITUTION

An Overview of the U.S. Constitution

Learn more about the U.S. Constitution:

http://www.constitution.org

Although virtually every constitutional issue and every court decision on a constitutional issue are complicated and detailed, the **U.S. Constitution** itself is a simple and short document. Contained within it is the entire structure of the federal government, its powers, the powers of the states, and the rights of all citizens. The exact language of the U.S. Constitution is presented in Appendix A.

Articles I, II, and III—The Framework for Separation of Powers

The first three articles of the U.S. Constitution set up the three branches of the federal government. Article I establishes the **legislative branch**. The two houses of Congress—the House of Representatives and the Senate—are created, their method of electing members is specified, and their powers are listed.

Article II creates the **executive branch** of the federal government. The office of president along with its qualifications, manner of election, term, and powers are specified.

Article III establishes the **judicial branch** of the federal government. This article creates only the U.S. Supreme Court and establishes its jurisdiction. Congress, however, is authorized to establish inferior courts, which it has done in the form of federal district courts, specialized federal courts, and U.S. courts of appeals (see Chapter 3, Exhibit 3.1).

The first three articles establish the nature of the federal government as involving the **separation of powers**. Each of the branches of government is given unique functions that the other branches cannot perform, but each branch also has curbing powers on the other branches through the exercise of its unique powers. For example, the judicial branch cannot pass laws, but it can prevent a law passed by Congress from taking effect by judicially interpreting the law as unconstitutional. The executive branch does not pass legislation but has veto power over legislation passed by Congress. The executive branch has responsibility for foreign relations and treaty negotiation. However, those treaties do not take effect until the Senate ratifies them. This system of different powers that can be used to curb the other branches' exercise of power is called a system of **checks and balances**.

The drafters of the U.S. Constitution designed the federal government this way to avoid the accumulation of too much power in any one branch of government. In *Nixon* v. *Administrator of General Services*, 433 U.S. 425 (1977), the Supreme Court held that former President Nixon was required to turn over to Congress any records and materials of the executive branch that were relevant to the congressional inquiry into the Watergate scandal (a break-in at the Democratic Party's national headquarters that was masterminded by members of the Nixon administration). In *Department of Commerce* v. *U.S. House of Representatives*, 525 U.S. 316 (1999), the Supreme Court ruled that an administrative agency under the executive branch could not ignore either congressional statute or constitutional mandate and conduct the U.S. Census by statistical sampling. The Court ruled that the Department of Commerce had to do a physical count of all U.S. citizens as required by statute and the Constitution. In *Clinton* v. *Jones*, 520 U.S. 681 (1997), the Supreme Court ruled that even the president is subject to the laws of the land and is accountable for civil wrongs alleged by private citizens. In the case, Paula Corbin Jones alleged that Mr. Clinton had sexually harassed her while he was governor of Arkansas. The Court ruled that the president cannot be above the law or judicial process when he has violated the rights of a citizen in his private conduct. In the case, the Court quoted the federal district judge who wrote, "Nowhere in the Constitution, congressional acts, or the writings of any judge or scholar, may any credible support for such a proposition be found. It is contrary to our form of government, which asserts as did the English in the Magna Carta and the Petition of Right, that even the sovereign is subject to God and the law."

Other Articles

Article IV deals with states' interrelationships. Article V provides the procedures for constitutional amendments. Article VI is the **Supremacy Clause** (discussed later in this chapter), and Article VII simply provides the method for state ratification of the Constitution.

The Bill of Rights

In addition to the seven articles, the U.S. Constitution has twenty-seven amendments, the first ten of which are the **Bill of Rights**. Although these rights originally applied only to federal procedures, the **Fourteenth Amendment** extended them to apply to the states as well. These amendments cover rights from freedom of speech (First Amendment) to the right to a jury trial (Sixth Amendment) to protection of privacy from unlawful searches (Fourth Amendment) to due process before deprivation of property (Fifth Amendment). The amendments as they apply to businesses are covered later in this chapter and in Chapter 9.

THE ROLE OF JUDICIAL REVIEW AND THE CONSTITUTION

The Supreme Court and its decisions are often in the news because the cases decided by the Court are generally significant ones that provide interpretations of the U.S. Constitution and also define the extent of the rights we are afforded under it. The role of the U.S. Supreme Court is to decide what rights are provided by the general language of the U.S. Constitution. For example, the Fifth Amendment guarantees that we will not be deprived of our life, liberty, or property without "due process of law." Due process of law, interpreted by the courts many times now, includes such rights as the right to a hearing before a mortgage foreclosure or at least the right of notice before property is sold after repossession as a result of nonpayment of the debt on it.

The First Amendment protects the simple right to freedom of speech, but the Supreme Court has been faced with issues such as whether limits on campaign contributions are a violation of that right to be heard. The Fourth Amendment, the privacy amendment, protects us from warrantless searches. This general idea has been analyzed in the context of garbage taken from cans waiting for pickup on the street and unannounced inspections by OSHA regulators of company workplaces (see Chapter 19 for more information on OSHA).

The U.S. Supreme Court has the responsibility of determining the extent and scope of the rights and protections afforded by the U.S. Constitution. In addition, the Supreme Court plays the unique role of reviewing the actions of the other branches of government. The Court is a crucial part of the checks-and-balances system set up in our Constitution. Recently, the Court reviewed the constitutionality of legislation passed by Congress granting the president line-item veto authority on the budget. The Court also reviews the constitutionality of actions taken by the other branches of government.

CONSTITUTIONAL LIMITATIONS OF ECONOMIC REGULATIONS

The Commerce Clause

The **Commerce Clause** is found in Article I, Section 8, Part 3, of the U.S. Constitution and provides Congress with the power "[t]o regulate Commerce with foreign Nations, and among the several States, . . ." Although the language is short and simple, the phrase "among the several states" has created much controversy. The clause limits Congress to the regulation of interstate commerce. Local commerce and intrastate commerce is left to the states for regulation. Defining interstate commerce has been the task of the courts. The standards are defined from two perspectives: federal regulation of state and local commerce, and state and local regulation of interstate commerce.

Standards for Congressional Regulation of State and Local Business Activity
The issue as defined by the U.S. Supreme Court is whether there is sufficient interstate contact or effects for the application of federal standards. The Constitution gives Congress authority to regulate interstate matters and vests all the remaining regulatory authority in the states.

BIOGRAPHY

A LOOK AT THE PHYSICAL SUPREME COURT

The U.S. Supreme Court has been an evolving body since the details of its duties were spelled out in the judiciary act of 1789. It began its session with the robes, wigs, pomp, and circumstance of the British courts. However, when young boys mocked justice William Cushing, an appointee from Massachusetts, as he walked along the streets of New York in his wig, the wig tradition was dropped. The robes remain still today.

Initially, the U.S. Supreme Court was a traveling court. Justices spent up to nineteen hours per day in coaches as they traveled from circuit to circuit to hear cases. Congress had mandated such a traveling court because of its fear that without such contact with the people, the court would become too detached. The justices grumbled sufficiently until the traveling requirement was dropped in 1793 in favor of a requirement that each justice make one trip per year to one circuit.

The Court has long maintained its detachment from political processes, hearing only cases with actual disputes. When President Washington sent the court twenty-nine questions on international law, begging for answers so that the United States could resolve its role in the wars between Britain and France, the Court refused. It explained it would decide questions only in the context of litigating parties. That restraint holds true today.

No one had even thought of moving the court to Washington, D.C. until there was a shouting match among spectators at a Supreme Court session in 1800. Offering its protection, Congress in 1801 gave the Court small quarters on the first floor of its buildings in Washington. One lawyer referred to these quarters as a "potato hole of a place." The Court has remained in Washington ever since but its digs have improved. In 1860 it moved to the old Senate chambers. The timing of the move to its present building could not have been worse. It was 1935—the Depression—and the Court had stood in the way of many of Roosevelt's reforms intended to help Americans through the Depression. Federal courts around the country felt public backlash and resentment as the building and its opulence became associated with the Court's initial refusals to allow Roosevelt's reform legislation.

That court building remains its home today and also a focal point for demonstrators on all the thorny issues that are brought before the Court—from those involving racial equality to abortion, and even to vote recounts in presidential elections.*

*For more history of the Court see http://www.supremecourthistory.org.

The U.S. Supreme Court has defined the extent of interstate commerce. The Court initially gave a very narrow interpretation to the scope of the Commerce Clause. For activity to be subject to federal regulation, there had to be a "direct and immediate effect" on interstate commerce. In 1918, the Court ruled that manufacturing was not "commerce" (was solely intrastate) and struck down an act of Congress that attempted to regulate goods manufactured in plants using child labor [*Hammer* v. *Dagenhart*, 247 U.S. 251 (1918)]. During the 1930s, Congress and President Roosevelt bumped heads with the Court many times in their attempts to legislate a recovery from the Depression. The Court consistently refused to validate federal legislation of manufacturing, operations, and labor [*Schechter Poultry* v. *United States*, 295 U.S. 495 (1935); *Carter* v. *Carter Coal*, 298 U.S. 238 (1936)]. Roosevelt refused to accept the roadblock to his legislation and initiated his court-packing plan to increase the number of members of the court with Roosevelt appointees.

The Court responded in *NLRB* v. *Laughlin Steel*, 336 U.S. 460 (1940), by ruling that intrastate activities, even though local in character, may still affect interstate commerce and thus be subject to federal regulation. The "affectation" doctrine thus expanded the authority of the federal government in regulating commerce. In the words of the Court, "If it is interstate commerce that feels the pinch, it does not matter how local the squeeze" (336 U.S. at 464). Today, judicial review of congressional action based on the Commerce Clause is perfunctory. Typically, there is always some connection between economic legislation and congressional authority.

The Commerce Clause has had a critical role in the elimination of discrimination because the Court's liberal definition of what constitutes interstate commerce has permitted the application of federal civil rights laws to local activities.

U.S. v. Morrison (Case 5.1) is a landmark case in which the U.S. Supreme Court defined the extent of interstate commerce.

CASE 5.1

U.S. v. *Morrison*
529 U.S. 598 (2000)

Economic Impact Is Not the Same as Commerce: Violence Is Intrastate Activity

FACTS

Christy Brzonkala (petitioner) enrolled at Virginia Polytechnic Institute (Virginia Tech) in the fall of 1994. In September of that year, Ms. Brzonkala met Antonio Morrison and James Crawford (respondents), who were both students at Virginia Tech and members of its varsity football team. Ms. Brzonkala alleges that, within 30 minutes of meeting Mr. Morrison and Mr. Crawford, they assaulted and repeatedly raped her. After the attack, Mr. Morrison allegedly told Ms. Brzonkala, "You better not have any . . . diseases." The court omitted portions of the quotes from the briefs in issuing its opinion, stating only that they "consist of boasting, debased remarks about what Morrison would do to women, vulgar remarks that cannot fail to shock and offend."

Ms. Brzonkala became severely emotionally disturbed and depressed. She sought assistance from a university psychiatrist, who prescribed antidepressant medication. Shortly after the rape, Ms. Brzonkala stopped attending classes and withdrew from the university.

In early 1995, Ms. Brzonkala filed a complaint against the respondents under Virginia Tech's Sexual Assault Policy. During the school-conducted hearing on her complaint, Mr. Morrison admitted having sexual contact with her despite the fact that she had twice told him "no." After the hearing, Virginia Tech's Judicial Committee found insufficient evidence to punish Mr. Crawford, but found Mr. Morrison guilty of sexual assault and sentenced him to immediate suspension for two semesters.

Virginia Tech's dean of students upheld the judicial committee's sentence. However, in July 1995, Virginia Tech informed Ms. Brzonkala that Mr. Morrison intended to initiate a court challenge to his conviction under the Sexual Assault Policy. University officials told her that a second hearing would be necessary to remedy the school's error in prosecuting her complaint under that policy, which had not been widely circulated to students. The university therefore conducted a second hearing under its Abusive Conduct Policy, which was in force prior to the dissemination of the Sexual Assault Policy.

Following this second hearing, the Judicial Committee again found Mr. Morrison guilty and sentenced him to an identical two-semester suspension. This time, however, the description of Mr. Morrison's offense was, without explanation, changed from "sexual assault" to "using abusive language."

Mr. Morrison appealed his second conviction through the university's administrative system. On August 21, 1995, Virginia Tech's senior vice president and provost set aside Mr. Morrison's punishment. She concluded that it was "excessive when compared with other cases where there has been a finding of violation of the Abusive Conduct Policy." Virginia Tech did not inform Ms. Brzonkala of this decision. After learning from a newspaper that Mr. Morrison would be returning to Virginia Tech for the fall 1995 semester, she dropped out of the university.

In December 1995, Ms. Brzonkala sued Mr. Morrison, Mr. Crawford, and Virginia Tech in Federal District Court. Her complaint alleged that Mr. Morrison's and Mr. Crawford's attack violated 42 U.S.C. § 13981, the Violence Against Women Act (VAWA). Mr. Morrison and Mr. Crawford moved to dismiss this complaint on the grounds that it failed to state a claim and that § 13981's civil remedy is unconstitutional.

The district court held that Congress lacked authority for the enactment of VAWA and dismissed the complaint against Mr. Morrison and Mr. Crawford. The court of appeals affirmed the finding that VAWA was unconstitutional, and Ms. Brzonkala appealed.

continued

JUDICIAL OPINION

REHNQUIST, Chief Justice

[We] consider the constitutionality of 42 U.S.C. § 13981, which provides a federal civil remedy for the victims of gender-motivated violence.

Section 13981 was part of the Violence Against Women Act of 1994. It states that "[a]ll persons within the United States shall have the right to be free from crimes of violence motivated by gender" 42 U.S.C. § 13981(b). To enforce that right, subsection (c) declares:

"A person (including a person who acts under color of any statute, ordinance, regulation, custom, or usage of any State) who commits a crime of violence motivated by gender and thus deprives another of the right declared in subsection (b) of this section shall be liable to the party injured, in an action for the recovery of compensatory and punitive damages, injunctive and declaratory relief, and such other relief as a court may deem appropriate."

Every law enacted by Congress must be based on one or more of its powers enumerated in the Constitution. Due respect for the decisions of a coordinate branch of Government demands that we invalidate a congressional enactment only upon a plain showing that Congress has exceeded its constitutional bounds. With this presumption of constitutionality in mind, we turn to the question whether § 13981 falls within Congress' power under Article I, § 8, of the Constitution. Brzonkala and the United States rely upon the third clause of the Article, which gives Congress power "[t]o regulate Commerce with foreign Nations, and among the several States, and with the Indian Tribes."

[M]odern Commerce Clause jurisprudence has "identified three broad categories of activity that Congress may regulate under its commerce power." "First, Congress may regulate the use of the channels of interstate commerce." "Second, Congress is empowered to regulate and protect the instrumentalities of interstate commerce, or persons or things in interstate commerce, even though the threat may come only from intrastate activities." "Finally, Congress' commerce authority includes the power to regulate those activities having a substantial relation to interstate commerce, . . . i.e., those activities that substantially affect interstate commerce."

Petitioners do not contend that these cases fall within either of the first two of these categories of Commerce Clause regulation. They seek to sustain § 13981 as a regulation of activity that substantially affects interstate commerce.

Since *U.S.* v. *Lopez,* 514 U.S. 564 (1995) most recently canvassed and clarified our case law governing this third category of Commerce Clause regulation, it provides the proper framework for conducting the required analysis of § 13981. In *Lopez,* we held that the Gun-Free School Zones Act of 1990, 18 U.S.C. § 922(q)(1)(A), which made it a federal crime to knowingly possess a firearm in a school zone, exceeded Congress' authority under the Commerce Clause.

First, we observed that § 922(q) was "a criminal statute that by its terms has nothing to do with 'commerce' or any sort of economic enterprise, however broadly one might define those terms." Reviewing our case law, we noted that "we have upheld a wide variety of congressional Acts regulating intrastate economic activity where we have concluded that the activity substantially affected interstate commerce." Although we cited only a few examples, including *Wickard* v. *Filburn,* 317 U.S. 111, 63 S.Ct. 82, 87 L.Ed. 122 (1942); *Katzenbach* v. *McClung,* 379 U.S. 294, 85 S.Ct. 377, 13 L.Ed.2d 290 (1964); and *Heart of Atlanta Motel,* we stated that the pattern of analysis is clear. "Where economic activity substantially affects interstate commerce, legislation regulating that activity will be sustained."

Both petitioners and Justice SOUTER's dissent downplay the role that the economic nature of the regulated activity plays in our Commerce Clause analysis. But a fair reading of *Lopez* shows that the noneconomic, criminal nature of the conduct at issue was central to our decision in that case. The possession of a gun in a local school zone is in no sense an economic activity that might, through repetition elsewhere, substantially affect any sort of interstate commerce. "[U]nlike the earlier cases to come before the Court here neither the actors nor their conduct has a commercial character, and neither the purposes nor the design of the statute has an evident commercial nexus. The statute makes the simple possession of a gun within 1,000 feet of the grounds of the school a criminal offense. In a sense any conduct in this interdependent world of ours has an ultimate commercial origin or consequence, but we have not yet said the commerce power may reach so far". *Lopez's* review of Commerce Clause case law demonstrates that in those cases where we have sustained federal regulation of intrastate activity based upon the activity's substantial effects on interstate commerce, the activity in question has been some sort of economic endeavor.

. . . [w]e noted that neither § 922(q) " 'nor its legislative history contain[s] express congressional findings regarding the effects upon interstate commerce of gun possession in a school zone.' " While Congress normally is not required to make formal findings as to the substantial burdens that an activity has on interstate commerce, the existence of such findings may "enable us to evaluate the legislative judgment that the activity in question substantially affect[s] interstate commerce, even though no such substantial effect [is] visible to the naked eye."

Finally, our decision in *Lopez* rested in part on the fact that the link between gun possession and a substantial effect on interstate commerce was attenuated. The United States argued that the possession of guns may lead to violent crime, and that violent crime "can be expected to affect the functioning of the national economy. . . ." The Government also argued that the presence of guns at schools poses a threat to the educational process, which in turn threatens to produce a less efficient and productive workforce, which will negatively affect national productivity and thus interstate commerce.

We rejected these "costs of crime" and "national productivity" arguments because they would permit Congress to "regulate not only all violent crime, but all activities that might lead to violent crime, regardless of how tenuously they relate to interstate commerce."

With these principles underlying our Commerce Clause jurisprudence as reference points, the proper resolution of the present cases is clear. Gender-motivated crimes of violence are not, in any sense of the phrase, economic activity. While we need not adopt a categorical rule against aggregating the effects of any noneconomic activity in order to decide these cases, thus far in our Nation's history our cases have upheld Commerce Clause regulation of intrastate activity only where that activity is economic in nature.

In contrast with the lack of congressional findings that we faced in *Lopez*, § 13981 is supported by numerous findings regarding the serious impact that gender-motivated violence has on victims and their families. " '[S]imply because Congress may conclude that a particular activity substantially affects interstate commerce does not necessarily make it so.' " Rather, " '[w]hether particular operations affect interstate commerce sufficiently to come under the constitutional power of Congress to regulate them is ultimately a judicial rather than a legislative question, and can be settled finally only by this Court.' "

Given these findings and petitioners' arguments, the concern that we expressed in *Lopez* that Congress might use the Commerce Clause to completely obliterate the Constitution's distinction between national and local authority seems well founded. The reasoning that petitioners advance seeks to follow the but-for causal chain from the initial occurrence of violent crime (the suppression of which has always been the prime object of the States' police power) to every attenuated effect upon interstate commerce. If accepted, petitioners' reasoning would allow Congress to regulate any crime as long as the nationwide, aggregated impact of that crime has substantial effects on employment, production, transit, or consumption. Indeed, if Congress may regulate gender-motivated violence, it would be able to regulate murder or any other type of violence since

gender-motivated violence, as a subset of all violent crime, is certain to have lesser economic impacts than the larger class of which it is a part.

Petitioners' reasoning, moreover, will not limit Congress to regulating violence but may, as we suggested in *Lopez*, be applied equally as well to family law and other areas of traditional state regulation since the aggregate effect of marriage, divorce, and childrearing on the national economy is undoubtedly significant. Congress may have recognized this specter when it expressly precluded § 13981 from being used in the family law context. Under our written Constitution, however, the limitation of congressional authority is not solely a matter of legislative grace.

We accordingly reject the argument that Congress may regulate noneconomic, violent criminal conduct based solely on that conduct's aggregate effect on interstate commerce. The Constitution requires a distinction between what is truly national and what is truly local. In recognizing this fact we preserve one of the few principles that has been consistent since the Clause was adopted. The regulation and punishment of intrastate violence that is not directed at the instrumentalities, channels, or goods involved in interstate commerce has always been the province of the States.

Affirmed.

DISSENTING OPINION

Justice SOUTER, with whom Justice STEVENS, Justice GINSBURG, and Justice BREYER join, dissenting

Our cases, which remain at least nominally undisturbed, stand for the following propositions. Congress has the power to legislate with regard to activity that, in the aggregate, has a substantial effect on interstate commerce. The fact of such a substantial effect is not an issue for the courts in the first instance, but for the Congress, whose institutional capacity for gathering evidence and taking testimony far exceeds ours. By passing legislation, Congress indicates its conclusion, whether explicitly or not, that facts support its exercise of the commerce power. The business of the courts is to review the congressional assessment, not for soundness but simply for the rationality of concluding that a jurisdictional basis exists in fact. Any explicit findings that Congress chooses to make, though not dispositive of the question of rationality, may advance judicial review by identifying factual authority on which Congress relied. Applying those propositions in these cases can lead to only one conclusion.

One obvious difference from *United States* v. *Lopez*, 514 U.S. 549, 115 S.Ct. 1624, 131 L.Ed.2d 626 (1995), is the mountain of data assembled by Congress, here

continued

showing the effects of violence against women on interstate commerce. Passage of the Act in 1994 was preceded by four years of hearings, which included testimony from physicians and law professors; from survivors of rape and domestic violence; and from representatives of state law enforcement and private business. The record includes reports on gender bias from task forces in 21 States, and we have the benefit of specific factual findings in the eight separate Reports issued by Congress and its committees over the long course leading to enactment.

Indeed, the legislative record here is far more voluminous than the record compiled by Congress and found sufficient in two prior cases upholding Title II of the Civil Rights Act of 1964 against Commerce Clause challenges. In *Heart of Atlanta Motel, Inc.* v. *United States,* 379 U.S. 241, 85 S.Ct. 348, 13 L.Ed.2d 258 (1964), and *Katzenbach* v. *McClung,* 379 U.S. 294, 85 S.Ct. 377, 13 L.Ed.2d 290 (1964), the Court referred to evidence showing the consequences of racial discrimination by motels and restaurants on interstate commerce. Congress had relied on compelling anecdotal reports that individual instances of segregation cost thousands to millions of dollars. Congress also had evidence that the average black family spent substantially less than the average white family in the same income range on public accommodations, and that discrimination accounted for much of the difference.

If the analogy to the Civil Rights Act of 1964 is not plain enough, one can always look back a bit further. In *Wickard,* we upheld the application of the Agricultural Adjustment Act to the planting and consumption of homegrown wheat. The effect on interstate commerce in that case followed from the possibility that wheat grown at home for personal consumption could either be drawn into the market by rising prices, or relieve its grower of any need to purchase wheat in the market. The Commerce Clause predicate was simply the effect of the production of wheat for home consumption on supply and demand in interstate commerce. Supply and demand for goods in interstate commerce will also be affected by the deaths of 2,000 to 4,000 women annually at the hands of domestic abusers. . . . Violence against women may be found to affect interstate commerce and affect it substantially.

All of this convinces me that today's ebb of the commerce power rests on error, and at the same time leads me to doubt that the majority's view will prove to be enduring law. There is yet one more reason for doubt. Although we sense the presence of *Carter Coal, Schechter,* and *Usery* once again, the majority embraces them only at arm's-length. Where such decisions once stood for rules, today's opinion points to considerations by which substantial effects are discounted. Cases standing for the sufficiency of substantial effects are not overruled; cases overruled since 1937 are not quite revived. As our predecessors learned then, the practice of such *ad hoc* review cannot preserve the distinction between the judicial and the legislative, and this Court, in any event, lacks the institutional capacity to maintain such a regime for very long. This one will end when the majority realizes that the conception of the commerce power for which it entertains hopes would inevitably fail the test expressed in Justice Holmes's statement that "[t]he first call of a theory of law is that it should fit the facts." The facts that cannot be ignored today are the facts of integrated national commerce and a political relationship between States and Nation much affected by their respective treasuries and constitutional modifications adopted by the people. The federalism of some earlier time is no more adequate to account for those facts today than the theory of laissez-faire was able to govern the national economy 70 years ago.

CASE QUESTIONS

1. What does VAWA do?
2. What did Congress do to establish the connection of VAWA to commerce?
3. What does the majority opinion say the test for the constitutionality of federal regulation under the Commerce Clause is?
4. What does the dissenting opinion say the test for the constitutionality of federal regulation under the Commerce Clause should be?
5. Is VAWA constitutional?
6. What rights does Ms. Brzonkala have other than those afforded by VAWA?

CONSIDER . . .   5 . 1

Ollie's Barbecue is a family-owned restaurant in Birmingham, Alabama, specializing in barbecued meats and homemade pies, with a seating capacity of 220 customers. It is located on a state highway eleven blocks from an interstate highway and a somewhat greater distance from railroad and bus stations. The restaurant caters to a family and white-collar trade, with a takeout service for "Negroes." (Note: The court uses this term in the opinion on the case.)

In the twelve months preceding the passage of the Civil Rights Act, the restaurant purchased locally approximately $150,000 worth of food, $69,683 or 46 percent of which was meat that it bought from a local supplier who had procured it from outside the state.

Ollie's has refused to serve Negroes in its dining accommodations since its original opening in 1927, and since July 2, 1964, it has been operating in violation of the Civil Rights Act. A lower court concluded that if it were required to serve Negroes, it would lose a substantial amount of business.

The lower court found that the Civil Rights Act did not apply because Ollie's was not involved in "interstate commerce." Will the Commerce Clause permit application of the Civil Rights Act to Ollie's? [*Katzenbach* v. *McClung,* 379 U.S. 294 (1964).]

THINK: What did the *Morrison* case require for the Commerce Clause to allow Congressional action on intrastate activities? If Congress was to have the authority to regulate seemingly intrastate activities, there had to be some underlying economic activity and whatever that economic activity was, it had to have some relation to or an impact on interstate activity.

APPLY: What is different about Ollie's Barbecue and the issue of violence against women?

Ollie's Barbecue is a commercial enterprise involved in producing and selling food. This is economic activity, and *Morrison* found that the underlying activity being regulated must be economic in nature before the findings of interstate economic activity can be made.

Ollie's has an impact on interstate commerce because it orders goods in interstate commerce, and it serves travelers who are moving from state to state. The impact may be smaller than that outlined in Congress for VAWA, but it is all pure economic activity.

ANSWER: Congress had the authority under the Commerce Clause to pass the Civil Rights Act and have it apply to intrastate businesses such as Ollie's Barbecue.

CONSIDER...   5 . 2

The Heart of Atlanta Motel, which has 216 rooms available to transient guests, is located on Courtland Street, two blocks from downtown Peachtree Street in Atlanta, Georgia. It is readily accessible to interstate highways 75 and 85 and state highways 23 and 41. The motel does advertise outside Georgia through various national advertising media, including magazines of national circulation; it maintains over fifty billboards and highway signs within the state, soliciting patronage for the motel; it accepts convention trade from outside Georgia; and approximately 75 percent of its registered guests are from out of state.

Prior to passage of Title II of the Civil Rights Act, the motel had followed a practice of refusing to rent rooms to Negroes, and it alleged that it intended to continue to do so. The motel filed suit, challenging Congress for passing this act in excess of its power to regulate commerce under Article I, Section 8, Part 3 of the Constitution of the United States.

Section 201 of Title II provides: "All persons shall be entitled to the full and equal enjoyment of the goods, services, facilities, privileges, advantages, and accommodations of any place of public accommodation, as defined in this section, without discrimination or segregation on the ground of race, color, religion, or national origin." There are listed in Section 201(b) four classes of business establishments, each of which "serves the public" and "is a place of public accommodation" within the meaning of Section 201(a) "if its operations affect commerce, or if discrimination or segregation by it is supported by State action." The covered establishments are:

> *(1) any inn, hotel, motel, or other establishment which provides lodging to transient guests, other than an establishment located within a building which contains not more than five rooms for rent or hire and which is actually occupied by the proprietor of such establishment as his residence;*
> *(2) any restaurant, cafeteria * * * (not here involved);*

continued

*(3) any motion picture house * * * (not here involved);*

*(4) any establishment * * * which is physically located within the premises of any establishment otherwise covered by this subsection, or * * * within the premises of which is physically located any such covered establishment * * * (not here involved).*

Section 201(c) defines the phrase "affect commerce" as applied to these establishments.

Is Title II of the Civil Rights Act constitutional? Is this case different from Ollie's Barbecue? from *Morrison*? [*Heart of Atlanta Motel, Inc.* v. *U. S.*, 379 U.S. 241 (1964).]

MAKING ETHICS PERSONAL

The More Subtle Forms of Discrimination: Make 'Em Wait

The days of discrimination are not yet over. Several large restaurant chains have entered into consent decrees and other settlements with federal agencies over charges that, for example, their employees did not wait on members of protected classes who entered their restaurants. The employees and management did not prohibit the potential customers from entering the restaurants but made them wait so long that they left.

Suppose that you work as a server at a restaurant where the manager has instructed you to wait before serving either Latino or African-American customers. His instructions are, "If you wait 20 minutes before going to their tables, I can almost guarantee they will leave. We don't have to do anything in violation of the law. We can just be slow."

Would you follow the manager's instructions? Why or why not? What are the consequences of following his instructions? What are the consequences of not following them? Is anyone really hurt if you refuse to follow his instructions?

Standards for State Regulation of Interstate Commerce

The Commerce Clause also deals with issues beyond those of federal power. The interpretation of the clause involves how much commerce the states can regulate without interfering in the congressional domain of interstate commerce. In answering this question, the courts are concerned with two factors: (1) whether federal regulation supersedes state involvement and (2) whether the benefits achieved by the regulation outweigh the burden on interstate commerce. These two factors are meant to prevent states from passing laws that would give local industries and businesses an unfair advantage over interstate businesses. There are, however, some circumstances in which the states can regulate interstate commerce. Those circumstances occur when the state is properly exercising its **police power**.

What Is the Police Power?   The police power is the states' power to pass laws that promote the public welfare and protect public health and safety. Regulation of these primary concerns is within each state's domain. It is, however, inevitable that some of the laws dealing with public welfare and health and safety will burden interstate commerce. Many of the statutes that have been challenged constitutionally have regulated highway use. For example, some cases have tested a state's power to regulate the length of trucks on state highways [*Raymond Motor Transportation* v. *Rice*, 434 U.S. 429 (1978)]. In *Bibb* v. *Navajo Freight Lines, Inc.*, 359 US. 520 (1959), the Supreme Court analyzed an Illinois statute requiring all trucks using Illinois roads to be equipped with contour mudguards. These mudguards were supposed to reduce the amount of mud splattering the windshields of other drivers and preventing them from seeing. Both cases revolved around the public safety purpose of the statutes.

The Balancing Test   A statute is not entitled to constitutional protection just because it deals with public health, safety, or welfare. Although the courts try to protect the police power, that protection is not automatic. The police power is upheld only so long as the benefit achieved by the statute does not outweigh the burden imposed on interstate commerce. Each case is decided on its own facts. States present evidence of the safety benefits involved, and the interstate commerce interests present evidence of the costs and effects for interstate commerce. The question courts must answer in these constitutional cases is whether the state interest in public health, welfare, or safety outweighs the federal interest in preventing interstate commerce from being unduly burdened. In performing this balancing test, the courts of course examine the safety, welfare, and health issues. However, the courts also examine other factors, such as whether the regulation or law provides an unfair advantage to intrastate or local businesses. For example, a prohibition on importing citrus fruits into Florida would give in-state growers an undue advantage.

Courts also examine the degree of the effect on interstate commerce. State statutes limiting the length of commercial vehicles would require commercial truck lines to buy different trucks for certain routes or in some cases to stop at a state's border to remove one of the double trailers being pulled. Such stops can have a substantial effect on interstate travel. On the other hand, a state law that requires travelers to stop at the border for a fruit and plant check is not as burdensome: Only a stop is required, and the traveler would not be required to make any further adjustments. Also, the state's health interest is great; most fruit and plant checks are done to keep harmful insects from entering the state and destroying its crops. In the *Bibb* case, the courts found that the evidence of increased safety was not persuasive enough to outweigh the burden on interstate commerce.

Another question courts answer in their analysis is whether there is any way the state could accomplish its health, welfare, or safety goal with less of a burden on interstate commerce. Suppose a state has a health concern about having milk properly processed. One way to cover the concern is to require all milk to be processed in-state. Such a regulation clearly favors that state's businesses and imposes a great burden on out-of-state milk producers. The same result, however, could be produced by requiring all milk sellers to be licensed. The licensing procedure would allow the state to check the milk-processing procedures of all firms and accomplish the goal without imposing such a burden on out-of-state firms.

In recent years, the most compelling police power issue has involved the states' authority to regulate hazardous waste disposal. *Fort Gratiot Sanitary Landfill, Inc. v. Michigan Dept. of Natural Resources* (Case 5.2) focuses on this issue and provides insights on evolving issues of waste disposal.

CASE 5.2

Fort Gratiot Sanitary Landfill, Inc. **v.** *Michigan Dept. of Natural Resources*
504 U.S. 353 (1992)

This Landfill Is Our Landfill

FACTS

In 1978, Michigan enacted its Solid Waste Management Act (SWMA), which required all Michigan counties to estimate the solid waste they would generate over the next 20 years and to develop plans for providing for its disposal.

St. Clair County adopted such a plan and required permits for the operation of solid waste landfills. Fort Gratiot Sanitary Landfill (petitioner) held such a permit for operation.

continued

On December 28, 1988, the Michigan legislature amended the SWMA by adopting two provisions concerning the "acceptance of waste or ash generated outside the county of disposal area." Those amendments (Waste Import Restrictions), which became effective immediately, provide:

A person shall not accept for disposal solid waste . . . that is not generated in the county in which the disposal area is located unless the acceptance of solid waste . . . that is not generated in the county is explicitly authorized in the approved county solid waste management plan. In order for a disposal area to serve the disposal needs of another county, state, or country, the service . . . must be explicitly authorized in the approved solid waste management plan of the receiving county.

On February 1, 1989, Fort Gratiot was denied a permit for operation because it accepted up to 1,750 tons per day of out-of-state waste. Fort Gratiot filed suit, seeking a declaration that the Waste Import Restrictions were unconstitutional. The district court dismissed the complaint and the court of appeals affirmed. Fort Gratiot appealed.

JUDICIAL OPINION

STEVENS, Justice

Before discussing the rather narrow issue that is contested, it is appropriate to identify certain matters that are not in dispute. Michigan's comprehensive program of regulating the collection, transportation, and disposal of solid waste, as it was enacted in 1978 and administered prior to the 1988 Waste Import Restrictions, is not challenged. No issue relating to hazardous waste is presented, and there is no claim that petitioner's operation violated any health, safety, or sanitation requirement. Nor does the case raise any question concerning policies that municipalities or other governmental agencies may pursue in the management of publicly owned facilities. The case involves only the validity of the Waste Import Restrictions as they apply to privately owned and operated landfills.

As we have long recognized, the "negative" or "dormant" aspect of the Commerce Clause prohibits States from "advanc[ing] their own commercial interests by curtailing the movement of articles of commerce, either into or out of the state." A state statute that clearly discriminates against interstate commerce is therefore unconstitutional "unless the discrimination is demonstrably justified by a valid factor unrelated to economic protectionism."

New Jersey's prohibition on the importation of solid waste failed this test. [T]he evil of protectionism can reside in legislative means as well as legislative ends. Thus, it does not matter whether that ultimate aim of [a law] is to reduce the waste disposal costs of New Jersey residents or to save remaining open lands from pollution, for we assume New Jersey has every right to protect its residents' pocketbooks as well as their environment. And it may be assumed as well that New Jersey may pursue those ends by slowing the flow of *all* waste into the State's remaining landfills, even though interstate commerce may incidentally be affected. But whatever New Jersey's ultimate purpose, it may not be accompanied by discriminating against articles of commerce coming from outside the State unless there is some reason, apart from their origin, to treat them differently. Both on its face and in its plain effect, [the law] violates this principle of nondiscrimination.

The Court has consistently found parochial legislation of this kind to be constitutionally invalid. . . .

The Waste Import Restrictions enacted by Michigan authorize each of its 83 counties to isolate itself from the national economy. Indeed, unless a county acts affirmatively to permit other waste to enter its jurisdiction, the statute affords local waste producers complete protection from competition from out-of-state waste producers who seek to use local waste disposal areas. In view of the fact that Michigan has not identified any reason, apart from its origin, why solid waste coming from outside the county should be treated differently from solid waste within the county, the foregoing reasoning would appear to control the disposition of this case.

Respondents Michigan and St. Clair County argue, however, that the Waste Import Restrictions—unlike the New Jersey prohibition on the importation of solid waste—do not discriminate against interstate commerce on their face or in effect because they treat waste from other Michigan counties no differently than waste from other States. Instead, respondents maintain, the statute regulates evenhandedly to effectuate local interests and should be upheld because the burden on interstate commerce is not clearly excessive in relation to the local benefits.

In *Dean Milk Co.* v. *Madison,* 340 U.S. 349, 71 S.Ct. 295, 95 L.Ed. 329 (1951), another Illinois litigant challenged a city ordinance that made it unlawful to sell any milk as pasteurized unless it had been processed at a plant "within a radius of five miles from the central square of Madison." We held the ordinance invalid, explaining:

[T]his regulation, like the provision invalidated in Baldwin *v.* Seelig, Inc., *[294 U.S. 511, 5 S.Ct. 497, 79 L.Ed. 1032 (1935)], in practical effect excludes from distribution in Madison wholesome milk produced and pasteurized in Illinois. "The importer . . . may keep his milk or drink it, but sell it he may not." In thus erecting an economic barrier protecting a major local industry against competition from without the State, Madison plainly discriminates against interstate commerce.*

The fact that the ordinance also discriminated against all Wisconsin producers whose facilities were more than five miles from the center of the city did not mitigate its burden on interstate commerce. As we noted, it was "immaterial that Wisconsin milk from outside the Madison area is subjected to the same proscription as that moving in interstate commerce."

In short, neither the fact that the Michigan statute purports to regulate intercounty commerce in waste nor the fact that some Michigan counties accept out-of-state waste provides an adequate basis for distinguishing this case. For the foregoing reasons, the Waste Import Restrictions unambiguously discriminate against interstate commerce and are appropriately characterized as protectionist measures that cannot withstand scrutiny under the Commerce Clause. The judgment of the Court of Appeals is therefore reversed.

DISSENTING OPINION

REHNQUIST, Chief Justice, and Blackmun, Justice
When confronted with a dormant Commerce Clause challenge "[t]he crucial inquiry . . . must be directed to determining whether [the challenged statute] is basically a protectionist measure, or whether it can fairly be viewed as a law directed to legitimate local concerns, with effects upon interstate commerce that are only incidental." Because I think the Michigan statute is at least arguably directed to legitimate local concerns, rather than improper economic protectionism, I would remand this case for further proceedings.

It is no secret why capacity is not expanding sufficiently to meet demand—the substantial risks attendant to waste sites make them extraordinarily unattractive neighbors. The result, of course, is that while many are willing to generate waste—indeed, it is

a practical impossibility to solve the waste problem by banning waste production—few are willing to help dispose of it. Those locales that do provide disposal capacity to serve foreign waste effectively are affording reduced environmental and safety risks to the States that will not take charge of their own waste.

In adopting this legislation, the Michigan Legislature also appears to have concluded that, like the State, counties should reap as they have sown—hardly a novel proposition. It has required counties within the State to be responsible for the waste created within the county. It has accomplished this by prohibiting waste facilities from accepting waste generated from outside the county, unless special permits are obtained. In the process, of course, this facially neutral restriction (i.e., it applies equally to both interstate and intrastate waste) also works to ban disposal from out-of-state sources unless appropriate permits are procured. But I cannot agree that such a requirement, when imposed as one part of a comprehensive approach to regulating in this difficult field, is the stuff of which economic protectionism is made.

CASE QUESTIONS

1. What type of restrictions has Michigan placed on solid waste disposal?

2. Of what significance is it that the restrictions apply both to outside counties and to other states?

3. Is economic protectionism involved?

4. Does this decision on the Michigan restrictions exacerbate the problem of waste and its disposal?

5. Does the dissenting opinion support the restrictions? Why, or why not?

ETHICAL ISSUES

Alabama is one of only sixteen states that have commercial hazardous waste landfills, and the Emelle, Alabama, facility is the largest of the twenty-one landfills of this kind located in these sixteen states.

The wastes and substances being disposed of at the Emelle facility "include substances that are inherently dangerous to human health and safety and to the environment. Such waste consists of ignitable, corrosive, toxic and reactive wastes which contain poisonous and cancer-causing chemicals and which can cause birth defects, genetic damage, blindness, crippling and death."

Increasing amounts of out-of-state hazardous wastes are shipped to the Emelle facility for permanent storage each year. From 1985 through 1989, the annual tonnage of hazardous waste received more than doubled, increasing from 341,000 tons in 1985 to 788,000 tons by 1989. Of this, up to 90 percent of the tonnage permanently buried each year is shipped in from other states.

Is it ethical for states to enjoy the economic benefits of production and then dispose of the resulting waste elsewhere? Are the extra fees charged unconscionable? Couldn't states monopolize the "dumping" market and enjoy a robust economy?

Congressional Regulation of Foreign Commerce

The Commerce Clause also grants Congress the power to regulate foreign commerce. The case of *Gibbons* v. *Ogden*, 9 Wheat. 1 (1824), defined foreign commerce as any "commercial intercourse between the United States and foreign nations." This power to regulate applies regardless of where the activity originates and where it ends. For example, many international trade transactions begin and end in the city of New York. Although the paperwork and delivery of the goods may be solely within one state (here within one city), the foreign commerce power is not restricted by intrastate standards. If there is foreign commerce, there can be congressional regulation regardless of the place of transaction.

Constitutional Standards for Taxation of Business

Article I, Section 8, Paragraph 1 of the Constitution gives Congress its powers of taxation: "The Congress shall have Power To lay and collect Taxes, Duties, Imposts and Excises. . . ." In addition, the Sixteenth Amendment to the Constitution gives this power: "The Congress shall have power to lay and collect taxes on incomes, from whatever source derived, without apportionment among the several States, and without regard to any census or enumeration."

It has been said that taxes are the price we pay for a civilized society. The U.S. Supreme Court has consistently upheld the ability of Congress, and local governments as well, to impose taxes. However, one area in taxation still results in considerable litigation. This area involves state and local taxation of interstate commerce. Interstate businesses are not generally exempt from state and local taxes just because they are interstate businesses. However, the taxes imposed on these businesses must meet certain standards.

First, the tax cannot discriminate against interstate commerce. A tax on milk could not be higher for milk that is shipped in from out of state than for milk produced within the state.

Second, the tax cannot unduly burden interstate commerce. For example, a tax on interstate transportation companies that is based on the weight of their trucks as measured upon entering and leaving the states would be a burdensome tax.

Third, there must be some connection—"a sufficient **nexus**"—between the state and the business being taxed. The business must have some activity in the state, such as offices, sales representatives, catalog purchasers, or distribution systems.

Finally, the tax must be apportioned fairly. This standard seeks to avoid having businesses taxed in all fifty states for their property. It also seeks to avoid having businesses pay state income tax on all their income in all fifty states. Their income and property taxes must be apportioned according to the amount of business revenues in each state and the amount of property located in that state. General Motors does not pay an inventory tax to all fifty states on all of its inventory, but it does pay an inventory tax on the inventory it holds in each state. Perhaps the most significant decision on state taxation in recent years is the U.S. Supreme Court case on catalog sales, *Quill Corporation v. North Dakota*, summarized in Case 5.3.

CASE 5.3

Quill Corporation v. North Dakota
504 U.S. 298 (1992)

Is North Dakota a Taxing State?

FACTS

Quill is a Delaware corporation with offices and warehouses in Illinois, California, and Georgia. None of its employees works or lives in North Dakota, and it owns no property in North Dakota.

Quill sells office equipment and supplies; it solicits business through catalogs and flyers, advertisements in national periodicals, and telephone calls. Its annual national sales exceed $200 million, of which almost $1 million are made to about three thousand customers in North Dakota. The sixth largest vendor of office supplies in the state, it delivers all of its merchandise to its North Dakota customers by mail or common carriers from out-of-state locations.

As a corollary to its sales tax, North Dakota imposes a use tax upon property purchased for storage, use, or consumption within the state. North Dakota requires every "retailer maintaining a place of business in" the state to collect the tax from the consumer and remit it to the state. In 1987, North Dakota amended its statutory definition of the term "retailer" to include "every person who engages in regular or systematic solicitation of a consumer market in th[e] state." State regulations in turn define "regular or systematic solicitation" to mean three or more advertisements within a 12-month period. Thus, since 1987 mail-order companies that engage in such solicitation have been subject to the tax even if they maintain no property or personnel in North Dakota.

Quill has taken the position that North Dakota does not have the power to compel it to collect a use tax from its North Dakota customers. Consequently, the state, through its tax commissioner, filed an action to require Quill to pay taxes (as well as interest and penalties) on all such sales made after July 1, 1987. The trial court ruled in Quill's favor.

The North Dakota Supreme Court reversed, and Quill appealed.

JUDICIAL OPINION

STEVENS, Justice
This case, like *National Bellas Hess, Inc. v. Department of Revenue of Ill.*, 386 U.S. 753, 87 S.Ct. 1389, 18 L.Ed.2d 505 (1967), involves a State's attempt to require an out-of-state mail-order house that has neither outlets nor sales representatives in the State to collect and pay a use tax on goods purchased for use within the State. In *Bellas Hess* we held that a similar Illinois statute violated the Due Process Clause of the Fourteenth Amendment and created an unconstitutional burden on interstate commerce. In particular, we ruled that a "seller whose only connection with customers in the State is by common carrier or the United States mail" lacked the requisite minimum contacts with the State.

In this case the Supreme Court of North Dakota declined to follow *Bellas Hess* because "the tremendous social, economic, commercial, and legal innovations" of the past quarter-century have rendered its holding "obsole[te]."

As in a number of other cases involving the application of state taxing statutes to out-of-state sellers, our holding in *Bellas Hess* relied on both the Due Process Clause and the Commerce Clause.

The Due Process Clause "requires some definite link, some minimum connection, between a state and the person, property or transaction it seeks to tax," and that the "income attributed to the State for tax purposes must be rationally related to 'values connected with the taxing State.'" Prior to *Bellas Hess*, we had held that that requirement was satisfied in a variety of circumstances involving use taxes. For example, the presence of sales personnel in the State, or the maintenance of local retail stores in the State, justified the exercise of that power because the seller's local activities were "plainly accorded the protection and services of the taxing State." We expressly declined to obliterate the "sharp distinction . . . between mail order sellers with retail outlets, solicitors, or property within a State, and those who do no more than communicate with customers in the State by mail or common carrier as a part of a general interstate business."

Our due process jurisprudence has evolved substantially in the 25 years since *Bellas Hess*, particularly in the area of judicial jurisdiction. Building on the seminal case of *International Shoe Co. v. Washington*, 326 U.S. 310, 66 S.Ct. 154, 90 L.Ed. 95 (1945), we have framed the relevant inquiry as whether a defendant had minimum contacts with the jurisdiction "such that the maintenance of the suit does not offend 'traditional notions of fair play and substantial justice.'"

Applying these principles, we have held that if a foreign corporation purposefully avails itself of the benefits of an economic market in the forum State, it may subject itself to the State's *in personam* jurisdiction even if it has no physical presence in the State.

continued

Comparable reasoning justifies the imposition of the collection duty on a mail-order house that is engaged in continuous and widespread solicitation of business within a State. In "modern commercial life" it matters little that such solicitation is accomplished by a deluge of catalogs rather than a phalanx of drummers: the requirements of due process are met irrespective of a corporation's lack of physical presence in the taxing State. Thus, to the extent that our decisions have indicated that the Due Process Clause requires physical presence in a State for the imposition of duty to collect a use tax, we overrule those holdings as superseded by developments in the law of due process.

In this case, there is no question that Quill has purposefully directed its activities at North Dakota residents, that the magnitude of those contacts are more than sufficient for due process purposes, and that the use tax is related to the benefits Quill receives from access to the State. We therefore agree with the North Dakota Supreme Court's conclusion that the Due Process Clause does not bar enforcement of that State's use tax against Quill.

Affirmed.

CASE QUESTIONS

1. Did Quill Corporation own any property in North Dakota?

2. Were any Quill offices or personnel located in North Dakota?

3. How did Quill come to have customers in North Dakota?

4. Will Quill be subject to North Dakota's use tax?

5. Is there a jurisdictional difference between pamphlets being present in a state and the presence of salespeople in that state?

CONSIDER...   5 · 3

J.C. Penney, a retail merchandiser, has its principal place of business in Plano, Texas. It operates retail stores in all fifty states, including ten stores in Massachusetts, and a direct-mail catalog business.

In connection with its catalog business, each year Penney issued three major seasonal catalogs, as well as various small sale or specialty catalogs, that described and illustrated merchandise available for purchase by mail order. The planning, artwork, design, and layout for these catalogs were completed and paid for outside of Massachusetts, primarily in Texas, and Penney contracted with independent printing companies located outside Massachusetts to produce the catalogs. The three major catalogs were generally printed in Indiana, while the specialty catalogs were printed in South Carolina and Wisconsin. Penney supplied the printers with paper, shipping wrappers, and address labels for the catalogs; the printers supplied the ink, binding materials, and labor. None of these materials was purchased in Massachusetts.

Printed catalogs, with address labels and postage affixed, were transported by a common carrier from the printer to a U.S. Postal Service office located outside Massachusetts, where they were sent to Massachusetts addressees via third- or fourth-class mail. Any undeliverable catalogs were returned to Penney's distribution center in Connecticut.

The catalogs advertised a broader range of merchandise than was available for purchase in Penney's retail stores. The purpose for mailing these catalogs, free of charge, to residents of, among other places, Massachusetts, was to solicit mail-order purchases from current and potential customers. Purchases of catalog merchandise were made by telephoning or returning an order form to Penney at a location outside Massachusetts, and the merchandise was shipped to customers from a Connecticut distribution center.

The Massachusetts Department of Revenue audited J.C. Penney in 1995 and assessed a use tax, penalty, and interest on the catalogs that had been shipped into Massachusetts. The use tax is imposed in those circumstances "in which tangible personal property is sold inside or outside the Commonwealth for storage, use, or other consumption within the Commonwealth." The position of the Department stated that there was a tax due of $314,674.62 on the catalogs used by Penney's Massachusetts customers. J.C. Penney said such a tax was unconstitutional in that it had no control or contact with the catalogs in the state. Can the state impose the tax? [*Commissioner of Revenue* v. *J.C. Penney Co., Inc.*, 730 N.E.2d 266 (Mass. 2001).]

BUSINESS STRATEGY

The Taxing Business of the Internet

The states continue their battle to collect sales taxes on all the commerce taking place over the Internet. When state budget deficits are expected all around the country, state treasurers see the collection of sales tax on purchases made over the Internet as a means of plugging the budget hole that most of them face.

Currently, the so-called bricks-and-mortar retailers such as Federated Department Stores and Macy's support state officials' drive to collect taxes because they already do so on their online sales and would like to level the playing field with their online competitors. Required to collect the taxes because their store facilities are in all states, chains such as J.C. Penney complain that the processes and formulas for collection are

© PHOTODISC/GETTY IMAGES

complex and increase their costs of doing business. Retailers such as Target, Wal-Mart, and Circuit City, part of the e-Fairness Coalition, argue that with their thin margins, giving e-retailers a pass on the 6–8 percent sales taxes is the difference between success and demise on the Internet.

The online retailers see such taxes as a cost increase. Congress has stayed out of the fray and, in fact, prohibited such taxation by states as unconstitutional because of an exercise of state authority over interstate commerce. The states plan to organize and ask Congress for the authority to tax.

Source: Norm Alster, "So Many Online Sales, So Little in Tax Revenue," *New York Times,* January 26, 2003, p. BU4.

STATE VERSUS FEDERAL REGULATION OF BUSINESS—CONSTITUTIONAL CONFLICTS: PREEMPTION AND THE SUPREMACY CLAUSE

Although the Constitution has sections that deal with the authority of the federal government and some that deal with state and local governments, some crossovers in the two sets of laws still occur. For example, both state and federal governments regulate the sale of securities and both have laws on the sale of real property. Such crossovers create conflicts and a constitutional issue of who has the power to regulate. These conflicts between state and federal laws are governed by Article VI of the Constitution, sometimes called the **Supremacy Clause**, which provides: "This Constitution, and the Laws of the United States which shall be made in Pursuance thereof; and all Treaties made, or which shall be made, under the Authority of the United States, shall be the supreme Law of the Land. . . ."

The Supremacy Clause provides that when state and local laws conflict with federal statutes, regulations, executive orders, or treaties, the federal statute, regulation, executive order, or treaty controls the state or local law. However, there are often cases in which a state law does not directly conflict with the federal law. Sometimes, the federal government just has extensive regulations in a particular area. In those areas of extensive federal regulation, the issue of which laws control can be resolved in Congress, which specifies its intent in an act. For example, Congress has provided that many federal credit laws can be circumvented by state law so long as the state law provides as much consumer protection as the federal law. In other words, Congress allows the states to regulate the field in some instances and sets the standards for doing so. Most statutes, however, do not include the congressional intent on **preemption**. Whether a field has been preempted is a question of fact, of interpretation, and of legislative history. The question of preemption is determined on a case-by-case basis using the following questions:

1. What does the legislative history indicate? Some hearings offer clear statements of the effect and scope of a federal law.

2. How detailed is the federal regulation of the area? The more regulation there is, the more likely a court is to find preemption. Volume itself indicates congressional intent.

3. What benefits exist from having federal regulation of the area? Some matters are more easily regulated by one central government. Airlines fly across state lines, and if each state had different standards there would be no guarantee of uniform standards. The regulation of aircraft and their routes is clearly better handled by the federal government.

4. How much does a state law conflict with federal law? Is there any way that the two laws can coexist?

Geier v. *American Honda Motor Co., Inc.* (Case 5.4) deals with a preemption issue.

CASE 5.4

Geier v. *American Honda Motor Co., Inc.*
529 U.S. 861 (2000)

Explosive Preemption Issues: Honda and Airbag Liability

FACTS

In 1992, Alexis Geier (petitioner) collided with a tree while driving a 1987 Honda Accord and was seriously injured. The car was equipped with manual shoulder and lap belts, which Geier had buckled up at the time. The car was not equipped with airbags or other passive restraint devices.

Geier and her parents (also petitioners), sued the car's manufacturer, American Honda Motor Company, Inc., and its affiliates (hereinafter American Honda), under District of Columbia tort law. They claimed, among other things, that American Honda had designed its car negligently and defectively because it lacked a driver's-side airbag. The District Court dismissed the lawsuit. The court noted that Federal Motor Vehicle Safety Standard (FMVSS) 208 gave car manufacturers a choice as to whether to install airbags. The court concluded that the petitioners' lawsuit, because it sought to establish a different safety standard—i.e., an airbag requirement—was expressly preempted by a provision of the act that preempts "any safety standard" that is not identical to a federal safety standard applicable to the same aspect of performance [15 U.S.C. § 1392(d) (1988 ed.)]. The Court of Appeals agreed with the District Court, and Geier appealed.

JUDICIAL OPINION

BREYER, Justice

This case focuses on the 1984 version of a Federal Motor Vehicle Safety Standard promulgated by the Department of Transportation under the authority of the National Traffic and Motor Vehicle Safety Act of 1966, 80 Stat. 718, 15 U.S.C. § 1381 et seq. (1988 ed.). The standard, FMVSS 208, required auto manufacturers to equip some but not all of their 1987 vehicles with passive restraints. We ask whether the Act pre-empts a state common-law tort action in which the plaintiff claims that the defendant auto manufacturer, who was in compliance with the standard, should nonetheless have equipped a 1987 automobile with airbags. We conclude that the Act, taken together with FMVSS 208, pre-empts the lawsuit.

Several state courts have held to the contrary, namely, that neither the Act's express pre-emption nor FMVSS 208 pre-empts a "no airbag" tort suit. All of the Federal Circuit Courts that have considered the question, however, have found pre-emption. We now hold that this kind of "no airbag" lawsuit conflicts with the objectives of FMVSS 208, a standard authorized by the Act, and is therefore pre-empted by the Act.

We first ask whether the Safety Act's express preemption provision pre-empts this tort action. The provision reads as follows:

> "*Whenever a Federal motor vehicle safety standard established under this subchapter is in effect, no State or political subdivision of a State shall have any authority either to establish, or to continue in effect, with respect to any motor vehicle or item of motor vehicle equipment[,] any safety standard applicable to the same aspect of performance of such vehicle or item of equipment which is not identical to the Federal standard.*" 15 U.S.C. § 1392(d) (1988 ed.).

We have found no convincing indication that Congress wanted to pre-empt, not only state statutes and regulations, but also common-law tort actions, in such circumstances. Hence the broad reading cannot be correct. The language of the pre-emption provision permits a narrow reading that excludes common-law actions. Given the presence of the saving clause, we conclude that the pre-emption clause must be so read.

Nothing in the language of the saving clause suggests an intent to save state-law tort actions that conflict with federal regulations. The words "[c]ompliance" and "does not exempt," 15 U.S.C. § 1397(k) (1988 ed.), sound as if they simply bar a special kind of defense, namely, a defense that compliance with a federal standard automatically exempts a defendant from state law, whether the Federal Government meant that standard to be an absolute requirement or only a minimum one. It is difficult to understand why Congress would have insisted on a compliance-with-federal-regulation precondition to the provision's applicability had it wished the Act to "save" all state-law tort actions, regardless of their potential threat to the objectives of federal safety standards promulgated under that Act. Nor does our interpretation conflict with the purpose of the saving provision, say by rendering it ineffectual. As we have previously explained, the saving provision still makes clear that the express pre-emption provision does not of its own force pre-empt common-law tort actions. And it thereby preserves those actions that seek to establish greater safety than the minimum safety achieved by a federal regulation intended to provide a floor.

On the one hand, the pre-emption provision itself reflects a desire to subject the industry to a single, uniform set of federal safety standards. Its pre-emption of all state standards, even those that might stand in harmony with federal law, suggests an intent to avoid the conflict, uncertainty, cost, and occasional risk to safety itself that too many different safety-standard cooks might otherwise create. This policy by itself favors pre-emption of state tort suits, for the rules of law that judges and juries create or apply in such suits may themselves similarly create uncertainty and even conflict, say, when different juries in different States reach different decisions on similar facts.

The basic question, then, is whether a common-law "no airbag" action like the one before us actually conflicts with FMVSS 208. We hold that it does. In petitioners' and the dissent's view, FMVSS 208 sets a minimum airbag standard. As far as FMVSS 208 is concerned, the more airbags, and the sooner, the better. But that was not the Secretary's view. DOT's comments, which accompanied the promulgation of FMVSS 208, make clear that the standard deliberately provided the manufacturer with a range of choices among different passive restraint devices. Those choices would bring about a mix of different devices introduced gradually over time; and FMVSS 208 would thereby lower costs, overcome technical safety problems, encourage technological development, and win widespread consumer acceptance—all of which would promote FMVSS 208's safety objectives.

The history of FMVSS 208 helps explain why and how DOT sought these objectives. See generally *Motor Vehicle Mfrs. Assn. of United States, Inc. v. State Farm Mut. Automobile Ins. Co.*, 463 U.S. 29, 34–38, 103 S.Ct. 2856, 77 L.Ed.2d 443 (1983). [See Chapter 6 for this case.] In 1967, DOT, understanding that seat belts would save many lives, required manufacturers to install manual seat belts in all automobiles. It became apparent, however, that most occupants simply would not buckle up their belts. DOT then began to investigate the feasibility of requiring "passive restraints," such as airbags and automatic seat belts. In 1970, it amended FMVSS 208 to include some passive protection requirements, while making clear that airbags were one of several "equally acceptable" devices and that it neither "'favored' [n]or expected the introduction of airbag systems." In 1971, it added an express provision permitting compliance through the use of nondetachable passive belts, and in 1972, it mandated full passive protection for all front seat occupants for vehicles manufactured after August 15, 1975, 37 Fed.Reg. 3911. Although the agency's focus was originally on airbags, FMVSS 208 was "'a de facto airbag mandate'" because of the state of passive restraint technology, [and] at no point did FMVSS 208 formally require the use of airbags. From the start, as in 1984, it permitted passive restraint options.

Read in light of this history, DOT's own contemporaneous explanation of FMVSS 208 makes clear that the 1984 version of FMVSS 208 reflected the following significant considerations. First, buckled up seat belts are a vital ingredient of automobile safety. Second, despite the enormous and unnecessary risks that a passenger runs by not buckling up manual lap and shoulder

continued

belts, more than 80% of front seat passengers would leave their manual seat belts unbuckled. Third, airbags could make up for the dangers caused by unbuckled manual belts, but they could not make up for them entirely. Fourth, passive restraint systems had their own disadvantages, for example, the dangers associated with, intrusiveness of, and corresponding public dislike for, nondetachable automatic belts. Fifth, airbags brought with them their own special risks to safety, such as the risk of danger to out-of-position occupants (usually children) in small cars. Sixth, airbags were expected to be significantly more expensive than other passive restraint devices, raising the average cost of a vehicle price $320 for full frontal airbags over the cost of a car with manual lap and shoulder seat belts (and potentially much more if production volumes were low). And the agency worried that the high replacement cost—estimated to be $800—could lead car owners to refuse to replace them after deployment. Seventh, the public, for reasons of cost, fear, or physical intrusiveness, might resist installation or use of any of the then available passive restraint devices. . . .

DOT explained why FMVSS 208 sought the mix of devices that it expected its performance standard to produce. DOT wrote that it had rejected a proposed FMVSS 208 "all airbag" standard because of safety concerns (perceived or real) associated with airbags, which concerns threatened a "backlash" more easily overcome "if airbags" were "not the only way of complying." It added that a mix of devices would help develop data on comparative effectiveness, would allow the industry time to overcome the safety problems and the high production costs associated with airbags, and would facilitate the development of alternative, cheaper, and safer passive restraint systems. And it would thereby build public confidence necessary to avoid another interlock-type fiasco.

The 1984 FMVSS 208 standard also deliberately sought a gradual phase-in of passive restraints. And it explained that the phased-in requirement would allow more time for manufacturers to develop airbags or other, better, safer passive restraint systems. It would help develop information about the comparative effectiveness of different systems, would lead to a mix in which airbags and other nonseatbelt passive restraint systems played a more prominent role than would otherwise result, and would promote public acceptance.

Finally FMVSS 208's passive restraint requirement was conditional. DOT believed that ordinary manual lap and shoulder belts would produce about the same amount of safety as passive restraints, and at significantly lower costs—if only auto occupants would buckle up. Thus, FMVSS 208 provided for rescission of its passive restraint requirement if, by September 1, 1989, two-thirds of the States had laws in place that, like those of many other nations, required auto occupants to buckle up. The Secretary wrote that "coverage of a large percentage of the American people by seat belt laws that are enforced would largely negate the incremental increase in safety to be expected from an automatic protection requirement." In the event, two-thirds of the States did not enact mandatory buckle-up laws, and the passive restraint requirement remained in effect.

In effect, petitioners' tort action depends upon its claim that manufacturers had a duty to install an airbag when they manufactured the 1987 Honda Accord. Such a state law—i.e., a rule of state tort law imposing such a duty—by its terms would have required manufacturers of all similar cars to install airbags rather than other passive restraint systems, such as automatic belts or passive interiors. It thereby would have presented an obstacle to the variety and mix of devices that the federal regulation sought. It would have required all manufacturers to have installed airbags in respect to the entire District-of-Columbia-related portion of their 1987 new car fleet, even though FMVSS 208 at that time required only that 10% of a manufacturer's nationwide fleet be equipped with any passive restraint device at all. It thereby also would have stood as an obstacle to the gradual passive restraint phase-in that the federal regulation deliberately imposed. In addition, it could have made less likely the adoption of a state mandatory buckle-up law. Because the rule of law for which petitioners contend would have stood "as an obstacle to the accomplishment and execution of" the important means-related federal objectives that we have just discussed, it is pre-empted.

The judgment of the Court of Appeals is affirmed.

CASE QUESTIONS

1. Why do you think the Supreme Court decided to grant *certiorari* and hear this case?

2. What in the history of the passive restraint system regulation supports a preemption finding?

3. What would happen if the states were permitted to set their own standards, via tort litigation, for auto safety devices?

4. Was there a duty to install an airbag at the time Geier purchased her Honda?

5. What standard did Honda meet in the design and safety devices of its car?

ETHICAL ISSUES

If you were an automobile manufacturer, would you install airbags in the cars you produce even though they are not required? Is it ethical not to do so? Volvo, Inc., installed airbags in its cars years ahead of the federal requirements. Why?

CONSIDER . . .   5 · 4

Myron Wolens and others (plaintiffs) are participants in American Airlines's frequent flyer program, AAdvantage. AAdvantage members earn mileage credits when they fly on American. The members can exchange those credits for flight tickets or class-of-service upgrades. Mr. Wolens complained that AAdvantage program modifications, instituted by American in 1988, devalued credits that AAdvantage members had already earned. The examples Mr. Wolens gave were American's imposition of capacity controls (limiting the number of seats per flight available to AAdvantage members) and blackout dates (restrictions on dates AAdvantage members could use their credits). Mr. Wolens brought suit alleging that these changes and cutbacks violated the Illinois Consumer Fraud and Deceptive Business Practices Act.

American Airlines challenged the suit on the grounds that the regulation of airlines was preempted by the Airline Deregulation Act (ADA) of 1978, which deregulated domestic air transportation but also included the following clause on preemption: "[N]o State . . . shall enact or enforce any law, rule, regulation, standard, or other provision having the force and effect of law relating to rates, routes, or services of any air carrier. . . ." [49 U.S.C. App. § 1305(a).] The Illinois Supreme Court found that the rules on the frequent flyer program were only tangentially related to rates, routes, and services and required American Airlines to defend the suit. American Airlines appealed. Who is correct? Is the litigation preempted? [*American Airlines, Inc.* v. *Wolens*, 513 U.S. 219 (1995).]

FOR THE MANAGER'S DESK

RE: A LOOK AT THE SUPREME COURT

The court does not operate in a vacuum, nor is it composed of Olympians. It functions as a legal, governmental, and political institution under a basic document that stands in constant need of interpretation against the backdrop of what Justice Oliver Wendell Holmes referred to as the "felt necessities of the times"—always provided the presence of explicit or implicit constitutional authority.

Our Founding Fathers created a magnificent Constitution. But they could hardly foresee some of the contemporary problems that have found their way to the Court for resolution. Indeed, whereas for most of our history we have made laws to help solve public issues, in recent years the byword has been "let's go to court." It is a regrettable development but one that is here to stay.

The nine Supreme Court justices who interpret the Constitution are steeped and trained in the law. But they respond to human situations: In Justice Cardozo's beautiful and telling words, "The great tides and currents which engulf the rest of mankind do not turn aside in their course and pass the judges idly by"; and in Justice

Frankfurter's parlance, the judges are "[m]en . . . not disembodied spirits, they respond to human emotions."

Moreover, the justices are well aware of two important facts of life: ultimately they do not have the power to enforce their decisions, for the purse is in the hands of the legislature and the sword in those of the executive; and the Court may be reversed by legislative action or by constitutional amendment. We should recognize that much of our reaction to the Court's ruling is highly subjective. A "good" decision is one that pleases us; a "poor" one is one that does not. All too often our response depends on "whose ox is gored." Nor is that bit of wisdom confined to laypersons. It includes political leaders, such as presidents whose calls for strict constructionists on the bench may be but a thinly disguised synonym for justices who agree with their philosophy of government and politics.

There is, of course, nothing wrong in a president's attempt to staff the Court with jurists who read the Constitution his way. All presidents have tried to pack the

continued

Court, to mold it in their images. Nothing is wrong with this, provided, however, that the nominees are professionally, intellectually, and morally qualified to serve.

The Supreme Court of the United States is, indeed, engaged in the political process; but, in Justice Frankfurter's admonition, it is "the Nation's ultimate judicial tribunal, not a super-legal aid bureau." Neither is the Court, in the second Justice Harlan's admonition, "a panacea for every blot upon the public welfare, nor should this Court ordained as a judicial body, be thought of as a general haven for reform movements." In other words, the Constitution of the United States was simply not designed to provide judicial remedies for every social or political ill.

The Supreme Court is much better at saying yes or no to the government than in prescribing policy; indeed, it should resolutely shun *prescriptive* policymaking. It has quite enough to do in constitutional and statutory interpretation and application. The Court is much better at saying what the government may *not* do or what it *may* do than in prescribing what public policy the government ought to chart and how to go about doing it. Paraphrasing Professor Paul A. Freund, the question is not whether the Court can do everything, but whether it can do something in its proper sphere.

Of course, all judging involves decision making, and the Court can escape neither controversy nor criticism, nor should it. In Justice Holmes's oft-quoted words: "We are very quiet up there, but it is the quiet of a storm center, as we all know." As an institution at once legal, politi-

cal, and human, it possesses both the assets and liabilities that attend these descriptive characteristics.

Yet, when all is said and done, the Court is the "living voice of the Constitution," as Lord Bryce once phrased it. As such it is both arbiter and educator and, in essence, represents the sole solution short of anarchy under the American system of government as we know it. Within the limits of procedure and deference to the presumption of the constitutionality of legislation, the Court—our sober second thought—is the natural forum in American society for the individual and small groups, what Madison, the father of the Bill of Rights, fervently hoped it would always be. The Court is infinitely more qualified to protect minority rights than the far more easily pressured, more impulsive, and more emotionally charged legislative and executive branches. All too readily do these two yield to the politically expedient and the popular, for they are close indeed to what Judge Learned Hand once called "the pressure of public panic, and public greed."

In general, if not unfailingly, the Supreme Court of the United States has evinced a remarkable degree of common constitutional sense in its striving, as a voice of reason, to maintain the blend of continuity and change that constitute the *sine qua non* for desirable stability in the basic governmental processes of a democracy. In that role it will—because it must—live in history.

Source: Henry J. Abraham, *Justices and Presidents: A Political History of Appointments to the Supreme Court*, 3rd ed. (New York: Oxford University Press), 1992, pp. 370–373. Copyright © 1974, 1985, 1992 by Henry J. Abraham. Used by permission of Oxford University Press, Inc.

APPLICATION OF THE BILL OF RIGHTS TO BUSINESS

Certain of the amendments to the U.S. Constitution have particular significance for business. This is especially true for the First Amendment on freedom of speech and the Fourteenth Amendment for its issues of substantive and procedural due process and equal protection. The Fourth, Fifth, and Sixth Amendments on criminal procedures also have significance for business; those issues are covered in Chapter 9.

Commercial Speech and the First Amendment

Review recent legal actions taken by the Media Institute, a nonprofit research foundation for the media's right to free speech:

http://www.mediainstitute.org

The area of First Amendment rights and freedom of speech is complicated and full of significant cases. The discussion here is limited to First Amendment rights as they apply to businesses. The speech of business is referred to as **commercial speech**, which is communication used to further the economic interests of the speaker. Advertising is clearly a form of commercial speech.

First Amendment Protection for Advertising

Until the early 1970s, the U.S. Supreme Court held that commercial speech was different from the traditional speech afforded protection under the First Amendment. The result was that government regulation of commercial speech was virtually unlimited. The Court's position was refined in the 1970s, however, to a view that commercial speech was entitled to First Amendment protection but not on the same level as noncommercial speech. Commercial speech was not an absolute freedom; rather, the benefits of commercial speech were to be weighed against the benefits achieved by government regulation of that speech. Several factors are examined in performing this balancing test.

1. Is a substantial government interest furthered by restricting the commercial speech?

2. Does the restriction directly accomplish the government interest?

3. Is there any other way to accomplish the government interest? Can it be accomplished without regulating commercial speech? Are the restrictions no more extensive than necessary to serve that interest?

Browse essays discussing the impact of the Internet on free speech:
http://www.scripting.com/ twentyFour

Under these standards, there is clearly authority for regulation of fraudulent advertising and advertising that violates the law. For example, if credit terms are advertised, Regulation Z requires full disclosure of all terms (see Chapter 15 for more details). This regulation is acceptable under the standards just listed. Further, restrictions on where and when advertisements are made are permissible. For example, cigarette ads are not permitted on television, and such a restriction is valid.

CONSIDER... 5·5

Mrs. Margaret Gilleo owns a single-family home in the area of Willow Hill in Ladue, Missouri. Mrs. Gilleo placed a 24-inch by 36-inch sign on her lawn that read, "SAY NO TO WAR IN THE PERSIAN GULF. CALL CONGRESS NOW." A Ladue ordinance prohibited such signs in residential areas, and Mrs. Gilleo was asked to remove it. She filed suit, claiming the ordinance violated her free speech rights. She said that other residents were permitted to put signs up advertising their homes for sale. Should Mrs. Gilleo's rights be protected? Does it make a difference that her speech was political and not commercial speech? [*City of Ladue* v. *Gilleo*, 512 U.S. 43 (1994).]

Exhibit 5.1 illustrates the degrees of protection afforded business speech. The overlapping area represents those cases in which the need to disseminate information conflicts with regulations on ad content or form.

EXHIBIT 5.1 Commercial Speech: First Amendment Protections and Restrictions

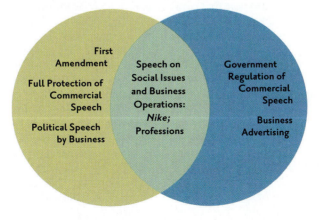

The 1970s brought in the overlapping area of the diagram with cases that re-formed the commercial speech doctrine by limiting restrictions on professional advertising. In *Virginia State Board of Pharmacy* v. *Virginia Citizens Consumer Council, Inc.*, 425 U.S. 748 (1976), the Supreme Court dealt with the issue of the validity of a Virginia statute that made it a matter of "unprofessional conduct" for a pharmacist to advertise the price or any discount of prescription drugs. In holding the statute unconstitutional, the Court emphasized the need for the dissemination of information to the public. In a subsequent case, the Court applied the same reasoning to advertising by lawyers [*Bates* v. *State Bar of Arizona*, 433 U.S. 350 (1977)].

An evolving area that is part of the overlapping portion of the two circles is that of corporate speech in defense of corporate decisions and policies—speech by corporations that is neither political speech nor advertising, but rather explains and defends corporate policies such as animal testing, outsourcing production to other countries, and environmental policies. The issues the companies are discussing have social and political implications, but they relate directly to the corporation's business and/or operations. Can the government regulate this form of speech? *Nike, Inc. v. Kasky* (Case 5.5) addresses such speech and provides the answers to the chapter's opening Consider.

CASE 5.5

Nike, Inc. v. *Kasky*
539 U.S. 654 (2003)

The Shoe and Mouth Writ of *Certiorari*

FACTS

Beginning in 1996, Nike was besieged with a series of allegations that it was mistreating and underpaying workers at foreign facilities. Nike responded to these charges in numerous ways, such as by sending out press releases, writing letters to the editors of various newspapers around the country, and mailing letters to university presidents and athletic directors. In addition, in 1997, Nike commissioned a report by former Ambassador to the United Nations Andrew Young on the labor conditions at Nike production facilities. After visiting 12 factories, "Young issued a report that commented favorably on working conditions in the factories and found no evidence of widespread abuse or mistreatment of workers."

In April 1998, Marc Kasky (respondent) a California resident, sued Nike for unfair and deceptive practices under California's Unfair Competition Law, Cal. Bus. & Prof.Code Ann. § 17200 et seq. (West 1997), and False Advertising Law, § 17500 *et seq*. Mr. Kasky asserted that "in order to maintain and/or increase its sales," Nike made a number of "false statements and/or material omissions of fact" concerning the working conditions under which Nike products are manufactured. Mr. Kasky alleged "no harm or damages whatsoever regarding himself individually," but rather

brought the suit "on behalf of the General Public of the State of California and on information and belief."

Nike filed a demurrer to the complaint, contending that Mr. Kasky's suit was absolutely barred by the First Amendment. The trial court sustained the demurrer and entered a judgment of dismissal. Mr. Kasky appealed, and the California Court of Appeal affirmed, holding that Nike's statements "form[ed] part of a public dialogue on a matter of public concern within the core area of expression protected by the First Amendment."

On appeal, the California Supreme Court reversed and remanded for further proceedings. The court held that "[b]ecause the messages in question were directed by a commercial speaker to a commercial audience, and because they made representations of fact about the speaker's own business operations for the purpose of promoting sales of its products, . . . [the] messages are commercial speech." However, the court emphasized that the suit "is still at a preliminary stage, and that whether any false representations were made is a disputed issue that has yet to be resolved."

The Supreme Court granted *certiorari* but later dismissed the case with a ***per curiam*** opinion (an unsigned opinion that comes from the majority of the court) that indicated only that *certiorari* was granted improvidently.

JUDICIAL OPINION

PER CURIAM

The writ of *certiorari* is dismissed as improperly granted.

Justice STEVENS, with whom Justice GINSBURG joins, and with whom Justice SOUTER joins

We granted *certiorari* to decide two questions: (1) whether a corporation participating in a public debate may "be subjected to liability for factual inaccuracies on the theory that its statements are 'commercial speech' because they might affect consumers' opinions about the business as a good corporate citizen and thereby affect their purchasing decisions"; and (2) even assuming the California Supreme Court properly characterized such statements as commercial speech, whether the "First Amendment, as applied to the states through the Fourteenth Amendment, permit[s] subjecting speakers to the legal regime approved by that court in the decision below." Today, however, the Court dismisses the writ of *certiorari* as improperly granted.

In my judgment, the Court's decision to dismiss the writ of *certiorari* is supported by three independently sufficient reasons: (1) the judgment entered by the California Supreme Court was not final within the meaning of 28 U.S.C. § 1257; (2) neither party has standing to invoke the jurisdiction of a federal court; and (3) the reasons for avoiding the premature adjudication of novel constitutional questions apply with special force to this case.

The first jurisdictional problem in this case revolves around the fact that the California Supreme Court never entered a final judgment. Congress has granted this Court appellate jurisdiction with respect to state litigation only after the highest state court in which judgment could be had has rendered a final judgment or decree.

Nike argues that this case fits within the . . . category of such cases . . . in which "the federal issue has been finally decided in the state courts with further proceedings pending in which the party seeking review" might prevail on nonfederal grounds, "reversal of the state court on the federal issue would be preclusive of any further litigation on the relevant cause of action," and "refusal immediately to review the state-court decision might seriously erode federal policy."

In Nike's view, this case fits within the category because if this Court holds that Nike's speech was noncommercial, then "reversal of the state court on the federal issue would be preclusive of any further litigation on the relevant cause of action." Notably, Nike's argument assumes that all of the speech at issue in this case is either commercial or noncommercial and that the speech therefore can be neatly classified as either absolutely privileged or not.

Theoretically, Nike is correct that we could hold that all of Nike's allegedly false statements are absolutely privileged even if made with the sort of "malice" defined in *New York Times Co. v. Sullivan*, 376 U.S. 254, 84 S.Ct. 710, 11 L.Ed.2d 686 (1964), thereby precluding any further proceedings or amendments that might overcome Nike's First Amendment defense. However, given the interlocutory posture of the case before us today, the Court could also take a number of other paths that would neither preclude further proceedings in the state courts, nor finally resolve the First Amendment questions in this case. For example, if we were to affirm, Nike would almost certainly continue to maintain that some, if not all, of its challenged statements were protected by the First Amendment and that the First Amendment constrains the remedy that may be imposed. Or, if we were to reverse, we might hold that the speech at issue in this case is subject to suit only if made with actual malice, thereby inviting respondent to amend his complaint to allege such malice. Or we might conclude that some of Nike's speech is commercial and some is noncommercial, thereby requiring further proceedings in the state courts over the legal standards that govern the commercial speech, including whether actual malice must be proved.

In short, because an opinion on the merits in this case could take any one of a number of different paths, it is not clear whether reversal of the California Supreme Court would "be preclusive of any further litigation on the relevant cause of action [in] the state proceedings still to come." Nor is it clear that reaching the merits of Nike's claims now would serve the goal of judicial efficiency. For, even if we were to decide the First Amendment issues presented to us today, more First Amendment issues might well remain in this case, making piecemeal review of the Federal First Amendment issues likely. Accordingly, in my view, the judgment of the California Supreme Court does not fall within the fourth Cox exception and cannot be regarded as final.

The second reason why, in my view, this Court lacks jurisdiction to hear Nike's claims is that neither party has standing to invoke the jurisdiction of the federal courts. Without alleging that he has any personal stake in the outcome of this case, respondent is proceeding as a private attorney general seeking to enforce two California statutes on behalf of the general public of the State of California. He has not asserted any federal claim; even if he had attempted to do so, he could not invoke the jurisdiction of a federal court because he failed to allege any injury to himself that is "distinct and palpable." . . . [r]espondent does not have

continued

Article III standing. For that reason, were the federal rules of justiciability to apply in state courts, this suit would have been "dismissed at the outset."

[T]he Court will not anticipate a question of constitutional law in advance of the necessity of deciding it. The novelty and importance of the constitutional questions presented in this case provide good reason for adhering to that rule.

This case presents novel First Amendment questions because the speech at issue represents a blending of commercial speech, noncommercial speech and debate on an issue of public importance. On the one hand, if the allegations of the complaint are true, direct communications with customers and potential customers that were intended to generate sales—and possibly to maintain or enhance the market value of Nike's stock—contained significant factual misstatements. The regulatory interest in protecting market participants from being misled by such misstatements is of the highest order. That is why we have broadly (perhaps overbroadly) stated that "there is no constitutional value in false statements of fact." On the other hand, the communications were part of an ongoing discussion and debate about important public issues that was concerned not only with Nike's labor practices, but with similar practices used by other multinational corporations. Knowledgeable persons should be free to participate in such debate without fear of unfair reprisal. The interest in protecting such participants from the chilling effect of the prospect of expensive litigation is therefore also a matter of great importance. That is why we have provided such broad protection for misstatements about public figures that are not animated by malice. See *New York Times Co. v. Sullivan*, 376 U.S. 254, 84 S.Ct. 710, 11 L.Ed.2d 686 (1964).

Whether similar protection should extend to cover corporate misstatements made about the corporation itself, or whether we should presume that such a corporate speaker knows where the truth lies, are questions that may have to be decided in this litigation. The correct answer to such questions, however, is more likely to result from the study of a full factual record than from a review of mere unproven allegations in a pleading. Indeed, the development of such a record may actually contribute in a positive way to the public debate. In all events, I am firmly convinced that the Court has wisely decided not to address the constitutional questions presented by the *certiorari* petition at this stage of the litigation.

Accordingly, I concur in the decision to dismiss the writ as improvidently granted.

DISSENTING OPINION

Justice BREYER, with whom Justice O'CONNOR joins, dissenting

During the 1990's, human rights and labor groups, newspaper editorial writers, and others severely criticized the Nike corporation for its alleged involvement in disreputable labor practices abroad. This case focuses upon whether, and to what extent, the First Amendment protects certain efforts by Nike to respond—efforts that took the form of written communications in which Nike explained or denied many of the charges made.

Does the First Amendment permit Kasky's false advertising "prosecution" to go forward? After receiving 34 briefs on the merits (including 31 amicus briefs) and hearing oral argument, the Court dismisses the writ of certiorari, thereby refusing to decide the questions presented, at least for now. In my view, however, the questions presented directly concern the freedom of Americans to speak about public matters in public debate, no jurisdictional rule prevents us from deciding those questions now, and delay itself may inhibit the exercise of constitutionally protected rights of free speech without making the issue significantly easier to decide later on.

Article III's "case or controversy" requirement does not bar us from hearing this case. Article III requires a litigant to have "standing"—i.e., to show that he has suffered "injury in fact," that the injury is "fairly traceable" to actions of the opposing party, and that a favorable decision will likely redress the harm. Kasky, the state-court plaintiff in this case, might indeed have had trouble meeting those requirements, for Kasky's complaint specifically states that Nike's statements did not harm Kasky personally. But Nike, the state-court defendant—not Kasky, the plaintiff—has brought the case to this Court. And Nike has standing to complain here of Kasky's actions.

These actions threaten Nike with "injury in fact." As a "private attorney general," Kasky is in effect enforcing a state law that threatens to discourage Nike's speech. This Court has often found that the enforcement of such a law works constitutional injury even if enforcement proceedings are not complete—indeed, even if enforcement is no more than a future threat.

Here, of course, an action to enforce California's laws—laws that discourage certain kinds of speech—amounts to more than just a genuine, future threat. It is a present reality—one that discourages Nike from engaging in speech. It thereby creates "injury in fact." Further, that injury is directly "traceable" to Kasky's pursuit of this lawsuit. And this Court's decision, if favorable to Nike, can "redress" that injury.

Since Nike, not Kasky, now seeks to bring this case to federal court, why should Kasky's standing problems make a critical difference[?]

No federal statute prevents us from hearing this case. The relevant statute limits our jurisdiction to "[f]inal judgments or decrees rendered by the highest court of a State in which a decision could be had." But the California Supreme Court determination before us, while technically an interim decision, is a "final judgment or decree" for purposes of this statute.

That is because this Court has interpreted the statute's phrase "final judgment" to refer, in certain circumstances, to a state court's final determination of a federal issue, even if the determination of that issue occurs in the midst of ongoing litigation.

The California Supreme Court thus "finally decided" the federal issue—whether the First Amendment protects the speech in question from legal attack on the ground that it is "false or misleading." According to the California Supreme Court, nothing at all remains to be decided with respect to that federal question. If we permit the California Supreme Court's decision to stand, in all likelihood this litigation will now simply seek to determine whether Nike's statements were false or misleading, and perhaps whether Nike was negligent in making those statements—matters involving questions of California law.

In my view, a proper resolution here favors application of the last mentioned public-speech principle, rather than the first mentioned commercial-speech principle. Consequently, I would apply a form of heightened scrutiny to the speech regulations in question, and I believe that those regulations cannot survive that scrutiny.

First, the communications at issue are not purely commercial in nature. They are better characterized as involving a mixture of commercial and noncommercial (public-issue-oriented) elements. The document least likely to warrant protection—a letter written by Nike to university presidents and athletic directors—has several commercial characteristics. As the California Supreme Court implicitly found, it was written by a "commercial speaker" (Nike), it is addressed to a "commercial audience" (potential institutional buyers or contractees), and it makes "representations of fact about the speaker's own business operations" (labor conditions).

But that letter also has other critically important and, I believe, predominant noncommercial characteristics with which the commercial characteristics are "inextricably intertwined." For one thing, the letter appears outside a traditional advertising format, such as a brief television or newspaper advertisement. It does not propose the presentation or sale of a product or any other commercial transaction. Rather, the letter suggests that its contents might provide "information useful in discussions" with concerned faculty and students. On its face, it seeks to convey information to "a diverse audience," including individuals who have "a general curiosity about, or genuine interest in," the public controversy surrounding Nike.

For another thing, the letter's content makes clear that, in context, it concerns a matter that is of significant public interest and active controversy, and it describes factual matters related to that subject in detail. In particular, the letter describes Nike's labor practices and responds to criticism of those practices, and it does so because those practices themselves play an important role in an existing public debate. This debate was one in which participants advocated, or opposed, public collective action. The First Amendment's protections of speech and press were "fashioned to assure unfettered interchange of ideas for the bringing about of political and social changes"). That the letter is factual in content does not argue against First Amendment protection, for facts, sometimes facts alone, will sway our views on issues of public policy.

These circumstances of form and content distinguish the speech at issue here from the more purely "commercial speech" described in prior cases. The speech here is unlike speech—say, the words "dolphin-safe tuna"—that commonly appears in more traditional advertising or labeling contexts. And it is unlike instances of speech where a communication's contribution to public debate is peripheral, not central. At the same time, the regulatory regime at issue here differs from traditional speech regulation in its use of private attorneys general authorized to impose "false advertising" liability even though they themselves have suffered no harm. In this respect, the regulatory context is unlike most traditional false advertising regulation. And the "false advertising" context differs from other regulatory contexts—say, securities regulation—where a different balance of concerns calls for different applications of First Amendment principles.

These three sets of circumstances taken together—circumstances of format, content, and regulatory context—warrant treating the regulations of speech at issue differently from regulations of purer forms of commercial speech, such as simple product advertisements, that we have reviewed in the past. And, where all three are present, I believe the First Amendment demands heightened scrutiny.

Second, I doubt that this particular instance of regulation (through use of private attorneys general) can survive heightened scrutiny, for there is no reasonable "fit" between the burden it imposes upon speech and the important governmental "interest served." Rather, the burden imposed is disproportionate.

I do not deny that California's system of false advertising regulation—including its provision for private causes of action—furthers legitimate, traditional, and important public objectives. It helps to maintain an honest commercial marketplace. It thereby helps that

continued

marketplace better allocate private goods and services. It also helps citizens form "intelligent opinions as to how [the marketplace] ought to be regulated or altered."

But a private "false advertising" action brought on behalf of the State, by one who has suffered no injury, threatens to impose a serious burden upon speech—at least if extended to encompass the type of speech at issue under the standards of liability that California law provides The delegation of state authority to private individuals authorizes a purely ideological plaintiff, convinced that his opponent is not telling the truth, to bring into the courtroom the kind of political battle better waged in other forums. Where that political battle is hard fought, such plaintiffs potentially constitute a large and hostile crowd freely able to bring prosecutions designed to vindicate their beliefs, and to do so unencumbered by the legal and practical checks that tend to keep the energies of public enforcement agencies focused upon more purely economic harm.

That threat means a commercial speaker must take particular care—considerably more care than the speaker's noncommercial opponents—when speaking on public matters. A large organization's unqualified claim about the adequacy of working conditions, for example, could lead to liability, should a court conclude after hearing the evidence that enough exceptions exist to warrant qualification—even if those exceptions were unknown (but perhaps should have been known) to the speaker. Uncertainty about how a court will view these, or other, statements, can easily chill a speaker's efforts to engage in public debate—particularly where a "false advertising" law, like California's law, imposes liability based upon negligence or without fault. At the least, they create concern that the commercial speaker engaging in public debate suffers a handicap that noncommercial opponents do not.

I do not see how "false advertising" regulation could suffer serious impediment if the Constitution limited the scope of private attorney general actions to circumstances where more purely commercial and less public-debate-oriented elements predominate. As the historical treatment of speech in the labor context shows, substantial government regulation can coexist with First Amendment protections designed to provide room for public debate.

These reasons convince me that it is likely, if not highly probable, that, if this Court were to reach the merits, it would hold that heightened scrutiny applies; that, under the circumstances here, California's delegation of enforcement authority to private attorneys general disproportionately burdens speech; and that the First Amendment consequently forbids it.

Returning to the procedural point at issue, I believe this discussion of the merits shows that not only will "reversal" of the California Supreme Court "on the federal issue" prove "preclusive of any further litigation on the relevant cause of action," but also such "reversal" is a serious possibility. Whether we take the words of the third condition literally or consider the circumstances pragmatically, that condition is satisfied.

If permitted to stand, the state court's decision may well "chill" the exercise of free speech rights. Continuation of this lawsuit itself means increased expense, and, if Nike loses, the results may include monetary liability (for "restitution") and injunctive relief (including possible corrective "counterspeech"). The range of communications subject to such liability is broad; in this case, it includes a letter to the editor of *The New York Times.* The upshot is that commercial speakers doing business in California may hesitate to issue significant communications relevant to public debate because they fear potential lawsuits and legal liability.

This concern is not purely theoretical. Nike says without contradiction that because of this lawsuit it has decided "to restrict severely all of its communications on social issues that could reach California consumers, including speech in national and international media." It adds that it has not released its annual Corporate Responsibility Report, has decided not to pursue a listing in the Dow Jones Sustainability Index, and has refused "dozens of invitations . . . to speak on corporate responsibility issues." Numerous amici—including some who do not believe that Nike has fully and accurately explained its labor practices—argue that California's decision will "chill" speech and thereby limit the supply of relevant information available to those, such as journalists, who seek to keep the public informed about important public issues.

At the same time waiting extracts a heavy First Amendment price. If this suit goes forward, both Nike and other potential speakers, out of reasonable caution or even an excess of caution, may censor their own expression well beyond what the law may constitutionally demand.

The position of at least one amicus—opposed to Nike on the merits of its labor practice claims but supporting Nike on its free speech claim—echoes a famous sentiment reflected in the writings of Voltaire: "I do not agree with what you say, but I will fight to the end so that you may say it."

I would not dismiss as improvidently granted the writ issued in this case. I respectfully dissent from the Court's contrary determination.

CASE QUESTIONS

1. What speech of Nike's is targeted?
2. Who is objecting to Nike's speech and how is the objection being voiced?
3. Why does the Supreme Court refuse to decide the case after taking *certiorari*?
4. Why does the dissenting justice believe the court should decide the case?

AFTERMATH: Nike settled the case with terms undisclosed by any of the parties. The case cannot now reach the point of justiciability in order for the Supreme Court to hear it and make a determination on this form of corporate speech. Another case will be required.

First Amendment Rights and Profits from Sensationalism

In the past few years, a number of book publishers and movie producers have pursued criminal figures for the rights to tell the stories of their crimes in books, television programs, and movies. Many of the victims of the crimes and their families have opposed such money-making ventures as benefits that encourage the commission of crimes. The state of New York, for example, passed a statute requiring that earnings from sales of such stories be used first to compensate victims of the crimes. Statutes such as the one in New York create dilemmas between First Amendment rights and public policy issues concerning criminal activities. In *Simon & Schuster, Inc.* v. *Members of the New York State Crime Victims Board*, 502 U.S. 105 (1991), the U.S. Supreme Court ruled that New York's statute on the profits from the books of criminal figures was overly broad and infringed on First Amendment rights. Called the "Son of Sam law," this statute was first proposed when a serial murderer, Sam Berkowitz, attempted to capitalize on his notoriety. Under the statute, the money earned on sales of books, move rights, and so on is deposited in an escrow account and payable to any victim of the crime who brings suit within five years from the establishment of the account.

Since its enactment in 1977, the Son of Sam law has been invoked only a handful of times. These include for Jean Harris, the convicted killer of "Scarsdale Diet" doctor Herman Tarnower; Mark David Chapman, the convicted assassin of John Lennon; and R. Foster Winans, the former *Wall Street Journal* columnist convicted of insider trading.

Simon & Schuster entered into a contract in 1981 with organized crime figure Henry Hill (who was arrested in 1980) and author Nicholas Pileggi for a book about Mr. Hill's life, *Wiseguy,* a book full of colorful details and the day-to-day workings of organized crime, primarily in Mr. Hill's first-person narrative. Throughout *Wiseguy,* Mr. Hill frankly admits to having participated in an astonishing variety of crimes.

The book was also a commercial success: Within nineteen months of its publication, more than a million copies were in print. A few years later, the book was converted into a film called *Goodfellas,* which won a host of awards as the best film of 1990.

When the Crime Victims Board requested that Simon & Schuster turn over all monies paid to Mr. Hill and that all future royalties be payable not to Mr. Hill but to the statutorily prescribed escrow account, Simon & Schuster brought suit maintaining that the Son of Sam law violated the First Amendment. The U.S. Supreme Court agreed and held that the statute was overly broad, would have a chilling effect on authors and publications, and required a redrafting of the statute to more narrowly tailor its scope so it could still accomplish the public purpose.

ETHICAL ISSUES

Orenthal James (O. J.) Simpson was charged with murder in June 1994 in the double homicide of his ex-wife, Nicole Brown Simpson, and her friend Ronald Goldman.

Because Mr. Simpson was charged with a capital crime, he was incarcerated upon being charged. California's version of the Son of Sam law prevents profits from crimes only after there has been a conviction. Mr. Simpson authored a book, *I Want to Tell You*, while he was incarcerated and his nine-month trial progressed. Mr. Simpson also signed autographs and sports memorabilia and sold them from the Los Angeles County jail. Mr. Simpson's cottage industry from jail netted him in excess of $3 million. Could a law that passes constitutional muster be implemented to prevent crime-related profits like those Mr. Simpson was able to obtain?

Mr. Simpson was acquitted of the murders. Following his acquittal, prosecutors in the case, Christopher Darden, Marcia Clark, and Hank Goldberg, signed multimillion-dollar book contracts to write about their experiences during the trial. Alan Dershowitz, Johnnie Cochran, and Robert Shapiro, members of the Simpson defense team, signed six-figure contracts to write books about the trial from the defense perspective. Daniel Petrocelli, the lawyer who represented the Goldmans in their civil suit against Mr. Simpson, also wrote a book, *Triumph of Justice: The Final Judgment on the Simpson Saga*. Mr. Simpson has not yet signed for a new book but did make a video detailing his side of the story.

Is it moral to profit from a crime and a trial? Are these contracts a form of making money from the deaths of two people? Many TV stations have refused to carry advertisements for Mr. Simpson's video. Would you have declined this advertising revenue?

First Amendment Rights and Corporate Political Speech

Not all commercial speech is advertising. Some businesses engage in **corporate political speech**. Corporate political speech takes form in three generalized ways:

1. Through financial support such as political candidate donations
2. Through financial support such as party donations
3. Through direct communications and ads about issues, ballot propositions, and funding proposals (such as bond elections)

For more than a century, both legislators and courts have grappled with the balancing of First Amendment rights and the influence of money in election campaigns. "More than a century ago the 'sober-minded Elihu Root' advocated legislation that would prohibit political contributions by corporations in order to prevent 'the great aggregations of wealth, from using their corporate funds, directly or indirectly,' to elect legislators who would 'vote for their protection and the advancement of their interests as against those of the public'" [*United States* v. *Automobile Workers*, 352 U.S. 567, 571, 77 S.Ct. 529, 1 L.Ed.2d 563 (1957)].

As a result, Congress, state legislatures, and the U.S. Supreme Court have all addressed corporate speech in all three of these categories. The first legislative prohibition came in 1907 when the Tillman Act completely banned corporate contributions of "money . . . in connection with" any federal election. Since that time corporations have been banned from making direct political donations to political candidates. In 1925 Congress extended the prohibition of contributions "to include 'anything of value,' and made acceptance of a corporate contribution as well as the giving of such a contribution a crime" (Federal Corrupt Practices Act, 1925, §§ 301, 313, 43 Stat. 1070, 1074). With corporate donations in tow, Congress realized through several election cycles that union contributions were equally as plentiful and powerful as corporate ones. Congress first restricted union contributions in 1940 with the passage of the Hatch Act. Congress later prohibited "union contributions in connection with federal elections . . . altogether" (18 U.S.C. § 610).

During the passage of these limitations, political action committees (PACs) began. PACs are independent of corporations and labor unions, although they may be formed by those affiliated with both. For example, Coors Brewing has its corporate PAC, known as the Six Pac. Employees of companies and members of labor unions make donations to their PACs. There are also trade association PACs (such as the American Medical Association and the American Association of Trial Lawyers), cooperative PACs, and PACs formed along ideological lines, such as the Right-to-Life PAC or Emily's List (Early Money Is Like Yeast, a PAC that supports prochoice candidates from the early primary stages of an election cycle).

As the Supreme Court has noted in its opinions on the topic of donations, "money is like water and it always finds an outlet," and the donations and PAC activity became a concern. As a result, in 1972 and 1974, Congress passed and amended the Federal Election Campaign Act (FECA), which limited individual donations to $1,000 per election cycle, with an overall annual limitation on donations of $25,000 by any contributor; imposed ceilings on spending by candidates and political parties for national conventions; required reporting and public disclosure of contributions and expenditures exceeding certain limits; and established the Federal Election Commission (FEC) to administer and enforce the legislation [2 U.S.C. § 431(8)(A)(i)].

The limitations in FECA were challenged and the U.S. Supreme Court ruled on their constitutionality in *Buckley* v. *Valeo*, 424 U.S. 1 (1976). The court struck down the expenditure limitations of the law but upheld the $1,000 donation limitation as being sufficiently narrowly tailored to address the corruption concerns without infringing on the speech elements of donation. Individuals remained free to spend as much as they wanted on their own campaigns, thus giving the court comfort on the availability of free speech during election campaigns. The court has described its decision in *Buckley* as follows.

> *Our opinion in Buckley addressed issues that primarily related to contributions and expenditures by individuals, since none of the parties challenged the prohibition on contributions by corporations and labor unions. We noted, however, that the statute authorized the use of corporate and union resources to form and administer segregated funds that could be used for political purposes.* [McConnell v. Federal Election Comm'n, 124 S.Ct. 619, at 648 (2003)].

The statute applied only to federal elections, and donations made solely for the purpose of influencing state or local elections are not subject to FECA's requirements and prohibitions. Under FECA, contributions made with funds that are subject to the act's disclosure requirements and source and amount limitations are thus known as "federal dollars" or "hard dollars." Corporations and unions, as well as individuals who had already made the maximum permissible contributions to federal candidates, could still contribute "nonfederal money"—also known as "soft money"—to political parties for activities intended to influence state or local elections. The FEC ruled that political parties could fund mixed-purpose activities—including get-out-the-vote drives and generic party advertising—in part with soft money. In 1995, the FEC concluded that the parties could also use soft money to defray the costs of "legislative advocacy media advertisements," even if the ads mentioned the name of a federal candidate, so long as they did not expressly advocate the candidate's election or defeat.

The so-called soft money donations became extensive. Of the two major parties' total spending, soft money accounted for 5 percent ($21.6 million) in 1984, 11 percent ($45 million) in 1988, 16 percent ($80 million) in 1992, 30 percent ($272 million) in 1996, and 42 percent ($498 million) in 2000. Many contributions of soft money were dramatically larger than the contributions of hard money permitted by FECA.

For example, in 1996, the top five corporate soft-money donors gave, in total, more than $9 million in nonfederal funds to the two national party committees. In 2002, the political parties raised almost $300 million—60 percent of their total soft-money fundraising—from just 800 donors, each of which contributed a minimum of $120,000. The largest corporate donors often made substantial contributions to both parties.

As a result, Congress passed the Bipartisan Campaign Reform Act of 2002 (BCRA, 2 U.S.C.A. § 431 et seq.). Often referred to as the McCain-Feingold law, Title I of the BCRA regulates the use of soft money by political parties, officeholders, and candidates. Title II primarily prohibits corporations and labor unions from using general treasury funds for communications that are intended to influence or have the effect of influencing the outcome of federal elections. The BCRA was immediately challenged by eleven different parties in different federal courts, and the cases were consolidated and eventually heard by the U.S. Supreme Court in *McConnell* v. *Federal Election Comm'n*, 124 S.Ct. 619 (2003). The Supreme Court concluded the following, in a 500-page opinion (including the dissents): (1) political parties and candidates could be banned from using soft money for federal election activities; (2) the ban on party donations to tax-exempt entities was generally valid; (3) soft money could not be used for issue ads that clearly identified candidate; (4) the statutory definition of "electioneering communications" was valid; (5) the cost of third-party issue ads coordinated with federal candidates' campaigns could validly be considered as contributions to those campaigns; (6) labor unions and corporations were generally required to pay for issue ads from separately segregated funds; (7) the prohibition on political donations by minors was invalid; and (8) the requirement that broadcasters disclose records of requests for air time for political ads was valid.

At present, corporate PACs and their donations and activities are substantially curtailed. However, new outlets for political activity, such as the so-called 527 groups, are emerging as parties form think tanks that issue substantive studies and reports on issues with the idea of those studies and reports being used by particular candidates. As the Supreme Court noted in *McConnell*, "We are under no illusion that BCRA will be the last congressional statement on the matter. Money, like water, will always find an outlet. What problems will arise, and how Congress will respond, are concerns for another day" (124 S.Ct. 619 at 707).

However, these Supreme Court decisions and federal legislation do not control activities at the state level and do not infringe on corporations' right to participate in the "public square" debates on issues. For example, many businesses participate in advertising campaigns against certain propositions or resolutions—for example, tax resolutions going before the voters. However, many states once restricted the political advertising allowed corporations and other businesses. The rationale for such a restriction was that corporate assets and funds were great and that corporations might be able to exercise too much power in influencing voters.

In *First National Bank of Boston* v. *Bellotti* (Case 5.6), the U.S. Supreme Court developed what has become known as the *Bellotti* doctrine, which gives corporations the same degree of First Amendment protection for their political speech that individuals enjoy in their political speech. Although commercial speech can be regulated, political speech enjoys full First Amendment rights. As you read this case, remember that it involves a state election and that it is an issue campaign, not an election of or support for a candidate for public office where the spending limitations and corruption issues arise.

CASE 5.6

First National Bank of Boston v. *Bellotti*
435 U.S. 765 (1978)

Banks Are People, Too: First Amendment Political Speech

FACTS

Massachusetts had passed a statute that prohibited businesses and banks from making contributions or expenditures "for the purpose of . . . influencing or affecting the vote on any question submitted to the voters, other than one materially affecting any of the property, business or assets of the corporation." The statute also provided that "no question submitted to the voters solely concerning the taxation of the income, property or transactions of individuals shall be deemed materially to affect the property, business or assets of the corporation." The statute carried a fine of up to $50,000 for the corporation and $10,000 and/or one year of imprisonment for corporate officers.

First National Bank and other banks and corporations (appellants) wanted to spend money to publicize their views on an upcoming ballot proposition that would permit the legislature the right to impose a graduated tax on individual income. Frances X. Bellotti, the attorney general for Massachusetts (appellee), told First National and the others that he intended to enforce the statute against them. First National and the others brought suit to have the statute declared unconstitutional. The lower courts held the statute constitutional, and First National appealed.

JUDICIAL OPINION

POWELL, Justice

"There is practically universal agreement that a major purpose of [the First] Amendment was to protect the free discussion of governmental affairs." If the speakers here were not corporations, no one would suggest that the State could silence their proposed speech. It is the type of speech indispensable to decision making in a democracy, and this is no less true because the speech comes from a corporation rather than an individual. The inherent worth of the speech in terms of its capacity for informing the public does not depend upon the identity of its source, whether corporation, association, union, or individual.

The court below nevertheless held that corporate speech is protected by the First Amendment only when it pertains directly to the corporation's interests. In deciding whether this novel and restrictive gloss on the First Amendment comports with the Constitution and the precedents of this Court, we need not survey the outer boundaries of the Amendment's protection of corporate speech, or address the abstract question whether corporations have the full measure of rights that individuals enjoy under the First Amendment. The question in this case, simply put, is whether the corporate identity of the speaker deprives this proposed speech of what otherwise would be its clear entitlement to protection.

Freedom of speech and the other freedoms encompassed by the First Amendment always have been viewed as fundamental components of the liberty safeguarded by the Due Process Clause, and the Court has not identified a separate source for the right when it has been asserted by corporations.

In the realm of protected speech, the legislature is constitutionally disqualified from dictating the subjects about which persons may speak and the speakers who may address a public issue. If a legislature may direct business corporations to "stick to business," it may also limit other corporations—religious, charitable, or civic—to their respective "business" when addressing the public. Such power in government to channel the expression of views is unacceptable under the First Amendment. Especially where, as here, the legislature's suppression of speech suggests an attempt to give one side of a debatable public question an advantage in expressing its views to people, the First Amendment is plainly offended. Yet the State contends that its action is necessitated by governmental interests of the highest order. We next consider these asserted interests.

Appellee . . . advances two principal justifications for the prohibition of corporate speech. The first is the State's interest in sustaining the active role of the individual citizen in the electoral process and thereby preventing diminution of the citizen's confidence in government. The second is the interest in protecting the rights of shareholders whose views differ from those expressed by management on behalf of the corporation.

Preserving the integrity of the electoral process, preventing corruption and "sustaining the active, alert responsibility of the individual citizen in a democracy for the wise conduct of government" are interests of the highest importance. Preservation of the individual citizen's confidence in government is equally important.

To be sure, corporate advertising may influence the outcome of the vote; this would be its purpose.

continued

But the fact that advocacy may persuade the electorate is hardly a reason to suppress it: The Constitution "protects expression which is eloquent no less than that which is unconvincing." We noted only recently that "the concept that government may restrict speech of some elements of our society in order to enhance the relative voice of others is wholly foreign to the First Amendment. . . ." Moreover, the people in our democracy are entrusted with the responsibility for judging and evaluating the relative merits of conflicting arguments. They may consider, in making their judgment, the source and credibility of the advocate. But if there be any danger that the people cannot evaluate the information and arguments advanced by appellants, it is a danger contemplated by the Framers of the First Amendment.

The statute is said to . . . prevent the use of corporate resources in furtherance of views with which some shareholders may disagree. This purpose is belied, however, by the provisions of the statute, which are both under- and over-inclusive.

The under-inclusiveness of the statute is self-evident. Corporate expenditures with respect to a referendum are prohibited, while corporate activity with respect to the passage or defeat of legislation is permitted, even though corporations may engage in lobbying more often than they take positions on ballot questions submitted to voters.

The over-inclusiveness of the statute is demonstrated by the fact that [it] would prohibit a corporation from supporting or opposing a referendum even if its shareholders unanimously authorized the contribution or expenditure.

Assuming, arguendo, that protection of shareholders is a "compelling" interest under the circumstances of this case, we find "no substantially relevant correlation between the governmental interest asserted and the State's effort" to prohibit appellants from speaking.

Reversed.

CASE QUESTIONS

1. What did the Massachusetts statute regulate?

2. What justification did Massachusetts offer for the statute? What were its concerns in passing the statute?

3. Why does the Court discuss under-inclusiveness and over-inclusiveness?

4. How does the Court respond to the fact that corporate speech might be more persuasive?

5. Is the statute constitutional?

BUSINESS STRATEGY APPLICATION

Go to the Web site and do the exercise on political action committees. Study who is donating to whom and how much money they are giving.

Eminent Domain: The Takings Clause

The right of a governmental body to take title to property for a public use is called **eminent domain**. This right is established in the Fifth Amendment to the Constitution and may also be established in various state constitutions. Private individuals cannot require property owners to sell their property, but governmental entities can require property owners to transfer title for public projects for the public good. The Fifth Amendment provides that "property shall not be taken for a public use without just compensation." Thus, for a governmental entity to exercise properly the right of eminent domain, three factors must be present: public purpose, taking (as opposed to regulating), and just compensation.

Public Purpose

To exercise eminent domain, the governmental authority must establish that the taking is necessary for the accomplishment of a government or public purpose. When eminent domain is mentioned, use of property for highways and schools is thought of most frequently. However, the right of the government to eminent domain extends much further. For example, the following uses have been held to con-

BUSINESS STRATEGY

Where the Money Flows

A look at the following list of top corporate and trade PACs indicates that those businesses whose markets or prices are controlled by the government are the most active political voices. Why do you think these particular PACs are so active?

© PHOTODISC, INC.

soft-dollar contributions as well as each group's perceived clout in Congress. Thus the rankings are based not on dollars alone but also on influence, including for independent issue and ideological campaigns. Compare this list with the previous one.

Rank/Name (2002 Election)

1. Realtors Political Action Committee
2. Association of Trial Lawyers of America Political Action Committee
3. American Federation of State, County, & Municipal Employees (AFSCME)
4. Dealers Election Action Committee of the National Automobile Dealers Association (NADA)
5. Democrat Republican Independent Voter Education
6. International Brotherhood of Electrical Workers Committee on Political Education
7. Machinists Nonpartisan Political League
8. UAW-V-CAP (UAW Voluntary Community Action Program)
9. American Medical Association Political Action Committee
10. Service Employees International Union Political Campaign Committee
11. National Beer Wholesalers' Association Political Action Committee (NBWA PAC)
12. Build Political Action Committee of the National Association of Home Builders
13. Laborers' Political League-Laborers' International Union of NA
14. United Parcel Service Inc. Political Action Committee (from Federal Election Commission, http://www.fec.gov)

Fortune magazine published its list of the 25 most powerful lobbying groups in the United States. The rankings shown here are based on both hard-dollar and

Rank 2001	Rank 1999	Name
1	2	National Rifle Association
2	1	AARP
3	3	National Federation of Independent Business
4	4	American Israel Public Affairs Committee
5	6	Association of Trial Lawyers
6	5	AFL-CIO
7	7	Chamber of Commerce
8	19	National Beer Wholesalers Association
9	15	National Association of Realtors
10	14	National Association of Manufacturers
11	16	National Association of Home Builders
12	13	American Medical Association
13	31	American Hospital Association
14	9	National Education Association
15	21	American Farm Bureau Association
16	17	Motion Picture Association of America
17	20	National Association of Broadcasters
18	8	National Right to Life Committee
19	25	Health Insurance Association
20	10	National Restaurant Association
21	12	National Governors' Association
22	40	Recording Industry Association
23	11	American Bankers Association
24	28	Pharmaceutical Research & Manufacturers
25	23	International Brotherhood of Teamsters

stitute public purposes: the condemnation of slum housing (for purposes of improving city areas), the limitation of mining and excavation within city limits, the declaration of property as a historic landmark, and the taking of property to provide a firm that is a town's economic base with a large enough tract for expansion.

According to the U.S. Supreme Court, the public purpose requirement for eminent domain is to be interpreted broadly, and "the role of the judiciary in determining whether that power is being exercised for a public purpose is an extremely narrow one" [*United States ex rel. TVA* v. *Welch*, 327 U.S. 546 (1946)].

Taking or Regulating

For a governmental entity to be required to pay a landowner compensation under the doctrine of eminent domain, it must be established that there has been a taking of the property. Mere regulation of the property does not constitute a taking, as determined by *Village of Euclid, Ohio* v. *Ambler Realty Co.*, 272 U.S. 365 (1926). Rather, a taking must go so far as to deprive the landowner of any use of the property. In the landmark case of *Pennsylvania Coal* v. *Mahon*, 260 U.S. 393 (1922), the Supreme Court established standards for determining a taking as opposed to mere regulation. At that time Pennsylvania had a statute that prohibited the mining of coal under any land surface where the result would be the subsidence of any structure used as a human habitation. The owners of the rights to mine subsurface coal brought suit challenging the regulation as a taking, and the Supreme Court ruled in their favor, holding that the statute was more than regulation and, in fact, was an actual taking of the subsurface property rights.

Because of the vast amount of technology that has developed since that case was decided, there are many new and subtly different issues in what constitutes a taking. For example, in some areas the regulation of cable television companies is an infringement on air rights. Such specialized areas of real estate rights are particularly difficult to resolve. In *Loretto* v. *Teleprompter Manhattan CATV Corp.*, 458 U.S. 100 (1982), the U.S. Supreme Court held that the small invasion of property by the placement of cable boxes and wires did constitute a taking, albeit very small, and required compensation of the property owners for this small but permanent occupation of their land. Recently, the courts have been faced with the issue of whether zoning or use regulations serve to limit the use of land so much that the result is a taking.

In recent years, the issue of taking has addressed local zoning restrictions on development. These restrictions focus on maintenance of beaches, wetlands, and other natural habitats. For example, in *Nollan* v. *California Coastal Commission*, 483 U.S. 825 (1987), the Nollans sought permission from the California Coastal Commission to construct a home on their coastal lot where they currently had only a small bungalow. The commission refused to grant permission to the Nollans for construction of their home unless they agreed to give a public easement across their lot for beach access. The Supreme Court held that the demand by the commission for an easement was a taking without compensation and, in effect, prevented the Nollans from using their property until they surrendered their exclusive use.

Yet another issue that arises in taking occurs when regulations take effect after owners have acquired land but before it is developed. In *Lucas* v. *South Carolina Coastal Council*, 505 U.S. 1003 (1992), the U.S. Supreme Court declared that *ex post facto* legislation that prevents development of previously purchased land is a taking. In *Lucas*, David Lucas purchased for $975,000 two residential lots on the Isle of Palms in Charleston County, South Carolina. In 1988, the South Carolina legislature enacted the Beachfront Management Act, which barred any permanent habitable structures on coastal properties. The court held South Carolina was required to compensate Mr. Lucas because his land was rendered useless.

Just Compensation

The final requirement for the proper exercise by a governmental entity of the right of eminent domain is that the party from whom the property is being taken be given **just compensation**. The issue of just compensation is difficult to determine and is always a question of fact. Basic to this determination is that the owner is to be compensated for loss and that the compensation is not measured by the governmental entity's gain. In *United States* v. *Miller,* 317 U.S. 369 (1943), the Supreme Court held that in cases where it can be determined, fair market value is the measure of compensation; and, in *United States ex rel. TVA* v. *Powelson,* 319 U.S. 266 (1943), the Supreme Court defined fair market value to be "what a willing buyer would pay in cash to a willing seller."

Possible problems in applying these relatively simple standards include peculiar value to the owner, consequential damages, and greater value of the land because of the proposed governmental project. Basically, the issue of just compensation becomes an issue of appraisal, which is affected by all the various factors involved. Thus, in determining just compensation, the courts must consider such factors as surrounding property values and the owner's proposed use.

Procedural Due Process

Both the Fifth and the Fourteenth Amendments require state and federal governments to provide citizens (businesses included) due process under the law. **Procedural due process** is a right that requires notice and the opportunity to be heard before rights or properties are taken away from an individual or business. Most people are familiar with due process as it exists in the criminal justice system: the right to a lawyer, a trial, and so on (Chapter 9). However, procedural due process is also very much a part of civil law. Before an agency can take away a business license, suspend a license, or impose a fine for a violation, there must be due process. This is true of both state and federal agencies.

Businesses encounter the constitutional protections of due process in their relationships with customers. For example, the eviction of a nonpaying tenant cannot be done unilaterally. The tenant has the right to be heard in the setting of a hearing. The landlord must file an action against the tenant, and the tenant will have the opportunity to present defenses for nonpayment of rent. The Due Process Clause of the U.S. Constitution provides protection for individuals before their property is taken. Property includes land (as in the case of eminent domain, discussed previously), rights of possession (tenants and leases), and even intangible property rights. For example, students cannot be expelled from schools, colleges, or universities without the right to be heard. Students must have some hearing before their property rights with respect to education are taken away.

All proceedings designed to satisfy due process requirements must provide notice and the right to be heard and present evidence (see Chapter 6 for more details). If these rights are not afforded, the constitutional right of due process has been denied and the action taken is rescinded until due process requirements are met. Suppose that OSHA charges a company with safety violations in its plants. Before a fine or order could be imposed, procedural due process requires that the company have the right to be heard and present evidence on the violations. In court cases, a matter reduced to a judgment entitles the victorious side to collect on that judgment. However, under due process, even the proceedings for collection allow the losing party or debtor to be notified of the proceedings and to be heard.

Substantive Due Process

Procedural rules deal with how things are done. All rules on the adjudication of agency charges are procedural rules. Similarly, all rules for the trial of a civil case,

CONSIDER...   **5 . 6**

When the Crafts moved into their residence in October 1972, they noticed that there were two separate gas and electric meters and only one water meter serving the premises. The residence had been used previously as a duplex. The Crafts assumed, based on information from the seller, that the second set of meters was inoperative.

In 1973, the Crafts began receiving two bills: their regular bill and another with an account number in the name of Willie C. Craft, as opposed to Willie S. Craft. In October 1973, after learning from a Memphis Light, Gas & Water (MLG&W) meter reader that both sets of meters were running in their home, the Crafts hired a private plumber and electrical contractor to combine the meters into one gas and one electric meter. Because the contractor did not combine the meters properly, they continued to receive two bills until January 1974. During this time, the Crafts' utility service was terminated five times for nonpayment.

Mrs. Craft missed work several times to go to MLG&W offices to resolve the "double billing" problem. She sought explanations on each occasion but was never given an answer.

In February 1974, the Crafts and other MLG&W customers filed suit for violation of the Due Process Clause. The district court dismissed the case. The court of appeals reversed, and MLG&W appealed.

Have the Crafts been given due process? [*Memphis Light, Gas & Water Div.* v. *Craft*, 436 U.S. 1 (1978).]

from discovery to jury instructions, are also procedural. These rules exist to make sure the substantive law is upheld. **Substantive law** consists of rights, obligations, and behavior standards. Criminal laws are substantive laws, and criminal procedure rules are procedural laws. **Substantive due process** is the right to have laws that do not deprive businesses or citizens of property or other rights without justification and reason.

Most of the early court cases dealing with substantive due process centered around economic issues. During the late nineteenth and early twentieth centuries, there was as much expansion of business regulation as there was expansion of business. Many of these regulations were challenged on grounds they were depriving businesses of economic rights without justification and unreasonably. In the landmark case of *Lochner* v. *New York,* 198 U.S. 45 (1905), the U.S. Supreme Court invalidated a New York statute that prohibited bakery employees from working more than ten hours a day and sixty hours a week. The Court found that in balancing the economic rights of the business against the health of employees, there was not enough evidence to show that the law accomplished its purpose. In other words, the statute was an unjustified invasion of the rights of bakeries without some "substantial showing" of benefits achieved.

Since *Lochner* and other early twentieth-century cases, the Court has broadened its standards for substantive due process. Now the Court uses a test of "some (more or less) relation" to the achievement of a government goal. A substantial showing is not required, only a tenuous connection. So long as the law is reasonably designed to correct a harm, it is substantively valid.

Equal Protection Rights for Business

The Fourteenth Amendment grants citizens the right to the **equal protection** of the law. Lawmakers, however, are often required to make certain distinctions in legislating and regulating that result in classes of individuals being treated differently.

CONSIDER... 5 · 7

Larry Collins was an employee in the sanitation department of Harker Heights, Texas (respondent). On October 21, 1988, he died of asphyxia after entering a manhole to unstop a sewer line. His widow, Myra Jo Collins (petitioner), brought suit alleging that Mr. Collins "had a constitutional right to be free from unreasonable risks of harm to his body, mind and emotions and a constitutional right to be protected from the city of Harker Heights's custom and policy of deliberate indifference toward the safety of its employees." Her complaint alleged that the city violated that right by following a custom and policy of not training its employees about the dangers of working in sewer lines and manholes, not providing safety equipment at job sites, and not providing safety warnings. The complaint also alleged that a prior incident had given the city notice of the risks of entering the sewer lines and that the city had systematically and intentionally failed to provide the equipment and training required by a Texas statute.

The district court dismissed the complaint, and the court of appeals affirmed. Mrs. Collins appealed on the grounds that the city substantively deprived her husband of his life through its lack of training.

Did the city violate the Collins's due process rights? [*Collins* v. *City of Harker Heights, Texas*, 503 U.S. 115 (1992).]

CONSIDER... 5 · 8

The Village of Hoffman passed an ordinance that requires a business to obtain a license if it sells any items that are "designed or marked for use with illegal cannabis or drugs." Guidelines define the items (such as "roach clips," "pipes," "paraphernalia"). Flipside is a merchant in the village selling, among other things, roach clips and pipes specially designed for smoking marijuana. Flipside filed suit challenging the ordinance as overly vague, broad, and violative of due process because of the inability to apply the ordinance consistently. Is the ordinance constitutional? [*Village of Hoffman Est.* v. *Flipside, Hoffman Est.*, 455 U.S. 191 (1982).]

Such different or **disparate treatment** is justified only if there is some rational basis for it. In other words, there must be a rational connection between the classifications and the achievement of some governmental objective. Most classifications survive the rational basis test. An example of a classification that would not survive is one requiring the manufacturers of soft drinks to use only nonbreakable bottles for their product but allowing juice manufacturers to use glass bottles; this is irrational. If there is a public safety concern about glass bottles, it must apply equally to all beverage manufacturers.

THE ROLE OF CONSTITUTIONS IN INTERNATIONAL LAW

Browse constitutions from around the world:
http://confinder.richmond.edu/

Although the U.S. Constitution is the basis for all law in the United States, not all countries follow a similar system of governance. The incorporation of other systems (such as a constitution or code) depends on a nation's history, including its colonization by other countries and those countries' forms of law. The United States and England (and countries established through English colonization) tend to follow a pattern of establishing a general set of principles, as set forth in a constitution, and of reliance on custom, tradition, and precedent for the establishment of law in particular legal areas.

CONSIDER...   5 · 9

Following a boom in cruise ship construction, the ships are now looking for ports at which they can dock in order to begin voyages, most of which start in the United States. With so many new ships, the companies are trying to establish connections with cities that are not ordinarily considered cruise ship docks. The companies pursue these alternatives because the traditional docking cities of New York, Seattle, Miami, Los Angeles, and Houston have become crowded with cruise ship traffic. The following issues have arisen.

- Some ports are not big enough for the larger cruise ships.
- Without proper scheduling and departures, cruise ships often end up waiting in the harbor for three to eight hours; as a result, ports such as Tampa, Florida, a nontraditional cruise ship port, are experiencing traffic jams of ships waiting to dock.
- The presence of the large boats and the number of tourists results in an overwhelming flooding of the often quaint alternative ports such as Charleston, South Carolina. Charleston residents worry that tourists from the cruise ships flooding their city will result in irreversible destruction of the town's preserved landmarks and quaint looks.
- Rising water levels in ports such as New Orleans mean that the tall ships cannot clear power lines and have to be redirected to ports nearby that are not prepared, as when New Orleans had to redirect a 2,974-passenger cruise ship to Gulfport, Mississippi.
- The ships do bring passengers with tourist dollars to spend and additional work for harbor pilots and service industries.
- The port facilities are not adequate to handle all the boats, the passengers, and even the fueling needs of the ships.

Most cruise ship lines are incorporated outside of the United States, do not pay federal income taxes, and are not subject to state income taxes even though the bulk of their passengers come from the United States. (See "Constitutional Standards for Taxation of Business" earlier in this chapter.)

Can the ships be taxed to cover the harbor expenses? Can they be required by states and cities to pay docking fees, or are they internationally exempt companies?

Source: Nicole Harris, Big Cruise Ships Cause Traffic Jams in Ports," *Wall Street Journal,* August 20, 2003, pp. B1, B6.

In countries such as France, Germany, and Spain (and nations colonized through their influences), a system of law that is dependent on code law exists. These countries have very specific codes of law that attempt to be all-inclusive and cover each circumstance that could arise under a particular provision. These nations do not depend on court decisions, and often there are inconsistent results in application of the law because of the lack of dependence on judicial precedent.

Approximately twenty-seven countries follow Islamic law in some way. When Islamic law is the dominant force in a country, it governs all aspects of personal and business life. The constitutions in these lands are the tenets of the nation's religion.

SUMMARY

What is the Constitution?

- U.S. Constitution—document detailing authority of U.S. government and rights of its citizens

What are the constitutional limitations on business regulations?

- Commerce Clause—portion of the U.S. Constitution that controls federal regulation of business; limits Congress to regulating interstate and international commerce
- Intrastate commerce—business within state borders
- Interstate commerce—business across state lines
- Foreign commerce—business outside U.S. boundaries

Who has more power to regulate business—the states or the federal government?

- Supremacy Clause—portion of the U.S. Constitution that defines relationship between state and federal laws

What individual freedoms granted under the Constitution apply to businesses?

- Bill of Rights—first ten amendments to the U.S. Constitution, providing individual freedoms and protection of individual rights
- First Amendment—freedom-of-speech protection in U.S. Constitution
- Commercial speech—ads and other speech by businesses
- Corporate political speech—business ads or positions on candidates or referenda
- Due process—constitutional guarantee against the taking of property or other governmental exercise of authority without an opportunity for a hearing
- Equal protection—constitutional protection for U.S. citizens against disparate treatment
- Substantive due process—constitutional protection against taking of rights or property by statute

QUESTIONS AND PROBLEMS

1. Oklahoma statute Title 29, Section 4–115(B), provides in part: "No person may transport or ship minnows for sale outside the state which were seined or procured within the waters of this state." William Hughes holds a Texas license to operate a commercial minnow business near Wichita Falls, Texas. Mr. Hughes was arrested by an Oklahoma game warden for transporting from Oklahoma to Texas minnows purchased from a licensed Oklahoma dealer.

He was charged with a violation of § 4–115(B), and he challenged the charges on the grounds that the statute was repugnant to the Commerce Clause. The lower court convicted and fined him, and he appealed. Is the Oklahoma statute constitutional or an impermissible burden on interstate commerce? [*Hughes* v. *Oklahoma*, 441 U.S. 322 (1979).]

2. Mrs. Florence Dolan owned a plumbing and electric supply store on Main Street in Portland. Fanno Creek flows through the southeastern corner of Mrs. Dolan's lot on which her store is located. She applied to the city for a permit to redevelop her lot. Her plans included the addition of a second structure.

The City Planning Commission granted Mrs. Dolan's permit but included the following requirement:

Where landfill and/or development is allowed within and adjacent to the 100-year floodplain, the city shall require the dedication of sufficient open land area for greenway adjoining and within the floodplain. This area shall include portions at a suitable elevation for the construction of a pedestrian/bicycle pathway within the floodplain in accordance with the adopted pedestrian/bicycle plan.

Mrs. Dolan maintained that the requirements were a taking of her property because she would be required to reserve a portion of her property for the pedestrian/bike path, and her plans would have to be redone to accommodate the city's requirements. The city maintains that its requirements are all simply part of a redevelopment plan for the city and a means of working with the flood plain created by Fanno Creek. Mrs. Dolan says the city has imposed additional expense and forced her to dedicate a large portion of her lot to public use. Who is correct? Is Portland taking property from Mrs. Dolan? Is the city required to pay compensation to her? [*Dolan* v. *City of Tigard*, 512 U.S. 374 (1994).]

3. Virginia had a series of statutes, Virginia's Alcoholic Beverage Control (ABC) laws, Va.Code § 4.1–100 *et seq.,* which barred out-of-state producers of alcoholic beverages from directly marketing and shipping such beverages to Virginia residents. Only Virginia producers could ship alcoholic beverages directly, while out-of-state producers could not obtain off-premises licenses or ship direct. The scheme required all liquor to pass through the hands of a Virginia-licensed entity. A group of citizens challenged the ABC statutes on the basis of the Commerce Clause, contending that the ABC laws favored local wine and beer manufacturers, who are permitted to sell directly to consumers, and discriminated against out-of-state wine and beer manufacturers, who must sell through the more costly multitiered structure. Virginia maintains that it has a public policy interest in ensuring the safety of alcoholic products and their distribution in Virginia. Are the ABC statutes constitutional? [*Bolick* v. *Danielson,* 330 F.3d 274 (4th Cir. 2003); see also *Dickerson* v. *Bailey,* 336 F.3d 388 (5th Cir. 2003).]

4. Bruce Church, Inc. is a company engaged in extensive commercial farming in Arizona and California. A provision of the Arizona Fruit and Vegetable Standardization Act requires that all cantaloupes grown in Arizona "be packed in regular compact arrangement in closed standard containers approved by the supervisor." Arizona, through its agent Pike, issued an order prohibiting Bruce Church from transporting uncrated cantaloupes from its ranch in Parker, Arizona, to nearby Blythe, California, for packing and processing.

It would take many months and $200,000 for Bruce Church to construct a processing plant in Parker. Further, Bruce Church had $700,000 worth of cantaloupes ready for transportation. Bruce Church filed suit in federal district court challenging the constitutionality of the Arizona statutory provision on shipping cantaloupes. The court issued an injunction against the enforcement of the act on the grounds that it was an undue hardship on interstate commerce. Will the regulation withstand Commerce Clause scrutiny? [*Pike* v. *Bruce Church, Inc.,* 397 U.S. 137 (1970).]

5. The International Longshoremen's Association refused to unload cargo shipped from the Soviet Union as a way of protesting the Soviet invasion of Afghanistan. Allied International, an importer of Soviet wood products, could not get its wood unloaded when its ship arrived in Boston. Allied sued on the basis of the National Labor Relations Act, claiming the conduct was an unlawful boycott. The union claims no commerce is involved and that federal law does not apply. Is there commerce? Does the National Labor Relations Act apply? [*International Longshoremen's Association* v. *Allied International, Inc.,* 456 U.S. 212 (1982).]

6. For the past sixty-two years, Pacific Gas & Electric (PG&E) has distributed a newsletter in its monthly billing envelopes. The newsletter, called *Progress,* reaches over 3 million customers and has contained tips on conservation, utility billing information, public interest information, and political editorials.

A group called TURN (Toward Utility Rate Normalization) asked the Public Utility Commission (PUC) of California to declare that the envelope space belonged to the ratepayers and that TURN was entitled to use the *Progress* space four times each year. The PUC ordered TURN's request, and PG&E appealed the order to the California Supreme Court. When the California Supreme Court denied review, PG&E appealed to the U.S. Supreme Court, alleging a violation of its First Amendment rights. Is PG&E correct? [*Pacific Gas & Electric* v. *Public Utility Commission of California,* 475 U.S. 1 (1986).]

7. The Minnesota legislature enacted a 1977 statute banning the retail sale of milk in plastic nonreturnable, nonrefillable containers but permitting such sale in other nonrefillable containers, such as paperboard milk cartons. Clover Leaf Creamery brought suit challenging the constitutionality of the statute under the Equal Protection Clause, alleging that there was no rational basis for the statute. The Minnesota legislature's purpose in passing the statute was to control solid waste, arguing that plastic containers take up more space in solid waste disposal dumps. The Minnesota Supreme Court found evidence to the contrary: The jugs took up less space and required less energy to produce. On appeal to the U.S. Supreme Court, can the statute survive a constitutional challenge? Is there a "rational basis" for the statute? What effect does the evidence to the contrary have on the statute's constitutionality? [*Minnesota* v. *Clover Leaf Creamery,* 449 U.S. 456 (1981).]

8. Iowa passed a statute restricting the length of vehicles that could use its highways. The length chosen was 55 feet. Semi trailers are generally 55 feet long; double or twin tracks (one cab pulling two trailers) are 65 feet long. Other states in the Midwest have adopted the 65-foot standard. Consolidated Freightways brought suit, challenging the Iowa statute as an unconstitutional burden on interstate commerce. The Iowa statute meant Consolidated could not use its twins in Iowa. The Iowa legislature claims the 65-foot doubles are more dangerous than the 55-foot singles. However, the statute did provide a border exception: Towns and cities along Iowa borders could make an exception to the length requirements to allow trucks to use their city and town roads. Can Iowa's statute survive a constitutional challenge? Is the statute an impermissible burden on interstate commerce? [*Kassel* v. *Consolidated Freightways Corp.,* 450 U.S. 662 (1981).]

9. In 1989, the city of Cincinnati authorized Discovery Network, Inc. to place sixty-two free-standing news-racks on public property for distributing free magazines that consisted primarily of advertising for Discovery Network's service. In 1990, the city became concerned about the safety and attractive appearance of its streets and sidewalks and revoked Discovery Network's permit on the ground that the magazines were commercial handbills whose distribution was prohibited on public property by a preexisting ordinance. Discovery Network says the prohibition is an excessive regulation of its commercial speech and a violation of its rights. The city maintains the elimination of the newsracks decreases litter and increases safety. Is the ban on newsracks constitutional? [*City of Cincinnati* v. *Discovery Network, Inc.*, 507 U.S. 410 (1993).]

10. In 1988, the voters of Escondido, California, approved Proposition K, an ordinance that set rents at their 1986 levels and prohibited increases without city council approval. John and Irene Yee own several mobile home parks in Escondido and have filed suit alleging that "the rent control law has had the effect of depriving [them] of all use and occupancy of [their] real property and granting to tenants the right to physically perma-nently occupy their land." Is the rent ordinance constitu-tional? [*Yee* v. *City of Escondido, California*, 503 U.S. 519 (1992).]

RESEARCH PROBLEM

Backgrounds and Dissenting Views

11. List the current justices of the Supreme Court, their ages, political affiliations, and number of years on the bench. Justice Stevens has written the most dissenting opinions for this court and is the most frequent lone dissenter. Why do you think his record is such?

6

Administrative Law

> **update** <

For up-to-date legal news and real-world business applications, click on **update** *at http://jennings.westbuslaw.com.*

The regulations of administrative agencies at the federal and state levels affect the day-to-day operations of all businesses. From permits to labor regulations, every business is affected. Agencies are the enforcement arm of governments. Created by one of the branches of government, they affect the way businesses operate. This chapter answers the following questions: What is an administrative agency? What does it do? What laws govern the operation of administrative agencies? How do agencies pass rules? How do agencies enforce the law?

Lord's Prayer	**66 words**
Gettysburg Address	**286 words**
Declaration of Independence	**1,322 words**
Federal regulations on the sale of cabbage	**26,911 words**
Internal Revenue Code	**6,200,000 words**

Grade A Fancy ketchup must flow no more than 9 centimeters in 30 seconds at 69 degrees Fahrenheit.
EXCERPT FROM A FOOD AND DRUG ADMINISTRATION REGULATION

Ninety percent of a 100-person panel, composed of people 50 to 70 years old, must be able to open and close the package within five minutes, then again within one minute.
CONSUMER PRODUCT SAFETY COMMISSION RULE
ON CHILD-PROOF CAPS

> Because of the Veterans Day holiday next Wednesday, this release will be published on Friday, November 13, instead of on Thursday, November 12. It will be issued on Thursday, November 19, its usual publication date, but will be delayed the following week until Friday, November 17, because of the Thanksgiving Day holiday on Thursday, November 26.
>
> FEDERAL RESERVE MEMO, 1992

> **DO NOT REMOVE UNDER PENALTY OF LAW.**
>
> WARNING PRINTED ON TAGS REQUIRED ON MATTRESSES SOLD IN THE UNITED STATES

> **THIS TAG NOT TO BE REMOVED EXCEPT BY THE CONSUMER**
>
> MODIFIED WARNING TAG REQUIRED ON MATTRESSES SO THAT AGENCY COULD REDUCE THE NUMBER OF CALLS FROM CITIZENS ABOUT REMOVING THEIR MATTRESS TAGS

CONSIDER...

A. Duda & Sons, Inc., has a plaque posted in the lobby of its company headquarters that reads: "But seek ye first the Kingdom of God, and his righteousness and all these things shall be added unto you." An employee complained to the Equal Employment Opportunity Commission (EEOC) about the plaque, stating that it constituted religious harassment in the workplace.

At the Montgomery County Middle School, the name of its December music event was changed from "Christmas Concert" to "Winter Concert" when a teacher complained that the use of the word "Christmas" constituted religious harassment.

Based on these complaints and others (a total of 538 religious harassment complaints), the EEOC proposed rules on religious harassment that prohibited verbal or physical contact that "denigrates or shows hostility or aversion toward individual because of his/her religion . . . or that of his/her relatives, friends or associates."

An executive in a Florida hospital asked, "These rules could prevent an employee from wearing a necklace with a crucifix to work. Would I have to control Bible reading by my employees when they're having a break? The rules are unmanageable. Where do I turn? How can I raise my concerns about them?"

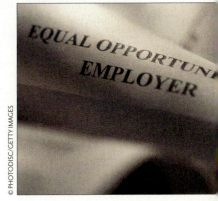

WHAT ARE ADMINISTRATIVE AGENCIES?

An **administrative agency** is best defined by what it is not: It is not a legislative or judicial body. An administrative agency is a statutory creation within the executive branch with the power to make, interpret, and enforce laws. Such agencies exist at practically every level of government, and their names vary considerably. Exhibit 6.1 is a list of all the federal administrative agencies and their acronyms.

EXHIBIT   6.1   Major Federal Administrative Agencies

Executive Office of the President
Executive Departments
Department of Agriculture
Department of Commerce
Department of Defense
Office of the Secretary of Defense
Department of the Air Force
Department of the Army
Department of the Navy
Department of Education
Department of Energy
Department of Health and Human
  Services
Department of Housing and Urban
  Development (HUD)
Department of the Interior
Department of Justice
Department of Labor
Department of State
Department of Transportation
Department of the Treasury

Independent Agencies
ACTION
Administrative Committee of the
  Federal Register
Advisory Committee on Intergovern-
  mental Relations
American Battle Monuments
  Commission
Appalachian Regional Council
Board for International Broadcasting
Civil Aeronautics Board (CAB)
Commission on Fine Arts (CFA)
Commodity Futures Trading Com-
  mission (CFTC)
Consumer Product Safety Commis-
  sion (CPSC)
Environmental Protection Agency
  (EPA)

Equal Employment Opportunity
  Commission (EEOC)
Export-Import Bank of the United
  States
Federal Aviation Administration
  (FAA)
Farm Credit Administration (FCA)
Federal Communications Commis-
  sion (FCC)
Federal Deposit Insurance Corpora-
  tion (FDIC)
Federal Election Commission (FEC)
Federal Emergency Management
  Agency (FEMA)
Federal Labor Relations Authority
  (FLRA)
Federal Maritime Commission
  (FMC)
Federal Mediation and Conciliation
  Service
Federal Mine Safety and Health
  Review Commission
Federal Reserve System
Federal Trade Commission (FTC)
General Services Administration
  (GSA)
Inter-American Foundation
International Communications
  Agency (ICA)
International Development Coop-
  eration Agency (IDCA)
Interstate Commerce Commission
  (ICC)
Merit Systems Protection Board
National Aeronautics and Space
  Administration (NASA)
National Credit Union Adminis-
  tration
National Foundation on the Arts
  and Humanities

National Highway Traffic Safety
  Administration
National Indian Gaming Com-
  mission
National Labor Relations Board
  (NLRB)
National Mediation Board
National Science Foundation
  (NSF)
National Transportation Safety
  Board (NTSB)
Nuclear Regulatory Commission
  (NRC)
Occupational Safety and Health
  Administration (OSHA)
Office of Personnel Management
  (OPM)
Overseas Private Investment
  Corporation
Patent and Trademark Office
Pension Benefit Guaranty Corpo-
  ration
Pennsylvania Avenue Development
  Corporation
Railroad Retirement Board (RRB)
Securities and Exchange Commis-
  sion (SEC)
Selective Service System (SSS)
Small Business Administration
  (SBA)
Tennessee Valley Authority (TVA)
U.S. Arms Control and Disarma-
  ment Agency
U.S. Commission on Civil Rights
U.S. International Trade Com-
  mission
U.S. Metric Board
U.S. Postal Service (USPS)
U.S. Water Resources Council
Veterans Administration (VA)

States also have administrative agencies that are responsible for such things as the licensing of professions and occupations. Architects, contractors, attorneys, accountants, cosmetologists, doctors, dentists, real estate agents, and nurses are all professionals whose occupations are regulated in most states by some administrative agency. Utility and securities regulation are also handled by administrative agencies in each of the states.

All these agencies at every level of government derive their authority from the particular legislature responsible for their creation. Congress creates federal agencies; state legislatures create state agencies; and city governments create their cities' administrative agencies.

EXHIBIT 6.2 SEC Organizational Chart

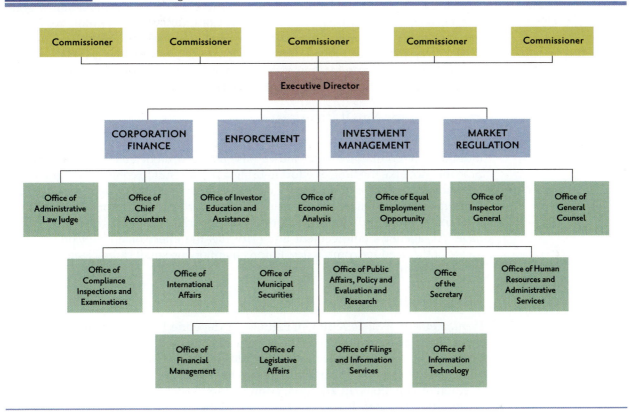

See the structure of the federal government, its agencies, and their contact numbers:

http://www.gpoaccess.gov/

The structures of agencies may differ significantly, but most will have an organizational chart to show how different departments operate. Exhibit 6.2 is an organizational chart for the Securities and Exchange Commission (SEC). The SEC consists of five commissioners, four divisions, and seventeen offices.

Legislators begin the administrative process leading to the creation of an agency with the recognition of a problem and the passage of a law designed to remedy the problem. The enacted law gives the overview—what the legislature wants to accomplish and the penalties for noncompliance with the law. The law may also establish an administrative agency with the power to adopt rules to deal with the problems of enforcement of the statute. The law, referred to as an **enabling act**, gives the agency the power to deal with the issues and problems the act addresses.

ROLES OF ADMINISTRATIVE AGENCIES

Specialization

Administrative agencies are specialists in their particular areas of law, and this type of specialization is needed not only because of the complexities of law but also because of the complexities of the regulated areas. For example, environmental regulation is complex because of both the chemical analyses involved in determining pollution levels and the types of equipment and technology needed for controlling pollution.

Visit the Federal Communi-
cations Commission:
http://www.fcc.gov

Visit the Commodity Futures
Trading Commission:
http://www.cftc.gov

Similarly, neither Congress nor the judiciary has the necessary specialization or expertise to deal with the highly technical matters handled by administrative agencies, such as broadcast frequencies (Federal Communications Commission), commodities trading (Commodity Futures Trading Commission), and mining (Federal Mine Safety and Health Review Commission). The people staffing these agencies, therefore, can be chosen for their expertise, which helps ensure adequate protection for the public and the members of the regulated industries.

Protection for Small Business

Administrative agencies have traditionally been protectors of small interests. An individual or competitor who finds a false advertisement in a newspaper would probably not take the time or effort to bring a private suit to collect damages for the false advertisement. But an agency created to oversee truth in advertising would undertake routine enforcement against such advertisements, affording small business competitors and consumers protection and rights they might not otherwise have. An agency's enforcement authority has the effect of making others more aware of the need for compliance. Enforcement of one small claim creates an atmosphere of compliance.

Faster Relief

If enforcement of all government regulations depended on court hearings, not only would there be a substantial increase in the caseload of the courts, but there would be a backlog for those hearings that would interfere with the goal of swift action and enforcement. Administrative agencies help expedite the investigation and disposition of violations. In addition, administrative agencies serve as review boards for granting licenses. If such license applications required legislative hearings, license and permit applications would be delayed substantially, and businesses would be left in limbo until a hearing could be held. An administrative agency provides an efficient way for fast licensing and timely enforcement.

Due Process

Administrative agencies provide the opportunity to be heard before any action to remove property, rights, or income can be taken. *Goldberg* v. *Kelly*, 397 U.S. 254 (1970), is often described as the judicial decision responsible for creating administrative agencies and procedures as we have them today. In *Goldberg*, the Supreme Court ruled that before a benefit (such as aid to dependent children) could be taken away, the agency must present its evidence and allow a response. Regulatory action thus requires due process, which includes the right to see the evidence and present your side of the story (see Chapter 5).

Social Goals

Visit the Environmental
Protection Agency:
http://www.epa.gov

Some experts see administrative agencies as a means for accomplishing social goals that might otherwise be delayed or debated until no resolution could be reached. For example, the Environmental Protection Agency is assigned the goal of creating a cleaner environment. If Congress had to debate every permit for a factory or rule on discharges, the goal might be lost in the political arena. Further, having judicial review and determination of these issues would result in a delay that might make the goal moot. Administrative agencies can be created and then permitted to function independently of the judicial and legislative branches. Very often, these agencies are created in response to a pressing social issue. For example, the Federal Home Loan Bank Board was established to regulate home mortgages after all the difficulties with foreclosures during the Great Depression. The goal was a more equitable system for mortgage lending and mortgage foreclosure, and an agency was created to accomplish those goals.

LAWS GOVERNING ADMINISTRATIVE AGENCIES

Apart from their enabling acts, administrative agencies are also subject to some general laws on the functioning of agencies. This section covers those laws.

The Administrative Procedures Act

Review the Administrative Procedures Act:
http://usgovinfo.about.com/ library/bills/blapa.htm

This act was the first to deal with administrative agency procedures. It was passed in 1946 after some agencies had been in existence long enough for some standard procedures to be established. The **Administrative Procedures Act (APA)** requires agencies to follow certain uniform procedures in making rules (those procedures are covered later in this chapter). The APA has been amended a number of times, by the Freedom of Information Act, the Federal Privacy Act, and the Government in the Sunshine Act, among others.

The Freedom of Information Act

For instructions on how to retrieve information from the Justice Department under the Freedom of Information Act, see:
http://www.usdoj.gov/ 04foia/

The **Freedom of Information Act (FOIA)** is an APA amendment passed in 1966. It allows access to certain information federal agencies possess and requires that the agencies publicly disclose their procedures and decisions. The types of procedures that must be publicly disclosed relate to agencies' structures: where the central and regional offices are located and which office or office division will respond to requests for information. Agencies must also publish their rules, regulations, procedures, policy statements, and reports.

Some agency information need not be published, but it must be available to the public upon request. This information includes the orders resulting from a hearing, any interpretations of unpublished rules the agency follows, and in-house management tools such as staff policies and manuals.

This information, not published but available to the public, can be obtained by a **FOIA request**, which must be written and must describe the documents sought. A general request for all the agency's research would not be a sufficient description, but a request, say, for the results of the Federal Trade Commission's study of coaching programs for college entrance exams would be allowable. The agency can charge for time and for copying costs in processing the request, although these charges must be published and applied uniformly to all requests. One exception allows an agency to waive fees for nonprofit public interest groups.

If an agency wrongfully refuses to supply the information requested, the party requesting it can bring a court action to enforce the request, with all costs paid by the agency.

Some information is exempt from FOIA requests. There are nine categories of exemptions, including requests that would reveal trade secrets or information about government workers' personnel records.

Agencies can refuse to release information that is exempt, but they can also decide to release that information if they wish to waive an exemption. Some requests have resulted in court cases brought by the parties protected by the exemptions. For example, suppose that one company requests the government bid contract submitted by another company (its competitor for the bid) to the Department of Defense. The bidding company could bring suit to stop the disclosure. Such suits are called "reverse FOIA suits." However, the U.S. Supreme Court has held in *Chrysler Corp.* v. *Brown*, 441 U.S. 281 (1979), that the right to stop or grant disclosure rests with the agency and not with the party who supplied the information to the agency.

Federal Privacy Act

Review the Federal Privacy Act:

http://www.law.cornell.edu/uscode/5/552a.html

By 1974, federal agencies had tremendous amounts of information about businesses and individuals. At least one, and usually more than one, agency could give an individual's name, occupation, address, Social Security number, and income. Furthermore, agencies were exchanging information among themselves to obtain more data for their files. All of this activity was going on without the knowledge of the persons involved. In 1974, Congress passed the **Federal Privacy Act (FPA)** to reduce exchanges of information between agencies about persons (individuals and businesses).

The FPA prohibits federal agencies from communicating any records to another agency or person without first obtaining the consent of the person whose record is being communicated. The FPA protects all records about individuals that might be in the possession of the agency, including medical and employment histories.

There are certain exemptions from the FPA. Because law enforcement agencies would have a difficult time trying to conduct investigations if they had to get permission from the individuals being investigated in order to obtain information, law enforcement agencies are exempt. Congress can also obtain information without consent. Routine agency tasks are also exempt from the prior permission requirement. For example, employees of the SEC need constant access to information about stock sales by directors to perform their duties regarding the control of insider trading.

Government in the Sunshine Act

Review the Government in the Sunshine Act:

http://www.law.cornell.edu/uscode/5/552b.html

The **Government in the Sunshine Act** is a 1976 amendment to the APA and is often called an **open meeting law**. Its purpose is to require prior public notice of meetings of those agencies with heads appointed by the president. All the agencies with the word *commission* in their names have agency heads appointed by the president.

This open meeting law applies only to meetings between or among agency heads. For example, when the commissioners of the FTC meet together, that meeting must be public and held only after there has been prior notice. Staff members can hold meetings in private without giving notice. Most states also have sunshine laws for state administrative government operations.

As with the other statutes, there are exemptions under the open meeting law. If an agency meeting will cover national defense, foreign policy, trade secrets, personnel, or law enforcement issues, the meetings need not be public. For example, the SEC commissioners could meet privately to discuss an enforcement program designed to curb insider trading (see Chapter 22).

The Federal Register Act

Although the **Federal Register Act (FRA)** is not a part of the APA, its provisions are necessary for all the acts under the APA to work. The FRA created the **Federal Register System**, which oversees publication of federal agency information. This system provides the means for Sunshine Act notices and publication of agency rules and procedures.

Three publications make up the Federal Register System. The first is the *U.S. Government Manual*. This publication is reprinted each year and lists all federal agencies and their regional offices along with addresses. In addition, the *Manual* contains statistics about the agencies and their sizes.

Review the Code of Federal Regulations: http://www.gpoaccess.gov

The second publication of the Federal Register Act is the *Code of Federal Regulations* (covered in Chapter 1). The *Code of Federal Regulations* contains all the regulations of all the federal agencies. The volumes are in paperback, and the entire Code is republished each year because of tremendous changes in the regulations. Exhibit 6.3 shows a sample excerpt from the Code.

The third publication under the Federal Register System provides a daily update on changes in the regulations. This publication, called the *Federal Register*, is published every government working day and contains proposed regulations, notices of meetings (under the Government in the Sunshine Act), notices of hearings on proposed regulations, and the final versions of amended or new regulations. The *Federal Register* totals about 70,000 pages a year, or about 250 pages every working day.

Search the Federal Register *and the* U.S. Government Manual: http://www.gpoaccess.gov/

FOR THE MANAGER'S DESK

RE: THE SIZE AND SCOPE OF FEDERAL REGULATION

In 2003, U.S. federal agencies issued 4,148 new rules in the 71,269-page *Federal Register*. This total amounts to 19 fewer rules than in 2002. For the past eight years, Clyde Wayne Crews Jr., vice president for policy at the Competitive Enterprise Institute, has issued a report each year on federal regulation: *Ten Thousand Commandments: An Annual Snapshot of the Federal Regulatory State.*

In 2003, Congress passed and the president signed into law 198 bills. Meanwhile, federal agencies have 4,266 pending regulations at various stages of the rulemaking process. Nearly half of the rules are promulgated by the Departments of Transportation, Treasury, Interior, and Commerce and the EPA.

For an economic analysis of the impact of regulation, go to http://www.cato.org.

EXHIBIT 6.3   Federal Regulations on Post–Mortem Inspection of Cattle, Excerpted from 9 C.F.R. § 310.1 [2001]

§310.1 Extent and time of post-mortem inspection; post-mortem inspection staffing standards.

(a) A careful post-mortem examination and inspection shall be made of the carcasses and parts thereof of all livestock slaughtered at official establishments. Such inspection and examination shall be made at the time of slaughter unless, because of unusual circumstances, prior arrangements acceptable to the Administrator have been made in specific cases by the circuit supervisor for making such inspection and examination at a later time.

(b)(1) The staffing standards on the basis of the number of carcasses to be inspected per hour are outlined in the following tables. Standards for multiple inspector lines are based on inspectors rotating through the different types of inspection stations during each shift to equalize the workload. The inspector in charge shall have the authority to require the establishment to reduce slaughter line speeds where, in his judgment, the inspection procedure cannot be adequately performed at the current line speed because of particular deficiencies in carcass preparation and presentation by the plant at the higher speed, or because the health condition of the particular animals indicates a need for more extensive inspection.

(2) *Cattle inspection.* For all cattle staffing standards, an "a" in the "Number of Inspectors by Stations" column means that one inspector performs the entire inspection procedure and a "b" means that one inspector performs the head and lower carcass inspection and a second inspector performs the viscera and upper carcass inspection.*

*The "Maximum Slaughter Rates" figures listed in paragraph (b)(2)(i) of this section for one (a) and two (b) inspector kills are overstated because the time required to walk from one inspection station to another is not included. To determine the proper adjusted maximum slaughter line speed, paragraph (b)(2)(i)(A) of this section for one inspector kills or paragraph (b)(2)(i)(B) of this section for two inspector kills must be used along with their accompanying rules.

(i) Inspection Using the Viscera Truck.

STEERS AND HEIFERS

Maximum slaughter rates (head per hour)	Number of inspectors by stations		
	Head	Viscera	Carcass
1 to 27	a	a	a
28 to 56	b	b	b
57 to 84	1	1	1
85 to 86	1	2	1
87 to 143	2	2	1

COWS AND BULLS

Maximum slaughter rates (head per hour)	Number of inspectors by stations		
	Head	Viscera	Carcass
1 to 27	a	a	a
28 to 55	b	b	b
56 to 77	1	1	1
78 to 81	1	2	1
82 to 134	2	2	1

(A) Rules for determining adjusted maximum slaughter rates for single-inspector kills considering walking distance according to the table in this subdivision: Determine the distances the inspector actually walks between the points shown in columns 2 through 14 of the following table. For each column, determine the deduction figure opposite the appropriate number of feet in column 1. Compute the total of the deduction figures for columns 2 through 14. The adjusted maximum rate is the maximum rate in paragraph (b)(2)(i) of this section minus total of the deduction figures. If the resultant number is not a whole number, it must be rounded off to the next *lowest* whole number.

THE FUNCTIONS OF ADMINISTRATIVE AGENCIES AND BUSINESS INTERACTION

Administrative agencies have three functions: promulgating regulations, enforcing rules, and adjudicating rules. Businesses will find themselves interacting with agencies in all three areas of operation.

Providing Input When Agencies Are Promulgating Regulations

The legislative function of administrative agencies has two forms: **formal rulemaking** and **informal rulemaking**. Some agencies combine these into a type of rulemaking that is a cross between formal and informal—**hybrid rulemaking**. This section focuses on formal rulemaking.

EXHIBIT 6.4   Steps in Formal Rulemaking by Administrative Agencies

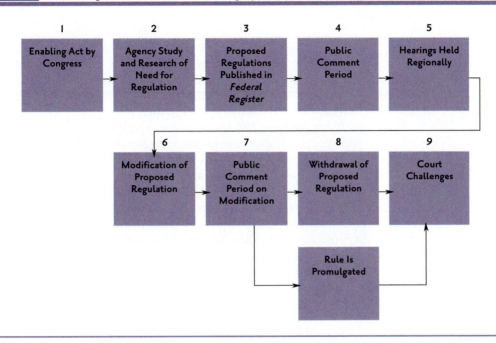

Formal Rulemaking

Exhibit 6.4 diagrams the steps involved in formal rulemaking.

Congressional Enabling Act   Congress is responsible for passing statutes designed to remedy a perceived problem that is within federal jurisdiction. At the point of legislation, constituents have an opportunity to voice their views and concerns about problem areas. For example, many people saw a problem with the way credit transactions were being handled in the early 1970s. There were concerns about disclosures, billings, and advertisements. In response to these concerns and problems, Congress passed the Consumer Credit Protection Act, or Truth in Lending Act. In addition, Congress authorized the Federal Reserve Board to promulgate rules covering the specifics of disclosure and gave the board the responsibility to enforce this new credit regulation. The actual details of credit disclosures are found in the Federal Reserve Board's regulations (called, as a group, **Regulation Z**).

After the 1929 stock market crash, Congress perceived problems with the way securities were being sold and traded on the national exchanges. To correct some of the problems and abuses in the trading of securities, Congress passed the 1933 and 1934 Securities Acts (see Chapter 22 for more details), the first of which created the SEC as the administrative agency responsible for the enforcement of the two acts. The following is an excerpt from the 1933 Securities Act, the enabling act for the SEC.

Review the Truth in Lending Act:
http://www.law.cornell.edu/ uscode/15/1601.html

Explore the 1933 and 1934 Securities Acts:
http://www.law.uc.edu/CCL

> *(a) There is hereby established a Securities and Exchange Commission (hereinafter referred to as the "Commission") to be composed of five commissioners to be appointed by the President by and with the advice and consent of the Senate. Not more than three of such commissioners shall be members of the same political party and in making appointments members of different political parties shall be appointed alternately as nearly as may be practicable. . . .*

(b) *The Commission is authorized to appoint and fix the compensation of such officers, attorneys, examiners, and other experts as may be necessary for carrying out its functions under this chapter. . . .*

Agency Research of the Problem   Any regulation passed by an administrative agency must have some purpose and evidence to show that the regulation will accomplish the purpose. Rules passed without some study and evidence supporting their need or effectiveness could be challenged by the persons or industries affected as arbitrary and capricious (discussed later in this chapter).

Agency staff can perform the study, or the agency can hire outside experts to conduct it. The study will examine issues such as whether the regulation will be cost effective. Some regulations may cost billions of dollars for industries to follow. Regulation Z, for example, requires lenders to send out a substantial amount of paperwork; the preparation of the paperwork and the cost of mailing, along with personnel costs for the work involved, are tremendous. However, full knowledge of the cost of consumer debt is an important goal specified by Congress in the Consumer Credit Protection Act. Although the study may reveal that the cost is great, it could also reveal that the cost outweighs the hazards to consumers. In other words, the study focuses not only on monetary costs but also on the problems the regulation is trying to correct and the cost of those problems to the individual and to society.

Proposed Regulations   Based on the needs and costs shown by the completed study, the agency will publish its proposed rules or rule changes in the *Federal Register*. By this time, the published form of the regulation has been through many departments and many hands. Legal counsel for the agency will review the regulation for language problems. Other experts within the agency will also review its content for problems and inaccuracies. Economists, financial analysts, and scientists are examples of experts used within an agency to review a regulation before publication.

To be valid, the notice in the *Federal Register* must contain certain information. If notice is not given or is given improperly, a court can set aside the action taken by the agency and require the rulemaking process to be repeated with proper notice. Requirements for a *Federal Register* notice include the following:

1. The name of the agency proposing the rules
2. The statutory authority the agency has for promulgating the rules (citing the enabling act)
3. Either the language of the proposed rules or an accurate summary or description of the proposed rules

Review the Regulatory Flexibility Act:
http://www.archives.gov/ federal_register/public_ laws/regulatory_flexibility_ act/601.html

Although not required to do so, some agencies provide background information in the notice so that some history and the function of the rules are given. In addition to publishing the notice of proposed rules in the *Federal Register,* an agency is required under the **Regulatory Flexibility Act** to publish a notice in the publications of those trades and industries that will be affected by the rule. For example, the regulation governing disclosures of sales of used vehicles was published in automobile dealers associations' publications. Exhibit 6.5 is a sample of a proposed rule publication from the SEC on shareholder input for director nominations.

The Public Comment Period   One of the purposes for publishing proposed rules is to allow the public an opportunity to review and provide input on the proposed rules. The period during which the agency accepts comments on the rule is called

| EXHIBIT | 6.5 | Sample Proposed SEC Rule on Shareholder Nominations of Directors |

PROPOSED RULE: SECURITY HOLDER DIRECTOR NOMINATIONS

SECURITIES AND EXCHANGE COMMISSION

17 CFR PARTS 240, 249 and 274

[RELEASE NOS. 34–48626; IC-26206; FILE NO. S7–19–03]

RIN 3235-AI93

SECURITY HOLDER DIRECTOR NOMINATIONS

Agency: Securities and Exchange Commission

Action: Proposed rule.

Summary: We are proposing new rules that would, under certain circumstances, require companies to include in their proxy materials security holder nominees for election as director. These proposed rules are intended to improve disclosure to security holders to enhance their ability to participate meaningfully in the proxy process for the nomination and election of directors. The proposed rules would not provide security holders with the right to nominate directors where it is prohibited by state law. Instead, the proposed rules are intended to create a mechanism for nominees of long-term security holders, or groups of long-term security holders, with significant holdings to be included in company proxy materials where there are indications that security holders need such access to further an effective proxy process. This mechanism would apply in those instances where evidence suggests that the company has been unresponsive to security holder concerns as they relate to the proxy process. The proposed rules would enable security holders to engage in limited solicitations to form nominating security holder groups and engage in solicitations in support of their nominees without disseminating a proxy statement. The proposed rules also would establish the filing requirements under the Securities Exchange Act of 1934 for nominating security holders.

Dates: Comments must be received by December 22, 2003.

Addresses: To help us process and review your comments more efficiently, comments should be sent by one method—U.S. mail or electronic mail—only. Comments should be submitted in triplicate to Jonathan G. Katz, Secretary, U.S. Securities and Exchange Commission, 450 Fifth Street, NW, Washington, DC 20549–0609. Comments also may be submitted electronically at the following e-mail address: rule-comments@sec.gov. All comment letters should refer to File No. S7–19–03. This number should be included in the subject line if sent via electronic mail. Electronically submitted comment letters will be posted on the Commission's Internet website (http://www.sec.gov). We do not edit personal information, such as names or electronic mail addresses, from electronic submissions. You should submit only information that you wish to make available publicly.

For Further Information Contact: Lillian C. Brown or Grace K. Lee, Division of Corporation Finance, at (202) 824-5250, or, with regard to investment companies, John M. Faust, Division of Investment Management, at (202) 942-0721, U.S. Securities and Exchange Commission, 450 Fifth Street, NW, Washington DC 20549–0402.

the **public comment period**. Under the APA, the public comment period cannot be fewer than 30 days, but most agencies make the public comment period much longer.

Private citizens, government officials, industry representatives, businesspeople, and corporations can all send in their public comments. This is the opportunity business has to provide information and express concerns about proposals. There is no formal format for a public comment; most just appear in letter form. Because comments are generally made by those who do not like the rule, most comment letters are negative. Anyone who wishes to challenge later the validity of a federal regulation must participate in the comment period and voice his or her concerns at that time.

Some agencies allow members of the public (and others who would be entitled to make comments) to participate in public hearings. These hearings are not for the purpose of challenging the agency's study that resulted in the rule; they are not trial

proceedings and are only informational in nature. The hearing officers or commissioners for the agency ask questions of witnesses, but no other parties can question
those who appear to make comments. The purpose of the hearings is to take input
on the proposals and consider additional evidence and factors relevant in promulgating the final version of the rule.

Exhibits 6.6, 6.7, and 6.8 are examples of letters sent to the SEC offering input on
the proposed rule on shareholder participation in the nomination and election of
directors. (See the proposal in Exhibit 6.5.)

EXHIBIT   6.6   Comments in Favor of the Proposal to Allow Shareholder Nominations for Directors

The SEC received e-mail comments such as the following.

> *"I think that shareholders should be able to nominate their own directors, and I think
> that they should not have to jump through hoops to do so. Give them proxy access,
> remove the triggers attached to your proposed rule, and watch corporate management
> scramble to reform itself under the accountability that follows."*

> *"I urge the SEC to pass the proposed rule giving shareholders the ability to nominate
> candidates for board elections. This is the right thing to do."*

The SEC received 4,128 letters of support similar to the following one.

> *Dear Jonathan G. Katz, Secretary,*
> *   I am writing in support of shareholders being able to better nominate candidates
> for corporate boards. I urge the SEC to support greater democracy in the corporate
> elections process, which has fallen victim to the special interests of the self-selected
> directors who now govern publicly held companies in the U.S. The SEC should sup-
> port investors' rights to nominate legitimate candidates for company boards, and to
> do so through the company's proxy ballot mailed out to all investors.*
>
> *****
>
> *   Until corporate governance is strengthened to make directors more accountable to
> shareholders and stakeholders, we'll continue to lose investors' confidence in markets
> and corporate management. I hope that this time, the SEC will stand by investors,
> including individual ones who have poured their life savings into the markets, and
> improve the system to allow for greater shareholder suffrage. Allowing the owners of
> companies to have a realistic say in the membership of the board is one of the best
> ways to begin cleaning up Corporate America, and restore our faith in its financial
> system.*

EXHIBIT 6.7 Comments That the Proposed Rules Are Not Enough

"This is too weak a reform, but it is better than nothing. If you are supposed to protect the rights of investors then DO IT. Quit wasting our tax dollars for the greedy corporations who you intend to work for after your country club stint at government."

". . . to approve SEC Proposed Rule #34–48626. This rule may not go quite as far as we might like it to go, requiring as it does that special conditions must occur before shareholders can nominate directors, but it is certainly a step in the right direction."

". . . The current proposal is better than nothing, but still far short of what is needed to clean up corporate governance abuses and restore investor confidence in the system."

"This proposal doesn't go nearly far enough to restore shareholder power, but it is a good first start."

EXHIBIT 6.8 Comments Opposing the Proposed Rule

Dear Mr. Katz:

I am a _____ of _____, as well as of two other public companies. I appreciate this opportunity to provide comments to the proposal of the Securities and Exchange Commission to require companies to include shareholder nominees for director in company proxy materials under certain circumstances.

*I **oppose** the proposal because I believe it is both bad for business and unnecessary. I conclude that for the following reasons.*

- *The recent corporate governance reforms initiated by the stock exchanges and the SEC will make boards of directors more independent and accountable. With the increased independence of boards of directors, the strengthened role and independence of nominating committees and the enhancement of shareholder-director communications, I believe that the issues that led to calls for reform have been addressed. The SEC should allow time for these reforms to work before deciding whether it needs to impose additional, unproven and onerous requirements on public companies. A contested election is not necessarily the best way to select qualified board members. An independent nominating committee is best suited to select qualified directors with the mix of skills and experience needed to oversee a public company.*

- *Shareholder nominees will inevitably represent the special interest agendas of the shareholders that nominated them rather than the interests of all shareholders as required under state law. Even though the nominee cannot be affiliated with the nominating shareholder, it is highly likely that the nominee would still be a special interest candidate. Moreover, there is no mechanism in the proposal that would provide for the removal of these directors if they are not acting in the best interest of all shareholders.*

- *Even companies that are performing well could face frequent contested elections. Annual election contests will be distracting and costly and could dissuade qualified individuals from serving as corporate directors.*

- *A proposal of this magnitude raises many issues and questions, and enactment could produce unintended consequences. The risks are far greater than the intended reward.*

- *If the SEC is going to adopt this proposal, companies should have a reasonable amount of time to anticipate and prepare for actions and events that may ultimately qualify as a triggering event for shareholder nominations. Many companies will have held their annual meeting in 2004, or will be well into the preparations for their annual meeting, before this proposal may be adopted, yet may be subject to the proposal and whatever changes are made to it prior to adoption. Therefore, shareholder action or voting results during the 2004 proxy season should not qualify as triggering events for shareholder nominations. In addition, there will be tremendous shareholder and company confusion with disclosures in 2004 proxy statements that attempt to provide information about a shareholder access process that has not been finalized.*

Thank you for considering these concerns about the proposed rules.

continued

Dear Mr. Katz:

I am on the Board of Directors of _____ publicly held corporations which would be impacted by the Commission's proposed shareholder access rules. I appreciate this opportunity to express my concerns with these proposed rules.

I understand the Commission's concern that the Boards and management of some U.S. corporations reportedly have not been very responsive to the views of their shareholders. However, for reasons described below, I believe that the proposed shareholder access rules miss the mark, could do considerably more harm than good and may, as a minimum, be premature.

Disruption of Director Elections. Once triggered, the proposed shareholder access requirements would be very disruptive and costly. They would permit shareholders to run an election contest through the company's own proxy statement. The resulting expense is sure to be substantial. Because of the importance of director elections, election contests always entail considerable management time and company resources. Another concern is that election contests would make it even more difficult to attract well-qualified director candidates—a task that is already challenging due to the recent wide-ranging corporate governance reforms and increased fear of personal liability. This outcome would directly contravene the intent of the newly approved NYSE listing standards and the spirit of sound corporate governance.

****

Premature and Perhaps Unnecessary Rule-Making. Since the Commission and the major stock exchanges have only recently completed a series of far-reaching corporate governance reforms (which I fully support), it would be sensible to allow time to observe how these reforms are working before adopting further changes. For example, we have not yet seen, for even one proxy season, how entirely independent Nominating Committees will perform and whether any improvements are required. Because the proposed shareholder access rules would carry significant risks and costs, both economic and non-economic, as outlined above, the Commission should be satisfied that they really are necessary and, if so, are well designed to address the problems remaining after the recent reforms. I suggest that it is too early to tell.

I appreciate the opportunity to offer my comments and express my concerns to the Commission. If you would like to discuss with me any of these issues or others, please contact me by telephone at _____.

CONSIDER...　　　　　　　　　　　　　　　　　6.1

This chapter's opening Consider described the EEOC's proposed guidelines on religious harassment in the workplace and the business concerns about those guidelines.

The U.S. Senate passed a resolution 94–0 urging the EEOC to drop the guidelines. The general public became actively involved in the rulemaking. Religious and business groups flooded the EEOC with more than 100,000 letters of protest.

Attorneys who examined the proposed rules issued opinions for their business clients that concluded the only way to avoid religious harassment lawsuits by employees or customers under the proposed rules was to ban all religious expression in the workplace, including the wearing or display of a yarmulke or a cross. The attorneys further concluded that banning such personal expression, a form of speech, would result in a flood of First Amendment suits.

The EEOC withdrew the proposed rules. EEOC spokesman Mike Widomski explained that "the public outcry and the number of comments that were received" triggered the reversal.

Public comments and input have an impact in the regulatory process. Is this a reasonable process? How do you feel about this particular rulemaking situation? Do you believe allowing comments is a fair process?

BUSINESS STRATEGY APPLICATION

On the book's Web site, the exercise for this chapter walks you through the rulemaking process for a rule on telemarketing calls that went into effect on October 1, 2003.

One of the important distinctions between the legislative process and the regulatory rulemaking process is the nature of the role of those involved. Legislators, such as representatives and senators, can accept campaign contributions and meals from lobbyists. However, those who work in administrative agencies fulfill both a rulemaking and enforcement role and cannot accept such gifts. Case 6.1 and the related Biography feature later in this chapter illustrate what can happen when businesses and regulators cross the fine line on influence. *U.S. v. Sun-Diamond Growers of California* (Case 6.1) is a criminal prosecution for alleged bribery of officials in order to persuade them to abandon or change proposed regulations before the agency.

CASE 6.1

U.S. v. Sun-Diamond Growers of California
526 U.S. 398 (1999)

Gratitude Can't Be in Cash or Kind

FACTS

Sun-Diamond Growers (Respondent) is a trade association that engaged in marketing and lobbying activities on behalf of its member cooperatives, which were owned by approximately 5,000 individual growers of raisins, figs, walnuts, prunes, and hazelnuts. The United States (Petitioner) is represented by Independent Counsel Donald Smaltz, who, as a consequence of his investigation of former Secretary of Agriculture Michael Espy (see p. 229), charged Sun-Diamond with making illegal gifts to Mr. Espy in violation of § 201(c)(1)(A). That statute provides, in relevant part, that anyone who

otherwise than as provided by law for the proper discharge of official duty . . . directly or indirectly gives, offers, or promises anything of value to any public official, former public official, or person selected to be a public official, for or because of any official act performed or to be performed by such public official, former public official, or person selected to be a public official . . . shall be fined under this title or imprisoned for not more than two years, or both.

Count One of the indictment charged Sun-Diamond with giving Mr. Espy approximately $5,900 in illegal gratuities: tickets to the 1993 U.S. Open Tennis Tournament (worth $2,295), luggage ($2,427), meals ($665), and a framed print and crystal bowl ($524). The indictment alluded to two matters in which Sun-Diamond had an interest in favorable treatment from the Secretary at the time it bestowed the gratuities. First, Sun-Diamond's member cooperatives participated in the Market Promotion Plan (MPP), a grant program administered by the Department of Agriculture to promote the sale of U.S. farm commodities in foreign countries.

Second, Sun-Diamond had an interest in the federal government's regulation of methyl bromide, a low-cost pesticide used by many individual growers. In 1992, the Environmental Protection Agency announced plans to promulgate a rule to phase out the use of methyl bromide in the United States. The jury convicted Sun-Diamond, and the District Court sentenced the respondent on this count to pay a fine of

continued

$400,000. The Court of Appeals reversed the conviction on Count One and remanded for a new trial, stating:

> Given that the "for or because of any official act" language in § 201(c)(1)(A) means what it says, the jury instructions invited the jury to convict on materially less evidence than the statute demands—evidence of gifts driven simply by Espy's official position.

The Supreme Court granted *certiorari*.

JUDICIAL OPINION

SCALIA, Justice

Talmudic sages believed that judges who accepted bribes would be punished by eventually losing all knowledge of the divine law. The Federal Government, dealing with many public officials who are not judges, and with at least some judges for whom this sanction holds no terror, has constructed a framework of human laws and regulations defining various sorts of impermissible gifts, and punishing those who give or receive them with administrative sanctions, fines, and incarceration. One element of that framework is 18 U.S.C. § 201(c)(1)(A), the "illegal gratuity statute," which prohibits giving "anything of value" to a present, past, or future public official "for or because of any official act performed or to be performed by such public official." In this case, we consider whether conviction under the illegal gratuity statute requires any showing beyond the fact that a gratuity was given because of the recipient's official position.

The first crime, described in § 201(b)(1) as to the giver, and § 201(b)(2) as to the recipient, is bribery, which requires a showing that something of value was corruptly given, offered, or promised to a public official (as to the giver) or corruptly demanded, sought, received, accepted, or agreed to be received or accepted by a public official (as to the recipient) with intent, inter alia, "to influence any official act" (giver) or in return for "being influenced in the performance of any official act" (recipient). The second crime, defined in § 201(c)(1)(A) as to the giver, and § 201(c)(1)(B) as to the recipient, is illegal gratuity, which requires a showing that something of value was given, offered, or promised to a public official (as to the giver), or demanded, sought, received, accepted, or agreed to be received or accepted by a public official (as to the recipient), "for or because of any official act performed or to be performed by such public official."

The distinguishing feature of each crime is its intent element. Bribery requires intent "to influence" an official act or "to be influenced" in an official act, while illegal gratuity requires only that the gratuity be given or accepted "for or because of" an official act. In other words, for bribery there must be a *quid pro quo*—a specific intent to give or receive something of value in exchange for an official act. An illegal gratuity, on the other hand, may constitute merely a reward for some future act that the public official will take (and may already have determined to take), or for a past act that he has already taken. The punishments prescribed for the two offenses reflect their relative seriousness: Bribery may be punished by up to 15 years' imprisonment, a fine of $250,000 ($500,000 for organizations) or triple the value of the bribe, whichever is greater, and disqualification from holding government office. Violation of the illegal gratuity statute, on the other hand, may be punished by up to two years' imprisonment and a fine of $250,000 ($500,000 for organizations).

The District Court's instructions in this case, in differentiating between a bribe and an illegal gratuity, correctly noted that only a bribe requires proof of a *quid pro quo*. The point in controversy here is that the instructions went on to suggest that § 201(c)(1)(A), unlike the bribery statute, did not require any connection between respondent's intent and a specific official act. It would be satisfied, according to the instructions, merely by a showing that respondent gave Secretary Espy a gratuity because of his official position—perhaps, for example, to build a reservoir of goodwill that might ultimately affect one or more of a multitude of unspecified acts, now and in the future.

In our view, this interpretation does not fit comfortably with the statutory text, which prohibits only gratuities given or received "for or because of any official act performed or to be performed." It seems to us that this means "for or because of some particular official act of whatever identity"—just as the question "Do you like any composer?" normally means "Do you like some particular composer?" It is linguistically possible, of course, for the phrase to mean "for or because of official acts in general, without specification as to which one"—just as the question "Do you like any composer?" could mean "Do you like all composers, no matter what their names or music?" But the former seems to us the more natural meaning, especially given the complex structure of the provision before us here. Why go through the trouble of requiring that the gift be made "for or because of any official act performed or to be performed by such public official," and then defining "official act" (in § 201(a)(3)) to mean "any decision or action on any question, matter, cause, suit, proceeding or controversy, which may at any time be pending, or which may by law be brought before any public official, in such official's official capacity," when, if the Government's interpretation were correct, it would have sufficed to say "for or because of such official's ability to favor the donor in executing the functions of his office"? The insistence upon an "official act," carefully defined, seems pregnant with the requirement that some particular official act be identified and proved.

Besides thinking that this is the more natural meaning of § 201(c)(1)(A), we are inclined to believe it correct because of the peculiar results that the Government's alternative reading would produce. It would criminalize, for example, token gifts to the President based on his official position and not linked to any identifiable act—such as the replica jerseys given by championship sports teams each year during ceremonial White House visits. Similarly, it would criminalize a high school principal's gift of a school baseball cap to the Secretary of Education, by reason of his office, on the occasion of the latter's visit to the school. That these examples are not fanciful is demonstrated by the fact that counsel for the United States maintained at oral argument that a group of farmers would violate § 201(c)(1)(A) by providing a complimentary lunch for the Secretary of Agriculture in conjunction with his speech to the farmers concerning various matters of USDA policy—so long as the Secretary had before him, or had in prospect, matters affecting the farmers. Of course the Secretary of Agriculture always has before him or in prospect matters that affect farmers, just as the President always has before him or in prospect matters that affect college and professional sports, and the Secretary of Education matters that affect high schools.

And the criminal statutes are merely the tip of the regulatory iceberg. In 5 U.S.C. § 7353, which announces broadly that no "employee of the executive, legislative, or judicial branch shall solicit or accept anything of value from a person . . . whose interests may be substantially affected by the performance or nonperformance of the individual's official duties," Congress has authorized the promulgation of ethical rules for each branch of the Federal Government. Pursuant to that provision, each branch of Government regulates its employees' acceptance of gratuities in some fashion.

All of the regulations, and some of the statutes, contain exceptions for various kinds of gratuities given by various donors for various purposes. Many of those exceptions would be snares for the unwary, given that there are no exceptions to the broad prohibition that the Government claims is imposed by § 201(c)(1). In

this regard it is interesting to consider the provisions of 5 CFR § 2635.202 (1999), issued by the Office of Government Ethics (OGE) and binding on all employees of the Executive Branch and independent agencies. The first subsection of that provision, entitled "General prohibitions," makes unlawful approximately (if not precisely) what the Government asserts § 201(c)(1)(B) makes unlawful: acceptance of a gift "[f]rom a prohibited source" (defined to include any person who "[h]as interests that may be substantially affected by performance or nonperformance of the employee's official duties," 5 CFR § 2635.203(d)(4) (1999)) or "[g]iven because of the employee's official position," § 2635.202(a)(2). We are unaware of any law empowering OGE to decriminalize acts prohibited by Title 18 of the United States Code. Yet it is clear that many gifts "accepted under the standards set forth in [the relevant] subpart" will violate 18 U.S.C. § 201(c)(1)(B) if the interpretation that the Government urges upon us is accepted.

More important for present purposes, however, this regulation, and the numerous other regulations and statutes littering this field, demonstrate that this is an area where precisely targeted prohibitions are commonplace, and where more general prohibitions have been qualified by numerous exceptions. Given that reality, a statute in this field that can linguistically be interpreted to be either a meat axe or a scalpel should reasonably be taken to be the latter. Absent a text that clearly requires it, we ought not expand this one piece of the regulatory puzzle so dramatically as to make many other pieces misfits.

We hold that, in order to establish a violation of 18 U.S.C. § 201(c)(1)(A), the Government must prove a link between a thing of value conferred upon a public official and a specific "official act" for or because of which it was given. We affirm the judgment of the Court of Appeals, which remanded the case to the District Court for a new trial on Count One.

Reversed and remanded.

CASE QUESTIONS

1. What violation is alleged?
2. Are administrative agency employees permitted to accept gifts from those affected by their regulations and policies?
3. What is required for proof of criminal wrongdoing in making a gift?
4. What happens with the conviction?

ETHICAL ISSUES

Three Chippewa Indian tribes submitted applications to the U.S. Department of the Interior seeking approval to convert a greyhound racing facility in Hudson, Wisconsin, to an off-reservation casino.

On June 8, 1995, the Indian Gaming staff in the department issued a draft report recommending approval of the Chippewa application.

While final decision on the application was pending in the agency, Harold Ickes (then White House Deputy Chief of Staff for Policy and Political Affairs) received a letter from Patrick O'Connor, a lobbyist for tribes that opposed the Chippewa application. The O'Connor letter explained the significance of the Chippewa decision, that the opposition tribes were important contributors to the Democratic Party, and that the Chippewa tribes were Republican supporters. In addition, Donald Fowler, the Democratic National Committee chairman, met with Mr. Ickes and "discussed the basis for the opposition to creating another gaming casino." Further, there were faxes regarding the application between White House staff and Department of the Interior staff.

On June 27, 1995, the Chippewa application was denied. The decision cited "community opposition" but did not incorporate or discuss the lengthy and detailed reports the staff had prepared for its June 8 recommendation of approval.

Interior Secretary Bruce Babbitt told Paul Eckstein, a lawyer for the Chippewas and a lifetime friend of Mr. Babbitt, that Mr. Ickes required him to issue the decision on June 27.

What ethical issues arise when political activities cross into administrative proceedings? How would the Chippewas perceive this series of events?

MAKING ETHICS PERSONAL

Getting Free Stuff For Doing Your Job

You work in a city office that handles the scheduling for construction inspections. Often, builders and contractors are in time crunches and want to move city inspections along as quickly as possible. You have never been offered cash, but builders and contractors, when calling in to get their projects inspected, have offered you the following:

- Tickets for a home game for your local NFL team
- Free movie tickets
- Free dinners
- Free lunches
- Free windshield replacement
- A set of luggage
- Two flights to Las Vegas
- A weekend at a local spa and resort
- A 10 percent discount on the purchase of a new home

Which would you accept? Why or why not? Are there distinctions among the gifts?

Deciding What to Do with the Proposed Regulation   After the comment period is over, the agency has three choices about what to do with the proposed rules. The first choice is simply to adopt the rules. The second choice is to modify the proposed rules and go through the process of public comment again. If the modification is minor, however, the APA allows the agency to adopt a modified version of the rule without going through the public comment period again. The final choice of the proposing agency is to withdraw the rule. Some rules have so many comments pointing out their impracticability, inflexibility, or prematurity that they are withdrawn from the promulgation process. For example, the Federal Trade Commission withdrew its proposed rules on regulating advertisements during children's programming hours because of strong industry opposition, the existence of a private industry code already controlling the area, and complicated legal issues involved in the regulation of commercial speech. Subsequently, modified rules were proposed and adopted.

Court and Legislative Challenges to Proposed Rules   Those parties who made comments on the rules during their proposal stage can challenge the validity of the rules in court. An administrative rule can be challenged on several different grounds.

The first ground on which to challenge an agency rule is that it is arbitrary, capricious, an abuse of discretion, or in violation of some other law. This standard is generally applied to informal rulemaking and simply requires the agency to show that there is evidence to support the proposed rule. Without such evidence, the rule can be held to be **arbitrary and capricious**. *Motor Vehicles Manufacturers Ass'n.* v. *State Farm Mutual Insurance Co.* (Case 6.2) addresses the issue of whether an agency's action is arbitrary and capricious.

CASE 6.2

Motor Vehicles Manufacturers Ass'n. v. *State Farm Mutual Insurance Co.*
463 U.S. 29 (1983)

Fasten Your Seatbelts: Rulemaking Is a Rough Ride

FACTS

The Department of Transportation (DOT), charged with the enforcement of the National Traffic and Motor Vehicle Safety Act of 1966 and the task of reducing auto accidents, passed Standard 208 in 1967. Standard 208 is the seatbelt requirement for motor vehicles, and its original form simply required that all cars be equipped with seatbelts. It soon became clear to the DOT that people did not use the belts, so the department began a study of passive restraint systems, which do not require any action on the part of the occupant other than operating the vehicle. The two types considered were automatic seatbelts and airbags. Studies showed that these devices could prevent approximately 12,000 deaths a year and over 100,000 serious injuries.

In 1972, after many hearings and comments, the Department of Transportation passed a regulation requiring some type of passive restraint system on all vehicles manufactured after 1975. The regulation allowed an ignition interlock system, which requires car occupants to have their seatbelts fastened before a car could be started. Congress, however, revoked the requirement of the ignition interlock.

Because of changes in directors of the DOT and the unfavorable economic climate in the auto industry, the requirements for passive restraints were postponed. In 1981, the department proposed a rescission of the passive restraint rule. After receiving written comments and holding public hearings, the agency concluded there was no longer a basis for reliably predicting that passive restraints increased safety levels or decreased accidents. Further, the agency found it would cost $1 billion to implement the rule, and they were unwilling to impose such substantial costs on auto manufacturers.

State Farm filed suit on the rescission of the rule on the basis that it was arbitrary and capricious. The court of appeals held that the rescission was, in fact, arbitrary and capricious. Auto manufacturers appealed.

JUDICIAL OPINION

WHITE, Justice

The ultimate question before us is whether NHTSA's [National Highway Traffic Safety Administration] rescission of the passive restraint requirement of Standard 208 was arbitrary and capricious. We conclude, as did the Court of Appeals, that it was.

The first and most obvious reason for finding the rescission arbitrary and capricious is that NHTSA apparently gave no consideration whatever to modifying the Standard to require that airbag technology be utilized. Standard 208 sought to achieve automatic crash protection by requiring automobile manufacturers to install either of two passive restraint devices: airbags or automatic seatbelts. There was no suggestion in the long rulemaking process that led to Standard 208 that if only one of these options were feasible, no passive restraint standard should be promulgated. Indeed, the agency's original proposed standard contemplated the installation of inflatable restraints in all cars. Automatic belts were added as a means of complying with the standard because they were believed to be as effective as airbags in achieving the goal of occupant crash protection.

The agency has now determined that the detachable automatic belts will not attain anticipated safety benefits because so many individuals will detach the mechanism. Even if this conclusion were acceptable in its entirety, standing alone it would not justify any more than an amendment of Standard 208 to disallow compliance by means of the only technology which will not provide effective passenger protection. It does not cast doubt on the need for a passive restraint standard or upon the efficacy of airbag technology. In its most recent rulemaking, the agency again acknowledged the life-saving potential of the airbag.

continued

Given the effectiveness ascribed to airbag technology by the agency, the mandate of the Safety Act to achieve traffic safety would suggest that the logical response to the faults of detachable seatbelts would be to require the installation of airbags. At the very least this alternative way of achieving objectives of the Act should have been addressed and adequate reasons given for its abandonment. But the agency not only did not require compliance through airbags, it did not even consider the possibility in its 1981 rulemaking. Not one sentence of its rulemaking statement discusses the airbags-only option. We have frequently reiterated that an agency must cogently explain why it had exercised its discretion in a given manner.

For nearly a decade, the automobile industry waged the regulatory equivalent of war against the airbag and lost—the inflatable restraint was proven sufficiently effective. Now the automobile industry has decided to employ a seatbelt system which will not meet the safety objectives of Standard 208. This hardly constitutes cause to revoke the standard itself. Indeed the Motor Vehicle Safety Act was necessary because the industry was not sufficiently responsive to safety concerns. The Act intended that safety standards not depend on current technology and would be "technology-forcing" in the sense of inducing the development of superior safety design.

It is not infrequent that the available data does not settle a regulatory issue and the agency must then exercise its judgment in moving from the facts and probabilities on the record to a policy conclusion. Recognizing that policy making in a complex society must account for uncertainty, however, does not imply that it is sufficient for an agency to merely recite the terms "substantial uncertainty" as a justification for its actions. The agency must explain the evidence which is available, and must offer a "rational connection between the facts found and the choice made."

In this case, the agency's explanation for rescission of the passive restraint requirement is not sufficient to enable us to conclude that the rescission was the product of reasoned decision making. We start with the accepted ground that if used, seatbelts unquestionably would save many thousands of lives and would prevent tens of thousands of crippling injuries. Unlike recent regulations we have reviewed, the safety benefits of wearing seatbelts are not in doubt and it is not challenged that were those benefits to accrue, the monetary costs of implementing the standard would be easily justified.

Since 20 to 50 percent of motorists currently wear seatbelts on some occasions, there would seem to be grounds to believe that seatbelt use by occasional users will be substantially increased by the detachable passive belts. Whether this is the case is a matter for the agency to decide, but it must bring its expertise to bear on the question.

An agency's view of what is in the public interest may change, either with or without a change in circumstances. But an agency changing its course must supply a reasoned analysis. We do not accept all of the reasoning of the Court of Appeals but we do conclude that the agency has failed to supply the requisite "reasoned analysis" in this case. Accordingly, we remand the matter to the NHTSA for further consideration consistent with this opinion.

CASE QUESTIONS

1. What regulation is at issue in the case?
2. When was the regulation first adopted?
3. What changes has the regulation undergone over the years?
4. What was done with the regulation to result in this judicial decision?
5. Who challenged the agency's actions, and what were the reasons for this challenge?
6. Is the agency's action valid?

FOR THE MANAGER'S DESK

RE: THE AIRBAG ISSUE THAT DOES NOT GO AWAY

The issue of passive restraints in vehicles and the Department of Transportation (DOT)'s rejection of them resurfaced in 1996. Following the *State Farm* case, passive restraint systems, including airbags, were mandated in passenger vehicles. However, in 1996, evidence of a problem—noted by General Motors in a 1979 comment to DOT and in DOT studies in 1981—emerged: Children were killed in auto accidents when the airbags in the vehicles in which they were riding deployed.

Engineers discovered that the force of an inflating bag (up to 200 mph) was sufficient to snap a child's neck or deform a child's head. In several of the accidents, children were decapitated by the inflated bags. Children involved in the accidents were properly restrained in their seatbelts or carseats. The cause of the fifty injuries or deaths involving children between 1991 and 1996 was the passenger-side airbag.

continued

Over a six-month period, the National Highway Traffic Safety Administration (NHTSA) studied the issue and considered the following options:

1. Elimination of airbags
2. Installation of switches to turn off passenger-side airbags
3. Warnings in vehicles on the dangers of passenger-side airbags
4. Recommendation that all children ride in the back seat of vehicles

Insurers and auto manufacturers opposed elimination of airbags and switches for fear of liability and misuse of switches. Consumers favored switches. NHTSA, following input, required warnings in all vehicles about airbags but did not require switches. The warning labels (three in all new cars beginning in February 1998) must be posted on the dashboard as well as on each side of the car visor. The dashboard label reads as follows:

WARNING

Children may be KILLED or INJURED by Passenger Airbag

The back seat is the safest place for children 12 and under.

Make sure all children use seat belts or child seats.

NHTSA will continue to study cut-off switches and will allow vehicle owners, by petition, to have airbags disconnected.

In September 1998 the DOT began a rulemaking process for modifying airbag requirements. Under the proposed rules, airbags must pass safety tests using all sizes of crash dummies. The current rule requires only the use of adult-size dummies. Also under review are side airbags and their effect on child passengers.

The first lawsuits for the airbag deaths of children have begun going to trial. A court in New York awarded a family $750,000 for the death of their 5-year-old son when the airbag deployed on the passenger side in the family's 1995 Dodge Caravan. The child was not wearing a seatbelt when the van was hit going 9–11 mph. Daimler Chrysler is appealing the verdict.

The airbag continues to be a lightning rod for discussion and controversy. One of the key researchers who testified of the need for airbags over twenty years ago recently testified that he was wrong and that passenger-side airbags don't save enough lives to justify their risk and expense. John Graham, the director of Harvard's Center for Risk Analysis, announced his change of heart at a National Transportation Safety Board hearing.

Side airbags have also been subject to safety questions because of their potential harm to children riding in back seats of cars. With the safety warnings against having children ride in the front passenger seat, their only place is in the back seat, and side airbags now appear to be a safety threat there.

The jury verdicts continue in cases involving children, with some of the latest cases presenting testimony that the children would have lived had the airbags not deployed.

In 2000, Congress directed the DOT to develop guidelines for airbags that would satisfy the safety requirements but would not result in injury to smaller occupants in cars. The NHTSA published a final rule in December 2001, but several consumer groups challenged the final rule as creating additional safety problems for vehicle occupants and being promulgated in defiance of existing evidence and studies, making the rules "arbitrary and capricious." The NHTSA continued with the rule, and the consumer groups took the agency to court in the Ninth Circuit, challenging the rules for being arbitrary and capricious. The Ninth Circuit heard the case but concluded that it did not have jurisdiction over the administrative law matter. The case was transferred and will be heard in the DC court of appeals. [*Public Citizen, Inc.* v. *Mineta*, 343 F.3d 1159 (9th Cir. 2003).]

BUSINESS STRATEGY

Why Insurers Pursue Federal Safety Regulations

In the *State Farm* case, it is an insurer, not an auto manufacturer, who is challenging the proposed regulation (or lack thereof). Certainly the insurer does not carry the responsibility of implementing the safety designs or perfecting the technology. However, because the implementation of such safety features helps reduce claims for accident injuries and damages, the insurer has

© PHOTODISC/GETTY IMAGES

a business interest in seeing that the regulations are passed. Very often, businesses, like the insurers here, must become involved in regulatory proceedings for rules that might not regulate them directly but will benefit or cost them indirectly. In regulatory proceedings, businesses that will experience indirect impact often take a position and use the process to their business benefit.

C O N S I D E R . . .   6 . 2

The use of snowmobiles in Yellowstone and Grand Teton National Parks was first permitted in 1963, and their use has been a topic of ongoing concern because of their impact on park resources. The National Park Service (NPS), part of the Department of the Interior, has been grooming snow-covered roads to allow for safe passage by snowmobiles for the past three decades. Snowmobile use has increased dramatically. In 2003, over 180 miles of park roads are groomed at least every other night, and historical use demonstrates that as many as 1,700 snowmobiles enter the parks on peak days.

Inevitably, a conflict arose between the NPS's mandate to protect park resources and the accommodation of visitors' desires to view the parks via snowmobiles during the winter season. Of particular concern were the effects of trail grooming and snowmobiling on the parks' wildlife, especially bison. During the winter of 1996–97, park officials documented that large numbers of bison left the parks, some traveling along the manmade groomed trails created to facilitate snowmobile use. As a consequence of this migration, over 1,000 bison had to be killed to prevent the spread of brucellosis to livestock in areas outside of the parks.

The Fund for Animals and other environmental groups objected to the snowmobile use, and in December 2000, the NPS issued a proposed rule that capped snowmobile use in the winters of 2001–02 and 2002–03 and completely eliminated snowmobile use by the 2003–04 winter season. The NPS received 5,273 comments during the thirty-day public comment period; over 4,300 of these comments supported the proposed phase-out rule. On January 22, 2001, the NPS published the final rule ("Snowcoach Rule" or "2001 Rule"), which allowed snowmobile use to continue in 2001–02 but mandated significant reductions in snowmobile use in 2002–03 and a complete elimination of snowmobile use, in favor of snowcoach ("snowcoach" is the NPS term intended to include all forms of mechanized snow vehicles, including snowmobiles) use, by the 2003–04 winter season. Neither the proposed rule nor the final rule made any changes in the groomed trail system, thus allowing trail grooming to continue unabated.

The 2001 Rule, promulgated by the Clinton administration, was published the day after President George W. Bush took office and was immediately stayed pending a review by the new administration. Meanwhile, the International Snowmobiler Manufacturers Association filed suit, challenging the 2001 Rule as an unsupported decision to ban snowmobiling. The lawsuit called for the NPS to set aside the rules. The NPS settled the litigation and agreed to consider data on new snowmobile technologies.

Pursuant to the settlement, in March 2002, the NPS issued another proposed rule. NPS received over 350,000 pieces of correspondence from the public; over 80 percent of the public comments supported the phase-out of snowmobiles. Despite this opposition, on November 18, 2002, one month before the phase-out was scheduled to go into effect, the NPS released a final rule delaying the implementation of the phase-out for an additional year. Snowmobile use was allowed to continue unabated during the 2002–03 winter season.

The Fund for Animals filed suit, challenging the postponement as arbitrary and capricious.

THINK: The decision in the *State Farm* case was that pending rules could not be revoked unless an agency followed the same types of processes used for promulgating rules. That process requires public disclosure of the intent to revoke the rule and a public comment period.

APPLY: In this case study, the Department of the Interior has proposed postponing the implementation of a regulation on snowmobiling. While the action taken by the agency is slightly different, a revocation versus a postponement, the agencies in both cases are doing so without notice or comment and without input from those affected.

ANSWER: The NPS cannot simply withdraw a rule. It must consider evidence, propose the withdrawal or postponement, and take comments. An agency cannot reverse a process unilaterally midstream. [*The Fund for Animals* v. *Norton*, 294 F.Supp.2d 92 (D.C. 2003) (memorandum opinion).]

A second theory for challenging an agency's regulation is that the regulation is unsupported by substantial evidence. This **substantial evidence test** is applied in the review of formal and hybrid rulemaking. Where the arbitrary and capricious standard simply requires some proof or basis for the regulation, substantial evidence requires that more convincing evidence exist in support of the regulation than against it. *Corn Products Co. and Derby Foods, Inc.* v. *Department of Health, Education, & Welfare and Food and Drug Administration* (Case 6.3) involves a business challenge to an administrative regulation based on the issue of whether substantial evidence was presented.

CASE 6.3

Corn Products Co. and Derby Foods, Inc. v. *Department of Health, Education, & Welfare and Food and Drug Administration*
427 F.2d 511 (3d Cir. 1970)

Skippy and Peter Pan Take On the FDA

FACTS

Corn Products Company (petitioner) manufactures peanut butter known as the Skippy brand and holds 22 percent of the peanut butter market. Derby (also a petitioner) holds 14 percent of the market with its product, Peter Pan.

Peanut butter originally was made of ground peanuts, salt, and sometimes sugar. This combination had the disadvantages of oil separation, short shelf life, and stickiness. These deficiencies have been diminished, if not eliminated, by the addition of stabilizing ingredients, mainly hydrogenated vegetable oils. Today, peanut butter is made of peanuts, an oil component, the stabilizer, and seasonings.

The Food and Drug Administration (FDA) adopted a regulation limiting the percentage (by weight) of optional ingredients that may be added to the peanut ingredients to 10 percent. The regulation allows for the addition or removal of peanut oil but limits the fat content to 55 percent.

Corn Products and Derby urged the adoption of a 13 percent standard as opposed to a 10 percent one and challenged the regulation as not being supported by substantial evidence.

JUDICIAL OPINION

STALEY, Circuit Judge

Using an affirmative approach to the order under consideration, the issue becomes whether the findings upon which the 90 percent standard is based are supported by substantial evidence. Corn Products' argument that the standard should have designated partially hydrogenated peanut oil as [a] peanut ingredient must be directed at those findings which equate them.

Skippy fails to comply with the standard because it contains 8½ percent of partially hydrogenated peanut oil and an amount of seasonings which together exceed the 10 percent limit on optional ingredients. No distinction is made in the standard between hydrogenated peanut oil and other hydrogenated vegetable oils.

Four expert witnesses, all chemists, testified to the dissimilarity between vegetable oil and hydrogenated oil. There was testimony that there is no nutritional variation between these oils. The basic function of the hydrogenated oil, to prevent oil separation in the product, is said to be served regardless of the source oil. The use of hydrogenated peanut oil does not add flavor to the product. From the foregoing, it is quite clear that there is substantial evidence to support a conclusion which makes no distinction between hydrogenated vegetable oils.

The standard reflects the practice of a number of manufacturers and to those not in compliance there will be no economic hardship in complying. The fact of exclusion of the leading producers does not make the regulation unreasonable. Skippy and Peter Pan will not be banned; merely a change in product formula will be required.

CASE QUESTIONS

1. What standard did the FDA pass for peanut butter?
2. Why didn't Corn Products and Derby meet the standard?
3. What arguments do they make in appealing the regulation?
4. Does it matter that the regulation excluded their substantial shares of the market?
5. Was there substantial evidence to support the rule changes?

A third ground on which to challenge an agency's regulation involves the rule that a regulation can be set aside if the agency did not comply with the APA requirements of notice, publication, and public comment or input. The procedures for rulemaking must be followed in order for the regulatory process and resulting rules to be valid. Thus, an agency that seeks public comment for the purposes of drafting legislation cannot then turn the legislation into rules after the comment period. The notice must specify that promulgated rules will be the result of the proceedings. *San Diego Air Sports Center, Inc.* v. *Federal Aviation Administration* (Case 6.4) addresses an agency's attempt to change a rule without following the APA requirements.

CASE 6.4

San Diego Air Sports Center, Inc. v. *Federal Aviation Administration*
887 F.2d 966 (9th Cir. 1989)

Are Parachutes Air Traffic?

FACTS

San Diego Air Sports Center (SDAS) operates a sports parachuting business in Otay Mesa, California. SDAS offers training to beginning parachutists and facilitates recreational jumping for experienced parachutists. It indicates that the majority of SDAS jumps occur at altitudes in excess of 5,800 feet.

The jump zone used by SDAS overlaps the San Diego Traffic Control Area (TCA). Although the aircraft carrying the parachutists normally operate outside the TCA, the parachutists themselves are dropped through it. Thus, each jump must be approved by the air traffic controllers.

In July 1987, an air traffic controller in San Diego filed an Unsatisfactory Condition Report complaining of the strain that parachuting was putting on the controllers and raising safety concerns. The report led to a staff study of parachute jumping within the San Diego TCA. In October 1987, representatives of the San Diego Terminal Radar Approach Control (TRACON) facility met with SDAS operators. In December 1987, the San Diego TRACON sent to SDAS a draft letter of agreement outlining agreed-upon procedures and coordination requirements. Nonetheless, the San Diego TRACON conducted another study between January 14, 1988, and February 11, 1988, and about two months after the draft letter was sent, the San Diego TRACON withdrew it.

SDAS states that the air traffic manager of the San Diego TRACON assured SDAS that it would be invited to attend all meetings on parachuting in the San Diego TCA. However, SDAS was not informed of or invited to any meetings.

In March 1988, the Federal Aviation Administration (FAA) sent a letter to SDAS informing SDAS that "[e]ffective immediately parachute jumping within or into the San Diego TCA in the Otay Reservoir Jump Zone will not be authorized." The FAA stated that the letter was final and appealable.

SDAS challenged the letter in federal court on grounds that it constituted rulemaking without compliance with required APA procedures.

JUDICIAL OPINION

BEEZER, Circuit Judge

The Federal Aviation Act requires that rules affecting the use of navigable airspace be issued in accordance with the Administrative Procedure Act (APA). 49 U.S.C. App. § 1348(d). The "principal purpose" of section 553 of the APA is "to provide that the legislative functions of administrative agencies shall so far as possible be exercised only upon public participation." Section 553 of the APA requires agencies to adhere to three steps when promulgating rules: Notice of the proposed rule, opportunity to comment, and an explanation of the rule ultimately adopted. 5 U.S.C. § (b),(c). These three requirements have been referred to as "the statutory *minima*" imposed by Congress.

Not every decision made by administrative agencies requires citizen participation. The APA lists four instances when the statutory *minima* do not apply: When the agency is promulgating (1) interpretive rules, (2) general statements of policy, or (3) rules of agency organization, procedure, or practice, or (4) when the requirement of notice and participation are impractical or contrary to public interest.

Congress was concerned that the exceptions to section 553, though necessary, might be used too broadly. The Senate noted that the courts have a "duty . . . to prevent avoidance of the requirements of the [Act] by any manner or form of indirection." We have stated that "[t]he exceptions to section 533 will be 'narrowly construed and only reluctantly countenanced.'"

The FAA letter does not come within either of the first two exceptions. The letter creates an immediate, substantive rule, i.e., that no parachuting will be allowed in the San Diego TCA.

The FAA argues that parachuting created an emergency to which it responded in the letter at issue. It is further argued that a response to an immediate emergency is covered by the fourth exception. This argument is not persuasive. The only accident known to the FAA occurred two years before it issued its letter. Furthermore, the FAA itself claims to have extensively studied the situation before issuing the letter. The FAA does not explain why public participation as required by the APA could not be included in its study.

Finally, the FAA argues that the letter is not a rule at all; rather, the FAA characterizes the letter as an order to which the requirements set forth in section 553 of the APA does [sic] not apply. We find this argument somewhat mystifying, as there are equally stringent participation requirements for orders. Furthermore, the FAA is wrong; the letter is a rule.

A time-honored principle of administrative law is that the label an agency puts on its actions "is not necessarily conclusive." Equally true, however, is the fact that agencies can issue rules through adjudication (the process by which orders are normally issued) and orders through rulemaking.

In this case no record was kept of the "process" that resulted in the FAA letter; we can only scrutinize the letter itself. The letter clearly promulgates a rule. It states that all parachuting by any party will be prohibited in the San Diego TCA from the time it is issued. This comports with this court's statement that "[s]ubstantive rules are those which effect a change in existing law or policy."

The Federal Aviation Act requires that rules affecting the use of navigable airspace be issued in accordance with the APA, 49 U.S.C.App. § 1348(d). In issuing this substantive rule, the FAA failed to do so. A substantive rule is invalid if the issuing agency fails to comply with the APA. Therefore, the petition for review is granted.

CASE QUESTIONS

1. What problem did the FAA have with SDAS?
2. How did the FAA attempt to control SDAS?
3. Was the letter an attempt to promulgate regulation?
4. Would the FAA letter shut down SDAS?
5. Was SDAS deprived of due process by the letter?

Another basis for challenging a regulation is that the regulation is unconstitutional. Many challenges based on constitutional grounds deal with regulations that give an agency authority to search records or that impose discriminatory requirements for licensing professionals. For example, a requirement of a minimum residency period before allowing an applicant to become licensed in a particular profession has been challenged successfully. Zoning board regulations that discriminate against certain classes or races as to the use of property have also been successfully challenged as unconstitutional. Further, broadcasters often depend on freedom of speech—the First Amendment—to challenge new Federal Communication Commission (FCC) regulations.

In *Rubin v. Coors Brewing Company* (Case 6.5), a business challenged a labeling rule on the grounds that its First Amendment rights were violated and that the agency was exceeding its authority.

Another theory for challenging a regulation in court is *ultra vires*, a Latin term meaning "beyond its powers." An *ultra vires* regulation is one that goes beyond the authority given to the agency in its enabling act. Although most agencies stay clearly within their authority, if an agency tries to change the substance and purpose of the enabling act through regulation, the regulations would be *ultra vires*. For example, the intent of the 1933 Securities Act was to provide full disclosure to investors about a securities sale. The SEC could not, on the basis of its authority, pass a rule that eliminated securities registration in favor of an unregulated securities market.

CASE 6.5

Rubin v. Coors Brewing Company
514 U.S. 476 (1995)

Rocky Mountain High: Alcohol Content on the Label

FACTS

Coors Brewing Company (respondent) brews beer. In 1987, it applied to the Bureau of Alcohol, Tobacco and Firearms (BATF) for approval of proposed labels and advertisements that disclosed the alcohol content of its beer. BATF refused to approve the disclosure under section 205(e)(2) of the Federal Alcohol Administration Act (FAAA), which prohibits the selling, shipping, or delivery of malt beverages, distilled spirits, or wines in bottles:

> unless such products are bottled, packaged, and labeled in conformity with such regulations, to be prescribed by the Secretary of the Treasury, with respect to packaging, marking, branding, and labeling and size and fill of container . . . as will provide the consumer with adequate information as to the identity and quality of the products, the alcoholic content thereof (except that statements of, or statements likely to be considered as statements of, alcoholic content of malt beverages are prohibited unless required by State law and except that, in case of wines, statements of alcoholic content shall be required only for wines containing more than 14 per centum of alcohol by volume), the net contents of the package, and the manufacturer or bottler or importer of the product.

Regulations related to this statutory restriction [27 C.F.R. § 7.26(a)] prohibit the disclosure of alcohol content on beer labels.

In addition to prohibiting numerical indications of alcohol content, the labeling regulations proscribe descriptive terms that suggest high content, such as "strong," "full strength," "extra strength," "high test," "high proof," "pre-war strength," and "full oldtime alcoholic strength" [27 C.F.R. § 7.29(f)]. The prohibitions do not preclude labels from identifying a beer as "low alcohol," "reduced alcohol," "non-alcoholic," or "alcohol-free."

When BATF (a division of the Department of the Treasury, headed by, at the time of the case, Robert Rubin) refused to approve the labels, Coors filed suit in federal district court challenging the regulation as a violation of the First Amendment. BATF (the government) argued that the ban on alcohol content in labels was needed to prevent "strength wars" among brewers who would then compete in the marketplace on the potency of their beers.

The district court found for Coors, but the U.S. Court of Appeals for the Tenth Circuit reversed, finding that the government's interest in suppressing strength wars was substantial. It remanded the case to the trial court for determining whether the ban was an appropriate means of avoiding strength wars. The lower court found there was no evidence of any relationship between the disclosure on labels of alcohol content and competition on the basis of content. The court of appeals (on the second appeal) concluded that BATF's regulation violated the First Amendment. Secretary Rubin appealed.

JUDICIAL OPINION

THOMAS, Justice

Both the lower courts and the parties agree that respondent seeks to disclose only truthful, verifiable, and nonmisleading factual information about alcohol content on its beer labels. Thus, our analysis focuses on the substantiality of the interest behind § 205(e)(2) and on whether the labeling ban bears an acceptable fit with the Government's goal. A careful consideration of these factors indicates that § 205(e)(2) violates the First Amendment's protection of commercial speech.

According to the Government, the FAAA's restriction prevents a particular type of beer drinker—one who selects a beverage because of its high potency—from choosing beers solely for their alcohol content. In the Government's view, restricting disclosure of information regarding a particular product characteristic will decrease the extent to which consumers will select the product on the basis of that characteristic.

Respondent counters that Congress actually intended the FAAA to achieve the far different purpose of preventing brewers from making inaccurate claims concerning alcohol content. According to respondent, when Congress passed the FAAA in 1935, brewers did not have the technology to produce beer with alcohol levels within predictable tolerances—a skill that modern beer producers now possess. Further, respondent argues that the true policy guiding federal alcohol regulation is not aimed at suppressing strength wars. If such were the goal, the Government would not pursue the opposite policy with respect to wines and distilled spirits.

Rather than suppressing the free flow of factual information in the wine and spirits markets, the Government seeks to control competition on the basis of strength by monitoring distillers' promotions and marketing. The respondent quite correctly notes that the general thrust of federal alcohol policy appears to favor greater disclosure of information, rather than less. This also seems to be the trend in federal regulation of other consumer products as well. See, e.g., Nutrition Labeling and Education Act of 1990, Pub. L. 101–535, 104 Stat. 2353, as amended (requiring labels of food products sold in the United States to display nutritional information).

The Government carries the burden of showing that the challenged regulation advances the Government's interest "in a direct and material way." That burden "is not satisfied by mere speculation and conjecture; rather, a governmental body seeking to sustain a restriction on commercial speech must demonstrate that the harms it recites are real and that its restriction will in fact alleviate them to a material degree."

The Government attempts to meet its burden by pointing to current developments in the consumer market. It claims that beer producers are already competing and advertising on the basis of alcohol strength in the "malt liquor" segment of the beer market. The Government attempts to show that this competition threatens to spread to the rest of the market by directing our attention to respondent's motives in bringing this litigation. Respondent allegedly suffers from consumer misperceptions that its beers contain less alcohol than other brands. According to the Government, once respondent gains relief from § 205(e)(2), it will use its labels to overcome this handicap.

Under the Government's theory, § 205(e)(2) suppresses the threat of such competition by preventing consumers from choosing beers on the basis of alcohol content. It is assuredly a matter of "common sense," that a restriction on the advertising of a product characteristic will decrease the extent to which consumers select a product on the basis of that trait. In addition to common sense, the Government urges us to turn to history as a guide. According to the Government, at the time Congress enacted the FAAA, the use of labels displaying alcohol content had helped produce a strength war. Section 205(e)(2) allegedly relieved competitive pressures to market beer on the basis of alcohol content, resulting over the long term in beers with lower alcohol levels.

We conclude that § 205(e)(2) cannot directly and materially advance its asserted interest because of the overall irrationality of the Government's regulatory scheme. While the laws governing labeling prohibit the disclosure of alcohol content unless required by state law, federal regulations apply a contrary policy to beer advertising. The failure to prohibit the disclosure of alcohol content in advertising, which would seem to constitute a more influential weapon in any strength war than labels, makes no rational sense if the government's true aim is to suppress strength wars.

While we are mindful that respondent only appealed the constitutionality of § 205(e)(2), these exemptions and inconsistencies bring into question the purpose of the labeling ban. To be sure, the Government's interest in combating strength wars remains a valid goal. But the irrationality of this unique and puzzling regulatory framework ensures that the labeling ban will fail to achieve that end. There is little chance that § 205(e)(2) can directly and materially advance its aim, while other provisions of the same act directly undermine and counteract its effects.

The Government argues that a sufficient "fit" exists here because the labeling ban applies to only one product characteristic and because the ban does not prohibit all disclosures of alcohol content—it applies only to those involving labeling and advertising. In response, respondent suggests several alternatives, such as directly limiting the alcohol content of beers, prohibiting marketing efforts emphasizing high alcohol strength (which is apparently the policy in some other Western nations), or limiting the labeling ban only to malt liquors, which is the segment of the market that allegedly is threatened with a strength war. We agree that the availability of these options, all of which could advance the Government's asserted interest in a manner less intrusive to respondent's First Amendment rights, indicates that § 205(e)(2) is more extensive than necessary.

We affirm the decision of the court below.

CASE QUESTIONS

1. What inconsistencies exist in BATF's regulatory scheme?

2. To survive a First Amendment challenge, what must a regulation of commercial speech accomplish?

3. What market perception is Coors trying to correct with its labels?

4. In what ways could BATF accomplish its goals of preventing strength wars other than the § 205(e)(2) complete ban?

5. Did the label restrictions prevent strength wars?

6. What are general government trends with respect to disclosure?

C O N S I D E R . . .   6 . 3

The National Credit Union Administration (NCUA) is the federal agency responsible for the regulation of credit unions in the United States. Credits unions were authorized and created under a 1934 congressional enactment that limited membership to "groups having a common bond of occupation or association, or to groups with a well-defined neighborhood, community, or rural district" (12 U.S.C. § 1759).

AT&T Family Federal Credit Union has 110,000 members nationwide, only 35 percent of whom are employees of AT&T. Several banks have brought suit, challenging NCUA's approval of AT&T's ongoing credit union when membership exceeds statutory authority. Are the banks correct? Has NCUA exceeded its statutory authority? [*Nat. Credit Union Adm.* v. *First Nat. Bank & Trust*, 522 U.S. 479 (1998).]

Proactive Business Strategies in Regulation

Some administrative regulations can be eliminated through the use of legislation. In an enabling act called a **sunset law**, Congress creates an agency for a limited period of time during which the agency must establish its benefits and other justification for its continuation. The enabling act may provide for an audit to determine effectiveness after the agency has been in existence for two years. Without renewal by Congress, the sun sets on the agency and it is terminated. Some businesses lobby for the creation of sunset agencies to better control the number of agencies and their effectiveness.

Some agencies' power is controlled through congressional purse strings. With **zero-based budgeting** the agency does not automatically receive a budget amount but rather starts with a zero budget each year and then is required to justify all its needs for funds. This type of control gives Congress some say each year in how the agency is operating. For example, the budget could be renewed only on the condition that the agency not promulgate certain regulations opposed by Congress.

Another tool for curbing regulation that has been used in recent years has been action by the executive branch. For example, former President George H. W. Bush imposed a ninety-day moratorium on all new regulations in 1992. During this period, regulators were not permitted to promulgate new regulations. Additionally, the Negotiated Rulemaking Act of 1990 helps businesses work with regulators and permits agencies to develop new methods for resolving controversies outside of the traditional rulemaking process.

Informal Rulemaking

The process for informal rulemaking is the same as that for formal rulemaking with the exception that no public hearings are held on the rule. The only input from the public comes in the form of comments, using the same procedures discussed earlier.

BUSINESS RIGHTS IN AGENCY ENFORCEMENT ACTION

Administrative agencies not only make the rules; they enforce them. In so doing, the agencies are also responsible for adjudicating disputes over the scope or interpretation of the rules. Exhibit 6.9 is a chart of the steps involved in agency enforcement and adjudication.

EXHIBIT 6.9 Steps for Administrative Agency Enforcement and Adjudication

Licensing and Inspections

Much of an administrative agency's role enforcement is carried out by requiring the submission of certain types of paperwork. Many agencies issue licenses or permits as a way to enforce the law. For example, state administrative agencies may require building contractors to be licensed so that their dues can finance a recovery fund for the victims of bankrupt or negligent contractors. The Environmental Protection Agency (EPA) carries out its function of protecting the environment in part by requiring licenses or permits for the discharge of foreign substances into the air or water and by requiring advance approval for the construction of projects substantially affecting the environment (see Chapter 12 for more details). The idea behind the licensing and permit method of enforcement is to curtail illegal activity up front and also to have records in case problems arise.

Visit the Occupational Safety and Health Administration:
http://www.osha.gov

Agencies also have the authority to conduct inspections, such as when an agency responsible for restaurant licenses inspects restaurant facilities to check for health code violations. The Occupational Safety and Health Administration (OSHA) at the federal level has the authority to inspect plants to check for violations of OSHA standards. This power of inspection at unannounced times is an enforcement tool by itself. There is strong incentive to comply with regulations when an inspection could happen at any time. A business can refuse an inspection, but an agency can obtain a warrant and return for a mandatory inspection.

Prosecution of Businesses

Administrative agencies are also given the authority to prosecute violators. These agency prosecutions, however, are not traditional criminal prosecutions; the sanctions imposed for agency violations are not jail terms but rather fines, penalties, and injunctions that are civil penalties, not criminal ones. For example, in the case of false advertising—a violation of Federal Trade Commission (FTC) rules—the agency could impose restitution as a sanction: The violator would have to reimburse all those individuals who bought the product based on false advertising. In some cases, an agency may merely want a violator to stop certain conduct and promise not to engage in that type of conduct again.

Beginning Enforcement Steps

Regardless of the remedy an agency seeks, all action begins when the agency issues a **complaint** against the violating party. The complaint describes when and what the company did and why it is a violation.

Once a complaint is filed, an agency can negotiate with a party for an order or proceed to a hearing to obtain an order from an administrative law judge. The remedies in an order vary according to the type of violation and whether it is ongoing. The FTC could, and typically does, order companies running deceptive ads to stop using the ads and promise not to use them again in the future. These sanctions usually come in the form of an **injunction**, which is a court order that prohibits specifically described conduct. Many statutes are unclear about the extent of authority an agency is given in enforcement proceedings and what types of sanctions an agency can impose for violations. The authority to assess civil penalties, for example, varies from agency to agency.

Consent Decrees

Rather than go through a hearing and the expense of the administrative process, some companies agree to penalties proposed by an agency. They do so in a document called a **consent decree**, which is comparable to a *nolo contendere* plea in the criminal system. The party does not admit or deny a violation but simply negotiates a settlement with the administrative agency. The negotiated settlement includes the same types of sanctions the agency would have the power to impose if the case went to a hearing. The agency may be willing to give up a little in exchange for the violator's willingness to settle and save the agency the time and costs of full prosecution. The consent decree is a contract between the charged party and the regulatory agency. Exhibit 6.10 provides an example of an FTC consent decree.

Hearings

If the parties cannot reach an agreement through a consent decree, the question of violations and penalties will go to an administrative hearing, which is quite different from the litigation procedures described in Chapter 4. Here there is no jury. The plaintiff or prosecutor is the administrative agency, represented by one of its staff attorneys. The defendant is the person or company accused of violating an administrative regulation. The judge is called an **administrative law judge (ALJ)** at the federal level, and in some state-level agencies is called a **hearing examiner** or **hearing officer**. The defendant can be represented by an attorney.

An ALJ has all the powers of a judge. He or she conducts the hearing, rules on evidentiary and procedural questions, and administers oaths. The ALJ also has certain unique powers, such as the ability to hold settlement conferences between the parties. The ALJ also has the responsibility of making the decision in the case. That decision is cast in the form of a written opinion that consists of findings of facts, conclusions of law, and an order specifying the remedies and sanctions.

The ALJ also has the ethical responsibilities of a trial judge; that is, the judges are prohibited from having *ex parte* **contacts**, which are contacts with one side or one of the parties in the dispute without the knowledge of the others. Staff members of the agency are prohibited from supplying information to the ALJ except when they are witnesses or attorneys in the hearings.

Administrative hearings can have as participants more than just the agency and the party charged with a violation. Other parties with an interest in the case can intervene. These **intervenors** file motions to intervene and are usually permitted to do so at any time before the start of a hearing. Typical intervenors are industry or-

EXHIBIT 6.10 Excerpts from an FTC Consent Decree

In the matter of the National Media Group, Inc. et al. Consent Order, etc., in regard to Alleged Violation of The Federal Trade Commission Act

This consent order, among other things, requires a King of Prussia, Pa. firm and a corporate officer, engaged in the advertising and sale of "Acne-Statin," an acne "treatment," to cease disseminating or causing the dissemination of advertisements that represent that Acne-Statin cures acne, eliminates or reduces the bacteria and fatty acids responsible for acne blemishes, and is superior to all other acne preparations and soap for the antibacterial treatment of acne. . . . Additionally, they are required to establish an independent, irrevocable trust account containing sixty thousand dollars ($60,000) to be used to pay half of all requests for restitution by Acne-Statin purchasers; and obligated to conduct and be totally responsible for the administration of the restitution program.

(The original complaint appeared here.)

Order

It is ordered, That respondents, The National Media Group, Inc. a corporation, . . . and the corporate respondent's officers, agents, representatives, and employees . . . do forthwith cease and desist from:

A. *Disseminating or causing the dissemination of any advertisement by means of the United States mails or by any means in or affecting commerce, . . . which directly or indirectly:*
   1. *Represents that use of Acne-Statin will cure acne or any skin condition associated with acne.*
   2. *Represents that Acne-Statin will eliminate or reduce the bacteria responsible for pimples, blackheads, whiteheads, or other acne blemishes or any skin condition associated with acne.*
   3. *Represents that Acne-Statin will eliminate or reduce the fatty acids responsible for pimples, blackheads, whiteheads, other acne blemishes or any skin condition associated with acne.*
   4. *Represents that Acne-Statin is superior to prescription or over-the-counter antibacterial acne preparations in the treatment of acne.*
   5. *Represents that Acne-Statin is superior to soap in the antibacterial treatment of acne.*

It is further ordered, That:

A. *Within thirty (30) days of final acceptance of this consent order by the Federal Trade Commission (hereinafter the "Commission"), respondent, The National Media Group, Inc., shall establish an interest-bearing trust account containing the sum of sixty thousand dollars ($60,000), for the purpose of paying restitution to Acne-Statin purchasers. . . .*

ganizations: Should the FCC hold hearings on charges against a television station on the content of ads on the station, the National Association of Broadcasters would probably want to intervene in the hearing.

The rules of evidence and procedure are somewhat relaxed in administrative hearings. Agencies involved in the hearings can issue subpoenas for documents, but the subpoenas can only be enforced by the courts. All of the investigation and adjudication processes of administrative agencies are subject to the constitutional standards of due process, which include the following rights: right to notification of the charges; right to notification of the hearing day; right to present evidence; right to be represented by an attorney; right to an impartial judge; right to a decision based on the law or regulation; and right to cross-examine the witnesses of the agency or intervenors.

Administrative Law of Appeals

Once the ALJ has issued a decision, the decision can be appealed. However, the appellate process in administrative law is slightly different. The first step in an appeal of an ALJ decision is not to a court but to the agency itself. This gives the agency a chance to correct a bad decision before the courts become involved.

The appeal is to the next higher level in the agency. For example, in the FTC an appeal of an ALJ's decision goes to the commissioners of the FTC for reconsideration.

In some agencies the structure is such that there may be appeals to more than one person in the structure. Those appealing an ALJ decision, however, must go through all the required lines of authority in the agency before they can go to court. This process is known as **exhausting administrative remedies**. If an appeal is made before administrative remedies are exhausted, the court will reject the case on those grounds.

There are some exceptions to the exhaustion rule. A decision by a zoning board to allow construction of a building project could go directly to court because, if the building is started but the decision to allow construction later overruled, the builder is damaged. Alternatively, if the building is not started, other purchasers of the land and the builder are harmed. In other words, fast action is required to maintain all parties' positions.

If an agency has gone beyond its enabling act, a party can also go directly to court. This is more of a challenge to a regulation than it is to the agency's decision, and direct appeal is therefore permitted.

Finally, an agency decision can be appealed directly to court if exhaustion of administrative remedies would be futile, as evidenced by public statements of officials of the agency. When the FTC was trying to develop rules on children's TV advertising, for example, a group of interested parties brought a court action to have then-FTC chairman Michael Pertschuk removed from the rulemaking process because he had indicated strong feelings in the press about his position. It would have been futile to try administrative remedies because the appeal would have been taken to the party they were trying to remove.

A decision of a federal administrative agency is appealed to one of the U.S. courts of appeals (as indicated in Chapter 3). In most states, appeals from state administrative agencies also go to state courts of appeals. However, some states require a **trial** *de novo*, which means the case is appealed to the state's general trial court, where it is tried. In other words, the hearing is repeated, but this time under strict rules of procedure and evidence.

An appellate court can simply affirm an agency action, find that an agency has exceeded its authority, find that an agency has violated the U.S. Constitution, or rule that an agency has acted arbitrarily or that an agency's decision or action is not

---

ETHICAL ISSUES

Some businesses take a backdoor approach to getting around administrative regulations. They go over an agency's head to its source of funding, namely, Congress. After the Association of National Advertisers succeeded in having Michael Pertschuk removed from the development of regulations for children's television advertising, its attention turned to Congress. As a result of strong lobbying efforts, Congress passed the FTC Improvements Act of 1980. In addition to cutting the FTC budget severely, one of the sections of the act provided that the FTC could not use section 5 (its general power in its enabling act to regulate "deceptive trade practices"; see Chapter 11) to regulate children's television advertising. Shortly after passage, the FTC withdrew all of its rulemaking procedures for children's television advertising. The organizations and businesses lobbying for the FTC Improvements Act contributed money to the political action committees of members of Congress.

Does the ability of businesses to circumvent administrative agencies hinder the agencies' effectiveness? Was the lobbying just an exercise of the businesses' rights? Was the lobbying a way to curtail forever the FTC's power in this area? Is such lobbying an ethical business practice? Does this type of circumvention allow businesses to operate unregulated?

Note: In 1990, the FTC was able to pass some rules on children's television advertising, and Congress held hearings in 1993 to determine whether more regulation of children's television was needed. The industry agreed to self-regulation in the form of clear delineations between programming and commercials.

BIOGRAPHY

THE RISING STAR WHO FELL

Mike Espy was elected to Congress as a representative from Mississippi in 1988. Bright and young, he was welcomed to the House and given substantial responsibilities. When Bill Clinton was elected president, he tapped Mr. Espy (only 40 at the time) for his cabinet as secretary of agriculture. Mr. Espy was described as a fast-rising political star.

Tyson Foods, Inc., the world's largest producer of fresh and processed poultry products, soon developed a close relationship with Mr. Espy. At the time of Mr. Espy's appointment, Tyson and other regulators were fighting proposed Department of Agriculture guidelines (ultimately not promulgated) that would have imposed a "zero tolerance" on the presence of fecal matter during processing. The proposed regulations would have substantially increased costs for Tyson and other processors.

Tyson offered and Mr. Espy accepted numerous benefits from Tyson, including a ride on a Tyson corporate jet, free lodging at a lakeside cabin owned by Tyson, and seats in Tyson's skybox at a Dallas Cowboys game. Additionally, Mr. Espy's girlfriend received a $1,200 college scholarship from Tyson Foods. Mr. Espy went to the 1994 Super Bowl at government expense, saying he made the trip because Smokey the Bear was being honored in public service announcements at the game.

When information about these corporate gifts and government spending was reported, there was tremendous public outcry. Mr. Espy paid back Tyson Foods for the jet rides and the tickets. However, a special prosecutor was appointed to look into these issues and others, including Quaker Oats' furnishing Mr. Espy a ticket to a Chicago Bulls playoff game after he contacted the company and made the request. In addition, a lobbyist for Sun-Diamond, a raisin and almond firm, sponsored a birthday party for Mr. Espy and 150 Department of Agriculture employees.

By December 1994, Mr. Espy, who had pledged that he would clean up the U.S. poultry business, resigned, saying, "It seemed as if I was just twisting in the wind."

Manley C. Molpus, president of the Grocery Manufacturers Association and a friend of Mr. Espy, said, "Clearly, there were some lapses of judgment in the administration of his affairs that should have been taken care of with greater sensitivity to the law as well as perception."

A former congressional colleague noted, "It seems as though he behaved as though he was still a member (of Congress). This is not a corrupt or venal guy."

Sun-Diamond was found guilty of making illegal gifts and fined $1.5 million. On appeal, the U.S. Supreme Court reversed the conviction, finding that there was not a sufficient connection between the gifts and alleged influence on various matters pending before Mr. Espy and his agency. Tyson Foods entered a guilty plea to making illegal gifts and paid a $6 million fine. Mr. Espy's former aide, Ronald H. Blackley, was tried and convicted of taking money from growers in exchange for the award of subsidies and also lying to federal agents in the subsequent investigation. Mr. Blackley was sentenced to two years in prison despite the federal sentencing guidelines recommending probation, because Judge Lambreth felt lying during an investigation was inexcusable. Richard Douglas, a lobbyist for Sun-Diamond, was also found guilty of making illegal gifts to Mr. Espy but appealed his case. (See Case 6.1.)

In 1996, Mr. Espy's brother Henry was indicated on charges related to campaign finance in his 1993 bid for his brother's vacant congressional seat. Sun-Diamond also pleaded guilty to illegal campaign contributions to Henry's campaign.

In 1997, Mr. Espy was charged, in a thirty-nine-count indictment, with accepting and soliciting gifts and favors from Tyson Foods, lying to the FBI, witness tampering, and soliciting NBA tickets from the chairman of Quaker Oats. A judge dismissed six counts, and, after a trial, Mr. Espy was acquitted on all thirty-three remaining counts and said, "I just expected each and every day that I would be found not guilty."

Mr. Espy now works for one of Mississippi's largest law firms as a trial attorney. He has been active in community service and has been mentioned as a possible candidate for the U.S. Senate as well as for lieutenant governor.

Mr. Douglas was found guilty of crimes related to his activities as a lobbyist and the resulting investigation, but the trial court did dismiss the gratuities charges against him. His appeal on these convictions was dismissed. [*U.S.* v. *Douglas,* 161 F.3d 15 (9th Cir. 1999).]

continued

ISSUES

1. Was Mr. Espy's role as an administrator different from his role in Congress?

2. Why wasn't paying back Tyson enough?

3. How did such a web of indictments develop? There were fifteen prosecutions, fifteen convic-

tions, and $11 million in fines resulting from the Espy investigation.

4. Why, for example, were Tyson, Mr. Blackley, and Sun-Diamond culpable but Mr. Espy was acquitted?

supported by the evidence. The *State Farm* seatbelt case (see Case 6.2 earlier in the chapter) is an example of a court's reversal of administrative agency action in the area of rulemaking.

Exhibit 6.11 provides a summary of the roles of administrative agencies.

EXHIBIT   6.11   The Roles of Administrative Agencies

ACTIVITY	STEPS	PARTIES	RESULTS
Passing rules	Rule proposed	Agency	New rules
	Comments	Consumers	Modified rules
	Modification,	Business	Withdrawn rules
	withdrawal, or	Congress	
	promulgation	Agency	
Enforcement	Licensing	Agency	
		Business	
	Inspections	Agency	Search and inspection
		Courts (if warrant	
		is required)	
		Business	
	Complaints	Agency	Fines
			Penalties
			Injunctions
			Consent decrees
			Hearings

THE ROLE OF ADMINISTRATIVE AGENCIES IN THE INTERNATIONAL MARKET

The United States wins the award for the most administrative agencies and regulations. Some businesses have argued that the amount of regulation hinders them in the international marketplace. For example, just the readability level of regulations, as shown in Exhibit 6.12, demands much time and energy as companies attempt to interpret and comply with the laws.

Many regulators, legislators, and businesses have advocated elimination and streamlining of existing regulations, as well as careful consideration before new regulations are promulgated.

EXHIBIT 6.12 Various Reading Levels of Documents and Populations

Documents and Populations	Grade Level
1. *Love Story*	7.64
2. Reading level of U.S. population over age 65	9.71
3. *Playboy*	11.46
4. Reading level of general U.S. population	11.68
5. *Sports Illustrated*	12.82
6. *Your Medicare Handbook*	14.94
7. *ERISA Summary Plan Description*	15.29
8. *Wall Street Journal*	16.34
9. *Social Security Handbook*	17.51
10. Reading level of lawyers	19.00
11. *Albermarle* (U.S. Supreme Court Ruling)	20.30
12. Occupational Safety and Health Act	30.79
13. Employment Retirement Income Safety Act	32.10
14. Section 18 of the Social Security Act	41.04

Sources: Warren S. Blumenfeld et al., "Readability of an ERISA Summary Plan Description vis-à-vis Intended Readership: An Empirical Test of Local Legal Compliance with a Federal Regulation." Paper presented at the Western American Institute for Decision Science Meeting, Reno, Nevada, March 1979. Warren S. Blumenfeld et al., "Readability of the Real Estate Settlement Procedures Act." Paper presented at the Southeastern Regional Business Law Association Meeting, Chapel Hill, North Carolina, October 1980.

ETHICAL ISSUE

Some businesses are able to take advantage of one government's regulations. For example, the Energy Policy Act of 1992 requires that toilets installed after the act took effect (1994) use only 1.6 gallons of water rather than the nearly century-old standard of 3.5 gallons. As of 2000, about one-fourth of the nation's toilets were the 1.6-gallon types.

As homeowners remodel and replace older toilets, they have learned that the 3.5-gallon toilets are no longer sold in the United States. However, just across the U.S./Canadian border near Detroit, Canadian hardware stores are doing a land office business selling 3.5-gallon tanks to U.S. citizens.

Those who are remodeling and even some building new homes generally install a $100 toilet from Home Depot in order to pass inspection. They then purchase a Canadian toilet, in the neighborhood of $500 to $1,000 for a standard fixture because the demand is so high, and install it. Plumbing stores all over Canada report sales are brisk. In a survey conducted in May 2000, owners of Canadian plumbing stores said that they sell, on average, one toilet per day to U.S. citizens either via direct sale or shipment.

Do the citizens break any laws by what they do? Is what they do ethical?

SUMMARY

What is an administrative agency?

- Administrative agency—statutory creature with the ability to make, interpret, and enforce laws

What laws govern the operation of administrative agencies?

- Administrative Procedure Act—general federal law governing agency process and operations

- Government in the Sunshine Act—federal law requiring public hearings by agencies (with limited exceptions)

- Federal Privacy Act—federal law protecting transfer of information among agencies unless done for enforcement reasons

- Freedom of Information Act—federal law providing individuals with access to information held by administrative agencies (with some exemptions such as for trade secrets)

What do administrative agencies do?

- Rulemaking—process of turning proposed regulations into actual regulations; requires public input
- *Federal Register*—daily publication that updates agency proposals, rules, hearing notices, and so forth
- *Code of Federal Regulations*—federal government publication of all agency rules
- Licensing—role in which an agency screens businesses before permitting operation
- Inspections—administrative agency role of checking businesses and business sites for compliance

How do agencies pass rules?

- Public comment period—period in rulemaking process when any individual or business can provide input on proposed regulations
- Promulgation—approval of proposed rules by heads of agencies

How do agencies enforce the law?

- Consent decree—settlement (*nolo contendere* plea) of charges brought by an administrative agency
- Administrative law judge (ALJ)—overseer of hearing on charges brought by administrative agency

QUESTIONS AND PROBLEMS

1. Residents of New York City who were receiving financial aid under the federally assisted program of Aid to Families with Dependent Children (AFDC) brought a class-action suit alleging that the New York officials responsible for the administration of the program were terminating aid to them without notice of the termination or without a hearing prior to the termination. The residents challenged the actions of the state officials as violative of their constitutional right to due process. The procedures for termination changed after the complaints of these residents, and notices and hearings were provided. What types of procedures would be necessary to protect the residents' due process rights? Must a court afford these procedures? [*Goldberg* v. *Kelly*, 397 U.S. 254 (1970).]

2. In 1979, Congress passed the Chrysler Corporation Loan Guarantee Act to keep the Chrysler Corporation in business and out of bankruptcy. The act established the Chrysler Corporation Loan Guarantee Board, made up of top federal officials, to oversee Chrysler's bailout. The meetings of this board necessarily involved sensitive discussions about Chrysler and its status. Would the meetings be covered under the Sunshine Act and thus open to the public? [*Symons* v. *Chrysler Corp. Loan Guarantee*, 670 F.2d 238 (D.C. 1981).]

3. Because of overcrowded conditions at the nation's airports during the late 1960s, the Federal Aviation Administration (FAA) promulgated a regulation to reduce takeoff and landing delays at airports by limiting the number of landing and takeoff slots at five major airports to sixty slots per hour. The airports were Kennedy, LaGuardia, O'Hare, Newark, and National. At National Airport (Washington), forty of the sixty slots were given

to commercial planes, and the commercial carriers allocated the slots among themselves until October 1980. In 1980, New York Air, a new airline, requested some of the forty slots, but the existing airlines refused to give up any. The secretary of transportation, in response and "to avoid chaos in the skies" during the upcoming holidays, proposed a rule to allocate the slots at National. The allocation rule was proposed on October 16, 1980, and appeared in the *Federal Register* on October 20, 1980. The comment period was seven days starting from the October 16, 1980, proposal date. The airlines and others submitted a total of thirty-seven comments to the secretary. However, Northwest Airlines filed suit on grounds that the APA required a minimum of thirty days for a public comment period. The secretary argued that the thirty-day rule was being suspended for good cause (the holiday season was upon them). Who is correct? Should an exception be made, or should the FAA be required to follow the thirty-day rule? [*Northwest Airlines, Inc.* v. *Goldschmidt*, 645 F.2d 1309 (8th Cir. 1981).]

4. Richardson-Vicks, Inc., is the manufacturer and seller of Vick's Pediatric Formula 44 (Pediatric 44), a cough medicine for children. In its ads for Pediatric 44, Vicks claims that the syrup contains active ingredients that enable it to begin working instantly. However, Pediatric 44 is considered to have only inactive ingredients, according to FDA regulations on "active" and "inactive" ingredients. A competitor has alleged that Vicks is "misbranding" its products. Can the FDA take any action? What steps could it take? Will the FDA be required to make an interpretation of the "active"/"inactive" regulation? [*Sandoz Pharmaceuticals* v. *Richardson-Vicks, Inc.*, 902 F.2d 222 (3d Cir. 1990).]

5. Read the following excerpt from the *Wall Street Journal.*

The smell of the greasepaint and the roar of the crowd, indeed.

The circus of yesteryear, loved by children and fondly remembered by older folk, keeps running smack into the modern world. In 1992, tents must fall within local fire codes. If the clown isn't a U.S. citizen, he had better have a valid work visa along with his makeup kit and big false nose. And the kid who wants to run away from home and join the circus? Forget it. . . .

Consider Carson & Barnes, the last of the five-ring road shows. The circus is traveling an 18-state route this year, from March 21 to Nov. 15, doing one-night stands. Each morning, about 200 performers and other employees, 150 animals, 80 trucks roll into town. Roustabouts race to erect the "Biggest Big Top On Earth." The circus performs two shows, packs, goes to sleep, rises at dawn and heads for the next stop.

With scheduling tight, satisfying the local tests is no mean feat. The 237 small towns where the circus is performing this year all usually require about half a dozen permits, with regulations varying from place to place.

This summer, the circus's soft-drink concession got shut down briefly because of bad water. An Illinois inspector found a high bacteria count and sent word to Wisconsin, so the water flunked inspection in Racine and Jefferson. . . .

If a sucker isn't born every minute, it is true that people are easily fooled and that can cause the circus trouble. While his circus was crossing Texas this year, someone complained about the stunt Argentine acrobat Sulliana Montes de Oca does with her French poodle. The dog sits on a platform as Ms. Montes de Oca appears to execute a handstand on the poor dog's head.

It's an illusion, of course, but a local inspector even came out to investigate an abuse complaint, circus officials say. They showed him the steel rod the circus crowd doesn't see that actually supports Ms. Montes de Oca when she does the trick. Dave Brandt, the show's press agent, says, "Who would ever think a nine-pound French poodle can hold up a 90-pound woman?" . . .

Local officials worry about the welfare of children as well as animals. About half a century ago, the Miller family circus actually did hire some young teenagers. And local kids willing to help set up the show got in free. But child-labor laws and insurance policy problems have put a stop to that. Applicants must be 18.

Nevertheless, Carson & Barnes has problems even with the only minors it does employ—those who perform in acts with their parents. Last year, California inspectors demanded that 14-year-old Dulce Vital quit holding target balloons for her father's archery act. Though the act is risky and Ms. Vital is young, she knew the routine. When she was replaced in Desert Hot Springs by a 19-year-old stand-in, Isabel Macias, the new girl caught an arrow in the forehead and today has a scar to show for it.

Then there is the foreign-performer problem. Carson & Barnes employs about 80 Latin Americans a year, and tangles for months with immigration officials to get papers for them. Last year, temporary-visa applications for the Chimals, a Mexican family of acrobats, got lost in the bureaucracy, say circus officials. The up-shot: For 10 days, the circus performed with an empty ring.

Certain towns make it harder on Carson & Barnes than others. "The fire marshall from hell is here today," reads the general manager's journal entry for Ojai, Calif. The fireman was concerned, among other things, that the inspector's ID number wasn't printed on fire extinguishers.

The hang-up forced the gathering afternoon audience to wait in the hot sun while circus officials jumped through hoops. Finally, at showtime, the fireman was willing to let the show go on if one fire extinguisher could be shown to function properly. One was tested, it worked, and the circus started half-an-hour late. . . .

Source: "Bunting & Red Tape: The Modern Circus Walks a High Wire," *Wall Street Journal,* August 31, 1992, pp. A1, A4.

Is too much regulation exerted upon the circus? Is all the regulation necessary?

6. Suppose that the SEC has proposed a new rule for the filing of registered companies' annual reports (see Chapter 22). One of the provisions of the rule requires the reports to be filed within three months after the close of the company's financial year. All of the companies commenting on the rule mentioned that the time for filing should be extended at least thirty days because most accounting firms require ninety days to complete their work for an annual report. After the comment period, the SEC changed the rule's time limit to 120 days. Is another public comment period required, or can the rule now be promulgated?

7. Hooked on Phonics is a reading program that departs from the current educational reading philosophy of "whole-language learning." The program emphasizes the more traditional reading process of having children sound out letters and combinations of letters. The Federal Trade Commission (FTC) filed a false advertising complaint against Gateway Educational Products, Inc., the owner of the Hooked on Phonics program. The FTC claimed that Gateway's television claims that those with reading disabilities would be helped "quickly and easily" and that Hooked on Phonics could "teach reading in a home setting without additional assistance" were misleading. Gateway does not feel the claims are false, but it does not want to have bad publicity. What advice can you give Gateway on handling the FTC charges?

8. In March 1992, the Federal Communications Commission (FCC) proposed rules that would increase the maximum number of radio stations a company could own from twelve AM stations and twelve FM stations to thirty of each. The FCC proposed the changes because more than half of the nation's 11,000 radio stations are unprofitable and larger ownership blocks would allow some economies of scale. Critics were vocal about domination and monopolization. As a result, the FCC changed the ownership maximums to eighteen FM and eighteen AM stations and issued its final rules on August 5, 1992. Describe the process the FCC employed to make these changes. Explain what public outcry accomplished.

9. The Food and Drug Administration (FDA) is concerned about laser eye surgery, noting that the industry concerned with correcting vision is spawning joint ventures, wine-and-cheese seminars to court potential investors, and databases of nearsighted consumers. There are 800 numbers and some dissatisfaction among the 700 patients who've had the surgery, including complaints of farsightedness. The corrective laser surgery costs $2,000 per eye and is not covered by insurance. Further, the only regulation the FDA has in the field covers granting permission to laser manufacturers, which has been given, to sell their machines to opthalmologists. The FDA would like to know more and perhaps control some aspects of patients' care. Describe the steps the FDA must take.

10. The following federal regulation—15 C.F.R. § 1511—governs the design and manufacture of pacifiers for babies. Read the regulation and then answer the following questions.
   a. What companies would be affected by this type of regulation?
   b. How could the companies provide input on the regulations?
   c. What types of tests must a pacifier pass under these regulations?
   d. What is done after the heat cycle deterioration? Why must a pacifier pass heat deterioration tests?

15 C.F.R. § 1511

§(a) A pacifier is an article consisting of a nipple that is intended for a young child to suck upon, but is not designed to facilitate a baby's obtaining fluid, and usually includes a guard or shield and a handle or ring.

(b) Guard or shield means the structure located at the base of the nipple used to prevent the pacifier from being completely drawn into the child's mouth.

(c) Handle or ring means the structure usually located adjacent to the guard or shield used for holding or grasping the pacifier. A hinged handle or ring is one that is free to pivot about an axis parallel to the plane of the guard or shield.

§ 1511.3. Guard or shield requirements.

(a) Performance requirements. Place the pacifier in the opening of the fixture illustrated in Figure 1(a) of this part so that the nipple of the pacifier is centered in the opening and protrudes through the back of the fixture as shown in Figure 1(b). For pacifiers with non-circular guards or shields, align the major axis of the guard or shield with the major axis of the opening in the fixture. Apply a tensile force to the pacifier nipple in the direction shown. The force shall be applied gradually attaining but not exceeding 2.0 pounds (8.9 newtons) within a period of 5 seconds and maintained at 2.0 pounds for an additional 10 seconds. Any pacifier which can be completely drawn through an opening with dimensions no greater than those of Exhibit 1(a) by such a force shall fail the test in this part.

(b) Ventilation holes. The pacifier guard or shield shall contain at least two holes symmetrically located and each being at least 0.20 inches (5 millimeters) in minor dimension. The edge of any hole shall be no closer than 0.20 inches (5 millimeters) to the perimeter of the pacifier guard or shield.

§ 1511.5 Structural integrity tests.

(a) Nipple. Hold the pacifier by the shield or guard, grasp the nipple end of the pacifier and gradually apply a tensile to the pacifier nipple in any possible direction. The force shall be applied gradually, attaining but not exceeding 10.0 pounds (44.5 newtons) within a period of 5 seconds and maintained at 10.0 pounds for an additional 10 seconds.

(b) Handle or ring. Hold the pacifier by the shield or guard or base of the nipple, and push or pull on the handle or ring in any possible direction. The force shall be applied gradually attaining but not exceeding 10.0 pounds (44.5 newtons) within a period of 5 seconds and maintained at 10.0 pounds for an additional 10 seconds.

(c) Heat cycle deterioration. After the testing prescribed in paragraphs (a) and (b) of this section, all pacifiers shall be subject to the following: submerge the pacifier in boiling water for 5 minutes and then remove the pacifier and allow it to cool for 5 minutes in room temperature air, 60° to 80° F. (16° to 27° C). After the cooling period, resubmerge the pacifier in the boiling water for 5 minutes. The process shall be repeated for a total of 6 boiling/cooling cycles. After the sixth cycle, the pacifier shall again be subjected to the structural tests in paragraphs (a) and (b) of this section and section 1511.3.

RESEARCH PROBLEM

Campaign Contributions Decisions Are Pending

11. Read *Sokaogon Chippewa Community* v. *Babbitt*, 961 F.Supp. 1276 (W.D. Wis. 1997), and discuss the issues, the role of the agency, and the role of politics.

International Law

update

For up-to-date legal news and real-world business applications, click on **update** *at* http://jennings.westbuslaw.com

Shakespeare was ahead of his time when he wrote that "the world is your oyster." Today's global business environment is the dream of economists, who have fostered the notion of free trade since the publication of Adam Smith's *The Wealth of Nations* about two hundred years ago. Trade barriers are down, resources are flowing, and even the smallest of businesses are involved in international trade. Trade across borders still involves additional issues and laws and carries risks that do not exist in transactions within nations. Businesses must understand the legal environment of international trade to enter into contracts and conduct operations in ways that minimize legal risks because, as noted in Chapter 4, litigation across borders can be difficult. This chapter covers the legal environment of international business. What laws affect businesses in international trade? What international agreements affect global businesses? What contract issues exist in international business?

> **It's not necessary to use chopsticks. A knife and fork are okay.**
> MAYOR ZHANG
> *Suzhou, China (in encouraging businesspeople to come to his town)*

> **If a foreign country can supply us with a commodity cheaper than we ourselves can make it, better buy it of them with some part of our own industry, employed in a way in which we have some advantage.**
> ADAM SMITH
> THE WEALTH OF NATIONS

> I don't believe you can run a major U.S. company from
> abroad. George III tried to run the United States
> from Britain and look what happened to him.
>
> SIR GORDON WHITE
> *Chairman, Hanson Industries, Inc.*

CONSIDER...

American Rice, Inc. (ARI), a Houston-based company, exports rice to foreign countries, including Haiti. Rice Corporation of Haiti, a wholly owned subsidiary of ARI, was incorporated in Haiti to represent ARI's interests and deal with third parties there. Haiti's customs officials assess duties based on the quantity and value of rice imported into the country. Haiti also requires businesses that deliver rice there to remit an advance deposit against Haitian sales taxes, based on the value of that rice, for which deposit a credit is eventually allowed on Haitian sales tax returns when filed. David Kay and Douglas Murphy, executives of ARI, were charged with violations of the Foreign Corrupt Practices Act (FCPA) for allegedly bribing Haitian officials to accept false bills of lading that reflected total rice imports to be about one-third of actual levels so that ARI would owe less in taxes. Is this type of an arrangement a bribe? Does it violate the FCPA?

© PHOTODISC/GETTY IMAGES

SOURCES OF INTERNATIONAL LAW

"When in Rome, do as the Romans do" is advice that can be modified for business: When in Rome, follow Roman law. In each country where a business has operations, it must comply with the laws of that nation. Just as each U.S. business must comply with all the tax, employment, safety, and environmental laws of each state in which it operates, each international business must comply with the laws of the countries in which it operates.

Types of International Law Systems

The various systems of laws can be quite different, and businesses are well advised to obtain local legal counsel for advice on the peculiarities of each nation's laws. Generally, a nation's laws are based on one of three types of systems. The United States has a **common law** system. Like England, our laws are built on tradition and precedent (see Chapter 1). Not every possible situation is codified; we rely on our courts to interpret and apply our more general statutes and, in many cases, to develop principles of law as cases are presented (as with the common-law doctrine of negligence; see Chapter 10).

Other countries rely on civil law or code law. This form of law is found in European nations that are not tied to England, and countries influenced through its colonial activities. France, Germany, Spain, and other countries with code law systems do not rely on court decisions but rely instead on statutes or codes that are intended to cover all types of circumstances and attempt to spell out the law so there is little need for interpretation.

A final system of law is Islamic law, which is followed in some form in twenty-seven countries. Islamic legal systems are based on religious tenets and govern all aspects of life, from appropriate dress in public to remedies for contract breaches. Many of the Islamic countries have a combination of civil and Islamic systems that result from the influences of both colonization and Islam.

Before its collapse in the former Soviet Union and Eastern Europe, communism was also classified as a legal system. Now the former communist nations struggle with evolving cultural, market, and governmental systems. In fact, much international work is being completed by U.S. lawyers, accountants, and other professionals, who are assisting in the development of constitutions, legislation, and even such issues as development of tax codes and collection systems.

The Roots of Commerce and Law: Nonstatutory Sources of International Law

Customs and values in a culture often have a controlling effect on negotiations, contracts, and performance in international business. The American Bar Association recommends that businesspeople and their lawyers examine seven cultural factors and do background work in these cultural areas before attempting negotiations and business in a particular country. Referred to as the LESCANT factors, the following issues should be researched as if they were legal background for doing business: language, environment and technology, social organization, contexting, authority, nonverbal behavior, and time concept.

For more information on the cultures of various countries, visit:

http://www.germanculture.com/ua

http://www.chineseculture.about.com
Click on articles to choose topic for background.

http://gomexico.about.com
Click on world heritage and explore from there.

http://www.jinjapan.org/

Language

Businesspeople should determine which language is preferred in a particular country for conducting business. Mexico and Latin American countries are accustomed to doing business in English. In Quebec, Canada, there are government regulations on the use of French in conducting business.

Environment and Technology

Communications systems vary in quality and universality in countries around the world. Because U.S. companies are used to rapid communication and verification of offers and acceptances (see Chapter 13 on contract formation), doing business in a country in which communication will be much slower and by different means requires advance knowledge and appropriate adjustments and provisions for negotiations.

Social Organization

Businesspeople should know the social order in the country: May women negotiate deals? Is it appropriate to discuss business during a meal?

Contexting

Low-context cultures are those that rely on the written word as the controlling factor in their relationship. Little weight is given to the context in which that agreement is reached. Low-context cultures include the North American countries, Switzerland, Germany, and Scandinavian countries (although not Finland). Mid-level-context cultures are France, England, and Italy; high-context cultures are Latin American countries, Arabic nations, and Asian countries, including Japan. In high-context cultures, how and in what setting an agreement is reached are as important as the words in the document itself.

Authority

Who has negotiating authority is important in a business meeting, and who is sent to a meeting sends a signal about importance in high-context cultures. Lawyers are not considered part of the negotiating team in Japan but are considered critical in the United States. Often, in Asian cultures, the negotiators do not have the authority to commit to a deal and must take proposals back to their companies and those who do have authority.

Nonverbal Behavior

In the United States, there is a tendency to interpret nonverbal behavior differently from the way it is perceived in other cultures. For example, silence during negotiations in the United States creates a compulsion for businesspeople to fill the awkward silence or interpret the silence as a rejection. In Asian cultures, such silence is simply a method of contemplating and considering and does not indicate a rejection.

Time Concept

The United States is a monochronic nation: Time is everything, and the goal of businesspeople is to get the deal done. Other monochronic nations include Great Britain, Germany, Canada, New Zealand, Australia, the Netherlands, Norway, and Sweden. Countries that operate with great flexibility in time and negotiate within the context of building a relationship as opposed to completing a deal are called polychronic nations. The remainder of the world operates within this flexible form of time culture.

Contracts for the International Sale of Goods (CISG)

Sometimes referred to as the Vienna Convention, the United Nations Convention on Contracts for the International Sale of Goods (CISG) began its development in

---

FOR THE MANAGER'S DESK

RE: NONVERBAL COMMUNICATION IN INTERNATIONAL BUSINESS

In his book *Gestures: The Do's and Taboos of Body Language around the World* (1991), Roger E. Axtell notes that body language can create problems in international trade negotiations. For example, while a "thumbs up" in the United States translates to "Good going!" such a hand signal in Bangladesh and Australia is the equivalent of a raised middle finger in the United States.

In many Latin American countries, the A-OK sign formed with the index finger and thumb in a circle is considered an insult. In France, the same gesture means "zero" or "worthless." In Japan, this same symbol is a means of asking for money. The use of the A-OK sign in Japan is particularly dangerous, because businesspeople there are likely to interpret the unintentional request for money as a request for a bribe.

Patting a child's head in India is offensive because the head houses the soul in India. Executives should not touch the heads of children when invited to dinner at the homes of executives in that country.

Rotating your index finger near your ear in the United States is a symbol for "crazy." In Argentina, the same signal means that you have a phone call.

Many U.S. businesspeople have tried to avoid any misinterpretation of their hand signals by consciously placing their hands in their pockets. However, such a gesture is considered impolite in Belgium, Finland, France, Indonesia, Japan, and Sweden.

FOR THE MANAGER'S DESK

RE: ENGLISH: THE LANGUAGE OF CONTRACTS

A new trend is emerging in international contracts. The dominant language for contracts has become English, even for contracts among natives of a country.

The trend is attributed by some to the Internet. Those in non–English speaking countries have become increasingly familiar with English as they have surfed the Net. One French businessman learned English so that he could enjoy the jokes his son sent to him over the Internet. The jokes were in English, and his son was stunned when he visited to find his father so fluent in English following several years of joke exchanges.

Others attribute the trend to, as H. L. Mencken once wrote, the "sheer weight of [the English language's] merit." Businesspeople appreciate the simplicity of grammar as well as the larger vocabulary available in English. English has also incorporated phrases from other languages and continues to evolve while other languages, such as French, prohibit change.

Others attribute the change to the rise of the EU. Because the EU needs one uniting language, most have landed upon English as the choice. Most new contracts being negotiated in Europe are choosing English as their language. The EU released the following information:

47% of Western Europeans speak English.
Only 32% speak German, and only 28% speak French.
77% of all Western European college students speak English.
69% of all Western European business managers speak English.
65% of those between the ages of 15 to 24 speak English.
91% of all school-age children study English.

One Italian CEO says, "The only business language worldwide is English."

Source: FORTUNE, Justin Fox, "The Triumph of English," September 18, 2000, pp. 209–212. © 2000 Time Inc. All rights reserved.

Visit the UNCITRAL:
http://www.uncitral.org
Click on international law

Review the CISG:
http://www.cisg.law.
pace.edu

1964 as an idea that was later discussed and formulated at the 1980 Vienna Convention. The CISG first became effective in 1988 with its adoption in the United States along with a small group of other countries. Today, CISG has been adopted in sixty countries, with ratification processes under way in many other countries.

The CISG is designed to provide for international contracts the convenience and uniformity that the Uniform Commercial Code provides for contracts across state lines in the United States. While there are some differences (see Chapters 13 and 14), the CISG is a reflection of the Uniform Commercial Code.

Treaties, Trade Organizations, and Controls on International Trade

In international trade, a number of treaties, tariffs, and organizations govern and guide international contracts. This section discusses some of the most important ones.

Whether supported or despised by economists, tariffs and restrictions on trade have existed for as long as trade itself. Duties, quotas, and tariffs have all been used to control the flow of goods over and across national boundaries. For most of history, these limits on trade have been imposed on a nation-by-nation basis. However, new forms of trade agreements are developing, and nations are organizing in larger groups in an attempt to eliminate many of the individually based barriers to trade.

Review GATT:
http://www.gatt.org

The General Agreement on Tariffs and Trade (GATT)

Adopted in 1994, the General Agreement on Tariffs and Trade (GATT) is a **multilateral treaty** (a treaty among more than two nations), currently subscribed to by 147 nations.

GATT is the most expansive attempt to negotiate free trade and boasts 147 member countries, including the United States. GATT has been able to reduce tariffs nearly 70 percent through meetings of its members, called "rounds." The president of the United States is authorized by Congress to participate in these rounds and agree to reductions in tariffs.

While there was a 1947 GATT, one of the principal differences between that original GATT and the 1994 GATT is the establishment of the World Trade Organization (WTO). The WTO is the body charged with the administration and achievement of the GATT objectives. GATT's primary objectives are trade without discrimination and protection through tariffs. Trade without discrimination is achieved through GATT's most-favored-nation clause. The issue of China's membership as a most favored nation was debated extensively, particularly along with the political and social context of human rights issues in that country, prior to its admission in 2001.

Under the most-favored-nation clause, subscribing countries treat each other equally in terms of import and export duties and charges. Subscribing countries do not give more favorable treatment to one country as opposed to another. Domestic production is protected by tariffs and not through any other commercial measures.

There are some exceptions under GATT for regional trading arrangements undertaken through other treaties, such as the North American Free Trade Agreement and the European Union.

The WTO has also established a Dispute Settlement Body (DSB), which is an international arbitration body created to bring countries together to resolve trade disputes rather than have those nations resort to trade sanctions. If a WTO panel finds that a country has violated the provisions of GATT, it can impose trade sanctions on that country. The sanctions imposed are generally equal to the amount of economic injury the country caused through its violation of GATT.

European Union (EU)

Visit the European Union:
http://europa.eu.int/index.htm
http://www.eurunion.org
(English)

The European Economic Community (EEC) was created by the Treaty of Rome and was formerly known as the Common Market; it is often referred to as the European Community (EC) and is now known as the European Union (EU). The EU15 members are Austria, Belgium, Denmark, Finland, France, Germany, Greece, Ireland, Italy, Luxembourg, the Netherlands, Portugal, Spain, Sweden, and the United Kingdom. Member states include Cyprus, Czech Republic, Estonia, Hungary, Layvia, Lithuania, Malta, Poland, Slovakia, and Slovenia. Candidate countries include Bulgaria, Croatia, Romania and Turkey. Macedonia has an application pending.

For up-to-date information on membership status, visit
http://eurunion.org/states/home.htm

Under the Single European Act, the EU, in an effort to provide for the free flow of goods, services, and human and financial capital, eliminated internal barriers to trade. The Maastricht Treaty (treaty on the European Union signed in Maastricht, the Netherlands) set the goals of the EU as single monetary and fiscal policies (including a common currency), common foreign policies, and cooperation in the administration of justice.

In addition, the EU has undertaken the ambitious goals of uniformity in laws, with proposals on product liability and litigation for member countries to ensure uniform costs and results. The EU has progressed to the point of having some enforceable international law. For example, the EU has created the European Commission, which has the authority to issue regulations and decisions that are binding on all EU members. The goal of the EU is to build one market of 340 million consumers. In January 1999, the EU introduced a single currency known as the euro.

In addition to the European Commission, the EU has created other institutions to assist it in carrying out its goal of unified European commercial operations. The European Council, which consists of the heads of state of the various members, is the policy-making body and establishes the broad directives for the operation of the EU. The next step below the council is the European Commission, the body charged with implementation of the Council policies. At the third level is the European Parliament, an advisory legislative body with some veto powers. Finally, the European Court of Justice (ECJ) is the judicial body created to handle disputes and any violations of regulations and the EU treaty itself. The EU has in place nearly 300 directives that govern everything from health and safety standards in the workplace to the sale of mutual funds across national boundaries.

Review NAFTA:
http://www.citizen.org/
trade/nafta/

The North American Free Trade Agreement (NAFTA)

The North American Free Trade Agreement (NAFTA) is a treaty among Canada, the United States, and Mexico, effective in 1994, which will eliminate all tariffs among the three countries in their trade over a fifteen-year period.

Products covered under NAFTA include only those that originate in these countries. All goods traded across the boundaries of these countries must carry a NAFTA certificate of origin, which verifies the original creation of the goods in that country from which they are being exported. NAFTA has eliminated nearly all of the barriers to trade among these three nations. However, NAFTA is unlike EU in that a common labor market, governing body, and currency were not created.

Prohibitions on Trade: Individual Nation Sanctions

In some countries, international tensions have resulted in trade sanctions being imposed so that commerce with certain nations is prohibited. Countries can impose two types of trade sanctions. With primary trade sanctions, companies based in the United States are prohibited from doing business with certain countries. For example, the United States has prohibited trade with Iraq since the time of the 1991 Gulf War. Primary boycotts can be limited to certain categories of goods. The status of "most favored nation" in trade (MFN) means that the country has no restrictions on the types of goods and services that can be imported and exported. Other category restrictions can include extreme limitations such as limiting trade to food and medical supplies. In some restrictions, the United States prohibits domestic companies from selling certain types of equipment to certain nations. For example, U.S. firms have severe restrictions on selling certain component parts to China. These parts are primarily those that could be used in the development of nuclear weapons and other military capabilities.

The second form of trade prohibition is the secondary boycott, which is a step beyond the primary boycott in that companies from other nations doing business with a sanctioned country will also experience sanctions for such activity. For example, in 1996, the United States passed the Iran and Libya Sanctions Act (ILSA) as a secondary boycott against two nations against which the United States already had imposed trade restrictions. This law was passed because of active lobbying by the families of those killed when Pan Am Flight 103 exploded over Lockerbie, Scotland, as a result of bombs planted on the flight by Libyan terrorists. Under the secondary boycott trade prohibition, the United States will not grant licenses to, permit its financial institutions to loan money to, award government contracts to, or allow imports from any company that finances, supplies, or constructs oil procurement in Iran or Libya. Generally, these types of secondary boycotts do not apply retroactively so that companies already invested need not divest themselves of their holdings in these countries. However, there can be no new business once the act takes effect if the companies wish to continue trading with the United States.

The International Monetary Fund (IMF) and the World Bank

Created at Bretton Woods, New Hampshire, the International Monetary Fund (IMF) was established following World War II with the goal of expanding international trade through a bank with a lending system designed to bring stability to national currencies. The IMF created the International Bank for Reconstruction and Development (commonly called the World Bank), which allows signing nations to have Special Drawing Rights (SDR) or the ability to draw on a line of credit in order to maintain the stability of their currency.

The idea of the IMF was to enhance and encourage international trade through assurances about monetary stability in various countries. Each time a particular nation, such as Japan or Russia, experiences a difficult economic swing, there is significant debate about the use of IMF funds to buoy that nation's currency so that international trade with that country is not destroyed.

The Kyoto Treaty

Review the Kyoto Treaty:
http://www.unfccc.de

The Kyoto Protocol, often called the Kyoto Treaty or the global-warming treaty, is a twenty-four-page document that focuses on the reduction of greenhouse gas emissions. All developed countries would be required to reduce their emissions "by at least 5% below 1990 levels," and the United States would be required to reduce its emissions by at least 7 percent below 1990 levels. China, India, and Mexico are excluded from the treaty's coverage. The EU will reduce emissions by 8 percent below 1990 levels, but their fulfillment can be met jointly and need not be on a country-by-country basis. An international body would be created to monitor emissions. For more information on the Kyoto Treaty, see Chapter 12.

OPEC

The Organization of Petroleum Exporting Countries (OPEC) is a cartel that works together to control oil supplies and production, prices, and taxes. The result of the OPEC cooperation has been increased royalties to those participating countries.

Trust, Corruption, Trade, and Economics

Perhaps the greatest activity in multilateral agreements among countries has been in the area of curbing bribes because of their devastating impact on trust and the resulting effects on the investment and economic environments of a country. In his departure speech as secretary of the U.S. Treasury, Robert Rubin cautioned government employees to never accept any sort of gift as part of their duties for, he noted, "Corruption and bribery benefit a few at the expense of many."

The Foreign Corrupt Practices Act

Perhaps the most widely known criminal statute affecting firms that operate internationally is the **Foreign Corrupt Practices Act** (FCPA; 15 U.S.C. §§ 78dd-1). The FCPA applies to business concerns that have their principal offices in the United States. It contains antibribery provisions as well as accounting controls for these firms, and it is meant to curb the use of bribery in foreign operations of companies.

The act prohibits making, authorizing, or promising payments or gifts of money or anything of value with the intent to corrupt for the purpose of *obtaining* or *retaining business* for or with, or *directing business*. Under the FCPA, payments designed to influence the official acts of foreign officials, political parties, party officials, candidates for office, any nongovernmental organization (NGO), or any person who will transmit the gift or money to one of the other types of persons are prohibited.

The 1998 changes added the NGO provision so that under the definitions section of the FCPA, foreign officials are now defined to include public international figures, such as officials with the United Nations or the IMF.

The FCPA is the result of an SEC investigation that uncovered questionable foreign payments by large stock issuers who were based in the United States. Approximately 435 U.S. corporations had made improper or questionable payments totaling $300 million in Japan, the Netherlands, and Korea. The most common type of payment was made to foreign government officials. Most of the payments were made in relation to tax valuation or assessments. First passed in 1977, the act was most recently amended in 1998. For a payment to a foreign official to constitute a violation of the FCPA, payment or something of value must have been given to a foreign official with discretionary authority, a foreign political candidate, or a foreign political party for the purpose of getting the recipient to act or refrain from acting to help business operations or, under the 1998 changes, to "secure any improper advantage" in doing business in that country. For example, if an American company trying to win a bid on a contract for the construction of highways in a foreign country paid a government official there who was responsible for awarding such construction contracts a "consulting fee" of $25,000, the American company would be in violation of the FCPA. The payment was of money, it was made to a foreign official, and it was made for the purpose of obtaining business within that country.

When the FCPA was passed initially, many companies tried to find ways around the bribery prohibitions. Companies would hire foreign agents or consultants to help them gain business in countries and allowed these "third parties" to act independently. However, many of these consultants then paid bribers. Under the FCPA, even these types of arrangements can constitute a violation if the consulting fees are high, there are odd payment arrangements, or the company has reason to know of a potential or actual violation. Companies must be able to establish that they have performed "due diligence" in investigating those hired as their agents and consultants in foreign countries. For example, if a U.S. company hired a consultant who charged the company $25,000 in fees and $250,000 in expenses, the U.S. company is, under Justice Department guidelines, on notice that the excessive expenses could signal potential bribes being paid. These types of expenses are known as "red flags" for U.S. companies. The Justice Department uses this information as a means of establishing intent event when the company may not know precisely what was done with the funds and what was paid to whom.

Payments to any foreign official for "facilitation," often referred to as "grease payments," are not prohibited under FCPA so long as these payments are made only to get these officials to do their normal jobs that they might not do or would do slowly without some payment. These grease payments can be made for obtaining permits, licenses, or other official documents; processing governmental papers, such as visas and work orders; providing police protection and mail pickup and delivery; providing phone service, power, and water supply; loading and unloading cargo, or protecting perishable products; and scheduling inspections associated with contract performance or transit of goods across the country.

Penalties for violations of the FCPA can run up to $100,000 and five years' imprisonment for individuals. Corporate fines are up to $2 million per violation. There are no civil penalties. Also, under the Alternative Fines Act, the Justice Department can seek to obtain two times the benefit that the bribe attempted to gain. For example, if a company paid a bribe to obtain a $100 million contract for computer services for a foreign government, the potential fine could be $200 million. The Justice Department can use the Alternate Fines Act to obtain civil penalties for violation of the FCPA.

U.S. v. *Kay* (Case 7.1) answers the chapter's opening Consider and deals with a violation of the FCPA.

CASE 7.1

U.S. v. *Kay*
359 F.3d 738 (5th Cir. 2004)

Throwing the Rice Market and Dodging Taxes

FACTS

David Kay (defendant) was an American citizen and a vice president for marketing of American Rice, Inc. (ARI) who was responsible for supervising sales and marketing in the Republic of Haiti. Douglas Murphy (defendant) was an American citizen and president of ARI.

Beginning in 1995 and continuing to about August 1999, Mr. Kay, Mr. Murphy, and other employees and officers of ARI paid bribes and authorized the payment of bribes to induce customs officials in Haiti to accept bills of lading and other documents that intentionally understated the true amount of rice that ARI shipped to Haiti for import, thus reducing the customs duties owed by ARI and RCH to the Haitian government.

In addition, beginning in 1998 and continuing to about August 1999, Mr. Kay and other employees and officers of ARI paid and authorized additional bribes to officials of other Haitian agencies to accept the false import documents and other documents that understated the true amount of rice being imported into and sold in Haiti, thereby reducing the amount of sales taxes paid by RCH to the Haitian government.

Mr. Kay directed employees of ARI to prepare two sets of shipping documents for each shipment of rice to Haiti, one that accurately reflected and another that falsely represented the weight and value of the rice being exported to Haiti.

Mr. Kay and Mr. Murphy agreed to pay and authorized the payment of bribes, calculated as a percentage of the value of the rice not reported on the false documents or in the form of a monthly retainer, to customs and tax officials of the Haitian government to induce these officials to accept the false documentation and to assess significantly lower customs duties and sales taxes than ARI would otherwise have been required to pay.

ARI, using official Haitian customs documents reflecting the amounts reported on the false shipping documents, reported only approximately 66 percent of the rice it sold in Haiti and thereby significantly reduced the amount of sales taxes it was required to pay to the Haitian government.

In 2001, a grand jury charged Mr. Kay with violating the FCPA and subsequently returned the indictment, which charges both Mr. Kay and Mr. Murphy with twelve counts of FCPA violations. Both Mr. Kay and Mr. Murphy moved to dismiss the indictment for the failure to state an offense, arguing that obtaining favorable tax treatment did not fall within the FCPA definition of payments made to government officials in order to obtain business. The district court dismissed the indictment, and the United States of America ("government") (appellant) appealed.

JUDICIAL OPINION

WIENER, Circuit Judge

The principal dispute in this case is whether, if proved beyond a reasonable doubt, the conduct that the indictment ascribed to defendants in connection with the alleged bribery of Haitian officials to understate customs duties and sales taxes on rice shipped to Haiti to assist American Rice, Inc. in obtaining or retaining business was sufficient to constitute an offense under the FCPA. Underlying this question of sufficiency of the contents of the indictment is the preliminary task of ascertaining the scope of the FCPA, which in turn requires us to construe the statute.

Because an offense under the FCPA requires that the alleged bribery be committed for the purpose of inducing foreign officials to commit unlawful acts, the results of which will assist in obtaining or retaining business in their country, the questions before us in this appeal are (1) whether bribes to obtain illegal but favorable tax and customs treatment can ever come within the scope of the statute, and (2) if so, whether, in combination, there are minimally sufficient facts alleged in the indictment to inform the defendants regarding the nexus between, on the one hand, Haitian taxes avoided through bribery, and, on the other hand, assistance in getting or keeping some business or business opportunity in Haiti.

None contend that the FCPA criminalizes every payment to a foreign official: It criminalizes only those

continued

payments that are intended to (1) influence a foreign official to act or make a decision in his official capacity, or (2) induce such an official to perform or refrain from performing some act in violation of his duty, or (3) secure some wrongful advantage to the payor. And even then, the FCPA criminalizes these kinds of payments only if the result they are intended to produce—their *quid pro quo*—will assist (or is intended to assist) the payor in efforts to get or keep some business for or with "any person."

The principal thrust of the defendants' argument is that the business nexus element, i.e., the "assist . . . in obtaining or retaining business" element, narrowly limits the statute's applicability to those payments that are intended to obtain a foreign official's approval of a bid for a new government contract or the renewal of an existing government contract. In contrast, the government insists that, in addition to payments to officials that lead directly to getting or renewing business contracts, the statute covers payments that indirectly advance ("assist") the payor's goal of obtaining or retaining foreign business with or for some person. The government reasons that paying reduced customs duties and sales taxes on imports, as is purported to have occurred in this case, is the type of "improper advantage" that always will assist in obtaining or retaining business in a foreign country, and thus is always covered by the FCPA.

Stated differently, how attenuated can the linkage be between the effects of that which is sought from the foreign official in consideration of a bribe (here, tax minimization) and the briber's goal of finding assistance or obtaining or retaining foreign business with or for some person, and still satisfy the business nexus element of the FCPA?

Invoking basic economic principles, the SEC reasoned in its amicus brief that securing reduced taxes and duties on imports through bribery enables ARI to reduce its cost of doing business, thereby giving it an "improper advantage" over actual or potential competitors, and enabling it to do more business, or remain in a market it might otherwise leave.

Section 78dd-1(b) excepts from the statutory scope "any facilitating or expediting payment to a foreign official . . . the purpose of which is to expedite or to service the performance of a routine governmental action by a foreign official. . . ." 15 U.S.C. § 78dd-1(b).

For purposes of deciding the instant appeal, the question nevertheless remains whether the Senate, and concomitantly Congress, intended this broader statutory scope to encompass the administration of tax, customs, and other laws and regulations affecting the revenue of foreign states. To reach this conclusion, we must ask whether Congress's remaining expressed desire to prohibit bribery aimed at getting assistance in retaining business or maintaining business opportunities was sufficiently broad to include bribes meant to affect the administration of revenue laws. When we do so, we conclude that the legislative intent was so broad.

Congress was obviously distraught not only about high profile bribes to high-ranking foreign officials, but also by the pervasiveness of foreign bribery by United States businesses and businessmen. Congress thus made the decision to clamp down on bribes intended to prompt foreign officials to misuse their discretionary authority for the benefit of a domestic entity's business in that country. This observation is not diminished by Congress's understanding and accepting that relatively small facilitating payments were, at the time, among the accepted costs of doing business in many foreign countries.

Obviously, a commercial concern that bribes a foreign government official to award a construction, supply, or services contract violates the statute. Yet, there is little difference between this example and that of a corporation's lawfully obtaining a contract from an honest official or agency by submitting the lowest bid, and—either before or after doing so—bribing a different government official to reduce taxes and thereby ensure that the under-bid venture is nevertheless profitable. Avoiding or lowering taxes reduces operating costs and thus increases profit margins, thereby freeing up funds that the business is otherwise legally obligated to expend. And this, in turn, enables it to take any number of actions to the disadvantage of competitors. Bribing foreign officials to lower taxes and customs duties certainly can provide an unfair advantage over competitors and thereby be of assistance to the payor in obtaining or retaining business. This demonstrates that the question whether the defendants' alleged payments constitute a violation of the FCPA truly turns on whether these bribes were intended to lower ARI's cost of doing business in Haiti enough to have a sufficient nexus to garnering business there or to maintaining or increasing business operations that ARI already had there, so as to come within the scope of the business nexus element as Congress used it in the FCPA. Answering this fact question, then, implicates a matter of proof and thus evidence.

Given the foregoing analysis of the statute's legislative history, we cannot hold as a matter of law that Congress meant to limit the FCPA's applicability to cover only bribes that lead directly to the award or renewal of contracts. Instead, we hold that Congress intended for the FCPA to apply broadly to payments intended to assist the payor, either directly or indirectly, in obtaining or retaining business for some person, and that bribes paid to foreign tax officials to secure illegally reduced customs and tax liability constitute a type of payment that can fall within this broad coverage. In 1977, Congress was motivated to prohibit rampant foreign bribery by domestic business entities, but nevertheless understood the pragmatic need to exclude innocuous grease payments from the scope of its proposals. The FCPA's legislative history instructs that Congress was concerned about both the kind of bribery that leads to discrete contractual arrangements and the kind that more generally helps a domestic payor obtain or retain business for some person in a foreign country; and that Congress was aware that this type includes illicit payments made to officials to obtain favorable but unlawful tax treatment.

Furthermore, by narrowly defining exceptions and affirmative defenses against a backdrop of broad applicability, Congress reaffirmed its intention for the statute to apply to payments that even indirectly assist in obtaining business or maintaining existing business operations in a foreign country. Finally, Congress's intention to implement the Convention, a treaty that indisputably prohibits any bribes that give an advantage to which a business entity is not fully entitled, further supports our determination of the extent of the FCPA's scope.

Thus, in diametric opposition to the district court, we conclude that bribes paid to foreign officials in consideration for unlawful evasion of customs duties and sales taxes could fall within the purview of the FCPA's proscription. We hasten to add, however, that this conduct does not automatically constitute a violation of the FCPA: It still must be shown that the bribery was intended to produce an effect—here, through tax savings—that would "assist in obtaining or retaining business."

(The court also found the indictment to sufficiently allege a violation of the FCPA.)

Reversed and remanded.

CASE QUESTIONS

1. What benefit did ARI obtain?
2. Why do Mr. Kay and Mr. Murphy argue that the FCPA does not apply to their conduct?
3. Why does the appellate court conclude differently?
4. What does the court look at in order to reach its conclusion?

CONSIDER... 7.1

A Philip Morris subsidiary, C. A. Tabacalera National, and a B.A.T. subsidiary known as C. A. Cigarrera Bigott entered into a contract with La Fundacion del Nino (the Children's Foundation) of Caracas, Venezuela. The agreement was signed on behalf of the foundation by the foundation's president, who also was the wife of the then president of Venezuela. Under the terms of the agreement, these two tobacco firms were to make periodic donations to the Children's Foundation totaling $12.5 million. In exchange, the two firms would receive price controls on Venezuelan tobacco, elimination of controls on retail cigarette prices in Venezuela, tax deductions for donations, and assurances that the existing tax rates applicable to tobacco companies would not be increased.

Is the donation to the charity a violation of the FCPA? [*Lamb* v. *Philip Morris, Inc.*, 915 F.2d 1024 (6th Cir. 1990; *cert. denied*, 498 U.S. 1086 (1995)).]

THINK: The FCPA prohibits payments to government officials for purposes of obtaining contracts/benefits. Third-party payments are also prohibited (i.e., a company cannot get around the FCPA by having someone else make the payment). The *Kay* case indicates that Congress wanted to be as broad as possible to cut back on bribes and corruption.

APPLY: What is different about this situation? The payment here is more indirect and more subtle—the benefit is not to a government official.

ANSWER: If the intent of Congress in passing the FCPA was to stop bribery, both direct and indirect payments should be covered. The *Kay* case covered indirect business benefits, and the statute is clear on the purposes for which payments are made. Here we have an indirect payment with the intent to secure a benefit. The situation is covered under the FCPA.

CONSIDER . . .   7 . 2

Robert R. King was an executive with Owl Securities and was charged with a violation of the FCPA because of a $1 million payment made to government officials when a land deal in Costa Rica closed. This "kiss" payment was made to secure certain benefits for the property. The payment was made through the bank at the closing and not done by Mr. King himself, but he was charged with a violation of the FCPA. The following is a transcription of conversations recorded when Mr. Kingsley, an undercover agent for federal officials, talked with Mr. King.

May 26, 2000
Kingsley: Well you've always known about the closing cost fees and that.
King: I've known what?
Kingsley: You've known about the closing costs.
King: The one million dollars?
Kingsley: Yeah.
King: I've known about that for five years, yeah. . . .

June 1 and 2, 2000
King: You see when they walk into the bank, you know, the bank is going to be curious as to what they're putting up a million dollars for. . . .
Kingsley: Well do they. . . .
King: . . . If they do a letter of credit.
Kingsley: . . . do the bank . . . do. . . .
King: Ah, my own bank does not ask for that. My own bank is going to take the Falcon. But if I go with these other people, a letter of credit, and the reason I may go to them for a letter of credit instead of my own letter of credit is that it's, it's going to get them involved in this.
Kingsley: Yeah. Do.
King: And we don't, we don't want just a million dollars, we want a hundred thirty-five million.
Kingsley: Yeah. Do they know what the million[']s for though?
King: Ah, probably . . . I think I told them yeah.
Kingsley: Yeah. Well.
King: They didn't bat an eye.
Kingsley: [coughs]
King: I put it in this letter as a closing cost.
Kingsley: Yeah, that's what Dick likes to call it, is a closing cost.

June 28, 2000
Kingsley: Well, look, what.
Halford: He irritated a lot of people.
Kingsley: Yeah, what, um, what Pablo had said, was why just pay, pay off the current politicians. Pay off the future ones.
King: That's right. Because we're gonna have to work with them anyway.
Kingsley: And so what he was saying was double, you know, give them more money. Buy the opposition. If you buy the current party and the opposition, then it doesn't matter who's in because there's only two parties.
King: The thing that really worries me is that, uh, if the Justice Department gets a hold of. Finds out how many people we've been paying off down there. Uh, or even if they don't. Are we gonna have to spend the rest of our lives paying off these petty politicians to keep them out of our hair? I can just see us, every, every day some politician on our doorstep down there wanting a hand out for this or that.
Kingsley: Well, I mean.
King: I'd like to. . . .

Kingsley: I. . . .

King: Think we could pay the top people enough, that the rest of the people won't bother us any. That's what I'm hoping this million and a half dollars does. I'm hoping it pays enough top people. . . .

August 17, 2000

Kingsley: Now Pablo's continued to talk to the politicians. They know about the toll, closing costs call it what you will. So he's still our biggest asset in place.

King: What do they know about the closing costs?

Kingsley: Who?

King: Does everybody agree to what we talked about recently?

Kingsley: Yeah, a million into escrow for the toll.

King: And then we get the property and then we do the [unintelligible]?

Kingsley: Um hum. Yeah now let me I'll, I'll, I'll come on to that because I'll explain how we work through that. Uh, essentially once the politicians see the money in escrow, they'll move. That's what it comes down to [clears throat]. Pablo's gonna send a list, an e-mail with a list of politicians already paid off and the ones he's gonna pay off.

King: Isn't that awfully dangerous?

Kingsley: No e-mail's probably the most secure form of communication.

King: From what I read it's not, number one and number two, there's got to be a better way.

Barquero: We have to make the politicians sure that they are going to get that. That is one thing that we have to make them feel comfortable that uh, we would get the full support.

King: I [unintelligible].

Did King violate the FCPA? Is there enough evidence here to prove intent? [*U.S. v. King,* 351 F.3d 859 (8th Cir. 2003).]

Many businesses have been critical of the FCPA because of the lack of uniformity among various nations concerning the propriety of facilitating (grease) payments and the legality of bribes. A foreign agent can legally receive the payment, but a U.S. corporation cannot make the payment. However, a survey by the U.S. Government Accounting Office of the companies affected by the FCPA found that the ability of companies from other countries to bribe officials did not give them a competitive advantage. The survey found that U.S. trade increased in fifty-one of fifty-six foreign countries after the FCPA went into effect. The increase was attributed to the position adopted by U.S. companies with respect to their competitors—if they could not bribe government officials, they would disclose publicly any information about bribes made by any of the companies from other nations.

Visit the U.S. Justice Department Web site on the FCPA:

http://www.usdoj.gov/criminal/fraud/fcpa.html

ETHICAL ISSUES

Drawing on materials from Chapter 2, make the argument as to why even facilitation or grease payments present problems for businesses and the countries in which they are made.

BUSINESS STRATEGY APPLICATION

See the exercise for this chapter on the book's Web site to review company policies on the FCPA.

FOR THE MANAGER'S DESK

RE: CORRUPTION, DEMOCRACY, AND WEALTH

In a review of the impact of bribes on economic activity, the *New York Times* quoted Mexico's anticorruption official as saying that graft results in increases in costs for government services that amount to 9.5 percent of Mexico's GDP, which is twice the amount of the country's education budget. The review of corruption and the impact of bribes reached the following conclusions.

- The most corrupt nations are the poor nations.
- Larger government structures tend to be less corrupt; however, more steps in processing can also lead to more corruption. For example, when there are sixteen steps required to get goods unloaded, there are often sixteen opportunities for government officials at customs to demand payments.
- Democracy helps cut down on corruption.
- How an economy is driven makes a difference, with oil corrupting more than other products.
- Keeping a registry of goods helps because then officials are aware of what is coming into the country. The most corrupt countries do not keep records as goods arrive, are inspected, and then are approved for entry.

Corruption discourages foreign investment and throws the countries into a never-ending circle of no economic development. Transparency International has published its annual Corruptions Perceptions Index (CPI). Transparency International is an NGO with the strategic goal of eliminating corruption in international business.

The CPI is determined by surveys of businesspeople, academics, and risk analysts in each of the countries. The survey ranks countries from 0 (highly corrupt) to 10 (highly clean). There are 91 countries on the list. (You can find the full survey at http://www.transparency.org.)

The report names Bangladesh (0.4), Nigeria (1.0), Uganda (1.9), Indonesia (1.9), Bolivia (2.0), Kenya (2.0), Cameroon (2.0), and Russia (2.3) as the countries most prone to corruption.

The following list shows the cleanest countries in the CPI.

Finland	9.9
Denmark	9.5
New Zealand	9.4
Iceland	9.2
Singapore	9.2
Sweden	9.0
Canada	8.9
Netherlands	8.8
Luxembourg	8.7
Norway	8.6
Australia	8.5
Switzerland	8.4
United Kingdom	8.3
Hong Kong	7.9
Austria	7.8
Israel	7.6
United States	7.6

Source: Corruption Perceptions Index 2002.

Why is there a concern about corruption in business transactions?

Source: Tina Rosenberg, "The Taint of the Greased Palm," *New York Times Magazine,* August 10, 2003, p. 28.

BUSINESS STRATEGY

The Costs of Slipping on the FCPA

In companies with 100,000 employees worldwide, supervision of employees with regard to the FCPA can be difficult. Without clear signals from executive management and strong policies, even companies with the best intentions in terms of compliance with the law can fall short. For example, IBM entered into a consent decree with the SEC on charges that it engaged in bribery in violation of the FCPA. The charges filed by the SEC alleged that an IBM subsidiary, IBM Argen-

© DIGITAL VISION/GETTY IMAGES

tina S. A., was awarded a $250 million contract for modernizing the systems of Banco de la Nacion Argentina (BNA), a government-owned commercial bank in Argentina. As part of the arrangement, the IBM subsidiary entered into a $37 million contract to do business with a corporation owned by directors of BNA, with the directors receiving $4.5 million of that $37 million contract as compensation. Those directors then voted to award IBM the contract.

The consent decree requires IBM to pay a $300,000 fine. The fine is minimal because IBM did conduct its own internal investigation to uncover what had happened and fired thirteen employees in its subsidiary when the preceding relationships were uncovered.

BNA revoked the contract after paying IBM $80 million, and IBM has agreed to reimburse BNA $34 million of that amount. Other Argentine agencies also revoked their contracts with IBM, with the total amount of business lost in the Argentina market estimated to be $500 million.

IBM has announced a new company policy that prohibits company bids for government projects that are not done in an open bidding process with full public access to documents.*

The costs to IBM in this situation, both in terms of its lost contracts and revenues and its reputation, are nearly incalculable. Many companies take the position that they will not even make facilitation payments so that their worldwide staff members understand a clear and definitive line. A Procter & Gamble executive explains that, once a government official knows that a company will pay to get things done or get them done quickly, the price keeps rising and that such payments never serve the shareholders well. Long-term growth in a country is limited when even facilitation payments become part of a company's operations there. Strategically, more than ethically and legally, these types of payments are questionable in their benefits and results.

*In the Matter of International Business Machines Corp., Administrative Proceeding File No 3–13097, Rel. No. 34–43761 (December 21, 2000).

The **Organization for Economic Cooperation and Development** (OECD) is now extremely supportive of the already existing U.S. position on bribery, and its member countries are enacting legislation for compliance with its international pact against bribery. The OECD passed an antibribery provision in December 1997 that, if accepted by the thirty member nations,[1] will result in a form of the FCPA being passed in those individual countries.[2]

When Congress amended the FCPA in order to implement the OECD Convention on Combating Bribery of Foreign Public Officials in International Business Transactions, the amendments expanded the act's jurisdiction to cover all U.S. citizens acting outside the United States and to all non-U.S. citizens acting inside the United States.

The convention basically adopts the standards of the United States under the FCPA and requires nations signing the agreement to: (1) criminalize bribery of foreign public officials; (2) define public officials to include officials in all branches of government, whether appointed or elected; any person exercising a public function, including for a public agency or public enterprise; and any official or agent of a public international organization; (3) include as public functions any activity in the public interest; (4) cover business-related bribes to foreign public officials made through political parties and party officials; (5) include as illegal those payments made to someone who will become a public official in anticipation of favorable treatment; (6) provide for "effective, proportionate and dissuasive criminal penalties" to those who bribe foreign public officials;[3] (7) authorize the seizure or confiscation of the bribe and bribe proceeds (i.e.,

BUSINESS PLANNING TIP

Compliance with the FCPA requires great effort and diligence on the part of companies involved in international operations.

1. Use great caution on any payments to government officials, even for things as simple as getting the phone lines in your office connected. The task may be administrative or bureaucratic, but the understanding of employees about what is and is not illegal is influenced by each choice to pay even so-called legal grease payments.

2. Do background checks on all your foreign employees and agents. Obtain financial information and personal references for them.

3. Publish your complete and unambiguous policy on FCPA payments. Include details and examples for employees, and post the policy in all offices.

4. Establish effective financial controls in all your offices and facilities. Send outside auditors to your international offices to make surprise visits and spot checks of the records.

5. Voluntarily report any slips or misunderstandings. Come forward with the information and disclose all relevant actions and records to the U.S. government.

net profit), or property of similar value, or impose monetary sanctions of comparable effect; (8) prohibit the establishment of off-the-books accounts and similar practices used to bribe foreign public officials or to hide such bribery; (9) establish jurisdiction over acts that take place in their countries even if there is not extensive physical contact by those paying the bribes; and (10) pledge to work together to provide legal assistance relating to investigations and proceedings and to make bribery of foreign public officials an extraditable offense. The United States was the first country to pass implementing procedures in its laws and did so by the end of 1998. Under these amendments to the existing FCPA, all officers, employees, agents, and even foreign nationals working for U.S. companies are covered under the act in order to comply with the OECD requirements.

OECD will continue to monitor its members' compliance with the policies in their laws as well as continue to study the impact of the convention on stopping corruption in international trade.

RESOLUTION OF INTERNATIONAL DISPUTES

Visit the International Court of Justice: **http://www.icj-cij.org**

As discussed in Chapters 1, 3, and 4, there really is no way to enforce international laws. The International Court of Justice established by the United Nations is a court of voluntary jurisdiction for disputes between nations; it is not a court for the resolution of business disputes between nations. More and more companies and individuals favor arbitration to resolve disputes. The most popular forum chosen for such arbitrations and quasi-trials is London's Commercial Court founded over 100 years ago on March 1, 1895, when it heard its first case, which involved a dispute over the quality of cloth sold by a Flemish manufacturer to a London agent. The court was perhaps the first to recognize the role of arbitration in deciding international business disputes; such innovation restored the confidence of business in the settlement of disputes by third parties. The London Commercial Court is viewed as a neutral forum with highly experienced judges who are also experienced commercial litigators.

PRINCIPLES OF INTERNATIONAL LAW

The sources of international law simply serve to govern businesses as they operate in a particular country, and the laws may vary from country to country. However, some principles of international law apply to all countries and people in the international marketplace. The principles of international law do affect the decisions and operations of businesses, regardless of the availability of court resolution of rights.

Sovereign Immunity

The concept of **sovereign immunity** is based on the notion that each country is a sovereign nation. This status means that each country is an equal with other countries; each country has exclusive jurisdiction over its internal operations, laws, and people; and no country is subject to the jurisdiction of another country's court system unless it so consents. Our court system cannot be used to right injustices in other countries or to subject other countries to penalties. For example, in *Schooner Exchange* v. *McFaddon*, 7 Cr. 116 (1812), a group of American citizens attempted to seize the vessel *Exchange* when it came into port at Philadelphia because the citizens believed that the ship had been taken improperly on the high seas by the French emperor Napoleon and that the ship rightfully belonged to them. The U.S. Supreme

Court held that the ship could not be seized because sovereign immunity applied, and France could not involuntarily be subjected to the jurisdiction of U.S. courts.

Review the Foreign Sovereign Immunities Act of 1976:
http://www.law.cornell.edu/uscode/28/1602.html

The Foreign Sovereign Immunities Act of 1976 clarified the U.S. government's position on sovereign immunity and incorporated the *Schooner Exchange* doctrine. Not only are countries immune, but the act also adds a clarification to the concept of sovereign immunity of sovereign nations for illegal acts. For example, in *Argentine Republic v. Amerada Hess Shipping Co.,* 488 U.S. 428 (1989), the Supreme Court dismissed a suit brought in a U.S. federal court by a Liberian-chartered commercial ship company against the government of Argentina for its unprovoked and illegal attack on a company ship that was in neutral waters when the war between Great Britain and Argentina broke out over the Falkland Islands. The attack by the Argentine navy was unprovoked and in clear violation of international law. However, the U.S. Supreme Court clarified that under the Sovereign Immunities Act and principles of international law, all sovereign nations are immune from suits in other countries, even for those acts—like that of Argentina's—that are clear violations of international law.

A distinction has been made, however, by both the Foreign Sovereign Immunities Act and the courts with respect to the commercial transactions of a sovereign nation. For example, the sale of services and goods; loan transactions; and contracts for marketing, public relations, and employment services entered into by a country are, in essence, voluntary agreements that subject that country's government to civil suits in another nation's courts according to the terms of the agreement or according to the basic tenets of judicial jurisdiction (see Chapter 3).

ETHICAL ISSUES

"You can't be a global player without a presence in the United States." James McDermott, president of the consulting firm Keefe, Bruyette & Woods, gave this advice while speaking of international banking. Many agreed with Mr. McDermott's assessment, including Daiwa Bank of Japan. Daiwa was established in Japan in 1918, and, as of November 2, 1995, was the tenth largest bank in Japan and the twenty-first largest bank in the world. Its 1994 assets were $183.5 billion, and its earnings for 1994 were booked as $1.3 billion. Daiwa set up its U.S. offices with headquarters in New York under the name of Daiwa Bank Trust Company. There were branches and offices of Daiwa Bank Trust in eleven states in the largest U.S. cities. The U.S. division of the bank employed about 400 people.

Toshihide Iguchi was the executive responsible for running the U.S. bank's trading operations. It would be the trading operations that would result in the bank's downfall. The losses in the bank's trading operations began in 1983 but were not entered on the books. Between 1983 and 1995, more than $1 billion in trading losses were not reported. Indeed, the records of the bank were falsified to conceal the losses. Records were also falsified to conceal another $97 million in losses from 1984 to 1987 in bank operations for the Manhattan offices.

Throughout this period, federal regulators had warned Daiwa officials to separate its trading activities from its record keeping and custody of funds. The functions were never separated.

In July 1995, Mr. Iguchi confessed his wrongdoing to senior management officials in Japan and urged them to buy back some of the Treasury bonds he had sold illegally to cover up the losses. His letter assured the senior management that there was "zero possibility" that federal regulators would discover what they were doing. In late July, an officer from Japan met with Mr. Iguchi in New York and told him to continue the cover-up until Daiwa issued its six-month financials for the period ending September 30, 1995.

But Daiwa officials reported the problems of the U.S. division and Mr. Iguchi's activities to Japanese regulators on August 8, 1995. The same report was made to U.S. regulators in Washington, D.C., on September 15, 1995.

In early November 1995, federal and state regulators "deported" Daiwa operations in the United States, requiring that all U.S. operations be shut down. In addition to deportation, the federal government issued a twenty-four-count indictment charging the bank with deception of federal regulators and cover-ups of losses. Daiwa paid a $345 million fine and settled shareholder suits for $775 million. Mr. Iguchi pleaded guilty to trying to conceal the losses. He converted $377 million in securities held to make up the losses. Mr. Iguchi was

continued

sentenced to four years in prison and paid a $2.6 million fine. Masahiro Tsuda, the general manager of the New York office, was also named in the indictments.

Takashi Kaiho, Daiwa's president, complained about the criminal charges and vowed to fight them, contending that "blaming Daiwa Bank for thievery and other unauthorized activities makes no sense."

Do you agree? Is it unfair to hold Daiwa accountable? If Daiwa is not responsible for what happened, who is? The term *rogue trader* has been used frequently in financial debacles. Barings Bank, the 200-year-old international bank that collapsed because of derivative trading, claimed its bankruptcy was the result of one trader. What signals and atmosphere allow a rogue trader to operate?

Expropriation, or the Act of State Doctrine

Under this doctrine, U.S. courts recognize the acts of governments of foreign nations as valid, even though under our system of legal rights there may be some question whether the acts were legal or appropriate. This doctrine has been challenged most frequently in cases in which a foreign country has expropriated or nationalized private property in a country by an order of attachment. In effect, the foreign government has seized control of private property. Under our standards of due process, such a taking would be unconstitutional without just compensation (see Chapter 5 for a discussion of eminent domain and just compensation), but the **act of state doctrine** provides that "the courts of one country will not sit in judgment on . . . the acts of another done within its own territory" [*Underhill* v. *Hernandez*, 168 U.S. 250 (1897)].

The effect of the act of state doctrine is to leave foreign affairs in the hands of the legislative and executive branches of government and keep courts out of the loop. There are many cases in which **expropriation** violates principles of international law. In most cases, expropriation or nationalization violates our notions of equity and justice. However, some protection exists for businesses and individuals who invest in foreign nations because the Sovereign Immunities Act exemption for commercial activity also applies in cases of expropriation. *Riedel v. Bancam* (Case 7.2) clarifies the distinction between expropriation and commercial activity, only one of which enjoys immunity.

CASE 7.2

Riedel v. *Bancam*
792 F.2d 587 (6th Cir. 1986)

Pesos to Dollars: Exchange Rates Can Kill Investments

FACTS

W. Christian Riedel, a resident of Ohio, had an account with Unibanco, S. A., and asked that it transfer $100,000 to Banca Metropolitana, S. A. (Bamesa) (predecessor to Bancam) for investment in a certificate of deposit (CD). Bamesa merged with another bank to form Bancam, and Mr. Riedel's CD was renewed with the newly merged bank.

Shortly after Mr. Riedel's renewal, the government of Mexico issued new rules governing accounts from foreigners in Mexican banks. The rules required the banks to pay the CDs in pesos at a rate that was substantially below exchange rates. A month after these rules were put into effect, Bancam was nationalized.

When Mr. Riedel's CD came due, the exchange rate was 74.34 pesos to the dollar. He was paid $53,276.23 for his $100,000 investment.

Mr. Riedel brought suit in a U.S. federal district court, alleging that Bancam had violated both federal and Ohio securities laws in selling the CDs in the United States without registration. Bancam filed a motion to dismiss the suit on the ground that the Sovereign Immunities Act of 1976 precluded U.S. courts from taking jurisdiction over the matter. Bancam also claimed protection under the act of state doctrine. Finally, Bancam claimed that the CD was not a security for purposes of U.S. securities laws.

The district court dismissed Mr. Riedel's suit on the grounds that it lacked jurisdiction over the claims under

Ohio law and also on grounds of sovereign immunity and the act of state doctrine. Mr. Riedel appealed.

JUDICIAL OPINION

KENNEDY, Circuit Judge

In this appeal, Riedel does not challenge the District Court's conclusion that the certificates of deposit that Bancam issued are not "securities" under federal securities law. Instead, Riedel argues that the "act of state doctrine" does not bar his breach of contract and Ohio securities law claims. The District Court, however, did not refer to the "act of state doctrine" in denying Riedel's motion for a new trial. In addition to holding, as a matter of law, that the certificate of deposit involved in this case was not a "security" under federal securities law, the District Court ruled that it did not have jurisdiction over Riedel's breach of contract and Ohio securities law claims. The District Court concluded that: "Diversity jurisdiction pursuant to 28 U.S.C. Section 1332 does not permit a citizen of this state to sue a foreign government, or agency thereof, in a federal district court."

We agree that the District Court did not have jurisdiction under 28 U.S.C. § 1332 over the breach of contract and Ohio securities law claims. Title 28 U.S.C. § 1332(a)(4) confers original jurisdiction on the district courts over civil actions between a foreign state, as plaintiff, and a citizen of a State. Title 28 U.S.C. § 1332(a)(4), however, does not apply to suits between a citizen of a State and a foreign state, as defendant. A "foreign state," under 28 U.S.C. § 1603(a), "includes a political subdivision of a foreign state or an agency or instrumentality of a foreign state. . . ." Since the Government of Mexico nationalized Bancam on September 1, 1982, Bancam qualifies as an "agency or instrumentality of a foreign state" under 28 U.S.C. § 1603(b)(2). Therefore, this action involves an Ohio citizen and a "foreign state," as a defendant. Consequently, 28 U.S.C. § 1332(a)(4) does not apply. Accordingly, we hold that the District Court properly concluded that it did not have jurisdiction under 28 U.S.C. § 1332 over the breach of contract and Ohio securities law claims.

We conclude, however, that the District Court may have had jurisdiction over the breach of contract and Ohio securities law claims under the [Foreign Sovereign Immunities Act (FSIA) 28 U.S.C. § 1330]. Although the FSIA ordinarily entitles foreign states to immunity from federal jurisdiction, 28 U.S.C. § 1605(a)(2) creates a "commercial activity" exception to this immunity. Title 28 U.S.C. § 1605(a)(2) provides in pertinent part:

A foreign state shall not be immune from the jurisdiction of courts of the United States or of the States in any case . . . in which the action is based upon commercial activity carried on in the United States by the foreign state; or upon an act performed in the United States in connection with a commercial activity of the foreign state elsewhere or upon an act outside the territory of the United States in connection with a commercial activity of the foreign state elsewhere and that act causes a direct effect in the United States.

Accordingly, 28 U.S.C. § 1605(a)(2) applies only when a foreign state's "commercial activity" has the required jurisdictional nexus with the United States.

We hold that the sale of the certificates of deposit in this case was a "commercial activity." . . .

The "act of state doctrine" precludes courts in this country from questioning the validity and effect of a sovereign act of a foreign nation performed in its own territory. . . .

Under the "act of state doctrine," courts exercise jurisdiction but prudentially "decline to decide the merits of the case if in doing so we would need to judge the validity of the public acts of a sovereign state performed within its own territory."

Accordingly, we affirm the portion of the District Court's order denying Riedel's motion for a new trial on the breach of contract claim. The "act of state doctrine," however, does not bar the Ohio securities law claim. Riedel bases that claim on Bancam's failure to register the certificate of deposit with the Ohio Division of Securities and not on Bancam's failure to repay dollars at the certificate's maturity.

Since the District Court may have had the subject matter jurisdiction, we remand the Ohio securities law claim for further proceedings consistent with this opinion. We also note that even if the District Court concludes that it has subject matter jurisdiction, Bancam has also argued that the District Court does not have personal jurisdiction. Assuming that the District Court decides that it has subject matter jurisdiction under the FSIA, the District Court will also have to make findings of fact to determine whether Bancam has sufficient "contacts" with the United States to satisfy due process.

Reversed in part.

CASE QUESTIONS

1. Describe Mr. Riedel's investment.
2. What did he get back from his original investment?
3. What are the bases for his suit against Bancam in Ohio?
4. Does the act of state doctrine apply?
5. Does Mexico have sovereign immunity for its expropriation of the bank?
6. What issues will the court be determining when the case is remanded?

CONSIDER...   7 · 3

Scott Nelson was employed at the Kingdom of Saudi Arabia, a hospital in Saudi Arabia. He had signed an employment contract to act as a monitoring systems engineer at the hospital. Mr. Nelson responded to an ad run in the United States, was hired, and began work in December 1983.

In the course of his employment, Mr. Nelson discovered numerous safety violations. When he brought them to the attention of hospital officials in March 1984, they told him to ignore it.

On September 27, 1994, Mr. Nelson was summoned to the security office, where agents of the Saudi government arrested him.

He was transported to a jail cell, where he was shackled, tortured, and beaten. He was kept for four days with no food and confined to an overcrowded cell area infested with rats. When food was provided, he had to fight other prisoners for it.

After thirty-nine days and U.S. intervention, Mr. Nelson was released from jail. He refused to return to the hospital and left for the United States.

Mr. Nelson and his wife brought a damages suit against his former employer for their failure to warn him about the government. The Saudi government sought to dismiss the suit under the Foreign Sovereign Immunities Act.

Was the activity commercial? Should the Nelsons be permitted to sue? [*Saudi Arabia* v. *Nelson*, 507 U.S. 349 (1993).]

CONSIDER...   7 · 4

What if a U.S. citizen were sexually harassed in the office of the Brazilian embassy located in Washington, D.C.? Would the Brazilian official be immune from suit for the harassment? What policy implications do you see in the decision in such a matter? [*Zveiter* v. *Brazilian National Superintendency of Merchant Marine*, 841 F. Supp. 111 (S.D.N.Y. 1993).]

Protections for U.S. Property and Investment Abroad

Review the Hickenlooper amendment:
http://www.law.cornell.edu/
uscode/22/2370.html

The effect of nationalization and expropriation combined with the act of state doctrine and sovereign immunity is to chill U.S. investments in foreign countries. To discourage expropriation, the Foreign Assistance Act of 1962 contained what has been called the Hickenlooper amendment, which requires the president to suspend all forms of assistance to countries that have expropriated the property of U.S. citizens or regulated the property in such a way as to effectively deprive a U.S. citizen of it (through taxation or limits on use).

Many trade treaties that have been negotiated or are being negotiated with other countries contain protections against expropriation. Some treaties provide U.S. companies and investors with the same levels of protection as the citizens of those countries. For example, if a country affords its citizens due process before taking over private property, U.S. citizens and companies must be afforded those same protections prior to expropriation.

Finally, Congress has created a federal insurer for U.S. investments abroad. The Overseas Private Investment Corporation (OPIC) is an insurer for U.S. investment in those countries in which the per capita annual income is $250 or less. OPIC will pay damages for expropriation, for inability to convert the currency of the country, or for losses from war or revolution.

Consumer protections in other countries depend on those countries' laws. For example, many U.S. citizens have constructed luxury homes along the coast near Ensenada in Baja California. They did so because the land and construction were so much cheaper than in the United States that they could afford large, luxurious homes. However, the land on which many of the homes were located was the subject of fourteen years of litigation and more than sixty court decisions over disputed ownership rights. With the Mexican Supreme Court's decision on land ownership, most of the current U.S. owners have been told that they must vacate their homes and leave everything behind. While there might be due process and property rights in the United States, the homeowners in Ensenada have no hope so long as the Mexican Supreme Court has declared the law for its country and land there.

Repatriation

Repatriation is the process of bringing back to your own country profits earned on investments in another country. In some nations, there are limits on repatriation; businesses can remove only a certain amount of the profits earned from the operations of a business within a country. Repatriation limits are considered acts of state and are immune from litigation in the United States.

> **BUSINESS PLANNING TIP**
>
> Limits on repatriation should be checked before an investment is made in a foreign country. Limits could be set strictly on amounts or on amounts over certain time periods. Financial planning requires foreknowledge of these types of limits.

Forum Non Conveniens, or "You Have the Wrong Court"

The doctrine of *forum non conveniens* is a principle of U.S. justice under which cases that are brought to the wrong court are dismissed. The doctrine allows judicial discretion whereby such issues as the location of the evidence, the location of the parties, and the location of the property that will be used to satisfy any judgment are examined. For example, when the Union Carbide disaster occurred at its Bhopal, India, plant, victims and families brought suit against Union Carbide in New York City. A U.S. court of appeals dismissed the case and sent it back to India on the grounds of *forum non conveniens* [*In re Union Carbide Corp. Gas Plant Disaster,* 809 F.2d 195 (2d Cir. 1987)].

Conflicts of Law

No two countries match in terms of the structure of their legal system or in their laws. For example, the law in the United States, codified by the widely adopted Uniform Commercial Code (UCC), is that all contracts and contract relationships are subject to a standard of good faith. In Canada, the good faith exists only if the parties place such a provision in their agreement. Under German law, protections are given not on the basis of good faith but, rather, on the basis of who is the weaker party. Just among three major commercial powers, laws on contracts are significantly different. The rules on conflicts of law in international transactions are as follows: (1) If the parties choose which law applies, that law will apply, and (2) if no provision is made, the law of the country where the contract is performed will be used. Agreeing to and understanding the set of laws to be applied in a contract is a critical part of international transactions. *Carnival Cruise Lines* v. *Shute* (Case 7.3) is the U.S. Supreme Court's decision on party agreements for resolution of disputes.

CASE 7.3

Carnival Cruise Lines v. *Shute*
499 U.S. 585 (1991)

Cruising for Forums: Contracts Clauses on the High Seas

FACTS

Through an Arlington, Washington, travel agent, Eulala and Russel Shute (respondents) purchased passage for a seven-day cruise on the *Tropicale*, a ship owned by Carnival Cruise Lines (petitioner). The Shutes paid the fare to the agent, who forwarded the payment to Carnival's headquarters in Miami, Florida. Carnival then prepared the tickets and sent them to the Shutes in Washington. The face of each ticket, at its left-hand lower corner, contained this admonition:

> SUBJECT TO CONDITIONS OF CONTRACT ON LAST PAGES IMPORTANT! PLEASE READ CONTRACT—ON LAST PAGES 1, 2, 3, App. 15

The following appeared on "contract page 1" of each ticket:

> TERMS AND CONDITIONS OF PASSAGE CONTRACT TICKET . . .
>
>   3. (a) The acceptance of this ticket by the person or persons named hereon as passengers shall be deemed to be an acceptance and agreement by each of them of all of the terms and conditions of this Passage Contract Ticket. . . .
>
>   8. It is agreed by and between the passenger and the Carrier that all disputes and matters whatsoever arising under, in connection with or incident to this Contract shall be litigated, if at all, in and before a Court located in the State of Florida, U.S.A., to the exclusion of the Courts of any other state or country.

The Shutes boarded the *Tropicale* in Los Angeles, California. The ship sailed to Puerto Vallarta, Mexico, and then returned to Los Angeles. While the ship was in international waters off the Mexican coast, Eulala Shute was injured when she slipped on a deck mat during a guided tour of the ship's galley. The Shutes filed suit against the petitioner in the U.S. District Court for the Western District of Washington, claiming that Mrs. Shute's injuries had been caused by the negligence of Carnival Cruise Lines and its employees.

Carnival moved for summary judgment, contending that the forum clause in the tickets required the Shutes to bring their suit in a court in the State of Florida. Carnival also contended that the District Court lacked personal jurisdiction over it because its contacts with the State of Washington were insubstantial. The District Court granted the motion, holding that Carnival's contacts with Washington were constitutionally insufficient to support the exercise of personal jurisdiction.

The Court of Appeals reversed. Reasoning that "but for" Carnival's solicitation of business in Washington, the Shutes would not have taken the cruise and Mrs. Shute would not have been injured, the court concluded that Carnival had sufficient contacts with Washington to justify the District Court's exercise of personal jurisdiction. Carnival appealed.

JUDICIAL OPINION

BLACKMUN, Justice

Turning to the forum-selection clause, the Court of Appeals acknowledged that a court concerned with the enforceability of such a clause must begin its analysis with *The Bremen* v. *Zapata Off-Shore Co.*, 407 U.S. 1, 92 S.Ct. 1907, 32 L.Ed.2d 513 (1972), where this Court held that forum-selection clauses, although not "historically . . . favored," are "prima facie valid." The appellate court concluded that the forum clause should not be enforced because it "was not freely bargained for." As an "independent justification" for refusing to enforce the clause, the Court of Appeals noted that there was evidence in the record to indicate that "the Shutes are physically and financially incapable of pursuing this litigation in Florida" and that the enforcement of the clause would operate to deprive them of their day in court and thereby contravene this Court's holding in *The Bremen*.

[R]espondents urge that the forum clause should not be enforced because, contrary to this Court's teachings in *The Bremen*, the clause was not the product of negotiation, and enforcement effectively would deprive respondents of their day in court. Additionally, respondents contend that the clause violates the Limitation of Vessel Owner's Liability Act, 46 U.S.C.App. § 183c.

Both petitioner and respondents argue vigorously that the Court's opinion in *The Bremen* governs this case, and each side purports to find ample support for its position in that opinion's broad-ranging language. This seeming paradox derives in large part from key factual differences between this case and *The Bremen*, differences that preclude an automatic and simple application of *The Bremen*'s general principles to the facts here.

In *The Bremen*, this Court addressed the enforce-ability of a forum-selection clause in a contract between two business corporations. An American corporation, Zapata, made a contract with Unterweser, a German corporation, for the towage of Zapata's oceangoing drilling rig from Louisiana to a point in the Adriatic Sea off the coast of Italy. The agreement provided that any dispute arising under the contract was to be resolved in the London Court of Justice.

After a storm in the Gulf of Mexico seriously dam-aged the rig, Zapata ordered Unterweser's ship to tow the rig to Tampa, Fla., the nearest point of refuge. Thereafter, Zapata sued Unterweser in admiralty in federal court at Tampa. Citing the forum clause, Unter-weser moved to dismiss. The District Court denied Un-terweser's motion, and the Court of Appeals for the Fifth Circuit, sitting en banc on rehearing, and by a sharply divided vote, affirmed.

This Court vacated and remanded, stating that, in general, "a freely negotiated private international agreement, unaffected by fraud, undue influence, or overweening bargaining power, such as that involved here, should be given full effect." The Court further generalized that "in the light of present-day commer-cial realities and expanding international trade we con-clude that the forum clause should control absent a strong showing that it should be set aside." The Court did not define precisely the circumstances that would make it unreasonable for a court to enforce a forum clause. Instead, the Court discussed a number of fac-tors that made it reasonable to enforce the clause at issue in *The Bremen* and that, presumably, would be pertinent in any determination whether to enforce a similar clause.

In this respect, the Court noted that there was "strong evidence that the forum clause was a vital part of the agreement, and [that] it would be unrealistic to think that the parties did not conduct their negotia-tions, including fixing the monetary terms, with the consequences of the forum clause figuring promi-nently in their calculations." Further, the Court ob-served that it was not "dealing with an agreement between two Americans to resolve their essentially local disputes in a remote alien forum," and that in such a case, "the serious inconvenience of the contrac-tual forum to one or both of the parties might carry greater weight in determining the reasonableness of the forum clause." The Court stated that even where the forum clause establishes a remote forum for resolu-tion of conflicts, "the party claiming [unfairness] should bear a heavy burden of proof."

[U]nlike the parties in *The Bremen*, respondents are not business persons and did not negotiate the terms of the clause with petitioner. Alternatively, the Court of Appeals ruled that the clause should not be enforced because enforcement effectively would deprive re-spondents of an opportunity to litigate their claim against petitioner.

The Bremen concerned a "far from routine transac-tion between companies of two different nations con-templating the tow of an extremely costly piece of equipment from Louisiana across the Gulf of Mexico and the Atlantic Ocean, through the Mediterranean Sea to its final destination in the Adriatic Sea." These facts suggest that, even apart from the evidence of negotia-tion regarding the forum clause, it was entirely reason-able for the Court in *The Bremen* to have expected Unterweser and Zapata to have negotiated with care in selecting a forum for the resolution of disputes arising from their special towing contract.

In contrast, respondents' passage contract was purely routine and doubtless nearly identical to every commercial passage contract issued by petitioner and most other cruise lines. In this context, it would be entirely unreasonable for us to assume that respon-dents—or any other cruise passenger—would negoti-ate with petitioner the terms of a forum-selection clause in an ordinary commercial cruise ticket. Com-mon sense dictates that a ticket of this kind will be a form contract the terms of which are not subject to ne-gotiation, and that an individual purchasing the ticket will not have bargaining parity with the cruise line. But by ignoring the crucial differences in the business contexts in which the respective contracts were exe-cuted, the Court of Appeals' analysis seems to us to have distorted somewhat this Court's holding in *The Bremen*.

In evaluating the reasonableness of the forum clause at issue in this case, we must refine the analysis of *The Bremen* to account for the realities of form pas-sage contracts. First, a cruise line has a special interest in limiting the fora in which it potentially could be sub-ject to suit. Because a cruise ship typically carries pas-sengers from many locales, it is not unlikely that a mishap on a cruise could subject the cruise line to liti-gation in several different fora. Additionally, a clause establishing *ex ante* the forum for dispute resolution has the salutary effect of dispelling any confusion about where suits arising from the contract must be brought and defended, sparing litigants the time and expense of pretrial motions to determine the correct forum and conserving judicial resources that otherwise would be devoted to deciding those motions. Finally, it stands to reason that passengers who purchase tickets containing a forum clause like that at issue in this case benefit in the form of reduced fares reflecting the

continued

savings that the cruise line enjoys by limiting the fora in which it may be sued.

Furthermore, the Court of Appeals did not place in proper context this Court's statement in *The Bremen* that "the serious inconvenience of the contractual forum to one or both of the parties might carry greater weight in determining the reasonableness of the forum clause." The Court made this statement in evaluating a hypothetical "agreement between two Americans to resolve their essentially local disputes in a remote alien forum." In the present case, Florida is not a "remote alien forum," nor—given the fact that Mrs. Shute's accident occurred off the coast of Mexico—is this dispute an essentially local one inherently more suited to resolution in the State of Washington than in Florida. In light of these distinctions, and because respondents do not claim lack of notice of the forum clause, we conclude that they have not satisfied the "heavy burden of proof" required to set aside the clause on grounds of inconvenience.

It bears emphasis that forum-selection clauses contained in form passage contracts are subject to judicial scrutiny for fundamental fairness. In this case, there is no indication that petitioner set Florida as the forum in which disputes were to be resolved as a means of discouraging cruise passengers from pursuing legitimate claims. Any suggestion of such a bad-faith motive is belied by two facts: Petitioner has its principal place of business in Florida, and many of its cruises depart from and return to Florida ports. Similarly, there is no evidence that petitioner obtained respondents' accession to the forum clause by fraud or overreaching. Finally, respondents have conceded that they were given notice of the forum provision and, therefore, presumably retained the option of rejecting the contract with impunity. In the case before us, therefore, we conclude that the Court of Appeals erred in refusing to enforce the forum-selection clause.

Respondents also contend that the forum-selection clause at issue violates 46 U.S.C.App. § 183c. That statute, enacted in 1936, see ch. 521, 49 Stat. 1480, provides:

> "It shall be unlawful for the . . . owner of any vessel transporting passengers between ports of the United States or between any such port and a foreign port to insert in any rule, regulation, contract, or agreement any provision or limitation (1) purporting, in the event of loss of life or bodily injury arising from the negligence or fault of such owner or his servants, to relieve such owner . . . from liability, or from liability beyond any stipulated amount, for such loss or injury, or (2) purporting in such event to lessen, weaken, or avoid the right of any claimant to a trial by court of competent ju-

risdiction on the question of liability for such loss or injury, or the measure of damages therefor. All such provisions or limitations contained in any such rule, regulation, contract, or agreement are hereby declared to be against public policy and shall be null and void and of no effect."

By its plain language, the forum-selection clause before us does not take away respondents' right to "a trial by [a] court of competent jurisdiction" and thereby contravene the explicit proscription of § 183c. Instead, the clause states specifically that actions arising out of the passage contract shall be brought "if at all," in a court "located in the State of Florida," which, plainly, is a "court of competent jurisdiction" within the meaning of the statute.

There was no prohibition of a forum-selection clause. Because the clause before us allows for judicial resolution of claims against petitioner and does not purport to limit petitioner's liability for negligence, it does not violate § 183c.

The judgment of the Court of Appeals is reversed.

DISSENTING OPINION

Justice STEVENS, with whom Justice MARSHALL joins, dissenting

The Court prefaces its legal analysis with a factual statement that implies that a purchaser of a Carnival Cruise Lines passenger ticket is fully and fairly notified about the existence of the choice of forum clause in the fine print on the back of the ticket. Even if this implication were accurate, I would disagree with the Court's analysis. But, given the Court's preface, I begin my dissent by noting that only the most meticulous passenger is likely to become aware of the forum-selection provision. I have therefore appended to this opinion a facsimile of the relevant text, using the type size that actually appears in the ticket itself. A careful reader will find the forum-selection clause in the 8th of the 25 numbered paragraphs.

Of course, many passengers, like the respondents in this case, will not have an opportunity to read paragraph 8 until they have actually purchased their tickets. By this point, the passengers will already have accepted the condition set forth in paragraph 16(a), which provides that "[t]he Carrier shall not be liable to make any refund to passengers in respect of . . . tickets wholly or partly not used by a passenger." Not knowing whether or not that provision is legally enforceable, I assume that the average passenger would accept the risk of having to file suit in Florida in the event of an injury, rather than canceling—without a refund—a planned vacation at the last minute. The fact that the cruise line can reduce its litigation costs, and therefore its liability insurance premiums, by forcing this choice on its passengers does not, in my opinion, suffice to render the provision reasonable.

Even if passengers received prominent notice of the forum-selection clause before they committed the cost of the cruise, I would remain persuaded that the clause was unenforceable under traditional principles of federal admiralty law and is "null and void" under the terms of Limitation of Vessel Owners Liability Act.

Exculpatory clauses in passenger tickets have been around for a long time. These clauses are typically the product of disparate bargaining power between the carrier and the passenger, and they undermine the strong public interest in deterring negligent conduct. For these reasons, courts long before the turn of the century consistently held such clauses unenforceable under federal admiralty law.

The stipulation in the ticket that Carnival Cruise sold to respondents certainly lessens or weakens their ability to recover for the slip and fall incident that oc-

curred off the west coast of Mexico during the cruise that originated and terminated in Los Angeles, California. It is safe to assume that the witnesses—whether other passengers or members of the crew—can be assembled with less expense and inconvenience at a west coast forum than in a Florida court several thousand miles from the scene of the accident.

CASE QUESTIONS

1. Explain where the parties are located and where the accident occurred.

2. What was the nature of the clause, and where was it located?

3. Does it make any difference to the court that this was a business-to-consumer and not a business-to-business contract?

4. Is the clause enforceable?

5. What problems do the dissenting justices see in the majority's decision?

C O N S I D E R . . .   **7 · 5**

International Ambassador Programs, Inc. is a Washington-based nonprofit organization that arranges tours and informational visits in foreign countries, including Russia. Archpexpo, once a Soviet state enterprise and now a Russian limited partnership, facilitates and expedites tours such as those sponsored by Ambassador to Russia and the other former Soviet republics.

Archpexpo and Ambassador entered into several agreements relating to tours. An April 1989 agreement provided that "all disputes and differences without recourse to courts of law shall be referred to the arbitration tribunal with the USSR Trade and Industry Chamber for resolution, such resolution acknowledged as final by the parties."

A dispute arose between the parties when Archpexpo alleged that it had not been paid certain fees due, and Ambassador claimed it was entitled to an offset of $20,000 for refunds it had to give to travelers who were dissatisfied with Archpexpo's service.

Archpexpo filed for arbitration, and Ambassador brought suit in federal district court in the United States. Does the federal district court have jurisdiction? Must Ambassador submit to arbitration in the USSR? What if Ambassador had more than one contract with Archpexpo and some of the contracts contained the arbitration clause and some did not? Would Ambassador be required to submit to arbitration then? [*International Ambassador Programs, Inc.* v. *Archpexpo*, 68 F.3d 337 (9th Cir. 1995).]

PROTECTIONS IN INTERNATIONAL COMPETITION

Although trade barriers are coming down and a global marketplace seems to be a reality, there is still much regulation of international competition. Regulation can be found in the forms of antitrust laws, protections for intellectual property, and trade treaties.

Antitrust Laws in the International Marketplace

All U.S. firms are subject to the antitrust laws of the United States, regardless of where their operations and anticompetitive behavior may occur. Firms from other countries operating in the United States or engaging in trade that has a substantial impact in the United States are also subject to U.S. antitrust laws. These firms are not covered under the act of state doctrine because they are not governmental entities and are engaging in commercial activity. For example, Go Video, a U.S. firm from Arizona, brought a successful antitrust suit against Japanese manufacturers for their alleged refusal to deal with the company in its attempt to develop a dual-deck VCR. U.S. courts and antitrust laws had jurisdiction because of the substantial impact the actions of the Japanese manufacturers would have on the VCR market in the United States.

The converse is also true. Firms outside the United States may enjoy the protections and benefits of our antitrust laws and bring suit for violations if it can be established that the violations they are alleging had a substantial impact on trade in the United States.

Review the Export Trading Company Act of 1982:
http://www.law.cornell.edu/uscode/15/4001.html

The Export Trading Company Act of 1982 carved an exception to the antitrust laws for U.S. firms that combine to do business in international markets. Large U.S. firms that would otherwise be prohibited from merging for anticompetitive reasons are permitted to form export trading companies (ETCs) for the purpose of participating in international trade. The Justice Department approves applications for ETCs in advance, provided the applicants can demonstrate that the proposed joint venture will not reduce competition in the United States, increase U.S. prices, or cause unfair competition. Thus, companies like Mobil and Exxon worked together to explore Siberian oil fields in a combination that would otherwise be prohibited both under the antitrust laws and for purposes of ongoing operations. These combinations allow effective negotiation of large foreign contracts. ExxonMobil is now one firm, a result of its joint drilling ventures.

Visit the Department of Justice:
http://www.usdoj.gov

Tariffs

Tariffs are taxes on goods as they move in and out of countries (import and export tariffs, respectively). Import tariffs are, in effect, a tax on goods coming into a country that increase the cost of those goods, particularly in comparison with domestic goods, and therefore limit the competitiveness of foreign goods within a country.

ETHICAL ISSUES

When the Taliban was in power in Afghanistan, it banned watching television. The result of the ban was the creation of a substantial market for smuggling television sets into Afghanistan. For example, a Sony TV set smuggled into Pakistan would cost about $400. The legal cost, paying tariffs, would be $440. The same set smuggled into Afghanistan could bring twice as much. Sony gets the same, or $220, for every set sold, regardless of where it is sold and what happens to it in terms of its final destination.

The Taliban decided to impose tariffs and taxes on TV sets even as it held to the ban because the ban pro-

duced the smuggling market from which they could extract substantial sums.

Do you think Sony had an ethical obligation to not sell to the Taliban? Does it have an ethical obligation to police what happens to its products? What happens when a company profits from a government making money from its own ban?

Source: Daniel Pearl and Steve Stecklow, "Taliban Banned TV But Collected Profits on Smuggled Sonys," *Wall Street Journal,* January 9, 2002, pp. A1, A8. (Note that the source for this article was a story coauthored by Daniel Pearl, the U.S. journalist who was kidnapped by terrorists and eventually killed by them with graphic coverage of the execution.)

In the United States, the U.S. Customs Service is responsible for developing the tariffs according to a tariff schedule and for enforcing the tariffs on imported goods. The tariff is based on the computed value of the goods coming into the country. That computed value depends on how the goods are classified under the schedule. For example, if potato chips are classified as bread, they are tariff or duty-free. If they are classified as snacks, they carry a tariff [*Sabritas* v. *U.S.*, 998 F. Supp. 1123 (Ct. Int'l Trade 1998)]. The federal government has created a specialized court to handle the many disputes that arise over the application of the tariffs and the underlying classification of goods.

Competition may also be controlled by import restrictions, a resulting control on trade balance and prices. By limiting the amounts of certain products or products from certain countries, supply and demand (and, through economic principles, price) are affected. These nontariff regulations also control competition and the flow of goods across borders.

As noted earlier, some countries also limit exports, particularly of technologies to certain countries that could use them to harm the United States and others through, for example, the development of nuclear technology.

Exhibit 7.1 provides a summary of international law principles and doctrines.

EXHIBIT 7.1 The Treaties, Principles, and Statutes of International Law

NAME	PURPOSE
North Atlantic Treaty North Atlantic Treaty Organization (NATO)	Treaty between U.S. and European nations that establishes a deployment of armed forces and security setup in Europe
Foreign Sovereign Immunities Act of 1976	U.S. statute that clarifies the immunity of foreign countries and officials from prosecution for crimes in the United States
Act of state doctrine (expropriation)	Recognition of foreign government's actions as valid; U.S. courts may not be used to challenge another country's actions, even toward U.S. citizens
Foreign Assistance Act of 1962 (Hickenlooper amendment)	Authorization given to president to cut off aid to countries where U.S. citizens' property has been taken by the government or regulated so as to deprive owner of use
Overseas Private Investment Corporation (OPIC)	Federal insurer for U.S. companies' investments in countries with low per capita income
Repatriation	Bringing back to your own country money earned on investments in other countries
Export Trading Company Act of 1982	Antitrust combination exemption for companies joining to compete in international markets
Maastricht Treaty	Agreement that created European Union
General Agreement on Tariffs and Trade (GATT)	Agreement among 100 countries to increase trade by reducing tariffs
North American Free Trade Agreement (NAFTA)	Agreement among United States, Canada, and Mexico that eliminates 65 percent of the tariffs across borders now, with the goal of tariff elimination by 2010

BIOGRAPHY

THE INTERNATIONAL CRUISE SHIP

With more people able to afford a cruise, the cruise line industry is booming. In 2000, nearly 7 million U.S. citizens took cruises, an increase of 51 percent from 1995. Thirty-eight cruise ships were delivered between 1999 and 2002, including two for the new Disney Cruise Lines. Many of these cruise ships hold in excess of 3,000 passengers each, with the industry estimating continuing increases in numbers of passengers at a rate of about 10 percent per year. Profit margins in the industry are high, with Carnival Cruise's net profits per day averaging about $3 million.* Gross revenue for the cruise ship industry in 2002 exceeded $14 billion.

One interesting issue that has arisen because of the increasing numbers of passengers and business-related issues, and litigation is what law applies to cruise ships? What country has jurisdiction over Royal Caribbean Cruise Lines, Inc., a company incorporated in Liberia with headquarters in Miami and boats registered in Norway? All cruise ships fly foreign country flags because the companies register their ships in other nations to avoid both the substantial U.S. taxes and the tighter labor and environmental regulations imposed on U.S. companies. There are five keys areas of law for cruise ships that have resulted in answers to the questions of which law applies and which countries have jurisdiction.

The first issue relates to the employees on the cruise ships. Workers on many cruise ships work twelve- to fourteen-hour days and are paid $400–$450 per month. The workers are not entitled to U.S. labor and wage protections. While nearly 90 percent of cruise ship passengers are U.S. citizens, the cruise lines are incorporated in countries where the companies can minimize their tax bills, such as Panama and Liberia. U.S. labor laws do not apply to the ships and their crews. The International Labor Organization of the United Nations suggests a workweek limit of seventy hours. Some of the workers do earn around $2,000 per month in tips. They work four to ten months per year and are not covered by medical insurance when they are not working on the ships. Most cruise ship workers are recruited from the Philippines, where average earnings are $1,000 per year.

A second problem is that of dumping. Cruise ships release effluent into the oceans because the cost of waste disposal for boats with 3,000 passengers can run into hundreds of thousands of dollars per day. Questions of jurisdiction arise: What country has authority to take action? Of the 111 complaints of cruise ship dumping (including everything from waifs to waste) brought in countries outside the United States, enforcement action was taken in only 2 of the cases. The U.S. Environmental Protection Agency (EPA) (see Chapter 12) has brought enforcement action against companies dumping in U.S. waters. For example, Holland America, a division of Carnival Cruises, pleaded guilty in 1998 to discharging waste into Alaska's Inside Passage and agreed to pay a fine of $2 million. In 1999, Royal Caribbean Cruises paid fines of $27 million for conspiracy to dump waste in the oceans. In 2002, Norwegian Cruise Lines paid a $1 million fine for dumping "oily waste," and Carnival paid an $18 million fine.† The EPA also accused both the cruise line companies of filing false records with the Coast Guard in order to cover up the dumping of materials that the EPA said consisted of some carcinogens.

A third problem is criminal activity, such as large numbers of thefts and sexual assaults aboard cruise ships. Litigation in federal district court in Miami resulted in revelations through discovery of a high number of sexual assaults on cruise ships with few of those reported to local law enforcement authorities. The lawsuit, against Carnival, produced records during discovery in which it was revealed that members of Carnival Cruise crews had sexually assaulted passengers and fellow crew members sixty-two times over a five-year period.

When such crimes were committed on the high seas, no country really had jurisdiction, and those aboard the ship were not even required to report the crimes. For example, a woman who was assaulted by a crew member she had invited to her cabin was asked not to report the incident by the ship's staff. When the ship docked in Miami, she reported the incident to the FBI. However, when FBI agents boarded the ship to investigate the crime, the ship's captain indicated that the crew member had been escorted to the airport and had boarded a flight for his native Italy.

The reporting stance of the cruise lines has, however, changed because of concerns passengers had about their safety; and prosecution for crimes not being possible, the cruise industry agreed to begin a practice of relaying all crimes reported on board ship to law enforcement agencies. The decision was made by the International Council of Cruise Lines, which is comprised of representatives from sixteen different cruise lines and 90 percent of the industry. The cruise industry had followed a policy of letting passengers decide whether to report these crimes, and the reporting level was low.

A fourth area of concern is that of consumer rights in cruise ship contracts. If there is misrepresentation or the cruise does not fulfill promised destinations, what rights do consumers have? Where can they litigate? Are arbitration clauses in cruise ship contracts valid? The *Carnival Cruise Line* v. *Shute* case (Case 7.3) answers these questions.

Finally, there is litigation. Passengers who are injured are bringing suit against the companies for their injuries. Several recent examples include a passenger who experienced a back injury in an organized pillow fight, a passenger who was injured while dancing the lindy as part of cruise activities, and a passenger who slipped and fell on a grape left behind from a passenger impersonating Carmen Miranda as part of a skit. Passengers are increasingly using long arm statutes

to require the companies to defend lawsuits in federal district court. Miami seems to be the most common location for such litigation because all major cruise lines have ships and offices there and meet the standards for minimum contacts. (See Chapter 3 for more discussion of long arm statutes.)

Are these ships subject to U.S. laws and courts? Are they floating cities? Sovereign nations? Congress held hearings on the safety issues and litigation questions surrounding cruises in 2002. What jurisdiction would the U.S. Congress have over these international carriers?

*Douglas Frantz, "For Cruise Ships' Workers, Much Toil, Little Protection," *New York Times*, December 24, 1999, pp. A1, A16.
†Marilyn Adams, "Cruise-ship dumping poisons seas, frustrates U.S. enforcers," *USA Today*, November 8–10, 2002, pp. 1A, 2A.
Source: Michael D. Goldhaber, "Ticket to Paradise or a Trip from Hell?" *National Law Journal*, March 22, 1999, p. C1.

Protections for Intellectual Property

Protections for intellectual property in the international marketplace are constantly undergoing refinements. Worldwide registration for patents, copyrights, and trademarks are goals that are within reach as the mechanisms for administration are being put into place. Details on international protections are found in Chapter 16.

Criminal Law Protections

All persons and businesses present within a country are subject to that nation's regulatory scheme for business as well as to the constraints of the country's criminal code. Compliance with the law is a universal principle of international business operations. Expulsion, fines, penalties, and imprisonment are all remedies available to governments when foreign businesses break the law in a particular nation.

Often, the complexities of international operations produce layers of business organizations throughout the world. These layers are often necessary for individual countries and proper business structure under the law. However, the layers of organizations may provide opportunities for laundering of money, concealment of transactions, and other complex transactions that can escape regulatory detection for a time. However, the activities are eventually discovered, and countries are cooperating more to be certain the complexities of international business do not conceal illicit activities.

MAKING ETHICS PERSONAL

Cruising Through Ethical Dilemmas

You have taken a job as a steward on a cruise ship for the summer. You are instructed to dump as much trash and waste off the ship as possible. "It reduces our costs in port, so let's get rid of it at sea. Look at the size of these waters. What could it hurt?" are the instructions from your manager. Would you follow the instructions? Would you report the activities? Would you report the activities once the summer was over and you no longer needed the job? Explain why or why not for each of your answers.

SUMMARY

What laws affect businesses in international trade?

- Foreign Sovereign Immunities Act of 1976
- Foreign Assistance Act of 1962 (Hickenlooper amendment)
- Overseas Private Investment Corporation (OPIC)
- Export Trading Company Act of 1982
- Contracts for the International Sale of Goods (CISG)

What treaties, agreements, practices, and principles affect international business and trade?

- North Atlantic Treaty
- North Atlantic Treaty Organization (NATO)
- Maastricht Treaty
- General Agreement on Tariffs and Trade (GATT)
- North American Free Trade Agreement (NAFTA)
- International Monetary Fund (IMF)
- Duties, quotas, tariffs—controls on prices and quantities of goods by nations with the goal of balancing imports and exports
- Foreign Corrupt Practices Act (FCPA)—controls on means of accessing governments

What principles of international law affect business?

- Sovereign immunity—freedom of one country from being subject to orders from another country
- Expropriation; act of state doctrine—recognition by U.S. courts of the actions of other governments as valid despite noncompliance with traditional U.S. rights and procedures
- Repatriation—returning profits earned in other countries to one's native land
- Conflict of laws—issue as to which country's law applies in international transactions
- Antitrust issues
- *Forum non conveniens*—doctrine requiring dismissal of cases that should be heard in another country's courts

What protections exist in international competition?

- Antitrust laws
- Protections for intellectual property
- Criminal law protections

QUESTIONS AND PROBLEMS

1. Tom Welch and Dave Johnson, two officials of the Salt Lake City Olympic Committee, were charged with bribery and racketeering for their alleged role in paying money to and giving rather large gifts to members of the International Olympic Committee (IOC) in order to win the bid for holding the winter Olympics in Salt Lake City in 2002. Salt Lake City did win the bid, but an anonymous letter to the IOC revealed that these types of payments and gifts had been offered. Following an investigation, nine members of the IOC were removed or resigned and others were sanctioned. The Salt Lake City Olympic Committee removed Mr. Welch and Mr. Johnson and replaced them with Mitt Romney as the head of its committee.

Utah declined prosecution under state law, and a federal district court judge dismissed the charges against Mr. Welch and Mr. Johnson. The U.S. Attorney for the case filed an appeal with the tenth circuit federal court of appeals asking that the charges be reinstated. He noted that the Olympics were an "international" event and mandated federal jurisdiction. He also argued in the brief that the payments, accommodations, and gifts were more than goodwill and amounted to bribery in violation of federal law.

Applying the cases and law presented in the discussion on the FCPA, determine whether there was or was not a violation of federal law. What jurisdiction do federal courts have over criminal charges? Describe the appellate process and what an appellate court can do in an appeal such as this. (Patrick O'Driscoll, "U.S. appeals in Olympics bribery case," *USA Today*, January 24, 2002, p. 2A.)

2. Suppose that the government of Brazil took possession of the cacao farms of a chocolate factory owned by a U.S. firm. What rights would the U.S. factory have? What limits exist on those rights?

3. LaFair Products, a company based in Mexico, manufactures and sells the bonnet type of hair dryer. The hair dryers are marketed in the United States through several catalog merchants who are based in the United States. One of the hair dryers was defective and severely burned Susan Queenan, a resident of North Carolina. Ms. Queenan has filed suit against LaFair in federal district court in North Carolina. Does this court have jurisdiction?

4. Between January 1983 and June 1987, Richard H. Liebo was vice president in charge of the Aerospace Division of NAPCO International, Inc. of Hopkins, Minnesota. NAPCO's primary business consisted of selling military equipment and supplies throughout the world.

In early 1983, the Niger government contracted with a West German company, Dornier Reparaturwerft, to service two Lockheed C-130 cargo planes. After the Niger Ministry of Defense ran into financial troubles, Dornier sought an American parts supplier in order to qualify the Ministry of Defense for financing through the U.S. Foreign Military Sales program. The Foreign Military Sales program is supervised by the Defense Security Assistance Agency of the U.S. Department of Defense. Under the program, loans are provided to foreign governments for the purchase of military equipment and supplies from U.S. contractors.

In June 1983, representatives from Dornier met with officials of NAPCO and agreed that NAPCO would become the prime contractor on the C-130 maintenance contracts. Under this arrangement, NAPCO would supply parts to Niger and Dornier, and Dornier would perform the required maintenance at its facilities in Munich.

Once NAPCO and Dornier agreed to these terms, Mr. Liebo and Axel Kurth, a Dornier sales representative, flew to Niger to get the president of Niger's approval of the contract. In Niger they met with Captain Ali Tiemogo, chief of maintenance for the Niger Air Force. Captain Tiemogo testified that during the trip, Mr. Liebo and Mr. Kurth told him that they would make "some gestures" to him if he helped get the contract approved. When asked whether this promise played a role in deciding to recommend approval of the contract, Captain Tiemogo stated, "I can't say 'no,' I cannot say 'yes,' at that time," but "it encouraged me." Following Captain Tiemogo's recommendation that the contract be approved, the president of Niger signed the contract.

Tahirou Barke, Captain Tiemogo's cousin and close friend, was the first consular for the Niger Embassy in Washington, D.C. Mr. Barke testified that he met Mr. Liebo in Washington sometime in 1983 or 1984. Mr. Barke stated that Mr. Liebo told him he wanted to make a "gesture" to Captain Tiemogo and asked Mr. Barke to set up a bank account in the United States. With Mr. Barke's assistance, Mr. Liebo opened a bank account in Minnesota in the name of "E. Dave," a variation of the name of Mr. Barke's then girlfriend, Shirley Elaine Dave. NAPCO deposited about $30,000 in the account, and Mr. Barke used the money to pay bills and purchase personal items and also gave a portion of the money to Captain Tiemogo.

In August 1985, Mr. Barke returned to Niger to be married. After the wedding, he and his wife honeymooned in Paris, Stockholm, and London. Before leaving for Niger, he informed Mr. Liebo of his honeymoon plans, and Mr. Liebo offered to buy, as a gift, Mr. Barke's airline tickets for both Mr. Barke's return to Niger and his honeymoon trip. Mr. Liebo made the flight arrangements and paid for the tickets, which cost $2,028, by charging them to NAPCO's Diners Club account. Mr. Barke considered the tickets a personal "gift" from Mr. Liebo.

Over a two-and-a-half-year period beginning in May 1984, NAPCO made payments totaling $130,000 to three "commission agents." The practice of using agents and paying them commissions on international contracts was acknowledged as a proper, legal, and accepted business practice in third-world countries. NAPCO issued commission checks to three "agents" identified as Amadou Mailele, Captain Tiemogo's brother-in-law; Fatouma Boube, Captain Tiemogo's sister-in-law; and

Miss E. Dave, Mr. Barke's girlfriend. At Captain Tiemogo's request, both Mr. Mailele and Ms. Boube set up bank accounts in Paris. Neither Mr. Mailele, Ms. Boube, nor Miss Dave, however, received the commission checks or acted as NAPCO's agent. These individuals were merely intermediaries through whom NAPCO made payments to Captain Tiemogo and Mr. Barke. NAPCO's corporate president, Henri Jacob, or another superior of Mr. Liebo's, approved these "commission payments." No one approved the payment for the honeymoon trip. Are there any violations of the FCPA? [*U.S. v. Liebo*, 923 F.2d 1308 (8th Cir. 1991).]

5. United Arab Shipping Company (UASC) is a corporation formed under the laws of Kuwait. Its capital stock is wholly owned by the governments of Kuwait, Saudi Arabia, the United Arab Emirates, Qatar, Iraq, and Bahrain. No single government owned more than 19.33 percent of UASC's shares, and the corporation was created by a treaty among the owner nations.

Three seamen who were injured while working for UASC brought suit against it in federal district court in the United States. UASC maintains it enjoys sovereign immunity. The seamen claim it is a commercial enterprise and not entitled to immunity. Who is correct? [*Mangattu* v. *M/V IBN Hayyan*, 35 F.3d 205 (5th Cir. 1994).]

6. Smith & Smith, a U.S. computer firm, contracted to install a computer system for Volkswagen, Germany, in the company's headquarters in Berlin. Smith's contract included the following liability limitation: "We are only liable for loss of data which is due to a deliberate action on our part. We are not responsible for lost profits in any event." The contract had no provisions on choice of law. A crash in the Smith & Smith system caused a loss of ninety-two days' worth of financial data. Volkswagen was required to use its auditors to restructure the database at a substantial cost. Smith & Smith says it did nothing deliberate and, therefore, is not liable. Volkswagen cites German law that mandates protection by sellers against such losses and permits recovery of lost profits. U.S. law would honor the Smith & Smith clause. Which law applies? Why?

7. In 1995, the French passed a law known as *Loi Toubon* that requires contracts in which performance will occur in France to be written in French. What disadvantages for foreign firms do you see in this policy?

8. The European Union has developed a directive on privacy and e-mail. Nations within the EU are permitted to use e-mail for commercial transactions and can exchange information via e-mail. However, businesses from countries outside the EU will not be permitted access to EU business information and EDI systems for contracting purposes unless they can guarantee that there are adequate privacy protections in place for the data transmitted via e-mail. Most legal experts believe the EU privacy directive applies to all forms of transmissions in business, including commercial contracts and ordering information.

What would happen if a business tapped into an EU business and began entering into transactions without an adequate privacy guarantee? Would there be criminal sanctions? Trade sanctions? How does this directive affect international trade with the EU? The EU has provided that trading privileges can be withdrawn from countries with businesses that violate the privacy standards on e-mail information and data transmission. What happens when trading privileges are withdrawn? Is the EU directive a commercial control of trade?

9. Walid Azab Al-Uneizi was an employee of the Ministry of Defense of Kuwait. Liticia Guzel was an employee of the Willard Inter-Continental Hotel in Washington, D.C. One of her duties was restocking minibars in guest rooms. Al-Uneizi approached Miss Guzel outside Rooms 610 and 612 and conferred with her about restocking Room 612. After Miss Guzel had finished restocking Room 612, Al-Uneizi assaulted and raped her. After the rape, Al-Uneizi gave her a Kuwaiti flag pin. Miss Guzel has brought suit against both Al-Uneizi and the Kuwaiti government, who seek a dismissal under the act of state doctrine. Should the case be dismissed against both? [*Guzel* v. *State of Kuwait*, 818 F. Supp. 6 (1993).]

10. When the Barings Bank bankruptcy occurred in 1995, Mr. Nick Leeson, the trader responsible for the immense losses the bank experienced after heavy derivative investments, fled to Germany. He was brought back to Hong Kong, the site of his trades, for trial. He is a British citizen who was arrested in Germany. Describe all the principles and issues of international law involved in his arrest, return, and eventual trial in Hong Kong.

RESEARCH PROBLEM

Selling Computer Arms Technology

11. IBM entered a guilty plea to selling sixteen computer workstations and a super computer to a Russian nuclear weapons laboratory. The sales occurred in 1996 and 1997 and were completed without IBM's having obtained the necessary federal licenses required to sell computers for military purposes. IBM agreed to pay an $8.5 million fine, and executives with IBM acknowledge that they knew the computers might be used for the building and testing of nuclear weapons.

U.S. officials requested assistance from Russian officials in conducting the investigation but were rebuffed. U.S. officials requested the return of the computers, but Russian officials refused. Russian officials say the U.S. officials promised them the computer hardware in exchange for the Russians signing the Comprehensive Test Ban Treaty. U.S. officials maintain no such promise was made.

Determine the answers to the following questions.

a. Can U.S. officials demand investigatory cooperation?
b. Can U.S. officials demand return of the computers?
c. Can U.S. officials take any action under the Comprehensive Test Ban Treaty?
d. Can IBM still be paid for the computers?

NOTES

1. The members are: Australia, Austria, Belgium, Canada, Czech Republic, Denmark, Finland, France, Germany, Greece, Hungary, Iceland, Ireland, Italy, Japan, Korea, Luxembourg, Mexico, Netherlands, New Zealand, Norway, Poland, Portugal, Slovak Republic, Spain, Sweden, Switzerland, Turkey, United Kingdom, United States.

2. OECD also has relationships with seventy countries and NGOs.

3. Some countries do not provide criminal penalties for corporations under their laws, and they are required only to provide for substantial civil penalties.

Cyber Law

In Chapters 1 through 7, you learned about all of the types and sources of law. This chapter is different because it draws on the laws from all of those sources that apply to business and personal activity in cyberspace.

Today, 80 percent of employees have a computer at work and use it as a part of their jobs. Nearly half of the homes in the United States also have a computer. Computers are a key part of the way we do business and live. They are tools of commerce and daily life. However, each eBay transaction and every wire transfer has legal issues. Every point and click has legal significance. This chapter covers those laws that deal with computer technology in our personal and business lives. Referred to as cyber law, this area consists of laws from different sources that are used to determine our rights, obligations, and protections in this era of computer technology and cyberspace.

Business managers, consumers, business students, and even some lawyers worry when they hear the term *cyber law* because they didn't have a course called "Cyber Law." This chapter was written to allay those fears. While laws have been created to address new technological systems, most people are surprised to learn that the law, with those qualities of flexibility and consistency discussed in Chapter 1, is quite capable of handling cyberspace issues without departing from the basic principles applied to all economic revolutions in the past. While the industrial revolution led to more contracts, the basic principles of contract formation did not change; and though the increased numbers of employees required new laws on safety and unions, the basic legal principles of fairness and disclosure remained. The basic principles of law that have seen

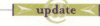

update

For up-to-date legal news and real-world business applications, click on **update** *at* http://jennings.westbuslaw.com

businesses through the many economic revolutions of the past still apply today. Cyberspace has just accelerated the pace at which law works to provide stability while fostering innovation in a flexible environment.

This chapter is called "Cyber Law," but its name is more accurately "The Law in Cyberspace." You will not be learning a whole new body of law. You will be learning how the principles of law apply to new ways of doing things. For example, you still have a right to privacy in your purchases and buying habits. The fact that an e-business can gather that information about you so easily does not change that right. Exhibit 8.1 provides a summary of cyber law in relation to other areas of law; as you can see, sometimes the legal issues are identical.

The purpose of this chapter is not to explore every possible legal issue in cyber law. Rather, its purpose is to acquaint you with the areas of focus in cyber law and provide a framework for analyzing cyberspace legal issues. This chapter answers two simple questions: What are the issues in cyber law? What laws affect business in cyberspace? You will explore both new-to-cyberspace laws and existing laws that apply in cyberspace. In addition to understanding the challenges of legal issues in cyberspace, you will gain a more complete appreciation for a legal system so capable of adjusting to and absorbing the changes created by business.

> **It's enough to send Cardinal Richelieu spinning, if not surfing, in his grave.**
> THE ACADEMIE FRANCAISE ON THE POLLUTION OF THE FRENCH LANGUAGE
> BY THE INVASION OF THE WORLD WIDE WEB (*LE WEB*)

> **The Internet presents age-old issues with a new face.**
> PROFESSOR TAMARA MADDOX
> *George Mason University*

> **For all the sophisticated work on firewalls, intrusion-detection systems, encryption, and computer security, e-businesses are at risk from a relatively simply technique that's akin to dialing a telephone repeatedly so that everyone else trying to get through will hear a busy signal.**
> BUSINESS WEEK, FEBRUARY 21, 2000

CONSIDER...

Steven Caspi, Ronald Jonas, Arden Cone, and Laurel Barrie were all Microsoft Network (MSN) subscribers. Microsoft rolled over its MSN memberships into more expensive plans without their knowledge or permission, a practice condemned by the attorneys general in twenty-one states. When the four objected, Microsoft offered no relief, and the four became representatives in a class action suit brought against Microsoft in New Jersey with approximately 1.5 million class members. Microsoft moved to have the complaint dismissed because of a clause that rolled through the screens of members as they signed up by clicking "I agree." All four had clicked "I agree" to the following clause.

This agreement is governed by the laws of the State of Washington, U.S.A., and you consent to the exclusive juris- *diction and venue of courts in King County, Washington, in all disputes arising out of or relating to your use of MSN or your MSN membership.*

Can Microsoft have the case dismissed in New Jersey? Did the MSN customers make a contract over the Internet? Are these Internet contract forum clauses enforceable?

EXHIBIT 8.1   Cyber Law Compared with Other Areas of Law

AREA OF LAW	LEGAL ISSUE	CYBERSPACE ISSUE	OTHER CHAPTER REFERENCES
Tort	Privacy	Monitoring of e-mails and Web access by employers to gather information about employees	10, 18
Tort	Privacy	Identification of people who post messages in chat rooms	9, 10
Tort	Privacy	File sharing, identity disclosure by server	10, 16
Tort	Appropriation	File sharing, getting around copyrights	10, 16
Tort	Trespass	File sharing, getting around copyrights, spam, use of company e-mail for nonwork purposes	8
Tort	Defamation	Same elements, but with wider damages and faster impact	10
Criminal	Wiretaps, eavesdropping	Access from third parties, server information employer disclosure	9
Contracts	Which contracts must be in writing	Sufficiency of electronic signatures, electronic proof	13, 14
Contracts	Formation	Determination of when a contract is formed, use of point-and-click agreements	13, 14
Contracts	Source of law: common law or Uniform Commercial Code	Uniform Computer Information Transaction Act, Uniform Electronic Transactions Act	13, 14
Criminal law Criminal procedure	Warrants—privacy	Same	9
Consumer protection	Restrictions on use of private information	Same	15
Intellectual property rights	Infringement	Peer-to-peer file sharing, domain names, links	10, 16
Commerce Clause	Regulation and taxation of interstate commerce	Regulation and taxation of Internet commerce	3, 5
Securities	Fraud, "pump and dump" tactics, insider trading	Fraud, "pump and dump" over the Internet	22
International	Jurisdiction, sources of law	Same	3, 5, 7

AN OVERVIEW OF LAW IN CYBERSPACE

Cyber law is best studied when it is broken down into existing areas of law. The laws affecting business in cyberspace fall into the following six categories: tort issues, contract issues, intellectual property issues, criminal violations, constitutional restraints and protections, and securities law issues. Also, because of the global nature of the Internet, international issues have already begun to arise in contract dis-

Visit a cyber law site:
http://www.cyberlaw.com

putes. Under each of these six categories of law (which cover the subareas listed in Exhibit 8.1) are a number of issues. For example, chat rooms are technologically sophisticated means of transferring damaging and often false information. While the transmission is faster and the damages perhaps greater, the underlying legal issue is still the tort of defamation.

The issues in intellectual property law related to cyberspace are no different in substance. We are still concerned with protecting copyrights and patents; however, now our concerns focus on issues such as copying software programs licensed for your employer onto your personal computer or even downloading music through Napster. Is burning CDs simply peer-to-peer file sharing or is it copyright infringement?

Cyber law is not so new. The breakdown of topics for this chapter into the same groups of law covered on a chapter-by-chapter basis in the book is a good indication that the existing body of law is working quite well in resolving issues that arise in cyberspace. Each of the following sections covers the law in cyberspace as it relates to specific topic areas. Before we cover those areas of law that apply to cyberspace, we must explore the notion of jurisdiction. Courts may know how to apply the law to cyberspace situations, but with parties located across the country and around the world, the issue of which court will apply what law must be resolved. Jurisdiction in cyberspace is an area of law that precedes all the substantive law discussion and application. The issue of jurisdiction crosses all areas of law involved in cyberspace. Jurisdiction of the federal government is the issue under the commerce clause. In contracts, which court has jurisdiction over the parties is a preliminary issue in all disputes. Resolving the issue of jurisdiction is step one in nearly all cyber-law areas.

JURISDICTION IN CYBERSPACE

As discussed in Chapter 4 under *in personam* jurisdiction, a continuing issue in cyberspace activity and transactions is which court has jurisdiction over the parties, and then, which law applies to those parties once they are in court. Also, as discussed in Chapter 5, there are limits to what states can do in terms of extending their sales tax reach to Internet sales.

Congress passed the Internet Tax Freedom Act (ITFA) in 1998 and has renewed it a number of times, with the most recent extension proposed to carry through until mid-2005.[1] The ITFA provides that states and local governments cannot tax Internet access. Contrary to popular belief, ITFA does not suspend sales taxes on transactions over the Internet. However, the same constitutional standards apply to taxation of sales over the Internet as apply to sales via catalog and phone to residents of other states. In order to tax such sales, the seller must have some physical presence in the state or a pattern of doing business there. For example, Nordstrom may not have stores located in a particular state, but it would be required to collect sales taxes from sales to residents of that state if Nordstrom had warehouse facilities in that state.

The following types of activities qualify as a presence for the purposes of states collecting sales taxes from Internet merchants:

- Having an office in the state
- Having an employee who works in the state
- Owning or leasing real property in the state (e.g., when a retailer buys land for purposes of constructing a store)

- Delivering merchandise in the state with vehicles owned by the Internet seller
- Having an independent contractor present in the state for two or more days each year for the purposes of establishing business contacts and sales

The usual constitutional standards on apportionment of taxation apply to collection of sales taxes over the Internet. States and local agencies may not overstep those bounds of protection.

Another jurisdictional issue that has arisen relates to the rights of employees who work off-site at home computers. What laws apply to them in terms of their employment benefits and rights? For example, what unemployment benefits do programmers who work from their homes in Denver for a company headquartered in San Francisco receive? Do Colorado or California laws apply? Laws exist to handle these jurisdictional questions; we simply must apply them to the facts and realities of cyberspace operations. *In the Matter of Maxine Allen* (Case 8.1) deals with the issue of employment rights and state jurisdiction for cyberspace employees.

CASE 8.1

In the Matter of Maxine Allen
763 N.Y.S.2d 237 (Sup.Ct. 2003)

The Fired Telecommuter:
Which Unemployment Line Do I Stand In?

FACTS

Maxine E. Allen (claimant) was employed by Reuters America, Inc., a financial information services provider, as a development technical specialist from October 21, 1996, until March 16, 1999. At the time Ms. Allen was hired, she worked and resided in New York. When Ms. Allen relocated to Florida in July 1997 for personal reasons, her employer agreed to allow her to "telecommute." She was able to do her job for her employer in New York from Florida via Internet connection over telephone lines.

Ms. Allen had an office in her Florida home, and Reuters paid for a second telephone line to her home and supplied her with a laptop computer, software, and an access code and security clearance for its mainframe computer located in New York. Working on the laptop computer from her home office in Florida, Ms. Allen would log on to her employer's mainframe computer each workday. She would monitor the performance of her employer's financial systems, troubleshoot, and recommend system changes and enhancements, just as she had done when she was physically located in New York.

Ms. Allen was required to be available during normal business hours (8:00 A.M. to 5:00 P.M., Monday through Friday) or after hours as circumstances dictated; to submit timesheets and requests for vacation time; and to call in sick and to seek permission to "come in" late or "leave" early. She maintained daily contact with her supervisor in New York and responded to her employer's directives by e-mail or telephone. She was required to make weekly status reports to her supervisor in New York, which she submitted electronically. She traveled from Florida to New York only once for two weeks when Reuters asked.

In March 1999, Reuters opted to end this telecommuting arrangement and offered Ms. Allen work in the New York office, which she turned down. On April 5, 1999, Ms. Allen filed a claim for unemployment insurance benefits in Florida.

When Ms. Allen was found eligible to receive unemployment insurance benefits at the rate of $275 per week, Reuters objected, contending that she had voluntarily quit her job without good cause. A claims adjudicator agreed on April 27, 1999, and this decision was affirmed by an appeals referee on June 2, 1999.

In the meantime, on May 5, 1999, the Florida Department of Labor and Employment Security advised Ms. Allen that she might qualify for benefits in New York at a weekly rate of $365. Ms. Allen filled out an interstate claim form and filed it on May 11, 1999. Ms. Allen stated on this form that she worked at her employer's New York address.

On October 7, 1999, the New York Commissioner of Labor issued an initial determination that Ms. Allen was ineligible for unemployment insurance benefits, effective April 5, 1999, because she had no covered employment in New York during the base period from April 6, 1998, to April 4, 1999, and thus could not file a valid original claim. The Commissioner concluded that Ms. Allen's employment was localized in Florida, where she performed all services for her employer. Further, Ms. Allen was charged with a recoverable overpayment of $8,395 for having made a false factual statement on her interstate claim form when she stated that she worked at her employer's New York address. Ms. Allen appealed.

On February 29, 2000, an administrative law judge determined that Ms. Allen had carried out job responsibilities for her employer simultaneously in New York and Florida and that she was eligible for unemployment insurance benefits in New York because her work was directed and controlled from New York. Having found Ms. Allen eligible for benefits, the administrative law judge overruled the overpayment determination. Both the employer and the Commissioner of Labor appealed to the Unemployment Insurance Appeal Board.

On August 23, 2000, the Board reversed the administrative law judge's decision and sustained the initial determination of ineligibility. The Board held that Ms. Allen did not work in New York. Rather, she carried out her job responsibilities entirely within Florida, where she was physically present and maintained an office. Ms. Allen, representing herself (*pro se*), appealed.

JUDICIAL OPINION

READ, Justice

We are asked to decide whether an employee who regularly works from her out-of-state residence by electronic linkup to her employer's workplace in New York is entitled to receive unemployment insurance benefits from New York. We conclude that, under the New York Unemployment Insurance Law (Labor Law art 18), the employee is ineligible for these benefits.

Unemployment insurance is temporary income for workers who become unemployed through no fault of their own; are ready, willing and able to work; and have earned sufficient wages during a specified time period in covered employment. Section 511 of the Labor Law, in relevant part, defines "employment" covered by unemployment insurance as follows:

> "2. Work localized in state. The term 'employment' includes a person's entire service performed within or both within and without this state if the service is localized in this state. Service is deemed localized within the state if it is performed entirely within the state or is performed both within and without the state but that performed without the state is incidental to the person's service within the state, for example, is temporary or transitory in nature or consists of isolated transactions.

> "3. Work within and without the state. The term 'employment' includes a person's entire service performed both within and without this state provided it is not localized in any state but some of the service is performed in this state, and

> "(a) the person's base of operations is in this state; or

> "(b) if there is no base of operations in any state in which some part of the service is performed, the place from which such service is directed or controlled is in this state; or

> "(c) if the base of operations or place from which such service is directed or controlled is not in any state in which some part of the service is performed, the person's residence is in this state."

In *Matter of Mallia*, 299 N.Y. 232, 86 N.E.2d 577 [1949], we explained that section 511 sets out four tests—localization, location of base of operations, source of direction or control, and employee's residence—to be applied successively to an employee's entire service performed for the employer both within and without the state. We added that the purpose of section 511 "is to bring within the scope of the New York act those employees who work both in New York and one or more other States. . . ."

To that end, the initial inquiry is whether the employee's entire service for the employer, with the exception of incidental work, is localized in New York or some other state. Here, claimant argues that her entire service was realized, and therefore localized, at her employer's mainframe computer in New York even though she initiated this service by making keystrokes on her laptop computer in Florida. The Commissioner takes the position that because claimant was physically present in Florida when she worked for her employer (with the exception of her two-week visit to New York), her entire service was localized in Florida.

We hold that physical presence determines localization for purposes of interpreting and applying section 511 to an interstate telecommuter. Because claimant was regularly physically present in Florida when she worked for her employer in New York, her work was localized in one state—Florida. Accordingly, the other tests specified in section 511 are not reached, and claimant was ineligible for unemployment insurance benefits from New York.

As we explained in *Mallia*, section 511 derives from a uniform definition of "employment" adopted by New York and most other states. This uniform definition advances two basic purposes:

> "(1) All the employment of an individual should be allocated to one State and not divided among the several States in which he might perform services, and such

continued

State should, of course, be solely responsible for benefits payable to him; (2) the State to which his employment is allocated should be the one in which it is most likely that the individual will become unemployed and seek work."

Thus, the uniform rule was intended to promote efficiency, and to ensure that unemployment benefits are paid by the state where an unemployed individual is physically present to seek new work. Unemployment has the greatest economic impact on the community in which the unemployed individual resides; unemployment benefits are generally linked to the cost of living in this area. While the drafters of the uniform rule could not have envisioned a world of interstate telecommuting, these underlying purposes remain valid, and are best served by tying localization to the state in which an interstate telecommuter is physically present.

No other state or federal court seems yet to have interpreted the uniform rule as applied to interstate telecommuters. As we further observed in *Mallia,* however, the purpose of the uniform rule was to create uniformity among states and to end uncertainty in the application of state unemployment compensation

rules. . . . In our view, physical presence is the most practicable indicium of localization for the interstate telecommuter who inhabits today's "virtual" workplace linked by Internet connections and data exchanges.

Finally, we conclude that the Board's assessment of a recoverable overpayment is supported by substantial evidence. [S]ection 597 (of the Labor Law) permits recovery of benefits received when the claimant has made a false statement of fact even though unintended. . . ."

Accordingly, the order of the Appellate Division should be affirmed, with costs.

CASE QUESTIONS

1. Describe Ms. Allen's working relationship and geographic location.

2. What uniform national policy does the court apply?

3. For the purposes of unemployment payments, which state is responsible for Ms. Allen?

4. Why does Ms. Allen owe money?

TORT ISSUES IN CYBER LAW

Four main tort issues arise in cyberspace commercial activity: privacy, appropriation, trespass, and defamation. Remember, for more background on these torts and related issues, refer to Chapters 9, 10, 16, and 18.

Privacy Issues in Cyber Law

E–Mail and Privacy

Ninety million American workers send 2.8 billion e-mail messages per day or an average of 190 e-mails per worker per day.[2] E-mail is a means of both commercial and personal communication. A cross between the written letter and the telephone call, e-mail does not have the boundaries of either of those forms of communication. A telephone call is a one-time interaction that depends on the memories of the parties for its recreation. A letter is tangible, but its one-copy existence means that it can be kept private. E-mail exists not only between the sender and receiver; it is also preserved within the computers' hard drives, the system in which it is transmitted, and also via any forwarding of the message to others. What may have been intended as a private exchange actually has several backup copies in a system that others can access. Are we entitled to privacy in our e-mail communications? Can the messages themselves be protected from disclosure on the basis of a right to privacy? Do sender and receiver have the same right to privacy? Does reading the e-mail messages of others intrude into private affairs? Is the right to privacy waived when the message is forwarded to someone else? And what are servers' and e-mail service providers' obligations in terms of privacy and disclosure of customers and users?

The law already exists to handle the question of invasion of privacy. The Electronic Communications Privacy Act of 1986 (ECPA)—prohibits the interception of

CHECK THE WEB

> This chapter has more updates than any other in the book because of its evolving nature and new surveys on employer practices on e-mail and Web usage.

"live" communications such as using a listening device to intercept a telephone conversation. However, with the advent of the Internet and e-mail, we have the intersection of privacy rights, First Amendment (freedom of speech) rights, and violations of other laws using this new technology. Is e-mail live communication so that the ECPA applies?

There may also be nonstatutory types of remedies for privacy protections in this new technological world. The tort of invasion of privacy, or intrusion into private affairs, applies to the issues of privacy in e-mail and Internet account information as much as it did when telephone service to private homes was first made available. The fact that the phone company could listen in to conversations did not mean it was entitled to do so. Privacy affords protection from both physical and technological invasion. For example, the Federal Trade Commission (FTC) recently ruled that information about consumers' purchasing history and activity cannot be used without their permission, even when that information was obtained over the Internet. In other words, the source of the information is not the issue; its use and disclosure, a breach of the consumers' right to privacy, is.

Three types of cases have arisen involving the intersection of these issues. The first are the employer/employee privacy cases that include issues of employers' access to employees' e-mails. The second are cases in which someone other than an employer is seeking the identity of those who have sent e-mails or posted information in chat rooms. The third are cases in which people with e-mail accounts are using servers for purposes of violating the law, such as infringing copyrights between two account holders (as when two AOL users share music or video files) or posting information on how to get around copyrights. Whether there has been a tortious invasion of privacy with regard to someone's e-mail depends on the nature of the e-mail system used for the message revealed to others. For example, employers do have a right to access their employees' e-mail.

Employer Rights to E–Mail and Employee Privacy

The courts have been consistent in their rulings that employees do not have an expectation of privacy in their employers' e-mail systems. To be certain that employees understand this limitation on privacy at work, most employers provide their employees with notice about the e-mail system and tell them that all e-mail is subject to review. That notice can be sent via e-mail to employees in some states. Most courts have also held that the lack of notice does not mean that the employee has an expectation of privacy. One court held that an employer did not breach an employee's privacy when it promised that it would not use the content of e-mails against employees and then used an e-mail as grounds for disciplining an employee.[3] However, employers must exercise caution in adopting this approach because they may find that they run afoul of federal and state wiretapping and electronic communications statutes that do impose both civil and criminal liability for violation. While there are exceptions for workplace monitoring in these statutes (see the discussion in the criminal law section later in this chapter), employers will want to be certain that any policy does not violate these statutes. Most statutes, including the federal statutes, are satisfied with a disclosure in the employee handbook or company policies and allow this one-sided consent to eliminate any civil or criminal liability. However, about ten states require that the consent be two-sided in order for the workplace exemption to apply.[4]

As a result of this clear mandate for employer monitoring, any messages sent or received on an employer's e-mail system can be retrieved and read by the employer, even messages of a personal nature.

Seventy-seven percent of all mid- to large-size firms do monitor employee's e-mail, and 84 percent of those firms tell their employees they will be monitoring their e-mails.[5] "While nearly 40 percent of employers allow personal use of office e-mail, only 12% allow unrestricted personal Internet access, and about 38% use blocking software to preclude access to certain Internet sites, usually adult and sexual sites. Nearly 24% of companies use key word searches of e-mails, but primarily to detect sexual and scatological phrases, as opposed to trade secrets and other proprietary information."[6] Most employers report that they have increased monitoring following the September 11, 2001, hijackings because of increased security provisions overall. *Garrity v. John Hancock Mut. Life Ins. Co.* (Case 8.2) deals with an issue of termination over an employee's e-mails that the boss read.

CASE 8.2

Garrity v. *John Hancock Mut. Life Ins. Co.*
2002 WL 974676 (D.Mass. 2002) (Memorandum Opinion)

The Boss Who Didn't Appreciate E-Mail Top Ten Lists

FACTS

Nancy Garrity and Joanne Clark (plaintiffs) were employees of John Hancock Mutual Life Insurance Company (defendant) for twelve and two years, respectively. Mrs. Garrity and Ms. Clark received on their office computers sexually explicit e-mails from Internet joke sites and other third parties, including Mrs. Garrity's husband, Arthur Garrity, which they then sent to coworkers. Examples included "The Top Ten Reasons Cookie Dough Is Better Than Men."

A fellow employee complained after receiving one such e-mail. Hancock investigated Mrs. Garrity's and Ms. Clark's e-mail folders, as well as the folders of those with whom they e-mailed on a regular basis. Based on the information gleaned from this investigation, Hancock determined that Mrs. Garrity and Ms. Clark had violated its E-Mail Policy, which states:

- Messages that are defamatory, abusive, obscene, profane, sexually oriented, threatening or racially offensive are prohibited.
- The inappropriate use of E-mail is in violation of company policy and may be subject to disciplinary action, up to and including termination of employment.
- All information stored, transmitted, received, or contained in the company's E-mail systems is the property of John Hancock. It is not company policy to intentionally inspect E-mail usage. However, there may be business or legal situations that necessitate company review of E-mail messages and other documents.
- [C]ompany management reserves the right to access all E-mail files.

Hancock periodically sent reminders, but it also provided information on how to keep e-mails private through password usage for the files.

Hancock fired both women, and they filed suit for invasion of privacy as well as wrongful termination. Hancock moved for summary judgment.

JUDICIAL OPINION

ZOBEL, District Judge

Plaintiffs' opposition states that "[i]t is uncontested . . . that Ms. Garrity, Mr. Garrity and Ms. Clarke believed that the personal e-mail correspondence they sent and received was private." While that may be true, the relevant inquiry is whether the expectation of privacy was reasonable. Any reasonable expectation on the part of plaintiffs is belied by the record and plaintiffs' own statements. According to deposition testimony, Mrs. Garrity and Ms. Clark assumed that the recipients of their messages might forward them to others. Likewise, Mr. Garrity testified that the e-mails he sent to his wife would eventually be sent to third parties. Although there is a dearth of case law on privacy issues with regard to office email, *Smyth* v. *Pillsbury Co., 914 F.Supp. 97 (E.D.Pa.1996)* is instructive here. In *Smyth*, the court held that even in the absence of a company e-mail policy, plaintiffs would not have had a reasonable expectation of privacy in their work e-mail:

Once plaintiff communicated the alleged unprofessional comments to a second person (his supervisor) over an e-mail system which was apparently utilized by the entire company, any reasonable expectation of privacy was lost. Significantly, the defendant did not require plaintiff, as in the case of urinalysis or personal property search to disclose any personal information about himself. Rather, plaintiff voluntarily communicated the alleged unprofessional comments over the company e-mail system. We find no privacy interests in such communications.

Both Mrs. Garrity and Ms. Clarke admit that they knew defendant had the ability to look at e-mail on the company's intranet system, and knew they had to be careful about sending e-mails. Nevertheless, they claim that their e-mails were private because the company had instructed them on how to create passwords and personal e-mail folders. Even so, any e-mail messages stored in [plaintiff's] personal folders were first transmitted over the network and were at some point accessible by a third party. Given these circumstances, we cannot conclude that [plaintiff], even by creating a personal password, manifested—and [defendant] recognized—a reasonable expectation in privacy in the contents of e-mail messages such that [defendant] was precluded from reviewing the messages.

Even if plaintiffs had a reasonable expectation of privacy in their work e-mail, defendant's legitimate business interest in protecting its employees from harassment in the workplace would likely trump plaintiffs' privacy interests. Both Title VII of the Civil Rights Act of 1964 and M.G.L. c. 151B require employers to take affirmative steps to maintain a workplace free of harassment and to investigate and take prompt and

effective remedial action when potentially harassing conduct is discovered. See *Faragher* v. *City of Boca Raton, 524 U.S. 775 (1998); Burlington Indus., Inc.* v. *Ellerth, 524 U.S. 742 (1998).*

Plaintiffs claim that, by reading their e-mails, defendant violated M.G.L. c. 272 § 99, which prohibits certain interceptions of wire and oral communications. Because the reading of e-mails, after they have been transmitted to the recipient, does not constitute "interception" within the wiretap statute, plaintiffs' claim fails. Although there is no case law directly on point under the Massachusetts wiretap statute, the conclusion set forth in *Eagle* v. *Investment Serv. Corp.* v. *Tamm, 146 F.Supp.2d 105 (D.Mass.2001),* is persuasive. The *Eagle* court held that the Electronic Communications Privacy Act of 1986, 18 U.S.C. §§ 2510 et seq. and 2701 et. seq. (the "ECPA"), requires that the acquisition of electronic communications occur during transmission. That is, the act of "interception" cannot proceed after the e-mail is received, as is the case here. Therefore, plaintiffs' wiretap claim fails as a matter of law.

Even if an employer's reading of employee e-mails constituted "interception," within the meaning of the statute, at least one Massachusetts court has held that an automatic e-mail back-up system is protected under the "ordinary business exemption" and therefore "does not constitute an unlawful interception in violation of G.L. c. 272 § 99."

Judgment may be entered for defendant.

CASE QUESTIONS

1. What type of e-mail did the employees send to one another?

2. What is Hancock's policy on its access to employee e-mail? Did the employees know about the policy?

3. Why does the violation of the wiretap argument fail?

4. What liability does Hancock have for not monitoring e-mail?

FOR THE MANAGER'S DESK

RE: A PROFILE OF THE OFFICE E-MAILER

A recent survey sponsored by the Ethics Officer Association provides insight into employee Internet use and employer monitoring of that use.* Employers have been concerned about such use because one estimate is that if 50 employees spend 3 hours per week on recreational surfing during work hours, the cost per week to a company is $3,322.50.† And the latest survey

indicates that employees spend about 2 hours per day surfing the Net.

E-mail use by employees is also controversial. A United Kingdom survey released the following data.

• 38% have used employer e-mail for political purposes.

continued

- 30% have sent racist, pornographic, sexist, or otherwise discriminatory e-mails while at work.‡

  The survey results (of 106 companies) indicate the following.

  - 92% of companies engage in monitoring.
  - 75% regularly record employees' e-mail transmissions.
  - Most allow "reasonable personal usage of e-mail and the Internet," but only 42% define what constitutes "reasonable personal usage."
  - Those activities considered "reasonable personal usage" are the following:
    - News—84%
    - E-mail to family—86%
    - 401(k) dealings—77%
    - Online banking—54%
    - Online shopping—51%

- Online trading—28%
- Job search—25%
- 86% of companies block certain Web sites.
- 19% monitor Web site traffic by employees.
- 69% use information technology for monitoring; 13% use the legal department; only 9% use the ethics office.
- 80% notify employees of monitoring by using the code of ethics, training, and the policy manual.

* W. Michael Hoffman, Laura P. Hartman, and Mark Rowe, "You've Got Mail . . . And the Boss Knows: A Survey by the Center for Business Ethics of Companies' Email and Internet Monitoring," 108 *Business and Society* 285, 2003.
† Elron Software, "Guide to Internet Usage and Policy," 2003, p. 12. See http://www.zixcorp.com for a look at the services companies can obtain for monitoring and securing their e-mail systems.
‡ Institute for Global Ethics, "U.K. survey finds many workers are misusing email," *Newsline*, 5(10), March 11, 2002.

Third-Party Access to E-Mails and Identity Disclosure

In this area of cyber law, it is not an employer who is taking action or disciplining an employee (although such discipline may follow) but a third party who seeks disclosure of the identity of an individual who is using a server or e-mail system and tries to obtain that identity through the server company. There are several different types of such third-party cases.

- Shareholders have brought suit seeking to halt users who post information that is false and defamatory but that results in damage to them and the company because the market reacts and the share price declines. When shareholders bring suit, they seek the identity of these chat room participants from the server. They generally seek the identity through the use of a civil subpoena.

- Private parties such as record companies and music publishers seek to determine the identity of those who are sharing files using a particular server.

- Government agencies seek the identity of Internet users and those posting notes in chat rooms, as well as the content of the communications, because crimes are being committed (as in the case of child pornography) or because information and notes related to terrorist activities are being posted. Under the USA Patriot Act, specific provisions relate to third-party access to private e-mail.[7] The government seeks this information with a warrant or criminal subpoena. The provisions in the Patriot Act liberalize the requirements for a warrant for access to e-mail, allowing such a warrant to be issued when there is probable cause (see Chapter 9) for any crime being committed as opposed to being required to allege specific types of crimes in order to obtain a warrant.

In these types of cases, courts must balance more than just privacy and employer and employee rights, as in the first type of cyber law privacy cases. They are also considering the First Amendment rights exercised in chat rooms and the Fourth Amendment protections against search and seizure. While the means for communication in these cases is electronic, more than one court has noted the "public square" quality of the Internet and these chat rooms. *Doe v. 2Themart.com, Inc.* and *U.S. v. Bailey*, (Cases 8.3 and 8.4), deal with the issues related to third-party access to e-mails and identity.

BUSINESS PLANNING TIP

Employers probably do need to monitor employee e-mails in order to protect themselves from liability. For example, both the *New York Times* and the U.S. Navy uncovered sexually suggestive e-mails among and between their employees. The presence of such e-mail can become part of a Title VII sexual harassment suit via employment atmosphere of harassment (see Chapter 20). Sexually suggestive e-mail circulating on e-mail systems can create an atmosphere of harassment. For example, one case involving e-mail and sexual harassment involved the circulation of a joke entitled "Why Beer Is Better Than Women."

Because liability results, employers need to provide warnings to employees and monitor to be certain that e-mails are not creating an atmosphere of harassment.

One of the lessons of cyberspace already discussed in Chapter 4 is that not only are e-mails not private for employees, they are also not private for the company. E-mails are completely discoverable if the company is a party to litigation. Opponents in litigation can review all of the jokes, correspondence, and other information employees put in their e-mails.

CASE 8.3

Doe v. *2Themart.com Inc.*
140 F Supp 2d 1088 (WD Wash 2001)

No Subpoena: NoGuano!

FACTS

The shareholders of 2Themart.com Inc. (TMRT) brought a shareholder derivative class action against the company and its officers and directors alleging fraud on the market. By subpoena, TMRT seeks to obtain the identity of twenty-three speakers who have participated anonymously on Internet message boards operated by InfoSpace.

InfoSpace is a Seattle-based Internet company that operates a Web site called Silicon Investor. The Silicon Investor site contains a series of electronic bulletin boards, and some of these bulletin boards are devoted to specific publicly traded companies. InfoSpace users can freely post and exchange messages on these boards. Many do so using Internet pseudonyms, the often fanciful names that people choose for themselves when interacting on the Internet. By using a pseudonym, a person who posts or responds to a message on an Internet bulletin board maintains anonymity.

One of the Internet bulletin boards on the Silicon Investor Web site is specifically devoted to TMRT. At the time of the case, "almost 1500 messages have been posted on the TMRT board, covering an enormous variety of topics and posters. Investors and members of the public discuss the latest news about the company, what new businesses it may develop, the strengths and weaknesses of the company's operations, and what its managers and its employees might do better." Past messages posted on the site are archived, so any new user can read and print copies of prior postings.

Some of the messages posted on the TMRT site have been less than flattering to the company. In fact, some have been downright nasty. For example, a user called "Truthseeker" posted a message stating "TMRT is a Ponzi scam that Charles Ponzi would be proud of. . . . The company's CEO, Magliarditi, has defrauded employees in the past. The company's other large shareholder, Rebeil, defrauded customers in the past." Another poster named "Cuemaster" indicated that "they were dumped by their accountants. . . . these guys are friggin liars. . . . why haven't they told the public this yet? ? ? Liars and criminals!!!!!" Another user, not identified in the exhibits, wrote, "Lying, cheating, thieving, stealing, lowlife criminals!!!!" Other postings advised TMRT investors to sell their stock. "Look out below!!!! This stock has had it. . . . get short or sell your position now while you still can." "They

[TMRT] are not building anything, except extensions on their homes . . . bail out now."

TMRT issued the present subpoena to InfoSpace for "[a]ll identifying information and documents, including, but not limited to, computerized or computer stored records and logs, electronic mail (e-mail), and postings on your online message boards," concerning a list of twenty-three InfoSpace users, including Truthseeker, Cuemaster, and the current J. Doe, who used the pseudonym NoGuano. These users have posted messages on the TMRT bulletin board or have communicated via the Internet with users who have posted such messages. The subpoena would require InfoSpace to disclose the subscriber information for these twenty-three users, thereby stripping them of their Internet anonymity.

InfoSpace notified these users by e-mail that it had received the subpoena, and the person who used the Internet pseudonym NoGuano asked to quash the subpoena. The court granted NoGuano's request to proceed under a pseudonym for the purposes of the motion.

JUDICIAL OPINION

ZILLY, District Judge

The Internet represents a revolutionary advance in communication technology. It has been suggested that the Internet may be the "greatest innovation in speech since the invention of the printing press." It allows people from all over the world to exchange ideas and information freely and in "real-time." Through the use of the Internet, "any person with a phone line can become a town crier with a voice that resonates farther than it could from any soapbox."

The rapid growth of Internet communication and Internet commerce has raised novel and complex legal issues and has challenged existing legal doctrine in many areas. This motion raises important and challenging questions of: (1) what is the scope of an individual's First Amendment right to speak anonymously on the Internet, and (2) what showing must be made by a private party seeking to discover the identity of anonymous Internet users through the enforcement of a civil subpoena?

The right to the freedom of speech is enshrined in the First Amendment to the United States Constitution, which provides that "Congress shall make no law . . .

continued

abridging the freedom of speech, or of the press[.]" U.S. Const. amend. I. This limitation on governmental interference with free speech applies directly to the federal government, and has been imposed on the states via the Fourteenth Amendment. See, e.g., *First Nat'l Bank* v. *Bellotti*, 435 U.S. 765, 779–80, 98 S.Ct. 1407, 55 L.Ed.2d 707 (1978).

First Amendment protections extend to speech via the Internet. "Through the use of web pages, mail exploders and newsgroups, [any person] can become a pamphleteer." A component of the First Amendment is the right to speak with anonymity.

The right to speak anonymously was of fundamental importance to the establishment of our Constitution. Throughout the revolutionary and early federal period in American history, anonymous speech and the use of pseudonyms were powerful tools of political debate. The Federalist Papers (authored by Madison, Hamilton, and Jay) were written anonymously under the name "Publius." The anti-federalists responded with anonymous articles of their own, authored by "Cato" and "Brutus." Anonymous speech is a great tradition that is woven into the fabric of this nation's history.

The right to speak anonymously extends to speech via the Internet. Internet anonymity facilitates the rich, diverse, and far ranging exchange of ideas. The "ability to speak one's mind" on the Internet "without the burden of the other party knowing all the facts about one's identity can foster open communication and robust debate." People who have committed no wrongdoing should be free to participate in online forums without fear that their identity will be exposed under the authority of the court.

The free exchange of ideas on the Internet is driven in large part by the ability of Internet users to communicate anonymously. If Internet users could be stripped of that anonymity by a civil subpoena enforced under the liberal rules of civil discovery, this would have a significant chilling effect on Internet communications and thus on basic First Amendment rights. Therefore, discovery requests seeking to identify anonymous Internet users must be subjected to careful scrutiny by the courts.

As InfoSpace has urged, "[u]nmeritorious attempts to unmask the identities of online speakers . . . have a chilling effect on" Internet speech. The "potential chilling effect imposed by the unmasking of anonymous speakers would diminish if litigants first were required to make a showing in court of their need for the identifying information."

. . . When the anonymous Internet user is not a party to the case, the litigation can go forward without the disclosure of their identity. Therefore, non-party disclosure is only appropriate in the exceptional case where the compelling need for the discovery sought outweighs the First Amendment rights of the anonymous speaker.

Accordingly, this Court adopts the following standard for evaluating a civil subpoena that seeks the identity of an anonymous Internet user who is not a party to the underlying litigation. The Court will consider four factors in determining whether the subpoena should issue. These are whether: (1) the subpoena seeking the information was issued in good faith and not for any improper purpose, (2) the information sought relates to a core claim or defense, (3) the identifying information is directly and materially relevant to that claim or defense, and (4) information sufficient to establish or to disprove that claim or defense is unavailable from any other source.

This test provides a flexible framework for balancing the First Amendment rights of anonymous speakers with the right of civil litigants to protect their interests through the litigation discovery process. The Court shall give weight to each of these factors as the court determines is appropriate under the circumstances of each case. This Court is mindful that it is imposing a high burden. "But the First Amendment requires us to be vigilant in making [these] judgments, to guard against undue hindrances to political conversations and the exchange of ideas." *Buckley,* 525 U.S. at 192, 119 S.Ct. 636.

In the present case, TMRT seeks information it says will validate its defense that "changes in [TMRT] stock prices were not caused by the Defendants but by the illegal actions of individuals who manipulated the [TMRT] stock price using the Silicon Investor message boards." This Court must evaluate TMRT's stated need for the information in light of the four factors outlined above.

1. Was the subpoena brought in good faith?

This Court does not conclude that this subpoena was brought in bad faith or for an improper purpose. TMRT and its officers and directors are defending against a shareholder derivative class action lawsuit.

They have asserted numerous affirmative defenses, one of which alleges that the defendants did not cause the drop in TMRT's stock value. TMRT could reasonably believe that the posted messages are relevant to this defense.

However, as originally issued the subpoena seeking the identity information was extremely broad. The subpoena would have required the disclosure of personal e-mails and other personal information that has no relevance to the issues raised in the lawsuit. This apparent disregard for the privacy and the First Amendment rights of the online users, while not demonstrating bad faith per se, weighs against TMRT in balancing the interests here.

2. Does the information sought relate to a core claim or defense?

Only when the identifying information is needed to advance core claims or defenses can it be sufficiently material to compromise First Amendment rights.

The information sought by TMRT does not relate to a core defense. Here, the information relates to only one of twenty-seven affirmative defenses raised by the defendant, the defense that "no act or omission of any of the Defendants was the cause in fact or the proximate cause of any injury or damage to the plaintiffs." This is a generalized assertion of the lack of causation.

3. Is the identifying information directly and materially relevant to a core claim or defense?

Even when the claim or defense for which the information is sought is deemed core to the case, the identity of the Internet users must also be materially relevant to that claim or defense. Under the Federal Rules of Civil Procedure discovery is normally very broad, requiring disclosure of any relevant information that "appears reasonably calculated to lead to the discovery of admissible evidence." But when First Amendment rights are at stake, a higher threshold of relevancy must be imposed. Only when the information sought is directly and materially relevant to a core claim or defense can the need for the information outweigh the First Amendment right to speak anonymously.

TMRT has failed to demonstrate that the identity of the Internet users is directly and materially relevant to a core defense.

According to the pleadings, the Internet user known as NoGuano has never posted messages on Silicon Investor's TMRT message board. At oral argument,

TMRT's counsel conceded this point but stated that NoGuano's information was sought because he had "communicated" via the Internet with Silicon Investor posters such as Truthseeker. Given that NoGuano admittedly posted no public statements on the TMRT site, there is no basis to conclude that the identity of NoGuano and others similarly situated is directly and materially relevant to TMRT's defense.

TMRT speculates that the users of the InfoSpace website may have been engaged in stock manipulation in violation of federal securities law. TMRT indicates that it intends to compare the names of the InfoSpace users with the names of individuals who traded TMRT stock during the same period to determine whether any illegal stock manipulation occurred. However, TMRT's innuendos of stock manipulation do not suffice to overcome the First Amendment rights of the Internet users. Those rights cannot be nullified by an unsupported allegation of wrongdoing raised by the party seeking the information.

4. Is information sufficient to establish TMRT's defense available from any other source?

TMRT has failed to demonstrate that the information it needs to establish its defense is unavailable from any other source. The chat room messages are archived and are available to anyone to read and print. TMRT obtained copies of some of these messages and submitted them to this Court. TMRT can therefore demonstrate what was said, when it was said, and can compare the timing of those statements with information on fluctuations in the TMRT stock price. The messages are available for use at trial, and TMRT can factually support its defense without encroaching on the First Amendment rights of the Internet users.

Doe's (NoGuano's pseudonym) motion to quash the subpoena is GRANTED.

CASE QUESTIONS

1. What type of information was posted to the site?

2. Why do the shareholders, officers, and directors want the identity of NoGuano revealed?

3. What tests does the court apply and in what other types of cases will these tests apply?

4. Will NoGuano's identity be revealed?

MAKING ETHICS PERSONAL

Weasels or Freedom Fighters: Anonymous Bloggers

How would you classify the ethics of those who post information without revealing their identity or being willing to be held accountable for that information? What do you think of its reliability? How would you evaluate their character? When do you think it is important to keep your identity concealed when it comes to disclosing information?

CASE 8.4

U.S. v. *Bailey*
272 F.Supp.2d 822 (M.D. Pa. 2004)

Kiddie Porn and Yahoo! The Feds Come Calling

FACTS

In 1998 the FBI launched the Innocent Images Crimes Against Children Initiative to investigate Internet criminal behavior directed against children, including the distribution, transmission, and possession of child pornography. Undercover FBI Agent Geoffrey Binney discovered and joined the Candyman online e-group. Upon entering the Candyman site, Agent Binney initially encountered the welcome page, which included only text and stated: "This group is for People who love kids. You can post any type of messages you like too or any type of pics and vids you like too."

While an undercover member of the group from January 2, 2001, through February 6, 2001, Agent Binney received 498 e-mails from the Candyman e-group. A little over 100 of these e-mails contained files depicting child pornography.

Upon joining the Candyman e-group, Agent Binney promptly attempted to obtain technical information regarding how the e-group operated. In January 2001, he informally asked Yahoo! for information but encountered significant resistance. When he asked to speak with a technical representative, its "compliance paralegal" told him he would "never speak to a technical representative" of Yahoo!. Therefore, on January 19, 2001, and while his undercover investigation was still ongoing, Agent Binney served a grand jury subpoena on Yahoo! for testimony and the production of documents related to the identity of Candyman e-group subscribers.

Yahoo!'s record revealed that "tbaile2@amfam.com" became a subscriber to the Candyman e-group on January 16, 2001 at 11:44 A.M. This was the e-mail address of Thomas Edward Bailey (defendant) at his place of employment. Since August 2000, Mr. Bailey had been employed by Bruce Southwell at an American Family Insurance in Omaha, Nebraska.

Based in part on information provided in Agent Binney's affidavit, and having identified "tbaile2@amfam.com" as the address assigned to Mr. Bailey, on December 21, 2001, Agent McMillion prepared an application for a warrant to search Mr. Bailey's work computer at the American Family Insurance office. Magistrate Judge Thalken issued a warrant to search Mr. Bailey's work computer and work space.

The American Family office contained three desks and three computers, one of which was used by Mr. Bailey. The computers were owned by American Family. Mr. Bailey needed a password to access American Family's computer network, which provided the defendant with Internet access and the Web base for his e-mail account. His boss did not know Mr. Bailey's password, which was changed every thirty days. Mr. Bailey used his work e-mail account to contact American Family personnel at its home office but also frequently used this e-mail address to send and receive personal messages.

American Family posted the following message to users when they logged in to the company's system.

These computer resources are solely owned by the Company. Unauthorized access or use is a violation of federal law and could result in criminal prosecution. Users agree not to disclose any company information except as authorized by the company. Your use of this computer system is consent to be monitored and authorization to search your personal computer to assure compliance with company policies.

Mr. Bailey acknowledged seeing the notice on his computer screen during his daily routine of logging in to the computer system but testified he believed it meant he could not share or disclose private information concerning clients.

Agent McMillion asked Mr. Bailey if he had access to other computers. Mr. Bailey explained that he and his girlfriend had a home computer and a home e-mail account through Yahoo!. Agent McMillion asked Mr. Bailey if the FBI could search the home computer to look for child pornography. The defendant did not object to any search of his home computer. He responded by contacting his girlfriend, Julie McEwen, at their home. Mr. Bailey told Ms. McEwen that the FBI was searching his work computer, FBI agents would be arriving at the house to look at the home computer, and she should cooperate with them.

Having completed a search of the work computer and office pursuant to the warrant, agents and an FBI photographer went to Mr. Bailey's home and his computer was removed from his home. Ms. McEwen never objected to any analysis of the computer in the home, nor to its later removal.

JUDICIAL OPINION

KOPF, District Judge

Defendant asserts he had a legitimate expectation of privacy in the information stored on his work computer, and the search of that computer pursuant to a warrant issued on the basis of false statements violated his Fourth Amendment rights. He seeks suppression of all evidence found on that computer and all evidence obtained as fruit of that search.

Employees may have reasonable expectations of privacy within their workplaces which are constitutionally protected against intrusions by police. "As with the expectation of privacy in one's home, such an expectation in one's place of work is 'based upon societal expectations that have deep roots in the history of the [Fourth] Amendment.'" However, an employee's expectation of privacy in the content of offices, desks, and files may be reduced by an employer's practices, procedures, and legitimate regulation over the use of the employer's property. The question of whether an employee has a reasonable expectation of privacy in his work area must be determined on a case-by-case basis.

Use of passwords and locking office doors to restrict an employer's access to computer files is evidence of the employee's subjective expectation of privacy in those files. Further, where the employer has no policy notifying employees that their computer use could be monitored, and there is no indication that the employer directs others to routinely access the employees' computers, the employees' subjective beliefs that their computer files are private may be objectively reasonable.

However, an employer's notice to an employee that workplace files, internet use, and e-mail may be monitored undermines the reasonableness of an employee's claim that he or she believed such information was private and not subject to search. An employee cannot claim a justified expectation of privacy in computer files where the employer owns the computer; the employee uses that computer to obtain access to the internet and e-mail through the employer's network; the employee was explicitly cautioned that information flowing through or stored on computers within the network cannot be considered confidential, and where computer users were notified that network administrators and others were free to view data downloaded from the internet.

Defendant Bailey could not access his e-mail account, or any other computer file or program, on the computer American Family provided to him for his work without first acknowledging that he understood the computer resources were solely owned by American Family, and his "use of this computer system [was] consent to be monitored and authorization to search" his computer. Although claiming he did not routinely read this screen notification, Bailey knew what it said. He nonetheless claims he did not believe American Family would look at his personal e-mail files, knew of no prior instance where they had, and believed his e-mails and personal files on the computer were private. However, despite the fact that his computer was password-protected, I conclude defendant's claim of a subjective expectation of privacy is not credible.

Defendant is an intelligent adult who was fully capable of reading and understanding the screen banner notifying him that his computer use could be searched by American Family. Bailey is a high school graduate, has successfully completed post high school education to become an ASC certified automotive technician, and has passed the licensing requirements to sell insurance. He offered no credible testimony explaining his alleged belief that his computer use was private when, to access his computer, he was required to acknowledge daily that American Family could monitor and search computer activity.

Even assuming defendant believed his workplace e-mail and files were private, he has failed to prove this subjective expectation of privacy was objectively reasonable and protected by the Fourth Amendment. In addition to the notice on his computer startup screen, American Family advised its computer users, including defendant, by e-mail letter and through its policies posted on its intranet that a worker's computer could be searched to assure employees were not using

continued

American Family equipment to violate the law or company policies, or in a way which could reflect negatively on American Family. A company can legitimately regulate the use of its property and is entitled to adopt policies and practices which place restrictions and conditions on the personal use of computer equipment. Employees have no objectively reasonable basis to believe that their activities on a company computer are private when, through the company's screen notification, they have actual knowledge that the computer can be searched and, through posted company policies and e-mail notifications, either know or should know they possess "no expectation of privacy associated with the information they store in or send through these systems."

Any expectation of privacy Bailey had in the contents of his American Family computer is not one that society is willing to accept and protect under the Fourth Amendment. Bailey cannot assert any Fourth Amendment violation from the search of his work computer provided to him by American Family to conduct Mr. Southwell's business on behalf of American Family. Bailey cannot successfully pursue a motion to suppress evidence found on his work computer, or arising from execution of a warrant to search that computer.

I therefore conclude the execution of the warrant to seize and search defendant's workplace computer did not violate defendant's Fourth Amendment rights. Therefore, I further conclude that Bailey's statements to the FBI agents performing the search and the evidence obtained from seizing and searching Bailey's home computer are not subject to suppression as fruit of an unconstitutional search of defendant's workplace.

CASE QUESTIONS

1. What crime was the FBI investigating?
2. Did Yahoo! cooperate with the FBI initially?
3. Did Mr. Bailey have an expectation of privacy on his work computer?
4. Did Mr. Bailey have an expectation of privacy on his home computer? How was the FBI able to search that computer?

 CONSIDER...   8.1

Discuss whether employees have the right to privacy in the following e-mail situations:
1. E-mail sent in a company in which there is no warning given about the lack of privacy in e-mails [*Smyth* v. *Pillsbury*, 914 F. Supp. 97 (E.D. Pa. 1996)]
2. E-mail sent by an employee to coworkers from home using the employee's AOL account
3. E-mail sent by an employee from a laptop while the employee is traveling for the company [*Muick* v. *Glenayre Electronics*, 280 F.3d 741 (7th Cir. 2002)]
4. E-mail sent by an employee to a coworker over a company Internet system in a company in which the employer has promised privacy in e-mail [*Commonwealth* v. *Proetto*, 771 A.2d 823 (Pa.Super.Ct. 2001)]
5. Employer monitoring the e-mails of any employee when those e-mails were stored in a file folder market "Personal" [*McLaren* v. *Microsoft Corp.*, 1999 WL 339015 (Tex.App.-Dallas 1999)]
6. Employees using company e-mail for union organization purposes [Pratt & Whitney, NLRB Gen. Couns. Adv. Mem. Cases 12-CA-18446, 12-CA-18722, 12-CS-18863 (Feb. 23, 1998)]
7. Government obtaining access to erased files containing pornography from a professor's computer located on his office computer, which was part of the university computer network [*United States* v. *Angevine*, 281 F.3d 1130 (10th Cir. 2002)]

Review the law, the cited cases, and the following principles to guide your discussion.
- Employees have no expectation of privacy regarding workplace computers and files.
- Employers should provide warnings and even if employees did not see the warnings that were there upon login, employees are covered.
- Government agencies can obtain access to workplace computers of employees through warrants served on employers because they have no expectation of privacy on workplace computers.

Here's an example of how to approach situation 1.

THINK: What's different about this scenario? The employer did not provide a warning. But the case discussion indicates that even without warning there is no expectation of privacy, only worries about violating federal and state laws. However, seeing an e-mail after its transmission is not a wiretap or an interception.

APPLY AND ANSWER: No right of privacy by employees in their workplace computers and e-mails.

Now follow the same approach to discuss situations 2 through 7.

Identifying Users Who Employ Servers for Infringement
In peer-to-peer file sharing (P2P), users help each other obtain copies of copyrighted materials. While these users have maintained an exemption from federal copyright law, the courts have found otherwise. (See Chapter 1 for a discussion of the Napster and Kazaa[8] cases and Chapter 16 for a discussion of intellectual property rights.) Music producers, songwriters, and publishers have successfully pursued injunctions and other remedies against the file sharers. However, there is the related privacy question of the server's revelation of the users' identities as well as the servers' liability for the use of their systems for P2P.

On the first question of the revelation of identity, the cases already covered in this section provide the answer. Criminal copyright infringement mandates disclosure of the users' identity. The question of the servers' liability for infringement is covered in the following section on appropriation.

The Tort of Appropriation in Cyberspace

Appropriation is the tort of taking an image, likeness, or name and then using it, without permission, for commercial advantage (see Chapter 10 for more information). Use of a name or image without permission, whether in a newspaper or in cyberspace, is still the tort of appropriation. For example, a screensaver program that uses a likeness of Richard, the million-dollar winner on CBS television's program *Survivor*, is the tort of appropriation. Using his likeness, in cartoon form for the *Conniver* screensaver program with the *Survivor* logo, without his permission, constitutes appropriation.

Appropriation has been applied to situations in which individuals are sharing files in order to obtain copies of copyrighted music. While federal laws protect copyrights and allow their owners to pursue remedies against P2P file sharers, those who hold copyrights know that stopping the infringement

BUSINESS PLANNING TIP

Because the law on Internet and e-mail privacy is evolving, taking the initiative not only can avoid future legal problems but also can help employees feel comfortable about company policies and their e-mail and Internet use. The following tips were provided by a lawyer for businesses interested in solving the issues of technology, the workplace, and cyberspace.

The Ten Commandments for Avoiding Workplace E-xposure

1. Publish policies regarding employee use of e-mail, the Internet, and any employer-issued hardware or software.
2. Have employees sign off on the policy each year.
3. Tell employees that the company will monitor e-mail, Internet use, and any other use of employer-issued computers. Be sure to cover all new technology, such as Palm Pilots, Blackberries, and two-way text-messagers.
4. Create a style guide for writing business e-mails.
5. Train all employees on how to write appropriate business e-mails.
6. Develop a document/e-mail retention policy.
7. Tell employees you will cooperate with law enforcement officials and turn over any evidence of illegal activities.
8. Enforce all policies in an even-handed manner.
9. Keep current on new technology in the market place and how it can be used and monitored.
10. Reevaluate all technology-related policies annually.

Source: Frank C. Morris, Jr., "The Electronic Platform: Email and Other Privacy Issues in the Workplace," *Computer & Internet Law*, 20(8).

requires cooperation from the owners of the servers used for P2P. Congress passed the **Digital Millennium Copyright Act** (DMCA, 17 U.S.C. § 512 *et seq.*), which provides servers with limited liability for the infringement activities of users. However, a requirement for that limited liability protection is that the server owner and operator periodically check to ensure that its cyberspace components are not being used for infringement. For example, under the DMCA, colleges and universities enjoy immunity from infringement liability for the downloading activities of students. However, colleges and universities must be able to show the following: (1) that they have warned students about P2P activities and prohibited them; (2) that they impose sanctions on students for violation of user conditions; and (3) that they have systems and checks designed to catch and stop users from infringement activities. *Recording Industry Ass'n of America, Inc. v. Verizon Internet Services, Inc.* (Case 8.5) deals with a server liability issue and P2P activities.

CASE 8.5

Recording Industry Ass'n of America, Inc. v. *Verizon Internet Services, Inc.*
351 F.3d 1229 (CA. D.C. 2003)

On the Blue Verizon: P2P File Sharers and Their ISPs

FACTS

The Recording Industry Association of America (RIAA) served two civil subpoenas under the DMCA on Verizon, an Internet service provider (ISP), seeking the identity of Internet users the RIAA believed were infringing the copyrights of its members. The RIAA specifically asked for the names of two Verizon subscribers who appeared to be trading large numbers of MP3 files of copyrighted music via P2P programs, such as Kazaa. Verizon refused to comply with the subpoenas.

The district court rejected Verizon's statutory and constitutional challenges to § 512(h) of the DMCA and ordered the ISP to disclose to the RIAA the names of the two subscribers. Verizon appealed.

JUDICIAL OPINION

GINSBURG, Chief Judge

Unlike Napster, which relied upon a centralized communication architecture to identify the .mp3 files available for download, the current generation of P2P file sharing programs allow an internet user to search directly the .mp3 file libraries of other users; no web site is involved. To date, owners of copyrights have not been able to stop the use of these decentralized programs. See *Metro-Goldwyn-Mayer Studios, Inc.* v. *Grokster, Ltd.*, 259 F.Supp.2d 1029 (C.D.Cal. 2003) (holding *Grokster* not contributorily liable for copyright infringement by users of its P2P file sharing program).

The RIAA now has begun to direct its anti-infringement efforts against individual users of P2P file sharing programs. In order to pursue apparent infringers the RIAA needs to be able to identify the individuals who are sharing and trading files using P2P programs. The RIAA can readily obtain the screen name of an individual user, and using the Internet Protocol (IP) address associated with that screen name, can trace the user to his ISP. Only the ISP, however, can link the IP address used to access a P2P program with the name and address of a person—the ISP's customer—who can then be contacted or, if need be, sued by the RIAA.

The RIAA has used the subpoena provisions of § 512(h) of the Digital Millennium Copyright Act (DMCA) to compel ISPs to disclose the names of subscribers whom the RIAA has reason to believe are infringing its members' copyrights. See 17 U.S.C. § 512 (h)(1) (copyright owner may "request the clerk of any United States district court to issue a subpoena to [an ISP] for identification of an alleged infringer"). Some ISPs have complied with the RIAA's § 512(h) subpoenas and identified the names of the subscribers sought by the RIAA. The RIAA has sent letters to and filed lawsuits against several hundred such individuals, each of whom allegedly made available for download by other users hundreds or in some cases even thousands of .mp3 files of copyrighted recordings. Verizon refused to comply with and instead has challenged the validity of the two § 512(h) subpoenas it has received.

The issue is whether § 512(h) applies to an ISP acting only as a conduit for data transferred between two internet users, such as persons sending and receiving e-mail or, as in this case, sharing P2P files. Verizon contends § 512(h) does not authorize the issuance of a subpoena to an ISP that transmits infringing material but does not store any such material on its servers. We conclude from both the terms of § 512(h) and the overall structure of § 512 that, as Verizon contends, a subpoena may be issued only to an ISP engaged in storing on its servers material that is infringing or the subject of infringing activity.

Section 512 creates four safe harbors, each of which immunizes ISPs from liability for copyright infringement under certain highly specified conditions. Subsection 512(a), entitled "Transitory digital network communications," provides a safe harbor "for infringement of copyright by reason of the [ISP's] transmitting, routing, or providing connections for" infringing material, subject to certain conditions, including that the transmission is initiated and directed by an internet user. See 17 U.S.C. §§ 512(a)(1)-(5). Subsection 512(b), "System caching," provides immunity from liability "for infringement of copyright by reason of the intermediate and temporary storage of material on a system or network controlled or operated by or for the [ISP]," § 512(b)(1), as long as certain conditions regarding the transmission and retrieval of the material created by the ISP are met. See 17 U.S.C. §§ 512(b)(2)(A)–(E). Subsection 512(c), "Information residing on systems or networks at the direction of users," creates a safe harbor from liability "for infringement of copyright by reason of the storage at the direction of a user of material that resides on a system or network controlled or operated by or for the service provider," as long as the ISP meets certain conditions regarding its lack of knowledge concerning, financial benefit from, and expeditious efforts to remove or deny access to, material that is infringing or that is claimed to be the subject of infringing activity. Finally, § 512(d), "Information location tools," provides a safe harbor from liability "for infringement of copyright by reason of the provider referring or linking users to an online location containing infringing material or infringing activity, by using information location tools" such as "a directory, index, reference, pointer, or hypertext link," subject to the same conditions as in §§ 512(c)(1)(A)-(C).

Infringing material obtained or distributed via P2P file sharing is located in the computer (or in an off-line storage device, such as a compact disc) of an individual user. No matter what information the copyright owner may provide, the ISP can neither "remove" nor "disable access to" the infringing material because that material is not stored on the ISP's servers. Verizon can not remove or disable one user's access to infringing material resident on another user's computer because Verizon does not control the content on its subscribers' computers.

In support of its claim that § 512(h) can—and should—be read to reach P2P technology, the RIAA points to congressional testimony and news articles available to the Congress prior to passage of the DMCA. These sources document the threat to copyright owners posed by bulletin board services (BBSs) and file transfer protocol (FTP) sites, which the RIAA says were precursors to P2P programs.

We need not, however, resort to investigating what the 105th Congress may have known because the text of § 512(h) and the overall structure of § 512 clearly establish, as we have seen, that § 512(h) does not authorize the issuance of a subpoena to an ISP acting as a mere conduit for the transmission of information sent by others. Legislative history can serve to inform the court's reading of an otherwise ambiguous text; it cannot lead the court to contradict the legislation itself.

In any event, not only is the statute clear (albeit complex), the legislative history of the DMCA betrays no awareness whatsoever that internet users might be able directly to exchange files containing copyrighted works. That is not surprising; P2P software was "not even a glimmer in anyone's eye when the DMCA was enacted." Furthermore, such testimony as was available to the Congress prior to passage of the DMCA concerned "hackers" who established unauthorized FTP or BBS sites on the servers of ISPs.

The Congress had no reason to foresee the application of § 512(h) to P2P file sharing, nor did they draft the DMCA broadly enough to reach the new technology when it came along. Had the Congress been aware of P2P technology, or anticipated its development, § 512(h) might have been drafted more generally. Be that as it may, contrary to the RIAA's claim, nothing in the legislative history supports the issuance of a § 512(h) subpoena to an ISP acting as a conduit for P2P file sharing.

Finally, the RIAA argues Verizon's interpretation of the statute "would defeat the core objectives" of the Act. More specifically, according to the RIAA there is no policy justification for limiting the reach of § 512(h) to situations in which the ISP stores infringing material on its system, considering that many more acts of copyright infringement are committed in the P2P realm, in which the ISP merely transmits the material for others, and that the burden upon an ISP required to identify an infringing subscriber is minimal.

We are not unsympathetic either to the RIAA's concern regarding the widespread infringement of its members' copyrights, or to the need for legal tools to protect those rights. It is not the province of the courts, however, to rewrite the DMCA in order to make it fit a new and unforeseen internet architecture, no matter how damaging that development has been to the music industry or threatens being to the motion picture

continued

and software industries. The plight of copyright holders must be addressed in the first instance by the Congress; only the "Congress has the constitutional authority and the institutional ability to accommodate fully the varied permutations of competing interests that are inevitably implicated by such new technology." See *Sony Corp.* v. *Universal City Studios, Inc.*, 464 U.S. 417, 431, 104 S.Ct. 774, 783, 78 L.Ed.2d 574 (1984).

The stakes are large for the music, motion picture, and software industries and their role in fostering technological innovation and our popular culture. It is not surprising, therefore, that even as this case was being argued, committees of the Congress were considering how best to deal with the threat to copyrights posed by P2P file sharing schemes. See, e.g., Privacy & Piracy: The Paradox of Illegal File Sharing on Peer-to-Peer Networks and the Impact of Technology on the Entertainment Industry: Hearing Before the Senate Comm.

On Governmental Affairs, 108th Congress (Sept. 30, 2003); Pornography, Technology, and Process: Problems and Solutions on Peer-to-Peer Networks: Hearing Before the Senate Comm. on the Judiciary, 108th Congress (Sept. 9, 2003).

[W]e remand this case to the district court to vacate its order enforcing the July 24 subpoena and to grant Verizon's motion to quash the February 4 subpoena.

CASE QUESTIONS

1. What is the difference between the Napster technology and P2P?

2. How does the DMCA protect P2P users?

3. What arguments does the RIAA make about requiring disclosure of the users?

4. What must the RIAA do to obtain access to the users' identity?

C O N S I D E R . . .   8 . 2

Apply the holding in the *Verizon* case to a slight variation in parties. In *Metro-Goldwyn-Mayer Studios, Inc.* v. *Grokster Ltd.*, 380 F. 3d 1154 (9th Cir. 2004), film studios filed suit against Grokster Ltd. and StreamCast Networks, Inc., two companies that freely distribute software that allows users to share computer files with each other, including digitized music and motion pictures. The film studios alleged vicarious copyright infringement by the software companies because they were aware of the use of their product. Grokster and StreamCast defended on the grounds that they had no control over how their products were used. Should the court hold the companies vicariously liable for copyright infringement?

F O R   T H E   M A N A G E R ' S   D E S K

RE: DOWNLOADING MUSIC AND COPYRIGHT ENFORCEMENT

The Recording Industry Association of America (RIAA) has undertaken an aggressive litigation strategy against music downloaders. The first wave of lawsuits consisted of suits against 261 people who were considered the most active sharers of music files. The lawsuits were accompanied by an offer of amnesty for those who are downloaders but turn themselves in prior to suits being filed against them.

Penalties for copyright infringement range from $750 to $150,000 per incident. In the past, the RIAA has settled the suits for an average of $3,000. However, four university students operating campus-wide file-sharing operations paid between $12,000 and $17,500 in July 2003.

The RIAA says that 300 million fewer albums were shipped between 1999 and 2002 and that 400 billion

software music files were shared free over the Internet during July 2003.

Sales are down 15 percent from 2002. RIAA estimates that 11 million home computers actively share music files in one month. Kazaa is the most frequently used system, carrying 7.2 million computers. WinMX has 2.3 million homes, and the remaining systems all have fewer than 1 million users. A survey showed that 67 percent of downloaders did not care whether the music they were downloading was copyrighted.

In an attempt to regain control of the record market, Universal reduced its prices on its CDs to $12.98, a price reduction of 24 to 32 percent.

Sources: Amy Harmon, "261 Lawsuits Filed on Music Sharing," *New York Times*, September 9, 2003, pp. A1, C6. Nick Wingfield, "The High Cost of Sharing," *Wall Street Journal*, September 9, 2003, pp. B1, B8.

ETHICAL ISSUES

Jesse Jordan, a 19-year-old student at Rensselaer Polytechnic Institute in New York, settled lawsuits with the RIAA for $12,000. The suit related to unauthorized "swapping" of songs over Kazaa and Morpheus that infringed the songs' copyrights. Two other students also settled their suits for amounts of $3,500 and $15,000. The settlement amounts were based on the amount of activity and downloading conducted by the three students.

The story of Mr. Jordan appeared on Slashdot.org's Web site, and donations began pouring in for him. He was able to raise the entire amount of the settlement from donations from Internet readers of the site. Mr. Jordan insists he did nothing wrong and simply created a search engine.

What are the copyright protections for the songs? Are the damages computed properly in this case? What do you make of the Internet users donating toward his settlement costs? Is it ethical to help the copyright infringer?

Sources: Jefferson Graham, "Fined student gets donations to tune of $12K," *USA Today,* June 25, 2003, p. 4D. Michelle Kessler, "Lawsuits may help Net song sellers," *USA Today,* June 30, 2003, p. 2B.

FOR THE MANAGER'S DESK

RE: EMPLOYEE INTERNET USE

Vault.com conducted a survey of workers and asked how they use the Internet at work for nonwork-related activity and found the following:

News reading	72%
Travel arrangements	45%
Shopping	40%
Job searching	37%
Special interests (hobbies)	37%
Stock-checking	34%
Planning social events	28%
Instant messaging	26%
Music downloads	13%
Games	11%
Chatting	9%
Pornography	4%

Employers have software that enables them to see which Web sites employees have visited, when they visited, and how long they stayed. Some employers issue reports that indicate which employees are spending large amounts of time. One employer warned an employee about too much online shopping during working hours and then blocked the sites so that the employee could no longer access them.

While employees are concerned about privacy, employers are concerned about productivity and the fact that downloading music, for example, can result in the employer's network jamming. Also, employers are concerned that some types of sites being visited, such as pornographic sites, may result in liability for the employer for an atmosphere of harassment.

The same Vault.com survey found that 90 percent of all employees surf the Net during work hours for things unrelated to their jobs, and 37 percent have used their computers at work to access the Internet to look for another job. About 13 percent say they spend two or more hours per working day surfing the Net for things unrelated to their jobs. Ten percent say that they receive twenty-one or more personal e-mails per day at work. However, 53 percent say that they limit their nonwork Internet access to 30 minutes per working day.

Some companies will police employee's Internet use for employers. Websense, Inc. serves this function for 12,000 companies, including 239 of the Fortune 500. The cost is approximately $15 per employee per year.

Source: FORTUNE, Alan Cohen, "Worker Watchers," *Fortune,* Summer 2001 (special issue *Fortune/CNET Technology Review*), p. 70. © 2001 Time Inc. All rights reserved.

Trespass in Cyberspace: Going Back to the Roots of Law and Commerce

Yet another tort that has developed as a means of stopping infringement and appropriation in cyberspace is the application of trespass to users. Unsolicited bulk e-mail or spam has burdened users and ISPs alike. Internet spiders are sent out to various Web sites to collect data that can then be used for spamming. Detection devices for blocking spam and spiders have not proven very effective because those employing spam and spiders simply find ways to get around the devices.

Lawyers, scholars, and lawmakers have creatively applied the traditional tort of trespass as a legal theory for stopping these invasions of cyberspace properties. While some have likened the use of the tort of trespass in cyberspace as the equivalent of driving a "horse and buggy on the information super highway," the application has worked in electronics prior to the advent of the Internet.[9] In *Thrifty-Tel, Inc. v. Bezenek,* 54 Cal. Rptr. 2d 468, 473 (Ct. App. 1996), a California court held that making 1,300 phone calls in an effort to gain access to phone card information was sufficient invasion of property to constitute a trespass. The court held that, given the history of trespass law and the findings that mere particles satisfied the invasion of property requirements, the infiltration of electronic systems via phone or computer was sufficient contact to satisfy the legal requirements for trespass. *Intel Corp. v. Hamidi* (Case 8.6) represents a landmark in cyber law, particularly in the application of trespass liability.

CASE 8.6

Intel Corp. v. *Hamidi*
71 P.3d 296 (Cal. 2003)

Hamidi's Code: Trespass or Protected Speech?

FACTS

Intel filed suit against Kourosh Hamidi because on six occasions during 1996, 1997, and 1998, Mr. Hamidi sent e-mail messages concerning Intel employment practices to over 30,000 Intel employees at their e-mail addresses on Intel's proprietary computer system. Intel had requested that Mr. Hamidi stop sending the messages, but he refused and employed surreptitious means to circumvent Intel's efforts to block entry of his messages into Intel's system.

Intel's e-mail system is part of its general proprietary computer system affording access to the Internet. The e-mail system is dedicated for use in conducting business, including communications between Intel employees and its customers and vendors. Employee e-mail addresses are not published for use outside company business. Mr. Hamidi was using an outdated employee e-mail address list not released for public use.

Reasonable personal use of the e-mail access to the Internet by employees is permitted but is subject to various restrictions, and communications are expressly not private. The company guidelines regarding e-mail, Internet, and computer use expressly provide that employees have no proprietary interest in any part of the system or its use.

Mr. Hamidi breached no computer security barriers in order to communicate with Intel employees. He offered to, and did, remove from his mailing list any recipient who so wished. Mr. Hamidi's communications to individual Intel employees caused neither physical damage nor functional disruption to the company's computers, nor did they at any time deprive Intel of the use of its computers. The contents of the messages, however, caused discussion among employees and managers.

The trial court granted Intel's motion for summary judgment and enjoined Mr. Hamidi from any further mailings. A divided Court of Appeal affirmed. Mr. Hamidi appealed.

JUDICIAL OPINION

WERDEGAR, Justice

After reviewing the decisions analyzing unauthorized electronic contact with computer systems as potential trespasses to chattels, we conclude that under California law the tort does not encompass, and should not be extended to encompass, an electronic communication that neither damages the recipient computer system nor impairs its functioning. Such an electronic communication does not constitute an actionable trespass to personal property, i.e., the computer system, because it does not interfere with the possessor's use or possession of, or any other legally protected interest in, the personal property itself. The consequential economic damage Intel claims to have suffered, i.e., loss of productivity caused by employees reading and reacting to Hamidi's messages and company efforts to block the messages, is not an injury to the company's interest in its computers—which worked as intended and were unharmed by the communications—any more than the personal distress caused by reading an unpleasant letter would be an injury to the recipient's mailbox, or the loss of privacy caused by an intrusive telephone call would be an injury to the recipient's telephone equipment.

Our conclusion does not rest on any special immunity for communications by electronic mail; we do not hold that messages transmitted through the Internet are exempt from the ordinary rules of tort liability. To the contrary, e-mail, like other forms of communication, may in some circumstances cause legally cognizable injury to the recipient or to third parties and may be actionable under various common law or statutory theories.

Nor does our holding affect the legal remedies of Internet service providers (ISP's) against senders of unsolicited commercial bulk e-mail (UCE), also known as "spam."

Dubbed by Prosser the "little brother of conversion," the tort of trespass to chattels allows recovery for interferences with possession of personal property "not sufficiently important to be classed as conversion, and so to compel the defendant to pay the full value of the thing with which he has interfered." (Prosser & Keeton, *Torts* (5th ed. 1984) § 14, pp. 85–86.)

Though not amounting to conversion, the defendant's interference must, to be actionable, have caused some injury to the chattel or to the plaintiff's rights in it. Under California law, trespass to chattels "lies where an intentional interference with the possession of personal property has proximately caused injury." (*Thrifty-Tel, Inc. v. Bezenek* (1996) 46 Cal.App.4th 1559, 1566, 54 Cal.Rptr.2d 468.)

Intel suggests that the requirement of actual harm does not apply here because it sought only injunctive relief, as protection from future injuries. But as Justice Kolkey, dissenting below, observed, "[t]he fact the relief sought is injunctive does not excuse a showing of injury, whether actual or threatened." Indeed, in order to obtain injunctive relief the plaintiff must ordinarily show that the defendant's wrongful acts threaten to cause irreparable injuries, ones that cannot be adequately compensated in damages.

The dispositive issue in this case, therefore, is whether the undisputed facts demonstrate Hamidi's actions caused or threatened to cause damage to Intel's computer system, or injury to its rights in that personal property, such as to entitle Intel to judgment as a matter of law. To review, the undisputed evidence revealed no actual or threatened damage to Intel's computer hardware or software and no interference with its ordinary and intended operation. Intel was not dispossessed of its computers, nor did Hamidi's messages prevent Intel from using its computers for any measurable length of time. Intel presented no evidence its system was slowed or otherwise impaired by the burden of delivering Hamidi's electronic messages. Nor was there any evidence transmission of the messages imposed any marginal cost on the operation of Intel's computers. In sum, no evidence suggested that in sending messages through Intel's Internet connections and internal computer system Hamidi used the system in any manner in which it was not intended to function or impaired the system in any way. Nor does the evidence show the request of any employee to be removed from FACE-Intel's mailing list was not honored. The evidence did show, however, that some employees who found the messages unwelcome asked management to stop them and that Intel technical staff spent time and effort attempting to block the messages. A statement on the FACE-Intel Web site, moreover, could be taken as an admission that the messages had caused "[e]xcited and nervous managers" to discuss the matter with Intel's human resources department.

In *Thrifty-Tel, Inc. v. Bezenek*, the California Court of Appeal held that evidence of automated searching of a telephone carrier's system for authorization codes supported a cause of action for trespass to chattels. The defendant's automated dialing program "overburdened the [plaintiff's] system, denying some subscribers access to phone lines" showing the requisite injury.

Following *Thrifty-Tel*, a series of federal district court decisions held that sending UCE through an ISP's equipment may constitute trespass to the ISP's computer system. The lead case, *CompuServe, Inc. v. Cyber Promotions, Inc.*, 962 F.Supp. 1015, 1021–1023 (*CompuServe*), was followed by *Hotmail Corp. v. Van$ Money Pie, Inc.* (N.D.Cal., Apr. 16, 1998, No. C 98–20064 JW) 1998 WL 388389, page *7, *America Online, Inc. v. IMS* (E.D.Va.1998) 24 F.Supp.2d 548, 550–551, and *America Online, Inc. v. LCGM, Inc.* (E.D.Va.1998) 46 F.Supp.2d 444, 451–452.

In each of these spamming cases, the plaintiff showed, or was prepared to show, some interference with the efficient functioning of its computer system. In *CompuServe*, the plaintiff ISP's mail equipment monitor stated that mass UCE mailings, especially from nonexistent addresses such as those used by the defendant, placed "a tremendous burden" on the ISP's equipment, using "disk space and drain[ing] the processing power," making those resources unavailable to serve subscribers.

Building on the spamming cases, in particular *CompuServe*, three even more recent district court decisions addressed whether unauthorized robotic data collection from a company's publicly accessible Web site is a trespass on the company's computer system. (*eBay, Inc. v. Bidder's Edge, Inc.*, 100 F.Supp.2d at pp. 1069–1072 (*eBay*); *Register.com, Inc. v. Verio, Inc.* (S.D.N.Y.2000) 126 F.Supp.2d 238, 248–251; *Ticketmaster Corp. v. Tickets.com, Inc.*, 2000 WL 1887522, at p. 4.) The two district courts

continued

that found such automated data collection to constitute a trespass relied, in part, on the deleterious impact this activity could have, especially if replicated by other searchers, on the functioning of a Web site's computer equipment.

Data search and collection robots, also known as "Web bots" or "spiders," are programs designed to rapidly search numerous Web pages or sites, collecting, retrieving, and indexing information from these pages. Their uses include creation of searchable databases, Web catalogs and comparison shopping services.

In the leading case, *eBay*, the defendant Bidder's Edge (BE), operating an auction aggregation site, accessed the eBay Web site about 100,000 times per day, accounting for between 1 and 2% of the information requests received by eBay and a slightly smaller percentage of the data transferred by eBay. The district court rejected eBay's claim that it was entitled to injunctive relief because of the defendant's unauthorized presence alone, or because of the incremental cost the defendant had imposed on operation of the eBay site, but found sufficient proof of threatened harm in the potential for others to imitate the defendant's activity.

These decisions do not persuade us to Intel's position here, for Intel has demonstrated neither any appreciable effect on the operation of its computer system from Hamidi's messages, nor any likelihood that Hamidi's actions will be replicated by others if found not to constitute a trespass.

That Intel does not claim the type of functional impact that spammers and robots have been alleged to cause is not surprising in light of the differences between Hamidi's activities and those of a commercial enterprise that uses sheer quantity of messages as its communications strategy. Though Hamidi sent thousands of copies of the same message on six occasions over 21 months, that number is minuscule compared to the amounts of mail sent by commercial operations.

Nor may Intel appropriately assert a property interest in its employees' time. "The Restatement test clearly speaks in the first instance to the impairment of the chattel. . . . But employees are not chattels (at least not in the legal sense of the term)." Whatever interest Intel may have in preventing its employees from receiving disruptive communications, it is not an interest in personal property, and trespass to chattels is therefore not an action that will lie to protect it. Nor, finally,

can the fact Intel staff spent time attempting to block Hamidi's messages be bootstrapped into an injury to Intel's possessory interest in its computers. To quote, again, from the dissenting opinion in the Court of Appeal: "[I]t is circular to premise the damage element of a tort solely upon the steps taken to prevent the damage. Injury can only be established by the completed tort's consequences, not by the cost of the steps taken to avoid the injury and prevent the tort; otherwise, we can create injury for every supposed tort."

Creating an absolute property right to exclude undesired communications from one's e-mail and Web servers might help force spammers to internalize the costs they impose on ISP's and their customers. But such a property rule might also create substantial new costs, to e-mail and e-commerce users and to society generally, in lost ease and openness of communication and in lost network benefits. In light of the unresolved controversy, we would be acting rashly to adopt a rule treating computer servers as real property for purposes of trespass law.

The Legislature . . . may see fit in the future also to regulate noncommercial e-mail, such as that sent by Hamidi, or other kinds of unwanted contact between computers on the Internet, such as that alleged in *eBay*. But we are not persuaded that these perceived problems call at present for judicial creation of a rigid property rule of computer server inviolability. We therefore decline to create an exception, covering Hamidi's unwanted electronic messages to Intel employees, to the general rule that a trespass to chattels is not actionable if it does not involve actual or threatened injury to the personal property or to the possessor's legally protected interest in the personal property. No such injury having been shown on the undisputed facts, Intel was not entitled to summary judgment in its favor.

CASE QUESTIONS

1. Describe the invasion of Intel's system.
2. What damages does Intel allege resulted?
3. What types of damages does the court say are required to prove trespass?
4. What fear does the court have of imposing "no trespassing" standards on servers and systems?

CONSIDER... 8.3

Companies have begun to compute the cost of spam, the junk mail of the Internet. The estimates of the cost per employee of dealing with spam vary from $49 per employee to $1,400 per employee, with the wide range resulting from what is included in the computation. The following costs are associated with handling spam, which sometimes reaches as high as 80 percent of a company's incoming mail.

- Purchase of additional computer capacity to handle the spam
- Employee time spent ferreting out and deleting spam
- Purchase of spam blockers
- Damage to computers and programs from spam and spam blockers

Estimates show that workers receive between ten and thirteen spam messages per day and that the time spent dealing with the messages ranges from 4 seconds to 84 seconds. The cost of sending a spam message is about $0.025 per message. As such, it continues to be a reliable marketing tool.

Spam blockers are not reliable because they can react to a "false positive," which means that they block out a good message. The problem with false positives is particularly acute on eBay, where those who win auction bids often can't get their message through to the auctioneer. Some companies, such as Amazon, have begun to file suits for trespass against the companies that use the spammers as advertisers for their products and services.

What are the rights of the parties who own computers? Can they stop spam? Why are these cost computations important?

Source: Saul Hansell, "Total Up the Bill for Spam," *New York Times,* July 28, 2003, pp. C1, C4.

 CONSIDER... 8.4

In April 2002, during the time when students are anxiously awaiting information about whether they have been accepted by a particular college, one Ivy League institution committed a cyberspace invasion against another. The associate dean and director of the Princeton admissions office used the names and Social Security numbers of students who had applied to Princeton to gain access to the Yale admissions Web site. While the motive was unclear, and the Princeton director of admissions was on administrative leave pending an investigation and unwilling to talk with reporters, the site was accessed on behalf of eighteen students.

The *Yale Daily News* uncovered the story and speculated that perhaps the Princeton director (and others from his staff because he was not acting alone) was trying to gain personal information about the students via the Yale Web site, the type of information that could provide an edge in recruiting.

Harvard does not use a Web site because its computer staff felt that e-mails sent directly to the students were less likely to experience the type of security breach involved in this situation.

What technology was Princeton using? Was it a trespass? Do you think the Princeton officials violated any laws? Was their conduct ethical?

Source: Karen W. Arenson, "Princeton Pries into Web Site for Yale Applicants," *New York Times,* July 26, 2002, pp. A1, A19.

BUSINESS STRATEGY

Automatic Electronic Shredding

While cyberspace has presented many legal difficulties for courts and businesses, the technology that created cyberspace has also developed solutions. Many companies are incorporating systems that automatically destroy e-mails

© PHOTODISC COLLECTION/GETTY IMAGES

after a selected period of time. The idea is to destroy the electronic trail of e-mail messages. Companies offering such technology have their own Web sites:

- http://www.authentica.com
- http://www.omniva.com

Defamation in Cyberspace

The only difference between **defamation** (see Chapter 10 for more details) in cyberspace and defamation in a newspaper is that the defamation in cyberspace may reach more people more quickly and perhaps increase the level of damages. The elements of defamation remain the same: that someone wrote or said something false that portrayed you in a bad light and that what was written or said was heard or read by others and understood. Chat rooms do not require any changes in the elements of defamation. Chat rooms only increase the likelihood that someone read and understood the defamatory remarks.

Perhaps one of the most costly cases of defamation occurred in an investor chat room. Mark S. Jakob was a day trader who had lost $100,000 in August 2000 through his poor predictions on how Emulex, Inc. stock options would perform. Desperate to recoup his losses, Mr. Jakob posted a fake press release on the Internet via a chat room that Emulex, Inc.'s earnings were overstated and that its CEO would resign. Various Web sites picked up the press release, and the impact was instantaneous. Emulex shareholders lost $2.5 billion in value before trading was stopped when company officials were able to convince the exchanges that the press release was phony. Mr. Jakob, however, was able to net $240,000 during the trading frenzy following his fake press release.[10] Mr. Jakob's statements about earnings and the resignation of the CEO constituted defamation. Damages for the defamation would be quite easy to establish because of the immediate and radical decline in the company's stock value, directly caused by frenetic trades quickly made following the posting of the press release. For more information on the issues surrounding securities trading and "pump and dump," refer to Chapter 22.

CONTRACT LAW IN CYBERSPACE

Formation Issues

Formation of contracts in cyberspace is the culmination of over two decades of effort by businesses to form contracts in an efficient manner. The technology available to businesses for communications has enabled them to move from complicated supply chain distribution systems that involved manufacturers, wholesalers, distributors, and eventually the customers in **business-to-**

BUSINESS PLANNING TIP

In an effort to prevent viruses from invading company systems and spam from overloading them, many employers are prohibiting employees from accessing their private e-mail accounts at work. For example, Merrill Lynch prohibits its employees from using AOL, Yahoo!, and other mail service providers from office computers. Some employers are eliminating Internet access from some employees' computers.

Other employers are taking less drastic steps, such as allowing Internet and e-mail access but prohibiting the downloading of files through these systems. These companies are employing security experts to monitor employees to stop the downloading. Some employers are asking employees to change their e-mail addresses every six months to cut back on spam.

Source: Jon Swartz, "More workers get shut out of e-mail," *USA Today*, September 29, 2003, p. IB.

ETHICAL ISSUES

Workers have developed a new type of corporate game using the new technologies such as computers, cell phones, and voicemail. Psychologists refer to the corporate game as "impression management." Some employees are using technology to give the impression that they are dedicated workers, that they are at work when they are not. Here are some of the components used for the "dedicated worker syndrome."

- E-mail timers can send e-mails late at night, something that suggests that you are burning the midnight oil and are a dedicated worker.
- By using a remote control to operate your office computer from outside the office, you can open documents and print them on the office printer. Workers seem to be in the office even when they are not.

- Instant messaging lets you respond immediately so it appears that you are always on alert and ready to work.
- Call forwarding allows you to get your office phone calls wherever you are.
- Reconfiguring your Blackberry can make it look as if you sent messages from your office computer, not your handheld device.
- Getting rid of the "idle" message on your computer eliminates a sign to coworkers and bosses that you are not there.

What ethical issues arise when using these devices to take three-hour lunches? To be late for work? To leave early?

Source: Jane Spencer, "Shirk Ethic: How to Fake a Hard Day at the Office," *Wall Street Journal,* May 15, 2003, pp. D1, D3.

Visit Georgetown's cyberspace law center:
http://www.cli.org

business (B2B) transactions where there is direct contact between manufacturers and customers. Under business's supply chain twenty years ago, Wal-Mart would have placed an order through a distributor when its supply of Pampers diapers was running low. Now Procter & Gamble and Wal-Mart have linked computers, and Procter & Gamble knows Wal-Mart's inventory and sales and knows exactly when to send Pampers and which stores need them.

This efficient means of orders and deliveries has evolved as technology has. Speed, direct communication, and simplicity have driven the reforms in contract formation. Twenty years ago, businesses negotiated contracts by sending drafts of agreements back and forth through the mail. With the advent of overnight delivery service, businesses were able to speed up their negotiation processes by sending contract proposals overnight. The fax machine—or telefax, as it was originally known—made for even faster negotiations and exchanges of drafts of contracts. However, the desire for less paper was still there. Paperless contracts actually have existed for some time in B2B transactions because of **electronic digital interchange (EDI)**. EDI has been such an integral part of business that companies using EDI actually have a set of contract formation guidelines that they follow. EDI was the forerunner of today's Internet contracting, and its concept was simple. EDI was the electronic exchange of business forms. Buyers sent purchase orders, and sellers sent receipts by computer.[11] Today, at least one high-tech company specializes in software that lets companies combine their EDI capability with the Internet in order to form contracts.

EDI still had transmission issues and problems with system capability and interchanges. E-mail and the ability to attach documents have provided greater clarity in document appearance and ease of transmission. In cyberspace, businesses have found both the speed and paperless nirvana they sought for contract formation.

However, the law was not quite ready for the new formation scenario businesses had created. How do we decide when a contract is formed? Do we still require signatures? What constitutes a signature in cyberspace? Businesses were ready to embrace a form of communication for negotiating contracts that the law had not anticipated and for which there were not yet definitive answers.

For Internet arbitration information, visit:

http://www.ombuds.org
or
http://www.squaretrade.com
or
http://www.CyberSettle.com

The same laws that apply when a contract is formed in a business office govern the formation of contracts in cyberspace. Was there an offer and acceptance? When did those two requirements come together? Some issues that arise in contract formation in the new economy are, for example, whether a contract is formed when someone downloads a program from the Internet. He may have paid for the program by credit card and simply downloaded it at his computer. Does the click of the mouse accepting the program mean that he has accepted all the terms of the contract? How does the seller of the program make sure that the buyer is aware of all the terms in the contract that governs the sale of the program? Can the click of the mouse constitute a signature for purposes of contracting? Is "point and click" enough to form a contract? Chapters 13 and 14 cover these issues in detail.

New Laws on Contract Formation

Several new laws govern the formation of contracts (see Chapters 13 and 14 for more information on formation of contracts in cyberspace). The **Electronic Signatures in Global and National Commerce Act** (E-sign) is a federal law that recognizes digital signatures as authentic for purposes of contract formation. While E-sign recognizes the validity of electronic signatures, states are responsible for passing laws regulating the authenticity and security of signatures. The important aspect of E-sign is that electronic signatures are in parity, or treated equally, with paper signatures.

View the ABA digital signature guidelines:

http://www.abanet.org/
scitech/ec/isc/dsg.html

States have begun to adopt two uniform laws that were drafted to provide the same uniformity in electronic contracts that the Uniform Commercial Code has provided for written contracts. The **Uniform Electronic Transactions Act** (UETA) and the **Uniform Computer Information Transaction Act** (UCITA) have been adopted in eighteen states and two states, respectively.[12]

Misrepresentation and Fraud in Cyberspace

Perhaps because there is no face-to-face contact, the Internet has proven to be fertile grounds for many types of frauds, schemes, and misrepresentations. The types of complaints consumers file about their contract experiences on the Web include everything from late delivery to lack of delivery to misstatements about the nature of goods being offered for sale.

Once again, misrepresentation, fraud, and nonperformance are not new legal issues. The forum for their occurrence is new and high tech, but the elements remain the same. Even federal regulation of retailers and their sales over the Internet are no different. For example, for the past ten years, the FTC has regulated catalog retailers with rules on performance and disclosure. Catalog retailers are not permitted to charge your credit card for merchandise you order until the merchandise is actually shipped. These retailers must also notify you if there will be a delay in shipping goods to you and also provide you with the opportunity to cancel the order in the event that the time required for shipment is unacceptable to you.

When retailers who had catalogs began doing business over the Internet, many of them did not follow the FTC rules on catalogs because they saw this as a different form of sale. However, the FTC saw the Internet as simply an electronic catalog to which the same rules on consumer rights applied. In 2000, the FTC issued a rule making the catalog rules applicable to Internet consumer sales. Using the rule as its enforcement tool, the FTC filed a complaint against seven Inter-

BUSINESS PLANNING TIP

To avoid an Internet scam:

1. Know your seller.

2. Check your seller's background.

3. Verify the seller's authenticity with your credit card company.

4. Check the brick-and-mortar address given on the Web site. If there is no address, be wary.

5. Check the business status of the seller. Use the Better Business Bureau, state attorney general fraud division, and even the secretary of state or other government agency responsible for receiving documents of organization for corporations, limited partnerships, and LLCs (see Chapter 21 for more information on these business organizations).

6. Trust, but verify.

net retailers for their failure to deliver Christmas merchandise on time. The retailers, including Macys.com, Toysrus.com, and CDNOW, entered into a consent decree (see Chapter 6 for more details on consent decrees) that required them to pay fines totaling $1.5 million.

Federal agency activity has stepped up because of fraudulent activity on the Web. The FBI reported that for the year 2000 its number one source of fraud complaints was the Internet. The FBI Internet Fraud Complaint Center receives an average of 6,255 complaints per month and referred about 4,000 of those cases in 2002 to federal and/or local authorities for prosecution. The FBI has even created an ethics Web site to provide information on the importance of honesty in business. One of the Internet fraud cases forwarded by the FBI for prosecution was the offer for sale of kidneys for transplantation, which was used to bilk thousands from those awaiting transplants before the scheme could be exposed as a fraud. The average loss per fraud complaint submitted to the FBI is $1,452.[13]

Another set of problems arises when search engine companies misrepresent the capabilities of their product or are not fully forthcoming about how they list subscribers' sites or how they provide links for those using the search engine. Companies relying on these search engine firms have the traditional remedies of misrepresentation and fraud available in all service contracts where the service provider has not performed as promised or has misrepresented the extent of or results from the service. (See Chapter 14 for more information on these traditional contract defenses.) Remedies for such misrepresentation and/or fraud include rescission of the agreement and/or compensation for monetary damages.

Take steps to prevent identity theft:
http://www.usdoj.gov/criminal/fraud/idtheft.html#What%20Can%201%20Do%20About%20Identity%20Theft

For information on what to do if someone has been using your Social Security number:
http://www.ssa.gov/pubs/10064.html

> ### BUSINESS PLANNING TIP
>
> Privacy and Internet theft of identity have become concerns for consumers who would like to purchase goods through the Internet but feel uncomfortable about the level of security. Leading retailers have been developing and perfecting "secure sites," or areas within their Web sites that are secure. These secure sites require some form of password to obtain the information they contain. In effect, retailers are locking up the information and giving access only to returning consumers. Several large accounting firms now offer certification programs under their names for secure business Web sites. Each firm provides its seal of approval for companies whose sites meet minimum standards for security of customers' identities, records, and financial information. These seals do not reflect approval for products or services; they certify only the adequacy of the format and protocol for the companies' secure sites.

One of the biggest areas of fraud that the Internet has facilitated is identity theft. A tremendous amount of personal and financial information is available over the Internet. Hackers can collect information on individuals and then piece together sufficient personal information on someone else to obtain credit; make purchases; and even secure government benefits, such as Social Security, using that individual's identity via his or her Social Security number, credit card numbers, and even bank accounts. In 1999, the Social Security Administration received 30,000 identity theft complaints. That number was nearly tripled from the 11,000 complaints received in 1998 and nearly quadrupled from the 7,868 complaints lodged in 1997. The FTC report indicated identity thefts of 210,000 for 2003.[14] Because the exponential growth parallels the Internet explosion, the Social Security administration attributes the increases to the ease with which information can be obtained.

BUSINESS STRATEGY APPLICATION

The exercise for this chapter on the book's Web site focuses on the FTC requirements for disclosure about Web site access and use of information and allows you to see the policies of several Web sites. You can then develop your own privacy policy for a Web site.

ETHICAL ISSUES

Concerned about their reputations as search engines, a small group of search engine companies has proposed a code of ethics for search engine firms. Mike Adams, founder and owner of WebSeed.com, has developed a code of ethics called the Search Engine Promotion Code of Ethics. Mr. Adams was concerned about companies that make technologically impossible claims about the number of Web sites and links their services provide. This code of ethics contains the following key provisions.

1. Search engine optimization services shall not impose undue bandwidth burdens on search engines.

2. Services shall abide by each search engine's page-submission guidelines and will not attempt to subvert them.

3. No service shall say it can submit pages to more search engines than actually exist.

4. No service shall engage in keyword repetition, page repetition, invisible HyperText Markup Language tags, or the use of robot pages.

Why would search engine companies want to have voluntary standards?

INTELLECTUAL PROPERTY ISSUES IN CYBERSPACE

The law on intellectual property rights has not changed. The Internet has simply facilitated the copying of everything from trademarks to songs to literary works. For universal access to the Internet, we necessarily opened the door universally to the downloading and copying of both patented and copyrighted software. Even some of the techniques and tools for accessing and using the Internet have been the subject of intellectual property right legal battles. For example, Jeff Bezos, the founder of Amazon.com, patented his one-click system for ordering and was met with great resistance because so many others wished to use such a system in their retail Internet sites.

The *Napster* case (see Chapter 1) was also a highly emotional battle over a technological revolution and its effect on copyrights. Rap star Dr. Dre argued that the unauthorized copying of his music via the Napster Web site deprived him of his royalties for his music and his means of making a living. Others called peer-to-peer file sharing no different from watching a video with a friend. Others saw new opportunities on the Internet because of Napster. Andy Grove, the CEO of Intel, noted, "The whole Internet could be re-architected by Napster-like technology."

Because of the innovation that surrounds the Internet, intellectual property rights require the same or perhaps greater protection so that the incentives for innovation because of resulting ownership are protected. The Internet has presented new challenges for interpretation and application of intellectual property law. For example, Mr. Bezos of Amazon.com has advanced the idea of changing the period for patent protection from twenty years to three to five years because he believes anything longer to be "a silly length of time for software patents."[15] These debates continue both in court and through new legislation written with the Internet in mind.

Copyright Infringement and Technology

The Internet and the nature of cyberspace have made the use, downloading, and copying of copyrighted materials in all forms very easy and very fast. Copyright holders continue to pursue clarifications about the application of federal copyright laws as well as the extent of any protection they have in cyberspace. Some of these issues are being addressed by litigation and others are requiring new legislation or amendments.

The Digital Millennium Copyright Act (DMCA), discussed earlier in this chapter, is an amendment to the federal copyright statute that was passed to address some of the new issues of copyright infringement that exist because of digital technology and cyberspace. (See Chapter 16 for more discussion of intellectual property rights in cyberspace.) The DMCA deals with the infringement liability of those who facilitate the infringement of copyrighted materials. As noted in *Verizon* (see Case 8.5), P2P usage of a server is not a violation of DMCA and does not result in liability, but storing data that is then used to infringe would be. For example, in *Sega Enterprises, Ltd.* v. *Maphia,* 857 F. Supp. 679 (N.D. Call. 1994), the court held that the creator of a bulletin board that permitted free downloading of computer games had committed a violation of federal copyright law because the DMCA applies to those who facilitate infringement as well as those who actually infringe.

Another issue developed when some Web site owners posted decryption code on their Web sites. These codes can be used to get around the encryption devices on CDs and DVDs so that music and films can be copied. At least one court has held that an injunction prohibiting the Web site owners from posting the code did burden their right to free speech more than was necessary to prevent unauthorized access to copyrighted materials [*Universal City Studios, Inc.* v. *Corley,* 273 F.3d 429 (2d Cir. 2001)].

Domain Names and Their Protection in Cyberspace

The name of a Web site carries certain appeal and marketability. While a "www._____" address may not fit the traditional definition of a trademark or trade name, it is intellectual property with some value. Because there is fierce competition for easy-to-remember as well as clever domain names, there have been many disputes over the use and registration of these names, called **domain registration**. Disputes over who owns a particular domain name are similar to the disagreements in the early days of the western United States over land ownership through squatter's rights. Numerous questions arise over domain ownership: If someone has registered a domain name for a site and then just sits on that name without using it, do they own the rights to the name? What if someone simply registers the name of a person or company and now that person or company wishes to use the domain name? Who owns it? There is now in place a means for owning a domain name and controlling its use as well as a way to resolve disputes over domain names.

View some of the disputes and pending litigation before ICANN:
http://www.icann.org/general/litigation.htm

In October 1999 the **Internet Corporation for Assigned Names and Numbers** (ICANN) approved the **Uniform Domain Name Dispute Resolution Policy** (UDRP). Prior to this policy, Network Solutions, Inc. had followed a policy of allowing trademark holders to halt the use of trademarked names for Web sites until the issue of ownership was resolved.

Explore the Web site with UDRP decisions:
http://www.icann.org/udrp/#proceedings

The UDRP provides for arbitration to resolve disputes over domain names. The current user of the disputed name is permitted to continue use of the name until the matter is resolved. The UDRP also does not require registration as a prerequisite for bringing a complaint against another for name use. The complaint can be based on a Web site's name being deceptively similar to the complainant's Web site name so that users are likely to be confused.

The first UDRP decision was issued in January 2000 and granted the rights to worldwidewrestlingfederation.com to the WWF. Since then, 5,000 UDRP disputes have been resolved by ICANN, with arbitration and mediation in most of the cases.

Trademarks and Cyberspace

While there are new ways to protect the new Internet intellectual property, many of the old laws and rights still apply. For example, the **Federal Trademark Dilution Act** permits a company whose name is harmed or diluted through its use by another to bring suit for injunctions and damages. Also, the FTC rules on trademark protection apply equally on the Internet and are self-enforcing. That is, the parties can bring actions against others for the deception caused by the use of similar domain names.

You can find more detail on intellectual property issues on the Internet in Chapter 16.

CRIMINAL LAW ISSUES IN CYBERSPACE

Just as fraud and misrepresentation have exploded on the Internet, so also has crime been committed using the Internet. The FBI calls the levels of cybercrime "epidemic."[16] Over 25 percent of the Fortune 500 corporations have fallen victim to computer crime.[17] Computer viruses cost companies $7.6 billion in lost productivity and repairs through August 1999.[18] In 1999, one man was able to perpetuate a fraud of $45 million by simply making credit card charges to various credit cards from around the world. He had obtained the credit card numbers and information simply by searching Web sites with consumer information.[19]

Most Internet or computer crime is just some form of a conventional crime carried out through the use of a computer. Whether you steal a wallet and use the credit cards in it to purchase goods and services for yourself or use the credit card number for Web transactions, the crime is still credit card fraud, obtaining goods by false pretenses, and other similar existing crimes as designated by each of the states.

However, some crimes have evolved because of the capabilities of the Internet. If a computer hacker can reroute users from the domain they were trying to access to a pornographic Web site, no existing crime exactly applies. While such activity may not rise to the level of a common law crime, it is perhaps a new crime often referred to as the wrongful use of a computer and its systems.[20] Special computer crime statutes have been developed to deal with the use of a computer in an unauthorized manner or to carry out fraud and take unfair advantage.[21] These statutes cover computer crimes committed when the computers are the tools of the crime (e.g., identity theft), are the targets of crime (e.g., hacking into a system), or are used incidentally to commit a crime (e.g., money laundering).

As noted earlier, specific statutes apply to monitoring e-mails. Two federal wiretapping statutes apply to monitoring of employee communications: the Wiretap Act (18 U.S.C. § 2510 *et seq.*) and the Stored Communications Act (§ 2701 *et seq.*). The Wiretap Act governs the monitoring of communications during their transmission and applies to surreptitious recording of or real-time listening to telephone conversations. The Stored Communications Act applies to monitoring e-mails and other forms of communication after they have already been transmitted, such as reading an e-mail message that has been printed out or forwarded. Employer e-mail monitoring policies, as noted earlier, must be in compliance with these statutes or the employers run the risk of violating federal law.

The Internet has been used to transport pornography across state lines and to children; to facilitate contacts with children by pedophiles; to harass employees via e-mail; to stalk victims; to make threats of harm or death; to commit fraud; to facilitate bets and other means of illegal gambling; to commit industrial and economic espionage; to extort money; to sell controlled substances without authorization; to pirate software; to vandalize, trespass, and steal; to shut down companies and services; and even to facilitate terrorism.

Browse Web sites on criminal law issues:

http://www.fbi.gov/
or http://www.cert.org
or http://cybercrimes.net

In all of these activities, there is either an underlying criminal statute to address the conduct (such as prohibitions on bribery, money laundering, and gambling) or there are computer-specific statutes passed to place criminal sanctions for such computer use. The criminal law statutes particularly applicable to computer crime are covered in Chapter 9 and include the Computer Fraud and Abuse Act [18 U.S.C. 1030 (1999)] and the Economic Espionage Act [18 U.S.C. 1831 *et seq.* (1999)].

Criminal Procedure and Rights in Cyberspace

The Fourth Amendment applies not only to searches of offices and homes but also to searches of computers. As noted earlier in the *Bailey* case (Case 8.4), the right to privacy does not change simply because technology permits invasion with ease. At least one court has ordered that the warrant be specific as to whether they are including home and/or office computers and files.[22] For more information on search warrants and the Fourth Amendment, refer to Chapter 9.

CONSTITUTIONAL RESTRAINTS AND PROTECTIONS IN CYBERSPACE

The constitutional issues that arise from cyberspace focus on many aspects of the Constitution. The following sections deal with some of those issues.

First Amendment Rights in Cyberspace

While some speech on the Internet is commercial, other forms of Internet speech are communications relating to voting and ballot initiatives. Speech on the Internet enjoys the same constitutional protections of the First Amendment as other forms of business, personal, and political speech. One of the first Internet speech–related cases to arise was the right of access by businesses to Internet service providers' networks. In *Cyber Promotions, Inc.* v. *American Online, Inc.,* 948 F.Supp. 436 (E.D. Pa. 1996), the court ruled that Internet servers are not required under the Constitution to give commercial advertisers unfettered access to their customers for purposes of distribution of e-mail to them. Another speech-related issue that has long been a subject of litigation is the right to publish and access pornographic materials. The Internet has also facilitated the transport of pornography in a forum to which children have easy access. The **Child Pornography Prevention Act** [18 U.S.C. 2252 *et seq.* (1999)] made it a crime to knowingly sell, possess, or distribute child pornography on the Web. However, the U.S. Supreme Court ruled that the statute was both void for vagueness and violative of First Amendment rights.[23]

The Commerce Clause in Cyberspace

The Commerce Clause has also come into play in the Internet because of the desire of both the states and the federal government to tax the transactions taking place via the Internet. The U.S. Constitution requires that there be some "nexus" between the taxing authority and the business paying the tax (see Chapter 5 for more information on constitutional issues in taxation), and many questions arise about the constitutionality of taxing Internet sales because of the lack of "bricks and mortar" in these businesses. Some Internet retailers are located in one state and have no physical contact with any other states. Their only contact is through the computers of their customers, who may be located in all fifty states. Is it constitutional for Colorado to tax a New Jersey company operating out of a small office in Trenton? While the nature of business has changed, the constitutional tests remain the same, and courts will simply apply the standards of fairness and allocation that they have in other eras as businesses grew in terms of reach even though their physical locations did not change.

Due Process in Cyberspace

Related to the "nexus" doctrine and taxation of Internet sales is the issue of whether an Internet business site with few physical facilities and no real presence in other states can be required to travel to the states where their customers are to litigate cases brought by those customers. The notion of long-arm jurisdiction (see Chapter 3) becomes even more critical because of the Internet. When does a company have a sufficient presence in a state to require it to defend a lawsuit in that state? The answer is the same as the answer for the presence of a brick-and-mortar business. Is requiring the Internet retailer to come to a state to defend a lawsuit fair, or does it offend notions of justice and fair play? Is reaching out to customers in a state through the Internet sufficient to require the Internet company to come to that state and defend a lawsuit brought by that customer, or should the customer be required to travel to the state where the Internet company is located? Refer to Chapters 3 and 5 for answers.

SECURITIES LAW ISSUES IN CYBERSPACE

The Internet has provided more information to more investors than at any other time in the capital markets' history. Day traders exist because of computers' ability to track stock prices and trade instantaneously. However, a universally accessible market and full information mean that some of the players may use tactics that are not entirely consistent with the existing legal framework or that discourage the level playing field necessary to preserve trust in the stock markets.

"**Pump and dump**" occurs when traders buy a certain stock and then post information on the Web to increase interest in it to drive up the price and hence their gain on that stock. It existed long before the Internet and day traders. However, as noted in the section on defamation earlier in the chapter, the rapid exchange of information makes the practice of pump and dump much easier. While the Internet is a new tool for pump and dump, it is still regulated the old-fashioned way with the Securities Exchange Act of 1934 and the regulations on securities fraud (see Chapter 22 for more details on fraud and insider trading). If the trader spreads false information in order to gain from sales of shares based on trading inspired by that information, the trader has committed fraud.

The SEC has also found that the very nature of new economy companies has created accounting and disclosure dilemmas and questions. When is revenue booked? What is the value of hits to a Web site, and how is that reflected? For example, America Online entered into a consent decree with the SEC for its accounting practices that had the company predicting sales on the basis of advertising expenses. The SEC found the model for predicting sales untested and misleading and the reporting of income based on the model, therefore, deceptive. The advertising methods, the company, and its technology were all new, but the

BIOGRAPHY

JONATHAN LEBED: THE 15-YEAR-OLD WHO ROARED ACROSS WALL STREET

Jonathan Lebed, a 15-year-old New Jersey middle-school student, shocked the investment world when the Securities and Exchange Commission came knocking at his parents' door with a charge of securities fraud. It seems that Jonathan had converted his $8,000 in savings and gifts from family members into nearly $900,000 in gains on stocks traded using a pump-and-dump strategy. Jonathan did so without ever missing a day of school.

Master Jonathan, using over twenty screen names on a computer his parents had given him as a gift, would buy shares of stock and then post positive information about the stock around the Internet in various chat rooms. When the price of his chosen stock would rise, he would then sell it and move on to another stock.

Mrs. Lebed said that Jonathan had always been fascinated with the market and would often sit by the television and watch the stock prices go across the screen on MSNBC and CNN. His mother also indicated he was not a bad stock picker, having given some of her friends and family members some good investment advice on stocks.

When the SEC stepped in to halt his trading and take his computer, Jonathan became the first minor ever prosecuted by the SEC for securities fraud. His father noted that his son did nothing more than what others in the market do and yet the SEC chose to come after "a kid." The Lebeds entered into a consent decree. They repaid all of the money Jonathan had made except for $273,000, a sum equal to about what is no doubt owed by his parents as taxes on the gains Jonathan made in his trading activity.

Mr. Lebed graduated from high school and has a Web site that touts stocks (http://www.lebed.biz).

Sources: Noelle Knox, "Teen settles stock-manipulation case for $285,000," *USA Today,* Sept. 21, 2000. Michael Schroeder and Ruth Simon, "Teenager in Stock-Fraud Case Kept $500,000 in Profits," *Wall Street Journal,* Oct 20, 2000, C1, C13. Gary Weiss, "The Kid Stays in the Picture," *Business Week,* April 2, 2003, p. 70. Gretchen Morgenson, "S.E.C. Says Teenager Had After-School Hobby: Online Stock Fraud," *New York Times,* September 21, 2000, pp. A1, C10.

same securities principles and laws applied: The financial projections must be based on adequate information.[24]

Insider trading issues (see Chapter 22) have been of particular concern in dot-com companies. The companies' sources of revenues and operations are very different, but the rule on insider trading remains the same: Insiders cannot trade on nonpublic information.

FOR THE MANAGER'S DESK

RE: THE PANIC THAT PRECEDED THE NASDAQ FREEFALL

In the month preceding the drop in the NASDAQ, many insiders at the so-called dot-com companies sold their stock and avoided the losses a 17 percent drop in NASDAQ had caused. Insider sales of stocks on the NASDAQ typically average $1 billion to $3 billion per month, but the average jumped to $12 billion per month from November 1999 to February 2000.

Some analysts are noting that the sell-offs by insiders may have prompted the drop in the market. Some examples of the trading include:

- Drugstore.com founder Jed Smith sold 150,000 of his 950,000 shares at a price of $23 per share. The price now is $9.88.

- MicroStrategy CEO Michael Saylor sold $80 million in his company's shares. The price of MicroStrategy shares dropped 62 percent within a few weeks of his sales.
- Beyond.com CEO Mark Breier (now ex-CEO) sold 80,000 shares of his company for $440,000 after he quit as CEO.
- Former Surgeon General C. Everett Koop sold $3 million in shares of his drkoop.com at about $9 per share in February. The spokespersons for drkoop.com indicated the insiders there were "diversifying their portfolios."

Source: Del Jones, "Net Execs Sold Stock before Big Drop," *USA Today.* Copyright April 6, 2000, p. B1. Reprinted with permission.

ETHICAL ISSUES

The following Web sites post information about the performance of companies.

- http://www.vault.com
- http://www.greedyassociates.com

Who is responsible for the postings? Those who post the information? Those who create the Web site? What if the information is incorrect? Would a disclaimer help? Can companies reference these Web sites in their own Web sites and caution users to be careful about going to these sites and relying on the information there?

CYBERSPACE AND INTERNATIONAL LAW

It is only natural that cyberspace would bring to a head international business questions and disputes. With the barriers of distance broken down by the Internet, people in Germany were easily doing business over eBay with those in Wisconsin. However, the courts are still left with the issues of which law applies and which courts have jurisdiction. In *Yahoo! Inc. v. La Ligue Contre le Racisme et L'Antisemitisme* (Case 8.7), a U.S. court grapples with issues of First Amendment protections, international jurisdiction, and the conflicts of law among and between countries.

CASE 8.7

Yahoo! Inc. v. La Ligue Contre le Racisme et L'Antisemitisme
145 F.Supp. 2d 1168 (N.D. Cal. 2001)
See also 2001 WL 1381157 (N.D. Cal. 2001)

Pardon My French: Rejecting an Order of a Foreign Court

FACTS

La Ligue Contre le Racisme et L'Antisemitisme (LICRA) and L'Union Des Etudiants Juifs De France (UEJF) are citizens (defendants) of France. Yahoo! is a corporation (plaintiff) organized under the laws of Delaware with its principal place of business in Santa Clara, California. Yahoo! is an Internet service provider that operates various Internet Web sites and services, which end users can access at the Uniform Resource Locater (URL) http://www.yahoo.com. According to Yahoo!'s complaint, Yahoo! services ending in the suffix ".com," without an associated country code as a prefix or extension (collectively, "Yahoo!'s U.S. Services"), use the English language and target users who are residents of, use servers based in, and operate under the laws of the United States. Yahoo! subsidiary corporations operate regional Yahoo! sites and services in twenty other countries, including, for example, Yahoo! France, Yahoo! India, and Yahoo! Spain.

Certain services provided by Yahoo! allow end users to post materials on Yahoo! servers, which then can be accessed by end users at Yahoo!'s Internet sites.

As relevant here, Yahoo! end users are able to post, and have in fact posted, highly offensive matter, including Nazi-related propaganda and memorabilia, the display and sale of which are illegal in France. While Yahoo! avers that its French subsidiary sites do not permit such postings, Yahoo!'s U.S.-based site ending in ".com" does not impose such a restriction because to do so might infringe upon the First Amendment to the United States Constitution. End users in France can access Yahoo!'s U.S. services via the Web site located at http://www.yahoo.com.

LICRA sent a "cease and desist" letter to Yahoo!'s headquarters in Santa Clara, California, stating that "unless you cease presenting Nazi objects for sale [on the U.S. auction site] within 8 days, we shall size [*sic*] the competent jurisdiction to force your company to abide by [French] law." The defendants then employed the United States Marshal's Office to serve process on Yahoo! in California and filed civil complaints against Yahoo! in the Tribunal de Grande Instance de Paris (the French Court) for alleged violation of a French criminal statute barring the public display in France of Nazi-related "uniforms, insignia or emblems" (the Nazi Symbols Act; see Le Nouveau Code Penal Art. R.645–2). On May 22, 2000, the French Court issued an order (the French Order) directing Yahoo! to "take all necessary measures" to "dissuade and render impossible" any access via "yahoo.com" by Internet users in France to the Yahoo! Internet auction service displaying Nazi artifacts. On November 20, 2000, the French Court "reaffirmed" its Order of May 22 for Yahoo to: (1) recognize French Internet Protocol (IP) addresses and block access to Nazi material by end users assigned such IP addresses; (2) require end users with "ambiguous" IP addresses to provide Yahoo! with a declaration of nationality when they arrive at Yahoo!'s home page or when they initiate any search using the word "Nazi"; and (3) comply with the Order within three months or face a penalty of 100,000 Francs (approximately U.S. $13,300) for each day of noncompliance. The Court denied the defendants' request to enforce its Order or impose any penalties directed at Yahoo! Inc. against Yahoo! France. Thereafter, the defendants again used the United States Marshal's Office to serve Yahoo! in Santa Clara with the French Order.

Yahoo challenged both the jurisdiction of the French Court and the applicability of French law to its activities.

JUDICIAL OPINION

FOGEL, Judge

This case presents novel legal issues arising from the global nature of the Internet. Yahoo! now seeks a declaration by this Court that the order of the French court is unenforceable in the United States because it contravenes the Constitution and laws of the United States. Defendants move for dismissal of this action on the ground that this Court lacks personal jurisdiction over them.

Personal jurisdiction over a nonresident of the forum state can be either "general" or "specific." If the nonresident defendant's contacts with the forum state are "substantial" or "continuous and systematic," the defendant is subject to "general jurisdiction" in the forum state even if the cause of action is unrelated to the defendant's activities within the state. See *Helicopteros Nacionales de Colombia, S.A.* v. *Hall,* 466 U.S. 408, 416 (1984). Where the defendant's activities within the forum are not so pervasive as to subject it to general jurisdiction, the defendant still may be subject to specific jurisdiction depending upon the nature and quality of its contacts in relation to the cause of action. The Court of Appeals for the Ninth Circuit applies a three-part test to determine whether a court may exercise specific jurisdiction: 1) the nonresident defendant must do

some act or consummate some transaction within the forum or perform some act by which the defendant purposefully avails itself of the privilege of conducting activities in the forum, thereby invoking the benefits and protection of its laws; 2) the claim must be one which arises out of or results from the defendant's forum-related activities; and 3) the exercise of jurisdiction must be reasonable.

The purposeful availment requirement is intended to give notice to a nonresident that it is subject to suit in the forum state, thereby protecting it from being haled into local courts solely as the result of "random, fortuitous or attenuated" contacts over which it had no control. Yahoo! asserts that Defendants' conduct meets this requirement under the "effects test" articulated by the United States Supreme Court in *Calder* v. *Jones,* 465 U.S. 783 (1984). "Under Calder personal jurisdiction can be based upon: '(1) intentional actions (2) expressly aimed at the forum state (3) causing harm, the brunt of which is suffered—and which the defendant knows is likely to be suffered—in the forum state.'"

This Court concludes that Yahoo! has made a sufficient prima facie showing of purposeful availment under the effects test. Yahoo! alleges that Defendants knowingly have engaged in actions intentionally targeted at its Santa Clara headquarters for the express purpose of causing the consequences of such actions to be felt in California, including 1) LICRA's "cease and desist" letter to Yahoo!'s Santa Clara headquarters; 2) Defendants' request of the French Court that Yahoo! be required to perform specific physical acts in Santa Clara (e.g., re-engineering of its Santa Clara–based servers); and 3) Defendants' utilization of United States Marshals to effect service of process on Yahoo! in California. Yahoo! further alleges that the conscious intent of these actions was to compel it to censor "constitutionally protected content on its U.S.-based Internet services."

This Court concludes, however, that the application of the effects test in the present case is fully consistent not only with the rationale of the test but also with traditional principles of personal jurisdiction and international law. While filing a lawsuit in a foreign jurisdiction may be entirely proper under the laws of that jurisdiction, such an act nonetheless may be "wrongful" from the standpoint of a court in the United States if its primary purpose or intended effect is to deprive a United States resident of its constitutional rights. Several of the cases discussing the purposeful availment have focused less on the characterization of the plaintiff's cause of action than on whether the defendant's

continued

forum-related acts evidenced intentional, or at the very least knowing, targeting of a forum resident(s).

In the present case, Yahoo! has alleged with particularity that Defendants "purposefully targeted" its Santa Clara headquarters and thus reasonably could have expected to be haled into a California forum in order to defend the Order they obtained from the French Court.

The second element of a specific jurisdiction analysis is a determination as to whether the plaintiff's claims arise out of the defendant's forum-related conduct. As to this element, the Court of Appeals for the Ninth Circuit employs a "but for" test. Accordingly, in the present case Yahoo! must demonstrate that it would have no need for a judicial declaration but for Defendants' forum-related activities. This requirement is easily met. But for Defendants' filing and prosecution of the French lawsuit, which in turn was obtained by Defendants' use of formal process in California, Yahoo! would have no need for a declaration that the French Order is unenforceable in the United States.

The final requirement for specific jurisdiction is that the exercise of jurisdiction be reasonable. For the exercise of jurisdiction to be reasonable it must comport with fair play and substantial justice [which] requires the consideration of several specific factors: (1) the extent of the defendant's purposeful interjection into the forum state; (2) the burden on the defendant in defending in the forum; (3) the extent of the conflict with the sovereignty of the defendant's state; (4) the forum state's interest in adjudicating the dispute; (5) the most efficient judicial resolution of the controversy; (6) the importance of the forum to the plaintiff's interest in convenient and effective relief; and (7) the existence of an alternative forum.

Here, Defendants' acts were aimed at Yahoo! in California. Defendants purposefully accessed Yahoo!'s U.S.-based web site, mailed a demand letter to Yahoo! in Santa Clara, used U.S. Marshals to serve Yahoo! in Santa Clara, and purposefully sought and obtained an order requiring Yahoo! to reconfigure its U.S.-based servers, specifically including servers located in California. The purposeful interjection factor thus weighs in favor of this Court's exercise of personal jurisdiction.

The Court recognizes that the burden on Defendants as non-profit organizations organized in France of litigating in California is not trivial. However, it does not appear that requiring Defendants to litigate this particular case in California is constitutionally unreasonable. Further, it is likely that this case will be resolved largely if not entirely by dispositive motions addressing issues of law which do not require extensive fact discovery in this forum. Defendants have made no factual showing as to the severity of their burden other than making a generalized reference to the financial expense of participating in litigation in a foreign country and noting correctly that the jurisdictional barrier is higher when the defendant is not a resident of the United States.

The instant action involves only the limited question of whether this Court should recognize and enforce a French Order which requires Yahoo! to censor its U.S.-based services to conform to French penal law. While this Court must and does accord great respect and deference to France's sovereign interest in enforcing the orders and judgments of its courts, this interest must be weighed against the United States' own sovereign interest in protecting the constitutional and statutory rights of its residents.

California has an interest in providing effective legal redress for its residents. This interest appears to be particularly strong in this case in light of Yahoo!'s claim that its fundamental right to free expression has been and will be affected by Defendants' forum-related activities. Many nations, including France, limit freedom of expression on the Internet based upon their respective legal, cultural or political standards. Yet because of the global nature of the Internet, virtually any public web site can be accessed by end-users anywhere in the world, and in theory any provider of Internet content could be subject to legal action in countries which find certain content offensive. Defendants' approach would force the provider to wait indefinitely for a determination of its legal rights, effectively causing many to accept potentially unconstitutional restrictions on their content rather than face prolonged legal uncertainty. California's interest in adjudicating this dispute thus weighs strongly in favor of the exercise of personal jurisdiction.

Yahoo! contends that only a United States court has jurisdiction to adjudicate the question of whether the French Order is enforceable in the United States. Defendants contend that Yahoo! could have challenged the Order's validity, scope and extraterritorial application in France. The Court concludes that even if it were to assume that Yahoo! could challenge the extraterritorial application of the French Order in either jurisdiction or in both, it would hold that this Court is the more efficient and effective forum in which to resolve the narrow legal issue in question: whether the French Order is enforceable in the United States in light of the Constitution and laws of the United States.

While the parties disagree as to whether the French Court offers an alternative forum for determining whether the French Order is enforceable in the United States, the point is moot in light of the superiority of a United States forum for addressing the limited legal question at issue here.

The Court concludes that Defendants have failed to make the "compelling case" necessary to rebut the presumption that jurisdiction is reasonable.

Accordingly, the motion to dismiss is denied.

CASE QUESTIONS

1. What is Yahoo! doing in France that is the subject of a French court order?
2. How have the French sought to enforce the order?
3. Can the U.S. court take jurisdiction over the French parties?
4. What interest does California have in resolving the parties' dispute?

SUMMARY

What is cyber law?

- More accurate to refer to the law in cyberspace
- Law as applied to issues that have arisen by doing business in cyberspace

What are the tort issues in cyber law?

- Privacy—e-mail
- Privacy and third-party information
- Privacy in the disclosure of buying information about consumers using the Internet for purchasing
- The Electronic Communications Privacy Act of 1986 (ECPA)—prohibits the interception of "live" communications such as using a listening device to intercept a telephone conversation and has been raised as a way to prevent e-mail "eavesdropping" if e-mail is considered "live" communications
- Appropriation—use of an image or likeness over the Internet
- Trespass—undue burdening of the servers and e-mail systems of others
- Defamation—the issues of identifying those who post information on Web sites and in chat rooms
- Trespass—the use of cyberspace facilities without permission of the owner of those facilities

What are the contract issues in cyber law?

- Business-to-business (B2B) transactions—trend wherein supplier and buyer have direct connections, for example, to let manufacturers know of customers' supply needs
- Electronic digital interchange (EDI)—precursor to the Internet and B2B transactions that permitted direct ordering and replenishment between manufacturers and their customers
- Point and click—process of using the Internet and a computer to form a contract; pointing to a box that indicates affirmation and clicking the mouse
- Electronic Signatures in Global and National Commerce Act (E-sign)—federal law that recognizes digital signatures as authentic for purposes of contract formation; puts electronic signatures on equal footing with paper contracts
- Uniform Electronic Transactions Act (UETA)—uniform law for states that provides the rules for formation of electronic contracts
- Uniform Computer Information Transaction Act (UCITA)—uniform law for states that provides requirements for disclosure in advance of formation
- Misrepresentation and fraud—false and misleading statements made in contract negotiation and

formation stages; both increased in Internet trans-actions because there is no face-to-face contact and more rapid dissemination of information

What are the intellectual property issues in cyber law?

- Digital Millennium Copyright Act (DMCA)—federal statute that amends existing copyright law in order to address some of the new issues of copyright infringement that exist because of digital technology and cyberspace, such as facilitating copyright infringement and whether linking to a copyrighted site can constitute an infringement

- Domain registration—public filing for ownership of the name for a Web site; names can be registered under an international umbrella and disputes are settled by arbitration

- Internet Corporation for Assigned Names and Numbers (ICANN)—organization that registers domain names for purposes of protection of that name as intellectual property

- Uniform Domain Name Dispute Resolution Policy (UDRP)—policy of ICANN that provides the means, timing, and rules for resolving disputes over domain names

- Federal Trademark Dilution Act—federal law that permits litigation to halt the use of a trademark that results in the loss of unique appeal for its owner

What are the criminal law issues in cyber law?

- Old statutes for crimes such as theft and credit card fraud—still apply to Internet crimes

- New statutes—some passed for types of activities that do not fit into traditional common-law crimes

- Burden of proof on all elements—still with the prosecutor regardless of whether the crime is under a new statute or an old common-law standard

- Fourth Amendment protections against search and seizure—still apply

What are the constitutional law issues in cyber law?

- First Amendment rights—no one can be forced to carry information over servers

- Child Pornography Prevention Act—federal law that prohibited the transmission of child pornography over the Internet; struck down as unconstitutional the infringement of right to free speech

- Commerce Clause—the issue of taxation and the requirement of a nexus or connection to a state for taxation to be imposed on Internet transactions

- Due process—issues on long-arm jurisdiction have already evolved; some courts permit jurisdiction over Web sites sponsors and others do not, depending on the level of contact within the state and the nature of the parties and claim

What are the securities law issues in cyber law?

- Pump and dump—practice of buying a stock, touting it to others so they'll buy it, and then selling the stock at an inflated price; not a new practice, but easier and faster over the Internet

- Laws on securities fraud and insider trading

- New securities fraud issues created by accounting policies of dot-coms

What are the international law issues in cyber law?

- Long-arm jurisdiction over foreign citizens

- Determination of which country's laws apply in case of a conflict between the laws of two nations when both are using the same Internet server with the same content

QUESTIONS AND PROBLEMS

1. In the midst of the litigation surrounding its program for downloading music, Napster, Inc. discovered that a company was using its logo for T-shirts and selling the T-shirts. Can Napster do anything to prevent the use of its logo? Is the use of the logo for T-shirts any different from the use of songs for purposes of downloading for individual listening? Do you see an inconsistency in the defense of downloading music and then taking offense at the copying of the Napster logo?

2. The *New York Times* discovered that twenty-four of its employees in its payroll-processing center were sending "inappropriate and offensive e-mail in violation of corporate policy." Do the employees have any right to privacy with regard to the jokes they send over their e-mail accounts at work? Does the *New York Times* have the right to review the e-mails of the employees to find out about the jokes?

3. California, Nevada, and Washington recently enacted antispam laws designed to protect Internet users from receiving unsolicited or unwanted junk e-mail. The growth of spam or junk e-mail has been so extensive that systems for companies and organizations are often incapacitated by its inflow.

California's legislation (Ca. Bus. and Prof. Code Sections 17538.4 and 17538.5 and Penal Code Section 502) prohibits commercial messages from being sent to those with whom the sender does not have an existing business relationship or from whom they have not received express consent. Some questions have already arisen because of the legislation: What constitutes a business relationship? Does a one-time transaction qualify for a business relationship?

In addition to controlling to whom the messages may be sent, advertisers must code their message on the subject line by beginning the text with "ADV." If there is adult material in the ad, the subject line must begin with "ADV:ADLT."

Do you think these statutes violate the First Amendment?

Under the California legislation, servers are permitted to adopt guidelines on the acceptance of ads and may adopt a policy of nonacceptance for unsolicited ads. These companies can then offer protections and screens to their customers, and customers can choose options on receipt of junk e-mail. Would this form of statute meet First Amendment standards?

4. Toys "Я" Us noted that Mohamad Ahmad Akkaoui created a Web site for the sale of his merchandise which consists of sexual devices and clothing. The name of his Web site is Adults "Я" Us Lingerienet. Toys "Я" Us worries that the use of " 'Я' Us" might confuse users and buyers at Mr. Akkaoui's site about its affiliation with Toys "Я" Us. What rights and protections exist here?

5. Michael Smyth worked at Pillsbury (defendant). Pillsbury's e-mail system was used for both intracompany and intercompany communication among and between employees and suppliers, customers, and others outside the company. Pillsbury repeatedly assured its employees, including Mr. Smyth, that all e-mail communications would remain confidential and privileged. Pillsbury also assured its employees that e-mail communications could not be intercepted and used against employees as grounds for termination or reprimand.

In October 1994, Mr. Smyth received e-mail communications from his supervisor over Pillsbury's e-mail system on his computer at home. Mr. Smyth responded and exchanged e-mails with his supervisor. Pillsbury employees did read the e-mail exchange. The e-mails concerned sales management and contained threats to "kill the backstabbing bastards" and referred to the planned holiday party as the "Jim Jones Koolaid affair."

As a result of what Mr. Smyth said, which Pillsbury executives called "inappropriate and unprofessional," he was terminated. Mr. Smyth sued for invasion of privacy. Pillsbury moved to have Mr. Smyth's complaint dismissed. What is the result? [Smyth v. Pillsbury Co., 914 F. Supp. 97 (E.D. Pa. 1996).]

6. The Melissa virus infected computers around the world and has the record for the fastest-moving virus to date. New Jersey law enforcement officials arrested 30-year-old David Smith for the creation of the now famous Melissa virus that has circulated and infected a number of computers. America Online helped the investigators determine the source of the original e-mail sent across the Internet that included the virus. The virus was part of a message that included an attachment. Mr. Smith's computer and disks were seized as part of the investigation.

Discuss the legal issues in America Online cooperating to reveal the identity and activities of one of its customers. Discuss the seizure of the computer and disks. Discuss what crimes Mr. Smith could be charged with.

What types of criminal charges could be brought against those who develop such viruses? Are there crimes beyond computer crimes that they may have committed?

7. The Cincinnati Enquirer ran a story called "Chiquita's Secrets Revealed," in which the reporter documented allegations about the company through the use of e-mail messages that had been obtained by tapping into the company's computer system. Chiquita alleges that Michael Gallagher, a reporter, illegally cracked the company's voicemail system. Mr. Gallagher was fired by the Enquirer.

Mr. Gallagher recorded over 2,000 voicemail messages, most of them from Chiquita's legal department. The messages also were delivered anonymously to the Securities and Exchange Commission (SEC). The SEC declined to reveal whether it was conducting an investigation of the company. The company's system logs more than 12,500 messages per week.

Mr. Gallagher submitted questions to the company and then listened to the voicemail of executives as they discussed their answers to his questions. The voicemail conversations were covered under the attorney-client privilege and would not have been discoverable in civil proceedings or usable in any type of criminal or regulatory proceedings.

The Enquirer printed an apology to Chiquita on the front page of its paper for three days and also agreed to pay $10 million.

Do you think Mr. Gallagher's conduct was legal? Ethical? What if Chiquita is found to have violated the law? Is his conduct then justified?

8. E-mail messages from a Microsoft executive, revealed as part of the antitrust case brought against it by the Justice Department, indicate that Microsoft engineers were working to program a software bug into an early version of Windows that would detect when a competitor's operating system was being used and then halt that use. One e-mail indicated that if such a program bug could be installed, it would "put competitors on a treadmill" and "crash at some point shortly later." One executive cautioned that the plan should be kept secret: "We need to make sure this doesn't distract the team for a couple of reasons. One, the pure distraction factor, and two, the less people know about exactly what gets done, the better." Are these e-mails private or can the government have access to them?

9. Two critics of the Mormon Church took portions of the Mormon Church's "church handbook" and placed them on their Web site, which is highly critical of Mormon doctrine and practices. Called *Church Handbook of Instructions,* the materials in the book are copyrighted and constitute the protocol, processes, and procedures for the lay clergy of the Mormon church.

On October 20, 1999, the Mormon Church filed suit in federal district court in Salt Lake City for copyright infringement and requested as a remedy that Jerald and Sandra Tanner be required to remove the excerpted portions of the handbook from their Web site.

Discuss why the suit was filed in federal district court when the Mormon Church is headquartered in Salt Lake City and the Tanners are Utah residents. (See also Chapter 3.)

If copies of the handbook are made regularly by members and shared with many, are there any problems with enforcing the copyright? (Also refer to Chapter 16.)

Should it make any difference that the materials were placed on the Internet rather than reprinted? How does the U.S. Supreme Court decision, *New York Times v. Tasini,* 533 U.S. 483 (2001) that allows authors to prevent their columns from being reprinted on newspapers' Web sites without their permission help in finding the answer in this case?

10. Douglas Colt was a second-year law student who developed a way to make money from the Internet. He set up a free Web site promising folks hot tips on stocks. However, Mr. Colt bought the stocks himself at low prices before trumpeting the stocks at his Web site. Once users of his site bought shares and thus pumped up the prices, he would then sell all of his shares, that is, dump them. Mr. Colt made over $345,000 using the old tool of pump and dump in the new technology, the Internet.

Mr. Colt had attracted 9,000 investors to his Web site (Fast-Trades.com). One of his shares, American Education Corporation, climbed 700 percent before he sold his holdings.

Those who participated in the pump-and-dump scam, including Mr. Colt's mother, a councilwoman from Colorado, agreed to a consent decree settlement. None will pay a fine and none will repay their profits. They have simply agreed not to violate federal securities laws in the future. Georgetown University, Mr. Colt's law school, said there would be no disciplinary action.

Did Mr. Colt violate insider trading laws or any federal securities laws? Was Mr. Colt's conduct ethical?

RESEARCH PROBLEM

Checking Out the Legal Liability of Your Favorite Web Sites and Chat Rooms

11. Go to any of your favorite Web sites or chat rooms and see if you find any of the following. List the examples you find.
  a. Defamation
  b. Unauthorized information about a company or its stock
  c. Private information about an individual
  d. Intellectual property issues of unauthorized use
  e. Criminal activity or suggestion of criminal activity
  f. Links to other sites and any issues of intellectual property or liability from those

---

NOTES

1. 47 U.S.C. § 151 Pub. L. No. 105–277, originally enacted on October 21, 1998.

2. Julie Cook, "Big Brother Goes to Work," *Office Systems,* August 1999, pp. 43–45.

3. *Smyth* v. *Pillsbury Co.,* 914 F. Supp. 97, 101 (E.D. Pa. 1996).

4. As of June 2004, those states are California, Florida, Illinois, Maryland, Massachusetts, Michigan, Montana, New Hampshire, Pennsylvania, and Washington.

5. See http://www.amanet.org. The data are from a 2003 survey of employers conducted by the American Management Association.

6. Lynne Bernabei, "Ethical and Legal Issues of Workplace Monitoring of Employee Communications," Georgetown University Law Center Continuing Legal Education, April 2003.

7. 18 U.S.C. §§ 2701–2709.

8. *A&M Records, Inc.* v. *Napster, Inc.,* 284 F.3d 1091 (9th Cir. 2002); *A&M Records, Inc.* v. *Napster, Inc.,* 239 F.3d 1004 (9th Cir. 2001).

9. R. Clifton Merrell, "Trespass to Chattels in the Age of the Internet," *Washington Quarterly Law Review,* Summer 2002, p. 675.

10. Alex Berenson, "Man Charged in Stock Fraud Based on Fake News," *New York Times,* September 1, 2000, pp. C1, C2.

11. L. J. Kutten, Bernard D. Reams, and Allen E. Strehler, *Electronic Contracting Law* (1991).

12. Virginia and Maryland have adopted UETA and UCITA. Both laws can be found online: see http://www.ncsl.org/ and http://www.arl.org/info/frn/copy/ucitapg.

13. See http://www.ifccfbi.gov/strategy/2002_IFCCReport. pdf. This is the 2002 annual report from the Internet Fraud Complaint Center, established by the FBI to process complaints related to Internet crimes.

14. See http://www.ftc.gov/os/2003/09/timelinereport.pdf.

15. Matt Richtel, "Chairman of Amazon Urges Reduction of Patent Terms," *New York Times,* March 11, 2000, p. B4.

16. See http://www.cybercrime.gov.

17. See http://www.usdoj.gov/criminal/cybercrime/ compcrime.html.

18. See http://www.crime-research.org.

19. See http://www.gocsi.com/press.

20. See http://www.zdnet.com.

21. *U.S.* v. *Peterson,* 98 F.3d 502 (9th Cir. 1996).

22. *U.S.* v. *Hunter,* 13 F. Supp. 2d 574 (D. Vt. 1998).

23. *U.S.* v. *Hilton,* 167 F.3d 61 (1st Cir. 1999), cert. denied, 120 S. Ct. 115 (1999); *U.S.* v. *Acheson,* 195 F.3d 645 (11th Cir. 1999); and *Free Speech Coalition* v. *Reno,* 1999 U.S. App. LEXIS 32704 (1999).

24. Floyd Norris, "AOL Pays a Fine to Settle a Charge That It Inflated Profits," *New York Times,* May 16, 2000, p. C6.

CHAPTER

9

Business Crime

Business and crime have jointly occupied the headlines of newspapers for much of the past decade. During 2004, the Securities and Exchange Commission (SEC) received over 1,000 complaints per day about stock frauds. In 2003, the SEC brought 430 enforcement actions in federal court against individuals and corporations for fraud, compared to 200 in 2000. In 2001, the FBI secured 2,702 convictions for financial fraud. The FBI estimates that economic espionage costs U.S. companies $250 billion per year.[1]

In its annual strategic plan for the year 2004, the FBI listed its ten priorities, and four of those ten focused on business-related crime: protect the United States against cyber-based attacks and high-technology crimes (third priority), combat public corruption at all levels (fourth), combat transnational and national criminal organizations and enterprises (sixth), and combat major white-collar crime (seventh). The increase in white-collar crime and the focus of law enforcement agencies on it demonstrate the need for every businessperson to have a solid background in the types and nature of business crimes. This chapter offers that background by answering the following questions: Why does business crime occur? Who is liable for crimes committed by businesses? What penalties are imposed for business crimes? What are the rights of corporate and individual defendants in the criminal justice system?

► update ◄

For up-to-date legal news and real-world business applications, click on **update** *at http://jennings.westbuslaw.com*

Did you ever expect a corporation to have a conscience,
when it has no soul to be damned and no body to be kicked?
LORD CHANCELLOR EDWARD THURLOW, 1731–1806

Your crimes show a pattern of skirting the law.
JUDGE KIMBA WOOD
On sentencing junk-bond king Michael Milken to prison

You don't put Michelangelo or da Vinci in jail. To lose that mind
for even a day would be a tragedy.
CHARLES KEATING
On the sentencing of Michael Milken

I haven't committed a crime. What I did was fail to comply with the law.
DAVID DINKINS, FORMER MAYOR OF NEW YORK CITY
On facing charges that he failed to pay taxes

I do not seek to justify my actions. I did not take these actions for personal
financial gain. It was a misguided effort to preserve the company."
SCOTT SULLIVAN, FORMER CFO OF WORLDCOM
*On entering his guilty plea to charges of securities fraud, conspiracy,
and making false and misleading statements*

To run him to earth and brand him, as long ago pirate and traitor were branded,
is the crying need of our time. . . . Every year that sees him pursue in insolent
triumph his nefarious career . . . hurries society toward moral bankruptcy.
EDWARD A. ROSS
On "criminaloids," his term for white-collar criminals in Sin and Society

I let down the company that I spent 30 years of my life helping to build.
I let down the shareholders, my family, and myself.
FRANK M. BERGONZI, FORMER CFO OF RITE AID
*During his guilty plea to conspiracy charges related to Rite Aid's
$1.6 billion accounting fraud, the largest in U.S. history*

CONSIDER...

John Park is the president of Acme Markets, a national retail food chain. Acme operated sixteen warehouses that were subject to inspection by the Food and Drug Administration (FDA). During 1970 and 1971, FDA inspectors found rodents in Acme's Philadelphia and Baltimore warehouses. The FDA's chief of compliance wrote to Mr. Park and asked that he direct his attention to cleaning up the warehouses. Mr. Park told a subordinate officer to take care of the problems. When the FDA inspected the warehouses again, rodent infestation was still evident. The FDA charged Acme and Mr. Park with criminal violations of the Federal Food, Drug, and Cosmetic Act. Mr. Park says he tried to clean up the warehouses but his subordinates failed and that he should not be liable. Is Mr. Park correct?

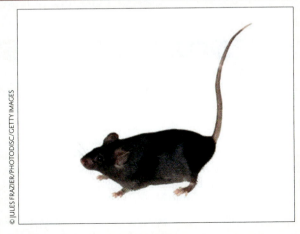

© JULES FRAZIER/PHOTODISC/GETTY IMAGES

WHAT IS BUSINESS CRIME?
THE CRIMES WITHIN A CORPORATION

Many business crimes are committed because the companies apply pressure to managers and employees to produce results. Economic pressure is responsible for much business crime. Upper- and middle-level managers feel the pressure to meet earnings goals or to reach incentive bonus plan figures, and they pass along the pressure they feel to employees. The drive to succeed or present a good earnings record can then lead many employees into crimes on behalf of the corporation. These crimes may not directly line employee pockets. The business benefits, and then employees benefit indirectly through profit sharing, salary increases, bonuses, or through just being able to keep their jobs.

For example, in January 2004, Andrew Fastow, the former CFO of the collapsed and bankrupt energy company Enron, entered a guilty plea to two counts of conspiracy to commit securities and wire fraud. His wife, Lea Fastow, pleaded guilty to filing a false joint tax return. Mr. and Mrs. Fastow were central executives at Enron who participated in the creation of off-the-book partnerships to which they transferred Enron's substantial debt. The result was that Enron's financial reports made the company seem very healthy because, under accounting rules that existed at that time, the debt in the entities, which included the Fastows as principals and officers, did not have to be reported on Enron's financial statements. The Fastows and other officers, including twenty-six executives who were indicted, have all explained that they were simply trying to meet projected earnings statements so that they could preserve shareholder value and share price on the market.

In addition to pressure to meet company goals, some individual employees feel personal financial pressure and resort to embezzlement as a means of remedying their own bleak financial positions. Estimates of losses from internal business thefts range from $4 billion to $44 billion a year.[2] Law enforcement officials claim that 90 percent of all crime occurs inside businesses. The FBI estimates that the amount lost in financial institution fraud is one hundred times the amount taken by bank robbers. The FBI also estimates that the losses attributable to business crimes are forty times greater than losses from crimes committed on the street.

These losses from business crimes do not include the indirect costs businesses now have because of the amount of crime—the costs of security (estimated at $30 billion) and of insurance against internal thefts. A 2001 survey found that 92 percent of employees interviewed admitted taking something from their employers, such as computer time or reimbursement for inflated travel expenses. A survey of busi-

MAKING ETHICS PERSONAL

Juggling Being a Parent With Felony Jail Time

Andrew and Lea Fastow are the parents of two small children. Part of their plea agreement permits Mrs. Fastow to serve her five months in prison (of a total ten-month sentence, with the remaining five months under house arrest) prior to Mr. Fastow reporting for his ten-

year sentence. Discuss the personal costs of white-collar crimes to families.

Source: Kurt Eichenwald, "Chief Financial Officer of Enron and Wife Plead Guilty," *New York Times*, January 15, 2004, pp. A1, C9.

nesses and government units found that the average amount each organization loses from check fraud such as forgeries and mail room thefts by employees is $624,000. Medical insurance fraud by employees is estimated at $3 million per company, and false expenses are put at $141,000 per company. These numbers are at least triple what they were in 1994.

From February to May 2004, the FBI opened over 90 cybercrime investigations involving 84,000 victims worldwide and losses exceeding $162 million. In that same period, the FBI made 97 arrests and obtained 64 separate indictments for cybercrime offenses uncovered in those investigations. A computer virus from a few years ago, ALove Bug, developed by a student from the Philippines, cost an estimated $3 billion worldwide for businesses to recover because millions of systems had been disrupted. Current estimates are that viruses cost businesses between $8 and $10 billion per year to prevent and then repair any resulting damage. This trend will increase as criminals discover new ways to exploit the Internet.

For up-to-date information on crimes, visit the Bureau of Justice statistics:

http://www.ojp.usdoj.gov/ bjs/dtdata.htm

and

http://www.ojp.usdoj.gov/ bjs/welcome.html

In 2001, various agencies in the federal government received 48,252 Internet fraud complaints. By 2003, that number was 75,063.[3] The Justice Department estimates that computer hackers steal $2 billion per year over the Internet and that Internet fraud losses for consumers totaled $54 million in 2002. The number of forensic accountants has increased from 200 in 1992 to 480 in the FBI today. Indeed, the forensic accounting field's professional organization now has 31,000 members, up from 5,000 in 1994, as everyone from internal auditors to special agents tries to ferret out fraud within corporations. Rated as the most secure job in America, forensic accountants are in demand.

Small businesses have higher employee theft costs because they cannot afford the sophisticated monitoring measures larger corporations adopt. Most employee theft is systematic: It goes on over a period of time and is well planned. For example, employees of an aircraft plant filled their pockets with nuts and bolts each day at the end of the shift. Over time, enough hardware was accumulated to fill kegs, which were then sold. Garment workers for apparel manufacturers have gone home with jeans in their purses. Nine out of every ten purchasing agents take kickbacks. All of these acts can be prosecuted under some criminal statute.

These crimes committed for and against a business are business crimes, often referred to as **white-collar crime**. Exhibit 9.1 provides a summary of companies and business executives that have had encounters with laws, regulators, and courts.

EXHIBIT   9.1   A Roster of Wrongdoing

COMPANY/PERSON	ISSUE	STATUS
Adelphia Communications (2002)	Company guaranteed loans to another entity controlled by the Rigas family (John Rigas and his sons held the top executive spots at Adelphia); result was $2.7 billion in guarantees and $1 billion in off-the-balance-sheet debt; overstatement of number of customers and cash	Annual report delayed; shares lost 70% of value from March 2002 to April 2002; in Chapter 11 bankruptcy; members of the Rigas family indicted and arrested on charges of "looting" the company of more than $1 billion in one of the largest corporate frauds ever; John Rigas and one son convicted.
Archer Daniels Midland (1996)	Price-fixing	Guilty plea; $100 million fine; $90 million to settle shareholder suits

continued

COMPANY/PERSON	ISSUE	STATUS
Arthur Andersen (2002)	Auditor for Sunbeam, Enron, Global Crossing, Dynegy, WorldCom, Qwest, and Waste Management	Found guilty of one felony count of obstruction of justice in Enron matter for destruction of documents; firm now defunct
Bausch & Lomb (1997)	Violation of federal securities law for overstatement of earnings	Fines paid by officers; shareholder suits
Boeing (2003)*	Charges of illicit use of competitor's proprietary documents; charges of recruiting government official	Loss of 7 government contracts worth $250 million; guilty plea by government official who was wooed; 9-month sentence
Ivan Boesky, arbitrager who worked with Michael Milken (1988)	Securities fraud	Guilty plea; 3-year prison sentence; $100 million in fines and restitution
Brown, Columbia, Cornell, Harvard, Penn, Princeton, and Yale universities and Dartmouth College (1992)	Monopolization in financial aid	Consent decrees agreeing to halt agreements on standard financial aid packages
Coca-Cola (2003)	Pending investigations over Coke's admissions that product marketing tests for Frozen Coke in Burger King were rigged	Coke settled issue with Burger King, with payments rumored to be $21 million; employee whistleblower suit pending
Columbia/HCA Health Care (1998)	Overbilling Medicare	$745 million fine; 53% profit drop; three executives indicted
Computer Associates (2004)	Securities fraud and obstruction following $2.2 billion restatement in sales	Top officers indicted for securities fraud
Drexel Burnham Lambert (1990)	Securities fraud	Plea bargain; $650 million for criminal charges; $1.6 billion settlement on investor suits; agreement to fire Michael Milken
Dynegy (2002)	Accounting issues surrounding Project Alpha that reduced taxes and inflated cash flow; adequacy of disclosures; off-the-books partnerships; issues on "round-trip" trading of energy, i.e., sham trading	CFO replaced; has halted online energy trading, citing poor credit; CEO quit when subpoenas from federal government regarding energy trading were announced; company paid $3 million fine to SEC
Jamie Olis, senior director of tax planning with Dynegy (2004)	Charged with fraud and conspiracy	Sentenced to 24 years without the possibility of parole
E. F. Hutton (1985)	Check kiting	Guilty plea; $2 million fine
Enron (2001)	Earnings overstated through mark-to-market accounting; off-the-book/special-purpose entities (SPEs) carried significant amounts of Enron debt not reflected in the financial statements; significant offshore SPEs (881 of 3,000 SPEs were offshore, primarily in Cayman Islands)	Company in bankruptcy (touted as the largest bankruptcy in U.S. history); shareholder litigation pending; Congressional hearings held; Justice Department and U.S. Attorney offices handling criminal investigations; numerous indictments

*By way of full disclosure, the author has performed consulting work on ethics for Boeing.

COMPANY/PERSON	ISSUE	STATUS
Andrew Fastow, former CFO of Enron (2004)	Multimillion-dollar earnings from serving as principle in SPEs of Enron created to keep debts off the company books; significant sales of shares during the time frame preceding company collapse	Resigned as CFO; multimillion-dollar home under construction in Houston; appeared before Congress and took the Fifth Amendment; entered guilty plea to securities and wire fraud; 10 years
Lea Fastow (2004)	Filing false income tax return	Guilty plea; 5 months prison; 5 months house arrest
Kenneth Lay, former chairman of Enron (2002)	Significant sales of shares during the time frame preceding Enron collapse; warning memo from one financial executive about possible implosion of company due to accounting improprieties	Resigned as CEO; appeared before Congress and took the Fifth Amendment; indicted for securities fraud, wire fraud
Jeffrey Skilling, former CEO of Enron (2004)	Resigned just prior to company's collapse	Testified before Congress; offered assurances that he did not understand what was happening at Enron and that he resigned when he became aware; indicted for securities and wire fraud
Exxon (1989)	Oil spill; felony pollution charges	$1.3 billion plus $100 million additional cleanup charges
Global Crossing (2004)	Deals made with CEO's son's companies; accounting questions surrounding booking of revenues (Arthur Andersen was auditor); also questions on booking of long-term leases	Filed for bankruptcy (fourth largest bankruptcy in U.S. history); investigation of related party transactions and sales of shares by officers; investigation into analysts' role by New York attorney general; shareholder suits settled for $325 million; former CEO Gary Winnick pledged $55 million to employees' retirement accounts
HealthSouth (2003)	$2.7 billion accounting fraud; overstatement of revenues	16 former executives indicted; 5 guilty pleas
Richard Scrushy, CEO of HealthSouth (2003)	85 federal felony counts, including violations of Sarbanes-Oxley financial certification provisions	Trial pending
Honda USA (1995)	Bribes; kickbacks	Guilty pleas and convictions of 16 officers
ImClone (2002)	Questions surrounding the timing of disclosure of FDA action relating to the company's anticancer drug, Erbitux, and its less-than-touted effectiveness	SEC notified the company that it will file a civil suit; shares dropped significantly after announcement of FDA action on December 28, 2001; shares dropped again on revelations of possible insider trading
Dr. Samuel Waksal, former CEO of ImClone (2002)	Sold $50 million in ImClone shares prior to releasing to public information that FDA had rejected marketing for Erbitux	Charged with insider trading; arrested by FBI at his SoHo residence; took the Fifth Amendment before Congress; investigations of others pending; guilty plea entered; 7 years and $3 million in fines

continued

COMPANY/PERSON	ISSUE	STATUS
Martha Stewart, CEO of Martha Stewart Living Omnimedia, Inc. and close friend of Dr. Waksal (2003)	Sold 5,000 shares of ImClone one day before public announcement of negative FDA action on Erbitux	Indicted and convicted, along with her broker at Merrill Lynch, of making false statements and conspiracy; 5-month sentence
Charles Keating, former CEO of Lincoln Savings and Loan (1991)	Securities fraud	Convicted; conviction reversed during his 10-year term; released from prison
Merck (2002)	Recorded $12.4 billion in revenue it never collected by counting co-pays received by pharmacies for drugs even though that money is not actually received by Merck; amount was 10% of Merck's overall revenue between 1999 and 2001	Stock price dropped 5% on revelation; SEC has not announced any investigation or requested changes in accounting treatment
Microsoft (1998)	Antitrust violations; monopolization	Case settled; Microsoft donated $80 million in software to schools
Frank Quattrone, investment banker for Credit Suisse First Boston (2004)	Document shredding	Found guilty of 3 counts of obstruction of justice for shredding of documents; sentenced to 18 months
Qwest (2004)	Conflicts of interest law violations	Indictments with some investigations pending
Joseph P. Nacchio, former CEO of Qwest (2003)	Allocation of IPO shares; friends and family conflicts	Settled with New York attorney general for $400,000
Rite Aid (2002)	Issues with earnings reports that resulted in the largest restatement of earnings in U.S. history: $1.6 billion	Chapter 11 restructuring; guilty pleas by executives; company settled with SEC
Martin Grass, former CEO of Rite Aid (2003)	Backdating documents; fraud; conspiracy	Guilty plea rejected by federal judge because 8 years' sentence was too lenient
Franklin Brown, former chief counsel of Rite Aid (2001–2004)	Falsifying documents	Trial
Frank Bergonzi, former CFO of Rite Aid (2001–2004)	Conspiracy	Guilty plea; sentenced to 28 months
U.S. Savings and Loans (1995)	Banking law violations; fraud	$45 million in fines; $2.9 billion in restitution; over 4,000 executives sent to prison
Sotheby's (2003)	Price-fixing	Chairman given 1 year and 1 day in prison and a $7.5 million fine; CEO placed under house arrest for 1 year
Sunbeam (1998–2001)	Revenues overstated; $62 million of $189 million were mythical; income had to be restated for a period of several years	Company in bankruptcy; shareholder suits pending; SEC actions pending for "fraudulent financial reporting"
Al Dunlap, former CEO of Sunbeam (1998–2001)	Fired by board in 1998	Settled shareholder suits by agreeing to pay $15 million; charged with fraud by SEC; Arthur Andersen, as auditor, settled shareholder suits for $110 million

COMPANY/PERSON	ISSUE	STATUS
Symbol (2004)	Inflated earnings of $200 million	Seven indictments of former officers; SEC fraud suit
Tyco International (2003)	Questions about accounting practices, particularly with regard to the booking of mergers and acquisitions; clandestine deals between CEO and board members for closing deals (one commission to board member was $20 million)	Stock dropped from almost $60 per share to around $20 on announcement of accounting issues; lost 27% value in one day following announcements about CEO; shareholder suits pending as well as other investigations; top lawyer for company fired for allegedly impeding probe on board payments
L. Dennis Kozlowski, former CEO of Tyco (2003)	Accused of improper use of company funds	Indicted in New York for failure to pay sales tax on transactions in fine art; hung jury on charges of looting Tyco
Tyson Foods (1993)	Making illegal gifts to government officials	Guilty plea; $6 million fine
ValuJet (1996–1997)	Unlawful transportation of tanks	$11.1 million fine
WorldCom (2003)	Accounting issues centered around swaps—selling to other telecommunications companies and hiding expenses, thereby overstating revenue	Workforce cut by 17,000 employees; revenues reversed for 2 years to reflect losses and not profits; ongoing and new SEC investigations; CEO Bernard Ebbers resigned with $366 million in loan forgiveness; share price dropped from over $60 per share in 1999 to less than $10 in 2002; WorldCom emerged from bankruptcy as MCI; four officers and managers entered guilty pleas; Ebbers indicted
Scott Sullivan, CFO of WorldCom (2004)	Securities fraud	Entered guilty plea to securities fraud and making false filings
Xerox (2003)	Improper booking of revenues ($6.4 billion)	Had settled charges with SEC in April 2003 for $10 million; inquiry expanded to KPMG

 C H E C K   T H E   W E B

Check the book's Web site updates for current status of the companies and individuals listed in Exhibit 9.1.

WHAT IS BUSINESS CRIME?
THE CRIMES AGAINST A CORPORATION

Interbusiness crime occurs among competitors and results in one business gaining a competitive advantage over others. The list of companies and misdeeds in Exhibit 9.1 provides examples of the wide variety of business crimes committed, from kickbacks to antitrust violations to securities fraud to obstruction.

ETHICAL ISSUES

For each of the companies and individuals listed in Exhibit 9.1, give a brief description of the competitive advantage they were trying to gain with their behaviors. What pressures would cause them to engage in these illegal behaviors?

Once again, it is competitive pressure that results in these types of crimes. Employees within one company engage in illegal behavior in order to achieve what they believe will be a competitive advantage. However, as the remainder of the chapter shows, any competitive advantage gained through criminal activity is only temporary.

BIOGRAPHY

MARTHA STEWART: SOMETIMES NOT SUCH A GOOD THING

Martha Helen Kostyra was born in 1941 in Jersey City, New Jersey, and worked her way through Barnard College with the money she earned from working as both a fashion model and a maid. She was married to Andy Stewart, a graduate of Yale Law School, in 1961, during her sophomore year. As Andy became a Manhattan lawyer, Martha completed her degree in Art History at Barnard. In 1965, she had her only child, a daughter, Alexis.

In 1968, she became a licensed securities broker and a member of the New York Stock Exchange. She had a successful five-year stint on Wall Street until she and Andy purchased a home in Westport, Connecticut, a home that would become known as Turkey Hill. Martha left Wall Street to become a full-time mother and homemaker in the quintessential suburban haven.

During this time, Martha became well known for her skills as a hostess, and friends began to ask her to handle their parties and receptions. Martha began a catering business, A Catered Affair, which continued to expand and grow. When she published her first book in the early 1980s, her now diverse business, known as Martha Stewart, Inc., included books, a retail store with prepared foods, a catering business, and endorsements for a line of products at Kmart.

In 1991, Martha ventured into both magazine publishing and television. *Martha Stewart Living* became a high successful monthly magazine, and she had one of the most successful syndicated television shows. Martha took her company public on the New York Stock Exchange in 1999, and it was one of the hottest IPOs of the decade. The value of her interest in her company doubled in just the opening minutes as the shares sold.

By 2001, she had four magazines, thirty-four books, a newspaper column, a radio show, a catalog sales company, and a weekly spot on *CBS This Morning*. A business icon, she was elected to the board of the New York Stock Exchange in June 2001. There seemed to be no end to Ms. Stewart's talent and success. Everything she touched brought returns. Some speculated that her name remaining with Kmart enabled it to survive bankruptcy.

However, it would be Ms. Stewart's investment in a friend's biotech company that would cause her empire to crash. Ms. Stewart's troubles began with her ownership of 5,000 ImClone shares.[a] ImClone Systems, Inc., a pharmaceutical company, was poised in December 2001 to market Erbitux, an anticancer drug; the company was just waiting for FDA approval. Oddly, Erbitux was developed at the Anderson Cancer Research Institute, located in Houston, Texas, and headed by Dr. John Mendelsohn, who served on the Enron board and its audit committee.[b] Enron and its chairman, Kenneth Lay, were significant donors to the center. Dr. Mendelsohn also served on ImClone's board.[c]

Ms. Stewart was a friend of Dr. Samuel D. Waksal's, the then-CEO of ImClone. She had invested in ImClone based on his recommendation.[d] However, there were ruminations during the fall of 2001 that the FDA approval might not be forthcoming. Some indications during this period hinted that both Dr. Waksal and Ms. Stewart were becoming anxious about their investments. Dr. Waksal owned 79,797 shares of ImClone stock, but, like so many other CEOs of this era, he had pledged the shares as collateral for loans and he was deeply in debt.

When Bristol-Myers-Squibb made a tender offer for ImClone shares in October 2001, at a price of $70 per share, Ms. Stewart had instructed her broker at Merrill Lynch, Peter Bacanovic, and his assistant, Douglas Faneuil, to accept the tender offer.[e] However, so many shareholders took the tender offer that Ms. Stewart was able to sell only about 1,000 of her ImClone shares. Her remaining interest was 3,928 shares, and the rumblings about ImClone and FDA approval only continued.

Employees at ImClone were aware by early December 2001 that FDA approval was not likely. In fact, an internal memo outlined the issues and suggested that FDA approval would not be granted.[f] Harlan Waksal, Sam's brother and also an officer of ImClone, sold $50,000,000 in ImClone shares shortly after the memo was written.[g]

The share price for ImClone was over $70 in early December 2001, but by December 26, 2001, the executive team at ImClone was "99% certain" that FDA approval would not be forthcoming. Their plan was to announce what would be the inevitable denial of approval on December 28, 2001, a Friday, after the markets had closed.[h] Dr. Waksal returned from a Caribbean vacation to sell his shares and also tipped family members to do the same. Using the same broker, Mr. Bacanovic, Dr. Waksal tried to sell his shares but was told that he would need approval from ImClone's general counsel to do so. Dr. Waksal then transferred his shares to his daughter and tried the sale through Bank of America but was given the same requirement. Dr. Waksal forged the approval of the ImClone general counsel and the shares were sold. (Later, Dr. Waksal entered a guilty plea to bank fraud and conspiracy and is now serving seven years in federal prison.[i]) Dr. Waksal's daughters were also attempting to sell their 40,000 shares of ImClone.[j]

Mr. Faneuil became concerned when Dr. Waksal was trying to transfer shares to his daughter in order to sell them and sought approval from a Merrill Lynch accountant, who indicated it was illegal.[k] At that point, Mr. Faneuil contacted Mr. Bacanovic, who was on vacation in Florida, and explained the rapid series of trading by the Waksal family. Mr. Bacanovic responded, "Oh my God, get Martha on the phone."[l] When Mr. Faneuil questioned whether telling Ms. Stewart was legal, Mr. Bacanovic responded, "Of course. You must. You've got to. That's the whole point."[m] Mr. Faneuil eventually reached Ms. Stewart, who was in the Houston airport on her way to a vacation in San Jose del Cabo, Mexico. The conversation was as follows.

> Ms. Stewart: Hi, This is Martha.
> Mr. Faneuil: Peter thought you'd like to act on the information that Sam is selling all his shares.
> Ms. Stewart: All of his shares?

> Mr. Faneuil: What he does have here, he's trying to sell.
> Ms. Stewart (later in the call): I want to sell.

Ms. Stewart's 3,928 shares of ImClone stock were sold at approximately $58 per share on December 27, 2001, for a total of $229,002. If Ms. Stewart had waited until the next day, December 28, 2001, when ImClone made the announcement about the FDA lack of approval, she could have sold the shares for a total of $189,495. The savings: $39,507.

When Dr. Waksal's illegal sales were uncovered and he entered his guilty plea (see Exhibit 9.1), the federal government turned its attention to others' sales of the stock, including Ms. Stewart's. Ms. Stewart was questioned by agents and attorneys and was ultimately charged, not with stock fraud, but with lying to federal investigators. When Mr. Bacanovic and Mr. Faneuil were confronted initially by an in-house investigation at Merrill Lynch with questions about Mr. Waksal's and Ms. Stewart's sales of ImClone stock, they offered their first explanation: "It was a tax-loss selling."[m] Mr. Faneuil told SEC investigators that Ms. Stewart had called for the price of the stock and then indicated to him to go ahead and sell it.

In early January 2002, one of Ms. Stewart's employees called Mr. Faneuil to complain that the sale of the ImClone stock, "completely screws up our tax-loss selling plan."[o]

At that point, Mr. Bacanovic and Mr. Faneuil changed their story on the tax-planning sale to following orders on a $60 stop-loss agreement that Ms. Stewart already had in place. By late January, Mr. Bacanovic was giving Mr. Faneuil instructions: "Listen, I've spoken to Martha. I've met with her. And everyone's telling the same story. Everyone's telling the same story. This was a $60 stop-loss order. That was the reason for her sale. We're all on the same page, and it's the truth. It's the true story. Everyone's telling the same story."[p]

However, paperwork was not on the same page. If a stop-loss order existed, it was one from October 2001 and related to Omnimedia's holdings of stock, not Ms. Stewart's personal holdings. The worksheet that Mr. Bacanovic produced also told a different story. The sheet detailed Ms. Stewart's stock holdings and had an "@ 60" written in next to ImClone, in what prosecution evidence showed as "scientifically distinguishable ink" from all the other notes on the worksheet.[q] The jury found the different ink to be proof of the obstruction charges and conspiracy to obstruct the government's investigation.[r] As a result, the second story, on the stop-loss order, did not fly.

continued

They were all faced with not just one false story, but two false stories among them. As even Ms. Stewart's lawyer noted, with the hope that the brokers would be blamed and not his client, "[Their] cover story has as many holes in it as a Swiss cheese."[s]

On March 5, 2004, a Manhattan jury found Ms. Stewart guilty of four felony counts, including conspiracy, obstruction of an investigation, and two counts of making false statements to federal investigators. Meg Crane, a graphic designer, one of the jurors in the case, summed up the feelings of her fellow panelists after the verdicts were announced: "We all felt terrible about it at the end. It felt like such a foolish mistake that was increased as it went along."[t] Another juror and the foreman, Rosemary McMahon, a schoolteacher, cried and lost sleep before the jury rendered its verdict and noted, "We thought of everything to try to find them not guilty of these charges. We just couldn't."[u]

Ms. Stewart was a billionaire at the time she sold the ImClone shares. The amount she saved seems insignificant, immaterial, and irrelevant in the grand scheme of her investment portfolio, including substantial holdings of her stock in her own company, Martha Stewart Omnimedia, Inc., which, on December 27, 2001, was selling for $70 per share. On December 19, 2003, just weeks before the start of her trial, Omnimedia was at $9.11. Trading in Omnimedia had to be halted when the Stewart verdict was announced, and the stock value fell to $7.10 per share in the week following. The share price as of March 12, 2004, was $10.13. For every $1 drop in the price of Omnimedia shares, Ms. Stewart has lost $30 million.[v]

Following revelations about the investigation into the sale of the ImClone stock, Ms. Stewart resigned from her position on the board of the New York Stock Exchange as well as from her position as chairman of the board of Omnimedia. Following her conviction, she resigned from her position on the board of Revlon, a position she had held for eight years. The New York Times Syndication services dropped her "askMartha" column, a loss of two hundred papers. Westwood One, the radio syndicator for the "askMartha" audio segments, lost affiliates immediately upon her conviction. Viacom pulled "Martha Stewart Living" from its CBS and UPN stations, and the show will have to be individually sold to independent stations.[w] Ad revenues for her publications, the single largest source of revenue for Omnimedia, began a steady decline when the investigation of the sale of ImClone shares became public.[x] From 2002 to 2003, ad revenues dropped 25.6%.[y] Ms. Stewart was forced to resign as CEO of the company she built from her home in Connecticut. Ms. Stewart served five months in a federal prison in West Virginia.

[a]Alessandra Stanley and Constance L. Hays, "Martha Stewart's To-Do List May Include Image Polishing," New York Times, June 23, 2003, pp. A1, A24.

[b]Andrew Pollack and David Cay Johnston, "Former Chief of ImClone Systems Is Charged with Insider Trading," New York Times, June 13, 2002, pp. C1, C6; Jerry Markon, "Active Inquiry Is Underway on Ms. Stewart," Wall Street Journal, June 14, 2002, pp. C1, C10.

[c]Jo Thomas and Reed Abelson, "How a Top Medical Researcher Became Entangled with Enron," New York Times, January 28, 2002, pp. C1, C2.

[d]Andrew Pollack and David Cay Johnston, "Former Chief of ImClone Systems Is Charged with Insider Trading, New York Times, June 13, 2002, pp. C1, C6; Constance L. Hays, "Prosecutor Says Martha Stewart Spun Web of Lies About Shares," New York Times, January 28, 2004, pp. C1, C11; Leslie Eaton, "The Ghost of Waksal Past Hovers Over the Stewart Trial," New York Times, February 17, 2004, pp. C1, C6.

[e]Constance L. Hays and Patrick McGeehan, "A Closer Look at Martha Stewart's Trade," New York Times, July 15, 2002, pp. C1, C9.

[f]Ibid.

[g]Ibid; Andrew Pollack, "ImClone's Cancer Drug Is Back, and U.S. Approval Is Expected," New York Times, February 11, 2004, pp. C1, C2.

[h]Atlas, Riva D, "ImClone Sues Former Chief to Recover $7 Million," New York Times, August 15, 2002, p. C3.

[i]Andrew Pollack and David Cay Johnston, "Former Chief of ImClone Systems Is Charged with Insider Trading," New York Times, June 13, 2002, pp. C1, C6; Andrew Pollack, "ImClone's Cancer Drug Is Back, and U.S. Approval Is Expected," New York Times, February 11, 2004, pp. C1, C2.

[j]Constance L. Hays, "Setback for Prosecutors in Martha Stewart Trial," New York Times, January 30, 2004, pp. C1, C4.

[k]Greg Farrell, "Faneuil describes ImClone stock sales," USA Today, February 4, 2004, p. 1B.

[l]Matthew Rose and Kara Scannell, "Stewart Trial Hears Key Witness," Wall Street Journal, February 4, 2004, pp. C1, C2.

[m]Ibid.

[n]Greg Farrell, "Faneuil: Broker changed stories," USA Today, February 5, 2004, p. 1B.

[o]Ibid.

[p]Ibid.

[q]Kara Scannell and Matthew Rose, "Worksheet's Importance Grows in Stewart Case," Wall Street Journal, February 17, 2004, pp. C1, C2.

[r]Kara Scannell and Matthew Rose, "In Stewart Case, Reluctant Jurors Found Guilt After Foolish Mistake," Wall Street Journal, March 8, 2004, pp. A1, A6.

[s]Constance L. Hays and Jonathan D. Glater, "More Tactics Than Theatrics at the Stewart Trial," New York Times, February 10, 2004, pp. A1, C9.

[t]Kara Scannell and Matthew Rose, "In Stewart Case, Reluctant Jurors Found Guilt After Foolish Mistake," Wall Street Journal, March 8, 2004, pp. A1, A6.

[u]Ibid.

[v]Karla Scannell and Matthew Rose, "Stewart Trial Gets Under Way," New York Times, January 28, 2004, pp. C1, C5.

[w]Theresa Howard, "Business partners shy from Stewart," USA Today, March 9, 2004, p. 1B.

[x]Gregory Zuckerman, "Martha: The Doyenne of Dilemmas," Wall Street Journal, March 8, 2004, pp. C1, C2.

[y]Suzanne Vranica, Matthew Rose, and Janet Adamy, "Living—Without Martha," Wall Street Journal, March 8, 2004, pp. B1, B11.

WHO IS LIABLE FOR BUSINESS CRIME?

One of the major differences between nonbusiness and business crimes is that more people can be convicted for business crimes. For nonbusiness crimes, only those actually involved in the planning or execution of the crime or assistance after it is committed can be convicted. In other words, those who were somehow involved in the criminal act or aftermath are criminally responsible. For business crimes, on the other hand, those in the management of firms whose employees actually commit criminal acts can be held liable if they authorized the conduct, knew about the conduct but did nothing, or failed to act reasonably in their supervisory positions. Liability for crimes also extends to employees who participate with the company and its management in illegal acts. For example, employees who help their employers establish fraudulent tax shelters for customers can be held liable along with the company and its officers. The key to liability is personal knowledge of wrongdoing.

U.S. v. *Park* (Case 9.1), a landmark case, discusses the liability standards for those who are in charge but may not themselves commit a criminal act. It also provides an answer to the chapter's opening Consider.

Browse the Law & Leading Attorneys (L&LA) Web site on white collar crime:
http://www.lawlead.com

CASE 9.1

United States v. *Park*
421 U.S. 658 (1975)

Is Chasing Rats from the Warehouse in My Job Description?

FACTS

Acme Markets, Inc., was a national food retail chain headquartered in Philadelphia, Pennsylvania. At the time of the government action, John R. Park (respondent) was president of Acme, which employed 36,000 people and operated sixteen warehouses.

In 1970, the Food and Drug Administration (FDA) forwarded a letter to Mr. Park describing, in detail, problems with rodent infestation in Acme's Philadelphia warehouse facility. In December 1971, the FDA found the same types of conditions in Acme's Baltimore warehouse facility. In January 1972, the FDA's chief of compliance for its Baltimore office wrote to Mr. Park about the inspection. The letter included the following language:

We note with much concern that the old and new warehouse areas used for food storage were actively and extensively inhabited by live rodents. Of even more concern was the observation that such reprehensible conditions obviously existed for a prolonged period of time without any detection, or were completely ignored.

We trust this letter will serve to direct your attention to the seriousness of the problem and formally advise you of the urgent need to initiate whatever measures are necessary to prevent recurrence and ensure compliance with the law.

After Mr. Park received the letter, he met with the vice president for legal affairs for Acme and was assured that he was "investigating the situation immediately and would be taking corrective action."

When the FDA inspected the Baltimore warehouse in March 1972, there was some improvement in the facility, but there was still rodent infestation. Acme and Mr. Park were both charged with violations of the Federal Food, Drug, and Cosmetic Act. Acme pleaded guilty. Mr. Park was convicted and fined $500; he appealed based on error in the judge's instruction, given as follows:

The individual is or could be liable under the statute even if he did not consciously do wrong. However, the fact that the Defendant is president and chief executive officer of the Acme Markets does not require a finding of guilt. Though he need not have personally participated in the situation, he must have had a responsible relationship to the issue. The issue is, in this case, whether the Defendant, John R. Park, by virtue of his position in the company, had a position of authority and responsibility in the situation out of which these charges arose.

The court of appeals reversed Mr. Park's conviction, and the government appealed.

continued

JUDICIAL OPINION

BURGER, Chief Justice

Central to the Court's conclusion [in *United States* v. *Dotterweich*], 320 U.S. 277 (1943), that individuals other than proprietors are subject to the criminal provisions of the Act was the reality that "the only way in which a corporation can act is through the individuals who act on its behalf."

At the same time, however, the Court was aware of the concern . . . that literal enforcement "might operate too harshly by sweeping within its condemnation any person however remotely entangled in the proscribed shipment." A limiting principle, in the form of "settled doctrines of criminal law" defining those who "are responsible for the commission of a misdemeanor," was available. In this context, the Court concluded, those doctrines dictated that the offense was committed "by all who have . . . a responsible share in the furtherance of the transaction which the statute outlaws."

The Act does not, as we observed in *Dotterweich*, make criminal liability turn on "awareness of some wrongdoing" or "conscious fraud." The duty imposed by Congress on responsible corporate agents is, we emphasize, one that requires the highest standard of foresight and vigilance, but the Act, in its criminal aspect, does not require that which is objectively impossible. The theory upon which responsible corporate agents are held criminally accountable for "causing" violations of the Act permits a claim that a defendant was "powerless" to prevent or correct the violation to "be raised defensively at a trial on the merits." *U.S.* v. *Wiesenfeld Warehouse Co.*, 376 U.S. 86 (1964). If such a claim is made, the defendant has the burden of coming forward with evidence, but this does not alter the Government's ultimate burden of proving beyond a reasonable doubt the defendant's guilt, including his power, in light of the duty imposed by the Act, to prevent or correct the prohibited condition.

Turning to the jury charge in this case, it is of course arguable that isolated parts can be read as intimating that a finding of guilt could be predicated solely on respondent's corporate position. . . . Viewed as a whole, the charge did not permit the jury to find guilt solely on the basis of respondent's position in the corporation; rather, it fairly advised the jury that to find guilt it must find respondent "had a responsible relation to the situation," and "by virtue of his position . . . had authority and responsibility" to deal with the situation. The situation referred to could only be "food . . . held in unsanitary conditions in a warehouse with the result that it consisted, in part, of filth or . . . may have been contaminated with filth."

Park testified in his defense that he had employed a system in which he relied upon his subordinates, and that he was ultimately responsible for this system. He testified further that he had found these subordinates to be "dependable" and had "great confidence" in them.

[The rebuttal] evidence was not offered to show that respondent had a propensity to commit criminal acts, that the crime charged had been committed; its purpose was to demonstrate that respondent was on notice that he could not rely on his system of delegation to subordinates to prevent or correct unsanitary conditions at Acme's warehouses, and that he must have been aware of the deficiencies of this system before the Baltimore violations were discovered. The evidence was therefore relevant since it served to rebut Park's defense that he had justifiably relied upon subordinates to handle sanitation matters.

Reversed.

CASE QUESTIONS

1. What problems did the FDA find in the Acme warehouses?

2. Over what period of time did the FDA find the problems?

3. Was Mr. Park warned about the problem?

4. What action did Mr. Park take?

5. What standard of liability did the instruction given by the judge impose?

6. Was the instruction correct?

7. Is Mr. Park guilty of a criminal violation?

 CHECK THE WEB

Be sure to visit the book's Web site updates for more statistics on convictions, types of charges, and guilty pleas in white-collar crime.

FOR THE MANAGER'S DESK

RE: THE SAVINGS AND LOANS STATISTICS

From 1988 to June 30, 1995, the federal government, through the Office of the Special Counsel of the Justice Department, conducted investigations into failed savings and loans "to find and prosecute those who looted our financial institutions." When the Office of Special Counsel concluded its work, the following statistics were released:

Number of defendants charged: 6,405

Types of crimes: 4,297 bank crimes; 1,852 savings and loans crimes; 256 credit union crimes

Convictions: 5,506 defendants convicted (96.5% conviction rate)

Types of persons convicted: Officers, directors, or CEOs: 29%; accountants, attorneys, and consultants: 71%

Types of persons charged: Directors and officers: 1,268 (97.5%) convicted; presidents or CEOs: 484 (95.1%) convicted

Prison time: Of the 5,506 defendants convicted: 75.5% sentenced to prison

Fines imposed: $45,000,000

Restitution ordered: $2.9 billion

James G. Richmond, who served as special counsel, noted that the 71 percent conviction rate of outsiders proves his point: "If you get an officer who goes bad, he isn't just going to do it with one guy. The most logical accomplice is the lawyer, accountant, or appraiser."

FOR THE MANAGER'S DESK

RE: WHO REALLY ENDS UP GOING TO JAIL FOR CORPORATE CRIME?

For the most part, those who are sentenced in federal court for white collar crimes tend to come from the middle classes rather than the upper classes. Criminal violations committed by Fortune 500 corporations over a two-year period showed that executives were convicted in only 1.5 percent of the cases. However, managers were more likely than not to be sentenced in such cases. And employees, particularly in securities fraud cases, were more likely to be sentenced to prison than the executives for whom they worked. Executives charged with securities violations were also less likely to even be prosecuted criminally than employees. However, executives are far more likely than both groups to be given civil sanctions.

White collar criminals are most likely to have committed their first offense with their business crime charges (72%).

They are older than most inmates, with 46 percent being over the age of 40.

The breakdown for federal offenders sent to prison is as follows.

Type of Crime	Percentage of Total White Collar Crime
Fraud	16.5%
Regulatory offenses	2.4%
Extortion, bribery	5.7%

Other types of federal crimes include tax evasion; Medicare and Medicaid overbilling; false reports; and environmental, antitrust, embezzlement, and other securities violations.

The conviction rate for federal prosecutors in the United States is 88 percent. In China, the rate is 99.7 percent.

CONSIDER...   9.1

Virginia T. Morris was the chief executive officer and chairman of the board of directors of Northwest National Bank, a financial institution located in Fayetteville, Arkansas. She was indicted on several counts of bank fraud, money laundering, making false entries in the books of a federally insured financial institution, and making false material statements to a federal bank examiner. Mrs. Morris was convicted and sentenced to prison. She appealed her case on grounds that all the paperwork for the loans, checks, and drafts involved in the case were completed and signed by employees at the bank and not by her. The government has responded by noting that all overdraft approvals were done orally by her. Can Ms. Morris be held criminally responsible for conduct completed on paper exclusively by others? [*United States* v. *Morris*, 18 F.3d 562 (8th Cir. 1994).]

CONSIDER...   9.2

Millennium Restaurants Group, Inc., doing business as Cabaret Royale, operates an adult entertainment club in Dallas, Texas. One of the dancers employed at the club was convicted of lewd conduct, and the city of Dallas sought to revoke Millennium's license because of the criminal conduct of its employees. Are the owners accountable for the conduct of their dancers and other employees? [*Millennium Restaurants Group, Inc.* v. *City of Dallas, Texas,* 191 F.Supp.2d 802 (N.D. Tex. 2002).]

Federal Laws Targeting Officers and Directors for Criminal Accountability

With each wave of accounting and fraud scandals, new legislation is passed at the federal level to provide increased penalties for those who are the masterminds of white-collar crimes. In 1990, Congress enacted what has been called the "white-collar kingpin" law. A response to the 1980s savings and loan scandals, the law imposes minimum mandatory sentences (ten years in most instances) for corporate officers who mastermind financial crimes such as bank and securities fraud. Following the collapses of Enron, WorldCom, Adelphia, and others in the period from 2001 to 2002, Congress passed Sarbanes-Oxley, also known as the White-Collar Criminal Penalty Enhancement Act of 2002. Under SOX, as it is known among businesspeople, penalties for mail and wire fraud increased from their former maximums of five years to twenty years in prison. (Refer to Exhibit 9.1 to see the number of wire and fraud charges that have been brought against executives.) Penalties for violation of the trust, reporting, and fiduciary duties under pension laws increased from one year to ten years, with fines increased from $5,000 to $100,000. SOX also provides for the specific crime of false financial statement certification, a crime directed at CEOs and CFOs, who are now required to certify the financial statements issued by their companies. Top officers who certify financials that they know contain false information now face a specific federal crime because of SOX reforms. Richard Scrushy, the former CEO of HealthSouth, became the first CEO charged with a violation of these new provisions (see Exhibit 9.1).

THE PENALTIES FOR BUSINESS CRIME

Statutes specify penalties for crimes. Some statutes have both business and individual penalties. Exhibit 9.2 provides a summary of the penalties under the major federal statutes.

Reforming Criminal Penalties

Some regulators and legislators argue that the difficulty with most criminal law penalties is that they were instituted with "natural" persons in mind, as opposed to "artificial" corporate persons. Fines may be significant to individuals, but a $10,000 fine to a corporation with billions in assets and millions in income is simply a cost of doing business.

A recommendation advanced for the reformation of criminal penalties is that the penalties must cost the corporation as much as a bad business decision would cost. For example, if a company develops a bad product line, net earnings could decline 10 to 20 percent. Penalties expressed in terms of net earnings, as opposed to set dollar amounts, are more likely to have a deterrent effect on business criminal behavior.

EXHIBIT 9.2 Penalties for Business Crime under Federal Law

ACT	PENALTIES
Internal Revenue Code 26 U.S.C. 7201	$100,000 ($500,000 for corporations) and/or 5 years For evasion (plus costs of prosecution as well as penalties and assessments: 5–50%) $350,000 and/or 3 years
Sherman Act (antitrust) 15 U.S.C. 1	$10,000,000 for corporations Injunctions Divestiture
Sarbanes-Oxley 15 U.S.C. §1512 (document destruction, concealment, alteration, mutilation during pending civil or criminal investigation)	20 years plus fines
Sarbanes-Oxley (certification of financial statements)	$1,000,000 and/or 10 years If willful: $5,000,000 and 20 years Officers who earn bonuses based on falsified financial statements must forfeit them
1933 Securities Act 15 U.S.C. 77x (as amended by Sarbanes-Oxley)	$100,000 and/or 10 years
Securities and Exchange Act of 1934 15 U.S.C. 78ff	$5,000,000 and/or 20 years $25,000,000 for corporations Civil penalties in addition of up to three times profit made or $1,000,000, whichever is greater
Clean Air Act 42 U.S.C. 7413	$1,000,000 and/or 5 years
Clean Water Act 33 U.S.C. 1319	For negligent violations: $25,000 per day and/or 1 year For knowing violations: $50,000 per day and/or 3 years For second violations: $100,000 per day and/or 6 years For false statements in reports, plans, or records: $10,000 per day and/or 2 years
Occupational Health Safety Act 29 U.S.C. 666	Willful violation causing death: $70,000 and/or 1 year; minimum of $5,000 per willful violation Giving advance notice of inspection: $1,000 and/or 6 months False statements or representations: $10,000 and/or 6 months
Consumer Product Safety Act 15 U.S.C. 2070	$50,000 and/or 1 year Tampering: up to $500,000 and/or 10 years

Another recommendation, one that has been implemented to a certain extent, requires prison sentences for officers and directors. The human element of the corporation—the action element—is then punished for the acts done in the name of the business.

A new type of sentence for corporations has emerged over the past five years. Judges are increasingly assigning monitors to corporations to follow up on corporate activity. For example, as its sentence in an environmental case, ConEd was assigned a Natural Resources Defense Council lawyer as a monitor for its asbestos activity.

While their cases were not criminal in nature, both Coca-Cola and Mitsubishi agreed to a panel of monitors as part of their settlements in discrimination cases.

A final recommendation for reforming criminal penalties would require corporations to stand criminally responsible under traditional criminal statutes for corporate wrongs. For example, when Ford Motor Company manufactured the Pinto automobile with a design flaw involving the gas tank location, many civil suits were brought for deaths and injuries caused by the exploding gas tank. However, Ford was indicted for a criminal charge of homicide. In 1999, the state of Florida charged ValuJet, Inc., with murder and manslaughter for carelessly handling deadly materials for shipment; their omissions resulted in an airplane crash and the deaths of 110 passengers and the crew. A traditional common-law crime was applied to corporations for the wrongful death of customers. The owner of Imperial Foods Company in North Carolina pled guilty to workplace hazards that resulted in the burn deaths of twenty-five employees at his chicken processing plant and received a nineteen-year prison sentence. While the crimes he was charged with were violations of business laws, the sentence was traditional in the sense that an individual within a company was held personally and criminally responsible for the crimes.

U.S. v. *Allegheny Bottling Co.* (Case 9.2) involves a creative sentence imposed by a judge on a corporation.

CASE 9.2

United States v. *Allegheny Bottling Co.*
695 F.Supp. 856 (E.D. Va. 1988) cert. denied, 493 U.S. 817 (1989)

Coke and Pepsi Wars Turn Criminal: Imprisonment for Price-Fixing

FACTS

Mid-Atlantic Coca-Cola Bottling Company and Allegheny Pepsi-Cola Bottling Company were charged with conspiracy to fix prices on Coke and Pepsi in order to avoid the ruinous competition that price wars were causing. Several officers pleaded guilty to the charges, and some were found guilty by a jury.

The trial evidence showed that in the Baltimore market, Coke sold from 6,200,000 to 7,000,000 cases of soft drinks a year. Prior to the price-fixing agreement, the price per case was $6.00 to $6.40. After the price-fixing agreement in 1982, the price was $6.80 per case, and it remained there for a full year. This additional 40 cents per case allowed the companies to earn over $1 million more. In pronouncing sentence on the corporate defendants, the judge used a creative solution (later affirmed by the appellate court).

JUDICIAL OPINION

DOUMAR, District Judge

The Lord Chancellor of England said some two hundred years ago, "Did you ever expect a corporation to have a conscience when it has no soul to be damned, and no body to be kicked?" Two hundred years have

passed since the Lord Chancellor espoused this view, and the whole area of what is and is not permitted or what is or is not prohibited, has changed both in design and application. Certainly, this Court does not expect a corporation to have a conscience, but it does expect it to be ethical and abide by the law. This Court will deal with this company no less severely than it will deal with any individual who similarly disregards the law.

. . . Allegheny Bottling Company [parent of Allegheny Pepsi] is sentenced to three (3) years imprisonment and a fine of One Million Dollars ($1,000,000). Execution of the sentence of imprisonment is suspended and all but $950,000 of said fine is suspended, and the defendant is placed on probation for a period of three years.

As special conditions of the probation, in addition to the normal terms of probation, the defendant, Allegheny Bottling Company, shall provide:

(a) An officer or employee of Allegheny of comparable salary and stature to Jerry Polino (former vice president of sales who pled guilty to the conspiracy charges) to perform forty (40) hours of community service per week in the Baltimore, Maryland area for a two (2) year period without compensation to the defendant. [The court required 40 hours of community service from someone of

equal stature for each of the four officers of Allegheny who had been convicted or pleaded guilty to the price-fixing conspiracy charges.]

Corporate imprisonment requires only that the Court restrain or immobilize the corporation. Such restraint of individuals is accomplished by, for example, placing them in the custody of the United States Marshal. The United States Marshal would restrain the corporation by seizing the corporation's physical assets or part of the assets or restricting its actions or liberties in a particular manner.

Cases in the past have *assumed* that corporations cannot be imprisoned, without any cited authority for that proposition. This Court, however, has been unable to find any case which actually held that corporate imprisonment is illegal, unconstitutional, or impossible. Considerable confusion regarding the ability of courts to order a corporation imprisoned has been caused by courts mistakenly thinking that imprisonment necessarily involves incarceration in jail. But since imprisonment of a corporation does not necessarily involve incarceration, there is no reason to continue the assump-

tion, which has lingered in the legal system unexamined and without support, that a corporation cannot be imprisoned. Since the Marshal can restrain the corporation's liberty and has done so in bankruptcy cases, there is no reason he cannot do so in this case as he himself has so stated prior to the imposition of this sentence.

Corporate imprisonment not only promotes the purposes of the Sherman Act, but also promotes the purposes of sentencing. The purposes of sentencing, according to the United States Sentencing Commission, include incapacitating the offender, deterring crime, rehabilitating the offender, and providing just punishment. The corporate imprisonment imposed today is specifically tailored to meet each of these purposes.

CASE QUESTIONS

1. Is corporate imprisonment illegal?

2. How will the corporation be imprisoned?

3. Is community service a sufficient punishment for the corporation?

4. Can the corporation's assets be imprisoned?

FOR THE MANAGER'S DESK

RE: ACCOUNTING FOR THE ACCOUNTING

A survey of 1,400 CFOs indicates the types of changes companies are making in order to change their accounting processes.

Reviewing and changing current accounting processes	44%
Creating and expanding internal audits	36%
Hiring independent firms for consulting work	23%
Restructuring executive compensation plans	8%

Source: Darryl Harralson and Adrienne Lewis, "Steps companies are taking to control accounting processes," *USA Today,* March 26, 2003, p. 1B.

BUSINESS STRATEGY APPLICATION

The exercise for this chapter on the book's Web site offers the opportunity to explore the various corporate crime statutes, their penalties, and the types of conduct covered.

"Shame punishment" has been on the increase in corporate criminal cases. Shame punishment involves public disclosure of an offense. For example, a Delaware federal judge ordered Bachetti Brothers Market to take out an ad for three weeks confessing to its crime of violating federal law by selling meat consisting "in whole or in part of filthy, putrid and contaminated substances."

Corporate Sentencing Guidelines: An Ounce of Prevention Means a Reduced Sentence

The U.S. Sentencing Commission, established by Congress in 1984, has developed both federal sentencing guidelines and a carrot-and-stick approach to fighting white-collar crime. Under the commission's guidelines, companies that take substantial steps to prevent, investigate, and punish wrongdoing and cooperate with federal investigators can be treated less harshly in sentencing. The goal of the commission was to ensure that companies would establish internal crime prevention programs.

Visit the U.S. Sentencing Commission:
http://www.ussc.gov

The sentencing guidelines permit judges to place guilty companies on probation for a period of up to five years if their offense or offenses occurred during a time when they had no crime prevention programs in place. The guidelines use a formula that takes into account the seriousness of the offense, the company's history of violations, its cooperation in the investigation, the effectiveness of its compliance program, and the role of senior management in the wrongdoing. The guidelines are a form of mandatory sentencing. If certain factors are present, the judge must order prison times. For example, corporate officers who are proven to have masterminded criminal activity must be sentenced to some prison time.

The federal sentencing guidelines provide for a score that determines the extent of the sentence of the company and individual officers, managers, and employees. A company's "culpability multiplier" can range from 0.05 to 4.00, which is then used to convert a business's culpability score (a number that ranges from 0 to 10 or above). Every company begins with a score of 5, which can be added to or subtracted from depending on various factors in the guidelines. The larger the organization, the greater the number of points added. Involvement of top officers in criminal conduct also adds to the score. Prior violations increase a company's score, as do attempts to cover up the conduct (obstruction of justice).

A company's score is decreased by the presence of effective compliance programs designed to prevent and detect violations. If a company comes forward and reports the violations voluntarily, the score is decreased. Cooperation with investigators and acceptance of responsibility also reduce the score.

These multipliers are also used in the computation of fines for a business and its employees and officers. Restitution made by a company before sentencing reduces penalties and fines. For example, a fine of $1 million to $2 million could be reduced to as low as $50,000 for a company with the following: (1) a code of conduct, (2) an ombudsman, (3) a hotline, and (4) mandatory training for executives. The sentencing guidelines have been referred to as a "quiet revolution" in changing corporate conduct.

In Re Caremark International, Inc. (Case 9.3), a landmark case, deals with the issue of the importance of compliance programs in a corporation and the responsibility of the board of directors for ensuring that the company's compliance program is in place and functioning effectively.

CASE 9.3

In Re Caremark International, Inc.
698 A.2d 959 (Del. Ch. 1996)

The Board's Supervision or Lack Thereof:
Kickbacks and Internal Controls

FACTS

Caremark International, Inc., a Delaware corporation with its headquarters in Illinois, was created in 1992 as a spin-off from Baxter International, Inc. It became a publicly held company, with its stock traded on the New York Exchange. Caremark operates two main health care segments: patient care and managed care services. In these two segments, a substantial portion of Caremark's revenues comes from third-party payments from insurers and Medicare and Medicaid reimbursements.

As part of its operations, Caremark paid physicians fees for monitoring in-home care for patients even though those physicians were not treating the patients. Caremark said the system was created to have outside physicians monitoring home care for quality. However, the federal government, through the Office of Inspector General, in its interpretation of applicable federal regulations, concluded that the fees paid to these physicians constituted referral fees or kickbacks paid with the idea of obtaining patient referrals from these physicians in exchange for their monitoring fees. Referral payments violate the Anti-Referral Payments Law (ARPL).

Caremark also had consulting and research payment arrangements with physicians for the promotion of the human growth hormone Protropin, a drug marketed by Caremark. (Originally the drug was marketed by Baxter.)

Caremark did disclose the ongoing federal investigation in 1992 (the investigation had begun before the 1992 spin-off), and, in 1993, Caremark received a clean opinion from Price Waterhouse on internal controls in the company.

In 1994, a federal grand jury in Minnesota issued a 47-page indictment charging Caremark, two of its officers, a physician, and a sales employee with violations of federal law in the forms of research grants, consulting fees, and other payments made by the company in exchange for the promotion of Protropin.

After the indictment became public, five shareholder derivative suits were filed against the company as well as its directors (director defendants). The shareholders petitioned the Delaware court for approval of a settlement with the company.

JUDICIAL OPINION

ALLEN, Chancellor

In relevant part the terms upon which these claims asserted are proposed to be settled are as follows:

1. That Caremark, undertakes that it and its employees, and agents not pay any form of compensation to a third party in exchange for the referral of a patient to a Caremark facility or service or the prescription of drugs marketed or distributed by Caremark for which reimbursement may be sought from Medicare, Medicaid, or a similar state reimbursement program;

2. That Caremark, undertakes for itself and its employees, and agents not to pay to or split fees with physicians, joint ventures, any business combination in which Caremark maintains a direct financial interest, or other health care providers with whom Caremark has a financial relationship or interest, in exchange for the referral of a patient to a Caremark facility or service

or the prescription of drugs marketed or distributed by Caremark for which reimbursement may be sought from Medicare, Medicaid, or a similar state reimbursement program;

3. That the full Board shall discuss all relevant material changes in government health care regulations and their effect on relationships with health care providers on a semiannual basis;

4. That Caremark's officers will remove all personnel from health care facilities or hospitals who have been placed in such facility for the purpose of providing remuneration in exchange for a patient referral for which reimbursement may be sought from Medicare, Medicaid, or a similar state reimbursement program;

5. That every patient will receive written disclosure of any financial relationship between Caremark and the health care professional or provider who made the referral;

6. That the Board will establish a Compliance and Ethics Committee of four directors, two of which will be non-management directors, to meet at least four times a year to effectuate these policies and monitor business segment compliance with the ARPL, and to report to the Board semiannually concerning compliance by each business segment; and

7. That corporate officers responsible for business segments shall serve as compliance officers who must report semiannually to the Compliance and Ethics Committee and, with the assistance of outside counsel, review existing contracts and get advanced approval of any new contract forms.

The complaint charges the director defendants with breach of their duty of attention or care in connection with the ongoing operation of the corporation's business. The claim is that the directors allowed a situation to develop and continue which exposed the corporation to enormous legal liability and that in so doing they violated a duty to be active monitors of corporate performance. The complaint thus does not charge either director self-dealing or the more difficult loyalty-type problems arising from cases of suspect director motivation, such as entrenchment or sale of control contexts. The theory here advanced is possibly the most difficult theory in corporation law upon which a plaintiff might hope to win a judgment.

As the facts of this case graphically demonstrate, ordinary business decisions that are made by officers and employees deeper in the interior of the organization can, however, vitally affect the welfare of the corporation and its ability to achieve its various strategic and financial goals. If this case did not prove the point itself, recent business history would. Recall for example the displacement of senior management and

continued

much of the board of Salomon, Inc.; the replacement of senior management of Kidder, Peabody following the discovery of large trading losses resulting from phantom trades by a highly compensated trader; or the extensive financial loss and reputational injury suffered by Prudential Insurance as a result [of] its junior officers' misrepresentations in connection with the distribution of limited partnership interests. Financial and organizational disasters such as these raise the question, what is the board's responsibility with respect to the organization and monitoring of the enterprise to assure that the corporation functions within the law to achieve its purposes?

Modernly this question has been given special importance by an increasing tendency, especially under federal law, to employ the criminal law to assure corporate compliance with external legal requirements, including environmental, financial, employee and product safety as well as assorted other health and safety regulations. In 1991, pursuant to the Sentencing Reform Act of 1984, the United States Sentencing Commission adopted Organizational Sentencing Guidelines which impact importantly on the prospective effect these criminal sanctions might have on business corporations. The Guidelines set forth a uniform sentencing structure for organizations to be sentenced for violation of federal criminal statutes and provide for penalties that equal or often massively exceed those previously imposed on corporations. The Guidelines offer powerful incentives for corporations today to have in place compliance programs to detect violations of law, promptly to report violations to appropriate public officials when discovered, and to take prompt, voluntary remedial efforts.

In 1963, the Delaware Supreme Court in *Graham* v. *Allis-Chalmers Mfg. Co.* addressed the question of potential liability of board members for losses experienced by the corporation as a result of the corporation having violated the anti-trust laws of the United States. There was no claim in that case that the directors knew about the behavior of subordinate employees of the corporation that had resulted in the liability. Rather, as in this case, the claim asserted was that the directors ought to have known of it and if they had known they would have been under a duty to bring the corporation into compliance with the law and thus save the corporation from the loss. The Delaware Supreme Court concluded that, under the facts as they appeared, there was no basis to find that the directors had breached a duty to be informed of the ongoing operations of the firm. In notably colorful terms, the court stated that "absent cause for suspicion there is no duty upon the directors to install and operate a corporate system of espionage to ferret out wrongdoing which they have no reason to suspect exists." The

Court found that there were no grounds for suspicion in that case and, thus, concluded that the directors were blamelessly unaware of the conduct leading to the corporate liability.

How does one generalize this holding today? Can it be said today that, absent some ground giving rise to suspicion of violation of law, that corporate directors have no duty to assure that a corporate information gathering and reporting system exists which represents a good faith attempt to provide senior management and the Board with information respecting material acts, events or conditions within the corporation, including compliance with applicable statutes and regulations? I certainly do not believe so. I doubt that such a broad generalization of the *Graham* holding would have been accepted by the Supreme Court in 1963. The case can be more narrowly interpreted as standing for the proposition that, absent grounds to suspect deception, neither corporate boards nor senior officers can be charged with wrongdoing simply for assuming the integrity of employees and the honesty of their dealings on the company's behalf.

Secondly, I note the elementary fact that relevant and timely information is an essential predicate for satisfaction of the board's supervisory and monitoring role under Section 141 of the Delaware General Corporation Law. Thirdly, I note the potential impact of the federal organizational sentencing guidelines on any business organization. Any rational person attempting in good faith to meet an organizational governance responsibility would be bound to take into account this development and the enhanced penalties and the opportunities for reduced sanctions that it offers.

In light of these developments, it would, in my opinion, be a mistake to conclude that our Supreme Court's statement in *Graham* concerning "espionage" means that corporate boards may satisfy their obligation to be reasonably informed concerning the corporation, without assuring themselves that information and reporting systems exist in the organization that are reasonably designed to provide to senior management and to the board itself timely, accurate information sufficient to allow management and the board, each within its scope, to reach informed judgments concerning both the corporation's compliance with law and its business performance.

Obviously the level of detail that is appropriate for such an information system is a question of business judgment. And obviously too, no rationally designed information and reporting system will remove the possibility that the corporation will violate laws or regulations, or that senior officers or directors may nevertheless sometimes be misled or otherwise fail reasonably to detect acts material to the corporation's compliance with the law. But it is important that the board exercise a good faith judgment that the corporation's information and reporting system is in concept and design adequate to assure the board that appropriate information will come to its attention in a timely manner as a matter of ordinary operations, so that it may satisfy its responsibility.

Thus, I am of the view that a director's obligation includes a duty to attempt in good faith to assure that a corporate information and reporting system, which the board concludes is adequate, exists, and that failure to do so under some circumstances may, in theory at least, render a director liable for losses caused by noncompliance with applicable legal standards.

CASE QUESTIONS

1. Was there any indication that the board was aware of the payment arrangements?
2. What does the court list as the responsibility of the board?
3. Why do you think the company settled the derivative suits? What did it agree to do?
4. What advice would you give to a board member on setting up and monitoring a compliance program?
5. When would directors be liable for criminal conduct by employees in the corporation?

FOR THE MANAGER'S DESK

RE: AN AGE PROFILE FOR CRIME

A new study released by the U.S. Federal Sentencing Commission offers some insight into who is committing crimes. The study also concludes that while the number of violent crimes has decreased significantly, white-collar crime is on the rise. The following are the average ages for the defendants by type of crime.

Crime	Age (years)
Burglary	24
Assault	29
Robbery	30

Murder	32
Fraud	37
Bribery	43
Tax offenses	48
Antitrust violations	50

Visit the Web site for the U.S. Sentencing Commission, http://www.ussc.gov, for more information.

Source: "My First Time in the Slammer, I Couldn't Even Spell Antitrust," *Forbes,* September 2, 2002, p. 56

BUSINESS STRATEGY

Much More Than Compliance

Businesses should learn the following from the basic principles of the sentencing guidelines.
1. Have a code of ethics in place.
2. Conduct training on the code of ethics.
3. Have a company hotline and ombudsperson for employees to use anonymously to report violations.
4. Protect employees who report violations.
5. Investigate all allegations regardless of their sources.

© GETTY IMAGES

6. Report all violations immediately and voluntarily.
7. Offer restitution to affected parties.
8. Cooperate and negotiate with regulators.
9. Admit your mistakes and shortcomings.
10. Be very public with your code of ethics. Discuss ethics with employees via Web site examples or illustrations of good ethical choices in the news among companies and employees.

ETHICAL ISSUES

Kevin Weber, a parolee who had committed two felonies, entered Eric's Gazebo, a restaurant in Santa Ana, California, through a rooftop vent on Mother's Day in May 1995. Mr. Weber's intention was to steal cash from the restaurant safe, but he tripped the burglar alarm and fled with four chocolate chip cookies. When he left the restaurant, police were already waiting outside for him.

In 1994, California had passed a "three-strikes" law. The statute requires a minimum sentence of 25 years on the third felony conviction. Mr. Weber was sentenced to 26 years, or 6½ years per cookie. Mr. Weber, 35, must serve at least 26 years before he will be eligible for parole. Is this a fair sentence?

In 2000, a Texas jury sentenced Kenneth Payne, 29, to 16 years in prison for stealing a $1 candy bar. Payne had ten previous convictions for theft, criminal mischief, assault, and possession of a controlled substance. The district attorney's office had recommended the sentence with the prosecuting attorney adding about the candy bar, "It was a king size." Do you think the sentence is fair? What do you think of the prosecuting attorney's comment?

ELEMENTS OF BUSINESS CRIME

The **elements**, or requirements for proof, of a business crime vary according to type. Crimes are violations of written laws, such as statutes or ordinances. But all crimes' specific elements can be classified into two general elements: *mens rea* (or *scienter*) and *actus reus*.

Mens Rea

A **crime** implies some voluntary action, which is to say that a criminal wrong is calculated or intentional; this element of criminal intent is the ***mens rea*** of a crime. *Mens rea* is the required state of mind for a crime—the intent to commit the act that is a crime. A criminal wrong is not based on an accident unless there was forewarning about the accident or the accident arose from criminal conduct. Driving while intoxicated is a crime, and an accident that happens while a driver is intoxicated is also a criminal wrong. Concealing income is intentional conduct calculated to avoid paying taxes; it is willful and criminal conduct. An oversight in reporting income is not a crime. *U.S.* v. *Ahmad* (Case 9.4) discusses the issue of intent in an environmental case.

CASE 9.4

United States v. *Ahmad*
101 F.3d 386 (5th Cir. 1996)

Gasoline, Drains, and Knowledge of the Two Together: A Crime?

FACTS

Mr. Ahmad owns a Spin-N-Market located in Conroe, Texas. Shortly after he purchased the combination gas and convenience store in 1992, a leak was discovered in one of the high-octane gasoline tanks at the location. The leak was at the top of the tank and did not present problems with gasoline seeping out. However, the leak did allow water to get into the tank and contaminate the gas. Because water is heavier than gas, the water sank to the bottom of the tank, and because the tank was pumped from the bottom, Mr. Ahmad was unable to sell gas from it.

In October 1993, Mr. Ahmad hired CTT Environmental Services, a tank-testing company, to examine the tank. CTT determined that the tank contained 800 gallons of water and the rest was mostly gasoline. Jewel McCoy, a CTT employee, told Mr. Ahmad that the leak could not be repaired until the tank was completely empty, which CTT offered to do for 65 cents per gallon plus $65 per hour of labor. After Ms. McCoy gave Mr. Ahmad this CIT estimate, he asked whether he could empty the tank himself. Ms. McCoy told him that it would be dangerous and illegal for him to do so. Mr. Ahmad then responded, "Well, if I don't get caught, what then?"

On January 25, 1994, Mr. Ahmad rented a handheld motorized water pump from a local hardware store, telling a hardware store employee that he was planning to use it to remove water from his backyard. Mr. Ahmad hooked the pump up to his tank at the Spin-N-Market and pumped 5,220 gallons of fluid into a manhole near the store and into Lewis Street alongside the store. Of the fluid pumped, 4,690 gallons were gasoline.

The gasoline from Lewis Street made its way to a storm drain and the storm sewer system and eventually into Possum Creek. When city officials discovered the gasoline in Possum Creek, several vacuum trucks were required to decontaminate it.

The gasoline from the manhole made its way to the city sewage treatment center. The gasoline was diverted into a different storage pool in order to avoid shutting down the plant altogether, but the plant had to evacuate all but essential personnel, and firefighters and hazardous materials crews from the city had to be called to restore the plant to a safe condition. While the crews worked, two area schools had to be evacuated for safety reasons.

The gasoline was traced back to Mr. Ahmad's Spin-N-Market, and Mr. Ahmad was indicted for three violations of the Clean Water Act (CWA), of knowingly discharging a pollutant into navigable waters without a permit, knowingly placing others in imminent danger through a pollutant, and knowingly operating a source in violation of pretreatment requirements. Mr. Ahmad did not dispute the conduct; he said he did not meet the "knowingly" requirements because he believed he was discharging water.

The jury found Mr. Ahmad guilty on two of the three charges and deadlocked on the charge of imminent danger. Mr. Ahmad appealed.

JUDICIAL OPINION

SMITH, Circuit Judge

One of the key pieces of evidence Ahmad attempted to introduce in support of this theory was the testimony of Mohammed Abassi and Shahid Latif, who would have told the jury that Ahmad was at the Spin-N-Market only until 7:30 or 8:00 P.M. on January 25, and not the entire evening as the government contended. The gist of this was an attempt to show that Ahmad did not knowingly discharge gasoline himself, but rather only negligently left the pump in the hands of his employees. The district court found Abassi's and Latif's testimony irrelevant and excluded it.

Ahmad contends that the jury should have been instructed that the statutory *mens rea*—knowledge—was required as to each element of the offenses, rather than only with regard to discharge or the operation of a source. Because Ahmad requested such instruction, we review the refusal to give it for abuse of discretion.

The language of the CWA is less than pellucid. Title 33 U.S.C. § 1319(c)(2)(A) says that "any person who knowingly violates" any of a number of other sections of the CWA commits a felony. One of the provisions that § 1319(c)(2)(A) makes it unlawful to violate is § 1311(a), which, when read together with a series of definitions in § 1362, prohibits the addition of any pollutant to navigable waters from a "point source." That was the crime charged in count one. Section 1319(c)(2)(A) also criminalizes violations of § 1317(d), which prohibits the operation of any "source" in a way that contravenes any effluent standard, prohibition, or pretreatment standard. That was the crime charged in count two.

The principal issue is to which elements of the offense the modifier "knowingly" applies. The matter is complicated somewhat by the fact that the phrase "knowingly violates" appears in a different section of the CWA from the language defining the elements of the offenses. Ahmad argues that within this context, "knowingly violates" should be read to require him knowingly to have acted with regard to each element of the offenses. The government, in contrast, contends that "knowingly violates" requires it to prove only that Ahmad knew the nature of his acts and that he performed them intentionally. Particularly at issue is whether "knowingly" applies to the element of the discharge's being a pollutant, for Ahmad's main theory at trial was that he thought he was discharging water, not gasoline.

The Supreme Court has spoken to this issue in broad terms. In *United States* v. *X-Citement Video, Inc.*, 513 U.S. 65, ___, 115 S.Ct. 464, 467, 130 L.Ed.2d 372 (1994), the Court read "knowingly" to apply to each element of a child pornography offense, notwithstanding its conclusion that under the "most natural grammatical reading" of the statute it should apply only to the element of having transported, shipped, received, distributed, or reproduced the material at issue. The Court also reaffirmed the long-held view that "the presumption in favor of a *scienter* requirement should apply to each of the statutory elements which criminalize otherwise innocent conduct."

Although *X-Citement Video* is the Court's most recent pronouncement on this subject, it is not the first. In

continued

Staples v. United States, 511 U.S. 600, 619–20, 114 S.Ct. 1793, 128 L.Ed.2d 609 (1994), the Court found that the statutes criminalizing knowing possession of a machinegun, 26 U.S.C. §§ 5845(a)(6) and 5861(d), require that defendants know not only that they possess a firearm but that it actually is a machinegun. Thus, an awareness of the features of the gun—specifically, the features that make it an automatic weapon—is a necessary element of the offense. More generally, the Court also made plain that statutory crimes carrying severe penalties are presumed to require that a defendant know the facts that make his conduct illegal.

Indeed, we find it eminently sensible that the phrase "knowingly violates" in § 1319(c)(2)(A), when referring to other provisions that define the elements of the offenses § 1319 creates, should uniformly require knowledge as to each of those elements rather than only one or two. To hold otherwise would require an explanation as to why some elements should be treated differently from others, which neither the parties nor the case law seems able to provide.

In support of its interpretation of the CWA, the government cites cases from other circuits. We find these decisions both inapposite and unpersuasive on the point for which they are cited. In *United States v. Hopkins,* 53 F.3d 533, 537–41 (2d Cir.1995), cert. denied, ___ U.S. ___, 116 S.Ct. 773, 133 L.Ed.2d 725 (1996), the court held that the government need not demonstrate that a § 1319(c)(2)(A) defendant knew his acts were illegal. The illegality of the defendant's actions is not an element of the offense, however. In *United States v. Weitzenhoff,* 35 F.3d 1275 (9th Cir.1994), cert. denied, ___ U.S. ___, 115 S.Ct. 939, 130 L.Ed.2d 884 (1995), the court similarly was concerned almost exclusively with whether the language of the CWA creates a mistake-of-law defense. Both cases are easily distinguishable, for neither directly addresses mistake of fact or the statutory construction issues raised by Ahmad.

The government also protests that CWA violations fall into the judicially created exception for "public welfare offenses," under which some regulatory crimes have been held not to require a showing of *mens rea.* On its face, the CWA certainly does appear to implicate public welfare.

As recent cases have emphasized, however, the public welfare offense exception is narrow. The *Staples* Court, for example, held that the statute prohibiting the possession of machine guns fell outside the exception, notwithstanding the fact that "[t]ypically, our cases recognizing such offenses involve statutes that regulate potentially harmful or injurious items." *Staples,* 511 U.S. at 607, 114 S.Ct. at 1794.

Though gasoline is a "potentially harmful or injurious item," it is certainly no more so than are machineguns. Rather, *Staples* held, the key to the public welfare

offense analysis is whether "dispensing with *mens rea* would require the defendant to have knowledge only of traditionally lawful conduct." The CWA offenses of which Ahmad was convicted have precisely this characteristic, for if knowledge is not required as to the nature of the substance discharged, one who honestly and reasonably believes he is discharging water may find himself guilty of a felony if the substance turns out to be something else.

The fact that violations of § 1319(c)(2)(A) are felonies punishable by years in federal prison confirms our view that they do not fall within the public welfare offense exception. As the *Staples* Court noted, public welfare offenses have virtually always been crimes punishable by relatively light penalties such as fines or short jail sentences, rather than substantial terms of imprisonment. Serious felonies, in contrast, should not fall within the exception "absent a clear statement from Congress that *mens rea* is not required." Following *Staples,* we hold that the offenses charged in counts one and two are not public welfare offenses and that the usual presumption of a *mens rea* requirement applies. With the exception of purely jurisdictional elements, the *mens rea* of knowledge applies to each element of the crimes.

At best, the jury charge made it uncertain to which elements "knowingly" applied. At worst, and considerably more likely, it indicated that only the element of discharge need be knowingly. The instructions listed each element on a separate line, with the word "knowingly" present only in the line corresponding to the element that something was discharged. That the district court included a one-sentence summary of each count in which "knowingly" was present did not cure the error.

The obvious inference for the jury was that knowledge was required only as to the fact that something was discharged, and not as to any other fact. In effect, with regard to the other elements of the crimes, the instructions implied that the requisite *mens rea* was strict liability rather than knowledge.

There was at least a reasonable likelihood that the jury applied the instructions in this way, so we conclude that the instructions misled the jury as to the elements of the offense. Because the charge effectively withdrew from the jury's consideration facts that it should have been permitted to find or not find, this error requires reversal.

Most of Ahmad's defense, after all, was built around the idea that he thought water, rather than gasoline, was being discharged. A rational jury could so have found, and at the same time could have found that he did not actually know that he was pumping gas.

Reversed and remanded.

CASE QUESTIONS

1. What was wrong with Mr. Ahmad's tank?
2. Of what significance is Jewel McCoy's testimony?
3. What is the difference between knowledge of the law and knowledge of conduct?
4. What does the court explain is required for the state of mind under the Clean Water Act?
5. Why is Mr. Ahmad's testimony that he thought he was discharging water significant?

Some crimes not only require "knowing" or "willful" conduct but also require a refined or specific intent in relation to the crime. Securities fraud, for example, requires proof of not just intentional conduct but of intentional conduct with the idea of defrauding another. An accountant who makes an error in preparing corporate financial statements, unintentionally defrauding stock purchasers, did not intend to defraud them, and his or her act is probably one of negligence or omission rather than a knowing or willful act. However, a deliberate overstatement of income to comply with a corporate management request would be an act showing intent to defraud.

CONSIDER...   9 · 3

Consider the following situation and discuss whether the appropriate *mens rea* is present.

A nineteen-year-old was acquitted of charges of vehicular manslaughter brought against him because he collided into the rear of a car on the shoulder of the road while he was driving 80–105 mph and talking on a cell phone.

Believed to be the first criminal case brought for manslaughter with a vehicle owing to cell-phone distraction, the case attracted national attention because Jason Jones killed John and Carole Hall when he struck their car. The accident occurred during Thanksgiving weekend in 1999. Mr. Jones is a Naval Academy midshipman and was found guilty of negligent driving. Negligent driving is a misdemeanor and carries a $500 fine.

Testimony by experts for the prosecution indicated that cell-phone use while driving is an enormous distraction. The increased accident rate during cell-phone use while driving is placed at between 34 and 300 percent by various experts.*

It is not illegal in Maryland to use a cell phone while driving. Three states do have restrictions on their use; and, since 1995, thirty-seven states have debated proposed legislation on controls for cell-phone use in vehicles. Can someone be convicted for conduct that is not illegal?

Nathan Hall, 21, was found guilty of criminally negligent homicide in a Colorado case that resulted from Mr. Hall's collision with Alan Cobb on the slopes in Vail, Colorado. Mr. Hall, who was eighteen at the time of the accident, worked as a lift operator at the Vail Resorts. At the end of his shift, he did a run at what witnesses described as a "much too high" rate of speed. Mr. Hall had been a member of his high school's ski racing team.†

The Vail Resorts settled a claim with Mr. Cobb's family. It was shortly after the Hall incident that Michael Kennedy and Sonny Bono were killed on ski slopes, the former playing football while skiing and the latter colliding with a tree on a downhill run. Following these accidents, the resorts increased their safety patrols as well as the number of warning signs on the slopes.

Mr. Hall said that the conditions caused the accident. The snow was slushy, and the result was moguls, or small hills, on the slopes that caused Mr. Hall to lose control.

In 1998–99, there were thirty-four fatalities on ski slopes in the United States. In 1999–2000, there were thirty, while the number of skier visits annually rose from 52.1 million in 1998–99 to 52.2 million in 1999–2000.

continued

Could the ski resort be held criminally liable for Mr. Cobb's death?

What was the prosecution required to prove for Mr. Hall's conviction of the crime of criminally negligent homicide?

*Jessie Halladay, "Driver Wins Cell-phone-Crash Verdict," *USA Today*, December 7, 2000, p. 10A.
†"Colorado Skier Is Convicted in Fatal Collision on Slopes," *New York Times*, November 18, 2000, p. A9.

ETHICAL ISSUES

In 2001, Arthur Andersen, one of the largest accounting firms in the world, already reeling from its role in the Enron collapse, agreed to pay a $7 million fine to the Securities and Exchange Commission (SEC), the largest fine ever assessed against an accounting firm. The SEC had charged Andersen with fraud for its role in the overstatement of earnings throughout the 1990s by Waste Management, Inc. Waste Management eventually had to restate its earnings in 1998, which amounted to a $3.5 billion charge. The company had overstated its earnings by $1.43 billion from 1992 to 1996.

The complaint filed by the SEC against Andersen and three of its audit partners alleged charges of fraud. In settling the case, neither Andersen nor the partners (who paid between $30,000 and $50,000 in fines) admitted or denied the allegations. The partners are also barred from doing audit work for publicly traded companies for periods ranging from one to five years. Andersen, now defunct, has already paid $220 million to settle the shareholder litigation that resulted from the overstatement.

The SEC's complaint in the case alleged that the auditors from Andersen had pleaded with Waste Management executives to make changes. While the executives promised future reforms, they refused each year to reduce the profits. Each year Andersen succumbed to pressure from the Waste Management executives and certified the financial statements. Andersen's internal records reveal that it considered Waste Management a "high risk client" and that it "actively managed reported results." When it was auditing Waste Management's 1993 earnings in early 1994, Andersen auditors discovered $128 million in earnings misstatements that it asked management to change, a change that would have resulted in a reduction in earnings of 12 percent. When Waste Management executives refused to restate earnings, Andersen certified the financial statements anyway, concluding that the misstatements were "not material."

The SEC issued the following statement on the announcement of the settlement.

> *Unless the auditor stands up to management the first time it discovers incorrect accounting, the auditor ultimately will find itself in an untenable position: it either must continue issuing unqualified audit reports on materially misstated financial statements and hope that its conduct will not be discovered or it must force a restatement or qualify its report and thereby subject itself to the liability that will likely result from the exposure of its role in the prior issuance of the materially misstated financial statements.*

Arthur Andersen's managing partner for North America released the following statement:

> *This settlement allows the firm and its partners to end a very difficult chapter and move on. There are important lessons to be learned from this settlement by all involved in the financial reporting process. The pressures on management to meet expectations are greater than ever in a market where information and capital move instantly.*

Do you think the auditors at Arthur Andersen had intent to mislead? What were they trying to accomplish? What would have helped Waste Management executives see the issue differently? What would have helped the auditors? Was this a sign of Andersen's fate? Its collapse?

Criminal intent has been a particularly significant issue in business crimes. The intent element is significant because there are actually two intents involved when a corporation is prosecuted for a crime: the intent of the corporation to commit the crime and the intent of those in charge of the corporation, officers, and directors to direct the corporation to commit the wrong.

Actus Reus

All crimes include, in addition to the mental intent, a requirement of some specific action or conduct, which is the ***actus reus*** of the crime. For example, in embezzlement the *actus reus* is the taking of an employer's money. Various types of criminal conduct, or *actus reus* examples, are found in subsequent sections on specific crimes.

C O N S I D E R . . .   9 · 4

Dennis Kozlowski and Mark Swartz, the former CEO and CFO, respectively, of Tyco International, had a hung jury with pledges from the prosecution for a retrial.*

Mr. Kozlowski and Mr. Swartz, indicted on thirty-three counts of felony violations of New York state law, enjoyed extensive personal benefits from Tyco, an embarrassment of personal acquisition at company expense. Additionally, former legal counsel for Tyco, Mark Belnick, whose trial had just begun in mid-2004, was charged with larceny and falsifying business records.† While the charges against the three men have been state charges, primarily related to the basic white-collar crime of embezzlement, prosecutors are still required to show *mens rea*, criminal intent. The defense that both men raised, apparently successfully enough to flummox some jurors in their first trial, was that none of what they obtained was done secretly. They argued that they had no criminal intent. Both men produced evidence related to board knowledge of their perks and approvals through the established and proper company procedures for personal loans and the use of company funds for refurbishing and furnishing homes. Along the lines of a "Why would I be such an idiot?" defense, the two approached their case as one in which the blatancy of their conduct worked in their favor.‡

None of the loans were made to the men without some form of authorization, however perfunctory. Many in the executive ranks and perhaps even some board members were aware of the loans, the officer loan policy, and the processes used for booking and forgiving the loans. The issue of board approval on the loans remains a question, and civil litigation is pending against the board, but compensation committee minutes from February 21, 2002, show that the committee was given a list of loans to officers and also approved Mr. Belnick's new compensation package. There was no public disclosure of these developments or the committee's review.§

Do you believe *mens rea* could be established given these facts?

*Andrew Ross Sorkin, "Judge Ends Trial When Tyco Juror Reports Threat," *New York Times*, April 3, 2004, pp. A1, B4; Andrew Ross Sorkin, "After a Mistrial, Choices to Make," *New York Times*, April 5, 2004, pp. C1, C6.
†Jonathan D. Glater, "Prosecutors See More Time in Another Tyco Case," *New York Times*, April 8, 2004, p. C4.
‡Mark Maremont, "Kozlowski's Defense Strategy: Big Spending Was No Secret," *Wall Street Journal*, February 9, 2004, pp. A1, A23.
§Andrew Ross Sorkin and Jonathan D. Glater, "Some Tyco Board Members Knew of Pay Packages, Records Show," *New York Times*, September 23, 2002, p. A1. Mr. Belnick does claim that the auditors knew, and he has filed an arbitration claim through the American Arbitration Association against Tyco for breach of his $10.6 million retention agreement and employment contract that applied if he were terminated before October 1, 2002. Laurie P. Cohen, "Tyco Ex-Counsel Claims Auditors Knew of Loans," *Wall Street Journal*, October 22, 2002, p. A6.

EXAMPLES OF BUSINESS CRIMES

Theft and Embezzlement

The action of employees who take their employers' property is **theft** or **embezzlement**. For theft, the following elements are necessary: (1) intent to take the property, (2) an actual taking of the property for permanent use, and (3) no authorization to take the property. These three elements are the *actus reus* of the crime. The *mens rea* is the taking of the property with the intent of permanently depriving the owner of use and possession.

For embezzlement, the elements are the same as for theft, with the addition of one more element: The person commits the crime while in the employ or position of trust of the property owner. In other words, embezzlement is theft from a specific type of person—an employer. Although it is usually limited to funds, embezzlement can cover such items as inventory and equipment of a business.

CONSIDER...   9 · 5

Darrin James was the manager of Allsup's Store in Clovis, New Mexico. Jay Finnell, his immediate supervisor, found $2,400 in cash below the checkstand, behind some books and papers. Mr. Finnell later discovered irregularities in the records of the store maintained by Mr. James. The sales receipts for the store were greater than the bank deposits. Is there sufficient evidence to convict Mr. James of embezzlement? [*State* v. *James,* 784 P.2d 1021 (N.M. App. 1989).]

Obstruction of Justice

Because of the cases involving the destruction of documents (see Exhibit 9.1, entries for Arthur Andersen, and Enron, and Frank Quattrone), Sarbanes-Oxley amended the federal law on obstruction of justice to make document destruction a specific crime and to increase its penalties. The new obstruction section makes it a felony for anyone, including company employees, auditors, attorneys, and consultants, *to alter, destroy, mutilate, conceal, cover up, falsify, or make a false entry with the "intent to impede, obstruct, or influence the investigation or proper administration of any matter within the jurisdiction of any department or agency of the United States."*[4] The statute also addressed audit records and requires auditors to retain their work papers related to a client's audit for at least five years. Any destruction of these documents prior to the expiration of that period would constitute a felony and carries a penalty of up to ten years.

Computer Crime

What Is a Computer Crime?

Review a summary of federal computer crimes:

http://www.davismccownlaw.com/articles/a-fedcc.htm

The term **computer crime** is used as though it were a completely separate body of law from criminal law. While certain crimes can only be committed using a computer, the nature of crime, with both *mens rea* and *actus reus,* does not change. Specific statutes addressing the unique means by which property is taken and covering the unique type of property found in computer software and hardware make establishing computer crimes easier than reliance on traditional crimes such as larceny and embezzlement.

Some computer crimes may involve a computer without making direct use of one. Ordinary criminal statutes can apply to these types of crimes. For example, a person who mails flyers that falsely advertise a service as computerized is guilty of committing the federal crime of using the mail to defraud.

For more serious and costly computer-related wrongs that do not fit the ordinary definitions of crime, there is a definite trend of adopting statutes that define specific computer crimes. These statutes are strictly construed: Only that conduct covered by the statute can be punished as the crime.

One of the problems with criminal law statutes has been making them sufficiently clear to be understood by ordinary persons of ordinary intelligence. If the statutes are unclear or cannot be understood or the terms defined, the statutes violate the standards of substantive due process. (See Chapter 5 for more discussion of these rights.) In some cases, statutes covering computer crimes have been held unconstitutional as too vague.

Computer Crimes That Involve the Computer as the Victim

A traditional crime may be committed by stealing or intentionally damaging a computer.

Theft of Hardware   When the computer itself is stolen, the ordinary law relating to theft crimes applies. Theft of a computer is subject to the same law as the theft of a typewriter or a desk. Whatever crime is committed when a disk is stolen is the same when a computer is the subject of the theft.

Theft of Software   When someone takes software, whether in the form of a program written on paper or a program on a disk or tape, a situation arises that does not fit common-law larceny because larceny covers only tangible property. Under this traditional concept of property, the intangible value of a software program would be ignored and the best charge that could be brought would be one of petty larceny. Now, however, virtually every state has amended its definition of larceny or theft so that stealing software is a crime. In some states, the unauthorized taking of information may constitute a crime under a trade secrets protection statute.

Intentional Damage   The computer may be the victim of a crime when it is intentionally destroyed or harmed. In the most elementary form of damage, the computer could be harmed if smashed with an ax or destroyed in an explosion or a fire. But the physical destruction is only one small part of the harm. The intent may actually be to cause the destruction of the information stored in the computer, a result with far greater financial implications and consequences for the computer owner.

Indeed, if the purpose is the destruction of software or the stored information on the computer, the simple act of gaining access to the hard drive or the files, without any physical destruction, is the criminal *actus reus* for this computer crime. Also, physical destruction can be accomplished without physical contact. For example, interfering with the air-conditioning needs for effective computer operation could result in computer malfunction, the loss of files, and perhaps even the future ability of the computer to process. The destruction occurs without touching the property, and specific statutes are needed to cover these types of acts that are committed with the intent of property destruction.

Intentionally planting a bug or virus in software, causing the program to malfunction, give incorrect output, or affect the hard drive and its content, is also conduct that fits under crimes to the computer itself. Even thought the virus or bug comes from outside the facility, the result is the same destruction or temporary disabling of the computer or its systems. For example, the 52,000 outside researchers hooked up to computers at NASA's Ames Center spent four to eight hours each month trying to determine whether their computers were infected with a virus. Their total time commitment in this task amounted to 142 person-years. The Melissa virus and the ILUVYOU virus that spread worldwide in just a day caused an estimated $3 billion damage to businesses.

Computer crime statutes in many states now make it a crime to damage software, computers, computer operations, or computer-stored information.

Computer Crimes That Involve Unauthorized Use of Computers

In contrast with conduct intended to harm a computer are the crimes that constitute the unlawful use of someone else's computer. There is no physical or program destruction. These crimes are committed by people who seek information and access. They do not wish to destroy the system. They want to use the system and the information in it for personal gain or advantage. In some states, the unlawful use of a computer is not a crime. Again, the traditional common-law crimes may not apply, and most states, as well as the federal government for its computers, have adopted statutes that make unauthorized use and access of computers a crime.

Computer Crimes That Involve Raiding for Information

A serious computer crime involves taking information from a computer without the consent of the owner of the information. Whether this is done by instructing the computer to make a printout of stored information or by tapping into the data bank of the computer by some electronic means is not important. In many instances, taking information from the computer constitutes the crime of stealing trade secrets. In some states, taking information is known as the crime of computer trespass.

Sometimes information is obtained from the printouts and receipts of computerized transactions. Scavenging is the name given to crimes perpetrated by collecting data from discarded materials. For example, ATM receipts can be recovered from trash bins, and the cardholder's account number and other printed information can then be used to acquire goods and services via computer.

Both Congress and state legislatures have adopted statutes that make it a crime to make any unauthorized use of a computer or to gain unauthorized access to a computer or the information stored in its database in order to cause harm to the computer or its rightful user.

Computer Crimes That Divert Delivery

In many industries, deliveries are controlled by a computer. The person in charge of that computer or someone who gains unlawful access may cause the computer to direct delivery to an improper place. That is, instead of shipping goods to the customers to whom they should go, the wrongdoer diverts the goods to a different place, where they will be received by the wrongdoer or a confederate.

In precomputer days, written orders were sent from the sales department to the shipping department. The shipping department would then send the ordered goods to the proper places. If the person in the sales department or the person in the shipping department was dishonest, either one could divert the goods from the proper destination. Today, this fraudulent diversion of goods may be effected by instructing the computer to give false directions. Basically, the crime has not changed. The computer is merely the new instrument by which the old crime is committed. This old crime has taken on a new social significance because of the amazingly large dollar value of the theft accomplished by means of it. In one case, several hundred loaded freight cars were made to disappear. In another case, a loaded oil tanker was diverted to unload into a fleet of tank trucks operated by an accomplice of the computer operator.

The crime of diverted delivery is not limited to goods. Diverted delivery can involve transferring money from a proper account to a wrong account. Computers can divert millions of dollars in a single criminal act. For example, a popular form of financial computer crime is the salami technique. In a bank computer system, changes can be made randomly to reduce accounts by a few cents and then transfer that money to one account from which the person who has changed the system can make a legitimate withdrawal. Because the reductions are so small and spread over so many accounts, those affected are unlikely to report any problems. The salami technique has also been used effectively in businesses with programs covering large amounts of inventory of various kinds. Small amounts of inventory are transferred to warehouses or fictitious firms. The employee making these changes in the system can then embezzle these inventory items.

The case of diverted delivery by computer does not require any new law because the appropriation of goods or money improperly delivered comes within the larceny-theft-embezzlement spectrum of crime. Statutes or courts may impose more severe penalties in these cases because of the huge dollar values involved.

Using Computers to Commit Economic Espionage

The Economic Espionage Act (EEA) is a federal law[5] passed in response to several cases in which high-level executives were taking downloaded proprietary information from their computers to their new employers. In one case, an executive was accused of taking General Motors' full plan for supply chain management in Europe. The EEA makes it a felony to steal, appropriate, or take a trade secret and also makes it a felony to copy, duplicate, sketch, draw, photograph, download, upload, alter, destroy, replicate, transmit, deliver, send, mail, or communicate a trade secret. The penalties for EEA violations are up to $500,000 and fifteen years in prison for individuals and $10 million for organizations. When employees take new positions with another company, their former employers are permitted to check the departing employees' computer e-mails and hard drives to determine whether the employees have engaged in computer espionage.

Using Computers to Commit Electronic Fund Transfer Crimes

The Electronic Fund Transfers Act (EFTA)[6] makes it a crime to use any counterfeit, stolen, or fraudulently obtained card, code, or other device to obtain money or goods in excess of a specified amount through an electronic fund transfer system. The EFTA also makes it a crime to ship in interstate commerce devices or goods so obtained or to knowingly receive goods that have been obtained by means of the fraudulent use of the transfer system.

Using Computers to Circumvent Copyright Protection Devices

The Digital Millennium Copyright Act (DMCA) (discussed further in Chapter 8) makes it a federal offense to circumvent or create programs to circumvent encryption devices that copyright holders place on copyrighted material to prevent unauthorized copying. For example, circumventing the encryption devices on software or CDs would be a violation of the DMCA. Dmitry Sklyarov, a Russian computer programmer, became the first person charged with a violation of DMCA. Mr. Sklyarov was arrested in early 2002 at a computer show after giving a speech on the product he developed that permits the circumvention of security devices on copyrighted materials. Specifically, his program unlocks password-protected eBooks and PDF files. He gave his speech in Las Vegas at the Defcon convention, a convention billed as "the largest hacker convention on the planet." He was returned to Russia in exchange for his agreement to testify in a case that will determine the constitutionality of the DMCA. The issues that will be tried in the case include the DMCA's interpretation as well as the issue of fair use and the right of individuals to copy materials for use in their own homes, including the right to use devices and programs that circumvent encryption devices.

Using Computer Access for Unauthorized Advertising: Spamming

Spamming, or the practice of sending out thousands of e-mails at once to many different computer users, is an ever-increasing problem. As noted in Chapter 8, the issues involved include First Amendment rights, privacy, and theft of property. Congress passed the **Controlling the Assault of Non-Solicited Pornography and Marketing (CAN-SPAM)** Act, which ordered the FTC to create a national do-not-e-mail list for e-mail marketers similar to the current do-not-call list that the FTC developed for consumers to use as a barrier for telemarketers. The FTC Chairman informed Congress that the FTC would not be developing such a list because it felt that spammers would use the national list to send more e-mail to individuals. Under CAN-SPAM, private companies can bring suit against spammers for their unauthorized use of ISPs. Microsoft filed suit against eight spammers under CAN-SPAM in January 2004. The suit alleges that the spammers sent millions of e-mails advertising everything from prescription drugs to dating services to products touted to enlarge body parts.

An industry group called the Anti-spam Technical Alliance has been formed and has endorsed several e-mail authentication technologies. Another of the group's proposals is to have ISPs limit outgoing e-mail traffic for each account. The group also endorses the Register of Known Spam Operations (ROKSO), operated by the Spamhaus Project. Under CAN-SPAM, the FTC is also authorized to bring suit against spammers, and it has brought two such complaints against spamming companies. Some states have made it a misdemeanor to send out e-mails with a misleading title line; Virginia was the first state to make spamming a criminal act. Under the Virginia statute, spamming becomes a felony when the volume of spam e-mails sent exceeds 10,000 in 24 hours, 100,000 in 30 days, or 1 million in one year.

CONSIDER...   9.6

In each of the following scenarios, determine which computer crimes were committed. The first scenario walks through a process you can use.

Selling Lists to Spammers

A software engineer at America Online was arrested on June 30, 2004, and charged with stealing AOL's subscriber list and selling it to a spammer. Jason Smathers entered AOL's computer system to steal a list of 92 million AOL customer account screen names and then sold them to Sean Dunaway, who is not an AOL employee. Mr. Dunaway then used the list to send e-mails for his Internet gambling business. Mr. Dunaway also sold the list to other spammers for $52,000. According to the charges, Mr. Dunaway paid Mr. Smathers $100,000 for the AOL customer list. AOL fired Mr. Smathers. What computer crimes were committed?

THINK: Refer back to the descriptions of computer crimes. Think of all the steps Mr. Smathers took.
- He took the screen names. (The list was AOL proprietary information, and the e-mail addresses were private, belonging to the AOL members, and could be released and used properly only with their permission.)
- He sold the information to someone outside AOL.
- Mr. Dunaway sent spam with the lists.
- Mr. Dunaway transferred the list to others.

APPLY: The possible crimes are unauthorized use by Mr. Smathers, theft of software, and raiding.

ANSWER: Both Mr. Smathers and Mr. Dunaway violated CAN-SPAM.

Now use the same process to apply the law to the following scenarios.

Creating Viruses

David L. Smith was charged with creating the Melissa virus that infiltrated computers worldwide in spring 1999, causing millions of dollars in damage. New Jersey state prosecutors charged Mr. Smith with interruption of public communication, theft of computer services, and wrongful access to computer systems. While there were federal crimes with which Mr. Smith could be charged, federal prosecutors deferred to the New Jersey authorities because the crimes carried a possible fine of $480,000 and/or forty years.

Mr. Smith had long been fascinated with hackers and viruses. He created the Melissa virus, named after a topless dancer he had met in Florida, as part of an e-mail attachment that, when opened, automatically spread to fifty other e-mail users. What computer crimes would Mr. Smith be charged with?

Violating Software Copyrights

David LaMacchia, a twenty-one-year-old student at the Massachusetts Institute of Technology (MIT) and a computer hacker, used MIT's computer network to gain entrance to the Internet. Using pseudonyms and an encrypted address, LaMacchia set up an electronic bulletin board, which he named Cynosure. He encouraged his correspondents to upload popular software applications (Excel 5.0 and WordPerfect 6.0) and computer games (Sim City 2000). These he transferred to a second encrypted address (Cynosure II), where they could be downloaded by other users with access to the Cynosure password. The worldwide traffic generated by the offer of free software attracted the notice of university and federal authorities.

On April 7, 1994, a federal grand jury returned a one-count indictment charging Mr. LaMacchia with conspiring with "persons unknown" to violate 18 U.S.C. § 1343, the wire fraud statute. According to the indictment, Mr. LaMacchia devised a scheme to defraud that had as its object the facilitation "on an international scale" of the "illegal copying and distribution of copyrighted software" without payment of licensing fees and royalties to software manufacturers and vendors. The indictment alleged that Mr. LaMacchia's scheme caused losses of more than $1 million to software copyright holders. The indictment did not allege that Mr. LaMacchia sought or derived any personal benefit from the scheme to defraud. What computer crimes could Mr. LaMacchia be charged with? [*U.S.* v. *LaMacchia*, 871 F. Supp. 535 (D. Mass. 1994).]

Some Specific Computer Crime Statutes

In addition to the general references to computer crimes discussed earlier, there are some specific well-known statutes often used for fighting computer crime.

Explore the Berne Convention for the Protection of Literary and Artistic Works (Paris text 1971):

http://www.law.cornell.edu/ treaties/berne/overview.html

International Conventions on Computer Crime The Berne (copyright) and Paris Conventions have provisions that permit businesses in member countries to obtain international copyright protection for their software products. Fifty-nine nations are members of one or more of the conventions (see Chapter 16).

Review the Copyright Act of 1976, as amended (1994):

http://www4.law.cornell. edu/uscode/17/index.html

Counterfeit Access Device and Computer Fraud and Abuse Act In 1984, Congress passed the Counterfeit Access Device and Computer Fraud and Abuse Act (CADCFA). This act makes it a federal crime to use or access federal or private computers without authorization in several types of situations. The CADCFA was amended in 1994 to cover additional new technologies, such as scanners, handheld computers, and laptops.

CADCFA prohibits unauthorized access to U.S. military or foreign policy information, FDIC financial institutions' data, or any government agency computer. For example, in *Sawyer* v. *Department of the Air Force,* 31 MPSR 193 (1986), a federal employee was terminated from his position for tampering with Air Force invoices and payments. Penalties under CADCFA range from five to twenty-one years' imprisonment.

Review the Counterfeit Access Device and Computer Fraud and Abuse Act:

http://www.law.cornell.edu/ uscode/18/1001.html

Federal Computer Fraud and Abuse Act The Federal Computer Fraud and Abuse Act (CFAA) classifies unauthorized access to a government computer as a felony and trespass into a federal government computer as a misdemeanor. CFAA covers "intentional" and "knowing" acts and includes a section that makes it a felony to cause more than $1,000 damage to a computer or its data through a virus program.

No Electronic Theft Act Passed at the end of 1997, this federal law makes it a criminal offense to willfully infringe copyrighted material worth over $1,000 using the Internet or other electronic devices even when the infringer does not profit from the use of the material. For example, many Internet users clip articles from subscriber services on the Internet and then send them along via e-mail to nonsubscriber friends. There is no transaction for profit, but the transfer of such copyrighted material is considered a violation of this federal law nonetheless. The act was lobbied for by the software and entertainment industries and was opposed by scientific and academic groups.

Economic Espionage Act   As mentioned earlier, the EEA, effective January 1, 1997, makes it a criminal offense to steal trade secrets from an employer. EEA includes fines of up to $500,000 for individuals and $5 million for corporations, as well as up to fifteen years in prison and possible property forfeitures. The EEA makes it a crime for employees to copy, download, or transmit in any fashion trade secrets of their employer. The EEA is largely the result of the Volkswagen/General Motors case in which an executive with General Motors was sued for allegedly taking proprietary information about General Motors's supply chain management system in its European operations for use in his new position with Volkswagen.

Criminal Fraud

Business crimes against individuals usually result from sales transactions. **Criminal fraud** is an example of this type of crime, the elements of which are the same as those the person defrauded would use to establish a contract defense: There was a false statement; the statement was material—that is, it was the type of information that would affect the buying decision; and there was reliance on the statement. The only differences between contract fraud and criminal fraud is that criminal fraud requires proof of intent that the seller intended to mislead the buyer for the purpose of effecting the transaction and making money. In most of the savings and loans cases in which charges were brought, fraud charges were included because often documents and appraisals were forged or falsified. Forgery provides proof of the level of intent needed for criminal fraud.

Commercial Bribery—Roots of Law and Commerce

Most states have provisions that govern both the giving and receiving of gifts or funds in exchange for a contract or favor. A supplier offering a purchasing agent of a company $25,000 in cash as an incentive or reward for choosing that supplier has committed commercial bribery. The purchasing agent has betrayed his employer's interest and compromised his judgment by accepting benefits for himself. This condemnation of bribery in commercial transactions dates back to the first eras of business activity because of concerns that quality and pricing would suffer if corruption was introduced into the bargaining process.

Racketeer Influenced and Corrupt Organizations (RICO) Act

Explore the Racketeer Influenced and Corrupt Organizations Act:
http://www.law.cornell.edu/ uscode/18/1961.html

The RICO Act (18 U.S.C. Sections 1961–1968), a complex federal statute, was passed with the intent of curbing organized crime activity. The ease of proof and severity of penalties for RICO violations have made it a popular charge in criminal cases in which organized crime may not actually be involved.

For RICO to apply, it must be established that there has been a "pattern of racketeering activity." That pattern is defined as the commission of at least two racketeering acts within a ten-year period. Racketeering acts are defined under the federal

ETHICAL ISSUES

Jim G. Locklear was a purchasing agent. His spectacular career as a buyer began in 1977 with Federated Stores in Dallas, Texas. Federated officers described him as a man with an eye for fashion and a keen ability to negotiate. In 1987, Mr. Locklear was offered a position with Jordan Marsh, in the Boston area, with an annual salary of $96,000.

Citing a desire to return to Dallas, Mr. Locklear left the Jordan Marsh position after only three months. He returned to Dallas as a buyer for J. C. Penney at an annual salary of $56,000. Mr. Locklear did a phenomenal job as the buyer for the J. C. Penney Home Collection. Penney was the first department store to feature coordinated lines of dinnerware, flatware, and glasses. Under Mr. Locklear's purchasing, annual sales in Penney's tabletop line went from $25 million to $45 million.

Based on an anonymous tip, Penney hired an investigator to look into Mr. Locklear's conduct. The investigator found and reported that Mr. Locklear had personal financial difficulties. He had a $500,000 mortgage on his home and child support payments of $900 a month for four children from four previous marriages. Mr. Locklear also had a country club membership, luxury vehicles, and large securities accounts; he was known to take vacations at posh resorts. Despite this puzzling lifestyle revealed by the investigator, Penney took no action.

In 1992, Penney received an anonymous letter disclosing a kickback situation between Mr. Locklear and a manufacturer's representative. Penney investigated a second time, referred the case for criminal prosecution, and filed a civil suit against Mr. Locklear.

The investigation conducted by authorities found that Mr. Locklear received payments from vendors through several corporations he had established. During the five-year period from 1987 to 1992, Mr. Locklear had received $1.5 million from vendors, manufacturers' representatives, and others.

Mr. Locklear was charged with commercial bribery and entered into a plea agreement. Mr. Locklear also served as a witness for the prosecution of those who paid him the bribes. A vendor described his payment of a $25,000 fee to Mr. Locklear as follows: "It was either pay it or go out of business." Mr. Locklear was sentenced to eighteen months in federal prison, less than the five-year maximum, due to his cooperation.

Should Penney have known of the difficulties earlier? Was Mr. Locklear's personal life responsible for his poor value choices at work? Is anyone really harmed by Mr. Locklear's activity? Wasn't he a good buyer?

---

statute to include murder; kidnapping; gambling; arson; robbery; bribery; extortion; dealing in pornography or narcotics; counterfeiting; embezzlement of pension, union, or welfare funds; mail fraud; wire fraud; obstruction of justice or criminal investigation; interstate transportation of stolen goods; white slavery; fraud in the sale of securities; and other acts relating to the Currency and Foreign Transactions Reporting Act (an act passed to prevent money laundering).

RICO provides for both criminal penalties and civil remedies. In a RICO civil suit, injured parties can recover treble damages, the cost of their suit, and reasonable attorney fees. According to the *Journal of Accountancy*, 91 percent of all RICO civil actions have been based on the listed pattern crimes of mail fraud, wire fraud, or fraud in the sale of securities. The statute has been used frequently against corporations. For example, Northwestern Bell Telephone Company lobbyists, who took public utility commissioners to dinner and hired two of them as consultants after they left their commission jobs, were sued under RICO. A lawyer representing phone company customers brought a RICO civil suit based on an alleged pattern of bribing the utility regulators [*H. J., Inc.* v. *Northwestern Bell Telephone Co.,* 492 U.S. 229 (1989)].

Another portion of the RICO statute permits prosecutors to freeze defendants' assets to prevent further crimes. When RICO charges are brought against corporations, the seizure of corporate assets can mean the termination of the business. The Justice Department has issued guidelines requiring prosecutors to seek a forfeiture of assets in proportion to the crime rather than seize all of the business assets. A growing number of states have enacted their own versions of the RICO statute for application at the state level. Some state RICO laws are specifically directed at narcotics, but over twenty include securities fraud as one of the covered acts.

CONSIDER... 9·7

Brigido Marmolejo Jr. and Mario Salinas, the former sheriff and chief deputy sheriff, respectively, of Hidalgo County, Texas, were convicted of various offenses arising from a series of bribes that Mr. Marmolejo received and Mr. Salinas aided and abetted in exchange for permitting conjugal visits for a federal prisoner, Homero Beltran-Aguirre, housed at the Hidalgo County Jail. The two operated the Hidalgo County Jail for local prisoners as well as under a contract with the U.S. Marshals Service for housing federal prisoners.

The bribes were paid during two different periods of incarceration of Mr. Beltran-Aguirre, from June 7, 1991, to April 14, 1992, and from November 6, 1992, to April 26, 1993. The federal prosecutor alleged the series of bribes comprised the pattern of racketeering charged in the indictment against Mr. Marmolejo and Mr. Salinas for RICO violations. The prosecutor also charged the two with money laundering. Mr. Marmolejo and Mr. Salinas were convicted, and they appealed, challenging the use of only federal crimes to establish a RICO violation. Are other kinds of underlying crimes required for RICO violation, or does violation of a federal statute satisfy the underlying crime requirement? Also, Mr. Marmolejo and Mr. Salinas appealed on the grounds that they were only local law enforcement officials and not involved in interstate commerce and therefore could not be charged with federal crimes. Are they correct? [*U.S. v. Marmolejo*, 89 F.3d 1185 (5th Cir. 1996).]

RICO violations have become added charges in many criminal cases. For example, if someone is charged with ongoing bribery of a state or local official, RICO charges can be added because of the pattern of corruption. Only one U.S. Supreme Court case has restricted RICO's application. In *Reves v. Ernst & Young*, 507 U.S. 170 (1993), the accounting firm of Arthur Young (later merged into Ernst & Young) was hired to conduct audits for the Farmer's Cooperative of Arkansas and Oklahoma. An investment by the coop in a gasohol plant proved to be a financial disaster, and the farmers who held coop notes that had served as the organization's means of financing over the years lost their investment when the coop filed for bankruptcy. The investors filed suit against Arthur Young for violations of federal securities laws (see Chapter 22) and RICO. However, the Supreme Court exempted the accounting firm from RICO charges because it found that the firm did not participate in the management of the coop. The auditor's participation was not that of directing the coop's affairs, only that of offering its opinions on the financial statements of the firm. The case represents one of the few restrictions on RICO application.

Over the past few years, businesses have been lobbying very heavily for reforms to the broad civil and criminal liabilities created by RICO. It seems unlikely that Congress will change the rights of plaintiffs to bring treble damage suits under the act's protective and deterrent mechanisms.

Business Crime and the USA Patriot Act

Prior to September 11, 2001, the federal government had the Money Laundering Control Act, 42 U.S.C. § 5301, that prohibited the knowing and willful participation in any type of financial transaction that was set up in order to conceal or disguise the source of funds. However, investigations into the backgrounds of those who had flown the planes that destroyed the World Trade Center and a portion of the Pentagon revealed intricate financial networks in which the sources of their funds were concealed through various business transactions in different types of industries. As a result, provisions of the USA Patriot Act, passed less than two months after the September 11 destruction, include substantial expansion of the Money Laundering Control Act as well as the Bank Secrecy Act. Under these changes, title and escrow companies; brokerage firms; travel agents; check-cashing firms; auto, plane, and boat dealers; branches of foreign banks located in the United States; and many other businesses are subject to disclosure and reporting requirements for transactions involving cash or more than $10,000 in transfers. In addition, the types of accounts covered under the disclosure requirements include not just savings accounts but also money market savings and brokerage accounts. With these changes, very few financial institutions are exempt from reporting and disclosure requirements for cash transactions.

Businesses affected by these amendments must develop new policies and procedures for preventing and detecting money laundering. Under the Federal Sentencing Guidelines, businesses subject to these anti–money laundering provisions must have a "Know Thy Customer" program that trains employees in how to spot money laundering and suspicious activities by customers.

Federal Crimes

Many of the statutes on business crimes are found at the federal level. Violations of the Securities Exchange Acts (Chapter 22), the Sherman Act (Chapter 17), the Internal Revenue Act, the Pure Food and Drug Act, the environmental statutes (Chapter 12), the Occupational Safety and Health Act (Chapter 19), and Consumer Product Safety statutes (Chapter 11) carry criminal penalties.

State Crimes

Similar criminal statutes at the state level cover such areas as criminal fraud and securities. In addition, states have particular regulations and laws for certain industries. The sale of liquor in most states is strictly regulated. The result is that there are many incidents of bribes and kickbacks in these highly regulated industries as businesses try to work around the regulatory restrictions. Since 2002, the state attorneys general have been very active in white-collar financial crimes. Eliot Spitzer (profiled in the Biography in Chapter 1) is feared in the business community for his use of state criminal fraud, embezzlement, and larceny statutes against corporations and executives.

PROCEDURAL RIGHTS FOR BUSINESS CRIMINALS

Business criminals are treated the same procedurally as other criminals. They have the same rights under the criminal justice system. The U.S. Constitution guarantees protection of certain rights. The **Fourth Amendment** protects the individual's privacy and is the basis for requiring warrants for searches of private property. The **Fifth Amendment** provides the protection against self-incrimination and is also the "due process" amendment, which guarantees that an accused individual has the right to be heard. The **Sixth Amendment** is meant to ensure a speedy trial; it is the basis for the requirement that criminal proceedings and trials proceed in a timely fashion. These constitutional rights are discussed in the following sections.

Fourth Amendment Rights for Businesses

The Fourth Amendment to the U.S. Constitution provides that "the right of the people to be secure in their persons, houses, papers, and effects, against unreasonable searches and seizures, shall not be violated." This amendment protects individual privacy by preventing unreasonable searches and seizures. Before a government

For more information on technology developing in this field, visit:
http://www.nlectc.org/

agency can seize the property of individuals or businesses, there must be a valid **search warrant**—or an applicable exception to the warrant requirement—which must be issued by a judge or magistrate and must be based on probable cause. In other words, there must be good reason to believe that instruments or evidence of a crime are present at the business location to be searched. The Fourth Amendment applies equally to individuals and corporations. In an unauthorized search, a corporation's property is given the same protection. If an improper search is conducted (without a warrant and without meeting an exception), any evidence recovered is inadmissible at trial for the purposes of proving the crime. *Kyllo* v. *U.S.* (Case 9.5) deals with the issues of privacy, warrants, and evolving technology for observation.

CASE 9.5

Kyllo v. *U.S.*
533 U.S. 27 (2001)

Thermal Marijuana Dynamics

FACTS

In 1991 Agent William Elliott of the United States Department of the Interior came to suspect that marijuana was being grown in the home belonging to Danny Kyllo (petitioner), part of a triplex on Rhododendron Drive in Florence, Oregon. Indoor marijuana growth typically requires high-intensity lamps. In order to determine whether an amount of heat was emanating from the petitioner's home consistent with the use of such lamps, at 3:20 A.M. on January 16, 1992, Agent Elliott and Dan Haas used an Agema Thermovision 210 thermal imager to scan the triplex.

Thermal imagers detect infrared radiation, which virtually all objects emit but which is not visible to the naked eye. The imager converts radiation into images based on relative warmth—black is cool, white is hot, shades of gray connote relative differences; in that respect, it operates somewhat like a video camera showing heat images.

The scan of Mr. Kyllo's home took only a few minutes and was performed from the passenger seat of Agent Elliott's vehicle across the street from the front of the house and also from the street in back of the house. The scan showed that the roof over the garage and a side wall of Mr. Kyllo's home were relatively hot compared to the rest of the home and substantially warmer than neighboring homes in the triplex. Agent Elliott concluded that Mr. Kyllo was using halide lights to grow marijuana in his house, which indeed he was. Based on tips from informants, utility bills, and the thermal imaging, a federal magistrate judge issued a warrant authorizing a search of Mr. Kyllo's home, and the agents found an indoor growing operation involving more than 100 plants. Mr. Kyllo was indicted on one count of manufacturing marijuana.

Mr. Kyllo unsuccessfully moved to suppress the evidence seized from his home and then entered a conditional guilty plea.

The Court of Appeals for the Ninth Circuit remanded the case for an evidentiary hearing regarding the intrusiveness of thermal imaging. On remand the District Court upheld the validity of the warrant that relied in part upon the thermal imaging and reaffirmed its denial of the motion to suppress. A divided Court of Appeals initially reversed, but that opinion was withdrawn and the panel affirmed. Mr. Kyllo appealed.

JUDICIAL OPINION

SCALIA, Justice

This case presents the question whether the use of a thermal-imaging device aimed at a private home from a public street to detect relative amounts of heat within the home constitutes a "search" within the meaning of the Fourth Amendment.

The Fourth Amendment provides that "[t]he right of the people to be secure in their persons, houses, papers, and effects, against unreasonable searches and seizures, shall not be violated." "At the very core" of the Fourth Amendment "stands the right of a man to retreat into his own home and there be free from unreasonable governmental intrusion." With few exceptions, the question whether a warrantless search of a home is reasonable and hence constitutional must be answered no.

On the other hand, the antecedent question of whether or not a Fourth Amendment "search" has occurred is not so simple under our precedent. The permissibility of ordinary visual surveillance of a home used to be clear because, well into the 20th century, our Fourth Amendment jurisprudence was tied to common-law trespass. Visual surveillance was unquestionably lawful because " 'the eye cannot by the laws of England be guilty of a trespass.' " We have since decoupled violation of a person's Fourth Amendment rights from trespassory violation of his property, but the lawfulness of warrantless visual surveillance of a home has still been preserved. "[T]he Fourth Amendment protection of the home has never been extended to require law enforcement officers to shield their eyes when passing by a home on public thoroughfares."

In assessing when a search is not a search, we have applied somewhat in reverse the principle first enunciated in *Katz* v. *United States*, 389 U.S. 347, 88 S.Ct. 507, 19 L.Ed.2d 576 (1967). *Katz* involved eavesdropping by means of an electronic listening device placed on the outside of a telephone booth—a location not within the catalog ("persons, houses, papers, and effects") that the Fourth Amendment protects against unreasonable searches. We held that the Fourth Amendment nonetheless protected Katz from the warrantless eavesdropping because he "justifiably relied" upon the privacy of the telephone booth. As Justice Harlan's oft-quoted concurrence described it, a Fourth Amendment search occurs when the government violates a subjective expectation of privacy that society recognizes as reasonable.

We have applied this test in holding that it is not a search for the police to use a pen register at the phone company to determine what numbers were dialed in a private home, and we have applied the test on two different occasions in holding that aerial surveillance of private homes and surrounding areas does not constitute a search.

The present case involves officers on a public street engaged in more than naked-eye surveillance of a home. We have previously reserved judgment as to how much technological enhancement of ordinary perception from such a vantage point, if any, is too much. While we upheld enhanced aerial photography of an industrial complex in *Dow Chemical* [see Case 9.6], we noted that we found "it important that this is not an area immediately adjacent to a private home, where privacy expectations are most heightened, . . ."

It would be foolish to contend that the degree of privacy secured to citizens by the Fourth Amendment has been entirely unaffected by the advance of technology. For example, as the cases discussed above make clear, the technology enabling human flight has exposed to public view (and hence, we have said, to official observation) uncovered portions of the house and its curtilage that once were private. The question we confront today is what limits there are upon this power of technology to shrink the realm of guaranteed privacy.

While it may be difficult to refine *Katz* when the search of areas such as telephone booths, automobiles, or even the curtilage and uncovered portions of residences are at issue, in the case of the search of the interior of homes—the prototypical and hence most commonly litigated area of protected privacy—there is a ready criterion, with roots deep in the common law, of the minimal expectation of privacy that exists, and that is acknowledged to be reasonable. To withdraw protection of this minimum expectation would be to permit police technology to erode the privacy guaranteed by the Fourth Amendment. We think that obtaining by sense-enhancing technology any information regarding the interior of the home that could not otherwise have been obtained without physical "intrusion into a constitutionally protected area," constitutes a search—at least where (as here) the technology in question is not in general public use. This assures preservation of that degree of privacy against government that existed when the Fourth Amendment was adopted. On the basis of this criterion, the information obtained by the thermal imager in this case was the product of a search. The dissent's comparison of the thermal imaging to various circumstances in which outside observers might be able to perceive, without technology, the heat of the home—for example, by observing snowmelt on the roof, is quite irrelevant. The fact that equivalent information could sometimes be obtained by other means does not make lawful the use of means that violate the Fourth Amendment. The police might, for example, learn how many people are in a particular house by setting up year-round surveillance; but that does not make breaking and entering to find out the same information lawful. In any event, on the night of January 16, 1992, no outside observer could have discerned the relative heat of Kyllo's home without thermal imaging.

The Government maintains, however, that the thermal imaging must be upheld because it detected "only heat radiating from the external surface of the house." The dissent makes this its leading point, contending that there is a fundamental difference between what it calls "off-the-wall" observations and "through-the-wall surveillance." But just as a thermal imager captures only heat emanating from a house, so also a powerful directional microphone picks up only sound emanating from a house—and a satellite capable of scanning from many miles away would pick up only visible light emanating from a house. We rejected such a mechanical interpretation of the Fourth Amendment in *Katz*, where the eavesdropping device picked up only sound waves that reached the exterior of the phone booth. Reversing that approach would leave the homeowner at the mercy of advancing technology—including imaging technology that could discern all human activity in the home. While the technology

continued

used in the present case was relatively crude, the rule we adopt must take account of more sophisticated systems that are already in use or in development. The dissent's reliance on the distinction between "off-the-wall" and "through-the-wall" observation is entirely incompatible with the dissent's belief that thermal-imaging observations of the intimate details of a home are impermissible.

The Government also contends that the thermal imaging was constitutional because it did not "detect private activities occurring in private areas." It points out that in *Dow Chemical* we observed that the enhanced aerial photography did not reveal any "intimate details." *Dow Chemical*, however, involved enhanced aerial photography of an industrial complex, which does not share the Fourth Amendment sanctity of the home. The Fourth Amendment's protection of the home has never been tied to measurement of the quality or quantity of information.

Limiting the prohibition of thermal imaging to "intimate details" would not only be wrong in principle; it would be impractical in application, failing to provide "a workable accommodation between the needs of law enforcement and the interests protected by the Fourth Amendment." To begin with, there is no necessary connection between the sophistication of the surveillance equipment and the "intimacy" of the details that it observes—which means that one cannot say (and the police cannot be assured) that use of the relatively crude equipment at issue here will always be lawful. The Agema Thermovision 210 might disclose, for example, at what hour each night the lady of the house takes her daily sauna and bath—a detail that many would consider "intimate"; and a much more sophisticated system might detect nothing more intimate than the fact that someone left a closet light on. We could not, in other words, develop a rule approving only that through-the-wall surveillance which identifies objects no smaller than 36 by 36 inches, but would have to develop a jurisprudence specifying which home activities are "intimate" and which are not. And even when (if ever) that jurisprudence were fully developed, no police officer would be able to know in advance whether

his through-the-wall surveillance picks up "intimate" details—and thus would be unable to know in advance whether it is constitutional.

We have said that the Fourth Amendment draws "a firm line at the entrance to the house." That line, we think, must be not only firm but also bright—which requires clear specification of those methods of surveillance that require a warrant. While it is certainly possible to conclude from the videotape of the thermal imaging that occurred in this case that no "significant" compromise of the homeowner's privacy has occurred, we must take the long view, from the original meaning of the Fourth Amendment forward.

Where, as here, the Government uses a device that is not in general public use, to explore details of the home that would previously have been unknowable without physical intrusion, the surveillance is a "search" and is presumptively unreasonable without a warrant.

Since we hold the Thermovision imaging to have been an unlawful search, it will remain for the District Court to determine whether, without the evidence it provided, the search warrant issued in this case was supported by probable cause—and if not, whether there is any other basis for supporting admission of the evidence that the search pursuant to the warrant produced.

Reversed.

CASE QUESTIONS

1. Describe how the federal agents were able to obtain a warrant to search Mr. Kyllo's home.

2. What is the general rule on searches of the home?

3. What does the court see as the difference between thermal scanning and observing patches of snow on a roof with some areas showing more melting than others?

4. Was the use of thermal scanning a search? Was it an invasion of privacy?

5. What does the court say about the issue of the method of invasion of privacy?

Exceptions to the warrant requirement are based on emergency grounds. For example, if an office building with relevant records is burning, government agents could enter the property without a warrant to recover the papers. Similarly, if the records are being destroyed, the government need not wait for a warrant. Another exception to the warrant requirement is the "plain view" exception. This exception allows police officers to seize evidence that is within their view. No privacy rights are violated when evidence is exposed to the view of others. The *Dow Chemical Co. v. U.S.* case (9.6) deals with a business issue and the Fourth Amendment exception.

CASE 9.6

Dow Chemical Co. v. *United States*
476 U.S. 1819 (1986)

Low-Flying Federal Agents: Photographic Searches

FACTS

Dow Chemical (petitioner) operates a two-thousand-acre chemical plant at Midland, Michigan. The facility, with numerous buildings, conduits, and pipes, is visible from the air. Dow has maintained ground security at the facility and has investigated fly-overs by other, unauthorized aircraft. However, none of the buildings or manufacturing equipment is concealed.

In 1978, the Environmental Protection Agency (EPA) conducted an inspection of Dow. EPA requested a second inspection, but Dow denied the request. The EPA then employed a commercial aerial photographer to take photos of the plant from 12,000, 3,000, and 1,200 feet. The EPA had no warrant, but the plane was always within navigable air space when the photos were taken.

When Dow became aware of the EPA photographer, it brought suit in federal district court and challenged the action as a violation of its Fourth Amendment rights. The district court found that the EPA had violated Dow's rights and issued an injunction prohibiting the further use of the aircraft. The court of appeals reversed, and Dow appealed.

JUDICIAL OPINION

BURGER, Chief Justice

The photographs at issue in this case are essentially like those used in map-making. Any person with an airplane and an aerial camera could readily duplicate them. In common with much else, the technology of photography has changed in this century. These developments have enhanced industrial processes, and indeed all areas of life; they have also enhanced enforcement techniques. Whether they may be employed by competitors to penetrate trade secrets is not a question presented in this case. Governments do not generally seek to appropriate trade secrets of the private sector, and the right to be free of appropriation of trade secrets is protected by law.

That such photography might be barred by state law with regard to competitors, however, is irrelevant to the questions presented here. State tort law governing unfair competition does not define the limits of the Fourth Amendment. The Government is seeking these photographs in order to regulate, not compete with, Dow.

Dow claims first the EPA has no authority to use aerial photography to implement its statutory authority of "site inspection" under the Clean Air Act.

Congress has vested in EPA certain investigatory and enforcement authority, without spelling out precisely how this authority was to be exercised in all the myriad circumstances that might arise in monitoring matters relating to clean air and water standards.

Regulatory or enforcement authority generally carries with it all the modes of inquiry and investigation traditionally employed or useful to execute the authority granted. Environmental standards cannot be enforced only in libraries and laboratories, helpful as those institutions may be.

The EPA, as a regulatory and enforcement agency, needs no explicit statutory provisions to employ methods of observation commonly available to the public at large; we hold that the use of aerial photography is within the EPA's statutory authority.

DISSENTING OPINION

POWELL, MARSHALL, BRENNAN, and BLACKMUN, Justices

The Fourth Amendment protects private citizens from arbitrary surveillance by their Government. Today, in the context of administrative aerial photography of commercial premises, the Court retreats from that standard. It holds that the photography was not a Fourth Amendment "search" because it was not accompanied by a physical trespass and because the equipment used was not the most highly sophisticated form of technology available to the Government. Under this holding the existence of an asserted privacy interest apparently will be decided solely by reference to the manner of surveillance used to intrude on that interest. Such an inquiry will not protect Fourth Amendment rights, but rather will permit their gradual decay as technology advances.

EPA's aerial photography penetrated into a private commercial enclave, an area in which society has recognized that privacy interests may legitimately be claimed. The photographs captured highly confidential information that Dow had taken reasonable and objective steps to preserve as private.

continued

CASE QUESTIONS

1. Of what significance is the fact that Dow's plant could be seen from the air?

2. Did Dow take any steps to protect its privacy?

3. Is the EPA specifically given aerial surveillance authority?

4. Did the EPA need a warrant for taking its aerial photographs?

5. What objections do the dissenting judges raise to the decision?

C O N S I D E R . . .   9 . 8

The IRS attached levies to the property and other assets of G.M. Leasing Corp. for non-payment of taxes. To satisfy the levy, the IRS seized several automobiles from the street in front of G.M.'s offices. Also, without a warrant, the IRS entered G.M.'s offices and seized business books and records. Has the Fourth Amendment been violated with the seizure of the cars? Of the books and records? [*G.M. Leasing Corp. v. United States,* 429 U.S. 338 (1977).]

In many business crimes, the records used to prosecute the defendant are not in the possession of the defendant. The records are, instead, in the hands of a third party, such as an accountant or a bank. Does the Fourth Amendment afford the defendant protection in documents that discuss the defendant or reflect the defendant's finances and transactions when those documents are in the hands of another? In some cases, there is a privilege between the third party and the defendants, and certain documents are protected and need not be turned over. Notes on trial strategy, audit procedures, and other plans and thoughts are not discoverable because such communications are privileged between lawyers and clients. Some states recognize an accountant-client privilege. The priest-parishioner privilege generally exists; however, there are exceptions in which reporting is required, such as in cases of abuse.

Fifth Amendment Rights for Businesses

The Fifth Amendment extends several protections to those facing criminal charges.

Self-Incrimination

The statement "I take the Fifth" is used so often that it has made the Fifth Amendment well known for its protection against self-incrimination. For example, Denise Rich took the Fifth Amendment when asked by both congressional committees and the U.S. Attorney's office in New York to explain her role in securing the presidential pardon for her ex-husband, Marc Rich. No one can be compelled to be a witness against herself. However, this protection applies only to natural persons; corporations are not given this privilege. A corporation cannot prevent the required disclosure of corporate books and records on grounds that they are incriminating.

Corporate officers cannot assert Fifth Amendment protection to prevent compulsory production of corporate records. Nor can corporate officers use the Fifth Amendment to prevent the production of corporate records on grounds that those records incriminate them personally. The rules applicable to corporate officers have been extended to apply to those involved in labor unions, close corporations, and even unincorporated associations. The same rule is applicable to sole shareholders of small corporations as well.

The FBI currently uses an Internet wiretapping system called Carnivore to conduct surveillance of Internet messages and activity. The American Civil Liberties Union says that such a device, even with a warrant, is a violation of the Fourth Amendment because the information and messages of those who are innocent are read by federal agents.

Technology has also facilitated wiretaps, and there were 1,350 authorized wiretaps in 1999, a 2 percent increase over 1998, a steady trend. However, Internet interception need only be authorized by an attorney and does not require a court order. Those seeking the interception need only show that the interception is related to the investigation.

Do you think there is a violation of privacy by Carnivore? Do you think warrants should be required? Why do you think wiretaps are treated differently from Internet interceptions?

Chapter 4 discusses the issues of attorney-client privilege and work product. Often, when a business is investigated for criminal activity, the issues all come together, as in *Upjohn Co.* v. *U.S.* (Case 9.7), the landmark case on the rights of corporate employees during a criminal investigation.

CASE 9.7

Upjohn Co. v. *United States*
449 U.S. 382 (1980)

The Upside and Downside of Internal Investigations

FACTS

Upjohn Company (petitioner) is a U.S. manufacturer and international seller of pharmaceuticals. In January 1976, independent auditors for the company notified Gerard Thomas, Upjohn's corporate secretary and general counsel, that they had discovered that an Upjohn subsidiary had made payments to foreign government officials in order to secure business for the company. Mr. Thomas, a member of the Michigan and New York bars, had been Upjohn's general counsel for twenty years.

After consulting with Upjohn's Chairman of the Board, Mr. Thomas began an internal investigation to determine whether "questionable payments" had been made. Mr. Thomas sent a memo to "All Foreign General and Area Managers" over the Chairman's signature and disclosed the "possibly illegal" payments and management's need for full information on any such payments made by Upjohn. Managers were asked to participate in an investigation to be conducted by "the company's General Counsel," to provide information on such payments, and to treat the information as "highly confidential."

Mr. Thomas received and compiled responses and interviewed thirty-three Upjohn officers and employees.

Mr. Thomas then submitted a voluntary report to the SEC disclosing certain questionable payments. A copy of the same report was also given to the IRS. The IRS began an investigation of the tax consequences of the payments and served Upjohn with a summons for:

> All files relative to the investigation conducted under the supervision of Gerard Thomas to identify payments to employees of foreign governments and any political contributions made by the Upjohn Company or any of its affiliates since January 1, 1971 and to determine whether any funds of the Upjohn Company had been improperly accounted for on the corporate books during the same period.
>
> The records should include but not be limited to written questionnaires sent to managers of the Upjohn Company's foreign affiliates, and memorandums or notes of the interviews conducted in the United States and abroad with officers and employees of the Upjohn Company and its subsidiaries.

Upjohn declined to turn over the documents requested in the summons on the grounds of attorney-client privilege and claims of work product. The U.S. filed a petition seeking enforcement of the summons.

continued

The District Court enforced the summons. The Court of Appeals found the work product claim not applicable and reversed the District Court's conclusion that the attorney-client privilege had been waived. Upjohn appealed.

JUDICIAL OPINION

REHNQUIST, Justice

Federal Rule of Evidence 501 provides that "the privilege of a witness . . . shall be governed by the principles of the common law as they may be interpreted by the courts of the United States in light of reason and experience." The attorney-client privilege is the oldest of the privileges for confidential communications known to the common law. Its purpose is to encourage full and frank communication between attorneys and their clients and thereby promote broader public interests in the observance of law and administration of justice. The privilege recognizes that sound legal advice or advocacy serves public ends and that such advice or advocacy depends upon the lawyer's being fully informed by the client.

The Court of Appeals, however, considered the application of the privilege in the corporate context to present a "different problem," since the client was an inanimate entity and "only the senior management, guiding and integrating the several operations, . . . can be said to possess an identity analogous to the corporation as a whole." The first case to articulate the so-called "control group test" adopted by the court below, *General Electric Co.* v. *Kirkpatrick,* 312 F. 2d 742 (CA3 1962) cert. denied, 372 U.S. 943 (1963), reflected a similar conceptual approach:

> Keeping in mind that the question is, Is it the corporation which is seeking the lawyer's advice when the asserted privileged communication is made?, the most satisfactory solution, I think, is that if the employee making the communication, of whatever rank he may be, is in a position to control or even to take a substantial part in a decision about any action which the corporation may take upon the advice of the attorney, . . . then, in effect, he is (or personifies) the corporation when he makes his disclosure to the lawyer and the privilege would apply.

Such a view, we think, overlooks the fact that the privilege exists to protect not only the giving of professional advice to those who can act on it but also the giving of information to the lawyer to enable him to give sound and informed advice.

In the case of the individual client the provider of information and the person who acts on the lawyer's advice are one and the same. In the corporate context, however, it will frequently be employees beyond the control group as defined by the court below—"officers and agents . . . responsible for directing [the company's] actions in response to legal advice"—who will possess the information needed by the corporation's lawyers. Middle-level—and indeed lower-level—employees can, by actions within the scope of their employment, embroil the corporation in serious legal difficulties, and it is only natural that these employees would have the relevant information needed by corporate counsel if he is adequately to advise the client with respect to such actual or potential difficulties.

The control group test adopted by the court below thus frustrates the very purpose of the privilege by discouraging the communication of relevant information by employees of the client to attorneys seeking to render legal advice to the client corporation. The attorney's advice will also frequently be more significant to noncontrol group members than to those who officially sanction the advice, and the control group test makes it more difficult to convey full and frank legal advice to the employees who will put into effect the client corporation's policy.

The narrow scope given the attorney-client privilege by the court below not only makes it difficult for corporate attorneys to formulate sound advice when their client is faced with a specific legal problem but also threatens to limit the valuable efforts of corporate counsel to ensure their client's compliance with the law. In light of the vast and complicated array of regulatory legislation confronting the modern corporation, corporations, unlike most individuals, "constantly go to lawyers to find out how to obey the law." . . .

But if the purpose of the attorney-client privilege is to be served, the attorney and client must be able to predict with some degree of certainty whether particular discussions will be protected. An uncertain privilege, or one which purports to be certain but results in widely varying applications by the courts, is little better than no privilege at all. The very terms of the test adopted by the court below suggest the unpredictability of its application. The test restricts the availability of the privilege to those officers who play a "substantial role" in deciding and directing a corporation's legal response. Disparate decisions in cases applying this test illustrate its unpredictability.

The communications at issue were made by Upjohn employees to counsel for Upjohn acting as such, at the direction of corporate superiors in order to secure legal advice from counsel. As the Magistrate found, "Mr. Thomas consulted with the Chairman of the Board and outside counsel and thereafter conducted a factual investigation to determine the nature and extent of the questionable payments *and to be in a position to give legal advice to the company with respect to the pay-*

ments." Information, not available from upper-echelon management, was needed to supply a basis for legal advice concerning compliance with securities and tax laws, foreign laws, currency regulations, duties to shareholders, and potential litigation in each of these areas. The communications concerned matters within the scope of the employees' corporate duties, and the employees themselves were sufficiently aware that they were being questioned in order that the corporation could obtain legal advice. The questionnaire identified Thomas as "the company's General Counsel" and referred in its opening sentence to the possible illegality of payments such as the ones on which information was sought.

The Court of Appeals declined to extend the attorney-client privilege beyond the limits of the control group test for fear that doing so would entail severe burdens on discovery and create a broad "zone of silence" over corporate affairs. Application of the attorney-client privilege to communications such as those involved here, however, puts the adversary in no worse position than if the communications had never taken place. The privilege only protects disclosure of communications; it does not protect disclosure of the underlying facts by those who communicated with the attorney.

Here the Government was free to question the employees who communicated with Thomas and outside counsel. Upjohn has provided the IRS with a list of such employees, and the IRS has already interviewed some twenty-five of them. While it would probably be more convenient for the Government to secure the results of petitioner's internal investigation by simply subpoenaing the questionnaires and notes taken by petitioner's attorneys, such considerations of convenience do not overcome the policies served by the attorney-client privilege. As Justice Jackson noted in his concurring opinion in *Hickman* v. *Taylor,* 329 U.S., at 516: "Discovery was hardly intended to enable a learned profession to perform its functions . . . on wits borrowed from the adversary."

Our decision that the communications by Upjohn employees to counsel are covered by the attorney-client privilege disposes of the case so far as the responses to the questionnaires and any notes reflecting responses to interview questions are concerned. The summons reaches further, however, and Thomas has testified that his notes and memoranda of interviews go beyond recording responses to his questions. To the extent that the material subject to the summons is not protected by the attorney-client privilege as disclosing communications between an employee and counsel, we must reach the ruling by the Court of Appeals that the work-product doctrine does not apply to summonses.

The Government concedes, wisely, that the Court of Appeals erred and that the work-product doctrine does apply to IRS summonses.

Rule 26 accords special protection to work product revealing the attorney's mental processes. The Rule permits disclosure of documents and tangible things constituting attorney work product upon a showing of substantial need and inability to obtain the equivalent without undue hardship. Rule 26 goes on, however, to state that "[i]n ordering discovery of such materials when the required showing has been made, the court shall protect against disclosure of the mental impressions, conclusions, opinions or legal theories of an attorney or other representative of a party concerning the litigation." Although this language does not specifically refer to memoranda based on oral statements of witnesses, the *Hickman* court stressed the danger that compelled disclosure of such memoranda would reveal the attorney's mental processes.

While we are not prepared at this juncture to say that such material is always protected by the work-product rule, we think a far stronger showing of necessity and unavailability by other means than was made by the Government or applied by the Magistrate in this case would be necessary to compel disclosure. Since the Court of Appeals thought that the work-product protection was never applicable in an enforcement proceeding such as this, and since the Magistrate whose recommendations the District Court adopted applied too lenient a standard of protection, we think the best procedure with respect to this aspect of the case would be to reverse the judgment of the Court of Appeals for the Sixth Circuit and remand the case to it for such further proceedings in connection with the work-product claim as are consistent with this opinion.

Accordingly, the judgment of the Court of Appeals is reversed, and the case remanded for further proceedings.

CASE QUESTIONS

1. What illegal activity was Upjohn investigating?
2. How did a criminal investigation start?
3. Why wasn't Upjohn charged with violations of the Foreign Corrupt Practices Act?
4. What is the difference between work-product protection and the attorney-client privilege?
5. What advice would you have for someone conducting an internal company investigation? What advice would you have for the employees involved?

Miranda *Rights*

The famous *Miranda* doctrine resulted from an interpretation of the Fifth Amendment by the U.S. Supreme Court in *Miranda* v. *Arizona*, 384 U.S. 436 (1966). ***Miranda* warnings** must be given to all people who are subjected to custodial interrogation. Custody does not necessarily mean "locked in jail," but it is generally based on an individual's perceptions of a situation. If a person feels he is without freedom to leave a place by choice, the level of custody at which *Miranda* rights must be issued has been reached. However, in *Missouri* v. *Seibert*, 124 S. Ct. 2601 (2004), the U.S. Supreme Court provided further clarification on when *Miranda* warnings must be given. A law enforcement official cannot coax a confession from an individual and then provide the warnings. If the individual then refuses to answer questions or offer the same information after the warnings are given, the law enforcement officials cannot use the prior confession, given before the warnings, as evidence in court. The warnings tell those in custody of their Fifth Amendment right to say nothing, as well as their right to an attorney. The failure to give *Miranda* warnings is not fatal to a case so long as the crime can be proved through evidence other than the statement of the defendant; the prosecution can still proceed based on other evidence.

Due Process Rights

The Fifth Amendment also contains due process language. The same language is found in the Fourteenth Amendment and made applicable to the states. **Due process**, as Chapters 5 and 6 discuss, means that no one can be convicted of a crime without the opportunity to be heard, to question witnesses, and to present evidence.

Due process in criminal proceedings guarantees certain procedural protections as a case is investigated, charged, and taken to trial. The Sixth Amendment complements due process rights by requiring that all these procedures be completed in a timely fashion. The following subsections discuss the basic steps in a criminal proceeding as diagrammed in Exhibit 9.3.

Warrant and/or Arrest   A criminal proceeding can begin when a crime is witnessed, as when a police officer attempts to apprehend a person who has just robbed a convenience store. When the convenience store is robbed but the robber escapes, and if the police can establish that a certain individual was probably responsible for the robbery, a **warrant** can be issued and the individual then arrested. Whether with or without a warrant, the due process steps begin with the arrest.

Initial Appearance   Once an arrest has been made, the defendant must have an opportunity to appear before a judicial figure within a short time period (usually twenty-four hours) to be informed of his charges, rights, and so on. This proceeding is generally referred to as an **initial appearance**. Dates for other proceedings are set at this time and, if the individual can be released, the terms of the release are also established. The individual may be required to post a bond to be released; others are held without release terms (release terms generally depend on the nature of the crime and the defendant). The terms *released on his own recognizance* and *released OR* mean the defendant is released without having to post a bond.

Preliminary Hearing or Grand Jury   Up to this step in the criminal proceedings, the defendant's charges are based on the word of a police officer; there has not yet

EXHIBIT 9.3 Steps in Criminal Proceedings

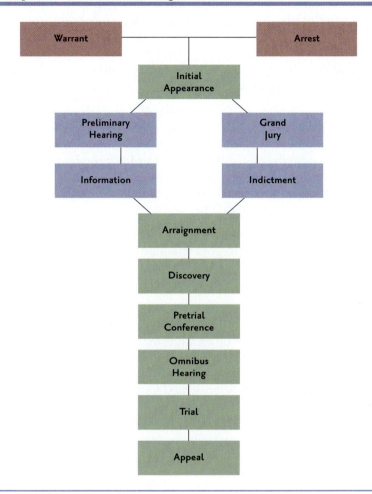

been any proof brought forth linking the crime and the defendant. The purpose of a preliminary hearing or grand jury proceeding is to require the prosecution to establish that there is some evidence that the defendant committed the crime.

In a **preliminary hearing**, the prosecution presents evidence to a judge to indicate that the accused committed the crime. The prosecution presents witnesses, and the defendant and the defendant's attorney are present for cross-examination of those witnesses. The defense does not present its case at this time but might make an offer of proof to show that the defendant could not have committed the crime. If the judge finds there is sufficient proof, an **information** is issued. The information is to a criminal proceeding what a complaint is to a civil proceeding: It establishes what the defendant did and when and what crimes were committed.

In some crimes, the evidence of the crime is presented to a **grand jury**, which is a panel of citizens who serve for a designated period of time (usually six months) and act as the body responsible for the review of evidence of crimes. If the grand jury finds that there is sufficient evidence that a crime was committed, it issues an **indictment**, which is similar to an information and serves the same function.

Grand jury proceedings are conducted secretly, whereas preliminary hearings are public. Grand juries also have the authority to conduct investigations to determine whether crimes were committed and who did so. Perhaps one of the most famous grand juries was the Washington, D.C., area grand jury that was investigating President Clinton and his wife Hillary for their involvement in a failed savings and loan and its assets. Mrs. Clinton is the only first lady to testify before a grand jury. Despite her public figure status, Mrs. Clinton's testimony remained a secret. In cases that are taken before a grand jury, the criminal process begins with an indictment followed by a warrant to arrest those charged.

The Arraignment   An **arraignment** is the proceeding at which the defendant enters a plea of guilty, not guilty, or no contest (***nolo contendere***). If a not guilty plea is entered, a date for trial is set. If the defendant enters a guilty or no contest plea, chances are the plea is the result of a **plea bargain**, which is the term used in criminal proceedings for a settlement. The defendant may plead guilty to a lesser offense in exchange for the prosecution's promise to support a lesser sentence, such as probation or minimum jail time.

Discovery   If a case is going to trial, there is a **discovery** period. Many states have mandatory criminal discovery laws that require each side to turn over certain types of information to the other side, including lists of witnesses they will call and lists of exhibits that will be used at trial. Exhibits include documents, murder weapons, and pictures.

Omnibus Hearing   In some cases, the defense attorney wishes to challenge the prosecution evidence on grounds that it was obtained in violation of any of the constitutional protections discussed earlier. Some documents, for example, may have been seized without a warrant. The **omnibus hearing** is the forum wherein all of these challenges can be presented for the judge's ruling as to the admissibility of evidence. It is held before the trial so the jury is not exposed to evidence that should

---

FOR THE MANAGER'S DESK

RE: INTERNATIONAL ORGANIZED CRIME

The 1999 Human Development Report of the United Nations concludes that organized crime has greater economic output than all but three of the world's nations. The U.N. report states that organized crime syndicates gross about $1.6 trillion per year. The total gross domestic product for the United Kingdom is $1.28 trillion.

The primary business of crime syndicates is drugs, and that industry is larger than auto manufacturing throughout the world. The report puts the gross revenue for drugs as $400 billion, which represents 8 percent of the world's total trade dollars.

The report points to three factors that have contributed to the growth in organized crime.

1. International trade facilitates greater activity across borders.
2. The lack of currency controls and trade barriers facilitates international monetary exchanges.
3. High-tech equipment and the presence of telecommunications in countries where phone services were

a problem for decades make transactions move rapidly but also facilitates forgeries, frauds, and computer theft.

Many of the crime families have also been able to establish legitimate business fronts in other nations such as the Chinese triads with restaurants in London and the Japanese yakuza selling pornography (legalized) in the Netherlands. Even the criminal segments have been exported with the Sicilian Mafia benefiting from its strong heroin presence in New York City.

What do you think regulators can do about the flow of organized crime funds? What can legitimate businesses and individuals, as well as regulators, do to prevent the technological types of crimes via phone, fax, and computer?

Source: Anthony Browne, "Organized Crime Prospers Globally, Tops Output of Most Nations," *London Observer,* as reported in *Washington Times,* July 12, 1999, p. 25. Reprinted by permission of Newspaper Enterprise Association, Inc.

not have been admitted. In the O. J. Simpson double-homicide trial, an omnibus hearing was held on the admissibility of evidence gathered at Mr. Simpson's estate without a warrant.

Trial   If no plea agreement is reached before trial, the case then proceeds to **trial**.

SUMMARY

Who is liable for business crimes?

- Vicarious liability—holding companies accountable for criminal conduct of their officers
- Elements—requirements of proof for crimes
- *Mens rea*—requisite mental state for committing a crime
- *Actus reus*—physical act of committing a crime

What penalties exist for business crimes?

- Penalties—punishments for commission of crimes; include fines and imprisonment
- Corporate sentencing guidelines—federal rules used to determine level of penalties for companies and officers; a system that decreases penalties for effort and increases penalties for lack of effort and other problems in company operations

What is the nature of business crime?

- Obstruction—under Sarbanes-Oxley, prohibits destruction of documents when civil or criminal investigations are pending
- Computer crime—crimes committed while using computer technology; includes such activities as transferring funds (salami technique) and collecting data without authorization (scavenging)
- Counterfeit Access Device and Computer Fraud and Abuse Act (CADCFA)—federal law making it a crime to access computers without authorization
- Electronic Espionage Act (EEA)—makes it a crime to take employer's proprietary information
- Criminal fraud—misrepresentation with the intent to take something from another without that person's knowledge; to mislead to obtain funds or property
- Racketeer Influenced and Corrupt Organizations (RICO) Act—federal law designed to prevent racketeering by making it a crime to engage in certain criminal activities more than once

- USA Patriot Act—federal law that deals with due process rights as well as substantive issues such as money laundering prohibitions and mandatory disclosures by those involved in financial transactions, including banks, escrow, and title companies and other financial institutions

What are the rights of corporate and individual defendants in the criminal justice system?

- Fourth Amendment—provision in U.S. Constitution that protects against invasions of privacy; the search warrant amendment
- Fifth Amendment—the self-incrimination protection of the U.S. Constitution
- Sixth Amendment—the right-to-trial protection of the U.S. Constitution
- Search warrant—judicially issued right to examine home, business, and papers in any area in which there is an expectation of privacy
- *Miranda* warnings—advice required to be given to those taken into custody; details right to remain silent and the right to have counsel
- Due process—right to trial before conviction
- Warrant—public document authorizing detention of an individual for criminal charges; for searches, a judicial authorization
- Initial appearance—defendant's first appearance in court to have charges explained, bail set, lawyer appointed, and future dates set
- Preliminary hearing—presentation of abbreviated case by prosecution to establish sufficient basis to bind defendant over for trial
- Information—document issued after preliminary hearing requiring defendant to stand trial
- Grand jury—secret body that hears evidence to determine whether charges should be brought and whether defendant should be held for trial
- Indictment—document issued by grand jury requiring defendant to stand trial

- Arraignment—hearing at which trial date is set and plea is entered
- Plea bargain—settlement of criminal charges

- Omnibus hearing—evidentiary hearing outside the presence of the jury
- Trial—presentation of case by each side

QUESTIONS AND PROBLEMS

1. In the summer of 1993, the United States experienced the great, but temporary, Pepsi syringe scare. In several areas throughout the country, "consumers" came forward and claimed they had found medication syringes in cans of Pepsi. The Food and Drug Administration (FDA) and officers of PepsiCo reeled for several days as they attempted to cope with the allegations. Within a short period of time from when the stories on the syringes first appeared, a film taken by a hidden store camera showed one of the "consumers" actually inserting a syringe into a Pepsi drink product prior to purchase.

Assume that a criminal charge of adulteration requires proof of an intentional act. Would the hidden camera film establish the intent element of the crime?

2. Borland International, Inc., and Symantec Corporation are software manufacturers based in Silicon Valley in California. A Borland executive, Eugene Wang, was planning to depart Borland to work for Symantec, considered Borland's archrival. Other Borland executives and its board uncovered evidence, on the evening of Mr. Wang's departure, that Mr. Wang had communicated trade secrets to Gordon Eubanks, Symantec's chief executive. Those secrets included future product specifications, marketing plans through 1993, a confidential proposal for a business transaction, and a memo labeled "attorney/client confidential" summarizing questions asked by the Federal Trade Commission (FTC) in its probe of restraint of trade allegations by Microsoft Corporation.

Mr. Wang had allegedly used his computer to communicate the information to Mr. Eubanks. The local police and Borland executives worked through the night, using Symantec's own software that reconstructs computer files after they have been destroyed.

When Mr. Wang reported for his exit interview, he was detained and questioned by investigators. Searches authorized by warrant of Mr. Eubanks' two homes and his office uncovered evidence that he had received Mr. Wang's information. Borland filed a civil suit against the two men.

Later during the day of the exit interview, Mr. Wang's secretary, who was transferring with him to Symantec, returned to copy from her computer what she called "personal files." A personnel official watched as she copied the files from her computer but became suspicious and notified plainclothes officers in the Borland parking lot. The secretary, Lynn Georganes, was stopped, and the two disks onto which she had copied materials were taken. The disks contained scores of confidential Borland documents, including marketing plans and business forecasts.

Do the actions of Mr. Wang and Mr. Eubanks fit any computer crime statutes? Was theft involved in their actions? Were Ms. Georganes's actions ethical? Can't a competitor always hire an executive away, and wouldn't Mr. Wang have had most of the information in his head anyway? Can Mr. Eubanks be certain Mr. Wang will not do the same thing to him?

3. Emma Mary Ellen Holley and David Holley, an interracial couple, tried to buy a house in Twenty-Nine Palms, California. A real estate corporation, Triad, Inc., had listed the house for sale. Grove Crank, a Triad salesman, is alleged to have prevented the Holleys from obtaining the house for racially discriminatory reasons.

The Holleys brought a lawsuit in federal court against Mr. Crank and Triad. They claimed, among other things, that both were responsible for a fair housing law violation. The Holleys later filed a separate suit against David Meyer, the sole shareholder of Triad and its president and CEO. They claimed that Mr. Meyer was vicariously liable in one or more of these capacities for Mr. Crank's unlawful actions, which were a violation of the Fair Housing Act. Are the Holleys correct? [*Meyer* v. *Holley*, 537 U.S. 280 (2003).]

4. The state of Ohio had a statute that provided criminal penalties for anyone who "with intent to defraud . . . make[s] a check . . . or, with like intent, utter[s] or publish[es] as true and genuine such false . . . matter, knowing it to be false. . . ." Could a violation be established by showing that an individual wrote a check drawn on a bank at which he had no checking account? Is the proper intent established? [*In re Clemons*, 151 N.E.2d 553 (Ohio 1958).]

5. Reuben Sturman was charged with income tax evasion based largely on evidence the Internal Revenue Service and the Justice Department gathered through records of a Swiss bank in which Mr. Sturman had made substantial deposits over the past five years. The U.S. officials obtained the records from the Swiss bank pursuant to a treaty arrangement the U.S. government has with the Swiss government regarding the exchange of bank and bank record information. Mr. Sturman challenged the charges and the evidence on grounds that he had an expectation of privacy in his Swiss bank account and that U.S. officials were required to have a warrant before obtaining information about specific accounts in the Swiss banking system. Is Mr. Sturman correct? [*United States* v. *Sturman*, 951 F.2d 1466 (6th Cir. 1991).]

6. Bernard Saul was a salesperson for A. P. Walter Company, a wholesale auto parts business, assigned to the D&S Auto Parts account. Mr. Saul took inventory at D&S each week and phoned in an order to Walter to cover the needed inventory replacements. Between 1976 and 1982, Mr. Saul ordered parts from Walter and invoiced D&S, but he actually kept a portion of the parts for himself, sold them to other dealers, and pocketed the money. Through an audit, D&S discovered that it had paid $155,445.20 for parts that were not received. Can Mr. Saul be charged with any crimes? Can Walter be charged with any crimes? [*D&S Auto Parts, Inc.* v. *Schwartz*, 838 F.2d 965 (7th Cir. 1988).]

7. Odessa Mae French operated the Pines Motel as a house of prostitution for seven years. During that time, Ms. French avoided any local law enforcement action by allowing the sheriff to have free services at the Pines. Eventually, the federal government brought charges against the operation for tax evasion and RICO violations. Would the services to the sheriff constitute a form of bribe that would support a RICO charge? [*United States* v. *Tunnell*, 667 F.2d 1182 (5th Cir. 1982).]

8. The New York City Department of Health is responsible for the inspection of Manhattan restaurants to determine whether they comply with the city's health code. Forty-six of the department's inspectors were inducing restaurateurs to pay money to them for permit approval or for a favorable inspection.

Is this activity a basis for a crime? What crime? What would a prosecutor be required to prove? Are the officers and the restaurateurs equally criminally liable? [*U.S.* v. *Tillem*, 906 F.2d 814 (2d Cir. 1990).]

9. John Blondek and Vernon Tull were employees of Eagle Bus Company, a company based in the United States. Both Mr. Blondek and Mr. Tull were indicted for violations of the FCPA for paying a $50,000 bribe to Donald Castle and Darrell Lowry, officials of the Saskatchewan (Canada) provincial government, to ensure

that their bid to provide buses to Saskatchewan would be accepted. Mr. Castle and Mr. Lowry were also indicted. Can they, as foreign officials, be prosecuted under the FCPA? [*United States* v. *Blondek*, 741 F. Supp. 116 (N.D. Tex. 1990).]

10. Harlan Nolte and others invested in IFC Leasing Company, a master music recording leasing program. The company was created to acquire and lease master music recordings. Jerry Denby, the executive vice president of IFC, contacted Stephen Weiss, a partner in the law firm of Rosenbaum, Wise, Lerman, Katz & Weiss, to draft the prospectus for investors. Mr. Weiss drafted four documents used in the recruitment of investors for IFC. The complex structure of the investments, according to the documents, would have substantial tax consequences (to their benefit) for the investors.

After Mr. Nolte and others had made their investments, the IRS issued an opinion that the deductions explained in the prospectus and other documents would not be allowed. Criminal fraud actions were brought against IFC and its officers, as well as Mr. Weiss. The Justice Department also indicted both Mr. Weiss's law firm and his partners. Mr. Weiss's partners and the firm, through its management committee, maintain they cannot be held criminally liable for the actions of one partner. The Justice Department maintains that the firm and the partners were negligent in their supervision of Mr. Weiss and should, therefore, be held criminally liable. Do you agree with the Justice Department's position? Why or why not? [*Nolte* v. *Pearson*, 994 F.2d 1311 (8th Cir. 1993).]

RESEARCH PROBLEM

Crime, the Internet, and Pornography

11. Read *Reno* v. *American Civil Liberties Union*, 521 U.S. 844 (1997), and determine the following.
   a. What criminal statutes were at issue?
   b. What provisions of the Constitution were at issue?
   c. What is the status of criminal prosecution for transmission of pornography over the Internet?

NOTES

1. From a speech by director Robert Mueller at the Detroit Economic Club, October 16, 2003. See http://www.fbi.gov/pressrel/speeches/director101603.htm.

2. See http://houston.bizjournals.com/houston/stories/2004/06/07/focus7.html.

3. See http://www.ifccfbi.gov/strategy/2002_IFCCReport.pdf.

4. 15 U.S.C. §1512.

5. 18 U.S.C. §§1831–1839.

6. 41 U.S.C. §1693.

10

Business Torts

Criminal wrongs require guilty parties to pay a debt to society through a fine, imprisonment, and/or community service. However, criminal wrongs have victims. A crime can harm an individual, a company, or society. Those harms are known as civil wrongs and entitle those who are harmed to recover damages. Torts are civil wrongs that provide a remedy for these victims. This chapter answers these questions: What types of civil wrongs create a right of recovery for harm? What are the types and elements of torts? What are the business costs and issues surrounding torts?

**The desire for safety stands against every
great and noble enterprise.**
TACITUS

**One does not seriously attack the expertise of a scientist
using the undefined phrase "Butt-head."**
JUDGE LOURDES G. BAIRD
*In dismissing the late Carl Sagan's lawsuit against Apple Computer for its code name
change from "Carl Sagan" to "Butt-Head Astronomer"*

In 1995, following a taped episode of *The Jenny Jones Show* Jonathan Schmitz shot and killed Scott Amedure. On the show, one on same-sex crushes, Mr. Amedure revealed that he had a crush on Mr. Schmitz.

Mr. Schmitz was convicted of murder, and Mr. Amedure's parents filed suit against Warner Brothers, the producer of the show, for its "ambush" of Mr. Schmitz. They alleged that because Mr. Schmitz was not told the subject matter of the show he was "ambushed" during the taping and that his humiliation resulted in the shooting death of their son. Warner Brothers said that it could not anticipate the criminal acts of others and had no duty to ensure the safety of Mr. Amedure. Who is correct?

WHAT IS A TORT? ROOTS OF LAW AND COMMERCE

Tort comes from the Latin term *tortus*, which means "crooked, dubious, twisted." Torts are civil wrongs, actions that are not straight but twisted. A **tort** is an interference with someone or with someone's property that results in injury to that person or to that person's property. For example, using someone else's land is interference with that person's property rights and is the tort of trespass. If you held a concert on someone else's land and the concert crowds destroyed the property's vegetation or left litter that had to be removed, then you have committed the tort of trespass with that damage. The law provides protection for us and our property through the law of torts, which is a way to recover for the damages done to us.

Tort versus Crime

A tort is a private wrong. When a tort is committed, the party who was injured is entitled to collect compensation for damages from the wrongdoer for the private wrong. A crime, on the other hand, is a public wrong and requires the wrongdoer to pay a debt to society through a fine or by going to prison. For example, the crime of assault results in imprisonment, probation, and/or a fine. However, the victim could bring suit against the charged assailant to recover damages, such as medical bills, lost wages, and pain and suffering. The suit would be for the tort of assault.

Types of Torts

There are three types of tort liability: **intentional torts**, **negligence**, and **strict tort liability**. Intentional torts are the harms that result when parties commit intentional acts. For example, battery, or the striking of another person, is an intentional tort. A person is injured because you chose to hit him or her. However, suppose that you are stretching your arms in a crowd and you strike a man in the nose and hurt him. You have not committed the tort of battery, but you may have committed the tort of negligence. You did not intentionally strike the man as you might if you were having an argument, but you were carelessly swinging your arms in a crowd of people. These careless actions, or actions done without thinking through the consequences, are torts and constitute negligence. Such accidental harms also impose liabilities on the parties. The key difference between intentional torts and negligence is state of mind. Under the intentional tort standard, the party intended to commit the act. Under negligence, the party may have been careless or may not have thought carefully through his or her actions, but the actions were not done with the intent to cause harm. Strict tort liability is a form of product liability and is discussed in Chapter 11.

Torts are also classified as *property torts* and *personal torts*. The example of trespassing given earlier is a property tort because the injury is done to someone's property. The tort of defamation is an example of a personal tort because it involves publishing untrue statements about a person, resulting in harm to that person. The tort of negligence can involve injury to person or property. For example, if someone runs a red light and bumps into your car, that driver has been careless and the tort of negligence has occurred. If you are injured and your car is damaged, you have experienced both personal and property damage. Regardless of the tort classification, the remedy for the tort is recovery for the damage done to you or your property.

THE INTENTIONAL TORTS

Defamation

Defamation is an untrue statement made by one party to another about a third party. It consists of either slander or libel; **slander** is oral or spoken defamation, and **libel** is written (or, in some cases, broadcast) defamation. The elements for defamation are:

1. A statement about a person's reputation, honesty, or integrity that is untrue
2. Publication
3. A statement that is directed at a particular person
4. Damages
5. In some cases, proof of malice

Publication

For defamation to occur, the statement must be communicated to a third party. An accountant who addresses a group of lawyers at a luncheon meeting and untruthfully states that another accounting firm has been involved in a securities fraud has met the publication element. So has a supplier who notifies other suppliers that a certain business is insolvent when it is not. Technically, the statement is published if it is communicated to one other person. The more publication, however, the greater the damages.

The Internet has provided a means for instant and international communication of defamatory information. Posting information on the Internet that is false is defamation if it harms another person or company. Internet messages do qualify as publication, and their electronic form qualifies as libel.

CONSIDER...   10.1

Pathologist Dr. Jonathan Oppenheimer anonymously posted a message on a Yahoo! Web site accusing Dr. Sam Graham, the chairman of the Department of Urology at the Emory University School of Medicine, of taking kickbacks. The message posted by "fbiinformant" read, "Urocor decided to underbid the Emory Pathology Department for pathology services and give Graham a cut of the money it got from doing pathology. This worked well until the poor SOB got caught with his hand in the cookie jar. Poor guy had to resign his prestigious position."

None of the information in the posting was true. Dr. Graham had left his position to go into private practice. Dr. Graham decided to file suit under the name "John Doe" so that he could then subpoena Yahoo! to determine the identity of the person who posted the message. Dr. Oppenheimer was not a Yahoo! subscriber, but Yahoo! was able to determine that Dr. Oppenheimer had connected to Yahoo! through AOL. Dr. Graham's lawyers were able to pursue identity from there.

Is the statement Dr. Oppenheimer made libel? Did the lawyers and AOL act properly in tracking down Dr. Oppenheimer's identity? What do you learn about privacy and the Internet from this case? [*Graham* v. *Oppenheimer*, 2000 WL 33381418 (E.D. Va. 2000).]

Statement about a Particular Person

The general statement "All accountants are frauds" is not sufficiently narrow to be defamatory. The defamatory statement must either be about a particular person or be narrow enough in scope to include only a small group of businesses. For example, the statement "All the accountants in the Parkland office complex are dishonest" is specific enough to meet this element.

Damages

The person who is defamed must be able to establish damages, such as lost business, lost profits, lost advertising, lost reputation, or some economic effect resulting from the defamatory statements.

Malice

Malice is not an element of defamation in every case. Malice must be established in those cases in which the defamation is about a public figure. Public figures are those who place themselves voluntarily in the public eye, for example, elected officials, recording artists, actors, and sports figures. Notoriety is often not a function of voluntary conduct. For example, witnesses in a case that has extensive media coverage are not public figures simply because they are in the public eye. However, should they then volunteer for exposure or capitalize on their fame as witnesses, they do become public figures. An example of someone who was a witness and then became a public figure by choice as part of a public relations boost to his career is Kato Kaelin, the once resident at O. J. Simpson's home who became a key witness in Simpson's trial for the murder of his ex-wife Nicole and her friend Ronald Goldman. An example of someone who was not a voluntary public figure is Richard Jewell, the man who was accused by several news sources as being a suspect in the blast that resulted in two deaths and hundreds of injuries at Olympic Park in Atlanta during the 1996 Summer Olympics. Mr. Jewell settled a defamation case with NBC without having to prove malice on its part because he was not a public figure, only a person with notoriety.

Because the First Amendment provides protections for the media, those who are public figures must prove, in addition to the other elements of defamation, that the

CONSIDER...   10.2

The basis for Richard Jewell's suit against NBC were the following sentences from Tom Brokaw: "Look, they probably got enough to arrest him. They probably have got enough to try him." Mr. Brokaw finished his on-air commentary by adding: "Everyone, please understand absolutely he is only the focus of this investigation—he is not even a suspect yet."

Decide whether Jewell was defamed by the remarks.

statements were made or printed with knowledge that they were false or with reckless disregard for whether they were true or false. For example, a newspaper that prints a story on the basis of an unconfirmed source who has been shown to be unreliable in the past would be acting with malice.

The Defenses to Defamation

There are certain times when defamatory statements are made or printed but the tort of defamation is not established because there is a valid defense. A statement may be damaging, but, if it is the truth, it is not defamation. For example, you could publicly disclose that your boss took LSD during the late 1960s when he was in college. The remark might hurt your employer's reputation, but, if it is the truth, it is not the tort of defamation despite the harm it may do to him.

One of the current issues in defamation cases is whether the statements made are protected when they are a columnist's analysis of a situation. That is, courts are trying to determine whether there is some protection for viewpoints when someone objects to the conclusions drawn rather than the statements of fact themselves. There is often a fine line between statements of fact and expressions of opinion. In business publications, those opinions can be devastating to companies and their stock performance. In *Wilkow* v. *Forbes, Inc.* (Case 10.1), involving an opinion column on litigation in Forbes, the court must analyze what is false versus what is true and what is analysis and opinion in order to determine whether a defamation suit can proceed.

CASE 10.1

Wilkow v. *Forbes, Inc.*
241 F.3d 552 (7th Cir. 2001)

"Pleading Poverty" May Not Be Enough for a Defamation Suit

FACTS

On October 5, 1998, *Forbes* magazine printed the following opinion piece in its biweekly magazine for the business community.

Have the courts gone too far in protecting debtors against creditors? In this case it sure looks like it.

   Stiffing the creditor
   By Brigid McMenamin
   IT HAPPENS EVERY DAY: Business seeks refuge in bankruptcy; owner and creditors make a deal—leaving owner in charge.

Presumably the creditors are satisfied that they got the best possible deal under the circumstances. But what if the owner tries to shaft them by offering only pennies on the dollar? These days, often as not, courts are siding with the bankrupt owners and forcing creditors to accept almost whatever deal the bankrupt party offers them.

In short, many judges, ever more sympathetic to debtors, are allowing unscrupulous business owners to rob creditors.

Unless a creditor is prepared to spend years battling it out in court, he usually caves in. Forget the old rule that in bankruptcy creditors enjoy "absolute priority" over debtors. The U.S. Supreme Court will soon test the limits of this leniency. It has agreed to review a case in which the Bank of America National Trust & Savings Association claims it was stiffed by a real estate partnership led by Marc Wilkow of M&J Wilkow, Ltd., a Chicago-based manager of strip malls and offices.

The bank is asking the Court to nix a bankruptcy plan under which it might receive as little as $55 million for its $93 million lien against a Chicago office building. Under Wilkow's plan the bank must give up as much as 40% of its claim while Wilkow and his partners get to keep the building.

A lot rides on an eventual Supreme Court decision. That's why eight outsiders have filed friend-of-the-court briefs, including the American Bankers Association, the American Council of Life Insurance, the American College of Real Estate Lawyers, and the Solicitor General.

The whole mess started in 1987 when Bank of America began lending 203 N. LaSalle Street Partnership $93 million to build a sleek building in Chicago with a 15-floor, 547,000-square-foot office space. The place was soon humming, 98% leased to everything from Coopers & Lybrand to the American Civil Liberties Union.

But by the mid-1990s, rents were not keeping up with costs. When the principal came due in January 1995, Wilkow and his partners pleaded poverty. To keep the bank from foreclosing, LaSalle Partnership filed for bankruptcy. Appraisals of the property came in at less than $60 million. In theory the bank was entitled to the entire amount. It suggested selling the property to the highest bidder. Determined to keep the building, LaSalle partners asked the bankruptcy court instead to accept a plan under which the bank would likely receive a fraction of what it was owed while the partners would keep the building. The bank, not the equity holder, would take the hit.

Yet federal judge Paul Plunkett blessed LaSalle's plan. Bank of America will get as little as $55 million plus interest—and even that in monthly payments over seven to ten years.

What happened to the old "absolute priority rule"? To get around that, the partners used a controversial "new value" concept in which the owners agree to kick in fresh capital in return for equity.

To validate the concept, the owners proposed to put in $6.1 million in fresh capital, over five years.

Nice deal—for the debtor. The bank takes an up-to-$38 million haircut, and the owner throws in just $4.1 million in present value.

In September 1997 the federal appeals court that heard the case deferred to the lower court's decision. So the bank petitioned the Supreme Court to step in. On May 4 it agreed.

Bank of America's argument has been boosted by a February ruling from a federal appeals court in New York that found in favor of the creditors in a similar situation. With two such recent conflicting rulings and so much at stake, arguments before the Supreme Court will be heard on Nov. 2.

Realizing the Court could rule against the partnership,

Wilkow says he is willing to sweeten his offer. "The time to talk settlement is when there's a cloud of uncertainty over everyone's head," he explains.

The article was accompanied by a photograph of the 203 North LaSalle Street building captioned "Chicago's 203 North LaSalle Street, Stiffing the bank with court approval."

The article ran in the magazine seven months prior to the U.S. Supreme Court's decision on the bankruptcy priority rule, a decision that required 8,000 words to explain [In re 203 North LaSalle Street Limited Partnership, 526 U.S. 450 (1999)].

Mr. Wilkow filed suit against Forbes, alleging that the article was defamatory and had caused him significant harm and damaged his reputation in the business community. The district court dismissed the suit, and Mr. Wilkow appealed.

JUDICIAL OPINION

EASTERBROOK, Circuit Judge

The majority opinion in the Supreme Court required about 8,000 words to resolve the case—and without reaching a final decision on the vitality of the new-value exception (though the majority's analysis hog-tied the doctrine).

The majority opinion in this court (on the priority rule prior to its appeal to the U.S. Supreme Court) ran about 9,500 words, with 5,200 more in a dissent. A 670-word article such as the one Forbes published could not present either the facts of the case or the subtleties of the law. What the article lacked in analysis, however, it made up for with colorful verbs and adjectives. Taking lenders' side, Forbes complained that "many judges, ever more sympathetic to debtors, are allowing unscrupulous business owners to rob creditors." According to the article, a partnership led by Marc Wilkow "stiffed" the bank, paying only $55 million on a $93 million loan while retaining ownership of the building.

Wilkow replied with this libel suit under the diversity jurisdiction, contending that Forbes and Brigid McMenamin, the article's author, defamed him by asserting that he was in poverty (or, worse, "pleaded poverty" when he was solvent) and had filched the bank's money. According to Wilkow, Forbes should at least have informed its readers that the bank had lent the money without recourse against the partners, so that a downturn in the real estate market, rather than legal machinations, was the principal source of the bank's loss.

The district court dismissed the complaint for failure to state a claim on which relief may be granted. That was a misstep. A complaint is sufficient whenever

continued

the plaintiff could prevail under facts consistent with the complaint's allegations, and defamation is a recognized legal claim. The body of this complaint was not self-defeating. Instead the district judge based her decision on the text of the article. But when "matters outside the pleading are presented to and not excluded by the court, the motion shall be treated as one for summary judgment and disposed of as provided in Rule 56, and all parties shall be given reasonable opportunity to present all material made pertinent to such a motion by Rule 56."

In the district court the parties wrangled about choice of law. *Forbes* is based in New York, and Wilkow's business has its headquarters in Chicago. The district judge split the difference, ruling that Illinois law supplies the claim for relief but that New York law supplies an absolute privilege for "the publication of a fair and true report of any judicial proceeding." According to the judge, McMenamin's story is privileged under New York law as a report of proceedings in 203 North LaSalle Street. The judge added, for good measure, that the article is protected by the first amendment because the forceful characterizations to which Wilkow objects are opinions rather than facts. *Forbes* did not misstate any of the details of the situation, and neither Illinois nor New York requires a reporter to include all facts (such as the nonrecourse nature of the loan) that put the subject in the best light.

We don't think it necessary to consider either constitutional limits on liability for defamation or privileges under New York law, because this article is not defamatory under Illinois law in the first place. In Illinois, a "statement of fact is not shielded from an action for defamation by being prefaced with the words 'in my opinion,' but if it is plain that the speaker is expressing a subjective view, an interpretation, a theory, conjecture, or surmise, rather than claiming to be in possession of objectively verifiable facts, the statement is not actionable."

Characterizations such as "stiffing" and "rob" convey McMenamin's objection to the new-value exception. She expostulates against judicial willingness to allow debtors to retain interests in exchange for new value, not particularly against debtors' seizing whatever opportunities the law allows. Nothing in the article implies that Wilkow did (or even proposed) anything illegal; *Forbes* informed the reader that the district court and this court approved Wilkow's proposed plan of reorganization. Every detail in the article (other than the quotation in the final paragraph) comes from public documents; the article does not suggest that McMenamin knows extra information implying that Wilkow pulled the wool over judges' eyes or engaged in other misconduct. Colloquialisms such as

"pleaded poverty" do not imply that Wilkow was destitute and failing to pay his personal creditors, an allegation that would have been defamatory. Read in context, the phrase conveys the idea that the partnership could not repay the loan out of rents received from the building's tenants. After all, inability to pay one's debts as they come due is an ordinary reason for bankruptcy, and 203 North LaSalle Street Partnership did file a petition in bankruptcy. Filing a bankruptcy petition is one way of "pleading poverty."

Although the article drips with disapproval of Wilkow's (and the judges') conduct, an author's opinion about business ethics isn't defamatory under Illinois law. Informing the reader about the nonrecourse nature of the loan might have made Wilkow look better, but it would not have drawn the article's sting: that the partners got to keep the property even though the bank lost $38 million. The original deal's fundamental structure was that the partnership would repay the loan from rental income, and that if revenue was insufficient the bank could choose to foreclose (cutting its loss and reinvesting at the market rate elsewhere), to renegotiate a new interest rate with the partners, or to forebear in the hope that the market would improve and the full debt could yet be paid. These options collectively would be worth more than the market value of the building on the date of default. Yet the partners refused to honor these promises to the bank. They persuaded judges to eliminate the bank's rights to foreclose, to renegotiate, or to forebear and retain the full security interest. The plan of reorganization stripped down the security interest, prevented the bank from foreclosing, and required it to finance the partnership's operations for the next decade, at a rate of interest below what the bank would have charged in light of the newly revealed riskiness of the loan. If the real estate market fell further during that time, so that the partnership could not repay even the reduced debt, then the bank was going to lose still more money. The present value of the promises made to the bank in the plan of reorganization therefore was less than the appraised value of the building. But the partners stood to make a great deal of money if the market turned up again (as it did), for they had shucked $38 million in secured debt while retaining most appreciation in the property's value. Whether that was a sound use of bankruptcy reorganization, independent of the plan's new-value aspects, is open to question.

A reporter is entitled to state her view that an ethical entrepreneur should have offered the lender a better bargain, such as allowing the bank to foreclose and take its $55 million with certainty, avoiding the additional risk that this plan fastened on the lender. Foreclosure would have had serious consequences for the partners, who would have lost about $20 million in recaptured tax benefits. These potential losses created room for negotiation. Armed with the new-value exception, however, the partners were able to retain the tax benefits, sharing none with the bank in exchange for its approval of a restructuring, while depriving the bank of a security interest that would have been valuable when the market recovered. Although a reader might arch an eyebrow at Wilkow's strategy, an allegation of greed is not defamatory; sedulous pursuit of self-interest is the engine that propels a market economy. Capitalism certainly does not depend on sharp practices, but neither is an allegation of sharp dealing anything more than an uncharitable opinion. Illinois does not attach damages to name-calling. Wilkow's current and potential partners would have read this article as an endorsement of Wilkow's strategy; they want to invest with a general partner who drives the hardest possible bargain with lenders. By observing that Wilkow used every opening the courts allowed, *Forbes* may well have improved his standing with in-

vestors looking for real estate tax shelters (though surely it did not help his standing with lenders). No matter the net effect of the article, however, it was not defamatory under Illinois law, so the judgment of the district court is AFFIRMED.

CASE QUESTIONS

1. What type of article did *Forbes* publish, and why is its nature important?

2. Is it defamation to express an opinion about the ethics of a businessperson?

3. What is the difference between the law and ethics, as this court discusses the question?

4. Does a writer have an obligation to disclose information that makes the subject matter of the piece look better than the writer did?

5. Is a writer expected to explain all the complexities of an issue before expressing an opinion?

Some speech is privileged; that is, there is a strong public interest in protecting the speech regardless of whether it is true. For example, members of Congress enjoy an **absolute privilege** when they are speaking on the floor of the Senate or House because there is a strong public policy to encourage free debate of issues. The same is true of judicial proceedings; in order to encourage people to come forward with the truth, witnesses enjoy an absolute privilege when testifying about the matters at hand. The media enjoy a **qualified privilege**, which is freedom to publish information even though it may be inaccurate, so long as it is not published with malice or with reckless disregard for whether the information published is true or false. Perhaps one of the most famous libel cases addressing the defense of the media privilege involved Carol Burnett and a story about her printed by the *National Enquirer*. The case decision on this incident follows in *Burnett* v. *National Enquirer* (Case 10.2).

CASE 10.2

Burnett v. *National Enquirer, Inc.*
144 Cal. App. 3d 991 (1983)

Only the *Enquirer* Didn't Know for Sure:
Carol Burnett, Henry Kissinger, and Defamation

FACTS

On March 2, 1976, the *National Enquirer* (appellant) published in its weekly publication a "gossip column" headlined "Carol Burnett and Henry K. in Row" that included the following four-sentence item:

In a Washington restaurant, a boisterous Carol Burnett had a loud argument with another diner, Henry Kissinger. Then she traipsed around the place offering everyone a bite of her dessert. But Carol really raised eyebrows

when she accidentally knocked a glass of wine over one diner and started giggling instead of apologizing. The guy wasn't amused and "accidentally" spilled a glass of water over Carol's dress.

Ms. Burnett (respondent) filed suit against the *Enquirer* alleging that the item was entirely false and libelous after the *Enquirer* printed the following retraction:

continued

An item in this column on March 2 erroneously reported that Carol Burnett had an argument with Henry Kissinger at a Washington restaurant and became boisterous, disturbing other guests. We understand these events did not occur and we are sorry for any embarrassment our report may have caused Miss Burnett.

After a jury trial, Ms. Burnett was awarded $300,000 compensatory damages and $1,300,000 punitive damages. The trial court reduced the amounts to $50,000 compensatory and $750,000 punitive damages. The *Enquirer* appealed.

JUDICIAL OPINION

ROTH, Presiding Justice

Prior to addressing the merits of appellant's contentions and in aid of our disposition, we set out the following further facts pertaining to the publication complained of. . . .

On the occasion giving rise to the gossip column item hereinabove quoted, respondent, her husband and three friends were having dinner at the Rive Gauche restaurant in the Georgetown section of Washington, D.C. The date was January 29, 1976. Respondent was in the area as a result of being invited to be a performing guest at the White House. In the course of the dinner, respondent had two or three glasses of wine. She was not inebriated. She engaged in banter with a young couple seated at a table next to hers, who had just become engaged or were otherwise celebrating. When curiosity was expressed about respondent's dessert, apparently a chocolate souffle, respondent saw to it the couple were provided with small amounts of it on plates they had passed to her table for the purpose. Perhaps from having witnessed the gesture, a family behind respondent then offered to exchange some of their baked alaska for a portion of the souffle, and they, too, were similarly accommodated. As respondent was later leaving the restaurant, she was introduced by a friend to Henry Kissinger, who was dining at another table, and after a brief conversation, respondent left with her party.

There was no "row" with Mr. Kissinger, nor any argument between the two, and what conversation they had was not loud or boisterous. Respondent never "traipsed around the place offering everyone a bite of her dessert," nor was she otherwise boisterous, nor did she spill wine on anyone, nor did anyone spill water on her and there was no factual basis for the comment she ". . . started giggling instead of apologizing."

The impetus for what was printed about the dinner was provided to the writer of the item, Brian Walker, by Couri Hays, a freelance tipster paid by the *National Enquirer* on an ad hoc basis for information supplied by

him which was ultimately published by it, who advised Walker he had been informed respondent had taken her Grand Marnier souffle around the restaurant in a boisterous or flamboyant manner and given bites of it to various other people; that he had further but unverified information respondent had been involved in the wine-water spilling incident; but that, according to his sources, respondent was "specifically, emphatically" not drunk. No mention was made by Hays of anything involving respondent and Henry Kissinger.

Having received this report, Walker spoke with Steve Tinney, whose name appears at the top of the *National Enquirer* gossip column, expressing doubts whether Hays could be trusted. Tinney voiced his accord with those doubts. Walker then asked Gregory Lyon, a *National Enquirer* reporter, to verify what Walker had been told by Hays. Lyon's inquiry resulted only in his verifying respondent had shared dessert with other patrons and that she and Kissinger had carried on a good-natured conversation at the restaurant.

In spite of the fact no one had told him respondent and Henry Kissinger had engaged in an argument, that the wine-water spilling story remained as totally unverified hearsay, that the dessert sharing incident was only partially bolstered, and that respondent was not under any view of the question inebriated, Walker composed the quoted item and approved the "row" headline.

The *National Enquirer* is a publication whose masthead claims the "Largest Circulation Of Any Paper in America." It is a member of the American Newspaper Publishers Association. It subscribes to the Reuters News Service. Its staff call themselves newspaper reporters.

By the same token the *National Enquirer* is designated as a magazine or periodical in eight mass media directories and upon the request and written representation of its general manager in 1960 that "In view of the feature content and general appearance [of the publication], which differ markedly from those of a newspaper . . ." its classification as a newspaper was changed to that of magazine by the Audit Bureau of Circulation. It does not subscribe to the Associated Press or United Press International news services. According to a statement by its Senior Editor it is not a newspaper and its content is based on a consistent formula of "how to" stories, celebrity or medical or personal improvement stories, gossip items, and TV column items, together with material from certain other subjects. It provides little or no current coverage of subjects such as politics, sports, or crime, does not attribute content to wire services, and in general does not make reference to time. Normal "lead time" for its subject matter is one to three weeks. Its owner allowed it did not generate stories "day to day as a daily newspaper does."

At appellant's request, the trial court herein made its determination after hearing and based on extensive evidence that the *National Enquirer* was not a newspaper for purposes of the application of Civil Code section 48a.

Seen in this light, the essential question is not then whether any publication is properly denominated a magazine or by some other designation, but simply whether it ought to be characterized as a newspaper or not.

Having so decided, we are also satisfied to conclude without extensive recitation of the evidence that the trial court consistently with the foregoing rationale correctly determined the *National Enquirer* should not be deemed a newspaper for the purposes of the instant litigation.

Nearly twenty years ago, it was announced in *New York Times Co.* v. *Sullivan*, 376 U.S. 254 (1964) that:

> *The constitutional guarantees [relating to protected speech] require, we think, a federal rule that prohibits a public official from recovering damages for a defamatory falsehood relating to his official conduct unless he proves that the statement was made with "actual malice"—that is, with knowledge that it was false or with reckless disregard of whether it was false or not.*

[W]e are of the opinion the award to respondent of $750,000 in order to punish and deter appellant was not justified.

In so concluding, we are persuaded the evidence fairly showed that while appellant's representatives knew that part of the publication complained of was probably false and that the remainder of it in substance might very well be, appellant was nevertheless determined to present to a vast national audience in printed form statements which in their precise import and clear implication were defamatory, thereby exposing respondent to contempt, ridicule and obloquy, and tending to injure her in her occupation. We are also satisfied that even when it was thought necessary to alleviate the wrong resulting from the false statements it had placed before the public, the retraction proffered was evasive, incomplete and by any standard, legally insufficient. In other words, we have no doubt the conduct of appellant respecting the libel was reprehensible and was undertaken with the kind of improper motive which supports the imposition of punitive damages.

Nevertheless, evidence on the point of appellant's wealth adequately established appellant's net worth to be some $2.6 million and its net income for the period under consideration to be about $1.56 million, such that the penalty award, even when substantially reduced by the trial court based on its conclusion the jury's compensatory verdict was "clearly excessive and . . . not supported by substantial evidence," continued to constitute about 35% of the former and nearly half the latter.

The judgment is affirmed except that the punitive damage award herein is vacated and the matter is remanded for a new trial on that issue only, provided that if respondent shall, within 30 days from the date of our remittitur, file with the clerk of this court and serve upon appellant a written consent to a reduction of the punitive damage award to the sum of $150,000, the judgment will be modified to award respondent punitive damages in that amount, and so as modified affirmed in its entirety. . . .

CASE QUESTIONS

1. Was malice established in the case? Why was it necessary to establish malice?

2. Is the *National Enquirer* a newspaper for purposes of the protection of the privilege?

3. Are the damages reduced? To what? Why?

4. Should tabloids like the *National Enquirer* enjoy the protection of the privilege?

CONSIDER...   10.3

Benjamin Paul, a personal injury lawyer with the firm of Benjamin Paul & Associates, was running for mayor of Philadelphia and was described by a city council member, Frank Rizzo, as a "slip-and-fall-lawyer running for mayor." *Philadelphia Magazine,* running a story on the candidates in the mayoral race, reprinted the comment about Mr. Paul. Mr. Paul filed suit against *Philadelphia Magazine* for libel. Mr. Paul said the term "slip-and-fall-lawyer" is similar in meaning to "shyster."

Does Mr. Paul have a case? Mr. Paul has handled some slip-and-fall cases, some on behalf of local members of the Fraternal Order of Police.

CONSIDER...   10.4

The *National Enquirer* published a supposed interview with actor Clint Eastwood. The interview had never taken place, and Mr. Eastwood said the publication of such an interview in a sensationalist newspaper made it seem as if he was "washed up as a movie star." Could Mr. Eastwood recover for the publication of the fake interview? What tort has occurred, if any?

THINK: Recall the elements for defamation: a false statement that impugns the integrity of a specific person.

APPLY: We don't have the content of the interview, but it is false that the interview occurred, and Mr. Eastwood argues that just the suggestion that he would be interviewed by the *National Enquirer* harms his career.

ANSWER: Mr. Eastwood took the case to trial and won, precisely because there was no interview and the content and even the suggestion of him granting an interview were false.

CONSIDER...   10.5

In the May 31, 2004, issue of *The Weekly Standard*, editor Fred Barnes wrote the following commentary.

> *A FEW YEARS AGO Michael Moore, who's now promoting an anti-President Bush movie entitled* Fahrenheit 9/11, *announced he'd gotten the goods on me, indeed hung me out to dry on my own words. It was in his first bestselling book,* Stupid White Men. *Moore wrote he'd once been "forced" to listen to my comments on a TV chat show,* The McLaughlin Group. *I had whined "on and on about the sorry state of American education," Moore said, and wound up by bellowing: "These kids don't even know what* The Iliad *and* The Odyssey *are!"*
>
> *Moore's interest was piqued, so the next day he said he called me. "Fred," he quoted himself as saying, "tell me what* The Iliad *and* The Odyssey *are." I started "hemming and hawing," Moore wrote. And then I said, according to Moore: "Well, they're . . . uh . . . you know . . . uh . . . okay, fine, you got me—I don't know what they're about. Happy now?" He'd smoked me out as a fraud, or maybe worse.*
>
> *The only problem is none of this is true. It never happened. Moore is a liar. He made it up. It's a fabrication on two levels. One, I've never met Moore or even talked to him on the phone. And, two, I read both* The Iliad *and* The Odyssey *in my first year at the University of Virginia. Just for the record, I learned what they were about even before college. Like everyone else my age, I got my classical education from the big screen. I saw the Iliad movie called* Helen of Troy *and while I forget the name of the Odyssey film, I think it starred Kirk Douglas as Odysseus.*
>
> *So why didn't I scream bloody murder when the book came out in 2001? I didn't learn about the phony anecdote until it was brought to my attention by Alan Wolfe, who was reviewing Moore's book for the* New Republic. *He asked, by email, if the story were true. I said no, not a word of it, and Wolfe quoted me as saying that. That was enough, I thought. After all, who would take a shrill, lying lefty like Moore seriously?*

Was Mr. Barnes defamed? Could he bring suit now?

BIOGRAPHY

OPRAH, MAD COW DISEASE, AND VEGGIE LIBEL LAWS

About thirteen states currently have "veggie libel" laws, statutes that permit suit when someone defames a generic product such as eggs, milk, or even broccoli. The laws provide a remedy for generic defamation of a natural food, thus not requiring a business to tie the defamatory remark directly to its particular product. Industry-wide damages can thus be recovered.

The veggie libel laws gained national public attention when Texas cattlemen filed an $11 million suit against talk show host Oprah Winfrey for her remarks during a show on mad cow disease. Following a presentation on the program by an anti-meat campaigner, Howard Lyman, Ms. Winfrey said, "It has just stopped me cold from eating another burger. I'm stopped." Using the Texas False Disparagement of Perishable Food Products Act of 1995, the ranchers and cattlemen alleged that the show presented a one-sided and inaccurate view of the issue of mad cow disease and caused a drop in sales of beef. Cattle futures prices dropped 10 percent on the day follow-ing the show, and beef prices went from 62 cents per pound to 55 cents per pound.

Following the judge's dismissal of many counts in the suit, the case proceeded to trial on the basis of a defamation claim, which the jury rejected. Ms. Winfrey emerged from the courthouse and noted, "The First Amendment isn't just alive. It rocks." The constitutionality of the veggie libel laws under the First Amendment has yet to be determined, but a case involving defamation of eggs in Pennsylvania is being taken up on appeal in order to obtain an opinion on that legal issue. In the case, a consumer's group was sued after it reported that an egg producer was washing and repackaging old eggs for sale.

ISSUES

1. How is vegetable defamation different from defamation of a person?
2. Could Ms. Winfrey have balanced her show?

Contract Interference

The tort of **contract interference** or **tortious interference with contracts** or tortious interference occurs when parties are not allowed the freedom to contract without interference from third parties. The tort developed in England before the twentieth century and still exists today.

While the elements of tortious interference are complex, a basic definition is that the law affords a remedy when someone intentionally persuades another to break a contract already in existence with a third party. Bryan A. Garner, the author of *Tortious Interference,* offers the following examples: "Say you had a contract with Joe Blow, and I for some reason tried to get you to break that contract. Or say that Pepsi has an exclusive contract with a hotel chain to carry Pepsi products, and Coke tries to get the hotel to carry Coke despite that contract. That's tortious interference."

One of the most famous cases involving the question of tortious interference was that of *Texaco, Inc. v. Pennzoil Co.,* 729 S.W.2d 768 (Tex. 1987). The board of directors of Getty Oil had agreed to sell a substantial portion of its oil to Pennzoil. While Getty and Pennzoil were drafting their agreement, Texaco stepped in and made a competing bid. The Getty board then accepted the Texaco offer. Pennzoil filed suit against Texaco for tortious interference. The trial court awarded Pennzoil $7.53 billion in actual damages and $3 billion in punitive damages. While the appellate court reduced the punitive damages by $2 billion, it did find that Texaco interfered with the Pennzoil contract because its officers described their conduct as "stop[ping] the train."

FOR THE MANAGER'S DESK

RE: A NEW TWIST ON THE TORT OF INTERFERENCE

The CBS news show *Sixty Minutes* pulled from a scheduled airing an interview with a former tobacco executive in a news story about the industry, when threats of both libel and tortious interference with contract suits arose. The former executive of Brown & Williamson, Jeffrey S. Wigand, agreed to have the interview run only if CBS News would indemnify him against the suits. Brown & Williamson lawyers notified CBS News that Wigand had signed a confidentiality agreement and that the company would sue CBS News for interference with that contract if the interview were run. *Sixty Minutes* ran a story on tobacco companies without the interview. CBS correspondents Mike Wallace and Morley Safer protested the decision of CBS News executives. However, the *Wall Street Journal* ran a story describing CBS News's unusual arrangements with Wigand, including the payment of a consulting fee of $12,000 and the promise of full indemnification. Many

lawyers commented that the promises CBS made to Wigand could be depicted as inducements for Wigand to breach his contract agreement of confidentiality with Brown & Williamson.

CBS eventually ran the story and interview with Mr. Wigand. The story of Mr. Wigand, CBS, and Brown & Williamson was made into a movie, based on the journalistic exposé of the events. The movie, *The Insider*, featured Russell Crowe as Mr. Wigand, and the role earned him an Academy Award nomination. The movie earned protests from many at CBS, particularly Mike Wallace, as an inaccurate depiction of his conduct. Mr. Wallace's producer, Lowell Bergman, left CBS and *Sixty Minutes* after the Wigand story ran. He now teaches journalism at the University of California at Berkeley and, on occasion, works as a producer for PBS's *Frontline*.

False Imprisonment

False imprisonment is often referred to as "the shopkeeper's tort" because it generally occurs as a result of a shoplifting accusation in a store. **False imprisonment** is the detention of a person for any period of time (even a few minutes) against his will. No physical harm need result; the imprisoned party can collect minimal damages simply for being imprisoned without consent. Because shopkeepers need the opportunity to investigate matters when someone is suspected of shoplifting, the tort of false imprisonment does carry the defense of the **shopkeeper's privilege**. This privilege allows a shopkeeper to detain a suspected shoplifter for a reasonable period of time while the matter or incident is investigated. In most states, the shopkeeper must have a reasonable basis for keeping the person; that is, the shopkeeper must have reason to suspect the individual even if it turns out later that the individual has an explanation or did not do what the shopkeeper suspected.

CONSIDER... 10.6

On November 16, 1986, Joseph Canto Jr., then eleven years old, and Samantha Canto, then sixteen, went shopping at the Ivey department store in Gainesville, Florida. After entering the store, they stopped at a display table to look at metallic chain-link belts. A videotape taken by a security camera shows the children stopping at the display table, handling the items, and exchanging conversation while looking around. The video also shows Samantha handing something to Joseph, which he placed in his pocket. Jo Ann Williams stopped the children as they were leaving the store and told them she had reason to believe that they had stolen something and to follow her to the security office. The sheriff's report discloses that Ms. Williams called the sheriff's office soon thereafter but that an officer did not arrive for another hour. Another employee, managing agent Kirsten Aalto, arrived at the security office and aided Ms. Williams. The children were released by the officer about two hours after they were initially detained by Ms. Williams. No merchandise was found on the children.

Joseph and Samantha said they were questioned in an intimidating manner, were not allowed to use the bathroom or call their parents, and were called "delinquents" and "shoplifters."

Through their parents, Joseph and Samantha filed suit for damages incurred for their psychological counseling and treatment and for punitive damages. Should they recover? Consider the applicable Florida statutes. Section 812.015(5), Florida Statutes (1989), provides:

> *A merchant, merchant's employee, or farmer who takes a person into custody, as provided in subsection (3) . . . shall not be criminally or civilly liable for false arrest or false imprisonment when the merchant, merchant's employee, or farmer has probable cause to believe that the person committed retail theft or farm theft.*

Subsection (3)(a) provides:

> *A law enforcement officer, a merchant, a merchant's employee, or a farmer who has probable cause to believe that retail or farm theft has been committed by a person and that he can recover the property by taking the person into custody may, for the purpose of attempting to effect such recovery or for prosecution, take the person into custody and detain him in a reasonable manner for a reasonable length of time. . . . In the event the merchant, merchant's employee, or farmer takes the person into custody, a law enforcement officer shall be called to the scene immediately after the person has been taken into custody.*

[*Canto v. J. B. Ivey & Co.*, 595 So. 2d 1025 (Fla. 1992).]

 CONSIDER . . .   **10.7**

Apply the same Florida Statutes mentioned in Consider 10.6 to the following facts.

Lyndon Silva was stopped by Kevin Rivera, an off-duty Houston police officer working as a security officer for Dillard's Department store. Mr. Silva was leaving Dillard's at the time. However, before questioning him, Mr. Rivera placed Mr. Silva on the floor, handcuffed him, and then dumped three shirts from his bag onto the floor. He had no receipts in the bag, but Mr. Silva asked Mr. Rivera to check his car for the receipts because he was returning the shirts. Mr. Rivera refused. Mr. Rivera then took Mr. Silva to the offices upstairs and detained him while they waited for the police. Mr. Silva was again placed on the floor while Mr. Rivera switched his handcuffs for those of the police. Mr. Silva was later able to produce a receipt.

Is Dillard's protected by the shopkeeper's privilege? [*Dillard Department Stores, Inc. v. Silva*, 106 S.W.3d 789 (Tex. App. 2003).]

Intentional Infliction of Emotional Distress

This tort imposes liability for conduct that goes beyond all bounds of decency and results in emotional distress in the harmed individual. One of the difficulties with this tort is that the only damage the plaintiff is required to prove is that of emotional distress. Although "pain and suffering" damages have been awarded for some time in negligence actions in which the plaintiff recovers damages for physical and property injuries, the awarding of damages for mental distress alone is a relatively new phenomenon. However, the tort of **intentional infliction of emotional distress** has been used quite often by debtors who are harassed by creditors and collection agencies in their attempts to collect funds.

For information on electronic privacy, see the Electronic Privacy Information Center:
http://www.epic.org

Invasion of Privacy

The intentional tort of *invasion of privacy* is actually three different torts: (1) intrusion into the plaintiff's private affairs; (2) public disclosure of private facts; and (3) appropriation of another's name, likeness, or image for commercial advantage. The appropriation tort is discussed subsequently, under competition torts. The two other components of the privacy tort represent rights to be left alone and not to have personal matters publicly disclosed. Intrusion simply requires proof that the defendant was present when the plaintiff was doing something normally considered private.

One of the most famous invasion of privacy cases was *Galella v. Onassis*, 353 F. Supp. 196 (S.D.N.Y. 1972). In the case, the late Mrs. Jacqueline Kennedy Onassis brought suit against Ron Galella, a photo journalist, for invasion of her privacy. As a result of the case, Mr. Galella was ordered to remain at least 50 yards from Mrs. Onassis and 100 yards from her children.

The issue of privacy has become more of a statutory one because of evolving technologies such as e-mail and Internet access. The computer provides efficient means for storing information, but that stored information also carries ease of access. One of the many privacy protections put into place by statute is that under the **Health Insurance Portability and Accountability Act of 1996** (HIPAA; 42 U.S.C. 1320d-1320d-8). Under HIPAA, health plans, health care clearinghouses, and health care providers who transmit in electronic form any health information that is related to medical care or condition are required to comply with the privacy requirements. Basically, those who use computers and are in the health care field are subject to HIPAA. The Department of Health and Human Services was directed to develop the enforcement processes for the privacy rules, and the final interim version of the rules was passed in April 2003. HIPAA has both civil and criminal penalties for violations. The criminal penalties include fines of up to $250,000 and up to ten years in prison. Those subject to HIPAA are now implementing the protections.

HIPAA requires the following:

- Patients must give permission before doctors can disclose patient information and data to employers, marketers, and life insurance companies.
- Patients have the right to examine their patient, medical, and health records and use a correction request process similar to that of the Fair Credit Reporting Act.
- Patients have the right to request restrictions on disclosures.

Here are some examples of changes in medical practice that will result from HIPAA.

- Doctors cannot use postcards to remind patients about the need for a checkup; the reminder must be in an envelope for privacy.
- If patients request, doctors cannot call them at work, or patients can request that doctors call them only at work. (This provision was included in order to help victims of domestic violence.)
- Patients can put restrictions on hospitals for discussing their treatment and condition, including restrictions on answering media questions.
- Patients can request a federal investigation when they file a complaint alleging a violation of their privacy under HIPAA.

Find out more about HIPAA at the Department of Health and Human Services:

http://www.hhs.gov/ ocr/hipaa/
and
http://www.cms.gov/ hipaa/hipaa2

HIPAA has resulted in the complex paperwork we sign when we receive medical care that discloses our rights to access our records. It also led to the marked lines at pharmacies behind which we must stand so that we cannot overhear the pharmacy worker's discussions with other customers.

HIPAA has made privacy front and center and introduced some new complexity. One patient services director explained HIPAA's impact as follows: "In the old days, a social workers could pick up the phone and ask Meals on Wheels to deliver lunch to Mrs. Jones five days a week. Under the federal rules, we'll now have to get a release from Mrs. Jones so we can tell Meals on Wheels that, as a diabetic with cardiac problems, she has special dietary needs."[1]

MAKING ETHICS PERSONAL

HIPAA on Wheels

You are a volunteer for Meals on Wheels. As a dedicated driver, you know your route and the people you serve very well. You have been warned by your supervisor not to talk about the people you serve, their health, or their diagnoses. The supervisor has explained their rights under HIPAA to you. One of the people you serve is an elderly gentleman who is suffering from incurable cancer. About twenty years ago, he had a falling out with his daughter, but she has been watching his home, trying to work up the nerve to go and talk with him. After watching you make three deliveries to her father, she approaches you and asks for information. "Is my father ill? What's wrong with him? Could you just give me some information?" What would you do? Think of ways that you might help without violating the law or breaching his privacy.

CHECK THE WEB

Check the book's Web site for updates on HIPAA and other privacy issues.

COMPETITION TORTS

Appropriation

For information on privacy rights, see the Privacy Rights Clearinghouse:

http://www.privacyrights.org

The appropriation of someone's name, likeness, or voice for commercial advantage without his or her permission constitutes the tort of **unauthorized appropriation**. For example, if a gas station used your picture in its window to show you as a satisfied customer, you might not be harmed greatly but your privacy is invaded because you have the right to decide when, how, and where your name, face, image, or voice will be used. The fact that you do use the gas station and are a satisfied customer is not the issue in appropriation—it is the use without your permission that constitutes the tort. *Midler* v. *Ford Motor Co.,* (Case 10.3) addresses the unauthorized appropriation of a singer's voice.

CASE 10.3

Midler v. *Ford Motor Co.*
849 F.2d 460 (9th Cir. 1988)

Ford to Bette, "Do You Wanna Dance?";
Bette to Ford, "Not Really!"

FACTS

In 1985, Ford Motor Company and its advertising agency, Young & Rubicam, Inc., advertised the Ford Lincoln Mercury with a series of nineteen 30- or 60-second television commercials in its "The Yuppie Campaign." The aim was to make an emotional connection with Yuppies, bringing back memories of when they were in college. The agency tried to get the "original people," that is, the singers who had popularized the songs, to sing them. When those efforts failed, the agency decided to go with "sound-alikes."

When Young & Rubicam was preparing the Yuppie Campaign, it presented the commercial to its client by playing an edited version of Bette Midler (plaintiff/appellant) singing "Do You Want to Dance?" taken from the 1973 Midler album, *The Divine Miss M.*

After Ford accepted the idea and the commercial, Young & Rubicam contacted Ms. Midler's manager, Jerry Edelstein. The conversation went as follows: "Hello, I am Craig Hazen from Young & Rubicam. I am calling you to find out if Bette Midler would be interested in doing . . . ?" Mr. Edelstein: "Is it a commercial?" "Yes." "We are not interested."

Undeterred, Young & Rubicam sought out Ula Hedwig, who had been one of the "Harlettes," backup singers for Midler for ten years. Ms. Hedwig was told by Young & Rubicam that "they wanted someone who could sound like Bette Midler's recording of ['Do You Want to Dance?']." She was asked to make a demo tape. She made an a cappella demo and got the job. At the direction of Young & Rubicam, Ms. Hedwig made a record for the commercial. She first had to listen to Ms. Midler's recording of it and was then told to "sound as much as possible like the Bette Midler record."

After the commercial aired, Ms. Midler was told by a number of people that it sounded exactly like her. Ms. Hedwig was told by friends that they thought it was Ms. Midler.

Ms. Midler, a nationally known actress and singer, won a Grammy in 1973 as Best New Artist of the Year. She has had both gold and platinum records. She was nominated in 1979 for an Academy Award for Best Female Actress in *The Rose*, in which she portrayed a pop singer. *Newsweek* described her as an "outrageously original singer/comedienne." *Time* hailed her as "a legend" and "the most dynamic and poignant singer-actress of her time."

Ms. Midler filed suit against Ford and Young & Rubicam for appropriation. Young & Rubicam had a license from the song's copyright holder to use it. Neither the name nor the picture of Ms. Midler was used in the commercial. The district court entered judgment for Ford and Young & Rubicam, and Ms. Midler appealed.

JUDICIAL OPINION

NOONAN, Circuit Judge

At issue in this case is only the protection of Midler's voice. The district court described the defendant's conduct as that "of the average thief." They decided, "If we can't buy it, we'll take it." The court nonetheless believed there was no legal principle preventing imitation of Midler's voice and so gave summary judgment for the defendants.

The First Amendment protects much of what the media do in the reproduction of likenesses or sounds. A primary value is freedom of speech and press. The purpose of the media's use of a person's identity is central. If the purpose is "informative or cultural" the use is immune; "if it serves no such function but merely exploits the individual portrayed, immunity will not be granted." It is in the context of these First Amendment and federal copyright distinctions that we address the present appeal.

Nancy Sinatra once sued Goodyear Tire and Rubber Company on the basis of an advertising campaign by Young & Rubicam featuring "These Boots Are Made for Walkin'," a song closely identified with her; the female singers of the commercial were alleged to have imitated her voice and style and to have dressed and looked like her. The basis of Nancy Sinatra's complaint was unfair competition; she claimed that the song and the arrangement had acquired "a secondary meaning" which, under California law, was protectible. This court noted that the defendants "had paid a very substantial sum to the copyright proprietor to obtain the license for the use of the song and all of its arrangements." To give Sinatra damages for their use of the song would clash with federal copyright law. Summary judgment for the defendants was affirmed. If Midler were claiming a secondary meaning to "Do You Want to Dance" or seeking to prevent the defendants from using that song, she would fail like Sinatra. But that is not this case. Midler does not seek damages for

Ford's use of "Do You Want to Dance," and thus her claim is not preempted by federal copyright law. What is put forward as protectible here is more personal than any work of authorship.

Bert Lahr once sued Adell Chemical Co. for selling Lestoil by means of a commercial in which an imitation of Lahr's voice accompanied a cartoon of a duck. Lahr alleged that his style of vocal delivery was distinctive in pitch, accent, inflection, and sounds. The First Circuit held that Lahr had stated a cause of action for unfair competition, that it could be found "that defendant's conduct saturated plaintiff's audience, curtailing his market." That case is more like this one.

A voice is as distinctive and personal as a face. The human voice is one of the most palpable ways identity is manifested. We are all aware that a friend is at once known by a few words on the phone. At a philosophical level it has been observed that with the sound of a voice, "the other stands before me." *A fortiori,* these observations hold true of singing, especially singing by a singer of renown. The singer manifests herself in the song. To impersonate her voice is to pirate her identity.

We need not and do not go so far as to hold that every imitation of a voice to advertise merchandise is actionable. We hold only that when a distinctive voice of a professional singer that is widely known is deliberately imitated in order to sell a product, the sellers have appropriated what is not theirs and have committed a tort in California. Midler has made a showing, sufficient to defeat summary judgment, that the defendants here for their own profit in selling their products did appropriate part of her identity.

CASE QUESTIONS

1. In what context was Ms. Midler's voice sought?
2. Did Ms. Midler agree to allow her voice to be used?
3. Was there some confusion about who was singing in the commercial?
4. What is the difference between this case and the Nancy Sinatra case?
5. What is the difference between this case and the Bert Lahr case?
6. Was the use of Ms. Midler's voice unfair competition?
7. Was the use of Ms. Midler's voice appropriation?

Aftermath: Ms. Midler's case was tried, and she recovered $400,000 from the defendants in October 1989.

NEGLIGENCE

The tort of **negligence** is one that applies in a variety of circumstances, but it is always used when the conduct of one party did not live up to a certain minimal standard of care we are all expected to use in driving, in our work, and in the care of our property. Negligence imposes liability on us when we are careless. The elements of and defenses to negligence are covered next.

Element One: The Duty

Each of us has the duty to act like an **ordinary and reasonably prudent person** in all circumstances. We do not always live up to the standard of the ordinary and reasonably prudent person; when we do not, we are negligent. The standard of the ordinary and reasonably prudent person is not always what everyone else does or what the law provides. For example, suppose you are driving on a curvy highway late at night and it is raining quite heavily. The posted speed limit is 45 mph. However, the ordinary and reasonably prudent person will not drive 45 mph because the road and the weather conditions dictate that slower driving is more appropriate. The level of care imposed on us by the ordinary and reasonably prudent person standard is one that requires an examination of all conditions and circumstances surrounding an event that leads to an injury. Many negligence cases struggle with the difficult task of determining whether a duty exists.

Duties, for purposes of negligence actions, can arise because of an underlying statute. Every traffic law carries a criminal penalty (fine and/or imprisonment) for violations of it. However, that law imposes a duty of obedience. A violation of that law is also a breach of duty for purposes of a civil or negligence action. When you run a red light, you have not only committed a crime; you have also breached a duty and are liable for injuries and damages resulting from that breach.

Professionals such as doctors, lawyers, and dentists have the duty of practicing their professions at the level of a reasonable professional. Failure to do so is a breach of duty and a basis for malpractice (negligence by professionals) lawsuits.

Landowners owe duties to people who enter their property. For example, the duty to trespassers, such as thieves, is not to intentionally injure them. Placing man traps would be a breach of this duty.

Randi W. v. *Muroc Joint Unified School District* (Case 10.4) involves one of the newer issues in whether a duty exists.

CASE 10.4

Randi W. **v.** *Muroc Joint Unified School District*
929 P.2d 582 (Cal. 1997)

The Glowing Letter of Recommendation That Forgot to Mention Sexual Misconduct with Minors

FACTS

Randi W. (plaintiff) is a thirteen-year-old minor who attended the Livingston Middle School where Robert Gadams served as vice principal. On February 1, 1992, while Randi was in Mr. Gadam's office, Mr. Gadams molested and sexually touched Randi.

Mr. Gadams had previously been employed at the Mendota Unified School District (from 1985 to 1988). During his time of employment there, Mr. Gadams had been investigated and reprimanded for improper conduct with female junior high students, including giving them back massages, making sexual remarks to them, and being involved in "sexual situations" with them.

Gilbert Rossette, an official with Mendota, provided a letter of recommendation for Mr. Gadams in May 1990. The letter was part of Mr. Gadams's placement file at Fresno Pacific College, where he had received his teaching credentials. The recommendation was extensive and referred to Mr. Gadams's "genuine concern" for students, his "outstanding rapport" with everyone, and concluded, "I wouldn't hesitate to recommend Mr. Gadams for any position."

Mr. Gadams had also previously been employed at the Tranquility High School District and Golden Plains Unified District (1987–1990). Richard Cole, an administrator at Golden Plains, also provided a letter of recommendation for the Fresno placement file that listed Mr. Gadams's "favorable" qualities and concluded that he "would recommend him for almost any administrative position he wishes to pursue." Mr. Cole knew, at the time he provided the recommendation, that Mr. Gadams had been the subject of various parents' complaints, including that he "led a panty raid, made sexual overtures to students, sexual remarks to students." Mr.

Cole also knew that Mr. Gadams had resigned under pressure because of these sexual misconduct charges.

Mr. Gadams's last place of employment (1990–1991) before Livingston was Muroc Unified School District, where disciplinary actions were taken against him for sexual harassment. When allegations of "sexual touching" of female students were made, Mr. Gadams was forced to resign from Muroc. Nonetheless, Gary Rice and David Malcolm, officials at Muroc, provided a letter of recommendation for Mr. Gadams that described him as "an upbeat, enthusiastic administrator who relates well to the students," and who was responsible "in large part," for making Boron Junior High School (located in Muroc) "a safe, orderly and clean environment for students and staff." The letter concluded that they recommended Mr. Gadams "for an assistant principalship or equivalent position without reservation."

All of the letters provided by previous administrators of Mr. Gadams were sent in on forms that included a disclosure that the information provided "will be sent to prospective employers."

Through her guardian, Randi W. filed suit against the districts, alleging that her injuries from Mr. Gadams's sexual touching were proximately caused by their failure to provide full and accurate information about Mr. Gadams to the placement service. The trial court dismissed the case, and the Court of Appeals reversed. The districts appealed.

JUDICIAL OPINION

CHIN, Associate Justice
In finding plaintiff's complaint stated a cause of action against defendants for fraud and negligent misrepre-

sentation, the Court of Appeal majority relied primarily on sections 310 and 311 of the Restatement Second of Torts. Section 310 involves intentional conduct and provides that "[a]n actor who makes a *misrepresentation* is subject to liability to another for *physical harm* which results from an act done by the other *or a third person* in reliance upon the truth of the representation, if the actor (a) intends his statement to induce or should realize that it is likely to induce action by the other, or a third person, which involves an unreasonable risk of physical harm to the other, and (b) knows (i) that the statement is false, or (ii) that he has not the knowledge which he professes." [Italics added.]

Section 311 of the Restatement Second of Torts, involving negligent conduct, provides that: "(1) One who negligently gives *false information* to another is subject to liability for physical harm caused by action taken by the other *in reasonable reliance upon such information,* where such harm results (a) to the other, or (b) *to such third persons as the actor should expect to be put in peril by the action taken.* (2) Such negligence may consist of a failure to exercise reasonable care (a) in ascertaining the accuracy of the information, or (b) in the manner in which it is communicated." [Italics added.]

Although ordinarily a duty of care analysis is unnecessary in determining liability for intentional misrepresentation or fraud, here we consider liability to *a third person* injured as a result of the alleged fraud, an extension of ordinary tort liability based on fraud. Accordingly, in deciding whether to adopt the two Restatement provisions in the circumstances of this case, we consider whether plaintiff has sufficiently pleaded that defendants owed her a *duty of care,* that they breached that duty by making *misrepresentations* or giving *false information,* and that Livingston's *reasonable reliance* on their statements *proximately caused* plaintiff's injury.

Did defendants owe plaintiff a duty of care? In defendants' view, absent some special relationship between the parties, or some specific and known threat of harm to plaintiff, defendants had no duty of care toward her, and no obligation to disclose in their letters any facts regarding the charges against Gadams.

Plaintiff does not argue that a special relationship existed between defendants and her or Gadams. [U]nder section 311 of the Restatement Second of Torts, a parole officer had a duty to exercise reasonable care in giving the victim information regarding the parolee who ultimately killed her. [A]lthough the parole officer had no duty to volunteer information regarding the released criminals he supervised, ". . . the absence of a duty to speak does not entitle one to speak falsely." [T]he parole officer, "having chosen to communicate information about [the parolee] to [the victim], had a duty to use reasonable care in doing so," and that the officer either knew or should have known that the victim's safety might depend on the accuracy of the information imparted.

[N]o California case has yet held that one who intentionally or negligently provides false information to another owes a duty of care *to a third person* who did not receive the information and who has no special relationship with the provider. Accordingly, the issue before us is one of first impression, and we apply the general analytical principles used to determine the existence of duty in particular cases.

In this state, the general rule is that all persons have a duty to use ordinary care to prevent others from being injured as the result of their conduct.

> *The major [considerations] are* the foreseeability of harm to the plaintiff, *the degree of certainty that the plaintiff suffered injury, the closeness of the connection between the defendant's conduct and the injury suffered, the moral blame attached to the defendant's conduct, the policy of preventing future harm, the extent of the burden to the defendant and consequences to the community of imposing a duty to exercise care with resulting liability for breach, and the availability, cost, and prevalence of insurance for the risk involved.*
>
> *The foreseeability of a particular kind of harm plays a very significant role in this calculus, but a court's task—in determining 'duty'—is not to decide whether a particular plaintiff's injury was reasonably foreseeable in light of a particular defendant's conduct, but rather to evaluate more generally whether the category of negligent conduct at issue is sufficiently likely to result in the kind of harm experienced that liability may appropriately be imposed on the negligent party.*

Applying these factors here, we first examine whether plaintiff's injuries were a *foreseeable* result of defendants' representations regarding Gadams's qualifications and character, coupled with their failure to disclose to the Fresno Pacific College placement office information regarding charges or complaints of Gadams's sexual misconduct. Could defendants reasonably have foreseen that the representations and omissions in their reference letters would result in physical injury to someone? Although the chain of causation leading from defendants' statements and omissions to Gadams's alleged assault on plaintiff is somewhat attenuated, we think the assault was reasonably foreseeable. Based on the facts alleged in the complaint, defendants could foresee that Livingston's officers would read and rely on defendants' letters in deciding to hire Gadams. Likewise, defendants could foresee that, had they not unqualifiedly recommended Gadams, Livingston would not have hired him. And,

continued

finally, defendants could foresee that Gadams, after being hired by Livingston, might molest or injure a Livingston student such as plaintiff. We must assume, for purposes of demurrer, that plaintiff was indeed *injured* in the manner she alleges, and that a *causal connection exists between defendants' conduct and the injury suffered.* As plaintiff's complaint alleges, her injury was a "direct and proximate result" of defendants' fraud and misrepresentations.

Whether defendants were guilty of any *moral blame* would depend on the proof adduced at trial, although it is certainly arguable that their unreserved recommendations of Gadams, together with their failure to disclose facts reasonably necessary to avoid or minimize the risk of further child molestations or abuse, could be characterized as morally blameworthy.

As for public policy, the law certainly recognizes a *policy of preventing future harm* of the kind alleged here. One of society's highest priorities is to protect children from sexual or physical abuse.

Defendants urge that *competing social or economic policies* may disfavor the imposition of liability for misrepresentation or nondisclosure in employment references. They observe that a rule imposing liability in these situations could greatly inhibit the preparation and distribution of reference letters, to the general detriment of employers and employees alike.

We have recently stated that "[w]hen deciding whether to expand a tort duty of care, courts must consider the potential social and economic consequences." Defendants argue that a rule imposing tort liability on writers of recommendation letters could have one very predictable consequence: employers would seldom write such letters, even in praise of exceptionally qualified employees.

In defendants' view, rather than prepare a recommendation letter stating all "material" facts, positive and negative, an employer would be better advised to decline to write a reference letter or, at most, merely to confirm the former employee's position, salary, and dates of employment. According to defendants, apart from the former employer's difficulty in deciding how much "negative" information to divulge, an employer who disclosed more than minimal employment data would risk a defamation, breach of privacy, or wrongful interference suit from a rejected job seeker. [C]ases involving only economic loss are subject to a more restrictive rule.

The Court of Appeal thus concluded that it was unnecessary under section 311 of the Restatement Second of Torts for plaintiff to plead her own reliance on defendants' misrepresentations, as long as the recipient of those misrepresentations (ultimately, Livingston) reasonably relied on them in hiring Gadams, as plaintiff

alleged here. Citing a comment to section 311, the court observed that "The Restatement, however, makes it clear that the plaintiff need not rely on the misrepresentation and may, indeed, not even know that it was made."

We agree with the Court of Appeal's reliance analysis. Under the Restatement provisions, plaintiff need only allege that her injury resulted from action that *the recipient* of defendants' misrepresentations took in reliance on them. In a case involving false or fraudulent letters of recommendation sent to prospective employers regarding a potentially dangerous employee, it would be unusual for *the person ultimately injured* by the employee actually to "rely" on such letters, much less even be aware of them.

In any event, as the Court of Appeal observed, failure to plead reliance would not be a ground for sustaining a demurrer without leave to amend. We note that questions concerning the reasonableness of Livingston's reliance on letters written well before Livingston allegedly received information regarding Gadams's misconduct are not before us in reviewing the trial court's ruling on demurrer.

As previously discussed, plaintiff's complaint alleges that her injury was a "proximate" result of defendants' fraud and misrepresentations. Defendants do not suggest that the complaint fails to state sufficient facts to establish proximate causation, assuming the remaining elements of duty, misrepresentation and reliance are sufficiently pleaded. Based on the facts alleged in the complaint, plaintiff's injury foreseeably and proximately resulted from Livingston's decision to hire Gadams in reliance on defendants' unqualified recommendation of him.

The judgment of the Court of Appeal is affirmed as to counts three and four (negligent misrepresentation and fraud), but reversed as to count five (negligence *per se*).

CASE QUESTIONS

1. Who provided the letters of recommendation for Mr. Gadams? What information was missing from the recommendations?

2. What concerns are raised about imposing liability on those who provide letters of recommendation?

3. What was the proximate cause of Randi W.'s injury?

4. Did the former employers owe a duty to anyone with respect to the letters of recommendation?

5. What issues should employers address, in light of this case, in providing letters of reference and recommendation?

FOR THE MANAGER'S DESK

Re: References, Risk, and Defamation

Paul Calden, a thirty-three-year-old, low-level manager, was fired from his job at Allstate Insurance Company in St. Petersburg, Florida, for carrying a gun to his job. His supervisors at Allstate would later describe him as a "total lunatic."

Mr. Calden applied for a job with Firemen's Fund Insurance in Tampa, Florida. Firemen's Fund contacted the Allstate offices for a reference. Allstate sent a letter signed by a vice president that was neutral in its description of Mr. Calden and did not disclose the true reasons for his termination. Mr. Calden had threatened litigation; there was some fear among the employees about him, and Allstate had agreed to a four-month severance package despite his having worked at Allstate for only nine months. Allstate also agreed to draft and send the neutral letter.

After Mr. Calden was terminated by Firemen's Fund, he shot and killed three executives of the company while they were having lunch at a café. One of the executives' wives filed suit against Firemen's Fund and Allstate. The suit against Allstate was based on its failure to disclose Mr. Calden's bizarre behavior and the risk that he was in the workplace.

Allstate defended its actions on the grounds that the average verdict in a defamation suit by a former employee against his former employer for a job reference is $57,000. In one Florida case, a former employee was awarded $25 million in damages. However, in an unpublished opinion, *Jerner v. Allstate Insurance Co.,* 94–03822 (Fla. App. 1995), the appellate court held that there could be an action against an employer for misrepresentation if the employer gives a neutral reference on an employee who is a danger, as in this case.

The majority of the states have some form of law that creates a privilege for employers in providing references. The privilege is designed to free managers in their discussions of former employees and their performances. A survey indicates that without such protection, disclosures about violent tendencies will not be made and the risk to employees at a new firm is high. Fifty-four percent of all employers indicate they would not disclose violent behavior when asked for a reference.

In nearly all states, there is a qualified privilege for those who have a moral obligation to speak. These types of privilege statutes provide protection for whistleblowers (see Chapter 18), in that a controlled (limited) disclosure of information made in good faith will not subject a businessperson to liability for defamation. However, verification of the truth of such statements is critical. Also adding to the complexity of the reference issue is a U.S. Supreme Court decision in which the court held that giving a negative reference on a former employee who has sued the company for discrimination can be considered retaliatory and a violation of Title VII [*Robinson v. Shell Oil Co.,* 519 U.S. 337 (1997)].

BUSINESS STRATEGY

A Reference on References

If you are assigned the task of developing a new reference policy for your company, remember the following guidelines.

1. Stick with factual disclosures: Use "There was an accusation of embezzlement and he resigned," not "He is an embezzler."
2. Stick with easily defined terms: Use "Angers easily," not "He is a lunatic."

3. Report what happened, not your view: Use "Other staff members complained about her conduct and work," not "She was a constant pain in the neck."
4. Implement an exit interview in which you disclose the information you have on file that will be given when references are requested.
5. Verify the protections offered under your state law, if any.

Element Two: Breach of Duty

Once the standard of care and the duty are established under element one, there must be a determination that the defendant fell short of that standard or breached that duty for the plaintiff to recover on the basis of negligence. For example, an accountant owes a duty to his client to perform an audit in a competent and professional manner and to conform the audit to the standards and rules established by the American Institute of Certified Public Accounts (AICPA). Failure to comply with these standards would be a breach of duty and would satisfy this second element of negligence.

In many cases, courts try to determine whether the duty was breached to determine whether the defendant's action satisfied the standard of care established in element one.

Graves v. *Warner Brothers* (Case 10.5) focuses on the issues of safety and the liability of businesses and property owners for injuries that result from the acts of third parties. This case provides the answer to the chapter's opening Consider.

CASE 10.5

Graves v. *Warner Brothers*
656 N.W.2d 195 (Mich. App. 2002)
cert. den. ___ U.S. ___, 2004 WL 1373288 (2004)

Shootout Following the *Jenny Jones* Showdown

FACTS

Scott Amedure (decedent; plaintiff's decedent; plaintiffs are decedent's parents) was shot and killed in March 1995 by Jonathan Schmitz (defendant), who was ultimately convicted of second-degree murder [*People* v. *Schmitz*, 231 Mich.App. 521, 523, 586 N.W.2d 766 (1998)].

Three days before the shooting, Mr. Schmitz appeared with Mr. Amedure and Donna Riley in Chicago for a taping of an episode of the *Jenny Jones* talk show, during which Mr. Schmitz was surprised by Mr. Amedure's revelation that he had a secret crush on him. After the taping, Mr. Schmitz told many friends and acquaintances that he was quite embarrassed and humiliated by the experience and began a drinking binge.

On the morning of the shooting, Mr. Schmitz found a sexually suggestive note from Mr. Amedure on his front door. Mr. Schmitz then drove to a local bank, withdrew money from his savings account, and purchased a 12-gauge pump-action shotgun and some ammunition. Mr. Schmitz then drove to Mr. Amedure's trailer, where he confronted Mr. Amedure about the note. When Mr. Amedure just smiled at him, Mr. Schmitz walked out of the trailer, stating that he had to shut off his car. Instead, he retrieved the shotgun and returned to the trailer. Standing at the front door, Mr. Schmitz fired two shots into Mr. Amedure's chest, leaving him with no chance for survival. Mr. Schmitz left the scene and telephoned 911 to confess to the shooting.

Following a jury trial and conviction, Mr. Schmitz was sentenced to twenty-five to fifty years' imprisonment for the murder conviction. Mr. Schmitz was dismissed from the suit as a result of a settlement agreement. The taped segment was never broadcast.

Mr. Amedure's parents (plaintiffs Patricia Graves and Frank Amedure) brought a wrongful death action against the *Jenny Jones Show*, its owner, Warner Brothers (defendants), and its producer, Telepictures. They alleged that the show and Warner Brothers knew or should have known that their actions would incite violence, with the sole purpose of the show being the increase in television ratings, and that they had an affirmative duty to prevent or refrain from placing Mr. Amedure in a position that would unnecessarily and unreasonably expose him to the risk of harm, albeit the criminal conduct of a third person. Mr. Amedure's parents argued that the show breached its duty and foreseeably subjected Mr. Amedure to an unreasonable risk of harm, ultimately resulting in his death.

Following an extensive trial, a jury returned a verdict of $29,332,686 in damages for the plaintiffs. The show and Warner Brothers appealed.

JUDICIAL OPINION

GRIFFIN, Judge
In determining standards of conduct in the area of negligence, the courts have made a distinction between

misfeasance, or active misconduct causing personal injury, and nonfeasance, which is passive inaction or the failure to actively protect others from harm. The common law has been slow in recognizing liability for nonfeasance because the courts are reluctant to force persons to help one another and because such conduct does not create a new risk of harm to a potential plaintiff. Thus, as a general rule, there is no duty that obligates one person to aid or protect another.

Social policy, however, has led the courts to recognize an exception to this general rule where a special relationship exists between a plaintiff and a defendant. . . . The rationale behind imposing a duty to protect in these special relationships is based on control. In each situation one person entrusts himself to the control and protection of another, with a consequent loss of control to protect himself. The duty to protect is imposed upon the person in control because he is best able to provide a place of safety.

A premises owner's duty is limited to responding reasonably to situations occurring on the premises because, as a matter of public policy, we should not expect invitors to assume that others will disobey the law. A merchant can assume that patrons will obey the criminal law. This assumption should continue until a specific situation occurs on the premises that would cause a reasonable person to recognize a risk of imminent harm to an identifiable invitee. It is only a present situation on the premises, not any past incidents, that creates a duty to respond.

Subjecting a merchant to liability solely on the basis of a foreseeability analysis is misbegotten. Because criminal activity is irrational and unpredictable, it is in this sense invariably foreseeable everywhere. However, even police, who are specially trained and equipped to anticipate and deal with crime, are unfortunately unable universally to prevent it. This is a testament to the arbitrary nature of crime. Given these realities, it is unjustifiable to make merchants, who not only have much less experience than the police in dealing with criminal activity but are also without a community deputation to do so, effectively vicariously liable for the criminal acts of third parties.

Logic compels the conclusion that defendants in this case had no duty to anticipate and prevent the act of murder committed by Schmitz three days after leaving defendants' studio and hundreds of miles away. Here, the only special relationship, if any, that ever existed between defendants and plaintiffs' decedent, or between defendants and Schmitz, was that of business invitor to invitee. However, any duty ends when the relationship ends, and in this instance the invitor/invitee relationship ended on March 6, 1995, three days before the murder, when Schmitz and Amedure peacefully left the Chicago studio following the taping of the episode. Because the evidence, even when viewed from a perspective most favorable to plaintiffs, revealed no ongoing special relationship at the time of the murder, defendants owed no duty to protect plaintiffs' decedent from Schmitz' violent attack on March 9, 1995. The present situation simply cannot, under any reasonable interpretation of the circumstances, be construed as involving an existing special relationship that required defendants to respond to a risk of imminent and foreseeable harm to an identifiable invitee on the premises. Consequently, the trial court erred as a matter of law in denying defendants' motions for summary disposition, a directed verdict, and judgment notwithstanding the verdict on the basis of lack of duty, an essential element of any negligence action.

DISSENTING OPINION

MURPHY, Presiding Judge

I respectfully dissent from the majority's opinion because the issue of foreseeability concerning the shotgun slaying was properly placed in the hands of the jury. Viewing the evidence in a light most favorable to plaintiffs, I believe that the issue was properly left to the jury where the evidence indicated that Jonathan Schmitz was humiliated and devastated on a show scheduled to be broadcast on national television by defendants through the revelation of a homosexual crush and lurid sexual fantasy by Scott Amedure after Schmitz told defendants that he did not want the crush to be that of another man, and where defendants nonetheless proceeded with the production of the show, using deceit, sensationalism, and outrageous behavior. I reach my conclusion taking into consideration Schmitz's personal history, which included mental illness, alcohol and drug abuse, suicide attempts, anger management problems, and sexual identity concerns. Certainly, reasonable men and women could differ on whether Schmitz's violent act foreseeably resulted from defendants' actions in manipulating and exploiting the lives, emotions, and sexual identities of individuals for the purpose of producing their television talk show.

Reversed.

CASE QUESTIONS

1. How did the victim and perpetrator meet?
2. Who is bringing the suit?
3. What constraints does the majority of the court put on liability for criminal acts?
4. What is the dissenting judge's position on liability for criminal acts?

ETHICAL ISSUES

Why do you think Warner Brothers never aired the segment of the *Jenny Jones Show* that featured Mr. Amedure and Mr. Schmitz?

CONSIDER...   10.8

Dorothy McClung went shopping at the Wal-Mart in the Delta Square Shopping Center in Memphis around noon. After she had completed her shopping and was returning to her car, she was abducted at gunpoint and forced into her car. She was later found dead in the trunk of her car, after it was spotted by some hunters in a remote area in Arkansas. Roger McClung, her husband, filed suit against Wal-Mart and the owner of the shopping center, Delta Square. Are these companies liable for the criminal acts of another when those acts occurred in their parking lot? [*McClung* v. *Delta Square Limited Partnership*, 937 S.W.2d 891 (Tenn. 1996).]

BUSINESS STRATEGY

The Post-9/11 Duty for Security and Safety

Corporate security advisers are in demand and growing as an industry. This increase in business began immediately after September 11, 2001, and the collapse of the World Trade Center in New York City. Corporate security advisers help companies with the following issues:

© GETTY IMAGES

- Emergency response—planning for evacuation of buildings as well as the shutdown and evacuation of operations in other countries
- Business continuity—planning for alternate sites in the event of destruction of buildings and the creation of emergency response systems should a company experience a problem at a site or factory
- Vulnerability assessments—identifying weak security points in a company's buildings and operations
- Background checks—doing private investigation work on employees in order to determine whether they present a security risk to the company

What liability would companies have for their failure to do any of the above processes, checks, and procedures?

Source: Paul Magnusson, "Your Jitters Are Their Lifeblood," *Business Week*, April 14, 2003, p. 41.

Element Three: Causation

After establishing a duty and breach of duty, the plaintiff in a negligence suit must also establish that the breach of the duty was the cause of the damages. A test often used to determine **causation** is the **"but for" test**—"but for the action or lack of action of the defendant, the plaintiff would not have been injured." For example, suppose that a guest is enjoying a scenic view of the ocean from a cliff near his hotel. At the edge of the cliff, the hotel had installed a fence, but the hotel does not keep it in good repair. When the guest leans against the fence to take a picture, the fence breaks and the guest falls over the cliff. The hotel breached its duty to keep its premises in reasonably safe condition, and its failure to do so caused the guest's injury.

FOR THE MANAGER'S DESK

RE: HOOTERS AND CAUSATION

A jury in San Diego returned a verdict that reflects an understanding of duty, breach of duty, and causation in negligence. The case involved a fight that began at an employee party for employees of Hooters. Robert Womack, a guest of one of the employees at the party, had been drinking and became disruptive. Evan Johnson, a security guard at the hotel where the party was held, asked Mr. Womack to leave. Mr. Womack then head-butted Mr. Johnson, and a fight began. Mr. Johnson suffered permanent neurological impairment as a result of the injuries he sustained in the fight.

Mr. Johnson sued both Mr. Womack and Hooters. The jury returned a verdict of $860,000, but only against Mr. Womack. The jury found that Hooters had done nothing to cause the altercation, that it did not know that Mr. Womack was causing trouble, and that it had no advance knowledge of any such tendencies on the part of Mr. Womack. The attorney for Hooters said, "We got by on causation."

Explain what the attorney meant with his statement.

Source: Randy Stewart, "Party fight leads to $860,000 award," *National Law Journal,* January 6, 2003, p. B1.

The "but for" test is limited by the so-called zone of danger rule, which requires that the plaintiff be in the zone of danger when the injury occurs. The zone of danger includes all those people who could foreseeably be injured if a duty is breached. For example, the hotel would also be liable to those injured by the guest as he fell through the weak fence because they are in the zone of danger.

Element Four: Proximate Cause

Some cutoff line must be drawn between the "but for" causation and events that contribute to the injury of the plaintiff—an element of a negligence case called *proximate cause.* Suppose that you have a tire replaced at a tire store and the technician fails to tighten the wheel sufficiently. As you drive down the street, the tire comes loose, rolls off, and strikes another car. Did the tire store cause the damage to the other car? Yes. Any accidents caused by that car? Yes. Suppose the tire comes off, rolls onto the sidewalk, and strikes a pedestrian. Did the tire store cause that injury? Yes. Suppose the pedestrian sees the tire coming and jumps out of the way but, in so doing, injures another pedestrian. Did the tire store cause that injury? Yes. In all of these accidents, the following statement can be made: "But for the failure to tighten the wheel, the accident would not have occurred." Suppose that the tire injures a pedestrian, although not fatally, but a doctor treating the pedestrian, through malpractice, causes the pedestrian's death. Did the tire store cause the death? No; another's negligence intervened.

Case 10.6, *Palsgraf* v. *Long Island Ry. Co.,* is a landmark case on the element of proximate cause.

BUSINESS PLANNING TIP

All businesses should help create a safe environment for their customers and discourage criminal acts with the following:

1. Good lighting
2. Access to public phones
3. Security patrols
4. Locked gates to parking lots; gate or security access
5. Escorts for customers and employees to their vehicles after closing hours
6. Camera security
7. Assigned parking spaces for tenants and employees
8. Warning signs to use caution and be alert

Many hotels change key access codes with each guest and post security personnel near guest elevators at night so that there is no access to the elevators unless you can show your room key. Some hotels have floors for women who are traveling alone, and extra security is provided on those floors.

CASE 10.6

Palsgraf v. *Long Island Ry. Co.*
162 N.E. 99 (N.Y. 1928)

Fireworks in the Passenger's Package
and Negligence in the Air

FACTS

Helen Palsgraf (plaintiff) had purchased a ticket to travel to Rockaway Beach on the Long Island Railway (defendant). While she was standing on a platform at the defendant's station waiting for the train, another train stopped at the station. Two men ran to catch the train, which began moving as they were running. One of the men made it onto the train without difficulty, but the other man, who was carrying a package, was unsteady as he tried to jump aboard. Employees of the defendant helped pull the man in and push him onto the train car, but in the process the package was dropped. The package contained fireworks, and when dropped, it exploded. The vibrations from the explosion caused some scales (located at the end of the platform on which Ms. Palsgraf was standing) to fall. As they fell, they hit and injured Ms. Palsgraf. She filed suit against the railroad for negligence.

JUDICIAL OPINION

CARDOZO, Chief Justice

The conduct of the defendant's guard, if a wrong in its relation to the holder of the package, was not a wrong in its relation to the plaintiff, standing far away. Nothing in the situation gave notice that the falling package had in it the potency of peril to persons thus removed. Negligence is not actionable unless it involves the invasion of a legally protected interest, the violation of a right. "Proof of negligence in the air, so to speak, will not do." The plaintiff, as she stood upon the platform of the station, might claim to be protected against intentional invasion of her bodily security. Such invasion is not charged. She might claim to be protected against unintentional invasion by conduct involving in the thought of reasonable men an unreasonable hazard that such invasion would ensue. These, from the point of view of the law, were the bounds of her immunity, with perhaps some rare exceptions, survivals for the most part of ancient forms of liability, where conduct is held to be at the peril of the actor. If no hazard was apparent to the eye of ordinary vigilance, an act innocent and harmless, at least to outward seeming, with reference to her, did not take to itself the quality of a tort because it happened to be a wrong, though apparently not one involving the risk of bodily insecurity, with reference to some one else.

A different conclusion will involve us, and swiftly too, in a maze of contradictions. A guard stumbles over a package which has been left upon a platform. It seems to be a bundle of newspapers. It turns out to be a can of dynamite. To the eye of ordinary vigilance, the bundle is abandoned waste, which may be kicked or trod on with impunity. Is a passenger at the other end of the platform protected by the law against the unsuspected hazard concealed beneath the waste? If not, is the result to be any different, so far as the distant passenger is concerned, when the guard stumbles over a valise which a truckman or a porter has left upon the walk? The passenger far away, if the victim of a wrong at all, has a cause of action, not derivative, but original and primary. His claim to be protected against invasion of his bodily security is neither greater nor less because the act resulting in the invasion is a wrong to another far removed. In this case, the rights that are said to have been violated, the interests said to have been invaded, are not even of the same order. The man was not injured in his person or even put in danger. The purpose of the act, as well as its effect, was to make his person safe. If there was a wrong to him at all, which may very well be doubted, it was a wrong to a property interest only, the safety of his package. Out of this wrong to property, which threatened injury to nothing else, there has passed, we are told, to the plaintiff by derivation or succession a right of action for the invasion of an interest of another order, the right to bodily security. The diversity of interests emphasizes the futility of the effort to build the plaintiff's right upon the basis of a wrong to some one else. The gain is one of emphasis, for a like result would follow if the interests were the same. Even then, the orbit of the danger as disclosed to the eye of reasonable vigilance would be the orbit of the duty. One who jostles one's neighbor in a crowd does not invade the rights of others standing at the outer fringe when the unintended contact casts a bomb upon the ground. The wrongdoer as to them is the man who carries the bomb, not the one who explodes it without suspicion of the danger. Life will have to be made over, and human nature transformed, before prevision so extravagant can be accepted as the norm of conduct, the customary standard to which behavior must conform.

The risk reasonably to be perceived defines the duty to be obeyed, and risk imports relation; it is risk to another or to others within the range of apprehension. Here, by concession, there was nothing in the situation to suggest to the most cautious mind that the parcel wrapped in newspaper would spread wreckage through the station. If the guard had thrown it down knowingly and willfully, he would not have threatened the plaintiff's safety, so far as appearances could warn him. His conduct would not have involved, even then, an unreasonable probability of invasion of her bodily security. Liability can be no greater where the act is inadvertent.

DISSENTING OPINION

ANDREWS, Justice

Assisting a passenger to board a train, the defendant's servant negligently knocked a package from his arms. It fell between the platform and the cars. Of its contents the servant knew and could know nothing. A violent explosion followed. The concussion broke some scales standing a considerable distance away. In falling, they injured the plaintiff, an intending passenger.

Upon these facts, may she recover the damages she has suffered in an action brought against the master? The result we shall reach depends upon our theory as to the nature of negligence. Is it a relative concept—the breach of some duty owing to a particular person or to particular persons?

Or, where there is an act which unreasonably threatens the safety of others, is the doer liable for all its proximate consequences, even where they result in injury to one who would generally be thought to be outside the radius of danger? This is not a mere dispute as to words. We might not believe that to the average mind the dropping of the bundle would seem to involve the probability of harm to the plaintiff standing many feet away whatever might be the case as to the owner or to one so near as to be likely to be struck by its fall. If, however, we adopt the second hypothesis, we have to inquire only as to the relation between cause and effect. We deal in terms of proximate cause, not of negligence.

Negligence may be defined roughly as an act or omission which unreasonably does or may affect the rights of others, or which unreasonably fails to protect one's self from the dangers resulting from such acts.

Where there is the unreasonable act, and some right that may be affected there is negligence whether damage does or does not result. That is immaterial. Should we drive down Broadway at a reckless speed, we are negligent whether we strike an approaching car or miss it by an inch. The act itself is wrongful. It is a wrong not only to those who happen to be within the radius of danger, but to all who might have been there—a wrong to the public at large.

Negligence does involve a relationship between man and his fellows, but not merely a relationship between man and those whom he might reasonably expect his act would injure; rather, a relationship between him and those whom he does in fact injure. If his act has a tendency to harm some one, it harms him a mile away as surely as it does those on the scene.

The proposition is this: Every one owes to the world at large the duty of refraining from those acts that may unreasonably threaten the safety of others. Such an act occurs. Not only is he wronged to whom harm might reasonably be expected to result, but he also who is in fact injured, even if he be outside what would generally be thought the danger zone.

As we have said, we cannot trace the effect of an act to the end, if end there is. Again, however, we may trace it part of the way. An overturned lantern may burn all Chicago. We may follow the fire from the shed to the last building. We rightly say the fire started by the lantern caused its destruction. A cause, but not the proximate cause. What we do mean by the word "proximate" is that, because of convenience, of public policy, of a rough sense of justice, the law arbitrarily declines to trace a series of events beyond a certain point. This is not logic. It is practical politics.

This last suggestion is the factor which must determine the case before us. The act upon which defendant's liability rests is knocking an apparently harmless package onto the platform. The act was negligent. For its proximate consequences the defendant is liable. If its contents were broken, to the owner; if it fell upon and crushed a passenger's foot, then to him; if it exploded and injured one in the immediate vicinity, to him. Mrs. Palsgraf was standing some distance away. How far cannot be told from the record—apparently 25 to 30 feet, perhaps less. Except for the explosion, she would not have been injured. . . . The only intervening cause was that, instead of blowing her to the ground, the concussion smashed the weighing machine which in turn fell upon her. There was no remoteness in time, little in space. And surely, given such an explosion as here, it needed no great foresight to predict that the natural result would be to injure one on the platform at no greater distance from its scene than was the plaintiff. Just how no one might be able to predict. Whether by flying fragments, by broken glass, by wreckage of machines or structures no one could say. But injury in some form was most probable.

Under these circumstances I cannot say as a matter of law that the plaintiff's injuries were not the proximate result of the negligence.

CASE QUESTIONS

1. Who was carrying the package?

2. How far away from the incident was Ms. Palsgraf?

3. What does Justice Cardozo find?

4. What point does the dissenting judge make?

Element Five: Damages

The plaintiff in a negligence case must be able to establish damages that resulted from the defendant's negligence. Such damages could include medical bills, lost wages, and pain and suffering, as well as any property damages. In many of the cases in this chapter, plaintiffs have also recovered punitive damages. Often referred to as "smart money," punitive damages are similar to civil penalties that are paid to plaintiffs because of the high level of carelessness involved on the defendant's part.

Defenses to Negligence

Contributory Negligence

In some cases, an accident results from the combined negligence of two or more people. A plaintiff who is also negligent gives the defendant the opportunity to raise the defense of **contributory negligence**. Contributory negligence is simply negligence by the plaintiff that is part of the cause of an accident. For example, suppose that a boat owner is operating his boat late at night on a lake in which the water is choppy and when he is intoxicated. An intoxicated friend is sitting at the bow of the boat trying to put her feet into the water when the owner takes the boat up to high speed. She falls in and is injured. The issue of causation becomes complicated here because there were breaches of duties by both parties. Did he cause the accident by driving at high speed late at night on a choppy lake while intoxicated? Or did she cause the accident by sitting without protection or restraint on the bow of the boat when the boat was being driven like that? The effect of the defense of contributory negligence is a complete bar to both from recovery.

BUSINESS STRATEGY APPLICATION

Be sure to do the exercise for this chapter, "Name That Tort!," found on the book's Web site. You can test your ability to apply the law to factual circumstances.

Comparative Negligence

Many states, in order to eliminate the harsh effect of contributory negligence, have adopted a defense of **comparative negligence**. Under this defense, the jury simply determines the level of fault for both the plaintiff and the defendant and, based on this assessment of fault, determines how much each of the parties will be awarded. Using our boat example, the jury could find that the boat owner was 75 percent at fault and the passenger was 25 percent at fault. Under comparative negligence, the passenger could recover for her injuries, but the amount recovered would be 25 percent less because of her fault in causing the accident.

The defense of comparative negligence was developed largely because of the perceived unfairness of contributory negligence, which was a complete bar to recovery. The concept of comparative negligence has resulted in more litigation and more verdicts for plaintiffs permitted to use the defense.

Assumption of Risk

The **assumption of risk** defense requires the defendant to prove that the plaintiff knew there was a risk of injury in the conduct he or she undertook but decided to go forward with it anyway. For example, there are some inherent dangers in activities such as skydiving, skiing, and roller skating. You assume the inherent risks in these activities, but you do not assume the risks caused by the owners of the premises or equipment. For example, when you ski, you assume the natural risks that exist in skiing, but you do not assume the risk of faulty equipment you rent. If the failure of that equipment causes your injuries, the rental company would be responsible for that injury. To assume the risk, you must be completely aware of the risk and you must assume the risk voluntarily. *Mosca* v. *Lichtenwalter* (Case 10.7) deals with the issue of assumption of risk.

CASE 10.7

Mosca v. *Lichtenwalter*
68 Cal. Rptr. 58 (Cal. App. 1997)

Hooked while Fishing

FACTS

Joseph Mosca and twenty-three others boarded a sportfishing boat for a day of fishing off San Clemente Island. David Lichtenwalter, one of the fishermen, was fishing off the stern near Mr. Mosca. Mr. Lichtenwalter's line became entangled in kelp and he was unable to get it released. A deckhand approached Mr. Lichtenwalter to help him. Mr. Lichtenwalter backed up and handed the pole to the deckhand just as the line "slingshotted" over the rail toward Mr. Mosca, who was struck in the eye with the sinker, which caused a partial vision loss.

Mr. Mosca filed suit against Mr. Lichtenwalter and others. The trial court, using the defense of assumption of risk, dismissed the case, and Mr. Mosca appealed.

JUDICIAL OPINION

WALEN, Acting Presiding Justice
The declaration of David Wilhite, a sportfishing expert, was submitted in opposition to the motion for summary judgment. He opined injury from hooks or sinkers when fishing lines slingshot may occur when an improper technique of freeing a stuck line is used.

He indicated the danger of injury when extricating a line caught on an underwater object can be minimized by reaching down near the waterline, wrapping the line around a hand, and pulling it at a low angle. Lichtenwalter apparently used that approach when he first tried to release it. When he stepped back for the deckhand to intervene, he allegedly pulled the line in a higher, upward direction.

Mosca contends the trial court erred in granting summary judgment based on assumption of risk.

In *Knight* v. *Jewett* (1992) 3 Cal.4th 296, 11 Cal.Rptr.2d 2, 834 P.2d 696, the Supreme Court discussed the difference between "primary" and "secondary" assumption of risk. Primary assumption of risk is a policy-driven legal concept where the courts declare there is no duty at all.

Primary assumption of risk has often been imposed where the plaintiff and defendant are engaged in a sport. "In the sports setting . . . conditions or conduct that otherwise might be viewed as dangerous often are an integral part of the sport itself."

continued

To decide whether a duty will be imposed on a participant in a sporting activity, the court must determine whether the injury suffered arises from an inherent risk in the activity, and whether imposing a duty "might chill vigorous participation in the implicated activity and thereby alter its fundamental nature."

The trial court, at least implicitly, determined the danger of injury from a hook or sinker flying toward a participant is an inherent risk in sportfishing, and imposing the specter of liability regarding the danger would chill or alter the sport. That determination was reasonable. Hooking and catching fish requires a great deal of knowledge, physical skill, and attention. A participant who worries whether he is hooked on a fish or kelp, and what method should be used to deal with the line in either instance, will not be an effective fisherman, and may be inclined to give up the sport.

Mosca argues that getting hit in the eye by a sinker is not an inherent danger in sportfishing because there was evidence none of the parties, witnesses or the expert had ever heard of this type of injury. The inquiry is not that narrow. The question involved is a broader inquiry: whether injury from flying hooks and sinkers is inherent in the sport.

Relying on expert witness Wilhite's declaration, Mosca also asserts the danger of being hit by a recoiling line which is stuck on an underwater object is not inherent in the sport if care is used to release it, by properly pulling it or even by cutting the line. He begs the question by making this argument. The question whether the sport can be made safer if certain techniques are used bears on the standard of care, and is a question that is reached only if the threshold question of duty is resolved against the defendant. Wilhite admits flying hooks and sinkers are risks in the sport. He merely indicated the danger can be minimized if care is taken and specific techniques to free a line are used.

Courts have recognized these principles in cases dealing with other sports activities. In *Regents of University of California* v. *Superior Court,* 41 Cal.App.4th 1040, 48 Cal.Rptr.2d 922, the court held rock climbers assume the risk climbing anchors may give way, even though it was a standard procedure to double check the anchors to maximize safety. "Falling, whether because of one's own slip, a coclimber's stumble, or an anchor system giving way, is the very risk inherent in the sport of mountain climbing and cannot be completely eliminated without destroying the sport itself." The court found an inherent risk of harm despite the presence of safety measures.

Mosca points out that *Knight* v. *Jewett,* Cal.4th 296, 11 Cal.Rptr.2d 2, 834 P.2d 696, and other cases where primary assumption of risk has been found involved contact sports or other sports where the defendant was

an opponent. But there is no such limitation on the doctrine. In *Staten* v. *Superior Court,* 45 Cal.App. 4th at p.1634, 53 Cal.Rptr.2d 657, the court applied the doctrine to figure skating, a "teamless" sport where one participates in close proximity with others so engaged. Sportfishing is the same type of close-proximity endeavor.

Cases declining to find primary assumption of the risk are distinguishable. In *Yancey* v. *Superior Court* (1994), 28 Cal.App.4th 558, 33 Cal.Rptr.2d 777, the court held a participant throwing a discus owes a duty of due care to check the field before throwing because "[n]othing about the inherent nature of the sport requires that one participant who has completed a throw and is retrieving his or her discus should expect the next participant to throw without looking toward the landing area." (See also *Lowe* v. *California League of Professional Baseball* (1997) 56 Cal.App. 4th 112, 123, 65 Cal.Rptr.2d 105 [antics of team mascot that distracted plaintiff who was struck by foul ball were not integral to the sport].) But Lichtenwalter, in attempting to free his line, was engaged in a typical adjunct of fishing.

In *Morgan* v. *Fuji Country USA, Inc.* (1995) 34 Cal.App.4th 127, 40 Cal.Rptr.2d 249, the court found assumption of the risk was not available to the defendants as grounds for summary judgment because their golf course design could be held by a trier of fact to have affirmatively increased the inherent risk of being struck by errant golf balls. Mosca neither claims, nor did he show, the fishing boat design or anything about the boat owners' fishing policy affirmatively increased the risk of harm. At most he alleges a deckhand was guilty of failing to ensure Lichtenwalter engaged in a preferred line retrieval technique.

Mosca notes that assumption of risk cannot be invoked in hunting accidents, but that is "because of the special danger to others posed by the sport of hunting." Indeed, that concept has been codified by the Legislature. Mosca makes no showing sportfishing has attained a similar status. Although fishing carries with it certain dangers, it does not involve the potentially mortal danger involved in hunting.

The judgment is affirmed.

CASE QUESTIONS

1. What happened on the boat, and how was Mr. Mosca injured?

2. Is the risk of being struck by a line inherent in the sport of fishing?

3. Was Mr. Mosca's injury typical?

4. What is the difference between assumption of risk in day-to-day activities and assumption of risk in sports?

> ## CONSIDER...   10.10
>
> Benjamin Dayries Wynne pledged the Sigma Alpha Epsilon fraternity at Louisiana State University in September 1997. To celebrate, Mr. Wynne and his fraternity brothers began drinking via "funneling," a process by which a hose from a keg shoots beer into the drinker's mouth.
>
> The fraternity brothers then moved on to a new drinking ritual, "The Three Wise Men," which is a 151-proof mix of rum, Crown Royal, and Jagermeister liqueur. At the end of this ritual, Mr. Wynne was staggering and had to be wheeled out of the bar in a shopping cart.
>
> By the next morning, Mr. Wynne was found dead of alcohol poisoning. Does the fraternity have liability? Does Louisiana State University have liability?
>
> According to a 1994 Harvard study, nearly half of all college students "binge" drink, or drink more than five drinks at one setting. A 1997 Harvard survey found that 52.3 percent of all college students who drink do so with the idea of getting drunk. In 1997, thirty-four students on college campuses died after excessive drinking. Would a complete prohibition on alcohol help? Would a prohibition on fraternity drinking help?

TORT REFORM

As noted in Chapter 3, the United States has a sizable court system equipped with sufficient lawyers for the support of litigation. The United States permits greater recovery for torts while requiring less in terms of proof than other nations. One study estimates tort costs to be 2.3 percent of the U.S. GDP, a cost of $721 per citizen.[2] Over the past decade, a number of reforms have been proposed, particularly with respect to tort litigation, to limit recovery or place other limitations on the amount of increasing tort litigation. For example, some reform proposals would limit damages. Those limitations may be general limitations on damage awards or limitations like the Canadian system of $200,000 for pain and suffering. Although nearly all states have adopted some form of limitations in tort recovery, these reforms are a maze of laws differing from state to state, have been subject to judicial challenges (in many cases successful), and have provided little hope for insurers as they try to forecast their risks in insuring businesses and their properties and agents.

Peter W. Huber, a senior fellow at the Manhattan Institute, a conservative New York think tank, maintains that judges should defuse confrontations in tort cases by encouraging the litigants to settle and by establishing rules that would hold defendants liable only in those cases in which they are at fault and a large recovery will deter future accidents that would not otherwise be deterred.

In *BMW of North America, Inc. v. Gore* (Case 10.8), the U.S. Supreme Court addressed the issue of large recoveries.

CASE 10.8

BMW of North America, Inc. v. Gore
517 U.S. 559 (1996)

The Fussy Doctor, the BMW, and Acid Rain

FACTS

Dr. Ira Gore, Jr. (respondent) purchased a new 1990 BMW 535i automobile from German Auto, Inc., a Birmingham, Alabama, dealership. Dr. Gore, a graduate of Harvard and Duke Medical School, signed a "Retail Buyers Order" and "Acknowledgment of Disclosure" in which he acknowledged that the car might have sustained damage, that he had inspected it, and that he agreed to accept it.

continued

Dr. Gore drove the car for nine months before taking it to "Slick Finish," an auto detail shop. Dr. Gore took the car in to make it "snazzier." The auto detailer told Dr. Gore that the car had been partially refinished. Dr. Gore later determined that the refinishing had been done because of acid rain damage to the paint on the car during transit from Germany (BMW AG) to the North American vehicle preparation center (BMW NA) in Brunswick, Georgia. The preparation center did not disclose any damage to a dealer or customer if the damage was less than 3 percent of the manufacturer's suggested retail price. The refinishing of Dr. Gore's auto cost $601.

Upon his discovery that the automobile had been refinished, Dr. Gore sued German Auto, BMW AG, and BMW NA, alleging that the failure to disclose the refinishing constituted fraud, suppression of a material fact, and breach of contract. With respect to the BMW defendants (BMW), only the suppression claim was submitted to the jury. The jury returned a verdict against all three defendants for $4,000 in compensatory damages, and it assessed $4,000,000 in punitive damages against BMW jointly, based on a determination that BMW had been guilty of gross, malicious, intentional, and wanton fraud. The trial court entered a judgment on that verdict. BMW appealed. The Alabama Supreme Court reduced the verdict to $2,000,000, and BMW appealed to the U.S. Supreme Court.

JUDICIAL OPINION

STEVENS, Justice

Punitive damages may properly be imposed to further a State's legitimate interests in punishing unlawful conduct and deterring its repetition.

Only when an award can fairly be categorized as "grossly excessive" in relation to these interests does it enter the zone of arbitrariness that violates the Due Process Clause of the Fourteenth Amendment. For that reason, the federal excessiveness inquiry appropriately begins with an identification of the state interests that a punitive award is designed to serve. We therefore focus our attention first on the scope of Alabama's legitimate interests in punishing BMW and deterring it from future misconduct.

No one doubts that a State may protect its citizens by prohibiting deceptive trade practices and by requiring automobile distributors to disclose presale repairs that affect the value of a new car. But the States need not, and in fact do not, provide such protection in a uniform manner. Some States rely on the judicial process to formulate and enforce an appropriate disclosure requirement by applying principles of contract and tort law. Other States have enacted various forms of legislation that define the disclosure obligations of automobile manufacturers, distributors, and dealers. The result is a patchwork of rules representing the diverse policy judgments of lawmakers in 50 states.

Alabama may insist that BMW adhere to a particular disclosure policy in that State. Alabama does not have the power, however, to punish BMW for conduct that was lawful where it occurred and that had no impact on Alabama or its residents. Nor may Alabama impose sanctions on BMW in order to deter conduct that is lawful in other jurisdictions.

In this case, we accept the Alabama Supreme Court's interpretation of the jury verdict as reflecting a computation of the amount of punitive damages "based in large part on conduct that happened in other jurisdictions."

When the scope of the interest in punishment and deterrence that an Alabama court may appropriately consider is properly limited, it is apparent—for reasons that we shall now address—that this award is grossly excessive.

Elementary notions of fairness enshrined in our constitutional jurisprudence dictate that a person receive fair notice not only of the conduct that will subject him to punishment but also of the severity of the penalty that a State may impose. Three guideposts, each of which indicates that BMW did not receive adequate notice of the magnitude of the sanction that Alabama might impose for adhering to the nondisclosure policy adopted in 1983, lead us to the conclusion that the $2 million award against BMW is grossly excessive: the degree of reprehensibility of the nondisclosure; the disparity between the harm or potential harm suffered by Dr. Gore and his punitive damages award; and the difference between this remedy and the civil penalties authorized or imposed in comparable cases. We discuss these considerations in turn.

Perhaps the most important indicium of the reasonableness of a punitive damages award is the degree of reprehensibility of the defendant's conduct. As the Court stated nearly 150 years ago, exemplary damages imposed on a defendant should reflect "the enormity of his offense."

In this case, none of the aggravating factors associated with particularly reprehensible conduct is present. The harm BMW inflicted on Dr. Gore was purely economic in nature. The presale refinishing of the car had no effect on its performance or safety features, or even its appearance for at least nine months after his purchase. BMW's conduct evinced no indifference to or reckless disregard for the health and safety of others. To be sure, infliction of economic injury, especially when done intentionally through affirmative acts of misconduct, or when the target is financially vulnerable, can warrant a substantial penalty. But this observation does not convert all acts that cause economic harm into torts that are sufficiently reprehensible to justify a significant sanction in addition to compensatory damages.

That conduct is sufficiently reprehensible to give rise to tort liability, and even a modest award of exemplary damages, does not establish the high degree of culpability that warrants a substantial punitive damages award. Because this case exhibits none of the circumstances ordinarily associated with egregiously improper conduct, we are persuaded that BMW's conduct was not sufficiently reprehensible to warrant imposition of a $2 million exemplary damages award.

The second and perhaps most commonly cited indicium of an unreasonable or excessive punitive damages award is its ratio to the actual harm inflicted on the plaintiff. The principle that exemplary damages must bear a "reasonable relationship" to compensatory damages has a long pedigree. Scholars have identified a number of early English statutes authorizing the award of multiple damages for particular wrongs. Some 65 different enactments during the period between 1275 and 1753 provided for double, treble, or quadruple damages.

The $2 million in punitive damages awarded to Dr. Gore by the Alabama Supreme Court is 500 times the amount of his actual harm as determined by the jury. Moreover, there is no suggestion that Dr. Gore or any other BMW purchaser was threatened with any additional potential harm by BMW's nondisclosure policy.

Of course, we have consistently rejected the notion that the constitutional line is marked by a simple mathematical formula, even one that compares actual *and potential* damages to the punitive award.

In most cases, the ratio will be within a constitutionally acceptable range, and remittitur will not be justified on this basis. When the ratio is a breathtaking 500 to 1, however, the award must surely "raise a suspicious judicial eyebrow."

Comparing the punitive damages award and the civil or criminal penalties that could be imposed for comparable misconduct provides a third indicium of excessiveness. As Justice O'CONNOR has correctly observed, a reviewing court engaged in determining whether an award of punitive damages is excessive should "accord 'substantial deference' to legislative judgments concerning appropriate sanctions for the conduct at issue."

The maximum civil penalty authorized by the Alabama Legislature for a violation of its Deceptive Trade Practices Act is $2,000; other States authorize more severe sanctions, with the maxima ranging from $5,000 to $10,000.

The sanction imposed in this case cannot be justified on the ground that it was necessary to deter future misconduct without considering whether less drastic remedies could be expected to achieve that goal. The fact that a multimillion dollar penalty prompted a change in policy sheds no light on the question whether a lesser deterrent would have adequately protected the interests of Alabama consumers.

The fact that BMW is a large corporation rather than an impecunious individual does not diminish its entitlement to fair notice of the demands that the several States impose on the conduct of its business. Indeed, its status as an active participant in the national economy implicates the federal interest in preventing individual States from imposing undue burdens on interstate commerce. While each State has ample power to protect its own consumers, none may use the punitive damages deterrent as a means of imposing its regulatory policies on the entire Nation.

Whether the appropriate remedy requires a new trial or merely an independent determination by the Alabama Supreme Court of the award necessary to vindicate the economic interests of Alabama consumers is a matter that should be addressed by the state court in the first instance.

The judgment is reversed, and the case is remanded for further proceedings not inconsistent with this opinion.

DISSENTING OPINION

Justice SCALIA, with whom Justice THOMAS joins, dissenting

Today we see the latest manifestation of this Court's recent and increasingly insistent "concern about punitive damages that 'run wild.'" *Pacific Mut. Life Ins. Co.* v. *Haslip,* 499 U.S. 1, 18, 111 S.Ct. 1032, 1043, 113 L.Ed.2d 1 (1991). Since the Constitution does not make that concern any of our business, the Court's activities in this area are an unjustified incursion into the province of state governments.

At the time of adoption of the Fourteenth Amendment, it was well understood that punitive damages represent the assessment by the jury, as the voice of the community, of the measure of punishment the defendant deserved. Today's decision, though dressed up as a legal opinion, is really no more than a disagreement with the community's sense of indignation or outrage expressed in the punitive award of the Alabama jury, as

continued

reduced by the State Supreme Court. It reflects not merely, as the concurrence candidly acknowledges, "a judgment about a matter of degree," but a judgment about the appropriate degree of indignation or outrage, which is hardly an analytical determination.

There is no precedential warrant for giving our judgment priority over the judgment of state courts and juries on this matter. The only support for the Court's position is to be found in a handful of errant federal cases, bunched within a few years of one another, which invented the notion that an unfairly severe civil sanction amounts to a violation of constitutional liberties.

One might understand the Court's eagerness to enter this field, rather than leave it with the state legislatures, if it had something useful to say. In fact, however, its opinion provides virtually no guidance to legislatures, and to state and federal courts, as to what a "constitutionally proper" level of punitive damages might be.

In Part III of its opinion, the Court identifies "[t]hree guideposts" that lead it to the conclusion that the award in this case is excessive: degree of reprehensibility, ratio between punitive award and plaintiff's actual harm, and legislative sanctions provided for comparable misconduct.

Of course it will not be easy for the States to comply with the new federal law of damages, no matter how willing they are to do so. In truth, the "guideposts" mark a road to nowhere; they provide no real guidance at all.

As to "degree of reprehensibility" of the defendant's conduct, we learn that "nonviolent crimes are less serious than crimes marked by violence or the threat of violence," and that "trickery and deceit" are "more reprehensible than negligence." As to the ratio of punitive to compensatory damages, we are told that a "general concern of reasonableness . . . enter[s] into the constitutional calculus," though even "a breathtaking 500 to 1" will not necessarily do anything more than "raise a suspicious judicial eyebrow" (an opinion which, when confronted with that "breathtaking" ratio, approved it). And as to legislative sanctions provided for comparable misconduct, they should be accorded "'substantial deference,'" *ibid.* One expects the Court to conclude: "To thine own self be true."

These criss-crossing platitudes yield no real answers in no real cases. And it must be noted that the Court nowhere says that these three "guideposts" are the *only* guideposts; indeed, it makes very clear that they are not—explaining away the earlier opinions that do not really follow these "guideposts" on the basis of *additional* factors, thereby "reiterat[ing] our rejection of a categorical approach." In other words, even these utter platitudes, if they should ever happen to produce an answer, may be overridden by other unnamed considerations. The Court has constructed a framework that does not genuinely constrain, that does not inform state legislatures and lower courts—that does nothing at all except confer an artificial air of doctrinal analysis upon its essentially ad hoc determination that this particular award of punitive damages was not "fair."

The elevation of "fairness" in punishment to a principle of "substantive due process" means that every punitive award unreasonably imposed is unconstitutional; such an award is by definition excessive, since it attaches a penalty to conduct undeserving of punishment. Indeed, if the Court is correct, it must be that every claim that a state jury's award of *compensatory* damages is "unreasonable" (because not supported by the evidence) amounts to an assertion of constitutional injury. And the same would be true for determinations of liability. By today's logic, *every* dispute as to evidentiary sufficiency in a state civil suit poses a question of constitutional moment, subject to review in this Court. That is a stupefying proposition.

For the foregoing reasons, I respectfully dissent.

CASE QUESTIONS

1. What was wrong with Dr. Gore's car, and how did he discover the problem?

2. What basis did the jury use for awarding $4,000,000 in punitive damages?

3. What arguments does the Court make in requiring that the award be reduced?

4. What constitutional issues are raised?

5. Why do Justices Scalia and Thomas dissent?

6. To whom would the dissent leave the issue of punitive damages?

AFTERMATH: In 1998, the Alabama Supreme Court (Alabama was the state in which the *BMW* case arose) placed restrictions on punitive damages. Now, in Alabama, no punitive damages are awarded without a showing of actual damages.

> ### CONSIDER . . . 10.11
>
> The Mathiases checked into a Motel 6 and were bitten extensively by bed bugs. Upon investigation, they learned that the managers and owners of the motel had been warned by guests, employees, and exterminators alike that there were bed bugs in the rooms. The exterminator offered to spray the motel each year for $600, but the motel refused. As a result, the bugs remained and propagated. The Mathiases filed suit, seeking punitive damages. The trial court awarded them $5,000 compensatory damages and $186,000 punitive damages. The motel appealed the punitive damage award as excessive. Is the award excessive? [*Mathias* v. *ACCR Economy Lodging, Inc.*, 347 F.3d 672 (7th Cir. 2003).]

New Verdicts on Tort Reform

Since the time of the *BMW* case, there have been a number of significant decisions on how much is too much in terms of damages awarded to plaintiffs. In *Cooper Industries, Inc.* v. *Leatherman Tool Group*, 532 U.S. 424 (2001), the U.S. Supreme Court held that the Eighth Amendment's prohibition on excessive fines and cruel and unusual punishment requires appellate courts to apply a *de novo* review standard (see Chapter 3) when determining the constitutionality of punitive damages awards made at the trial court level. Several cases that followed the *Leatherman* decision ordered a reduction of punitive damages. In *State Farm Mutual Auto Insurance Co.* v. *Campbell*, 123 S.Ct. 1513 (2003), the U.S. Supreme Court held that a punitive damage award of $145 million in punitive damages and $1 million in compensatory damages against an insurance company for its wrongful refusal to pay a claim violated the due process clause. The court found that the Utah Supreme Court had not applied properly the standards of the *Gore* case. The court also added to the *Gore* case some additional factors for the determination of punitive damages:

(a) Punitive damages awards serve the same purpose as criminal penalties. However, because civil defendants are not accorded the protections afforded criminal defendants, punitive damages pose an acute danger of arbitrary deprivation of property, which is heightened when the decisionmaker is presented with evidence having little bearing on the amount that should be awarded. Thus, this Court has instructed courts reviewing punitive damages to consider (1) the degree of reprehensibility of the defendant's misconduct, (2) the disparity between the actual or potential harm suffered by the plaintiff and the punitive damages award, and (3) the difference between the punitive damages awarded by the jury and the civil penalties authorized or imposed in comparable cases. Gore, at 575, 116 S.Ct. 1589. A trial court's application of these guideposts is subject to de novo *review.* Cooper Industries, supra, *at 424, 121 S.Ct. 1678. Pp. 1519–1521.*

(b) Under Gore's *guideposts, this case is neither close nor difficult. (1) To determine a defendant's reprehensibility—the most important indicium of a punitive damages award's reasonableness—a court must consider whether: the harm was physical rather than economic; the tortious conduct evinced an indifference to or a reckless disregard of the health or safety of others; the conduct involved repeated actions or was an isolated incident; and the harm resulted from intentional malice, trickery, or deceit, or mere accident. It should be presumed that a plaintiff has been made whole by compensatory damages, so punitive damages should be awarded only if the defendant's culpability is so reprehensible to warrant the imposition of further sanctions to achieve punishment or deterrence.*

Because the highest criminal penalty available for fraud in Utah was $10,000 the court could not find a justification for the large punitive damage award. In addition, the court noted that including out-of-state activities of a company when determining damage awards for plaintiffs for conduct within the state was not proper.

The tort reform battle continues in the courts, through legislation, and through continuing studies about how high verdicts really are. A study published in *Cornell Law Review* raises questions about tort reform and the allegations of runaway juries.[3] The jury may be out still on how extensive the problem of excessive jury verdicts is. The study, conducted by two Cornell professors and the National Center for State Courts, concludes that, particularly with regard to punitive damages, juries are not as generous as once believed. The study looked at 8,724 civil cases in forty-five courts around the nation and found the following.

Type of Case	% of Time Jury Awarded Punitive Damages	% of Time Judge Awarded Punitive Damages
All cases	4.0%	4.0%
Individual versus individual	3.5%	5.3%
Individual versus government	2.4%	0.0%
Individual versus corporation	4.7%	6.7%
Individual versus hospital	3.1%	0.0%
Premises liability	1.1%	10.8%
Product liability	7.1%	8.3%
Intentional tort	21.4%	23.8%
Fraud	15.0%	12.6%
Rental/lease	7.3%	0.7%

Source: Theodore Eisenberg, Neil LaFountain, Brian Ostrom, David Rottman, and Martin T. Wells, "Juries, Judges, and Punitive Damages: An Empirical Study," 87 *Cornell Law Review* 743 (2002). Used with permission.

The study also concludes that there is no difference between the amounts of punitive damages awarded by juries versus those awarded by judges. Others who have studied punitive damages immediately raised questions about the study because it runs contra to existing data.

FOR THE MANAGER'S DESK

RE: STATE REFORMS ON PUNITIVE DAMAGES: SPLIT VERDICTS

Governor Arnold Schwarzenegger has proposed that California become the ninth state to have "split-recovery laws." These laws allocate part of the punitive damage awards in product liability and negligence cases to state treasuries. Sometimes specific state programs are designated as beneficiaries of the funds from punitive damages.

As of 1993, ten states had enacted split-recovery statutes: Colorado, Florida, Georgia, Illinois, Iowa, Kansas, Missouri, New York, Oregon, and Utah.*

However, Colorado struck down its statute as an unconstitutional taking of private property. In addition, the Alabama Supreme Court has recognized such a split-recovery proposal as being within the powers

granted the judiciary, in a case that held punitive damage distribution of half to the plaintiff and half to the American Medical Association to be constitutional [*Smith* v. *States Gen. Life Ins. Co.,* 592 So. 2d 1021, 1023 (Ala. 1992)].

In 1987, the American Bar Association introduced a proposal to award a portion of punitive damage awards to "public purposes" as a method of tort reform. Although brought to public attention in 1987, the concept of split-recovery arose at least as early as 1983.

Do you think that requiring the sharing of punitive damages will reduce the amount of those damages? Will it reduce the number of cases brought seeking punitive damages?

For More Information

Justice Janie L. Shores, A Suggestion for Limited Tort Reform: Allocation of Punitive Damage Awards to Eliminate Windfalls, 44 Ala. L. Rev. 61, 90 (1992).

Clay R. Stevens, Split-Recovery: A Constitutional Answer to the Punitive Damage Dilemma, 21 Pepp. L. Rev. 857 (1994).

"Split-Recovery" Survives: The Missouri Supreme Court Upholds the State's Power to Collect One-Half of Punitive Damage Awards, *Fust* v. *Attorney General of Missouri,* 63 Mo. L. Rev. 511, 535 (1998).

The Practical Effects of Split-Recovery Statutes and Their Validity as a Tool of Modern Day "Tort Reform," 50 Drake L. Rev. 593, 610 (2002).

*Colo. Rev. Stat. Ann. S 13–21–102(4) (West 1989); Fla. Stat. Ann. S 768.73(1)(a) (West Supp. 1992); Ga. Code Ann. S 51–12–5.1(e)(2) (Michie Supp. 1992); Ill. Ann. Stat. ch. 110, para. 2–1207 (Smith-Hurd Supp. 1992); Iowa Code S 668A.1.2.b (1991); Kan. Stat. Ann. S 60–3402(e) (Supp. 1992); Mo. Rev. Stat. S 537.675.2 (Supp. 1992); N.Y. Civ. Prac. L. & R. S 8701(1) (McKinney Supp. 1993); Or. Rev. Stat. S 18.540(1)(c) (1991); Utah Code Ann. S 78–18–1(3) (1992)].

STRICT LIABILITY

Sometimes the law imposes strict liability on parties for their conduct. **Strict liability** is absolute liability for conduct with few, if any, defenses available. Strict liability can result from violation of a statute. For example, any violation of federal laws on disposal of biomedical waste would result in strict liability. Strict liability can also result because of public policy issues. For example, strict liability is available as a theory for recovery of injury and damages resulting from a defective product (see Chapter 11). The public policy is to afford few defenses to product liability so that manufacturers take the appropriate steps in design, production, and packaging to ensure that their products are safe to use with adequate instructions. With few defenses available, companies take extra precautions knowing the strict liability that results. For more details, refer to Chapter 11 and the discussion of product liability there.

SUMMARY

What types of civil wrongs create a right of recovery for harm?

- Tort—a civil wrong; action by another that results in damages that are recoverable

- Intentional tort—civilly wrong conduct that is done deliberately

- Negligence—conduct of omission or neglect that results in damages

- Strict tort liability—imposition of liability because harm results

What are the types and elements of torts?

- Defamation—publication of untrue and damaging statements about an individual or company

- Product disparagement—the tort of defamation for products

- Malice—publication of information knowing it is false or with reckless disregard for whether it is false

- Privilege—a defense to defamation that protects certain statements because of a public interest in having information such as testimony in a trial or media coverage protected from suit

- Interference—the wrong of asking a party to breach a contract with a third party

- False imprisonment—wrongful detention of an individual; shopkeepers have a privilege to reasonably detain those they have good cause to believe have taken merchandise

- Shopkeeper's privilege—defense to torts of defamation, invasion of privacy, and false imprisonment for merchants who detain shoppers when shopkeepers have reasonable cause to believe merchandise has been taken without payment

- Intentional infliction of emotional distress—bizarre and outrageous conduct that inflicts mental and possible physical harm on another

- Invasion of privacy—disclosing private information, intruding upon another's affairs, or appropriating someone's image or likeness

- Appropriation—the use, without permission, of another's likeness, image, voice, or trademark for commercial gain

- Reasonable and prudent person—the standard by which the conduct of others is measured; a hypothetical person who behaves with full knowledge and alertness

- Causation—the "but for" reason for an accident

- Proximate cause—the foreseeability requirement of causation

- Contributory negligence—negligence on the part of a plaintiff that was partially responsible for causing injuries

- Comparative negligence—newer negligence defense that assigns liability and damages in accidents on a percentage basis and thus reduces a plaintiff's recovery by the amount his negligence contributed to the cause of the accident

- Assumption of risk—plaintiff's voluntary subjection to a risk that caused injuries

What is the business issue surrounding torts?

- Tort reform—political and legislative process of limiting damages and changing methods of recovery for civil wrongs

QUESTIONS AND PROBLEMS

1. Sylvia Salek is a teacher at Passaic Collegiate School. The yearbook contained a section entitled "The Funny Pages," consisting of pictures of students and faculty accompanied by purportedly humorous captions. One of the pages in this section contained a picture of Ms. Salek sitting next to and facing another teacher, John DeVita, who had his right hand raised to his forehead. The photograph is captioned "Not tonight, Ms. Salek. I have a headache." Another page in the yearbook contains a picture of Mr. DeVita eating, with the caption, "What are you really thinking about, Mr. DeVita?"

Ms. Salek brought suit against the school on grounds that the photographs and captions made it seem that Mr. DeVita was refusing to engage in a sexual relationship with her. What tort(s) is Ms. Salek alleging? [*Salek* v. *Passaic Collegiate School*, 605 A.2d 276 (N.J. 1992).]

2. Douglas Margreiter was severely injured in New Orleans on the night of April 6, 1976. He was the chief of the pharmacy section of the Colorado Department of Social Services and was in New Orleans to attend the annual meeting of the American Pharmaceutical Association.

On Tuesday evening, April 6, Mr. Margreiter had dinner at the Royal Sonesta Hotel with two associates from Colorado who were attending the meeting and were staying in rooms adjacent to Mr. Margreiter's in the New Hotel Monteleone. Mr. Margreiter returned to his room between 10:30 P.M. and 11:00 P.M.; one of his

friends returned to his adjoining room at the same time. Another friend was to come by Mr. Margreiter's room later to discuss what sessions of the meetings each would attend the next day.

About three hours later, Mr. Margreiter was found severely beaten and unconscious in a parking lot three blocks from the Monteleone. The police who found him said they thought he was highly intoxicated, and they took him to Charity Hospital. His friends later had him moved to the Hotel Dieu.

Mr. Margreiter said two men had unlocked his hotel room door and entered his room. He was beaten about the head and shoulders and had only the recollection of being carried to a dark alley. He required a craniotomy and other medical treatment and suffered permanent effects from the incident.

Mr. Margreiter sued the hotel on grounds that the hotel was negligent in not controlling access to elevators and hence to the guests' rooms. The hotel says Mr. Margreiter was intoxicated and met his fate outside the hotel. Is the hotel liable? [*Margreiter* v. *New Hotel Monteleone*, 640 F.2d 508 (5th Cir. 1981).]

3. Carolyn Dolph was shopping at the Dumas, Arkansas, Wal-Mart at 3:00 P.M. on Friday, June 16, 1989. She had just gone through the checkout line and was attempting to leave the store when she was accosted near the exit by the loss-prevention officer for the store, Loretta McNeely. Ms. Dolph testified that Ms. McNeely told her that she knew that Ms. Dolph had been apprehended for shoplifting in the McGehee Wal-Mart the week before, and because of that she was not allowed to shop at any Wal-Mart store. According to Ms. Dolph, Ms. McNeely made the accusation four times. Ms. Dolph countered that Ms. McNeely was mistaken. Ms. McNeely did not believe her; instead, she thought Ms. Dolph was going through typical shoplifter's denial. They were arguing the point, according to Ms. Dolph, where people could overhear, and she felt as if she were on display "right in front of the store."

To resolve the matter, Ms. Dolph and Ms. McNeely moved to a nearby service area, and Ms. McNeely went into a mezzanine office to call the McGehee store. After telephoning McGehee, Ms. McNeely then "hollered down" questions to Ms. Dolph from the office, according to Ms. Dolph. During the time that Ms. McNeely was calling, Ms. Dolph believed that she was being watched by Wal-Mart employees and that she was not free to leave. Ms. McNeely then requested that Ms. Dolph come up to the office, but she refused and asked to see the manager. It turned out that Ms. McNeely was in error and that Ms. Dolph's sister—not Ms. Dolph—had been apprehended in McGehee for shoplifting. Ms. Dolph sued Wal-Mart for slander and was awarded $25,000. Wal-Mart appealed because Ms. Dolph did not produce anyone at the trial who could testify about hearing the "hollered" exchange. Why is this evidence important? Should Wal-Mart win the appeal? [*Wal-Mart Stores, Inc. v. Dolph*, 825 S.W.2d 810 (Ark. 1992).]

4. A woman used the women's restroom at a roller-skating rink run by Abate. She discovered that the restroom had see-through panels in the ceiling that allowed observation of those in the restroom. Is this an invasion of privacy? [*Harkey v. Abate*, 346 N.W.2d 74 (Mich. 1983).]

5. Two disc jockeys at WPYX-FM radio in Albany, New York, have been sued for intentional infliction of emotional distress by Annette Esposito-Hilder, who was identified on the air by the two disc jockeys as the "winner" of the "ugliest bride" contest. The two disc jockeys sponsor an ugliest bride contest based on the wedding pictures in the daily newspaper. Viewers are invited to call in with their guesses as to which bride has been chosen. Generally, the disc jockeys did not reveal last names of the brides. However, in Ms. Esposito-Hilder's case, they broke with past practice and revealed her name.

On appeal of the case from an earlier dismissal, the court held that there was no defamation involved in their statements because they were "pure, subjective opinion." The court did hold, however, that a suit for intentional infliction of emotional distress could go forward. The court held, "Comedic expression does not receive absolute First Amendment protection."

Is opinion protected by the First Amendment? Does it make any difference that Ms. Esposito-Hilder was employed by a competing radio station in the area at the time she "won" the contest? [*Esposito-Hilder* v. *SFX Broadcasting, Inc.*, 665 N.Y.S.2d 697 (1997).]

6. Mae Tom went to Kresge's store on November 15, 1977, slipped, and fell on a clear substance on the floor. No one ever determined what the substance was, but Kresge's did sell soft drinks in the store, and customers could walk around with their drinks. Ms. Tom wishes to recover for her injuries. Can she do so? [*Tom v. S. S. Kresge Co., Inc.*, 633 P.2d 439 (Ariz. App. 1981).]

7. Peoples Bank and Trust Company is the conservator of the estate of Nellie Mitchell, a 96-year-old resident of Mountain Home, Arkansas, who has operated a news-stand on the town square since 1963. Before that, she delivered newspapers on a paper route and, according to the evidence, still makes deliveries to certain "downtown" business establishments and select customers.

It appears that Nellie, as she is known to almost everyone in this small Ozark Mountain town, is a town "landmark" or "treasure." She has cared for herself and raised a family as a single parent for all these years on what must have been the meager earnings of a "paper girl."

Her newspaper stand was in a short, dead-end alley between two commercial buildings on the town square. She received permission to put a roof over the alley, and this newsstand was her sole means of support. Her tenacity was evident at trial when she was asked whether she lived with her adult daughter, Betty. She replied, "No, Betty lives with me."

In the October 2, 1990, edition of the *Sun*, published by Globe International, Inc., there was a photograph of Nellie with a story entitled:

Special Delivery

World's oldest newspaper carrier, 101, quits because she's pregnant! I guess walking all those miles kept me young.

The "story" purports to be about a "paper-gal Audrey Wiles" in Stirling, Australia, who had been delivering papers for ninety-four years. Readers are told that Miss Wiles became pregnant by "Will," a "reclusive millionaire" she met on her newspaper route. "I used to put Will's paper in the door when it rained, and one thing just kind of led to another."

In words that could certainly have described Nellie Mitchell, the article, which was in the form and style of a factual newspaper account, in part said:

[S]he's become like a city landmark because nearly everyone at one time or another has seen her trudging down the road with a large stack of papers under her arm.

The photograph used in the October 2 edition of the *Sun,* of Nellie apparently "trudging down the road with a large stack of papers under her arm," had been used by the defendant in a reasonably factual and accurate article about Nellie published in another of the defendant's publications, the *Examiner,* in 1980.

Peoples Bank, on behalf of Nellie, filed suit against Globe for invasion of privacy and intentional infliction of emotional distress. The jury awarded Nellie $650,000 in compensatory damages and $850,000 in punitive damages. Globe asked the court to reverse the verdict or, in the alternative, reduce the damages. Have any torts been committed? Describe them. Are the damages reasonable? [*Peoples Bank & Trust Co. v. Globe Int'l, Inc.,* 786 F. Supp. 791 (W.D. Ark. 1992).]

8. Benjamin VonBehren, then two years old, and his mother paid a visit to their neighbors Edward and Diane Bradley. Mr. and Mrs. Bradley were not home, but Benjamin and his mother were invited into the Bradley home by the Bradleys' sixteen-year-old daughter, who was at home babysitting her nine-year-old brother, Andy. Andy and Benjamin went to the backyard to play with the Bradleys' dog, a labrador retriever. The Bradleys' dog had a bird in its mouth, which was disturbing to Benjamin. Benjamin hit the dog and pulled its ears and tail to get it to spit out the bird. The dog instead bit Benjamin, who had severe lacerations on his face.

The VonBehrens sued the Bradleys, and the trial court dismissed the case because Benjamin had provoked the dog. The VonBehrens have appealed. What should the appellate court do? Should the Bradleys be held liable? [*VonBehren v. Bradley,* 640 N.E.2d 664 (Ill. 1994).]

9. KSL Recreation Corp. and Boca Partnership signed an agreement on February 23, 1994, to form a joint venture to renovate and expand the 356-acre Boca Raton Hotel & Club resort in Palm Beach County, Florida. The joint venture did not go through because KSL demanded an additional $3.5 million in expenses and fees. Boca then negotiated a loan with Olympus Real Estate Corporation. Boca was about to close on the financing of the renovation with Olympus when KSL faxed a copy of a lawsuit against Boca to Olympus. The lawsuit was not yet filed. Boca had a litigation clause in its agreement with Olympus, and it was required to pay more fees and a higher interest rate. Did KSL interfere with Boca's contract with Olympus?

10. Michael Boone was assaulted in the Palace Bar in Albert Lea, Minnesota, by Aristeo Martinez. Mr. Boone suffered a laceration and multiple stab wounds. The fight lasted three minutes and was already ended by the time employees arrived to break up the two warring patrons. Mr. Boone sued both Mr. Martinez and the Palace Bar. Prior to the fight, Mr. Martinez was quite obviously intoxicated, and bar patrons indicated that he was quite loud.

What would Mr. Boone have to establish in order to hold the Palace Bar liable for his injuries? [*Boone v. Martinez,* 567 N.W.2d 508 (Minn. 1997).]

RESEARCH PROBLEM

Avoiding Permanent Damage From Temporary Help

11. Because employers have become dependent on temporary workers and the agencies that provide them, an interesting issue has developed with regard to liability: Who is responsible for checking the temporary worker's background, especially when the temporary worker is offered a permanent position following a temporary stint?

For example, Robert Half International, Inc., had recruited T'Challa Ross as a bookkeeper, and she was placed with Fox Associates, Inc., in Chicago. She did so well at the temporary position that Fox hired her permanently.

However, Robert Half had failed to uncover the fact that Ms. Ross had entered a guilty plea to charges that she embezzled $192,873 from a former employer and had been sentenced to four years' probation and community service. Once hired by Fox, Ms. Ross took blank checks and forged signatures, which resulted in her taking over $70,000 from the company. Her annual salary was $35,000 when she was hired by Fox.

Fox brought suit against Robert Half to recover the $70,000 plus its $6,600 fee, alleging that Robert Half was negligent in that it failed to verify that Ms. Ross, who had checked "No felony convictions" on her application, indeed had no felony convictions. However, two previous employers had given good recommendations and never mentioned any issues of dishonesty or embezzlement.

However, a judge dismissed the case, ruling that Robert Half was in the talent business and not the background check or investigation business.

The issue is not limited to staff level. Sunbeam discovered that the executive search firm it used to recruit Al Dunlap did not discover that Mr. Dunlap had been dismissed from two previous executive positions. Sunbeam is reeling from losses resulting from Mr. Dunlap's tenure as CEO there.

Do you think there is a duty on the part of the temporary agency to check backgrounds? Do you think Fox should have done its own background check? Why do you think the former employers said nothing about her history and gave her good recommendations?

Develop some recommendations and policies for your company on background checks for employees hired through a search firm or temp agency. Be sure to consider what you have learned in this chapter on references, defamation, and negligence. Also, refer to the Web sites of various law firms and others advising clients on this issue: http://www.bakerbotts.com.

You can also refer to the statutes of various states that have passed laws on privilege with regard to references: Alaska, Arizona, Arkansas, California, Colorado, Delaware, Florida, Georgia, Idaho, Illinois, Indiana, Kansas, Louisiana, Maine, Maryland, Michigan, Nebraska, New Mexico, North Carolina, North Dakota, Ohio, Oklahoma, Oregon, Rhode Island, South Carolina, South Dakota, Tennessee, Texas, Utah, Wisconsin, and Wyoming. For example, you could go to http://www.capitol.state.tx.us to look for the Texas statute.

NOTES

1. Robert Pear, "Health System Warily Prepares for Privacy Rules," *New York Times,* April 6, 2003, pp. A1, A19.

2. Melanie Stanley, "Very expensive suits," *Fortune,* March 3, 2003, p. 40.

3. William Glaberson, "A Study's Verdict: Jury Awards Are Not Out of Control," *New York Times,* August 6, 2001, p. A9.

11

Product Advertising and Liability

The first jury verdict over $1,000,000 in a product liability suit occurred in 1962. Today, the top ten verdicts each year in the United States exceed $50,000,000, and there are more than 400 multimillion-dollar verdicts a year. Business payments to claimants are estimated to be $129–136 billion per year.[1] In 2002, the median award in product liability cases was $520,000.

Product liability cases today are common, the judgments and settlements are large, and insurance coverage costs are now a major expense for businesses. Buyers seem increasingly willing to have matters concerning defective products settled in court.

Product liability is a unique area of law. It has social roots in that it attempts to lessen the burden of losses by requiring a manufacturer or manufacturer's insurer to pay for a defective product. It also has contract roots in that if a product does not do what it is supposed to do, a breach of contract has occurred. Finally, it also has roots in tort law insofar as there is an injury resulting from someone else's carelessness. In these senses, product liability is a combination of contract law, tort law, and social responsibility.

This chapter answers the following questions: How did product liability law develop? What are the contract theories for recovery? What is required for a tort-based recovery on a defective product? How does advertising create liability for a business? What is strict tort liability for products? What reforms are proposed for cutting back liability? Are international product liability standards different?

> **update**
>
> *For up-to-date legal news and real-world business applications, click on* **update** *at* http://jennings.westbuslaw.com

Caution: This product can burn eyes.
WARNING ON A CURLING IRON

Advertising may be described as the science of arresting human intelligence long enough to get money out of it.
STEPHEN LEACOCK

Advertisements contain the only truths to be relied on in a newspaper.
THOMAS JEFFERSON

Caution: Cape does not enable user to fly.
INSTRUCTIONS ON KENNER PRODUCTS' BATMAN COSTUME

If you do not understand, or cannot read, all directions, cautions and warnings, do not use this product.
WARNING ON A BOTTLE OF DRAIN CLEANER AND WINNER OF
LAWSUIT ABUSE WATCH'S ANNUAL "WACKY LABEL CONTEST," 2004

Do not use massage chair without clothing . . . and, never force any body part into the backrest area while the rollers are moving.
WARNING ON A MASSAGE CHAIR AND WINNER, 2003

Fireplace log may cause fire.
WARNING ON A FIREPLACE LOG AND WINNER, 2001

Never iron clothes while they are being worn.
WARNING ON AN IRON AND WINNER, 2000
RUNNERS-UP AND WINNERS FROM OTHER YEARS:

Not for highway use.
ON A WHEELBARROW TIRE

Never use hair dryer while sleeping.
ON A BLOW DRYER

Remove child before folding.
ON A STROLLER

Do not use as a ladder.
ON A 12-INCH-HIGH STORAGE RACK FOR COMPACT DISKS

CONSIDER...

In November 1993, QVC Network advertised, as part of a one-day Thanksgiving promotion, the "T-Fal Jumbo Resistal Roaster." The QVC ad described the roaster as suitable for roasting a 25-pound turkey. At the time that T-Fal and QVC entered into an agreement for the sale of the roasting pan, T-Fal did not have a pan in its line large enough to roast a 25-pound turkey. T-Fal asked its parent company in France to provide a suitable roasting pan as soon as possible. The parent company provided a larger pan to which it added two small handles.

Loyda Castro ordered the roasting pan and used it for roasting her turkey on Thanksgiving Day, 1993. Mrs. Castro was injured when she tried to remove the turkey from the oven. Using two large insulated oven mitts, Mrs. Castro tried to lift the pan from the oven, placing two fingers on each handle on the pan. Two fingers were the maximum grip permitted by the small handles. As the turkey tipped toward her, she lost control of the pan, spilling the hot drippings and fat that had accumulated in the pan during the cooking and basting process. Mrs. Castro suffered second- and third-degree burns to her foot and ankle, which have led to scarring, paresthesia, and swelling. Can she recover from QVC for her injuries? From T-Fal?

DEVELOPMENT OF PRODUCT LIABILITY

For some time, courts followed the principle of *caveat emptor*—"Let the buyer beware." This theory meant that sellers were not liable for defects in their products and that it was the buyer's responsibility to be on the alert for defects and take the appropriate precautions.

Following a series of court decisions in which buyers were allowed recovery and courts questioned the public policy wisdom of *caveat emptor,* the *Restatement (Second) of Torts* adopted its now famous Section 402A on strict tort liability (discussed later in this chapter). With this adoption, the area of product liability had gone full swing from no liability *(caveat emptor)* to an almost *per se* standard of liability for defective products.

Learn about advertising law:
http://www.adlaw.org

ADVERTISING AS A CONTRACT BASIS FOR PRODUCT LIABILITY

Express Warranties

Review UCC § 2–313:
http://www.law.cornell.edu/
ucc/2/2%2d313%2ehtml

An **express warranty** as provided in the Uniform Commercial Code (UCC) is an express promise (oral or written) by the seller as to the quality, abilities, or performance of a product (UCC § 2–313). The seller need not use the words *promise* or *guarantee* to make an express warranty. Such a warranty is made when a seller uses a sample or model or provides a description of the goods. Promises of how the goods will perform are also express warranties. Examples of express warranties are: "These goods are 100% wool"; "This tire cannot be punctured"; "These jeans will not shrink."

While advertisements are one means by which express warranties arise, they are not the only means. The process of negotiations can find the seller making express warranties to the buyer. For example, if a seller tells the buyer that a dog is a

EXHIBIT 11.1 Statements of Fact versus Opinion

STATEMENT	FACT OR OPINION?
This car gets twenty miles per gallon.	Fact
This car gets great gas mileage.	Opinion
These goods are 100% wool.	Fact
This is the finest wool around.	Opinion
This truck has never been in an accident.	Fact
This truck is solid.	Opinion
This mace stops assailants in their tracks.	Fact (promise of performance)
This mace is very effective.	Opinion
This makeup is hypoallergenic.	Fact
This makeup is good for your skin.	Opinion
This ink will not stain clothes.	Fact
This ink is safe to use.	Opinion
This computer is IBM-compatible.	Fact
This computer is as good as any IBM.	Opinion
This watch is waterproof.	Fact
This watch is durable.	Opinion

For more on business law and the UCC, go to the ABA's Business Law Web site (go to Legal Resources and search for UCC):

http://www.abanet.org/
buslaw/home.shtml

pure bred or that a horse is "disease-free," the seller has made an express warranty. Any statements made by the seller to the buyer before the sale that are part of the basis of the sale or bargain are express warranties. Also, the information included on the product packaging constitutes an express warranty if those are statements of fact or promises of performance.

Opinions, however, are not considered a basis for transactions and are therefore not express warranties. For example, the statement "These jeans are the best on the market" is sales puffing and not an express warranty. Exhibit 11.1 gives some examples of statements of fact versus opinion.

In some cases, such as *Castro* v. *QVC Network, Inc.* (Case 11.1), the issue of product liability is one of representations via ad statements. This case provides the answer for the chapter's opening Consider.

CASE 11.1

Castro v. *QVC Network, Inc.*
139 F.3d 114 (2d Cir. 1998)

A Turkey of a Pan: Liability on Thanksgiving Day

FACTS

In November 1993, QVC Network (appellee), an operator of a cable television home-shopping channel, advertised, as part of a one-day Thanksgiving promotion, the "T-Fal Jumbo Resistal Roaster." The roaster was manufactured by U.S.A. T-Fal Corporation. The QVC ad described the roaster as suitable for roasting a 25-pound turkey. At the time that T-Fal and QVC entered into an agreement for the sale of the roasting pan, T-Fal did not have a pan in its line large enough to roast a 25-pound turkey. T-Fal asked its parent company in France to provide a suitable roasting pan as soon as possible. The parent company provided a larger pan to which it added two small handles.

Loyda Castro (appellant) ordered the roasting pan and used it for roasting her turkey on Thanksgiving Day, 1993. Mrs. Castro was injured when she tried to remove the turkey from the oven. Using two large insulated oven mitts, Mrs. Castro tried to lift the pan from the oven, placing two fingers on each handle. Two fingers were the maximum grip permitted by the small handles. As the turkey tipped toward her, she lost control of the pan, spilling the hot drippings and fat that had accumulated in the pan during the cooking and basting process. Mrs. Castro suffered second- and third-degree burns to her foot and ankle, which have led to scarring, paresthesia, and swelling.

Mrs. Castro filed suit for strict liability and breach of warranty. The warranty charge was dismissed, and the jury returned a verdict for QVC and T-Fal. Mrs. Castro appealed.

JUDICIAL OPINION

CALABRESI, Circuit Judge

Products liability law has long been bedeviled by the search for an appropriate definition of "defective" product design. Over the years, both in the cases and in the literature, two approaches have come to predominate. The first is the risk/utility theory, which focuses on whether the benefits of a product outweigh the dangers of its design. The second is the consumer expectations theory, which focuses on what a buyer/user of a product would properly expect that the product would be suited for.

Not all states accept both of these approaches. Some define design defect only according to the risk/utility approach.

One of the first states to accept both approaches was California, which in *Barker* v. *Lull Engineering Co.*, 20 Cal.3d 413, 143 Cal.Rptr. 225, 573 P.2d 443 (1978), held that "a product may be found defective in design, so as to subject a manufacturer to strict liability for resulting injuries, under either of two alternative tests"—consumer expectations and risk/utility. Several states have followed suit and have adopted both theories.

Prior to the recent case of *Denny* v. *Ford Motor Co.*, 87 N.Y.2d 248, 639 N.Y.S.2d 250, 662 N.E.2d 730 (1995), it was not clear whether New York recognized both tests. In *Denny,* the plaintiff was injured when her Ford Bronco II sports utility vehicle rolled over when she slammed on the brakes to avoid hitting a deer in the

continued

vehicle's path. The plaintiff asserted claims for strict products liability and for breach of implied warranty, and the district judge—over the objection of defendant Ford—submitted both causes of action to the jury. The jury ruled in favor of Ford on the strict liability claim, but found for the plaintiff on the implied warranty claim. On appeal, Ford argued that the jury's verdicts on the strict products liability claim and the breach of warranty claim were inconsistent because the causes of action were identical.

This court certified the *Denny* case to the New York Court of Appeals to answer the following questions: (1) "whether, under New York law, the strict products liability and implied warranty claims are identical"; and (2) "whether, if the claims are different, the strict products liability claim is broader than the implied warranty claim and encompasses the latter."

In response to the certified questions, the Court of Appeals held that in a products liability case a cause of action for strict liability is not identical to a claim for breach of warranty.

Moreover, the court held that a strict liability claim is not per se broader than a breach of warranty claim such that the former encompasses the latter. Thus, while claims of strict products liability and breach of warranty are often used interchangeably, under New York law the two causes of action are definitively different. The imposition of strict liability for an alleged design "defect" is determined by a risk-utility standard. The notion of "defect" in a U.C.C.-based breach of warranty claim focuses, instead, on consumer expectations.

Since *Denny*, then, it has been settled that the risk/utility and consumer expectations theories of design defect can, in New York, be the bases of distinct causes of action: one for strict products liability and one for breach of warranty. This fact, however, does not settle the question of when a jury must be charged separately on each cause of action and when, instead, the two causes are, on the facts of the specific case, sufficiently similar to each other so that one charge to the jury is enough.

While eminent jurists have at times been troubled by this issue, the New York Court of Appeals in *Denny* was quite clear on when the two causes of action might meld and when, instead, they are to be treated as separate. It did this by adding its own twist to the distinction—namely, what can aptly be called the "dual purpose" requirement. Thus in *Denny,* the Court of Appeals pointed out that the fact that a product's overall benefits might outweigh its overall risks does not preclude the possibility that consumers may have been misled into using the product in a context in which it was dangerously unsafe. And this, the New York court emphasized, could be so even though the benefits in other uses might make the product sufficiently reasonable so that it passed the risk/utility test.

In *Denny,* the Ford Bronco II was not designed as a conventional passenger automobile. Instead, it was designed as an off-road, dual purpose vehicle. But in its marketing of the Bronco II, Ford stressed its suitability for commuting and for suburban and city driving. Under the circumstances, the Court of Appeals explained that a rational fact-finder could conclude that the Bronco's utility as an off-road vehicle outweighed the risk of injury resulting from roll-over accidents (thus passing the risk/utility test), but at the same time find that the vehicle was not safe for the "ordinary purpose" of daily driving for which it was also marketed and sold (thus flunking the consumer expectations test).

That is precisely the situation before us. The jury had before it evidence that the product was designed, marketed, and sold as a multiple-use product. The pan was originally manufactured and sold in France as an all-purpose cooking dish without handles. And at trial, the jury saw a videotape of a QVC representative demonstrating to the television audience that the pan, in addition to serving as a suitable roaster for a twenty-five pound turkey, could also be used to cook casseroles, cutlets, cookies, and other low-volume foods. The court charged the jury that "[a] product is defective if it is not reasonably safe[,] [t]hat is, if the product is so likely to be harmful to persons that a reasonable person who had actual knowledge of its potential for producing injury would conclude that it should not have been marketed in that condition." And, so instructed, the jury presumably found that the pan, because it had many advantages in a variety of uses, did not fail the risk/utility test.

But it was also the case that the pan was advertised as suitable for a particular use—cooking a twenty-five pound turkey. Indeed, T-Fal added handles to the pan in order to fill QVC's request for a roasting pan that it could use in its Thanksgiving promotion. The product was, therefore, sold as appropriately used for roasting a twenty-five pound turkey. And it was in that use that allegedly the product failed and injured the appellant.

In such circumstances, New York law is clear that a general charge on strict products liability based on the risk/utility approach does not suffice. The jury could have found that the roasting pan's overall utility for cooking low-volume foods outweighed the risk of injury when cooking heavier foods, but that the product was nonetheless unsafe for the purpose for which it was marketed and sold—roasting a twenty-five pound turkey—and, as such, was defective under the consumer expectations test. That being so, the appellants were entitled to a separate breach of warranty charge.

In light of the evidence presented by appellants of the multi-purpose nature of the product at issue, the district court, applying New York law, should have granted appellants' request for a separate jury charge on the breach of warranty claim in addition to the charge on the strict liability claim.

Reversed.

CASE QUESTIONS

1. How was the turkey pan purchased?

2. Who designed the turkey pan?

3. Was the pan represented as suitable for roasting a turkey?

4. What is the relationship between tort liability and warranty liability?

5. What is the risk/utility test?

CONSIDER...   11.1

John R. Klages was employed as a night auditor at Conley's Motel on Route 8 in Hampton Township. He worked from 11 P.M. until 7 A.M., five days a week. On March 30, 1968, at approximately 1:30 A.M., two individuals entered the motel and announced, "This is a stickup. Open the safe." Mr. Klages indicated that he was unable to open the safe because he did not know the combination. One of the individuals then pointed a gun at his head and pulled the trigger. Fortunately for Mr. Klages, the gun was a starter pistol, and he was not seriously injured.

The next day, Mr. Klages and a fellow employee, Bob McVay, decided that they needed something to protect themselves against the possibility of future holdups. After reading an article concerning the effects of mace, Mr. McVay suggested that they consider using mace for their protection and secured from the Mark1 Supply Company four leaflets describing certain mace weapons.

After reading and discussing the literature with their employer, Mr. McVay purchased an MK-II mace weapon from Mark1 Supply Company, which described the mace as follows.

Rapidly vaporizes on face of assailant effecting instantaneous incapacitation. . . . *It will* instantly stop and subdue *entire groups . . .* instantly stops assailants in their tracks. . . . *[A]n attacker is* subdued instantly, *for a period of 15 to 20 minutes. . . .* Time Magazine *stated the Chemical Mace is "for police the first, if not the final, answer to a nationwide need—a weapon that* disables as effectively *as a gun and yet does no permanent injury." . . . The effectiveness is the result of a unique,* incapacitating formulation (*patent pending), projected in a shotgun-like pattern of heavy liquid droplets that, upon contact with the face, cause extreme tearing, and a stunned, winded condition, often accompanied by dizziness and apathy.*

At approximately 1:40 A.M. on September 22, 1968, while Mr. Klages was on duty, two unknown individuals entered the motel office, requested a room, and announced a stickup. One of the intruders took out a gun and directed Mr. Klages to open the safe. Using the cash register as a shield, Mr. Klages squirted the mace, hitting the intruder "right beside the nose." Mr. Klages immediately ducked below the register, but the intruder followed him down and shot him in the head. The intruders immediately departed, and Mr. Klages called the police. The bullet wound caused complete loss of sight in Mr. Klages's right eye. He claims a breach of an express warranty. Is he right? [*Klages* v. *General Ordnance Equipment Corp.,* 19 UCC Rep. Serv. (Callaghan) 22 (Pa. 1976).]

THINK: The requirements for an express warranty are a statement of fact or a promise of performance.

APPLY: What statements of fact or promises of performance are made in the ad or on the product packaging?

continued

"[I]nstantly stops assailants in their tracks" is a promise of performance; *"subdued instantly, for a period of 15 to 20 minutes"* is also a promise of performance.

ANSWER: The product failed to live up to those promises, so there was a breach of express warranty, and the company is liable for the injury Mr. Klages sustained after using the mace against his attackers.

Review Exhibit 11.1 and then apply your knowledge and analysis skills to the problem presented in Consider 11.2.

CONSIDER...   11.2

Lawrence Dorneles purchased a used 1972 Buick GSX from Mr. Carpenito. Mr. Dorneles had seen Mr. Carpenito's ad that contained a picture of the vehicle and that read as follows: "Buick 1972 GSX, not an original, as close as you can get, all new body parts, 5,000 miles on a new rebuilt 455 Stage 1, car show winner, new exhaust system, mint, tires, never seen rain or snow, garage kept, needs minor interior work, 12 bolt posi rear, hood, tachometer, rear spoiler, all replica details, must sell, $4,500.00. . . ."

Mr. Dorneles answered the ad and spoke with Mr. Carpenito, who reiterated the items in the ad and specifically assured Mr. Dorneles that the rebuilt engine had less than 5,000 miles and that the car had been "babied," among other things. Mr. Dorneles neither test-drove the vehicle nor had a mechanic inspect the vehicle prior to purchasing it. The seller provided no written warranty.

Mr. Dorneles paid $4,000.00 for the car and drove it from Port Chester to his home in Pelham. He left the car at home until July 17, when he registered it and was going to drive the car to Valhalla to have a mechanic inspect the car. July 17 was a hot summer day; on the way to Valhalla, some 15 miles from Pelham, the car began to overheat. The car's engine apparently seized because of the extreme heat and had to be towed back to Pelham. The engine was removed from the Buick at a cost of $450.00, and another new rebuilt engine was installed at a cost of $1,152.00. Additional work has to be done on the car, including repairing broken rear suspension springs ($600.00), installing a new transmission ($750.00), and replacing a corroded chain cover ($174.25).

Was an express warranty given that can be the basis of recovery? Do you waive the express warranty when you do not inspect a car? [*Dorneles* v. *Carpenito*, 521 N.Y.S.2d 967 (1987).]

Federal Regulation of Warranties and Advertising

Express warranties are advertisements for goods. Advertising is crucial to both business success and consumers. Because accurate advertising is necessary to ensure full information to support a competitive environment, it is important that advertising be policed for its fairness and accuracy.

Visit the Federal Trade Commission:
http://www.ftc.gov

In 1914, Congress passed the **Federal Trade Commission Act**, which authorized the **Federal Trade Commission** (FTC) to prevent "unfair and deceptive trade practices." Initially, the FTC used its power to regulate all forms of deceptive advertising. However, the Supreme Court, in interpreting the 1914 act, severely restricted the FTC to the regulation of false advertising that adversely affected competition. In reaction to this Court ruling, Congress passed the **Wheeler-Lea Act** of 1938, giving the FTC the power to regulate "unfair and deceptive acts or practices" whenever the public is being deceived, regardless of any effects on competition.

Review the Federal Trade Commission Act and the Wheeler–Lea Act:
http://www.law.cornell.edu/uscode/15/ch2.html#s45

With the Wheeler-Lea Act, the FTC has expanded its authority over the years. Unsubstantiated or ambiguous advertising claims have been challenged, and deceptive techniques in television ads have also been reviewed by the FTC. The only restriction the FTC has experienced since passage of the Wheeler-Lea Act came after the agency attempted to regulate the content and number of ads on children's television programming. In that case, the FTC ran into powerful opposition by broadcaster, advertising, and producer groups. These groups brought court actions in an attempt to halt the proceedings and at one point disqualified the FTC chairman from the proceedings. This struggle ended with congressional passage of the **FTC Improvements Act of 1980**. The act actually terminated the FTC's authority in the children's television case and put general restrictions on the FTC. In 1990, some children's television regulations were passed.

FOR THE MANAGER'S DESK

RE: ADS ON THE INTERNET

In May 2000, the FTC issued a working paper titled "Dot Com Disclosures" about online advertising. In addition to offering guidelines for Internet advertising, the FTC used the paper to confirm its jurisdiction over Internet advertising. The FTC view is that, just as with all other forms of advertising, online advertising claims must be truthful and not misleading, must be properly substantiated, and must not be unfair to consumers.

The guidelines for Internet advertising include the following.

1. Disclosure in Internet advertisements must be close to the claims to which they relate.

2. If the consumer must scroll down to view a disclosure, the page should be designed to encourage the consumer to scroll down.

3. If hyperlinks are used to make disclosures, the hyperlink should be clearly labeled so that consumers know the hyperlink contains information related to the advertising claim.

4. Wherever the disclosures are made, they must be made to consumers before they make a purchase.

5. The prominence of the disclosure is important. The factors the FTC considers for prominence are:

   • Size, contrasting color, and graphics
   • Other items on the Web page should not distract from disclosures.
   • Repetition may be required for lengthy disclosures.
   • Disclosures should be in clear and simple language.

There are special rules for disclosures related to banner ads.

Because advertising is moving away from media such as television and magazines to the Internet, these rules will become more and more important for sellers.

Source: http://www.ftc.gov/ (click on e-commerce and the Internet).

FOR THE MANAGER'S DESK

RE: ONLINE SPENDING

Online advertising works. New research on online spending indicates a substantial increase in consumer use of the Internet for making purchases. The following chart shows the increased growth.

YEAR	SPENDING (in billions)
2001	$51
2002	$76
2003	$114
2004	$145

Source: Darryl Harralson and Adrienne Lewis, "Online spending grows," *USA Today,* Aug. 18, 2004, 1B.

Content Control and Accuracy

The FTC has regulated the accuracy of ads in several ways. First, the FTC has challenged certain types of price claims. If an ad announces "50% off," the prices must actually be half the original prices charged for the products or services prior to the sale; that price cannot be inflated to cover the markdown. If an ad quotes a "normal" price, that price must reflect what most sellers in the area are charging.

For more information regarding ad–blocking software, visit:

http://www.junkbusters.com
http://www.zeroknowledge.com
http://www.guidescope.com

The FTC has also challenged the accuracy of ads. Claims that goods are "100% wool" are not only the basis for express warranty recovery but also the basis for an FTC challenge. Also, the FTC challenges advertising methods. For example, using "marbles" in soup to make it look thicker as it pours is deceptive. The FTC has used its powers to ensure that ads accurately depict the product as it exists. The regulations also apply to the terms of the contract and the time for performance. For example, the FTC, through its Mail or Telephone Order Merchandise Rule, requires that catalog merchants disclose delays in delivering ordered goods to consumers and that consumers be informed up front about custom product delays, special order delays, and direct-from-the-manufacturer delays. The ads, pamphlets, catalogs, and mailings must disclose delays known up front, and the consumer must be notified after an order is placed if the delay will exceed the maximum amount of time allowed under the rules for delivery. The FTC has enforced those disclosure requirements against Internet merchants as well. In *In the Matter of Macys.com, KBkids.com, and CDnow, Inc.,* the FTC settled charges with these three e-retailers who were alleged to have violated the Mail or Telephone Order Merchandise Rule by failing to provide buyers with adequate notice of shipping delays or had continued to promise specific delivery dates when they were aware that they were unlikely to meet those deadlines.

FTC Control of Performance Claims

Any claims of the ability or efficacy of a product must be supportable. If a sunburn-relief product claims to "anesthetize nerves," the advertiser must be able to prove that claim.

Where an advertising claim cannot be substantiated, the FTC has used **corrective advertising** as a remedy. Corrective advertising requires a seller to correct the unsubstantiated claims made in previous ads. The landmark case *Warner-Lambert Co. v. FTC* (Case 11.2) involves an issue of corrective advertising.

CASE 11.2

Warner-Lambert Co. v. FTC
562 F.2d 749 (D.C.Cir. 1977)
cert den. 435 U.S. 950 (1978)

Does Listerine Prevent Colds?

FACTS

Listerine, a product of the Warner-Lambert Company (petitioner), has been on the market since 1879 and has been represented through advertising to be beneficial for colds, cold symptoms, and sore throats. After a 1972 complaint about Warner-Lambert advertising for Listerine, the FTC held four months of hearings on the ad issues and then ordered Warner-Lambert to do the following.

1. Cease and desist representing that Listerine will cure colds or sore throats, that it will prevent colds or sore throats, or that users of Listerine will have fewer colds than nonusers.

2. Cease and desist representing that Listerine is a treatment for, or will lessen the severity of, colds or sore throats; that it will have any significant beneficial effect on the symptoms of sore throats or any beneficial effect on symptoms of colds; or that the ability of Listerine to kill germs is of medical significance in the treatment of colds or sore throats or their symptoms.

3. Cease and desist disseminating any advertisement for Listerine unless it is clearly and conspicuously disclosed in each advertisement, in this exact language, that "Contrary to prior advertising, Listerine will not help prevent colds or sore throats or lessen their severity." This requirement extended only to the next $10 million Listerine would spend on advertising after the order.

Warner-Lambert appealed the order.

JUDICIAL OPINION

WRIGHT, Circuit Judge

The first issue on appeal is whether the Commission's conclusion that Listerine is not beneficial for colds or sore throats is supported by the evidence.

First, the Commission found that the ingredients of Listerine are not present in sufficient quantities to have any therapeutic effect.

Second, the Commission found that in the process of gargling it is impossible for Listerine to reach critical areas of the body in medically significant concentration.

Third, the Commission found that even if significant quantities of the active ingredients of Listerine were to reach critical sites where cold viruses enter and infect the body, they could not interfere with the activities of the virus because they could not penetrate the tissue cells.

. . . [T]he Commission found that the ability of Listerine to kill germs by millions on contact is of no medical significance in the treatment of colds or sore throats.

. . . [T]he Commission found that Listerine has no significant beneficial effect on the symptoms of sore throat. The Commission recognized that gargling with Listerine could provide temporary relief from a sore throat by removing accumulated debris irritating the throat. But this type of relief can also be obtained by gargling with salt water or even warm water.

Petitioner contends that even if its advertising claims in the past were false, the portion of the Commission's order requiring "corrective advertising" exceeds the Commission's statutory power. The Commission's position is that the affirmative disclosure that Listerine will not prevent colds or lessen their severity is absolutely necessary to give effect to the prospective cease and desist order; a hundred years of false cold claims have built up a large reservoir of erroneous consumer belief that would persist, unless corrected, long after petitioner ceased making the claims.

If the Commission is to attain the objectives Congress envisioned, it cannot be required to confine its road block to the narrow lane the transgressor has traveled; it must be allowed effectively to close all roads to the prohibited goal, so that its order may not be bypassed with impunity.

We turn next to the specific disclosure required: "Contrary to prior advertising, Listerine will not help prevent colds or sore throats or lessen their severity." Petitioner is ordered to include this statement in every future advertisement for Listerine for a defined period. In printed advertisements it must be displayed in type size at least as large as that in which the principal portion of the text of the advertisement appears and it must be separated from the text so that it can be readily noticed. In television commercials the disclosure must be presented simultaneously in both audio and visual portions. During the audio portion of the disclosure in television and radio advertisements, no other sounds, including music, may occur.

These specifications are well calculated to assure that the disclosure will reach the public. It will necessarily attract the notice of readers, viewers and listeners, and be plainly conveyed. Given these safeguards, we believe the preamble "Contrary to prior advertising" is not necessary. It can serve only two purposes: either to attract attention that a correction follows or to humiliate the advertiser. The Commission claims only the first purpose for it, and this we think is obviated by other terms of the order. The second purpose, if it were intended, might be called for in an egregious case of deliberate deception, but this is not one. While we do not decide whether petitioner proffered its cold claims in good faith or bad, the record compiled could support a finding of good faith. On these facts, the confessional preamble to the disclosure is not warranted.

Accordingly, the order, as modified, is affirmed.

CASE QUESTIONS

1. What claims does the FTC make about Listerine?

2. What proposals for corrective advertising are made in the order?

3. What modifications in the order does the court make?

4. What happens to the preamble, "Contrary to prior advertising"?

5. Is Listerine still required to make disclosures in future ads? For how long?

CONSIDER...   **11.3**

Doan's over-the-counter back pain products had been marketed for over ninety years. Ciba-Geigy Corporation, manufacturer of Doan's, conducted a marketing study that concluded: "Doan's has a weak image in comparison to the leading brands of analgesics and would benefit from positioning itself as a more effective product that is strong enough for

continued

the types of backaches sufferers usually get." To strengthen the Doan's image, Ciba-Geigy undertook an aggressive television and newspaper advertising campaign, which lasted from May 1988 through June 1996. The new advertisements characterized Doan's as a remedy effective specifically for back pain and as containing a special ingredient (magnesium salicylate) not found in other over-the-counter analgesics. Some of the ads compared Doan's with other over-the-counter back pain remedies.

The FTC issued a complaint against Ciba-Geigy, requiring that the ads end and that Ciba-Geigy run new ads for an equivalent amount of time with the following statement: "Although Doan's is an effective pain reliever, there is no evidence that Doan's is more effective than other pain relievers for back pain." Ciba-Geigy and its new owner, Novartis, challenged the FTC order for its excessive requirements. Will Ciba-Geigy prevail in its challenge? [*Novartis Corp. v. F.T.C.*, 223 F.3d 783 (D.C. Cir. 2000).]

MAKING ETHICS PERSONAL

Wondering If You Can Make Those Ad Claims

You work for the ad agency that has landed the advertising account for Interstate Bakeries, the producer of Wonder Bread. Your supervisor has emphasized, of course, that the bread campaign must have a focus on children. As you sat together brainstorming with executives from Interstate about a possible ad campaign, your supervisor noticed that Wonder Bread has calcium in it. An Interstate executive commented, "All breads have calcium in them because milk is an ingredient in bread." But another executive from Interstate exclaimed, "That's our angle!" Your supervisor asked, "Can we make claims on such a small amount of calcium?" The executive replied, "It's true, isn't it? The calcium is in there, right? Calcium is good for kids. Let's run with it." You and your supervisor then developed a series of ads that represented that calcium in

Wonder Bread helps children's minds work better and helps their memory.

As she prepared the boardroom for the final presentation of the campaign, your supervisor seemed distracted. "I just don't know if we can really say this, but it's what the client wants." You asked her, "If it turns out that we have overstepped on our claims, a little like the Doan's back pill case, are we responsible? I mean, the agency? Can we be held liable?" Your supervisor seemed perplexed at your question: "And what exactly can we do about it?"

Discuss both the law and the ethical issues you and your supervisor face in this situation. Suppose you were a Web designer and were asked to include statements on the Web site that you knew were not true. Would you do it? Could you be held responsible?

FTC Control of Celebrity Endorsements

During the 1980s, the FTC entered a new aspect of ad content control—namely, the use of **celebrity endorsements** for products. At the time the FTC became involved, its director of consumer protection stated:

> The effectiveness of having a product touted by a well-known movie star or sports figure is apparent from the increasing use of celebrity endorsements in advertising. A sales pitch by a celebrity may be more believable than the same message delivered by an unknown spokesperson. The endorsement can be an important part of sales strategy, and is often quite handsomely rewarded. The endorser may profit from a false advertisement just as much as the manufacturer, and thus it is not unreasonable to obligate him to ascertain the truthfulness of the claims he is being paid to make.[2]

With a celebrity endorsement, the FTC requires several steps. First, as the quote indicates, the celebrity must ascertain the truth of the ad claims. Second, the celebrity cannot make any claims about product use unless the celebrity has actually used and experienced the product. Finally, if any claims are being made that are not the celebrity's, the source of the information must be disclosed as part of the ad.

FTC Control of Bait and Switch

Read the FTC's advice on purchasing a computer for a low cost in exchange for signing up for Internet service:

http://www.ftc.gov/ bcp/conline/pubs/alerts/ pcalrt.htm

One of the better-known FTC ad regulations prohibits the use of **bait and switch**, a sales tactic in which a cheaper product than the one in stock is advertised to get customers into a store. The seller has no intention of selling the product and in some cases might not even have the product in stock; but the ad is used as "bait" to get the customers in and present them with a "better," more expensive product. Such ad tactics are considered deceptive and subject to FTC remedy.

ETHICAL ISSUES

The FTC has been focusing on the concept of "free," particularly as it relates to ads for computers. Many companies have advertised "free computers" or "low-cost computers" with fine-print disclosure on requirements such as having to subscribe to CompuServe, Prodigy, or MSN for three-year periods to qualify for the $400 rebates or computer discounts. If the fees for these Internet services are factored in at an average cost of $21.95 per month, the total cost for those services for three years is $790.20; and there is usually a penalty of $400 if the computer purchaser cancels the Internet service contract before the three-year term expires. Further, some consumers in certain areas must pay long-distance costs to access the Internet service provider they choose in order to qualify for the rebate or computer price discount.

While most computer retailers do disclose all the terms of the discount or rebate, the FTC notes that some of the disclosures in the ads are "microscopic." The FTC is considering a rule that would require a conspicuous up-front disclosure of the total cost of purchasing the computer.

Presently, there are no regulations that apply specifically to these discounts and rebates for computer sales other than the generic accuracy in advertising regulations. Refer to Chapter 2 and the discussion of the social, regulatory, and litigation cycle (Exhibit 2.3). Is this an issue that has moved into the awareness and activism stage? Is regulation likely? What could the computer retailers do? Do you think they should make more obvious disclosures about the total package cost of these discount computers? Won't they sell more computers with the hook of the $400 rebate and fine-print disclosure?

FTC Control of Product Comparisons

Visit the Better Business Bureau:

http://www.bbb.org

Another aspect of active enforcement by the FTC is in the area of product comparisons. The FTC permits and even welcomes comparisons of products, but such comparisons must be accurate. Results of surveys must be supportable, and product preference tests must be done fairly. In the past few years, the FTC has taken a laissez-faire approach in ad regulation. Other agencies, such as the offices of state attorneys general, the Better Business Bureau, and private companies and individuals, have undertaken public and private enforcement of deceptive ad claims.

The bulk of litigation over comparative ads is now conducted by and against competitors. The FTC generally focuses on deception by companies about their own products. However, federal trademark law permits competitors to recover from companies for ads that include such misrepresentations. Companies can also be held liable for misrepresentations regarding other companies' products. Litigation over comparative ads is somewhat rewarding because plaintiffs can recover treble damages, the defendant company's profits, and, in some cases, attorney fees. Suits that have been filed for competitor misrepresentations include an action by MCI against AT&T for claims that AT&T is cheaper than MCI and a suit by Gillette against Wilkinson for claims that men preferred Wilkinson's Ultra Glide razor to Gillette's Ultra Plus. *Verizon Directories Corp.* v. *Yellow Book USA, Inc.* (Case 11.3) presents a competitor litigation over misrepresentation.

CASE 11.3

Verizon Directories Corp. v. *Yellow Book USA, Inc.*
309 F.Supp.2d 401, (E.D. N.Y. 2004)

I Say They're Just Yellow Customers

FACTS

Yellow Book USA (YB USA) publishes a yellow pages directory, the Yellow Book, which competes with Verizon's yellow pages directory, the SuperPages, in a number of major markets. YB USA promotes the Yellow Book in commercials on local and national broadcast and cable television and through sales representatives.

Verizon alleges that YB USA's commercials falsely represent that more people use the Yellow Book than use the SuperPages. Verizon claims that more people use the SuperPages than use the Yellow Book and that it has been irreparably harmed by YB USA's misrepresentations in three television commercials.

The first commercial, the "Senior Focus Group," starts with three marketing men who work for the "Other Book" directory—which Verizon alleges is a thinly veiled pseudonym for Verizon's SuperPages—holding a focus group session with nine senior citizens. The men ask the senior citizens which book they use, the Yellow Book or the Other Book. Each senior responds that he or she uses the Yellow Book. The men then ask whether the seniors ever look at the Other Book. In response they receive only blank stares. The commercial closes with an image of the Yellow Book standing on end next to the Other Book, as a voiceover says, "More people choose Yellow Book, not the Other Book."

The second commercial, the "Apartment Lobby," opens with the same three men who work for the Other Book in the back of a van spying on an apartment building lobby. On the side of the van is a picture of the Other Book yellow pages directory and the words "The Other Book by the Phone Company." In the lobby are two large stacks of new yellow pages directories, one stack of the Yellow Book and one of the Other Book. The men watch as, one by one, residents of the apartment building come into the lobby to pick up a directory. The stack of Yellow Books quickly disappears, while all of the Other Books remain unclaimed. A voiceover says, "Today, people are choosing the Yellow Book, not that Other Book."

The third and final commercial, the "Wind Tunnel," opens on one of the marketing men from the Phone Company. He is carrying a copy of the Yellow Book and a copy of a yellow pages directory clearly titled "The Other Book by the Phone Company." He brings them into a wind tunnel that is identified as "The Phone Company Secret Test Site." The man says in disgust, "Consumers keep choosing Yellow Book yellow pages!" He holds up the Yellow Book. Two people dressed as scientists are behind a window in a control room; one says, "We'll find out which directory has the right stuff!" The marketing man places the two directories side-by-side on a platform. The scientists increase the speed of the wind machine. The Other Book gets blown away by a light wind, while the Yellow Book remains firmly in place even as the intensity of the wind increases to the point where the Other Book's marketer is blown off the screen.

Verizon moved for a preliminary injunction, a permanent injunction, and treble damages. YB USA moved to dismiss.

JUDICIAL OPINION

WEINSTEIN, Senior District Judge
YB USA moves for a judgment on the pleadings to dismiss all of Verizon's claims as to the television commercials on the ground that the commercials constitute nonactionable puffery as a matter of law. It also seeks dismissal of Verizon's product disparagement claim on the ground that Verizon has failed to plead special damages.

Section 43(a) of the Lanham Act provides that

any person who . . . in commercial advertising or promotion, misrepresents the nature, characteristics, qualities, or geographic origin of his or her or another person's goods, services, or commercial activities, shall be liable in a civil action by any person who believes that he or she is likely to be damaged by such act.

15 U.S.C. § 1125(a)(1)(B).
A plaintiff must allege that: (1) the defendant made false or misleading representations regarding the nature, characteristics, or quality of the plaintiff's services or commercial activities; (2) the representations were used in commerce; (3) the representations were made in the context of commercial advertising or promotion;

and (4) the defendant's actions made the plaintiff believe it would be damaged by the representations.

An advertisement must be: "(1) . . . literally false as a factual matter, or (2) although . . . literally true, . . . likely to deceive or confuse customers." *McNeil-P.C.C., Inc. v. Bristol-Myers Squibb Co.,* 938 F.2d 1544, 1549 (2d Cir. 1991); see also *Johnson & Johnson Merck Consumer Pharmaceuticals Co. v. Smithkline Beecham Corp.,* 960 F.2d 294, 297 (2d Cir.1992).

Context of the advertisement is critical, for it is "fundamental to any task of interpretation . . . that text must yield to context." *Avis Rent A Car Sys., Inc. v. The Hertz Corp.,* 782 F.2d 381, 385 (2d. Cir.1986) ("[T]he Supreme Court long ago inveighed against the tyranny of literalness."). In addition to its text, a commercial's visual images will be considered in determining falsity. *S.C. Johnson & Son, Inc. v. The Clorox Co.,* 241 F.3d 232, 238 (2d Cir.2001).

False representations of fact are distinguished from puffery. Puffery is a somewhat amorphous concept. In the Lanham Act context, puffery has been defined alternately as "an exaggeration or overstatement expressed in broad, vague, and commendatory language," as "a general claim of superiority over comparable products that is so vague that it can be understood as nothing more than a mere expression of opinion," *Pizza Hut, Inc. v. Papa John's Int'l, Inc.,* 227 F.3d 489, 497 (5th Cir.2000); and as an "exaggerated, blustering, and boasting statement upon which no reasonable buyer would rely," *Southland Sod Farms v. Stover Seed Co.,* 108 F.3d 1134, 1145 (9th Cir.1997).

Puffery is not actionable under the Lanham Act because it "cannot be proven either true or false." [S]ee *Bologna v. Allstate Insurance Co.,* 138 F.Supp.2d 310, 322–23 (E.D.N.Y.2001) (granting motion to dismiss Lanham Act claim on ground that slogan "you're in good hands with Allstate" was mere puffery).

YB USA urges review and evaluation of each television commercial separately, while Verizon insists that the commercials should be viewed together as part of a coordinated and comprehensive campaign. Even assuming that defendant's commercials should be evaluated separately, plaintiff has alleged facts sufficient to make out a prima facie claim as to each of the commercials under section 43(a) of the Lanham Act. YB USA moves to dismiss Verizon's Lanham Act claim on the ground that its commercials consist of mere puffery. A viewing of YB USA's commercials in toto and with consideration of their visual imagery as well as their sound suggests that they might be interpreted by consumers to mean that more people use the Yellow Book than use the Verizon SuperPages.

On a literal level the commercials are merely playful and absurd. No one would believe that an adult finding two free directories at the doorstep would leave one; both would almost certainly be taken. Even a young child would know that a blast of air that could blow away both a yellow pages directory and an adult would not leave another directory of similar heft unaffected. Cf., Alison Gopnick, Finding Our Inner Scientist, Daedalus, Winter 2004, at 21, 27 ("[B]y the time children are four they will . . . uncover causal structure.").

Literalness is not what these commercials are about. They are skillfully crafted and shown at great expense to subtly but firmly communicate an idea—that the Yellow Book is preferred by users to Verizon's book and that, more to the point, advertisers will reach more potential consumers if they put their names and money in the former rather than the latter.

Publishers of yellow pages directories generate revenue through the sale of advertising in their pages. Potential advertisers make the decision to purchase space within a directory based largely on that directory's usage rate. A higher usage rate means more advertising revenue for the directory favored by the public. The creators of television commercials are well paid for their ability to subtly communicate specific messages while appearing to say almost nothing.

A federal trial judge, with a background and experience unlike that of most consumers, is hardly in a position to declare, "Because I appreciate that the television campaign is just expressing a far-fetched opinion and not making a statement of fact, all viewers must appreciate it as well." Yet, that is what the court is expected to do when it is asked to characterize a video as "mere puffery." Arguably, the communication intended by YB USA and understood by the viewer is defendant's—to wit, "The Yellow Book is preferred by potential users over the competitor's." It may, however, mean something quite different to the viewer. This central issue cannot be resolved without surveys, expert testimony, and other evidence of what is happening in the real world of television watchers and advertisers in yellow pages.

At the level of a motion directed to the pleadings, the extensive citations submitted by the parties to widely disparate cases where the communication was characterized as "puffery" or "fact" are almost useless. The characterization is similar to that of proximate cause, a rule that the court applies on an ad hoc basis where it thinks recovery should not be permitted for largely unexpressed reasons of policy and repressed biases.

Analytical transparency begins with an accurate assessment of the facts—here what the defendant-communicator intended to communicate and what was communicated to the intended communicant, not what

continued

a communication means to a judge. In the present case the court is not prepared to say how users and advertisers would be affected by these commercials and what YB USA's salespersons are saying to prospective advertisers who have seen them. Evidence is required on a motion for summary judgement (sic) or at trial. The motion to dismiss on the pleadings on the theory of puffery cannot be granted.

CASE QUESTIONS

1. What is the basic thrust of the comparative ads?
2. Are the ads puffery?
3. Why doesn't the judge grant a judgment on the pleadings?
4. What will Verizon need to prove in order to recover?

 CONSIDER...   **II. 4**

In August 1999, Clorox (defendant/appellant) introduced a 15-second television commercial and a 30-second one ("Goldfish I"), each depicting an S. C. Johnson (plaintiff/appellee) Ziploc Slide-Loc resealable storage bag side-by-side with a Clorox Glad-Lock bag. The bags are identified in the commercials by brand name. Both commercials show an animated, talking goldfish in water inside each of the bags.

In the commercials, the bags are turned upside-down, and the Slide-Loc bag leaks rapidly while the Glad-Lock bag does not leak at all. In both the 15- and 30-second Goldfish I commercials, the Slide-Loc goldfish says, in clear distress, "My Ziploc Slider is dripping. Wait a minute!," while the Slide-Loc bag is shown leaking at a rate of approximately one drop per one to two seconds. In the 30-second Goldfish I commercial only, the Slide-Loc bag is shown leaking while the Slide-Loc goldfish says, "Excuse me, a little help here," and then, "Oh, dripping, dripping." At the end of both commercials, the Slide-Loc goldfish exclaims, "Can I borrow a cup of water!!!"

On November 4, 1999, S. C. Johnson brought an action against Clorox under section 43(a) of the Lanham Act, 15 U.S.C. § 1125(a), for false advertising in the Goldfish I commercials.

Dr. Phillip DeLassus, an outside expert retained by S. C. Johnson, conducted "torture testing," in which Slide-Loc bags were filled with water, rotated for 10 seconds, and held upside-down for an additional 20 seconds. He testified about the results of the tests he performed, emphasizing that 37% of all Slide-Loc bags tested did not leak at all. Of the remaining 63% that did leak, only a small percentage leaked at the rate depicted in the Goldfish I television commercials. The vast majority leaked at a rate between two and twenty times slower than that depicted in the Goldfish I commercials. Can the comparative ads be halted? What is different about this case and these ads from the Verizon case? [*S. C. Johnson & Son, Inc. v. Clorox Company*, 241 F.3d 232 (2d Cir. 2001).]

FTC Remedies

As noted in the previous sections, the FTC has a wide range of remedies available in the event of deceptive advertising, including corrective ads, injunctions to prevent deceptive ads from being run, and reimbursement by companies and endorsers for purchasers who were misled by ads.

More often than not, these remedies come about through a consent decree. A **consent decree** is a negotiated settlement between the FTC and the advertiser. It is the equivalent of a *nolo contendere* or no contest plea. The FTC and the advertiser, endorser, and/or agency or Web site designer agree to remedies, and the case is disposed of through the decree without further action.

Ad Regulation by the FDA

The Food and Drug Administration (FDA) also has authority over some forms of advertising. For example, the FDA has control over direct advertising to the public of prescription medications. Products such as Retin A have had direct ads and news releases subject to FDA regulation. For example, in the case of Retin A, the FDA warned Ortho, its manufacturer, that Retin A had been approved as an anti-acne cream, not as an anti-aging cream, and that it could not be advertised to the public as such.

FOR THE MANAGER'S DESK

RE: BETTER BUSINESS AND ADS

The National Advertising Division of the Council of Better Business Bureaus has undertaken a role of private scrutiny of television ad content. Most particularly, the ad division is focusing on the infomercial, the thirty-minute show-type formats for advertising products. Direct response television advertising attracted 163 million American viewers in 200 or about 63 percent of Americans.* Worldwide revenues are estimated to be $2 trillion per year, an amount that exceeds the revenues of the motion picture industry. About 25 to 30 percent of the complaints on infomercial content come from local Better Business Bureaus, with the remaining 70–75 percent of the claims coming from competitors. Only five of those cases were referred to federal regulators, with the remaining cases resolved by discussions with the product manufacturer or ad sponsor.

The ad division has not taken any action against the psychic reader infomercials because whether a reading "brings joy" to humans is difficult to define, let alone prove a breach of any type of express promise. Further, the ad division does not become involved in puffery. An example cited by the division is the claim by BMW that its cars are "the ultimate driving machine." Such a claim is not actionable.

One product the ad division investigated is a thirty-minute infomercial for the DeLonghi America Caffe Sienna espresso/cappuccino machine. The ad included this statement from the host/announcer:

> *Brew cappuccino just like the pros do right at home.*
> *Up until now, the home machines, they just didn't work.*

The ad division approached Jim McCrusker, the president of the U.S. unit of DeLonghi, on the grounds that the ad was misleading. The ad division, reacting to complaints from competitors, wanted Mr. McCrusker to add language that indicated it wasn't that other machines didn't work. The machines worked, but their frothing processes were not good.

Mr. McCrusker brought in other machines and consumers to talk with the ad division. The presentation of competitors' machines along with testimonials from consumers about the problems with other machines convinced the ad council that the statement "They didn't work" was indeed accurate for more than just the frothing process.

What lessons are learned from Mr. McCrusker's experience? Is documentation for ad claims important? Is it appropriate for competitors to complain to a regulatory body about ad content?

*Data are from the Electronic Retailing Association.

Professional Ads

Most states have limitations on the types of ads professionals (such as doctors, lawyers, dentists, and accountants) can use in reaching the public. At one time, states had complete bans on ads by professionals. However, the U.S. Supreme Court held such bans to be too restrictive and violative of First Amendment protections on commercial speech. (See Chapter 5.) Restrictions may include requirements on fee disclosures or caveats on distinctions in individual cases and needs. The extent and validity of the restrictions continue to be refined through judicial application of First Amendment rights.

CONTRACT PRODUCT LIABILITY THEORIES: IMPLIED WARRANTIES

The UCC's Article 2 governs contracts for the sale of goods and includes several provisions for implied warranties. The following sections cover the requirements for each of the implied warranties.

The Implied Warranty of Merchantability

The **implied warranty of merchantability** (UCC § 2–314) is given in every sale of goods by a merchant seller. The warranty is not given by all sellers, only by merchant sellers. Briefly defined, merchants are those sellers who are engaged in the business of selling the good(s) that are the subject of the contract. The revisions to the UCC changed the wording of this warranty slightly so that it now provides that goods sold by a merchant "(c) are fit for the ordinary purposes for which goods of that description are used." The warranty means the goods are of fair or average quality and are fit for ordinary purposes. Under this warranty, basketballs must bounce, book bindings must hold together, and food items must be free of foreign objects.

For example, in *Metty v. Shurfine Central Corp.*, 736 S.W.2d 527 (Mo. 1987), the court found that a breach of the implied warranty of merchantability occurred because part of a grasshopper in a can of green beans was eaten by a pregnant woman who purchased the beans. Shurfine was liable to the woman for resulting complications in her pregnancy. But what happens if there is something naturally present, such as a cherry pit in a cherry pie, that harms someone? Is there still a breach of warranty? *Mitchell* v. *T.G.I. Friday's* (Case 11.4) provides an answer to these questions.

CASE 11.4

Mitchell v. *T.G.I. Friday's*
748 N.E.2d 89 (Ohio App. 2000)

Clamming Up Because of Shell-Shock

FACTS

On April 11, 1996, Sandra Mitchell (appellant) was having dinner at Friday's restaurant (appellee). Ms. Mitchell was eating a fried clam strip when she bit into a hard substance that she believed to be a piece of a clam shell. She experienced immediate pain and later sought dental treatment. Some time later, the crown of a tooth came loose. The crown could not be reattached, and an oral surgeon removed the remaining root of the tooth.

Ms. Mitchell filed a product liability action against Friday's, which had served her the meal, and Pro Source Distributing (also appellee), the supplier of the fried clams. Both Friday's and Pro Source filed motions for summary judgment, which the trial court granted without explanation. Ms. Mitchell appealed.

JUDICIAL OPINION

WAITE, Judge

Appellant argues that in light of Ohio's product liability legislation, the trial court should have applied the "reasonable-expectation test" to her claim and in doing so the court should not have granted appellees' motions for summary judgment. R.C. 2307.74 provides

that "[a] product is defective [if] [i]t deviated in a material way from the design specifications, formula, or performance standards of the manufacturer." R.C. 2307.75(A)(2) provides that a product is defective in design or formulation if "[i]t is more dangerous than an ordinary consumer would expect when used in an intended or reasonably foreseeable manner." According to appellant, by the enactment of these statutes the "reasonable-expectation" test supersedes the traditional "foreign-natural test" applied in cases where injury is caused by substances in food. Appellant asserts that there is a reasonable expectation that clams are completely cleaned of their shells and free of foreign materials.

Before addressing the merits of this argument, we begin by noting that the trial court's journal entries granting summary judgment to appellees failed to delineate any basis for the decisions. Such practice has become common in courts subject to our review. While on review, we must and do conduct a meticulous *de novo* review on appeal, a trial court that gives careful consideration to a motion for summary judgment along with a concise explanation of its decision will benefit the whole of the judicial process. The trial court will not only serve the parties by providing the basis for more expeditious appeals, but may encourage the termination of claims by use of conspicuous and irrefutable logic. The interests of justice are only well served if the parties are informed as to the basis for decisions that affect them.

In the present case, Friday's set forth in its motion for summary judgment appellant's deposition testimony to the effect that while eating a clam strip, she bit down on "a hard, foreign substance." Appellant stated that she assumed it was a piece of a clam shell. Appellant described the size of the object as about a quarter of the size of a small fingernail or about a quarter of an inch or smaller and irregular in shape. Moreover, Friday's attached an affidavit from its manager, Eric Hicks, who immediately responded to appellant's report of the incident. In that affidavit, Hicks confirmed that the object appellant presented to him was indeed a piece of clam shell and that it was approximately one-quarter inch in length and irregularly shaped. In its motion for summary judgment, Pro Source adopted and incorporated the statement of Friday's, appellant's deposition testimony, and the affidavit of Eric Hicks. In her response, appellant set forth no facts to dispute that the object in the clam strip was in fact a piece of clam shell.

Both Friday's and Pro Source presented essentially the same argument, that regardless of whether the foreign-natural test or reasonable-expectation test was applied, appellant has no claim against appellees.

The basis of appellant's argument for application of the reasonable-expectation test is found in R.C. 2307.75, which provides that a product is defective if it is more dangerous than an ordinary consumer would reasonably suspect. However, appellant has not set forth any case law or analysis that would suggest that food products fall under the purview of the statute. We can find no case that has analyzed a food item in that context. Indeed, the weight of product liability cases deal with synthetic products, for example, a cargo door hinge, a glass bottle, or a prosthetic hip joint. Thus, we see no compelling reason to abandon any established test due to the enactment of Ohio's product liability legislation.

However, it does not appear necessary to determine which test applies to the present case. Save for reference to the product liability statute, a similar argument was addressed in *Mathews* v. *Maysville Seafoods, Inc.* (1991), 76 Ohio App.3d 624, 602 N.E.2d 764. In *Mathews*, the plaintiff suffered a bowel injury when he swallowed a fish bone while eating a fish fillet served by the defendant. The trial court granted the defendant's motion for summary judgment. On appeal, the defendant argued for the adoption of the reasonable-expectation test as opposed to the foreign-natural test.

The *Mathews* court set forth both tests. Under the foreign-natural test:

> Bones which are natural to the type of meat served cannot legitimately be called a foreign substance, and a consumer who eats meat dishes ought to anticipate and be on his guard against the presence of such bones.

[Q]uoting *Mix* v. *Ingersoll Candy Co.* (1936), 6 Cal.2d 674, 682, 59 P.2d 144, 148.

The reasonable-expectation test states:

> The test should be what is "reasonably expected" by the consumer in the food as served, not what might be natural to the ingredients of that food prior to preparation.*** As applied to the action for common-law negligence, the test is related to the foreseeability of harm on the part of the defendant. The defendant is not an insurer but has the duty of ordinary care to eliminate or remove in the preparation of the food he serves such harmful substances as the consumer of the food, as served, would not ordinarily anticipate and guard against.

Mathews, 602 N.E.2d at 765.

The *Mathews* court looked to *Allen* v. *Grafton* (1960), 164 N.E.2d 167, where the plaintiff was injured after swallowing a piece of oyster shell contained in a serving of fried oysters. The Supreme Court held:

> The presence in one of a serving of six fried oysters of a piece of oyster shell approximately 3×2 centimeters (about 1⅛ inches by ⅖ of an inch) in diameter will not justify a legal conclusion either (a) that that serving of fried oysters constituted "food" that was "adulterated" within the meaning of Section 3715.59, Revised Code, or (b) that that serving constituted food not "reasonably fit for" eating.

The *Mathews* court further noted:

> In the instant case, it is not necessary to hold * * * that, because an oyster shell is natural to an oyster and thus not a substance "foreign" to an oyster, no liability can be predicated upon the sale of a fried oyster containing a piece of oyster shell. However, the fact, that something that is served with food and that will cause harm if eaten is natural to that food and so not a "foreign substance," will usually be an important factor in determining whether a consumer can reasonably anticipate and guard against it.
>
> In our opinion, the possible presence of a piece of oyster shell in or attached to an oyster is so well known to anyone who eats oysters that we can say as a matter of law that one who eats oysters can reasonably anticipate and guard against eating such a piece of shell, especially where it is as big a piece as the one described in plaintiff's petition.

Most courts which have relied on *Allen* conclude that the Ohio Supreme Court has adopted the

continued

foreign-natural test. However, other courts have found that *Allen* endorses the reasonable-expectation test.

Despite the opposing interpretations of *Allen*, the *Mathews* court stated that "it is not necessary to decide whether the 'reasonable expectation' test or the 'foreign-natural' test holds sway in Ohio." The court stated that it must be reasonably expected that even a fish fillet may contain fish bones, citing *Polite* v. *Carey Hilliards Restaurants, Inc.* (1985). The *Mathews* court noted that in *Polite*, the court applied the foreign-natural test in affirming a summary judgment for the defendant where the plaintiff swallowed an obviously naturally occurring one-inch fish bone concealed in a fish fillet.

> *An occasional piece of clam shell in a bowl of clam chowder is so well known to a consumer that we can say the consumer can reasonably anticipate and guard against it.*
>
> *Courts cannot and must not ignore the common experience of life and allow rules to develop that would make sellers of food or other consumer goods insurers of the products they sell.*

In the present case, it cannot be disputed that the piece of clam shell that caused appellant's injury was natural to the clam strip she consumed. Turning to the question of whether appellant should have reasonably anticipated the presence of the clam shell, we are reminded of the Ohio Supreme Court's holding in *Allen, supra*, that "the possible presence of a piece of oyster shell in or attached to an oyster is so well known to anyone who eats oysters that we can say as a matter of law that one who eats oysters can reasonably anticipate and guard against eating such a piece of shell." The facts of the present case are virtually indistinguishable from *Allen* except for the type of injury and that, here, appellant was eating fried clams rather than fried oysters. We therefore hold that, as a matter of law, one who eats clams can reasonably anticipate and guard against eating a piece of shell.

As appellant's claim fails under both tests, we overrule her assignment of error and affirm the judgment of the trial court.

Judgment affirmed.

CASE QUESTIONS

1. What did Ms. Mitchell eat, and what were her resulting injuries?

2. What did the lower court do in the case that caused an admonition from the appellate court?

3. What test does Ohio follow—the foreign-natural or the reasonable-expectation test?

4. Does the court think the Ohio test makes a difference in this case?

5. Is the reasonable-expectation test one that makes the food producer or provider an insurer?

CONSIDER...   11.5

Jack A. Clark ordered a chicken enchilada at Mexicali Rose restaurant (defendants). Because of a one-inch-long chicken bone in the enchilada, Mr. Clark choked and received throat injuries. He brought suit for breach of implied warranty, negligence, and strict liability. Should he recover? [*Mexicali Rose* v. *Superior Court*, 822 P.2d 1292 (Cal. 1992).]

CONSIDER...   11.6

On November 11, 1994, Loretta Jones was injured when she bit into a meatball at an Olive Garden Restaurant owned by GMRI, Inc. in Pineville, North Carolina. When Ms. Jones attempted to take her first bite of the meatball, she bit down into an unidentified metal object. At that time, she experienced an "incredible stabbing pain in [her] tooth and [her] jaw," caused by a broken tooth. Because she was startled, she "sucked in and immediately sucked down the food" and the object. Ms. Jones said that she cut the meatball into eight pieces prior to taking the bite and that she did not detect any foreign object in the meatball at that time.

She filed suit against GMRI and Rich Products Corporation, which allegedly supplied or manufactured the meatball, asserting claims of negligence, breach of implied warranty, and loss of consortium. GMRI asserted as a defense to the implied warranty claim that it did not have a reasonable opportunity to inspect the meatball in a way that would have discovered the defect.

GMRI said that most of the restaurant's meatballs come into the store frozen and in sealed bags. The restaurant does a visual inspection of the sealed bags of meatballs and sends back those that do not meet the inspection. The meatballs are put into the freezer at the restaurant until needed, then put into a plastic holding container and placed in a refrigerator. The meatballs, which are slightly larger than a golf ball, are then mixed with a tomato sauce, heated, and served whole. Restaurant personnel indicated that they do not poke or slice the meatballs, other than to check the temperature with a probe.

Is GMRI liable to Ms. Jones? [*Jones v. GMRI, Inc.,* 2001 WL 747812 (N.C.App. 2001).]

CONSIDER...   11.7

Sylvia Lewis purchased an ice cream cone from Handel's Homemade Ice Cream and Yogurt in Liberty Township, Ohio. The ice cream cone consisted of one scoop of banana ice cream and one scoop of pistachio nut ice cream. As Ms. Lewis walked away from the counter where she ordered the cone, she began to consume the ice cream. After taking her third bite of pistachio nut ice cream, Ms. Lewis claims she bit into a pistachio nut with the shell still intact. Ms. Lewis returned to the counter and notified the owner of the incident. She was then given a vanilla ice cream cone in exchange for her original cone. As a result of biting into the shell, she alleged that she suffered injuries to both her tooth and jaw. She filed suit against Handel's. Should she recover? [*Lewis v. Handel's Homemade Ice Cream and Yogurt,* 2003 WL 21509258 (Ohio App. 2002).]

CONSIDER...   11.8

Ms. Hubbs, 80, suffered from arthritis and osteoporosis. She purchased the Clapper, a device designed to turn electrical appliances on by responding to sound, namely, the clapping of hands.

Ms. Hubbs did not follow the instructions in the product to adjust its sensitivity. As a result of continual hard clapping, Ms. Hubbs broke her wrists. Ms. Hubbs also did not follow the product instructions to use (buy) a clicker available for the product if clapping is a chore. She has sued the Clapper's manufacturer for breach of the warranty of merchantability. Should she recover? [*Hubbs v. Joseph Enterprises,* 604 N.Y.S.2d 292 (1993).]

CONSIDER...   11.9

Wendi James was already eating her taco when she noticed that there was a bloody thumbprint on the flour tortilla shell. She and her brother, who had just obtained their food from a Taco Bell drive-through restaurant, then examined all of their food purchases and discovered that they were spattered with blood. Wendi became ill.

Wendi and her brother, James, then called the Taco Bell restaurant requesting an explanation. A cook there told them that he had cut his finger and had not realized it. He then volunteered that he had recently been tested for the HIV virus and that the test had come back negative. Wendi asked why he had been tested for the virus, and the cook refused to provide an explanation.

Wendi and James have filed suit against Taco Bell. What bases could they allege for liability?

The Implied Warranty of Fitness for a Particular Purpose

The **implied warranty of fitness for a particular purpose** (UCC § 2–315) arises when the seller promises a buyer that the goods will be suitable for a use the buyer has proposed. For example, the owner of a nursery makes an implied warranty for a particular purpose when telling a buyer that a weed killer will work in the buyer's rose garden without harming the roses. An exercise enthusiast is given this warranty when the seller recommends a particular shoe as appropriate for aerobics.

The requirements for this warranty are:

1. The seller has skill or judgment in use of the goods.
2. The buyer is relying on that skill or judgment.
3. The seller knew or had reason to know of the buyer's reliance.
4. The seller makes a recommendation for the buyer's use and purpose.

CONSIDER...   11.10

Cynthia Rubin went to Marshall Field's department store on April 5, 1986. While browsing, she got into a conversation with Julianna Reiner, a salesclerk, and told Ms. Reiner that she used Vaseline to remove her eye makeup. Ms. Reiner said Vaseline could clog her eye ducts and cause cataracts or other permanent eye damage, and she recommended Princess Marcella Borghese Instant Eye Make-Up Remover, manufactured by Princess Marcella Borghese, Inc. Ms. Rubin asked if the product was safe. Ms. Reiner showed her the box, which said, "Recommended for all skin types." Ms. Reiner said, "If it wouldn't be safe for you, it wouldn't say this on the box." Relying on Ms. Reiner's representations, Ms. Rubin purchased the product.

That night she used the product to remove her eye makeup. Her eyelids and the skin around her eyes turned red, became taut and rough, and started to sting. She washed her skin repeatedly and kept a cold washrag on her eyes all night. Two days later, when the burning did not subside, she called an ophthalmologist and went to see him the next day. He told her that she had contact dermatitis and prescribed an ointment.

A few weeks later, because the burning and roughness of her eyelids persisted, Ms. Rubin decided to see Dr. Katherine Wier, a dermatologist. Dr. Wier prescribed a similar ointment and told Ms. Rubin that the chemical causing the burning would remain in her system for three or four months. The stinging subsided, but Ms. Rubin could not wear eye makeup again regularly until summer 1987. When she tried to wear makeup again before that, her eyelids turned bright red and began swelling upon removal of the makeup.

Ms. Rubin filed suit for breach of implied warranty of fitness for a particular purpose. Should she recover? [*Rubin* v. *Marshall Field & Co.*, 597 N.E.2d 688 (Ill. 1992).]

Eliminating Warranty Liability by Disclaimers

Warranties can be eliminated by the use of **disclaimers**. The proper method for disclaiming a warranty depends on the type of warranty. Express warranties, however, cannot be given and then taken back. Basically, an express warranty cannot be disclaimed. Exhibit 11.2 includes a summary of the means for disclaiming warranties.

The implied warranty of merchantability and the implied warranty of fitness for a particular purpose can be disclaimed by using a phrase such as "WITH ALL FAULTS," or "AS IS." Either warranty alone can be disclaimed by using the name of the warranty: "There is no warranty of merchantability given" or "There is no implied warranty of fitness for a particular purpose." Under Revised Article 2, the disclaimer for the implied warranty of merchantability must include the following language: "The seller undertakes no responsibility for the quality of the goods except as otherwise provided in this contract." Also under the Revised Article 2 provisions, a warranty can be disclaimed in a record. "*Record*" is new to the Revised

UCC and expands the definition of writing to include electronic communications such as e-mails and faxes. For those warranty disclaimers required to be in writing, their presence in a record satisfies the writing requirements.

Even though the UCC is clear on the language to be used for warranty disclaimers and the process seems to be easy, even the warranty disclaimers are subject to the general UCC constraint of good faith. **Unconscionable** disclaimers of warranties or waiver of warranties when one party has no bargaining power may not be valid. For example, a disclaimer of liability for personal injury resulting from a breach of the warranty of merchantability for a consumer good would be unconscionable. Consider 11.11 deals with a warranty disclaimer and whether it is valid.

 CONSIDER...   **11.11**

Nunes Turfgrass, Inc. was the largest independent sod grower in California. Based in Modesto with outlets in seven other California cities, it had been in business since 1962. Vaughan-Jacklin Seed Company was a corporate grower, developer, and commercial retailer of grass seed and was based in Post Falls, Idaho. At the time of the dispute, Vaughan-Jacklin had been in business for fifty years and was one of the largest seed companies in the world.

Nunes sold its sod fields and seed mixes under the Nunes name to landscapers, golf courses, and the general public. In 1980, Nunes began to notice that its customers wanted a hardier, more drought-resistant type of grass (bluegrass-perennial ryegrass blend). Nunes contacted Doyle Jacklin, the sales and marketing manager for Vaughan-Jacklin, and discussed its needs. Mr. Jacklin researched the needs and recommended to Nunes the Jackpot perennial ryegrass. Nunes relied on the recommendation and ordered 8,000 pounds of Jackpot in September 1981.

Before the seed was shipped, Vaughan-Jacklin sent a written confirmation of sale with this warranty and disclaimer:

JACKLIN SEED COMPANY, DIVISION OF VAUGHAN-JACKLIN CORPORATION, warrants that seed it sells conforms to the label description as required by State and Federal Seed Laws. IT MAKES NO OTHER WARRANTIES, EXPRESS OR IMPLIED, OF MERCHANTABILITY, FITNESS FOR PURPOSE, OR OTHERWISE, AND IN ANY EVENT ITS LIABILITY FOR BREACH OF ANY WARRANTY OR CONTRACT WITH RESPECT TO SUCH SEEDS IS LIMITED TO THE PURCHASE PRICE OF SUCH SEEDS. JACKLIN SEED COMPANY FURTHER LIMITS TO SUCH PURCHASE PRICE ITS LIABILITY OF ANY KIND ON ACCOUNT OF ANY NEGLIGENCE WHATSOEVER ON ITS PART WITH RESPECT TO SUCH SEEDS.

The seed bags had the same language, to which was added the following:

LIABILITY for damages for any cause, including breach of contract or breach of warranty, with respect to this sale of seeds IS LIMITED TO A REFUND OF THE PURCHASE PRICE OF THE SEEDS. THIS REMEDY IS EXCLUSIVE. IN NO EVENT SHALL THE LABELER BE LIABLE FOR ANY INCIDENTAL OR CONSEQUENTIAL DAMAGES, INCLUDING LOSS OF PROFIT.

In September and October 1981, Nunes overseeded fifty-six acres with the Jackpot seed. Within weeks of overseeding, large clumps of off-colored ryegrass appeared in the fields, rendering them unfit for sod production. The result was that Nunes could not make sod sales and was forced to liquidate its business in 1984.

Can Nunes recover for breach of warranty? [*Nunes Turfgrass, Inc.* v. *Vaughan-Jacklin Seed Co.*, 246 Cal. Rptr. 823 (1988).]

Privity Standards for UCC Recovery

If you have a contract to buy a car and the seller breaches the contract by refusing to deliver, you can bring suit for breach of contract. There is **privity** between you and the seller. The people in your carpool, however, could not sue the seller for breach if you no longer have a car to use (even though they are affected) because they have no privity of contract with the seller. Traditionally, a recovery for a breach of contract requires privity of contract. A breach of warranty is a breach of contract, and until the time of the UCC, privity was required to be able to recover on a breach of warranty theory.

Revised Section 2–318 of the UCC establishes three alternatives that states can adopt, each of which provides warranty protections for *more* than the buyer. For example, Alternative A extends warranty protection to "any natural person who is in the family or household . . . of the remote purchaser or who is a guest in the home [of the remote purchaser]." Alternative B extends coverage to "any natural person who is reasonably expected to use, consume, or be affected by the goods" or who is "injured in person" by the goods. Alternative C extends the warranty protection to "any person that may be reasonably expected to use, consume, or be affected by the goods" and is injured by them or their use. Alternative C also prohibits the disclaimer of liability for personal injury to those covered by the warranty.

Exhibit 11.2 summarizes the UCC warranty protections and disclaimers.

EXHIBIT   11.2 UCC Warranties: Creation, Restrictions, and Disclaimers

TYPE	CREATION	RESTRICTION	DISCLAIMER
Express	Affirmation of fact or promise of performance (samples, models, descriptions)	Must be part of the basis of the bargain	Cannot make a disclaimer inconsistent with an express warranty
Implied Warranty of Merchantability	Given in every sale of goods by a merchant ("fit for ordinary purposes")	Only given by merchants	(1) Must use disclaimer of quality or use "merchantability" or general disclaimer "as is" or "with all faults" (2) if written—(record) must be conspicuous
Implied Warranty of Fitness for a Particular Purpose	Seller knows of buyer's reliance for a particular use (buyer is ignorant)	Seller must have knowledge— Buyer must rely	(1) Must be in writing (record) (2) Must be conspicuous (3) Must be clear there are no warranties (using specific language) or (4) Also disclaimed with "as is" or "with all faults"
Title	Given in every sale	Does not apply in circumstances where apparent warranty is not given	Must state "There is no warranty of title"

STRICT TORT LIABILITY: PRODUCT LIABILITY UNDER SECTION 402A

The discussion to this point has focused on the statutory and contract theories of product liability. There is liability for making false statements about products, either under UCC warranty provisions or under federal and state advertising and consumer protection statutes. But these theories are grounded in contract relationships and limited statutory authority. A broader focus to product liability is grounded in tort law. There is strict liability in tort for defective products as well as recovery in negligence for products that were created or sold with defects.

The first tort theory for recovery for defective products is **strict liability** in tort. This tort was created and defined by Section 402A of the *Restatement (Second) of Torts*. Restatements of the law are developed by the American Law Institute, an educational group of professors and practicing attorneys. Restatements are not the law, even though they are adopted and recognized in many states as the controlling statement of law in that state. The adoption of a restatement generally comes in the form of judicial acceptance of the doctrines provided.

Visit the American Law Institute:
http://www.ali.org

Restatement § 402A:

-402A. Special Liability of Seller of Product for Physical Harm to User or Consumer

(1) One who sells any product in a defective condition unreasonably dangerous to the user or consumer or to his property is subject to liability for physical harm thereby caused to the ultimate user or consumer, or to his property if
   (a) the seller is engaged in the business of selling such a product, and
   (b) it is expected to and does reach the user or consumer without substantial change in the condition in which it is sold.
(2) The rule stated in Subsection (1) applies although
   (a) the seller has exercised all possible care in the preparation and sale of his product, and
   (b) the user or consumer has not bought the product from or entered into any contractual relations with the seller.

Part 2 of 402A spells out the distinction between negligence and strict tort liability. Liability results for physical harm even when sellers have exercised all possible care in developing, producing, and selling the product. The fact that the seller is in the business of making and/or selling the product and someone is injured results in the liability. No negligent error or omission is required as an element of proof for recovery. Section 402A applies to defective conditions regardless of the precautions taken by the manufacturer. Manufacturers or food processors that take great precautions in their procedures could overcome a charge of negligence; however, strict liability focuses on the fact that a defect exists, not whether the manufacturer could or could not have prevented the problem. The *Restatement (Third) of Product Liability* has been proposed and would clarify the definition of "defective" with regard to knowledge requirements and recovery.

Section 402A has no privity requirements and is not subject to the disclaimers that can eliminate warranty liability.

Unreasonably Dangerous Defective Condition

The requirement of proof of an unreasonable defective condition can be produced in many different ways. Unreasonable defects can come from everything from the materials used to the manufacturing processes. Every product liability suit finds a different type of defect. A product can be unreasonably dangerous because it contains a foreign substance. Most product liability cases relating to food are based on this tenet. Rats in pop bottles, moldy bananas in cereal, parts of a snake in frozen vegetables, and stones in soup are all factual circumstances that have been recognized as Section 402A defective conditions.

The most common types of product liability cases are based on the following types of defects:

1. Design defects
2. Dangers of use due to lack of warnings or unclear use instructions
3. Errors in manufacturing, handling, or packaging of the product

Design Defects

A product with a faulty design exposes its users to unnecessary risks, and products must be designed with all foreseeable uses in mind. Thus, cars must be designed in view of the probability of accidents. A design that creates an otherwise unnecessary explosion upon a rear-end collision is a faulty design.

To make the best possible case in the event of a product liability suit, it is helpful for the manufacturer to have complied with all federal and state regulations on the product. It is also helpful if the manufacturer has used the latest technology and designs available within the industry and has met industry standards in designing its product.

One of the evolving product liability issues is whether sellers and manufacturers can be held liable for the dangers inherent in their products, placed there not by design but by nature. For example, eggs that contain a harmful disease or that were injected with a virus would be unreasonably dangerous and subject to product liability recovery claims. However, could there be recovery from egg producers because of the effects of eggs on body cholesterol levels? And is McDonald's liable because its high-calorie, high-fat foods have resulted in weight gains and obesity in those who frequent this restaurant chain? Or can gun and bullet manufacturers be held liable for the crimes, deaths, and injuries that result from the inherently dangerous nature and uses of their products? The courts have been fairly consistent in ruling that the use of a nondefective product with adequate warnings does not result in liability for the manufacturer because such a result would hold manufacturers liable for the criminal conduct of others, for example, in the case of guns, a result that would be a shift in public policy.[3]

CHECK THE WEB

Check the book's Web site for updates for continuing information on the gun and McDonald's lawsuits.

Greif v. *Anheuser-Busch Companies, Inc.* (Case 11.5) deals with a related issue of whether beer producers are liable for accidents caused by those who are drunk from imbibing the product.

CASE 11.5

Greif v. Anheuser–Busch Companies, Inc.
114 F. Supp.2d 100 (D.Conn.2000)

Is Beer Inherently Dangerous?

FACTS

Christine Mary Greif was stopped on a bicycle on the edge of Route 4 in Farmington, Connecticut, when a motor vehicle driven by Elmer Michaud crossed over the roadway and struck her, causing serious injuries to her. Mr. Michaud had consumed Anheuser-Busch (defendants) products and was under their influence. Mr. Michaud was found guilty of assault in the second degree with a motor vehicle and served two years in prison. The Greifs filed a civil suit against him for damages but do not indicate the status of that suit. Mr. Michaud may be judgment-proof or close to it.

The products in question are beer and beer-type beverages (e.g., light beer, malt liquor, and other alcoholic beverages). Mr. Michaud was driving while intoxicated and was charged with a violation of Connecticut General Statutes § 14–227.

Mrs. Greif, and her husband, Robert Charles Greif (plaintiffs), filed suit under Connecticut's Products Liability Act, maintaining that the beer was defective because it contained alcohol, which can lead to intoxication and thereby impair the consumer's ability to drive, and that the manufacturers have breached warranties made to consumers. The Greifs also alleged that Anheuser-Busch failed to warn about the dangers of drinking their products and has made misrepresentations about them.

JUDICIAL OPINION

GOETTEL, District Judge

The defendants move to dismiss the plaintiffs' action in Connecticut State Court and removed to the federal court by them on diversity grounds.

Beer has been brewed for tens of thousands of years, although the method of making beer in ancient times varied greatly from place to place. Beer is brewed by fermentation in which microscopic fungi known as yeast consume sugars in the grain, converting them to alcohol and carbon dioxide gas. Typically, a beer contains from two to six percent alcohol.

While beer is a relatively mild form of alcoholic beverage, the complaint alleges, and everyone knows, that anyone who consumes enough of any product containing alcohol will become, to some degree, inebriated. Indeed, the complaint alleges that the defendants should have known that some consumers like Mr. Michaud would drink to excess and that intoxication

impairs motor skills including driving. According to paragraph 22 of the complaint, the defendants should reduce the intoxicating effects of the products by lowering or removing the alcohol content. In effect, the complaint alleges that the defendants produced a product that can and does have anti-social effects and should be banned or, at the least, the manufacturer should be responsible for all ultimate misuse of the product by consumers. This essentially is a call for the return of Prohibition, the "great experiment" which not only failed seventy years ago but, according to some, actually led to a substantial increase in the drinking of alcoholic beverages.

At first blush, the theories of the complaint are so bizarre that one is tempted not to treat them seriously. However, similar types of suits have been brought in recent years concerning other products with at least some degree of success. For example, suits against gun manufacturers brought by the estates of persons killed by criminals using legally manufactured guns (or brought by those who had supplied medical assistance to those injured in such events) are a recent phenomenon. See, e.g., *Hamilton v. Beretta U.S.A. Corp.,* Nos. 99–7753, 7785, 7787, 2000 WL 1160699 (2d Cir. August 16, 2000) (certifying certain questions to the New York Court of Appeals).

There is of course no way in which a product containing alcohol can be marketed so as to prevent the type of criminal conduct engaged in by Michaud in this case. Moreover, the Connecticut Products Liability Act, on which the plaintiffs rely, requires proof that the product is unreasonably dangerous, i.e., that it must be dangerous to an extent beyond that which would be contemplated by the ordinary consumer who purchases it, with the ordinary knowledge common to the community as to its characteristics.

That comment addresses and rejects the very design defect claim made in this case, stating "Good whiskey is not unreasonably dangerous merely because it will make some people drunk, and is especially dangerous to alcoholics. . . ." A beverage is not unreasonably dangerous because it contains alcohol, providing that its presence is disclosed. The Connecticut courts have consistently held that the potential risks of alcohol intoxication and drunk driving are matters of common knowledge. Consumers expect there to be

continued

alcohol in beer and should anticipate that, if they have more than one or two, they will experience a degree of intoxication. The product was not, therefore, defective.

Turning to the plaintiffs' failure to warn claim, it too mimics another new style of case. In recent tobacco litigations, plaintiffs have claimed that, while they were aware of the serious health risks involved in smoking (indeed, they could hardly deny it, since the Surgeon General's warnings have been on cigarette packages for many years), the manufacturers knew of dangerous aspects of their products beyond those commonly understood and therefore were responsible for the smokers' continued addiction. Such cases were not generally successful until a recent huge Florida class action verdict which has now been removed to federal court. *Engle* v. *R. J. Reynolds Tobacco Co.*, No. 00-CV-2641 (removal on July 24, 2000 following July 14, 2000 jury verdict awarding $145 billion punitive damages in state court, No. 94–8273–CA–22 (Fla.Cir.Ct.)). Plaintiffs maintain that while there may have been a common understanding about the risks of consuming alcohol and driving, recent studies have indicated the dangers to be greater than had previously been understood and that therefore the existing case law should be ignored. Plaintiffs cite no new breakthrough in the study of alcoholic beverages which could produce such a change. Plaintiffs rely on *Burton* v. *R. J. Reynolds Tobacco Co.*, 884 F.Supp. 1515 (D.Kan.1995), but that case rests on the fact that the plaintiff began smoking some sixty years ago, so that, the Court held, the state of knowledge concerning smoking's dangers were not as well known. (Perhaps they were not, but even in the thirties, cigarettes were referred to as "coffin nails.")

Among other things, the plaintiffs claim the defendants failed to warn consumers and the general public that consumption level effects of products differ from person to person, so that an amount which may not cause inebriation in one consumer might do so to another. We doubt that there is any practical way of conveying such a warning in a meaningful way, but there is clearly no claim that any doubts in that regard were the proximate cause of Mr. Michaud's drunkenness.

Those who drink a substantial amount of alcohol within a relatively short period of time are given clear warning that to avoid possible criminal behavior they must refrain from driving.... Considering also today's heightened level of public awareness regarding the problem, we cannot believe that any person who drives after drinking would be unaware of the possibility that his blood-alcohol level might equal or exceed the statutory standard....

As if the foregoing were not enough, pursuant to the Alcohol Beverage Labeling Act of 1988, 27 U.S.C. §§ 213 *et seq.*, every bottle or can of beer brewed and sold in the United States contains a federally mandated warning that "consumption of alcohol beverages impairs your ability to drive a car . . . ." 27 U.S.C. § 215(a). That warning was required not because of newly discovered evidence of the effects of alcohol but rather as a "reminder" of such hazards. 27 U.S.C. § 213.

In the final analysis, the plaintiffs cannot prevail against the defendants, because the sole proximate cause of their injuries was the conduct of the drunken driver whose excessive use of alcoholic beverages intoxicated him but who nevertheless drove in a dangerous condition causing injury to the plaintiffs. While the dram shop laws under appropriate circumstances can create liability on the part of those who serve alcoholic beverages, a claim cannot be made against the manufacturer "for the reason that the subsequent injury has been held to have been proximately caused by the intervening act of the immoderate consumer whose voluntary and imprudent consumption of the beverage brings about intoxication and the subsequent injury." Consequently we GRANT the motion to dismiss.

CASE QUESTIONS

1. What accident led to this litigation?
2. What product is alleged to be defective?
3. Is beer defective because it makes people drunk?
4. Is beer defective because of a lack of warning?
5. Is beer inherently dangerous?

Improper Warnings and Instructions

Manufacturers have a duty to warn buyers when there is a foreseeably dangerous use of a product that buyers are not likely to realize is dangerous. They also have a duty to supplement the warnings. For example, as defects are discovered in autos, the manufacturers send recall notices to buyers. Similarly, manufacturers of airplanes have sent warnings on problems and proper repair procedures to airlines throughout the life of a particular plane design's use.

Manufacturers must also give adequate instructions to buyers on the proper use of the product. Over-the-counter drugs carry instructions about proper dosages and the limitations on dosages.

The quotes in the chapter opening give an indication of the levels of warnings required on products.

BUSINESS STRATEGY

Nestlé and the Infant Formula and Product Marketing

Reprinted with permission from Marianne M. Jennings, *Case Studies in Business Ethics*, 5th ed., 2004.

While the merits and problems of breast-feeding versus using infant formula are debated in the United States and other developed countries, the issue is not so balanced in Third World nations. Studies have demonstrated the difficulties and risks of bottle-feeding babies in such places.

First, refrigeration is not generally available, so the formula, once it is mixed or opened (in the case of premixed types), cannot be stored properly. Second, the lack of purified water for mixing with the formula powder results in diarrhea or other diseases in formula-fed infants. Third, inadequate education and income, along with cultural differences, often lead to the dilution of formula and thus greatly reduced nutrition.

Medical studies also suggest that regardless of the mother's nourishment, sanitation, and income level, an infant can be adequately nourished through breast-feeding.

In spite of medical concerns about using their products in these countries, some infant formula manufacturers heavily promoted bottle-feeding.

These promotions, which went largely unchecked through 1970, included billboards, radio jingles, and posters of healthy, happy infants, as well as baby books and formula samples distributed through the health care systems of various countries.

Also, some firms used "milk nurses" as part of their promotions. Dressed in nurse uniforms, "milk nurses" were assigned to maternity wards by their companies and paid commissions to get new mothers to feed their babies formula. Mothers who did so soon discovered that lactation could not be achieved and the commitment to bottle-feeding was irreversible.

In the early 1970s, physicians working in nations where milk nurses were used began vocalizing their concerns. For example, Dr. Derrick Jelliffe, the then director of the Caribbean Food and Nutrition Institute, had the Protein-Calorie Advisory Group of the United

© RONDA OLIVER/ISTOCKPHOTO

Nations place infant formula promotion methods on its agenda for several of its meetings.

Journalist Mike Muller first brought the issue to public awareness with a series of articles in the *New Internationalist* in the 1970s. He also wrote a pamphlet on the promotion of infant formulas called "The Baby Killer," which was published by a British charity, War on Want. The same pamphlet was published in Switzerland, the headquarters of Nestlé, a major formula maker, under the title "Nestlé Kills Babies." Nestlé sued in 1975, which resulted in extensive media coverage.

In response to the bad publicity, manufacturers of infant formula representing about 75% of the market formed the International Council of Infant Food Industries to establish standards for infant formula marketing. The new code banned the milk nurse commissions and required the milk nurses to have identification that would eliminate confusion about their "nurse" status.

The code failed to curb advertising of formulas. In fact, distribution of samples increased. By 1977, groups in the United States began a boycott against formula makers over what Jelliffe called "comerciogenic malnutrition."

One U.S. group, Infant Formula Action Coalition (INFACT), worked with the staff of Senator Edward Kennedy of Massachusetts to have hearings on the issue by the Senate Subcommittee on Health and Human Resources, which Kennedy chaired. The hearings produced evidence that 40% of the worldwide market for infant formula, which totaled $1.5 billion at the time, was in Third World countries. No regulations resulted, but Congress did tie certain forms of foreign aid to the development by recipient countries of programs to encourage breast-feeding.

Boycotts against Nestlé products began in Switzerland in 1975 and in the United States in 1977. The boycotts and Senator Kennedy's involvement heightened

continued

media interest in the issue and led to the World Health Organization (WHO) debating the issue of infant formula marketing in 1979 and agreeing to draft a code to govern it.

After four drafts, and two presidential administrations (Carter and Reagan), the 118 member nations of WHO finally voted on a code for infant formula marketing. The United States was the only nation to vote against it; the Reagan administration opposed the code being mandatory. In the end, WHO made the code a recommendation only, but the United States still refused to support it.

The publicity on the vote fueled the boycott of Nestlé, which continued until the formula maker announced it would meet the WHO standards for infant formula marketing. Nestlé created the Nestlé Infant Formula Audit Commission (NIFAC) to demonstrate its commitment to and ensure its implementation of the WHO code.

In 1988, Nestlé introduced a new infant formula, Good Start, through its subsidiary, Carnation. The industry leader, Abbott Laboratories, which held 54% of the market with its Similac brand, revealed Carnation's affiliation: "They are Nestlé," said Robert A. Schoellhorn, Abbott's chairman and CEO. Schoellhorn also disclosed that Nestlé was the owner of Beech-Nut Nutrition Corporation, officers of which had been indicted and convicted (following one reversal) for selling adulterated apple juice for babies.

Carnation advertised Good Start in magazines and on television. The American Academy of Pediatrics (AAP) objected to this direct advertising, and grocers feared boycotts.

The letters "H.A." came after the name "Good Start," indicating the formula was hypoallergenic. Touted as a medical breakthrough by Carnation, the formula was made from whey and advertised as ideal for babies who were colicky or could not tolerate milk-based formulas.

Within four months of Good Start's introduction in November 1988, the FDA was investigating the formula because of six reported cases of vomiting due to the formula. Carnation then agreed not to label the formula hypoallergenic and to include a warning that milk-allergic babies should be given Good Start only with a doctor's approval and supervision.

In 1990, with its infant formula market share at 2.8%, Carnation's president, Timm F. Crull, called on the AAP to "examine all marketing practices that might hinder breast-feeding." Crull specifically cited manufacturers' practices of giving hospitals education and research grants, as well as free bottles, in exchange for having exclusive rights to supply the hospital with formula and to give free samples to mothers. He also called for scrutiny of the practice of paying pediatricians' expenses to attend conferences on infant formulas.

The AAP looked into prohibiting direct marketing of formula to mothers and physicians' accepting cash awards from formula manufacturers for research.

The distribution of samples in Third World countries continued during this time. Studies by the United Nations Children's Fund found that a million infants were dying every year because they were not breast-fed adequately. In many cases, the infant starved because the mother used free formula samples and could not buy more, while her own milk dried up. In 1991, the International Association of Infant Food Manufacturers had agreed to stop distributing infant formula samples by the end of 1992.

In the United States in 1980, the surgeon general established a goal that the nation's breast-feeding rate be 75% by 1990. The rate remains below 60%, however, despite overwhelming evidence that breast milk reduces susceptibility to illness, especially ear infections and gastrointestinal illnesses. The AAP took a strong position that infant formula makers should not advertise to the public, but as a result, new entrants into the market (such as Nestlé with its Carnation Good Start) were disadvantaged because long-time formula makers Abbott and Mead Johnson were well established through physicians. In 1993, Nestlé filed an antitrust suit alleging a conspiracy among AAP, Abbott, and Mead Johnson.

Some 200 U.S. hospitals have voluntarily stopped distributing discharge packs from formula makers to their maternity patients because they felt it "important not to appear to be endorsing any products or acting as commercial agents." A study at Boston City Hospital showed that mothers who receive discharge packs are less likely to continue nursing, if they nurse at all. UNICEF and WHO offer "Baby Friendly" certification to maternity wards that take steps to eliminate discharge packs and formula samples.

Discussion Questions

1. If you had been an executive with Nestlé, would you have changed your marketing approach after the boycotts began? Didn't the first mover approach make sense?

2. Did Nestlé suffer long-term damage because of its Third World marketing techniques?

3. How could a marketing plan address the concerns of the AAP and WHO?

4. Is anyone in the infant formula companies morally responsible for the deaths of infants described in the United Nations study?

5. Is the moratorium on distributing free formula samples voluntary? Would your company comply?

6. If you were a hospital administrator, what policy would you adopt on discharge packs?

7. Should formula makers advertise directly to the public? What if their ads read, "Remember, breast is best"?

Sources

"Breast Milk for the World's Babies." *New York Times,* 12 March 1992, A18.

Burton, Thomas B. "Methods of Marketing Infant Formula Land Abbott in Hot Water." *Wall Street Journal,* 25 May 1993, A1, A6.

Freedman, Alix M. "Nestlé's Bid to Crash Baby-Formula Market in the U.S. Stirs a Row." *Wall Street Journal,* 6 February 1989, A1, A10.

Garland, Susan B. "Are Formula Makers Putting the Squeeze on the States?" *Business Week,* 18 June 1990, 31.

Gerlin, Andrea. "Hospitals Wean from Formula Makers' Freebies." *Wall Street Journal,* 29 December 1994, B1.

Meier, Barry. "Battle over the Market for Baby Formula." *New York Times,* 15 June 1993, C1, C15.

"Nestlé Unit Sues Baby Formula Firms, Alleging Conspiracy with Pediatricians." *Wall Street Journal,* 1 June 1993, B4.

Post, James E. "Assessing the Nestlé Boycott: Corporate Accountability and Human Rights." *California Management Review* 27 (1985): 113–31.

Star, Marlene G. "Breast Is Best." *Vegetarian Times,* June 1991, 25–26.

Errors in Manufacturing, Handling, or Packaging

This breach of duty is the most difficult form of negligence to prove. There are usually so many handlers in the process of manufacturing and packaging a product that it becomes difficult to prove when and how the manufacturer was negligent. One of the issues in drug manufacturing cases is whether the packaging for the materials is sufficient. Does it protect against tampering? Is it childproof? These types of dangers are foreseeable and require special duties with regard to packaging drugs.

BUSINESS STRATEGY APPLICATION

Be sure to do the exercise for this chapter on the book's Web site. You can walk through the full manufacture and distribution of a product to determine areas of vulnerability to product liability claims.

CONSIDER... 11.12

Classify the following as design, manufacture, or warning defects:
- Failure to disclose changes in fuel and operations for a helicopter in hot weather and higher altitudes
- A polio vaccine that produces not immunity but polio in a child
- Teflon-induced autoimmune system disease caused by Teflon used in the manufacture of an implanted TMJ jaw device
- Diamond represented as a grade V.V.S. that is actually a lower grade
- Infant swing that causes infants to fall out backward if they fall asleep and their weight shifts
- Tobacco that causes lung cancer
- Fondue pot tipping over and burning a 2-year-old child
- Bleeding of pizza-box ink onto pizza

Reaching the Buyer in the Same Condition

The requirement that a product reach the buyer without "substantial change" is a protection for the seller. A seller will not be liable for a product that has been modified or changed. The reason for this requirement is that once a product is modified or changed, it becomes unclear whether the original product or the modifications caused the unreasonably dangerous condition. Volkswagen would not be held liable for a dune buggy accident just because the builder and owner of the dune buggy happened to use a Volkswagen engine in building the vehicle. Because Volkswagen's product has been taken apart and modified, its liability has ended. One issue that arises in airplane crash cases is whether the air carrier followed the manufacturer's repair procedures. The failure to follow these procedures could eliminate the manufacturer's liability because the aircraft may have been altered. In *Austin* v. *Will-Burt Company* (Case 11.6), the court deals with a product liability claim related to a much-used and older product.

CASE 11.6

Austin v. *Will-Burt Company*
361 F.3d 862 (5th Cir. 2004)

The Shocking Reality of Used Products and Liability

FACTS

Will-Burt builds steel masts that are used by the military, border control, firefighters, and the television broadcast industry for transmission purposes. Will-Burt built one such mast in 1982 and sold it to Quality Coach of Elkhart, Indiana. Somehow the mast made its way into the hands of Haines Custom Construction, and in 1989, Haines sold a "completely rebuilt" mast to Mississippi Telecasting Company, also called WABG-TV.

Barksdale Austin was a 24-year-old college graduate employed by WABG-TV as a production manager. One of his jobs was to set up the TV station's van for remote broadcasts, which included operating the telescopic mast on the van. Mr. Austin did take safety training on raising and using the mast. In that training he was warned about keeping the mast at least twenty feet from any power lines.

During a broadcast assignment at the Greenville City Hall, Mr. Austin parked the van beneath transformers and power lines. When the mast was raised, it hit an 8,000-volt power line. When Mr. Austin later touched the van, which had been energized from the contact with the wires, he was electrically shocked to death.

The estate and heirs of Mr. Austin (appellants) settled with all parties except Will-Burt. Will-Burt maintained that it was not liable because too many years had passed since it built the mast and that alterations had been made. The mast still did contain its original warnings: "DANGER! PLEASE READ INSTRUCTIONS BEFORE RAISING!" and "DANGER! WATCH FOR WIRES. YOU CAN BE KILLED IF THIS PRODUCT COMES NEAR ELECTRICAL WIRES." The court granted summary judgment for Will-Burt, and the estate and family of Mr. Austin appealed.

JUDICIAL OPINION

GARWOOD, Circuit Judge

WABG had a 1985 ENG van which it had purchased from a third party (Will-Burt did not and does not make or sell such vans). In 1990, WABG, through its own employees, "integrated" into its ENG van the mast and separate "payload components, which included a Quick Set pan-and-tilt and a microwave antenna." That process involved cutting a hole in the top of the van, affixing the mast to the floor of the van where it could extend through that hole, and attaching the separate "pan-and-tilt and the antenna to the top of the mast." The WABG employee that performed this work was at that time "aware of the risk that the telescoping mast could be raised into overhead power lines" and he "therefore placed two warning plaques on the van," one "on the dashboard of the van" and the other "near the lever that activated the telescoping mast," stating "something to the effect of 'check around the van before raising the mast and look for all overhead obstructions.'" These two plaques were in addition to the "warnings [sic] sign[s] that came affixed to the Will-Burt telescoping mast that warned of overhead danger as well."

Although Will-Burt originally sold the mast with a constant pressure switch, which required an operator to continuously depress the switch in order to raise or lower the mast, when WABG integrated the mast into its ENG van, it rigged a bungee cord to hold down the pressure switch. The bungee functioned as a crude remote control, enabling the mast to be raised and lowered without a person physically applying constant pressure.

Austin's surviving mother, individually and as Administratrix of his estate, father, and sister, filed this wrongful death and survival products liability action in 2000 against Will-Burt alleging . . . that at the time the mast left Will-Burt's control, it was defective in design, and that Will-Burt failed to provide adequate warnings or instructions. They further alleged respecting Will-Burt that it breached its post-sale duty to warn end-users like WABG about the dangers posed by its product, in light of its knowledge of five or six post-1982 deaths by electrocution involving its masts.

The appellants claim that the mast at issue was defectively designed and unreasonably dangerous when it left Will-Burt's control in May 1982 because of inadequate warnings. The district court dismissed this claim, noting that the warning labels that were placed on the mast specifically cautioned the operator that he or she could be killed if the mast were raised "near" power lines. In Mississippi, a warning may be held adequate as a matter of law where the adverse effect was one that the manufacturer specifically warned against. There were also warnings in product manuals which Will-Burt supplied with its masts not to raise the mast under or near power lines and to check for overhead obstructions in proximity to the mast's line of extension and maximum height.

The warnings on the mast clearly connected contact with power lines and risk of death. Moreover, to the extent this danger was not already obvious, we refer to the testimony of Donnie Reid, the operations manager at WABG who conducted Austin's safety training and trained him in setting up the "live truck." Reid warned Austin that before raising the mast he should check that the truck was on level ground, check for obstacles overhead such as trees and power lines, never raise the mast if there were overhead obstacles, and maintain a twenty-foot clearance from any power lines. Furthermore, on the day in question Reid specifically told Austin that he did not need to raise the mast to do the shot from the City Hall location.

The warnings on the mast seem clearly adequate. . . . In any event, the uncontradicted evidence establishes that Austin was adequately warned of the danger he encountered using the mast and that that danger was either "known" or "open and obvious" to him (and certainly "should have been known or open and obvious" to him)."

Appellants claim that the Will-Burt mast was defectively designed in two respects, namely that it did not have a proximity warning device (PWD) and that it was not insulated. Appellants also assert that the mast's design was defective because it lacked a remote control device. The district court concluded that, because the bungee cord attached to the lever operated as remote control by overriding the constant pressure switch and allowed Austin to raise the mast while sufficiently outside of the truck to adequately observe the power lines above the mast as it rose, and Austin raised the mast by using the bungee cord while outside the truck, that accordingly there was no evidence to sustain a finding that the lack of remote control device was a proximate cause of the accident.

Appellants claim that the mast should have had a PWD which would have either given a warning sound or signal, or stopped the mast from continuing to rise, when the mast came within a certain distance of a power line. Will-Burt has manufactured and sold such a device, called a D-Tec, starting in 1998; it commenced attempting to develop the D-Tec in 1996 and produced a prototype which it exhibited at the April 1997 National Association of Broadcasters convention. Thereafter, it made some improvements to the D-Tec and began selling it in September 1998. The only other PWD referenced in the evidence is the Sigalarm, manufactured by another company. It was first used in the broadcast industry in 1995 or 1996. PWDs used in the broadcast industry or in ENG vans are and were sold by the manufacturer either to van assembling companies, which then sell the van with mast, payload, and PWD to broadcasters, or are sold directly to the station, which does its own integration. The PWD is a separate item, not a part of the mast itself, and is affixed on top of the mast payload (the pan-and-tilt and antenna) which itself sits on the top of the mast. The pan-and-tilt and antenna are likewise items separate from the mast itself and are manufactured by companies other than mast manufacturers. The cost of a PWD is and has been approximately 28 to 30% of the cost of the mast. In 1998 Will-Burt unsuccessfully attempted to sell its D-Tec PWD to WABG, which declined to purchase it and continued to use its van without a PWD.

With respect to insulation, the summary judgment evidence showed that telescoping masts were not and never had been insulated. The only exception to this was that commencing in 1985 Will-Burt made some telescoping masts, through not for ENG vans, the top tube of which was of fiberglass (rather than metal, which the rest of the mast was). This was apparently done for military surveillance devices. Although fiberglass is nonconductive (at least unless dirty or wet) it was not used to avoid anticipated problems of electricity coming into the mast, or for related safety reasons, but to avoid interference with separate communications devices that were placed on top of the mast. In the late 1990s Will-Burt began working on the development of an entirely non- metallic, non-conductive telescoping mast, a prototype being first built in 1999 or 2000, but the project was abandoned and no such masts were produced or sold. Moreover, if the pan-and-tilt and antenna, which sit on top of the mast and extend horizontally from it a distance considerably greater than the diameter of the mast, came into contact with a live electrical wire the current would pass down wires (contained in the "nycoil" that runs around the mast and connects with the camera and antenna on the pan-and-tilt) to the base of the mast and the van. The summary judgment evidence showed without contradiction that neither telescoping masts used in the broadcast industry or in ENG vans, nor pan-and-tilt devices, nor their cameras or antennas, were or had ever been insulated.

continued

Here, the evidence is that at the relevant time—May 1982, when the mast left Will-Burt's control—no telescoping masts (or their "payloads"), whether in the broadcast industry or any other, were insulated so as not to conduct electricity or were either equipped or used with any sort of PWD, and the danger of electrocution if the mast was raised so that it or its "payload" came into contact with an overhead power line was well recognized. There is no contrary evidence. This not only continued to be the case in the broadcast industry until the tragic 1997 accident in question but apparently still continues to be the case. There is no evidence that anyone in the industry ever—in 1982 or 1997 or at any other time—did not realize that a telescoping mast such as this, if raised when under a power line, would not extend to the height of the power line so that the "payload" on top of the mast (or even the mast itself) would come into contact with the power line with serious resultant electric shock, or that any device on or used with the mast, or any characteristic of the mast or of any such device, would prevent such a result or give a prior warning signal of it. The evidence is that Austin had been made aware of these dangers, and there is no contrary evidence. There is simply no evidence that the mast "failed to function as expected." That a truly tragic accident occurred in

using the mast does not mean that the mast failed to function as expected. The mast did nothing unusual or unexpected. An ordinary revolver functions as expected if, when loaded and off-safety, the trigger is normally pulled and a bullet is expelled, and this is no less so because, quite unintentionally, someone is struck by the bullet. So also with a cigarette lighter normally ignited and applied to flammable material, notwithstanding that a tragic fire results, or an intact hatchet which strikes a hand placed or left on the target wood.

Because there is no evidence that the mast "failed to function as expected," recovery against Will-Burt for design defect is precluded. For the reasons stated, the judgment of the district court is AFFIRMED.

CASE QUESTIONS

1. When was the product manufactured?
2. Who is seeking recovery?
3. What privity issues are involved?
4. What does the court hold about the warnings on the mast?
5. What does the court hold about modifications for the mast?
6. Can Mr. Austin's estate recover from Will-Burt?

The Requirement of a Seller Engaged in a Business

Section 402A requires the seller to be "engaged in the business of selling the product." This requirement sounds like the merchant requirement for the UCC warranty of merchantability. However, the meaning of "selling the product" is slightly broader under Section 402A than the UCC meaning of merchant. For example, a baseball club is not a merchant of beer, but, if the club sells beer at its games, it is a seller for purposes of Section 402A. Section 402A covers manufacturers, wholesalers, retailers, food sellers, and even those who sell products out of their homes.

In recent years, some courts have allowed recovery from groups of sellers. For example, in the controversy over diethylstilbestrol (DES, a drug taken by pregnant women), the plaintiffs could show that their harms resulted from DES but could not show exactly who manufactured the drug their mothers took. The courts permitted recovery against the group of manufacturers of DES during that time period [*Sindell* v. *Abbott Lab.*, 607 P.2d 924 (Cal. 1980)].

NEGLIGENCE: A SECOND TORT FOR PRODUCT LIABILITY

A suit for product defects can also be based in negligence. The elements for establishing a negligence case are the same as those for a Section 402A case with one addition: establishing that the product seller or manufacturer either knew of the defect before the product was sold or allowed sales to continue with the knowledge that the product had a defect. Establishing this knowledge is difficult in an evidentiary sense in court, but a plaintiff in a product liability suit who shows that the defendant-seller knew of the problem and sold or continued to sell the product can collect punitive damages in addition to damages for personal injury and property damage. Establishing knowledge in a product liability case usually produces a multimillion-dollar verdict because punitive damages are awarded in addition to compensatory ones.

Examples of cases in which establishing knowledge has been an issue include the Ford Pinto exploding gas tank cases (in which the plaintiffs used internal memos from engineers to establish the company's knowledge of defects) and the Dow Corning breast implant suits (in which an engineer, Thomas Talcott, who worked for Dow Corning in 1976, testified for the plaintiffs regarding his feelings during the product's development that leakage was possible).

Exhibit 11.3 compares product liability theories, and Exhibit 11.4 details the basis for product liability.

EXHIBIT 11.3 Comparison of Product Liability Theories

TYPE	PRIVITY REQUIRED	KNOWLEDGE OF PROBLEM REQUIRED?	WARRANTY PROMISE REQUIRED?
Negligence	No	Yes	No
Section 402A/ strict tort liability	No	No	No
Express warranty	Yes	No	Yes
Implied warranty of merchantability	Yes	No	No
Implied warranty of fitness for a particular purpose	Yes	No	Yes

EXHIBIT 11.4 Legal Basis for Product Liability

CONTRACT	TORT
Express warranty	402A—Strict Tort Liability
Implied warranty of merchantability	Elements
Implied warranty of fitness for particular purpose	(1) Defective condition unreasonably dangerous: design; manufacturing defect; or inadequate warning (2) Defendant in business of using, selling, or manufacturing product (3) Condition of product is the same Negligence Same; and add (4) Knowledge of defect

CONSIDER... 11.13

Firestone ATX, ATX II, and Wilderness tires have come under fire in the media because of complaints about the failure of those tires being linked to so many accidents. In May 2002, following a report by a Houston television station on a correlation between the tires and accidents in that area, the National Highway Traffic Safety Administration (NHTSA) received a flurry of complaints about the tires.

continued

The treads on about 48 million tires, found on many trucks and SUVs and used mostly on Ford Explorers, seem to suddenly separate, although no one yet understands why. One theory is heat and poor tire maintenance. A former Firestone tire engineer, however, theorizes that these particular tires lack nylon caps between their steel belts and the rubber to keep the belts from sawing through the treads. Such caps are common in other tires and cost about $1.00 and make the treads on the tires less likely to separate.

Currently, 100 lawsuits are pending around the country that involve accidents resulting from the tires separating. Records for the agency reveal that it has documented four deaths as well as 193 accidents from the tires. Reports of tread failure have been documented at speeds of 20 mph, and the vehicle appearing most often in the reported crashes is the Ford Explorer. Many of the tire failures have occurred in vehicles with fewer than 2,000 odometer miles.

The NHTSA has known of the Firestone tire issues for at least ten years. At least six other nations have issued product recall notices on the tires. Ford has replaced tires in Venezuela, Ecuador, Thailand, Malaysia, Colombia, and Saudi Arabia. Ford referred to the replacements in those nations as a "customer satisfaction issue."

What theories of liability could the plaintiffs in the litigation use? Against whom would they be bringing their suits? Is Firestone liable to the drivers? Does prior knowledge of the tire issue with no action to correct the problem present additional problems for defending against the suits?*

Bridgestone/Firestone, Inc. issued a recall of its defective tires for a total of 6.5 million tires, the largest ever in the United States. However, the company did not have the inventory to replace the tires at one time, and many drivers and car owners would have had to wait for replacements. The company upped production to 500,000 per month, but that rate still would have required a year for completing all the replacements. As a result, the company provided dealers with a list of ten acceptable substitutes for the tires, including tires from other manufacturers, for which there will be reimbursement.

Does the company have any liability during the waiting period? What if customers wanted substitute transportation during the time they were waiting for tire replacements? What liability would the company have for the substitute tires authorized for the replacements?

Most of the tires were on Ford Explorers, and Ford has distanced itself from the recall, saying it did not know until the time of the recall of the tire problems and that it wants the recall accelerated. Why is Ford concerned?†

*For more information, see James R. Healey and Sara Nathan, "More Deaths Linked to Tires," *USA Today*, August 2, 2000, p. 1A; and Healey and Nathan, "Officials Have Known SUV Tire Suspicions for Decade," *USA Today*, August 2, 2000, p. 1B.

†For more information, see Norihiko Shirouzu and Timothy Aeppel, "Firestone Says It Acted to Improve Problem Tires," *Wall Street Journal*, August 18, 2000, p. A3; and David Kiley, "Ford Chief Wants to Speed Tire Recall," *USA Today*, August 17, 2000, p. 1A.

PRIVITY ISSUES IN TORT THEORIES OF PRODUCT LIABILITY

Privity is not the standard for recovery in negligence actions. The standard for recovery in negligence actions is whether the injury that resulted was foreseeable and foreseeable to that particular party. For example, a manufacturer of toasters can foresee use by children and would have a duty to warn that they should not use the equipment unless supervised by adults. A manufacturer of a weed killer could foresee the presence of dogs, cats, and other pets in a yard sprayed with the killer and should either make the product not harmful to them or warn of the need to keep them away from the sprayed area for a certain period of time. Children and pets certainly have

---

John Evraets underwent eye surgery in September 1983 at a hospital in Long Beach, California. He had a cataract removed and an artificial lens implanted. The lens was manufactured, designed, tested, distributed, and sold by Intermedics Intraocular, Inc., and Pharmacia Opthalmics, Inc.

After the operation, Mr. Evraets suffered pain; irritation; decreased vision; light sensitivity; deterioration of his eye structures, including macular, retinal, and corneal damage; edema; and a detached retina and vitreous humor. He was ultimately obliged to undergo another surgery to replace the lens. In addition to his physical suffering, Mr. Evraets experienced emotional distress, shock, and fright.

In August 1991, Mr. Evraets read a published article in which he learned that defects in Intermedic's and Opthalmic's lenses were the source of his injuries. Could Mr. Evraets recover from these companies? On what basis? [*Evraets v. Intermedics Intraocular, Inc.,* 34 Cal. Rptr. 2d 852 (1994).]

---

no privity with the manufacturers, but they can recover from the manufacturer (or their parents and owners can) on the basis of the foreseeability of the children's and pets' presence and the foreseeability of the danger causing their injuries.

Likewise, parties other than the product manufacturer may be responsible for defective conditions in the products and can be held liable for their participation. For example, parts manufacturers may be held liable if it can be shown that defects in their parts resulted in a product's defect and the injury to the plaintiff.

DEFENSES TO PRODUCT LIABILITY TORTS

Three defenses are available to a defendant in a product liability tort:

1. Misuse or abnormal use of a product
2. Contributory negligence
3. Assumption of risk

Misuse or Abnormal Use of a Product

Any use of a product that the manufacturer has specifically warned against in its instructions is a **misuse**. Using a forklift to lift 25,000 pounds when the instructions limit its capacity to 15,000 pounds is a misuse of the product, and any injuries resulting from such misuse will not be the liability of the manufacturer. Product misuse also occurs when a plaintiff has used the product in a manner that the defendant could not anticipate and warn against.

Contributory Negligence

Contributory negligence is traditionally a complete defense to a product liability suit in negligence. For example, although a front loader might have a design failure of no protective netting around the driver, a driver who is injured while using the front loader for recreational purposes is contributorily negligent. Contributory negligence overlaps greatly with product misuse.

Some states, as discussed in Chapter 10, have adopted a standard of **comparative negligence**, under which the plaintiff's negligence is not a complete defense: The negligence of the plaintiff merely serves to reduce the amount the plaintiff is

ETHICAL ISSUES

Cell-phone controversy continues on several fronts. Vehicle safety issues surround the use of cell phones while driving, with some states and cities prohibiting their use while operating a vehicle. Other people are concerned about a possible link between cell phones and cancer.

New York became the first state to pass restrictions on cell-phone use in cars. Except for emergencies, and effective December 1, New York drivers will not be permitted to use cell phones next to their ears while driving. Dialing a phone that is in a cradle or attached to a headset will be legal. There are similar bills pending in 35 other states.

In response to the growing legislative trend, cell-phone companies are scrambling to develop technology to permit continued use of cell phones even when regulations are imposed. The companies fear a decline in business; currently, the cell-phone industry makes sales worth $53 billion per year. They are developing voice dialing and other hands-free technology for cell-phone users. For a New York–type statute, cell-phone users need only use a headset, and Sprint in New York is already offering customers such a headset at a discount. Sprint also offers voice command dialing for an extra $10 per month, and about 10% of its customers have signed on for the technology.

In addition, automakers are working to develop in-auto systems with phone companies. Ford has a joint venture with one cellular phone company in an attempt to develop a cell-phone system that will meet the most stringent forms of proposed cell-phone legislation.

Statistically, cell-phone usage is not the most common cause of driver distraction, as noted in the following list.

What Distracts Drivers?

Something outside the vehicle	29.4%
Adjusting the radio	11.4%
Other occupants of vehicles	10.9%
A moving object in the car	4.3%
Other device or object	2.9%
Adjusting vehicle climate	2.9%
Eating, drinking	1.7%
Using cell phone	1.5%
Smoking	0.9%

As mentioned earlier, the other controversy is whether cell phones cause cancer. Some studies conclude that they do not, but the Wireless Technology Research program, a program funded by the cellular-phone industry, has concluded that there are enough questions about their safety that no one should assure users that the phones are absolutely safe.

The FDA's Center for Devices and Radiological Health has concluded that there are no adverse health effects from cell phones and that no additional warnings are needed. Following a lawsuit filed by a cell-phone user in 1993 that alleged a cell phone caused his cancer, the industry placed $27 million into a blind trust for research projects supported by the funding. The Wireless Technology Research program was one of the beneficiaries of the trust.

Review the findings on cell-phone safety at http://www.medscape.com. If you were a cell-phone manufacturer, would you take any action? Would you provide warnings? What about those who drive with cell phones and cause accidents? Are cell-phone manufacturers liable to those who are injured by drivers using cell phones?

Source: Gregory L. White and Andrea Peterson, "Cell Phone Firms Make Adjustments," *Wall Street Journal*, July 4, 2001, p. B1.

---

entitled to recover. For example, a jury might find that the defendant is 60 percent at fault and the plaintiff is 40 percent at fault. The plaintiff recovers, but the amount of that recovery is reduced by 40 percent.

Assumption of Risk

When a plaintiff is aware of a danger in the product but goes ahead and uses it anyway, **assumption of risk** occurs. If a car manufacturer recalled your car for repair and you failed to have the repair done, despite full opportunity to do so, you have assumed the risk of driving with that problem.

Binakonsky v. *Ford Motor Co.* (Case 11.7) involves issues of assumption of risk in a product liability suit.

CASE 11.7

Binakonsky v. Ford Motor Co.
133 F.3d 281 (4th Cir. 1998)

The Sliding Gas Tank Hits a Brick Wall

FACTS

In February 1988, David Binakonsky purchased a 1988 E-150 Ford Econoline van equipped with a 5.8-liter fuel-injected engine. Like most full-size vans, the Ford E-150 contained a shortened engine compartment, which was located between the driver and passenger seats. The engine was encased in an insulated, fiberglass cover, often called a "doghouse." The fuel system of the van consisted of fuel lines and plastic "snap-together" fuel line connectors. The plastic fuel lines carried fuel from two 20-gallon fuel tanks through a high-pressure electronic fuel pump and up to the fuel-injection rail at the rear of the engine. The van also had a cutoff switch to stop the flow of fuel to the engine in the event of an accident.

On August 20, 1992, Mr. Binakonsky drove his van off the road into a large tree. Upon impact, the engine was pushed into the passenger compartment. Gasoline ignited an intense fire, and Mr. Binakonsky, unable to escape, was killed. Accident reconstruction experts put the speed of the vehicle between 40 and 47 mph at the time of the crash (the speed limit was 30 mph in the area). A postmortem examination of Mr. Binakonsky revealed that he had a blood-alcohol content between .14% and .16% and that he died as a result of the fire (thermal injury to the larynx and fourth-degree burns over 100% of his body as well as a carbon monoxide level of 8%). Mr. Binakonsky was an alcoholic with a long history of serious traffic violations. At the time of the accident, he did not have a valid license.

Mr. Binakonsky's widow, Charlotte, and his four children (plaintiffs) brought suit against Ford Motor Company on the basis of the crashworthiness doctrine—that the van was defectively designed because it caused or aggravated injuries in an accident.

The lower court held that the design of the van was reasonable and granted summary judgment for Ford. Charlotte and the children appealed.

JUDICIAL OPINION

BUTZNER, Senior Circuit Judge

The plaintiffs contend that the fuel delivery system was defectively designed. The defendant contends that the system was safe.

[T]he plaintiffs, through the use of Ford documents and by cross-examination of Ford's designated corporate representative, established that gasoline siphoned from the gas tanks into the engine and passenger compartments when the fuel line ruptured.

This is not the first time Ford has addressed the Econoline fuel system. A Ford employee in 1986 commented: "Design should consider getting rid of plastic connectors to improve overall integrity of the system." A Ford 1987 "Concern Analysis Report: Econoline Fuel Line Leaks" addressed problems with the fuel line leaks in the 1985–87 E-series vans. The same plastic fuel system, consisting of plastic fuel lines and plastic connectors, was incorporated into the 1988 E150 van Binakonsky drove.

The plaintiffs' expert testified that the plastic fuel connectors in the Binakonsky van unsnapped during the accident, either by vibration from the accident or by the movement of the various components of the fuel system. He testified that if the fuel lines had been made of braided stainless steel and held together with nut and feral connectors, the fire would not have been fed by fuel and would have been much more manageable. He also testified that in his opinion Ford should not use nylon 11 or 12 within the heat distribution zone of the engine.

The plaintiffs produced sufficient evidence to show a likelihood that the fuel delivery system in the event of an accident was unreasonably dangerous and caused serious injury.

The fact that metal components of the fuel delivery system were relatively undamaged and intact after the collision, while the plastic components succumbed to fire, gives rise to a reasonable inference that steel lines and connectors would have been safer than plastic. Because the evidence disclosed that other 1988 Ford trucks and cars were using steel rather than plastic fuel lines, steel lines and connectors were available as a suitable substitute for the plastic.

Section 402A provides: "A product is not in a defective condition when it is safe for normal handling and consumption." Maryland has relied on comment h to fashion a defense to strict liability known as "misuse" of the product. This defense is explained in *Ellsworth* v. *Sherne Lingerie, Inc.*, 303 Md. 581, 495 A.2d 348 (1985):

> *Misuse of a product may also bar recovery where the misuse is the sole proximate cause of damage, or where it is the intervening or superseding cause.*

continued

Maryland courts have held that whether an accident was so unusual as to be unforeseeable is an issue for the jury. In none of those cases did the court rule that the accident was so bizarre that it was unforeseeable as a matter of law.

We cannot say that a car crashing into a tree at as high as 47 miles per hour is "unquestionably bizarre." The same 40–47 mile per hour single car collision could have been produced by a myriad of other events, such as a car veering off the road to avoid an oncoming collision, or a car losing control on a patch of ice or because of drowsiness.

The fact that Binakonsky was drunk does not make the physical aspects of the crash any more bizarre. In this respect, care must be exercised not to confuse contributory negligence with misuse. On this issue, Maryland law is clear. "The fact that a negligent driver may be the initial cause of an accident does not abrogate the manufacturer's duty to use reasonable care in designing an automobile to reduce the risk of 'secondary impact injuries.'"

Assumption of risk, sometimes called a form of contributory negligence, is a defense to claims based on strict liability. The defense is available against a plaintiff who unreasonably uses a product despite a known risk of danger. Drunk driving is an unreasonable use of a car, and it is common knowledge that a driver who strikes a tree will cause damage. For this reason, a drunk driver, such as Binakonsky, assumes the risk of injury from the initial impact.

It is not generally known, however, that plastic lines and connectors and the lack of an antisiphoning device will cause a vehicle to burst into a devastating postcollision fire. Moreover, Ford gave no warning about the likelihood of such a fire. For these reasons the plaintiffs are entitled to the reasonable inference that Binakonsky did not assume the risk of a lethal fire. To reiterate, Binakonsky assumed the risk of injury from the initial impact. For the purpose of summary judgment, it cannot be inferred that he assumed the risk of an allegedly defective fuel delivery system.

Plaintiffs must prove that a defectively designed fuel system caused the postcollision fire and that the fire was the cause of death.

Dr. Margarita Korella, the assistant medical examiner who performed the autopsy, testified that her examination indicated no nonthermal fractures to the extremities and no evidence of external bleeding. She also testified that there was no "internal evidence of blunt force or penetrating injury to the thoracoabdominal area." Based upon burns found in the larynx, she concluded that the specific thermal injury that caused Binakonsky's death was "the inhalation of superheated hot air."

We reverse that aspect of the summary judgment pertaining to the van's fuel delivery system and remand the case for trial.

DISSENTING OPINION

NIEMEYER, Circuit Judge, dissenting

The majority opinion rules, by implication, that an automobile manufacturer has a duty to design its automobiles to withstand risks of injury from a head-on collision with an oak tree at a speed of 40–47 miles per hour. Because I believe that the majority's holding in this case imposes a duty far greater than that imposed by Maryland law, I dissent.

The impact occurred in the center front of the van so that the sides of the van wrapped around the tree, forming a sharp V in the center front bumper area. The tree penetrated the front of the vehicle two to three feet, driving the engine rearward, seriously damaging all of the major components of the vehicle and rupturing the fuel line. The spilling gasoline caught fire, and Binakonsky was dead by the time he was removed from the vehicle. His family contends that the fire caused his death, while Ford contends that he was killed upon impact with the tree.

The majority opinion also correctly notes that Maryland recognizes a misuse defense to strict liability.

To rule that this case presents a jury question, the majority states, "We cannot say that a car crashing into a tree at as high as 47 miles per hour is 'unquestionably bizarre.'" This, I respectfully submit, misses the issue. The question is not whether an accident is so bizarre as not to be foreseeable, but whether the risk of injury or death is reasonably foreseeable if a design feature is not adopted. Applied to this case, the question is whether it was foreseeable that a slide valve, which has never been used in any motor vehicle, could reasonably have prevented Binakonsky's death. I submit that as a matter of law we must say that this goes beyond foreseeability and into rank speculation. In order to anticipate that such a valve would reasonably have participated in Binakonsky's death, Ford would have had to assume:

1. That Binakonsky could survive a head-on crash with a tree at 47 miles per hour;
2. That the gas tank would survive such a crash and retain the gasoline in it;
3. That the slide valve would survive sufficiently intact as to contain the gasoline;
4. That the fuel pump would not shut off; and
5. That a fire from some other source or that some other post-collision condition would not have killed Binakonsky.

In speculating about such remote possibilities, and others, we would then have to decide whether such a duty applies if the vehicle were driven into a tree, say, at 65 miles per hour, or 85 miles per hour. There must be a legally established limit to a manufacturer's duty. I believe that that limit should be set at a speed where the risk of death can meaningfully be addressed by the design feature at issue.

I find it difficult to conclude that we must assume, in imposing duties of design, that any human-being will survive the impact of a fall from a seven-story window—the force that Binakonsky was exposed to in this case. If we cannot reasonably foresee that Binakonsky would, except in freakish circumstances, have survived such an impact, we certainly cannot impose a duty on a manufacturer to design a vehicle to prevent post-collision injury from a cause other than the collision itself.

I believe that the holding made by the majority applies a clinical rule in a formulaic way, without considering the common sense factors that must come into play. Rules developed in this manner are antagonistic to the law's role in preserving the manufacturer's duty to produce practicable and desirable safety devices without destroying their ability to continue to develop consumer products. No product can withstand the scrutiny of an absolute safety standard. Yet, that is the direction in which the majority opinion unfortunately is headed.

CASE QUESTIONS

1. How did the accident occur?

2. How did Mr. Binakonsky die?

3. What role does Mr. Binakonsky's blood-alcohol level play in the case? If Mr. Binakonsky would have died regardless of the design, should there be recovery under product liability?

4. How does the majority define the issue in the case? How does the dissent define it?

5. Does this case impose liability regardless of the cause of the crash?

 CONSIDER...   11.15

In early 1994, Sergio Jimenez (Mr. Jimenez), young Sergio's father, purchased a used 1985 Dodge Caravan from a used car dealer in North Charleston, South Carolina. A few months later, on April 10, Mr. Jimenez's wife, Denise Barrientos, was driving the vehicle on an errand with her 8-year-old daughter, Maria, riding in the front seat and young Sergio in the back seat. As Ms. Barrientos exited a shopping center parking lot, she drove through a red light and was struck in the left rear by an oncoming car traveling at 30 mph. The impact caused Ms. Barrientos's vehicle to flip over and spin around. Young Sergio, who was not wearing a seatbelt, was thrown through the rear liftgate, which had opened during the accident. He sustained fatal injuries. Ms. Barrientos and Maria, both of whom were wearing seatbelts, were not seriously injured. Young Sergio's estate sued Ms. Barrientos for negligence in running the red light and settled with her for $15,000, the limit of her insurance coverage. The estate also filed suit against DaimlerChrysler, the manufacturers of the Dodge Caravan. Following a four-week trial, the jury returned a verdict finding in favor of young Sergio's estate, awarding it $12.5 million in compensatory damages and $250 million in punitive damages. The district court remitted the compensatory damage award to $9 million.

At trial, the estate contended that DaimlerChrysler's 1985 Dodge Caravan included a defectively designed rear door latch. DaimlerChrysler did not deny the defective latch problem but defended on the grounds of Ms. Barrientos running the red light and the contributory negligence of her failure to buckle young Sergio in a seatbelt. Discuss the issues in the case, applying the *Binakonsky* standard to the facts. [*Jimenez* v. *DaimlerChrysler Corp.*, 269 F.3d 439 (4th Cir. 2001).]

ETHICAL ISSUES

In 1994, a group of Chrysler engineers met to review proposals and recommendations for improving their Chrysler Minivan lines in order to make them more competitive. Paul Sheridan, one of the engineers on Chrysler's Minivan Safety Team, raised the number one issue on the lists of proposals and recommendations: The latches on the minivan rear doors appeared to be popping open even in low-speed crashes. The Chrysler Minivan latches did not appear to have the strength of either the Ford Windstar minivan or the Chevy minivan rear door latches. Mr. Sheridan proposed that Chrysler make the latches stronger and use that strength as a marketing tool.

After Mr. Sheridan made his proposal, and according to testimony in a subsequent product liability suit, a top production engineer told Mr. Sheridan, "That ship has sailed. We told you that last time. Next subject."

In *Jimenez* v. *Chrysler Corporation,* the jury deliberated only 2.5 hours before returning a verdict for the Jimenez family of $262.5 million, $250 million of which was punitive damages.

Chrysler agreed with the National Highway Traffic Safety Administration (NHTSA) to replace the latches on 4.3 million minivans manufactured since 1984. Chrysler has spent $115 million for that replacement program on everything from notification to installation and estimates that about 61 percent of the van latches have now been replaced.

The number of deaths from ejection through the rear minivan doors is 37, which is 11 more than the fatalities from the Ford Pinto exploding gas tank defect but well short of GM's 168 fatalities in side-saddle gas tank collisions in that company's pickups. Chrysler has forty lawsuits pending around the country that involve rear-door ejection deaths and injuries.

However, damaging evidence brought out in the *Jimenez* case tends to be the focus of jury interest and awards.

- Chrysler initially used a latch in its vans that the rest of the industry had abandoned.
- When it switched to a better latch, still not meeting federal standards for passenger vehicles, it did not notify the owners of existing vans of the change and safety issues.
- Chrysler destroyed documentation on minivan crash tests, including films and computer records. (The company says that such destruction was part of its routine document destruction program; however, a juror noted, following the trial, that only the documentation on the collisions in which the rear door was affected was destroyed. Chrysler still had the documentation on the vans' front-end collision tests.)

- Engineers proposed adding a latch strengthener for a cost of about $0.25 per vehicle in 1990, but the plan was vetoed by Chrysler executives because it was believed such an addition would be tantamount to an admission to regulators that the latches were not safe, and Chrysler had been taking the position that the latches were indeed safe.
- Chrysler used political clout to prevent a 1994 recall by NHTSA of the vehicles for latch replacement; a letter from Chrysler Vice Chairman Tom Denomme to Chairman Robert Eaton and President Robert Lutz read, "If we want to use political pressure to try to quash a recall letter, we need to go now." Chrysler officials helped staff members for Representative John Dingell of Michigan (the ranking Democrat on the House Commerce Committee, which supervises the NHTSA) draft a letter objecting to the recall. NHTSA postponed the recall. When the recall was made in 1995, there was no acknowledgment that the latches were defective or that there was any safety issue.

Following the verdict, one juror said the evidence painted a picture of corporate indifference and added, "We want people to understand why we made the decision we did. We knew what we were doing. When you speak to a company as big as Chrysler, you've got to speak on terms they understand." Another juror said that the political interference with the recall was an 8 on a scale of 10 for damage to the company. Still another juror noted that executives answered, "I don't know. I don't remember. I can't recall," too often to have much credibility.

Chrysler had been the first mover in the minivan market. Its product filled a niche in the family auto market, and it occupied a unique position in terms of federal regulation in that there were no applicable federal standards for the lifting rear door on the van. Chrysler used latch designs and parts that had been banned in passenger vehicles for years precisely because of the risk of ejection and associated high fatality rates. However, the lack of federal regulations on the minivan meant that Chrysler violated no law in using the outmoded systems and parts.

When Chrysler began to receive notice of accidents and began holding design and marketing meetings in 1993, lawyers ordered that no notes be taken at meetings, and minutes of meetings were collected and destroyed.

Why were punitive damages appropriate in this case? Are they too high? What message do the punitive damages send to businesses? What should Chrysler do internally to be certain such a series of events does not happen again?

BIOGRAPHY

The Space Shuttle, NASA and O-Rings

On January 28, 1986, NASA launched the space shuttle *Challenger* in 30°F weather. Seventy-four seconds into the launch, the low temperature caused the O-ring seals on the *Challenger*'s booster rockets to fail. The *Challenger* exploded, killing all seven persons aboard (six astronauts and Christa McAuliffe, a school teacher chosen and trained for the mission).

Morton Thiokol was the NASA subcontractor responsible for the booster rocket assembly. Roger Boisjoly was an engineer at Morton Thiokol who had raised concerns about the O-rings. Boisjoly had given a presentation on the O-ring issue at a conference, but Thiokol took no action. Boisjoly noted the problems in his activity report and finally, in July 1985, wrote a confidential memo to R. K. Lund, Thiokol's vice president for engineering. Excerpts appear below:

> This letter is written to insure that management is fully aware of the seriousness of the current O-ring erosion problem . . . The mistakenly accepted position on the joint problem was to fly without fear of failure . . . [This position] is now drastically changed as a result of the SRM [shuttle recovery mission] 16A nozzle joint erosion which eroded a secondary O-ring with the primary O-ring never sealing. If the same scenario should occur in a field joint (and it could), then it is a jump ball as to the success or failure of the joint . . . The result would be a catastrophe of the highest order—loss of human life . . .
>
> It is my honest and real fear that if we do not take immediate action to dedicate a team to solve the problem, with the field joint having the number one priority, then we stand in jeopardy of losing a flight along with all the launch pad facilities.

In October 1985, Boisjoly presented the O-ring issue at a conference of the Society of Automotive Engineers and requested suggestions for resolution.

On January 27, 1986, the day before the launch, Boisjoly attempted to halt the launch. However, four Thiokol managers, including Lund, voted unanimously to recommend the launch. One manager urged Lund to "take off his engineering hat and put on his management hat." The managers then developed the following revised recommendations. Engineers were excluded from the development of these findings and the final launch decision.

- Calculations show that SRM-25 [the designation for the *Challenger*'s January 28 flight] O-rings will be 20° colder than SRM-15 O-rings
- Temperature data not conclusive on predicting primary O-ring blow-by
- Engineering assessment is that:
  - Colder O-rings will have increased effective durometer [that is, they will be harder]
  - "Harder" O-rings will take longer to seat
  - More gas may pass primary [SRM-25] O-ring before the primary seal seats (relative to SRM-15)
  - If the primary seal does not seat, the secondary seal will seat
  - Pressure will get to secondary seal before the metal parts rotate
  - O-ring pressure leak check places secondary seal in outboard position which minimizes sealing time
  - MTI recommends STS-51L launch proceed on 28 January 1986_SRM-25 will not be significantly different from SRM-15

After the decision was made, Boisjoly returned to his office and wrote in his journal:

> I sincerely hope this launch does not result in a catastrophe. I personally do not agree with some of the statements made in Joe Kilminster's [Kilminster was one of the four Thiokol managers who voted to recommend the launch] written summary stating that SRM-25 is okay to fly.

The subsequent investigation by the presidential commission placed the blame for the faulty O-rings squarely with Thiokol. Charles S. Locke, Thiokol's CEO, maintained, "I take the position that we never agreed to the launch at the temperature at the time of the launch. The Challenger incident resulted more from human error than mechanical error. The decision to launch should have been referred to headquarters. If we'd been consulted here, we'd never have given clearance, because the temperature was not within the contracted specs."

Boisjoly testified before the presidential panel regarding his opposition to the launch and the decision of his managers (who were also engineers) to override his recommendation. Boisjoly, who took medical

continued

leave for post-traumatic stress disorder, has left Thiokol, but he does receive disability pay from the company. Currently, Mr. Boisjoly operates a consulting firm in Mesa, Arizona. He speaks frequently on business ethics to professional organizations and companies.

In May 1986, then-CEO Locke stated, in an interview with the *Wall Street Journal*, "This shuttle thing will cost us this year 10¢ a share." Locke later protested that his statement was taken out of context.

Roger Boisjoly offers the following advice on whistle-blowing:

a. You owe your organization an opportunity to respond. Speak to them first VERBALLY. Memos are not appropriate for the first step.

b. Gather collegial support for your position. If you cannot get the support, then make sure you are correct.

c. Then spell out the problem in a letter.

ISSUES

1. Do you think Mr. Boisjoly feels some responsibility for the *Challenger* accident?
2. Would you have done anything differently?
3. What can companies do to be certain they listen to a Roger Boisjoly?

PRODUCT LIABILITY REFORM

Visit FMC Corporation:
http://fmc.com

"Our product liability system discourages innovation because of unforeseeable potential liability," says Robert Malcott, CEO of FMC Corporation. Mr. Malcott issued this statement as the chair of the Business Roundtable's task force on product liability. This task force and others have proposed several changes, including limiting punitive damages; meeting government standards as a defense; instituting liability shields for drugs, medical devices, and aircraft; and requiring higher standards of proof for recovery of punitive damages.

Visit THOMAS, a service of the U.S. Congress, for the status of current congressional bills:
http://thomas.loc.gov

In each session since 1977, a bill on product liability reform has been introduced in Congress. However, such a bill faces significant opposition from consumer groups and trial lawyers. As trade barriers fall, the ability of the United States to compete with nations with limits on product liability will be hindered. The Business Roundtable and other business groups continue to work for reform at the federal and state levels. Further, businesses continue to emphasize total quality management as a tool for minimizing product liability.

The American Law Institute (ALI) has proposed the *Restatement (Third) of Torts*, which would change the current strict liability standard to a negligence standard for defective design and informational defect cases. In other words, plaintiffs who bring product liability cases based on defective design and instruction would have to establish negligence to recover. The strict liability standard would be eliminated under this new proposal. Strict liability would still be the standard for manufacturing defects.

FEDERAL STANDARDS FOR PRODUCT LIABILITY

Consumer Product Safety Commission

Visit the Consumer Product Safety Commission:
http://www.cpsc.gov

The federal level of government generally is not involved in product liability issues. However, the **Consumer Product Safety Commission** (CPSC) is a regulatory agency set up under the Consumer Product Safety Act to regulate safety standards for consumer products. The commission has several responsibilities in carrying out its purposes.

1. *To protect the public against unreasonable risks of injury from consumer products*—To perform this function, the CPSC has been given the authority to recall products and order their repair or correction. The commission also has the power to ban products completely. This ban can apply only if a product cannot be made less dangerous. The ban on asbestos is an example of the commission's powers. In another example, in 1994, the CPSC recalled nearly all types of metal bunk beds.

2. *To develop standards for consumer product safety*—These standards take the form of regulations and minimum requirements for certain products.

3. *To help consumers become more informed about evaluating safety*—Certain regulations require disclosure of the limits of performance and hazards associated with using a particular product.

4. *To fund research in matters of product safety design and in product-caused injuries and illnesses*

The act carries civil penalties of up to a maximum of $500,000. Knowing or willful violations carry a criminal fine of up to $50,000 and/or one year imprisonment, and willful repeat violations carry penalties of up to $500,000 and ten years. In addition, consumers have a right to sue in federal district court for any damages they sustain because of a violation of a regulation or law.

Uniform Product Liability Act

Visit the Department of Commerce:
http://www.commerce.gov

In a number of different attempts, the Department of Commerce has tried to issue drafts and recommendations to the states on a set of uniform product liability laws. The proposed act would change the law substantially by establishing several defenses, such as state-of-the-art manufacturing or design. In addition, the proposed law establishes how a product can be defective. In view of the confusion as to standards in product liability, the high awards for damages, and the high insurance premiums paid by businesses, a change seems necessary but has been slow in coming. Tort reform efforts continue at both federal and state levels.

INTERNATIONAL ISSUES IN PRODUCT LIABILITY

In 1985, the European Community Council of Ministers adopted a directive on product liability. The directive limits liability to "producers"; this is not as inclusive as U.S. law, which holds all sellers liable. There is a ten-year limit on liability, and the "state-of-the-art" defense applies to most member countries: If a product upon its release was as good as any available, there is no product liability.

Visit the International Organization for Standardization:
http://www.iso.org/iso/
en/ISOOnline.frontpage

In addition to the council's guidelines are the International Standards Organization's 9000 Guidelines for Quality Assurance and Quality Management. These directives require products to carry a stamp of compliance with standards and procedures as a means of limiting product defects.

Under the CISG (see Chapter 7 for more details), there are similar provisions to the UCC warranty protections for goods sold in international transactions. However, disclaimers are made more easily under the CISG and the notions of consequential damages are limited because the United States' level of damages in product liability cases far exceeds the levels for any other country in the world. Further, the notion of strict liability for products is unique to the United States, and under EU guidelines the notion of knowledge is used as a standard for imposing liability.

ETHICAL ISSUES

In some cases, products outlawed in the United States are sold outside the United States. Referred to as dumping, the products are sold without mention of the U.S. litigation pending. What can be done about firms that sell defective products in third-world countries? For example, IUDs and non-flame-retardant pajamas were dumped after problems developed in the United States. Discuss the ethical issues.

SUMMARY

How does advertising create liability for a business?

- Express warranty—contractual promise about nature or potential of product that gives right of recovery if product falls short of a promise that was a basis of the bargain

- Bait and switch—using cheaper, unavailable product to lure customers to store with a more expensive one then substituted or offered instead

- Federal Trade Commission (FTC)—federal agency responsible for regulating deceptive ads

- Wheeler-Lea Act—federal law that allows FTC to regulate "unfair and deceptive acts or practices"

- Celebrity endorsements—FTC area of regulation wherein products are touted by easily recognized public figures

- Consent decree—voluntary settlement of FTC complaint

What are the contract theories of product liability?

- Implied warranty of merchantability—warranty of average quality, purity, and adequate packaging given in every sale by a merchant

- Implied warranty of fitness for a particular purpose—warranty given in circumstances in which the buyer relies on the seller's expertise and acts to purchase according to that advice

- Disclaimer—act of negating warranty coverage

- Privity—direct contractual relationship between parties

What is required for tort-based recovery on a defective product? What is strict tort liability for products?

- Strict liability—standard of liability that requires compensation for an injury regardless of fault or prior knowledge

- Restatement (Second) § 402A—American Law Institute's standards for imposing strict liability for defective products

- Negligence—standard of liability that requires compensation for an injury only if the party responsible knew or should have known of its potential to cause such injury

- Punitive damages—damages beyond compensation for knowledge that conduct was wrongful

What defenses exist in product liability?

- Misuse—product liability defense for plaintiff using a product incorrectly

- Contributory negligence—conduct by plaintiff that contributed to plaintiff's injury; serves as a bar to recovery

- Comparative negligence—negligent conduct by plaintiff serves as a partial defense by reducing liability by percentage of fault

- Assumption of risk—defense to negligence available when plaintiff is told of product risk and voluntarily uses it

What reforms have occurred and are proposed in product liability?

- Consumer Product Safety Commission—federal agency that regulates product safety and has recall power

- Uniform Product Liability Act—proposed federal statute that would limit product liability suits and recovery

QUESTIONS AND PROBLEMS

1. Roger Gonzales purchased a Volvo station wagon for himself and his family. While the Volvo was pulling a U-Haul trailer and Mrs. Gonzales was driving, there was an accident in which the Volvo rolled over. Mrs. Gonzalez was killed, and the Gonzalez's daughter was severely injured. The trailer hitch used on the Volvo was unsuitable for the Volvo's bumper. Mr. Gonzalez brought suit against Volvo for its failure to warn him not to use certain trailer hitches on the bumper that could cause accidents. Is Volvo liable? What is U-Haul's liability? [*Gonzalez* v. *Volvo of America Corp.*, 752 F.2d 295 (7th Cir. 1985).]

2. Joyce Payne got a permanent wave from a beautician, Ms. Thrower. Ms. Thrower used a permanent wave product called Soft Sheen, and she carefully read and followed all instructions on the wave kit. While Ms. Thrower applied one step ("rearranger") in the process, Ms. Payne complained of a burning sensation in her back. The wave was completed, but two days later Ms. Payne was diagnosed in a hospital emergency room as having second degree burns on her back. She brought suit against the manufacturer of the wave and Ms. Thrower. Ms. Thrower says there were no warnings about the rearranger possibly burning skin. Who is liable? [*Payne* v. *Soft Sheen Products, Inc.*, 486 A.2d 712 (D.C. 1985).]

3. Seven-Up Co. began distributing its soft drinks, including its lemon-lime 7UP, in the 1920s, and by the time Coca-Cola introduced its lemon-lime soft drink, Sprite, in 1961, 7UP dominated the market.

Coca-Cola had been trying for years to break 7UP's hold on the market. In 1991, it launched a sales presentation known as "The Future Belongs to Sprite." The sales presentation consisted of charts, graphs, and overhead displays comparing the relative sales performance of Sprite and 7UP during the 1980s. After the sales presentation had been made to eleven bottlers, five of them decided to switch their lemon-lime soft drink from 7UP to Sprite.

7UP filed suit, alleging that Coca-Cola had skewed the data in its presentations and misrepresented what was happening with 7UP's market share. Is the presentation a form of advertising for which 7UP has a remedy? Is there damage from a competitor through misleading ads? [*Seven-Up Co.* v. *Coca-Cola Co.*, 86 F.3d 1379 (5th Cir. 1996).]

4. Wade Lederman, 31, was at a Fourth of July pool party at a relative's house in 1991. At about 10:30 P.M., Mr. Lederman, his brother, and two others decided to go swimming. They jumped from the sides of the pool into the water and also dove from the pool's diving board. At about midnight, Mr. Lederman dove into the pool from the side and struck his head on the bottom, sustaining permanent physical and neurological injuries.

The pool in which Mr. Lederman was injured is a residential swimming pool that is in-ground and oval-shaped, with a shallow end and a deep end. The pool has three steps at the shallow end by which swimmers can enter the pool. There is a white line one foot wide painted on the bottom of the pool between the shallow end and the deep end. At the start of that line, the depth increases to 7 feet and then slowly descends to a depth of 10 feet at the diving-board end of the pool.

Mr. Lederman filed suit against Pacific Industries, Inc., the pool manufacturer, for its failure to display water depths in and around the pool; failure to warn as to which areas were not appropriate for diving; failure to warn that at night, with pool lights on, the depth of the pool was deceptive; and failure to warn that the white line was just the start of the deep end and not a line for diving versus nondiving areas of the pool.

Should Mr. Lederman recover from Pacific? [*Lederman* v. *Pacific Industries Inc.*, 119 F.3d 551 (7th Cir. 1997).]

5. On August 6, 1998, Mr. Ruvolo purchased two chicken gordita sandwiches from Taco Bell. While eating the second sandwich, he felt a sharp pain in his throat and dislodged a chicken bone. The bone caused a scrape in his throat, and, as a result, he was treated at an emergency room. The following day, Mr. Ruvolo was diagnosed with acute tonsillitis, pharyngitis, sinusitis, and gastritis.

Mr. Ruvulo sued Taco Bell and its food distributors, alleging that the infections were due to the chicken bone's scratching his throat and causing an opening where germs and bacteria could enter. He further alleged that Taco Bell and its food distributors were liable because of their failure to properly inspect the chicken. Discuss the theories Mr. Ruvulo might use for recovery and who the defendants might be. [*Ruvolo* v. *Homovich*, 778 N.E.2d 661 (Ohio App. 2002).]

6. On September 6, 1986, Floyd Simeon, 63, and his son, Edward Simeon, 38, went to the Sweet Pepper Grill, a restaurant at the River Walk in New Orleans. They ordered a dozen and a half raw oysters. Floyd ate six oysters, and Edward ate nine or ten. The men had eaten raw oysters before, and these looked and smelled "good."

Two days later, Mr. Floyd Simeon began running a fever and complained of pain in his ankle. Several physicians were consulted, and it was determined that Mr. Simeon was suffering from vibrio vulnificus septicemia, an infection resulting from eating raw oysters with vibrio vulnificus bacteria. As the disease progressed,

Mr. Simeon developed severe blisters on his legs and began to lose subcutaneous tissue. Plastic surgeons and other physicians tried to stop the spread of the disease, but they were unsuccessful, and Mr. Simeon died on September 23, 1986.

Mrs. Simeon brought a suit against Sweet Pepper Grill for breach of the warranty of merchantability. Should the restaurant be held liable? [*Simeon* v. *Doe*, 618 So. 2d 848 (La. 1993).]

7. Roy E. Farrar Produce Co. ordered a shipment of boxes from International Paper Company that were to be suitable for the packing and storage of tomatoes. The dimensions of the two sizes of boxes were to be such that either 20 or 30 pounds of tomatoes could be packed without the necessity of weighing each box. Mr. Farrar requested that the boxes be the same type as those supplied to Florida packers for shipping tomatoes. Mr. Farrar told Mr. Wilson, an agent for International, to obtain the correct specifications for the Florida-type box.

International shipped Mr. Farrar 21,500 unassembled boxes at a unit price of 64 cents per box. The boxes were not tomato boxes, were not Florida boxes, did not have adequate stacking strength, and would not hold up during shipping. Mr. Farrar had to repack 3,624 boxes (at a cost of $1.92 per box). Substitute boxes were purchased for 10 cents above the International price. The replacement boxes were Florida boxes and did not collapse. Mr. Farrar was also forced to pay growers $6 a box for tomatoes damaged during shipping. He could not use 6,100 boxes, and his sales dropped off, resulting in financial deficiencies in his operation. Can Mr. Farrar recover for his damages? Why or why not? [*International Paper Co.* v. *Farrar*, 700 P.2d 642 (N.M. 1985).]

8. Cindi Cott, her husband, Charles Price, and her father, John Cott, joined friends for an evening at the Peppermint Twist bar nightclub in Topeka, Kansas, on September 23, 1989. That evening, Peppermint Twist advertised watermelon shots for one dollar by posting it on a portable sign in the nightclub's parking lot. A watermelon shot contains Southern Comfort, Creme de Noyaux, and orange juice. Mary Cottrell was the Peppermint Twist waitress assigned to the table where Ms. Cott, Mr. Price, Mr. Cott, and their friends were sitting. Three shots were ordered. Ms. Cottrell poured the watermelon shots from a pour-and-serve container on her tray.

Unbeknownst to Ms. Cottrell, the bar staff had confused a pour-and-serve container with Eco-Klene—a heavy-duty commercial dishwasher detergent that contains lye. Eco-Klene is red in color like the watermelon shots, and the bartenders had been using Eco-Klene near their sinks because they had run out of the normal dishwashing liquid they used. Eco-Klene contains sodium hydroxide, a cause of severe chemical burns that can be fatal.

Ms. Cott took a drink of the Eco-Klene, became very ill, and went to the restroom. Her father, curious, then tasted his Eco-Klene. Both were rushed to the hospital, experienced permanent physical damage, lost work time, and endured extensive rehabilitation. The Cotts have sued Peppermint Twist. Can they recover? Are the manufacturers of Eco-Klene liable? [*Cott* v. *Peppermint Twist Management Co., Inc.*, 856 P.2d 906 (Kan. 1993).]

9. On February 14, 1999, Garry O. Hickman opened a pack of Big Red gum, which is manufactured by Wrigley. Mr. Hickman purchased the gum at a grocery store on the evening of February 13, 1999. Mr. Hickman unwrapped the package, which was still sealed, and put two pieces of the gum into his mouth. Mr. Hickman provided the following description of the events that occurred after he began to chew the gum:

> [A]fter I started chewing the gum I bit down on it, uh, when I bit down on it the tooth exploded in my mouth. I begin to get all of this stuff out of my mouth, tooth fragments all over my mouth and everything. The screw turned up and stuck up in the top of my gum. I had to pull it out which caused me a lot of pain and all and everything and it was very uncomfortable there for a while.

Mr. Hickman sought treatment from Dr. Conly on February 18, 1999. One of Mr. Hickman's bottom teeth was fragmented. Those fragments chipped his top front teeth. Dr. Conly recommended that Mr. Hickman have surgery, which would total approximately $905.00, to remove the fractured tooth. However, Mr. Hickman had been unable to do so because he could not afford the surgery. His gums stayed sore for several weeks.

Mr. Hickman filed suit against Wrigley. Can he recover? What theories might he try? [*Hickman* v. *Wm. Wrigley, Jr. Co., Inc.*, 768 So.2d 812) (La. App. 2000).]

10. On August 11, 1995, David Lyall was adding chlorine to his swimming pool in the backyard of his home. The chlorine was in a tablet form called Leslie's Chlorinator Tablets 1. The tablets were contained in a 5.5-gallon bucket-like container with a childproof lid. Plastican, Inc., was the designer of the container.

When Mr. Lyall attempted to open the container, the lid blew off, allegedly due to the buildup of nitrogen trichloride gas. The lid, chlorine, and chlorine gas blew into his face, causing him to lose his right eye and suffer several chemical burns and cuts to his face, which resulted in scarring and permanent disfigurement. Mr. Lyall's right eye has been replaced with a prosthetic device.

Mr. Lyall filed suit against both Leslie's and Plastican for the defective container and the failure to warn about the effects of gas buildup. What theories of liability do you think Mr. Lyall used and why? [*Lyall* v. *Leslie's Poolmart*, 984 F.Supp. 587 (E.D. Mich. 1997).]

RESEARCH PROBLEM

Coffee Talk

11. Review the following hypotheticals as well as the cited case and develop a policy for your chain of restaurants on serving coffee, including coffee temperatures, types of cups, and any related issues. Write a memo discussing your new policies and explain why you are implementing them.

Stella Liebeck, 81, suffered third-degree burns when coffee spilled on her lap inside her car after she went through a McDonald's drive-through in Albuquerque, New Mexico. The temperature of the coffee, according to corporate guidelines, is 180 to 190 degrees

Fahrenheit. Ms. Liebeck has sued McDonald's to recover for her injuries resulting from the coffee spill. Should Ms. Liebeck be allowed to recover? What theories could she use to recover?

George Morgan, 58, purchased coffee at a Burger King drive-through. He suffered third-degree burns when the bottom of his coffee cup collapsed, spilling hot coffee over his legs and groin. What is different about Mr. Morgan's accident from Ms. Liebeck's accident? Are there different liability issues?

For some insight, read *Austin* v. *W. H. Braum, Inc.*, 249 F.3d 805 (8th cir. 2001).

NOTES

1. AEI-Brookings Joint Center for Regulatory Studies, Senior Fellow Judyth W. Pendell with cost analysis conducted by Paul J. Hinton, 2004; White House Study on U.S. Tort System, conducted by the President's Council on Economic Advisors, 2002.

2. *FTC News Summary,* May 19, 1978, pp. 1–2.

3. See *McCarthy* v. *Olin,* 119 F.3d 148 (2d Cir. 1997). A series of cases dealt with negligent distribution of guns. Those cases too have been dismissed as issues of public policy to be handled by legislatures. See *Hamilton* v. *Beretta U.S.A. Corp.,* 727 N.Y.S.2d 7 (N.Y. App. 2001); *Hamilton* v. *Beretta U.S.A. Corp.,* 264 F.3d 21 (2d Cir. 2001). A new line of cases focuses on public nuisance as a theory for recovery from gun manufacturers. Courts are divided on these cases, with one procedural dismissal for standing, *N.A.A.C.P.* v. *AcuSport, Inc.,* 271 F.Supp.2d 435 (E.D.N.Y.), and one certification for trial, *City of New York* v. *Beretta U.S.A. Corp.,* 315 F.Supp.2d 256 (E.D.N.Y. 2004).

CHAPTER

12

Environmental Regulation

▶ update ◀

For up-to-date legal news and real-world business applications, click on **update** *at http://jennings.westbuslaw.com*

■ When producing its products or providing its services, a firm has an obligation to do so in a manner that does not illegally affect the environment. Apart from the damage claims and penalties that can result from unlawful pollution of the environment, social responsibility is a major issue. Keeping a clean environment is a long-range goal not only for a society but also for the businesses that hope to continue operating in that society. This chapter answers the following questions: What are the public and private environmental laws? What protections and requirements are present in environmental laws? Who enforces environmental laws? What are the penalties for violations?

> By the shores of Gitche Gumee,
> By the shining Big-Sea-Water, . . .
> How they built their nests in summer,
> Where they hid themselves in winter,
> How the beavers built their lodges,
> Where the squirrels hid their acorns,
> How the reindeer ran so swiftly,
> Why the rabbit was so timid . . .
>
> HENRY WADSWORTH LONGFELLOW
> *"Hiawatha's Childhood"*

> The landscape and the language are the same
> For we ourselves are landscape and land.
>
> CONRAD AIKEN
> *A Letter from Li Po and Other Poems* (1955)

Klamath Irrigation Project, one of the oldest of the federal reclamation projects, is a series of lakes, rivers, dams, and irrigation canals in northern California and southern Oregon. Environmental groups have pointed out that the operation of the project might impact on the Lost River sucker (*Deltistes luxatus*) and shortnose sucker (*Chasmistes brevirostris*) species of fish, which were listed as endangered in 1988. Brad Bennett and other ranchers operate their ranches within the areas designated to receive less water because the biological opinion issued on the Klamath Project made that recommendation. Mr. Bennett filed suit, alleging that the Klamath biological opinion was incorrect in its conclusions on the impact of the project on the two species of fish. Mr. Bennett also argued that the opinion did not take into account the resulting economic impact of lessening the water levels for the ranchers. Mr. Bennett's complaint alleged that the Endangered Species Act (ESA) and the Administrative Procedures Act (APA) required the federal government to take his interests into account in making the determination about what to do about the project. The federal district court dismissed the complaint, and the court of appeals affirmed the dismissal. Mr. Bennett appealed. Does Mr. Bennett have any rights under the ESA?

How much environmental regulation do we need? When can development be curtailed through regulation?

© PAT POWERS AND CHERRYL SHAFER/PHOTODISC/GETTY IMAGES

COMMON LAW REMEDIES AND THE ENVIRONMENT

Visit an environmental educational site:
http://www.enn.com

From earliest times, landowners have enjoyed the protections of the courts and various doctrines to prevent bad smells, noises, and emissions. Common law affords relief to adjoining landowners and communities when activities rise to the level of a **nuisance**. A nuisance exists when the activities of one landowner interfere with the use and enjoyment of their properties by other landowners or by members of the community in which the nuisance occurs. Bad smells, ongoing damage to paint on buildings, excessive noise, polluted air, and the operation of facilities that present health problems can all be enjoined as nuisances. In many environmental problems, concerned parties do not want money for damages as much as they want the harmful activity halted. The courts have the power to issue **injunctions** against those who are harming land, individuals, or the environment. Injunctions are granted in those cases in which the party (or parties) requesting the injunctive relief can establish ongoing harm as a result of the defendant's activities. In *T & E Industries, Inc.* v. *Safety Light Corp.* (Case 12.1), the New Jersey Supreme Court was faced with an issue of contamination of property and the liability of the transferors and transferees for the hazard created.

CASE 12.1

T & E Industries, Inc. v. Safety Light Corp.
587 A.2d 1249 (N.J. 1991)

Toxic Waste Radiates: You Can't Bury the Past

FACTS

United States Radium Corporation (USRC) owned an industrial site on Alden Street in Orange, New Jersey, where it processed radium from 1917 until 1926. USRC sold the radium for medical purposes and also used it to manufacture luminous paint for instrument dials, watches, and other products. Radium processing permitted recovery of only 80% of the radium from the carnotite ore transported to the plant from Colorado and Utah. The unextracted radium was contained in "tailings" that USRC discarded onto unimproved portions of the Alden Street site.

Through a complex series of chemical processes, the discarded radium emits radon, which can cause lung cancer when inhaled. Epidemiological studies had not been done at the time the tailings were discarded, and the federal government did not regulate the disposal of tailings until 1978. However, many people had suspicions about handling radium, and as early as 1917 USRC employees measured the radioactivity of radium. One story told of how Dr. Van Sochocky, the president of USRC, "hacked" off his fingertip when radium lodged beneath his fingernail because he feared the effects of radium.

Radium processing ceased at the Alden Street site in 1926, and the site was leased to various commercial tenants until it was sold in 1943 to Arpin, a plastics manufacturer. The tailings were not removed from the site in spite of continually developing evidence about the danger. In fact, Arpin constructed a new portion of its plant that rested on the discarded tailings. The property changed hands several times. T&E (plaintiff), a manufacturer of electronic components, leased the premises in 1969 and purchased it in 1974.

The Uranium Mill Tailings Radiation Control Act (1978) calls for the evaluation of inactive mill-tailing sites. New Jersey's Department of Environmental Protection (DEP) inspected the plaintiff's site and found radon levels exceeding state and federal standards. In spite of soil removal and other actions, the site could not be brought into compliance; T&E was forced to move its operations. The site could not be sold until cleanup of the tailings was complete.

In 1981, T&E sued Safety Light Corporation (a successor corporation to USRC) (defendant) and others (all corporations that bought from USRC or its transferees) based on nuisance, negligence, misrepresentation, fraud, and strict liability for abnormally dangerous activity. The trial court dismissed the strict liability claim and found that USRC had no knowledge of the dangers when the tailings were disposed of. The jury found for T&E, but the trial court entered a judgment NOV for Safety Light. T&E appealed. The appellate court reversed the trial court's decision, and Safety Light appealed.

JUDICIAL OPINION

CLIFFORD, Justice

The abnormally dangerous-activity doctrine emphasizes the dangerousness and inappropriateness of the activity. Despite the social utility of the activity, that doctrine imposes liability on those who, for their own benefit, introduce an extraordinary risk of harm into the community.

Because some conditions and activities can be so hazardous and of "such relatively infrequent occurrence," the risk of loss is justifiably allocated as a cost of business to the enterpriser who engages in such conduct. Although the law will tolerate the hazardous activity, the enterprise must pay its way.

Because the former owner of the property whose activities caused the hazard might have been in the best position to bear or spread the loss, liability for the harm caused by abnormally dangerous activities does not necessarily cease with the transfer of property.

A real-estate contract that does not disclose the abnormally dangerous condition or activity does not shield from liability the seller who created that condition or engaged in that activity.

The *Restatement* sets forth six factors that a court should consider in determining whether an activity is "abnormally dangerous."

(a) existence of a high degree of risk of some harm to the person, land, or chattels of others;

(b) likelihood that the harm that results from it will be great;

(c) inability to eliminate the risk by the exercise of reasonable care;

(d) extent to which the activity is not a matter of common usage;

(e) inappropriateness of the activity to place where it is carried on; and

(f) extent to which its value to the community is outweighed by its dangerous attributes.

Defendant does not dispute that liability can be imposed on enterprisers who engage in abnormally dangerous activities that harm others; but it contends that such liability is contingent on proof that the enterpriser knew or should have known of the "abnormally dangerous character of the activity." According to defendant, absent such knowledge, that enterpriser "is in no position to make the cost-benefit calculations that will enable him to spread the risk and engage in the optimal level of activity." Defendant argues that absent such an opportunity, the policy basis for imposing strict liability on those who engage in abnormally dangerous activities, namely, cost spreading, cannot be realized.

We need not, however, determine whether knowledge is a requirement in the context of a strict-liability claim predicated on an abnormally dangerous activity. Even if the law imposes such a requirement, we are convinced, for the reasons set forth more fully below, that defendant should have known about the risks of its activity, and that its constructive knowledge would fully satisfy any such requirement.

Radium has always been and continues to be an extraordinarily dangerous substance. Although radium processing has never been a common activity, the injudicious handling, processing, and disposal of radium has for decades caused concern; it has long been suspected of posing a serious threat to the health of those who are exposed to it.

Furthermore, although the risks involved in the processing and disposal of radium might be curtailed, one cannot safely dispose of radium by dumping it onto the vacant portions of an urban lot. Because of the extraordinarily hazardous nature of radium, the processing and disposal of that substance is particularly inappropriate in an urban setting. We conclude that despite the usefulness of radium, defendant's processing, handling, and disposal of that substance under the facts of this case constituted an abnormally dangerous activity, plaintiff's property is befouled with radium because of defendant's abnormally dangerous activity. Radiation levels at the site exceed those permitted under governmental health regulations. Moreover, the property has been earmarked as a Superfund site. Because plaintiff vacated the premises in response to the health concern posed by the radium-contaminated site and because the danger to health is "the kind of harm, the possibility of which [made defendant's] activity abnormally dangerous," defendant is strictly liable for the resulting harm.

Here defendant knew that it was processing radium, a substance concededly fraught with hazardous potential. It knew that its employees who handled radium should wear protective clothing; it knew that some employees who had digested radium had developed cancer, and prior to the sale of the property, it knew that the inhalation of radon could cause lung cancer. Despite that wealth of knowledge concerning the harmful effects of radium exposure, defendant contends that it could not have known that disposal of the radium-saturated by-products behind the plant would produce a hazard. That contention appears to rest on the idea that somehow the radium's potential for harm miraculously disappeared once the material had been deposited in a vacant corner of an urban lot, or at the least that one might reasonably reach that conclusion— a proposition that we do not accept.

Surely someone engaged in a business as riddled with hazards as defendant's demonstrably was should realize the potential for harm in every aspect of that dangerous business. If knowledge be a requirement, defendant knew enough about the abnormally dangerous character of radium processing to be charged with knowledge of the dangers of disposal.

Finally, we reflect on the "parade of horribles" argument, namely, that our decision will create such uncertainty as to render it impossible for today's business community to regulate its affairs effectively. We have already noted the limited scope of our holding in that it extends only to that rare form of conduct that meets the criteria of an abnormally dangerous activity. Second, we note that almost without exception any conveyance of industrial property today would be made not in a vacuum but in full appreciation of regulatory requirements that would surely embrace a condition such as the one on the Alden Street property.

Affirmed.

CASE QUESTIONS

1. Who originally owned the property?

2. How was the property originally used?

3. How did the original owners feel about handling radium?

4. What was disposed of on the site?

5. What made the disposal an abnormally dangerous activity?

6. What does the court say about the "parade of horribles" argument?

CONSIDER...   12.1

Spur Industries has operated a feedlot in an area about 20 miles from the city of Phoenix since 1956. Del E. Webb began the development of Sun City, a retirement community, in 1959. Spur expanded its operations in 1960 from 35 acres to 115 acres. Spur was feeding between 20,000 and 30,000 cattle, each of which produced 35 to 40 pounds of wet manure per day. Residents of Sun City are complaining about the odors and flies. Webb has been unable to sell 1,300 lots located next to the feedlot. Could the residents win a nuisance suit against Spur? Does it matter that Spur was there first? [*Spur Industries, Inc.* v. *Del E. Webb Dev. Co.*, 494 P.2d 700 (Ariz. 1972).]

MAKING ETHICS PERSONAL

NIMBYs Unite!

Cellular-phone service is growing at a rate of 34 percent per year. There are an estimated 51 million cell-phone users and 38,000 wireless tower sites.* However, the sites for those towers continue to cause problems for local zoning boards. To cope with so-called NIMBYs, an acronym for people who say "Not in my back yard" and oppose locating things like wireless towers near their homes, local authorities have been declining requests by telecommunications companies for new towers.†

Recognizing the need for reliable telecommunications service, Congress intervened with Section 332(c) of the Telecommunications Act of 1996, which covers "Mobile Services" [47 U.S.C.A. § 332(c)]. The federal law does not preempt local zoning authority over tower locations, but it does place some limitations on that local government authority over siting. The limitations are imposed in discreet ways. For example, state and local governments cannot engage in unreasonable discrimination among "providers of functionally equivalent services." If they allow telephone wires and cables, they must allow towers. The act also prevents state and local governments from prohibiting "the provision of personal wireless services."

Denials for towers must be based on scientific or medical facts under the federal law. For example, if the denial is based on health claims, the state and local authority must provide something more than community hysteria when issuing its denial on that basis. A denial on the basis of aesthetics has been deemed to not meet the standards of the act.

While cell-phone towers have resulted in legislation, other issues—including placement of power plants, prisons, and even Wal-Marts—have also drawn NIMBY protests. NIMBYs bring nuisance suits, ask for special initiatives on ballots, or lobby for legislation to halt approval for these economic developments.

What issues must courts and local authorities balance when making decisions about telecommunications towers, power plants, and Wal-Marts? What economic issues are at stake? If you use cell-phone service, can you be a NIMBY about the towers? If you shop at Wal-Mart, should you object if your local government approves of building a new one?

*"U.S. FCC Moves to Boost Phone Subscribership Levels," Reuters Financial Service, July 13, 1995.
†David W. Hughes, "When NIMBYs Attack: The Heights to Which Communities Will Climb to Prevent the Siting of Wireless Towers," 23 *Journal of Corporation Law* 469 (Spring 1998).

Because any electrical current sets up a magnetic field, computers and wire transmissions to and from computers set up magnetic fields that might affect electrical equipment in buildings on neighboring land; the stronger the current, the greater the magnetic field. Also, if a loose or broken circuit sparks, the interference with neighbors increases. If that interference rises to an unreasonable level, it may be stopped as a nuisance and damages recovered for the harm. The issue of electromagnetic fields has produced litigation against electric utilities for their placement of overheads wires, transformers, and power plants. The litigation has focused on many legal theories, including trespass and nuisance.

For example, the Meridian Data Processing Center was an independent contractor that performed all the data processing for a large number of banks and stockbrokers within the state. Because of the large number of computers and direct wire lines to its customers, the center's operation set up a substantial magnetic field that interfered with some of the electronic display equipment in several neighboring stores. The stores sued the data processing center to obtain an injunction against it for nuisance.

Because of the social utility of the activity, it is unlikely a court would enjoin this form of activity. It might, however, impose some limitations on hours of operation or require investment in technology to find a means around the problem.[1]

STATUTORY ENVIRONMENTAL LAWS

At the federal level, most environmental laws can be placed in one of three categories: those regulating air pollution, those regulating water pollution, and those regulating solid waste disposal on land. In addition, the federal regulatory scheme has several laws affecting property rights that do not fit into these categories but are discussed in this subsection nonetheless.

Air Pollution Regulation

Early Legislation

The first legislation dealing with the problem of air pollution, the **Air Pollution Control Act**, passed in 1955. However, the 1955 act did very little to control or even to take steps to control the problem of air pollution.

Little action was taken to encourage greater involvement in the air pollution issue until Congress passed the **Air Quality Act** in 1967. Under this act, the Department of Health, Education, and Welfare (HEW, now HHS) was authorized to oversee the states' adoption of air quality standards and the implementation of those plans. Again, this legislation proved ineffective, for by 1970 no state had adopted a comprehensive plan.

Review the Clean Air Act and Amendments:
http://www.law.cornell.edu/uscode/42/ch85.html#s7401

Visit the Environmental Protection Agency:
http://www.epa.gov

1970 Amendments to the Clean Air Act: New Standards

Because the states did not take action concerning air pollution, Congress passed the 1970 amendments to the original but ineffective 1963 **Clean Air Act** (42 U.S.C. § 7401); these amendments constituted the first federal legislation with any real authority for enforcement. Under the act, the **Environmental Protection Agency** (EPA) was authorized to establish air quality standards; once those standards were developed, states were required to adopt implementation plans to achieve the federally developed standards. These **state implementation plans** (SIPs) had to be approved by the EPA, and adoption and enforcement of the plans were no longer discretionary but mandatory. To obtain EPA approval, the SIPs had to meet deadlines for compliance with the EPA air quality standards, and thus the Clean Air Act established time periods for achieving air quality.

The air quality standards set by the EPA specify how much of a particular substance in the air is permissible. It was up to each state to devise methods for meeting those standards. First the states measured existing air content of substances such as sulfur dioxide, carbon monoxide, and hydrocarbons. Based on the results, the states then took appropriate steps to reduce the amounts of any substances that exceeded federal standards. The EPA required those state standards to mandate the development of air pollution devices. Lack of technology could not be used as a defense to air pollution.

1977 Amendments

With the 1977 amendments came authority for the EPA to regulate business growth in an attempt to achieve air quality standards. With this authority, the EPA classified two types of areas in which business growth could be contained. **Nonattainment areas**, as originally defined under these amendments, included those areas with existing, significant air quality problems, the so-called dirty areas. Today, the number of nonattainment areas has been reduced significantly. The EPA now has nonattainment areas classified according to categories of pollutants. Some areas, such as Los Angeles, have achieved air quality for certain pollutants, but are classified as nonattainment areas for others. There are now six classifications of pollutants for designating nonattainment areas. In some categories there are no longer any nonattainment areas. Clean areas designated under the amendments were labeled **prevention of significant deterioration (PSD) areas**.

EPA Economic Controls for Nonattainment Areas

For information on development of solar technology, see:
http://www.ncsc.ncsu.edu

For nonattainment areas, the EPA developed its **emissions offset policy**, which requires three elements before a new facility can begin operation in a nonattainment area: (1) The new plant must have the greatest possible emissions controls; (2) the proposed plant operator must have all its other operations in compliance with standards; and (3) the new plant's emissions must be offset by reductions from other facilities in the area.

In applying these elements, the EPA follows the **bubble concept**, which examines all the air pollutants in the area as if they came from a single source. If it can be shown that a new plant will have no net effect on the air in the area (after offsets from other plants), the new facility will not be subject to a veto.

Although the EPA initially did not regulate the construction of plants in areas that already meet air quality standards, environmentalists' protests and suits brought about the application of EPA regulations to PSD areas. Basically, the purpose of PSD regulations is to permit the EPA to have the right to review proposed plant constructions prior to their construction. In their submissions for EPA review, the plant operators are required to establish that there will be no significant effect on air quality and that emissions will be controlled with appropriate devices.

New Forms of Control: The 1990 Amendments to the Clean Air Act

The Clean Air Act was revised substantially with the **Clean Air Act Amendments of 1990**. These amendments focus on issues such as **acid rain**, urban smog, airborne toxins, ozone-depleting chemicals, and the various regional economic concerns and political problems attendant to these issues.

As of 1990, ninety-six cities were already three years late in achieving the attainment levels mandated by their SIPs in 1977, and forty-one cities had carbon monoxide levels exceeding the goals in their SIPs. Under the 1990 amendments, the EPA was authorized to establish a **federal implementation plan** (FIP) within two years of a state's failure to submit to the EPA an adequate SIP. New deadlines were established for polluted areas according to current levels of pollution. Except for Los Angeles, which was given a more flexible deadline, compliance deadlines were set for the year 2000, with annual pollution reduction goals for cities set at 3–4 percent per year. There is increasing progress but EPA estimates are that 60 percent of Americans still live in some form of nonattainment areas. (Go to *http://www.epa.gov/oar/oaqps/peg_caa/pegcaa10.html* for more information.)

FOR THE MANAGER'S DESK

RE: THE EMISSIONS PERMIT MARKET

The market for emissions permits continues to expand. Under EPA guidelines, over 200 utilities are permitted to sell and buy on an open market. The market has created an incentive for utilities to reduce their sulfur dioxide emissions, which the EPA capped with the 1990 statute. No one can gain any more rights to emit sulfur dioxide, there are substantial penalties for utilities that do not meet their maximums, and the opportunity to sell any emissions reductions achieved. The result has been that sulfur dioxide emissions have fallen faster than even the EPA anticipated; they are now at one-half their 1980 levels. While the cost has been $1 billion in lost production, most experts figure there is a net gain because of the sales and also because of the reduced health costs.

As in all free markets, the system of buying and selling emissions permits encouraged creativity. Environmentalist groups that purchase permits retire them so that the air is permanently cleaner—these permits will not go back into the market.

The emissions trading system exists in other countries as well. Canada has a market for sulfur dioxide, nitrogen oxides, and volatile organic compounds. The Chinese market is for sulfur dioxide. Chile's market is for suspended particulates. Most anticipate greenhouse gases will be the next step.

Source: Cait Murphy, "Hog Wild for Pollution Trading," *Forbes,* September 2, 2002, p. 137.

To meet the new EPA standards and deadlines that resulted from the 1990 amendments, cities and counties imposed even residential regulations such as "no-burn" days for fireplaces and restrictions on charcoal barbeques.

The 1990 amendments have had a substantial impact on smaller businesses, such as dry cleaners, paint shops, and bakeries, because the definition of a major source of pollution was changed from those businesses emitting 100 tons or more a year to those emitting 50 tons or more per year.

One of the effects of the Clean Air Act Amendments of 1990 has been the buying and selling of EPA permits for sulfur dioxide emissions. If, for example, a utility has an EPA permit to discharge one ton of sulfur dioxide per year, but its equipment permits it to run "cleaner" so that it discharges less than the one ton, the utility can sell the emissions savings portion of its permit to another utility. In fact, the Chicago Board of Trade conducts a national auction for the sale of such permits. The price for a permit for one ton of sulfur dioxide ranges from $122 to $450. The first day of trading these permits—March 30, 1993—produced sales of 150,000 permits worth $21.4 million; 1 percent of the bids were from environmental groups seeking to prevent use of the permits.

The nine worst nonattainment areas were required to use reformulated gasolines to reduce emissions by 25 percent by 2000. Tighter tailpipe standards for autos were phased in to require emissions reductions ranging from 30 to 60 percent for various pollutants. Plants that are major sources of toxic emissions must use **maximum achievable control technology** (MACT), or the best available methods for limiting emissions, regardless of cost.

Penalties under the act allow field citations and civil penalties of up to $25,000 a day in general fines. The $5,000-per-day penalty applies to even minor violations, including those related to record keeping. The EPA is also authorized under the 1990 amendments to pay $10,000 rewards to people who provide information leading to criminal convictions or civil penalties. Stiffer criminal penalties were added, with a possibility of up to two years imprisonment for false statements or failures to report violations. Willful violations carry penalties of up to fifteen years and/or $1 million in fines. The act specifically holds as criminally liable any responsible corporate officers.

CONSIDER...   12.2

Union Electric Company is an electric utility serving St. Louis and large portions of Illinois and Iowa. It operates three coal-fired generating plants in metropolitan St. Louis that are subject to sulfur dioxide restrictions under Missouri's SIP. Union Electric did not seek review of the implementation plan but applied for and obtained variances from the emissions limitations. When an extension for the variances was denied, Union Electric challenged the implementation plan on the grounds that it was technologically and economically infeasible and should therefore be amended. Will Union Electric succeed in having the plan amended? Consider the question in light of the 1990 Clean Air Act Amendments. [*Union Electric Co. v. EPA,* 427 U.S. 246 (1976).]

ETHICAL ISSUES

Clean Air and the Popular SUV

In 1990, the SUV/light truck market consisted of approximately 4 million units sold out of 14 million total vehicle sales in the United States. By 1999, the percentage of the total market had increased, and total sales were higher: SUV/light truck sales were 8.2 million of 16.4 million units sold. Of Ford Motor Company's sales, 47.6 percent are of SUVs, primarily its Ford Explorer and larger Expedition models, but also its even larger Excursion.

In 1997, most auto manufacturers entered the luxury SUV market. These SUVs, with prices around $50,000, featured in-vehicle televisions and VCRs, leather interiors, and all the amenities of luxury cars.

Market data on SUV buyers indicate that the primary reasons for purchasing an SUV are safety (44 percent), need (due to family size—33 percent), desire to go off-roading (10 percent), and desire "to be with the latest trend" (10 percent).

The SUV has proven to be a lightning rod for public discussion in areas as diverse as environmentalism and safety. Focusing on safety concerns and the use of fuel and resulting emissions, there has been intense media coverage of SUVs.

In 1997, the *New York Times* ran a report titled "License to Pollute: Light Trucks, Darlings of Drivers, Are Favored by Law, Too." The article concluded that, because of a loophole, these vehicles, including SUVs, had emissions 20–100 percent higher than cars. The article noted that if Americans had continued buying just cars instead of light trucks and SUVs, carbon dioxide emissions would have been "down by 9.3 percent."

Later in 1997, California air quality officials revealed a proposal to require trucks, minivans, and most SUVs to meet the same emissions standards as passenger cars by the year 2004. That proposal is now law.

Following the Kyoto treaty of December 12, 1997, would have required the United States to reduce its emissions to its 1990 levels by the year 2012. The United States did not ratify the treaty. Ford and Chrysler announced on January 5, 1998, that they would cut the emissions of their SUVs and minivans. At a cost of $100 per vehicle or $100 million per year, Ford announced that its Windstar vans would immediately meet the same emissions standards as its passenger vehicles. The *New York Times* reported on the Ford decision as follows:

> ... Jacques Nasser [Ford's president of worldwide automotive operations] made clear in an interview that Ford wanted to maintain the acceptability of sports utility vehicles as alternatives to cars, while gaining an advantage over rival automakers in catering to environmentally aware families. "Anybody who has concerns about the environment can set them aside," Nasser said adding that Ford was also influenced by recent articles in the New York Times *on the environmental problems of light trucks.*

USA Today ran a series of articles during 1999 on the following topics: the disadvantages of driving a small car in an SUV-dominated market; the high center of gravity in small SUVs and the danger of rollovers; and the automakers' detours around Corporate Average Fuel Economy (CAFE) rules. CAFE rules are the mileage standards the federal government requires each automaker to attain when the fuel economies of all the vehicles they sell in a model year are averaged together. The standard for cars is 27.5 mpg in combined city and highway driving, and the standard for trucks and SUVs is 20.7 mpg. The fine for failing to meet CAFE rules is $5.50 for each 0.1 mpg short of the standard, multiplied by the number of such cars sold. For example, if an automaker sells 1 million cars that average 27 mpg instead of 27.5 mpg, the fine is $27.5 million. Foreign automakers generally ignore the CAFE standards and simply pay the fines as a cost of doing business. U.S. automakers strive for compliance because criminal sanctions include prison time for officers and managers. *USA Today* concluded, however, that U.S. automaker compliance was meaningless because automakers are permitted to carry credits forward when they exceed CAFE standards, and by juggling model years through mid-year introduction of vehicles, companies can exclude substantial numbers of sales of larger vehicles that would decrease their average mileage statistics.

Following the series in the *New York Times* and *USA Today,* Ford announced that it would escalate its emissions standards for its trucks and SUVs. Jacques Nasser announced on May 17, 1999, that Ford's trucks, including its Explorer and Expedition models, would meet EPA emissions standards for 2004 by the year 2000. Mr. Nasser said he wants customers to have the option to select from a full range of Ford products rather than choosing "between the one that is environmentally friendly and the one that isn't."

In early 2000, Ford released its social responsibility report, called "Corporate Citizenship Report," and its chairman announced it to the shareholders at Ford's annual meeting in May 2000. William Clay Ford Jr. read the Sierra Club's description of the Ford Excursion at the meeting as "a gas-guzzling rolling monument to environmental destruction." Mr. Ford promised that his company would do better. Sales of the Excursion in 1999 were 15,838 units, in excess of the 15,000 produced. There is a waiting list for buyers. The following day, the *Detroit Free Press* carried the story of the Ford announcement with the following headline in its business section: "Ford admits its trucks hurt the earth." The Associated Press headline was "Ford admits dilemma: SUVs vs. environment." Environmental groups said they would use the report to lobby in Washington for more stringent regulations. Debbie Zemke, director of Ford's corporate governance, said Ford still stood by its decision to be forthright: "We just said: 'For heaven's sake, everybody else is talking about it, so why shouldn't we?'"

GM and DaimlerChrysler announced that while they would not be accelerating their emissions reductions programs, they were working on alternative fuel vehicles. "We have different objectives on how we get to lower emissions," was the DaimlerChrysler response. GM noted, "It is taking its own path to lower vehicle emissions in the U.S. and around the world."

The following events have resulted in continuing emotion and changes in the SUV market.

- The Energy Department began releasing its list of the "worst gas guzzlers," with these models leading the list:
  - Hummer H2: 12 mpg
  - Lincoln Navigator: 13.25 mpg
  - Mercedes-Benz G500: 13.45 mpg
  - GMC Yukon XL, Cadillac Escalade: 13.8 mpg
  - Land Rover Discovery Series II: 13.8 mpg
- GM introduced a new hybrid electric engine that it plans to put in 1 million vehicles to increase fuel efficiency, from an average of 20.7 mpg to 22.2 mpg. CEO G. Richard Wagoner noted, "We have a responsibility to provide cleaner emissions and better fuel efficiency."[a]

- Auto industry officials indicate they cannot meet new government fuel efficiency standards, but the National Academy of Science notes that Japanese manufacturers have met those standards already. "The Big Three always say they can't do anything," notes MaryAnn Keller, a member of the academy.[b]
- Sales of the larger SUVs dropped during 2002, about 2 percent, the same drop rate for all vehicles. Sales of the car-based SUVs were, however, up 23 percent in 2002.[c] Other figures show SUV sales up 6.9 percent for 2002.
- SUVs and pickups produced 90 percent of the Big Three automakers' profits in 2002.
- The new auto is the "family-size crossover vehicle," which includes features of a car, a minivan, and an SUV. Nissan launched its Murano. Honda introduced its Element. GM introduced its Saturn Vue. Ford introduced the Freestyle in 2004. Acura has its MDX, Volvo its new XC90, Infinity its FX 45, Lexus its RX 330, Honda its Pilot, Buick its Rendezvous, and Toyota its Highlander. Women have driven the change, as it were, in the design because they did not like the truck feel of traditional SUVs and were concerned about the safety issues. Many of the new models feature airbags for knees.[d]
- A book by the editor of *Road & Track* calls the new Hummer H2 SUV Satan's station wagon. John Lamm documents in his book *HUMMER H2* that only 5–10 percent of sales of the vehicle are to ranchers and others who use the vehicle for off-road driving. The other 90–95 percent of sales are to "successful achievers" whose only brush with off-roading is "with the landscape architect."[e]
- New safety studies indicate that there is a higher fatality rate in SUV rollover accidents, but in those accidents, nearly all drivers and passengers were not wearing their seatbelts.[f]
- The Ford Explorer had a driver death rate of 56 per 1 million registered vehicles. But of the 89 car models for which death rates are available, 74 had higher death rates. Of 34 pickups, 32 had higher death rates, and the death rates for 7 sports cars (including the Mazda Miata and Ford Mustang) were all higher.[g]
- There are 750 million cars and trucks on the road around the world; 4 million vehicles sold last year were SUVs.[h]
- The Ford Expedition and Lincoln Navigator were redesigned so that their bumpers will not override most cars.[i]
- *USA Today* released a study in which it concluded that automakers were making the fronts of SUVs extra stiff to meet government safety standards,

continued

with the intended result being that the occupants of SUVs are extra safe. However, the study notes that the the the deadly impact comes to passengers in other cars when SUVs hit them.[j]

- Law enforcement officials have noticed an increasing trend around the country in which SUVs on dealership lots are set afire during the night, with calling cards left by environmental groups.[k] Generally, the fires are started by the Earth Liberation Front; thirty SUVs were burned at an Oregon dealership in 2001.

- The Detroit Project announced its "What would Jesus drive?" campaign in which priests, ministers, and rabbis denounced the SUVs as evidence of an uncaring soul insensitive to God's earth.[l]

- Antiwar activists introduced ads, paid for by Ariana Huffington, that linked driving an SUV to funding terrorists through the use of so much oil.[m]

- New stealth bumper sticker campaigns emerged with environmental activists placing on SUVs slogans that read, "I'm changing the environment. Ask me how."[n]

- Jeffrey W. Runge, head of the National Highway Safety Administration, in a speech before automakers indicated that SUVs pose a great danger of rollover accidents, and consumers' safety perceptions are misplaced. Rollover accidents accounted for 3 percent of all auto accidents in 2001. Deaths were mostly in pick-ups. Dr. Runge indicated that his agency would be drafting new safety standards for these vehicles. Many SUVs have been redesigned to reduce rollover risk.[o]

- In response to Dr. Runge's speech, a Ford spokesperson said, "As a general rule, we don't believe the way to introduce new technologies is to have it mandated. We believe it should be customer driven." Dr. Runge responded, "Responsible car companies will do this in the absence of the federal government. They're already at work."[p]

- A *New York Times* exposé shows regulators already pursuing redesign mandates for SUVs.[q]

- Some see a shift of automakers away from large SUVs, but automakers call it a response to consumer demand.[r]

If you were the head of an automaker, would you admit your best-selling products were dangerous for the environment? How would you deal with all these issues surrounding SUVs?

[a]David Welch and Kathleen Kerwin, "Detroit Is Wrecking Its SUV Edge," *Business Week,* March 3, 2003, p. 42.

[b]Ibid.

[c]Ibid.

[d]Sholnn Freeman, "SUVs for People Ashamed to Buy One," *Wall Street Journal,* March 4, 2003, pp. D1, D4.

[e]David Kiley, "Book chronicles making of an urban legend," *USA Today,* March 10, 2003, p. 7B.

[f]Jerry Flint, "The Holy War on SUVs," *Forbes,* March 3, 2003, p. 74.

[g]Ibid.

[h]Ibid.

[i]Ibid.

[j]Jayne O'Donnell, "Crash tests may make SUVs even more deadly," *USA Today,* February 26, 2003, pp. 1A, 2A.

[k]John Cloud, "Why the SUV Is All the Rage," *Time,* February 24, 2003, pp. 35–42.

[l]Ibid.

[m]Ibid.; Karen Lundegaard, Jeffrey Ball, and Gregory L. White, "Auto Makers Start to Back Away from Big SUVs," *Wall Street Journal,* January 27, 2003, pp. A1, A8.

[n]Karen Lundegaard, Jeffrey Ball, and Gregory L. White, "Auto Makers Start to Back Away from Big SUVs," *Wall Street Journal,* January 27, 2003, pp. A1, A8.

[o]Karen Lundegaard, "Auto-Safety Czar Warns Drivers of SUV Dangers," *Wall Street Journal,* January 15, 2003, pp. A1, A2.

[p]Ibid.

[q]Danny Hakim, "Regulators Seek Ways to Make S.U.V.s Safer," *New York Times,* January 30, 2002, pp. C1, C4.

[r]Lundegaard, "Auto-Safety Czar Warns Drivers of SUV Dangers."

Source: Adapted with permission from Marianne M. Jennings, *Case Studies and Readings in Business Ethics,* 5th ed., West, 2004.

Water Pollution Regulation

Early Legislation

In 1965, the first federal legislation on water quality standards was passed—the **Water Quality Act**. The act established a separate enforcement agency—the **Federal Water Pollution Control Administration** (FWPCA)—and required states to establish quality levels for the waters within their boundaries. Because the act contained few expeditious enforcement procedures, only about half of the states had developed their zones and standards by 1970, and none of the states were engaged in active enforcement of those standards with their implementation plans.

The **Rivers and Harbors Act of 1899,** which prohibits the discharge into navigable rivers and harbors of refuse that causes interference with navigation, was used for a time to enforce water standards since state action was minimal. Specifically, the act prohibited the release of "any refuse matter of any kind or description" into navigable waters in the United States without a permit from the Army Corps of Engineers. For a time, the act was used to prosecute industrial polluters that were discharging without permit.

Present Legislation

Review the Clean Water Act:
http://www.law.cornell.edu/
uscode/33/ch26.html

Not until 1972 was meaningful and enforceable federal legislation enacted with the passage of the **Federal Water Pollution Control Act of 1972** (33 U.S.C. § 1401). Under this act, two goals were set: (1) swimmable and fishable waters by 1983 and (2) zero discharge of pollutants by 1985. The act was amended in 1977 to allow extensions and flexibility in meeting the goals and was renamed the **Clean Water Act**. One of the major changes brought about by the act was the move of water pollution regulation from local to federal control. Federal standards for water discharges were established on an industry-wide basis, and all industries, regardless of state location, are required to comply.

Under the act, all direct industrial dischargers are placed into twenty-seven groups, and the EPA—now responsible for water pollution control since the FWPCA was merged into it—establishes ranges of discharge allowed for each industrial group. The ranges for pulp mills, for example, differ from those for textile manufacturers, but all plants in the same industry must comply with the same ranges.

*For information on
wetlands, visit:*
http://www.bergen.org/
AAST/Projects/ES/WL

The ranges of discharges permitted per industrial group are referred to as **effluent guidelines**. In addition, the EPA has established within each industrial group a specific amount of discharge for each plant, which is the effluent limitation. Finally, for a plant to be able to discharge wastes into waterways, it must obtain from the EPA a **National Pollution Discharge Elimination System** (NPDES) permit. This type of permit is required only for direct dischargers, or **point sources**, and is not required of plants that discharge into sewer systems (although these secondary dischargers may still be required to pretreat their discharges). Obtaining a permit is a complicated process that requires not only EPA approval but also state approval, public hearings, and an opportunity for the proposed plant owners to obtain judicial review of a permit decision.

In issuing permits, the EPA may still prescribe standards for release. Generally, the standards set depend on the type of substance the discharger proposes to release. For setting standards, the EPA has developed three categories of pollutants: **conventional**, **nonconventional**, and **toxic pollutants**. If a discharger is going to release a conventional pollutant, the EPA can require it to pretreat the substance with the **best conventional treatment** (BCT). If the pollutant to be discharged is either toxic or nonconventional, the EPA can require the **best available treatment** (BAT), which is the highest standard imposed. In issuing permits and requiring these various levels of treatment, the EPA need only consider environmental effects and not the economic effects on the applicant discharger.

CONSIDER...   1 2 . 3

Inland Steel Company applied for a permit from the EPA under the Federal Water Pollution Control Act of 1972. Although Inland was granted the permit, the EPA made the permit modifiable, as new standards for toxic releases and treatment were being developed. Inland filed suit, claiming the modification restriction on the permit was invalid because the EPA did not have such authority and also because Inland would be subject to every technological change or discovery made during the course of the permit. Was the restriction invalid? [*Inland Steel Co.* v. *EPA*, 547 F.2d 367 (7th Cir. 1978).]

Review the Safe Water Drinking Act:
http://www.law.cornell.edu/ uscode/42/300g-1.html

In 1986, Congress passed the **Safe Drinking Water Act** (42 U.S.C. §300f), which provides for the EPA to establish national standards for contaminant levels in drinking water. The states are primarily responsible for enforcement and can have higher standards than the federal standards, but they must at least enforce the federal standards for their drinking water systems.

Review the Oil Pollution Act:
http://www.law.cornell.edu/ uscode/33/ch40.html

In 1990, Congress passed the **Oil Pollution Act** (OPA; 33 U.S.C. §1251). The act was passed in response to large oil tanker spills, such as the one resulting from the grounding of the *Exxon Valdez* in Prince William Sound, Alaska, that resulted in a spill of 11 million gallons of crude oil that coated 1,000 miles of Alaskan coastline. Another example was the 1990 explosion aboard the *Mega Borg* in Galveston Bay that resulted in a 4-million-gallon spill and a fire that burned for more than a week.

FOR THE MANAGER'S DESK

RE: THE *EXXON VALDEZ*

On March 24, 1989, the oil tanker *Exxon Valdez* ran aground on Bligh Reef, south of Valdez, Alaska, and spilled approximately 10.8 million gallons of oil into Prince William Sound. The captain of the tanker was Joseph Hazelwood.

Captain Hazelwood had a history of drinking problems and had lost his New York driver's license after two drunk-driving convictions. In 1985, with the knowledge of Exxon officials, Captain Hazelwood joined a twenty-eight-day alcohol rehabilitation program. Almost a week after the Prince William Sound accident, Exxon revealed that Captain Hazelwood's blood-alcohol reading was 0.061 in a test taken 10½ hours after the spill occurred. When announcing the test results, Exxon also announced Captain Hazelwood's termination.

The U.S. Interior Secretary at the time, Manual Lujan, called the spill the oil industry's "Three Mile Island." After ten days, the spill covered 1,000 square miles and leaked out of Prince William Sound onto beaches along the Gulf of Alaska and Cook Inlet. A cleanup army of 12,000 people was sent in with hot water and oil-eating microbes. The workers found more than 1,000 dead otters among a local otter population of 15,000 to 22,000. Approximately 34,400 sea birds died, as did 151 bald eagles that ate the oil-infested remains of the sea birds.

Captain Hazelwood was indicted by the state of Alaska on several charges, including criminal mischief, operating a watercraft while intoxicated, reckless endangerment, and negligent discharge of oil. He was found innocent of all charges except the negligent discharge of oil, was fined $50,000, and was required to spend 1,000 hours helping in the cleanup of the Alaskan beaches.

Following the spill, critics of Exxon maintained that the company's huge personnel cutbacks during the 1980s affected the safety and maintenance levels aboard the tankers. Subsequent hearings revealed that the crew of the *Valdez* was overburdened with demands of speed and efficiency. The crew was working ten- to twelve-hour days and often had interrupted sleep. Lookouts were often improperly posted, and junior officers were permitted control on the bridge without the required supervision. Robert LeResche, oil-spill coordinator for the state of Alaska, said, "It wasn't Captain Ahab on the bridge. It was Larry and Curly in the Exxon boardroom." In response to Exxon's critics, then-CEO Lawrence Rawl stated, "And we say, 'We're sorry, and we're doing all we can.' There were 30 million birds that went through the sound last summer, and only 30,000 carcasses have been recovered. Just look at how many ducks were killed in the Mississippi Delta in one hunting day in December! People have come up to me and said, 'This is worse than Bhopal.' I say, 'Hell, Bhopal killed more than 3,000 people and injured 200,000 others!' Then they say, 'Well, if you leave the people out, it was worse than Bhopal.'"

Late in February 1990, Exxon was indicted by a grand jury in Anchorage on federal felony charges of violations of maritime safety and antipollution laws. The charges were brought after negotiations between Exxon and the Justice Department had been terminated. Both the state of Alaska and the Justice Department also brought civil suits against Exxon for the costs associated with cleaning up the spill.

By May 1990, Exxon had resumed its cleanup efforts, using 110 employees at targeted sites. In 1991, Exxon reached plea agreements with the federal government and the state of Alaska on the criminal charges. In the agreements, Exxon consented to plead guilty to three misdemeanors and pay a $1.15 billion fine.

At the end of 1991, an Alaska jury awarded sixteen fishermen more than $2.5 million in damages and established a payout formula for similar plaintiffs in future litigation against Exxon. The jury awarded $5 billion in punitive damages, the largest verdict in history, but the Ninth Circuit called the award excessive in 2001 and remanded the case for a redetermination of the damages.

Eight hundred other civil cases remained pending at the time of the verdict.

Upon remand, the federal district judge reduced the verdict to $4 billion. Upon appeal, the Ninth Circuit again determined that the award was excessive and sent the case back to the federal district court. The $4 billion award was changed to $4.5 billion by the federal district judge, and the case remains on appeal, again, at the Ninth Circuit.

As part of amendments to the Oil Pollution Act of 1990, Congress banned the *Valdez* from ever sailing into Prince William Sound again. The *Valdez* is not named in the act specifically, but the language of the statute is as follows:

> *Notwithstanding any other law, tank vessels that have spilled more than 1,000,000 gallons of oil into the marine environment after March 22, 1989, are prohibited from operating on the navigable waters of Prince William Sound, Alaska.*

(33 U.S.C.A. § 2737)

What was Exxon's "attitude" with regard to the spill? What was the company's purpose in cutting back on staff and maintenance expenditures? Was Captain Hazelwood morally responsible for the spill? Was Exxon management morally responsible for the spill?

View a letter from Judge Holland, the judge in the Exxon case, to a student regarding the Exxon litigation and the rights of the parties. Go to http://www.exxonmobil.com/corporate/files/corporate/letterholland.pdf to download the judge's letter as a PDF file.

The OPA applies to all navigable waters up to 200 miles offshore and places the federal government in charge of all oil spills. Once full liability for cleanup is imposed on the company responsible for the spill, the federal government may step in and clean up a spill and then demand compensation for the costs incurred. The Oil Spill Liability Trust Fund, established by a five-cent-per-barrel tax, covers cleanup costs when the party responsible is financially unable to do the cleanup.

Those responsible for spills are liable for penalties of $25,000 per day or $1,000 per barrel spilled. If the spill is the result of negligence or willful misconduct, the penalties are $3,000 per barrel spilled. Failure to report a spill can bring a $250,000 fine for an individual (sole proprietor or officer, according to agency and criminal liability principles) and up to five years imprisonment or $1 million for a corporation. Civil penalties run higher and include the full cost of cleanup (up to $50 million) should those responsible not clean up the oil spill.

FOR THE MANAGER'S DESK

RE: WAS EXXON RIGHT TO LET THE SPILL SELF-CORRECT?

Questions about oil spills and the role of Exxon in the *Valdez* spill in 1991 arose again in 2002 as the oil tanker *Prestige* sank off the coast of Arteixo, Spain. In dealing with the 85,000-ton spill (the *Exxon Valdez* spilled 250,000 tons), officials have been using the usual methods such as straw foam but have discovered that the treatment seems to make the spill worse, gumming the oil and causing more damage to the water, fowl, flora, and fauna. Many experts are now wondering whether the best approach may not be one advocated by Exxon at the time of the *Valdez* spill, which was to let Mother Nature take its course by absorbing the oil itself and performing its natural cleansing process.

The experts believe that there is some benefit to initial cleanup but that there comes a point when the cleanup efforts actually make things worse. The demand for immediate cleanup, particularly by fishers in the area, is great but may not be in the best interests of long-term recovery.

Source: Keith Johnson and Gautam Nair, "For Spain, *Exxon Valdez* Offers Some Surprising Lessons," *Wall Street Journal,* November 23, 2002, pp. B1, B4.

CHECK THE WEB

Check the book's Web site updates for new developments on the *Exxon Valdez* case and new issues related to oil transport and spills.

Solid Waste Disposal Regulation

Early Regulation

During the 1970s, two major toxic waste debacles resulted in a new federal regulatory scheme of toxic waste disposal. In 1978, "Love Canal," as it came to be called, made national news as 80,000 tons of hazardous waste were found in the ground in an area that was primarily residential and included an elementary school. Epidemiological studies of cancer and illness rates in the area led to the discovery and eventual cleanup. Also, in Sheppardsville, Kentucky, an area that came to be called "Valley of the Drums," 17,000 drums of hazardous waste leaked tons of chemicals into the ground and water supply before their removal.

The emotional reaction to these two problem areas and the public outcry resulted in the passage of legislation that provided the federal government with some enforcement power for improper solid waste disposal. The **Toxic Substances Control Act** (TOSCA; 15 U.S.C. § 601) was passed in 1976 and authorized the EPA to control the manufacture, use, and disposal of toxic substances. Under the act, the EPA is authorized to prevent the manufacture of dangerous substances and stop the manufacture of substances subsequently found to be dangerous.

Also passed by Congress in reaction to dangerous dumping practices was the **Resource Conservation and Recovery Act of 1976** (RCRA; 42 U.S.C. § 6901). The two goals of the act are to control the disposal of potentially harmful substances and to encourage resource conservation and recovery. A critical part of the act's control is a manifest or permit system that requires manufacturers to obtain a permit for the storage or transfer of hazardous wastes so that the location of such wastes can be traced through an examination of the permits issued.

The Superfund

In 1980, Congress passed the **Comprehensive Environmental Response, Compensation, and Liability Act** (CERCLA; 42 U.S.C. § 9601), which authorized the president to issue funds for the cleanup of areas that were once disposal sites for hazardous wastes. Under the act, a **Hazardous Substance Response Trust Fund** was set up to provide funding for cleanup. If funds are expended in such a cleanup, then, under the provisions of the act, the company responsible for the disposal of the hazardous wastes can be sued by the federal government and required to repay the amounts expended from the trust fund. Often called the **Superfund**, the funds are available for governmental use but cannot be obtained through suit by private citizens affected by the hazardous disposals.

In 1986, CERCLA was amended by the **Superfund Amendment and Reauthorization Act**. Under the amendments in that act, liability provisions were included, and the EPA is now permitted to recover cleanup funds from those responsible for the release of hazardous substances. Approximately 700 hazardous substances are now covered. (They are listed at 40 C.F.R. § 302.) Since the passage of the 1986 amendments, there has been judicial expansion of the concept of "responsibility." Clearly, those who release the substances are liable, but that liability has been expanded to include those who purchase the property and did not perform adequate checks on the property's history.

CERCLA Lender Liability   One of the more intriguing issues that resulted from CERCLA liability was whether a lender has the responsibility of cleanup because it was back in possession of the property due to a foreclosure sale or a deed in lieu of foreclosure. In *U.S. v. Fleet Factors Corp.*, 901 F.2d 1550 (11th Cir. 1990), the court held

Review the Toxic Substances Control Act:

http://www.law.cornell.edu/
uscode/15/ch53.html

Review the Resource Conservation and Recovery Act of 1976:

http://www.law.cornell.edu/
uscode/42/ch82.html

Review the Comprehensive Environmental Response, Compensation, and Liability Act and Amendments:

http://www.law.cornell.edu/
uscode/42/ch103.html

For Superfund information, try:

http://www.monitor.net/
monitor/free/luftcleanup.
html
or
http://www.epa.gov/
superfund/index.htm

For an industry view of CERCLA, go to:

http://www.chemalliance.
org/Handbook/background/
back-cercla.asp

that a lender could be held responsible and liable for the cleanup of real property it finds itself holding due to a loan default. The finding of the court appeared to create great liability for lenders when they did not have control over the conduct of the mortgagor prior to their repossession or foreclosure. The result was that the EPA promulgated rules on lender liability in 1992. However, the rules did not provide lenders with sufficient guidelines for managing property obtained through default or foreclosure. To clarify liability issues, Congress passed the **Asset Conservation, Lender Liability, and Deposit Insurance Protection Act of 1996**. This statute provides a specific exclusion for lenders in that the definition of "owner/operator" does not include someone who "holds indicia of ownership primarily to protect his security interest." This new provision has been labeled the "secured lender exemption" from CERCLA liability. However, the new act does provide that a lender can lose its status if it "actually participate[s] in the management or operational affairs of a vessel or facility." But, the "capacity" to assert control does not result in lender liability as the *Fleet Factors* case held. A lender can do the following and still not be subject to environmental liability:

- Monitor or enforce terms of the security agreement
- Monitor or inspect the premises or facility
- Mandate that the debtor take action on hazardous materials
- Provide financial advice or counseling
- Restructure or renegotiate the loan terms
- Exercise any remedies available at law
- Foreclose on the property
- Sell the property
- Lease the property

ETHICAL ISSUES

Environmental concerns have prompted many voluntary actions within the U.S. business community. Consider the programs initiated by the following companies.

Amana: Initiated company-wide recycling program for newspapers, plastic jugs, and motor oil; proceeds donated to nonprofit environmental groups

Arco Chemical: Promotes the antifreeze agent propylene glycol over the more toxic ethylene glycol

AT&T: Publishes annual environmental report

Chevron: Publishes annual environmental report

Conoco: Ordered two double-hulled tankers and plans to add more to fleet

Du Pont: Will reduce air emissions on an ongoing basis and explore new technologies for doing so; publishes annual environmental report

General Mills: Requires use of recycled paper in all cereal boxes; banned use of metals in heavy printing ink

H. J. Heinz: Developed easy-to-recycle ketchup bottles; will not buy tuna caught with dolphins in nets

Herman Miller: Stopped using rainforest mahogany in Eames signature chair; gave employees mugs and stopped using Styrofoam cups

Johnson & Johnson: Eliminated use of Styrofoam cups in the workplace; started company-wide recycling program at employee desks

Kodak: Established camera recycling program

McDonald's: Shortened straws; uses recycled paper for napkins and trays

Polaroid: Publishes annual environmental report

Procter & Gamble: Is developing recycling of disposable diapers

Scott Paper: Sponsors tree-planting programs

Union Carbide: Will spend $310 million over four years on environmental and recycling programs; publishes annual environmental report

None of the programs initiated by these companies is mandated by law. Why are the companies taking such steps? Discuss the benefits each company derives from its programs. Do some of the benefits meet Milton Friedman's test for social responsibility (see Chapter 2)?

CERCLA—Four Classes of Liability Rules There are four classes of parties that can be held liable under CERCLA. The present owners and operators of a contaminated piece of property comprise one group. While *owner* is self-explanatory, *operator* includes those who lease property and then contaminate it, such as those who lease factories, operate storage facilities, and so forth. The owners and operators at the time the property was contaminated form the second group. This group brings under CERCLA jurisdiction those who were responsible for the property contamination, as opposed to present owners who had the problem deeded to them. For example, many gas stations have been converted to other businesses. Suppose that one of the underground gas tanks once used by the gas station has been leaking hazardous materials into the surrounding soil. Not only would the present owners be liable; so also would be all those who owned the gasoline station previously.

The final two groups consist of those who transport hazardous materials and those who arrange for the transportation of hazardous materials. There are virtually no liability exemptions for those who fit into these four groups. Further, it is important to understand that the liability exists under CERCLA for both corporations and corporate officers. For example, the EPA has been successful in criminal prosecutions against officers of corporations who have been ordered to conduct a cleanup but who failed to do so.

CERCLA and Corporate Liability CERCLA liability has also extended to corporate board members, successors, and officers in cases in which a company is purchased by another firm. Those who merge or buy corporations also buy into CERCLA liability—liability under CERCLA cannot be avoided by a transfer of ownership. The U.S. Supreme Court ruled in *U.S. v. Bestfoods,* 524 U.S. 51 (1998) that a parent corporation is not automatically liable under CERCLA for a subsidiary corporation's conduct but may be responsible if the subsidiary is simply a shell (see Chapter 21). In other words, CERCLA liability of parent corporations for the actions of their subsidiaries is governed by corporate law on piercing the corporate veil. Under the *Bestfoods* case, liability of the parent corporation for actions of a subsidiary results if any of the following are true.

1. The parent corporation operates the facility, is a joint venturer in the operation of the facility, or works side by side with the subsidiary in operations.

2. The parent and subsidiary corporations share officers and directors such that it becomes impossible to separate out the decision-making processes.

3. An officer of the parent corporation (or other designated or authorized employee) operates the facility of the subsidiary.[2]

CERCLA and Buying Land The best safeguard for lenders against CERCLA liability is screening the property carefully before accepting it as collateral. The lender's sale to another is not covered, and the lender is in the position of trying to sell property with a CERCLA problem. The value of the collateral is reduced substantially. The lender and any purchaser of a piece of property should conduct a *due diligence review* of the property. There are three phases in a due diligence review. Phase 1 consists of a search to determine whether there is evidence of past or current environmental problems on the property. Evidence reviewed in a Phase 1 search would be private and public records, aerial photographs, and a site inspection. If Phase 1 reveals some concerns, the parties proceed to Phase 2, which consists of chemical analysis of soil, structures, and water from the property. If Phase 2

CONSIDER... **1 2 . 4**

Grand Auto Parts Stores receives used automotive batteries from customers as trade-ins. Grand Auto drives a screwdriver through spent batteries and then sells them to Morris Kirk & Sons, a battery-cracking plant that extracts and smelts lead. Tons of crushed battery casings were found on Kirk's land. The EPA sought to hold Grand Auto liable for cleanup. Can Grand Auto be held liable? [*Catellus Dev. Corp.* v. *United States,* 34 F.3d 748 (9th Cir. 1994).]

finds the presence of contaminants, the report for Phase 2 estimates the cost of cleanup. Phase 3 is the actual cleanup plan.

New Developments under CERCLA

Judicial Developments   One issue that courts continue to face with respect to CERCLA cleanup efforts is whether insurance policies for comprehensive general liability apply to a company's cost of cleanup. The wording of individual policies and intent of the parties are controlling in these cases.

Other issues within CERCLA are developing in various types of CERCLA cases. One federal district court declared CERCLA unconstitutional for its retroactive effect (*U.S.* v. *Olin Corp.,* 927 F.Supp. 1502 S.D. Ala. 1996)), but it was reversed [*U.S.* v. *Olin Corp.,* 107 F.3d 1506 (11th Cir. 1997)]. Other courts have begun to examine the issue of causation between the contaminants present on a piece of property and its relation to any injury as a means of a cost-benefit analysis. For example, in *Licciardi* v. *Murphy Oil U.S.A.,* 111 F.3d 396 (5th Cir. 1997), one federal circuit court held that some causation must be established between the cleanup and what the owner or operator is alleged to have dumped at the site. However, not all the federal circuit courts have followed that line of reasoning in their decisions [*Johnson* v. *James Langley Operation Co., Inc.,* 226 F.3d 957 (8th Cir. 2000)].

Another basis for CERCLA challenges has been one grounded in the basic administrative law principle of an arbitrary and capricious challenge to an EPA demand for cleanup of a site when the demand for cleanup is not linked to any danger. The EPA order for cleanup was upheld in *U.S.* v. *Broderick Investment Co.,* 200 F.3d 679 (10th Cir. 1999), despite the cleanup being very costly, because the EPA ordered a cleanup to the point that the cancer rate in the area would be reduced to one in 100,000, a rate higher than in non-Superfund sites. However, because a day-care center was planned for the land, the court held that the cleanup level was not arbitrary or capricious.

> **BUSINESS PLANNING TIP**
>
> Due diligence is necessary not only when buying property but also when buying companies with land holdings. Liability under CERCLA is transferred via land ownership or corporate ownership.

These types of challenges to CERCLA, including causation and the application of administrative law, including challenges on the basis of arbitrary and capricious action, represent the first constraints on EPA actions regarding solid waste cleanup.

The Self-Audit   Companies have been responding to CERCLA liability with voluntary disclosures through the EPA's self-audit procedures. The EPA encourages companies to self-identify problem lands and areas in exchange for reduced fines. Companies have hired executive-level managers such as vice presidents for environment or vice presidents for health, safety, and environment to manage a staff of in-house professionals who do everything from supervising a company's current activities to investigating past activities to determine environmental problems. These problems are then reported to the EPA, and the company and agency work together to solve the problem and be certain cleanup is done where warranted. These self-audits and disclosures also help the companies be more accurate in their disclosures to shareholders and analysts. "The In-House Investigation and the EPA" gives background on the requirements for self-audits.

FOR THE MANAGER'S DESK

RE: THE IN-HOUSE INVESTIGATION AND THE EPA

In 1997, the EPA initiated 562 criminal investigations and referred 256 cases to the U.S. Justice Department for criminal prosecution. Both environmental investigations and referrals for prosecutions under federal law have been increasing each year. The criminal investigation staff for the EPA has grown from 150 in 1996 to 200 in 1997.

The definition of criminal intent or *mens rea* (see Chapter 9) required for prosecution of environmental crimes is quite broad, and even the barest degree of knowledge can result in the imposition of liability for corporate officers. Those who should have known and could have prevented environmental violations are held accountable, even though they may not have had complete knowledge about a problem.

This potential level of liability has created an atmosphere of self-investigation and self-reporting among corporations, in-house legal counsel, and officers designated as environmental officers. Concerns developed about privilege issues and self-incrimination as the companies, employees, and officers tried to determine whether there have been any violations within companies.

To encourage self-reporting and self-investigation, the EPA developed a policy on recommending *against* criminal prosecutions. Companies complying with the steps provided in the policy enjoy some guarantee that the officers and companies will not be prosecuted criminally. These steps include the following.

1. The company must fully cooperate with the EPA, including turning over to EPA officials all information and materials from the investigation, audit, or due diligence studies that led to the discovery of the criminal violation.

2. The reported violation must have come from the company's own self-discovery processes, and it must not be reported because of another's discovery or threat of disclosure.

3. The voluntary disclosure must be made before the EPA has launched a criminal investigation.

4. The voluntary disclosure must be made before the EPA—while not having yet opened an investigation—is talking with citizens, whistle-blowers, or others about potential violations.

5. The voluntary disclosure must be made in a timely fashion (generally ten days from the time of discovery).

6. The company making the voluntary disclosure must remedy the problem within sixty days and provide verification of such closure or, if additional time is needed, make a request with accompanying justification for extended time.

7. The company must agree to take whatever steps are necessary to prevent a recurrence.

8. The reported violation must not be a repeat of previous conduct.

Decisions on criminal prosecution under environmental statutes will be made by a Voluntary Disclosure Board comprised of employees from both the EPA and the Department of Justice.

Source: Adapted from an in-house memo from Earl Devaney, director of the EPA's Office of Criminal Enforcement, Forensics, and Training.

 CHECK THE WEB

Check the book's Web site updates for new approaches to environmental management by companies.

ETHICAL ISSUES

The following chart is a summary of environmental issues in various industries, the solutions companies developed, and the resulting benefits from the changes made pursuant to environmental regulation.

What stakeholders benefit from these types of environmentally motivated production changes? Were benefits to the environment the same as benefits to the shareholders? Should companies consider innovation in environmental modifications beyond just what the law requires? Why or why not?

SECTOR/ INDUSTRY	ENVIRONMENTAL ISSUES	INNOVATIVE SOLUTIONS	INNOVATION OFFSETS
Pulp and paper	Dioxin released by bleaching with chlorine	Improved cooking and washing processes Elimination of chlorine by using oxygen, ozone, or peroxide for bleaching Closed-loop processes (still problematic)	Lower operating costs through greater use of by-product energy sources 25% initial price premium for chlorine-free paper
Paint and coatings	Volatile organic compounds (VOCs) in solvents	New paint formulations (low-solvent-content paints, water-borne paints) Improved application techniques Powder or radiation-cured coatings	Price premium for solvent-free paints Improved coatings quality in some segments Worker safety benefits Higher coatings-transfer efficiency Reduced coating costs through materials savings
Electronics manufacturing	Volatile organic compounds (VOCs) in cleaning agents	Semiaqueous, terpene-based cleaning agents Closed-loop systems No-clean soldering where possible	Increase in cleaning quality and thus in product quality 30% to 80% reduction in cleaning costs, often for one-year payback periods Elimination of an unnecessary production step
Refrigerators	Chlorofluorocarbons (CFCs) used as refrigerants Energy usage Disposal	Alternative refrigerants (propane-isobutane mix) Thicker insulation Better gaskets Improved compressors	10% better energy efficiency at same cost 5% to 10% initial price premium for "green" refrigerator
Dry cell batteries	Cadmium, mercury, lead, nickel, cobalt, lithium, and zinc released in landfills or to the air (after incineration)	Rechargeable batteries of nickel-hydride (for some applications) Rechargeable lithium batteries (now developed)	Nearly twice as efficient at same cost Higher energy efficiency Expected to be price competitive in the near future
Printing inks	VOCs in petroleum inks	Water-based inks and soy inks	Higher efficiency, brighter colors, and better printability (depending on application)

BUSINESS STRATEGY APPLICATION

Be sure to do the exercise for this chapter provided on the book's Web site. You can see the policies and practices of companies with regard to environmental issues.

Environmental Quality Regulation

Review the National Environmental Policy Act:
http://www.law.cornell.edu/uscode/42/ch55.html

Environmental controls of air, water, and waste are directed at private parties in the use of their land. However, as part of the environmental control scheme, Congress also passed an act that regulates what governmental entities can do in the use of their properties. The **National Environmental Policy Act** (NEPA) of 1969 (42 U.S.C. § 4321) was passed to require federal agencies to take into account the environmental impact of their proposed actions and to prepare an **environmental impact statement** (EIS) before taking any proposed action.

An EIS must be prepared and filed with the EPA whenever an agency sends a proposed law to Congress and whenever an agency will take major federal action significantly affecting the quality of the environment. The information required in an EIS is as follows:

1. The proposed action's environmental impact
2. Adverse environmental effects (if any)
3. Alternative methods
4. Short-term effects versus long-term maintenance, enhancement, and productivity
5. Irreversible and irretrievable resource uses

Examples of federal agency actions that have faced the issue of preparation of EISs include the Alaskan oil pipeline, the extermination of wild horses on federal lands, the construction of government buildings, the NAFTA treaty, and highway construction.

Sierra Club v. *United States Dep't of Transportation* (Case 12.2) involves the question of whether an EIS was needed.

CASE 12.2

Sierra Club v. *United States Dep't of Transportation*
753 F.2d 120 (D.C. 1985)

Skiing and Landing at Jackson Hole

FACTS

In 1983, the Federal Aviation Administration (FAA) issued two orders amending the operations specifications for Frontier Airlines, Inc., and Western Airlines, Inc. These amendments gave the airlines permanent authorizations to operate Boeing 737 jet airplanes (B-737s) out of Jackson Hole Airport, which is located within the Grand Teton National Park in Wyoming. These two airlines are the only major commercial carriers that schedule flights to and from Jackson Hole.

Private jets have flown into the airport since 1960, and Western Airlines has been flying into Jackson Hole since 1941. The airport is the only one in the country located in a national park, and Congress has continually funded expansions and improvements of the once single-dirt-runway airport.

In 1978, Frontier applied for permission to fly B-737s into the Jackson Hole Airport. The FAA released its EIS on the application in 1980, which found that B-737s were comparable with C-580 propeller aircraft (the type then being used by Western and Frontier) for noise intrusion but were substantially quieter than the private jets using the airport. The study also showed that fewer flights would be necessary because the B-737 could carry more passengers and that different flight paths could reduce noise. Based on this EIS, Frontier was given the right to use B-737s for two years. When Frontier applied for permanent approval, the FAA used the 1980 EIS and found that with flight time restrictions, the impact would not harm the environment.

Following FAA orders allowing the runway expansion, the Sierra Club (petitioner), a national conservation organization, brought suit for the FAA's failure to file an EIS for the 1983 amendments and for the use of national park facilities for commercial air traffic without considering alternatives. (Because this is an appeal of an administrative agency's order, the case goes directly to the federal appellate level.)

JUDICIAL OPINION

BORK, Circuit Judge

We do not think the FAA violated NEPA by failing to prepare an additional EIS. Under NEPA, an EIS must be prepared before approval of any major federal action that will "significantly affect the quality of the human environment." The purpose of the Act is to require agencies to consider environmental issues before taking any major action. Under the statute, agencies have the initial and primary responsibility to determine the extent of the impact and whether it is significant enough to warrant preparation of an EIS. This is accomplished by preparing an Environmental Assessment (EA). An EA allows the agency to consider environmental concerns, while reserving agency resources to prepare full EIS's for appropriate cases. If a finding of no significant impact is made after analyzing the EA, then preparation of an EIS is unnecessary. An agency has broad discretion in making this determination, and the decision is reviewable only if it was arbitrary, capricious or an abuse of discretion.

This court has established four criteria for reviewing an agency's decision to forego preparation of an EIS. First, the agency must have accurately identified the relevant environmental concern. Second, once the agency has identified the problem, it must take a "hard look" at the problem in preparing the EA. Third, if a finding of no significant impact is made, the agency must be able to make a convincing case for its finding. Last, if the agency does find an impact of true significance, preparation of an EIS can be avoided only if the agency finds that changes or safeguards in the project sufficiently reduce the impact to a minimum.

The first test is not at issue here. Both the FAA and Sierra Club have identified the relevant environmental concern as noise by jet aircraft within Grand Teton National Park. The real issues raised by Sierra Club are whether the FAA took a "hard look" at the problem, and whether the methodology used by the agency in its alleged hard look was proper.

We find that the FAA did take a hard look at the problem. The FAA properly prepared an EA to examine the additional impact on the environment of the plan. The EA went forward from the 1980 EIS. The 1980 EIS, which was based on extensive research by Dr. Hakes of the University of Wyoming, noise testing by the FAA, and data derived from manufacturer information, showed that noise intrusions of B-737 jets over the level caused by C-580 propeller aircraft amounted to only 1 dbl near the Airport and decreased in proportion to the distance from the Airport. The agency, exercising its expertise, has found that an increase this minute is not significant for any environment. In addition, the EIS and Hakes studies were based on a worst case scenario, and it was determined that if certain precautions were taken the actual noise levels could be diminished greatly.

Petitioner argues that because Jackson Hole Airport is located within national parkland a different standard—i.e., individual event noise level analysis—is mandated. Both individual event and cumulative data were amassed in preparing the 1980 EIS on which the EAs were based. The fact that the agency in exercising its expertise relied on the cumulative impact levels as being more indicative of the actual environmental disturbance is well within the area of discretion given to the agency. We agree with petitioner that although noise is a problem in any setting, "airplane noise is fundamentally inconsistent with the type of recreational experience Park visitors are seeking" and should be minimized. Here the FAA found that a cumulative noise increase of 1 dbl or less is not significant—even for the pristine environment in which Jackson Hole Airport is located.

Given all of these facts, we think the FAA was not required to prepare yet another EIS before granting permanent authorizations for the use of B-737s.

The orders of the FAA are hereby affirmed.

CASE QUESTIONS

1. What airport noise is at issue?
2. Who is involved in the case?
3. Was an EIS prepared?
4. What is the basis for the appeal?
5. What has the FAA allowed? Will the authorizations stand?

Other Federal Environmental Regulations

In addition to the previously discussed major environmental laws, many other specific federal statutes protect the environment.

Surface Mining

The **Surface Mining and Reclamation Act of 1977** (42 U.S.C. § 6907) requires those mining coal to restore land surfaces to their original conditions and prohibits surface coal mining without a permit.

Noise Control

Under the **Noise Control Act of 1972** (42 U.S.C. § 4901), the EPA, along with the FAA, can control the amount of noise emissions from low-flying aircraft for the protection of landowners in flight paths.

Pesticide Control

Review an environmental group's pesticide Web site:
http://www.beyondpesticides.org

Under the **Federal Environmental Pesticide Control Act**, the use of pesticides is controlled. All pesticides must be registered with the EPA before they can be sold, shipped, distributed, or received. Also under the act, the EPA administrator is given the authority to classify pesticides according to their effects and dangers.

Review the Environmental Pesticide Control Act:
http://www.law.cornell.edu/uscode/7/ch6.html

OSHA

The **Occupational Safety and Health Administration** (OSHA) is responsible for workers' environments. OSHA controls the levels of exposure to toxic substances and requires safety precautions for exposure to such dangerous substances as asbestos, benzene, and chloride.

Asbestos

Review the Asbestos Hazard Emergency Response Act:
http://www.law.cornell.edu/uscode/15/2641.html

Buildings that contain asbestos materials remain a problem for buyers, sellers, and occupants. The **Asbestos Hazard Emergency Response Act** (AHERA), passed in 1986, required all public and private schools to arrange for the inspection of their facilities to determine whether their buildings had asbestos-containing materials. Schools are required to develop plans for containment, but other buildings are not regulated. The Clean Air Act does, however, define airborne asbestos as a toxic pollutant, and liability may result from the release of fibers from this known carcinogen. Further, an amendment to the Superfund Act classified asbestos as a **community-right-to-know substance**, which means that there is probably a duty to disclose the presence of asbestos to buyers, tenants, and employees. Numerous ethical questions arise with respect to the presence of asbestos and the obligations of landowners to replace the asbestos given that the phaseout of its use did not end until 1997. Questions such as the impact of the release of asbestos from the walls when tenants, employees, and others hang photos and other objects by nailing them into the walls remain. The issues of the degree of harm and the cost of replacement continue to be debated among property owners.

Endangered Species

Review the Endangered Species Act:
http://www.law.cornell.edu/uscode/22/2151q.html

In 1973, Congress passed the **Endangered Species Act** (ESA), a law that has been a powerful tool for environmentalists in protecting certain species through their advocacy of restrictions on commercial use and development when the habitats of certain species are interfered with. Under the act, the secretary of the interior is re-

For information on forests, see: http://forests.org

sponsible for identifying endangered terrestrial species, and the secretary of commerce identifies endangered marine species. In addition, these cabinet members must designate habitats considered crucial for these species if they are to thrive. In many instances, there is litigation concerning which species should or should not be on the list. Once a species is on the list, its critical habitat cannot be disturbed by development, noise, or destruction. *Babbitt* v. *Sweet Home Chapter of Communities for a Great Oregon* (Case 12.3) has given federal agencies broad authority in protecting endangered species.

CASE 12.3

Babbitt v. *Sweet Home Chapter of Communities for a Great Oregon*
515 U.S. 687 (1995)

Jobs versus Owls: Lumber versus Endangered Species

FACTS

Two U.S. agencies halted logging in the Pacific Northwest because it endangered the habitat of the northern spotted owl and the red-cockaded woodpecker, both endangered species. Sweet Home Chapter (respondents) is a group of landowners, logging companies, and families dependent on the forest products industries in the Pacific Northwest. They brought suit, seeking clarification of the authority of the secretary of the interior and the director of the Fish and Wildlife Service (petitioners) to include habitation modification as a harm covered by the ESA.

The federal district court found for the secretary and director and held that they had the authority to protect the northern spotted owl through a halt to logging. The court of appeals reversed. Bruce Babbitt, the secretary of the interior, appealed.

JUDICIAL OPINION

STEVENS, Justice

Section 9(a)(1) of the Endangered Species Act provides the following protection for endangered species:

Except as provided in sections 1535(g)(2) and 1539 of this title, with respect to any endangered species of fish or wildlife listed pursuant to section 1533 of this title it is unlawful for any person subject to the jurisdiction of the United States to—(B) take any such species within the United States or the territorial sea of the United States[.]

16 U.S.C. § 1538(a)(1).

Section 3(19) of the Act defines the statutory term "take":

The term 'take' means to harass, harm, pursue, hunt, shoot, wound, kill, trap, capture, or collect, or to attempt to engage in any such conduct.

16 U.S.C. § 1532(19).

The Act does not further define the terms it uses to define "take." The Interior Department regulations that implement the statute, however, define the statutory term "harm":

Harm in the definition of 'take' in the Act means an act which actually kills or injures wildlife. Such act may include significant habitat modification or degradation where it actually kills or injures wildlife by significantly impairing essential behavioral patterns, including breeding, feeding, or sheltering.

50 CFR § 17.3 (1994).

We assume respondents have no desire to harm either the red-cockaded woodpecker or the spotted owl; they merely wish to continue logging activities that would be entirely proper if not prohibited by the ESA. On the other hand, we must assume *arguendo* that those activities will have the effect, even though unintended, of detrimentally changing the natural habitat of both listed species and that, as a consequence, members of those species will be killed or injured. Under respondents' view of the law, the Secretary's only means of forestalling that grave result—even when the actor knows it is certain to occur—is to use his § 5 authority to purchase the lands on which the survival of the species depends. The Secretary, on the other hand, submits that the § 9 prohibition on takings, which Congress defined to include "harm," places on respondents a duty to avoid harm that habitat alteration will cause the birds unless respondents first obtain a permit pursuant to § 10.

The text of the Act provides three reasons for concluding that the Secretary's interpretation is reasonable. First, an ordinary understanding of the word "harm" supports it. The dictionary definition of the

continued

verb form of "harm" is "to cause hurt or damage to: injure." Webster's Third New International Dictionary 1034 (1966). In the context of the ESA, that definition naturally encompasses habitat modification that results in actual injury or death to members of an endangered or threatened species.

Respondents argue that the Secretary should have limited the purview of "harm" to direct applications of force against protected species, but the dictionary definition does not include the word "directly" or suggest in any way that only direct or willful action that leads to injury constitutes "harm." Moreover, unless the statutory term "harm" encompasses indirect as well as direct injuries, the word has no meaning that does not duplicate the meaning of other words that § 3 uses to define "take." A reluctance to treat statutory terms as surplusage supports the reasonableness of the Secretary's interpretation.

Second, the broad purpose of the ESA supports the Secretary's decision to extend protection against activities that cause the precise harms Congress enacted the statute to avoid. As stated in § 2 of the Act, among its central purposes is "to provide a means whereby the ecosystems upon which endangered species and threatened species depend may be conserved."

Third, the fact that Congress in 1982 authorized the Secretary to issue permits for takings that § 9(a)(1)(B) would otherwise prohibit, "if such taking is incidental to, and not the purpose of, the carrying out of an otherwise lawful activity," 16 U.S.C. § 1539(a)(1)(B), strongly suggests that Congress understood § 9(a)(1)(B) to prohibit indirect as well as deliberate takings. The permit process requires the applicant to prepare a "conservation plan" that specifies how he intends to "minimize and mitigate" the "impact" of his activity on endangered and threatened species, 16 U.S.C. § 1539(a)(2)(A), making clear that Congress had in mind foreseeable rather than merely accidental effects on listed species.

The Court of Appeals made three errors in asserting that "harm" must refer to a direct application of force because the words around it do. First, the court's premise was flawed. Several of the words that accompany "harm" in the § 3 definition of "take," especially "harass," "pursue," "wound," and "kill," refer to actions or effects that do not require direct applications of force. Second, to the extent the court read a requirement of intent or purpose into the words used to define "take," it ignored § 9's express provision that a "knowing" action is enough to violate the Act. Third, the court employed *noscitur a sociis* to give "harm" essentially the same function as other words in the definition, thereby denying it independent meaning. The canon, to the contrary, counsels that a word "gathers meaning from the words around it." The statutory context of "harm" suggests that Congress meant that term to serve a particular function in the ESA, consistent with but distinct from the functions of the other verbs used to define "take." The Secretary's interpretation of "harm" to include indirectly injuring endangered animals through habitat modification permissibly interprets "harm" to have "a character of its own not to be submerged by its association."

When it enacted the ESA, Congress delegated broad administrative and interpretive power to the Secretary. See 16 U.S.C. §§ 1533, 1540(f). The task of defining and listing endangered and threatened species requires an expertise and attention to detail that exceeds the normal province of Congress. Fashioning appropriate standards for issuing permits under § 10 for takings that would otherwise violate § 9 necessarily requires the exercise of broad discretion. The proper interpretation of a term such as "harm" involves a complex policy choice. When Congress has entrusted the Secretary with broad discretion, we are especially reluctant to substitute our views of wise policy for his. In this case, that reluctance accords with our conclusion, based on the text, structure, and legislative history of the ESA, that the Secretary reasonably construed the intent of Congress when he defined "harm" to include "significant habitat modification or degradation that actually kills or injures wildlife."

In the elaboration and enforcement of the ESA, the Secretary and all persons who must comply with the law will confront difficult questions of proximity and degree; for, as all recognize, the Act encompasses a vast range of economic and social enterprises and endeavors. These questions must be addressed in the usual course of the law, through case-by-case resolution and adjudication.

The judgment of the Court of Appeals is reversed.

CASE QUESTIONS

1. Is habitat modification harming endangered species?
2. Does the Court's interpretation mean no intent is required to violate ESA?
3. Did Congress intend to give the secretary authority to shut down an industry?
4. Is logging prevented now?
5. What ethical issues arise from this case?

Aftermath: In August 1995, Congress passed, as a rider to a budget-reduction bill, a provision that suspended environmental laws in some national forest areas in Washington and Oregon through 1996.

Since the time of these head-on confrontations, the logging and paper industries have adopted a Sustainable Forestry Initiative. The Initiative, adopted by 200 members of the American Forest and Paper Association, supports ecofriendly logging. The Nature Conservancy supports the initiative, which has had the effect of negotiated solutions to the issue of logging versus environmental protection. No further legislation has been needed at the federal level because of the cooperation among these groups.

In *Bennett* v. *Spear* (Case 12.4), the U.S. Supreme Court interpreted the ESA as also permitting lawsuits by landowners affected by the statute's application. The case provides the answer to the chapter's opening Consider.

CASE 12.4

Bennett v. *Spear*
520 U.S. 154 (1997)

Falling for the Lost River Sucker: Ranchers, ESA, and Water Levels

FACTS

The Fish and Wildlife Services issued an opinion on the operation of the Klamath Irrigation Project and the project's impact on two varieties of endangered fish. The Klamath Project, one of the oldest federal reclamation projects, is a series of lakes, rivers, dams, and irrigation canals in northern California and southern Oregon. The opinion concluded that the operation of the project might impact on the Lost River sucker (*Deltistes luxatus*) and shortnose sucker (*Chasmistes brevirostris*) species of fish that were listed as endangered in 1988. The opinion further provided for alternative means of operation for the project, including the maintenance of minimum water levels in certain portions of the project.

Brad Bennett and other ranchers (petitioners) operate their ranches within the areas designated to receive less water pursuant to the biological opinion issued. Mr. Bennett filed suit, alleging that the opinion was incorrect in its conclusions on the impact of the project on the two species of fish and that the opinion failed to take into account the resulting economic impact of lessening the water levels. Mr. Bennett's complaint alleged that the Endangered Species Act (ESA) and the Administrative Procedures Act (APA) required the federal government to take his interests into account in making the determination about what to do about the project. The federal district court dismissed the complaint, and the court of appeals affirmed the dismissal. Mr. Bennett appealed.

JUDICIAL OPINION

SCALIA, Justice
We first turn to the question the Court of Appeals found dispositive: whether petitioners lack standing by virtue of the zone-of-interests test. Although petitioners contend that their claims lie both under the ESA and the APA, we look first at the ESA because it may permit petitioners to recover their litigation costs, and because the APA by its terms independently authorizes review only when "there is no other adequate remedy in a court," 5 U.S.C. § 704.

The question of standing "involves both constitutional limitations on federal-court jurisdiction and prudential limitations on its exercise."

Numbered among these prudential requirements is the doctrine of particular concern in this case: that a plaintiff's grievance must arguably fall within the zone of interests protected or regulated by the statutory provision or constitutional guarantee invoked in the suit.

We have made clear, however, that the breadth of the zone of interests varies according to the provisions of law at issue, so that what comes within the zone of interests of a statute for purposes of obtaining judicial review of administrative action under the "generous review provisions" of the APA may not do so for other purposes.

The first question in the present case is whether the ESA's citizen-suit provision negates the zone-of-interests test (or, perhaps more accurately, expands the zone of interests). We think it does. The first operative portion of the provision says that "any person may commence a civil suit"—an authorization of remarkable breadth when compared with the language Congress ordinarily uses. Even in some other environmental statutes, Congress has used more restrictive formulations, such as "[any person] having an interest which is or may be adversely affected," or "any person having a valid legal

continued

interest which is or may be adversely affected . . . whenever such action constitutes a case or controversy." And in contexts other than the environment, Congress has often been even more restrictive. In statutes concerning unfair trade practices and other commercial matters, for example, it has authorized suit only by "[a]ny person injured in his business or property."

Our readiness to take the term "any person" at face value is greatly augmented by two interrelated considerations: that the overall subject matter of this legislation is the environment (a matter in which it is common to think all persons have an interest) and that the obvious purpose of the particular provision in question is to encourage enforcement by so-called "private attorneys general"—evidenced by its elimination of the usual amount-in-controversy and diversity-of-citizenship requirements, its provision for recovery of the costs of litigation (including even expert witness fees), and its reservation to the Government of a right for first refusal to pursue the action initially and a right to intervene later. Given these factors, we think the conclusion of expanded standing follows.

It is true that the plaintiffs here are seeking to prevent application of environmental restrictions rather than to implement them. But the "any person" formulation applies to all the causes of action authorized by § 1540(g)—not only to actions against private violators of environmental restrictions, and not only to actions against the Secretary asserting underenforcement under § 1533, but also to actions against the Secretary asserting overenforcement under § 1533. As we shall discuss below, the citizen-suit provision does favor environmentalists in that it covers all private violations of the Act but not all failures of the Secretary to meet his administrative responsibilities; but there is no textual basis for saying that its expansion of standing requirements applies to environmentalists alone. The Court of Appeals therefore erred in concluding that petitioners lacked standing under the zone-of-interests test to bring their claims under the ESA's citizen-suit provision.

By the Government's own account, while the Service's Biological Opinion theoretically serves an "advisory function," 51 Fed.Reg. 19928 (1986), in reality it has a powerful coercive effect on the action agency:

> The statutory scheme . . . presupposes that the biological opinion will play a central role in the action agency's decision-making process, and that it will typically be based on an administrative record that is fully adequate for the action agency's decision insofar as ESA issues are concerned. . . . [A] federal agency that chooses to deviate from the recommendations contained in a biological opinion bears the burden of "articulat[ing] in its administrative record its reason for disagreeing with the conclusions of a biological opinion."

51 Fed.Reg. 19, 956 (1986).

What this concession omits to say, moreover, is that the action agency must not only articulate its reasons for disagreement (which ordinarily requires species and habitat investigations that are not within the action agency's expertise), but that it runs a substantial risk if its (inexpert) reasons turn out to be wrong. A Biological Opinion of the sort rendered here alters the legal regime to which the action agency is subject. When it "offers reasonable and prudent alternatives" to the proposed action, a Biological Opinion must include a so-called "Incidental Take Statement"—a written statement specifying, among other things, those "measures that the [Service] considers necessary or appropriate to minimize [the action's impact on the affected species]" and the "terms and conditions . . . that must be complied with by the Federal agency . . . to implement [such] measures."

The Service itself is, to put it mildly, keenly aware of the virtually determinative effect of its biological opinions. The Incidental Take Statement at issue in the present case begins by instructing the reader that any taking of a listed species is prohibited unless "such taking is in compliance with this incidental take statement," and warning that "[t]he measures described below are nondiscretionary, and must be taken by [the Bureau]." Given all of this, and given petitioners' allegations that the Bureau had, until issuance of the Biological Opinion, operated the Klamath Project in the same manner throughout the twentieth century, it is not difficult to conclude that petitioners have met their burden—which is relatively modest at this state of the litigation—of alleging that their injury is "fairly traceable" to the Service's Biological Opinion and that it will "likely" be redressed—i.e., the Bureau will not impose such water level restrictions—if the Biological Opinion is set aside.

Whether a plaintiff's interest is "arguably . . . protected . . . by the statute" within the meaning of the zone-of-interests test is to be determined not by reference to the overall purpose of the Act in question (here, species preservation), but by reference to the particular provision of law upon which the plaintiff relies. It is difficult to understand how the Ninth Circuit could have failed to see this from our cases. As we said with the utmost clarity in *National Wildlife Federal*, "the plaintiff must establish that the injury he complains of . . . falls within the 'zone of interests' sought to be protected by the statutory provision whose violation forms the legal basis for his complaint."

The Court of Appeals erred in affirming the District Court's dismissal of petitioners' claims for lack of jurisdiction. Petitioners' complaint alleges facts sufficient to meet the requirements of Article III standing, and none of their ESA claims is precluded by the zone-of-interests test. Petitioners' § 1533 claim is reviewable under ESA's citizen-suit provision, and petitioners' remaining claims are reviewable under the APA.

The judgment of the Court of Appeals is reversed.

CASE QUESTIONS

1. Who has brought the suit, and why?

2. Can those affected by the protection of an endangered species bring suit under the ESA?

3. How does the court deal with the issue raised by the government that the opinion is only an opinion and not government action?

4. Do the ranchers have standing to challenge the endangered species protection under the ESA?

5. The court's opinion was unanimous. Do you agree that both sides in an environmental case, those representing the interests of the species and those representing economic interests, should have the right to challenge a finding by the federal government?

CONSIDER...   **1 2 . 5**

Arizona Cattle Growers' Association and Jeff Menges, a rancher seeking a grazing permit on the lands at issue (together called "ACGA"), sued the Fish and Wildlife Service and the Bureau of Land Management to challenge Incidental Take Statements (ITSs) issued by the Fish and Wildlife Service in a biological opinion for certain grazing lands. Mr. Menges sought livestock grazing permits for land within the area supervised by the Bureau of Land Management's Saffold and Tucson, Arizona, field offices, and the Association represented members who claimed to be harmed by the government action. The Bureau of Land Management's livestock grazing program for this area affects 288 separate grazing allotments that in total comprise nearly 1.6 million acres of land. The Fish and Wildlife Service's biological opinion, issued on September 26, 1997, analyzed twenty species of plants and animals and concluded that the livestock grazing program was not likely to jeopardize the continued existence of the species affected, nor was it likely to result in destruction or adverse modification of the designated or proposed critical habitat. The Fish and Wildlife Service did, however, issue ITSs for various species of fish and wildlife listed or proposed as endangered.

ACGA's suit challenged both the ITSs and their terms and conditions. The challenge was based on the fact that the razorback sucker and the cactus ferruginous pygmy-owl were in abundance and not endangered. The environmental groups challenged ACGA's right to challenge the conclusions of the agency. Who is correct?

THINK: The conclusion in the *Bennett* case was that those who sought to protect the species as well as those who were harmed by the protection had the right to challenge the agency's determination. Chapter 6 described the basis for challenging administrative agency actions, including that the action taken was not based on study and information but was arbitrary and capricious.

APPLY: The cattle growers here are the equivalent of Mr. Bennett in that case and therefore have standing to challenge the determination of endangered species status and the resulting impact on grazing lands. If the ACGA can show that the species are not endangered and challenge the factual findings of the agency, the rule can be set aside.

ANSWER: The federal district court found that the Fish and Wildlife Service's issuance of an ITS for both the razorback sucker and the pygmy-owl was arbitrary and capricious, reasoning that the Fish and Wildlife Service "failed to provide sufficient reason to believe that listed species exist in the allotments in question." [*Arizona Cattle Growers' Ass'n* v. *U.S. Fish and Wildlife, Bureau of Land Management,* 273 F.3d 1229 (9th Cir. 2001).]

Now apply your skills to Considers 12.6 and 12.7.

CONSIDER...   12.6

The Natural Resources Defense Council, Inc., the Humane Society of the United States, Cetacean Society International, League for Coastal Protection, Ocean Futures Society, and Jean-Michel Cousteau filed suit in federal district court to obtain a preliminary injunction against federal officials to prevent the United States Navy's peacetime use of a low-frequency sonar system for training, testing, and routine operations. This new technology, Surveillance Towed Array Sensor System (SURTASS) Low Frequency Active Sonar (LFA), sends out intense sonar pulses at low frequencies that travel hundreds of miles in order to timely detect increasingly quiet enemy submarines. Their complaint alleges that the National Marine Fisheries Service improperly approved use of SURTASS LFA in as much as 75 percent of the world's oceans in violation of the Marine Mammal Protection Act, the Endangered Species Act, the National Environmental Policy Act, and the Administrative Procedures Act. The complaint claims that these violations will cause irreparable injury by harassing, injuring, and killing marine mammals with sensitive hearing and other sea creatures, many of them rare and endangered, including whales, dolphins, seals, sea turtles, and salmon.

The Navy indicates that it is in full compliance with the law and that enjoining the peacetime use of LFA sonar would harm national security, even though the Navy would still be free to use it during wartime or periods of heightened threat, because training and testing are necessary for military readiness.

Do the groups and Mr. Cousteau have standing to challenge the Navy's work? Can the Navy's work be enjoined? [*Natural Resources Defense Council, Inc. v. Evans,* 232 F.Supp.2d 1003 (N.D. Cal. 2002).]

CONSIDER...   12.7

American Rivers, a national river conservation organization; Environmental Defense, a national conservation organization; National Wildlife Federation (NWF), a national conservation advocacy and education organization; state affiliates of NWF (Iowa Wildlife Federation, Kansas Wildlife Federation, Montana Wildlife Federation, Nebraska Wildlife Federation, North Dakota Wildlife Federation, and South Dakota Wildlife Federation); Izaak Walton League of America, a national conservation organization in Maryland; and a number of national and local environmental organizations brought suit against the U.S. Army Corps of Engineers, the Secretary of the Army, the U.S. Fish and Wildlife Service (FWS), and the Secretary of the Interior, seeking to protect the endangered least tern, the endangered pallid sturgeon, and the threatened Great Plains piping plover, all of which are protected by the ESA.

The groups allege that the manner in which the Corps has operated the extensive dam and reservoir system on the Missouri River and the manner in which the FWS has carried out its statutory responsibilities under the ESA have adversely impacted the three species. Do the groups have the right to assert the claim? What response can the government agencies offer? What should the court do? [*American Rivers* v. *U.S. Army Corps of Engineers,* 271 F.Supp.2d 230 (D.D.C. 2003).]

BUSINESS STRATEGY APPLICATION

The exercise for this chapter on the book's Web site gives you the chance to study the environmental, health, and safety policies of several companies and then develop such a policy for your company.

STATE ENVIRONMENTAL LAWS

In addition to federal enactments, all the states have enacted some form of environmental law and have established their own environmental policies and agencies. Some states may require new industrial businesses to obtain a state permit along with the required federal permits for the operation of their plants. Some states regulate the types of fuels that can be used in vehicles and offer incentives for carpooling.

All states have some form of regulation on hazardous waste, a sort of CERCLA statute at the state level. The statutes are creative in their fines and remedies. For example, Oregon imposes a fine for each animal destroyed as a result of hazardous waste dumping and the failure to clean up in a timely manner. The death of one mountain goat due to hazardous waste carries a $3,500 fine under the Oregon statute. Other states require property sellers to disclose to buyers the history of the property's use. The purpose of these disclosure statutes is to provide the buyer with a history of activity that will result in the Phase 1, Phase 2, and Phase 3 activities that might not occur to the buyer unless, for example, the buyer learned through the disclosure that the land was used at one time for chemical production or storage.

ENFORCEMENT OF ENVIRONMENTAL LAWS

Federal environmental laws can be enforced through criminal sanctions, penalties, injunctions, and suits by private citizens. In addition to federal enforcement rights, certain common-law remedies, such as nuisance or trespass, exist for the protection of property rights. This portion of the chapter discusses the various remedies available for environmental violations.

Parties Responsible for Enforcement

Although many federal agencies are involved with environmental issues, the EPA, established in 1970, is the agency responsible for the major environmental problems of air and water pollution, solid waste disposal, toxic substance management, and noise pollution. The EPA is responsible for the promulgation of specific standards and the enforcement of those standards with the use of the remedies discussed in the following subsections. The federal EPA may work in conjunction with state EPAs in the development and enforcement of state programs.

The **Council on Environmental Quality** (CEQ) was established in 1966 under the National Environment Act and is part of the executive branch of government. Its role in the environment regulatory scheme is that of policymaker. The CEQ is responsible for formulating national policies on the quality of the environment and then making recommendations to lawmakers regarding its policy statements.

In addition to these major environmental agencies, other federal agencies are involved in enforcement of environmental issues, such as the Atomic Energy Commission, the Federal Power Commission, the Department of Housing and Urban Development, the Department of the Interior, the Forest Service, the Bureau of Land Management, and the Department of Commerce. Basically, all federal agencies that deal with the use of land, water, and air are involved in compliance with and enforcement of environmental laws.

BIOGRAPHY

The EPA Administrators

1971–1973: William D. Ruckelshaus

Served as the first EPA administrator, appointed by Richard Nixon. Continued to serve under Gerald Ford and was responsible for the implementation of both the Clean Water Act and the Clean Air Act. By the time of his departure, the EPA had 9,077 employees.

1973–1977: Russell E. Train

Established close congressional relationships. Agency size ranged from 9,200 to 10,200 employees during his tenure.

1977–1981: Douglas M. Costle

The first EPA administrator under a Democratic president; appointed by Jimmy Carter. Saw the role of the EPA as that of a health agency. Often credited for the beginning of environmental activism. Responsible for the Superfund Amendments being passed in Congress. Agency grew to 11,000 employees. Budget of EPA went from $1 billion in 1971 to $5.4 billion in 1981.

1981–1983: Anne Burford Gorsuch

Appointed by Ronald Reagan. Questions arose about how effective the EPA had been in Superfund cleanup. Constitutional confrontation with Congress on executive privilege regarding documents relating to Superfund cleanups. Agency was reduced from 13,000 employees to 12,000.

1983–1985: William D. Ruckelshaus

Appointed by Ronald Reagan. His seasoned experience was required in order to restore the EPA's reputation following the Burford years. Pursued an asbestos-removal program in schools. Began global environmental relations and meetings. Agency grew to 13,000 employees.

1989–1993: William K. Reilly

Key figure in getting the Clean Air Act of 1990 through Congress. Issues with contractors and subcontractors in Superfund cleanups plagued his administration. Pushed for the 1992 Earth Summit in Rio de Janeiro. Agency grew to 17,000 employees during his tenure.

1993–2001: Carol M. Browner

Formerly head of Florida's environmental agency. Pushed "environmental justice." Implemented strictest air quality standards to date. Agency budget was increased to $7.5 billion and employees to 18,375 during her tenure.

2001–03: Christine Todd Whitman

Appointed by George W. Bush in early 2001; formerly the governor of New Jersey. Her first EPA budget was for $7.2 million. EPA employees at the end of 2001 were 18,050. Indicating that she had no one to talk to in Washington except her plants, Mrs. Whitman resigned as EPA director to return to her family and native New Jersey in 2003.

2003 to present: Michael Leavitt

Sworn in on November 6, 2003; formerly the governor of Utah. Achieved zero emissions during the Salt Lake City Winter 2002 Olympics as the environmental administrator for that event. The budget for the EPA for 2005 is $7.76 billion, and as of July 2004, the agency had 17,094 employees.

Criminal Sanctions for Violations

Most of the federal statutes previously discussed carry criminal sanctions for violations. Exhibit 12.1 summarizes the various penalties provided under each of the discussed acts. In exercising its enforcement power, the EPA may require businesses to maintain records or to install equipment necessary for monitoring the amounts of pollutants being released into the air or water.

United States v. *Johnson & Towers, Inc.* (Case 12.5) deals with the issue of criminal liability for environmental law violations.

EXHIBIT 12.1 Penalties for Violation of Federal Environmental Laws

ACT	PENALTIES	PRIVATE SUIT
Clean Air Act	$25,000 per day, up to one year imprisonment; fifteen years for willful or repeat violations; $10,000 rewards	Citizen suits; authorized EPA suit for injunctive relief
Clean Water Act	$25,000 per day, up to one year imprisonment, or both; $50,000/three years for violations with knowledge; $100,000/six years for subsequent violations	Citizen suits; authorized EPA suit for injunctive relief
Resource Conservation and Recovery Act (Solid Waste Disposal Act)	$250,000 and/or fifteen years for intentional; $1,000,000 for corps; $50,000 and/or five years for others	Citizen and negligence suits after EPA refuses to handle
Oil Pollution Act	$25,000 per day, or $1,000 per barrel; $3,000 per barrel if willful or negligent; $250,000 and/or five years for failure to report	Hazardous Substance/Response Trust Fund for cleanup; EPA suit for injunctive relief and reimbursement of trust funds; private actions in negligence

CASE 12.5

United States v. *Johnson & Towers, Inc.*
741 F.2d 662 (3d Cir. 1984)

Changing Your Oil: It Can Be Criminal

FACTS

Johnson & Towers (Johnson) repairs and overhauls large motor vehicles. In its operations, Johnson uses degreasers and other industrial chemicals that contain methylene chloride and trichlorethylene, classified as "hazardous wastes" under the Resource Conservation and Recovery Act (RCRA) and as pollutants under the Clean Water Act.

The waste chemicals from Johnson's cleaning operations were drained into a holding tank and, when the tank was full, pumped into a trench. The trench flowed from the plant's property into Parker's Creek, a tributary of the Delaware River. Under RCRA, generators of such wastes must obtain a permit from the EPA, but Johnson had not received or even applied for such a permit.

Jack Hopkins, a foreman, and Peter Angel (defendants) the service manager for Johnson, were charged with criminal violations of the RCRA and the Clean Water Act. Johnson was also charged and pled guilty. Mr. Hopkins and Mr. Angel pled not guilty on grounds that they were not "owners" or "operators" as required for RCRA violations. The trial court agreed and dis-

missed all charges against the two men except for the criminal conspiracy charges.

The government appealed the dismissal.

JUDICIAL OPINION

SLOVITER, Circuit Judge
The single issue in this appeal is whether the individual defendants are subject to prosecution under RCRA's criminal provision, which applies to:

> any person who— . . . (2) knowingly treats, stores, or disposes of any hazardous waste identified or listed under this subchapter either—(A) without having obtained a permit under Section 6925 of this title . . . or (B) in knowing violation of any material condition or requirement of such permit.

If we view the statutory language in its totality, the congressional plan becomes . . . apparent. First, "person" is defined in the statute as "an individual, trust, firm, joint stock company, corporation (including a government corporation), partnership, association, State, municipality, commission, political subdivision

continued

of a State, or any interstate body." Had Congress meant to take aim more narrowly, it could have used more narrow language. Second, under the plain language of the statute, the only explicit basis for exoneration is the existence of a permit covering the action. Nothing in the language of the statute suggests that we should infer another provision exonerating persons who knowingly treat, store or dispose of hazardous waste but are not owners or operators.

Finally, though the result may appear harsh, it is well established that criminal penalties attached to regulatory statutes intended to protect public health, in contrast to statutes based on common law crimes, are to be construed to effectuate the regulatory purpose.

In summary, we conclude that the individual defendants are "persons" within the RCRA, that all elements of that offense must be shown to have been knowing, but that such knowledge, including that of the permit requirement, may be inferred by the jury as to those individuals who hold the requisite responsible positions with the corporate defendant. For the foregoing reasons, we will reverse the district court's dismissal and we will remand for further proceedings consistent with this opinion.

CASE QUESTIONS

1. Who is charged with criminal violations?
2. What violations are charged?
3. What violations did the lower court dismiss?
4. Did Congress intend to prosecute corporate employees?
5. Does the appellate court reinstate the charges?
6. What proof is required to show violations by the "persons"?

Group Suits: The Effect of Environmentalists

In many circumstances, private suits have had the most effect either in terms of obtaining compliance with environmental regulations or in terms of abating existing nuisances affecting environmental quality. The reason for the success of these suits may be the ultimate outcome of the litigation—possible business shutdowns and, at the least, the payment of tremendous amounts of damages and costs.

Private suits have been brought by environmental groups that have both the organizational structure and sufficient funding to initiate and complete such suits. In some cases, environmental groups are formed to protest one specific action, as is the case of Citizens Against the Squaw Peak Parkway; other groups are national organizations that take on environmental issues and litigation in all parts of the country. Examples of these national groups include the Sierra Club, the Environmental Defense Fund, Inc., the National Resources Defense Council, and the League of Conservation Voters. Some environmental groups represent business interests in environmental issues, as does the Mountain States Legal Foundation, which becomes involved in presenting business issues when private organizations and individuals bring environmental suits.

Visit the Sierra Club:
http://www.sierraclub.org

These environmental groups have been successful not only in bringing private damage and injunctive relief suits but also in forcing agencies to promulgate regulations and to enjoin projects when EISs should have been filed but were not.

INTERNATIONAL ENVIRONMENTAL ISSUES

The EU and Environmentalism

Visit the European Environment Agency:
http://www.eea.eu.int

By the end of 1992, the European Union (EU) had passed more than 200 environmental directives that focus on noise restrictions; protection of endangered species; energy efficiency; recycling; and air, land, and water quality. The view of the EU is that environmental planning is to be conducted by member states as part of their economic development plans and processes. In 1990, the EU created the European

Environment Agency to serve as a clearinghouse for environmental information; eventually the agency will operate for members in a manner similar to the EPA.

Many EU directives are designed to eliminate the need for regulation by encouraging different business choices and educating consumers. One directive required manufacturers to make 90 percent of all packaging materials recyclable by the year 2000. Another directive awards companies the use of an "eco-audit" sticker on their labels and stationeries if they comply with an annual environmental audit of their manufacturing, waste management, materials use, and energy choices. The audits can be done in-house or conducted by registered eco-auditors, but results must be released to the public. An innovative directive of the EU has created an EU-wide "eco-label" to be placed on all consumer goods to provide information about the environmental impact of a product's production, distribution, life, and disposal. Germany has had such a label, called the "Blue Angel," for a number of years, and the EU has adopted the concept for its continental marketplace.

ISO 14000

Visit the International Organization for Standardization:
http://www.iso.org/iso/en/ISOOnline.frontpage

The International Organization for Standardization (ISO) has developed its ISO 14000 series of international environmental standards. Some environmental scholars have predicted that the ISO standards will become the model for regulators and prosecutors in their enforcement and sentencing activities for environmental violations.

Information about ISO 14000 is available at:
http://www.iso.org/iso/en/iso9000-14000/iso14000index.html

Under ISO 14000, companies can become ISO certified, which will permit them to place special insignias on their materials, correspondence, and products to indicate their ISO standing. ISO standards emphasize not only compliance but also self-audits and self-correction. Genuine dedication to improvement is a key standard for this environmental certification.

Visit the CERES organization and review its principles:
http://www.ceres.org

The Kyoto Protocol

The United Nations Framework Convention for Climate Change (UNFCCC) is a group of government officials and nonprofit leaders who have been meeting regularly about the issues of global warming, air pollution, acid rain, and other environmental concerns. Citing automobile production as the world's leading industry and oil production as the second, the UNFCCC, in its Kyoto meeting, adopted the Kyoto Treaty, which proposes the reduction of six greenhouse gases (mostly carbon dioxide) in the United States and other industrialized nations. The year 1990 was the baseline for omissions under the treaty. The Kyoto Treaty has not yet been adopted in the United States, and the Bush (43rd) administration has taken a strong position against the treaty.

Visit the Business Roundtable site for its Kyoto Treaty report:
http://www.businessroundtable.org

The Precautionary Principle

The **precautionary principle** has become a dominant force in environmental regulation in Canada, Australia, and Europe. The precautionary principle requires those who propose change to demonstrate that their proposed actions will not cause serious or irreversible harm to the environment. The standard is used, for example, in Australia as the burden of proof for anyone who seeks to obtain a permit to dump hazardous waste. The government will not issue the permit unless and until the applicant demonstrates that the action will not cause serious or irreversible harm. It has been used in applications for logging permits and building construction.

BUSINESS STRATEGY

Can U.S. Businesses Do Well under Kyoto?

When some businesses consider the UN global-warming treaty, known as the Kyoto Protocol, and what it would mean for them if adopted by the United States, they see red. The treaty would require dramatic cuts in the use of fossil fuels. Conventional estimates place the costs of implementing the treaty at over $100 billion per year in the United States alone. A new study by the Energy Information Administration estimates that it could increase retail electricity prices anywhere from 20 to 80 percent.

But still other companies—in a development that may bode ill for treaty opponents—see green, green as in profits. Joseph Romm, an energy consultant who once oversaw alternative-energy programs at the Energy Department, had glad tidings for members of the Energy Efficient Building Association at a recent Washington, D.C., conference. "It's going be great business for everyone at this conference," Romm said of the treaty. "By 2010, climate change will be driving every major energy-related investment." And that, he explained, creates great economic opportunities for EEBA members and other companies producing "green" products.

Romm is not alone in predicting tremendous profits from the Kyoto Protocol. In recent months, several Fortune 500 firms have come out in favor of immediate action to curb greenhouse gas emissions, despite lingering scientific uncertainty about the threat of global warming and clear indications that emissions controls will entail substantial costs to consumers. British Petroleum, one of the world's largest petroleum companies, resigned from the anti-Protocol Global Climate Coalition and called upon industry to play a "positive and responsible part in identifying solutions." Honeywell CEO Michael Bonsignore likewise proclaimed that industry "can't sit back and wait for the perfect, obvious solutions to present itself" and must instead begin to act.

Earlier this year, the Pew Charitable Trusts launched the Center for Climate Change to bolster support for greenhouse gas controls. Recognizing the political value of getting business leaders to support new regulatory measures, the Center, in one of its first actions, created the Business Environmental Leadership Council. In addition to Honeywell and BP, Council members include Enron, United Technologies, International Paper, 3M, and DuPont.

The Council hails the Kyoto Protocol as a "first step in the international process" and is already receiving wide media attention. . . .

Companies such as Enron and BP are revered as role models of the new corporation citizen who places the demands of ecological sustainability ahead of revenues, profits—and shareholders. . . .

Yet the companies are hardly acting out of enlightened concern for the earth. As Clemson economist Bruce Yandle notes, "Actions that might be seen as attempts by industries to restrict output and raise rivals' costs are encouraged rather than frowned upon in the name of global environmental protection. . . ." For years, many corporations have sought to turn government intervention in the economy to their benefit. All the better when, as in the climate-change debate, they can pretend to be on the side of the angels in the bargain.

Yet not all corporate leaders pretend they are jumping on the greenhouse bandwagon for altruistic reasons. "We're a beneficiary of environmental regulations because we have for a long time invested in providing energy-efficient services," Enron's John Palmisano told *Investor's Business Daily.* "Our main product, natural gas, is relatively clean. This market is emerging for technologies not just because of Kyoto but also because of domestic regulations and regulations worldwide."

Companies that do not stand to profit from the Kyoto Protocol are still hedging their bets to ensure a "place at the table," if and when the United States begins to issue new emissions-control regulations. A General Motors official pledged that the company would "constructively address the global-climate issue" while still opposing the Kyoto Protocol and higher fuel-economy standards. Similarly, many companies that are lukewarm about the treaty are endorsing a proposal by the International Climate Change Partnership (ICCP)—a business group devoted to finding a middle ground with environmentalists before the treaty is in place.

If you were in charge of your company's environmental program, what position would you take on Kyoto? Would it matter what the nature of your company's business is? Where should political activity be focused?

Source: Reprinted with permission. Copyright © 1998 by National Review Inc., 215 Lexington Ave., New York, NY 10016, "Greenbacks" by Jonathan H. Adler.

Advocates of the precautionary principle urge that it be used to initiate legislation. That is, if new regulations and/or legislation are not passed, there will be serious or irreversible harm to the environment. Many also see it as a potential application to particular products that may harm the environment and as a means to force the development of more environmentally friendly products if the burden of proof for the precautionary principle were not met.[3]

SUMMARY

What are the public and private environmental laws? What protections and requirements are there in environmental laws?

- Nuisance—bad smells, noises, or dirt from one property that interferes with another's use and enjoyment of their own property

- Nonattainment areas—areas with significant air pollution problems

- Emissions offset policy—new plants not built until new emissions are offset by reductions elsewhere

- Bubble concept—EPA policy of maximum air emissions in one area

- Clean Air Act—federal law that controls air emissions

- Maximum Achievable Control Technology (MACT)—best means for controlling emissions

- Clean Water Act—federal law that regulates emissions in various water sources

- Effluent guidelines—EPA maximum allowances for discharges into water

- Safe Drinking Water Act—federal law establishing standards for contaminants

- Oil Pollution Act (OPA)—federal law imposing civil and criminal liability for oil spills

- Resource Conservation and Recovery Act (RCRA)—federal law controlling disposal of hazardous waste through a permit system

- Superfund—funds available for government to use to clean up toxic waste sites

- Comprehensive Environmental Response, Compensation, and Liability Act (CERCLA)—federal law providing funds and authority for hazardous waste site cleanups

- Endangered Species Act (ESA)—powerful federal law that can curb economic activity if it presents harm to endangered species or their habitat

Who enforces environmental laws?

- Environmental Protection Agency (EPA)—federal agency responsible for enforcement of environmental laws at the federal level

- National Environmental Policy Act (NEPA)—federal law that requires federal agencies to assess environmental issues before taking actions

- Environmental impact statement (EIS)—report by federal agency on study of proposed action's effect on the environment

What are the penalties for violations?

- Injunction—judicial order halting an activity
- Fines and criminal penalties

QUESTIONS AND PROBLEMS

1. Philip Carey Company owned a tract of land in Plymouth Township, Pennsylvania, on which it deposited a large pile of manufacturing waste containing asbestos. Carey sold the land to Celotex, and Celotex sold the land to Smith Land & Improvement Corporation. The EPA notified Smith in July 1984 that unless Smith took steps to eliminate the asbestos hazard, the EPA would do the work and pursue reimbursement. Smith proceeded with the cleanup to the EPA's satisfaction at a total cost of $218,945.44. Smith then turned to Celotex and Carey, as previous owners of the property, for reimbursement. These firms say they have no liability under CERCLA. Which firms are liable? [*Smith Land & Improvement Corp.* v. *Celotex*, 851 F.2d 86 (3rd Cir. 1988).]

2. A group of landowners situated near the Sanders Lead Company brought suit to recover for damages to their agricultural property from accumulations of lead particulates and sulfur oxide deposits released in Sanders' production process. The landowners' property had increased in value because of its commercial potential in being close to the plant. Sanders employs most of the town's residents in its operations. What common-law and statutory rights do the landowners have, and what relief can be obtained? [*Borland* v. *Sanders Lead Co., Inc.*, 369 So. 2d 523 (Ala. 1979).]

3. In 1985, Manufacturers National Bank of Detroit issued a letter of credit for Z&Z Leasing, Inc., an industrial firm, in order to enable Z&Z to obtain bond financing from Canton Township, Michigan.

After six years of operation, Z&Z was not doing well and had defaulted on its bond obligations. A consultant for the bank found underground storage tanks on Z&Z's site. The tanks contained a yellowish liquid that was found to be a solvent and a hazardous substance. The bank paid off the Canton township bond obligation and foreclosed on the Z&Z property. By 1993, Z&Z had still not sold the property, and the EPA sought to hold the bank liable as an operator for the costs of cleaning up the tanks.

Can the bank be held liable? [*Z&Z Leasing, Inc.* v. *Graying Reel, Inc.*, 873 F. Supp. 51 (E.D. Mich. 1995).]

4. Reynolds Metal has been held to the same technological standards in its pollution control for can-manufacturing plants as those applied to aluminum manufacturers. Reynolds claims the processes are different and that the technology for pollution control in can manufacturing is not yet available. Does Reynolds have a point? [*Reynolds Metals Co.* v. *EPA*, 760 F.2d 549 (D.C. 1985).]

5. The Mitchells lived in a residential section of Beverly Hills, Michigan, and sought to enjoin the operation of a nearby piggery. The pigs were fed in an open field, and any garbage not eaten by the pigs was plowed under by tractors. The odors from the operation, particularly in the spring and summer, were such that the use and enjoyment of the Mitchells' property was impaired. Could the Mitchells file a suit? On what basis? Could they win? Are any federal statutory violations involved? [*Mitchell* v. *Hines*, 9 N.W. 2d 547 (Mich. 1943).]

6. Peabody Mine No. 47 was located one-fourth mile from Walter Patterson's land. Mr. Patterson used his land for farming and operated on a low-maintenance schedule. His house had never been painted. Mr. Patterson said that gas, smoke, fumes, and dust traveled to his property, and he complained his clothes turned black, his bedclothes were dusty, his food was covered in coal dust, and his throat and nostrils were affected. Mr. Patterson said he was forced to sleep with the windows closed, even in the summer, to avoid blowing coal dust. The coal mine facilities operated twenty-four hours a day, six days each week. Does Mr. Patterson have any remedy? [*Patterson* v. *Peabody Coal Co.*, 122 N.E.2d 48 (Ill. 1954).]

7. A federal regulation promulgated by the EPA restricts the amout of water than can flow from showerheads to a rate of 2.5 gallons per minute. When the regulation took effect, many hotel chains had complaints from their guests about the slow water flow and the difficulty they had in bathing. Westin Hotels and Resorts announced that it would install two showerheads in the baths and showers of its hotel rooms to accommodate its guests. Each showerhead will meet federal requirements, but if the two are both turned on, the guests will have water at a rate of 5 gallons per minute. Westin maintains that it is in compliance with the law. A federal employee responded, "But we didn't anticipate the loophole of 2 shower heads per shower."[4] Discuss the Westin approach to compliance with the law.

8. The Nuclear Regulatory Commission (NRC) was responsible for the decision to allow the once-crippled Three Mile Island Unit I nuclear plant to resume operation. Pursuant to the NEPA, the NRC considered the impact on the surrounding community and determined that there would be no adverse impact. A group, People Against Nuclear Energy (PANE), intervened in the action by the NRC and asked that the court require the NRC to consider whether the risk of a nuclear accident (as had been experienced with the original shutdown of the plant) might harm the community in a psychological sense. The NRC says the risk of an accident is not an effect on the environment. Is psychological health a factor in EIS evaluations? [*Metropolitan Edison Co.* v. *People Against Nuclear Energy*, 460 U.S. 766 (1983).]

9. The Tennessee Valley Authority (TVA) proposed the construction of Tellico Dam. If the dam is constructed, the known population of snail darters will be eradicated. A snail darter is a three-inch-long fish protected by the Endangered Species Act, which requires all federal agencies (like the TVA) not to fund, authorize, or carry out projects that would jeopardize the continued existence of an endangered species. At the time an environmental group brought the issue to light, the TVA had already expended $100 million in the construction of the dam, which would bring great economic benefits to the area.

What factors are important in resolving such a dispute? Is it a matter of the significance of the species? Should an EIS have discussed this problem? [*Tennessee Valley Authority* v. *Hill*, 437 U.S. 153 (1978).]

10. Albert J. Hubenthal operated a fifty-five-acre worm-farming operation in Winona County, Minnesota. Mr. Hubenthal maintained that large amounts of scrap materials, such as tires, wood, metal, leather, and solid waste, were necessary for a successful worm operation. The fifty-five acres were "messy, smelly, and germy," as described by the neighbors. The county attorney called the farm a nuisance and warned Mr. Hubenthal that he had thirty days to clean up the farm. He refused, and the county removed all materials from the worm farm. Could the county do this? Was the farm a nuisance? [*Hubenthal* v. *County of Winona*, 751 F.2d 243 (8th Cir. 1984).]

RESEARCH PROBLEM

Have It PETA's Way At Burger King

11. People for the Ethical Treatment of Animals (PETA) has been a powerful force in demanding changes in corporate behavior. Its latest target has been Burger King for its treatment of chickens—the group wants the company to stop removing the beaks of laying hens and also to enlarge the animals' cages. Also, PETA would like Burger King to ensure that its animals are stunned before they are slaughtered. PETA has developed a new logo and name for the company, MURDER KING. Burger King is suffering from flat sales and does not welcome the negative publicity. How would you respond to PETA's concerns? Visit the Web sites of both PETA and Burger King for more information on these issues: http://www.bk.com and http://www.peta.org.

NOTES

1. E-commerce selection reprinted with permission from *Anderson's Business Law and the Legal Environment* (2002) by David Twomey, Marianne Jennings, and Ivan Fox. West, p. 1011.

2. The work of Professors Cindy A. Schipani and Lynda J. Oswald is an excellent resource for discussions on parent liability for CERCLA violations as well as a history of the development and scope of CERCLA. See, for example, Oswald and Schipani, "CERCLA and the 'Erosion' of Traditional Corporate Law Doctrine," 86 *Northwestern Law Review* 259 (1990). Their work was referred to in the *Bestfoods* case.

3. For more information on the precautionary principle, see Charmian Barton, "The Status of the Precautionary Principle in Australia: Its Emergence in Legislation as a Common Law Doctrine," 22 *Harvard Environmental Law Review* 509 (1998).

4. Chris Woodyard, "Dual Shower Heads Land Hotel in Hot Water," *USA Today*, May 22, 2001, 1B.

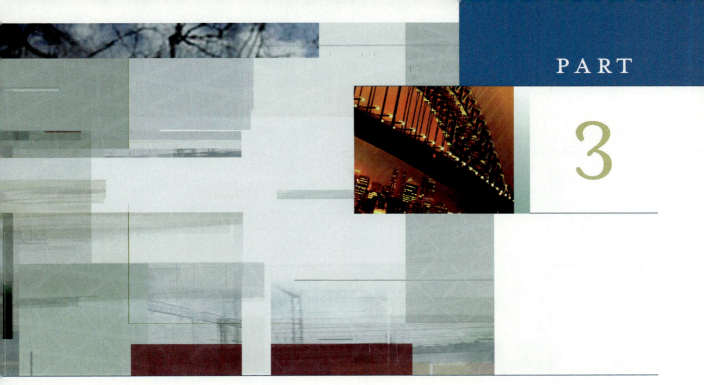

Business Competition and Sales

This section of the book covers the laws and regulations on what a business sells, how it sells its product, and how the sales are set up and financed. Do you have the right to sell a product?—or have you appropriated someone else's idea? What can you say and write in your advertising? What is fair and legal in competition? When do you have a contract, and what kinds of terms do you need to have in it? In this era of electronic commerce, what exactly is a contract, and when is it formed? When has a contract been performed, and what is a breach? Can you be compensated if the other side fails to perform? How are transactions financed, and what forms do you need? What are your rights as a seller for collecting from buyers?

This portion of the text covers all the preliminary aspects of contracts, contract performance and collection. The materials walk through the heart of business operations: sales, competition, property rights, advertising, contract formation and performance, and receivable collection.

Contracts and Sales: Introduction and Formation

Contracts have been necessary in business since business began. They allow businesses to count on money, supplies, and services. Contracts are the private law of business; the parties develop their own private set of laws through their contracts. These private laws can be enforced by the courts in all states. This chapter covers contract basics: What is a contract? What laws govern contracts? What are the types of contracts? How are contracts formed? What contracts must be in writing?

update

*For up-to-date legal news and real-world business applications, click on **update** at http://jennings.westbuslaw.com*

A verbal contract isn't worth the paper it's written on.
SAMUEL GOLDWYN

In the summer of 1996, Pepsico, Inc. ran a marketing campaign involving Pepsi Points. The Pepsi Points, obtained by drinking Pepsi, could be redeemed for prizes. One television ad promoting Pepsi Points shows a Harrier jet outside a school yard with the campaign's slogan beneath it: DRINK PEPSI GET STUFF. The jet pictured in the ad was generated by computer. The ad said the jet could be yours for 7 million Pepsi Points. Pepsico maintains the ad was a spoof. John Leonard, then a 21-year-old business student, saw the ad and delivered to Pepsi 15 original Pepsi Points plus a check for $700,008.50—sufficient for the cost of a Harrier jet, plus shipping and handling.

Pepsi refused to deliver the jet. Pentagon spokesman Kenneth Bacon (famous now for the release of Linda Tripp's personnel records from the Pentagon) indicated that no Harrier jets were available at that time because the jets must be demilitarized before a member of the public can buy one.

Pepsi also said the ad was a joke and not an offer. Mr. Leonard said that the ad induced conduct on his part, as would all Pepsi Points ads, and that Pepsi was required to deliver to him a Harrier jet. Who was correct? Was the ad an offer?

© JOHN H. CLARK/CORBIS

WHAT IS A CONTRACT?

Businesses cannot expand and grow without being able to rely on commitments; resources are wasted if promises are not fulfilled. For example, suppose that Aunt Hattie's Bread Company constructs a new wing and buys new equipment to expand production, but, when the wing is ready to operate, the wheat supplier backs out of the supply contract with Aunt Hattie's. Aunt Hattie's has wasted resources and will lose the opportunity and motivation to expand because of the problems created by unenforceable agreements. These strong economic considerations brought about the involvement of the courts in enforcing contractual promises.

"A **contract** is a promise or set of promises for breach of which the law gives a remedy, or the performance of which the law in some way recognizes as a duty." This definition comes from the *Restatement (Second) of Contracts*, a statement of contract law by the American Law Institute (ALI), which recognizes a contract as a set of voluntary promises that the law will enforce for private parties. The remainder of this chapter focuses on the creation, performance, and enforcement of those promises.

SOURCES OF CONTRACT LAW

There are three general sources of contract law for contracts entered into in the United States: common law, the Uniform Commercial Code, and the new sources of law evolving in response to e-commerce—the Uniform Electronic Transactions Act, the Uniform Computer Information Transactions Act, and the Electronic Signatures in Global and National Commerce Act of 2000 (E-sign).

497

Common Law

Common law was the first law of contracts. As discussed in Chapter 1, common law consists today of those traditional notions of law and that body of law developed by judicial decisions dealing with contract issues. Although it is not statutory law, the traditional English common law of contracts has been modified by statute in some states. Certain types of contracts have unique and specific content requirements—for example, listing agreements for real estate agents, insurance policies, and consumer credit contracts (see Chapter 15 for a more complete discussion of the statutory requirements in consumer credit contracts); but, however much specific language and statutory requirements these contracts have, their formation and enforcement are still governed by common law. Common law applies to contracts that have land or services as their subject matter. Contracts for the construction of a home or an employment contract are governed by common law. A rental agreement for an apartment may be covered by specific landlord–tenant statutes in addition to common law.

A general treatment of the common law for contracts can be found in the *Restatement (Second) of Contracts.* A group of legal scholars wrote the *Restatement,* and changes have been made to reflect the changes in contract law over the years.

The Uniform Commercial Code[1]

One of the problems with common law is its lack of uniformity. The states do not follow the same case decisions on contract law, and some states do not follow the *Restatement;* the result is that different rules apply to contracts in different states.

Consequently, businesses experienced great difficulty and expense when they contracted across state lines because of differences in state contract common law. To address the need for uniformity, the National Conference of Commissioners on Uniform State Laws and the American Law Institute worked to draft a set of commercial laws appropriate for businesspeople, lawyers, and lawmakers. The result of their efforts was the **Uniform Commercial Code** (UCC). The final draft of the UCC first appeared in the 1940s. With several revisions and much time and effort, the Code was adopted, at least in part, in all the states.

Review Article 2 of the UCC:
http://www.law.cornell.edu/ucc/2/overview.html

Article 2 of the UCC governs contracts for the sale of goods and has been adopted in all states except Louisiana. Although sections of Article 2 may have various forms throughout the states, the basic requirements for contracts remain consistent; businesses now have uniform requirements that have expedited interstate contracts. Article 2 is more liberal than common law: contracts are more easily formed and performed, and remedies are easier to determine under Article 2. The remaining sections of the chapter cover specific differences. (Excerpts of Article 2 are reproduced in Appendix G.) Determining which contracts are UCC contracts and which are common law contracts is often difficult. With the rise in electronic commerce and computer transactions, the issue has become the focus of an intense debate. For example, following passage of substantial revisions to the UCC Article 2, the American Law Institute and National Conference of Commissioners on Uniform State Laws voted, in 2003, to amend those changes to exclude the sale of "information" as being a good subject to Article 2's provisions.[2] *Cook* v. *Downing* (Case 13.1) addresses an interesting factual issue involving a question of goods and the application of UCC Article 2.

Examine drafts of proposed changes to the UCC, published by the National Conference of Commissioners on Uniform State Laws:
http://www.law.upenn.edu/bll/ulc/ulc.htm

CASE 13.1

Cook v. Downing
891 P.2d 611 (Ok. Ct. App. 1995)

The Dentures Sold Were a "Bill of Goods," but Were They UCC Goods?

FACTS

Dr. Cook (appellant) is a licensed dentist who devotes less than 50 percent of his practice to the work of fitting and making dentures. Mrs. Downing (appellee) is a patient of Dr. Cook who was fitted for dentures. Mrs. Downing filed suit against Dr. Cook after she took delivery of her dentures because she said they were ill-fitting and produced sore spots in her mouth. Dr. Cook's expert witness testified that Mrs. Downing's problems were probably due to candidas, an autoimmune reaction, or an allergy to the dental material. No expert testified that her problems were due to ill-fitting dentures.

The trial court awarded damages to Mrs. Downing on the basis of a breach of UCC Article 2, implied warranty of fitness for a particular purpose. Dr. Cook appealed, maintaining that the dentures were not a sale of goods.

JUDICIAL OPINION

HUNTER, Judge

Section 2–105(1) defines goods as meaning "all things (including specially manufactured goods) which are movable at the time of identification to the contract for sale other than the money in which the price is to be paid, investment securities (Article 8) and things in action. 'Goods' also includes the unborn young of animals and growing crops and other identified things attached to realty. . . ." The law of implied warranty in the commercial code is found in § 2–315 which states:

> *Where the seller at the time of contracting has reason to know any particular purpose for which the goods are required and that the buyer is relying on the seller's skill or judgment to select or furnish suitable goods, there is unless excluded or modified under the next section an implied warranty that the goods shall be fit for such purpose.*

We agree with Appellant's position that any claim Appellee might have sounds in tort. In Oklahoma, dentists, professionals who are regulated by the state, furnish dentures. In general, dentists must use ordinary skill in treating their patients. A patient does not establish the elements of legal detriment by only showing nonsuccess or unsatisfactory results. A dentist is not a merchant and the Uniform Commercial Code is not the law to apply to these facts. Finding no Oklahoma law on point, we align ourselves with the reasoning stated by the Court of Appeals of North Carolina in *Preston v. Thompson*, 53 N.C.App. 290, 280 S.E.2d 780 (1981). In the *Preston* case, the patient determined through her research in the yellow pages that the dentist was a specialist in dentures. The patient claimed the doctor made oral assurances that the dentures would fit satisfactorily. The dentures did not fit well and subsequent attempts at correcting the problem were not successful. The patient sued the dentist on an implied warranty theory pursuant to the Uniform Commercial Code. The court held that the transaction was not of "goods" and that a dentist was not a "merchant" under the UCC. We adopt the rule as enunciated by the North Carolina court that "those who, for a fee, furnish their professional medical services for the guidance and assistance of others are not liable in the absence of negligence or intentional misconduct." The court further held that "the fact that defendant holds himself out as specializing in the preparing and fitting of dentures does not remove him from the practice of dentistry and transform him into a merchant." We hold that under the laws of Oklahoma, a dentist is not a merchant and dentures, furnished by a dentist, are not goods under the UCC.

A dentist could be sued for breach of contract, if such contract were alleged to exist, but that is not the fact as revealed in the record in our case. Appellee presented evidence of an advertisement guaranteeing dentures to fit, but testified that she did not see this ad until after she had begun her treatment with Appellant. The evidence does not support any breach of contract action.

As a matter of law, Appellee erroneously based her cause of action on the Uniform Commercial Code rather than negligence. The court erred in entering judgment in favor of Appellee based on this law. For this reason, we reverse the judgment of the trial court and remand the matter with directions to enter judgment in favor of Appellant.

Reversed and remanded with directions.

DISSENTING OPINION

JONES, Judge, dissenting

As is typical of small claims cases, there were no pleadings here to define the issues. At trial, however, issues were raised as to dental malpractice and breach of implied warranties under the UCC. Although the trial

continued

court based its decision on a finding of a breach of the implied warranty of fitness for a particular purpose, the trial court's decision must be affirmed if sustainable on any ground.

The decision cannot be affirmed on the basis of professional negligence as the necessary evidence of such negligence was lacking. But neither can the trial court's decision's [sic] be affirmed on the basis of implied warranty of fitness for a particular purpose. There was no particular or special purpose involved as is required by § 2–315. The use Appellee was to make of the dentures was their ordinary use, and that they may not have been suitable for the ordinary purpose for which they were to be used is the concept of "merchantability".

The implied warranty of merchantability is codified at 12A O.S.1991 § 2–314 and deserves a closer look.

> "(1) . . . a warranty that the goods shall be merchantable is implied in a contract for their sale if the seller is a merchant with respect to goods of that kind. * * * *
>
> (2) Goods to be merchantable must be at least such as . . .
>
> (c) are fit for the ordinary purposes for which such goods are used; * * * * ".
>
> A "merchant" is defined as:
>
> ". . . a person who deals in goods of the kind or otherwise by his occupation holds himself out as having knowledge or skill peculiar to the practices or goods involved in the transaction or to whom such knowledge or skill may be attributed by his employment of an agent or broker or other intermediary who by his occupation holds himself out as having such knowledge or skill."
>
> "Goods" means "all things (including specially manufactured goods) which are movable at the time of identification to the contract for sale other than the money in which the price is to be paid, investment securities . . . and things in action. * * * * ".
>
> "Dentists" and "dentures" appear to be included in the definitions of merchants and goods.

The transaction of a patient being fitted for and purchasing dentures from a dentist is actually a hybrid. It is not purely a sale of goods by a merchant, nor is it purely the providing of a service by a health care pro-

fessional. Whether implied warranties under Article 2 of the U.C.C. apply to such a transaction should depend on whether the predominant element of the transaction is the sale of goods or the rendering of services. If the sale of goods predominates, it would be within the scope of Article 2 and the implied warranties contained therein. However, if the service aspect predominates, there would be no implied warranties. Although the record contains no specific findings of fact, the record does contain evidence from which it could be concluded that this transaction was principally a sale of goods and that the implied warranty of merchantability applies thereto. The evidence was also sufficient that the trier of fact could have concluded that the dentures were not fit for their ordinary purpose as required to establish a prima facie case for breach of the implied warranty of merchantability. We must affirm a law action tried to the court if there is any competent evidence to support the judgment.

In contemporary society the old distinctions separating health care professionals from other businessmen are blurring in many respects. This Court's holding that a dentist is not a merchant, and dentures, furnished by a dentist, are not goods ignores the fact that nothing excludes them from the statutory definitions of merchant and goods. It also ignores the fact that health care professionals in some instances are selling goods to their "patients", with the providing of professional services being secondary to the sale. To such transactions there is no reason Article 2 of the UCC should not apply. I respectfully dissent.

CASE QUESTIONS

1. Did the fitting for dentures constitute a sale of goods?

2. Does classifying the dentures as something other than the sale of goods deprive Mrs. Downing of a remedy?

3. Do you think eyeglasses and contact lenses should be classified as sales of goods? Why or why not?

4. What public policy issues does the dissenting judge raise?

 CONSIDER...   13.1

In September of 1988, Jane Pittsley contracted with Hilton Contract Carpet Co. for the installation of carpet in her home. The total contract price was $4,402. Hilton paid the installers $700 to put the carpet in Ms. Pittsley's home. Following installation, Ms. Pittsley complained to Hilton that some seams were visible, that gaps appeared, that the carpet did not lie flat in all areas, and that it failed to reach the wall in certain locations. Although Hilton tried several times to fix the installation by stretching the carpet and other methods, Ms. Pittsley was not satisfied with the work. Eventually, Ms. Pittsley refused to allow Hilton to try to fix the carpet. Ms. Pittsley had paid Hilton $3,500, but she refused to pay the remaining balance of $902.

Ms. Pittsley filed suit, seeking rescission of the contract, return of her $3,500, and incidental damages. Hilton answered and counterclaimed for the balance remaining on the contract. Hilton also defended on the grounds that the only issue was the installation and that the damages were minimal. Ms. Pittsley argued that the contract was under the UCC and that she was entitled to remedies because the carpet was defective. Hilton disagreed on the application of the UCC. Who is correct? Does the UCC apply to the contract for the carpet sale and installation? Is Ms. Pittsley entitled to the warranty protection of the UCC? [*Pittsley* v. *Houser*, 875 P.2d 232 (Idaho 1994).]

THINK: The discussion of UCC versus common law has us examine the following:
- The cost of goods versus the cost of service in the contract
- The role of the seller in performing the contract
- The nature of the service component

APPLY: In this case, the cost of the carpet is clearly the largest part of the contract price. While the buyer wanted the carpet installed (rather than just delivered to her home), the installation is incidental to the purchase itself. The contract was made for the purchase of the carpet, a good, and the agreement to install the carpet was then tacked onto the contract. Goods such as carpet were intended as part of the UCC to have full warranty protection.

ANSWER: The contract is covered by the UCC.

Now apply these reasoning skills to Consider 13.2.

CONSIDER...   13.2

Determine whether the following subject matters would be governed by the UCC or by common law.
- Software licensing agreements [*NMP Corp.* v. *Parametric Technology Corp.*, 32 U.C.C. Rep. Serv. 2d 687, 958 F. Supp. 1536 (N.D. Okla. 1997)]
- Natural gas [*New Bremen Corp.* v. *Columbia Gas Transmission Corp.*, 29 U.C.C. Rep. Serv. 2d 442, 913 F. Supp. 985 (S.D. Tex. 1995)]
- Electricity [*Gordonsville Energy, L.P.* v. *Virginia Electric & Power Co.*, 29 U.C.C. Rep. Serv. 2d 849 (Va. Cir. 1996)]
- Boats [*Standing* v. *Midgett*, 22 U.C.C. Rep. Serv. 2d 472, 850 F. Supp. 396 (E.D.N.C. 1993)]
- Software to provide voice messaging, described as a "turnkey" system, that is, it operates without additional work [*Pentagram Software Corp.* v. *Voicetek Corp.*, 22 U.C.C. Rep. Serv. 2d 646 (Mass. Super. 1993)]
- Golf irrigation systems [*Champion Turf, Inc.* v. *Rice, Papuchis Const. Co.*, 21 U.C.C. Rep. Serv. 2d 519, 853 S.W.2d 323 (Mo. App. 1993)]
- Wheat [*Mogan* v. *Cargill, Inc.*, 21 U.C.C. Rep. Serv. 2d 661, 259 Mont. 400, 856 P.2d 973 (1993)]
- Water [*Gall* v. *Allegheny County Health Dept.*, 8 U.C.C. Rep. Serv. 2d 379, 521 Pa. 68, 555 A.2d 786 (1989)]
- Standing timber [*Bohle* v. *Thompson*, 8 U.C.C. Rep. Serv. 2d 897, 78 Md. App. 614, 554 A.2d 818 (1989)]
- Animals [*Andersen* v. *Koss*, 7 U.C.C. Rep. Serv. 2d 42, 173 Ill. App. 3d 872, 527 N.E.2d 1098 (1988)]
- Potatoes [*H.C. Schmieding Produce Co., Inc.* v. *Cagle*, 7 U.C.C. Rep. Serv. 2d 676, 529 So. 2d 243 (Ala. 1988)]
- Mobile homes [*Aslakson* v. *Home Sav. Ass'n*, 6 U.C.C. Rep. Serv. 2d 35, 416 N.W.2d 786 (Minn. App. 1987)]
- Extracted oil [*Texas American Energy Corp.* v. *Citizens Fidelity Bank & Trust Co.*, 5 U.C.C. Rep. Serv. 2d 184, 736 S.W.2d 25 (Ky. 1987)]
- Barges [*In re Merritt Dredging Co., Inc.*, 5 U.C.C. Rep. Serv. 2d 900, 839 F.2d 203 (4th Cir. 1988)]

continued

- Ships [*Mahler* v. *Allied Marine*, 4 U.C.C. Rep. Serv. 2d 1427, 513 So. 2d 677 (Fla. App. 1987)]
- Diamonds [*Wixon Jewelers, Inc.* v. *Di-Star, Ltd.*, 218 F.3d 913, 42 U.C.C. Rep. Serv. 2d 94 (8th Cir. 2000)]
- Feed [*Sherman* v. *Sherman*, 2000 SD 117, 616 N.W.2d 393, 42 U.C.C. Rep. Serv. 2d 491 (S.D. 2000)]
- Livestock [*Flanagan* v. *Consolidated Nutrition, L.C.*, 627 N.W.2d 573 (Iowa Ct. App. 2001)
- Degas painting [*Weil* v. *Murray*, 161 F. Supp. 2d 250, 44 U.C.C. Rep. Serv. 2d 482 (S.D. N.Y. 2001)]
- Grape plants from a nursery [*Gladhart* v. *Oregon Vineyard Supply Co.*, 40 U.C.C. Rep. Serv. 2d 722, 164 Or. App. 438, 994 P.2d 134 (1999)]
- Ticket to an amusement park ride [*Dantzler* v. *S.P. Parks, Inc.*, 40 U.C.C. Rep. Serv. 2d 955, 1988 WL 131428 (E.D. Pa. 1988)]
- Computer hardware [*Klocek* v. *Gateway, Inc.*, 41 U.C.C. Rep. Serv. 2d 1059, 104 F. Supp. 2d 1332 (D. Kan. 2000)]
- Concert tickets [*State* v. *Cardwell*, 38 U.C.C. Rep. Serv. 2d 1158, 246 Conn. 721, 718 A.2d 954 (1998)]

Article 2A—Leases

The UCC has added a new section called Article 2 Leases, which applies to leases of goods. Over the past ten years, many new forms of goods transactions have developed, such as the long-term auto lease, which appears to be more of a sale than a lease. Because of the nature of these agreements, leases did not fit well under common law or traditional Article 2. The new section, drafted for these types of contracts, covers such issues as the statute of frauds (leases in which payments exceed $1,000, for example, must be in writing), contract formation, and warranties associated with a lease. The Article 2 Leases section of the UCC has been adopted in most states.

Evolving E-Commerce Contract Laws

Uniform Electronic Transactions Act (UETA)

Visit the UETA online for updates on legislation: **http://www.uetaonline.com**

The **Uniform Electronic Transactions Act** (UETA) is a uniform law drafted in 1999. As of the end of 2003, it has been adopted in forty-two states and the District of Columbia and remains on the agenda of state legislatures in the remaining states.

The UETA was promulgated in response to contracts being formed over the Internet and includes provisions on issues such as electronic signatures. However, state adoptions of the UETA are not nearly as uniform as those of the UCC, and the issues of what constitutes a valid signature and the effect of electronic verification continue to evolve.

Electronic Signatures in Global and National Commerce Act of 2000

The UETA is state recognition of the **Electronic Signatures in Global and National Commerce Act of 2000 (E-sign)**, 15 U.S.C. §7001, the federal law that mandates the

▶ update ◀ **CHECK THE WEB**

> You can check the current status of states' adoptions of UETA at http://www.ncsl.org/programs/lis/cip/ueta.htm#State. Also, be sure to check the book's Web site updates for the latest on UETA.

recognition of electronic signatures for the formation of contracts (see p. 534 for more information). While states may vary in their specifics under the UETA, it is clear from E-sign that all states cannot deny legal effect to contracts that are entered into electronically and that bear electronic signatures. (See Chapter 15 for more discussion of how consumer contracts are formed electronically.)

Visit the UCITA online for updates on legislation:

http://www.ucita.org

Find more details on the UCITA at the site for the National Conference of Commissioners on Uniform States Laws:

http://www.nccusl.org

Read about the objections some consumer groups have to the UCITA:

http://www.cpsr.org/ program/UCITA/ ucita-fact.html

Uniform Computer Information Transactions Act (UCITA)

The **Uniform Computer Information Transactions Act** (UCITA) was promulgated in 1999 and has been adopted in two states (Virginia and Maryland) and proposed in eight others (as of September 2004).[3] The UCITA would govern all contracts involving the sale, licensing, maintenance, and support of computer software. Those contracts not involving software that are contracts for the sale of other goods would still be governed by the UCC along with the UETA, if adopted in the state.

The UCITA recognizes as terms of the contract those terms that are not revealed to the buyer until after payment and delivery. Typically, these terms are presented in what are often called "shrinkwrap" or "clickwrap" contracts. Once you open the shrinkwrap on the product, you have agreed to the terms, or, once you click "OK" in an electronic transaction, you have agreed to the terms. The UCITA also treats software and digital content contracts as "licenses" rather than sales of goods or sales of copies of software. This classification and treatment creates some questions about these types of contracts: Does the UCC apply, or are these common law contracts? And can the post-transaction terms take away rights of the parties afforded under UCC or common law? As noted in Chapter 8, these cyber law issues continue to evolve.

TYPES OF CONTRACTS

Contracts exist in many different forms, and these forms can control many of the parties' rights and remedies with respect to the relationship. The following sections cover the various types of contracts and offer an introduction to contract terminology.

Bilateral versus Unilateral Contracts

A contract can result from two parties exchanging promises to perform or from one party exchanging a promise for the other party's actions. A **bilateral contract** is one in which both parties promise to perform certain things. For example, if you sign a contract to buy a used pink Cadillac for $2,000, you have entered into a bilateral contract with the seller. The seller has promised not to sell the car to anyone else and will give you the title to the car when you pay the $2,000. You have promised to buy that pink Cadillac and will turn over the $2,000 to the seller in exchange for the title. The contract consists of two promises: your promise to buy and the seller's promise to sell.

Some contracts have one party issuing a promise and the other party simply performing. This type of contract is called a **unilateral contract**. For example, suppose that your uncle said, "I will pay you $500 if you will drive my new Mercedes to San Francisco for me within the next five days." Your uncle has promised to pay, but you have not promised to do anything. Nonetheless, you can hold your uncle to his promise if you drive his car to San Francisco. Your agreement is a promise in exchange for performance. If you drive the car to San Francisco, your uncle's promise will be enforceable as a unilateral contract.

FOR THE MANAGER'S DESK

RE: A UNILATERAL TATTOO

In a case bound to leave an imprint in the halls of justice, David Winkleman and Richard Goddard filed suit against the owner of a Davenport radio station (KORB-FM), Cumulus Broadcasting, because they allege that they had "93 Rock" tattooed on their foreheads in response to a disc jockey's promise. According to the permanently tattooed men, they heard disc jockey Ben Stone say on November 29, 2000, that the radio station would pay anyone who got "93 Rock" tattooed on their foreheads $30,000 per year for five years plus concert tickets, backstage passes, and a TV satellite dish.

Mr. Winkleman and Mr. Goddard say that when they called to confirm the offer, someone at the station referred them to a tattoo parlor. The station refused to pay the men, asserting that the statements by Mr. Stone were simply a joke and no one would assume otherwise.

The two men also say that they have been unable to get jobs since the tattoos and that they have been "publicly scorned and ridiculed for their greed and lack of common good sense."

The case was dismissed in 2003 because the court found no evidence that such an offer had been made. The audiotapes from the interchange indicated that the disc jockey actually said the men could go ahead and tattoo all they wanted, but that there "wasn't even a free CD in it for you." Subsequently, the two men were involved in dramatic incidents at their trailer park homes, including attempted murder of one by a neighbor wielding a ball peen hammer and accusations of arson of one's mobile home following a garage sale in which all of his personal items were sold.

Source: Annie Hsia, "Here's my tattoo. Where's the cash?" *National Law Journal,* June 24–July 1, 2002, p. A4.

Express versus Implied Contracts (Quasi Contracts)

Some contracts are written, signed (even notarized), and very formal in appearance. Others are simply verbal agreements between the parties (see p. 531 for a discussion of the types of contracts that can be oral). Still others are electronic contracts entered into via e-mail and the Internet. A contract that is written or orally agreed to is an **express contract**. In still other situations, the parties do not discuss the terms of the contract but nonetheless understand that they have some form of contractual relationship. A contract that arises from circumstances and not from the express agreement of the parties is called an **implied contract**, as when you go to a doctor for treatment of an illness. You and the doctor do not sit down and negotiate the terms of treatment, the manner in which the doctor will conduct the examination, or how much you will pay. You understand that the doctor will do whatever examinations are appropriate to determine the cause of your illness and that there is a fee associated with the doctor's work. The payment and treatment terms are implied from general professional customs. You have an **implied-in-fact contract**.

A second type of implied or enforceable agreement is called an **implied-in-law contract** or a **quasi contract**. The term *quasi* means "as if" and describes the action of a court when it treats parties who do not have a contract "as if" they did. The courts enforce a quasi contract right if one party has conferred a benefit on another, both are aware of the benefit, and the retention of the benefit would be an enrichment of one party at the unjust expense of the other.

It is important to understand that the theory of quasi contracts does not apply to what has been referred to as "the officious meddler." The officious meddler is someone who performs unrequested work or services and then, based on a quasi contract theory, seeks recovery. For example, you could not be required to compensate a painting contractor who came by and painted your house without your permission because the contractor acted both without your knowledge and without your consent. However, if you are aware the painting is going on and you do nothing to stop it, you would be held liable in quasi contract.

Void and Voidable Contracts

A **void contract** is an agreement to do something that is illegal or against public policy, or one that lacks legal elements (see Chapter 14). For example, a contract to sell weapons to a country under a weapons ban is a void contract. Neither side can enforce the contract, even if the weapons have already been delivered, because allowing the seller to collect payment would encourage further violations of the law banning the weapons sales.

A contract may be partially void; that is, only a portion of the contract violates a statute or public policy and is therefore unenforceable. For example, in many states, it is illegal to charge excessive rates of interest (known as usury; see Chapter 15 for more discussion). In a usurious loan contract, the loan repayment would be enforceable, but the interest terms would not be. As another example, suppose that an owner has sold her business and in the contract has agreed never to start another similar business. Although the buyer deserves some protection for the payment of goodwill, the complete elimination of the seller's right to start a business is an excessive restraint of trade that is against public policy and would not be enforced, even though the actual sale of the business would be enforced.

A **voidable contract** is a contract that can be unenforceable at the election of one of the parties. For example, if there has been misrepresentation, the party who is the victim can elect to void the contract. Likewise, a minor who signs a contract can choose to be bound by the agreement or can choose to disaffirm the contract. These types of contracts are voidable at the option of one of the parties.

Unenforceable Contracts

An **unenforceable contract** is a contract that cannot be enforced because of some procedural problem. A contract that should be in writing to comply with the statute of frauds but is not written is unenforceable. When a suit to enforce a contract is not brought within the statute of limitations, the contract becomes unenforceable.

Executed versus Executory Contracts

Contracts are **executed contracts** when the parties have performed according to their promises or required actions (under unilateral agreements). Contracts are **executory contracts** when the promise to perform is made but the actual performance has not been done. A contract could be wholly executed, wholly executory, or partially executed. For example, referring to the offer your uncle made about the Mercedes trip to California, the contract is wholly executory at the time your uncle makes the offer. If you drive the car to San Francisco, your performance is complete but your uncle's is not; hence, the contract is partially executed. When your uncle pays you, the contract is wholly executed because both of you have performed your responsibilities under this unilateral contract. Courts often distinguish between executed and executory contracts in determining both the rights of the parties (particularly with respect to issues of public policy and capacity) and the remedies available to the parties.

FORMATION OF CONTRACTS

A contract is formed when two parties with the correct mental intent, under the correct circumstances, within the boundaries of the law, and with some detriment to each of them agree to do certain acts in exchange for the other's acts. This formation

EXHIBIT   13.1   Overview of Contracts

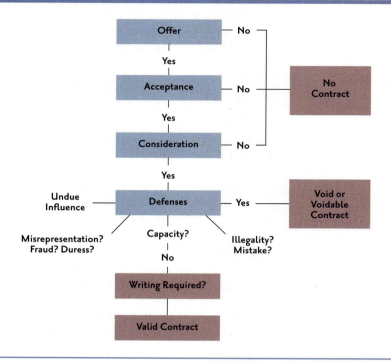

---

requires the presence of all of these elements; the lack of one element or the presence of a problem, such as illegality, can invalidate the contract. The elements necessary for the formation of a valid contract are outlined in Exhibit 13.1.

Offer

The **offer** is the first part of a contract. The person who makes the offer is called the **offeror**, and the person to whom the offer is made is called the **offeree**. The requirements for a valid offer are covered in the following sections.

Intent to Contract versus Negotiation

The offeror must intend to contract at the time the offer language is used. This requirement distinguishes offers from negotiations. For example, a letter from a businessperson may contain the following: "I am interested in investing in a franchise. I have heard about your opportunities. Please send me all necessary information." The letter expresses an interest in possibly contracting in the future, but it does not express any present intent to enter into a contract. But suppose this letter of inquiry was followed by another letter with the following language: "I have decided to invest in one of your franchises. Enclosed are the necessary documents, signatures, and a deposit check." Here the parties have passed the negotiation stage and entered into part one of the contract—there is an offer.

Courts use an objective standard in determining the intent of the parties, which means that courts look at how a reasonable person would perceive the language, the surrounding circumstances, and the actions of the parties in determining whether a contract was formed. For example, a businessperson who is exasperated with the poor financial performance of her firm may say jokingly to someone over

CONSIDER... 13.3

Review the following language and determine whether an offer has been made.

TO: Brit Ripley
FROM: Yachts International
RE: Sailing Vessel *Infinity*

We are prepared to make an offer to purchase the U.S. Coast Guard Documented Vessel *Infinity* for the price of $600,000 on the following terms and conditions:
Price: $600,000

Terms: Cash $300,000 at close of escrow
Note: $300,000 (unsecured) due in one year
Interest: 0.5% per month on unpaid balance versus 100,000 shares of stock of a public company
Will guarantee $3.00 per share in one year. Buyer reserves the right to repurchase shares at $3.00 in one year if guarantee given.
Escrow: ASAP
Conditions:
1. All insurance to remain in effect until close.
2. Seller to deliver to Port of San Francisco in seaworthy and sailable condition.

/s./ J. P. Morgan
Yachts International

For a look at auction sales on the Internet, see:
http://www.ebay.com
http://www.haggle.com
http://www.priceline.com

lunch, "I'd sell this company to anyone willing to take it." If that statement is made in the context of a series of complaints about the firm and the workload, it would not be an offer. That same language used in a luncheon meeting with a prospective buyer would create a different result.

In many situations, one party has simply requested bids or is inviting offers. The frustrated business owner could say, "I am interested in selling my firm. If you run into anyone who is interested, have them call me." The owner has not made an offer to sell but, rather, has made an invitation for an offer.

Ads are simply invitations for offers. *Leonard* v. *Pepsico* (Case 13.2) provides the answer for the chapter's opening Consider.

CASE 13.2

Leonard v. *Pepsico*
210 F.3d 88 (2d Cir. 2000)*

Does "Pepsi Stuff" Include a Harrier Jet?

FACTS

Pepsico (defendant/appellee), the producer and distributor of the soft drinks Pepsi and Diet Pepsi, ran a promotion titled "Pepsi Stuff," which encouraged consumers to collect Pepsi Points from specially marked packages of Pepsi or Diet Pepsi and redeem these points for merchandise featuring the Pepsi logo. John Leonard (plaintiff/appellant) is a resident of Seattle, Washington, who saw the Pepsi Stuff commercial that he contends constituted an offer for obtaining a Harrier Jet as part of the

Pepsi Stuff. The commercial opens on an idyllic, suburban morning, where birds chirping in sun-dappled trees welcome a paperboy on his morning route. As the newspaper hits the stoop of a conventional two-story house, the tattoo of a military drum introduces the subtitle, "MONDAY 7:58 AM." The stirring strains of a martial air mark the appearance of a well-coiffed teenager preparing to leave for school, dressed in a shirt emblazoned with the Pepsi logo, a red-white-and-blue ball.

continued

While the teenager confidently preens, the military drumroll again sounds as the subtitle "T-SHIRT 75 PEPSI POINTS" scrolls across the screen. Bursting from his room, the teenager strides down the hallway wearing a leather jacket. The drumroll sounds again, as the subtitle "LEATHER JACKET 1450 PEPSI POINTS" appears. The teenager opens the door of his house and, unfazed by the glare of the early morning sunshine, puts on a pair of sunglasses. The drumroll then accompanies the subtitle "SHADES 175 PEPSI POINTS." A voiceover then intones, "Introducing the new Pepsi Stuff catalog," as the camera focuses on the cover of the catalog. At this point, the following message appears at the bottom of the screen: "Offer not available in all areas. See details on specially marked packages."

The scene then shifts to three young boys sitting in front of a high school building. The boy in the middle is intent on his Pepsi Stuff Catalog, while the boys on either side are each drinking Pepsi. The three boys gaze in awe at an object rushing overhead as the military march builds to a crescendo. The Harrier Jet is not yet visible, but the observer senses the presence of a mighty plane as the extreme winds generated by its flight create a paper maelstrom in a classroom devoted to an otherwise dull physics lesson. Finally, the Harrier Jet swings into view and lands by the side of the school building, next to a bicycle rack. Several students run for cover, and the velocity of the wind strips one hapless faculty member down to his underwear. While the faculty member is being deprived of his dignity, the voiceover announces: "Now the more Pepsi you drink, the more great stuff you're gonna get."

The teenager opens the cockpit of the fighter and can be seen, helmetless, holding a Pepsi. Looking very pleased with himself, the teenager exclaims, "Sure beats the bus," and chortles. The military drumroll sounds a final time, as the following words appear: "HARRIER FIGHTER 7,000,000 PEPSI POINTS." A few seconds later, the following appears in more stylized script: "Drink Pepsi—Get Stuff." With that message, the music and the commercial end with a triumphant flourish.

Inspired by this commercial, Mr. Leonard set out to obtain a Harrier Jet. The Catalog specifies the number of Pepsi Points required to obtain promotional merchandise. The Catalog includes an Order Form that lists, on one side, fifty-three items of Pepsi Stuff merchandise redeemable for Pepsi Points. Conspicuously absent from the Order Form is any entry or description of a Harrier Jet. The amount of Pepsi Points required to obtain the listed merchandise ranges from 15 for a "Jacket Tattoo" ("Sew 'em on your jacket, not your arm.") to 3,300 for a "Fila Mountain Bike" ("Rugged. All-terrain. Exclusively for Pepsi.").

The rear foldout pages of the Catalog contain directions for redeeming Pepsi Points for merchandise. These directions note that merchandise may be ordered "only" with the original Order Form. The Catalog notes that in the event that a consumer lacks enough Pepsi Points to obtain a desired item, additional Pepsi Points may be purchased for ten cents each; however, at least 15 original Pepsi Points must accompany each order.

Although Mr. Leonard initially set out to collect 7,000,000 Pepsi Points by consuming Pepsi products, it soon became clear to him that he "would not be able to buy (let alone drink) enough Pepsi to collect the necessary Pepsi Points fast enough." Reevaluating his strategy, Mr. Leonard realized that buying Pepsi Points would be a more promising option. Through acquaintances, Mr. Leonard ultimately raised about $700,000.

On March 27, 1996, Mr. Leonard submitted an Order Form, 15 original Pepsi Points, and a check for $700,008.50. At the bottom of the Order Form, Mr. Leonard wrote in "1 Harrier Jet" in the "Item" column and "7,000,000" in the "Total Points" column. In a letter accompanying his submission, Mr. Leonard stated that the check was to purchase additional Pepsi Points "expressly for obtaining a new Harrier jet as advertised in your Pepsi Stuff commercial." On May 7, 1996, Pepsico rejected Mr. Leonard's submission and returned the check, explaining that:

> The item that you have requested is not part of the Pepsi Stuff collection. It is not included in the catalogue or on the order form, and only catalogue merchandise can be redeemed under this program.
>
> The Harrier jet in the Pepsi commercial is fanciful and is simply included to create a humorous and entertaining ad. We apologize for any misunderstanding or confusion that you may have experienced and are enclosing some free product coupons for your use.

Mr. Leonard responded via his lawyer:

> Your letter of May 7, 1996 is totally unacceptable. We have reviewed the video tape of the Pepsi Stuff commercial . . . and it clearly offers the new Harrier jet for 7,000,000 Pepsi Points. Our client followed your rules explicitly. . . .
>
> This is a formal demand that you honor your commitment and make immediate arrangements to transfer the new Harrier jet to our client. If we do not receive transfer instructions within ten (10) business days of the date of this letter you will leave us no choice but to file an appropriate action against Pepsi. . . .

After some complex maneuvers related to diversity jurisdiction, Mr. Leonard filed suit, and Pepsico moved for summary judgment. The court granted summary judgment, and Mr. Leonard appealed.

JUDICIAL OPINION

PER CURIAM

Plaintiff-appellant John D. R. Leonard alleges that the ad was an offer, that he accepted the offer by tendering the equivalent of 7 million points, and that Pepsico has breached its contract to deliver the Harrier jet. Pepsico characterizes the use of the Harrier jet in the ad as a hyperbolic joke ("zany humor"), cites the ad's reference to offering details contained in the promotional catalog (which contains no Harrier fighter plane), and argues that no objective person would construe the ad as an offer for the Harrier jet.

The United States District Court for the Southern District of New York (Wood, J.) agreed with Pepsico and granted its motion for summary judgment on the grounds (1) that the commercial did not amount to an offer of goods; (2) that no objective person could reasonably have concluded that the commercial actually offered consumers a Harrier Jet; and (3) that the alleged contract could not satisfy the New York statute of frauds.

We affirm for substantially the reasons stated in Judge Wood's opinion. See 88 F.Supp.2d 116 (S.D.N.Y. 1999). [To help you understand the issues in the case, portions of Judge Wood's opinion follow.]

WOOD, District Judge

The general rule is that an advertisement does not constitute an offer. The Restatement (Second) of Contracts explains that

> *Advertisements of goods by display, sign, handbill, newspaper, radio or television are not ordinarily intended or understood as offers to sell. The same is true of catalogues, price lists and circulars, even though the terms of suggested bargains may be stated in some detail.*
>
> *It is of course possible to make an offer by an advertisement directed to the general public, but there must ordinarily be some language of commitment or some invitation to take action without further communication.*

Restatement (Second) of Contracts § 26 cmt. b (1979).

An advertisement is not transformed into an enforceable offer merely by a potential offeree's expression of willingness to accept the offer through, among other means, completion of an order form.

Under these principles, plaintiff's letter of March 27, 1996, with the Order Form and the appropriate number of Pepsi Points, constituted the offer. There would be no enforceable contract until defendant accepted the Order Form and cashed the check.

The exception to the rule that advertisements do not create any power of acceptance in potential offerees is where the advertisement is "clear, definite, and explicit, and leaves nothing open for negotiation," in that circumstance, "it constitutes an offer, acceptance of which will complete the contract." *Lefkowitz* v. *Great Minneapolis Surplus Store*, 251 Minn. 188, 86 N.W.2d 689, 691 (1957). In *Lefkowitz*, defendant had published a newspaper announcement stating: "Saturday 9 AM Sharp, 3 Brand New Fur Coats, Worth to $100.00, First Come First Served $1 Each." Mr. Morris Lefkowitz ar-

rived at the store, dollar in hand, but was informed that under defendant's "house rules," the offer was open to ladies, but not gentlemen. The court ruled that because plaintiff had fulfilled all of the terms of the advertisement and the advertisement was specific and left nothing open for negotiation, a contract had been formed.

The present case is distinguishable from *Lefkowitz*. First, the commercial cannot be regarded in itself as sufficiently definite, because it specifically reserved the details of the offer to a separate writing, the Catalog. The commercial itself made no mention of the steps a potential offeree would be required to take to accept the alleged offer of a Harrier Jet. The advertisement in *Lefkowitz*, in contrast, "identified the person who could accept." Second, even if the Catalog had included a Harrier Jet among the items that could be obtained by redemption of Pepsi Points, the advertisement of a Harrier Jet by both television commercial and catalog would still not constitute an offer.

The Court finds, in sum, that the Harrier Jet commercial was merely an advertisement.

[P]laintiff largely relies on a different species of unilateral offer, involving public offers of a reward for performance of a specified act. Because these cases generally involve public declarations regarding the efficacy or trustworthiness of specific products, one court has aptly characterized these authorities as "prove me wrong" cases. The most venerable of these precedents is the case of *Carlill* v. *Carbolic Smoke Ball Co.*, 1 Q.B. 256 (Court of Appeal, 1892), a quote from which heads plaintiff's memorandum of law: "[I]f a person chooses to make extravagant promises . . . he probably does so because it pays him to make them, and, if he has made them, the extravagance of the promises is no reason in law why he should not be bound by them."

The case arose during the London influenza epidemic of the 1890s. Among other advertisements of the time, for Clarke's World Famous Blood Mixture, Towle's Pennyroyal and Steel Pills for Females, Sequah's Prairie Flower, and Epp's Glycerine Jube-Jubes, appeared solicitations for the Carbolic Smoke Ball. The specific advertisement that Mrs. Carlill saw, and relied upon, read as follows:

> *£100 reward will be paid by the Carbolic Smoke Ball Company to any person who contracts the increasing epidemic influenza, colds, or any diseases caused by taking cold, after having used the ball three times daily for two weeks according to the printed directions supplied with each ball. £1000 is deposited with the Alliance Bank, Regent Street, shewing our sincerity in the matter.*

During the last epidemic of influenza many thousand carbolic smoke balls were sold as preventives

continued

against this disease, and in no ascertained case was the disease contracted by those using the carbolic smoke ball.

Mrs. Carlill purchased the smoke ball and used it as directed, but contracted influenza nevertheless. The advertisement was construed as offering a reward because it sought to induce performance, unlike an invitation to negotiate, which seeks a reciprocal promise. As Lord Justice Lindley explained, "advertisements offering rewards . . . are offers to anybody who performs the conditions named in the advertisement, and anybody who does perform the condition accepts the offer." Because Mrs. Carlill had complied with the terms of the offer, yet contracted influenza, she was entitled to £100.

Other "reward" cases underscore the distinction between typical advertisements, in which the alleged offer is merely an invitation to negotiate for purchase of commercial goods, and promises of reward, in which the alleged offer is intended to induce a potential offeree to perform a specific action, often for noncommercial reasons.

In the present case, the Harrier Jet commercial did not direct that anyone who appeared at Pepsi headquarters with 7,000,000 Pepsi Points on the Fourth of July would receive a Harrier Jet. Instead, the commercial urged consumers to accumulate Pepsi Points and to refer to the Catalog to determine how they could redeem their Pepsi Points. The commercial sought a reciprocal promise, expressed through acceptance of, and compliance with, the terms of the Order Form. As noted previously, the Catalog contains no mention of the Harrier Jet. Plaintiff states that he "noted that the Harrier Jet was not among the items described in the catalog, but this did not affect [his] understanding of the offer."

In evaluating the commercial, the Court must not consider defendant's subjective intent in making the commercial, or plaintiff's subjective view of what the commercial offered, but what an objective, reasonable person would have understood the commercial to convey.

If it is clear that an offer was not serious, then no offer has been made. . . .

An obvious joke, of course, would not give rise to a contract. On the other hand, if there is no indication that the offer is "evidently in jest," and that an objective, reasonable person would find that the offer was serious, then there may be a valid offer.

Plaintiff's insistence that the commercial appears to be a serious offer requires the Court to explain why the commercial is funny. Explaining why a joke is funny is a daunting task; as the essayist E. B. White has

remarked, "Humor can be dissected, as a frog can, but the thing dies in the process. . . ." The commercial is the embodiment of what defendant appropriately characterizes as "zany humor."

First, the commercial suggests, as commercials often do, that use of the advertised product will transform what, for most youth, can be a fairly routine and ordinary experience. The commercial in this case thus makes the exaggerated claims similar to those of many television advertisements: that by consuming the featured clothing, car, beer, or potato chips, one will become attractive, stylish, desirable, and admired by all. A reasonable viewer would understand such advertisements as mere puffery, not as statements of fact. Second, the callow youth featured in the commercial is a highly improbable pilot, one who could barely be trusted with the keys to his parents' car, much less the prize aircraft of the United States Marine Corps. Rather than checking the fuel gauges on his aircraft, the teenager spends his precious preflight minutes preening. The youth's concern for his coiffure appears to extend to his flying without a helmet. Finally, the teenager's comment that flying a Harrier Jet to school "sure beats the bus" evinces an improbably insouciant attitude toward the relative difficulty and danger of piloting a fighter plane in a residential area, as opposed to taking public transportation.

Third, the notion of traveling to school in a Harrier Jet is an exaggerated adolescent fantasy. In this commercial, the fantasy is underscored by how the teenager's schoolmates gape in admiration, ignoring their physics lesson. The force of the wind generated by the Harrier Jet blows off one teacher's clothes, literally defrocking an authority figure. As if to emphasize the fantastic quality of having a Harrier Jet arrive at school, the Jet lands next to a plebeian bike rack. This fantasy is, of course, extremely unrealistic. No school would provide landing space for a student's fighter jet, or condone the disruption the jet's use would cause.

Fourth, the primary mission of a Harrier Jet, according to the United States Marine Corps, is to "attack and destroy surface targets under day and night visual conditions." [D]epiction of such a jet as a way to get to school in the morning is clearly not serious even if, as plaintiff contends, the jet is capable of being acquired "in a form that eliminates [its] potential for military use."

Fifth, the number of Pepsi Points the commercial mentions as required to "purchase" the jet is 7,000,000. To amass that number of points, one would have to drink 7,000,000 Pepsis (or roughly 190 Pepsis a day for the next hundred years—an unlikely possibility), or one would have to purchase approximately $700,000 worth of Pepsi Points. The cost of a Harrier Jet is roughly $23 million dollars, a fact of which plaintiff was aware when he set out to gather the amount he believed necessary to accept the alleged offer.

In light of the obvious absurdity of the commercial, the Court rejects plaintiff's argument that the commercial was not clearly in jest.

The absence of any writing setting forth the alleged contract in this case provides an entirely separate reason for granting summary judgment. Under the New York Statute of Frauds, a contract for the sale of goods for the price of $500 or more is not enforceable by way of action or defense unless there is some writing sufficient to indicate that a contract for sale has been made between the parties and signed by the party against whom enforcement is sought or by his authorized agent or broker.

There is simply no writing between the parties that evidences any transaction. Plaintiff argues that the commercial, plaintiff's completed Order Form, and perhaps other agreements signed by defendant which plaintiff has not yet seen, should suffice for Statute of Frauds purposes, either singly or taken together.

The commercial is not a writing; plaintiff's completed order form does not bear the signature of defendant, or an agent thereof.

For the reasons stated above, the Court grants defendant's motion for summary judgment. Summary judgment granted and affirmed.

CASE QUESTIONS

1. What offer does Mr. Leonard allege was made?
2. When does the court think an offer was made?
3. Why is whether the ad is funny an important issue?
4. Does the commercial satisfy the statute of frauds?
5. Will Mr. Leonard get his Harrier jet? Why or why not?

*The appellate court affirmed the federal district court opinion in a very brief affirmation. The bulk of the facts and discussion presented here are taken from the lower court's decision, 88 F. Supp.2d 116 (S.D.N.Y. 1999).

C O N S I D E R . . .   **1 3 . 4**

Procter & Gamble (P & G) began a Pampers catalog promotional offer in 1981. A statement on each box of Pampers explained that by saving the teddy bear proof-of-purchase symbols (Teddy Bears points) on packages of Pampers diapers, a customer could order various baby items from the Pampers Softouches Baby Catalog at a reduced cost. The catalog would be sent free to consumers upon request. Included in the catalog were pictures of the items for sale and the designated amount of Teddy Bears points and cash necessary for purchase. All sale terms, including the dates during which the offer was in effect, were described in each catalog. The only method for ordering merchandise was the use of the specific order form included in each catalog.

Around April 1989, P & G sent out its final catalog. On the front of the catalog was a statement that it was the final catalog and that the offer would expire on February 28, 1990.

Ms. Alligood and others had cut out and saved the teddy bear symbols. The diaper purchasers claim that each package of Pampers contained an offer to enter into a unilateral contract, which they accepted by purchasing Pampers and saving the teddy bear proof-of-purchase symbols.

The precise language of the advertisement printed on packages of Pampers states:

Save these Teddy Bears points and use them to save money on toys, clothes, furniture, and lots of other baby things when you shop the Pampers Baby Catalog. For your free copy of the Catalog, send your name, complete address and youngest baby's date of birth to:

> *Pampers Baby Catalog*
> *P.O. Box 8634,*
> *Clinton, Iowa 52736.*

If P & G refused to redeem the Teddy Bears points, would the purchasers have any contract rights to force P & G to deliver the catalog merchandise? [*Alligood* v. *Procter & Gamble Co.*, 594 N.E.2d 668 (Ohio App. 1991).]

MAKING ETHICS PERSONAL

Disappointing Ad Hype

As you look at the Pepsi and Pampers cases, you may be thinking, "Somehow it doesn't seem fair." While the law sets the minimum legal requirements and standards for contract formation, it does not address the issue of disappointment when consumers believe they can rely on even the humorous word of the company. What standards would you use in your company or ad agency if you were running these promotions and ads? Would you run the ads differently or make disclaimers?

Certain and Definite Terms

One of the ways to determine whether there is intent to contract is also the second requirement for a valid offer. The offer must contain certain and definite language and cover all the terms necessary for a valid contract, which include the following:

- Parties
- Subject matter of the contract
- Price
- Payment terms
- Delivery terms
- Performance times

Under the UCC, the requirements for an offer are not as stringent as the requirements under common law. So long as the offer identifies the parties and the subject matter, the Code sections can cover the details of price, payment, delivery, and performance (see § 2–204 in Appendix G).

Also under the UCC, courts give great weight to industry custom and the previous dealings of the parties in determining whether the terms are certain and definite enough to constitute an offer (see § 2–208 in Appendix G). For example, the parties may have done business with each other for ten years and their agreement simply contains a quantity and a price. Whatever payment and delivery terms have been used in their relationship in the past (their **course of dealing**) will be the terms for their ongoing relationship.

Communication of the Offer

An offer must be communicated to the offeree before it is valid. A letter in which an offer is made is not an offer until the letter reaches the offeree. For example, suppose Office Max had prepared an offer letter to be sent to Renco Rental Equipment and other customers. The letter included an offer for a substantial price discount for computers so that Renco and its regular customers might buy computers at that discount. Before the letter is mailed to Renco, Office Max decides that because the computers are in such high demand it will not send the offer and will just sell them at their full retail price. The letter to Renco and other Office Max customers is never mailed. Renco, realizing the value of the computers and learning of the unmailed letter, cannot accept the discount computer offer because it was never communicated to them.

Some forms of communication are not treated as offers. For example, as the *Leonard* v. *Pepsico* case indicates, television ads are generally not offers. Mass communications of information about deals and prices are generally treated as invitations for offers.

BUSINESS STRATEGY

The Art and Law of Negotiations: Rocky, Bullwinkle, and Binding Contracts

Jay Ward Productions owns the copyrights and trademarks for the cartoon characters Rocky the Flying Squirrel, Bullwinkle the Moose, Boris, Natasha, and Dudley Do-Right (the Ward characters). I.R.V. licenses characters, copyrights, and trademarks for a variety of businesses.

On March 27, 1991, Mrs. Ramona Ward and Ms. Tiffany Ward, the principals of Jay Ward Productions, met with Mr. Irving Handelsman, I.R.V.'s president, to discuss I.R.V. serving as the licensing agent for the Ward characters. I.R.V. had previously been the licensing agent for several of the Ward characters from 1969 through 1991.

Before the March 27 meeting, I.R.V. had held telephone discussions with Ramona and Tiffany Ward, outlining its proposal for obtaining the licensing work for the Ward characters. Mr. Handelsman claims that he was assured by Ramona that I.R.V. would continue to represent the Ward characters.

At the meeting, the Wards emphasized that they wished to maximize their licensing income and that Mr. Handelsman should proceed quickly in order to obtain licensing agreements. At the meeting, Tiffany Ward typed a memo on Jay Ward Productions letterhead, which provided as follows:

© GEOFF MANASSE/PHOTODISC/GETTY IMAGES

March 27, 1991

Dear Irv:

This is to signify our intention to do business with I.R.V. Merchandising on an exclusive merchandising basis with the exception of three companies listed below. When we receive our lawyers go ahead per a contract to be signed and official written release from Peter Piech regarding merchandising rights we are prepared to pay at 25% commission on the first $500,000.00; 30% *on the next million; 35% on the next $500,000.00 and 40% on everything over $2,000,000.00.*

Details of payments, accounting details, etc. to be included in the contract. This contract is to be effective March 27, 1991, for two years.

This intention to do business pertains only to Bullwinkle, Rocky, Boris, Natasha, Mr. Peabody, Sherman, Dudley Do-Right, Aesop, Fractured Fairy Tales. [Hoppity Hooper]

Sincerely,
/s/ Ramona C. Ward

EXCLUSIONS TO CONTRACT; KRAFT FOODS [pasta], RALSTON PURINA [10%], KENTUCKY FRIED CHICKEN

[Note: grammatical errors unchanged]

The Wards told Mr. Handelsman to proceed and that their attorney would be in touch in a few days with the final agreement. Mr. Handelsman negotiated several licensing agreements over the next few days. He notified Ramona Ward of such agreements and indicated that she expressed pleasure.

On April 4, 1991, I.R.V. received a letter from Jay Ward Productions indicating that it had reconsidered its "preliminary feeling" and decided against entering into an agreement with I.R.V. Jay Ward Productions eventually granted the licensing rights to MCA, and MCA subsequently signed up those clients Mr. Handelsman had obtained between the time of the March 27 meeting and the April 4 letter of withdrawal. Jay Ward Productions did not pay Mr. Handelsman license fees on any of these arrangements.

Do you think Mr. Handelsman is entitled to the license fees? List the errors you think the parties made in trying to establish a contractual relationship. Refer to the language, the timing, and the assumptions.

ETHICAL ISSUES

David Pelzman owns a restaurant called "David's on the Main" in Columbus, Ohio. It is a trendy and popular restaurant that is always fully booked for New Year's Eve. Jeff Burrey of Columbus called and made a reservation for New Year's Eve at David's, but did not go to David's as he had planned.

Mr. Pelzman sued Mr. Burrey for breach of contract. Mr. Pelzman says he paid for food and scheduled staff based on the number of reservations he had received. In his suit, Mr. Pelzman asked for $440 in damages or the price of the two-person package for New Year's Eve that parties who wish to participate pay.

Mr. Burrey, upon being served with the suit for his failure to arrive, said, "Never in a million years did I think it was a contract. If they can sue a customer for not showing up for a reservation, then a customer can sue the restaurant for having to wait 15 minutes to be seated when they have a reservation."

Do you think that Mr. Burrey and David's had a contract? Was it fair of Mr. Burrey to make a reservation and then not show up? Was it ethical for Mr. Burrey to do so? Is it a proper use of the courts to have Mr. Pelzman filing this type of suit?

Termination of an Offer by Revocation

Because an offer is one-sided, it can be revoked anytime before acceptance by the offeree. **Revocation** occurs when the offeror notifies the offeree that the offer is no longer good.

There are some limitations on revocation. One such limitation has already been mentioned: Acceptance by the offeree cuts off the right to revoke. Also, under common law, **options** cannot be revoked. An option is a contract in which the offeree pays the offeror for the time needed to consider the offer. For example, suppose that Yolanda's Yogurt is contemplating opening a new restaurant, and Yolanda has a property location in mind but is uncertain about the market potential.

Yolanda does not want the property to be sold to someone else until she can complete a market study. Yolanda could pay the seller (offeror) a sum of money to hold the offer open for thirty days. During that thirty-day period, the offeror can neither revoke the offer nor sell to anyone else.

Under the UCC, there is a form of an option that, without the offeree's payment, makes an offer irrevocable. Under a **merchant's firm offer** (see § 2–205 in Appendix G), the offer must be made by a merchant, put in some form of record,[4] and signed by the merchant. If these requirements are met, the merchant must hold the offer open for a definite time period (but no longer than three months). A merchant is someone who is in the business of selling the goods that are the subject matter of the contract or who holds particular skills or expertise in dealing with the goods. A rain check for sale merchandise from a store is an example of this type of offer. The firm offer cannot be revoked if the requirements are met, and money or consideration is not one of those requirements.

Termination of an Offer by Rejection

An offer carries no legally binding obligation for the offeree, who is free to accept or reject the offer. Once the offeree rejects the offer, the offer is ended and cannot later be accepted unless the offeror renews the offer.

Rejection by Counteroffer under Common Law
An offer also ends when the offeree does not fully reject the offer but rejects some portion of the offer or modifies it before acceptance. These changes and rejections are called **counteroffers**.

The effect of a counteroffer is that the original offer is no longer valid, and the offeree now becomes the offeror as the counteroffer becomes the new offer. Consider the following dialogue as an example:

CONSIDER... 13.5

December 30, 1977: John Hancock Insurance Company sends a commitment letter to Houston Dairy offering to loan Houston $800,000 at 9.25 percent interest; acceptance must be in writing within seven days and must be accompanied by a $16,000 letter of credit or cashier's check.

January 17, 1978: The president of Houston Dairy sends a letter of acceptance to Hancock along with a cashier's check.

January 23, 1978: Hancock cashes the check, which went through standard company processing.

Hancock claims there is no contract because the acceptance occurred after the offer had expired. Houston Dairy maintains that its letter of acceptance was a new offer that was accepted by Hancock with the cashing of the check. Who is correct? Is there a contract?

> Alice: I will pay you $50 to paint the trim on my house.
> Brad: I will do it for $75.

Alice made the first offer. Brad's language is a counteroffer and a rejection at the same time. Alice is now free to accept or reject the $75 offer. If Alice declines the $75 counteroffer, Brad cannot then force Alice to contract for the original $50 because the offer ended. Consider 13.5 deals with an issue of offers and counteroffers.

Rejection by Counteroffer under the UCC   Under the UCC, modification by offerees was seen as a necessary part of doing business, and Section 2–207 (see Appendix G) allows flexibility for such modifications. Under the previous Section 2–207 (which may still be the law in some states because the adoption of the new UCC is not yet universal), there are two separate rules for modifications: one governs merchants, and the other governs nonmerchant transactions. Exhibit 13.2 shows a chart of the rules.

EXHIBIT 13.2 UCC Rules for Additional Terms in Acceptance under Former Article 2

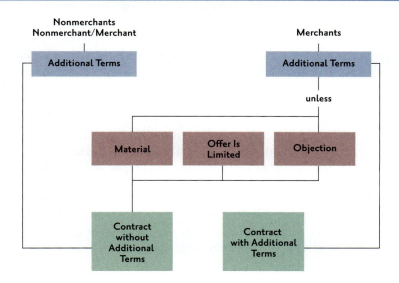

For nonmerchants, the addition of terms in the counteroffer does not result in a rejection; there will still be a contract if there is a clear intent to contract, but the additional terms will not be a part of the contract.

For example, consider the following dialogue:

Joe: I will sell you my pinball machine for $250.
Jan: I'll take it. Include $10 in dimes.

Joe and Jan have a contract, but the $10 in dimes is not a part of the contract. If Jan wanted the dimes, she should have negotiated before formally accepting the offer.

For merchants (both parties must be merchants), former Section 2–207 has more complicated rules and details on additional terms in acceptance. Sometimes called the **battle of the forms**, Section 2–207 covers situations in which offerors and offerees send purchase orders and invoices back and forth with the understanding that they have a contract. Under Section 2–207, if the parties reach a basic agreement but the offeree has added terms, there will be an enforceable contract; the added terms are not a rejection under Section 2–207. Whether the added terms will become a part of the contract depends on the following questions.

1. Are the terms material?
2. Was the offer limited?
3. Does one side object?

If the terms the offeree adds to the original offer terms are *material,* they do not become a part of the contract. For example, suppose that Alfie sent a purchase order to Bob for twelve dozen red four-inch balloons at 4 cents each. Bob sends back an invoice that reflects the quantity and price, but Bob's invoice also has a section that states, "There are no warranties express or implied on these goods." Do Alfie and Bob have a contract with or without warranties? The waiver of warranties is a material change in what Alfie gets: now a contract without warranties. Because it is material, Section 2–207 protects Alfie and the warranty waiver is not part of the contract.

Terms that can be added but are not considered material are such payment terms as "30 days same as cash." Shipment terms are generally immaterial unless the method of shipment is unusually costly.

An offeror can avoid the problems of form battles and Section 2–207 by simply *limiting* the offer to the terms stated. The following language could be used: "This offer is limited to these terms." If the offeree attempts to add terms in the acceptance, there will be a contract, but the added terms will not be part of the contract. For example, suppose Alfie's offer on the balloons was limited and Bob accepted but added that the payment terms were "30 days same as cash." They would still have a contract but without the additional payment term.

A final portion of Section 2–207 allows the parties to take action to eliminate additional terms. They can do so by *objecting* to any added terms within a reasonable time. For example, if Alfie's offer was not limited and Bob accepted the payment terms, Alfie could object to the payment terms and they would then not be a part of the contract. Exhibit 13.2, as already noted, summarizes the UCC's Section 2–207 rules. As noted earlier, the most significant changes under Revised Article 2 deal with Section 2–207. The new language for Section 2–207 provides:

If (i) conduct by both parties recognizes the existence of a contract although their records do not otherwise establish a contract, (ii) a contract is formed by an offer and acceptance, (iii) a contract formed in any manner is confirmed by a record that contains terms additional to or different from those in the contract being confirmed, the terms of the contract, subject to Section 2–202, are:

(a) terms that appear in the records of both parties;
(b) terms, whether in a record or not, to which both parties agree; and
(c) terms supplied or incorporated under any provision of this Act.

Because so many confusing circumstances arose under the merchant/nonmerchant rules, materiality issues, and other concerns because of additional terms, the effect of the new Section 2–207 is to leave the issues of what is or is not included in a contract not to rigid rules and exceptions set forth in old Section 2–207 but to the courts that can determine the intent of the parties. The courts will determine, on a case-by-case basis, what is included as part of the contract, in some cases regardless of what the "record" provides. Revised Section 2–207 applies to merchants and nonmerchants alike and regardless of whether the parties use forms. The new UCC Section 2–207 is often called the "terms later" provision because it permits parties to go forward with contract performance and decide on terms later or resolve any disputes only if they arise during the course of performance. One writer has referred to "terms later" as bad economics because of the inability of parties to rely on definitive laws in making contracts and then performing under them.[5] *ProCD, Inc. v. Zeidenberg* (Case 13.3), the "terms later"/shrinkwrap acceptance case that began the great Section 2–207 reform debate, follows.

CASE 13.3

ProCD, Inc. v. *Zeidenberg*
86 F.3d 1447 (7th Cir. 1996)

When the Terms Are Not Wrapped Up

FACTS

At a cost of $10 million, ProCD created a comprehensive national directory of residential and business listings in its CD-ROM product, Select PhoneTM. The directory CD developed by ProCD included over 95,000,000 residential and commercial listings that ProCD had obtained from approximately 3,000 publicly available telephone books. While the telephonic information itself was not copyrightable, there was a copyright associated with the format of the CD and accessing information. ProCD wanted to be certain that purchasers of Select Phone (trademark) did not use the data to become competitors, so it included a restrictive use contract, or "license," as part of its sales transaction. However, this competitive restriction and others were not disclosed prior to the time of the purchase of the CD. ProCD included the covenants and restrictions in shrink-wrapped boxes that were shipped to cus-

tomers and that contained a user guide and the discs. The user guide contained the terms prohibiting copying of the data for other than personal use. The discs were programmed so that upon installation the purchaser was alerted that the use of the product and the data was subject to the Single User License Agreement. One of the terms of the agreement provided that by using the discs and the listings, purchasers agreed to be bound by the terms of the license. Purchasers who did not agree to the terms were required to return the discs and the user guide, along with all copies of the software and listings that had been exported, promptly, to the place where the product had been obtained.

Matthew Zeidenberg had purchased an earlier version of Select Phone at a local retail store. Some months later he purchased an updated version of Select Phone to download telephone listings from it so that he could

continued

incorporate them into a larger database he was developing and planned to market. Mr. Zeidenberg indicated in testimony he was aware from the computer screen warnings that Select Phone was subject to the agreement contained in the user guide, but he disregarded them because he did not believe the license was binding. ProCD brought suit in federal district court to enjoin competitive commercial use by Mr. Zeidenberg, asserting that such use constituted copyright infringement and breach of the license agreement.

The district court rejected ProCD's copyright challenge, finding that using the software to access the noncopyrighted listings and then subsequently making copies of the listings without further use of the ProCD software did not constitute a copyright infringement.

ProCD appealed.

JUDICIAL OPINION

EASTERBROOK, Circuit Judge

Must buyers of computer software obey the terms of shrinkwrap licenses? The district court held not, for two reasons: first, they are not contracts because the licenses are inside the box rather than printed on the outside; second, federal law forbids enforcement even if the licenses are contracts. [W]e disagree with the district judge's conclusion. Shrinkwrap licenses are enforceable unless their terms are objectionable on grounds applicable to contracts in general (for example, if they violate a rule of positive law, or if they are unconscionable). Because no one argues that the terms of the license at issue here are troublesome, we remand with instructions to enter judgment for the plaintiff.

If ProCD had to recover all of its costs and make a profit by charging a single price—that is, if it could not charge more to commercial users than to the general public—it would have to raise the price substantially over $150. The ensuing reduction in sales would harm consumers who value the information at, say, $200. They get consumer surplus of $50 under the current arrangement but would cease to buy if the price rose substantially. If because of high elasticity of demand in the consumer segment of the market the only way to make a profit turned out to be a price attractive to commercial users alone, then all consumers would lose out—and so would the commercial clients, who would have to pay more for the listings because ProCD could not obtain any contribution toward costs from the consumer market.

To make price discrimination work, however, the seller must be able to control arbitrage. An air carrier sells tickets for less to vacationers than to business travelers, using advance purchase and Saturday-night-stay requirements to distinguish the categories. A producer of movies segments the market by time, releasing first to theaters, then to pay-per-view services, next to the videotape and laserdisc market, and finally to cable and commercial tv. Vendors of computer software have a harder task. Anyone can walk into a retail store and buy a box. Customers do not wear tags saying "commercial user" or "consumer user." Anyway, even a commercial-user-detector at the door would not work, because a consumer could buy the software and resell to a commercial user. That arbitrage would break down the price discrimination and drive up the minimum price at which ProCD would sell to anyone.

Instead of tinkering with the product and letting users sort themselves—for example, furnishing current data at a high price that would be attractive only to commercial customers, and two-year-old data at a low price—ProCD turned to the institution of contract. Every box containing its consumer product declares that the software comes with restrictions stated in an enclosed license. This license, which is encoded on the CD-ROM disks as well as printed in the manual, and which appears on a user's screen every time the software runs, limits use of the application program and listings to non-commercial purposes.

The district court held the licenses ineffectual because their terms do not appear on the outside of the packages. The court added that the second and third licenses stand no different from the first, even though they are identical, because they might have been different, and a purchaser does not agree to—and cannot be bound by—terms that were secret at the time of purchase.

Following the district court, we treat the licenses as ordinary contracts accompanying the sale of products, and therefore as governed by the common law of contracts and the Uniform Commercial Code. Whether there are legal differences between "contracts" and "licenses" (which may matter under the copyright doctrine of first sale) is a subject for another day. Zeidenberg does argue, and the district court held, that placing the package of software on the shelf is an "offer," which the customer "accepts" by paying the asking price and leaving the store with the goods. In Wisconsin, as elsewhere, a contract includes only the terms on which the parties have agreed. One cannot agree to hidden terms, . . . So far, so good—but one of the terms to which Zeidenberg agreed by purchasing the software is that the transaction was subject to a license. Zeidenberg's position therefore must be that the printed terms on the outside of a box are the parties' contract—except for printed terms that refer to or incorporate other terms. But why would Wisconsin fetter the parties' choice in this way? Vendors can put the entire terms of a contract on the outside of a box only by using microscopic type, removing other information that buyers might find more useful (such as what the software does, and on which computers it works), or both. The "Read Me" file included with most software, describing system requirements and potential incompatibilities, may be equivalent to ten pages of type; warranties and license restrictions take still more space. Notice on the outside, terms on the inside, and a right to return the software for a refund if the terms are unacceptable (a right that the license expressly extends), may be a means of doing business valuable to buyers and sellers alike. Doubtless a state could forbid the use of standard contracts in the software business, but we do not think that Wisconsin has done so.

Transactions in which the exchange of money precedes the communication of detailed terms are common. Consider the purchase of insurance. The buyer goes to an agent, who explains the essentials (amount of coverage, number of years) and remits the premium to the home office, which sends back a policy. On the district judge's understanding, the terms of the policy are irrelevant because the insured paid before receiving them. Yet the device of payment, often with a "binder" (so that the insurance takes effect immediately even though the home office reserves the right to withdraw coverage later), in advance of the policy, serves buyers' interests by accelerating effectiveness and reducing transactions costs. Or consider the purchase of an airline ticket. The traveler calls the carrier or an agent, is quoted a price, reserves a seat, pays, and gets a ticket, in that order. The ticket contains elaborate terms, which the traveler can reject by canceling the reservation. To use the ticket is to accept the terms, even terms that in retrospect are disadvantageous. Just so with a ticket to a concert. The back of the ticket states that the patron promises not to record the concert; to attend is to agree. A theater that detects a violation will confiscate the tape and escort the violator to the exit. One could arrange things so that every concertgoer signs this promise before forking over the money, but that cumbersome way of doing things not only would lengthen queues and raise prices but also would scotch the sale of tickets by phone or electronic data service.

Consumer goods work the same way. Someone who wants to buy a radio set visits a store, pays, and walks out with a box. Inside the box is a leaflet containing some terms, the most important of which usually is the warranty, read for the first time in the comfort of home. By Zeidenberg's lights, the warranty in the box is irrelevant; every consumer gets the standard warranty implied by the UCC in the event the contract is silent; yet so far as we are aware no state disregards warranties furnished with consumer products. Drugs come with a list of ingredients on the outside and an elaborate package insert on the inside. The package insert describes drug interactions, contraindications, and

other vital information—but, if Zeidenberg is right, the purchaser need not read the package insert, because it is not part of the contract.

Next consider the software industry itself. Only a minority of sales take place over the counter, where there are boxes to peruse. A customer may place an order by phone in response to a line item in a catalog or a review in a magazine. Much software is ordered over the Internet by purchasers who have never seen a box. Increasingly software arrives by wire. There is no box; there is only a stream of electrons, a collection of information that includes data, an application program, instructions, many limitations. The user purchases a serial number, which activates the software's features. On Zeidenberg's arguments, these unboxed sales are unfettered by terms—so the seller has made a broad warranty and must pay consequential damages for any shortfalls in performance, two "promises" that if taken seriously would drive prices through the ceiling or return transactions to the horse-and-buggy age.

According to the district court, the UCC does not countenance the sequence of money now, terms later. One of the court's reasons—that by proposing as part of the draft Article 2B a new UCC § 2–2203 that would explicitly validate standard-form user licenses, the American Law Institute and the National Conference of Commissioners on Uniform Laws have conceded the invalidity of shrinkwrap licenses under current law, . . . To propose a change in a law's text is not necessarily to propose a change in the law's effect. New words may be designed to fortify the current rule with a more precise text that curtails uncertainty. To judge by the flux of law review articles discussing shrink-wrap licenses, uncertainty is much in need of reduction—although businesses seem to feel less uncertainty than do scholars, for only three cases (other than ours) touch on the subject, and none directly addresses it. As their titles suggest, these are not consumer transactions.

What then does the current version of the UCC have to say? We think that the place to start is § 2–204(1): "A contract for sale of goods may be made in any manner sufficient to show agreement, including conduct by both parties which recognizes the existence of such a contract." A vendor, as master of the offer, may invite acceptance by conduct, and may propose limitations on the kind of conduct that constitutes acceptance. A buyer may accept by performing the acts the vendor proposes to treat as acceptance. And that is what happened. ProCD proposed a contract that a buyer would accept by using the software after having an opportunity to read the license at leisure. This Zeidenberg did. He had no choice, because the software

continued

splashed the license on the screen and would not let him proceed without indicating acceptance. So although the district judge was right to say that a contract can be, and often is, formed simply by paying the price and walking out of the store, the UCC permits contracts to be formed in other ways. ProCD proposed such a different way, and without protest Zeidenberg agreed. Ours is not a case in which a consumer opens a package to find an insert saying "you owe us an extra $10,000" and the seller files suit to collect. Any buyer finding such a demand can prevent formation of the contract by returning the package, as can any consumer who concludes that the terms of the license make the software worth less than the purchase price. Nothing in the UCC requires a seller to maximize the buyer's net gains.

Section 2–606, which defines "acceptance of goods", reinforces this understanding. A buyer accepts goods under § 2–606(1)(b) when, after an opportunity to inspect, he fails to make an effective rejection under § 2–602(1). ProCD extended an opportunity to reject if a buyer should find the license terms unsatisfactory; Zeidenberg inspected the package, tried out the software, learned of the license, and did not reject the goods. We refer to § 2–606 only to show that the opportunity to return goods can be important; acceptance of an offer differs from acceptance of goods after delivery, but the UCC consistently permits the parties to structure their relations so that the buyer has a chance to make a final decision after a detailed review.

ProCD has rivals, which may elect to compete by offering superior software, monthly updates, improved terms of use, lower price, or a better compromise among these elements. As we stressed above, adjusting terms in buyers' favor might help Matthew Zeidenberg today (he already has the software) but would lead to a response, such as a higher price, that might make consumers as a whole worse off.

REVERSED AND REMANDED.

CASE QUESTIONS

1. What was the buyer doing with the CD and information?

2. When did the buyer learn of restrictions on the use of the CD?

3. Why does the court find that the UCC allows post-contract terms?

4. What problems do you see resulting from post-contract terms?

5. Are post-contract terms part of the old Section 2–207 or the new Section 2–207?

 CONSIDER...   **13.6**

Mary DeFontes, Nicholas Long, and others purchased computers from Dell Computers. The following notice appeared on the boxes in which the computers were sent.

TERMS AND CONDITIONS AGREEMENT

PLEASE READ THIS DOCUMENT CAREFULLY! IT CONTAINS VERY IMPORTANT INFORMATION ABOUT YOUR RIGHTS AND OBLIGATIONS, AS WELL AS LIMITATIONS AND EXCLUSIONS THAT MAY APPLY TO YOU. THIS DOCUMENT CONTAINS A DISPUTE RESOLUTION CLAUSE.

This Agreement contains the terms and conditions that apply to purchases by Home, Home Office, and Small Business customers from the Dell entity named on the invoice ("Dell"). By accepting delivery of the computer systems, related products, and/or services and support, and/or other products described on that invoice. [sic] You ("Customer") agrees [sic] to be bound by and accepts [sic] these terms and conditions. . . . These terms and conditions are subject to change without prior written notice at any time, in Dell's sole discretion. . . .

2. Governing law. THIS AGREEMENT AND ANY SALES THEREUNDER SHALL BE GOVERNED BY THE LAWS OF THE STATE OF TEXAS, WITHOUT REGARD TO CONFLICTS OF LAWS RULES. . . .

*2)

13. Binding Arbitration. ANY CLAIM, DISPUTE, OR CONTROVERSY (WHETHER IN CONTRACT, TORT, OR OTHERWISE, WHETHER PREEXISTING, PRESENT OR FUTURE, AND INCLUDING STATUTORY, COMMONLAW, INTENTIONAL TORT AND EQUITABLE CLAIMS) AGAINST DELL, its agents, employees, successors, assigns or affiliates . . . arising from or relating to this Agreement, its interpreta-

tion, or the breach, termination or validity thereof, the relationships which result from this Agreement (including, to the full extent permitted by applicable law, relationships with third parties who are not signatories to this Agreement), Dell's advertising, or any related purchase SHALL BE RESOLVED EXCLUSIVELY AND FINALLY BY BINDING ARBITRATION ADMINISTERED BY THE NATIONAL ARBITRATION FORUM (NAF) under its Code of Procedure then in effect. . . . The arbitration will be limited solely to the dispute or controversy between Customer and Dell. Any award of the arbitrator(s) shall be final and binding on each of the parties, and may be entered as a judgment in any court of competent jurisdiction. Information may be obtained and claims may be filed with the NAF at P.O. Box 50191, Minneapolis, MN 55405. . . .

Ms. DeFontes and the others say they cannot be bound by an arbitration clause given to them after they purchased the computer and in circumstances in which they had no choice if they wanted to use the computer they had purchased.

Are they bound by the arbitration clause and other provisions? [*Defontes v. Dell Computers Corp.,* 2004 WL 253560 52 UCC Rep 2d 795 (R.I.Super. 2004).]

 CONSIDER. . . **1 3 . 7**

Schulze and Burch Biscuit Company (Schulze) purchased low-moisture 16-mesh dehydrated apple powder from Tree Top, Inc. to use in making strawberry and blueberry "Toastettes," which it sells to Nabisco, Inc.

On April 27, 1984, E. Edward Park, Schulze's director of procurement, telephoned Rudolph Brady, a broker for Tree Top, and ordered 40,000 pounds of Tree Top's apple powder. Mr. Park told Mr. Brady that the purchase was subject to a Schulze purchase order and gave Mr. Brady the number of the purchase order, but Mr. Park did not send the purchase order or a copy of it to Mr. Brady or to Tree Top. On the front of the purchase order was the following clause:

> **Important:** *The fulfillment of this order or any part of it obligates the Seller to abide by the terms, conditions and instructions on both sides of this order. Additional or substitute terms will not become part of this contract unless expressly accepted by Buyer; Seller's acceptance is limited to the terms of this order, and no contract will be formed except on these terms.*

Shortly after the telephone conversation, Mr. Brady sent Schulze a form entitled simply "Confirmation" that listed Mr. Brady as broker, Schulze as buyer, and Tree Top as seller as well as the quantity, price, shipping arrangements, and payment terms. It also showed the purchase order number that Mr. Park had given to Mr. Brady. Several preprinted provisions, including an arbitration clause, stood on the lower portion of the form:

> *Seller guarantees goods to conform to the national pure food laws. All disputes under this transaction shall be arbitrated in the usual manner. This confirmation shall be subordinate to more formal contract, when and if such contract is executed. In the absence of such contract, this confirmation represents the contract of the parties. If incorrect, please advise immediately.*

Mr. Brady had sent a similar confirmation form to Schulze in each of at least ten previous transactions between Tree Top and Schulze. Schulze had never objected to any of the preprinted provisions. Schulze had sent Mr. Brady a purchase order in two of those transactions; in each of the other transactions, as in the present case, Schulze simply informed Mr. Brady of the number of the appropriate purchase order.

Subsequently, Schulze brought suit seeking damages for breach of contract, alleging that the dehydrated apple powder had been so full of apple stems and wood splinters that it clogged the machinery of Schulze's Toastette assembly line, causing the line to shut

continued

down, with various financial losses. Schulze alleged that the powder thus failed to meet Schulze's specifications, which had governed the previous sales of apple powder. Tree Top alleged that the dispute was subject to arbitration because of the arbitration clause in the confirmation sent by Mr. Brady to Schulze. Does the arbitration clause apply? Decide under both old and new UCC Section 2–207. [*Schulze and Burch Biscuit Co.* v. *Tree Top, Inc.,* 831 F.2d 709 (7th Cir. 1987).]

FOR THE MANAGER'S DESK

RE: CHECKLIST FOR CONTRACT PRELIMINARIES

1. Do your contract homework.

   a. Do background checks—check references, complaints at state and private agencies, court dockets.

   b. Learn the nature of the business and industry custom—learn to use the language.

2. Negotiate details.

   a. Agree on terms that help you accomplish your purpose ("apple powder for bakery equipment," not just "apple powder").

   b. Make sure your written agreement is complete.

RE: CHECKLIST FOR DRAFTING CONTRACTS

1. Identify both parties clearly. Be certain corporate names are correct. Make sure the parties have the proper authority to enter into the transaction. (Are copies of board resolutions approving the contract available?)

2. Define the terms used in the contract, including industry terms.

3. List all terms: price, subject matter, quantity, delivery, payment terms.

4. Answer "what if" questions. (What if payment is not made? What if deliveries are late?)

Exhibit 13.3 shows the new way terms added under new Section 2–207 are treated.

EXHIBIT 13.3 Additional Terms under New UCC Section 2–207

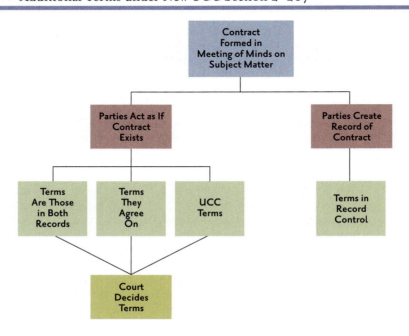

C O N S I D E R . . .   **1 3 . 8**

In the following three dialogues, determine whether there would be a contract under both new and old Section UCC 2–207.

1. A: "I'll sell you my Peugeot bicycle for $100."
   B: "I'll take it. Include your tire pump."
   Result:
   OLD UCC _____
   NEW UCC _____

2. A: "I'll sell you my white 1974 Ford Torino for $358. This offer is limited to these terms."
   B: "I'll take it. Furnish a history of repairs."
   Result:
   OLD UCC _____
   NEW UCC _____

3. A: "I'll sell you my antique Coca-Cola sign."
   B: "I'll take it if you will deliver it."
   Result:
   OLD UCC _____
   NEW UCC _____

Termination by Offer Expiration

An offer can end by expiring and, once expired, can no longer be accepted by the offeree. For example, if an offer states that it will remain open until November 1, it automatically terminates on November 1, and no one has the power to accept the offer after that time. The death of the offeror also ends the offer, unless the offeree holds an option. Even offers without time limits expire after a reasonable time has passed. For example, an offer to buy a home is probably only good for one or two weeks because the offeror needs to know whether to try for another house. The offeror's offer terminates naturally if the offeree fails to accept within that time frame.

Acceptance: The Offeree's Response

An **acceptance** is the offeree's positive response to the offeror's proposed contract, and only persons to whom the offer is made have the power of acceptance. That acceptance must be communicated to the offeror using the proper method of communication, which can be controlled by the offeror or left to the offeree. In either case, the method of communication controls the effective time of the acceptance.

Acceptance by Stipulated Means

Some offerors give a required means of acceptance that is called a specified or **stipulated means**. If the offeree uses the stipulated means of acceptance, the acceptance is effective sooner than the offeror's receipt; the acceptance is effective when it is properly sent. For example, if the offeror has required the acceptance to be mailed and the offeree properly mails the letter of acceptance, the acceptance is effective when it is sent. This timing rule for acceptance is called the **mailbox rule**, and it applies in stipulated means offers so long as the offeree uses the stipulated means to communicate acceptance.

Acceptance with No Stipulated Means

If the offeror does not stipulate a means of acceptance, the offeree is free to use any method for communication of the acceptance. If the offeree uses the same method

EXHIBIT   13.4   Timing Rules for Acceptance

TYPE OF OFFER	METHOD OF ACCEPTANCE	ACCEPTANCE EFFECTIVE?
No means given	Same or reasonable method of communication*	When properly mailed, dispatched (mailbox rule)
No means given	Slower or unreasonable method of communication	When received, if offer still open
Means specified (specified or stipulated means)	Stipulated means used	Mailbox rule
Means stipulated (specified or stipulated means)	Stipulated means not used	Counteroffer and rejection

*Some states still follow the common law rule that requires the same UCC rule.

of communication or a reasonable means, the mailbox rule also applies. If the offeree uses a slower method of acceptance, the acceptance is not effective until it is received. Exhibit 13.4 summarizes the timing of acceptance rules. *Cantu* v. *Central Education Agency* (Case 13.4) deals with an issue of timing on offer and acceptance.

CASE 13.4

Cantu v. *Central Education Agency*
884 S.W. 2d 565 (Tex. App. 1994)

The Teacher's Lesson on Acceptance

FACTS

Ms. Cantu had a teaching contract with the San Benito Consolidated Independent School District. She hand-delivered to her supervisor a written offer to resign. Three days later the superintendent of schools mailed her a letter accepting the offer of resignation. Ms. Cantu then changed her mind and the next day hand-delivered a letter withdrawing her resignation. The superintendent refused to recognize the attempted rescission of the resignation. Ms. Cantu appealed to the state district court. It decided against her, and she again appealed.

JUDICIAL OPINION

SMITH, Justice

. . . Cantu was hired as a special-education teacher by the San Benito Consolidated Independent School District under a one-year contract for the 1990–91 school year. On Saturday, August 18, 1990, shortly before the start of the school year, Cantu hand-delivered to her supervisor a letter of resignation, effective August 17, 1990. In this letter, Cantu requested that her final paycheck be forwarded to an address in McAllen, Texas, some fifty miles from the San Benito office where she tendered the resignation. The San Benito superintendent of schools, the only official authorized to accept resignations on behalf of the school district, received Cantu's resignation on Monday, August 20. The superintendent wrote a letter accepting Cantu's resignation

the same day and deposited the letter, properly stamped and addressed, in the mail at approximately 5:15 P.M. that afternoon. At about 8:00 A.M. the next morning, August 21, Cantu hand-delivered to the superintendent's office a letter withdrawing her resignation.

This letter contained a San Benito return address. In response, the superintendent hand-delivered that same day a copy of his letter mailed the previous day to inform Cantu that her resignation had been accepted and could not be withdrawn.

The State Commissioner of Education concluded that, because the school district's acceptance of Cantu's resignation was effective when mailed, an agreement to rescind Cantu's employment contract was in force when she attempted to withdraw her offer of resignation and the school district's refusal to honor her contract was not unlawful.

The sole legal question presented for our review is the proper scope of the "mail-box rule" under Texas law and whether the rule was correctly applied. . . . Cantu contends . . . that the trial court erred in ruling that the agreement to rescind her contract of employment became effective when the superintendent deposited his letter accepting Cantu's resignation in the mail. Cantu argues that, under Texas law, an acceptance binds the parties in contract on mailing only if the offeror has sent the offer by mail or has expressly authorized acceptance by mail. There was no express authorization for the school district to accept Cantu's offer by mail. The question presented is whether authorization to accept by mail may be implied only when the offer is delivered by mail or also when the existing circumstances make it reasonable for the offeree to so accept.

The aphorism "the offeror is the master of his offer" reflects the power of the offeror to impose conditions on acceptance of an offer, specify the manner of acceptance, or withdraw the offer before the offeree has effectively exercised the power of acceptance. However, more often than not, an offeror does not expressly authorize a particular mode, medium, or manner of acceptance. Consequently, particularly with parties communicating at a distance, a rule of law is needed to establish the point of contract formation and allocate the risk of loss and inconvenience that inevitably falls to one of the parties between the time that the offeree exercises, and the offeror receives, the acceptance. See 1 Arthur L. Corbin, *Contracts* § 78 (1963).

As Professor Corbin notes, courts could adopt a rule that no acceptance is effective until received, absent express authorization by the offeror; however, the mailbox rule, which makes acceptance effective on dispatch, closes the deal and enables performance more promptly, and places the risk of inconvenience on the party who originally has power to control the manner of acceptance. . . . "Even though the offer was not made by mail and there was no [express] authorization, the existing circumstances may be such as to make it reasonable for the offeree to accept by mail and to give the offeror reason to know that the acceptance will be so made." . . . In short, acceptance by mail is impliedly authorized if reasonable under the circumstances.

The *Restatement* approves and adopts this approach: an acceptance by any medium reasonable under the circumstances is effective on dispatch, absent a contrary indication in the offer. *Restatement (Second) of Contracts* §§ 30(2), 63(a), 65, 66 (1979). In addition, the *Restatement* specifically recognizes that acceptance by mail is ordinarily reasonable if the parties are negotiating at a distance or *even if a written offer is delivered in person to an offeree in the same city*. . . . The same standard, *viz.*, whether the manner of acceptance is reasonable under the circumstances, governs offer and acceptance in commercial transactions under the Texas Business and Commerce Code. (Uniform Commercial Code § 2–206.)

Cantu relies primarily on a 1903 opinion of the Texas Supreme Court to support her contention that an offeree is impliedly authorized to accept by mail only if the offer is submitted through the mail. *Scottish-American Mortgage Co. v. Davis*, 96 Tex. 504, 74 S.W. 17 (1903).

A more recent opinion of the supreme court, *McKinney v. Croan*, 144 Tex. 9, 188 S.W.2d 144 (1945), suggests that circumstances indicating the reasonableness

of an acceptance be considered in determining whether an acceptance by mail is impliedly authorized and effective on mailing. In holding that a reply to a request for admissions was effective when mailed, the *McKinney* court specifically noted that the "parties resided about 350 miles apart," in addition to noting that the request was sent by mail. . . . The court also cited to 17 C.J.S. *Contracts* § 52, which reads: The request or authorization to communicate the acceptance by mail is implied in two cases, namely: (1) Where the post is used to make the offer . . . (2) *Where the circumstances are such that it must have been within the contemplation of the parties that according to the ordinary usages of mankind the post might be used as a means of communicating the acceptance.* . . .

The *McKinney* court's express mention of the distance between the parties as a circumstance making acceptance by mail reasonable and its affirmation of an authority following the modern trend that *either* mail delivery of the offer *or* reasonable circumstances might impliedly authorize communication by mail convince us that Texas law is not frozen into the rigid 1903 position urged by appellant. As we noted earlier, Texas courts are directed by statute to consider whether acceptance by mail is reasonable under the circumstances in commercial transactions. . . . § 2.206 . . . We hold that it is proper to consider whether acceptance by mail is reasonably implied under the circumstances, whether or not the offer was delivered by mail.

. . . It was reasonable for the superintendent to accept Cantu's offer of resignation by mail. Cantu tendered her resignation shortly before the start of the school year—at a time when both parties could not fail to appreciate the need for immediate action by the district to locate a replacement. In fact, she delivered the letter on a Saturday, when the Superintendent could neither receive nor respond to her offer, further delaying matters by two days. Finally, Cantu's request that her final paycheck be forwarded to an address some fifty miles away indicated that she could no longer be reached in San Benito and that she did not intend to return to the school premises or school-district offices. The Commissioner of Education and district court properly considered that it was reasonable for the school district to accept Cantu's offer by mail. . . .

Judgment affirmed.

CASE QUESTIONS

1. Who was the offeror? Does the UCC apply in this case?

2. Why did the court refer to the fact that Ms. Cantu's forwarding address was fifty miles away from the place where she delivered her offer to resign?

3. What is the distinction between the *Davis* case and the *McKinney* case?

E-Commerce and Contract Formation

The Internet has provided a means for contracting online. However, the courts have been left to deal with the issue of whether and when a contract has been formed. The new rules that have emerged regarding cyberspace contracts focus on whether the parties knew the terms and whether they voluntarily accepted those terms once aware of them. In other words, the rules on contract formation in cyberspace require that the parties prove that a click was something more than an accidental action and that the click was made after there had been full disclosure of the terms.

A new section of revised Article 2 deals with electronic communication of acceptance, including the timing issues. Section 2–213 provides that "receipt of an electronic communication has a legal effect, it has that effect even though no individual is aware of its receipt," and that acknowledgment of the receipt of an electronic communication is receipt but, "in itself, does not establish that the content sent corresponds to the content received." So, receipt is required for electronic communication and receipt occurs when the e-mail arrives, even if the receiver does not know it has arrived. Also, the parties are left to use other means of proof to establish that all of the message made it from one party to another because acknowledging receipt does not mean that all terms arrived.

Sellers generally accomplish these two goals by establishing on their Web sites "clickon," "clickthrough," or "clickwrap" agreements. The company or offeror simply lists all the terms of the agreement that the visitor/offeree is about to enter into. The visitor/offeree must click on "I agree" or "I agree to these terms," or he or she cannot proceed to the completion of the contract segments of the site. The terms include cost, payment, warranties, arbitration provisions, and so on, and all applicable terms must be spelled out in advance of the "I agree" click point.

Because this type of contract formation is so new, case law is rare, but *M.A. Mortenson Co., Inc. v. Timberline Software Corp.* (Case 13.5) is one example of a "clickwrap" dispute.

CASE 13.5

M.A. Mortenson Co., Inc. v. Timberline Software Corp.
998 P.2d 305 (Wash. 2000)

Wrapping Up the Acceptance on Shrinking Liability

FACTS

M.A. Mortenson Company, Inc. (Mortenson) (petitioner), a general construction contractor, purchased licensed computer software from Timberline Software Corporation (Timberline) (respondent) through Softworks Data Systems, Inc. (respondent), Timberline's local authorized dealer.

Since at least 1990, Mortenson has used Timberline's Bid Analysis software to assist with its preparation of bids. Mortenson had used Medallion, an earlier version of Bid Analysis, at its Minnesota headquarters and its regional offices. In early 1993, Mortenson installed a new computer network operating system at its Bellevue, Washington, office and contacted Mark Reich, president of Softworks, to reinstall Medallion.

Mr. Reich discovered, however, that the Medallion software was incompatible with Mortenson's new operating system. Mr. Reich informed Mortenson that Precision, a newer version of Bid Analysis, was compatible with its new operating system.

After Mr. Reich provided Mortenson with a price quote, Mortenson issued a purchase order dated July 12, 1993, confirming the agreed-upon purchase price, setup fee, delivery charges, and sales tax for eight copies of the software. The purchase order indicated that Softworks, on behalf of Timberline, would "[f]urnish current versions of Timberline Precision Bid Analysis Program Software and Keys" and "[p]rovide assistance in installation and system configuration for Mortenson's Bellevue Office." The purchase order also contained the following notations:

—Provide software support in converting Mortenson's existing Bid Day Master Files to a format accepted by the newly purchased Bid Day software. This work shall be accomplished on a time and material basis of $85.00 per hour. Format information of conversion of existing D-Base Files to be shared to assist Mortenson Mid-West programmers in file conversion.

—System software support and upgrades to be available from Timberline for newly purchased versions of Bid Day Multi-User.

—At some future date should Timberline upgrade "Bid Day" to a windows version, M.A. Mortenson would be able to upgrade to this system with Timberline crediting existing software purchase toward that upgrade on a pro-rated basis to be determined later.

Below the signature line the following was stated: "ADVISE PURCHASING PROMPTLY IF UNABLE TO SHIP AS REQUIRED. EACH SHIPMENT MUST INCLUDE A PACKING LIST. SUBSTITUTIONS OF GOODS OR CHANGES IN COSTS REQUIRE OUR PRIOR APPROVAL." The purchase order did not contain an integration clause.

Mr. Reich signed the purchase order and ordered the requested software from Timberline. When Mr. Reich received the software, he opened the three large shipping boxes and checked the contents against the packing invoice. Contained inside the shipping boxes were several smaller boxes, containing program diskettes in plastic pouches, installation instructions, and user manuals. One of the larger boxes also contained the sealed protection devices for the software.

All Timberline software is distributed to its users under license. Both Medallion and Precision Bid Analysis are licensed Timberline products. In the case of the Mortenson shipment, the full text of Timberline's license agreement was set forth on the outside of each diskette pouch and the inside cover of the instruction manuals. The first screen that appears each time the program is used also references the license and states, "[t]his software is licensed for exclusive use by: Timberline Use Only." Further, a license to use the protection device was wrapped around each of the devices shipped to Mortenson. The following warning preceded the terms of the license agreement:

CAREFULLY READ THE FOLLOWING TERMS AND CONDITIONS BEFORE USING THE PROGRAMS. USE OF THE PROGRAMS INDICATES YOUR ACKNOWLEDGEMENT THAT YOU HAVE READ THIS LICENSE, UNDERSTAND IT, AND AGREE TO BE BOUND BY ITS TERMS AND CONDITIONS. IF YOU DO NOT AGREE TO THESE TERMS AND CONDITIONS, PROMPTLY RETURN THE PROGRAMS AND USER MANUALS TO THE PLACE OF PURCHASE AND YOUR PUR-

CHASE PRICE WILL BE REFUNDED. YOU AGREE THAT YOUR USE OF THE PROGRAM ACKNOWLEDGES THAT YOU HAVE READ THIS LICENSE, UNDERSTAND IT, AND AGREE TO BE BOUND BY ITS TERMS AND CONDITIONS.

Under a separate subheading, the license agreement limited Mortenson's remedies and provided:

LIMITATION OF REMEDIES AND LIABILITY

NEITHER TIMBERLINE NOR ANYONE ELSE WHO HAS BEEN INVOLVED IN THE CREATION, PRODUCTION OR DELIVERY OF THE PROGRAMS OR USER MANUALS SHALL BE LIABLE TO YOU FOR ANY DAMAGES OF ANY TYPE, INCLUDING BUT NOT LIMITED TO, ANY LOST PROFITS, LOST SAVINGS, LOSS OF ANTICIPATED BENEFITS, OR OTHER INCIDENTAL, OR CONSEQUENTIAL DAMAGES ARISING OUT OF THE USE OR INABILITY TO USE SUCH PROGRAMS, WHETHER ARISING OUT OF CONTRACT, NEGLIGENCE, STRICT TORT, OR UNDER ANY WARRANTY, OR OTHERWISE, EVEN IF TIMBERLINE HAS BEEN ADVISED OF THE POSSIBILITY OF SUCH DAMAGES OR FOR ANY OTHER CLAIM BY ANY OTHER PARTY. TIMBERLINE'S LIABILITY FOR DAMAGES IN NO EVENT SHALL EXCEED THE LICENSE FEE PAID FOR THE RIGHT TO USE THE PROGRAMS.

In December 1993, Mortenson used the Precision Bid Analysis software to prepare a bid for a project at Harborview Medical Center in Seattle. On the day of the bid, the software allegedly malfunctioned multiple times and gave the following message: "Abort: Cannot find alternate." Mortenson received this message nineteen times that day. Nevertheless, Mortenson submitted a bid generated by the software. After Mortenson was awarded the Harborview Medical Center project, it learned its bid was approximately $1.95 million lower than intended.

Mortenson filed an action in King County Superior Court against Timberline and Softworks, alleging breach of express and implied warranties. After the suit was filed, a Timberline internal memorandum surfaced, dated May 26, 1993. The memorandum stated, "[a] bug has been found [in the Precision software] . . . that results in two rather obscure problems," and explained, "[t]hese problems only happen if the following [four] conditions are met." The memorandum concluded, "[g]iven the unusual criteria for this problem, it does not appear to be a major problem." Apparently, other Timberline customers had encountered the same problem and a newer version of the software was sent to some of these customers. After an extensive

continued

investigation, Timberline's lead programmer for Precision Bid Analysis acknowledged if the four steps identified in the memo were "reproduced as accurately as possible," Mortenson's error message could be replicated.

Timberline moved for summary judgment of dismissal in July 1997, arguing the limitation on consequential damages in the licensing agreement barred Mortenson's recovery. Mortenson countered that its entire contract with Timberline consisted of the purchase order and it never saw or agreed to the provisions in the licensing agreement. The trial court granted Timberline's motion for summary judgment. The trial judge stated, "if this case had arisen in 1985 rather than 1997, I might have a different ruling" but "the facts in this case are such that even construing them against the moving party, the Court finds as a matter of law that the licensing agreements and limitations pertaining thereto were conspicuous and controlling and, accordingly, the remedies that are available to the plaintiff in this case are the remedies that were set forth in the licensing agreement. . . ."

Mortenson appealed the summary judgment order to the Court of Appeals. The Court of Appeals affirmed the trial court and held (1) the purchase order was not an integrated contract; (2) the license terms were part of the contract; and (3) the limitation of remedies clause was not unconscionable and, therefore, enforceable. Mortenson appealed.

JUDICIAL OPINION

JOHNSON, Justice

This case presents the issue of whether a limitation on consequential damages enclosed in a "shrinkwrap license" accompanying computer software is enforceable against the purchaser of the licensed software.

Mortenson contends because the purchase order fulfilled the basic requirements of contracting under the U.C.C., it constituted a fully integrated contract. As a result, Mortenson argues the terms of the license, including the limitation of remedies clause, were not part of the contract and, thus, are not enforceable. Timberline counters that the parties did not intend the purchase order to be an exclusive recitation of the contract terms, and points to the absence from the purchase order of several key details of the agreement. Timberline argues, and the trial court and Court of Appeals agreed, that the purchase order did not prevent the terms of the license from becoming part of the contract or render the limitation of remedies clause unenforceable.

Whether the parties intend a written document to be a final expression of the terms of the agreement is a question of fact. Whether the purchase order qualifies as a contract at all does not resolve the issue of whether

it is an integrated contract. Even if we assume the purchase order could, standing alone, constitute a complete contract under the U.C.C., such was not the case here. The language of the purchase order makes this clear. For example, the purchase order sets an hourly rate for Timberline's provision of "software support," but does not specify how many hours of support Timberline would provide. The purchase order also states: "[a]t some future date should Timberline upgrade 'Bid Day' to a windows version, M.A. Mortenson would be able to upgrade to this system with Timberline crediting existing software purchase toward that upgrade on a pro-rated basis to be determined later." Finally, the purchase order does not contain an integration clause. The presence of an integration clause "strongly supports a conclusion that the parties' agreement was fully integrated. . . ." Here, the absence of such a clause further supports the conclusion that the purchase order was not the complete agreement between the parties. The trial court and the Court of Appeals correctly determined the purchase order did not constitute an integrated contract.

Mortenson next argues even if the purchase order was not an integrated contract, Timberline's delivery of the license terms merely constituted a request to add additional or different terms, which were never agreed upon by the parties. Mortenson claims the additional terms did not become part of the contract because they were material alterations. Timberline responds that the terms of the license were not a request to add additional terms, but part of the contract between the parties. Timberline further argues that so-called "shrinkwrap" software licenses have been found enforceable by other courts, and that both trade usage and course of dealing support enforcement in the present case.

For its section 2–207 analysis, Mortenson relies on *Step-Saver Data Sys., Inc.* v. *Wyse Tech.*, 939 F.2d 91 (3d Cir.1991). There, Step-Saver, a value added retailer, placed telephone orders for software and confirmed with purchase orders. The manufacturer then forwarded an invoice back to Step-Saver. The software later arrived with a license agreement printed on the packaging. Finding the license "should have been treated as a written confirmation containing additional terms," the Third Circuit applied U.C.C. section 2–207 and held the warranty disclaimer and limitation of remedies terms were not part of the parties' agreement because they were material alterations. Mortenson claims *Step-Saver* is controlling, as "virtually every element of the transaction in the present case is mirrored in *Step-Saver*." We disagree.

First, *Step-Saver* did not involve the enforceability of a standard license agreement against an end user of the software, but instead involved its applicability to a value added retailer who simply included the software in an integrated system sold to the end user. In fact, in *Step-Saver* the party contesting applicability of the licensing agreement had been assured the license did not apply to it at all. Such is not the case here, as Mortenson was the end user of the Bid analysis software and was never told the license agreement did not apply.

Further, in *Step-Saver* the seller of the program twice asked the buyer to sign an agreement comparable to their disputed license agreement. Both times the buyer refused, but the seller continued to make the software available. In contrast, Mortenson and Timberline had utilized a license agreement throughout Mortenson's use of the Medallion and Precision Bid Analysis software. Given these distinctions, we find *Step-Saver* to be inapplicable to the present case. We conclude this is a case about contract formation, not contract alteration.

[T]he Seventh Circuit held software shrinkwrap license agreements are a valid form of contracting under Wisconsin's version of U.C.C. section 2–204, and such agreements are enforceable unless objectionable under general contract law such as the law of unconscionability. The court stated, "[n]otice on the outside, terms on the inside, and a right to return the software for a refund if the terms are unacceptable (a right that the license expressly extends), may be a means of doing business valuable to buyers and sellers alike."

The UCITA embraces the theory of "layered contracting," which acknowledges while "some contracts are formed and their terms fully defined at a single point in time, many transactions involve a rolling or layered process. An agreement exists, but terms are clarified or created over time." UCITA § 208 cmt. 3 (Approved Official Draft).

We, therefore, hold under RCW 62A.2–204 the terms of the license were part of the contract between Mortenson and Timberline, and Mortenson's use of the software constituted its assent to the agreement, including the license terms.

The terms of Timberline's license were either set forth explicitly or referenced in numerous locations. The terms were included within the shrinkwrap packaging of each copy of Precision Bid Analysis; they were present in the manuals accompanying the software; they were included with the protection devices for the software, without which the software could not be used. The fact the software was licensed was also noted on the introductory screen each time the software was used. Even accepting Mortenson's contention it never saw the terms of the license, as we must do on summary judgment, it was not necessary for Mortenson to actually read the agreement in order to be bound by it.

Furthermore, the U.C.C. defines an "agreement" as "the bargain of the parties in fact as found in their lan-

guage or by implication from other circumstances including course of dealing or usage of trade or course of performance. . . ." Mortenson and Timberline had a course of dealing; Mortenson had purchased licensed software from Timberline for years prior to its upgrade to Precision Bid Analysis. All Timberline software, including the prior version of Bid Analysis used by Mortenson since at least 1990, is distributed under license. Moreover, extensive testimony and exhibits before the trial court demonstrate an unquestioned use of such license agreements throughout the software industry. Although Mortenson questioned the relevance of this evidence, there is no evidence in the record to contradict it. While trade usage is a question of fact, undisputed evidence of trade usage may be considered on summary judgment.

Mortenson contends even if the limitation of remedies clause is part of its contract with Timberline, the clause is unconscionable and, therefore, unenforceable.

Limitations on consequential damages are generally valid under the U.C.C. unless they are unconscionable. Whether a limitation on consequential damages is unconscionable is a question of law.

Mortenson asserts Timberline's failure to inform it of the "defect" in the software prior to its purchase renders the licensing agreement substantively unconscionable.

Comment 3 to [U.C.C.] § 2–719 generally approves consequential damage exclusions as "merely an allocation of unknown or undeterminable risks." Thus, the presence of latent defects in the goods cannot render these clauses unconscionable. The need for certainty in risk-allocation is especially compelling where, as here, the goods are experimental and their performance by nature less predictable.

Mortenson also contends the licensing agreement is procedurally unconscionable because "the license terms were never presented to Mortenson in a contractually-meaningful way."

Procedural unconscionability has been described as the lack of a meaningful choice, considering all the circumstances surrounding the transaction including "'[t]he manner in which the contract was entered,' whether each party had 'a reasonable opportunity to understand the terms of the contract,' and whether 'the important terms [were] hidden in a maze of fine print. . . .'"

Examining the contracting process between the parties based on the above factors, we hold the clause to be procedurally conscionable. The clause was not hidden in a maze of fine print. The license was set forth in capital letters on each diskette pouch and on the inside cover of the instruction manuals. A license to use

continued

the protection device was wrapped around each such device. The license was also referenced in the opening screen of the software program. This gave Mortenson more than ample opportunity to read and understand the terms of the license. Mortenson is also not an inexperienced retail consumer, but a nationwide construction contractor that has purchased licensed software from Timberline in the past.

We find Mortenson's unconscionability claim unpersuasive and, therefore, find the limitation of remedies clause to be enforceable.

Affirmed.

CASE QUESTIONS

1. When did Mortenson agree to the limitation on damages?

2. Where does the liability limitation clause fit in the Section 2–207 scenario?

3. What choices do software buyers have when they read a screen that limits the software company's liability?

4. Is the damage limitation clause unconscionable?

Consideration

Consideration is what distinguishes gifts from contracts and is what each party—offeror and offeree—gives up under the contract; it is sometimes called **bargained-for exchange**. If you sign a contract to buy a 1980 Mercedes for $17,000, your consideration is the $17,000 and is given in exchange for the car. The seller's consideration is giving up the car and is given in exchange for your $17,000. On the other hand, if your grandmother tells you that she will give you her Mercedes, there is no consideration, and your grandmother's promise (unfortunately) is not a contract and is not enforceable.

The courts are not concerned with the amount or nature of consideration so long as it is actually passed from one party to the other. A contract is not unenforceable because a court feels you paid too little under the contract terms. The amount of consideration is left to the discretion of the parties, but one party cannot demand greater consideration once the contract is finalized.

CONSIDER... 13.9

In 1977, George Lucas granted Kenner Toys the exclusive right to produce *Star Wars* toys—the action figures and other replicas from the movie—in perpetuity for $100,000 per year. At the time the contract was negotiated, no one understood how valuable the contract rights were.

In 1991, Hasbro Toys purchased Kenner. By this time, the sales of Princess Leia dolls and R2D2 replicas were nonexistent. Because there was no market for the toys, the toys were no longer produced, and an accountant with Kenner decided to save $100,000 and not send the check to Mr. Lucas.

In 1992, an employee of Mr. Lucas saw a line of Galoob toys at a trade show and asked if Galoob was interested in making the *Star Wars* toy line. Galoob jumped at the chance and did quite well marketing the toys. Some executives believe that the popularity of the toys motivated Mr. Lucas to rerelease the movies, which turned out to be a money-maker for Mr. Lucas as well as for the Galoob toy line.

In 1996, Mr. Lucas did grant some rights to Hasbro, but it has lost market share and footing to Galoob. Was the failure to make the payment a failure of consideration? Has Hasbro lost its rights?

Unique Consideration Issues

The concept of consideration and its requirement for contract formation has presented courts with some unique problems. Often an element of fairness and reliance exists in circumstances in which there is an offer and acceptance but no consideration. For example, many nonprofit organizations raise funds through pledges. Such pledges are not supported by consideration, but the nonprofit organizations rely on those pledges. Called **charitable subscriptions**, these agreements are enforced by courts despite the lack of consideration.

The doctrine of **promissory estoppel** is also used as a substitute for consideration in those cases in which someone acts in reliance on a promise that is not supported by consideration. For example, suppose an employer said, "Move to Denver and I'll hire you." There is no detriment on your part until you begin work. The employer has no detriment either. However, if you sold your home in Phoenix and incurred the expense of moving to Denver, it would be unfair to allow the employer to claim the contract did not exist because of no consideration. You have acted in reliance on a promise, and that reliance serves as a consideration substitute.

 C O N S I D E R . . .   1 3 . 1 0

Alan Fulkins, who owns a construction company that specializes in single-family residences, is constructing a small subdivision with twenty-three homes. Tretorn Plumbing, owned by Jason Tretorn, was awarded the contract for the plumbing work on the homes at a price of $4,300 per home.

Plumbing contractors complete their residential projects in three phases. Phase 1 consists of digging the lines for the plumbing and installing the pipes that are placed in the foundation of the house. Phase 2 involves the placement of pipes within the walls of the home, and phase 3 handles the surface plumbing, such as sinks and tubs. However, industry practice dictates that the plumbing contractor receive one-half of the contract amount after completion of phase 1.

Mr. Tretorn completed the digs of phase 1 for Mr. Fulkins and received payment of $2,150. Mr. Tretorn then went to Mr. Fulkins and demanded an additional $600 per house for completion of the work. Mr. Fulkins said, "But you already have a contract for $4,300!" Mr. Tretorn responded, "I know, but the costs are killing me. I need the additional $600."

Mr. Fulkins explained the hardship of the demand: "Look, I've already paid you half. If I hire someone else, I'll have to pay them two-thirds for the work not done. It'll cost me $5,000 per house." Mr. Tretorn responded, "Exactly. I'm a bargain because the additional $600 I want only puts you at $4,900. If you don't pay it, I'll just lien the houses and then you'll be stuck without a way to close the sales. I've got the contract all drawn up. Just sign it and everything goes smoothly."

Should Mr. Fulkins sign the agreement? Does Mr. Tretorn have the right to the additional $600? Was it ethical for Mr. Tretorn to demand the $600? Is there any legal advice you can offer Mr. Fulkins?

BUSINESS STRATEGY APPLICATION

Do the exercise for this chapter on the book's Web site to see if you can determine from a collection of documents whether a contract has been formed.

Contract Form: When Writing Is Required

Some contracts can exist just on the basis of an oral promise. Others, however, must be in writing to be enforceable, and these contracts are covered under each state's **statute of frauds**.

Common Law Statute of Frauds

To view the Federal Trade Commission's report on progress on e-signatures, visit: **http://www.ftc.gov/opa/2001/06/esign.htm**

The term *statute of frauds* originated in 1677 when England passed the first rule dealing with written contracts: the Statute for the Prevention of Frauds and Perjuries.

The purpose of the first statute and the descendant statutes today is to have written agreements for the types of contracts that might encourage conflicting claims and possible perjury if oral agreements were allowed. The following is a partial list of the types of contracts required to be in writing under most state laws.

1. **Contracts for the sale of real property.** This requirement includes sales, certain leases, liens, mortgages, and easements.

2. **Contracts that cannot be performed within one year.** These contracts run for long periods and require the benefit of written terms.

3. **Contracts to pay the debt of another.** Cosigners' agreements to pay if a debtor defaults must be in writing. A corporate officer's personal guarantee of a corporate note must be in writing to be enforceable.

UCC Statute of Frauds

Under the UCC, there is a separate statute of frauds for contracts covering the sale of goods. Contracts for the sale of goods costing $500 or more must be evidenced by a record to be enforceable. As noted earlier, a record can be in the form of an electronic communication. Under Revised Article 2, the amount has been increased from $500 to $5,000.

C O N S I D E R . . .   13.11

Which of the following contracts must be in writing to be enforceable? Answer for both the old and revised UCC for those problems that involve UCC subject matter.
1. A contract for the sale of an acre of land for $400
2. A contract for management consulting for six months for $353,000
3. A contract for the sale of a car for $358
4. A contract for a loan cosigned by a corporation's vice president
5. A contract for the sale of a mobile home for $12,000

Exceptions to the Statute of Frauds

Some exceptions to the UCC and common law statute of frauds provisions were created for situations in which the parties have partially or fully performed their unwritten contract. Under both the UCC and common law, if the parties perform the oral contract, courts will enforce the contract for what has already been done. For example, if Alan agreed to sell land to Bertha under an oral contract and Bertha has paid, has the deed, and has moved in, Alan cannot use the statute of frauds to remove Bertha and get the land back.

For a summary of electronic signature legislation, visit:
http://www.mbc.com/ ecommerce/ecommerce.asp

What Form of Writing Is Required?

The form of writing required under the statute of frauds is not formal. Evidence of a written agreement can be pieced together from memos and letters. With E-sign now in place, contracts can be evidenced by electronic communications such as e-mail and Web site communications. New Section 2–211 of the UCC makes electronic communication and forms of contracts in that mode equal with paper contracts. Under the UCC, merchants can meet the statute of frauds by sending confirmation memos (see § 2–201 in Appendix G). These **merchants' confirmation memoranda** summarize the oral agreement and are signed by only one party, but they can be used to satisfy the statute of frauds so long as the memo has been sent to the non-signing party for review and there is no objection upon that party's receipt. The confirmation memoranda could be done via e-mail. Exhibit 13.5 provides a summary of provisions for contract formation under UCC and common law.

For a summary of proposed electronic signature legislation, visit:
http://www.ilpf.org

EXHIBIT   13.5   Common Law versus UCC Rules on Formation

AREA	UCC	COMMON LAW
Application	Sales of goods	Services, real estate, employment contracts
Offers	Need subject matter (quantity); code gives details	Need subject matter, price, terms, full details agreed upon
Options	Merchant's firm offer—no consideration needed	Need consideration
Acceptance	Can have additional terms	Mirror image rule followed
	Mailbox rule works for reasonable means of acceptance	Must use same method to get mailbox rule*
Consideration	Required for contracts but not for modification or firm offers	Always required
Writing requirement	Sale of goods for $500 or more	Real estate, contracts not to be performed in one year; paying the debt of another
Defenses†	Must be free of all defenses for valid contract	Must be free of all defenses for valid contract

* Some courts have adopted the UCC rule for common law contracts.
† See Chapter 14.

Rosenfeld v. *Basquiat* (Case 13.6) discusses the sufficiency of the contract writing.

CASE 13.6

Rosenfeld v. *Basquiat*
78 F.3d 184 (2d Cir. 1996)

The Artist, the Crayon, and the Contract

FACTS

Michelle Rosenfeld, an art dealer, alleges she contracted with artist Jean-Michel Basquiat to buy three of his paintings. The works that she claims she contracted to buy were entitled *Separation of the K, Atlas,* and *Untitled Head.* Ms. Rosenfeld testified that she went to Mr. Basquiat's apartment on October 25, 1982; while she was there, he agreed to sell her three paintings for $4,000 each, and she picked out three. Mr. Basquiat asked for a cash deposit of 10 percent; she left his loft and later returned with $1,000 in cash, which she paid him. When she asked for a receipt, he insisted on drawing up a contract and got down on the floor and wrote it out in crayon on a large piece of paper, remarking that some day this contract would be worth money. The handwritten document listed the three paintings, bore Ms. Rosenfeld's signature and Mr. Basquiat's signature, and stated: "$12,000—$1,000 DEPOSIT—Oct 25 82." Ms. Rosenfeld later returned to Mr. Basquiat's loft

to discuss delivery, but Mr. Basquiat convinced her to wait for at least two years so that he could show the paintings at exhibitions.

After Mr. Basquiat's death, the estate argued that there was no contract because the statute of frauds made the agreement unenforceable. The estate contended that a written contract for the sale of goods must include the date of delivery. From a judgment in favor of the estate, Ms. Rosenfeld appealed.

JUDICIAL OPINION

CARDAMONE, J.

. . . Because this case involves an alleged contract for the sale of three paintings, any question regarding the Statute of Frauds is governed by the U.C.C. (applicability to "transactions in goods") (contract for $500 or more is unenforceable "unless there is some writing sufficient to indicate that a contract for sale has been

continued

made between the parties and signed by the party [charged]"). Under the U.C.C., the only term that *must* appear in the writing is the quantity. See N.Y.U.C.C. § 2–201.

Beyond that, "[a]ll that is required is that the writing afford a basis for believing that the offered oral evidence rests on a real transaction." The writing supplied by the plaintiff indicated the price, the date, the specific paintings involved, and that Rosenfeld paid a deposit. It also bore the signatures of the buyer and seller. Therefore, the writing satisfied the requirements of § 2–201.

Citing *Berman Stores Co.* v. *Hirsh,* 240 N.Y. 209 (1925), the estate claims that a specific delivery date, if agreed upon, must be in the writing. *Berman Stores* was decided before the enactment of the U.C.C. and was based on the principle that "the note or memorandum . . . should completely evidence the contract which the parties made." 240 N.Y. at 214 (quoting *Poel* v. *Brunswick-Balke-Collender Co.,* 216 N.Y. 310, 314 [1915]). The rule that a specific delivery date is "an essential part of the contract and must be embodied in the memorandum," *Berman Stores,* 240 N.Y. at 215, was rejected by the legislature—at least for sale-of-goods cases—when it enacted the U.C.C. That rule and the statute upon which it was based were repealed to make way for the U.C.C.

. . . Because the writing, allegedly scrawled in crayon by Jean-Michel Basquiat on a large piece of paper, easily satisfied the requirements of § 2–201 of the U.C.C., the estate is not entitled to judgment as a matter of law. It is of no real significance that the jury found Rosenfeld and Basquiat settled on a particular time for delivery and did not commit it to writing. . . . As a consequence, . . . the alleged contract is not invalid on Statute of Frauds grounds. . . .

Judgment reversed.

CASE QUESTIONS

1. Why was the contract required to be in writing?
2. Did the contract comply with the statute of frauds?
3. Does a writing that does not comply with the statute of frauds make the alleged contract void?

The Writing Requirement in the Electronic Contract

As noted earlier in the chapter, the UETA is the proposed uniform law on making contracts via electronic means. However, whatever form of law the states adopt individually for signature requirements for electronic contacts, those laws cannot violate the federal E-sign provisions. Under E-sign, states must provide parity for electronic and paper signatures. That is, electronic contracts and signatures must be held to meet the statute of frauds requirements in the same way that paper contracts and signatures do. However, some documents are exempt from this equal treatment, including wills, trusts, checks, letters of credit, court documents, and cancellation of health and life insurance policies. States may require paper documentation for protection of legal rights in these transactions.

E-sign does not deal with the issues of digital signatures and security. Each of the states must grapple with these issues in adopting their legislation giving e-contracts parity in terms of the writing requirement. Some companies are not comfortable without some form of **digital signature**. A digital signature can be accomplished in different ways. Encryption is used to encode messages so that they cannot be read without the code. This process allows a form of electronic or digital signature that can have the same authenticity and verification of source as a notarized document. A digital signature is defined as a "transformation of a message using an asymmetric cryptosystem such that a person having the initial message and the signer's public key can accurately determine whether (a) the transformation was created using the private key that corresponds to the signer's public key; and (b) the message has been altered since the transformation was made." In other words, using a public/private electronic code system, the authenticity of transmissions codes can be determined.

Problems faced by businesses and those working to draft effective legislation and uniform laws on encryption commerce include the concerns of law enforce-

---

BUSINESS PLANNING TIP

Many businesses are relying on fax machines for offers and acceptances. These machines offer the benefit of quick, written documents. However, clarity is often sacrificed, and fax paper can fade. Further, in several recent cases signatures had been taped onto faxed copies. There was no authentic signature, and the taped signature could not be detected on the fax. Always follow up your faxes with actual documents for signature.

ment officials with the use of encryption devices. Law enforcement officials want the capacity to decode messages because of the national security issues that arise when communications include illegal activities and information. The FBI has asked for some controls on encryption.

The Effect of the Written Contract: Parol Evidence

Once a contract is reduced to its final written form and is complete and unambiguous, the parties to the contract are not permitted to contradict the contract terms with evidence of their negotiations or verbal agreements at the time the contract was executed. This prohibition on extrinsic evidence for fully integrated contracts is called the **parol evidence** rule and is a means for stopping ongoing contradictions to contracts that have been entered into and finalized. It is a protection for the application of the document to the parties' rights as well as a reminder of the need to put the true nature of the agreement into the contract.

There are some exceptions to the parol evidence rule. If a contract is incomplete or the terms are ambiguous, extrinsic evidence can be used to clarify or complete the contract, as in the case of UCC contracts in which price, delivery, and payment terms can be added (see § 2–202 in Appendix G). Also, if one of the parties to the contract is alleging a defense to the contract's formation, evidence of the circumstances creating that defense can be used as evidence. Evidence of lack of capacity or fraud does not violate the parol evidence rule.

ISSUES IN FORMATION OF INTERNATIONAL CONTRACTS

International business contracts are very similar to domestic contracts. However, the unique aspect of international contracts is that additional risks and questions arise over the choice of currency, the impact of culture on contract interpretation and performance, and the stability of the governments of the parties involved in the contract. In other words, international contracts carry certain risks that are not part of contracts between businesses in the same country. Over the past few years, the increased number of international transactions has resulted in recognition of the need for a more uniform law on international contract formation and performance. The United Nations has developed such a set of laws, called the **United Nations Convention on Contracts for the International Sale of Goods** (CISG) (see Chapter 7).

The CISG, which applies to those contracts in which buyer and seller have their businesses in different countries (unless the parties agree otherwise), has four parts: Part I: Application; Part II: Formation;

Visit the Institute of International Commercial Law, sponsored by the Pace University School of Law, to review the CISG:
http://law.pace.edu/pilr/ reviewofcisg.html

BUSINESS PLANNING TIP

Avoiding Legal Pitfalls in International Transactions

1. Use short, simple contracts. The tendency to place all possibilities in a contract is a U.S. tradition. In Germany, for example, the parties have a one-page agreement that references and incorporates terms and conditions of one of the parties.

2. Watch unconscionability protections. While the United States focuses its unfairness protections on consumers, other countries afford these same protections to commercial transactions.

3. Some disclaimers are void in other countries. For example, the clause, "We are only liable for loss of data which is due to a deliberate act on our part. We are not responsible for lost profits in any event," would be valid in the United States but void in Germany. In Germany, sellers of software must assume liability for at least gross negligence.

4. One party's attempt to limit liability would be void in Germany. Any liability limitation must be specifically addressed and negotiated for such a clause to be valid.

5. Unusually long periods for performance are typical in the United States but void in Germany.

6. Price increase limitations are typical in non-U.S. contracts.

7. In other countries, parties can refuse to pay on a current contract if performance on an earlier contract was less than satisfactory and damages are owed.

Part III: Sale of Goods; and Part IV: Final Provisions. Part II includes provisions for the requirements for offers and acceptance, including a merchant's firm offer provision. Acceptance is effective only upon receipt; and, whenever forms do not match, there is no contract unless the nonmatching terms are immaterial.

Party autonomy continues to remain a priority. The parties can always choose the applicable law, the nation for the location of courts for resolving disputes, and remedies. You can find details on global contracts in Chapter 7.

There are several significant differences between the UCC and the CISG. For example, the CISG follows the common law mirror image rule and not the more liberal UCC "battle of the forms" modification exception. The CISG also requires the presence of a price for an offer to be definite enough to be valid. Merchants' firm offers exist under the CISG, but there are no time limitations on their validity, as with the UCC three-month limit. Parties in international trade need to be familiar with the hybrid nature of the CISG in order to protect their contract rights.

Those firms and countries not relying on the CISG should be familiar with the nuances of commercial law in the countries in which they are doing business. The tendency of many U.S. businesses is to draft a form contract using the home country legal concepts and carry them over to other countries. As the earlier planning tips indicate, such a practice and reliance on form contracts can be dangerous.

One of the content and interpretation issues in international contracts focuses on the method of payment. Currently, many contracts specify that payment is to be made in deutsche marks or pounds. On January 1, 1999, the EU began the use of one currency. Payment under various contracts will become more of an issue for parties to negotiate in international transactions. Some parties are negotiating now to put substitutes into their contracts, and all parties working on new agreements are covering the issue in their negotiations. In *Intershoe, Inc.* v. *Bankers Trust* (Case 13.7), confusion on payment issues proved expensive for one party.

CASE 13.7

Intershoe, Inc. v. *Bankers Trust*
569 N.Y.S.2d 33 (1991)

Lira, Shoes, and Exchange Rates

FACTS

Intershoe, Inc. (plaintiff), is a shoe importer that uses various foreign currencies, including Italian lira, in its business.

On March 3, 1985, Intershoe phoned Bankers Trust (defendant) and entered into several foreign currency transactions, one being a futures transaction involving lira. On March 13, Bankers Trust sent Intershoe a confirmation slip with the following terms: "WE [Bankers] HAVE BOUGHT FROM YOU [Intershoe] ITL 537,750,000" and "WE HAVE SOLD TO YOU USD 250,000.00."

The confirmation slip specified a rate of 2,151 lira per dollar and called for delivery of the lira approximately seven and a half months later, between October 1 and October 31, 1985. Intershoe's treasurer signed the slip and returned it to Bankers Trust on March 18, 1985.

By letter dated October 11, 1985, Bankers Trust notified Intershoe that it was awaiting instructions as to Intershoe's delivery of the lira. Intershoe responded in a letter dated October 25, 1985, that the transaction was a mistake and that it would not go through with it. To cover commitments in other currency transactions, Bankers Trust was forced to purchase lira on the open market at a higher price than that on March 13, 1985, resulting in a loss of $55,014.85. Intershoe filed suit claiming that it had purchased, not sold, lira and that it had sustained damages of $59,336.40. Bankers Trust counterclaimed for its damages.

The trial court held that there were issues of fact. Bankers Trust maintained that the case should be decided in its favor by summary judgment because of the parol evidence rule and appealed.

JUDICIAL OPINION

HANCOCK, Jr., Justice

We turn to defendant's argument that UCC § 2–202 bars the parol evidence submitted in opposition to its motion.

There seems to be no question that the UCC applies to foreign currency transactions. Plaintiff does not dispute this point. Instead, plaintiff simply asserts that UCC § 2–202 has no application because defendant has not made a sufficient showing that the confirmation slip was "intended by the parties as a final expression of their agreement with respect to such terms as are included therein." Something more is required, plaintiff says, either language in the confirmation slip indicating that it was intended to be the final expression of the parties' agreement or uncontroverted evidence that the writing was so intended. Otherwise, according to plaintiff, there are factual issues as to the effect the parties intended the confirmation slip to have and summary judgment must be denied. We disagree.

Here, the essential terms of the transaction are plainly set forth in the confirmation slip: that plaintiff had sold lira to defendant, the amount of the lira it sold, the exchange rate, the amount of dollars to be paid by defendant for the lira, and the maturity date of the transaction. The signature of plaintiff's agent who signed and returned the confirmation slip five days later on March 18, 1985, signifies plaintiff's acceptance of these terms. Nothing in the confirmation slip suggests that it was to be a memorandum of some preliminary or tentative understanding with respect to these terms. On the contrary, it is difficult to imagine words which could more clearly demonstrate the final expression of the parties' agreement than "WE HAVE BOUGHT FROM YOU ITL 537,750,000" and "WE HAVE SOLD TO YOU USD 250,000.00."

The confirmation is not of some bargain to be made in the future but expresses the parties' meeting of the minds as to a completed bargain's essential terms—a sale of 537,750 lira at a rate of 2151 for 250,000 dollars—made in a telephone conversation on March 13, 1985. The only evidence plaintiff has tendered does no more than contradict the stated terms of the confirmation slip—the very evidence which UCC § 2–202 precludes.

It does not address the critical question of whether the terms in the confirmation slip were intended to represent the parties' final agreement on those matters. We conclude that where, as here, the form and content of the confirmation slip suggest nothing other than that it was intended to be the final expression of the parties' agreement as to the terms set forth and where there is no evidence indicating that this was not so, UCC § 2–202 bars parol evidence of contradictory terms.

We reject plaintiff's contentions that UCC § 2–202 requires that there be some express indication in the writing itself or some other evidence that the parties intended it to be the final expression of their agreement. . . . To require that the record include specific extraneous evidence that the writing constitutes the parties' final agreement as to its stated terms would in many instances impose a virtually insurmountable obstacle for parties seeking to invoke UCC § 2–202, particularly in cases involving large commercial banks and other financial institutions, which typically close hundreds of transactions over the telephone during a business day. As a practical matter, a confirmation slip or similar writing is usually the only reliable evidence of such transactions, given the unlikely prospect that one who makes scores of similar deals each day will remember the details of any one particular agreement. Indeed, this case is illustrative inasmuch as neither of the participants had a specific recollection of the March 13, 1985, telephone conversation.

Plaintiff also argues that UCC § 2–202 does not bar the parol evidence submitted in opposition to defendant's motion because it is offered to show that there was never a contract between the parties. This argument is unavailing. Plaintiff does not dispute that it entered into a foreign currency transaction with defendant; its only contention is that the transaction called for it to purchase and not sell lira. Hence, the parol evidence is being used to contradict a term of the contract, not to show that there was no contract, and UCC § 2–202 applies.

Reversed.

CASE QUESTIONS

1. Describe the transaction.
2. Who sold, according to the memo?
3. Who sold, according to Intershoe?
4. Is the memo a final writing?
5. What dangers would the court introduce if orders such as this were contradicted by oral testimony?
6. Did someone fail to read a document carefully before signing? Does the parol evidence rule allow "failure to read" as a defense?

*For the United Nations'
model law on electronic
commerce, visit:*

http://www.un.org

*For information on law,
contracts, and contract forms
in international transactions,
visit the Web site for the
National Law Center for
Inter–American Free Trade:*

http://www.natlaw.com

In negotiating an international contract, parties should determine which country's laws will govern the transaction. Courts will not interfere with this decision so long as the law chosen has some relation to the transaction. The parties should also agree to submit to the jurisdiction of a particular court so that litigation does not begin with the issue of whether or not there is jurisdiction in a particular court. If the parties wish to submit to arbitration prior to litigation, the terms and nature of arbitration should be delineated in the contract.

International contracts carry peculiar and additional risks. One of the lessons of the 1991 war in the Persian Gulf, for example, is that international contracts should have provisions for war, interruption of shipping lines, and other political acts. Often referred to as *force majeure* clauses, these provisions in international contracts allow the parties to agree what will happen in the event of sudden changes in government or in the global political climate rather than rely on a court to determine after the fact what rights, if any, the parties had. (See Chapter 14 for more details on contract issues.)

In addition to the risks of political changes, international contracts have the risks of changing currency exchange rates, long distances in transportation, and difficulties with collection of payments. Most international contracts have built-in performance guarantees. For example, a seller ships goods with a **bill of lading** (a document of title that the carrier will have). To be able to pick up the goods from the carrier, the buyer must have a copy of the bill of lading. The seller can have a bank release the bill of lading to the buyer when the buyer has paid or when the buyer's bank issues a letter of credit (which is the bank's commitment to pay) to the seller for the amount due for the goods. The effect of these two documents is that the seller or carrier does not release the goods until the payment is made or assured. The flow of goods is controlled across borders through documents that travel with the goods and through banks that will issue the payment. At the same time, the buyer is assured that the goods are there before payment is made or authorized.

CONSIDER...   13.12

Terrorist acts, such as the September 11, 2001, destruction of the World Trade Center towers in New York City, have become more frequent over the past few years. What happens when there is a substantial interruption in a business's operations because a bombing destroys or damages its leased facilities? Would you add provisions and protections to your lease? What terms would you want if you were the landlord?

BIOGRAPHY

THE STORY OF TELEVISION CONTRACTS

In 1996, the six stars of the cast of the NBC-TV situation comedy *Friends* (Jennifer Aniston, Courtney Cox, Lisa Kudrow, Matt LeBlanc, Matthew Perry, and David Schwimmer) each demanded a salary increase from $40,000 per episode to $100,000 per episode, which was more than double their contract salaries. Further, the six stars threatened to walk out on the beginning of the fall season if their salary demands were not met.

Friends was one of a handful of highly successful programs on NBC, indeed, on any network. The six actors had examined the ad revenues for their show and concluded that with their short-lived careers and fame, they needed to negotiate as much salary as possible. The six stars were successful in renegotiating their contracts, but they also created a new phenomenon in the television industry whereby stars can command high salaries when nervous executives feel their departure is imminent.

Some sample salaries are as follows.

Tim Allen	*Home Improvement*	$1.25 million per episode
Paul Reiser	*Mad about You*	$1 million per episode
Helen Hunt	*Mad about You*	$1 million per episode

(Note: Both Mr. Reiser and Ms. Hunt received an increase from $750,000 to $1 million per episode following the end of the *Seinfeld* series, which was the heart of NBC's successful Thursday night lineup. Mr. Seinfeld had been the first and only television actor to receive $1 million per episode—Mr. Allen's contract was negotiated at about the same time as Mr. Reiser's and Ms. Hunt's, and Mr. Allen's show was with ABC Television.)

Julia Louis-Dreyfuss	*Seinfeld*	$600,000 per episode
Jason Alexander	*Seinfeld*	$600,000 per episode
Michael Richards	*Seinfeld*	$600,000 per episode
Kelsey Grammer	*Frasier*	$250,000 per episode
John Lithgow	*Third Rock from the Sun*	$150,000 per episode
Tom Selleck	*The Closer*	$150,000 per episode
David Duchovny	*The X-Files*	$110,000 per episode
Gillian Anderson	*The X-Files*	$100,000 per episode
Roma Downey	*Touched by an Angel*	$75,000 per episode
Drew Carey	*Drew Carey Show*	$60,000 per episode
Della Reese	*Touched by an Angel*	$55,000 per episode
Calista Flockhart	*Ally McBeal*	$40,000 per episode
Jenna Elfman	*Dharma & Greg*	$40,000 per episode
Sarah Michelle Geller	*Buffy the Vampire Slayer*	$30,000 per episode

Just recently, the actors who work two days each week to do the voices of the characters for *The Simpsons* received an increase from $15,000–$25,000 per episode to $50,000 per episode. These voice actors work only two days each week, whereas actors in television series work five days per week. Julie Kavner, the voice of Marge Simpson, has a separate deal and did not participate in the threatened walkout by the voice talents for the show.

ISSUES

Are the actors justified in threatening to walk out if they do not receive pay increases? Is there a legal basis for their walkouts? Some of the actors point to the earnings for the shows as justification for the walkouts. The net profits for the eight-year run of *The Simpsons* have been $500 million. Reruns for the *Drew Carey Show* recently sold for $2 million each. Are unanticipated earnings and success a reason for increased payments under existing contracts?

When Jay Leno was asked about the tactics of the *Friends* stars, he responded, "You have to get what you can while you can in this business." Is Mr. Leno right? Is such an attitude ethical? The *Friends* show ended in 2004, and only one of the actors from the show has a new television series.

SUMMARY

What are contracts?

- Contract—promise or set of promises for breach of which the law gives a remedy, or the performance of which the law in some way recognizes as a duty

What laws govern contracts?

- Common law—traditional notions of law and the body of law developed in judicial decisions
- *Restatement (Second) of Contracts*—general summary of the common law of contracts
- Uniform Commercial Code (UCC)—set of uniform laws (forty-nine states) governing commercial transactions

What are the types of contracts?

- Bilateral contract—contract of two promises; one from each party
- Unilateral contract—contract made up of a promise for performance
- Express contract—written or verbally agreed-to contract
- Implied contract—contract that arises from parties' voluntary conduct
- Quasi contract—theory for enforcing a contract even though there is no formal contract because the parties behaved as if there were a contract
- Implied-in-fact contract—contract that arises from factual circumstances, professional circumstances, or custom
- Implied-in-law contract—legally implied contract to prevent unjust enrichment
- Void contract—contract with illegal subject matter or against public policy
- Voidable contract—contract that can be avoided legally by one side
- Unenforceable contract—agreement for which the law affords no remedy
- Executed contract—contract that has been performed
- Executory contract—contract not yet performed

How are contracts formed?

- Offer—preliminary to contract; first step in formation

- Offeror—person making the offer
- Offeree—recipient of offer
- Course of dealing—UCC provision that examines the way parties have behaved in the past to determine present performance standards
- Revocation—offeror canceling offer
- Options—offers with considerations; promises to keep offer open
- Merchant's firm offer—written offer signed by a merchant that states it will be kept open
- Counteroffer—counterproposal to offer
- Battle of the forms—UCC description of merchants' tendency to exchange purchase orders, invoices, confirmations, and so on; under Revised UCC, the court determines terms after the fact looking at intent, forms used, and the UCC terms
- Acceptance—offeree's positive response to offer
- Mailbox rule—timing rule for acceptance
- Consideration—something of value exchanged by the parties that distinguishes gifts from contracts
- Charitable subscriptions—enforceable promises to make gifts
- Promissory estoppel—reliance element used to enforce otherwise unenforceable contracts

When must contracts be in writing?

- Statute of frauds—state statutes governing the types of contracts that must be in writing to be enforceable
- Merchants' confirmation memorandum—UCC provision that allows one merchant to bind another based on an oral agreement with one signature
- Parol evidence—extrinsic evidence that is not admissible to dispute an integrated unambiguous contract

What issues for contracting exist in international business?

- CISG—Contracts for the International Sale of Goods; a proposed uniform law for international commercial transactions

QUESTIONS AND PROBLEMS

1. L. A. Becker Co., Inc., sent D. A. Clardy a $100 down payment along with a merchandise order. Clardy deposited the check, as was its usual daily practice for payments. After examining the offer, Clardy sent a rejection letter along with a check for $100 to Becker, which claims Clardy accepted by cashing the check. Is Becker correct? [*L. A. Becker Co. v. Clardy*, 51 So. 211 (Miss. 1910).]

2. Consider the following proposal description:

Attached are an original and two (2) carbon copies of our Proposal No. 620-M-86R covering the subject as agreed upon in your office last Friday, June 20, 1986. Please sign the original and one (1) copy on the lower left corner of page 9 and return to us for our execution. We will return one (1) executed copy for your files.

Again we thank you for selecting us for this project. We assure you it is receiving our best attention. Our Engineering Department is proceeding with the designs, fabrication drawings, and material orders.

We look forward to your receiving the necessary permits.

The "proposal" consists of five pages of typewritten terms, setting forth specifications for the manufacture, assembly, and erection of a television tower and related items, and four pages of preprinted "Terms and Conditions of Sale." The printed portion includes the following relevant terms:

Acceptance of Proposal
This proposal is for immediate acceptance and prior to such acceptance is subject to modification or withdrawal without notice.

Acceptance of this proposal will evidence Buyer's intent that the sale be governed solely by the terms and conditions of this proposal.

Any modifying, inconsistent or additional terms and conditions of Buyer's acceptance shall not become a part of any contract resulting from this proposal unless agreed to in writing by Kline.

Any order or offer by Buyer as a result of this proposal shall not be binding upon Kline until accepted by Kline in writing by an officer of Kline. If accepted by Kline, this proposal shall constitute the agreement between the Buyer and Kline.

At the bottom of the final page are the following signature spaces:

KLINE IRON & STEEL CO., INC.
By _____
Its   (Seller)

GRAY COMMUNICATIONS, INC.
By _____
Its   (Buyer)

Is there an offer? When would the earliest acceptance be? [*Kline Iron & Steel Co., Inc. v. Gray Communications Consultants, Inc.*, 715 F. Supp. 135 (D.S.C. 1989).]

3. Would an arbitration clause added to the reverse side of a buyer's purchase order be a material change for purposes of the merchant's battle of the forms under Section 2–207 of the UCC? [*Berquist Co. v. Sunroc Corp.*, 777 F. Supp. 1236 (E.D. Pa. 1991).]

4. Mace Industries, Inc., sent a quotation to Paddock Pools for water treatment equipment. Paddock responded with a purchase order that had the following written on its reverse side:

"THE SELLER AGREES TO ALL OF THE FOLLOWING TERMS AND CONDITIONS."

The clause was then followed by language stating that acceptance was expressly conditional upon Mace's acceptance of the terms.

Problems between the parties developed. Paddock says there is no contract because of its conditional acceptance. Mace maintains that Section 2–207 applies and that there was a contract, with the only issues being the additional terms Paddock wrote on its purchase order and whether they are part of the contract. Who is correct? [*Mace Industries, Inc. v. Paddock Pool Equipment Co., Inc.*, 339 S.E.2d 527 (S.C. 1986).]

5. Consider the following sequences of offers and acceptances and determine whether in each case there would be a contract.

a. September 1, 2004: A mails an offer to B.
September 2, 2004: B receives the offer.
September 3, 2004: A mails a revocation.
September 4, 2004: B mails an acceptance.
September 5, 2004: B receives the revocation.
September 6, 2004: A receives the acceptance.
RESULT: _____

b. September 1, 2004: A mails an offer to B.
September 2, 2004: B receives the offer.
September 3, 2004: B wires an acceptance.
September 4, 2004: B wires a rejection.
September 4, 2004 (later): A receives the acceptance.
September 5, 2004: A receives the rejection.
RESULT: _____

c. September 1, 2004: A mails an offer to B.
September 2, 2004: B receives the offer.
September 3, 2004: A wires a revocation.
September 3, 2004: B wires an acceptance.

September 4, 2004:   B receives the revocation.
September 5, 2004:   A receives the acceptance.
RESULT: _____

Would your answers be different under the UCC from those under common law?

6. Corinthian Pharmaceuticals Systems, Inc., placed a telephone order with Lederle Laboratories for 1,000 vials of vaccine. Corinthian then followed the telephonic/computer order with two written confirmations. Neither the phone order nor the confirmations mentioned a price. Is there a valid offer? [*Corinthian Pharmaceuticals Systems, Inc.* v. *Lederle Lab.*, 724 F. Supp. 605 (S.D. Ind. 1989).]

7. Hillcrest Country Club contacted N. D. Judds Company about replacement of the roof on its clubhouse. Rick Langill served as Judds's representative in negotiating the contract. Hillcrest managers had a brochure that described the RS-18 roofing manufactured by Roof Systems made of galvanized steel laminated with acrylic film called Korad.

Judds maintains Hillcrest received the brochure by calling Roof Systems. Hillcrest managers maintain Mr. Langill gave them the brochures. Mr. Langill generally stamps brochures and attaches a cover letter before mailing them out, but Hillcrest's brochure was not stamped, although it was used as a basis for Hillcrest's specification sheet. The brochure touted a twenty-year warranty and promised no chalking, fading, chipping, peeling, or other forms of coating deterioration.

Judds submitted a bid with language that waived all warranties once final payment was made. Hillcrest accepted Judds's bid, and the roof was installed in July 1982.

By September 1984, the roof panels on the Hillcrest clubhouse were flaking and required replacement. Judds cited the warranty waiver. Hillcrest replaced the roof at a cost of $80,000 and filed suit against Judds and Roof Systems.

Did Roof Systems's warranty extend to Hillcrest? Was there privity of contract? Is this a UCC Section 2–207 problem? Was a contract formed? Does Hillcrest have a warranty? [*Hillcrest Country Club* v. *N. D. Judds Co.*, 12 U.C.C.2d Rep. Serv. (Callaghan) 990, 236 Neb. 233 (1990).]

8. Ben Diskin, a clothing manufacturer, placed an order with J. P. Stevens for 290 pieces of all-wool flannel material. Mr. Diskin issued a check to Stevens for $151,380. On the reverse side of the check, Mr. Diskin wrote: "In full payment for 290 pcs. of flannel as per contract, less anti. to be figured upon billing. Final total subject to adjustment."

Stevens sent to Mr. Diskin its standard sales contract that was initialed as approved by the sales and credit departments, but there were no signatures. Do the parties have a contract? [*Diskin* v. *J. P. Stevens & Co.*, 652 F. Supp. 553 (D. Mass. 1987).]

9. Thomas Koenen signed a car-purchase order form to buy a limited edition Buick Regal. GM would manufacture only 500 of these Regals. The order form was also signed by the car dealer's salesman and sales manager. Mr. Koenen gave Royal Buick Company (the dealer) a check for $500. No price is mentioned on the order form. Is there a contract? [*Koenen* v. *Royal Buick Co.*, 783 P.2d 822 (Ariz. 1989).]

10. Nation Enterprises, Inc., purchased a large (36 by 3 feet) gas-fired convection oven from Enersyst, Inc., to make its pizza crusts. The oven had problems that the parties were working to resolve, but Nation needed a second oven. It was going to purchase one from someone else, but Enersyst orally promised to fix the first oven if Nation bought the second oven from it. (Oven 1 was beyond its sixty-day warranty.) Nation bought the second oven, but Enersyst did not fix the first one. Nation sued, but Enersyst claims its promise on the first oven is inadmissible under the parol evidence rule. Is this correct? [*Nation Enterprises, Inc.* v. *Enersyst, Inc.*, 749 F. Supp. 1506 (N.D. Ill. 1990).]

RESEARCH PROBLEM

A Draft of a Beer Contract

11. On March 23, 1994, Northern Distributing Company made two offers to purchase two brands of beer carried by Keis Distributors, Inc.: 683,136 cases of Genesee beer at $1.75 per case and 95,632 cases of LaBatt's/Rolling Rock beer at $2 per case. The offer contained a termination date of April 11, 1994, and directed Keis to "accept this offer by signing below." Keis countersigned as requested and sent the offer back to Northern with a cover letter that stated both sides should retain counsel to work out "the wording of the final details." A proposed "closing and consulting agreement" was drafted but never signed, and Keis then withdrew from these distribution areas. Northern did purchase some of Keis's inventory after the distributorship termination, and a dispute arose as to the price due on that inventory. Northern claimed the contract price, and Keis said they had no contract so the price was higher. Who is correct? Read the case and decide. [*Keis Distributors, Inc.* v. *Northern Distributing Co.*, 641 N.Y.S. 2d 417 (App. Div. 1996).]

NOTES

1. The roots of law and commerce are evident here in the discussion of businesses working to develop uniform laws for trade across state lines. More information on the roots of law and commerce can be found on the Website, the updates, and in the instructor's manual.

2. The debate over software, computers, and transactions that mix both had been intense and confusing. Up through 1999, Article 2B had been proposed. Article 2B would have been a new addition to Article 2 to govern those transactions that involve information such as software or a combination of goods and software. With the exclusion of information from Article 2's scope, there remain many issues to be resolved with regard to those contracts.

3. UCITA was formerly Article 2B of the Uniform Commercial Code. It was separated out because reforms for the UCC on Article 2 were pending and the controversy related to Article 2B (now UCITA) was isolated with its separate promulgation as a uniform law. UCITA remains controversial. See Americans for Fair Electronic Commerce at http://www.ucita.com for a summary of the concerns and issues.

4. With the UCC modifications and E-sign, a writing is no longer required. However, there must be some type of record, which could come in the form of an electronic submission.

5. Roger C. Bern, "'Terms Later' Contracting: Bad Economics, Bad Morals, and a Bad Idea for a Uniform Law, Judge Easterbrook Not Withstanding," 12 *Journal of Law and Policy* 641 (2004).

CHAPTER

14

Contracts and Sales: Performance and Remedies

Once the parties have formed a contract with an offer, acceptance, and consideration (as discussed in Chapter 13), it would seem that their troubles are over and that all they need is performance. However, their agreement may be challenged if new issues about formation arise. And how does someone know what is sufficient performance? What may be sufficient performance to one party may not be sufficient to another. This chapter focuses on contract problems and answers the following questions: What if the assumptions made in formation turn out to be untrue? Must the parties go through with the contract? If one party does not perform, is the other excused? When is performance required, and when is it sufficient? What remedies exist? Do third parties have rights in a contract?

> **update** <

*For up-to-date legal news and real-world business applications, click on **update** at http://jennings.westbuslaw.com*

> For want of a nail the shoe was lost;
> For want of a shoe the horse was lost;
> And for want of a horse the rider was lost;
> For the want of a rider the battle was lost;
> For the want of the battle the kingdom was lost
> And all for the want of a horseshoe-nail.
> POOR RICHARD'S ALMANAC (1758)

CONSIDER...

Dorris Reed purchased a home from Robert King for $76,000. After Mrs. Reed moved in, she learned that the house had been the site of the murders of a mother and her four children. Mr. King and the real estate agents were aware of these events but did not disclose them to Mrs. Reed prior to the sale. The neighbors told Mrs. Reed of the murders after she moved into her home. Is Mrs. Reed stuck with the house? Is there any way she can get out of the contract?

© NANCY LOUIE/ISTOCKPHOTO

DEFENSES IN CONTRACT FORMATION

Even though a contract may have been formed with the three elements of offer, acceptance, and consideration, one of the elements may be flawed. The result is a contract that may be void, voidable, or unenforceable. When one of the required elements of formation is flawed, the contract is subject to a defense. A **contract defense** is a situation, term, or event that makes an otherwise valid contract invalid. These defenses ensure that the parties enter into contracts voluntarily and on the basis of accurate information. The defenses, displayed in Exhibit 14.1, are discussed in the following sections.

EXHIBIT 14.1 Defenses in Contract Formation

545

Capacity

Both parties to a valid contract must have **capacity**, which includes both age and mental capacity.

Age Capacity

Age capacity means the parties must have reached the age of majority. In most states, that age is 18, but in some states the age of contractual capacity is 21. Before the time a party reaches the age of capacity, his or her contracts are voidable: A **voidable contract** of a minor allows the party lacking the necessary age (**minor** or **infant**) to choose not to honor the contract, in which case the other party to the contract will have no remedy. But there are some exceptions to the minors' contracts rules. Some statutes make such contracts enforceable; for example, student loan agreements are enforceable against minors. Minors' contracts for necessities such as food and clothing are still voidable, but courts do hold minors liable for the reasonable value of those necessities. *Schmidt* v. *Prince George's Hospital* (Case 14.1) deals with an issue of a minor's liability under a contract.

CASE 14.1

Schmidt v. *Prince George's Hospital*
784 A.2d 1112 (Md. 2001)

The Concussion That Netted a Car

FACTS

Michelle Schmidt, 16 (petitioner), was injured in a car accident and taken to Prince George's Hospital (respondent). Ms. Schmidt was treated for a scalp wound and a concussion. Total costs for the medical treatment were $1,756.24, and the hospital billed Ms. Schmidt's father's insurance company because she was covered under his policy. The insurance company issued a check for the hospital bill to Ms. Schmidt, who used the funds to buy a car with the assumption that, as a minor, she could not be held liable for the costs of her medical treatment.

The hospital filed suit when Ms. Schmidt refused to pay, and she asserted her rights as a minor to disaffirm the obligation to pay. The trial court granted summary judgment and issued an order to attach Ms. Schmidt's wages. Ms. Schmidt appealed.

JUDICIAL OPINION

HARRELL, Judge

In the absence of a statute to the contrary, the prevailing modern rule is that a minor's contracts are voidable; nevertheless, it also is well established that a minor may be liable for the value of necessaries furnished to him or her. This doctrine, eponymously referred to as the doctrine of necessaries, is well recognized in Maryland law.

By common law, persons, under the age of twenty-one years, are not bound by their contracts, except for necessaries, nor can they do any act, to the injury of their property, which they may not avoid, when arrived at full age. Infants have this indulgence from their supposed want of judgment in their transactions with others, and the law takes this care of them to prevent them from being imposed upon, or overreached by persons of more years and experience.

They are allowed to contract for their benefit with power in most cases, to recede from their contract when it may prove prejudicial to them, but in their contract for necessaries, such as board, apparel, medical aid, teaching and instruction, and other necessaries, they are absolutely bound, and may be sued and charged in execution; but it must appear that the things were absolutely necessary, and suitable to their circumstances, and whoever trusts them does so at his peril, or as it is said, deals with them at arms' length.

Their power, thus to contract for necessaries, is for their benefit, because the procurement of these things is essential to their existence, and if they were not permitted so to bind themselves they might suffer.

[A]lthough we decline to vest a right to recover medical expenses in a minor in all cases, we agree that the doctrine of necessaries is sufficient to hold a minor child liable for medical expenses incurred by him or her if it can be shown that his or her parent is unwilling or truly unable to pay them. This liability will, in turn, give a minor the right to claim medical expenses on his or her own behalf. It would be manifestly unjust to hold a child liable for medical expenses but to deny that child the opportunity to recover those expenses from a wrongdoer.

[I]t would be patently unfair to disallow a claim by a minor child for medical expenses, but to then subject that minor child's recovery to the hospital lien. Under such a circumstance, the minor must be allowed to recover medical expenses to the extent that the minor will be liable for such expenses.

Petitioner next asks us to repudiate the common law doctrine of necessaries in its entirety and to hold that "this principle should never be accepted as valid Maryland law." According to Petitioner, the doctrine of necessaries creates a "patently unfair scenario" and provides Maryland judges with the opportunity to "ignore the existing Maryland law," specifically, Maryland Rule 1–202(l), which includes "an individual under the age of 18 years" in its definition of an "Individual under disability."

. . . [w]e find no reason either to abandon or abjure the doctrine of necessaries.

Petitioner repeatedly chants the mantra that a minor does not possess the legal capacity to enter into a binding promise or contract. Specifically, Petitioner asserts that any implied or express contract she may have entered into by receiving Respondent's care should be considered void ab initio in light of her disability as a minor at the time.

"Generally, the law regards contractual obligations of minors as voidable, giving the minor child the choice whether to avoid the contract, or to perform it." . . . [a]lthough parents are required by law to provide for their children's necessaries, a contract entered into by a minor child is presumed to be for non-necessaries and, therefore, voidable and, in some cases, even void ab initio . . .

Contracts entered into by minor children for non-necessaries, therefore, ordinarily are only voidable. Thus, only after a minor has disaffirmed the contract for non-necessaries may the contract ordinarily be considered null and void. Notwithstanding this, a minor can be held to a contract for necessaries under certain circumstances. Under the facts of this case, Petitioner is incorrect in arguing that she, while a minor child, inherently did not possess the legal capacity to promise or contract for payment of her medically-necessitated hospital bill.

Lastly, Petitioner offers us the following hypothetical as a means of demonstrating why the doctrine of necessaries places minors unreasonably at risk for future lawsuits. A newborn child receives emergency medical care soon after birth which resulted in its sur-

vival. As counsel for the hospital I could immediately file suit, without notice, to hold the newborn liable for the unpaid bill alleging the necessaries doctrine as a basis for liability. The parent or guardian fails to establish that it is unable to pay the bill. A judgment is entered personally against the newborn infant in favor of the hospital. Alternatively, as counsel I could wait for a period of 18 years and sue the former newborn infant as an adult, obtain judgment, and then attach this child's wages to satisfy the judgment as was done exactly in this case. As counsel for the hospital I could file suit in all such cases to avoid collection efforts and hiring an accounts representative.

If no wrongdoer existed, as in Petitioner's hypothetical, then the minor ultimately would be responsible for the debt. Should the hypothetical hospital wait until the minor reached the age of majority to sue to recover the medical expenses under the doctrine of necessaries, the defendant could defend on the basis that his or her parents had been able or willing to pay for his or her medical necessaries at the time of incursion while he or she was a minor. Failing such proof, the greater public policy dictates that the former patient pay for the benefits received when given the medically-necessary care by the hospital. Whatever unfairness may inhere in this principle is overweighed by the consideration of not placing hospitals and other emergency health care providers in a situation where financially-able individuals might avoid paying for necessary medical treatment.

JUDGMENT AFFIRMED.

DISSENTING OPINION

RAKER, Judge, dissenting, joined by BELL, Chief Justice, and ELDRIDGE, Justice. I disagree with the majority's holding for two reasons. First, the majority finds the petitioner's father unwilling to pay for her medical bills without discussing what constitutes unwillingness. Indeed, the majority's reasoning is based largely on cases that do not touch on the meaning or import of unwillingness. Second, this State's common law and statutory law does not support the proposition that a child, supported by his or her parents, should be held responsible for isolated necessary medical costs that the parents fail to pay. Despite the fact that parents are obligated by statute to support their children, the majority leaves minors who are supported by their parents liable for their parents' choices, regardless of what those choices are or whether the choices actually reflect unwillingness to pay for necessary medical care.

We agree that the hospital should be paid. The hospital, however, should have sought recovery from petitioner's father rather than waiting to sue petitioner.

continued

The majority's decision to protect the hospital despite the hospital's failure to determine whether petitioner's father was actually unwilling to pay for petitioner's medical bills will leave children liable even where it is the parent and not the child who contrives to avoid paying an isolated medical cost.

It is sensible to hold that a parent who has truly abandoned a child is unwilling to pay for anything for the child, including medical care (sic).

It is also reasonable to find a parent unwilling to pay for the child's medical care where the parent contributes nothing to the child's support. . . . [C]ases do not hold the child liable where the parents, who otherwise support their child, fail to pay for isolated medical expenses. This makes sense because basing a finding of unwillingness on the parents' conduct after medical expenses are incurred would enable parents who otherwise support their children to selectively avoid paying for costs of necessary medical expenses.

Here, . . . it does not appear from the record that the father was contacted by the hospital until the time his daughter had reached majority and was sued by the hospital. So far as I can tell from the record, the father never affirmatively refused to pay the hospital. Since the father was otherwise supporting his daughter, without further proof, there is no basis for concluding that his failure to use insurance proceeds to pay for her medical care reflects unwillingness to pay.

. . . [t]he majority's result would enable petitioner's father to spend the insurance proceeds on whatever he pleased, leaving his daughter liable to the hospital. Despite the fact that the father supported petitioner during her childhood, the father could have, in this instance, used the funds for his own purposes rather than pay his daughter's medical bills, thereby rendering her responsible for this necessary cost.

In keeping with the statutory view of a parent's duty to provide for a child's care, petitioner's father should not be allowed to escape liability for the costs of medical care merely because he decided, after the care was rendered, not to transfer insurance proceeds to the care provider. This is particularly true where the record indicates that the hospital never contacted the father to determine whether he was willing to pay. The majority altogether ignores that the respondent agreed at oral argument that under this statute, even if the parents are truly unwilling to pay for medical care given their child, the parents, not the child, should be sued because liability is a statutory responsibility, irrespective of unwillingness.

Under the majority's reasoning, a child, upon turning age eighteen, may become liable for any necessary medical cost that the child's parents neglected to pay. The child is liable whether or not the claimant ever asks the parents if they are willing to pay. The child is liable even where the parent inexplicably chooses a single occasion on which they will not pay for their child's needs. This manner of piercing the shield of disability stands in stark contrast to the cases discussed above, where there was strong evidence that no one other than the child was or would be willing to pay for the medical care. In those cases, it was almost certain that the medical care provider would not be able to recover from anyone if the child was not forced to pay. The majority's reasoning transforms disability from a shield protecting those too young to be bound to contracts into a starting gate, after which medical care providers are free to sue children for even the most isolated cost that the child's parents inexplicably fail to pay.

I would not hold the child responsible for the parents' choices.

CASE QUESTIONS

1. What type of contract and amount is at issue?
2. When were the services rendered and when was payment demanded?
3. Is Ms. Schmidt liable for the medical expenses?
4. What concerns the dissenting judges about the court's decision?

MAKING ETHICS PERSONAL

Picking Up the Tab When You Aren't Required To

If you were Ms. Schmidt, regardless of legal obligation, would you pay for the medical care? If you were her parents, and regardless of legal obligation, would you pay for the medical care? Are Ms. Schmidt and her parents ethically and morally responsible for the costs of the medical care?

CONSIDER...   14.1

Because of a domestic relations problem, on May 9, 1983, John D. Gilbert canceled, on the advice of counsel, a Visa card held jointly with his wife. Mr. Gilbert made a new application, and a new credit card was issued to him.

The card was mailed to Mr. Gilbert at his business address. After a month, he received a Visa bill for $1,341.54 in purchases. Mr. Gilbert acknowledges that his married daughter Christine charged $85.44 and that he charged $89.88. The remaining $1,166.22 was charged by Ann Gilbert, Mr. Gilbert's minor daughter.

Mr. Gilbert refused to pay Ann's share of the bill, and Visa brought suit. Can Visa recover from Ann? Can Visa recover from Mr. Gilbert? [*Fifth Third Bank/Visa* v. *Gilbert*, 478 N.E. 2d 1324 (Ohio 1981).]

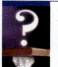

ETHICAL ISSUES

LeAnn Rimes, a country western singer, signed a contract at age 12 with Curb Records. Curb Records is owned by Mike Curb, a longstanding presence in the music industry who began his career with a group known as The Mike Curb Congregation. Ms. Rimes will be 35 before she has delivered the twenty-one albums required under the terms of the agreement. "At 12, I didn't understand everything in my contract. All I know is that I really wanted to sing." Ms. Rimes testified at a hearing of the California Senate Select Committee on the Entertainment Industry looking into the labor issues surrounding long-term album requirements contracts.

Other artists testified about their lack of health insurance benefits under these contracts. Singer Courtney Love testified, in reference to her minimal insurance coverage, "I can maybe get six days in rehab."

Don Henley, a solo artist formerly with The Eagles, testified, "The deck is stacked and has been stacked for sixty years in the recording companies' favor."

Record industry executives testified that the long-term contracts are necessary because of the time, money, and effort required to build young artists. One executive said, "There is one thing that all labels have in common and that's risk."

The Dixie Chicks are in litigation with their label, Sony, and Ms. Love is in litigation with her label, Vivendi Universal, for what they say are questionable accounting practices in arriving at the artists' share of the profits. Both companies have responded with countersuits alleging that the artists have not produced the albums required under their contracts.

Does Ms. Rimes have a possible defense? Are the recording contracts binding, or are they unconscionable? Are the long-term contracts and their requirements ethical?

Mental Capacity

Contracting parties must also have *mental capacity*, which is the ability to understand that contracts are enforceable, that legal documents have significance, and that contracts involve costs and obligations. Contracts of those lacking mental capacity are voidable. Moreover, if a party to a contract has been declared legally incompetent, that person's contracts are void. A **void contract** is one the courts will not honor, and neither party is obligated to perform under that agreement.

Misrepresentation

When one party to a contract is not given full or accurate information by the other party about the contract subject matter, **misrepresentation** occurs. Misrepresentation allows **rescission** of the contract, which means the contract is rescinded or set aside. Misrepresentation occurs when a seller makes inaccurate statements about its product or fails to disclose pertinent information about its product that should be disclosed. Misrepresentation or innocent misrepresentation is not an intentional act (see fraud). For example, failing to disclose that a deluxe model car has a standard car engine is misrepresentation if the seller is mistaken. It would be fraud if the seller withheld the information in order to deceive the buyer. The elements required for innocent misrepresentation are as follows:

1. Misstatement of a material fact (or the failure to disclose a material fact)

2. Reliance by the buyer on that material misstatement or omission

3. Resulting damages to the buyer

To be a basis for rescission, the misrepresentation must have been one regarding a **material fact**. A material fact is the type of information that would affect someone's decision to enter into the contract. For example, if a buyer for your stock in XYZ Corporation failed to disclose that a takeover was pending, there would be misrepresentation of a material fact. A takeover affects the price of stock, and the price of stock in the future affects your decision to buy and sell presently.

Misrepresentation cannot be based on sales **puffing**, which is opinion about the subject matter of a contract. For example, suppose that a real estate agent told you a house you were considering buying was located in the "best area in town." Such a statement is an opinion and cannot be a basis for misrepresentation.

CONSIDER...   **14.2**

Analyze the following statements. Are they opinion, or could they be the basis for a misrepresentation claim?

This light bulb will last 200 hours.

THINK: Misrepresentation requires a statement of fact or a promise of performance that is a basis for entering into a contract.

APPLY: This statement about the light bulb is a promise of performance. It is the type of information someone relies on when making a buying decision.

ANSWER: The statement is a basis for claiming misrepresentation if it turns out to be false.

These suits are 100 percent wool.

THINK: Misstatement of a material fact that the buyer relies on when making decisions can be the basis for a claim of misrepresentation

APPLY: Saying that the suits are 100 percent wool is a statement of fact about the goods.

ANSWER: If the goods are not 100 percent wool, the statement is a basis for claiming misrepresentation.

Now use this approach to analyze the following statements.

This fabric is the finest money can buy.

This sweater is 50 percent cashmere.

This toothpaste reduces cavities by 20 percent.

This car gets 22 miles to the gallon.

This stock has never decreased in value.

This house has no easements running through the backyard.

This car has not been in an accident.

These bicycle locks are theft-proof.

This carpet-cleaning machine will remove every type of spot on your rugs.

CHECK THE WEB

Check the book's Web site updates for examples of cases involving misrepresentation.

The buyer must rely on or attach some importance to the statement that was made. For a buyer of stock to claim financial misrepresentation, the buyer must have actually examined the false financial statements of the company selling the stock and based the buying decision on the company's financial condition. A buyer who is buying cars only to take them apart for their used parts does not rely on a misrepresentation that the car has not been in an accident. Whatever information is given must be part of the reason the buyer has agreed to enter into the contract.

Fraud or Fraudulent Misrepresentation

Although misrepresentation can result simply because of inaccurate information, **fraud** is the knowing and intentional disclosure of false information or the knowing

ETHICAL ISSUES

Beech-Nut Nutrition Corporation was a division of Squibb Corporation. Its chewing gum segment was profitable but was sold in 1973. Beech-Nut's baby food division, which had 15 percent of the baby food market, had never been profitable, and by 1978 creditors were increasingly anxious.

Beech-Nut had entered into a contract in 1977 with Interjuice Trading Corporation for Interjuice to furnish apple juice concentrate to Beech-Nut at a price that was 20 percent below market prices. This contract was a huge break for Beech-Nut since it used apple concentrate in 30 percent of its baby food products. The Interjuice contract attracted enough attention that Nestlé purchased Beech-Nut in 1979.

Jerome J. LiCari was the director of research and development for Beech-Nut. Mr. LiCari and the chemists in his department were concerned about the Interjuice contract for two reasons: (1) rumors of adulteration (substituted product or inferior product) in the apple juice concentrate market were rampant, and (2) the price was simply too good to be true.

At that time there were no tests to determine adulteration, but Mr. LiCari sent two of his employees to the Interjuice plant in Queens, New York. Interjuice officials refused to allow them to see processing operations but did provide them access to the plant storage tanks.

Mr. LiCari then tried, in 1981, to develop a test for adulteration. He could not, but he took his circumstantial evidence and concerns for Beech-Nut's reputation to John F. Lavery, Beech-Nut's head of operations. Mr. LiCari suggested Beech-Nut adopt Gerber's policy requiring suppliers to establish authenticity or lose their contracts. Mr. Lavery called Mr. LiCari "Chicken Little" and told him he had no proof.

In late 1981, Mr. LiCari, feeling that his tests showed the Interjuice concentrate had no apple juice, wrote a memo to Mr. Lavery suggesting Beech-Nut switch suppliers. Mr. Lavery did not respond.

Mr. LiCari then took his cost and chemical analysis to Neils Hoyvald, the president and CEO of Beech-Nut, who told Mr. LiCari, "I'll look into it." He did nothing and told Mr. LiCari he had great technical ability but that his judgment was "colored by naivete and impractical ideals."

Mr. LiCari resigned from Beech-Nut and wrote a letter to the FDA disclosing the Interjuice adulteration, signing it "Johnny Appleseed."

Mr. LiCari's letter started an FDA inquiry and the eventual discovery that Interjuice concentrate was a chemical concoction with no apple juice at all. After what the FDA called a cat-and-mouse game of shipping juice lots to avoid regulatory testing, the FDA found and tested a lot with no juice.

Mr. Hoyvald and Mr. Lavery were indicted. (Following two trials and appeals, Mr. Hoyvald entered a guilty plea.) Mr. LiCari, located as a witness through company files, testified at their trials, "I thought apple juice should be made from apples."

Beech-Nut still struggles with market share and consumer loyalty.

Issues

Was there misrepresentation in the sale of Beech-Nut baby food? Was there fraud? Was Mr. LiCari harmed by his discovery and disclosure? Was Beech-Nut's conduct with respect to the Interjuice contract ethical? Was Beech-Nut's conduct with respect to Mr. LiCari ethical?

failure to disclose relevant information. Fraud has the same elements of proof as misrepresentation, with the added element of *scienter*, or knowledge that the information given is false. An example of the distinction is a situation in which the seller of a home obtains an exterminator's report that says the house is clear of termites and passes the report along to the buyer. If the house actually has termites, there has been misrepresentation but not fraud because the seller was simply passing along the information without knowledge of its accuracy. If, however, that same seller received a report from an exterminator that indicated there were termites and then found another exterminator to report there were no termites, and the seller passed only that second report along to the buyer, there would be fraud because there was knowledge of the false report and the intent to defraud the buyer. *Reed* v. *King* (Case 14.2) includes a discussion of the elements of misrepresentation, when misrepresentation becomes fraud, and provides the answer for the chapter's opening Consider.

CASE 14.2

Reed v. *King*
193 Cal. Rptr. 130 (1983)

Buying Property from the Addams Family: How Scary Must It Be?

FACTS

Dorris Reed (plaintiff) purchased a home from Robert King for $76,000. Mr. King and his real estate agents did not disclose to Mrs. Reed that ten years before, the house had been the site of the murders of a mother and her four children. After Mrs. Reed moved into the home, neighbors disclosed to her the story of the murders and the fact that the house carried a stigma. Because of its history, appraisers evaluated the true worth of the house to be $65,000. Mrs. Reed filed suit on the basis of misrepresentation and sought rescission and damages. Her complaint was dismissed by the trial court, and she appealed.

JUDICIAL OPINION

BLEASE, Associate Justice

In the sale of a house, must the seller disclose it was the site of a multiple murder?

Does Reed's pleading state a cause of action? Concealed within this question is the nettlesome problem of the duty of disclosure of blemishes on real property which are not physical defects or legal impairments to use.

Reed seeks to state a cause of action sounding in contract, i.e., rescission, or in tort, i.e., deceit. In either event her allegations must reveal a fraud. "The elements of actual fraud, whether as the basis of the remedy in

contract or tort, may be stated as follows: There must be (1) a *false representation* or concealment of a material fact (or, in some cases, an opinion) susceptible of knowledge, (2) made with *knowledge* of its falsity or without sufficient knowledge on the subject to warrant a representation, (3) with the *intent* to induce the person to whom it is made to act upon it; and such person must (4) act in *reliance* upon the representation (5) to his *damage*."

The trial court perceived the defect in Reed's complaint to be a failure to allege concealment of a material fact. "Concealment" and "material" are legal conclusions concerning the effect of the issuable facts pled. As appears, the analytic pathways to these conclusions are intertwined.

Reed's complaint reveals only nondisclosure despite the allegation King asked a neighbor to hold his peace. There is no allegation the attempt at suppression was a cause in fact of Reed's ignorance. Accordingly, the critical question is: does the seller have duty to disclose here? Resolution of this question depends on the materiality of the fact of the murders.

In general, a seller of real property has a duty to disclose: "where the seller knows of facts *materially* affecting the value or desirability of the property which are known or accessible only to him and also knows that such facts are not known to, or within the reach of the diligent attention and observation of the buyer, the seller is under a duty to disclose them to the buyer."

Whether information "is of sufficient materiality to affect the value or desirability of the property . . . depends on the facts of the particular case." Materiality "is a question of law, and is part of the concept of right to rely or justifiable reliance." Accordingly, the term is essentially a label affixed to a normative conclusion. Three considerations bear on this legal conclusion: the gravity of the harm inflicted by nondisclosure; the fairness of imposing a duty of discovery on the buyer as an alternative to compelling disclosure, and its impact on the stability of contracts if rescission is permitted.

Numerous cases have found nondisclosure of physical defects and legal impediments to use of real property are material. However, to our knowledge, no prior real estate sale case has faced an issue of nondisclosure of the kind presented here. Should this variety of ill-repute be required to be disclosed? Is this a circumstance where "nondisclosure of the fact amounts to a failure to act in good faith and in accordance with reasonable standards of fair dealing"[?]

The paramount argument against an affirmative conclusion is it permits the camel's nose of unrestrained irrationality admission to the tent. If such an "irrational" consideration is permitted as a basis of rescission the stability of all conveyances will be seriously undermined. Any fact that might disquiet the enjoyment of some segment of the buying public may be seized upon by a disgruntled purchaser to void a bargain. In our view, keeping this genie in the bottle is not as difficult a task as these arguments assume. We do not view a decision allowing Reed to survive a demurrer in these unusual circumstances as endorsing the materiality of facts predicating peripheral, insubstantial, or fancied harms.

The murder of innocents is highly unusual in its potential for so disturbing buyers they may be unable to reside in a home where it has occurred. This fact may foreseeably deprive a buyer of the intended use of the purchase. Murder is not such a common occurrence that *buyers* should be charged with anticipating and discovering this disquieting possibility. Accordingly, the fact is not one for which a duty of inquiry and discovery can sensibly be imposed upon the buyer.

Reed alleges the fact of the murders has a quantifiable effect on the market value of the premises. We cannot say this allegation is inherently wrong and, in the pleading posture of the case, we assume it to be true.

Reputation and history can have a significant effect on the value of realty. "George Washington slept here" is worth something, however physically inconsequential that consideration may be. Ill-repute or "bad will" conversely may depress the value of property. Failure to disclose such a negative fact where it will have a foreseeably depressing effect on income expected to be generated by a business is tortious. Some cases have held that *unreasonable* fears of the potential buying public that a gas or oil pipeline may rupture may depress the market value of land and entitle the owner to incremental compensation in eminent domain.

Whether Reed will be able to prove her allegation, the decade-old multiple murder has a significant effect on market value we cannot determine. If she is able to do so by competent evidence she is entitled to a favorable ruling on the issues of materiality and duty to disclose. Her demonstration of objective tangible harm would still the concern that permitting her to go forward will open the floodgates to rescission on subjective and idiosyncratic grounds.

CASE QUESTIONS

1. What information about the house was not disclosed to Mrs. Reed before she purchased it?

2. How did she discover the information and when?

3. Is the information material?

4. What does Mrs. Reed need to establish to be entitled to rescission and damages?

5. Is Mrs. Reed's case dismissed, or will she be permitted to go forward with the suit?

6. Would the information about the house make a difference to you in making a buying decision?

7. Should Mr. King and the real estate agents have disclosed the information to Mrs. Reed? Was there an ethical obligation to do so?

The failure to disclose material information about the subject matter of a contract can also constitute fraud. For example, a car dealership that fails to disclose to a customer that the car he is buying was in an accident is misrepresentation. If the car dealership performed the body work on the car in its own body shop, the failure to disclose the accident and repairs would be fraud.

With respect to real estate transactions, most states have passed some form of disclosure statutes. In some states, the history of criminal activity on a property must be disclosed. In other states, there are prohibitions on disclosure. Some of

> ## CONSIDER...   14.3
>
> On December 5, 1997, Michael Dekofsky and Christopher Vrakelos sold Brea Range, Inc., an indoor shooting range, to Hansen for $140,000. Hansen paid $70,000 cash and assumed two promissory notes due and owing from the corporation to Mr. Dekofsky and Mr. Vrakelos. After escrow closed, Hansen discovered that two patrons committed suicide at Brea Range, in 1995 and March 1997.
>
> Hansen made interest payments on the promissory notes until January 1, 1999, defaulted on the first principal payment, and ceased making payments on June 1, 1999. Mr. Dekofsky and Mr. Vrakelos sued for the balance due. Hansen defended on the theory that the sellers had unclean hands and breached a duty to disclose material facts. In a cross-complaint Hansen sued for conspiracy, fraud, misrepresentation, and rescission. Does Hansen have a valid defense to the contract's formation? Was there misrepresentation? Was there fraud? [*Dekofsky* v. *Brea Range, Inc.*, 2001 WL 1613509, (Cal.App. 2 Dist.) (not printed in Cal. Rptr.—unpublished opinion).]

these states prohibit disclosure of information, such as whether an occupant of the property died of AIDS. For example, a California statute provides the following.

PART 3. OBLIGATIONS IMPOSED BY LAW

§ 1710.2. Occupant of property afflicted with or who died from AIDS; failure to disclose to transferee; no cause of action; state preemption of AIDS disclosure

(a) No cause of action arises against an owner of real property or his or her agent, or any agent of a transferee of real property, for the failure to disclose to the transferee the occurrence of an occupant's death upon the real property or the manner of death where the death has occurred more than three years prior to the date the transferee offers to purchase, lease, or rent the real property, or that an occupant of that property was afflicted with, or died from, Human T-Lymphotropic Virus Type III/Lymphadenopathy-Associated Virus.

However, even in states with protections and immunity from disclosure, the truth must be revealed if the buyer asks specifically about the occupants and their health.

FOR THE MANAGER'S DESK
RE: THE INSURER WHO FELT OVERDRAWN

American Insurance Group, Inc. (AIG) has a reputation for taking on any client the company believes has filed an unjust claim.

Now, AIG and several other insurers are taking on Mary Poppins. More to the point, they appear to be questioning her truthfulness.

The central issue: Did Julie Andrews—renowned as the beloved Miss Poppins, the heroic Maria Von Trapp, and the gender-bending Victoria Grant—fib when she filled out medical forms needed for an insurance policy for the musical "Victor/Victoria"? According to a suit filed in a New York state court in Manhattan by the producers of the play, the insurers have rescinded a policy they wrote on "Victor/Victoria." The insurers claim Ms. Andrews falsely answered questions about her medical past, the suit says.

The policy was purchased in March 1995 from a group of insurers led by Lexington Insurance Co., an AIG subsidiary, for a premium of $157,985. For that, the producers say, they thought they were getting coverage that would pay as much as $2 million for missed appearances by Ms. Andrews and $8.5 million if Ms. Andrews was forced to abandon the show altogether. The policy carried a two-show deductible—standard procedure in show business—that meant the insurers wouldn't have to pay until two consecutive performances were missed. AIG shared much of the liability with eight other insurance companies but remained the lead underwriter, according to the lawsuit.

Broadway shows with superstars generally offer ticketholders the option of leaving the theatre and taking a refund if the star can't make it. Seldom is a show, other than a one-person performance, canceled. Well-trained understudies are usually waiting in the wings for such a chance to strut their stuff—as was the case in "Victor/Victoria."

"Most people have adjusted to the fact that if the star is out they'll still watch a darn good show," says Carol Bressi-Cilona, who brokered the insurance policy for the play through her employer, the DeWitt Stern Group.

That wasn't entirely the case for this musical, heavily dependent on Ms. Andrews's star power. In fact, most of the times it was announced that Ms. Andrews wouldn't appear, dozens of patrons headed for the exits—with a stop at the refund window.

Ms. Andrews had a spate of rough spells during the show's run. The musical opened in October 1995, but the following January, she came down with a sore throat and a hacking cough. At her doctors' request, the suit says, she missed 10 performances, resulting in losses of $442,435.

Several weeks later, according to the suit, she had a gallbladder operation and missed 21 shows: Cost: $980,850.

A few months down the road, she missed several more performances because of a bad larynx. Those losses amounted to about $183,000, according to the suit, which says that insurers refused to pay any of these claims.

Indisputably, Ms. Andrews worked hard. And to the tens of thousands of theatergoers who watched her sing and dance her way through the strenuous routines as a cross-dressing cabaret star, she is a hero. To take on that role at her age—she is 61 years old—was no mean feat.

"It's a very demanding part. There are only two scenes Julie is not in," says Ms. Bressi-Cilona. "One costume is so heavily beaded they have to lift it onto her. First she's running around with practically no clothes, and then she has lots of clothes and she's sweating."

To date, Ms. Andrews has performed in nearly 600 performances of the musical, which shows eight times a week, Tuesday through Saturday, with matinees three days a week. Her husband, Blake Edwards, directs the show and, according to an interview Ms. Andrews gave to Newsday, he put up $2 million of the family's money to fund the show.

According to the lawsuit, the insurers rescinded the policy on the grounds that Ms. Andrews had allegedly falsely answered two questions in an affidavit submitted when the producers applied for the policy.

One question asked if she ever had suffered from tuberculosis, asthma, emphysema, persistent cough or any other disease or abnormality of the lungs or respiratory system, according to the suit. Her answer was "no," the suit says. The second question asked if she had had "any disease, disorder or injury of the bones, joints, muscles, back, spine, or neck." Again, the suit says, the answer was "no."

It isn't clear what the insurers think was incorrect about those responses—and New York-based AIG wouldn't comment yesterday. About the only thing the producers say in the suit about Ms. Andrews's health is that she "occasionally experiences mild bronchial symptoms solely in response to specific external factors such as infection, smog or other environmental factors, and occasionally has mild osteoarthritic symptoms in her hands."

As for Ms. Andrews, she couldn't comment yesterday afternoon. Peter Cromarty, publicist for "Victor/Victoria," says she was in "vocal rest." "When you sing seven or eight times a week for two hours," he says, "the only way you can humanly do that is not talking between shows."

Source: "Maybe Julie Andrews Could Offer Insurers a Spoonful of Sugar," *Wall Street Journal,* April 4, 1997, A1, by Leslie Scism. Copyright © 1997 Dow Jones & Company, Inc. Reprinted by permission of Dow Jones & Company, Inc. via the Copyright Clearance Center.

Duress

Duress occurs when a party is physically forced into a contract or deprived of a meaningful choice when deciding whether to enter into a contract. Requiring employees to sell company stock holdings in order to keep their jobs is an example of duress because of a lack of choice. If there has been duress, the contract is voidable. The party who experienced the duress has the right to rescind the agreement, but rescission is a choice; the law does not make the contract illegal or unenforceable because duress was present. The choice of enforcement or rescission is left to the party who experienced the duress.

Undue Influence

Undue influence occurs when one party uses a close personal relationship with another party to gain contractual benefits. Before undue influence can be established, a **confidential relationship** of trust and reliance must exist between the parties.

Attorneys and clients have a confidential relationship. Elderly parents who rely on a child or children for their care have a confidential relationship with those children. To establish undue influence, there must be an abuse of this confidential relationship. For example, conditioning an elderly parent's care upon the signing over of his land to a child is an abuse of the relationship. An attorney who offers advice on property disposition to his benefit is abusing the confidential relationship. Again, contracts subject to undue influence defenses are voidable. They can be honored if the party who experienced the influence desires to honor the contract.

Illegality and Public Policy

A contract that violates a statute or the general standards of public policy is void and cannot be enforced by either party. To enforce contracts that violate statutes or public conscience would encourage the commission of these illegal acts, so contract law is controlled by the statutory prohibitions and public policy concerns of other areas of law.

Contracts in Violation of Criminal Statutes

Contracts that are agreements to commit criminal wrongs are void. For example, the old saying that "there is a contract out on his life" may be descriptive, but it is not accurate in the legal sense. There could never be a valid contract to kill someone because the agreement is one to commit a criminal wrong and is therefore void. No one is permitted to benefit from contracts to commit illegal acts. For example, a beneficiary for a life insurance policy will not collect the proceeds from the insured's policy if the beneficiary arranged for the death of the insured (contract for murder). Consider 14.4 deals with the issue of benefits from an illegal contract.

Contracts in Violation of Licensing Statutes

In some cases, contracts are not contracts to commit illegal acts but are simply contracts for a legal act to be done by one not authorized to perform such services. Every state requires some professionals or technicians to be licensed before they can perform work for the public. For example, a lawyer must be admitted to the bar be-

---

CONSIDER...   1 4 . 4

Robert Hackett became a substitute fireman for the city of New Britain, Connecticut, in 1949. In 1950, he was made a full-time fireman and in 1968 became a lieutenant. After earning the highest mark on the captain's examination, he was promoted to captain in 1974. He then scored the highest score on the deputy chief exam and was promoted to that rank in 1977.

Mr. Hackett had paid an employee in the city department responsible for administering the exams to ensure that he earned the highest grades (which he did). He had, in effect, purchased his last two promotions. When these acts were discovered (after Mr. Hackett had retired), criminal charges were brought against him and the city employee. Both were convicted of felonies.

The pension board of New Britain then met and voted to reduce Mr. Hackett's pension by $5,483.97 a year because that reduction placed his pension at the level it would have been without the last two promotions. The board said the reduction was necessary because the last two promotions were obtained through illegal conduct. Mr. Hackett filed suit. Is illegality a defense to Hackett's suit for his full pension? [*Hackett* v. *City of New Britain*, 477 A.2d 148 (Conn. 1984).]

fore representing clients. A lawyer who contracts to represent a client before having been admitted to the practice of law has entered into a void contract. Even if the lawyer successfully represents the client, no fee could be collected because the agreement violated the licensing statute, and to allow the lawyer to collect the fee, even in a quasi contract, would encourage others to violate the licensing requirements.

In some cases, licensing requirements are in place not for competency reasons but to raise revenues. For example, an architect may be required to pass a competency screening to be initially licensed in a state, and after that the license may be renewed simply by paying an annual fee. Suppose that the architect forgot to pay the annual renewal fee and, after the license had lapsed, entered into a $300,000 contract with a developer. The developer discovers the renewal problems after the work is completed and wants to get out of paying the architect. In this case, the issue is not one of competency screening but of financial oversight, and the architect would be permitted to collect the fee.

Contracts in Violation of Usury Laws

These contracts are credit or loan contracts that charge interest in excess of the state's limits for interest or finance charges. These statutes are discussed in detail in Chapter 15.

Contracts in Violation of Public Policy

Some contracts do not violate any criminal laws or statutory provisions but do violate certain standards of fairness or encourage conduct in violation of public policy. For example, many firms include **exculpatory clauses** in their contracts that purport to hold the firms completely blameless for any accidents occurring on their premises. Most courts consider a firm's trying to hold itself completely blameless for all accidents, regardless of the degree of care or level of fault, against public policy and will not, therefore, enforce such clauses. One court has defined an unconscionable contract as one "such as no man in his senses and not under delusion would make on the one hand, and as no honest and fair man would accept on the other" [*Waters* v. *Min. Ltd.*, 412 Mass. 64, 587 N.E.2d 231 (1992)].

Also grouped into the public policy prohibition are contracts that restrict trade or employment. For example, when a business is sold, part of the purchase price is paid for the business's goodwill. The benefit of that payment is lost if the seller moves down the street and starts another similar business. Hence, the courts have permitted **covenants not to compete** to be included in these contracts so long as they are reasonable in time and geographic scope. These covenants and their legality are discussed in detail in Chapter 17.

Some contracts are not actually contracts for criminal or illegal activities, but the terms of the contract are grossly unfair to one party. A contract that gives all the benefits to one side and all the burdens to the other is an **unconscionable** contract. The standards for determining whether a contract is unconscionable are the public policy standards for fairness that cover all types of contract provisions and negotiations. Many consumer rental contracts have been declared unconscionable because the consumers were paying more in rent than it would cost to buy the rented appliance outright.

The standards for unconscionability are set on a case-by-case basis. The courts have not given a firm definition of unconscionability. Even the UCC does not specifically define unconscionability, although one section (2–302) prohibits the enforcement of unconscionable contracts.

BIOGRAPHY

MORAL ROLE MODELS IN ADS

The morals issue has touched endorsement contracts and affected actual performance contracts. For example, the CNN Web site (http://www.cnn.com) ran the following report of the half-time show with Janet Jackson and Justin Timberlake at the 2004 Super Bowl.

> *"The decision to have a costume reveal at the end of my halftime show performance was made after final rehearsals," Jackson said in a statement.*
>
> *"MTV was completely unaware of it. It was not my intention that it go as far as it did. I apologize to anyone offended —including the audience, MTV, CBS and the NFL."*
>
> *MTV produced the halftime show, which was broadcast by CBS. Both had issued their own apologies.*
>
> *On Monday, Federal Communications Commission Chairman Michael Powell ordered an investigation of the incident.*
>
> *An estimated 140 million people were watching the show when at the end, pop star Justin Timberlake popped off part of Jackson's corset, exposing her breast.*
>
> *Powell told CNN he was not convinced the incident was an accident.*
>
> *"Clearly somebody had knowledge of it. Clearly it was something that was planned by someone," he said. "She probably got what she was looking for."*
>
> *Jackson spokesman Stephen Huvane said the incident "was a malfunction of the wardrobe; it was not intentional. . . . He was supposed to pull away the bustier and leave the red-lace bra."*

Mr. Powell said he "expressed my great displeasure" over the incident in a telephone call Monday with CBS President and CEO Mel Karmazin, who "promised to cooperate" with the investigation.

Although Mr. Karmazin expressed "a great deal of regret," Mr. Powell said those sentiments would not deter the investigation.

The stock price of Viacom, the parent of CBS, rose more than 1 percent Monday.

"CBS deeply regrets the incident that occurred during the Super Bowl halftime show," the network said in a statement. "We attended all rehearsals throughout the week, and there was no indication that any such thing would happen.

"The moment did not conform to CBS broadcast standards, and we would like to apologize to anyone who was offended."

A statement from MTV said the tearing of Ms. Jackson's costume "was unrehearsed, unplanned, completely unintentional and was inconsistent with assurances we had about the content of the performance.

"MTV regrets this incident occurred, and we apologize to anyone who was offended by it."

Despite its apology, MTV did not hesitate to promote the incident after the fact. A Web page headline said: "Janet Jackson Got Nasty at the MTV-Produced Super Bowl Halftime Show."

Performing together in a routine that had included a number of bump-and-grind moves, Mr. Timberlake reached across Ms. Jackson and flicked off the molded right cup of the bustier, leaving her breast bare except for a starburst-shaped decoration held in place by a nipple piercing.

Mr. Timberlake issued his own apology. "I am sorry if anyone was offended by the wardrobe malfunction during the halftime performance at the Super Bowl," he said. "It was not intentional and is regrettable."

The White House also weighed in on the issue. "Our view is that it's important for families to be able to expect a high standard when it comes to programming," White House spokesman Scott McClellan said.

NFL Commissioner Paul Tagliabue joined the chorus. "The show was offensive, inappropriate and embarrassing to us and our fans. We will change our policy, our people and our processes for managing the halftime entertainment in the future in order to deal far more effectively with the quality of this aspect of the Super Bowl."

AOL, owned by CNN parent company Time Warner, attempted to distance itself from the dispute.

"While AOL was the sponsor of the Super Bowl Halftime Show, we did not produce it. In deference to our membership and the fans, AOL and AOL.com will not be presenting the halftime show online as originally planned."

CBS canceled Ms. Jackson's appearance on the Grammy awards and introduced tape delay broadcast for that event as well as the Oscars. Ms. Jackson resigned from playing Lena Horne in a movie that had not yet gone into production, following discussions with 86-year-old Ms. Horne and her daughter. The FCC fined CBS $550,000 for the Janet Jackson incident.

ISSUES

1. Is there an implied morals clause in endorsement contracts?

2. Should there be?

3. Is private life subject to scrutiny in endorsement contracts?

4. How can morals clauses be important when such conduct causes the stock price to increase?

Waters v. *Min Ltd.* (Case 14.3) deals with a contract that involves several different defenses.

CASE 14.3

Waters v. *Min Ltd.*
587 N.E.2d 231 (Mass. 1992)

Young, Drugged, and Wealthy: Capable of Contracting?

FACTS

Gail A. Waters (plaintiff) was injured in an accident when she was 12 years old. At age 18 she settled a negligence claim with Commercial Union Insurance Company and purchased an annuity contract, the income from which was her support.

At age 21, Ms. Waters became romantically involved with Thomas Beauchemin (defendant), an ex-convict who introduced her to drugs and to Min Ltd., a partnership consisting of David and Robert DeVito and Michael D. Steamer (defendants), and suggested that she sell her annuity contract to them.

Ms. Waters signed a contract to sell her policy, with a cash value of $189,000, to the defendants for $50,000. The contract was signed on the hood of a car in the parking lot of a restaurant. The guaranteed return to the owner of the policy over its 25-year life was $694,000.

Ms. Waters filed suit to rescind the contract. The trial court found, among other things, that the contract was unconscionable. The DeVitos, Mr. Steamer, and Mr. Beauchemin appealed.

JUDICIAL OPINION

LYNCH, Justice

The defendants contend that the judge erred by (1) finding the contract unconscionable (and by concluding the defendants assumed no risks and therefore finding the contract oppressive); (2) refusing them specific performance; and (3) failing to require the plaintiff to return all the funds received from them.

Unconscionability. The defendants argue that the evidence does not support the finding that the contract

was unconscionable or that they assumed no risks and therefore that the contract was oppressive.

The doctrine of unconscionability has long been recognized by common law courts in this country and in England. "Historically, a [contract] was considered unconscionable if it was 'such as no man in his senses and not under delusion would make on the one hand, and as no honest and fair man would accept on the other.' Later, a contract was determined unenforceable because unconscionable when 'the sum total of its provisions drives too hard a bargain for a court of conscience to assist.'"

The doctrine of unconscionability has also been codified in the Uniform Commercial Code (code), G.L.C. 106, § 2–302 (1990 ed.), and, by analogy, it has been applied in situations outside the ambit of the code.

Unconscionability must be determined on a case-by-case basis, with particular attention to whether the challenged provision could result in oppression and unfair surprise to the disadvantaged party and not to allocation of risk because of "superior bargaining power." Courts have identified other elements of the unconscionable contract. For example, gross disparity in the consideration alone "may be sufficient to sustain [a finding that the contract is unconscionable]," since the disparity "itself leads inevitably to the felt conclusion that knowing advantage was taken of [one party]." High pressure sales tactics and misrepresentation have been recognized as factors rendering a contract unconscionable. If the sum total of the provisions of a contract drive too hard a bargain, a court of conscience will not assist its enforcement.

continued

The judge found that Beauchemin introduced the plaintiff to drugs, exhausted her credit card accounts to the sum of $6,000, unduly influenced her, suggested that the plaintiff sell her annuity contract, initiated the contract negotiations, was the agent of the defendants, and benefited from the contract between the plaintiff and the defendants. The defendants were represented by legal counsel; the plaintiff was not. The cash value of the annuity policy at the time the contract was executed was approximately four times greater than the price to be paid by the defendants. For payment of not more than $50,000 the defendants were to receive an asset that could be immediately exchanged for $189,000, or they could elect to hold it for its guaranteed term and receive $694,000. In these circumstances the judge could correctly conclude the contract was unconscionable.

The defendants assumed no risk and the plaintiff gained no advantage. Gross disparity in the values exchanged is an important factor to be considered in determining whether a contract is unconscionable. "[C]ourts [may] avoid enforcement of a bargain that is shown to be unconscionable by reason of gross inadequacy of consideration accompanied by other relevant factors."

We are satisfied that the disparity of interests in this contract is "so gross that the court cannot resist the inference that it was improperly obtained and is unconscionable."

Amount of repayment order. The defendants also argue that the judge erred in failing to require the plaintiff to return the full amount paid by them for the annuity.

The defendants paid $18,000 cash after deducting $7,000 for a debt which was owed to them by Beauchemin. The remaining $25,000 due on the contract was never paid.

The judge's order was consistent with his findings that Beauchemin was the agent of the defendants, and that the plaintiff only received $18,000 for her interest in the annuity.

Judgment affirmed.

CASE QUESTIONS

1. List the possible defenses to this contract.

2. What made the contract unconscionable?

3. What protections for Ms. Waters could have been built into the annuity contract?

4. Is there any criminal conduct here?

CONTRACT PERFORMANCE

Once parties have contracted, they have the obligation of performance. The following subsections cover when performance is due, what constitutes performance, and when performance is excused.

When Performance Is Due

Performance is due according to the times provided in the contract. In some contracts, however, prescribed events must occur before there is an obligation of performance. These events are called **conditions**. **Conditions precedent** are events that give rise to performance. Suppose that Zelda has agreed to buy Scott's house and their contract provides that Zelda does not have to pay until she is able to obtain a reasonable loan to finance the purchase. This financing clause is a condition precedent to contract performance. If Zelda is denied financing, she is not required to perform under the contract. Another example of a condition precedent is in a contract for construction of jackets out of a material to be furnished by the seller. Unless the seller gives the manufacturer the fabric to work with, the manufacturer has no obligation to perform. **Conditions concurrent**, or **conditions contemporaneous**, exist in every contract; there is an exchange of benefits at the same time. One is willing to perform because the other side does.

Standards for Performance

The contract details what the parties are required to do for complete performance. In some contracts, performance is easily determined. If there is a contract between

BUSINESS STRATEGY

Dealing with High-Powered Talent

Paula Zahn was under contract with the Fox News Channel as the anchor of a nightly news show called "The Edge." She was hired by Fox News in 1999 after her stint as a cohost of the CBS Morning Show ended. Her contract with Fox News ran through February 2002. Her 10 P.M. talk show earned the lowest ratings of any of Fox News' evening talk shows.

CNN has been in a tight competitive battle with Fox News because Fox has ousted CNN from the number one position in terms of news networks.

© GETTY IMAGES

Through Ms. Zahn's agent, Richard Liebner, who also represents Diane Sawyer of ABC and Dan Rather of CBS, CNN approached Ms. Zahn about jumping to CNN. Mr. Liebner then asked Fox News if it could begin contract negotiations early for Ms. Zahn. Fox News refused, and Mr. Liebner disclosed the third-party offer from CNN.

Ms. Zahn's contract with Fox News includes a provision that prohibits her from talking with other news networks and programs while her contract with Fox News is still in effect.

When Fox News learned of the negotiations and discussions with CNN, Roger Ailes, the chairman of Fox News, fired Ms. Zahn, calling the discussions and negotiations a breach of contract. Mr. Ailes also alleges that CNN induced the breach.

Shortly after her termination at Fox, Ms. Zahn was hired by CNN. Walter S. Isaacson, chairman of CNN, said, "We're totally jazzed that Paula is out of her contract and is now available."

Ms. Zahn had been making $600,000 per year with Fox News and was hired by CNN for $2.1 million.

Did negotiating with CNN constitute a breach? Is such a prohibition on negotiations legal? Did CNN commit the tort of interference with contract relations? Is there any way for networks to protect themselves against such anchor-hopping? Could you develop a strategy for them?

Ms. Zahn is not the only example of difficulties with talent. George Michael, an English recording artist, rocketed to international fame in the 1980s as the lead singer with the pop group Wham! Mr. Michael was signed in 1988 by Sony Music Entertainment for a fifteen-year exclusive recording contract. His first solo album with Sony was "Faith," which sold 14 million copies worldwide. Mr. Michael conducted a year-long world tour to promote the "Faith" album. After the tour, he became dissatisfied with his lack of privacy. Sony wanted him to do more tours, but he felt the tours would only create more privacy problems for him.

Mr. Michael also became dissatisfied with the image Sony had created for him. Mr. Michael said that Sony had created a "sex-saturated" image of him and that his music and the quality of his songs were lost in the promotion of him as a sex symbol.

Mr. Michael brought suit, alleging Sony had breached its contract with him through its insistence on the cultivated image. At the trial of the case in London, Sony barristers introduced evidence that Mr. Michael's agent had sought more money from Sony between 1988 and 1990. Sony barristers also established that Mr. Michael did not complain to Sony about his marketing during the 1988 "Faith" tour, nor did Mr. Michael's agents express any concerns.

Was Mr. Michael's suit about artistic freedom? Was there any breach of contract by Sony? Did Mr. Michael want more money than the original contract provided? Why can't he just be paid more? Didn't Sony make Mr. Michael a star? Is it ethical for him to leave Sony after its investment in his debut album?

Note: Mr. Michael lost his suit. But Dreamworks SKG and Virgin Records purchased his record contract from Sony for $40 million. [*Panayiotou* v. *Sony Music Entertainment (UK) Ltd.*, 8711 (1993).]

Some artists try a different route from contract litigation. The music group TLC (T-Boz, Left-Eye, and Chili), a three-woman group based in Atlanta, rose to the top of the music charts in 1993 and has since had two multiplatinum albums along with six top singles. (Note: Lisa "Left-Eye" Lopes was killed in a car accident in 2002.)

At the end of 1995, all three women filed for bankruptcy. If the bankruptcy judge grants their petition, the three women will be excused from the record contracts they signed five years ago with independent producers. When groups are unknown, as TLC was five years ago, the major record producers will not sign them. These groups rely on independent producers.

continued

The contracts negotiated with "new kids" are extremely lopsided in the producer's favor. For example, a producer has the right to drop an artist at any time, but the artist has no right to leave the contract relationship. However, when groups' music takes off and they begin selling records, the stars want renegotiated contracts or contracts with other producers. They want more than the customary industry figure of 12 percent royalties for new artists.

From 1995 to 1996, three other groups filed for bankruptcy after achieving success in the pop music charts. Section 365 of the Federal Bankruptcy Code permits the bankruptcy court to release a debtor from contracts that are burdensome or onerous or that impair the ability of the debtor to make a fresh start.

The lawyer for TLC maintains that the women have debts and meet the test for bankruptcy. The lawyer for their producer says the women face only a cash-flow problem and that $2.2 million in royalties is in the system for them. He also adds, "I think they wanted to be bankrupt because they think they can get out of their contract on the basis of bankruptcy."

Is it ethical to run up debts in order to declare bankruptcy to get out of a contract? Is it ethical to declare bankruptcy to obtain a higher royalty percentage on your sales through another contract? Could you develop a strategy for the record companies to use in their contracts to avoid these bankruptcy evasions by stars?

Do you think highly visible contracts and employees must be handled differently from regular employee contracts? Do you think the high visibility affords less rights under the contract? Do the issues of the fairness of contracts and public visibility make contract enforcement more difficult? What do you learn about celebrity contracts from these examples and those given in the ethical issue on morals clauses?

---

an employment agency and a potential employee to find work for the employee, performance is complete once the work is found.

But in some contracts, performance is complicated, and there may be errors in its execution. For example, construction contracts are long-term, complicated agreements. During the construction of a building, it is possible that some mistakes might be made. Is an owner allowed to not pay a contractor because there is a mistake or two? The doctrine of **substantial performance** applies in construction contracts, and it means that the constructed building is for practical purposes just as good as the one contracted for. For example, a builder might have substituted a type of pipe when the brand name specified in the contract was not available. The substitution is a technical breach of contract, but it is a substitute that is just as good. The builder will be paid for the construction, but the owner will be entitled to damages.

E-Commerce: Payments Have Changed

One aspect of contract performance is payment. Internet and online transactions have changed dramatically how we pay for goods and services. The following methods have been developed for electronic payment. Parties choose these methods largely on the basis of their perceptions about the security in the method of payment.

1. *Digital cash.* Retailers create their own currency on the Internet, and customers with the right software can purchase the currency and then pay for items with their currency account. It is a virtual phone card and is good for those who do not have credit cards or would prefer not to use those credit cards on the Web.

2. *Digital wallets.* The one-stop payment location authorized by a buyer. Retailers can be paid from the wallet when given access by the buyer. Some digital wallet programs also include shipping information so that buyers can shop faster because they need not fill out all the seller's forms and information.

3. *Virtual points.* This is an Internet frequent flyer program. Web users accumulate points and then can make purchases using those points. These systems

FOR THE MANAGER'S DESK

RE: KILLER PERFORMANCE REQUIREMENTS IN RETAIL

It's called "the Squeeze." The Squeeze refers to the increasingly onerous logistical demands retailers place on clothing suppliers. The logistical demands add tremendous costs to suppliers, they are rigid, they are complex (some retailers' rules run fifty pages), and they carry penalties. Noncompliance with logistical requirements allows the retailer to take a "chargeback," or a deduction from its payment.

Here are some sample logistical requirements:

Shipping and Packing Guidelines from Retailers to Vendors

Packing Hanging Garments

You must have written authorization from Federated to ship GOH. All ready-to-wear merchandise should be shipped in conveyable cartons in order to maximize the use of UCC-128 shipping container label. . . .

Lazarus, unit of Federated Department Stores

Routing Instructions

Determine your RPS Zone number on the Zone Chart. . . . Determine your LTL [less than truckload] Zone number from the Zone Chart and follow the LTL Routing for that zone.

Kaufmann's, unit of May Department Stores

Paperwork Documentation

Provide a separate packing list for each store and for each purchase order, detailed as to purchase order #, department #, store # and two letter code, style #, color (when ordered by color), size (when ordered by size), number of cartons, and total units shipped.

Hecht's, unit of May Department Stores

Charges include $300 for incorrect labels, $500 for incorrect packing materials, and a 5 percent penalty if a shipment arrives late.

Schwab Co., the manufacturer of "Little Me" infants clothes, was charged $400 for late delivery of a $500 shipment.

A buyer for Federated Department Stores says, ". . . [I]t's not our responsibility to keep vendors afloat. We have a separate philanthropy program." Small vendors complain they must hire extra people to handle special boxing and that retailers' chargebacks are reversed if they offer proof of compliance.

Smaller vendors are taking their products to specialty stores and boutiques. Large retailers say, "This is all still negotiable." Some vendors say that retailers are wrong on their charges about 25–50 percent of the time, but "They throw it up to see what will stick." Vendors note that their cash flow is affected and that until the disputes are resolved, it often takes a year for them to be paid on their invoices.

Discussion Questions

1. Is there a problem with unconscionability?
2. Would you deal with large retailers?
3. Is this kind of behavior anticompetitive?
4. Do you feel the guidelines and chargeback fees are truly negotiable?
5. Are the chargeback levels of fees ethical?

---

must have a sufficient number of retailers to make them work well and entice consumers.

4. *Person-to-person payment.* Most commonly called PayPal, this is a system in which the buyer authorizes payment and the seller then drops by a site to give information needed in order to authorize the payment. The amount is taken from the buyer's bank account.

5. *Virtual escrow.* A third party handles the Internet transaction and makes sure that the seller has performed according to the contract before releasing payment to the buyer.

6. *Virtual credit card.* A system for those who doubt the security of the Internet. This system creates a new credit card number for each transaction that cannot be reused.

When Performance Is Excused

There are times when all conditions of a valid contract are met but performance of the contract is excused. Under common law, the parties are excused from performance if performance has become impossible. **Impossibility** means that the contract cannot be performed by the parties or anyone else. For example, performance under a contract for the purchase and sale of land that has been washed away into a lake is impossible. Completing a year of dance lessons is impossible for someone who has had a paralyzing accident.

Under the UCC (and under the *Restatement*), performance can be excused if there is commercial impracticability. **Commercial impracticability** (see § 2–615 in Appendix G) excuses performance if the basic assumptions the parties made when they entered into the contract have changed. Although this definition makes it seem that the UCC excuses performance when wars, embargoes, and unusually high price increases occur, courts have been reluctant to apply the excuse of commercial impracticability. The standard of commercial impracticability has been interpreted to mean nothing more or less than the common law standard of impossibility.

Parties can protect themselves from unusual events by putting in their contracts *force majeure* clauses, which excuse the parties from performance in the event of such problems as wars, depression, or embargoes. Following the attack on the World Trade Center in New York City, many contracts were excused for impossibility. For example, because air traffic was halted, all overnight shipping contract performances were excused.

CONSIDER...   **14.6**

In December 1983, the Department of Energy agreed that it would take possession of 100,000 metric tons of spent radioactive fuel rods from nuclear power plants around the country beginning February 1, 1998. In order to be able to take possession of the nuclear waste from the plants, the Department of Energy agreed to construct a nuclear waste repository. The utilities with nuclear plants agreed to pay in funds for the construction of such a site. Over the years, seventy-two utilities in thirty-four states paid in $13.5 billion for construction of such a site, with the funds for the storage plan collected in rates from customers. The site was to be the Yucca Mountain facility, located near Yucca Mountain in Nevada. However, presently Yucca Mountain has a five-mile-long tunnel and there are no storage bays or concrete walls. It is estimated that it will take another fifteen years before the site is ready to accept the spent nuclear fuel.

The utilities are running out of storage room at their plant sites, and the fuel rods remain radioactive for 20,000 years. Has the federal government breached its contract? What damages would the utilities have?

In *Sons of Thunder, Inc.* v. *Borden, Inc.* (Case 14.4), there are issues of performance and termination of a contract in a case that some experts have labeled a landmark one in terms of imposing a duty of good faith in performance.

CASE 14.4

Sons of Thunder, Inc. v. Borden, Inc.
690 A.2d 575 (N.J. 1997)

Ships and Liability Passing in the Night?

FACTS

Borden, Inc., owned Snow Food Products Division, a leading producer of clam products, including Snow's Clam Chowder. Borden had used its own four-vessel fleet as well as independent boats in order to obtain clams for processing. Boats delivered the clams to Borden's Cape May plant, where the shell stock was processed into clam meat. From there the meat was shipped to Pine Point, Maine, where final products were made and canned.

In 1978, Borden hired Donald DeMusz to be the captain of the *Arlene Snow,* one of Borden's four boats. Eventually, Mr. DeMusz was hired as an independent contractor to manage Borden's boats, and Mr. DeMusz formed Sea Labor, Inc., as the company responsible for the management of those boats. Sea Labor received five cents per bushel of clams harvested by the four boats. Mr. DeMusz still also received his compensation as captain of the *Arlene Snow.*

At about the same time Mr. DeMusz was hired, Borden began its "Shuck-at-Sea" program, which enabled the fishermen to shuck the clams on the boat, thus allowing the boats to bring back larger amounts of clams, thereby reducing costs and eliminating the need for more plant and facilities. However, the existing boats were not large enough for the shucking equipment.

Wayne Booker, a manager for Borden and Snow's, discussed with Mr. DeMusz the possibility that Mr. DeMusz might buy a larger boat and undertake the Shuck-at-Sea program. Mr. DeMusz submitted a proposal that Mr. Booker and other executives approved. Along with two partners, Mr. DeMusz formed Sea Works, Inc., and for $750,000 purchased the *Jessica Lori,* a clam-fishing boat with shucking equipment. Mr. DeMusz financed the purchase through a bank loan.

An internal company memo from Mr. Booker included the following paragraph along with a description of how Mr. DeMusz's purchase of a boat would save money:

> [W]e still have a significant mutual interest with De-Muse [sic]. His principal business will still be in chartering the Snow fleet and in captaining Arlene. He needs a dependable customer for the clams that he catches, either shell stock or meat. If we terminate our agreement with him, he would have a hard time making the payments on his boat.

continued

Mr. DeMusz drafted a one-page contract, and Mr. Booker approved it with one small change. Mr. DeMusz then formed Sons of Thunder, Inc., with Bill Gifford and Bob Dempsey in order to purchase the second boat. The final contract was entered into on January 15, 1985, and included the following provision:

IT IS understood and Agreed to by the parties hereto that Snow Food Products shall purchase shell stock from Sons of Thunder Corp. for a period of one (1) year, at the market rate that is standardized throughout the industry. The term of this contract shall be for a period of one (1) year, after which this contract shall automatically be renewed for a period up to five years. Either party may cancel this contract by giving prior notice of said cancellation in writing Ninety (90) days prior to the effective cancellation date.

Sons of Thunder Corp. will offer for sale all shell stock that is landed to Snow Food.

In March 1985, Sons of Thunder bought a boat, which it named *Sons of Thunder.* The cost to rig and purchase the boat was $588,420.26. Sons of Thunder sought financing from First Jersey National Bank but was unable to obtain a loan until Mr. Booker intervened in the negotiations. Mr. Booker told the bank representative that Mr. DeMusz had a solid relationship with Borden and that although the contract could be terminated within one year, Borden expected the contract to run for five years. Moreover, Mr. Booker explained to the representative that the five-year term of the contract would be sufficient to pay back the loan. Ultimately, Mr. DeMusz obtained a $515,000 loan, which he, Mr. Gifford, Mr. Dempsey, and their spouses personally guaranteed. Mr. DeMusz used a personal note to cover the remaining balance.

Meanwhile, in August 1984, Mr. Booker and Mr. DeMusz had begun negotiations about Mr. DeMusz purchasing a second boat that would provide clams to Borden. If the Shuck-at-Sea project was successful, Borden would want a second vessel shucking at sea. Moreover, a second large boat would give Borden the advantage of receiving clam meat in bad weather because small boats generally cannot go out to sea in bad weather.

After some preliminary testing, the *Sons of Thunder* started to operate and to fulfill its contract with Borden. For most weeks, the records show that Borden did not buy the minimum amount specified in the contract.

Problems continued with the Shuck-at-Sea program, and the original boat, the *Jessica Lori,* had to be rerigged with resulting delays. At the same time problems with the program were being worked through, there were changes in Borden's management. Mr. DeMusz explained to new managers that Borden was not purchasing the amounts it had promised but received no assurances that the contract would be honored. Also

at this time, Borden was experiencing difficulties with plant managers in terms of conflicts and kickbacks with resulting terminations.

The relationship between Mr. DeMusz and his companies and Borden began to deteriorate. When Borden discovered that a $500,000 accounting error had actually overstated the benefits of the Shuck-at-Sea program, Borden elected to exercise its termination rights under the contracts and sent Mr. DeMusz (through the various companies) notice of termination. Mr. DeMusz and his companies experienced substantial losses as a result of the termination of contracts. Mr. DeMusz filed suit. Borden moved for summary judgment on the grounds that it had properly exercised its termination rights. The jury found for Mr. DeMusz, the court of appeals affirmed, and Borden appealed.

JUDICIAL OPINION

GARIBALDI, Justice

The question whether Borden performed its obligations in good faith appears before the Court. . . .

The obligation to perform in good faith exists in every contract, including those contracts that contain express and unambiguous provisions permitting either party to terminate the contract without cause. See *United Roasters, Inc.* v. *Colgate-Palmolive Co.,* 649 F2d 985 (4th Cir.), cert. denied, 454 U.S. 1054, 102 S.Ct. 599, 70 L. Ed.2d 590 (1981). In *United Roasters,* United Roasters gave Colgate the right to manufacture and distribute Bambeanos, its roasted soybean snack. The contract governing the relationship allowed Colgate to terminate its performance at any time during the test-marketing period so long as it gave United Roasters thirty days notice. After two years of testing Bambeanos, Colgate announced plans to merge with Riviana Foods, Inc., and in the next five months, it ceased producing Bambeanos, stopped advertising them, sold its entire inventory of raw soybeans and Bambeanos, and transferred its product manager to another project. Eventually, Colgate terminated the contract.

Interpreting North Carolina law in the diversity action, the Fourth Circuit concluded that North Carolina had not decided whether there was a good faith limitation on an unconditional right to terminate a contract. The Fourth Circuit did, however, evaluate United Roaster's claim that Colgate violated the covenant of good faith and fair dealing. The panel stated

What is wrong with Colgate's conduct in this case is not its failure to communicate a decision to terminate. . . . , but its cessation of performance. Clearly it had an obligation of good faith performance up until its right of termination was actually effective. The contract expressly obliged it to use its best efforts in the promotion of Bambeanos. Instead of doing that, it simply ceased perfor-

mance. . . . *Quite simply, it broke its contract when it terminated its performance, which was United Roasters' contractual due.*

In *Bak-A-Lum Corp.,* supra, 69 N.J. 123 (1976), this Court reached a similar conclusion even though the contract was oral and the parties had not discussed how the contract could be terminated. In that case, Bak-A-Lum and Alcoa made an oral agreement, which gave Bak-A-Lum an exclusive distributorship of aluminum siding and related products manufactured by Alcoa. Alcoa eventually terminated the exclusive part of the agreement by appointing four additional distributors. Even though Alcoa planned on terminating the distributorship, it encouraged Bak-A-Lum to expand its warehouse facilities, which substantially increased its operating costs.

Despite acknowledging Alcoa's unconditional right to terminate the contract, the Court upheld the verdict for Bak-A-Lum because it found that Alcoa had breached the implied covenant of good faith and fair dealing by withholding its plans to terminate the contract while encouraging the plaintiff to expand its facilities. As the Court explained: "While the contractual relation of manufacturer and exclusive territorial distributor continued between the parties an obligation of reciprocal good-faith dealing persisted between them." The Court found that the implied covenant of good faith and fair dealing required the defendant to give the plaintiff reasonable notice of its termination. Ultimately, the Court concluded that "a reasonable period of notice of termination of the distributorship . . . would have been twenty months."

The case most heavily relied on by Borden and the majority at the Appellate Division, *Karl's Sales & Service, Inc.* v. *Gimbel Brothers Inc.,* 249 N.J.Super. 487 (App. Div.), cert. den., 127 N.J. 548 (1991), is distinguishable from this matter. In that case, the Appellate Division stated that where the contractual right to terminate is express and unambiguous, the motive of the terminating party is irrelevant. As stated previously, we agree with that view of the law. However, in *Karl's Sales,* unlike this case and *Bak-A-Lum,* there were no allegations of bad faith or dishonesty on the part of the terminating party. Accordingly, *Karl's Sales* did not address the issue we are concerned with here.

Borden knew that Sons of Thunder depended on the income from its contract with Borden to pay back the loan. Yet, Borden continuously breached that contract by never buying the required amount of clams from the Sons of Thunder. Furthermore, after Gallant took Booker's place, he told DeMusz that he would not honor the contract with Sons of Thunder. Nicholson also told DeMusz that he did not plan to honor that contract. Borden's failure to honor the contract left

Sons of Thunder with insufficient revenue to support its financing for the Sons of Thunder.

Borden was also aware that Sons of Thunder was guaranteeing every loan that Sea Work had taken to finance the rerigging and purchasing costs for the [boat]. Thus, Borden knew that the corporations were dependent on each other, and that if one company failed, the other would most likely fail. Borden, however, fulfilled its obligations to Sea Work only for a short time before it began to breach that agreement. Eventually, Borden terminated its contract with Sea Work even though it knew that terminating the contract would leave Sea Work with no market to fish the *Jessica Lori.*

The final issue is whether the jury's assessment of $412,000, approximately one year's worth of additional profits, for the breach of the implied covenant of good faith and fair dealing was a reasonable verdict. Specifically, can a plaintiff recover lost profits for a breach of the implied covenant of good faith and fair dealing? We agree with Judge Humphreys that the jury's award of one year's additional profits "is a reasonable and fair estimate of 'expectation damages.'" Moreover, we agree with the trial court that lost profits are an appropriate remedy when a buyer breaches the implied covenant of good faith and fair dealing.

> *In order to recover for lost profits under [Section 2–708(2)], the plaintiffs must prove the amount of damages with a reasonable degree of certainty, that the wrongful acts of the defendant caused the loss of profit, and that the profits were reasonably within the contemplation of the parties at the time the contract was entered into.*

The jury's award of $412,000, approximately one year's profit, for the breach of the implied covenant of good faith and fair dealing is reasonable and fair.

CASE QUESTIONS

1. Explain the nature of the relationships between Mr. DeMusz and Borden.

2. Were all the DeMusz corporations completely dependent on Borden?

3. What is the effect of following a termination clause in a contract?

4. What impact does "good faith" have on termination of a contract?

5. What are the damages when there is a lack of good faith in the termination of a contract?

6. What provisions would you suggest be added to a contract such as this in which the relationship is one of contract but also one of dependence?

*To look at form
contracts, go to:*
http://www.legaldocs.com
or
http://www.lectlaw.com/

Often the obligation to perform is discharged by agreement of the parties. In some cases, the parties agree to substitute someone else for the obligation in an agreement called a **novation**. For example, suppose that before forming a corporation, a business owner had signed a lease for store premises and then incorporates the business. The landlord agrees to substitute the new corporation as the tenant. All three parties (landlord, owner, and corporation) sign a novation. The owner is excused from individual liability and performance, and the corporation is substituted. Note that the landlord must agree; the owner cannot discharge his performance obligations by unilaterally substituting the corporation.

In other situations, the parties reach an agreement for payment in full on a contract; such an agreement is called an **accord and satisfaction**. The amount they agree to pay may be less than the original contract amount, but disputes over warranties, repairs, and other issues change the value of the contract. The accord and satisfaction serves to discharge the performance of both parties.

CONTRACT REMEDIES

If performance is not excused and there is a valid contract, the nonbreaching party can recover for damages from the nonperforming party. The purpose of such **compensatory damages** is to put the nonbreaching party in the same position he would have been in had there not been a breach. The law has formulas to calculate the amount of compensatory damages for breach of every type of contract. For example, if a seller has agreed to sell a buyer a car for $5,000 and the seller breaches, the buyer could collect the extra $1,000 it would cost to buy a substitute car priced at $6,000.

In addition to compensatory damages, nonbreaching parties are entitled to collect the extra damages or **incidental damages** involved because of the breach. If a seller must run an ad in a newspaper to sell a car a buyer has refused to buy, the costs of the ad are incidental damages.

Some parties agree in their contracts on the amounts they will pay in the case of nonperformance. Damages agreed upon in advance are **liquidated damages**, and the contractual clauses containing them are enforceable so long as they are not excessive and compensatory damages are not awarded in addition to the liquidated damages.

In some cases, the nonbreaching party may be able to collect **consequential damages**. Consequential damages are damages that result because of the breach and generally involve such damages as lost business, lost profit, or late penalties. For example, if a contractor must pay a penalty of $200 for each day a building is late after the completion date stipulated in the contract and the contractor is late because the steel supplier did not meet its deadline, the $200-per-day penalty would be a consequential damage that the steel supplier would be required to pay. Whether a party will be able to collect consequential damages depends on whether the breaching party knew or should have known what the consequences of the breach would be.

 CONSIDER...   **1 4 . 7**

Boeing Company was scheduled to deliver several of its 747–400 jumbo jetliners to Northwest Airlines by December 31, 1988. Northwest set that deadline because it needed the $16 million in investment tax credits the planes would bring. Boeing missed the December 31 deadline, and Northwest wants to recover compensation from Boeing for the lost tax credits. Could Northwest recover for these lost credits?

> ### CONSIDER... 14.8
>
> Dan O'Connor paid $125 to have Notre Dame University's leprechaun mascot tattooed on his upper arm with the words "Fighting Irish" inscribed above the little gnome. The tattoo parlor inscribed the chosen leprechaun and "Fighing Irish."
>
> Mr. O'Connor's girlfriend pointed out the spelling error, and Mr. O'Connor filed suit against the Tattoo Shoppe in Carlstadt, New Jersey, seeking unspecified damages.
>
> Mr. O'Connor noted, "I was irate, and for a minute or two after I cooled down I kind of giggled. But I can't just live with this. You're not talking about a dented car where you can get another one . . . you're talking about flesh."
>
> What damages should Mr. O'Connor receive? Would a refund of $125 be enough? What if the Tattoo Shoppe had a clause in its contract limiting damages to a refund? Would it be valid?

THIRD-PARTY RIGHTS IN CONTRACTS

Generally, a contract is a relationship between or among the contracting parties and is not enforceable by others who happen to benefit. For example, suppose a landowner and a commercial developer enter into an agreement for the construction of a shopping mall. Such a project means jobs for the area and additional business for restaurants, hotels, and transportation companies, but these businesses would not have the right to enforce the contract or collect damages for breach if the developer pulled out of the project. However, certain groups of people do have rights in contracts even though they may not have been parties to the contracts. A good example is a beneficiary of a life insurance policy. The beneficiary does not contract with the insurance company and does not pay the premiums, but the beneficiary has contract rights because the purchaser of the policy directed so.

In other types of third-party contract rights, the third parties are not part of the original contract, as is the life insurance beneficiary, but are brought in after the fact. For example, suppose that a homebuilder owes a plumbing contractor $5,000 for work done on homes in the builder's subdivision. In the sales contracts for the homes, the homebuilder is the seller, and the buyer's purchase monies will go to the homebuilder. However, the homebuilder could assign payment rights to the plumber as a means of satisfying the debt. This process, called **assignment**, gives the plumber the right to collect the contract amount from the buyer. The plumber takes the place of the homebuilder in terms of contract rights.

In some cases, the duty or obligation to perform under a contract is transferred to another party. The transfer of contractual duties and obligation is called a **delegation**. Generally, a delegation of duties carries with it an assignment of benefits. For example, suppose that Neptune Fisheries, Inc. has a contract with Tom Tuna, Inc. to sell thirty fresh lobsters each day. Neptune is stopping its lobster line and delegates its duties under the Tom Tuna contract to Louie's Lobsters, Inc. Louie's takes over Neptune's obligation to furnish the thirty lobsters and is assigned the right to benefits (payment for the lobsters) under the contract. Both Louie's and Neptune are liable to Tom Tuna for performance. A delegation, unlike a novation, does not release the original contracting party.

INTERNATIONAL ISSUES IN CONTRACT PERFORMANCE

Assuring Payment

Review bills of lading:
http://www.itds.treas.gov/
bills_lading.htm

International contract transactions for goods involve extensive shipment requirements. To control access to the goods and, payment for them, many sellers use a **bill of lading** for transacting business. The bill of lading is a receipt for shipment issued by the carrier to the seller. It is also a contract for the shipment of the goods and provides evidence of who has title to the goods. If a bill of lading is used, the buyer will not gain access to the goods unless and until the seller provides the necessary documents for release of the goods. Once the seller has the bill of lading, the seller can choose to transfer title to the goods by transferring the bill of lading. The seller could also pledge the bill of lading as security for the payment of a debt. A bill of lading can be made directly to the buyer, or it can be a negotiable bill of lading that can be transferred to anyone.

The bill of lading is often used in conjunction with a line of credit in international transactions because the two together offer the seller assurance of payment and the buyer assurance of arrival of the goods. In international transactions, in which resolution of disputes over great distances can be difficult, this means of controlling access to goods and payment is very helpful.

In this type of transaction, the seller delivers goods to a carrier for transportation and receives a bill of lading. The seller then sends the bill of lading through its bank to the buyer's bank to give the buyer's bank title to the goods, which will be turned over to the buyer once the funds are deducted from the line of credit established by the bank for the buyer.

The buyer may also arrange for a **letter of credit** to be used in conjunction with the bill of lading. The letter of credit is issued by the buyer's bank and is sent to a corresponding bank where the seller is located. The letter of credit lists the terms and conditions under which the seller can draw on the letter of credit or be paid. For example, turning the bill of lading over to the corresponding bank may be the condition of drawing on the letter of credit; the bill of lading is then used by the corresponding bank and the buyer's bank to allow the buyer to take possession of the goods. Because banks are involved in these transactions through credit assurances, the seller enjoys more of an assurance of payment prior to shipment because a letter of credit is actually a confirmation of payment.

Assuring Performance: International Peculiarities

International contracts have a particular need for a *force majeure* clause. Wars, revolutions, and coups are often included in international contracts as justification for noncompletion. The *force majeure* clauses are summaries of potential international events that could hamper production or trade.[1]

One other risk of international contracts is the stability of various currencies and their possible devaluation. The method and means of payment should be specified in the contract, and a clause covering devaluation may also be included so that full payment is ensured.

Lakeway Co. v. *Bravo* (Case 14.5) illustrates what can happen between the negotiation of an international contract and the time for contract payment.

CASE 14.5

Lakeway Co. v. *Bravo*
576 S.W.2d 926 (Tex. 1979)

Falling Pesos: Negotiating an Exchange Rate

FACTS

Lakeway and Bravo (in a contract drawn and executed in both English and Spanish) agreed that Bravo would buy a certain Lakeway lot in Travis County, Texas. The purchase price was $25,820, with payment by Bravo to be in pesos. The agreement was executed July 31, 1976.

By the time the check was presented for final payment, it was August 30, 1976. The Mexican government devalued the peso on August 31, 1976, and the result was that Lakeway received $8,188.45 less than it would have had the transaction not been subject to an interim devaluation. Lakeway brought suit. Summary judgment was granted for Bravo, and Lakeway appealed.

JUDICIAL OPINION

SUMMERS, Chief Justice

Appellant (Lakeway) contends that the intention of the parties, as set forth in the contract, was for a total purchase price of $25,820.00; that how it was paid, whether in dollars or in pesos, was immaterial so long as the result to the seller was the required number of dollars; and that the peso figure in parenthesis was simply for the convenience of the buyer to let him know how many pesos would be required to buy the property. It urges that this intention is supported by the fact that

the contract provides that "Seller agrees to notify Buyers in writing of the total amount due in Mexican pesos if a change in the official exchange rate occurs prior to such payment." We agree with these contentions.

However, in the instant case a check payable in the correct amount of pesos for final payment under the contract was delivered to Lakeway by the Bravos on August 18, 1976; such check was received by Lakeway without objection; said check was honored and cleared appellees' bank account on August 30, 1976, prior to the devaluation of the peso, which occurred on August 31, 1976; and when honored and paid in due course, the payment became absolute and related back to the date of delivery of the check on August 18, 1976; and as of said date of delivery it produced the specified value in dollars and satisfied the terms of the contract.

The judgment of the trial court is affirmed.

CASE QUESTIONS

1. What was the land purchase price?
2. How much did Lakeway lose once there was devaluation?
3. Will Lakeway get more money?
4. How did the contract address the issue of devaluation?

SUMMARY

What if the assumptions made and the information given turn out to be untrue? Must the parties still go forward with the contract?

- Contract defense—situation, term, or event that excuses performance
- Capacity—mental and age thresholds for valid contracts
- Voidable contract—one party can choose not to honor the contract
- Puffing—statements of opinion
- Material fact—basis of the bargain

- Void contract—contract that courts will not honor
- Misrepresentation—incomplete or inaccurate information prior to contract execution
- Rescission—setting aside of contract as a remedy
- Fraud—intentional misrepresentation
- *Scienter*—knowledge that information given is false
- Duress—physical or mental force that deprives party of a meaningful choice with respect to a proposed contract
- Undue influence—exerting control over another party for purposes of gain

- Confidential relationship—trust, confidence, reliance in a relationship
- Public policy—standards of decency
- Exculpatory clauses—attempt to hold oneself harmless for one's own conduct
- Unconscionable contract—contract that is grossly unfair

If one party does not perform, is the other side excused? When is performance required and when is it excused?

- Conditions precedent—advance events that must occur before performance is due, for example, obtaining financing
- Substantial performance—performance that, for practical purposes, is just as good as full performance
- Commercial impracticability—defense to performance of sales contract based on objective impracticability
- Novation—agreement to change contract among all affected, for example, agreement to substitute parties
- Accord and satisfaction—agreement entered into as settlement of a disputed debt

- Obligation of good faith—must perform in a reasonable fashion; performance must meet commercial standards

What remedies exist?

- Compensatory damages—amount required to place party in as good a position as before breach
- Incidental damages—costs of collecting compensatory damages
- Liquidated damages—agreement clause in contract that preestablishes and limits damages
- Consequential damages—damages owed to third parties from a breach

What are the contract performance issues in international business?

- Bill of lading—title document used to control transfer of goods
- Letter of credit—pledge by bank of availability of funds for a transaction
- Exchange rate and risk issues in contracts

QUESTIONS AND PROBLEMS

1. Robert G. Rawlinson was employed by Germantown Manufacturing in Marple Township as its assistant controller. He embezzled $372,113.21 from the company, which discovered the theft, though not the exact amount, on May 21, 1982. Mr. Rawlinson admitted his wrongdoing and was fired. He did not tell his wife, and it was not until she eavesdropped on a telephone conversation between her husband and Peter Kulaski that she discovered something was amiss. Mr. Rawlinson told her (after his phone conversation) that he had taken $20,000 from the company and was fired. Mrs. Rawlinson testified that her "whole world fell apart" upon hearing the news. She was already depressed and tired because of a miscarriage she had suffered in late April.

The following day, Mr. Kulaski came to the Rawlinson home and asked them to sign two judgment notes. The first note was for $160,000, the amount Mr. Rawlinson admitted taking from the company. The second note was for any amounts above and beyond the $160,000 that would be established by the company president as having been taken by Mr. Rawlinson. Mrs. Rawlinson's name was on the documents, and she asked if they should not have an attorney. Mr. Kulaski told them they did not need an attorney because the company was acting in good faith and that no criminal charges would

be brought if the Rawlinsons would cooperate. Mrs. Rawlinson felt that if she signed the notes, her husband would not go to jail.

Mrs. Rawlinson had never before seen a judgment note and cried while trying to read these. She thought she was signing only for $160,000 and, because her husband had a check for $150,000 ready to turn over, that they could easily come up with the remaining $10,000.

In August 1982, the president of the company verified that the total amount taken was $212,113.21 more than the $160,000 already paid. When demand for payment was made, Mrs. Rawlinson requested that the confession of judgment be opened and disallowed on the basis of misrepresentation. The lower court found for Mrs. Rawlinson, and Germantown Manufacturing appealed. Give a list of defenses Mrs. Rawlinson could use. [*Germantown Mfg. Co.* v. *Rawlinson*, 491 A.2d 138 (Pa. 1985).]

2. Tony Curtis, a respected actor, entered into a contract to write a novel for Doubleday & Company, publishers. Because of complex divorce proceedings and other personal factors, Mr. Curtis was unable to submit a satisfactory manuscript. Doubleday demanded a return of the $50,000 advance Mr. Curtis had received. Is Doubleday entitled to it? [*Doubleday & Co. v. Curtis,* 763 F.2d 495 (2d Cir. 1985).]

3. Bernina Sewing Machines imports sewing machines and parts for U.S. distribution. Its contract prices are in francs. Because of the devaluation of the U.S. dollar, Bernina wants to be excused from its contracts. Can it be excused under any contract doctrine? [*Bernina Distributors, Inc. v. Bernina Sewing Machines,* 646 F.2d 434 (10th Cir. 1981).]

4. Would failure to disclose a delinquency on your mortgage on a loan application be a misrepresentation? [*Barrer v. Women's National Bank,* 761 F.2d 752 (D.C. 1985).]

5. Orkin investigated Helen M. Clarkson's home for termites and found none, but continued routine inspections. After one monthly inspection, Ms. Clarkson hired another firm to inspect for termites. The firm found termite tunnels and damage. Ms. Clarkson had to spend approximately $1,200 for repairs. Could she recover that amount from Orkin? [*Clarkson v. Orkin Exterminating Co., Inc.,* 761 F.2d 189 (4th Cir. 1985).]

6. Northland Ford Dealers sponsored a hole-in-one contest at the Moccasin Creek Country Club in South Dakota. The contest winner would receive a new Ford Explorer. Jennifer Harms registered for the contest. She stood at the women's marker for teeing off and hit a hole-in-one. She was denied her car because the dealers' insurance policy for the event indicated the following, "ALL AMATEUR MEN AND WOMEN SHALL UTILIZE THE SAME TEE." That tee was established in the policy as 170 yards. However, the men and women participating in the contest were not told of this rule or restriction. Must the dealers give Ms. Harms her Ford Explorer, or will she remain "tee'd off"? [*Harms v. Northland Ford Dealers,* 602 N.W. 2d 58 (S.D. 1999).]

7. Amy was a 78-year-old widow who lived alone. She drove an hour each day to take care of her disabled sister, Mary. When Mary died, Amy drove to take care of Mary's husband, Bill. Bill left Amy a fourth of his estate when he died. Was there undue influence? [*Totman v. Vernon,* 494 A.2d 97 (R.I. 1985).]

8. On February 21, 1990, Robert Barto and his wife signed an agreement with Estate Motors, Ltd., of Birmingham, Michigan, to purchase a Mercedes Benz 500 SL automobile. They signed the agreement that follows.

Retail Buyers Order

ESTATE MOTORS LTD.
464 S. Woodward Telephone 644-8400
BIRMINGHAM, MICHIGAN 48011

Purchasers Name ___ Robert Barto ___ Date Feb. 21, 1990

— NEW — CAR

PLEASE ENTER MY ORDER FOR ONE Mercedes Benz — USED —
TRUCK
AS FOLLOWS

Year	Make	Model or Series	Body Type	Color	Trim
1991	Mercedes Benz	500SL	2 Door	199 Black Pearl	Gray Leather

MVI or Serial No.   Stock No.   To Be Delivered On or About ___ 19 ___

CASH PRICE OF VEHICLE

199 BLACK PEARL—
Gray Leather—
740 Black Soft Top

TOTAL
TAX
TOTAL CASH DELIVERED PRICE
CASH DEPOSIT SUBMITTED WITH ORDER   500—

SALESMAN /s/ (Doug MacFarlane)   SIGNED /s/ (Robert Barto)
PURCHASER
PURCHASER'S NAME   Robert Barto
STREET ADDRESS 1 Winward Place
THIS ORDER IS NOT VALID UNLESS SIGNED BY DEALER OR HIS AUTHORIZED REPRESENTATIVE.
CITY & STATE Gross Pointe Farms   ZIP 48236
APPROVED ___
Dealer or Authorized Representative
BUS. PHONE ___
RES. PHONE 886-2277

THIS ORDER IS NOT A BINDING CONTRACT
CASH OR CASHIER'S CHECK UPON DELIVERY

Doug MacFarlane, their salesman, told the Bartos that because of high demand, their car might not be delivered for eighteen months.

In mid-August 1991, Mr. MacFarlane telephoned Mr. Barto and informed him that his Mercedes would be at the dealership and ready for pickup on August 30. Mr. MacFarlane also informed Mr. Barto in that telephone conversation for the first time that he would have to pay a luxury tax on his new car (in addition to the purchase price, state sales tax, and license/title fees) when he came to pick it up.

Mr. Barto was angry about having to pay the luxury tax because he believed that his car fell within the scope of the preexisting binding contract exception, as his order for the car had been placed before September 30, 1990. During the ensuing weeks before his car arrived at Estate Motors, Mr. Barto telephoned the Mercedes-Benz district sales representatives and legal counsel and was informed that Mercedes-Benz was advising their dealers that the new luxury tax was not to be assessed on cars ordered before September 30, 1990. Mr. Barto also learned that of the 114 Mercedes-Benz dealers within the midwest region, only Estate Motors was assessing the tax on cars ordered before September 30, 1990.

Mr. Barto attempted to negotiate a manner of payment of the tax with Estate Motors. He first proposed that he bring with him two checks when he picked up his car—one check payable to Estate Motors for everything but the amount of the luxury tax, and one check for the luxury tax payable to the IRS. The dealer refused this arrangement. Mr. Barto then suggested that he pay the luxury tax into an escrow account. Again the dealer refused. Because Mr. Barto wanted his new car, he ultimately agreed to pay Estate Motors the full purchase price, including the luxury tax assessment.

On August 30, 1991, when Mr. Barto went to Estate Motors to pick up his Mercedes-Benz, he tendered to the dealer his check for $111,446 to cover the $99,950 purchase price of the car, the sales tax/license/title fees of $4,501, and the 10 percent luxury tax amounting to $6,995. Mr. Barto and the dealer also executed on August 30 Estate Motors' "Statement of Vehicle Sale," which reflected the breakdown of his $111,946 total purchase price, license/title transfer and proof of insurance information, and the odometer disclosure.

Mr. Barto continued to protest having to pay the $6,995 luxury tax on his new Mercedes after picking up the car. The dealer provided Mr. Barto with a blank IRS 843 form for a tax refund. When the IRS denied Mr. Barto's claim a refund, he filed suit against Estate.

Mr. Barto wished to rescind the agreement. He wanted his $500 back. Is Mr. Barto entitled to it? Is there a contract at all? [*Barto* v. *United States*, 823 F. Supp. 1369 (E.D. Mich. 1993).]

9. Betty Lobianco had a burglar alarm system installed in her home by Property Protection, Inc. The contract for installing the system provided:

> *Alarm system equipment installed by Property Protection, Inc. is guaranteed against improper function due to manufacturing defects or workmanship for a period of 12 months. The installation of the above equipment carries a 90-day warranty. The liability of Property Protection, Inc., is limited to repair or replacement of security alarm equipment and does not include loss or damage to possessions, persons, or property.*

On November 22, 1975, Ms. Lobianco's home was burglarized and $35,815 in jewelry was taken. The alarm system, which had been installed less than ninety days earlier, included a standby source of power in case the regular source of power failed. On the day of the fateful burglary, the alarm did not go off because the batteries installed in the system had no power.

Ms. Lobianco brought suit to recover the $35,815. She claimed that the liability limitation was unconscionable and unenforceable under the UCC. Property Protection claimed that the UCC did not apply to the installation of a burglar alarm system. Who is correct? [*Lobianco* v. *Property Protection, Inc.*, 437 A.2d 417 (Pa. 1981).]

10. Northrup King Company produces and sells seeds to farmers and others throughout the United States. Northrup placed the following disclaimer on its product:

> *NOTICE: Northrup King Co. warrants that seeds sold have been labeled as required under State and Federal Seed Laws and that they conform to the label description. No liability hereunder shall be asserted unless the buyer or user reports to the warrantor within a reasonable period after discovery (not to exceed 30 days), any condition that might lead to a complaint. <u>Our liability on this warranty is limited in amount to the purchase price of the seeds. This warranty is in lieu of all other warranties, express or implied, including warranties of merchantability and fitness for a particular purpose. There are no warranties which extend beyond the face hereof.</u>*

The underlined language was in red print on containers. Northrup sold pepper seeds to Floyd Ammons, whose pepper crop developed bacterial rust-spotting disease. Mr. Ammons brought suit for damages (loss of his crop), saying the disclaimer is unconscionable and void. Is he right? [*Northrup King Co.* v. *Ammons*, 9 U.C.C.2d Rep. Serv. (Callaghan) 836 (4th Cir. 1989).]

RESEARCH PROBLEM

Click, Point, Contract

11. Visit the following Web sites and determine how the companies have computer users enter into contracts. Determine how the computer user knows that a contract has been formed and what the terms of that contract are. Also, watch for liability limitation clauses (when they are disclosed) and what types of liability limitations companies use.

> http://www.fedex.com
> http://www.hertz.com
> http://www.dell.com
> http://www.ups.com

NOTE

1. International history has played a role in the development of *force majeure* clauses because wars, trade, and international relations influence contract rights and performance. For more information, see the course Web site and the Instructor's Manual.

CHAPTER

15

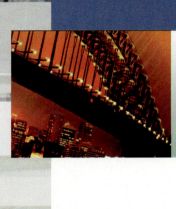

Financing of Sales and Leases: Credit and Disclosure Requirements

update

For up-to-date legal news and real-world business applications, click on **update** *at http://jennings.westbuslaw.com*

The English refer to credit sales as "buying on the never never" because you never really pay for everything; there is always some outstanding credit. Credit sales are a way of life in the United States. Nearly all sellers advertise not only their products but also the availability of credit terms for buyers. Credit is used so often that both Congress and state legislatures have enacted statutes regulating credit contracts. This chapter covers those regulations and credit contracts. How is a credit contract set up? What are the requirements? What statutes affect the credit contract? How are credit contracts enforced?

> Neither a borrower nor a lender be,
> For a loan oft loses both itself and friend
> And borrowing dulls the edge of husbandry.
> HAMLET
> *Act 1, Scene 3*

Consumer Credit Outstanding (per American Bankers Association)

1993	$850 million
2000	$1.550 billion
2001	$1.590 billion
2002	$1.915 billion
2003	$1.986 billion
2004	$2.039 billion (through July)

Delinquency Rate of Consumer Loans

Year	Percent of Loans Outstanding
1992	2.74%
1993	2.60%
1994	2.66%
1995	2.10%
1999	2.11%
2000	2.45%
2001	2.41%
2003	1.93%
2004	1.52% (through 2nd quarter)

Upon first exposure to the subject of credit regulation, the impression of the average attorney might be that the field is a maze, if not a mess, and probably both.

CHRISTOPHER L. PETERSON

In "Truth, Understanding, and High-Cost Consumer Credit: The Historical Context of the Truth in Lending Act," 55 *Fla. L. Rev. 807 (2003)*

CONSIDER...

In February 1995, A.B.&S., an auto repair shop owned by Jerry L. Bonner, an African-American, applied for a $230,000 business loan from the South Shore Bank. Mr. Bonner submitted the required Small Business Administration Loan Form 912 on December 27, 1994. In response to the question about arrests and convictions, Mr. Bonner noted the following:

1. Domestic matter between 1982 and 1984
2. Conviction for aggravated battery and assault in 1983 (claims self-defense)
3. Possession of a controlled substance in 1985
4. Disorderly conduct between 1985 and 1990
5. Possession of a controlled substance in 1990
6. Possession of a stolen car in September 1994

The bank denied the loan.

Mr. Bonner filed suit under the Equal Credit Opportunity Act, alleging that the bank's practice of considering criminal records has an unlawful disparate impact on African-American men. Can the bank consider Mr. Bonner's criminal record in making a loan decision?

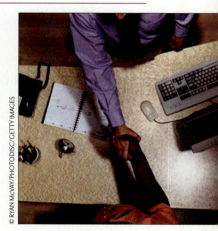

ESTABLISHING A CREDIT CONTRACT

For information on consumer debt levels, see http://www.federalreserve. gov/releases/housedebt/ default.htm

A credit contract not only needs the usual elements of a contract (as covered in Chapter 13), including offer, acceptance, and consideration, but also requires additional information for the credit agreement to be valid. The following list covers the extra details needed in a credit contract:

1. How much the buyer/debtor is actually carrying on credit or financing
2. The rate of interest the buyer/debtor will pay
3. How many payments will be made, when they will be made, and for how long
4. Penalties and actions for late payments
5. Whether the creditor will have collateral
6. The necessary statutory disclosures on credit transactions

Gather consumer credit protection information: http://www. federalreserve.gov *Click on Consumer Information*

STATUTORY REQUIREMENTS FOR CREDIT CONTRACTS

The following statutes affect and, in some cases, control the terms in a credit contract. Exhibit 15.1 summarizes the federal statutes.

EXHIBIT   15.1   Summary of Federal Laws on Consumer Credit

CREDIT STATUTE (FEDERAL)	PURPOSE AND SCOPE
Equal Credit Opportunity Act 15 U.S.C. § 1691 (1974)	Prohibits discrimination on the basis of sex, race, age, or national origin in credit extension decision
Consumer Credit Protection Act (CCPA) 15 U.S.C. § 1601 (1968)	Umbrella statute passed to deal with fairness of consumer credit transactions
Truth in Lending Act 15 U.S.C. § 1601 (1968)	Part of CCPA that governs disclosure of credit terms
Amendments (1995) 15 U.S.C. § 1605	Closes loopholes for avoiding loan repayments based on clerical errors in loan documents
Fair Credit and Charge Card Disclosure Act 15 U.S.C. § 1646 (1988)	Provides for disclosure requirements in the solicitation of credit cards
Regulation Z 12 C.F.R. § 226 (1981)	Federal Reserve Board regulations providing details for all disclosure statutes
Home Equity Loan Consumer Protection Act 15 U.S.C. § 1647 (1988)	Disclosure requirements for home equity loans and a rescission period
Home Ownership and Equity Protection Act 15 U.S.C. § 1637 (1994)	Disclosure requirements on payment amounts for home equity loans and cancellation rights
Fair Credit Billing Act 15 U.S.C. § 1637 (1974)	Rights of debtors on open-end credit billing disputes
Fair Credit Reporting Act 15 U.S.C. § 1681 (1970)	Right of debtors with respect to reports of their credit histories
Consumer Leasing Act 15 U.S.C. § 1667 (1976)	Disclosure requirements for leases of goods by consumers
Fair Debt Collections Practices Act 15 U.S.C. § 1692 (1977)	Regulation of conduct of third-party bill collectors and attorneys

State Usury Laws

Usury is charging an interest rate higher than the maximum permitted by law. If the maximum rate of interest permitted by statute is 24 percent, a creditor charging 28 percent has violated a statute and created a void contract.

The usury rate varies from state to state, and many states have different usury rates for the various types of transactions. For example, the usury rate for real estate loans may be lower than the usury rate for credit cards or installment credit transactions. Some states' usury rates are just a percentage figure, whereas other states include loan origination charges, finders' fees, service charges, and other fees paid by the debtor in determining the actual rate of interest charged.

The Federal Deposit Insurance Corporation (FDIC) has undertaken a program to educate consumers about these types of loans; you can find its brochure online at http://www.fdic.gov/consumers/consumer/predatorylending/index.html

Penalties for charging a usurious rate also vary. Some states treat the usurious agreement as completely void, and the penalty for the creditor is forfeiture of interest and principal. Other states allow the creditor to recoup the principal but deny any interest. Some states simply require the creditor to forfeit any interest above the maximum; others also impose a penalty on the creditor by allowing the debtor to collect two or three times the amount of excess interest charged as damages.

Over the past few years, there have been increasing numbers of high-interest loans secured by titles to cars and homes. These loans are made instantly, but at high interest rates with title to the car or home pledged as security for the loan. Referred to as the *subprime lending market*, or *predatory lending*, it is an area where regulation is pending in some form at federal and state levels. With title loans, upon default, the lender gains title to the car or home.

FOR THE MANAGER'S DESK

RE: ATM FEES AND OTHER CREATIVE BANK AND CREDIT CARD CHARGES

In California, there is a heated battle between banks and consumers over ATM fees. Consumers have been upset recently with ATM usage charges that can be as much as $3.50 for the withdrawal of $20. For example, a bank can charge $2.00 when a customer uses an ATM from a different bank. The bank the customer uses can also charge money, generally $1.50, for the foreign customer using its system. The result is a total charge for the consumer of $3.50.

When ATMs were first gaining popularity, banks waived such fees in order to encourage use of the electronic forms of banking as opposed to the labor-intensive and costly physical tellers. In fact, the two major ATM systems had joined together to fight charging fees. However, legislatures in fifteen states passed statutes permitted the ATM surcharges.

Now states are swinging the other way, with Connecticut and Iowa being two examples of states that do not permit the surcharges. The litigation in the San Francisco area involves the issue of whether states can regulate banking surcharges. The issue of preemption has been raised with respect to state statutes on ATM fees.

Credit card holders have discovered new and creative fees being assessed to them by their credit card companies. The following is a list of the latest new forms of charges on credit card bills:

- Foreign transaction fees have increased from 1 percent to 3 percent.
- Cash advance fees have increased from 1% to between 3 percent and 5 percent, and the minimum fee has increased from $1 to between $5 and $10.
- Balance transfer fees for transferring the balance from one credit card to another with lower interest is typically 3 percent of the balance, with minimum transfer fees ranging from $5 to $50.
- On some credit cards, cancellation of the card can lead to an accelerated interest rate such as the 26.99 percent charged by Fleet Financial.

The fees are in response to a new consumer trend to pay off their credit card balances. With so little interest income from the cards, the cards are generating revenue in other ways, such as by these new fees and charges.

The Federal Reserve Bank imposed new rules with greater disclosure requirements. You can see those rules at http://www.federalreserve.gov.

CONSIDER...   15.1

The mail-order business is a large part of the retail industry. With more companies, more catalogs, and more customers, consumer protection issues are increasing.

Currently, the Federal Trade Commission (FTC) regulates catalog forms and disclosures about merchandise availability and costs. However, some areas are not regulated and do present costly problems for consumers. For example, a Talbots catalog sets the shipment cost for a pair of $12.00 ragg trouser socks as $5.50, or 45.8 percent of the purchase price. If a shopper wanted to send those socks to a daughter at college and thus to a different address than the catalog shopper's, there is an additional $3.00 for a "shipped to" address. Then the customer would pay shipping costs of 70.8 percent of the purchase price. Further, shipping and handling costs are not related to item weights or sizes; they are related to total ordered amount, and the shipping and handling costs decrease as a percentage of total price the more the customer buys. The following chart is from a Talbots catalog.

Shipping and handling

Total merchandise (exclude tax)	Add	Shipping and Handling (%)
$20.00 and under	$5.50	27.5%
$20.01 to $30.00	$6.50	22–32.5%
$30.01 to $50.00	$7.50	15–25%
$50.01 to $100.00	$8.50	8.5–17%
$100.01 to $150.00	$9.50	6.3–9.5%
$150.01 to $200.00	$10.50	5.25–7%
$200.01 and over	$11.50	5.7% and less

Please add $3.00 for each additional shipping address.

Some companies, such as LL Bean, base their shipping and handling charges on actual weight, and each item in the catalog carries the weight of the item beside the price. What do you think the basis for catalog shipping and handling charges is? Is it to encourage customers to order more? Do you think companies have determined the most common price ranges for orders and charged the most in those ranges? Could this be considered usury? Why or why not? Do you think this area will be a new focus for consumer protection?

The Equal Credit Opportunity Act

Review the Equal Credit Opportunity Act:
http://www.law.cornell.edu/ uscode/15/1691.html

The **Equal Credit Opportunity Act** (ECOA) was passed to ensure that credit was denied or awarded on the applicant's merits—the ability to pay—and not on such extraneous factors as sex, race, color, religion, national origin, or age. (See Exhibit 15.1 on p. 578.) Creditors may ask about these for record-keeping purposes, but the decision to extend or deny credit must be based on factors other than these. The following types of information also cannot be considered in making the credit decision:

1. Marital status of the applicant
2. Applicant's receipt of public assistance income
3. Applicant's receipt of alimony or child support payments
4. Applicant's plans for having children

The ECOA also provides married persons the right to have individual credit applications, lines, and ratings. Credit applications must specify that a spouse's income need not be disclosed unless the applicant is relying on that income to qualify for credit. Further, even on joint accounts, debtors can require creditors to report credit ratings individually for the spouses.

BUSINESS STRATEGY

How to Evaluate Credit Risk

Lawrence B. Lindsey, then 41, who earns $123,100 a year, applied for a Toys "Я" Us credit card through the Delaware division of the Bank of New York. He pays his mortgage on time each month and has a clean credit record and job security. Mr. Lindsey's application was rejected; the letter from the bank explained as follows: "We have received your new account application. We regret that we are not able to approve it at this time."

The bank used a computerized scoring system to evaluate credit applications, and Mr. Lindsey's was rejected, according to his letter, because "Multiple companies requested your credit report in the past six months."

Mr. Lindsey was, at the time, a member of the Federal Reserve Board, the federal agency that sets interest rates and regulates banks. (From 2001 to 2003, he was an economic advisor in the Bush administration.) He has expressed concerns about computerized credit

© TAN KIAN KHOON/ISTOCKPHOTO

scoring and has said: "I would expect credit-scoring type procedures to be overwhelmingly dominant by the end of the decade. We will obtain the fairness of the machine but lose the judgments, talents, and sense of justice that only humans can bring to decision making."

Discussion Questions

1. How is computer scoring more fair in credit applications?
2. What are the advantages of credit scoring?
3. Are lenders using computer screening to ensure compliance with the ECOA?
4. Are people unfairly affected by that use?
5. What problems does it create?
6. Do you foresee a time when computer scoring is regulated?
7. Would you use computer scoring for credit extension in your business?

MAKING ETHICS PERSONAL

Speaking Up When Credit Discussions Turn Ugly

What would you do if you were discussing a credit application and someone said, "Yes, but she just got a divorce," or "Yes, but he's from the barrio." What are your legal obligations? What are your ethical obligations?

Visit the Federal Trade Commission:
http://www.ftc.gov

Violations of the ECOA carry statutory penalties. The ECOA is enforceable by the Federal Trade Commission (FTC), by the U.S. attorney general, and by private actions by debtors. Debtors can recover their actual damages for embarrassment and emotional distress and also for punitive damages of up to $10,000. If a group of debtors brings a class action against a creditor, they can collect punitive damages of up to the lesser of $500,000 or 1 percent of the creditor's net worth. Punitive damages are recoverable even when there are no actual damages. *A.B.&S. Auto Service, Inc.* v. *South Shore Bank of Chicago* (Case 15.1) involves an issue of an ECOA violation and also provides the answer to the chapter's opening Consider.

CASE 15.1

A.B.&S. Auto Service, Inc. v. South Shore Bank of Chicago
962 F.Supp. 1056 (N.D.Ill. 1997)

Do the Crime, Forget the Loan

FACTS

A.B.&S. Auto Service, Inc. (AB&S) is an automobile repair shop located in Chicago, Illinois. Jerry L. Bonner is AB&S's president, and he is an African-American. South Shore is a commercial bank that maintains three branches on Chicago's South Side and a loan office in the Austin neighborhood of Chicago's West Side. South Shore participates in the Small Business Administration's (SBA) loan guarantee program.

The SBA requires all applicants for the loan guarantee program to fill out an SBA Form 912 Statement of Personal History. SBA Form 912 asks applicants if they have ever been charged with or arrested or convicted for any criminal offense other than a minor motor vehicle violation and, if so, asks applicants to provide details. Form 912 also provides:

> *The fact that you have an arrest or conviction record will not necessarily disqualify you.*

Before submitting a loan package for SBA approval, the bank is expected to make an independent determination regarding the criminal record in evaluating the applicant's character.

In February 1995, AB&S applied for a $230,000 business loan from the bank after having a similar SBA request denied by La Salle Bank Lakeview. Mr. Bonner submitted a Form 912 on December 27, 1994. In response to the question about arrests and convictions, Mr. Bonner noted the following:

1. Domestic matters between 1982 and 1984
2. Conviction for aggravated battery and assault (1983) (claims self-defense)
3. Possession of a controlled substance in 1985
4. Disorderly conduct between 1985 and 1990
5. Possession of a controlled substance in 1990
6. Possession of a stolen car in September 1994

Leslie Davis, an African-American vice president at South Shore Bank, recommended approval of Mr. Bonner's application. However, the loan committee agreed that because of Mr. Bonner's criminal record, the application should be denied. The bank then decided to deny the loan.

During the last fifteen years, the South Shore Bank has made at least three business loans to applicants with criminal records. One of these three applicants was an African-American. South Shore evaluates each application on an individual basis and examines criminal record and other information for purposes of determining character.

Mr. Bonner and his company (plaintiffs) filed suit under the ECOA, alleging that the bank's practice of considering criminal record has an unlawful disparate impact on African-American men. South Shore Bank (defendants) moved for summary judgment because Mr. Bonner did not establish a case of discrimination. Mr. Bonner also moved for summary judgment on the grounds that consideration of criminal record without tying it to creditworthiness violated the ECOA.

JUDICIAL OPINION

WILLIAMS, Anne Claire, District Judge

The court must determine whether South Shore Bank's policy of inquiring about a credit applicant's criminal record, in compliance with SBA's requirements, violates the ECOA. The ECOA provides, in relevant part, that:

> *it shall be unlawful for any creditor to discriminate against an applicant, with respect to any aspect of a credit transaction—*
>
> *(1) on the basis of race, color, religion, national origin, sex or marital status, or age (provided the applicant has the capacity to contract)*

15 U.S.C. § 1691(a)(1). A credit applicant can prove discrimination under the ECOA by using any one of the following three different approaches used in the employment discrimination context: 1) direct evidence of discrimination; 2) disparate impact analysis, also called the "effects" test; or 3) disparate treatment analysis.

In order to prove discrimination under the disparate impact analysis or "effects" test, an applicant must show how "a policy, procedure, or practice specifically identified by the [applicant] has a significantly greater discriminatory impact on members of a protected class." Plaintiffs traditionally establish this prima facie case by making "a statistical comparison of the representation of the protected class in the applicant pool with representation in the group actually accepted from the pool. "If the statistical disparity is significant, then plaintiff is deemed to have made out a prima facie case." However, courts have found that "proof of disparate impact need not be shown by statistics in every case nor need it be shown by proof of actual disproportionate exclusion from the applicant pool."

Once the plaintiff has made the prima facie case, the defendant-lender must demonstrate that any policy, procedure, or practice has a manifest relationship to the creditworthiness of the applicant. In other words, the onus is on the defendant to show that the particular practice makes defendant's credit evaluation system more predictive than it would be otherwise.

Courts have held that the use of general population statistics is insufficient to make out a prima facie case under the ECOA.

In *Saldana* v. *Citibank,* 1996 WL 332451 (N.D.Ill. 1996), the plaintiff, loan-applicant, sued Citibank claiming it denied her loan based on its policy of redlining. Saldana tried to make her case under the disparate impact theory. Specifically, she claimed that Citibank had an unwritten policy that set the minimum amount for a rehab loan at $100,000. This policy, she claims, disproportionately impacted the African-American community because few African-Americans could meet this financial test based on their income and net worth. Saldana offered statistical evidence regarding 1) the bank's loan approval rate for loans over $100,000 in the Austin area; 2) the bank's loan rejection rate for white and African-American applicants in comparison with their representation in the greater Chicago community; and 3) the bank's average refinancing approval and average rejection rate in Austin in comparison to the City of Chicago's average approval and rejection rates. While the court found that this last set of statistics successfully presented some statistical evidence comparing the Austin community to the greater Chicago community, the court still found that "these statistics are of a very general nature and do not relate specifically to the policy identified as having a discriminatory impact. Thus, Saldana has failed to establish her claim under a disparate impact analysis."

Similarly, in *Cherry* v. *Amoco Oil Co.,* 490 F.Supp. 1026 (N.D.Ga. 1980), the credit-card applicant sued Amoco Oil Company, alleging that Amoco's use of zip code ratings in Atlanta, which assigned low-ratings to those zip code areas where Amoco had unfavorable delinquency experience, adversely effected [*sic*] black applicants disproportionately.

Plaintiffs claim that South Shore Bank's practice of considering an applicant's criminal record in making commercial lending decisions has a disparate impact on African-Americans. To make the prima facie case plaintiffs offer the testimony of Dr. Jaslin U. Salmon. Dr. Salmon testified that any decision that is based on arrest records would militate against people of color. He suggests that, based on his research, there are many cases in which the black applicant is qualified, credit worthy, but was not given the loan for other reasons and among those reasons, arrest records had been taken into consideration. However, the bank disputes this point because Dr. Salmon was unable to identify a single study showing that consideration of arrest records has a disproportionate impact on African-American

applicants for any type of credit, much less any study addressing the impact on business loan applicants.

In addition to Dr. Salmon's testimony, plaintiffs offer the general population statistics of arrest by race in 1990. Considering these general population statistics, the court finds that these statistics are insufficient to make out a prima facie case under the ECOA. The court recognizes that the ECOA prohibits creditors from inquiring into the race, sex, or marital status of an applicant. This in turn places plaintiffs in a difficult position of trying to prove disproportionate impact without any access to a creditor's statistical lending profile. Plaintiffs can refer to the general population as long as plaintiffs clearly demonstrate that the applicant pool would possess approximately the same characteristics. Considering the statistical proof and the testimony of Dr. Salmon, the court finds that plaintiffs have not made this showing that the applicant pool possesses approximately the same characteristics as the general population.

Both the statistics and Dr. Salmon's supporting testimony do not answer the following questions: 1) how many African-Americans with convictions or arrests are otherwise qualified for the loan; and 2) how many African-Americans are deterred from applying because of the bank's practice. Plaintiffs' evidence is further undermined, as it was in *Hill,* by the fact that the bank's practice of considering an applicant's criminal record was not consistently applied to disqualify applicants with criminal records. Rather, the bank has made at least three business loans to applicants with criminal records. One of these three applicants with criminal records is African-American.

South Shore Bank's practice of inquiring into a credit applicant's criminal history is legitimately related to its extension of credit for two reasons. First, the regulations require the SBA, in evaluating a loan guarantee application, to consider "the character, reputation, and credit history of the applicant, its associates, and guarantors." 13 C.F.R. § 120.150. As a participant in the SBA loan guarantee program, South Shore Bank is obligated to consider an applicant's criminal record provided on SBA Form 912 in its evaluation of a loan applicant's character.

Secondly, the bank's inquiry into an applicant's criminal record provides relevant information about an applicant's creditworthiness, particularly his judgment and character. Plaintiff Bonner admits that several of the incidents described in his completed SBA Form 912: possession of a controlled substance, domestic abuse, and disorderly conduct, reflected negatively on his judgment and character. Specifically, Bonner admits that these incidents involved an exercise of bad judgment. Therefore, because an applicant's judgment and character may legitimately be considered in making

continued

commercial lending decisions, South Shore Bank's practice of considering criminal history as it relates to character and judgment bears a legitimate and manifest relationship to the extension of credit. Therefore, the court finds that the bank has successfully demonstrated that its practice of inquiring into a credit applicant's criminal record is legitimately related to the extension of credit.

For the foregoing reasons, the court grants defendant South Shore Bank's motion for summary judgment and denies plaintiff Bonner and AB&S's motion for summary judgment.

CASE QUESTIONS

1. Who asked for the information about the loan applicant's criminal record?
2. What, according to Mr. Bonner's expert, is the impact of considering criminal records of applicants?
3. Is the use of the criminal record in making a decision to extend credit a violation of the ECOA?
4. Do you think a criminal record is an indication of character?

CONSIDER...   15.2

Nash Cooley is a 66-year-old African-American male who lives in Montgomery, Alabama. Since the mid-1980s, Mr. Cooley had earned a living from his ownership of residential rental properties in the Montgomery area. Mr. Cooley owns approximately fifteen apartment units and twenty-four houses.

In order to have the financial flexibility to invest in new real estate ventures, Mr. Cooley maintained active lines of credit with various financial institutions. By the summer of 2000, Mr. Cooley had $100,000 in unsecured lines of credit at two separate banks. He ultimately hoped to establish five $100,000 lines of credit in order to complete a real estate project that he began in 1992. To meet his financial goals, Mr. Cooley approached Sterling Bank in September 2000 about another $100,000 unsecured line of credit. He chose Sterling because he had a prior business relationship with Kenny Hill, who had worked at another bank where Mr. Cooley had a line of credit. In early 2000, Mr. Hill had spoken with Mr. Cooley about bringing some of his business to Sterling. Mr. Cooley opened a checking account with Sterling and maintained a balance of approximately $15,000 in the account, then deposited a $100,000 insurance settlement several months before applying for his credit line.

In September 2000, Mr. Cooley met with Mr. Hill to apply for a $100,000 unsecured line of credit with Sterling. He submitted a credit application and provided Mr. Hill with all of his relevant financial information, including tax returns and a personal financial statement. On September 15, 2000, Mr. Hill conducted a credit check on Mr. Cooley that revealed a "Beacon Score" of 749. Although this score was commensurate with an "excellent credit rating," Mr. Hill became concerned about Mr. Cooley's income level after reviewing the remainder of Mr. Cooley's financial information. His most recent tax return indicated that Mr. Cooley and his wife had a joint pretax income of $106,214. Of this amount, Mr. Hill calculated that the income attributable to Mr. Cooley was $51,483. Because Mr. Cooley was applying for an unsecured line of credit in his name only, Mr. Hill was worried that the income level was insufficient for him to obtain a $100,000 line of credit. Additionally, Mr. Hill was apprehensive about approving Mr. Cooley's request knowing that Mr. Cooley had two existing $100,000 lines of credit.

After Mr. Hill compiled Mr. Cooley's loan materials, he presented them to Bob Ramsey, Sterling's Executive Vice President in charge of lending. Because Mr. Hill did not have the authority to approve a loan in excess of $50,000, he met with Mr. Ramsey to discuss the Cooley loan application. During this meeting Mr. Ramsey reviewed Mr. Cooley's financial statement and tax return. Mr. Hill expressed his concerns about Mr. Cooley's financial situation, and Mr. Ramsey concurred. In short, Mr. Ramsey concluded that Mr. Cooley's "individual income of $51,464 simply did not justify adding another $100,000 unsecured debt on top of the two existing lines of credit at other banks totaling $200,000." Instead of denying Mr. Cooley's request outright, Mr. Ramsey suggested making either a secured loan in the same amount or an unsecured loan for $25,000. After Mr. Ramsey and Mr. Hill agreed that a counteroffer was the best solution, Mr. Hill informed Mr. Ramsey that Mr. Cooley was

"African American and might claim racism." In response, Mr. Ramsey suggested discussing the matter with Alan Worrell, Sterling's Chief Executive Officer. Mr. Worrell agreed with Mr. Hill and Mr. Ramsey's assessment of Mr. Cooley's financial situation and indicated his preference to find an alternative way to establish a credit relationship with Mr. Cooley.

On September 18, 2000, Mr. Hill informed Mr. Cooley of Sterling's decision and gave him a document entitled "Notice of Action Taken." The document explained that Sterling could not provide Mr. Cooley with a $100,000 unsecured line of credit but was willing to offer "a $25,000 unsecured line of credit or a larger secured line." In response, Mr. Cooley immediately requested a list of the individuals on Sterling's Board of Directors so he could contact them about his loan denial. Mr. Cooley also expressed his belief that Sterling was discriminating against him on the basis of race.

Mr. Worrell met with Mr. Cooley and told him that he had "good credit" but expressed concerns about his income level and existing lines of credit. At the conclusion of the meeting, Mr. Worrell emphasized that he wanted to do business with Mr. Cooley.

During Sterling's Board of Directors meeting on September 20, 2000, and, according to Greg Calhoun, an African-American member of Sterling's Board of Directors, individual Board members began discussing Mr. Cooley's application during the meeting. Mr. Calhoun stated in his deposition that the Board "didn't think [Mr. Cooley] could qualify for a hundred thousand dollar line of credit being . . . that he was a retired school teacher." Moreover, Board members "jok[ed] about [Mr. Cooley's application]" and "laughed about Cooley." In response, Mr. Calhoun told the other Board members that he believed they were putting Mr. Cooley down. Mr. Calhoun then "told them they was [*sic*] all Republicans, and they're all members of the Montgomery Country Club. And there's no way that a black man can come in here and get money from the bank." Following this statement, Mr. Calhoun informed the Board that he was resigning. In Mr. Calhoun's opinion, Sterling denied the loan application "because of [Mr. Cooley's] skin color."

Mr. Cooley filed suit for violation of the ECOA. Should he prevail in the suit? [*Cooley* v. *Sterling Bank,* 280 F.Supp.2d 1331 (M.D. Ala. 2003).]

THINK: The ECOA requires that the decision to not extend credit be related to creditworthiness and not factors such as race, marital status, age, gender, and so on.

APPLY: In this case, the applicant (Mr. Cooley) already had two lines of credit, income that did not meet the bank's requirements, and no security for the new line of credit. However, Mr. Cooley also had an excellent credit history. It is problematic that his race was mentioned.

ANSWER: The bank was applying credit risk tests for making its decisions, and it was not denying Cooley credit altogether. It wanted to do business with him, either by offering a lesser amount for an unsecured line of credit or a greater amount for a secured line of credit. His race was not an issue until Mr. Hill raised it as a possible motivation for Mr. Cooley to file a lawsuit. Even so, the door was still open for his business. The court held the discussion of his race did not change the basic character of the numbers-based decision on his loan application.

CONSIDER...   15.3

In 1994 Joyce Sallion contacted Beverly Wittler, a loan originator, to discuss the possibility of qualifying in advance for a loan to construct a house on a lot she and her husband purchased. After reviewing Mrs. Sallion's financial information, Ms. Wittler recommended Mrs. Sallion apply for a loan in the amount of $108,000, but Mrs. Sallion submitted a loan application for $132,000.

continued

On August 3, 1994, Nancy Wallis, a SunTrust underwriter, denied Mrs. Sallion's application for the finally submitted amount of $132,250 because she did not qualify for the loan due to (1) insufficient verifiable income, (2) an unacceptable debt-to-income ratio, (3) delinquent credit obligations, and (4) insufficient closing funds. This determination rested in part on the finding Mrs. Sallion had failed to verify monthly income of $1,500 from a recent divorce. Ellen Lighton, also a SunTrust underwriter, reviewed the application and agreed with Ms. Wallis's decision. Ms. Wittler then obtained Mrs. Sallion's handwritten explanation of her credit history and resubmitted Mrs. Sallion's application to underwriting.

Ms. Lighton denied the resubmitted application on August 18, noting that even if Mrs. Sallion could submit sufficient verification of her alleged $1,500 monthly alimony income, her debt-to-income ratios would still exceed banking guidelines. Based on the loan amount and Mrs. Sallion's slow payment credit history, Ms. Lighton also concluded the bank required more closing funds and reserve funds than Mrs. Sallion possessed.

Mrs. Sallion admits she cannot show receipt of alimony payment for twelve months but argues the verification requirement violates ECOA's proscription of discrimination based on marital status because it establishes more stringent standards of verification for alimony than other types of income. Mrs. Sallion admits her credit report contained some late payments and one charged-off debt but contends SunTrust did not deny her loan application based on her alleged poor credit history. SunTrust's statement of credit denial sent to Mrs. Sallion when SunTrust rejected the loan application for the second time states, "The Credit Reporting Agency information on you did not influence our decision." SunTrust's loan files allegedly show the bank extended credit to many white applicants with poorer credit histories. After SunTrust concluded Mrs. Sallion's alimony payment of $1,500 was unverifiable and thus could not be considered for purposes of the loan application, it recalculated Mrs. Sallion's debt-to-income ratios and found they exceeded SunTrust's guidelines. Mrs. Sallion does not attack the correctness of the calculations but advances instead the argument described above, that SunTrust's verification requirements for alimony payments violate ECOA.

SunTrust moved for summary judgment. Is there a violation of the ECOA? [*Sallion* v. *SunTrust Bank, Atlanta*, 87 F.Supp.2d 1323 (N.D. Ga. 2000).]

CONSIDER... 15.4

Medmark, Inc., a small corporation, requested a loan from Merchant's Bank. Merchant's Bank agreed to make the loan if Bruce Shalberg, a director of the company, obtained his wife's signature on the loan guaranty he had agreed to make. Merchant's Bank had made an independent investigation of Mr. Shalberg and found him to be creditworthy.

When Merchant's Bank failed, the Federal Deposit Insurance Corporation (FDIC) took over all accounts and filed against Medmark as well as Mr. and Mrs. Shalberg on their guaranty of the note. Mrs. Shalberg filed a motion for summary judgment on the grounds that she had been required, in violation of the ECOA, to sign as a guarantor for an obligation for which her husband qualified independently. Why did Merchant's Bank require Mrs. Shalberg to sign? Had the bank violated the ECOA? [*Federal Deposit Insurance Corporation* v. *Medmark, Inc.*, 897 F.Supp. 511 (Kan. 1995).]

The Truth in Lending Act

The **Truth in Lending Act** (TILA) is actually part of the **Consumer Credit Protection Act** passed in 1968 by Congress (15 U.S.C. § 1601), which was the first federal statute to deal with credit issues. Its purpose was to make sure debtors were treated fairly through adequate disclosure of credit terms. The Federal Reserve Board was delegated the responsibility for enforcing the TILA and has promulgated various

ETHICAL ISSUES

Credit Cards and Privacy

The Federal Trade Commission (FTC) found through an investigation that credit card companies were selling lists of their credit card holders, including their purchasing patterns, to marketing firms so they could engage in targeted marketing. As a result, all credit card companies are now required to send out disclosure and election forms to all customers. The disclosure form explains how the company might use information about the credit card holder and purchasing patterns. The election form permits credit card holders to choose options on disclosure ranging from full disclosure to anyone to complete removal of the customer's name from all mailing lists used for promotional materials.

In its annual report for 1999, Yahoo!, Inc. included a disclosure notice to say the company was cooperating with the FTC in its inquiry into how Internet sites gather personal information about users. Yahoo! also filed a Form 8 disclosure with the SEC indicating its cooperation. Yahoo! said that it made the disclosure in its financial reports because it is "extremely conservative in legal documents" and downplayed the significance of the FTC inquiry. By 2003, Yahoo! and the FTC had closed the investigation, and Yahoo! disclosed in its annual report that its privacy policies and practices were in compliance with FTC rules that resulted from its investigation of Yahoo! and others. The rules apply to the practices used for gathering information via the Internet and for curtailing the current activities of many Internet companies. The change has had an impact on companies that mine the Internet for information. With restrictions on use of consumer information obtained through the Internet, the marketing lists are far less target-directed. Advertisers are willing to pay seven to ten times as much for ad space that goes to prescreened audiences. Internet providers are able to mine users and provide just such access. If denied that ability, ad revenues would drop.

The FTC also investigated DoubleClick, Inc. for its data-gathering processes. One industry analyst said, "DoubleClick is not doing anything that anyone else isn't doing."

Evaluate the ethical implications of that last statement. Analyze the strategic choices of Yahoo! and others in waiting for the FTC to take action as opposed to taking voluntary action themselves.

regulations to carry out the details of the act. One of them, **Regulation Z** (12 C.F.R. § 226), is perhaps better known than the statute that gave rise to it.

TILA Applications

The TILA does not apply to all credit transactions; it is limited to consumer credit transactions, which are contracts for goods or services for personal or home use. A computer purchased for use in a law office is not covered by TILA, but a computer purchased for personal use at home is.

Wherever consumer credit is extended, the TILA applies regardless of the type of credit transaction. **Open-end credit transactions**, like the use of a credit card, are covered under the TILA. **Closed-end transactions**, also covered under the TILA, are those in which the debtor is buying a certain amount and repaying it. A loan to buy a car that will be paid back over a fixed time, such as four years, is a closed-end transaction.

Open-End Disclosure Requirements

In charge card credit arrangements, the creditor has several responsibilities at different stages in the transaction. When a debtor is first sent the credit card, the creditor must include the following information: what

BUSINESS PLANNING TIP

The following questions of credit applicants are prohibited under ECOA.

1. Are you receiving public assistance income?
Comment: Applicant may voluntarily disclose income if relying on it to obtain credit but need not disclose it.

2. Are you planning to start a family?
Comment: Questions about family and marital status are prohibited.

3. Are you pregnant?
Comment: Questions about family and marital status are prohibited.

4. Are you married?
Comment: Applicant can voluntarily disclose marriage if relying on spouse's income to obtain credit.

5. Please circle: Miss, Ms., Mrs., Mr.
Comment: Questions cannot ask about marital status.

6. Will your spouse serve as a guarantor?
Comment: Answering this question would reveal marital status.

7. Do you have alimony or child support income?
Comment: Questions cannot require disclosure of this information; applicant could reveal it if relying on such income to qualify for credit.

the interest (finance) charges and annual percentage rate are for charges on the credit card; when bills will be sent; what to do about questions on the bills; and when payments are due.

The monthly bill that the creditor is required to send must contain the balance from the last statement, payments and credits made during the billing period, new charges made during the billing period, and computation of finance charges.

Other required information on credit card bills includes the following: the dates of the billing period, the free-ride period or the time the debtor has to pay the balance to avoid any finance charges, and where to inquire about billing errors. Any changes in credit terms, billing, or charges must be sent to the debtor at least one month in advance of the change. Exhibit 15.2 is a sample billing statement.

In 1988, the Board of Governors of the Federal Reserve promulgated rules to comply with the **Fair Credit and Charge Card Disclosure Act of 1988** for the solicitation of credit card customers. The rules require the disclosure up front of certain information to these potential customers, such as the fees for issuing the card, the annual percentage rate for the card, any finance or transaction charges, and whether a grace period for payment exists. In addition, potential customers must

EXHIBIT   15.2 Sample Billing Statement

BUSINESS STRATEGY APPLICATION

Be sure to do the exercise for this chapter on the book's Web site so that you have the chance to develop a credit policy for a company that covers all areas of credit solicitation, disclosure, and enforcement.

be told how the average daily balance is computed, when payments are due, whether there is a late payment fee, and whether there are charges for going over the credit limit.

The federal law focuses on the need for disclosure of all possible charges that can occur if a customer accepts the card, charges that may entail much more than the finance charges on the balance. Model forms are available for these disclosures and must be given in writing to a customer at the time of application or solicitation.

Roberts v. *Fleet Bank* (Case 15.2) indicates that creditors and regulators are still thrashing out what constitutes full disclosure in credit card solicitation.

CASE 15.2

Roberts v. *Fleet Bank*
342 F.3d 260 (C.A.3 2003)

The Introductory and Not-So-Annual Fees

FACTS

In May 1999, Fleet Bank sent Denise Roberts a credit card solicitation, encouraging her to apply for its new "Titanium MasterCard."

The solicitation contained an introductory flyer, a solicitation letter, a "pre-qualified . . . invitation," and an initial disclosure statement. The introductory flyer stated in two places that the credit card would have a "7.99% Fixed APR" for both purchases and balance transfers. The solicitation letter also stated that the card would offer a "7.99% Fixed APR." In two places, the letter claimed that the 7.99% APR was "NOT an introductory rate," promising that "[i]t won't go up in just a few short months."

In order to obtain the Fleet credit card, Ms. Roberts had to complete the invitation form. The front side of the form stated that the credit card carried a "7.99% Fixed APR." On the back of the invitation, Fleet included the "TERMS OF PRE-QUALIFIED OFFER" and the "CONSUMER INFORMATION SECTION." The terms section stated that the terms of the credit card agreement were "subject to change." The consumer information section contained the so-called Schumer Box, the table of information required by TILA (see Exhibit 15.3 for an example of the Schumer Box). This box contained a column with the headings "Annual Percentage Rate (APR) for Purchases and Balance Transfers." The box beneath that heading stated that "7.99% APR" was the applicable rate. Inside the box, Fleet listed two circumstances under which the rate could change: (1) if the cardholder failed to meet repayment

requirements or (2) if the account was closed. Fleet listed no other circumstances that would merit a rate change. The initial disclosure statement also stated that the APR for the card would be 7.99% and listed the same two conditions under which the rate could change.

Ms. Roberts completed and returned the invitation and in June 1999, she received her Fleet Titanium MasterCard, along with the cardholder agreement. Section 10 of this agreement indicated that the APR would be 7.99%. Section 24, however, stated that Fleet had "the right to change any terms of this agreement at any time." Thirteen months after she first obtained the card, Fleet sent Ms. Roberts a letter notifying her that Fleet would be increasing the APR on her Titanium MasterCard to 10.5%. Ms. Roberts and others filed a class action suit against Fleet for its violation of the TILA disclosure requirements for solicitation of credit card customers. The lower court entered summary judgment for Fleet, and Ms. Roberts appealed.

JUDICIAL OPINION

FUENTES, Circuit Judge

The stated purpose of the TILA is "to assure a meaningful disclosure of credit terms so that the consumer will be able to compare more readily the various credit terms available to him and avoid the uninformed use of credit, and to protect the consumer against inaccurate and unfair credit billing and credit card practices." 15 U.S.C. § 1601(a). In 1988, concerned that consumers were still not receiving accurate information about the

continued

potential costs of credit cards, Congress strengthened the TILA's protections for credit card consumers through enactment of the Fair Credit and Charge Card Disclosure Act, "a bill to provide for more detailed and uniform disclosure by credit and charge card issuers, at the time of application or solicitation, of information relating to interest rates and other costs which may be incurred by consumers through the use of any credit or charge card."

In particular, Congress determined that consumers were being inundated with credit card solicitations that failed to disclose basic cost information about the cards being promoted. Prior to the passage of the Fair Credit and Charge Card Disclosure Act, the TILA did not require issuers to provide such information until the consumer actually received the card. Congress decided that demanding early disclosure of relevant cost information from credit card companies would enable consumers to shop around for the best cards.

Congress delegated the responsibility of "prescrib[ing] regulations to carry out the purposes of" the TILA to the Federal Reserve Board. 15 U.S.C. § 1604(a). In response to this mandate, the Board promulgated "Regulation Z," 12 C.F.R. § 226, and it also published a comprehensive "Official Staff Interpretation," 12 C.F.R. Pt. 226 Supp. 1. Both of these measures were published in accordance with "the broad powers that Congress delegated to the Board to fill gaps in the statute." In light of Congress' explicit delegation of authority, we defer quite broadly to the Board's interpretation.

The TILA requires a credit card provider to disclose certain information in "direct mail applications and solicitations," including "annual percentage rates." 15 U.S.C. § 1637(c)(1)(A)(i). The Board's regulations also require "[a] credit card issuer" to disclose the applicable "annual percentage rate." 12 C.F.R. § 226.5a(b)(1) (requiring disclosure of "[e]ach periodic rate that may be used to compute the finance charge on an outstanding balance for purchases . . . expressed as an annual percentage rate."). The TILA requires that information described in 15 U.S.C. § 1637(c)(1)(A), such as "annual percentage rates," must be "clearly and conspicuously disclosed" in a "tabular format." Likewise, the Board's regulations mandate that disclosures required under 12 C.F.R. § 226.5a(b)(1) through (7) "be provided in a prominent location on or with an application or a solicitation, or other applicable document, and in the form of a table with headings, content, and format substantially similar to any of the applicable tables found in Appendix G." 12 C.F.R. § 226.5a(a)(2). [See Exhibit 15.3.]

The Board's regulations also dictate that a "creditor shall make the disclosures required by this subpart clearly and conspicuously in writing." Hence, both the TILA and Board-promulgated regulations require a credit card issuer to disclose the applicable annual per-

centage rate clearly and conspicuously in a table, commonly referred to as the Schumer Box.

Roberts asserts that Fleet failed to clearly and conspicuously inform consumers that the 7.99% APR was subject to change at any time. The IDS and the Schumer Box included in Fleet's solicitation materials stated only two conditions under which Fleet could raise Roberts' APR. A reasonable consumer could read this list as exhaustive and conclude that the 7.99% APR could be raised only under those two described circumstances. Construing the TILA strictly against the creditor and liberally in favor of the consumer, as we must, we believe that the TILA disclosures in this case, read in conjunction with the solicitation materials, present a material issue of fact as to whether Fleet clearly and conspicuously disclosed its right to change the APR. We therefore conclude that the District Court erred in granting summary judgment to Fleet on Roberts' TILA claim.

In the Schumer Box, Fleet stated that the 7.99% APR could change in the event of nonpayment or closure of the account. Fleet listed no other conditions under which the 7.99% APR could change. We believe that it would be just as reasonable, if not more reasonable, for a consumer to conclude from the information contained in the Schumer Box that the 7.99% APR could be changed only under the two listed circumstances as it would be for a consumer to conclude that Fleet could change the APR at any time. Roberts has raised a genuine issue of material fact as to the adequacy of Fleet's disclosures and should have been permitted to proceed to trial on the matter.

Fleet argues that it adequately disclosed the necessary information in the Schumer Box and that the Board's regulations prevent it from including a "change in terms" provision in the Schumer Box.

. . . [t]he issue is not Fleet's obligation to disclose the change-in-terms provision, but its obligation to disclose the APR. Our inquiry focuses on whether Fleet's disclosures in the Schumer Box provided "an accurate representation of the legal obligation of the parties . . . when the relevant solicitation was mailed." As we explained above, we believe Roberts raised a question of material fact as to whether Fleet clearly and conspicuously provided an accurate representation of the APR.

Congress created the Schumer Box to assist consumers in accessing such information, not to shield credit card companies from liability for information placed outside of the Schumer Box. As a result, while we recognize that the TILA only applies the "clear and conspicuous" standard to required disclosures, we conclude that the TILA permits us to consider materials outside of the Schumer Box in determining whether the credit issuer disclosed the required information clearly and conspicuously.

In its defense, Fleet relies on Paragraph 24 of the Cardholder Agreement that states "[w]e have the right to change any of the terms of this Agreement at any time." This provision, however, fails to cure any of the TILA defects in the initial mailing. To begin with, Fleet only mails the Cardholder Agreement after a consumer has accepted the invitation. Thus, a consumer will not learn, until after the acceptance of the invitation, that the APR can be changed by Fleet at any time. Indeed, Fleet's practice of mailing the Cardholder Agreement containing important rate change information, after the consumer accepts the card, is contrary to the TILA mandate that credit card solicitations disclose all required information. Nonetheless, Fleet argues that it is prohibited from including "change in terms" information in the Schumer Box. However, as we previously stated, this argument avoids the central issue in this case, which is whether the APR was adequately disclosed. Additionally, we note that the "right to change" language in Paragraph 24 contradicts the statement in the introductory letter that this APR "won't go up in just a few short months."

Accordingly, we reverse the entry of summary judgment and remand for further proceedings.

CASE QUESTIONS

1. Describe the Schumer Box and what was in it in the Fleet solicitation.
2. What was different about the credit terms from what was in the Schumer Box?
3. Were the differing terms disclosed in the solicitation?
4. What happens with the case now?

ETHICAL ISSUES

Since the mid-1980s, the noninterest income from credit card fees has risen to almost one-half of the operating income of many commercial banks. Late fees, fees for exceeding the approved credit line, and other sources of credit card income are not subject to usury limits and are lucrative sources of revenue. In 1990, 1.1 billion credit card solicitations were sent to consumers in the United States. In 2001, credit card solicitations hit an all-time high of 5.01 billion, or 39 solicitations per home. There were 28 million applications filed in response to these mail solicitations, and both consumer debt in the United States and credit card company charge-offs have increased dramatically during the same period. With the still lucrative results from such small returns and a direct-mail response rate of only 0.58 percent, the competition for credit card users has become fierce. Banks and other credit card companies have been using aggressive marketing techniques such as "preapproved" credit card solicitations that offer "low introductory" interest rates or no annual fees. Consumer activists call these types of offers "bait and switch" or "shark in the mailbox" tactics that they believe are designed to trick unwary consumers.* In many situations, the banks are partnering with airlines, hotels, and other businesses that offer consumers incentives for signing up for the credit cards.

Evaluate the ethics of the solicitation, the fine print in terms of statutory requirements for disclosure in solicitation, the temptation of consumers for more debt, and earning so much revenue from fees that result from the inability of the consumer to pay.

* John A. Marold, "Third Circuit's Decision in *Roberts* v. *Fleet Bank:* Thinking Outside of the 'Schumer Box' or 'Consumerism Gone Berserk'?" 8 *N.C. Banking Inst.* 399 (2004).

Closed-End Disclosure Requirements

In a closed-end contract, in which the amount to be paid is definite from the beginning, the creditor must include in the credit contract the following terms:

1. The amount the debtor is financing
2. The **finance charges**, that is, the rate of interest charged for repayment
3. The **annual percentage rate** (APR), which is the finance charge reflected in a percentage figure
4. The number and amount of payments and when they are due

5. The total cost of financing (a total of the actual price of the goods or services along with all interest charges that will be paid over the scheduled repayment time)

6. Whether there are any additional penalties such as prepayment penalties or late payment penalties

7. Any security interest (lien or collateral) the creditor has in the goods sold by credit

8. The cost of credit insurance if the debtor is paying for credit insurance

Exhibit 15.3 is an example of a closed-end credit contract.

EXHIBIT   15.3 Sample Closed-End Credit Contract

Big Wheel Auto   Alice Green

ANNUAL PERCENTAGE RATE The cost of your credit as a yearly rate.	FINANCE CHARGE The dollar amount the credit will cost you.	Amount Financed The amount of credit provided to you or on your behalf.	Total of Payments The amount you will have paid after you made all payments as requested.	Total Sales Price The total cost of your purchase on credit including your down payment of $ *1500 —*
14.84%	$ *1496.80*	$ *6107.50*	$ *7604.30*	*9129.30*

You have the right to receive at this time an itemization of the Amount Financed.
☐ I want an itemization. ☒ I do not want an itemization.

Your payment schedule will be:

Number of Payments	Amount of Payments	When Payments are Due
36	$ *211.23*	*Monthly beginning 6-1-95*

Insurance
Credit life insurance and credit disability insurance are not required to obtain credit, and will not be provided unless you sign and agree to pay the additional cost.

Type	Premium*	Signature
Credit Life	$ *120 —*	I want credit life insurance. *Alice Green* ___ Signature
Credit Disability		I want credit disability insurance. ___ Signature
Credit Life and Credit Disability		I want credit life and disability insurance. ___ Signature

Security: You are giving a security interest in: ☒ the goods being purchased.
☐ _____.

Filing fee $ *12.50*   Non-filing Insurance $_____
Late charge: If a payment is late you will be charged $10.00

Prepayment: If you pay early, you
☐ may   ☐ will not   have to pay a penalty.
☒ may   ☐ will not   be entitled to a refund of part of the finance charge.

See your contract documents for any additional information about nonpayment, default, any required repayment in full before the scheduled date, and prepayment refunds and penalties.

I have received a copy of this document.

Alice Green _____   *5-1-99*
Signature   Date

*Means an estimate

Errors on the form or disclosure are viewed in light of their seriousness as well as the overall picture presented to the consumer. Recent amendments to the TILA eliminated the once petty and highly technical violations so costly to creditors for an inconsequential omission.

In addition to ensuring adequate disclosures in credit contracts, Regulation Z covers advertising that includes credit terms. If any part of the credit arrangement is mentioned in an advertisement, all terms must be disclosed. For example, if a creditor advertises payments "as low as $15 per month," the ad must also disclose the APR, the down payment required, and the number of payments.

State v. *Terry Buick, Inc.* (Case 15.3) deals with credit advertising.

CASE 15.3

State v. *Terry Buick, Inc.*
520 N.Y.S.2d 497 (1987)

$99 per Month plus Fine Print

FACTS

Terry Buick, Inc. is an automobile retailer that displayed across the street-side face of its building large yellow signs in block letters that read:

NO MONEY DOWN INSTANT CREDIT! $99/MO.

Terry Buick was located on Route 9, a very busy public highway in Poughkeepsie, New York. The actual credit terms of the sales were printed on 2¼" × 3⅜" stickers, which could be read only by close inspection and were attached to the windshields of cars that were for sale. These small stickers showed the price of the car, the down payment, the term in months, and the average interest rate applied to installment payments. The state of New York brought suit for violation of the credit advertisement regulations of TILA.

JUDICIAL OPINION

BENSON, Justice

This action for an injunction under 15 U.S.C. § 1664 (Truth in Lending Act), General Business Law Article 22-A and CPLR § 6301 enjoining Terry Buick, Inc. from continuing to advertise the terms for credit on vehicles it is selling in an illegal, false and deceptive manner is determined as follows:

The Court viewed the defendant's place of business with the attorneys and examined a number of the windshield stickers. They were legible only upon inspection from a distance of a few feet and set forth the financial details of each offer. Examination of the stickers showed that almost every offering required a down payment to obtain $99 per month financing. Other used cars had only "99/MO" painted on their windshields. According to the testimony of one witness, the salesman did not know the price of several of such cars. He testified that no cars were offered for sale for $2,000 down and $99 per month.

The plaintiff relied heavily upon the testimony of an undercover agent, a woman in the employ of the Attorney General who went to the defendant's place of business in the guise of a prospective purchaser and engaged a salesman in conversation about the cars. She recorded the conversation secretly and offered the tape, which the Court admitted into evidence. The plaintiff emphasized in argument a statement which the salesman made to the plaintiff's agent in which he admitted that the purpose of the advertising was to capture people's attention as they drove by and get them into the dealership.

The Truth in Lending statutes which govern the defendant's conduct are 15 U.S.C. § 1664(d) and New York General Business Laws §§ 350 and 350-a. The Federal statute is amplified by Regulation Z, 12 C.F.R. § 226.24. State courts have concurrent jurisdiction to enforce the Federal statute.

§ 1664(d) reads as follows:

If any advertisement . . . states the amount of the downpayment, if any, the amount of any installment payment, the dollar amount of any finance charge, or the number of installments or the period of repayment, then the advertisement shall state all of the following items . . .
1. the downpayment, if any;
2. the terms of repayment;
3. the rate of the finance charge expressed as an annual percentage rate.

The regulation adopted pursuant to the statute requires that "The creditor shall make the disclosures required by this subpart clearly and conspicuously."

continued

The Court's inspection of the defendant's place of business and its advertising material showed beyond question that the announcement signs were a "come on" designed to lure the eager seeker of a good deal. It also showed that "what you see is not what you get." We have not given the testimony of the undercover agent much weight. It was a contrived tactic practiced upon a relatively guileless salesman by a young woman who pretended to be a purchaser. Her testimony is not necessary, however, to convince the Court that defendant's public announcement of its deals fell far short of the candid display which the law requires. The law requires full disclosure described in the plain language of the statute. A look at the defendant's advertising scheme leads directly to the conclusion that it was designed to attract customers by half truths or falsity. No customer could buy a car on the terms boldly announced on the face of the building. The defendant's intentions did not have to be explained by testimony. No undercover agent was needed to obtain admissions. The message spoke for itself and could not be misread. It was "misleading in a material respect."

Truth in lending laws were not adopted for the canny shopper. They were made for the gullible and those easily led. . . . "In weighing a statement's capacity, tendency or effect in deceiving or misleading customers, we do not look to the average customer but to the vast multitude which the statutes were enacted to safeguard, including the ignorant, the unthinking and the credulous who, in making purchases, do not stop to analyze but are governed by appearances and general impressions." The plaintiff was not required to show that anyone had been deceived or that the advertising had injured anyone. It met its burden by showing its misleading effect.

The defendant's violation of Federal and New York State truth in lending laws has been demonstrated.

The motion for an order granting a preliminary injunction enjoining the defendant Terry Buick, Inc. from continuing to advertise the terms for credit on vehicles it is selling in an illegal, false and deceptive manner is granted.

CASE QUESTIONS

1. Describe the location of the large signs about the credit terms.

2. Where were the details of the credit transaction explained?

3. Did the court need the testimony concerning the salesman's words?

4. Did it matter that no one was deceived by the ads?

5. What will the court order Terry Buick to do?

Credit Card Liabilities

Regulation Z provides protection for credit card holders in addition to the required open-end disclosures. These additional protections are designed to limit the liability of a debtor for unauthorized use of a credit card.

First, a creditor cannot send an unsolicited credit card to a debtor. The debtor must have applied for the card or consented to have one sent. This protection is necessary so that debtors will be aware of what cards are coming and will know when to report losses or thefts.

Second, even if a credit card is stolen, Regulation Z provides dollar limitations for debtor liability. The maximum amount of liability a debtor can have for the misuse of a credit card is $50, including cases of identity theft. This liability limitation applies only if the debtor takes the appropriate steps for notifying the creditor of the theft or loss. The procedures for notification are given when the credit card is first sent to the debtor.

The Department of Justice has information on its Web site for avoiding identity theft:

http://www.usdoj.gov/

Click on fraud and go to identity theft.

CONSIDER...   15.5

Suppose an employee of a firm forged a credit application for his company and then used the card for personal purchases. Would the credit card issuer be liable? Should the issuer verify the request and check references? [*Transamerica Ins. Co. v. Standard Oil Co.*, 325 N.W.2d 210 (N.D. 1981).]

FOR THE MANAGER'S DESK

RE: IDENTITY THEFT

The largest identity theft ring in the history of the United States was broken up in December 2002 when federal authorities arrested those responsible for stealing the credit identities of at least 30,000 people. The total amount obtained through the identity theft is believed to be about $3 million. One example given was of an identity thief opening a line of credit in another person's name, using another's good credit. When the line of credit was funded for $35,000, the thief wrote a check for $34,000.

Ford Motor Credit was a key player in the arrests when it noticed that it was being billed for credit reports it did not order. The thieves used access codes to obtain credit reports and then had the companies billed. Other companies are now checking their bills, and consumers whose reports were ordered are being notified so that they can check for possible fraudulent charges and uses

of their credit ratings to obtain credit cards and lines of credit.

USA Today offers the following insights on what identity thieves do:

- Open new charge accounts and run up bills to the maximum credit level
- Change the mailing address on your credit cards so you don't notice the lack of bills or the charges
- Purchase cell phones in your name so that they can give creditors a phone number
- Open bank accounts and, with a line of credit, write checks
- Buy cars with loans in your name and then sell the cars for cash

Source: Greg Farrell, "Ring of identity thieves busted," *USA Today,* November 26, 2002, 1A. Copyright 2004. Reprinted with permission.

CHECK THE WEB

Check the book's Web site updates for information about recent issues in identity theft.

Canceling Credit Contracts: Regulation Z Protections

In addition to all the usual disclosures for a closed-end contract, certain types of credit contracts must include a **three-day cooling-off period** for the debtor, which is a buyer's protection for "cold feet." The buyer has the right to rescind certain types of credit contracts anytime during the seventy-two hours immediately following execution of a credit contract.

The types of credit contracts covered by the cooling-off period are those in which the creditor takes a security interest in the debtor's home. For example, if Alfie is installing a solar hot water system in his home, has purchased it on credit, and is giving the solar company a lien on his house, the three-day period applies; Alfie has three days to change his mind after he signs the contract. The three-day period also applies to **home solicitation sales**, in which sellers/creditors first approach consumers in the buyers' homes. The protection here allows buyers to recoup from any sales pressure that might have been used.

Where the three-day rescission period applies, the creditor must include both a description of the rights in the contract and a full explanation of the procedures the debtor should follow to rescind the contract during the three-day period.

Under the **Home Equity Loan Consumer Protection Act of 1988**, additional disclosures are required for those transactions in which consumers use their homes as security for the credit. These additional disclosures must explain that consumers who do not pay these debts could lose their dwellings, which could be sold to pay the debts. The three-day rescission period also applies to home equity credit lines. If notice of this three-day rescission right is not given to the homeowner/debtor, the right of rescission will continue for three years. Variable rate loans require specific disclosures on maximum increases in interest rates and the impact on payments.

Exhibit 15.4 is an example of a three-day cancellation provision.

TILA Penalties

The TILA provides specific penalties for violations of disclosure provisions. A creditor is liable to an individual for twice the amount of finance charges and for the debtor's attorney fees. The minimum recovery for an individual is $100 and the maximum, $1,000. A group of debtors bringing a class action against a creditor can collect the lesser of $500,000 or 1 percent of the creditor's net worth as damages.

EXHIBIT   15.4 Sample Three-Day Cancellation Notice

H-9 Rescission Model Form (Refinancing)

NOTICE OF RIGHT TO CANCEL

Your Right to Cancel

You are entering into a new transaction to increase the amount of credit provided to you. We acquired a [mortgage/lien/security interest] [on/in] your home under the original transaction and will retain that [mortgage/lien/security interest] in the new transaction. You have a legal right under federal law to cancel the new transaction, without cost, within three business days from whichever of the following events occurs last:

(1) the date of the new transaction, which is _____ ; or

(2) the date you received your new Truth-in-Lending disclosures; or

(3) the date you received this notice of your right of cancel.

If you cancel the new transaction, your cancellation will apply only to the increase in the amount of credit. It will not affect the amount that you presently owe or the [mortgage/ lien/security interest] we already have [on/in] your home. If you cancel, the [mortgage/lien/security interest] as it applies to the increased amount is also cancelled. Within 20 calendar days after we receive your notice of cancellation of the new transaction, we must take the steps necessary to reflect the fact that our [mortgage/lien/security interest] [on/in] your home no longer applies to the increase of credit. We must also return any money you have given to us or anyone else in connection with the new transaction.

You may keep any money we have given you in the new transaction until we have done the things mentioned above, but you must then offer to return the money at the address below. If we do not take possession of the money within 20 calendar days of your offer, you may keep it without further obligation.

How to Cancel

If you decide to cancel the new transaction, you may do so by notifying us in writing, at
                              (creditor's name and business address).

You may use any written statement that is signed and dated by you and states your intention to cancel, or you may use this notice by dating and signing below. Keep one copy of this notice because it contains important information about your rights.

If you cancel by mail or telegram, you must send the notice no later than midnight of   (date)   (or midnight of the third business day following the latest of the three events listed above). If you send or deliver your written notice to cancel some other way, it must be delivered to the above address no later than that time.

I WISH TO CANCEL

_____   _____

Consumer's Signature   Date

FOR THE MANAGER'S DESK

RE: E-SIGN AND CREDIT

The Census Bureau has estimated that U.S. e-commerce sales by retail establishments in the first quarter of 2001 rose 33 percent from the first quarter of 2000. According to Forrester Research, U.S. online retail revenues hit approximately $38 billion in 2000. Forrester projects that North America will lead global e-commerce to $6.9 trillion by 2004.

E-sign allows e-retailers and creditors to rely on Internet transactions and signatures. However, E-sign's requirements also mean that creditors must have con-

sumers point and click their ways through the detailed information of TILA, the ECOA, and any state disclosure laws. Consumers must give electronic consent or confirmation. Once this digital interchange of consent is given, the creditor can send the consumer the required credit disclosures. If the consumer remains online at this point, goods can be purchased on credit, or an e-loan can be executed, through a credit agreement or promissory note, electronically.

A sample interchange appears below.

PLEASE READ THE FOLLOWING TO COMPLETE THE APPLICATION PROCESS ON-LINE

By clicking the Submit Application button below, you are submitting your application for credit, and you are consenting to receive the following notices and disclosures electronically:

(a) Disclosures and notices detailing acceptance or denial of credit, including those required by the Equal Credit Opportunity Act;

(b) Cost of credit disclosures, including those required by the Truth in Lending Act.

You may withdraw your consent to receive these electronic disclosures at any time prior to signing the Credit Sale Agreement by canceling this electronic transaction and selecting an alternative payment option. You may cancel this electronic application now by clicking here.

You may obtain a paper copy of any disclosure or notice provided electronically to you by calling _____, Inc. at 888-333-9999. You will be charged $2.50 for each copy requested.

Before consenting to receive electronic disclosures, we will ask you to print or download a copy of this application to ensure that you can access the electronic disclosures we will provide to you.

To print any notice or disclosure we provide to you electronically, you will need a printer available to your operating system with letter-sized paper or larger. To download any notice or disclosure, you will need an available storage medium such as a hard drive or floppy drive, with at least 2 KB available. [FN40]

Please print or download a copy of your credit application now to confirm that you can access and retain subsequent disclosures, which will be provided in the same format as this credit application. If you CANNOT print or store your application properly or you do not wish to accept electronic notices and disclosures, please click here to select an alternative payment option.

By clicking the [Submit Application] button below, I understand that I am:

1. Submitting my application for credit to _____, Inc.
2. Consenting to receive the disclosures and notices described above, electronically.
3. Confirming that I have successfully printed or downloaded my credit application.

Source: Adapted from Robert A. Cook and Nicole F. Munro, "Giving Consumer Disclosures On-Line: Is ESIGN the Path to the Paperless Loan?" 57 *Bus. Law.* 1187, (2002).

Fair Credit Billing Act

The **Fair Credit Billing Act** affords debtors the opportunity to challenge the figures on an open-end transaction monthly statement. Errors on credit card accounts are covered by this act and, to a lesser degree, by Regulation Z. Creditors are required to supply on the monthly statement an address or phone number to write or call in the event a debtor has questions or challenges regarding the bill. The language must read: "IN CASE OF ERRORS, CALL OR WRITE. . . ."

Under the act, debtors can collect damages if they comply with all the act's procedural requirements. First, a debtor must notify the creditor of any errors within sixty days of the receipt of the statement. The notification must be in writing for the damage sections to apply. If a creditor supplies a phone number for inquiries, the notice must explain that oral protests do not preserve all Regulation Z rights. The written protest of the debtor must include the debtor's name, the account number, and a brief explanation of the claimed error.

Once the creditor has received the written protest, thirty days are allotted for the creditor to acknowledge to the debtor receipt of the protest. The creditor has ninety days from receipt of the protest to take final action, either giving the debtor's account a credit or reaffirming that the charges are valid.

During the time the creditor is considering the debtor's protest, the debtor is not required to pay the questioned amount or any finance charges on that amount. If the charges are in fact accurate, the debtor will be charged for the finance charges during this time period. If the creditor fails to comply with any of the requirements or deadlines on bill protests, the debtor can be excused from payment even if the charges disputed were actually accurate.

Fair Credit Reporting Act

For information on debtor's rights and credit issues, visit the National Foundation for Credit Counseling:
http://www.nfcc.org

The **Fair Credit Reporting Act** (FCRA) is designed to provide debtors some rights and protections regarding the credit information held by third parties about them. Before the passage of the FCRA, many debtors were denied the right to see their credit reports and were often victims of inaccurate reports. The FCRA brought credit reports out in the open.

When the FCRA Applies

Review the Fair Credit Reporting Act:
http://www.law.cornell.edu/uscode/
Enter Title 15 and Section 1681 in search box.

The FCRA applies to consumer reporting agencies, which are third parties (not creditors or debtors) that compile, evaluate, and sell credit information about consumer debt and debtors. Commercial credit reporting agencies and commercial debtors are not subject to FCRA standards.

Limitations on FCRA Disclosures

Under the FCRA, consumer reporting agencies can disclose information only to the following:

1. A debtor who asks for his own report
2. A creditor who has the debtor's signed application for credit
3. A potential employer
4. A court pursuant to a subpoena

Phillips v. *Grendahl* (Case 15.4) deals with an issue of disclosure of credit information.

CASE 15.4

Phillips v. *Grendahl*
312 F.3d 357 (C.A. 8 2002)

Credit and In-Law Trouble

FACTS

Mary Grendahl's daughter Sarah became engaged to marry Lavon Phillips and moved in with him. Mary Grendahl became suspicious that Mr. Phillips was not telling the truth about his past, particularly about whether he was an attorney and whether he had done legal work in Washington, D.C. She also was confused about who his ex-wives and girlfriends were and where they lived. She contacted Kevin Fitzgerald, a family friend who worked for McDowell Agency, a private investigation agency. She asked Mr. Fitzgerald to do a "background check" on Mr. Phillips, and she also gave him the name of the woman Mr. Phillips had lived with before Sarah Grendahl.

Mr. Fitzgerald began his search by obtaining Mr. Phillips's Social Security number from a computer database. He also searched public records in Minnesota and Alabama, where Mr. Phillips had lived earlier. He discovered one suit against Mr. Phillips for delinquent child support in Alabama, a suit to establish child support for two children in Minnesota, and one misdemeanor conviction for writing dishonored checks.

Mr. Fitzgerald then supplied the Social Security information to Econ Control and asked for "Finder's Reports" on Mr. Phillips and his former girlfriend. Econ Control was in the business of furnishing credit reports, Finder's Reports, and credit scoring for credit grantors and for private investigators.

Robert McDowell, on behalf of McDowell Agency, had signed an Econ Control registration agreement, titled "Agreement for Consumer Credit Services." One clause of the registration agreement stated:

> 3. I certify that I will order consumer reports, as defined by the Fair Credit Reporting Act, only when they are intended to be used as a factor in establishing a consumer's eligibility for new or continued credit, collections of an account, insurance, licensing, employment purposes, or otherwise in connection with a legitimate business transaction involving the consumer. Such reports will be used for no other purpose. Each time I request a report I intend to use for employment purposes, I will specifically identify it to [Econ Control] at the time I request the report.

Econ Control did not ask why McDowell wanted the report, and McDowell did not disclose his purpose in requesting it. Econ Control obtained a report from Computer Science Corporation on Mr. Phillips and passed it on to McDowell and Mr. Fitzgerald.

Mr. Fitzgerald met with Mary Grendahl and gave her the results of his investigation, including the Finder's Report.

Mr. Phillips eventually found out about the background check and became angry, as did Sarah. Mary Grendahl then telephoned and left the following voicemail for Sarah: "Sarah, this is mom. I didn't directly do a credit report. I hired a PI and they have every right to do that."

Mr. Phillips brought suit against Mary Grendahl, McDowell Agency, and Econ Control, alleging violations of the Fair Credit Reporting Act. Mr. Phillips appealed the lower court's summary judgment for Mary Grendahl and the others on the grounds that what they had obtained was not a consumer report in violation of the FCRA.

JUDICIAL OPINION

GIBSON, Circuit Judge

The Fair Credit Reporting Act, 15 U.S.C. §§ 1681b–1681u (2000), prohibits the disclosure of consumer credit reports by consumer credit reporting agencies, except in response to the following kinds of requests: (1) court order or subpoena, § 1681b(a)(1); (2) request by governmental agencies involved in setting or enforcing child support awards, § 1681b(a)(4) and (5); (3) request authorized in writing by the consumer about whom the report is made, § 1681b(a)(2); or (4) request by a person whom the reporting agency has reason to believe intends to use the consumer report for one of a number of specific, permissible business reasons, § 1681b(a)(3).

The first step in establishing liability under section 1681n(a) or section 1681o for obtaining a consumer report without a permissible purpose is to show that the document at issue was a "consumer report." The statutory definition is complex. Section 1681a(d) defines a consumer report as (1) any written, oral, or other communication of information (2) by a consumer reporting agency (3) bearing on a consumer's credit worthiness, credit standing, credit capacity, character, general reputation, personal characteristics, or mode of living (4) which is used or expected to be used or collected in whole or in part for the purpose of serving as a factor in establishing the consumer's eligibility for (A) credit or insurance to be used primarily for personal, family, or

continued

household purposes; (B) employment purposes; or (C) any other purposes authorized under section 1681b. Section 1681b in turn lists five major purposes, two of which have many subparts.

In this case, there is no dispute that the Finder's Report was (1) a written communication (2) by a consumer reporting agency, Computer Science Corporation. The two issues in dispute pertaining to whether the Finder's Report is a consumer report are (3) whether it contained the sort of personal information that would bring it within the definition and (4) whether anyone "expected" the Finder's Report or the information in it to be used for one of the purposes listed in the definition or "collected" the information in it for that purpose.

A consumer report must contain information "bearing on a consumer's credit worthiness, credit standing, credit capacity, character, general reputation, personal characteristics, or mode of living." The Finder's Report listed "Trade line Information," consisting of the names of several creditors with whom Phillips had credit accounts and the existence of a child support obligation, with dates for "last activity," but no other details such as amount of obligation or payment history. The Finder's Report also lists Phillips's former employers, which also would bear on his mode of living by showing that he has been employed. We conclude that the Finder's Report contains the kind of personal information required by the definition of consumer report.

The second question, whether the putative consumer report or the information in it was "used or expected to be used" or "collected for" one of the listed purposes, such as use in a credit or employment decision, is more difficult. Three statutory ambiguities in this clause could affect what communications are covered by the clause: the statutory language does not specify who must do the using, collecting or expecting; whether those verbs describe a specific or habitual action; or whether those actions must be done with regard to "information" or with regard to the consumer report itself.

We need not choose among the competing interpretations of the clause urged by the parties, because we conclude that the Finder's Report fell within the "used, expected to be used, or collected" clause even under the interpretation urged by McDowell Agency. The record demonstrates that the Finder's Report, not just the information in it, was actually intended by the credit reporting agency that prepared it to be used for a statutory purpose. The sample Finder's Report supplied by Econ Control to McDowell Agency states: "FINDERS delivers skip-locate power in a cost-effective, easy-to-use format. This remarkable product was de-

signed by and for collections professionals who need timely debt-recovery support at an economical price."

We next determine whether each of the defendants "obtained or used" the consumer report. There is no dispute that McDowell Agency and Econ Control obtained a consumer report, for each of them requested a Finder's Report.

Mary Grendahl, on the other hand, testified that she did not request the release of any credit information on Phillips. Mere passive receipt of the report would not be enough to satisfy the statutory element that she "use or obtain" a consumer report. However, Phillips argues that the phone machine message Grendahl left for Sarah is evidence that she asked Fitzgerald to obtain credit information: "Sarah, this is mom. I didn't directly do a credit report. I hired a PI and they have every right to do that." This evidence is ambiguous. On the one hand, it could mean that Grendahl hired a private investigator because she thought he was entitled to do a credit report. On the other hand, it could mean that she simply hired a private investigator who ordered a credit report on his own initiative, which she now understood he was entitled to do. Because this case was disposed of on summary judgment, we must resolve any ambiguities in the evidence in favor of Phillips. In this procedural posture, the ambiguous telephone message is sufficient to create a genuine issue of fact as to whether Mary Grendahl asked Fitzgerald to obtain a consumer report on Phillips.

The next inquiry is whether any of the defendants had a permissible statutory purpose for obtaining the consumer report. The only purpose for obtaining the report was to obtain information on Mary Grendahl's prospective son-in-law. Investigating a person because he wants to marry one's daughter is not a statutory consumer purpose under section 1681b(a). Even if getting married can be characterized as a consumer transaction under section 1681b(a)(3), it was not Mary Grendahl, but her daughter, whom Phillips was engaged to marry. He had no business transaction pending with Mary Grendahl. There was no permissible purpose for obtaining or using a consumer report.

Section 1681n(a) provides civil liability for willful noncompliance with any requirement of the Fair Credit Reporting Act.

The statute's use of the word "willfully" imports the requirement that the defendant know his or her conduct is unlawful.

Here, there is evidence that none of the three defendants believed their conduct to be covered by the Fair Credit Reporting Act. William Porter of Econ Control testified that a representative of Computer Science

Corporation told him that a Finder's Report was not a "credit report." Kevin Fitzgerald of McDowell Agency knew of Econ Control from the Minnesota Private Investigators Association meeting, where Porter had told the attendees that they could obtain Finder's Reports without the authorization of the subject.

Fitzgerald testified, "To the best of my knowledge, a finder's report is not considered a credit history." He also testified: "I did not do anything that I know to be illegal, unethical, or outside the standard practice of private investigators." Mary Grendahl testified that she only asked Fitzgerald to look into Phillips's background and that she gave him no instructions on how to do the investigation. She stated: "At no time did I ask Mr. Fitzgerald to try to obtain credit information or a 'credit report,' and it is my understanding that he did not do so."

On the other hand, there is also evidence that each defendant had some experience in dealing with credit reports and either knew of the Fair Credit Reporting Act or at least knew that such reports can only be ob-tained legally under certain circumstances. This kind of experience can support an inference that the defendants knew that their actions were impermissible. These facts are sufficient to create a genuine issue of material fact as to whether defendants acted knowingly and with conscious disregard for Phillips's legal rights.

We reverse the entry of summary judgment on Phillips's Fair Credit Reporting Act claim. . . . We remand for further proceedings in accordance with this opinion.

CASE QUESTIONS

1. Who sought the credit report?
2. What was contained in it?
3. Does the report qualify for protection under the FCRA?
4. Is there enough factual basis for the case to go forward?

When consumers file applications for credit with lenders, they have the right to know where a credit report came from. However, the creditor cannot show the report to the debtor, who must get the report through a credit reporting agency.

Consumer agencies are limited not only as to whom disclosures can be made but also as to what can be disclosed. The following are the general limitations on debtor disclosures:

1. No disclosure of bankruptcies that occurred more than ten years ago
2. No disclosure of lawsuits finalized more than seven years ago
3. No disclosure of criminal convictions and arrests that have been disposed of more than seven years ago

When a debtor applies for a loan of more than $50,000 or a job that pays more than $20,000, these limitations on disclosures do not apply.

Visit two sites for companies that handle credit reports:
http://www.equifax.com
http://www.transunion.com

Under the FCRA, debtors have not only the right to see reports but also the right to make corrections of inaccurate information included in those reports. A debtor simply notifies the reporting agency of the alleged error. If the agency acknowledges the error, the debtor's report must be corrected, and anyone who has received a report on that debtor during the previous two years must be notified.

If the agency still stands by the information challenged by the debtor, the debtor has the right to have included in the credit report a 100-word statement explaining his position on the matter. This statement is then included with the actual credit report in all future reports sent to third parties.

Stevenson v. *TRW, Inc.* (Case 15.5) deals with a problem of an inaccurate credit report.

CASE 15.5

Stevenson v. *TRW, Inc.*
987 F.2d 288 (5th Cir. 1993)

The Father with the Prodigal Son's Credit Rating

FACTS

TRW, Inc. is one of the nation's largest credit reporting agencies. Subscribing companies report to TRW both the credit information they obtain when they grant credit to a consumer and the payment history of the consumer. TRW then compiles a credit report on that consumer to distribute to other subscribers from whom the consumer has requested credit.

John M. Stevenson is a 78-year-old real estate and securities investor. In late 1988 or early 1989, Mr. Stevenson began receiving numerous phone calls from bill collectors regarding arrearages in accounts that were not his. Mr. Stevenson first spoke with TRW's predecessor, Chilton's, to try to correct the problem. When TRW purchased Chilton's, Mr. Stevenson began calling TRW's office in Irving, Texas. In August 1989, he wrote TRW and obtained a copy of his credit report dated September 6, 1989. He discovered many errors in the report. Some accounts belonged to another John Stevenson living in Arlington, Texas, and some appeared to belong to his estranged son, John Stevenson, Jr. In all, Mr. Stevenson disputed approximately sixteen accounts, seven inquiries, and much of the identifying information.

The reverse side of the credit report contained a printed notice describing how consumers could send a written dispute of the accuracy of their credit reports to the local TRW office. Mr. Stevenson, however, called TRW to register his complaint and then wrote TRW's president and CEO on October 6, 1989, requesting that his credit report be corrected. His letter worked its way to TRW's consumer relations department by October 20, 1989, and on November 1, 1989, that office began its reinvestigation by sending consumer dispute verification forms (CDVs) to subscribers that had reported the disputed accounts. The CDVs ask subscribers to check whether the information they have about a consumer matches the information in TRW's credit report. Subscribers who receive CDVs typically have 20 to 25 working days to respond. If a subscriber fails to respond or indicates that TRW's account information is incorrect, TRW deletes the disputed information. Mr. Stevenson understood from TRW that the entire process should take three to six weeks.

As a result of its initial investigation, TRW removed several of the disputed accounts from Mr. Stevenson's report by November 30, 1989. TRW re-tained one of the remaining accounts on the report because the subscriber insisted that the account was Mr. Stevenson's. The others were still either pending or contained what TRW called "positive information." It also began to appear that Mr. Stevenson's estranged son had fraudulently obtained some of the disputed accounts by using his father's Social Security number. This information led TRW to add a warning statement in December 1989, advising subscribers that Mr. Stevenson's identifying information had been used without his consent to obtain credit. Meanwhile, Mr. Stevenson paid TRW a fee and joined its Credentials Service, which allowed him to monitor his credit report as each entry was made. TRW finally completed its investigation on February 9, 1990. By then, TRW claimed that all disputed accounts containing "negative" credit information had been removed. Inaccurate information, however, either continued to appear on Mr. Stevenson's reports or was reentered after TRW had deleted it.

Mr. Stevenson filed suit in Texas state court alleging both common law libel and violations of the Fair Credit Reporting Act (FCRA). TRW removed the case to federal court, and on October 2, 1991, the case was tried before a federal court without a jury. The district court granted judgment for Mr. Stevenson on both the libel and FCRA claims, and TRW appealed.

JUDICIAL OPINION

WILLIAMS, Circuit Judge

Congress enacted FCRA "to require that consumer reporting agencies adopt reasonable procedures for meeting the needs of commerce for consumer credit, personnel, insurance, and other information in a manner which is fair and equitable to the consumer, with regard to the confidentiality, accuracy, relevancy, and proper utilization of such information. . . ." To guard against the use of inaccurate or arbitrary information in evaluating an individual for credit, insurance, or employment, Congress further required that consumer reporting agencies "follow reasonable procedures to assure maximum possible accuracy of the information concerning the individual about whom" a credit report relates.

Consumers have the right to see their credit information and to dispute the accuracy or completeness of their credit reports. When it receives a complaint, a consumer reporting agency must reinvestigate the disputed information "within a reasonable period of time" and "promptly delete" credit information that has been found to be inaccurate or unverifiable. (15 U.S.C. § 1681i(a).) The parties here stipulated that TRW began its reinvestigation within a reasonable period of time after receiving Stevenson's written dispute. Nevertheless, the court found that TRW had negligently and willfully violated § 1681i(a) by not deleting inaccurate and unverifiable information promptly and by allowing deleted information to reappear.

The record, however, contains evidence from which the district court could find that TRW did not delete unverifiable or inaccurate information promptly. First, TRW did not complete its reinvestigation until February 9, 1990, although TRW's subscribers were supposed to return the CDVs by December 4, 1989. Second, § 1681i(a) requires prompt deletion if the disputed information is inaccurate or unverifiable. If a subscriber did not return a CDV, TRW claims that it deleted the disputed information as unverifiable. Yet, some disputed accounts continued to appear on Stevenson's credit report for several weeks. One subscriber failed to return the CDV, but its account appeared on the report issued on February 9, 1990. Another subscriber returned its CDV by December 4, 1989, indicating that TRW's information was inaccurate, yet the information was not deleted until after February 9, 1990.

Allowing inaccurate information back onto a credit report after deleting it because it is inaccurate is negligent. Additionally, in spite of the complexity of Stevenson's dispute, TRW contacted the subscribers only through the CDVs. Although testimony at trial revealed that TRW sometimes calls subscribers to verify information, it made no calls in Stevenson's case. TRW relied solely on the CDVs despite the number of disputed accounts and the allegations of fraud. TRW also relied on the subscribers to tell TRW whether to delete information from Stevenson's report. In a reinvestigation of the accuracy of credit reports, a credit bureau must bear some responsibility for evaluating the accuracy of information obtained from subscribers.

The bureau had exhibited no ill will toward the plaintiff and had acted to fix the problem. Likewise, TRW provided Stevenson's credit report on request, did not conceal information about his report, investigated the disputed accounts, and attempted to resolve the complaints. TRW moved slowly in completing its investigation and was negligent in its compliance with the prompt deletion requirement. The record does not reveal, however, any intention to thwart consciously Stevenson's right to have inaccurate information removed promptly from his report.

TRW maintains that most of Stevenson's distress was the result of the many calls he received from creditors of the fraudulently obtained accounts. TRW correctly questions the relevance of these creditors' calls to violations of FCRA. Nearly all of these calls occurred before Stevenson filed his written dispute and TRW began its reinvestigation. Only after that did the FCRA violations occur. Stevenson's distress because of creditors' calls arose before TRW's FCRA violations.

The record reveals evidence, however, that Stevenson suffered mental anguish over his lengthy dealings with TRW after he disputed his credit report. First, Stevenson testified that it was a "terrific shock" to him to discover his bad credit rating after maintaining a good credit reputation since 1932. Second, Stevenson was denied credit three times during TRW's reinvestigation: by Bloomingdale's, by Bank One, and by Gabbert's Furniture Company. Stevenson testified that he had to go "hat in hand" to the president of Bank One, who was a business associate and friend, to explain his problems with TRW. As a result, he obtained credit at Bank One. Third, Stevenson had to explain his credit woes to the president of the First City Bank Colleyville when he opened an account there. With a new president at First City Bank, Stevenson had to explain his situation again. Despite the fact that he was ultimately able to obtain credit, Stevenson testified to experiencing "considerable embarrassment" from having to detail to business associates and creditors his problems with TRW. Finally, Stevenson spent a considerable amount of time since he first disputed his credit report trying to resolve his problems with TRW.

The district court properly found that Stevenson had suffered humiliation and embarrassment from TRW's violations of FCRA. We affirm the award of $30,000 in actual damages based upon the finding of mental anguish. We also affirm the award of $20,700 in attorney's fees.

CASE QUESTIONS

1. What caused Mr. Stevenson's anguish? Was it the correction process?

2. What suggestions could you offer to TRW to prevent the problems with Mr. Stevenson's credit report?

3. What would you do differently if you were trying to correct your report?

4. Are the damages reasonable?

> ### CONSIDER...   15.6
>
> Jennifer Cushman has a permanent residence in Pennsylvania but attended college in Vermont. In the summer of 1993, an unknown person, possibly a member of her household in Philadelphia, applied under Ms. Cushman's name for credit cards from three credit grantors: American Express (Amex), Citibank Visa, and Chase Manhattan Bank. The person provided the credit grantors with Ms. Cushman's Social Security number, address, and other identifying information. Credit cards were issued to that person in Ms. Cushman's name, and that person accumulated balances totaling approximately $2,400 on the cards between June 1993 and April 1994. All this occurred without Ms. Cushman's knowledge.
>
> In August 1994, an unidentified bill collector informed Ms. Cushman that TUC was publishing a consumer credit report indicating that she was delinquent on payments to these three credit grantors. Ms. Cushman notified TUC that she had not applied for or used the three credit cards in question and suggested that a third party had fraudulently applied for and obtained the cards. In response, a TUC clerk called Amex and Chase to inquire whether the verifying information (such as Ms. Cushman's name, Social Security number, and address) in Amex's and Chase's records matched the information in the TUC report. The TUC clerk also asked if Ms. Cushman had opened a fraud investigation with the credit grantors. Because the information matched, and because Ms. Cushman had not opened a fraud investigation, the information remained in the TUC report. TUC was unable to contact Citibank, so TUC deleted the Citibank entry from the report. TUC's investigations are performed by clerks who are paid $7.50 per hour and are expected to perform ten investigations per hour.
>
> There is no evidence that TUC took the necessary steps to obtain access to pertinent documents from the credit grantors that would enable TUC to perform a handwriting comparison. Ms. Cushman was denied credit because of the report. She filed suit under the FCRA. Did TUC violate the law? [*Cushman* v. *Trans Union Corp.*, 115 F.3d 220 (3d Cir. 1997).]

Consumer Leasing Act

Get information on issues in auto leasing:
http://www.leasetips.com

The **Consumer Leasing Act** is an amendment to TILA that provides disclosure protection for consumers who lease goods. Under this act, the lessor must disclose how much will be paid over the life of the lease, whether any money will be owed at the end of the lease, and whether the lease can be terminated.

In 1998, the Federal Trade Commission (FTC) and the Federal Reserve Board developed a new disclosure form for consumer leases. The new form requires disclosure of the following:

1. The amount due at the lease signing (must be itemized, too)
2. Total of payments
3. Monthly payments and other charges
4. Capitalized cost (shows the actual price of the goods—was previously missing from most lease agreements so as to discourage consumer shopping, especially for cars)
5. Residual value (value at the end of the lease, which helps determine the monthly payments)

View a sample lease form with the required disclosures:
http://www.fdic.gov/
regulations/laws/rules/
6500-2000.html#6500
appendixatopart213

6. Rent charge (which really is the interest rate)
7. Trade-ins, rebates, and other credits given at signing
8. Early termination conditions and terms
9. Excessive wear, use, and mileage provisions

Examine Article 2A of the UCC:
http://www.law.cornell.edu/ucc/2A/overview.html

Consumer leasing has become an important part of our economy. As noted in Chapter 13, Article 2A, of the Uniform Commercial Code, which immediately follows the sales article, covers all aspects of consumer leases. Article 2A covers lease contracts, warranties, and remedies.

ENFORCEMENT OF CREDIT TRANSACTIONS

Although a debtor has the benefit of paying over time, a creditor has the worry of trying to ensure payment. A creditor may be able to increase sales by extending credit, but risks of nonpayment also increase with each extension of credit. Fortunately, the law affords creditors some additional protections that can be used to guarantee repayment.

The Use of Collateral: The Security Interest

One way a creditor can have additional assurances of repayment is to obtain a pledge of collateral from the debtor. For goods, this collateral pledge is called a **security interest**. The creation of security interests is governed by Article 9 of the Uniform Commercial Code.

A security interest is created by a written agreement called a **security agreement**. Once a security interest is created, the creditor is given the right to repossess the pledged goods in the event the debtor defaults on repayment. When a debtor purchases a car on credit, there is nearly always a security interest in that car that allows the lender the right to repossess the car and sell it to satisfy the loan in the event the debtor defaults. This right to sell gives the creditor some additional assurances that the debt will be repaid. For more information on security interests, see Chapter 16.

Collection Rights of the Creditor

If a debtor falls behind on payments, the creditor has the right to proceed with collection tactics. Many creditors refer or sell their delinquent credit accounts to collection agencies. There was a time when some of these agencies engaged in questionable conduct in the collection of debts, including harassing debtors with phone calls and embarrassing them by contacting their friends and relatives. To control abuses in the collection process, Congress passed the **Fair Debt Collections Practices Act** (FDCPA) in 1977. The FDCPA became effective in 1978 and controls a great deal of debt collection. About two-thirds of the states have adopted some form of debt collection statutes. If state law, relative to the federal act, provides the same or greater protection for debtors in the collection process, the state law governs. In states without a collection law, the FDCPA applies.

Review the Fair Debt Collection Practices Act:
http://www.law.cornell.edu/uscode/15/1692.html

When the FDCPA Applies

The FDCPA applies to consumer debts and debt collectors. Consumer debts are defined here as they are under the TILA: debts for personal, home, or family purposes. Debt collectors are third-party collectors. The FDCPA does not apply to original creditors collecting their own debts; for example, Sears collecting Sears' debts is not governed by the FDCPA. However, if Sears referred its collection accounts to Central Credit Collection Agency, Central Credit would be under the FDCPA. If Sears created its own collection agency with a name other than Sears, the FDCPA would apply to that agency as well.

> **CONSIDER...** 15.7
>
> Telecredit Service Corporation's business is the collection of dishonored checks. Telecredit purchases these checks and then contacts the drawers to collect the funds. Stanley Holmes wrote a $315 check to Union Park Pontiac that was dishonored. Union Park sold the check to Telecredit, and Telecredit sent letters and made contacts to collect the check. Some contacts would be violations of FDCPA, but Telecredit says it is not covered by FDCPA because it is not collecting the debts of another. Is this correct? [*Holmes* v. *Telecredit Service Corp.*, 736 F. Supp. 1289 (D. Del. 1990).]

The FDCPA does not apply to the collection of commercial accounts or to banks and the Internal Revenue Service. In a rule revision, attorneys collecting debts for clients were made subject to coverage of the FDCPA.

Collector Requirements under the FDCPA

One of the requirements for collectors under the FDCPA is written verification of debt. A collector must provide such verification if a debtor asks. The collector must also automatically provide written verification within five days after contacting the debtor. Written verifications must include the following information:

1. The amount of the debt
2. The name of the creditor
3. The debtor's right to dispute the debt and the procedures for doing so

If a debtor disputes a debt, the collector has thirty days to verify the debt and its amount before any collection contact can continue.

Collector Restrictions under the FDCPA

In addition to affirmative disclosure requirements, collectors are subject to certain prohibitions under the FDCPA. The following subsections cover the prohibitions.

Debtor Contact   One of the most frequent abuses of collectors prior to the FDCPA was constant debtor contact and harassment. The FDCPA curbs the amount of contact: Debtors cannot be contacted before 8:00 A.M. or after 9:00 P.M., and debtors who work night shifts cannot be disturbed during their sleeping hours in the daytime.

The place of contact is also controlled by the FDCPA: Collectors must avoid contact at inconvenient places. Home contact is permitted, but contact in club, church, or school meetings is prohibited. Collectors can approach debtors at their places of employment unless employers object or have a policy against such contact.

To prevent harassment, the FDCPA gives debtors a chance to "call off" a collector. If a debtor tells the collector that he wants no more contact, the collector must stop and take other steps, such as legal action, to collect the debt. If the debtor is represented by an attorney and gives the name of the attorney to the collector, the collector can contact only the attorney from that point.

Third-Party Contact   The FDCPA also prohibits notifying other parties of the debtor's debts and collection problems. However, the debtor's spouse and parents can be contacted regarding the debt. Other parties can be contacted for information, but the collector cannot disclose the reason for the contact. Further, the only information that can be obtained from these third parties is the address, phone number, and place of employment of the debtor.

These third parties cannot be told about the debt, the amount, delinquencies, or any other information about the debtor. The collector must even be careful to use appropriate stationery when writing for information so that the letterhead does not disclose the nature of the collector's business. Postcard contact with the debtor or third parties is prohibited because of the likelihood that others will see the information about the debtor.

Prohibited Acts Collectors have certain other restrictions on their conduct under the FDCPA. The general prohibition in the FDCPA is that collectors cannot "harass, oppress, or abuse" the debtor. Using abusive language or physical force is prohibited. Misrepresenting the authority of a collector is also prohibited, as is posing as a law enforcement official or producing false legal documents. Debtors cannot be threatened with prison or other actions not authorized by law.

Trull v. *GC Services Ltd. Partnership* (Case 15.6) involves an issue of FDCPA violations.

CASE 15.6

Trull v. *GC Services Ltd. Partnership*
961 F. Supp. 1199 (N.D. Ill. 1997)

Debts, Threats, and FDCPA

FACTS

Lisa Trull (plaintiff) owed $68.05 to BMG Music Service. BMG Music Service referred the account to GC Services Limited Partnership (defendant) for collection. GC Services sent the following pieces of correspondence to Ms. Trull.

LETTER #1

FOR : L A TRULL
DATE : MAY 23, 1995
SUBJECT : BMG MUSIC SERVICE'S CLAIM
AGAINST L A TRULL

Your account has now been referred to GC Services and we intend to obtain payment from you.

In the process of writing this memorandum to you, this firm has accessed the computer information on you provided by BMG MUSIC SERVICE, which is now contained in our National Database. Please be advised that this information will be used by GC Services, including my office, to proceed with our formal collection procedures to settle your account with BMG MUSIC SERVICE.

If you do not think this debt is a just one, you may want to obtain advice on this question. Otherwise, we will expect payment promptly to remedy this claim. When remitting your payment, detach and return the upper portion of this notice. A return envelope is enclosed for your convenience.

LETTER #2

YOU OWE : BMG MUSIC SERVICE
ACCOUNT# : 3683915395
BALANCE DUE : $68.05
June 13, 1995

The debt listed above has been placed with us for collection. (Since you ignored our previous notice, we assume this debt is correct.) We intend to take all appropriate steps to see that you pay it.

Your failure to pay has been listed by BMG MUSIC SERVICE with a National Credit Reporting Bureau as an outstanding delinquency. This delinquent credit report will be maintained and available as part of your personal file by the National Credit Reporting Bureau. This may be used by interested consumer product and service companies, or other creditors in case you should attempt to obtain goods or credit from them.

Pay what you owe and further collection activities on your account will stop. Failure to resolve this delinquent account will result in continued collection activity.

LETTER #3

July 5, 1995
WARNING!

Don't even think about ignoring this notice as you've ignored others in the past requesting you to pay what you owe BMG MUSIC SERVICE.

continued

Buying on credit can be highly convenient. Why run the risk of losing that privilege? You need to take action immediately in order to avoid being labeled as a bad credit risk by BMG MUSIC SERVICE.

Pay your bill and wipe your record clean today!

IMPORTANT NOTICE

YOUR ACCOUNT HAS BEEN TRANSFERRED FROM BMG MUSIC SERVICE TO GC SERVICES' AGENCY MASTER DEBTOR FILE. YOUR PAYMENT MUST BE RECEIVED BY GC SERVICES AT THE ADDRESS INDICATED ABOVE IN ORDER TO ENSURE PROPER CREDIT OR ADJUSTMENT TO YOUR ACCOUNT.

LETTER #4

August 15, 1995

This is the last effort I will be making to settle your account with BMG MUSIC SERVICE.

Your lack of response to date indicates to us that you do not intend to pay for the merchandise you received from BMG MUSIC SERVICE. Your name will be retained as part of our records along with others who, despite their good name and reputation, have shirked their payment responsibility.

Is it not about time you settled this matter, especially in view of the consequences? We are anxious to clear your record as well as ours. Send your payment!

IMPORTANT NOTICE

YOUR ACCOUNT HAS BEEN TRANSFERRED FROM BMG MUSIC SERVICE TO GC SERVICES' AGENCY MASTER DEBTOR FILE. YOUR PAYMENT MUST BE RECEIVED BY GC SERVICES AT THE ADDRESS INDICATED ABOVE IN ORDER TO ENSURE PROPER CREDIT OR ADJUSTMENT TO YOUR ACCOUNT.

Further, each letter concludes with the following sentence: "NOTICE: see reverse side for important consumer information." The reverse side then provides the following in all capital letters:

"This is an attempt to collect a debt and any information obtained will be used for that purpose. Consumer information:

"Unless you, within thirty (30) days after your receipt of GC Services' initial written notice to you concerning this debt, dispute the validity of the debt, or any portion hereof, the debt will be assumed to be valid by GC Services. If you notify GC Services in writing within the above described thirty (30) day period that the debt, or any portion thereof, is disputed, GC Services will obtain verification of the debt or a copy of a judgment against you and a copy of such verification or judgment will be mailed to you by GC Services upon your written request within the above described thirty (30) day period, GC Services will provide you with the name and address of the original creditor, if different from the current creditor.

"The demands for payment in this letter do not reduce your rights to dispute this debt, or any portion thereof, and/or to request verification within the thirty (30) day period as set forth above."

Ms. Trull brought suit against GC alleging violations of the FDCPA. GC filed a motion to dismiss Ms. Trull's claim.

JUDICIAL OPINION

NORDBERG, District Judge

Plaintiff complains that the correspondence from Defendant violates [the FDCPA].

The Seventh Circuit has identified the "unsophisticated consumer" as "the hypothetical consumer whose reasonable perceptions will be used to determine if collection messages are deceptive or misleading." This standard is designed to protect consumers who are of below-average sophistication or intelligence, uninformed, naive, or trusting, while incorporating an objective element of reasonableness that "shields complying debt collectors from liability for unrealistic or peculiar interpretations of collection letters."

Applying the standard to this case, the Court concludes that an unsophisticated consumer, who has been informed that "This is the last effort I will be making to settle your account with BMG MUSIC SERVICE," reasonably could interpret the statement, "Your name will be retained as part of our records along with others who, despite their good name and reputation, have shirked their payment responsibility," followed by a reference to (1) the need to "settle[ ] this matter, especially in view of the consequences," (2) the statement that "[w]e are anxious to clear your record as well as ours," and (3) the "***IMPORTANT NOTICE***" that "YOUR ACCOUNT HAS BEEN TRANSFERRED TO GC SERVICES' AGENCY MASTER DEBTOR FILE," to imply that GC operates a consumer reporting agency that assembles consumer credit information for the purpose of furnishing consumer reports to third parties.

[In] the present case, GC Services has implied that, despite the letter being its last effort to settle the debt, Plaintiff's inclusion in GC Services' "master debtor file" will have "consequences." The reasonable unsophisticated consumer could construe the furnishing of this master debtor file to third parties to be among those vague consequences and, therefore, the purpose behind the "master debtor file." Thus, Trull has sufficiently stated a claim upon which relief may be granted.

Plaintiff further claims in Count II that Exhibit C (Letter #3) simulates a telegram, thus deceptively overstating and misrepresenting the urgency of the communication, in violation of the Act.

Plaintiff's Complaint merely alleges that the letter simulates a telegram, without specifying in what manner. Nevertheless, as the letter is attached to the Complaint, the Court may consider the letter in determining whether Plaintiff states a claim upon which relief may be granted. Plaintiff argues in her responsive brief that the letter of June 13, 1995 simulates a telegram because it is on yellow paper and headed "STAR High Priority Communication" and because of the layout and type face.

The Staff Commentary on the Fair Debt Collection Practices Act advises that "A debt collector may not communicate by a format or envelope that misrepresents the nature, purpose, or urgency of the message. It is a violation to send any communication that conveys to the consumer a false sense of urgency." The only case cited by Plaintiff that held a simulated telegram violates Section 1692e(10) is distinguishable, as the letter was headed "Tell-A-Gram." Nevertheless, assuming, without purporting to decide, that simulating a telegram violates the Act, the Court finds that Plaintiff cannot state such a claim, as even an unsophisticated consumer could not reasonably construe the letter at issue to be a telegram. First, unlike a telegram, the letter was sent through the mail. One who lacks the information to appreciate the distinction would be similarly unaware of the expense that attaches to a telegram and, thus, would not interpret the letter with the same urgency as one who believed it was hand delivered. Further, no derivation of the word telegram appears on the letter; rather, a sentence appears below the heading, stating in all capital letters that "This star high priority letter is being sent to you by GC Services," clearly identifying it as a letter. This is a situation where the standard's objective element of reasonableness "shields complying debt collectors from liability for unrealistic or peculiar interpretations of collection letters." Accordingly, that claim is dismissed, with prejudice.

Plaintiff claims that the correspondence violated Section 1692g in two ways: (1) each letter contained a validation notice, diluting the meaning of the warning and confusing the consumer, and (2) the second letter was sent within 30 days of the initial communication, overshadowing and effectively invalidating the validation notice.

Drawing all reasonable inferences in favor of Plaintiff, the Court finds that it appears beyond doubt that she can prove no set of facts in support of the claim arising from repeated validation notices that would entitle her to relief. The validation notice defines the validation period as being "within thirty (30) days after your receipt of GC Services' *initial* written notice to you concerning this debt." It is unreasonable for even the consumer of below-average sophistication or intelligence, who is uninformed, naive, or trusting, to ignore the word "initial," and, the standard protects the compliant debt collector from a peculiar interpretation.

In contrast, Plaintiff states a claim arising from the letter of June 13, 1996, because it states "Since you ignored our previous notice, we assume this debt is correct," contradicting notice of the thirty-day period before which the debt will be assumed to be valid. The Court finds that an unsophisticated consumer reasonably could be misled reading that statement within the validation period.

CASE QUESTIONS

1. How much money did Ms. Trull owe?
2. What was the nature of the four pieces of correspondence?
3. What violations of FDCPA does the court find?
4. Will Ms. Trull be permitted to go forward with her suit?

Penalties for FDCPA Violations

The Federal Trade Commission (FTC) is responsible for enforcement of the FDCPA. The FTC can use its cease and desist orders to stop collectors from violating the FDCPA and can also assess penalties for violations. However, the greatest power of enforcement under the FDCPA lies with individual debtors. Debtors who can prove collector violations can collect for actual injuries and mental distress. Debtors can also collect up to $1,000 in addition to actual damages for actions by collectors that are extreme, outrageous, malicious, or repeated. Attorney fees incurred by debtors in bringing their suits are also recoverable.

> **BUSINESS PLANNING TIP**
>
> Generating form collection letters by computer must be carefully monitored. The FDCPA imposes notice and content requirements that must flow in sequence. Threatened actions must be taken, or the threat is a violation.

BIOGRAPHY

JOEL KRISOLOFSKY: HAVE SKILLS, WILL COLLECT

Joel Krisolofsky dials the phone about 300 times a day. Nobody he calls wants to hear from him.

"I want to give you some information that you might not have been aware of," Mr. Krisolofsky tells a Minnesota woman who answers the phone. He cites a figure—$3,271—the charges she and her husband ran up on a credit card and never repaid.

"We're dealing with unemployment," the woman says, as a baby cries in the background. "That's why it's hard to meet that."

After 15 minutes of cajoling, Mr. Krisolofsky persuades her to accept a payment schedule in which $75 a month will be deducted automatically from the family's checking account. Hanging up the phone, he notes the easy time he had. "This is like taking candy from a baby," he says.

Mr. Krisolofsky loves collecting debt, and why not? The more than $1 million a year of repayments he reels in makes him the star performer at Abacus Financial Management Services LP, a collection agency here. "He's a very driven individual—no doubt about it," says Bradford J. Gustin, the executive vice president.

And he earns good money. Abacus pays collectors $24,000 plus commission. "This year I will make 95 grand and next year $120,000," says Mr. Krisolofsky, who is 31. "Where else can you make this kind of money without a college degree?"

As more Americans fail to repay debt, collecting has become lucrative work. Bad debt placed with collection agencies soared 39 percent to $117 billion in 1995 from $84 billion in 1994, according to the latest estimates by the American Collectors Association in Minneapolis. During that period, debt collected by agencies rose 40 percent to $31 billion, says M. Kaulkin & Associates, Inc., a Bethesda, Md., firm that advises on mergers and acquisitions in the industry.

With the field growing so rapidly, the nation's 6,000 collection agencies need more and more collectors. Between 1994 and 2005, agency employment will rise 37 percent, according to a study by the Bureau of Labor Statistics, more than double the 14 percent average growth the bureau projected for all other industries.

Some agencies are growing even faster. Anderson Financial Network, Inc., of Bloomington, Ill., expects to quadruple its collection force by the end of next year to about 2,400. In Phoenix, the workforce at Associated Creditors Exchange, Inc., has increased to 350 from 150 in 18 months and soon will grow by another 75.

Driving this growth is the rising delinquency rate on credit cards. In the second quarter, bank credit card losses climbed to 5.2 percent of total credit card debt outstanding, the highest annualized level in the 14 years that the Federal Deposit Insurance Corp. has tabulated the numbers. Among retailers feeling the pinch, Sears, Roebuck & Co. has said rising credit card charge-offs will hurt fourth-quarter earnings.

MANY KINDS OF DEBT

Besides credit card debt, collection agencies are pursuing the receivables of utilities, wireless-phone companies, and government agencies for such matters as parking tickets, court judgments, child support, and state and municipal taxes. An especially fast-growing category: medical facilities stiffed by uninsured patients.

The industry isn't popular. "If I had a dime for everyone who says they are going to blow us up, I would have a million dollars," says Bruce Passen, president of Abacus Financial.

Debt collectors have been around as long as debt. Many of them resort to intimidation, though the 1977 Fair Debt Collection Practices Act put some limits on it. It restricted collection calls to the hours of 8 A.M. to 9 P.M. and prohibited harassing language and idle threats, such as litigation.

"There are still agencies out there twisting people's arms and making false representations," says Gary Klein, a staff attorney at the National Consumer Law Center, a consumer-advocacy group in Boston. "But there is a sophisticated end of the business that has cleaned up its act quite a bit."

The industry also has an economic incentive to mind its manners: competition. Most debtors have multiple creditors and receive calls from a number of collectors, each wanting the money due it to get top priority. And pleasantry usually works better than intimidation.

The industry is nearly invisible because its clients, the creditors, demand confidentiality, and the law protects the identity of debtors. But several days at Abacus Financial offer some insight into the growth potential and operating procedures of the collection industry.

Abacus collects debt for some major credit card companies, retailers, and medical organizations. Its 150 collectors work in tiny cubicles with two main tools: a telephone, with headset, and a computer screen that pulls up debtor names, phone numbers, credit records, and even neighbors' phone numbers.

The room gets noisy as the collectors talk to debtors, joke with each other and, on rare occasions, lose their temper with someone on the other end of the line. "Why do you have to use that kind of language with me?" one collector bellows into his headset. "Did your dog die, or has your wife been on your back?"

Mr. Krisolofsky scoffs at the collector: "I'll show you someone who is butting heads during a call. I'll show you somebody who does not make a commission."

Unlike many collectors, who often go to the vending room to guzzle beverages, Mr. Krisolofsky rarely leaves his desk. He sometimes goes three hours between breaks, making call after call. "You got to get into a zone," he says. He doesn't mind the grind. "It beats manual labor," he says. "You get to use your brains and communicate with customers." A Buddha paperweight sits on his desk, beside pinned-up slogans such as "Values: Integrity, Love, Friendship, Money."

Mr. Krisolofsky, a muscular 235-pounder with the loudest and most animated voice in the office, nonetheless says the most important part of the job is to listen and offer counsel, even when debtors are swearing. "Even angry people tell you their problems," he says. "You have to read between the lines."

He favors positive reinforcement.

"It's that you want to pay, but you just can't pay now," he says to a woman who owes $5,440 in credit card debt.

"I had perfect credit until this year," she confides. "I am a single parent. I'm the one I have to depend on. I got divorced."

He suggests paying $100 a month on the debt, on which the creditor, after writing it off, is no longer charging interest. "At least there is no interest, and all this will go toward your balance," he says. After she agrees to the plan, he ends the call with, "Best of luck to you, ma'am."

Not that he can't get tough. "If we can't work out something temporarily, I am going to have to recommend further action," he says to a South Carolina woman who owes $5,893 in credit card debt. (Although he doesn't expressly threaten litigation, because Abacus doesn't sue debtors, a debtor could infer that that might be the next step—and the creditor could eventually decide to file suit.)

Even here, though, Mr. Krisolofsky is quick to soften his tone and add: "I just want to know where you

stand and put our heads together to create a win-win situation." After he describes the benefits of cleaning up her credit record, the woman agrees to make four $150 payments over four months via Western Union.

Collectors try to get the full balance first. They also sometimes offer settlements at 85 cents on the dollar. But if they see no hope of getting even that, they negotiate monthly payments because some money is better than nothing. In October, Mr. Krisolofsky brought in $66,251 in such payments, either through Western Union, postdated checks, or direct drafts from checking accounts—payments he calls "my annuities."

Mr. Krisolofsky, a collector since age 22, mainly seeks payments for one major credit card company and for issuers of student loans. Last year, he collected $1,180,000 and expects to hit $1.5 million this year. The son of a debt collector, he says the business is in his blood.

Most of his calls get an answering machine. "This is Mr. Kay from Abacus Financial," Mr. Krisolofsky usually says. "It's important that you return my call." He uses the alias "Mr. Kay" because it is easier to pronounce and remember than his real name and to protect himself from vindictive debtors.

A recent call on a delinquent student loan is answered by the debtor's mother in Illinois. The debtor isn't home. His mother asks why Mr. Krisolofsky is calling, but the law allows collectors to say that only to the debtor. She says she is suffering from cancer and asks him not to call back.

"Ma'am, I'm sorry, but I am going to have to keep calling," he says. She screams hysterically into the phone and hangs up.

That prompts calls of complaint first from the woman's husband and then from the debtor himself, who swears loudly into the phone. "If you are going to talk to me like that, you better start with Mister," says Mr. Krisolofsky, grinning. "Sometimes you have to fight a nasty attitude with a sense of humor," he says later. Mr. Krisolofsky is confident that he will collect the debt because the man has a good credit record and probably won't want an unpaid student loan to spoil it.

Abacus's second-highest-performing collector, Jerome Bridges, is empathetic with debtors. Seven years ago, he and his wife had a premature baby that saddled the family with $70,000 in medical debt. His credit card bills soared because his wife stopped working to care for the baby.

continued

"I got a lot of calls from bill collectors," recalls Mr. Bridges, now 39. He himself was a collector at the time. "It humbles you. It makes you want to treat people like you want to be treated."

Compared with Mr. Krisolofsky, Mr. Bridges uses a low-key approach. "I call it seasoning," he says. He gives a demonstration after tracking down a debtor at the bookstore where the man works. Mr. Bridges tells the debtor, "It sounds like you are a person who wants to take care of their responsibility but is a little stressed because you have some bills that are behind." He adds that his bad credit will hurt him in applying for jobs.

The man concedes that much, saying he couldn't get a better-paying job because employers did credit checks on him. He earns $18,000 a year, has $18,000 in bad debt on seven credit cards and $19,000 in student loans outstanding.

Mr. Bridges asks the man what he can pay per month. The man begrudgingly says $75. Mr. Bridges raises it to $100 and sets up a $100 direct draft from the man's bank account. Hanging up, Mr. Bridges excitedly pumps one arm in the air.

On another call, Mr. Bridges learns that the debtor has scheduled a meeting with a bankruptcy attorney. This news is discouraging because collection activity must stop once a debtor files for bankruptcy-court protection, as record numbers of people are doing these days.

But most debtors don't, and Mr. Bridges says that assures him, and many others, of a job. By next March, Abacus plans to more than double its number of collectors to nearly 400. And just wait until a recession hits, says Mr. Passen, its president. "There are not going to be enough of us to go around."

Source: "Dun Deals: As Many People Sink into Debt, One Group of Workers Prospers," *Wall Street Journal,* November 20, 1997, A1, A15, by Robert Berner. Copyright © 1997 Dow Jones & Company, Inc. Reprinted by permission of Dow Jones & Company, Inc. via the Copyright Clearance Center.

Suits for Enforcement of Debts

Occasionally, collection is ineffective and there is no collateral to repossess. The creditor has few options left but to bring suit to enforce collection of the debt. In bringing a successful suit, the creditor will obtain a **judgment**, which is the court's official document stating that the debtor owes the money and the collector is entitled to that money. However, in debt cases, the judgment is only the beginning. Once the creditor has the judgment, it must be executed to obtain funds.

A judgment is executed by having it attach to various forms of the debtor's property. For example, a judgment can attach to real property. A judgment can also attach to funds by **garnishment**, which is the attachment of a judgment to an account, paycheck, or receivables. Once there is attachment, the creditor is entitled to those funds. The third party holding the funds must comply with the terms of the garnishment and release the appropriate amount of funds to the creditor.

Employees are given some protection under the Consumer Credit Protection Act with respect to garnishments. One such protection is the limitation on the employer's ability to fire employees who have their wages garnisheed by a single creditor.

CONSIDER...   15.8

Clarence J. Ellis was employed by Glover & Gardner as a laborer and carpenter from August 1979 until June 18, 1980. On June 18, 1980, Charles Gardner, the president and owner of Glover & Gardner, received a notice of garnishment of Mr. Ellis's wages and fired Mr. Ellis that day. It was Mr. Ellis's first garnishment. Mr. Gardner said he fired Mr. Ellis because of alcoholism, poor job performance, insubordination, and dishonesty. However, Mr. Ellis's separation notice, which was sent to the Tennessee Department of Employment Security, gave as the reason for termination the garnishment. Did Mr. Gardner violate the law? [*Ellis v. Glover & Gardner Construction Co.,* 562 F. Supp. 1054 (M.D. Tenn. 1983).]

Under the Consumer Credit Protection Act, the amount that consumer creditors can garnishee on debtor wages is limited to 25 percent of the net wages. Garnishment for past-due child support is limited to 50 percent of net wages.

THE END OF THE LINE ON ENFORCEMENT OF DEBTS: BANKRUPTCY

Visit the American Bankruptcy Institute for more about bankruptcy:
http://www.abiworld.org

Federal laws afford debtors shelter when their obligations cannot be paid. *Bankruptcy* is the legal process of having a debtor—individual, partnership, corporation, LLC (see Chapter 21)—turn over all nonexempt assets in exchange for a release from debts following the distribution of those assets to creditors. There are three forms of bankruptcy. *Chapter 7* bankruptcy is the liquidation form in which the entity is dissolved or the individual's debts are discharged. *Chapter 11* is the reorganization form in which a business enjoys protection from collection and creditors until a new plan for satisfying the business obligations is approved. *Chapter 13* is the consumer debt adjustment plan under which consumers can be given a new repayment plan for their debts.

Once an individual or business voluntarily declares bankruptcy, all collection efforts must stop. A voluntary petition in bankruptcy provides the debtor with immediate relief from creditors. A debtor can be involuntarily petitioned into bankruptcy by creditors. In an involuntary petition case, the debtor has the opportunity for a hearing. The standard for declaring voluntary bankruptcy is that the individual or business has debts. The standard for creditors petitioning a debtor into involuntary bankruptcy is that the debtor is unable to pay debts as they become due.

Not all debts are discharged in bankruptcy. Alimony, child support, student loans, and taxes are examples of debts that survive bankruptcy.

For an update on the status of the bankruptcy bill, visit:
http://www.clla.org

Bankruptcy reform has been passed in the House and Senate and awaits joint conference committee approval as well as the president's signature. The reforms under the new law include limitations on the exemptions debtors can claim, more stringent requirements for declaring bankruptcy, and more types of debts surviving bankruptcy. Also, the reforms would require consumers to first go through the Chapter 13 process before going to Chapter 7 liquidation.

INTERNATIONAL CREDIT ISSUES

With the problems in the world economy, bankruptcies are increasing substantially.[1] However, there are significant differences between declaration of bankruptcy in the United States and other countries. In Japan, for example:

- Debtors can keep only kitchen utensils and $1,500 in cash.

- A meeting, called *dogeza*, is held wherein the company owner sits on the floor among creditors and begs for forgiveness while the creditors are permitted to yell abusive epithets at the debtor.

Other aspects of Japanese law make a company's failure and the impact on individual businesspeople very different. Japanese creditors routinely require guarantors, even on business debts, and most businesspeople rely on family for such guarantors. As a result, many in-laws find themselves responsible for debt when the business of their son-in-law fails. The divorce rate for executives of bankrupt Japanese businesspeople is twice that of the national average.

The suicide rate for failed Japanese businesspeople is 50 percent greater than in the general population. Under Japanese law, insurance companies do pay benefits even when death results from suicide so long as the policy has been in effect for at least one year. And the suicide rate for people with insurance policies is 50 percent higher than in the general population.

SUMMARY

What statutes affect credit contracts?

- Usury—charging interest in excess of the statutory maximum
- Equal Credit Opportunity Act (ECOA)—federal law prohibiting denial of credit on the basis of sex, race, color, religion, national origin, age, marital status, public assistance income, alimony, or child support income and plans for additional family
- Truth in Lending Act (TILA)—federal law governing disclosures in credit contracts
- Consumer Credit Protection Act (CCPA)—first federal statute on credit disclosure requirements
- Open-end transactions—credit card transactions
- Closed-end transactions—finance contracts for preestablished amounts, as in the financing of a television purchase
- Fair Credit and Charge Card Disclosure Act of 1988—federal law governing solicitation of credit card customers
- Regulation Z—federal regulation governing credit disclosures
- Three-day cooling-off period—right of rescission on credit contracts initiated in the home
- Home Equity Loan Consumer Protection Act of 1988—federal law requiring disclosures for home equity consumer loans

- Fair Credit Billing Act—federal law governing rights of debtors to dispute credit card charge
- Fair Credit Reporting Act (FCRA)—federal law regulating disclosure of credit information to and by third parties
- Consumer Leasing Act—federal law governing consumer lease transactions

How are credit contracts enforced?

- Security interest—pledge of collateral for credit
- Fair Debt Collections Practices Act (FDCPA)—federal law regulating collection of consumer debt by third parties
- Judgment—court order authorizing collection of money from party
- Garnishment—attachment of account, paycheck, or receivables to collect judgment
- Bankruptcy—federal process of collecting assets to pay creditors and discharge debts
- Chapter 7—liquidation bankruptcy
- Chapter 11—reorganization bankruptcy
- Chapter 13—consumer debt adjustment plan

QUESTIONS AND PROBLEMS

1. In May 1976, TRW (a credit reporting agency) issued a consumer report on Bennie E. Bryant in connection with his application for a federally insured home loan under the Veterans Administration. The consumer report had several inaccuracies, and Mr. Bryant went to TRW to point out the matters needing correction. For unrelated reasons, the mortgage did not close.

In August 1976, Mr. Bryant applied for another mortgage. On September 28, TRW called the mortgage company to let them know his credit report would be unfavorable. When the mortgage company notified Mr. Bryant, he again went to TRW offices and explained that the September report contained new inaccuracies in addition to those that were part of the May report. After this meeting, a memo about possible inaccuracies was placed in Mr. Bryant's file. However, the credit report without corrections was issued to the mortgage company on September 30. No follow-through had been done on the file memo.

Mr. Bryant's August mortgage application was originally denied. After personal efforts on his part, however, the credit report was corrected and the mortgage was eventually given.

Does Mr. Bryant have any rights and protections? [*Bryant v. TRW, Inc.,* 689 F.2d 72 (6th Cir. 1982).]

2. Michael S. Lamar had held a First USA Bank credit card for five years. He paid the entire balance each month. In July 1998, he missed the July 26th due date for his payment. He was assessed a $29 late fee on charges of $21.66. Upon complaint, First USA rescinded the charge but warned that it does so only once each year. Are these charges legal?

3. Maurice Miller obtained an American Express credit card in 1966, and his wife, Virginia, was given a supplementary card. Her card had a different number, was issued in her name, and had a separate annual fee. When Mr. Miller died in 1979, American Express canceled both credit cards. Mrs. Miller sued for violation of the ECOA. Has there been a violation? [*Miller v. American Express Co.,* 688 F.2d 1235 (9th Cir. 1982).]

4. In community property states, signatures of both spouses are required on real property transactions. Would a mortgagee that requires both spouses' signatures on a mortgage application be violating the ECOA? [*McKenzie v. U.S. Home Corp.,* 704 F.2d 778 (5th Cir. 1983).]

5. Would the collection of a dishonored check for $23.15 written by a consumer to a Circle-K Store by a collection agency be covered under the FDCPA? [*Wade v. Regional Credit Association,* 87 F.3d 1098 (9th Cir. 1996).]

6. James A. Swanson received a letter from a collection agency, the Southern Oregon Credit Service, indicating that if payment in full or definite arrangements for payment of his account were not made within forty-eight hours, the agency would begin a complete investigation into his employment and assets. Is the agency's threat a violation of the FDCPA? [*Swanson v. Southern Oregon Credit Service, Inc.,* 869 F.2d 1222 (9th Cir. 1988).]

7. A loan agreement provided for total number of payments as "one × $128.00 and 24 × $128.00." Is this sufficient disclosure of the total number of payments? Is it too confusing to be disclosure? Would it make any difference if the agreement showed how much would be paid in total? [*Sunamerica Finance Corp. v. Williams,* 442 N.E.2d 83 (Ohio 1982).]

8. American Future Systems, Inc. (AFS) sells china, cookware, crystal, and tableware, and extends credit to its customers for such purchases. Sales on a credit basis amount to over 95 percent of AFS sales. First National Acceptance Corporation (FNAC) is AFS's credit company and is wholly owned by AFS. AFS affords young people and minorities a chance to obtain credit in spite of their lack of prior credit histories.

Its general standards for credit are (1) a telephone in the residence, (2) positive credit experience of at least $100, and (3) employment with regular income. AFS has three specific marketing programs: a summer program; a winter program for single white females; and a winter program for minorities, married persons, and males.

Under the summer program, target customers are single white females living at home with a parent who could cosign for the credit. AFS does not always require the parent's signatures and might ship goods to this group without checking credit histories. This market is reached by salespeople who are sent only to white neighborhoods and instructed to avoid neighborhoods where there might be a racial mix.

If salespeople encounter a minority customer in their presentations, AFS will sell the goods and extend credit to them, but a credit check is done on both the applicant and cosigner before goods are shipped. About 20 percent of the applications of minority applicants are denied.

The winter program has two parts. The preferred part of the winter program consists of sales to single white women who are sophomores, juniors, or seniors in four-year colleges or nursing schools. The other part of the program focuses on minorities, males, and married persons attending college or vocational schools. Shipment to preferred customers is immediate, with automatic credit approval. Shipment to the nonpreferred winter group is deferred until the applicant makes three timely monthly payments.

AFS presented evidence that minority customers are, as a group, less creditworthy than their white counterparts. However, the statistics presented did not account for AFS's failure to solicit in minority neighborhoods.

The U.S. government brought suit for violation of the ECOA. Is the AFS program a violation of ECOA? [*United States v. American Future Systems, Inc.,* 743, F2d 169 (3d Cir. 1984).]

9. In 1984, Jean Mayes purchased Albert L. Silva, d/b/a Rainbow Motors, a Nantucket car dealership. In May 1985, Mr. Mayes entered into financing arrangements with Chrysler Credit Corporation to finance his car inventory. The borrower was Rainbow Motors, with Mr. Mayes as president and sole shareholder.

Chrysler demanded that Mr. Mayes and his wife, Michele Mayes, sign a "continuing guaranty" before it would extend credit. Mrs. Mayes, a well-compensated corporate attorney, was listed as a director and officer of Rainbow, but she did not participate in managing it. Rainbow defaulted, and Chrysler brought suit against Mrs. Mayes, seeking $750,126.41. Mrs. Mayes said Chrysler was estopped from collecting the debt because of the ECOA. Is she correct? [*Mayes v. Chrysler Credit Corp.,* 37 F.3d 9 (1st Cir. 1994).]

10. In late 1999, Paula Rossman received a "Pre-Qualified Invitation" to obtain a credit card from defendant Fleet Bank. The solicitation was for a "Fleet Platinum Master-Card" with a low annual percentage rate and "no annual fee." If interested, the recipient of this offer was to check a box next to which was written, "YES! I want the top card for genuine value and superior savings, the no-annual-fee Platinum MasterCard." An asterisk directed the recipient to a note that stated, "See the TERMS OF PRE QUALIFIED OFFER and CONSUMER INFORMA-TION for detailed rate and other information."

The enclosure entitled "Consumer Information" contained the Schumer Box, the table of basic credit card information required under the Truth in Lending Act, 15 U.S.C. § 1601 et seq., as amended by the Fair Credit and Charge Card Disclosure Act of 1988. Within the Schumer Box was a column with the heading "Annual Fee"; the box beneath that heading contained only the word "None." On the "Consumer Information" enclosure, but outside the Schumer Box, Fleet listed other fees. Also in that location was the statement, "We reserve the right to change the benefit features associated with your Card at any time."

Ms. Rossman responded to Fleet's offer, and soon thereafter received her "no-annual-fee Platinum Master-Card." Along with the card, Ms. Rossman was sent Fleet's "Cardholder Agreement," which contained the following provision concerning annual fees: "No annual membership fee will be charged to your Account."

The agreement provided for various applicable annual percentage rates charged on outstanding balances, including the standard rate for purchases (7.99 percent) and several higher rates that could be triggered by certain acts or omissions on the part of the card-holder. Among these was a rate of 24.99 percent that Fleet was entitled to impose "upon any closure of [the] Account." The Agreement also contained a change-in-terms provision, which stated:

> We have the right to change any of the terms of this Agree-ment at any time. You will be given notice of a change as required by applicable law. Any change in terms governs your Account as of the effective date, and will, as permit-ted by law and at our option, apply both to transactions made on or after such date and to any outstanding Account balance.

In May 2000, Fleet sent a letter to Ms. Rossman an-nouncing its intention to change the terms of the agree-ment.

Soon thereafter, Fleet notified Ms. Rossman that the annual fee would be imposed almost immediately:

> We are modifying the terms of your Fleet Cardholder Agreement only to correct the timing of the annual mem-bership fee previously disclosed. That fee will first be charged to your Account in your billing cycle that closes in July, 2000, and will be charged in that billing cycle each year thereafter.

A $35 fee was charged to Ms. Rossman's account by July 6, 2000, in accordance with the second letter. Ms. Rossman filed a class action suit against Fleet for viola-tions of the TILA. The District Court dismissed the case. Ms. Rossman has appealed. Should the case have been dismissed? [*Rossman v. Fleet Bank Nat. Ass'n,* 280 F.3d 384 (C.A.3, 2002).]

RESEARCH PROBLEM

Burgeoning Credit, Burgeoning Debt, Burgeoning Bankruptcies

11. Consumers' available credit limits on their credit cards have jumped significantly. Between 1996 and 1998, credit limits on consumer credit cards in-creased by 50.3 percent to a total of $1.78 trillion dol-lars of available credit lines for consumers. This increase means that consumers could be in total debt up to 4.2 times their current outstanding debt balance—a figure that increased from 3.4 times the current outstanding debt in March 1996.

The most common credit card line is now $3,500, as opposed to the typical $2,000 limit just two years ago. The average account balance has also increased from $1,479 to $1,987. On gold card credit cards, the increase in account balances is not as significant: from $2,334 to $2,497.

Meanwhile, consumer bankruptcies also continue at an all-time high, largely fueled by excessive credit card debt, according to the Consumer Federation of America. The proposed Bankruptcy Act reforms would make declaration of bankruptcy more difficult. The Consumer Federation of America has also issued a report on what it calls the "irresponsible" promotion of credit cards and credit card debt and points to the increase in limits as an example of banks' willingness to lure consumers into an often dangerous path of credit dependency.

Are banks acting in a responsible fashion with their solicitations of consumers for credit cards and increases in credit card lines? What responsibility do consumers have with regard to credit card debt? What disclosure rules apply in banks' solicitation of credit card customers? What should the banks do to influence legislation?

For More Information

Robert D. Hershey Jr., "The Sky Is Becoming the Only Limit for Credit Card Users," *New York Times,* August 9, 1998, Money & Business, p. 11.

Also see the Chamber of Commerce News: http://www.uschamber.org

For House debate on this issue: http://thomas.loc.gov

For a look at the American Bankruptcy Institute: http://www.abiworld.org

NOTE

1. Bankruptcy is a universal process that has a deep history. See the course Web site and Instructor's Manual for more background.

16

Business Property

The Vatican Library. The House of Windsor. Princess Diana. Spuds McKenzie. NASCAR. "Shrek." The common thread? They all have lucrative arrangements for the licensing of their images and symbols. The law affords protection for these images and symbols even though the property right is a bundle of images and feelings about a person, business, or logo. According to the *National Law Journal,* intellectual property, particularly with the rise of Internet commerce, remains the fastest-growing legal specialty.

This chapter covers the rights of businesses and their property. Property comes in different forms: personal, intellectual, and real; and the rights and protections differ for each type. What does a business own? What are the types of business property? What are the rights and issues in personal property owned by a business? What statutory protections exist for intellectual property? What issues of property protection exist in international business operations? What are real property interests, and what rights are included? Protecting the goodwill that symbols, names, and motifs provide for a business is an important part of the ongoing success of a business.[1]

> Possession is nine points of the law.
> No, it's not. Paperwork is.
> Harvard Business Review
> *September/October 1995*

> We must take care to guard against two extremes equally preju-
> dicial: the one, that men of ability, who have employed their
> time for the service of the community, may not be deprived
> of their just merits, and the reward for their ingenuity and
> labour; the other, that the world may not be deprived of
> improvements, nor the progress of the arts retarded.
> Sayre v. Moore, 102 Eng. Rep. 138, 140 (1785)

CONSIDER...

Victor and Cathy Moseley owned and operated an adult toy, gag gift, and lingerie shop that they called Victor's Little Secret near Elizabethtown, Kentucky. The store advertised its grand opening in a publication for the Fort Knox base, and an army colonel notified Victoria's Secret of the shop's name and merchandise. Victoria's Secret owns 750 stores around the country and distributes 400 million catalogs each year via U.S. mail. Two of Victoria's Secret's stores were located in Louisville, Kentucky, a short drive from Elizabethtown and Fort Knox.

Legal counsel for Victoria's Secret asked the Moseleys to stop using the name Victor's Secret because of possible confusion over the trademark and resulting dilution. Is Victoria's Secret correct? Are the Moseleys infringing the trademark, image, and name of Victoria's Secret?

© SCOTT ROTHSTEIN/ISTOCKPHOTO

WHAT CAN A BUSINESS OWN?
PERSONAL PROPERTY: THE TANGIBLE KIND

When we see a Dreyer's Ice Cream truck driving along beside us, we understand that Dreyer's Ice Cream owns that truck; it is a part of the Dreyer's fleet and is carried as business equipment on the books of the Dreyer's corporation. If someone took that truck, it would be theft, and Dreyer's would be entitled to compensation if the truck were damaged or destroyed by the theft. Dreyer's would also be entitled to compensation if someone hit the truck in an accident and damaged it. Because the truck is Dreyer's property, Dreyer's enjoys certain rights of ownership in it. The delivery truck is **tangible property**. Tangible property is the type of property we can see and touch. Delivery trucks, desks, computers, inventory, and the building and land in which a business is located are all forms of tangible property. We have specific laws governing real and personal property rights for tangible property. We have laws to protect us against theft of our property and laws that provide remedies if someone harms or destroys that property.

Types of Personal Property

The Dreyer's truck would be an example of one form of personal property that businesses own—equipment. Everything from the laser printer in the office to the Thermos brand watercoolers that construction crews have attached to their company trucks is included as a form of business equipment. Businesses also have personal property interests in the form of inventory or the goods they hold for sale to customers.

Transfer of Personal Property

Business property that is equipment or inventory may or may not have **documents of title** associated with it. Vehicles in a company's fleet have the standard title documents for motor vehicles. Other types of tangible personal property that would have title documents include airplanes, helicopters, and even purebred animals. Title to these forms of personal property is transferred by the transfer of the document of title.

Many other forms of business property do not have any formal documents of title. Computers, desks, and file cabinets are typical forms of business property that do not have title documents. These forms of personal property are transferred by a **bill of sale**. A bill of sale is simply a contract that reflects the sale of personal property and provides all the proof necessary to establish ownership.

Leases and Bailments of Personal Property

Many businesses choose to lease their equipment. A **lease** is a right of use and possession of property for a fixed or open-ended period of time. The key difference between a lease of personal property and ownership is that in a lease the possession of the property transfers, but ownership does not. Upon termination of the lease, possession reverts back to the lessor.

In some circumstances, personal property is rented for a short period of time. A temporary transfer of possession of personal property is called a **bailment**. If you rent an extra bed for company, you are the **bailee** in the bailment relationship. The rental store is the **bailor**. If you check your coat at the coatroom in a Broadway theater, a bailment is created. The coat-check person as an agent for the theater is the bailee, and you are the bailor. If you leave your watch at a jeweler's for repair, you are the bailor and the jeweler is the bailee.

The bailment relationship is created with very simple requirements: The bailor turns possession over to the bailee with the understanding that the personal property will be returned, and both parties intend to create a bailment relationship. The intention to create a bailment distinguishes the bailment relationship from a **license**. For example, if you park your car yourself in a parking lot and pay for parking upon entry or departure, you have been given a license, the right to park on a lot owned by another. If you drive to a lot and a valet takes your keys and car and parks it for you, a bailment is created because possession of your car has been turned over to another. In those circumstances, you are the bailor and the parking lot owner is the bailee.

The bailment relationship carries duties and responsibilities. The bailee has the duty to return the bailment at the end of the agreed-upon period of possession. The bailee also has the duty of using reasonable care to protect the bailor's property while it is in his possession. In a parking valet situation, the bailee has a duty to take reasonable care to protect your car. A bailee cannot eliminate its liability for damage to the bailor's property. Often, parking stubs issued by valets read: "RESTAURANT ASSUMES NO LIABILITY FOR DAMAGE TO PROPERTY." Such a disclaimer of liability is called an **exculpatory clause**, but it is generally not valid because it is against public policy to allow someone to hold himself completely harmless for his negligent acts. It is, however, valid for the restaurant to limit its liability. For a parking stub from a valet that reads, "RESTAURANT NOT LIABLE FOR ITEMS VALUED AT OVER $50 LEFT IN VEHICLE," the bailee is not disclaiming all liability but, rather, is letting the bailor know in advance not to leave valuable items in the car. Many parking valet stubs now disclaim liability for theft of cellular phones and stereo systems. Such disclaimers are valid because they limit but do not eliminate liability.

> **BUSINESS PLANNING TIP**
>
> Businesses that rent equipment to others should follow a regular maintenance schedule for their equipment. Also, their rental forms should include disclosures about the nature of activities for which their equipment is used. For example, businesses that rent ski equipment have disclosures on their rental forms about the risks inherent in skiing.

In rental bailments, the bailor has the duty of checking the rented equipment to be certain it is in working order and has no defects that could injure the bailee. For example, if you leased a snowblower from a rental equipment franchise and a loose belt on the snowblower caused it to injure you, the franchise would have liability for your injuries because of its failure to maintain the equipment. The franchise that rents equipment, however, is not responsible for injuries that you experience because an activity for which you use their equipment is dangerous. If you rent in-line skates from a rental franchise, the franchise is not responsible for any injuries you experience because of the inherent dangers of in-line skating. They would, however, be responsible if a defective buckle caused your skate to come loose and you fell and were injured as a result.

Creditors' Rights and Personal Property

Often, a business may not have enough cash available to purchase equipment or inventory. Many businesses rely on the extension of credit to purchase both these forms of business personal property. Creditors, on the other hand, are concerned about the ability of a business to pay for property, particularly in those situations where the business is new and the capitalization is small. To provide more security for a creditor, a business can provide a **lien or security interest** to the creditor in the property that is purchased. Sometimes called a **chattel mortgage**, this form of security is created under Article 9 of the **Uniform Commercial Code** (UCC). The UCC is a near-universal uniform law in the United States that governs commercial transactions, including contracts (see Chapters 13 and 14) and financial transactions such as notes, checks, and drafts.

Review Article 9 of the UCC:
http://www.law.cornell.edu/ucc/9/overview.html

Article 9 of the UCC, revised in 2000, allows creditors to take a security interest in debtors' personal property. That security interest is created when a debtor authenticates a **security agreement** in exchange for the extension of credit or as security for an underlying debt. Once the creditor has a security interest in the personal property, that creditor has priority above other unsecured creditors in the event of the debtor's bankruptcy as well as the right of repossession of the secured property, often referred to as the **collateral**, if the debtor fails to make the necessary payments. Repossession under Article 9 can take place without court action. The creditor is permitted to take back the property from the debtor without first going to court to obtain a foreclosure. The only restrictions on creditors' repossession of debtors' property when there has been a **default**, or nonpayment of the debt, is that the creditor cannot "breach the peace." A breach of the peace is a violation of the law. A creditor cannot trespass or use physical force to repossess the property. Perhaps the most common example of repossession is taking back cars for which payment has not been made. Those responsible for the actual repossession may take the car from a public place, but they cannot enter the debtor's private property to repossess the car because that would be a trespass, a violation of the law, and thus a breach of the peace.

One additional protection that an Article 9 creditor can obtain is through **perfection**, generally accomplished by the filing of a **financing statement**. A financing statement is filed with a public agency (generally either the secretary of state or county recorder or clerk) to provide public notice that the creditor has an interest in the debtor's property. Under the 2000 revisions to Article 9, these financing statements generally are filed in a central location; the move is toward an electronic system that permits easy access to information. The process of perfection is important because it often gives the creditor priority over subsequent creditors who might take a security interest in the same equipment or inventory.

WHAT CAN A BUSINESS OWN? PERSONAL PROPERTY: THE INTANGIBLE OR INTELLECTUAL KIND

In addition to the Dreyer's truck itself, referred to earlier, you also see painted on the truck the signature brown and white stripes that are part of the ice cream's packaging. You see the distinctive writing, "Dreyer's Grand Ice Cream." You recognize the truck from its distinctive paint and writing probably before you even read the name "Dreyer's." That distinctive color scheme, name, and writing are also business property that belongs to Dreyer's. The recognition and goodwill that come from those brown stripes and the name are forms of **intangible property** that also enjoys statutory protections, which include Dreyer's right to prevent others from using its distinctive name and colors and taking from it the goodwill those items have come to symbolize. The symbols represent a bundle of very valuable rights for the business.

Forms of intangible property include patents, copyrights, trademarks, trade names, and trade dress. Protections include federal rights, international protections, and common-law rights of action for the damage to or taking of these forms of intangible property.

Protection for Business Intellectual Property

Federal law provides competitive protection for ideas, formulas, and trademarks. This section of the chapter covers these statutory protections of competition.

Patents

Visit the U.S. Patent and Trademark Office: http://www.uspto.gov

Patents are a type of legal monopoly obtained by filing certain information and forms with the U.S. Patent Office. So fundamental is the protection of new products and processes that the protection for inventors is found in Article 1, Section 8, of the U.S. Constitution.

While there are several types of patents, the most common are utility or functional patents and design patents. *Utility or function patents* are those that cover machines, processes, and improvements to existing devices. For example, a computerized method for tracking a dry cleaner's inventory of clothing is protected by a patent. Prior to 1995, a patent was valid for seventeen years. However, in order to bring the U.S. laws into compliance with GATT (see Chapter 7 for more information on this treaty) provisions, the protection was extended to twenty years in 1995. *Design patents* are those that protect the features of a product. The lace configuration on Eve of Milady bridal gowns and Procter & Gamble's method for elasticized legs on its disposable diapers are examples of product designs protected by patent. Design patents are granted for fourteen years.

During these exclusive rights periods of fourteen and twenty years, the patent holder has the sole rights for profits on sales. Because protection is so extensive, an idea is patentable only if it is nonobvious, novel, and useful; and the idea must be reduced to some tangible form. For example, a discovery of a reproductive hormone in the male body is not patentable, but a product to stop production of that hormone for birth control purposes can be patented.

Anyone who sells or uses a patented product or process without the consent of the patent holder has committed patent **infringement**. Infringement entitles the patent holder to a statutory action for damages. The patent holder (the plaintiff) in such a case need only show that a patent was held and that the defendant infringed that patent. A Patent Office registration for a product or process, however, is not a guarantee of recovery. A court must still agree with the Patent Office determination that the product or process is nonobvious, useful, and novel.

Amazon.com has had an ongoing battle with Barnes & Noble over the "One Click" shopping method. Amazon.com obtained a patent for its buyers' shopping

> ### BUSINESS PLANNING TIP
>
> To be certain federal protection for your intangible property rights is maximized, put either the "®" by the trade name or trademark or on the packaging or product, or place the words "Registered in U.S. Patent and Trademark Office" or "Reg. U.S. Pat. & TM. Off." Once you are registered with the U.S. Patent and Trademark Office, obtaining registrations in other countries becomes much easier. Also, a registered product enjoys protection at the borders of the United States. Customs officials can exclude products that are being imported if they infringe a registered property right.

BUSINESS STRATEGY

The Best Defense to Infringement Is a Good Offense of Disparagement

Gucci brought suit against Duty Free America (DFA) for trademark infringement. Gucci alleges that DFA sells knock-off goods such as purses, wallets, and shirts with the Gucci logo but that the goods are not authentic. Gucci discovered the sales when DFA customers came to Gucci stores to return or exchange their Gucci items without a receipt. When Gucci filed suit against DFA for infringement, DFA filed a counterclaim for disparagement. DFA

© RENE MANSI/ISTOCKPHOTO

alleges that its Gucci goods are indeed authentic and that it has been damaged because its customers are told by Gucci personnel that anything purchased at DFA is not authentic Gucci.

What will Gucci need to establish for infringement? What will DFA need to establish for disparagement? To show that its goods are authentic? [*Gucci America, Inc.* v. *Duty Free Apparel, Ltd.*, 277 F.Supp.2d 269 (S.D.N.Y. 2003).]

CONSIDER...   **16.1**

Procter & Gamble (P&G) was issued patent #4,455,333 on June 19, 1984, for an invention entitled "Doughs and Cookies Providing Storage-Stable Texture Variety." The patent covers a method of manufacturing ready-to-serve cookies that remain crispy on the outside and chewy on the inside for an extended shelf life. P&G markets these cookies under the Duncan Hines label.

P&G brought a patent infringement action against Nabisco Brands, Inc., which markets its own line of dual-textured cookies called "Almost Home" and "Chewy Chips Ahoy." P&G also sued Keebler Company for its dual-textured cookie called "Soft Batch" and Frito-Lay, Inc. for its "Grandma's Rich and Chewy." Each of the defendants denies infringement. They have moved for dismissal of the case on grounds that the patent is invalid because baking cookies is not patentable. Do you agree? Would you protect P&G's process? [*Procter & Gamble Co.* v. *Nabisco Brands, Inc.*, 604 F. Supp. 1485 (D.C. Del. 1985).]

---

method that permits shoppers to place items in a virtual shopping cart and then click just one button when they are ready to purchase. The buyers need not go through the time of filling in shipping, billing, and credit information for each purchase.

Barnes & Noble created a similar "One Click" shopping experience for its online customers, and Amazon.com sued for patent infringement. On appeal, a court held that Barnes & Noble could continue to use the "One Click" method while the parties proceeded to trial on the issue of whether the "One Click" patent was a valid one or simply an obvious convenience for online shoppers. While the outcome of the case is unknown, Barnes & Noble at least introduced enough evidence to prevent the court from issuing an injunction against it pending the trial [*Amazon.com, Inc.* v. *Barnes & Noble.com*, 239 F.3d 1343 (Fed. Cir. 2001)].

Copyrights

Visit the issue of fair use at the Copyright and Fair Use site:

http://www.copyright.gov/he lp/faq/faq-fairuse.html

Patents protect inventors. **Copyrights** protect authors of books, magazine articles, plays, movies, songs, dances, recordings, and so on, as well as the creators of photographs. A copyright protects the expression of ideas. A copyright gives the holder of the copyright the exclusive right to sell, control, or license the copyrighted work. A copyright exists automatically for works created after 1989. While the placement of the traditional C or copyright symbol (©) is not required, it is recommended. Further, the existence of a copyright in the United States is recognized in all nations that have signed the Berne Convention. Under the terms of the Berne Convention and U.S. law, copyright registration is not required, but it is recommended. Registration is a means of preventing someone violating the copyright from claiming a lack of knowledge about the work's protection. In order to register a copyright, the creator need only file two copies of the work with the Copyright Office in Washington, D.C. Without copyright registration, the owner cannot bring a suit for copyright infringement.

A copyright runs for the life of the creator plus 70 years. If the work produced was done in the employ of a business, the business then registers the copyright. These types of copyrights run for 120 years from the time of creation or 95 years from publication of the work, whichever is shorter. These time limits for protection have been expanding over the years with the most recent extension, from 50 to 70 years, passed with the **Sonny Bono Copyright Term Extension Act** (CTEA). The late Representative Bono was concerned because copyrights he held and many others, such as the copyright on the cartoon character Mickey Mouse, were about to expire. While the Constitution prohibits granting copyrights in perpetuity, there has been a clear trend in congressional actions to keep extending that protection period.

A copyright holder has control over the use of the created work. That control includes control over reproduction, distribution, public performances, derivative works, and public displays. Some copyright holders assign or license these rights to others in exchange for royalties. For example, most songwriters assign their rights for public performances of their songs to the American Society of Composers, Authors, and Publishers (ASCAP) and Broadcast Music, Inc. (BMI), who then pay the writers each time their song is used, according to a previously determined schedule of fees. There is an international fee schedule for payment for tapes, CDs, and records; it could be a flat fee, a per-minute fee, a per-record fee, or a per-song fee.

Visit the "Copyright Website" for more information on copyrights:
http://www.benedict.com

> **BUSINESS PLANNING TIP**
>
> Be certain your employees understand the copyrighted nature of computer software and the protections afforded the owners of those programs. Be sure they understand that there are both criminal and civil penalties for infringement of software programs.

Damages for copyright infringement include the profits made by the infringer, actual costs, attorney fees, and any other expenses associated with the infringement action. All illegal copies can be obtained through court injunction and any distribution of the illegal copies halted by the same court order.

In addition to the civil suits that can be brought for infringement and resulting damages to a business owner, there are federal criminal penalties for copyright infringement. Criminal penalties are available when infringement is willful and for "commercial advantage or private financial gain."

Technology has created new issues in copyright infringement, particularly in the areas of copyrighted software and music, with the availability of digital technology. For example, an MIT student uploaded and downloaded copyrighted software programs and then gave fellow students passwords for access. The result was that students at MIT enjoyed free access to the Internet at a cost of $1 million to the system's owners. However, the student did not charge for the access and thus realized no personal financial gain from the project. Technically, there was no violation of the copyright laws.

For a copyright quiz, visit:
http://www.cyberbee.com

> **BUSINESS PLANNING TIP**
>
> Most employers acquire site licenses for computer software programs so that they enjoy a type of discount by not being required to purchase a full program for each employee. Have appropriate controls in place for the master disks and access to the programs so that the site license is not violated. Be certain employees understand the content of and reasons for the site license agreements.

As a result of this case, music producers and software developers added protection technology to their copyrighted products and lobbied for a change in copyright law, which came with the **Digital Millennium Copyright Act** in 1998. This act criminalizes the circumvention of protection technology in order to make copies of copyrighted materials as well as assisting others, providing expertise, or manufacturing products to circumvent protection technology. This act is at the root of the *Napster* case (see Chapter 1), in which music was downloaded without charge via peer-to-peer file sharing. Shawn Fanning, Napster's founder, argued that his technology did not violate copyright laws because his service was a nonprofit enterprise. However, the acts of circumvention and facilitating circumvention are now violations of copyright laws. The liability has also been extended to those who facilitate the infringement via these downloading programs. There are criminal sanctions for those who maneuver around encryption devices and those who hire them to avoid those devices, as in the case of industrial espionage.

Under the **Computer Software Copyright Act of 1980**, all software can be copyrighted, whether it is written in ordinary language (source code) or machine language (object code). While software copyrights do not cover methods of operation (such as menus), they do cover the underlying programs themselves.

Fair Use and Copyrights

Review the Copyright Act of 1976, as amended (1994):
http://www.law.cornell.edu/topics/copyright.html

When the copyright laws were amended in 1976, one change permitted "fair use" of copyrighted materials. **Fair use** is occasional and spontaneous use of copyrighted materials for limited purposes—for example, a short quote from a copyrighted work. Fair use also allows instructors to reproduce a page or chart from a copyrighted work to use in the classroom; and copies of book pages can be made for research purposes. One interesting question that has arisen is the relationship between the notion of fair use and the prohibitions under the Digital Millennium Copyright Act. Can a professor circumvent protection technology for fair use in the classroom? Some feel the professor can do so if he has purchased the work. In other words, the professor can use an excerpt from the Beatles' *White Album* if the professor owns that album.

Another issue in fair use involves questions about such use and the First Amendment. For example, satirical works use the lyrics and speech of others as a form of social commentary such as those found in *Mad Magazine* and *Saturday Night Live*. The First Amendment protects social commentary, and the copyright laws protect original work. *Campbell* v. *Acuff-Rose Music, Inc.* (Case 16.1) involves an issue of a parody of copyrighted material being used for commercial gain, dealing with the balancing of First Amendment rights and copyright protection.

CASE 16.1

Campbell v. *Acuff–Rose Music, Inc.*
510 U.S. 569 (1994)

Justice Souter Does the Pretty Woman Rap

FACTS

2 Live Crew, a popular rap musical group, recorded and performed "Pretty Woman," a rap music version of Roy Orbison's famed 1964 "Oh, Pretty Woman" rock ballad. The song was written by Mr. Orbison and William Dees, and the rights to the song were assigned to Acuff-Rose Music, Inc. (respondent). Rap music is a style of black American popular music that consists of often-improvised rhymes performed to rhythmic accompaniment. 2 Live Crew's manager had written to Acuff-Rose to request permission to do the parody and offered to pay for rights to do so. Acuff-Rose's response: "I am aware of the success enjoyed by the '2 Live Crew,' but I must inform you that we cannot permit the use of a parody of 'Oh, Pretty Woman.'"

2 Live Crew recorded the parody anyway and named Mr. Orbison and Mr. Dees as the songwriters and Acuff-Rose as the publisher on the CD cover. After over 250,000 copies of the CD had been sold and over one year later, Acuff-Rose filed suit against Luther Campbell (also known as Luke Skywalker), Christopher Wongwon, Mark Ross, and David Hobbs, members of the 2 Live Crew group, for infringement. 2 Live Crew maintained that its song was a parody and thus protected under the fair use exceptions of the copyright laws. The district court granted summary judgment for 2 Live Crew. The court of appeals held that the commercial nature of the parody rendered it presumptively unfair. 2 Live Crew (petitioners) appealed.

JUDICIAL OPINION

SOUTER, Justice

We are called upon to decide whether 2 Live Crew's commercial parody of Roy Orbison's song, "Oh, Pretty Woman," may be a fair use within the meaning of the Copyright Act of 1976, 17 U.S.C. § 107 (1988 ed. and Supp. IV).

It is uncontested here that 2 Live Crew's song would be an infringement of Acuff-Rose's rights in "Oh, Pretty Woman," under the Copyright Act of 1976, 17 U.S.C. § 106 (1988 ed. and Supp. IV), but for a finding of fair use through parody.

The first factor in a fair use enquiry is "the purpose and character of the use, including whether such use is of a commercial nature or is for nonprofit educational purposes." The central purpose of this investigation is to see whether the new work merely "supersede[s] the objects" of the original creation, or instead adds something new, with a further purpose or different character, altering the first with new expression, meaning, or message; it asks, in other words, whether and to what extent the new work is "transformative." Although such transformative use is not absolutely necessary for a finding of fair use, *Sony Corp. of America* v. *Universal City Studios, Inc.*, 464 U.S. 417 (1984), the goal of copyright, to promote science and the arts, is generally furthered by the creation of transformative works. Such works thus lie at the heart of the fair use doctrine's guarantee of breathing space within the confines of copyright and the more transformative the new work, the less will be the significance of other factors, like commercialism, that may weigh against a finding of fair use.

Suffice it to say now that parody has an obvious claim to transformative value, as Acuff-Rose itself does not deny. Like less ostensibly humorous forms of criticism, it can provide social benefit, by shedding light on an earlier work, and, in the process, creating a new one. We thus line up with the courts that have held that parody, like other comment or criticism, may claim fair use under § 107.

Parody needs to mimic an original to make its point, and so has some claim to use the creation of its victim's (or collective victims') imagination, whereas satire can stand on its own two feet and so requires justification for the very act of borrowing.

The fact that parody can claim legitimacy for some appropriation does not, of course, tell either parodist or judge much about where to draw the line. Like a book review quoting the copyrighted material criticized, parody may or may not be fair use, and petitioner's suggestion that any periodic use is presumptively fair has no more justification in law or fact than the equally hopeful claim that any use for news reporting should be presumed fair.

As the District Court remarked, the words of 2 Live Crew's song copy the original's first line, but then "quickly degenerate[e] into a play on words, substituting predictable lyrics with shocking ones . . . [that] derisively demonstrate[e] how bland and banal the Orbison song seems to them." Judge Nelson, dissenting below, came to the same conclusion, that the 2 Live Crew song "was clearly intended to ridicule the white-bread original" and "reminds us that sexual congress with nameless streetwalkers is not necessarily the stuff of romance and is not necessarily without its consequences. The singers (there are several) have the same thing on their minds as did the lonely man with the nasal voice, but here there is no hint of wine and roses." Although the majority below had difficulty discerning any criticism of the original in 2 Live Crew's song, it assumed for purposes of its opinion that there was some.

We have less difficulty in finding that critical element in 2 Live Crew's song than the Court of Appeals did, although having found it we will not take the further step of evaluating its quality. The threshold question when fair use is raised in defense of parody is whether a periodic character may reasonably be perceived. Whether, going beyond that, parody is in good taste or bad does not and should not matter to fair use. As Justice Holmes explained, "[i]t would be a dangerous undertaking for persons trained only to the law to constitute themselves final judges of the worth of [a work], outside of the narrowest and most obvious limits. At the one extreme some works of genius would be sure to miss appreciation. Their very novelty would make them repulsive until the public had learned the new language in which their author spoke."

While we might not assign a high rank to the periodic element here, we think it fair to say that 2 Live Crew's song reasonably could be perceived as commenting on the original or criticizing it, to some degree. 2 Live Crew juxtaposes the romantic musings of a man whose fantasy comes true, with degrading taunts, a bawdy demand for sex, and a sigh of relief from paternal responsibility. The later words can be taken as a comment on the naivete of the original of an earlier day, as a rejection of its sentiment that ignores the ugliness of street life and the debasement that it signifies. It is this joinder of reference and ridicule that marks off the author's choice of parody from the other types of comment and criticism that traditionally have had a claim to fair use protection as transformative works.

The use, for example, of a copyrighted work to advertise a product, even in a parody, will be entitled to less indulgence under the first factor of the fair use enquiry, than the sale of a parody for its own sake, let alone one performed a single time by students in school.

We agree with both the District Court and the Court of Appeals that the Orbison original's creative expression for public dissemination falls within the core of the copyright's protective purposes. This fact, however, is not much help in this case, or ever likely to help much in separating the fair use sheep from the infringing goats in a parody case, since parodies almost invariably copy publicly known, expressive works.

We think the Court of Appeals was insufficiently appreciative of parody's need for the recognizable sight or sound when it ruled 2 Live Crew's use unreasonable as a matter of law. It is true, of course, that 2 Live Crew copied the characteristic opening bass riff (or musical phrase) of the original, and true that the words of the first line copy the Orbison lyrics. But if quotation of the opening riff and the first line may be said to go to the "heart" of the original, the heart is also

continued

what most readily conjures up the song for parody, and it is the heart at which parody takes aim. Copying does not become excessive in relation to parodic purpose merely because the portion taken was the original's heart. If 2 Live Crew had copied a significantly less memorable part of the original, it is difficult to see how its parodic character would have come through.

This is not, of course, to say that anyone who calls himself a parodist can skim the cream and get away scot free. In parody, as in news reporting, context is everything, and the question of fairness asks what else the parodist did besides go to the heart of the original. It is significant that 2 Live Crew not only copied the first line of the original, but thereafter departed markedly from the Orbison lyrics for its own ends. 2 Live Crew not only copied the bass riff and repeated it, but also produced otherwise distinctive sounds, interposing "scraper" noise, overlaying the music with solos in different keys, and altering the drum beat. This is not a case, then, where "a substantial portion" of the parody itself is composed of a "verbatim" copying of the original. It is not, that is, a case where the parody is so insubstantial, as compared to the copying, that the third factor must be resolved as a matter of law against the parodists.

It was error for the Court of Appeals to conclude that the commercial nature of 2 Live Crew's parody of "Oh, Pretty Woman" rendered it presumptively unfair. No such evidentiary presumption is available to address either the first factor, the character and purpose of the use, or the fourth, market harm, in determining whether a transformative use, such as parody, is a fair one. The court also erred in holding that 2 Live Crew had necessarily copied excessively from the Orbison original, considering the parodic purpose of the use. We therefore reverse the judgment of the Court of Appeals.

The case was remanded for trial.

APPENDIX A

"Oh, Pretty Woman," by Roy Orbison and William Dees

Pretty Woman, walking down the street,
Pretty Woman, the kind I like to meet,
Pretty Woman, I don't believe you,
you're not the truth,
No one could look as good as you
Mercy
Pretty Woman, won't you pardon me,
Pretty Woman, I couldn't help but see,
Pretty Woman, that you look lovely as can be
Are you lonely just like me?
Pretty Woman, stop a while,
Pretty Woman, talk a while,
Pretty Woman give your smile to me

Pretty Woman, yeah, yeah, yeah
Pretty Woman, look my way,
Pretty Woman, say you'll stay with me
'Cause I need you, I'll treat you right
Come to me baby, Be mine tonight
Pretty Woman, don't walk on by,
Pretty Woman, don't make me cry,
Pretty Woman, don't walk away,
Hey, O.K.
If that's the way it must be, O.K.
I guess I'll go on home, it's late
There'll be tomorrow night, but wait!
What do I see
Is she walking back to me!
Oh, Pretty Woman.

APPENDIX B

"Pretty Woman," as recorded by 2 Live Crew

Pretty woman walkin' down the street
Pretty woman girl you look so sweet
Pretty woman you bring me down to that knee
Pretty woman you make me wanna beg please
Oh, pretty woman
Big hairy woman you need to shave that stuff
Big hairy woman you know I bet it's tough
Big hairy woman all that hair it ain't legit
'Cause you look like "Cousin It"
Big hairy woman
Bald headed woman girl your hair won't grow
Bald headed woman you got a teeny weeny afro
Bald headed woman you know your hair could look nice
Bald headed woman first you got to roll it with rice
Bald headed woman here, let me get this hunk of biz for ya
Ya know what I'm saying you look better than rice a roni
Oh bald headed woman
Big hairy woman come on in
And don't forget your bald headed friend
Hey pretty woman let the boys
Jump in
Two timin' woman girl you know you ain't right
Two timin' woman you's out with my boy last night
Two timin' woman that takes a load off my mind
Two timin' woman now I know the baby ain't mine
Oh, two timin' woman
Oh pretty woman

CASE QUESTIONS

1. What constitutes fair use?

2. What is the significance of 2 Live Crew's commercial gain from the parody?

3. Why is the *Sony* case cited?

4. Why did 2 Live Crew's manager seek permission first?

5. Do you agree with the court's decision? Was it a fair use? Should the owner of the rights be allowed to decide how a song will be parodied for commercial gain?

6. Does the court comment on bad taste and parody quality? Why?

Aftermath: The 2 Live Crew case began a trend in the music parody industry, based on what has become known as "Footnote 10." In Footnote 10 in the Supreme Court opinion, the Court noted its concern for the use of injunctions in parody cases. The footnote indicates that automatic injunctive relief when the parody goes beyond fair use is wrong because there may be a strong public interest in the publication of the secondary work, as in the 2 Live Crew parody, in which social commentary is present.

CONSIDER...   16.2

The San Diego Chicken, a mascot at professional baseball games, has a portion of his act in which he grabs a purple dinosaur and stomps it, stamps it, pounds it, and pummels it. Lyons Partnership, L.P. produces the *Barney the Dinosaur* television show, which features a purple dinosaur, and holds all its product licenses. Lyons filed suit against Ted Giannoulas (the man beneath the San Diego Chicken costume) for copyright infringement.

A Texas court classified the portion of Mr. Giannoulas's act that involved a purple dinosaur as a form of parody or satire that was thereby protected by the First Amendment. Kenneth Fitzgerald, the lawyer for Mr. Giannoulas, said Mr. Giannoulas will seek to recover his attorney's fees in the case.

Mr. Fitzgerald noted during the case that Barney has been spoofed by Jay Leno as well as on the television show *Saturday Night Live,* but Lyons chose only to pursue Mr. Giannoulas.

What is wrong with selective enforcement of one's copyright protections? Is Barney the Dinosaur something that can be copyrighted?

CONSIDER...   16.3

Jesse "The Body" Ventura, the former professional wrestler who became governor of Minnesota, was concerned when Garrison Keillor announced that he was so inspired by Mr. Ventura's election that he had written a comic novel. The novel, with a lead character of Jimmy "Big Boy" Valente, is also the story of a professional wrestler's life and rise to a governorship. Then-Governor Ventura accused Mr. Keillor of "cheating" because he was "making money off of me." At the time, Governor Ventura was writing a book about himself, but Mr. Keillor's book was to appear long before the Ventura autobiography.

Did Governor Ventura have any grounds for stopping Mr. Keillor's efforts? Did he have the right to protect his life story? Did he have exclusive rights on that story? Is it protectable under any intellectual property provisions? What effect does his being elected governor have on his rights?

ETHICAL ISSUES

In the summer of 1996, the dance song "Macarena" hit the pop music scene and charts in the United States. The line-type dance inspired by the song is called the Macarena. At camps around the country, the song was played and children were taught the dance.

The American Society of Composers, Authors, and Publishers (ASCAP) serves as a clearinghouse for fee payments for use of copyrighted materials belonging to its members. ASCAP sent a letter to the directors of camps and nonprofit organizations sponsoring camps (Girl Scouts, Boy Scouts, Camp Fire Girls, American Cancer Association, and so forth) that warned them that licensed songs should not be used without paying

continued

ASCAP the licensing fees and that violators would be pursued. ASCAP's prices for songs are, for example, $591 for the camp season for "Edelweiss" (from *The Sound of Music*) or "This Land Is Your Land."

Some of the nonprofit-sponsored camps charge only $44 per week per camper. The directors could not afford the fees, and the camps eliminated their oldies dances and dance classes. ASCAP declined to offer discounted licensing fees for the camps.

Why did ASCAP work so diligently to protect its rights? What ethical and social responsibility issues do you see with respect to the nonprofit camps? Some of these camps are summer retreats for children who suffer from cancer, AIDS, and other terminal illnesses. Does this information change your feelings about ASCAP's fees? What would you do if you were an ASCAP member and owned the rights to a song a camp wished to use?

Trademarks

Review the Lanham Act:
http://www.law.cornell.edu/
topics/trademark.html

Trademarks are words, pictures, designs, or symbols that businesses place on goods to identify those goods as their product. "Xerox," the Mercedes-Benz triangle, and "M and M's" are all examples of trademarks. The **Lanham Act** of 1946 is a federal law passed to afford businesses protection of their trademarks. This law is really a protection of a company's goodwill. A trademark becomes associated with that company and is used as a means of identifying that company's goods or services. The Lanham Act assures the right to retain that unique identification.

To obtain protection, goods must move in interstate commerce. When this requirement is met, a trademark is registered on the *Principal Register*. The trademark must be unique and nongeneric. For example, "cola" is a generic term; "Coca-Cola" is a trademark. Before recent changes in the law, a trademark must have been in use before registration, but a recent amendment to the Lanham Act allows preregistration, a practice followed in Europe for many years.[2] Once a trademark is registered, its registration can be challenged for five years. If no challenge is brought, the trademark becomes incontestable and is protected as long as its owner enforces it.

Once a trademark is registered, the holder has the obligation of maintaining the unique nature of that trademark. To do so, there must be a generic term that can be associated with the trademark so the public does not turn the trademark itself into a generic term. For example, there are "Band-Aid brand adhesive strips" instead of "Band-Aids." There is "Jell-O brand gelatin dessert" instead of "Jell-O." There are "Formica brand kitchen countertops" instead of "Formica" and "Rollerblade in-line skates" instead of "Rollerblades." Parker Brothers recently lost its "Monopoly" trademark because there is no generic term for the type of board game it was. Other examples of generics are "aspirin" and "cellophane."

Harley-Davidson, Inc. v. *Grottanelli* (Case 16.2) deals with an issue of generic or protectable use.

BUSINESS PLANNING TIP

Before you pay for a copyright or a trademark, be sure the seller owns the intellectual property and has the authority to sell it. The Lyons Group, owner and developer of Barney, the large, childlike purple dinosaur of PBS fame, purchased the rights to Barney's "I Love You" theme song from Lee Bernstein. Jean Warren, a music publisher from Everett, Washington, surfaced in 1995 and told the Lyons Group that Ms. Bernstein had sold her the rights in 1983. The result was litigation involving all the parties.

CASE 16.2

Harley–Davidson, Inc. v. *Grottanelli*
164 F.3d 806 (2d Cir. 1999)
cert. denied 531 U.S. 1103 (2001)

When Is a Hog Generic?

FACTS

Harley-Davidson (Harley-Davidson, Harley, or the company), a corporation based in Milwaukee, Wisconsin, manufactures and sells motorcycles, motorcycle parts and accessories, apparel, and other motorcycle-related merchandise. It brought suit against The Hog Farm, owned by Ronald Grottanelli (Grottanelli), for its use of the word "hog" in its business name and in reference to other products. Harley maintains that "hog" is a trademark associated with its motorcycles.

The lower court enjoined Mr. Grottanelli from

using the term "hog" in his store except as to his store's name, which he could keep so long as confined to a narrow geographic area. Mr. Grottanelli appealed, as did Harley-Davidson (the latter to request a more narrow geographic scope for use of "The Hog Farm" name by Mr. Grottanelli).

JUDICIAL OPINION

NEWMAN, Circuit Judge

This appeal primarily involves trademark issues as to whether the mark "HOG" as applied to large motorcycles is generic. [We] conclude that the word "hog" had become generic as applied to large motorcycles before Harley-Davidson began to make trademark use of "HOG" and that Harley-Davidson's attempt to withdraw this use of the word from the public domain cannot succeed.

In the late 1960s and early 1970s, the word "hog" was used by motorcycle enthusiasts to refer to motorcycles generally and to large motorcycles in particular. The word was used that way in the press at least as early as 1965, and frequently thereafter, prior to the 1980s when Harley first attempted to make trademark use of the term. Several dictionaries include a definition of "hog" as a motorcycle, especially a large one. The October 1975 issue of *Street Chopper* contained an article entitled "Honda Hog," indicating that the word "hog" was generic as to motorcycles and needed a trade name adjective.

See *The Oxford Dictionary of Modern Slang* (1992) ("hog noun U.S. A large, often old, car or motorcycle. 1967–."); *American Heritage Dictionary* (3d ed. 1992) ("hog . . . 4. Slang. A big, heavy motorcycle"); Eric Partridge, *A Dictionary of Slang and Unconventional English* (8th ed. 1984) ("hog n . . . 8. a homebuilt motorcycle . . ."); see also Glossary of Sportscycle Terms, *Bike and Rider*, Aug. 1992, at 84 ("HOG Old fashioned, heavyweight sportscycle").

A likely etymology of "hog" to mean a motorcycle is suggested in the entry for "road-hog" in Eric Partridge, *A Dictionary of Slang and Unconventional English* (6th ed. 1996), which reports that in the United States as early as 1891 "road-hog" was applied to an "inconsiderate" cyclist and somewhat later to motorists.

Beginning around the early 1970s and into the early 1980s, motorcyclists increasingly came to use the word "hog" when referring to Harley-Davidson motorcycles. However, for several years, as Harley-Davidson's Manager of Trademark Enforcement acknowledged, the company attempted to disassociate itself from the word "hog." The Magistrate Judge drew the reasonable inference that the company wished to distance itself from the connection between "hog" as applied to motorcycles and unsavory elements of the population, such as Hell's Angels, who were among those applying the term to Harley-Davidson motorcycles.

In 1981, Harley-Davidson's new owners recognized that the term "hog" had financial value and began using the term in connection with its merchandise, accessories, advertising, and promotions. In 1983, it formed the Harley Owners' Group, pointedly using the acronym "H.O.G." In 1987, it registered the acronym in conjunction with various logos. It subsequently registered the mark "HOG" for motorcycles. That registration lists Harley-Davidson's first use as occurring in 1990.

Grottanelli opened a motorcycle repair shop under the name "The Hog Farm" in 1969. Since that time his shop has been located at various sites in western New York. At some point after 1981, Grottanelli also began using the word "hog" in connection with events and merchandise. He has sponsored an event alternatively known as "Hog Holidays" and "Hog Farm Holidays," and sold products such as "Hog Wash" engine degreaser and a "Hog Trivia" board game.

Though the Magistrate Judge made no ultimate finding as to whether "hog" was generic as applied to large motorcycles prior to Harley-Davidson's trademark use of the word, his subsidiary findings point irresistibly toward that conclusion. He found that there was "substantial evidence which would indicate that in those years the term referred to motorcycles (or motorcyclists) generally." He cited the various press and dictionary usages of the word that we have set forth above. Though not conclusive, dictionary definitions of a word to denote a category of products are significant evidence of genericness because they usually reflect the public's perception of a word's meaning and its contemporary usage. In this case, one dictionary cites a generic use of "hog" to mean a large motorcycle as early as 1967, long before Harley's first trademark use of the word, and the recent dictionary editions continuing to define the word to mean a large motorcycle indicate that the word has not lost its generic meaning. We have observed that newspaper and magazine use of a word in a generic sense is "a strong indication of the general public's perception" that the word is generic.

However, rather than recognize that the word "hog," originally generic as applied to motorcycles, cannot subsequently be appropriated for trademark use, the Magistrate Judge upheld Harley-Davidson's anti-dilution claim on the ground that its "HOG" mark has become a strong trademark. This was error. Even the presumption of validity arising from federal registration, . . . cannot protect a mark that is shown on strong evidence to be generic as to the relevant category of products prior to the proprietor's trademark use and registration.

continued

Supporting the generic nature of "hog" as applied to motorcycles is Harley-Davidson's aversion to linking the word with its products until the early 1980s, long after the word was generic. Harley's Manager of Trademark Enforcement acknowledged that in the past Harley had attempted to disassociate itself from the term "hog." As the Magistrate Judge noted, Harley's own history of the company, "The Big Book of Harley-Davidson," makes no reference to "hog" as relating to its products before the early 1980s. Though Harley-Davidson was not shown to have used the word "hog" in a generic sense, its deliberate resistance to linking the word to its products is nonetheless probative.

Harley-Davidson cites the rulings in *Harley-Davidson Motor Co.* v. *Pierce Foods Corp.*, 231 U.S.P.Q. 857 (T.T.A.B.1986), and *Harley-Davidson, Inc.* v. *Seghieri*, 29 U.S.P.Q.2d 1956 (N.D.Cal.1993), but we are not bound by those decisions, and, more significantly, there is no indication that the bodies making those rulings had the extensive record of early generic usage that we have. In *Pierce Foods,* the litigation did not even raise the issue of the genericness of "hog." Seghieri apparently had scant evidence of genericness; the Court relied on articles from Harley's own newsletter, which indicated that "hog" meant Harley-Davidson motorcycles.

Professor McCarthy contends that, in some contexts, there might be a doctrine whereby trademark use can be reacquired in a generic term, and he cites the "SINGER" and "GOODYEAR" marks as examples. But Professor McCarthy recognizes that his examples are words that were originally proper names of the manufacturer and that the cases he enlists, *Singer Mfg. Co.* v. *Briley*, 207 F.2d 519 (5th Cir.1953), and *Goodyear Tire & Rubber Co.* v. *H. Rosenthal Co.*, 246 F.Supp. 724 (D.Minn.1965), "do not stand for the proposition that a commonly used name of an article like 'computer,' 'typewriter' or 'flashlight' can be appropriated by one seller as a trademark." Moreover, if a generic word could ever be infused with trademark significance, the word must have ceased to have current generic meaning. The recent editions of the dictionaries cited by the District Court demonstrate that generic usage of "hog," applied to motorcycles, still exists.

Nor does Professor McCarthy's discussion of so-called "dual usage" terms provide any help to Harley-Davidson. "Dual usage" in trademark law refers to a mark that starts out as proprietary and gradually become [*sic*] generic as to some segments of the public. If such a mark "retains" trademark significance, injunctive relief must be carefully tailored to protect only the limited trademark use and not to bar the generic use. Our case, however, concerns a mark that starts out generic and is sought to be given trademark significance by a manufacturer.

Harley-Davidson suggests, albeit in a footnote, that it is entitled to trademark use of "HOG" as applied to motorcycles because a substantial segment of the relevant consumers began to use the term specifically to refer to Harley-Davidson motorcycles before the company made trademark use of the term. Some decisions have invoked this principle to accord a company priority as to its subsequent trademark use of a term. Whether or not we would agree with these decisions, they present a significantly different situation. Neither "ACE" nor "BUG" was a generic term in the language as applied, respectively, to a category of film editors or a category of automobiles prior to the public's use of the terms to refer to the American Cinema Editors and Volkswagen cars. By contrast, "hog" was a generic term in the language as applied to large motorcycles before the public (or at least some segments of it) began using the word to refer to Harley-Davidson motorcycles. The public has no more right than a manufacturer to withdraw from the language a generic term, already applicable to the relevant category of products, and accord it trademark significance, at least as long as the term retains some generic meaning.

The public may also take a trademark and give it a generic meaning that is new. See *Lucasfilm, Ltd.* v. *High Frontier*, 622 F. Supp. 931 (D.D.C.1985) ("Strategic Defense Initiative" referred to as "Star Wars Program" without infringing movie trademark STAR WARS).

For all of these reasons, Harley-Davidson may not prohibit Grottanelli from using "hog" to identify his motorcycle products and services. Like any other manufacturer with a product identified by a word that is generic, Harley-Davidson will have to rely on all or a portion of its tradename (or other protectable marks) to identify its brand of motorcycles, e.g., "Harley Hogs."

Reversed.

CASE QUESTIONS

1. Who used the term "hog" first among the two parties?

2. When did the term "hog," as applied to motorcycles, appear in the dictionary?

3. Did Harley-Davidson reclaim the term "hog" from its generic standing?

4. Is the term "hog" generic now?

CONSIDER . . . 16 . 4

Wordspy.com is a site that specializes in noting newly coined words. The site noted that the popularity of the search engine, Google, has netted a verb, such as when someone says, "I went in and googled it." A lawyer from Google has asked that the new term be deleted from Wordspy's site. Why does Google want to stop its use as a verb?

Trade Names

Not all commonly used terms, however, are generic because they may be trade names. In *San Francisco Arts & Athletics, Inc.* v. *United States Olympic Committee*, 483 U.S. 522 (1987), the Supreme Court held that the term *Olympic* belongs to the U.S. Olympic Committee and could not be used by San Francisco Arts & Athletics, Inc. (SFAA) in promoting its "Gay Olympic Games."

The SFAA did not have permission to use the term *Olympic.* Use of a **trade name** without the registered owner's permission is infringement. Suit can be brought for injunctive relief to stop the use of the trade name. The plaintiff owner can also recover all damages and attorneys' fees. If the plaintiff can show a willful infringement, the Lanham Act allows the plaintiff to recover treble damages. Relief by a suit seeking an injunction is also available for using a trademark without authorization in advertising. Recent changes in the law allow a competitor to seek treble damages when its product is used deceptively in a comparative ad.

Federal Trademark Dilution Act and Confused Consumers

In 1995, Congress passed the **Federal Trademark Dilution Act**, a statute that permits recovery and injunctions for "dilution" of distinctive trademarks. The purpose of the law was to prevent others from capitalizing on the recognition, familiarity, and reputation of a distinctive trademark. This is protection for the trademark owner who can establish confusion, that is, that buyers assumed they were purchasing goods or services with the trademark and from the company who owns that trademark. The act covers the problem of blurring or creating confusion among consumers about the source of a product and tarnishing or portraying a product in an unsavory manner.

Moseley, dba Victor's Little Secret, v. *V Secret Catalogue, Inc* (Case 16.3) deals with a trademark dilution issue and also provides the answer to the chapter's opening Consider.

CASE 16.3

Moseley, dba Victor's Little Secret, v. *V Secret Catalogue, Inc.*
537 U.S. 418 (2003)

The Bare Essentials on Trademark Law:
Victor or Victoria's Secret?

FACTS

Victor and Cathy Moseley (petitioners) owned and operated an adult toy, gag gift, and lingerie shop that they called Victor's Little Secret near Elizabethtown, Kentucky. In the February 12, 1998, edition of a weekly publication distributed to residents of the military installation at Fort Knox, Kentucky, the Moseleys advertised the "GRAND OPENING Just in time for Valentine's Day!" of their store "VICTOR'S SECRET" in Elizabethtown. The ad featured "Intimate Lingerie for every woman"; "Romantic Lighting"; "Lycra Dresses"; "Pagers"; and "Adult Novelties/Gifts."

continued

An army colonel, who saw the ad and was offended by what he perceived to be an attempt to use a reputable company's trademark to promote the sale of "unwholesome, tawdry merchandise," sent a copy to Victoria's Secret, Inc. (respondents).

Victoria's Secret owns 750 stores around the country and distributes 400 million catalogs each year via U.S. mail. Victoria's Secret spends $55 million annually on advertising "the VICTORIA'S SECRET brand—one of moderately priced, high quality, attractively designed lingerie sold in a store setting designed to look like a wom[a]n's bedroom." Two of Victoria's Secret's stores were located In Louisville, Kentucky, a short drive from Elizabethtown and Fort Knox.

Legal counsel for Victoria's Secret asked the Moseleys to stop using the name Victor's Secret because of possible confusion over the trademark and resulting dilution. The Moseleys changed the name of their store to Victor's Little Secret. Not satisfied, Victoria's Secret filed suit for dilution of its trademark under the Federal Trademark Dilution Act (FTDA).

The District Court granted summary judgment for Victoria's Secret under the FTDA, and the Sixth Circuit affirmed, finding that the respondents' mark was "distinctive" and that the evidence established "dilution" even though no actual harm had been proved. The Moseleys appealed.

JUDICIAL OPINION

STEVENS, Justice

The record contained uncontradicted affidavits and deposition testimony describing the vast size of respondents' business, the value of the VICTORIA'S SECRET name, and descriptions of the items sold in the respective parties' stores. Respondents sell a "complete line of lingerie" and related items, each of which bears a VICTORIA'S SECRET label or tag. Respondents described their business as follows: "Victoria's Secret stores sell a complete line of lingerie, women's undergarments and nightwear, robes, caftans and kimonos, slippers, sachets, lingerie bags, hanging bags, candles, soaps, cosmetic brushes, atomizers, bath products and fragrances." Petitioners sell a wide variety of items, including adult videos, "adult novelties," and lingerie. In answer to an interrogatory, petitioners stated that they "sell novelty action clocks, patches, temporary tattoos, stuffed animals, coffee mugs, leather biker wallets, zippo lighters, diet formula, diet supplements, jigsaw puzzles, whyss, handcufs [sic], hosiery bubble machines, greeting cards, calendars, incense burners, car air fresheners, sunglasses, ball caps, jewelry, candles, lava lamps, blacklights, fiber optic lights, rock and roll prints, lingerie, pagers, candy, adult video tapes, adult novelties, t-shirts, etc."

Victor Moseley stated in an affidavit that women's lingerie represented only about five percent of their sales. In support of their motion for summary judgment, respondents submitted an affidavit by an expert in marketing who explained "the enormous value" of respondents' mark. Neither he, nor any other witness, expressed any opinion concerning the impact, if any, of petitioners' use of the name "Victor's Little Secret" on that value.

However, the Sixth Circuit held, "While no consumer is likely to go to the Moseleys' store expecting to find Victoria's Secret's famed Miracle Bra, consumers who hear the name 'Victor's Little Secret' are likely automatically to think of the more famous store and link it to the Moseleys' adult-toy, gag gift, and lingerie shop. This, then, is a classic instance of dilution by tarnishing (associating the Victoria's Secret name with sex toys and lewd coffee mugs) and by blurring (linking the chain with a single, unauthorized establishment). Given this conclusion, it follows that Victoria's Secret would prevail in a dilution analysis, even without an exhaustive consideration of all ten of the Nabisco factors."

In reaching that conclusion the Court of Appeals expressly rejected the holding of the Fourth Circuit in *Ringling Bros.-Barnum & Bailey Combined Shows, Inc.* v. *Utah Div. of Travel Development*, 170 F.3d 449 (1999). In that case, which involved a claim that Utah's use on its license plates of the phrase "greatest snow on earth" was causing dilution of the "greatest show on earth," the court had concluded "that to establish dilution of a famous mark under the federal Act requires proof that (1) a defendant has made use of a junior mark sufficiently similar to the famous mark to evoke in a relevant universe of consumers a mental association of the two that (2) has caused (3) actual economic harm to the famous mark's economic value by lessening its former selling power as an advertising agent for its goods or services." Because other Circuits have also expressed differing views about the "actual harm" issue, we granted certiorari to resolve the conflict.

Infringement law protects consumers from being misled by the use of infringing marks and also protects producers from unfair practices by an "imitating competitor."

. . . [w]e decide the case on the assumption that the Moseleys' use of the name "Victor's Little Secret" neither confused any consumers or potential consumers, nor was likely to do so. Neither the absence of any likelihood of confusion nor the absence of competition, however, provides a defense to the statutory dilution claim alleged. . . .

Unlike traditional infringement law, the prohibitions against trademark dilution are not the product of common-law development, and are not motivated by an interest in protecting consumers.

In 1988, when Congress adopted amendments to the Lanham Act, it gave consideration to an antidilution provision. During the hearings on the 1988 amendments, objections to that provision based on a concern that it might have applied to expression protected by the First Amendment were voiced and the provision was deleted from the amendments. The bill, that was introduced in the House in 1995, and ultimately enacted as the FTDA, included two exceptions designed to avoid those concerns: a provision allowing "fair use" of a registered mark in comparative advertising or promotion, and the provision that noncommercial use of a mark shall not constitute dilution.

The relevant text of the FTDA provides that "the owner of a famous mark" is entitled to injunctive relief against another person's commercial use of a mark or trade name if that use "causes dilution of the distinctive quality" of the famous mark. This text unambiguously requires a showing of actual dilution, rather than a likelihood of dilution.

This conclusion is fortified by the definition of the term "dilution" itself. That definition provides:

"The term 'dilution' means the lessening of the capacity of a famous mark to identify and distinguish goods or services, regardless of the presence or absence of—

"(1) competition between the owner of the famous mark and other parties, or

"(2) likelihood of confusion, mistake, or deception."§ 1127.

The contrast between the initial reference to an actual "lessening of the capacity" of the mark, and the later reference to a "likelihood of confusion, mistake, or deception" in the second caveat confirms the conclusion that actual dilution must be established.

Of course, that does not mean that the consequences of dilution, such as an actual loss of sales or profits, must also be proved. To the extent that language in the Fourth Circuit's opinion in the Ringling Bros. case suggests otherwise, we disagree. We do agree, however, with that court's conclusion that, at least where the marks at issue are not identical, the mere fact that consumers mentally associate the junior user's mark with a famous mark is not sufficient to establish actionable dilution. As the facts of that case demonstrate, such mental association will not necessarily reduce the capacity of the famous mark to identify the goods of its owner, the statutory requirement for dilution under the FTDA. For even though Utah drivers may be reminded of the circus when they see a license plate referring to the "greatest snow on earth," it by no means follows that they will associate "the greatest show on earth" with skiing or snow sports, or associate it less strongly or exclusively with the circus. "Blurring" is not a necessary consequence of mental association. (Nor, for that matter, is "tarnishing.")

The record in this case establishes that an army officer who saw the advertisement of the opening of a store named "Victor's Secret" did make the mental association with "Victoria's Secret," but it also shows that he did not therefore form any different impression of the store that his wife and daughter had patronized. There is a complete absence of evidence of any lessening of the capacity of the VICTORIA'S SECRET mark to identify and distinguish goods or services sold in Victoria's Secret stores or advertised in its catalogs. The officer was offended by the ad, but it did not change his conception of Victoria's Secret. His offense was directed entirely at petitioners, not at respondents. Moreover, the expert retained by respondents had nothing to say about the impact of petitioners' name on the strength of respondents' mark.

Noting that consumer surveys and other means of demonstrating actual dilution are expensive and often unreliable, respondents and their amici argue that evidence of an actual "lessening of the capacity of a famous mark to identify and distinguish goods or services" may be difficult to obtain. It may well be, however, that direct evidence of dilution such as consumer surveys will not be necessary if actual dilution can reliably be proved through circumstantial evidence—the obvious case is one where the junior and senior marks are identical. Whatever difficulties of proof may be entailed, they are not an acceptable reason for dispensing with proof of an essential element of a statutory violation. The evidence in the present record is not sufficient to support the summary judgment on the dilution count. The judgment is therefore reversed, and the case is remanded for further proceedings consistent with this opinion.

CASE QUESTIONS

1. Describe the connection between the two companies.

2. What is Victoria's Secret concerned about?

3. What do they have to prove to get an injunction under the FTDA?

4. Why does Victoria's Secret argue against that burden of proof?

FOR THE MANAGER'S DESK

Re: Surveys and Trademark Confusion

Consumer surveys have become a critical part of infringement trials. Where the issue is whether the public has been misled by a trademark infringement, the responses of a representative sample are critical evidence in a case. One such case involved a survey of consumers in twenty-four shopping malls nationwide. The Baltimore Colts had become the Indianapolis Colts, and the Canadian Football League proposed calling one of its teams the Baltimore CFL Colts. The survey showed consumers were confused, and the data carried the case for the former Baltimore Colts's owners.

CONSIDER . . .   16.5

Nautilus and ICON are direct competitors in the market for home exercise equipment. Both produce resistance training systems that use bendable rods. In Nautilus's product, the Bowflex exerciser, the rods are arranged vertically; when a user pulls on a cable connected to the upper ends of the rods, the rods curve or "bow" outward. The rods are structured to resist this outward movement, requiring exertion by the user.

Nautilus has continuously produced the Bowflex exerciser since 1984 and holds two patents on related technology. Nautilus registered the trademark for the Bowflex brand in 1986. Since 1993, when Nautilus began to directly market its Bowflex exerciser to consumers, the company has invested in excess of $233 million in promotion efforts. Nautilus's advertising has focused on infomercials, the Internet, and print publications. As a result, over 780,000 machines have been sold, with total revenues to Nautilus of $900 million.

In 2002, ICON introduced a competing rod-based resistance training system it called CrossBow. In the CrossBow exerciser, the bendable rods are arranged horizontally so that they bend downward, in an inverted U-shape, rather than outward, as in Bowflex's vertical rod configuration. According to ICON, the product's resemblance to the medieval crossbow weapon inspired the brand name. In ICON's two-line logo for the machine, the "o" in "Cross" is replaced by a circular crosshairs. Beneath the mark, in smaller type, appears an additional line, "by Weider," signaling the machine's source. Since it introduced the CrossBow exerciser, ICON has spent $13 million on marketing in many of the same advertising channels as Nautilus, including infomercials and the Internet.

Nautilus commenced a suit for patent infringement against ICON. Is there infringement? What must Nautilus establish? [*Nautilus Group, Inc. v. ICON Health and Fitness, Inc.,* 372 F.3d 1330 (Fed.Cir. 2004).]

MAKING ETHICS PERSONAL

A Hairy Situation on Knock-Off Goods

At your hair salon, you notice collections of Gucci, Louis Vuitton, and Fendi handbags, wallets, and briefcases in several glass display cases. As you examine them, you find that no article is priced over $68. You know that no item in any of the genuine collections is priced at or below $68 (key chains and small change purses excluded). Would you buy any of the items for yourself? For gifts? Would you report the salon to anyone? Is it fair to those foreign manufacturers to have these sales of knock-off goods?

Trade Dress

A more recent and critical aspect of the Lanham Act is the concept of **trade dress**. Trade dress consists of the colors, designs, and shapes associated with a product. If someone copies the color schemes and shapes, they are likely to benefit from the goodwill of the owner and developer of the trade dress. The subtle copying of trade dress dilutes the value of the company's goodwill and reputation. In *Two Pesos, Inc. v. Taco Cabana, Inc.*, 505 U.S. 763 (1992), the U.S. Supreme Court resolved issues related to trade dress infringement. In the case, Taco Cabana, Inc., which operated a chain of fast-food restaurants in Texas that serve Mexican food, had opened in San Antonio and had the following trade dress:

> *A festive eating atmosphere having interior dining and patio areas decorated with artifacts, bright colors, paintings and murals. The patio includes interior and exterior areas with the interior patio capable of being sealed off from the outside patio by overhead garage doors. The stepped exterior of the building is a festive and vivid color scheme using top border paint and neon stripes. Bright awnings and umbrellas continue the theme.*

Two Pesos opened its first restaurant in Houston. Its motif was very similar to Taco Cabana's motif. Two Pesos expanded rapidly in Houston, and Taco Cabana entered the Houston and Austin markets. The two chains also ended up in head-to-head competition in Dallas, and a trade dress infringement suit resulted. The U.S. Supreme Court held that a claim of trade dress infringement requires proof of the same elements as trademark infringement. That is, a company must show that its trade dress is distinctive and that consumers are likely to be confused by the similarity.

In *Wal-Mart v. Samara*, 529 U.S. 205 (2000), the U.S. Supreme Court limited its ruling in *Two Pesos* to product packaging and held that there is no trade dress protection for product design absent some form of registration under federal law such as trademark or patent or the product design having achieved some level of distinctiveness. In the case, Samara designed, produced, and sold a line of seersucker children's clothes with bold appliques and large collars. Wal-Mart had introduced its own line of clothing that was similar. Product design trade dress enjoys no inherent protection. Product packaging, which the court noted was involved in *Two Pesos*, does enjoy protection, as in the shape of a Coca-Cola bottle. However, absent some other statutory protection, product design, with the exception of famous designers such as Tommy Hilfiger, Ralph Lauren, and Izod, requires legislative change for protection.

High–Tech Infringement and Reverse Engineering: Special Status for Semiconductor Chips

The Semiconductor Chip Protection Act of 1984 (17 U.S.C. §§ 901 *et seq.*) provides intellectual property protection for a new form of property in the computer age: the semiconductor chip. The act permits civil recovery and penalties of up to $250,000 for chip piracy, which includes infringing the design of another's chip during the ten-year period in which the chip design and manufacturing stencils enjoy exclusive protection under federal law. Reverse engineering of chips themselves is not prohibited so long as any new products developed as a result are not simply a product of that process of examining a competitor's work. Any design based on reverse engineering must build on the examined design and offer some new innovation or capability.

Trademarks and the Internet: Infringement

What are the rights of search engines such as Netscape and Excite to use the symbols and trademarks of companies to direct Internet users to sites that are not affiliated with the trademark owners? Playboy Enterprises filed suit against Netscape to stop that search engine's use of the Playboy Bunny symbol in ads that directed Internet users to sites oriented toward sexual content. Netscape benefits when users click onto those sites. However, the use of the Playboy symbol allows Netscape and the sites to capitalize on Playboy's name, advertising, and goodwill. In *Playboy Enterprise, Inc.* v. *Netscape Communications,* 354 F.3d 1020 (9th Cir. 2004), a unanimous Ninth Circuit ruled that such use was an infringement.

Cybersquatting

Cybersquatting is registering sites and domain names that are deceptively or confusingly similar to existing trademarks that belong to others. While the Federal Trademark Dilution Act had been used to halt cybersquatting, Congress enacted the Federal Anticybersquatting Consumer Protection Act (ACPA) in 1999 to prohibit cybersquatting and to offer clear standards of proof as well as remedies for this activity. The remedies available include injunctions to stop use of the name, forfeiture of the name, and recovery of money damages and costs of litigation. While there is a defense of good faith, cybersquatters may not use the intent to compete in good faith as a defense to using a deceptively similar name. For example, in *Victoria's Secret Stores Inc.* v. *Artco,* 194 F. Supp.2d 704 (S.D. Ohio 2002), the court held that the use of the name www.victoriassecrets.net was too confusing with www.victoriassecret.com, and the cybersquatter must halt its use even though his stated intention was simply to get people to come to his site and look at this very competitive lingerie.

The **Internet Corporation for Assigned Names and Numbers** (ICANN) has been the provider of arbitration services for disputes between trademark owners and Internet sites.

C O N S I D E R . . .   1 6 . 6

They can be spotted from a distance. The classic Ferrari design with its lined side panels and hidden headlights is unique. Although the Ferrari name is a registered trademark, the design of the Ferrari is not. Roberts Motor Company designed a car with a look similar to the Ferrari, but the Roberts car would sell for a much lower price. Ferrari brought suit against Roberts, alleging infringement. Is Ferrari correct? Can a nonpatented, noncopyrighted design belong exclusively to Ferrari? [*Ferrari* v. *Roberts Motor Co.,* 944 F.2d 1235 (6th Cir. 1991), *cert. denied,* 505 U.S. 1219 (1992).]

THINK: The protections for design require proof that consumers would be confused about the product, that they would likely think the Roberts car was a Ferrari. Also, where the products are the same and one company seeks to draw upon the advertising and goodwill of the other, the confusion and damages are more easily established.

APPLY: If Ferrari is able to show confusion, it can halt the design and seek damages. But proof of that confusion is necessary to seek a remedy for design infringement. Would your answer be the same if Avanti Motor Corporation designed and built a new vehicle that looks like General Motors' Hummer?

ANSWER: The court held that (1) the automobile designs had acquired secondary meaning; (2) there was likelihood of confusion between plaintiff's cars and defendant's replicas; and that (3) injunction granted by district court was proper.

C O N S I D E R . . .   **1 6 . 7**

During his double-homicide trial, Orenthal James Simpson applied for trademark registration for his widely used nicknames, O.J. and Juice. Joseph J. Gleason, vice president and general counsel of Florida Citrus Mutual, a trade group, responded, "I'd question if he could copyright something that generic."

Are the nicknames entitled to trademark and trade name protection? The trade names and trademarks will be used for the merchandising of Simpson products. Mr. Simpson was acquitted of the double homicide charges against him for the killing of his ex-wife, Nicole Brown, and her friend Ronald Goldman but was later held liable monetarily in a civil suit for wrongful death. His name and nicknames became household words because of the notoriety of the trial. Evaluate the likelihood of Mr. Simpson obtaining the trademarks.

C O N S I D E R . . .   **1 6 . 8**

Jim Henson Productions created a new character, Spa'am, a high priest of the wild boars, which is a group of boars that worship Miss Piggy, another Henson creation and a pig puppet. The movie *Muppet Treasure Island* introduced Spa'am as a character and also as a stuffed animal toy for children to purchase. Spa'am acts childish.

Hormel Foods Corporation brought suit against Henson Productions, alleging that the new character will cause the public to spurn Spam, Hormel's popular luncheon meat. Hormel's suit asked for an injunction against Henson Productions to prohibit it from releasing the movie until the character's name was changed. Hormel spokesman Alan Krejci notes, "Henson Productions is seeking to use our trademark . . . for monetary gain." Should the injunction be granted? Are the puppet and its name infringements of the Spam trademark?

Exhibit 16.1 provides a summary of intellectual property rights and protections.

EXHIBIT   16.1   Summary of Intellectual Property Rights

TYPE OF INTELLECTUAL PROPERTY	TRADEMARKS	COPYRIGHTS	PATENTS	TRADE SECRETS
Protection	Words, names, symbols, or devices used to identify a product or service	Original creative works of authorship, such as writings, movies, records, and computer software	Utility, design, and plant patents	Advantageous formulas, devices, or compilation of information
Applicable standard	Identifies and distinguishes a product or service	Original creative works in writing or in another format	New and non-obvious advances in the art	Not readily ascertainable, not disclosed to the public
Where to apply	Patent and Trademark Office	Register of Copyrights	Patent and Trademark Office	No public registration necessary
Duration	Indefinite so long as it continues to be used	Life of author plus 70 years; corporate is 120 years from creation or 95 years from publication of the work	Utility and plant patents, 20 years from date of application; design patents, 14 years	Indefinite so long as secret is not disclosed to public

Source: Adapted from *Anderson's Business Law,* © 2001 by David Twaney, Marianne Jennings, and Ivan Fox.

BUSINESS STRATEGY APPLICATION

Be sure to do the exercise for this chapter on the book's Web site. Based on your knowledge of protections discussed in this chapter, you have a chance to develop policies for a company to help it protect its intellectual property rights.

INTERNATIONAL INTELLECTUAL PROPERTY ISSUES

Patent Protection

A patent in the United States affords protection for inventors only in the United States. To ensure international protection, the inventor needs to register the patent in each country where he will be selling the product or idea.

The period for patent protection varies from country to country. The United States does not permit patent protection for products until the patent is granted, whereas other countries afford protection from the time application is made. Procedures for obtaining patents also vary significantly from country to country. For example, many countries hold **opposition proceedings** as part of the patent process. Much like the federal regulatory promulgation steps (see Chapter 6), the description of the patent is published, and the public is invited to study the description and possibly oppose the granting of a patent.

Some countries impose **working requirements** on the patent holder, which means that the idea or product must be produced commercially within a certain period of time or the patent protection is revoked.

Trademark Protection

In the United States, trademarks are registered to afford protection. However, like patents, the U.S. registration is effective only in the United States. For protection in other countries, a trademark must be registered (if the country affords the protection of registration). In some countries, known as common law countries, trademark protection is established through use in that country and through the recognition by others of the use and distinction provided by the trademark. In the United States, protection for trademarks is afforded without actually introducing the product on the market. Beginning on November 16, 1989, companies could register trademarks without first marketing the product. This change was made for purposes of competition in international markets because European protection begins at the time of application, which can be before the product is used or marketed.

Visit the World Intellectual Property Organization:
http://www.wipo.int

Several international registries attempt to offer international protection. For example, the 1891 **Madrid Agreement** Concerning the International Registration of Trademarks provides a central form of registration through the International Bureau, which is part of the World Intellectual Property Organization (WIPO) in Geneva, Switzerland. Registrations with the bureau are effective for five years in all member countries unless one of the members objects to the trademark registration, in which case the registration is not effective in that country. In addition, the United States is a party to the 1929 **Pan American Convention**, which includes a provision affording trademark protection in all member countries.

In 1989, a diplomatic convention in Madrid resulted in the adoption of the Madrid Protocol Concerning the International Registration of Marks, which created WIPO. WIPO would serve, for those countries participating in the Madrid Protocol

BIOGRAPHY

CALVIN KLEIN AND LINDA WACHNER: A BATTLE OF JEANS AT PRICE CLUB

One of the most dramatic intellectual property suits of this era involved Calvin Klein and Linda Wachner, head of the Warnaco Group. Mr. Klein sued Warnaco, the licensed manufacturer for Calvin Klein jeans, because he said that Warnaco exceeded its licensing authority for the trademark jeans by selling them to warehouse clubs where they were sold at discount prices. Mr. Klein said the sales diminished the value of the Calvin Klein trademark, and he called Ms. Wachner "a cancer on the value and integrity of my business." He also referred to Ms. Wachner as "vulgar and unprofessional."

Ms. Wachner says that Mr. Klein was simply disturbed by the public revelation that most designers do not manufacture their own clothing but, rather, have mass-market manufacturers handle the production and distribution.

At the time the suit was filed in 2000, Warnaco's stock had declined 83 percent since 1998 and the company was carrying debt of $1.2 billion.

Mr. Klein hired the firm of David Boies (of the Microsoft litigation and *Bush* v. *Gore*) to represent him in his suit to have the license for his jeans returned to him.

Warnaco responded to the suit by alleging that Mr. Klein took action only after he failed to sell his company and that his financial problems could not be solved by "throwing stones at Warnaco." Mr. Klein responded that he could not sell the company because of its affiliation with Warnaco.

By January 2001, the two settled their litigation. The terms of the settlement, announced as the parties left the courtroom just prior to selecting a jury in the case, were sealed, but the parties did disclose that Warnaco agreed to substantially curb its sales of the jeans to warehouse clubs.

However, Warnaco's stock continued to tumble and its troubles mounted as its auditors rebelled on disclosures and its canceled calls with analysts. Its losses mounted and banks were attempting to unload their Warnaco debt for as little as 35 cents on the dollar. By the summer of 2001, Warnaco was in bankruptcy, which many industry insiders called "poetic justice" for Ms. Wachner, Warnaco's CEO since 1986.

Why would Mr. Klein worry about the sales to warehouse clubs? Does a trademark owner have the right to restrict the number of sales and the types of buyers? What business lessons should both sides learn from the dispute and litigation?

For more information: Leslie Kaufman, "Calvin Klein Suit against Warnaco Is Settled," *New York Times*, January 23, 2001, pp. C1, C7.

System established in 1891, as a central clearinghouse for all trademarks. National or local application would also result in WIPO application for participating nations. The system is designed to simplify, streamline, and reduce the costs of international trademark protection.

In 1996, the European Union began its one-stop trademark registration known as Community Trademark (CTM). Under the provisions of this program, U.S. companies register their trademarks once and enjoy protection in all countries that are part of the European Union. The trademark and backup materials are filed with the Office of Harmonization of the Internal Market (OHIM). The OHIM will then notify the trademark offices in each of the member states of the European Union.

Visit BUFETE AF, a Spanish intellectual property law firm, to learn more about the Community Trademark:
http://www.bufeteaf.es

Many countries have permitted the unauthorized use of trademarks in an effort to develop local economies. These countries permit the production of **knock-off goods**, which are goods that carry the trademark or trade name of a firm's product but are not actually produced by that firm. A costly problem for trademark holders is the **gray market**. Manufacturers in foreign countries are authorized to produce a certain amount of goods, but many foreign manufacturers exceed their licensed quota and dump the goods into the market at a much lower price and thereby reduce the trademark owner's market. Such excessive use is an infringement.

CONSIDER...   16.9

Congoleum Corporation holds the American patents for the manufacture of chemically embossed vinyl floor covering and owns corresponding patents in twenty-six foreign countries. Mannington is also involved in the manufacture of vinyl flooring and is authorized to use Congoleum patents in the United States. However, Mannington has just expanded its operations to other countries and is using its license rights in them. Congoleum claims that the patent license for the other countries must be obtained in those countries as well as in the United States. Is Congoleum correct? [*Mannington Mills, Inc.* v. *Congoleum Corp.,* 595 F.2d 1287 (3d Cir. 1979).]

CONSIDER...   16.10

Illia Lekach and Simon Falic are brothers-in-law who founded Perfumania, Inc. Perfumania is a chain of no-frills stores that sells 170 brands of upscale perfumes, such as Estée Lauder, Calvin Klein, and Chanel, at prices 20–70 percent below department store prices. Mr. Lekach referred to the company as the Toys "Я" Us of perfume sales.

Manufacturers of the expensive perfumes like to sell only to their full-price department store customers. Perfumania must get its supplies from the gray market—unauthorized and authorized distributors in other countries where manufacturers charge less than in the United States.

Givenchy, Boucheron, and Cosmair have sued Perfumania for copyright infringement and patent violations. The manufacturers maintain that they must pay the promotion fees on the perfumes and Perfumania enjoys the benefits of the expensive promotions without paying costs. One manufacturer notes, "I don't want to sell to the gray market. It's not a strategy. You kill your name."

Evaluate the legalities and ethics of Perfumania's gray market purchases and discount sales.

Copyrights in International Business

Review the Berne Convention for the Protection of Literary and Artistic Works (Paris Text 1971):

http://www.law.cornell.edu/treaties/berne/overview.html

The United States was a party to the 1986 Berne Convention agreement and made it a part of U.S. copyright law through the **Berne Convention Implementation Act of 1988**. Under the convention and the act, a collective work can bear its own notice of copyright and still afford protection for the individual contributions within the work. Under prior copyright law, each contribution had to carry its own notice to be afforded full protection. These new provisions apply to books, magazines, and records. The purpose of the Berne Convention, called the Convention for the Protection of Literary and Artistic Works, was to establish international uniformity in copyright protection. The convention was signed on September 9, 1986, and became effective in the United States on March 1, 1989. Twenty-four countries are members of Berne, which is administered by WIPO. However, the Berne Convention gives backdoor copyright protection to works originating in non-Berne member countries if the work is simultaneously published in a Berne member country. Presently, some copyright holders are governed under previous U.S. copyright laws, which required separate and collective copyrights for full protection.

Differing International Standards

The protection of intellectual property in other countries is a difficult task, particularly when the standards of those countries do not recognize computer software as a property right.

China has led the world with software piracy. In 1994, the U.S. Trade Representative placed China on its Special 301 Priority Watch List. By February 1995, the United States threatened to impose more than $1 billion in trade sanctions if China did not take action to curb software pirating. In August 1995, the United States and China reached an agreement to prevent the sanctions. China agreed to take immediate action against known software pirates and to confiscate software packages without seals that U.S. companies would place on their software packages and materials. China remains on the trade watch list as the cultural change for appreciation of ownership rights with respect to computer programs takes place.

ENFORCING BUSINESS PROPERTY RIGHTS

Product Disparagement

When an untrue statement is made about a business product or service, the defamation is referred to as **disparagement** and is either **trade libel** (written) or **slander of title** (oral). These business torts occur when one business makes untrue statements about another business, its product, or its abilities. The elements for disparagement follow:

1. False statement about a business product or about its reputation, honesty, or integrity
2. Publication
3. Statement that is directed at a business (in many cases, businesses are considered public figures, and the statement must be made with malice and the intent to injure that business)
4. Damages

These elements are the same as those discussed in Chapter 10 for the personal tort of defamation (see pp. 368–376). *Bose Corporation* v. *Consumers Union of United States, Inc.* (Case 16.4) deals with the tort of disparagement.

Palming Off

Palming off, one of the oldest unfair methods of competition, occurs when one company sells its product by leading buyers to believe it is really another company's product. For example, there were many cases of palming off during the 1980s, when Cabbage Patch dolls were popular, in demand, and scarce. Many replicas were made and called "Cabbage Patch dolls" even though they were not manufactured by Coleco, the original creator.

Establishing that someone is palming off requires proof that there is likely to be confusion because of the appearance or name of the competing product. For

CASE 16.4

Bose Corporation v. *Consumers Union of United States, Inc.*
466 U.S. (1984)

Woofers, Tweeters, and Disparagement

FACTS

Bose Corporation manufactures the Bose 901, a stereo loudspeaker. In May 1970, the Consumers Union publication *Consumer Reports* analyzed and evaluated the middle-range price group of loudspeaker systems, including the Bose 901. It was described in a two-page boxed-off section as "unique and unconventional," but the description also pointed out that a listener could "pinpoint the location of various instruments much more easily with a standard speaker than with the Bose system." The following is an excerpt from the boxed description:

> Worse, individual instruments heard through the Bose system seemed to grow to gigantic proportions and tended to wander about the room. For instance, a violin appeared to be ten feet wide and a piano stretched from wall to wall. With orchestral music, such effects seemed inconsequential. But we think they might become annoying when listening to soloists. . . .
>
> We think the Bose system is so unusual that a prospective buyer must listen to it and judge it for himself. We would suggest delaying so big an investment until you were sure the system would please you after the novelty value had worn off.

The article was not written by the same people who made the observation of the speakers. The observers described the sound as moving around the room and the article described the sounds as wandering back and forth.

Bose Corporation took exception to many of the statements made and asked *Consumer Reports* to publish a retraction. *Consumer Reports* would not retract the statements, and Bose sued for disparagement. The district court found that Bose was a public figure and, as such, was required to prove that the statements were made with knowledge they were false (malice). However, the court did find that some of the remarks constituted disparagement and held for Bose (petitioner). The court of appeals reversed on the grounds that the statements were not made with malice, that the article did not accurately reflect what evaluators heard but

was written for a mass audience and not with reckless disregard for the truth. Bose appealed.

JUDICIAL OPINION

STEVENS, Justice

Respondent (Consumers Union) correctly reminds us that in cases raising First Amendment issues we have repeatedly held that an appellate court has an obligation to "make an independent examination of the whole record" in order to make sure "that the judgment does not constitute a forbidden intrusion on the field of free expression."

. . . There are categories of communication and certain special utterances to which the majestic protection of the First Amendment does not extend because they "are no essential part of any exposition of ideas, and are of such slight social value as a step to truth that any benefit that may be derived from them is clearly outweighed by the social interest in order and morality." Libelous speech has been held to constitute one such category. . . .

We agree with the Court of Appeals that the difference between hearing violin sounds move around the room and hearing them wander back and forth fits easily within the breathing space that gives life to the First Amendment. We may accept all of the purely factual findings of the District Court and nevertheless hold as a matter of law that the record does not contain clear and convincing evidence that [Consumers Union] prepared the loudspeaker article with knowledge that it contained a false statement, or with reckless disregard for the truth.

The judgment of the Court of Appeals is affirmed.

CASE QUESTIONS

1. Who prepared the *Consumer Reports* article?
2. Why is malice an important part of the case?
3. What classes of speech are exceptions to First Amendment protection?
4. Is disparagement a difficult tort to prove?

example, labeling a diamond DeBiers instead of DeBeers is likely to cause confusion. Competitors' packaging with the same colors and design as an original product creates confusion. Potential buyers are likely to be confused as to who actually made the product and who has what market and quality reputation.

Misappropriation

Some businesses have a **trade secret**—chemical formula, procedure, customer list, data, or device that only that business has. Generally, these types of secrets should be given patent or copyright protection. However, those that do not qualify for these federal statutory protections (discussed earlier in this chapter) have only the tort of **misappropriation** as protection. Misappropriation occurs when a competitor figures out the formula for a product or takes a customer list or other data and puts the product or information to use competitively. Misappropriation is conversion of a trade secret, and proof of misappropriation requires that there be some theft, industrial espionage, or bribery as the means used for obtaining the trade secret. These tort actions are in addition to the criminal issues discussed earlier.

WHAT CAN A BUSINESS OWN? REAL PROPERTY

The Nature of Real Property

Land

Real property consists of more than just land itself; it is a bundle of rights. An old saying in property law is, "The owner of the soil owns also to the sky and to the depths." When you own real property, you own the surface that we actually see and upon which buildings are placed, but you also own **air rights** and **mineral rights**.

Air Rights

Air rights in real property consist of the right to use the air above the surface land that is described as your real property interest. Your land interest can actually be separated into two interests so that you can keep the surface rights and transfer the air rights. The ownership of air rights is important in large cities because building up is the only way to expand available space in cities limited in opportunities for expansion on the ground. For example, in New York City, the Met Life building is built in the air rights above Grand Central Station. This fifty-nine-story building occupies the air rights above the station. The foundation of the building rests on the surface of the land through an **easement**, or a right to use the land of another for a limited purpose.

The sale of the air space above one's surface land can be profitable. In cities in which horizontal growth is limited, the only means of expansion for businesses is to build vertically. Excessive demand coupled with a finite supply make air space rights extremely valuable. In Los Angeles, the air space above the owned surface rights has its own value for which property taxes are assessed. Some businesses purchase air rights for possible future expansion and simply hold the rights until their expansion occurs.

There are limitations on air rights. All property owners take their air rights subject to the right of flight. Airplanes may use the air lots over your property in travel without committing trespass and without being required to pay compensation.

Mineral Rights

Mineral rights are rights to what rests below the surface of land. Examples of valuable commodities that a landowner can own beneath a property's surface include oil, gas, coal, geothermal energy pockets, and water. Just as with air rights, these subsurface rights can be transferred separately. The right to drill for oil and gas can be conveyed to another (possibly in exchange for royalty payments) and the surface rights retained. Those who purchase the mineral rights are again given an easement for access to the property for drilling.

Fixtures

Yet another form of real property rights crosses personal property with real property. **Fixtures** are a part of the property that were once personal property but have become a part of the land or a structure on the land. For example, a microwave oven is personal property when it is purchased from a store. But if that oven is installed in a home in a place built especially for it and is bolted to the walls or cabinets in the kitchen, it becomes a part of the real property. Fixtures often create confusion in the transfer of real property, as the parties disagree over whether the personal property was intended to become a part of the real property. The following important questions can help determine whether an item is personal property or a fixture and thus part of the real property.

1. What did the parties intend? If the parties have agreed that an item is a fixture, it will be treated as such. For example, draperies in a home are a frequent source of disagreement among buyers and sellers over whether they stay with the home or go with the seller. If the contract includes draperies, they are treated as fixtures and will transfer with the home to the buyer.

2. How is the item attached to the real property? The greater the degree of attachment and the more the item has become a part of the real property, the greater the likelihood that it will be classified as a fixture. One exception to this general rule is the classification of **trade fixtures**. Many forms of personal property that a business uses will be attached to the real property, but they are a part of the business and are not intended to remain a part of the real property. Retail stores have counters bolted to the floor. These counters are an integral part of the store, but they are trade fixtures and would be classified as personal property and not a part of the real property.

3. What is the relationship between the attacher and the property? Who attached the fixture to the real property, and is the attacher a tenant or a landowner? Shelves attached by a tenant are probably not intended to remain as part of the real property. Those same shelves attached by a homeowner would probably

---

 CONSIDER...   16.11

Consider the following items and determine whether the items would be fixtures or personal property. Assume that the parties have not reached an agreement on the nature of the fixtures.

1. A pipe organ installed in a building owned and operated by Organ Stop Pizza. Organ Stop Pizza features an organist each night who works with the patrons to play appropriate music and offer entertainment to children. What additional information would help you determine whether the organ would be a fixture and real property or just personal property?

2. Refrigerators, washers, and dryers found in the apartments of a twenty-unit complex a buyer has just purchased.

3. The garage door opener and keys to a house just purchased.

4. A neon sign purchased by a tattoo parlor and installed above the door of its leased premises in a strip mall.

5. The color-coordinated bedspreads and curtains in a hotel just sold.

be classified as a fixture. A commercial tenant is different from a residential tenant because of the rules about trade fixtures being personal property.

4. **Who wants to know?** Courts vary in their classifications of fixtures according to who is asking whether an item is a fixture. If an insurer is seeking classification of an item as personal property so that an insurance claim for damage to the real property is less, the courts will probably find in favor of the insured and classify the item as a fixture. For assessments of value for property tax purposes, the courts label items as fixtures more frequently because of the increased value to the real property they bring.

Interests in Real Property

There are various forms of ownership interests in real property. The highest degree of land ownership is called a **fee simple** interest. If a company or individual has a fee simple interest in property, it owns full rights to the property and has the freedom to mortgage the property, sell the property, and, in the case of individuals, transfer the property by will.

A lesser degree of real property ownership is the **life estate**. In this form of real property interest, one person is given the right to use and occupy the property for life. When that person, the **life tenant**, dies, the property either goes back to the grantor (the person who originally transferred it) or, in most cases, to another person—called the **remainderman**. Generally, the remainderman receives a fee simple interest. The life estate is used often in estate planning. A surviving spouse is given a life estate in the family residence with the couple's children (remaindermen) receiving the fee simple interest when the spouse passes away.

> **BUSINESS PLANNING TIP**
>
> Before purchasing property, check the area for noise and other activity. Determine flight paths and plans for construction of airports, runways, and possible expansion of airport capacity and facilities.

Another real property interest is the **easement**, which is a right to use another's property. *Access easements* permit the owner of the easement to use a path or road on another's property in order to gain access to her own real property. In *negative easements,* a property owner promises the easement holder that he will not, for example, plant trees that will block sunlight from the solar panels on the easement holder's property. *Easements in gross,* which run through most properties, are held by utility companies and give them the right to run wires and pipes through segments of property so individual property owners and the surrounding community can enjoy utility service.

A final form of real property interest is the **lease**, which is temporary possession of real property. A lease can be a fixed lease in which there is a beginning and ending date, or the lease can be a **periodic tenancy** in which the landlord and tenant go from period to period renewing the lease. For example, a month-to-month tenancy is a form of periodic tenancy in which a tenant pays rent on a given day each month and thereby renews the lease. To end a periodic tenancy, the other party must be given a full period's notice of termination. If the rent in a periodic tenancy is paid on the first day of each month and the tenant wishes to end the lease, notice must be given on the first of the month. If, for example, a tenant notified the landlord on October 15 that the tenant wished to terminate the lease, the tenant's obligation to pay rent continues through November because the tenant will not have given a full period's notice until the end of November.

A lease for a fixed period has the benefit of fixed rent that cannot be changed until the lease is over. A periodic tenant's rent can be raised at any time once a full period's notice is given.

FOR THE MANAGER'S DESK

RE: SOLAR EASEMENTS

One form of easement that is negotiated in more and more sales contracts today is the solar easement. Under common law, there is no "right to light"; someone can build a building next to your property that blocks all of your light and not be liable for any damages. In the case of *Fontainebleau Hotel Corp. v. Forty-Five Twenty-Five, Inc.*, 114 So.2d 357 (Fla. 1959), a Miami hotel could not obtain relief from a court when the neighboring property owner constructed a fourteen-story addition to its existing hotel that blocked the afternoon sun from the plaintiff hotel's swimming pool and sunbathing areas. The court held that absent an agreement, there were no restrictions on the blockage of light.

However, with a properly negotiated contract, the right to light can be obtained and protected. The contract can specify that the seller gives a solar easement or right of light to the buyer, or neighbors can agree to a solar easement among themselves. Even residential property owners can benefit from solar easement clauses, particularly when they have a solar heating system that requires the panels of the system to be near direct sunlight to maximize efficiency.

Some cities have passed ordinances that prevent solar panel obstruction. Often a part of zoning laws, these ordinances give the solar system owner a statutory right of light. In these cities, title insurance companies physically inspect neighboring properties for solar systems so that they can exclude solar easements from their policy or offer additional insurance for increased "solar premium."

Most states have full statutory provisions on residential leases, and many have requirements on commercial leases. These statutory provisions cover such issues as the condition of the property when the lease begins, maintenance, security deposits, and when lease agreements must be in writing to be enforceable.

Transferring Real Property

The transfer of real property is more complex than the transfer of personal property. Real property is transferred through a document called a **deed**. A deed must be in writing, it must be signed by the owner (grantor) of the property, and it must contain a full legal description of the property in order to transfer title to real property.

There are several different types of deeds. The type of deed determines the degree of title protection the transferor or grantor gives the transferee. A **warranty deed** or **general warranty deed** provides the highest degree of title protection from the grantor. When the grantor gives the grantee a warranty deed, he promises that he has good title, that he has the authority to transfer title, and that there are no liens or title problems other than anything noted on the deed. A deed may include a qualification, "subject to public utility easements," which means that the grantee takes the title subject to the utility easements through the property.

A **special warranty deed** or **bargain and sale deed** is one in which the grantor makes the same promises as under a warranty deed but does so only for the time during which she held title to the property. In this form of deed, the grantor is simply saying that she did nothing during her ownership of the property to cloud the title. Most buyers elect to purchase **title insurance**, a policy that affords reimbursement to the buyer in the event a title defect arises after the purchase. Title insurance is protection in addition to the grantor's promises, but it covers only defects in title that are of record, such as tax liens and easements.

A **quitclaim deed** carries no warranties about the title to the land. In effect, the grantor in a quitclaim deed is saying, "I hereby transfer whatever interest I have in this real property, but there is no guarantee that I hold any interest in this property." The quitclaim deed is often used in situations where someone is trying to clear title to property and obtains quitclaim deeds from many individuals who might or might not have a claim on title.

While the delivery of a complete and signed deed is all that is necessary to transfer title to real property, the process of **recording** is done in nearly all property transfers. Recording is the filing of the deed with a government agency, usually a county recorder or county clerk, so that public notice is given of the transfer of ownership. The risk of not recording a deed is that the grantor could make a subsequent transfer of the land, and, depending upon particular state statutes, the original grantee could lose title to the land to that subsequent transferee.

Title to real property can be transferred in other ways. Real property can be transferred by will, and heirs obtain title through the probate of the estate (still by use of a deed). Title to land can also be transferred through **adverse possession**. Adverse possession is use of another's land for a statutory period of time (generally ranging from ten to twenty years) in an open manner. In effect, what begins as a trespass can ripen into title if the owner of the land takes no action to remove a trespasser from the land. Often called *squatter's rights,* adverse possession can occur in situations as simple as placing a fence incorrectly along a property's border. If the fence encroaches on a neighbor's land by six inches, and the fence remains there for twenty years, the fence builder acquires title to those extra six inches by adverse possession. Parties who succeed each other in land interests, such as a daughter inheriting from a father or a buyer purchasing from a seller, can add together their years of adverse possession to qualify for ownership. This is called *tacking.* A buyer who buys land from a seller who has owned it for ten years and used adjoining property adversely needs only ten more years to claim ownership in a twenty-year jurisdiction.

Financing Real Property Purchases

The purchase of real property is a major transaction for individuals and businesses. Most property buyers are unable to pay cash for their property. Financing arrangements that allow the creditor to take a lien on the purchased property have existed since English common law. The most common form of property security for a creditor is the **mortgage**. In this form of security, a borrower pledges property to the lender as security for the debt that arises because the lender advances the money for purchase of the property. In the event the buyer/borrower does not make the necessary payments to the lender, the lender can foreclose on the mortgage. **Foreclosure** is a judicial process in which the lender takes possession and title of mortgaged property and then sells it to satisfy the unpaid debt.

Another form of creditor security for real property purchases is the **deed of trust**. Popular in the western states, this form of security places title to property in the hands of a trustee, who holds title until a debtor repays the creditor the full amount of the debt. If the debtor defaults on payments, the trustee may then proceed to sell the property to satisfy the debt. The deed of trust financing arrangement is beneficial to lenders because judicial foreclosure is not required in order to hold a property sale.

Because of the importance of these interests and the need to have priority over subsequent real property creditors, mortgages and deeds of trust are also recorded in the public offices where deeds and other land interests are recorded.

SUMMARY

What does a business own? What are the types of business property?

- Tangible property—physical: real and personal property
- Intangible property—bundles of rights with respect to goodwill, trade names, copyrights, patents, trade dress, and trade secrets
- Real property—bundles of rights with respect to land, attachments, air space, and subsurface materials

What are the rights and issues in personal property owned by a business?

- Documents of title—formal legal document that serves to prove and transfer title to tangible personal property
- Bill of sale—informal document or contract that serves to prove and transfer title to tangible personal property
- Lease—right of use and possession of property for fixed or open-ended period
- Bailment—temporary transfer of possession of personal property
- Bailor—party who owns property and surrenders possession
- Bailee—party who has temporary possession of the property of another
- License—right granted of access; generally oral; personal right that is nontransferrable
- Exculpatory clause—clause that attempts to hold a party harmless in the event of damage or injury to another or another's property
- Lien—creditor's right in property to secure debt
- Security interest—UCC lien on personal property
- Chattel mortgage—term for lien on personal property
- Uniform Commercial Code (UCC)—uniform statute governing commercial transactions adopted in forty-nine states
- Security agreement—contract that creates a security interest
- Collateral—property subject to lien, security interest, or chattel mortgage
- Financing statement—publicly filed document reflecting security interest

What statutory protections exist for intellectual property?

- Patents—statutory protection for products and processes
- Copyrights—statutory protection for words, thoughts, ideas, music
- Trademarks—statutory protection for product symbols
- Trade names—statutory protection for unique product labels and names
- Trade dress—statutory protection for product colors and motifs
- Trade secrets—criminal sanctions for unauthorized transfer or use

What issues of intellectual property protection exist in international operations?

- OPTH—European Community Trademark registration
- WIPO—World Intellectual Property Organization

What private remedies exist for property protections?

- Product disparagement—false and damaging statements
- Misappropriation—use of another's ideas or trade secrets
- Palming off—causing deception about the maker or source of a product

What are real property interests, and what rights are included?

- Air rights—rights of surface owner to air above land surface
- Mineral rights—rights of surface owner to materials beneath the land surface
- Easement—right or privilege in the land of another
- Fixtures—property that was once personal in nature that is affixed to real property and becomes a part of it
- Trade fixtures—personal property used in a trade or business that is attached to real property but is considered personal property
- Fee simple—highest degree of land ownership; full rights of mortgage and transferability

- Life estate—right to use and occupy property for life
- Remainderman—interest in third party following a life estate
- Lease—temporary possession and use of real property
- Periodic tenancy—lease that runs from period to period such as month to month
- Warranty deed—highest level of title protection in real property transfer
- Special warranty deed—promises of title protection only for grantor's period of ownership

- Bargain and sale deed—a special warranty deed
- Title insurance—insurance purchased for buyer's benefit of land title
- Quitclaim deed—transfer of title with no warranties
- Recording—public filing of land documents
- Adverse possession—acquisition of land title through use for statutory period
- Mortgage—lien on real property
- Foreclosure—process of creditor's acquiring mortgaged land for resale
- Deed of trust—alternative form of creditor security in land purchase

QUESTIONS AND PROBLEMS

1. Lotus 1–2–3 is a spreadsheet program that enables users to perform accounting functions electronically on a computer. Users manipulate and control the program with a series of menu commands such as "Copy," "Print," and "Quit." Lotus 1–2–3 has 469 commands arranged into more than 50 menus and submenus and includes what is known as a "macro" feature. Users can write a series of command choices that can then be executed with a single keystroke.

Borland introduced its Quattro spreadsheet program in 1987, after three years of development work by its engineers. Borland's objective was to build a superior spreadsheet program and take over the market, but its product contains an identical copy of the entire Lotus 1–2–3 menu tree. Borland does not dispute its inclusion; it simply notes that the Quattro system builds on the Lotus commands.

Lotus filed suit against Borland for infringement. Borland removed the interface part of its program, but Lotus contends the commands in the Quattro program are virtually the same as the Lotus program—just the first letters are different. Borland maintains the menus are not protected by copyright. Should they be protected? [*Lotus Dev. Corp.* v. *Borland Int'l., Inc.*, 49 F.3d 807 (1st Cir. 1995); *cert. granted*, 515 U.S. 1191 (1995). The Supreme Court deadlocked on the merits, resulting in an affirmance by an equally divided court; 516 U.S. 233 (1996).]

2. Storck Candy manufactures Werther's Original Butter Toffee Candy. The toffee is sold in an eight-ounce bag with a brown background, a picture of a mound of unwrapped candy, an Alpine village, and an old-fashioned container pouring white liquid.

Farley Candy Company introduced its butter toffee candy in a bag the same size and shape as Werther's, with a pair of containers pouring liquid.

Storck says that Farley is using its trade dress to sell the Farley candy. Has Farley done anything that is a tort? Do federal laws offer protection? [*Storck USA, L.P.* v. *Farley Candy Co., Inc.*, 785 F. Supp. 730 (N.D. Ill. 1992).]

3. Tommy Hilfiger Licensing, Inc. ("Hilfiger") is the owner of the world-famous TOMMY HILFIGER and flag design trademarks used in connection with the sale of numerous high-end products, including fragrances. The flag design mark is comprised of a combination of red, white, and blue geometric shapes. These marks are federally registered trademarks. Nature Labs, LLC manufactures, markets, and sells a line of pet perfumes whose names parody elegant brands sold for human consumption—Timmy Holedigger (Tommy Hilfiger), CK-9 (Calvin Klein's cK-1), Pucci (Gucci), Bono Sports (Ralph Lauren's Polo Sports), Miss Claybone (Liz Claiborne), and White Dalmations (Elizabeth Taylor's White Diamonds). Nature Labs' initial spoof of Hilfiger was called Tommy Holedigger and had a flag-shaped label with side-by-side red and white squares bordered on top and bottom by a blue stripe with white letters. Hilfiger complained that this use infringed its marks. Nature Labs then changed the name to Timmy Holedigger and changed the label to its present form: inverted side-by-side yellow and red triangles bordered on top and bottom by a blue stripe with white letters. Beneath the new logo design, the following phrase appears: "If You Like Tommy Hilfiger Your Pet Will Love Timmy Holedigger." Neither party performed a disciplined olfactory comparison or chemical analysis, but John Harris, the general partner of Nature Labs, testified at his deposition that the two scents are similar, based on his recollection of Hilfiger cologne. An asterisk following the words "Tommy Hilfiger" references a disclaimer in red type on the back label, which states, "This imitation fragrance is not related to Tommy Hilfiger Licensing, Inc." Another current version of the product, a two-ounce bottle being marketed primarily to PetCo, changes the flag-shape label to a bone with red and yellow triangles and a thick blue border. Tommy Hilfiger Licensing, Inc. brought suit for trademark infringement, trademark dilution, false designation of origin, and false advertising. Can Tommy Hilfiger stop the production and sale of the Nature Labs' Timmy Holedigger? [*Tommy Hilfiger Licensing, Inc.* v. *Nature Labs, LLC* 221 F.Supp.2d 410 (S.D. N.Y. 2002).]

4. Robert Conroy invented and holds the patent for "inflatable bladders used in athletic footgear." The patent is called "Athletic Armor and Inflatable Bag Assembly." The "Bladders" can be inflated with air to cushion and protect the feet of athletic shoe wearers.

Reebok International, Ltd., manufactures a basketball shoe with inflatable bladders that it sells under the name of the PUMP. Mr. Conroy brought suit, claiming Reebok infringed his patent. Reebok says the design and method of inflation are different from Mr. Conroy's patented system. Mr. Conroy says the idea of an inflatable shoe is his and he is entitled to royalties from Reebok. Is Mr. Conroy correct? [*Conroy* v. *Reebok International, Ltd.,* 29 U.S. P. Q.2d 1373 (Mass. 1994).]

5. Roger Burten submitted his "Triumph" electronic game to Milton Bradley for possible mass production, but it was rejected twice after review. One year later, however, Milton Bradley began marketing a new electronic board game under the name of "Dark Tower." There were structural and design similarities between "Triumph" and "Dark Tower." Mr. Burten brought suit for fraud, breach of contract, and trade secret misappropriation. Can Mr. Burten recover under any of these theories? [*Burten* v. *Milton Bradley Co.,* 763 F.2d 461 (1st Cir. 1985).]

6. Vanna White is the hostess of *Wheel of Fortune*, one of the most popular game shows in television history. An estimated 40 million people watch the program daily. Capitalizing on the fame that her participation in the show has bestowed on her, Ms. White markets her identity to various advertisers.

Samsung Electronics ran a series of ads in at least six publications with widespread, and in some cases national, circulation. Each of the advertisements in the series followed the same theme: Each depicted a current item from popular culture and a Samsung electronic product. Each was set in the twenty-first century and conveyed the message that the Samsung product would still be in use at that future time. By hypothesizing outrageous future outcomes for the cultural items, the ads created humorous effects. For example, one lampooned current popular notions of an unhealthy diet by depicting a raw steak with the caption: "Revealed to be health food. 2010 A.D." Another depicted irreverent

"news" show host Morton Downey Jr. in front of an American flag with the caption: "Presidential candidate. 2008 A.D."

The advertisement that prompted a dispute was for Samsung video cassette recorders (VCRs). The ad depicted a robot dressed in a wig, gown, and jewelry that was consciously selected to resemble Ms. White's hair and dresses. The robot was posed next to a game board instantly recognizable as the *Wheel of Fortune* game show set in a stance for which Ms. White is famous. The caption of the ad read: "Longest-running game show. 2012 A.D." Samsung executives referred to the ad as the "Vanna White ad." Unlike the other celebrities used in the campaign, Ms. White neither consented to the ads nor was paid. Have Ms. White's rights been violated? Did Samsung violate federal law? [*White* v. *Samsung Elect. Am., Inc.,* 971 F.2d 1395 (9th Cir. 1992).]

7. Spuds MacKenzie is a ring-eyed dog known as the mascot/trademark for Bud Light beer. Beneath Spuds's picture, the following line appears: "The original Party Animal." Another company has begun using the slogan. Anheuser-Busch claims the slogan is a trademark for Bud. Is Anheuser-Busch correct? [*In Re Anheuser-Busch,* No. 17,939, slip op. (May 16, 1990).]

8. Freddie Fuddruckers, Inc. uses glass-enclosed bakeries and butcher areas exposed to the public to emphasize its freshness as a decor theme in all its Fuddruckers restaurants. Fuddruckers floors are checkered, walls tiled, and lighting bright to communicate cleanliness and quality. Ridgeline opened its restaurants with nearly identical decor. Does Fuddruckers have any rights? [*Freddie Fuddruckers, Inc.* v. *Ridgeline, Inc.,* 589 F. Supp. 72 (1984).]

9. Do the following slogans constitute protectable business properties?
  a. MetLife: "Get Met, It Pays"
  b. General Electric: "GE Brings Good Things to Life"
  c. Nike: "Just Do It"
  d. Toys "Я" Us: "Я Us"

10. Starbucks, Inc., the international coffee house, is an aggressive defender of its name as well as the names for its coffees. It has ongoing litigation for infringement.

- A & D Café of Brooklyn, New York, uses the name "Warbucks" for its coffee, and Starbucks has filed suit against the Café for dilution of its trade name.

- Sambuck's Coffee House of Astoria, Oregon, has been sued by Starbucks for dilution. However, the owner of the café is Samantha Buck-Lundberg, and she explains that the name of the café is a play on her name.

- Black Bear Monster Roastery in New Hampshire uses the name "Charbucks Blend" for one of its coffees, and Starbucks has filed suit for disparagement.

- Backwash.com had a link to Starbucks on its Web site. Starbucks filed suit to have the link removed, which Backwash did, citing "unappreciative" reasons.

- Coffee Bean & Tea Leaf Co. of Los Angeles has sued Starbucks for trademark infringement for the com-

pany's use of the term "ice blended," a term that the LA company claims it coined.[3]

What protections exist for trade names? For trademarks? Do you think there is infringement in these cases?

RESEARCH PROBLEM

It's a Wonderful Life, but Whose Is It? Using Property Rights to Preserve Earnings

11. In 1946, director Frank Capra produced *It's a Wonderful Life,* a movie based on a short story by Philip Van Doren Stern called "The Greatest Gift." The movie, starring Jimmy Stewart, did not perform well at the box office, and, although it received five Academy Award nominations, it won no awards. The movie's copyright was allowed to lapse. Television stations showed the classic without paying fees since the copyright had lapsed.

However, the U.S. Supreme Court decision in *Stewart* v. *Abend,* 495 U.S. 207 (1990), offering an extension of the copyright protection of the underlying story to the movie, affected Jimmy Stewart's life once again. The original story owner, Mr. Stern, had the rights to

the story since the movie rights had lapsed. With his story copyright in place, royalties for its use in the movie had to be paid once again. The owners of *It's a Wonderful Life* began charging fees to cover their fees to Mr. Stern, and the result was costly access. *It's a Wonderful Life* was seen on television day and night during the holiday season when the copyright on the movie had lapsed. Now, with the copyright clarification, the movie rights have been reprotected. The story's continuing protection and the high royalty fees make *It's a Wonderful Life* a singular holiday event.

What is the relationship between movie copyrights and the rights to the underlying story? Who owns what between story authors and movie producers? What should businesses negotiating movie rights and royalties be certain about before signing an agreement?

NOTES

1. The protection of intellectual property has been important to commercial development both here and in other countries for centuries. See the course Web site and the *Instructor's Manual* for more information.

2. Some states do have provisions for registration of trade names for businesses, such as when a company is named Carla's Hair Salon, DBA (doing business as) "The Mane Place."

3. Emily Lambert, "The Buck Stops Here," *Forbes,* January 6, 2003, p. 52.

Trade Practices: Antitrust

Economic power is an inevitable result of the free enterprise system. Building a better mousetrap should result in attracting more customers and developing economic power. But gaining economic power through other means destroys the free enterprise system and often precludes purchasers from buying the better mousetrap. They are stuck with a mousetrap that may be mediocre but is built by a firm with perhaps ill-gained economic power and resulting market control.

Antitrust law exists to regulate the growth of economic or market power; it does so in part by ensuring that competition remains an aspect of the free enterprise system. This chapter answers the following questions: What restraints of trade are permissible? What antitrust laws exist? What penalties can be imposed for violations? What are the forms of horizontal trade restraints and defenses? What are the forms of vertical trade restraints and defenses?

> update

For up-to-date legal news and real-world business applications, click on **update** *at http://jennings.westbuslaw.com*

> People of the same trade seldom meet together, even for merriment and diversion, but the conversation ends in some contrivance to raise prices. It is impossible indeed to prevent such meetings, by any law which would be consistent with liberty and justice. But though the law cannot hinder people of the same trade from sometimes assembling together, it ought to do nothing to facilitate such assemblies.
> ADAM SMITH
> *The Wealth of Nations*

> While the law of competition may be sometimes hard for the individual, it is best for the race, because it ensures the survival of the fittest in every department.
> ANDREW CARNEGIE

CONSIDER...

Microsoft Corporation virtually controls the software market for personal computers. Over 90 percent of the operating systems used in personal computers have Microsoft software. Rival Novell CEO Robert J. Frankenberg says, "There is no doubt Microsoft is out to kill us. This is not paranoia. They really are out to get us."

Bill Gates, CEO of Microsoft, has responded, "This is a fiercely competitive business."

Microsoft requires its customers that manufacture computers to pay a fee for each computer they ship, even if the computer contains another software maker's operating system. These manufacturers thus have an incentive to use Microsoft because they must pay double royalties if they do not.

The Justice Department and Microsoft entered into a consent decree under which Microsoft halted the payment requirements, but Microsoft then refused to sell Windows to manufacturers using other Internet browser systems. Can Microsoft do this?

COMMON LAW PROTECTIONS AGAINST RESTRAINT OF TRADE

Early Common Law of Trade Restraints

In the sixteenth century, the earliest trade restraint cases held that it was void *per se* for parties to agree that one party would not engage in a lawful trade or profession. Oddly enough, the void *per se* rule was not followed with the intent of encouraging competition; rather, it was followed out of fear that those not able to practice their trade would become a burden to society.[1]

In the seventeenth and eighteenth centuries, the courts began to recognize that certain circumstances required some form of trade restraint. The first permissible type of restraint was allowed in the sale of a business: In the sale provisions, the seller agreed not to open a competing business. This trade restraint, called a **covenant not to compete**, was valid so long as it was reasonable in its length and scope. For example, in *Mitchell* v. *Reynolds*, 24 Eng. Rep. 347 (1711), a baker who sold his bakery agreed not to compete in the immediate area for five years, and a court held the covenant valid because it was limited in time and geographic scope.

BUSINESS PLANNING TIP

When negotiating valid covenants not to compete, follow these guidelines.

1. Be certain the covenant is necessary.

2. Be certain the covenant is reasonable.

   a. It covers only the geographic scope necessary. (A five-mile radius for the sale of a dry cleaning business is reasonable; a worldwide prohibition is not.)

   b. It covers only the time necessary. (Five years is reasonable; a lifetime prohibition is not.)

3. Make the covenant part of the agreement of sale, lease, or employment. Separate agreements not to compete arouse suspicions.

4. Be certain both parties initial the noncompete clause or paragraph.

5. Legal representation helps ensure validity by assumed understanding.

Modern Common Law of Trade Restraints

Under common law, contracts and covenants that restrain trade are not illegal *per se.* Such contracts are enforceable so long as they are not unreasonable—that is, they go no further than necessary for protection. Exceeding reasonable time and geographic limits would be examples of unreasonable trade restraints. For example, a covenant in a contract for the sale of a dry cleaning business that prohibits the seller from opening another dry cleaning business anywhere in the state is unreasonably broad, but a similar covenant limited to the town where the business is located is probably reasonable. The reasonable restraint is related to the sale of a business and preservation of its goodwill.

Restraints in leases are also related to a business transaction and are valid. For example, a restriction in a shopping center lease that prohibits a lessee from operating a business that competes with other tenants is appropriate so long as the purpose of the restriction is to obtain a proper mix in the shopping center with the idea of attracting more business. Partners' and employees' restrictions that prevent them from competing for a certain time period after they leave a partnership or corporation are also reasonable so long as they are not excessive.

In *Child World, Inc.* v. *South Towne Centre, Ltd.* (Case 17.1), the court addresses the issue of a shopping center lease covenant and its reasonableness under common law standards.

CASE 17.1

Child World, Inc. v. *South Towne Centre, Ltd.*
634 F.Supp. 1121 (S.D. Ohio 1986)

Toys "Я" Us Only

FACTS

Child World, Inc. (plaintiff) operates large retail toy stores throughout Ohio and other states called Children's Palace. South Towne Centre, Ltd. (defendant) is a limited partnership in Ohio that leases space in its South Towne Centre shopping complex to a Children's Palace store. Section 43(A) of the lease, executed in February 1976, provided as follows:

Except insofar as the following shall be unlawful, the parties mutually agree as follows:

A. Landlord shall not use or permit or suffer any other person, firm, corporation or other entity to use any portion of the Shopping Center or any other property located within six (6) miles from the Shopping Center and owned, leased, or otherwise controlled by the landlord (meaning thereby the real property or parties in interest and not a "straw" person or entity) or any person or entity having a substantial identity of interest, for the operation of a toys and games store principally for the sale at retail of toys and games, juvenile furniture and sporting goods such as is exemplified by the Child World and Children's Palace stores operated by Tenant's parent company, Child World, Inc. at the demised premises and elsewhere.

The lease was for 20 years and was signed by Barbara Beerman Weprin, the sole general partner of South Towne. Mad River, Ltd. is another limited partnership in which Ms. Weprin is the sole general partner. Mad River owns another parcel of land approximately one-half mile from the South Towne Centre. On December 24, 1985, Mad River entered into an agreement to sell the parcel of land to Toys "Я" Us, Inc. Toys "Я" Us intends to construct a retail facility similar to the description in the above-noted lease clause. When Children's Palace was informed of the sale, they brought suit, seeking to enforce the covenant not to lease or sell to a competitor of Children's Palace.

JUDICIAL OPINION

RICE, Circuit Judge

The consensus of the federal courts which have considered covenants in shopping center leases is one with which this Court can agree; namely, that the varying terms, conditions, and economic justifications for such restrictions render them inappropriate subjects for application of the *per se* rule. Defendants have not alleged nor proven anything about Section 43(A) of the lease which would indicate that it has only anticompetitive consequences. Indeed, in Finding of Fact #9, Defendants agree that Section 43(A) was negotiated as an inducement for Plaintiff to erect a Children's Palace store on Defendants' premises and to enter into a 20-year lease. This economic justification for exclusivity clauses is among the primary reasons that clauses such as Section 43(A) have not been found to be *per se* illegal, but rather have been found consistent with the public interest in economic development. Such laws can induce tenants to establish stores and to enter into a particular marketplace, often then encouraging the entry of other, often smaller, merchants.

A number of factors have been considered by the courts which have excluded restrictive covenants in shopping center leases: (1) the relevant product and geographic markets, together with the showing of unreasonable impact upon competition in these markets, due to the restrictive covenant; (2) the availability of alternate sites for the entity excluded by the operation of such a covenant; (3) the significance of the competition eliminated by the exclusivity clause, and whether present or future competitors were the parties excluded; (4) the scope of the restrictive covenant and whether it varied depending on particular circumstances; and (5) the economic justifications for the inclusion of the restrictive covenant in the lease.

Due to the particular facts of this case, however, the Court needs not, and specifically does not, reach the validity of the six-mile limitation contained in Section 43(A). Regardless of possible overbreadth, a restrictive covenant challenged as unreasonable . . . will be upheld to the extent that a breach of the covenant has occurred or is threatened to occur within a reasonable geographic area and time period. The parties have agreed, in Finding of Fact #12, that the parcel which Defendants seek to convey to Toys "Я" Us is approximately one-half mile from the Children's Palace store covered by the Lease. The Court finds that Section 43(A) is lawful and enforceable to the extent of one-half mile, as required by the facts of this case.

Turning to the impact which enforcement of Section 43(A), as applied in this case, would have upon the Defendants, the burdens of enforcement are not unduly great. As noted *supra*, Section 43(A) does not appear to preclude rental or sale, even within a one-half mile radius, to any number of stores which can compete with a Children's Palace toy and game store but which are not "copycat" stores. On the financial level, there is testimony from a representative of Defendants in the record to the effect that the value of the parcel in question increases almost daily. Moreover, Defendants believe that they will have no difficulty in finding another purchaser, should Section 43(A) preclude their sale of the parcel to Toys "Я" Us.

Enforcement of Section 43(A) to the extent of one-half mile would also not appear to foreclose the entry of Toys "Я" Us into competition with Plaintiff's store in the environs of the South Towne Centre shopping center. In his deposition, J. Tim Logan indicated that, even were Section 43(A) upheld, presumably in its entirety, Toys "Я" Us would still establish a store in the vicinity of Plaintiff's store.

Other courts have believed that restrictive covenants of a scope of one-half mile or more, albeit less than six miles, are legitimate lures by landlords in order for shopping center tenants to enter particular marketplaces and to thereby enhance the economic development of the community. The public has surely benefitted from the development of South Towne Centre. As a restriction of six miles appeared reasonable to Defendants' predecessors at the time of bargaining, enforcement of Section 43(A) of the Lease to the extent of one-half mile is consistent with that original calculation of value, and certainly reasonable.

CASE QUESTIONS

1. Who leased what from whom?
2. What restrictions were placed in the lease agreement?
3. How did Toys "Я" Us become involved?
4. Is the sale a violation of the anticompetition clause?
5. Is the same shopping center involved?

 CONSIDER. . . **17.1**

In April 1965, Berkeley Heights Shopping Center leased 11,514 square feet of space to A&P Supermarkets. Under the terms of the lease, Berkeley agreed not to lease any other shopping center space to another grocery store. On April 16, 1977, A&P informed Berkeley that it was ceasing operations and subleasing the premises to Drug Fair, a modern drug store chain that sells foodstuffs. In 1985, Berkeley sought to lease other space in the center to another grocery store, and Drug Fair objected on the grounds of the covenant not to compete. Berkeley maintains the covenant only applies when the premises Drug Fair occupies are used as a grocery store operation. Who is correct? [*Berkeley Dev. Co.* v. *Great Atlantic & Pacific Tea Co.*, 518 A.2d 790 (N.J. 1986).]

FEDERAL STATUTORY SCHEME ON RESTRAINT OF TRADE

During the last half of the nineteenth century, the United States experienced a tremendous change in its economy. A primarily agricultural economy changed to an industrial economy. Law on business combinations was largely undeveloped and unsuitable for the types of predatory business practices this new industrial age brought. Furthermore, because common law was the only source of law for dealing with these business problems, those laws that did exist were nonuniform. In reaction to the lack of laws and the public outcry over business abuses, Congress became involved, passing federal statutes on antitrust issues in the late nineteenth and early twentieth centuries. With some amendments and changes, this scheme still exists and applies today. Exhibit 17.1 summarizes the general federal statutory antitrust statutes covered in detail in the following topic sections.

EXHIBIT   17.1   Federal Antitrust Statutes

STATUTE	ORIGINAL DATE	JURISDICTION	COVERAGE	PENALTIES
Sherman Act 15 U.S.C. § 1	1890	Commerce Clause	Monopolies; attempts to monopolize; boycotts; refusals to deal; price fixing; resale price maintenance; division of markets	Criminal; $100,000,000 if a corporation, or, individual, $1,000,000, or by imprisonment not exceeding 10 years, or by both private suits
Clayton Act 1914 15 U.S.C. § 12	1914	Persons engaged in commerce	Tying; treble damages; mergers; interlocking directorates	Private suits
Federal Trade Commission Act 15 U.S.C. § 41	1914	Commerce Clause	Unfair methods of FTC competition	
Robinson-Patman Act 15 U.S.C. § 13	1936	Persons engaged in commerce and selling goods across state lines	Price discrimination	Private suits and criminal for international acts
Celler-Kefauver (part of Clayton Act) 15 U.S.C. § 18	1950		Asset acquisitions	
Hart-Scott-Rodino Antitrust Improvements Act 15 U.S.C. § 1311	1976 amended 1980, 1994	Gives greater authority to Justice Department for prosecution; requires premerger notification to Justice Department		
Antitrust Modernization Commission Act PL 107–273, November 2, 2002, 116 Stat 1758	2002	Gives authority to study antitrust laws and their impact and to provide proposals for updating the statutes; commission appointed at end of 2003		

In study stages

Chapter 17 Trade Practices: Antitrust 659

BUSINESS STRATEGY

Keeping Employees in Place When You're Selling the Subsidiary

In July 1995, AT&T decided to sell one of its affiliates, Paradyne Corp., a manufacturer of network access products for the telecommunications industry. AT&T wanted to ensure that Paradyne remained a viable entity because AT&T and its other affiliates, including Lucent Technologies, purchased many of the network access products Paradyne manufactured. To make Paradyne more attractive to buyers as an ongoing business, AT&T adopted a human resource plan that placed restrictions on Paradyne employees' ability to transfer to other divisions of AT&T. Specifically, the Preliminary Net (the initial restriction agreement) precluded an employee who voluntarily left Paradyne from being hired by any other division of AT&T. AT&T believed that one of Paradyne's most marketable assets was its skilled employees. The retention of Paradyne's employees, therefore, was considered essential for the sale of Paradyne.

© CHAD BAKER/RYAN McVAY/ISTOCKPHOTO

On July 31, 1996, Lucent sold Paradyne to Texas Pacific Group. Before closing, Lucent agreed, on behalf of itself and the other former AT&T affiliates, that it would not hire, rehire, retain, or solicit the services of any Paradyne employee or consultant whose annual income exceeded $50,000. This "Pre Closing Net" (another version of the restriction agreement) was consistent with the understanding that Texas Pacific Group's interest in purchasing Paradyne was based on its desire to acquire the technical skills of Paradyne's employees for a sufficient period of time to ensure a successful transition of ownership.

Once the deal was closed, Lucent and Texas Pacific Group entered a post-closing agreement in which Lucent warranted on behalf of itself and the other AT&T affiliates that for 245 days (8 months) following the sale and the expiration of the Pre Closing Net, it would not seek to hire, solicit, or rehire any Paradyne employee or consultant whose compensation exceeded $50,000. The employees filed suit, contending that the effect of the covenant in the agreements was to reduce competition as well as their ability to work for other companies. Is the covenant enforceable? [*Eichorn* v. *AT&T Corp.*, 248 F.3d 131 (3d Cir. 2001).]

Jurisdiction of Federal Antitrust Laws

Federal laws cannot apply to business conduct unless interstate commerce is involved. (See Chapter 5 for a complete discussion of interstate commerce.) All federal antitrust statutes define interstate commerce for purposes of applying the statutes to businesses and are discussed in the following subsections.

Sherman Act Jurisdiction

The standards for **Sherman Act** jurisdiction are the same as the standards established under the Commerce Clause (see Chapter 5). Even if an activity is purely intrastate, it is subject to Sherman Act jurisdiction if the activity has a substantial economic effect on interstate commerce. Even if the activity of a business is purely local in nature, its economic impact and resources are examined to determine whether interstate commerce has been affected. There are very few times when interstate commerce is not found under the Sherman Act standard.

In *McClain* v. *Real Estate Board of New Orleans*, 441 U.S. 942 (1980), for example, an antitrust action against real estate brokers who worked only in the New Orleans area was permitted under the Sherman Act because the U.S. Supreme Court found that the brokers facilitated the loans and insurance for the properties they sold. The loans and insurance were provided by national firms, and funding came from out-side the state. This involvement of interstate commerce, even in an indirect fashion, is sufficient for Sherman Act jurisdiction.

Clayton Act Jurisdiction

The jurisdictional standard for the **Clayton Act** is different from the broad Sherman Act jurisdiction of any interstate commerce. The Clayton Act can be applied *only* to transactions and persons *engaged* in interstate commerce, not just businesses *affect-ing* interstate commerce.

Robinson–Patman Act Jurisdiction

The **Robinson-Patman Act** has the most stringent jurisdictional requirements. The seller accused of price discrimination must be engaged in interstate commerce, and at least one of two claimed discrimination sales must be across state lines. A firm that sells only to in-state customers is not subject to Robinson-Patman jurisdiction.

Antitrust Penalties and Remedies

The federal antitrust laws have powerful incentives for compliance that include substantial penalties and remedies. The following subsections discuss these provi-sions, and a summary appears in Exhibit 17.2.

Criminal Penalties

The Sherman Act carries felony criminal penalties. For individuals, the penalties are fines of up to $1 million and/or up to ten years in prison. For corporations, there are fines of up to $100 million. These criminal penalties require proof that the viola-tor intended the anticompetitive conduct and realized the consequences of the ac-tion taken.

The FTC and Clayton Acts do not carry criminal penalties. However, Section 4 of the Robinson-Patman Act makes criminal certain forms of intentional price dis-crimination. It is important to note that officers and directors of violating corpora-tions can also be held criminally liable for antitrust violations. The Antitrust Division

---

EXHIBIT 17.2 Antitrust Remedies				
	SHERMAN ACT	**CLAYTON ACT**	**ROBINSON-PATMAN ACT**	**FTC ACT**
Criminal	$350,000 and/or three years in prison for individuals; $10 million for corporations; directors and officers also liable as to intent and knowledge	None	Section 4 for intentional price discrimination	None
Civil	Treble damages plus costs and attorney fees	Same	Same	None
Equitable	Injunctions, divestitures, asset distributions, sales	Same	Same	Same
Enforcers	Justice Department; U.S. attorney; state attorneys general; private persons	Same	Same	FTC

of the Department of Justice or the local U.S. attorney's office is responsible for bringing criminal actions under the antitrust laws.

Equitable Remedies

Equitable remedies can be obtained by either the government or private parties. Equitable relief is an order from a court that restrains or prevents anticompetitive conduct. An **injunction** is a frequent form of antitrust relief; it is a court order prohibiting a violating party from engaging in anticompetitive conduct.

Equitable remedies are also affirmative in nature. They can require parties to take appropriate steps to eliminate the results of anticompetitive behavior. A firm can be ordered to divest itself of an acquired firm, for example; or in an unlawful asset acquisition, a court order can require that the assets be divided with a competing firm. Contracts whose terms violate the antitrust laws can be canceled by court order.

Equitable remedies give the courts discretion to fashion remedies that will eliminate the results of anticompetitive behavior.

Private Actions for Damages

Section 4 of the Clayton Act allows any person whose business or property is injured as a result of an antitrust violation to recover "threefold the damages by him sustained"—commonly referred to as **treble damages**—along with the costs of the suit and reasonable attorney fees. This section, with its substantial recovery provisions, is strong incentive for private enforcement of antitrust laws. Consumers, businesses, and state attorneys general can all bring private damage actions under Section 4.

The types of damages that can be recovered include lost profits, increased costs, and decreased value in property. These damage suits have a four-year statute of limitations; that is, suit must be brought within four years of the alleged violation. Those who bring private damage suits enjoy a proof benefit: If the government has brought suit and a violation is found, that judgment can be used in a private suit as *prima facie* evidence against the violating defendant. A ***prima facie* case** allows a plaintiff to survive a directed verdict and entitles the plaintiff to a judgment if the defendant offers no contradictory evidence (see Chapter 4 for more discussion).

Visit the Corporate Counsel Web site for information on current antitrust issues:
http://www. corpcounselor.com

HORIZONTAL RESTRAINTS OF TRADE

Horizontal restraints of trade are designed to lessen competition among a firm's competitors. For example, Ford's and GM's fixing prices to drive Chrysler out of business would be a horizontal restraint. The Sherman Act covers the horizontal restraints of **price fixing**, market division, **group boycotts** and refusals to deal, **joint ventures**, and monopolization. The Clayton Act also covers the problem of anticompetitive horizontal mergers or mergers with competitors.

Sherman Act Restraints

Monopolization

Section 2 of the Sherman Act prohibits the act of **monopolizing**. Notice that the Sherman Act does not prohibit monopolies—certain types of monopolies are recognized as exceptions to Section 2. For example, in a small town there is usually only enough economic base to support one newspaper; such an operation is not a Section 2 violation. Some businesses simply produce a product that is superior or unique; this type of monopoly is not a violation. When a business has obtained a large market share by **superior skill, foresight, and industry**, it has simply put its product in the market in a superior way and is entitled to its market share.

Acquiring a large market share through methods other than legitimate competition is prohibited under Section 2. To prove such monopolization, the following elements must be established:

1. The possession of **monopoly power** in the relevant market
2. The willful acquisition or maintenance of that power

Monopoly Power   Judicial decisions have defined monopoly power under Section 2 as the power to control prices or exclude competition in a relevant market. To determine whether a firm has this ability, or monopoly power, the courts have examined the firm's **market power**, which is an economic term that means the firm has a relatively inelastic demand curve. An elastic demand curve means that the firm's products have competition from other firms or from firms with substitute products. For example, cosmetic firms have an elastic demand; buyers can switch to other products when there are price increases in one line or can even give up the use of cosmetics. On the other hand, the demand curve for gasoline is less elastic. Although there are substitute means of transportation, most drivers need to use their cars and hence need gasoline.

At some point, ever-increasing market power will turn into monopoly power. High profits and the lack of substitute goods are indications that market power has made this transition. Some courts examine the firm's market share to determine whether it has monopoly power. There is, however, no set percentage figure used to make this determination. Most of the cases dealing with the percentage-of-market approach have involved firms with market shares greater than 50 percent.

Relevant Market   In determining market share, a court must first determine a firm's market. The context in which market share is measured is called the **relevant market**; and each product has a relevant **geographic market**. For example, a beer producer may have 50 percent of all nationwide beer sales, but, in a suit involving a local competitor, the producer's share might be only 20 percent because of the local beer's popularity. This local or **submarket** could be used as the relevant geographic market. A product may have an international market but may have only 10 percent market share in a particular area.

Each firm also has its own relevant **product market**, which is determined by consumers' preferences and their willingness to substitute other products for the product at issue. For example, a market could be defined as plastic wrapping materials, or it could be defined as food storage materials and include such wraps as wax paper, aluminum foil, and plastic storage bags. The product market is determined by the **cross-elasticity** of demand. Cross-elastic demand means consumers are willing to substitute other products in the event of unavailability or price changes.

The definition of relevant market is one of the key elements in monopolization cases. There will always be contradictory testimony from expert economists. As a result, the decisions on relevant market vary widely.

Purposeful Act Requirement   Proving that a firm has monopoly power is only half of an antitrust monopolization case. The second element requires showing that the firm acquired or is maintaining monopoly power by some purposeful or deliberate act that is not "superior skill, foresight, and industry" (which in short is the ability to build a better mousetrap). Some examples of prohibited purposeful conduct are **predatory pricing** and **exclusionary conduct**. Predatory pricing is pricing below actual cost for a temporary period to drive a potential competitor out of business. Exclusionary conduct is conduct that prevents a potential competitor from entering the market. For example, interfering with the purchase of a factory by a competitor would be improper exclusionary conduct. The landmark case *U.S.* v. *Microsoft* (Case 17.2), both judicially and economically, deals with nearly all legal issues under the Sherman Act and other federal antitrust laws.

CASE 17.2

U.S. v. *Microsoft*
253 F.3d 34 (C.A. D.C. 2001)

You Have Performed an Illegal Operation

FACTS

Microsoft Corporation, a company based in Washington that does business in all 50 states and around the world, is the leading supplier of operating systems for personal computers (PCs). Although Microsoft licenses its software programs directly to consumers, the largest part of its sales consists of licensing the products to manufacturers of personal computers.

Microsoft was concerned about its strategic position with respect to the Internet and whether it would be able to maintain a dominant market position there similar to the one it enjoyed in software and operating systems.

The United States Justice Department had an ongoing inquiry into the market shares and practices of Microsoft, and 23 state attorneys general were also looking into the company's practices. The concerns of the Justice Department and attorneys general (plaintiffs) include the following:

1. Microsoft's position in the market as a monopolist (90 percent market share for operating systems).
2. Microsoft's barriers to entry for operating systems and Web browsers. Microsoft has refused to sell its software operating system to computer companies that installed the competitive browser, Netscape, which was gaining popularity as Microsoft's Internet Explorer (IE) struggled.
3. Microsoft worked to inhibit the efforts of Netscape with its browser by first trying to acquire Netscape and then working to "cut off [its] air supply" by retarding Sun Corporation's development and implementation of the Java program. When Microsoft altered the portions of Sun's Java program that allowed it to work without Windows, Sun notified Microsoft that such was a violation of its licensing agreement. Microsoft's response was, "Sue us." Sun sued Microsoft one week before the Justice Department brought its suit against Microsoft. Sun's suit then ran parallel with the Justice Department's.

In issuing a three-part opinion, Judge Thomas Penfield Jackson of the district court found that Microsoft had violated the antitrust laws and ordered a remedy of breaking up the company. Microsoft appealed the decision.

JUDICIAL OPINION

PER CURIAM

What is somewhat problematic . . . is that just over six years have passed since Microsoft engaged in the first conduct plaintiffs allege to be anticompetitive. As the record in this case indicates, six years seems like an eternity in the computer industry. By the time a court can assess liability, firms, products, and the marketplace are likely to have changed dramatically. This, in turn, threatens enormous practical difficulties for courts considering the appropriate measure of relief in equitable enforcement actions, both in crafting injunctive remedies in the first instance and reviewing those remedies in the second. Conduct remedies may be unavailing in such cases, because innovation to a large degree has already rendered the anticompetitive conduct obsolete (although by no means harmless). And broader structural remedies present their own set of problems, including how a court goes about restoring competition to a dramatically changed, and constantly changing, marketplace. That is just one reason why we find the District Court's refusal in the present case to hold an evidentiary hearing on remedies—to update and flesh out the available information before seriously entertaining the possibility of dramatic structural relief—so problematic.

We do not mean to say that enforcement actions will no longer play an important role in curbing infringements of the antitrust laws in technologically

continued

dynamic markets, nor do we assume this in assessing the merits of this case. Even in those cases where forward-looking remedies appear limited, the Government will continue to have an interest in defining the contours of the antitrust laws so that law-abiding firms will have a clear sense of what is permissible and what is not. And the threat of private damage actions will remain to deter those firms inclined to test the limits of the law.

The second matter of note is more theoretical in nature. We decide this case against a backdrop of significant debate amongst academics and practitioners over the extent to which "old economy" § 2 monopolization doctrines should apply to firms competing in dynamic technological markets characterized by network effects. In technologically dynamic markets, however, such entrenchment may be temporary, because innovation may alter the field altogether. Rapid technological change leads to markets in which "firms compete through innovation for temporary market dominance, from which they may be displaced by the next wave of product advancements." Microsoft argues that the operating system market is just such a market.

Whether or not Microsoft's characterization of the operating system market is correct does not appreciably alter our mission in assessing the alleged antitrust violations in the present case.

Moreover, it should be clear that Microsoft makes no claim that anticompetitive conduct should be assessed differently in technologically dynamic markets. It claims only that the measure of monopoly power should be different. For reasons fully discussed below, we reject Microsoft's monopoly power argument.

II. Monopolization

Section 2 of the Sherman Act makes it unlawful for a firm to "monopolize." The District Court found that Microsoft possesses monopoly power in the market for Intel-compatible PC operating systems. Focusing primarily on Microsoft's efforts to suppress Netscape Navigator's threat to its operating system monopoly, the court also found that Microsoft maintained its power not through competition on the merits, but through unlawful means.

A. Monopoly Power

While merely possessing monopoly power is not itself an antitrust violation, it is a necessary element of a monopolization charge. Because direct proof is only rarely available, courts more typically examine market structure in search of circumstantial evidence of monopoly power.

The District Court considered these structural factors and concluded that Microsoft possesses monopoly power in a relevant market. Defining the market as Intel-compatible PC operating systems, the District Court found that Microsoft has a greater than 95% share. It also found the company's market position protected by a substantial entry barrier.

Microsoft argues that the District Court incorrectly defined the relevant market. It also claims that there is no barrier to entry in that market. Alternatively, Microsoft argues that because the software industry is uniquely dynamic, direct proof, rather than circumstantial evidence, more appropriately indicates whether it possesses monopoly power. Rejecting each argument, we uphold the District Court's finding of monopoly power in its entirety.

1. Market Structure
a. Market definition

In this case, the District Court defined the market as "the licensing of all Intel-compatible PC operating systems worldwide," finding that there are "currently no products—and . . . there are not likely to be any in the near future—that a significant percentage of computer users worldwide could substitute for [these operating systems] without incurring substantial costs."

The District Court found that consumers would not switch from Windows to Mac OS in response to a substantial price increase because of the costs of acquiring the new hardware needed to run Mac OS (an Apple computer and peripherals) and compatible software applications, as well as because of the effort involved in learning the new system and transferring files to its format. The court also found the Apple system less appealing to consumers because it costs considerably more and supports fewer applications.

Microsoft's challenge to the District Court's exclusion of non-PC based competitors, such as information appliances (handheld devices, etc.) and portal websites that host server-based software applications, suffers from the same defect: the company fails to challenge the District Court's key factual findings. In particular, the District Court found that because information appliances fall far short of performing all of the functions of a PC, most consumers will buy them only as a supplement to their PCs.

Operating systems also function as platforms for software applications. They do this by "exposing"—i.e., making available to software developers—routines or protocols that perform certain widely-used functions. These are known as Application Programming Interfaces, or "APIs."

Every operating system has different APIs. Ultimately, if developers could write applications relying exclusively on APIs exposed by middleware, their applications would run on any operating system on which the middleware was also present. Netscape Navigator and Java—both at issue in this case—are middleware products written for multiple operating systems.

Microsoft argues that, because middleware could usurp the operating system's platform function and might eventually take over other operating system functions (for instance, by controlling peripherals), the District Court erred in excluding Navigator and Java from the relevant market. The District Court found, however, that neither Navigator, Java, nor any other middleware product could now, or would soon, expose enough APIs to serve as a platform for popular applications, much less take over all operating system functions. Again, Microsoft fails to challenge these findings, instead simply asserting middleware's "potential" as a competitor.

Microsoft claims that even a predominant market share does not by itself indicate monopoly power. Although the "existence of [monopoly] power ordinarily may be inferred from the predominant share of the market," we agree with Microsoft that because of the possibility of competition from new entrants, looking to current market share alone can be "misleading." In this case, however, the District Court was not misled. Considering the possibility of new rivals, the court focused not only on Microsoft's present market share, but also on the structural barrier that protects the company's future position. That barrier—the "applications barrier to entry"—stems from two characteristics of the software market: (1) most consumers prefer operating systems for which a large number of applications have already been written; and (2) most developers prefer to write for operating systems that already have a substantial consumer base. This "chicken-and-egg" situation ensures that applications will continue to be written for the already dominant Windows, which in turn ensures that consumers will continue to prefer it over other operating systems.

The consumer wants an operating system that runs not only types of applications that he knows he will want to use, but also those types in which he might develop an interest later. Also, the consumer knows that if he chooses an operating system with enough demand to support multiple applications in each product category, he will be less likely to find himself straitened later by having to use an application whose features disappoint him. Finally, the average user knows that, generally speaking, applications improve through successive versions. He thus wants an operating system for which successive generations of his favorite applications will be released—promptly at that. The fact that a vastly larger number of applications are written for Windows than for other PC operating systems attracts consumers to Windows, because it reassures them that their interests will be met as long as they use Microsoft's product.

2. Direct Proof

Having sustained the District Court's conclusion that circumstantial evidence proves that Microsoft possesses monopoly power, we turn to Microsoft's alternative argument that it does not behave like a monopolist. Claiming that software competition is uniquely "dynamic," the company suggests a new rule: that monopoly power in the software industry should be proven directly, that is, by examining a company's actual behavior to determine if it reveals the existence of monopoly power. According to Microsoft, not only does no such proof of its power exist, but record evidence demonstrates the absence of monopoly power. The company claims that it invests heavily in research and development.

Microsoft's argument fails because, even assuming that the software market is uniquely dynamic in the long term, the District Court correctly applied the structural approach to determine if the company faces competition in the short term.

Even if we were to require direct proof, moreover, Microsoft's behavior may well be sufficient to show the existence of monopoly power. Certainly, none of the conduct Microsoft points to—its investment in R&D and the relatively low price of Windows—is inconsistent with the possession of such power. The R&D expenditures Microsoft points to are not simply for Windows, but for its entire company, which most likely does not possess a monopoly for all of its products. Moreover, because innovation can increase an already dominant market share and further delay the emergence of competition, even monopolists have reason to invest in R&D. Microsoft's pricing behavior is similarly equivocal. The company claims only that it never charged the short-term profit-maximizing price for Windows. Microsoft does argue that the price of Windows is a fraction of the price of an Intel-compatible PC system and lower than that of rival operating systems, but these facts are not inconsistent with the District Court's finding that Microsoft has monopoly power.

More telling, the District Court found that some aspects of Microsoft's behavior are difficult to explain unless Windows is a monopoly product. For instance, according to the District Court, the company set the price of Windows without considering rivals' prices, something a firm without a monopoly would have been unable to do. The District Court also found that Microsoft's pattern of exclusionary conduct could only be rational "if the firm knew that it possessed monopoly power." It is to that conduct that we now turn.

B. Anticompetitive Conduct

Whether any particular act of a monopolist is exclusionary, rather than merely a form of vigorous competition, can be difficult to discern: the means of illicit exclusion, like the means of legitimate competition, are myriad. The challenge for an antitrust court

continued

lies in stating a general rule for distinguishing between exclusionary acts, which reduce social welfare, and competitive acts, which increase it.

1. Licenses Issued to Original Equipment Manufacturers [OEMs]

Microsoft's efforts to gain market share in one market (browsers) served to meet the threat to Microsoft's monopoly in another market (operating systems) by keeping rival browsers from gaining the critical mass of users necessary to attract developer attention away from Windows as the platform for software development.

[T]he District Court condemned the license provisions prohibiting the OEMs from: (1) removing any desktop icons, folders, or "Start" menu entries; (2) altering the initial boot sequence; and (3) otherwise altering the appearance of the Windows desktop.

The District Court concluded that the first license restriction—the prohibition upon the removal of desktop icons, folders, and Start menu entries—thwarts the distribution of a rival browser by preventing OEMs from removing visible means of user access to IE. The OEMs cannot practically install a second browser in addition to IE, the court found, in part because "[p]reinstalling more than one product in a given category . . . can significantly increase an OEM's support costs, for the redundancy can lead to confusion among novice users."

The second license provision at issue prohibits OEMs from modifying the initial boot sequence—the process that occurs the first time a consumer turns on the computer. Upon learning of OEM practices including boot sequence modification, Microsoft's Chairman, Bill Gates, wrote: "Apparently a lot of OEMs are bundling non-Microsoft browsers and coming up with offerings together with [Internet access providers, IAPs] that get displayed on their machines in a FAR more prominent way than MSN or our Internet browser." Microsoft does not deny that the prohibition on modifying the boot sequence has the effect of decreasing competition against IE by preventing OEMs from promoting rivals' browsers. Because this prohibition has a substantial effect in protecting Microsoft's market power, and does so through a means other than competition on the merits, it is anticompetitive.

b. Microsoft's justifications for the license restrictions

Microsoft argues that the license restrictions are legally justified because, in imposing them, Microsoft is simply "exercising its rights as the holder of valid copyrights." Microsoft's primary copyright argument borders upon the frivolous. The company claims an absolute and unfettered right to use its intellectual property as it wishes: "[I]f intellectual property rights have been lawfully acquired," it says, then "their subsequent exercise cannot give rise to antitrust liability."

That is no more correct than the proposition that use of one's personal property, such as a baseball bat, cannot give rise to tort liability. As the Federal Circuit succinctly stated: "Intellectual property rights do not confer a privilege to violate the antitrust laws."

* * *

Microsoft denies, as a factual matter, that it commingled browsing and non-browsing code, and it maintains the District Court's findings to the contrary are clearly erroneous. According to Microsoft, its expert "testified without contradiction that '[t]he very same code in Windows 98 that provides Web browsing functionality' also performs essential operating system functions—not code in the same files, but the very same software code."

Microsoft's expert did not testify to that effect "without contradiction," however. A Government expert, Glenn Weadock, testified that Microsoft "design[ed] [IE] so that some of the code that it uses co-resides in the same library files as other code needed for Windows." Another Government expert likewise testified that one library file, SHDOCVW.DLL, "is really a bundle of separate functions. It contains some functions that have to do specifically with Web browsing, and it contains some general user interface functions as well." One of Microsoft's own documents suggests as much.

In view of the contradictory testimony in the record, some of which supports the District Court's finding that Microsoft commingled browsing and non-browsing code, we cannot conclude that the finding was clearly erroneous.

3. Agreements with Internet Access Providers

The District Court also condemned as exclusionary Microsoft's agreements with various IAPs. The IAPs include both Internet Service Providers, which offer consumers internet access, and Online Services ("OLSs") such as America Online ("AOL"), which offer proprietary content in addition to internet access and other services. The District Court deemed Microsoft's agreements with the IAPs unlawful because: Microsoft licensed [IE] and the [IE] Access Kit to hundreds of IAPs for no charge. Then, Microsoft extended valuable promotional treatment to the ten most important IAPs in exchange for their commitment to promote and distribute [IE] and to exile Navigator from the desktop. Finally, in exchange for efforts to upgrade existing subscribers to client software that came bundled with [IE] instead of Navigator, Microsoft granted rebates— and in some cases made outright payments—to those same IAPs.

Although offering a customer an attractive deal is the hallmark of competition, the Supreme Court has indicated that in very rare circumstances a price may be unlawfully low, or "predatory." The rare case of price predation aside, the antitrust laws do not condemn even a monopolist for offering its product at an attractive price, and we therefore have no warrant to condemn Microsoft for offering either IE or the IEAK [IE Access Kit] free of charge or even at a negative price. Likewise, as we said above, a monopolist does not violate the Sherman Act simply by developing an attractive product.

4. Dealings with Internet Content Providers [ICPs], Independent Software Vendors [ISVs], and Apple Computer

The District Court held that Microsoft engages in exclusionary conduct in its dealings with ICPs, which develop websites; ISVs, which develop software; and Apple, which is both an OEM and a software developer.

With respect to the deals with ICPs, the District Court's findings do not support liability. After reviewing the ICP agreements, the District Court specifically stated that "there is not sufficient evidence to support a finding that Microsoft's promotional restrictions actually had a substantial, deleterious impact on Navigator's usage share." Because plaintiffs failed to demonstrate that Microsoft's deals with the ICPs have a substantial effect upon competition, they have not proved the violation of the Sherman Act.

As for Microsoft's ISV agreements, however, the District Court did not enter a similar finding of no substantial effect.

In dozens of "First Wave" agreements signed between the fall of 1997 and the spring of 1998, Microsoft has promised to give preferential support, in the form of early Windows 98 and Windows NT betas, other technical information, and the right to use certain Microsoft seals of approval, to important ISVs that agree to certain conditions. One of these conditions is that the ISVs use Internet Explorer as the default browsing software for any software they develop with a hypertext-based user interface.

Another condition is that the ISVs use Microsoft's "HTML Help," which is accessible only with Internet Explorer, to implement their applications' help systems.

[T]he effect of these deals is to "ensure . . . that many of the most popular Web-centric applications will rely on browsing technologies found only in Windows," and that Microsoft's deals with ISVs therefore "increase [ ] the likelihood that the millions of consumers using [applications designed by ISVs that entered into agreements with Microsoft] will use Internet Explorer rather than Navigator."

When Microsoft entered into the First Wave agreements, there were 40 million new users of the internet. Because, by keeping rival browsers from gaining widespread distribution (and potentially attracting the attention of developers away from the APIs in Win-

dows), the deals have a substantial effect in preserving Microsoft's monopoly, we hold that plaintiffs have made a *prima facie* showing that the deals have an anticompetitive effect.

Of course, that Microsoft's exclusive deals have the anticompetitive effect of preserving Microsoft's monopoly does not, in itself, make them unlawful. A monopolist, like a competitive firm, may have a perfectly legitimate reason for wanting an exclusive arrangement with its distributors. Accordingly, Microsoft had an opportunity to, but did not, present the District Court with evidence demonstrating that the exclusivity provisions have some such procompetitive justification.

5. Java

Java, a set of technologies developed by Sun Microsystems, is another type of middleware posing a potential threat to Windows' position as the ubiquitous platform for software development. Programs calling upon the Java APIs will run on any machine with a "Java runtime environment," that is, Java class libraries and a JVM [Java Virtual Machine].

In May 1995 Netscape agreed with Sun to distribute a copy of the Java runtime environment with every copy of Navigator, and "Navigator quickly became the principal vehicle by which Sun placed copies of its Java runtime environment on the PC systems of Windows users." Microsoft, too, agreed to promote the Java technologies—or so it seemed.

When specifically accused by a *PC Week* reporter of fragmenting Java standards so as to prevent cross-platform uses, Microsoft denied the accusation and indicated it was only "adding rich platform support" to what remained a crossplatform implementation. An e-mail message internal to Microsoft, written shortly after the conversation with the reporter, shows otherwise:

> [O]k, i just did a followup call. . . . [The reporter] liked that i kept pointing customers to w3c standards [(commonly observed internet protocols)]. . . . [but] he accused us of being schizo with this vs. our java approach, i said he misunderstood [—] that [with Java] we are merely trying to add rich platform support to an interop layer. . . . this plays well. . . . at this point its [sic] not good to create MORE noise around our win32 java classes. instead we should just quietly grow j++ [(Microsoft's development tools)] share and assume that people will take more advantage of our classes without ever realizing they are building win32-only java apps.

Finally, other Microsoft documents confirm that Microsoft intended to deceive Java developers, and predicted that the effect of its actions would be to generate

continued

Windows-dependent Java applications that their developers believed would be cross-platform; these documents also indicate that Microsoft's ultimate objective was to thwart Java's threat to Microsoft's monopoly in the market for operating systems. One Microsoft document, for example, states as a strategic goal: "Kill cross-platform Java by grow[ing] the polluted Java market."

Microsoft's conduct related to its Java developer tools served to protect its monopoly of the operating system in a manner not attributable either to the superiority of the operating system or to the acumen of its makers, and therefore was anticompetitive. Unsurprisingly, Microsoft offers no procompetitive explanation for its campaign to deceive developers. Accordingly, we conclude this conduct is exclusionary, in violation of § 2 of the Sherman Act.

d. The threat to Intel

In 1995 Intel was in the process of developing a high-performance, Windows-compatible JVM. Microsoft wanted Intel to abandon that effort because a fast, cross-platform JVM would threaten Microsoft's monopoly in the operating system market. At an August 1995 meeting, Microsoft's Gates told Intel that its "cooperation with Sun and Netscape to develop a Java runtime environment . . . was one of the issues threatening to undermine cooperation between Intel and Microsoft." Three months later, "Microsoft's Paul Maritz told a senior Intel executive that Intel's [adaptation of its multimedia software to comply with] Sun's Java standards was as inimical to Microsoft as Microsoft's support for non-Intel microprocessors would be to Intel."

Intel nonetheless continued to undertake initiatives related to Java. By 1996 "Intel had developed a JVM designed to run well . . . while complying with Sun's cross-platform standards." In April of that year, Microsoft again urged Intel not to help Sun by distributing Intel's fast, Suncompliant JVM. And Microsoft threatened Intel that if it did not stop aiding Sun on the multimedia front, then Microsoft would refuse to distribute Intel technologies bundled with Windows.

Intel finally capitulated in 1997.

Microsoft's internal documents and deposition testimony confirm both the anticompetitive effect and intent of its actions. Microsoft does not deny the facts found by the District Court, nor does it offer any procompetitive justification for pressuring Intel not to support cross-platform Java. Microsoft lamely characterizes its threat to Intel as "advice." The District Court, however, found that Microsoft's "advice" to Intel to stop aiding cross-platform Java was backed by the threat of retaliation, and this conclusion is supported by the evidence cited above. Therefore we affirm the conclusion that Microsoft's threats to Intel were exclusionary, in violation of § 2 of the Sherman Act.

REMEDIES

The District Court's remedies-phase proceedings are a different matter. It is a cardinal principle of our system of justice that factual disputes must be heard in open court and resolved through trial-like evidentiary proceedings. Any other course would be contrary "to the spirit which imbues our judicial tribunals prohibiting decision without hearing."

This rule is no less applicable in antitrust cases. Despite plaintiffs' protestations, there can be no serious doubt that the parties disputed a number of facts during the remedies phase. In two separate offers of proof, Microsoft identified 23 witnesses who, had they been permitted to testify, would have challenged a wide range of plaintiffs' factual representations, including the feasibility of dividing Microsoft, the likely impact on consumers, and the effect of divestiture on shareholders.

The reason the court declined to conduct an evidentiary hearing was not because of the absence of disputed facts, but because it believed that those disputes could be resolved only through "actual experience," not further proceedings. But a prediction about future events is not, as a prediction, any less a factual issue. Indeed, the Supreme Court has acknowledged that drafting an antitrust decree by necessity "involves predictions and assumptions concerning future economic and business events." Trial courts are not excused from their obligation to resolve such matters through evidentiary hearings simply because they consider the bedrock procedures of our justice system to be "of little use."

In sum, we vacate the District Court's remedies decree for three reasons. First, the District Court failed to hold an evidentiary hearing despite the presence of remedies-specific factual disputes. Second, the court did not provide adequate reasons for its decreed remedies. Finally, we have drastically altered the scope of Microsoft's liability, and it is for the District Court in the first instance to determine the propriety of a specific remedy for the limited ground of liability which we have upheld.

The judgment of the District Court is affirmed in part, reversed in part, remanded in part. We vacate in full the Final Judgment embodying the remedial order, and remand the case to the District Court for reassignment to a different trial judge for further proceedings consistent with this opinion.

CASE QUESTIONS

1. Make a list of the conduct Microsoft engaged in that the court finds indicated it was a monopoly.

2. What is the relevant market? What does Microsoft say the relevant market is?

3. What intellectual property argument does Microsoft make as a defense to the antitrust charges?

4. What error did the trial judge make with respect to the remedies?

5. Did Microsoft violate the Sherman Act?

6. Why is the case remanded?

Aftermath: The Justice Department reached a settlement of the case with Microsoft near the end of 2001. There would be no breakup of Microsoft as part of the remedies for the antitrust violation. Microsoft agreed to pay penalties, the majority of which ($180 million) would be in software donations to schools. Several states had not yet agreed to the settlement.

FOR THE MANAGER'S DESK

RE: E-COMMERCE, E-MAIL, AND TECHNOLOGY

E-mail is redefining the way cases are tried.

In the U.S. Justice Department's case against Microsoft, a lawyer commented, "The Government does not need to put Mr. Gates on the stand because we have his e-mail and memoranda." The lawyer's comment reflects the tendency of e-mail to speak for itself. Witnesses can shrug and assert they cannot remember, but an e-mail from them is always available for recollection purposes as well as admission as evidence. At Microsoft, e-mail supplanted the telephone as the primary means of communication, and the Government was able to tap into the entire e-mail system. There are 30 million pages of e-mail used as evidence in the Microsoft trial.

E-mail provides what is known as a contemporaneous record of events and has the added bonus that, for whatever psychological reason, those communicating with e-mail tend to be more frank and informal than they would be in a memo. E-mail can also contradict a witness's testimony and serve to undermine credibility. For example, when asked whether he recalled discussions with a subordinate about whether Microsoft should offer to invest in Netscape, Mr. Gates responded in his deposition, "I didn't see that as something that made sense." But Mr. Gates's e-mail included an urging to his subordinates to consider a Netscape alliance: "We could even pay them money as part of the deal, buying a piece of them or something."

E-mail is discoverable, it is admissible as evidence, and it is definitely not private. Employees should follow the admonition of one executive whose e-mail was used to fuel a million-dollar settlement by his company with a former employee: "If you wouldn't want anyone to read it, don't send it in e-mail." The impact of e-mail in the Microsoft antitrust case on companies and their e-mail policies was widespread. For example, Amazon.com launched a company-wide program called "Sweep and Keep," under which employees are instructed to purge e-mail messages no longer needed for conducting business. Amazon.com is offering employees who purge immediately free lattes in the company cafeteria.

The company had a two-part program. The first portion included instructions on document retention and deletion. The second part of the program was on document creation and included the following warning for employees: "Quite simply put, there are some communications that should not be expressed in written form. Sorry, no lattes this time."

Eliot Spitzer, New York's attorney general, used e-mails as critical parts of his cases against analysts and investment bankers. When asked to speak at an analyst's meeting he began by saying, "It's nice to be able to put faces with so many of your e-mails that I have read." (A biography of Mr. Spitzer appears in Chapter 1.)

Employees around the country report that they are now holding back on their e-mail communications and being careful about their choices of words.

Sources: Steve Lohr, "Antitrust Case Is Highlighting Role of E-Mail," *New York Times,* November 2, 1998, pp. C1, C4; John R. Wilke, "Old E-Mail Dogs Microsoft in Fighting Antitrust Suits," *Wall Street Journal,* August 27, 1998, p. B1.

BUSINESS STRATEGY APPLICATION

In the exercise for this chapter on the book's Web site, you have the chance to correct the activities and memos of employees for the antitrust violations you find in them, stopping the violations before they occur.

ETHICAL ISSUES

The Running Fox is a small running-shoe manufacturer well known among professional runners for its high-quality, highly protective shoes. Athletic Feet is a manufacturer of a full line of running shoes, from track to long-distance running. Athletic Feet also publishes *Runner's Monthly,* a top magazine in the field of running with a circulation almost exclusively composed of runners. For the past three years, *Runner's Monthly* has published its "annual shoe survey" in which all the running shoes on the market are rated. Athletic Feet's shoes have been ranked as the top three in every category. Running Fox did not perform well in the ratings and has brought a monopolization suit against Athletic Feet. Athletic Feet says the relevant market is athletic shoewear because it not only manufactures running shoes but also tennis, basketball, baseball, and other types of sport shoes. In the athletic shoe market, Athletic Feet holds a 20 percent share of the market; but in the running-shoe market, it holds an 80 percent share. Obviously, Running Fox wants to argue that running shoes are the relevant market. Who is correct? What is the relevant market? Does *Runner's Monthly* have a conflict of interest?

Attempts to Monopolize

Section 2 of the Sherman Act can be violated even though actual monopolization might not be the result. In other words, attempts at monopolization are also part of Section 2. There need not be an actual successful effort so long as it can be shown that the conduct created a "dangerous probability" of monopolization.

CONSIDER...   17.2

Amanda Reiss had completed her residency in ophthalmology in Portland, Oregon, and was moving to Phoenix, Arizona, to start her practice. She began looking for office space and met with a leasing agent who showed her several complexes of medical suites. Dr. Reiss was ready to sign for one of them when the leasing agent turned to her and said, "Oh, by the way, you're not one of those advertising doctors, are you? Because they don't want that kind in any of my complexes." Has there been a violation of the antitrust laws?

Price Fixing

Any agreement or collaboration among competitors "for the purpose and with the effect of raising, depressing, fixing, pegging, or stabilizing the price of a commodity" is the Supreme Court's definition of price fixing. Under Section 1 of the Sherman Act, price fixing is a *per se* violation, which means that the conduct is illegal and unreasonable as a matter of law. The effect of a *per se* violation of the antitrust laws is to shorten trials substantially because a *per se* violator has no defenses to present in the case. Some antitrust scholars feel the Supreme Court is moving away from its *per se* standard for price fixing. Price fixing can result from several different activities, covered in the following subsections.

For an update on the Intel antitrust litigation, visit:
http://www.zdnet.com/

Minimum Prices   A minimum fee or price schedule discourages competition, puts an artificial restriction on the market, and provides a shield from market forces. There is no defense to this type of agreement. Even proof that the minimum price is a reasonable price is irrelevant once there is proof of an agreement.

Maximum Prices   Although establishing maximum prices sounds like an excellent benefit for consumers, the effect is to stabilize prices, which translates into a restriction on free-market forces.

List Prices   An agreement among competitors to use list prices as a guideline in sale prices is also a *per se* violation. There is still a violation even though the agreement was not mandatory and even though the list price was just a starting point in price negotiations. Just the exchange of price information has an effect on the market and interferes with the ability to price in relation to demand, supply, and competition.

Production Limitations

An agreement to limit production is an agreement to fix prices because the parties are controlling the supply, which in turn controls the right to demand the resulting price.

Limitations on Competitive Bidding

Some competitors have tried to avoid "ruinous competition" by eliminating bidding. In *National Soc'y of Professional Engineers* v. *United States*, 435 U.S. 679 (1978), a professional society agreed that there should not be bidding on engineering projects because the bidding process encouraged cost cutting and posed possible safety risks in the construction of the projects bid. Although its motives were well intentioned, it was still found to have committed a violation because the agreement was price fixing and a *per se* violation of the Sherman Act.

Credit Arrangement Agreements

The cost of credit is part of the price of goods and services. Any agreement among creditor-competitors to limit credit terms or to charge a universal credit fee is an agreement relating to price and a *per se* violation.

BUSINESS PLANNING TIP

The following tips can help keep trade associations free of anticompetitive behavior.

1. Do not exchange price information, including disclosures about credit terms, shipping fees, and so on.

2. Do not reveal future plans with respect to customers (e.g., "I'm not going to deal with that company anymore.").

3. Do not define or reveal territories (e.g., "I'm not interested in the Yuma region anymore.").

4. Do not agree to uniform pricing, commissions, or refusals to deal.

FOR THE MANAGER'S DESK

RE: WHY DO COMPANIES SUCCUMB TO PRICE FIXING?

Down through the centuries social analysts have frequently charged, "Laws are like spiderwebs, which may catch small flies but let wasps and hornets break through." As more and more corporations have been caught in the web of price fixing laws, however, this charge has lost its punch. Senior business managers in industries that have never before known these problems, as well as previous offenders, are probably more concerned now about their corporate exposure to being indicted and convicted of price fixing than they were in any other recent period.

The costs of violating price fixing laws are very high: lawyers' fees, government fines, poor morale, damaged public image, civil suits, and now prison terms. Justice Department statistics indicate that 60 percent of antitrust felons are sentenced to prison terms. Thus, for very pragmatic reasons as well as for personal convictions, America's top executives are searching for fail-safe ways of meeting legal requirements.

One CEO well expressed the frustration common to executives in convicted companies:

We've tried hard to stress that collusion is illegal. We point out that anticompetitive practices hurt the company's
ethical standards, public image, internal morale, and earnings. Yet we wind up in trouble continually. When we try to find out why employees got involved, they have the gall to say that they "were only looking out for the best interests of the company." They seem to think that the company message is for everyone else but them. You begin to wonder about the intelligence of these people. Either they don't listen or they're just plain stupid.

General Management Signals

Some executives talked very explicitly about the problem of changing the culture of a problem division. Having been burned in the past, the financial vice president of a convicted company has adopted an inventive approach. He has communicated new acquisition criteria to his investment brokers. He is now at least as interested in information about a company's ethical practices as in its financial performance. One chief executive officer said that he and his top managers learned the hard way from troubles soon after making an acquisition. He felt that retraining management is helpful.

continued

Some managers have been reviewing their practices and making tighter definitions of who can legitimately take part in pricing decisions. It takes careful analysis of the multiple sources of relevant information concerning prices as well as an explicit commitment procedure to make such rules both workable and prudent.

Attempts to move beyond top-level role modeling have led some executives to prepare codes of ethics on company business practices. In some companies this document circulates only at top levels and, again, the word seems to have trouble getting down the line. Even those documents that were sent to all employees seemed to have been broadly written, toothless versions of the golden rule. One company tried to get more commitment by requiring employees to sign and return a pledge.

For codes to really work, substantial specificity is important. One executive said his company's method was successful because the code was tied in with an employee's daily routine:

> There is a code of business conduct here. To really make it meaningful, you have to get past the stage of endorsing motherhood and deal with the specific problems of policy in the different functional areas. We wrote up 20 pages on just purchasing issues.

Auditing for Compliance

Once these more specific codes of business conduct are distributed, top managers may want more than a signed statement in return. Individuals can be held responsible if they have been informed on how to act in certain gray areas. The company can show its commitment to the code by checking to see that it is respected and then disciplining violators.

Several companies are developing ways to implement internal policing. Some executives think that audits could hold people responsible for unusual pricing successes as well as for failures. Market conditions, product specifications, and factory scheduling could be coded, put on tables, and compared to prices. High variations could be investigated. One division vice president also plans to audit expense accounts to see that competitor contact is minimized.

Source: Reprinted by permission of *Harvard Business Review.* From "Why Do Companies Succumb to Price Fixing?" by Jeffrey A. Sonnenfeld and Paul R. Lawrence, July–August 1978. Copyright © 2002 by the Harvard Business School Publishing Corporation; all rights reserved.

BIOGRAPHY

CHRISTIE'S AND SOTHEBY'S: ARTISTIC PRICE FIXING

Christie's International and Sotheby's are international auction houses for art and estate items known for their handling of the estates and property of the rich and famous, such as the estate of Jacqueline Kennedy Onassis; the gowns of Diana, Princess of Wales; and the effects of Marilyn Monroe. Together, the two firms controlled 95 percent of the international auction market. They became the subject of a price fixing investigation by the Federal Trade Commission and the Justice Department in 1997.

The allegations of price fixing against the auction houses involve "conscious parallelism." That is, the two federal agencies were investigating why the two auction houses raised their commissions in lock step over the years with virtually no price competition in auction commissions.

The drama and media coverage surrounding the Christie's and Sotheby's antitrust investigation continued, but the case seemed to have no substance until the end of 1999.

In December 1999, Christopher M. Davidge, the CEO of Christie's, was terminated. Upset about what he called his "paltry" severance package and what others say was his concern that he might have been set up to take the blame for any antitrust charges, Mr. Davidge demanded all of his business records from Christie's. He took everything from his files, including handwritten notes he had sent to Sotheby's CEO, Diana (Dede) Brooks. Also implicated in his files was then chairman of Sotheby's, A. Alfred Taubman.

Mr. Davidge had initially denied, when questioned by the Justice Department, that he had any inappropriate communications with Sotheby's and Ms. Brooks. However, Mr. Davidge's former assistant, Irmgrad Pickering, told the Justice Department that she believed Mr. Davidge and Ms. Brooks had held meetings.

He turned the records over to his lawyer who, in turn, turned them over to the Justice Department. The records have been described as establishing "classic cartel behavior—price fixing pure and simple" between Christie's and Sotheby's. The correspondence in his files was between him and Ms. Brooks, CEO of Sotheby's. The correspondence reflects a pattern of the two auction houses matching their commission rates. For example, in March 1995, Christie's announced it was increasing its sellers' fees from a flat rate to a sliding scale ranging from 2 percent to 20 percent. Sotheby's made an announcement of the same change in sellers' rates one month later.

Soon after Christie's became aware of the documents and correspondence in the hands of the Justice Department, it announced its cooperation with the federal government and was given amnesty. At the same time, Christie's announced that it was raising its buyer's commission from 17.5 percent to 18 percent (for buyers spending up to $80,000 and 10 percent for buyers above that amount) and charging its sellers less, taking its commission for sales down 1 percent to 5 percent and as low as 1.25 percent for amounts greater than $1,000.

Both changes placed Sotheby's, Christie's prime competitor, in the position of charging higher commissions. The disparity in commissions was the first time there was any difference in the competitors' prices in over a decade.

Mr. Taubman denied any involvement in the price fixing and offered a lie detector test conducted by a former FBI agent to establish that he did not know of the arrangements and communications between Ms. Brooks and Mr. Davidge. The two key questions in the polygraph exam, which Mr. Taubman passed, were:

> *Did you tell Dede Brooks to try and reach an agreement with Davidge regarding amounts to be charged to buyers or sellers?*

> *Did Dede Brooks ever tell you that she had reached an agreement with Davidge about amounts to be charged to buyers and sellers?*

Mr. Taubman's answers of "no" to each of these questions were found to be truthful by the polygraph examiner. The test was conducted without any law enforcement agents present.

At nearly the same time, Christie's agreed to pay $256 million, one-half of a $512 million civil suit brought against the company, and settled a shareholder lawsuit for $30 million. Sotheby's also agreed to pay its $256 million of the suit amount to settle civil claims. Mr. Taubman agreed to be responsible for paying $156 million of that corporate obligation. Representing the plaintiffs in the antitrust suit against the two auction houses was David Boies, the lawyer who represented Al Gore in the 2000 presidential election litigation, Shawn Fanning and Napster in their copyright litigation, and the federal government in the Microsoft antitrust case.

Mr. Davidge got immunity in exchange for his cooperation. Ms. Brooks entered a guilty plea on October 5, 2000, and declined all of her stock options. Her friends say she refused the options so as to put all of the case behind her. Others say she declined them so that she will not be held responsible for any of the costs the company has incurred related to the antitrust activities. In exchange for favorable sentencing, Ms. Brooks, Mr. Taubman's one-time protégé, turned state's evidence and cooperated with the Justice Department in its investigation.

In May 2001, four years after the investigation began, the Justice Department announced the indictment of Mr. Taubman as well as his counterpart at Christie's, Sir Anthony Tennant. The indictment charged price fixing over a six-year period involving over 13,000 customers. The criminal case proceeded to trial near the end of 2001. Ms. Brooks testified against Mr. Taubman. Mr. Taubman was found guilty of price fixing and related charges.

Both Christie's and Mr. Davidge are immune from prosecution for antitrust violations because of their cooperation.

Following the settlements, Sotheby's, a 256-year-old company, hired Michael I. Sovern, the former president of Columbia University, as chairman of the board. Sotheby's stock suffered during the time of the daily disclosures about the investigations, the evidence, and the resulting litigation. At the beginning of the investigation, Sotheby's stock was trading in March 1999 at $42 per share. By March 2000, it was down to $15 per share.

Why do we worry that two auction houses were agreeing on increases in their commission rates? What do you think of Mr. Davidge's ethics? Did his intent to sue Christie's for terminating him turn out to provide Christie's with a break in the antitrust case? What do you think of Ms. Brooks providing evidence on her former mentor?

SOURCES

Alexandria Peers and Ann Davis, "Christie's Overhauls Commissions," *Wall Street Journal,* February 8, 2000, pp. A3, A10.

Douglas Frantz, with Carol Vogel and Ralph Blumenthal, "Files of Ex-Christie's Chief Fuel Inquiry into Art Auction," *New York Times,* October 8, 2000, pp. A1, A28.

CONSIDER . . .   17 · 3

General Electric, through its GES (General Electric Superabrasives) subsidiary, and De-Beers are both diamond processors and sellers. In 1991, both GES and DeBeers announced a price increase for their diamonds.

Edward Russell was a former GES employee who, in 1986, was promoted to the position of vice president in charge of GES. During this period Mr. Russell exchanged notes and held meetings with the managing director of a customer who also served as a board member for DeBeers. Following the meetings, both companies announced a 1991 price increase. There was some evidence that the customer indicated to GES that DeBeers would be increasing its prices. However, the customer who offered the information about the forthcoming price increase was not authorized to negotiate contracts or agreements on behalf of DeBeers.

Mr. Russell held his position as vice president of GES until November 11, 1991, when General Electric terminated his employment. In early 1992, Mr. Russell contacted the government, alleging that General Electric employees had committed various acts of wrongdoing, including antitrust violations.

Soon after contacting the government, Mr. Russell filed a civil wrongful termination action against General Electric. He alleged that General Electric fired him because he was a whistle-blower. Mr. Russell settled his wrongful termination suit against General Electric on February 16, 1994, one day before the grand jury handed down an indictment against General Electric (GE) for price fixing in violation of the Sherman Act. Mr. Russell was a key witness for the government. His testimony was that there was advance contact between GES and DeBeers before the announcement of the price increases. GE and DeBeers do not deny the advance contact but assert that there was no agreement to increase prices. [*U.S.* v. *General Elec. Co.*, 869 F.Supp. 1285 (1994).]

THINK: The elements for price fixing are that competitors act together to keep prices at a certain level or agree to charge a certain price. The statute does require an agreement between the parties.

APPLY: There must be evidence of an agreement to fix prices.

ANSWER: The court held that the fact that the managing director of the customer was also the director of a company that manufactured industrial diamonds did not establish that the managing director was acting on behalf of the competitor and that the industrial diamond manufacturer knew this when the managing director and the manufacturer exchanged advance list pricing information, for purposes of establishing that the manufacturer and the competitor conspired to raise list prices of industrial diamonds, where there was no evidence that the managing director's corporate links were used by the director or the competitor to form or facilitate an agreement with the manufacturer to fix prices.

ANSWER: Just because a managing director of customer, who was also director of company which manufactured industrial diamonds under a joint venture between the customer and a competitor, supported an industrial diamond price increase did not establish that the managing director was acting on behalf of the competitor. Any exchange of information took place with both parties aware that the managing director had no authority to act on behalf of the competitor.

CONSIDER . . .   17 · 4

If the three major cereal manufacturers or car manufacturers all raised their prices at the same time, would that be a price fixing violation of the Sherman Act?

Division of Markets

Any agreement between competitors to divide up an available market is a *per se* violation under the Sherman Act. The result of such an agreement is to give the participants monopolies in their particular area. Such a market division introduces an unnatural force into the competitive market. For example, office product supply companies agreeing to operate only in certain cities throughout a state would be a division of markets and a *per se* violation.

CONSIDER...   **17·5**

BRG of Georgia, Inc. (BRG), and Harcourt Brace Jovanovich Legal and Professional Publications (HBJ) are the nation's two largest providers of bar review materials and lectures. HBJ began offering a Georgia bar review course on a limited basis in 1976 and was in direct, often intense competition with BRG from 1977 to 1979. BRG and HBJ were the two main providers of bar review courses in Georgia during this period. In early 1980, they entered into an agreement that gave BRG an exclusive license to market HBJ's materials in Georgia and to use its trade name "Bar/Bri." The parties agreed that HBJ would not compete with BRG in Georgia and that BRG would not compete with HBJ outside of Georgia.

Under the agreement, HBJ received $100 per student enrolled by BRG and 40 percent of all revenues over $350. Immediately after the 1980 agreement, the price of BRG's course was increased from $150 to over $400.

Is this an illegal division of markets? [*Palmer* v. *BRG of Georgia, Inc.*, 498 U.S. 46 (1990).]

Group Boycotts and Refusals to Deal

A group of competitors that agrees not to deal with buyers unless those buyers agree to standard credit or arbitration clauses has committed a *per se* violation.

Some group boycotts appear to have the best intentions. Many garment manufacturers once agreed not to sell to buyers who sold discount or pirated designer clothing. Certainly their intentions were good, but the result still has the anticompetitive effect of controlling the marketplace. Competitors cannot enforce the law through boycotts; other avenues of relief are available. The American Medical Association's rules that prohibited salaried medical practices and prepaid medical plans are illegal boycotts in spite of the protection motivations behind the restrictions.

Visit the American Medical Association:
http://www.ama-assn.org

FTC v. *Superior Court Trial Lawyers Ass'n* (Case 17.3) involves an issue of a well-intentioned but still illegal boycott.

CASE 17.3

FTC v. *Superior Court Trial Lawyers Ass'n*
493 U.S. 411 (1990)

A Legal Boycott: Legal Aid, Legal Fees

FACTS

The U.S. Constitution requires that legal counsel be provided to indigent defendants. The District of Columbia, like other local governments, fulfills this responsibility through a program that hires private lawyers at a rate of $30 per hour. In 1982 these lawyers handled 25,000 indigent defendant cases at a cost of $4,579,572 to the District. Over 1,200 lawyers were reg-

istered for the indigent defendant program, with 100 lawyers classified as "regulars." Three of these 100 lawyers derived all of their income from indigent representation cases.

The Superior Court Trial Lawyers Association (SCTLA) had been concerned about the low fees paid in the program and had met with the mayor to encourage

continued

higher fees to ensure quality representation. The mayor was sympathetic but indicated that no funds were available for an increase.

In 1983 SCTLA formed a strike committee that recommended, as the only way to increase fees, encouraging members to stop signing indigent representation agreements until a rate schedule of $45 for out-of-court time and $55 for in-court time was achieved. About 100 lawyers signed a petition to this effect and agreed not to accept new cases. The result was that 90 percent of the regulars refused to accept new cases.

Within ten days of the September 6, 1983, petition, the criminal justice system in the District of Columbia was in chaos; the mayor met with the SCTLA strike committee and, declaring a crisis, increased the fees to the $45–$55 per hour rates. The agreement was approved by the city council on September 21, 1983.

The Federal Trade Commission (FTC) filed a complaint against SCTLA alleging that SCTLA's conduct was a conspiracy to fix prices and conduct a boycott and that it violated Section 5 of the FTC Act as an unfair method of competition. The administrative law judge (ALJ) found for the FTC, and the FTC found that a boycott had occurred that caused harm. The court of appeals remanded the case for a determination of whether SCTLA (respondents) had market power. The FTC appealed.

JUDICIAL OPINION

STEVENS, Justice

Respondents' boycott may well have served a cause that was worthwhile and unpopular. We may assume that the preboycott rates were unreasonably low, and that the increase has produced better legal representation for indigent defendants. Moreover, given that neither indigent criminal defendants nor the lawyers who represent them command any special appeal with the electorate, we may also assume that without the boycott there would have been no increase in District fees at least until Congress [acted]. These assumptions do not control the case, for it is not our task to pass upon the social utility or political wisdom of price fixing agreements.

It is of course true that the city purchases respondents' services because it has a constitutional duty to provide representation to indigent defendants. It is likewise true that the quality of representation may improve when rates are increased. Yet neither of these facts is an acceptable justification for an otherwise unlawful restraint of trade. As we have remarked before, the "Sherman Act reflects a legislative judgment that ultimately competition will produce not only lower prices, but also better goods and services." *National Society of Professional Engineers* v. *United States*, 435 U.S. 679 (1978). This judgment recognizes that all elements

of a bargain—quality, service, safety, and durability—and not just the immediate cost, are favorably affected by the free opportunity to select among alternative offers. That is equally so when the quality of legal advocacy, rather than engineering design, is at issue.

The social justifications proffered for respondents' restraint of trade thus do not make it any less unlawful. The statutory policy underlying the Sherman Act "precludes inquiry into the question whether competition is good or bad." Respondents' argument, like that made by petitioners in *Professional Engineers*, ultimately asks us to find that their boycott is permissible because the price it seeks to set is reasonable. But it was settled shortly after the Sherman Act was passed that it "is no excuse that the prices fixed are themselves reasonable." Respondents' agreement is not outside the coverage of the Sherman Act simply because its objective was enactment of favorable legislation.

The lawyers' association argues that if its conduct would otherwise be prohibited by the Sherman Act and the Federal Trade Act, it is nonetheless protected by the First Amendment rights.

The activity the FTC order prohibits is a concerted refusal by [the] lawyers to accept any further assignments until they receive an increase in their compensation; the undenied objective of their boycott was an economic advantage for those who agreed to participate. No matter how altruistic the motives of respondents may have been, it is undisputed that their immediate objective was to increase the price that they would be paid for their services.

Respondents' concerted action in refusing to accept further assignments until their fees were increased was thus a plain violation of the antitrust laws.

Affirmed as to the finding of a violation. Reversed for further proceedings on the issue of market power.

CASE QUESTIONS

1. Explain the District of Columbia system for providing legal representation for indigent defendants.
2. What was the rate of compensation for lawyers in the program?
3. What fees did the lawyers want?
4. What was the effect of the refusal to take new cases?
5. How long did the boycott last?
6. Did the lawyers get the fees they desired?
7. Of what relevance is the motivation of the lawyers in staging the boycott?
8. Was the boycott a violation of antitrust laws?
9. Was the violation *per se*?

ETHICAL ISSUES

The Federal Trade Commission (FTC) has charged AOL Time Warner, Inc., and its subsidiaries, Warner Music Group and Vivendi Universal SA, with price fixing in connection with the sales of the Three Tenors' audio and video CDs and tapes. (The three tenors are Luciano Pavarotti, Placido Domingo, and Jose Carreras.)

The Three Tenors make a record of their live performances together—done once every four years. The first two CDs and videos in the series sold millions, with both becoming two of the highest sales volume opera recordings in history. However, by the third live performance and its CD and video, the public demand was not as great. The FTC charges that Warner felt the first two releases would cannibalize the sales for the third. As a result, all parties involved in the sales of these CDs and tapes had to agree not to discount the first two performance tapes so that the third would have an opportunity to sell. The FTC also alleges that there were agreements on when advertisements could run for the third series sales and availability.

The FTC stumbled across a memo on the marketing plan and advertising constraints as it was reviewing documents in connection with the Warner/EMI Music merger proposal, a merger that fell through after European officials balked at the idea. The FTC pursued the case, and Warner settled the charges by agreeing not to restrain competition or set prices in the future.

Is it permissible for an agency investigating one issue to use evidence it comes across related to another issue? What lessons does this situation offer on the percolating nature of the truth? Is establishing a minimum price a violation of the Sherman Act? Is restricting advertising a violation of the Sherman Act?

CONSIDER...   17.6

The Federal Trade Commission is conducting an investigation into the informal agreements reached between Toys "Я" Us and toy manufacturers. Toys "Я" Us holds a 19.4 percent share of the U.S. toy market and has informal agreements with Mattel and Hasbro with respect to the sale of their toys to discount warehouse clubs such as Costco and Sam's Club. The clubs are sold toys only in more expensive packaging arrangements. For example, Hollywood Hair Barbie can be purchased at Toys "Я" Us for $10.95 but at warehouse clubs can be purchased only in a package with a dress for $15.95. Some of the most popular toy items are never sold to the warehouse clubs. For example, Hasbro has not sold its Hall of Fame GI Joe action figures to warehouse clubs, and Mattel will not sell its Fisher Price pool table to the clubs.

The FTC commissioners voted 5 to 3 to begin the investigation because toy manufacturers are put into a situation of choosing between selling to Toys "Я" Us and other retailers. Toys "Я" Us maintains that the warehouse clubs do not have the overhead of advertising the toys and simply choose those items that sell the best at very low margins. The low margins can be maintained because, for example, Costco took in more in membership fees over the last ten years than its total net profit.

Is there illegal restraint of trade? Is there price fixing? Have the antitrust laws been violated?

Joint Ventures

A **joint venture** is an undertaking by two or more businesses for a limited purpose. An oil corporation working with an engineering firm for the development of a new drill would be a joint venture; they would be business partners for that limited purpose and project.

Competitors who become involved in joint ventures are a natural concern. These combinations are subject, not to a *per se* violation standard, but to the **rule of reason**, which allows a court to consider the various benefits and detriments involved in a joint venture. For example, in one case all coal producers formed a joint venture sales agency during a time of a depressed coal market to increase sales and save selling costs. This joint venture was held to be reasonable under the Sherman Act [*United States* v. *Appalachian Coal*, 228 U.S. 334 (1933)].

FOR THE MANAGER'S DESK

Re: The Rule of Reason versus *Per Se* Violations

The rule of reason became the standard for judging antitrust cases as early as 1911 and is used for cases that do not fall in the *per se* category. Under the rule of reason "the anticompetitive consequences of a challenged practice are weighed against the business justifications upon which it is predicated and its putative procompetitive impact, and a judgment with respect to its reasonableness is made." Conduct that does not unambiguously injure competition ordinarily is not subject to the *per se* rule but instead is analyzed under the rule of reason. Unlike *per se* cases, rule of reason analysis considers whether there may be legitimate justifications for the restraint.

For example, the Supreme Court held that an association of dentists that required its members to withhold X-rays from dental insurers evaluating patient benefit claims, even though evaluated under the rule of reason, violated section 1 of the Sherman Act. The Court explained:

A refusal to compete with respect to the package of services offered to customers, no less than a refusal to compete with respect to the price term of an agreement, impairs the ability of the market to advance social welfare by ensuring the provision of goods and services to consumers at a price approximating the marginal cost of providing them.

Because the rule of reason focuses on anticompetitive effects, factors unrelated to the restraint's effect on competition are generally irrelevant to the analysis. In *National Society of Professional Engineers* v. *United States,* the defendants argued unsuccessfully that price competition among professional engineers could potentially result in inferior engineering work and create hazards to public safety and welfare. The Court stated that its function was "not to decide whether a policy favoring competition is in the public interest" because the "Sherman Act reflects a legislative judgment that ultimately competition will not only produce lower prices, but also better goods and services."

Source: Nancy J. White and Theodore R. Bolema, "Federal Antitrust Law Implications of Bid Shopping," 24 *Construction Lawyer* 37 (2004).

In another case, a joint venture between movie producers and movie theaters was held to be unreasonable because it gave the theaters exclusive showing rights to the producers' movies [*United States* v. *Paramount Pictures,* 334 U.S. 131 (1948)].

Exceptions to Sherman Act Violations

Some activities by competitors are protected even though the competitors are acting as a group and even though the effect may be to reduce competition. One such exception is the **Noerr-Pennington doctrine**, under which competitors are permitted to work together for the purpose of governmental lobbying and other political action.[2] Their conduct cannot be restrained under the Sherman Act because their activity enjoys the protection of the First Amendment. Competitors who work together to influence legislators and administrative agencies are protected even though they may be working for anticompetitive benefits. For example, competitors can make appearances at new licensee hearings and oppose the granting of a license. The resulting reduction in competition is done within the confines of the First Amendment and is not subject to Sherman Act jurisdiction.

The *Noerr-Pennington* doctrine strikes a delicate balance between anticompetitive behavior and First Amendment rights. That balance often fluctuates as new issues in regulation, lobbying, and licensing arise. In some instances, market domination is at issue in regulatory proceedings. In *City of Columbia* v. *Omni Outdoor Advertising,* 499 U.S. 365 (1991), a company that was controlling the outdoor advertising market in one city attempted to use its lobbying First Amendment rights to protect its market control. An objection and suit by a competitor still resulted in the protection of *Noerr-Pennington* and First Amendment rights. Courts are hesitant to intervene in a business's right to lobby and petition government agencies even if the purpose is preservation of market superiority.

CONSIDER...   **1 7 . 7**

In Arizona, fees for title insurance searches and policies were established by rating bureaus established by the title companies. The bureaus recommended rates to the state, and the state adopted those rates unless some specific objection was made. The result was that title search and insurance fees were the same for all companies within the state. The FTC filed a complaint against the title companies, alleging that they were engaged in price fixing. The companies responded that government regulation of prices is not price fixing. Do you agree? [*FTC v. Ticor Title Ins. Co.*, 504 U.S. 621 (1992).]

MAKING ETHICS PERSONAL

Bid Shopping

Bid shopping is a practice in which a prime contractor, who has been awarded a contract based upon bids from subcontractors, contacts those subcontractors in an effort to induce the subcontractors to reduce a previously quoted price. Bid peddling is a similar practice but occurs when a subcontractor contacts the prime who has been awarded a contract and attempts to get the work by lowering its original bid. In general, bid shopping seems to draw the greatest objections from the construction industry when it involves prime contractors revealing the current low bid to potential subcontractors in order to induce them to lower their bids.

Bid shopping can take place both before a contractor submits its bid to the owner as well as after the prime has already submitted its bid and been awarded the job. While both acts are "generally condemned as unethical by construction industry associations," the latter tends to be more offensive as a matter of law, as will be discussed later. In addition, contractor groups have lobbied for Congress and state legislatures to enact legislation to discourage bid shopping. California's "Subletting and Subcontracting Fair Practices Act" is an example of such a law that has been enacted.

The practice of bid shopping by prime contractors seeking to obtain bids from subcontractors is often condemned by groups within the construction industry as unethical or as leading to poorer quality of work. For example, the American Institute of Contractors' (AIC) Web site contains an article condemning the practices of bid shopping and bid peddling as "usurp[ing] the business opportunities that ethically should accrue to the sub-bidder who submitted the lowest, responsive price on or before bid day." The same article also points out that the AIC, the American Subcontractors Association, and the American Specialty Contractors in 1995

issued a joint statement and quotes the joint statement as follows:

> Bid shopping or bid peddling are abhorrent business practices that threaten the integrity of the competitive bidding system that serves the construction industry and the economy so well.
>
> The bid amount of one competitor should not be divulged to another before the award of the subcontract or order, nor should it be used by the contractor to secure a lower proposal from another bidder on that project (bid shopping). Neither should the subcontractor or supplier request information from the contractor regarding any subbid in order to submit a lower proposal on that project (bid peddling).
>
> The Associated General Contractors of America, the American Subcontractors Association, and the Associated Specialty Contractors oppose these practices.

The Mechanical Contractors Association's Web site contains a similar condemnation of bid shopping. The National Electrical Contractors Association (NECA) policy statement makes the claim that NECA has sought to prevent these practices:

> For many years NECA has taken an active role in attempting to prevent such practices as complimentary bidding, bid shopping, bid peddling, blacklisting of selected contractors, product boycotts, operation of exclusive bid depositories or activities of a like nature by individuals, groups or entire chapters.

The objections to bid shopping raise a number of concerns, some of which include "promoting lower standards of work, clouding ability to pinpoint responsibility for system performance, legal disputes, overall

continued

job safety, minority/female set asides, and higher orig-inal bid costs."

Regardless of the merits of the reasons for opposing these practices, such condemnations of bid shopping by private groups run a serious risk of being found in violation of federal antitrust laws, especially if accom-panied by additional evidence that construction inter-ests have sought on their own to suppress this practice. Such evidence may include the statement on the NECA Web site. Whether or not these practices are unethical is probably beside the point. On the other hand, actions

by these construction groups to lobby states to enact prohibitions against bid shopping, in and of them-selves, are unlikely to violate the antitrust laws, al-though they may nonetheless attract the attention of the federal antitrust authorities.

Would you engage in bid shopping? What would happen if you organized subcontractors to lobby to make bid shopping illegal? Doesn't bid shopping in-crease competition and reduce prices?

Source: Nancy J. White and Theodore R. Bolema, "Federal Antitrust Law Implications of Bid Shopping," 24 *Construction Lawyer* 37 (2004).

Review the Local Government Antitrust Act of 1984:
http://www.law.cornell.edu/uscode/15/34.html

There are additional exceptions to the antitrust laws. The Local Government Antitrust Act of 1984 was passed to eliminate the effects of several Supreme Court decisions that would not allow state and local governments to be exempted from the application of federal antitrust laws unless there was a state policy that specifi-cally exempted such activities. The Local Government Antitrust Act has provided an exemption for these localities, which were facing over 300 antitrust lawsuits at the time the act was passed.

In order to compete effectively in the international market, U.S. businesses have been permitted to form selling cooperatives or joint ventures with prior approval from the Justice Department. The Joint Venture Trading Act of 1983 allows joint ventures of competitors for the purpose of competing with foreign competitors (with Justice Department approval). The Shipping Act of 1984 allows carriers to enter into joint venture shipping arrangements so shippers can more effectively compete in the international market, where rates are set and routes and shipments are divided among competitors.

Clayton Act Restraints

Interlocking Directorates

The first Clayton Act horizontal restraint concerns the use of directors on the boards of competitive firms to lessen the effects of competition—**interlocking directorates**. Section 8 prohibits a director of a firm with $10 million or more in capital from being a director of a competing company. The intent of this prohibition is to lessen the likelihood of the exchange of anticompetitive information about price, markets, and other competitors.

Horizontal Mergers

Horizontal mergers are mergers between competitors. To determine when they have taken place, courts have applied a test of "presumptive illegality": Any merger that produces an undue percentage share of the market or significantly increases market concentration is a violation. In these cases, the courts examine market share and the relevant markets to determine whether there is undue con-centration.

There are some defenses that justify a horizontal merger. One is the **failing-company doctrine**, which allows the acquisition of a competitor that is clearly fail-ing if it is an asset or inventory acquisition. Another defense is the **small-company doctrine**, which applies when two small companies merge with the hope of being better able to compete with the larger businesses in that market.

In *United States* v. *Von's Grocery Co.,* 384 U.S. 270 (1966), the Supreme Court held that a merger between Von's Grocery Company and Shopping Bag Food Stores, which would have given the two companies together a 7.5 percent share of the retail grocery market in Los Angeles, violated the Clayton Act because its effect would be to substantially lessen competition. In 1988, the Justice Department approved the merger of Von's and Safeway in southern California. The merger made the new Von's the largest competitor in terms of market percentage as well as in the number of stores. Justice Department attitudes and guidelines on mergers have changed largely because geographic markets have changed. Geographic markets are now defined in light of international trade. Some domestic combinations that would have been illegal in 1966 are now permissible because of size requirements for companies in international competition.

VERTICAL TRADE RESTRAINTS

Various steps are involved in getting a product from its creation to its ultimate consumer. For example, producing packaged sandwich meats requires the manufacturer to obtain bulk-butchered meat (originally from a ranch) through a distributor and turn it into packaged sandwich meat that is sold to another distributor. This distributor sells to a grocery wholesaler, who sells to grocery stores, where consumers buy the packaged meat. This entire process has different levels of production and distribution, but there is one vertical chain from start to finish.

The types of vertical restraints, discussed in the following subsections, are:

- Resale price maintenance
- Sole outlets and exclusive distributorships
- Customer and territorial restrictions
- Tying arrangements
- Exclusive dealing or requirements contracts
- Price discrimination

Resale Price Maintenance

Resale price maintenance is an attempt by a manufacturer to control the price that retailers charge for the manufacturer's product. Resale price maintenance is a rule-of-reason violation of Section 1 of the Sherman Act (see *State Oil* v. *Khan,* Case 17.4). Resale price maintenance includes either minimum or maximum prices, or both. A minimum price encourages a retailer to carry a certain product because its profit margin will be higher. One explanation offered to justify minimum prices is that, without them, dealers who advertise and offer service may be used by consumers for information only, after which these consumers actually buy at discount houses.

A manufacturer who attempts to set a maximum price is trying to prevent retailers with market power from charging a price higher than that set for the manufacturer's goods, thereby reducing the number of sales. The economic theory is that fewer goods would be sold under such circumstances than if there were open competition.

Resale price maintenance can also occur in ways other than actual price controls—for example, through the use of consignments. If the packaged-sandwich-meat manufacturer required all grocery stores to act as agents for the sale of its meats and paid a commission on each sale, there would be a consignment. The manufacturer could control the price through such an arrangement, but such price-controlled consignments are violations of Section 1 of the Sherman Act.

Manufacturers can offer a "suggested retail price" without violating Section 1, although any attempt to enforce that suggested price would be a violation. For example, a manufacturer who refuses to sell to a retailer who does not use the suggested price is engaging in resale price maintenance.

At one time, states were permitted to allow resale price maintenance by statute. That power was taken away in 1975, and states cannot, by statute, allow minimum price schedules or require dealers to adhere to **fair trade contracts**, which are agreements on maximum or minimum prices.

State Oil v. *Khan* (Case 17.4) deals with the issue of resale price maintenance and the change from its *per se* violation to a rule-of-reason standard.

CASE 17.4

State Oil v. *Khan*
522 U.S. 3 (1997)

Fill It Up, but Only at My Price

FACTS

Barkat U. Khan and his corporation (respondents) entered into an agreement with State Oil (petitioner) to lease and operate a gas station and convenience store owned by State Oil. The agreement provided that Mr. Khan would obtain the gasoline supply for the station from State Oil at a suggested retail price set by State Oil, less a margin of 3.25 cents per gallon. Mr. Khan could charge any price he wanted, but if he charged more than State Oil's suggested retail price, the excess was rebated to State Oil. Mr. Khan could sell the gasoline for less than State Oil's suggested retail price, but the difference came out of his allowed margin.

After a year, Mr. Khan fell behind on his lease payments, and State Oil began proceedings for eviction. The court had Mr. Khan removed and appointed a receiver to operate the station. The receiver operated the gas station without the price constraints and received an overall profit margin above the 3.25 cents imposed on Mr. Khan.

Mr. Khan filed suit, alleging that the State Oil agreement was a violation of Section 1 of the Sherman Act because State Oil was controlling prices. The district court held that there was no *per se* violation and that Mr. Khan had failed to demonstrate antitrust injury. The Court of Appeals reversed, and State Oil appealed.

JUDICIAL OPINION

O'CONNOR, Justice
Under § 1 of the Sherman Act, 26 Stat. 209, as amended, 15 U.S.C. § 1, "[e]very contract, combination . . . , or conspiracy, in restraint of trade" is illegal. In *Albrecht* v.

Herald Co., 390 U.S. 145, 88 S.Ct. 869, 19 L.Ed.2d 998 (1968), this Court held that vertical maximum price fixing is a per se violation of that statute. In this case, we are asked to reconsider that decision in light of subsequent decisions of this Court. We conclude that *Albrecht* should be overruled.

Although the Sherman Act, by its terms, prohibits every agreement "in restraint of trade," this Court has long recognized that Congress intended to outlaw only unreasonable restraints.

As a consequence, most antitrust claims are analyzed under a "rule of reason," according to which the finder of fact must decide whether the questioned practice imposes an unreasonable restraint on competition, taking into account a variety of factors, including specific information about the relevant business, its condition before and after the restraint was imposed, and the restraint's history, nature, and effect.

Some types of restraints, however, have such predictable and pernicious anticompetitive effect, and such limited potential for procompetitive benefit, that they are deemed unlawful per se.

Thus, we have expressed reluctance to adopt per se rules with regard to "restraints imposed in the context of business relationships where the economic impact of certain practices is not immediately obvious."

In *White Motor Co.* v. *United States,* 372 U.S. 253, 83 S.Ct. 696, 9 L.Ed.2d 738 (1963), the Court considered the validity of a manufacturer's assignment of exclusive territories to its distributors and dealers. The Court determined that too little was known about the competitive impact of such vertical limitations to warrant treating them as per se unlawful.

Four years later, in *United States v. Arnold, Schwinn & Co.*, 388 U.S. 365, 87 S.Ct. 1856, 18 L.Ed. 2d 1249 (1967), the Court reconsidered the status of exclusive dealer territories and held that, upon the transfer of title to goods to a distributor, a supplier's imposition of territorial restrictions on the distributor was "so obviously destructive of competition" as to constitute a per se violation of the Sherman Act. In *Schwinn*, the Court acknowledged that some vertical restrictions, such as the conferral of territorial rights or franchises, could have procompetitive benefits by allowing smaller enterprises to compete, and that such restrictions might avert vertical integration in the distribution process. The Court drew the line, however, at permitting manufacturers to control product marketing once dominion over the goods had passed to dealers.

Albrecht, decided the following Term, involved a newspaper publisher who had granted exclusive territories to independent carriers subject to their adherence to a maximum price on resale of the newspapers to the public. Influenced by its decisions in *Socony-Vacuum, Kiefer-Stewart*, and *Schwinn*, the Court concluded that it was per se unlawful for the publisher to fix the maximum resale price of its newspapers. The Court acknowledged that "[m]aximum and minimum price fixing may have different consequences in many situations," but nonetheless condemned maximum price fixing for "substituting the perhaps erroneous judgment of a seller for the forces of the competitive market."

Albrecht was animated in part by the fear that vertical maximum price fixing could allow suppliers to discriminate against certain dealers, restrict the services that dealers could afford to offer customers, or disguise minimum price fixing schemes. The Court rejected the notion (both on the record of that case and in the abstract) that, because the newspaper publisher "granted exclusive territories, a price ceiling was necessary to protect the public from price gouging by dealers who had monopoly power in their own territories."

In a vigorous dissent, Justice Harlan asserted that the majority had erred in equating the effects of maximum and minimum price fixing.

Nine years later, in *Continental T.V., Inc. v. GTE Sylvania, Inc.*, 433 U.S. 36, 97 S.Ct. 2549, 53 L.Ed.2d 568 (1977), the Court overruled *Schwinn*, thereby rejecting application of a per se rule in the context of vertical nonprice restrictions. The Court acknowledged the principle of *stare decisis*, but explained that the need for clarification in the law justified reconsideration of *Schwinn*:

> Since its announcement, Schwinn *has been the subject of continuing controversy and confusion, both in the scholarly journals and in the federal courts. The great weight of scholarly opinion has been critical of the decision, and a number of the federal courts confronted*

with analogous vertical restrictions have sought to limit its reach.

Thus, our reconsideration of *Albrecht*'s continuing validity is informed by several of our decisions, as well as a considerable body of scholarship discussing the effects of vertical restraints. Our analysis is also guided by our general view that the primary purpose of the antitrust laws is to protect interbrand competition. See, e.g., *Business Electronics Corp. v. Sharp Electronics Corp.*, 485 U.S. 717, 726, 108 S.Ct. 1515, 1520–1521, 99 L.Ed.2d 808 (1988). "Low prices," we have explained, "benefit consumers regardless of how those prices are set, and so long as they are above predatory levels, they do not threaten competition." Our interpretation of the Sherman Act also incorporates the notion that condemnation of practices resulting in lower prices to consumers is "especially costly" because "cutting prices in order to increase business often is the very essence of competition." *Matsushita Elec. Industrial Co. v. Zenith Radio Corp.*, 475 U.S. 574, 594, 106 S.Ct. 1348, 1360, 89 L.Ed.2d 538 (1986).

So informed, we find it difficult to maintain that vertically-imposed maximum prices could harm consumers or competition to the extent necessary to justify their per se invalidation. As Chief Judge Posner wrote for the Court of Appeals in this case:

> As for maximum resale price fixing, unless the supplier is a monopsonist he cannot squeeze his dealers' margins below a competitive level; the attempt to do so would just drive the dealers into the arms of a competing supplier. A supplier might, however, fix a maximum resale price in order to prevent his dealers from exploiting a monopoly position.... [S]uppose that State Oil, perhaps to encourage ... dealer services ... has spaced its dealers sufficiently far apart to limit competition among them (or even given each of them an exclusive territory); and suppose further that Union 76 is a sufficiently distinctive and popular brand to give the dealers in it at least a modicum of monopoly power. Then State Oil might want to place a ceiling on the dealers' resale prices in order to prevent them from exploiting that monopoly power fully. It would do this not out of disinterested malice, but in its commercial self-interest. The higher the price at which gasoline is resold, the smaller the volume sold, and so the lower the profit to the supplier if the higher profit per gallon at the higher price is being snared by the dealer.

93 F.3d, at 1362.

See also R. Bork, The Antitrust Paradox 281–282 (1978) ("There could of course, be no anticonsumer effect from [the type of price fixing considered in *Albrecht*], and one suspects that the paper has a legitimate

continued

interest in keeping subscriber prices down in order to increase circulation and maximize revenues from advertising").

Further, although vertical maximum price fixing might limit the viability of inefficient dealers, that consequence is not necessarily harmful to competition and consumers.

After reconsidering *Albrecht*'s rationale and the substantial criticism the decision has received, however, we conclude that there is insufficient economic justification for per se invalidation of vertical maximum price fixing. That is so not only because it is difficult to accept the assumptions underlying *Albrecht*, but also because *Albrecht* has little or no relevance to ongoing enforcement of the Sherman Act.

Despite what Chief Judge Posner aptly described as *Albrecht*'s infirmities, [and] its increasingly wobbly, moth-eaten foundations, there remains the question whether *Albrecht* deserves continuing respect under the doctrine of *stare decisis*. The Court of Appeals was correct in applying that principle despite disagreement with *Albrecht*, for it is this Court's prerogative alone to overrule one of its precedents.

We approach the reconsideration of decisions of this Court with the utmost caution. *Stare decisis* reflects "a policy judgment that 'in most matters it is more important that the applicable rule of law be settled than that it be settled right.'"

But "[s]tare decisis is not an inexorable command." In the area of antitrust law, there is a competing interest, well-represented in this Court's decisions, in recognizing and adapting to changed circumstances and the lessons of accumulated experience. Thus, the general presumption that legislative changes should be left to Congress has less force with respect to the Sherman Act in light of the accepted view that Congress "expected the courts to give shape to the statute's broad mandate by drawing on common-law tradition." *National Soc. of Professional Engineers v. United States*, 435 U.S. 679, 688, 98, S.Ct. 1355, 1363, 55 L.Ed.2d 637 (1978). As we have

explained, the term "restraint of trade," as used in § 1, also "invokes the common law itself, and not merely the static content that the common law had assigned to the term in 1890." Accordingly, this Court has reconsidered its decisions construing the Sherman Act when the theoretical underpinnings of those decisions are called into serious question.

In overruling *Albrecht*, we of course do not hold that all vertical maximum price fixing is per se lawful. Instead, vertical maximum price fixing, like the majority of commercial arrangements subject to the antitrust laws, should be evaluated under the rule of reason. In our view, rule-of-reason analysis will effectively identify those situations in which vertical maximum price fixing amounts to anticompetitive conduct.

There remains the question whether respondents are entitled to recover damages based on State Oil's conduct. Although the Court of Appeals noted that "the district judge was right to conclude that if the rule of reason is applicable, Khan loses," its consideration of this case was necessarily premised on *Albrecht*'s per se rule. Under the circumstances, the matter should be reviewed by the Court of Appeals in the first instance. We therefore vacate the judgment of the Court of Appeals and remand the case for further proceedings consistent with this opinion.

Remanded.

CASE QUESTIONS

1. What were the terms of Mr. Khan's lease?
2. Could Mr. Khan charge a different price?
3. What happened when a receiver operated the station without the State Oil lease constraints?
4. Is vertical price fixing a *per se* violation?
5. What does the court say about inefficient retailers and vertical price controls?
6. What does the court say about a long-standing precedent and *stare decisis*?

Sole Outlets and Exclusive Distributorships

A **sole outlet** or **exclusive distributorship** agreement is one in which a manufacturer appoints a distributor or retailer as the sole or exclusive outlet for the manufacturer's product. This type of arrangement can be a violation of Section 1 but is subject to a rule of reason analysis. When the rule of reason is applied to alleged antitrust violators, the alleged violators have an opportunity to present justifications for their conduct.

In a rule of reason analysis of sole outlets or exclusive distributorships, courts examine several factors. One factor is a manufacturer's freedom to pick and choose

CONSIDER... 17.8

Department 56 is a company that manufactures and sells collectible Christmas village houses and other replica items to allow collectors to create the whimsical "Snow Village" town or "Dickens Christmas." Department 56 has only authorized dealers. Sam's Club, a division of Wal-Mart Stores, Inc., began selling Department 56 pieces from The Heritage Village Collection.

Susan Engel, president and CEO of Department 56, attempted to contact Wal-Mart because it is not an authorized Department 56 dealer. Wal-Mart did not respond, and Ms. Engel sent by Federal Express to National Collector clubs a letter that contained the following language:

> *Sam's Club should not have any Department 56 merchandise. In a marketing environment where most companies are fighting to get their merchandise into the Wal-Marts of the world, we are fighting to get our merchandise out. While we recognize there is surely a place for mass market and warehouse stores, Department 56 Villages enjoy a strong heritage of dealer sales and service support. Our products simply do not fit the warehouse-style selling environment of Sam's Club.*
>
> *Of strong importance to us—and we hope to you too—is the tradition of selling our villages through an exclusive dealer network made up almost entirely of independent retailers. Wal-Mart Stores, Inc., and its subsidiaries are predators on these hard working individuals. Sales of our products mean virtually nothing to the bottom line of a company the size of Wal-Mart. But to many of our loyal dealers, healthy Department 56 product sales mean survival.*
>
> *Do you really need to shop at Sam's Club or Wal-Mart? Let's refuse to purchase villages or any other products from local Wal-Mart owned stores.*

The letter asked collector club members to write Wal-Mart executives and local store managers. Names, mailing addresses, and telephone and fax numbers were offered.

Has Ms. Engel violated any laws? How do you think Sam's Club obtained the Department 56 products?

ETHICAL ISSUES

Evaluate Ms. Engel's conduct in sending out the letter. Were her statements about Wal-Mart and calls to action fair? Should Wal-Mart respond? How?

certain buyers to deal with. However, the extent of the manufacturer's freedom is limited by the amount of **interbrand competition**, which is the competition available for the manufacturer's product. For example, in the case of the sandwich-meat manufacturer, so long as there are other manufacturers selling their products in the area, the manufacturer could agree to sell to only one chain of grocery stores. But if there is little interbrand competition, the antitrust laws require that **intrabrand competition** be more available. Thus, if the manufacturer were the only one distributing sandwich meats in the area, dealing with only one grocery chain might not be reasonable and could not survive an antitrust challenge.

The rule of reason also allows a court to consider other factors involved in a manufacturer's arrangements. For example, if the manufacturer agrees to limit outlets merely to benefit one of the outlets, there may be a violation.

Customer and Territorial Restrictions

Sole outlets allow manufacturers to decide (within limitations) to whom they will sell goods. However, manufacturers are not given the right to control what the buyer does with goods and how those goods are sold. Under Section 1 of the Sherman Act, restricting to whom and where a buyer of a manufacturer's goods can sell is a rule-of-reason violation. The restrictions are subject to the rule of reason because interbrand competition may be increased even though intrabrand competition is reduced.

In applying the rule of reason to **customer and territorial restrictions**, there are several issues to be considered. The first is whether there is an increase in interbrand competition because of decreased intrabrand competition. A second consideration is whether the manufacturer imposing the restriction has market power. The more market power the manufacturer has, the fewer substitute goods consumers have, resulting in less interbrand competition.

Vertical restrictions are likely to be judged reasonable when the manufacturer is new to the market or is having financial or sales difficulties. If the restrictions will help the manufacturer get started or keep going, the objective of interbrand competition is met by the restrictions on intrabrand competition.

Tying Arrangements

Tying sales require buyers to take an additional product in order to buy a needed product. For example, requiring the buyer of a copier machine to buy the seller's paper when there are other brands of paper suitable for use in the machine is a tying arrangement. The copier machine is the tying product or the desired product, and the paper is the tied product or the required product.

Tying is usually an illegal *per se* violation of Section 3 of the Clayton Act (for goods contracts) and Section 1 of the Sherman Act (for services, real property, and intangibles). Both acts prohibit tying but cover different subject matters. Whether there is a violation depends on whether market power results from the tying arrangement and whether there are any defenses.

Market power is established if the tying product is unique. For example, requiring the purchase of inferior movie films in order to buy copyrighted quality films is an example of the presence of market power. Because the seller is the only one with the copyrighted films, market power is being used to sell another unnecessary, low-demand product.

Two defenses have been recognized in tying cases. The first is the *new industry defense.* Under this defense, the manufacturer of the tying product is permitted to have a tied product to protect initially the quality control in the start-up of a business. For example, a cable television antenna manufacturer required purchasers to take a service contract also. The tying was upheld during the outset of the business so that the system could begin functioning properly and this new cable television industry could catch hold.

A second defense is *quality control for the protection of goodwill.* This defense is rarely supportable. The only time it would apply is if the specifications for the tied goods were so detailed that they could not possibly be supplied by anyone other than the manufacturer of the tying product.

Jefferson Parish Hosp. Dist. No. 2 v. *Hyde* (Case 17.5) involves an issue of whether a tying arrangement was valid.

CASE 17.5

Jefferson Parish Hosp. Dist. No. 2 v. Hyde
466 U.S. 2 (1984)

B.Y.O. Anesthesiologist: Tying Hospital Arrangements

FACTS

Dr. Edwin G. Hyde, a board-certified anesthesiologist, applied for permission to practice at East Jefferson Hospital (petitioners) in Louisiana. An approval was recommended for his hiring, but the hospital's board denied him employment on grounds that the hospital had a contract with Roux & Associates for Roux to provide all anesthesiological services required by the hospital's patients. Dr. Hyde filed suit, which the district court dismissed. The court of appeals reversed that decision and held that the contract for the services with Roux was illegal *per se*. The hospital appealed.

JUDICIAL OPINION

STEVENS, Justice

The exclusive contract had an impact on two different segments of the economy: consumers of medical services, and providers of anesthesiological services. Any consumer of medical services who elects to have an operation performed at East Jefferson Hospital may not employ any anesthesiologist not associated with Roux. No anesthesiologists except those employed by Roux may practice at East Jefferson.

There are at least twenty hospitals in the New Orleans metropolitan area and about 70 percent of the patients living in Jefferson Parish go to hospitals other than East Jefferson. Because it regarded the entire New Orleans metropolitan area as the relevant geographic market in which hospitals compete, this evidence convinced the District Court that East Jefferson does not possess any significant "market power"; therefore it concluded that petitioners could not use the Roux contract to anticompetitive ends. The same evidence led the Court of Appeals to draw a different conclusion. Noting that 30 percent of the residents of the Parish go to East Jefferson Hospital, and that, in fact, "patients tend to choose hospitals by location rather than price or quality," the Court of Appeals concluded that the relevant market was the East Bank of Jefferson Parish. The conclusion that East Jefferson Hospital possessed market power in that area was buttressed by the facts that the prevalence of health insurance eliminates a patient's incentive to compare costs, that the patient is not sufficiently informed to compare quality, and that family convenience tends to magnify the importance of location.

The Court of Appeals held that the case involves a "tying arrangement" because the "users of the hospital's operating rooms (the tying product) are also compelled to purchase the hospital's chosen anesthesia service (the tied product)."

It is clear, however, that every refusal to sell two products separately cannot be said to restrain competition. For example, we have written that "if one of a dozen food stores in a community were to refuse to sell flour unless the buyer also took sugar it would hardly tend to restrain competition if its competitors were ready and able to sell flour by itself." Buyers often find package sales attractive; a seller's decision to offer such packages can merely be an attempt to compete effectively—conduct that is entirely consistent with the Sherman Act.

Accordingly, we have condemned tying arrangements when the seller has some special ability—usually called "market power"—to force a purchaser to do something that he would not do in a competitive market. When "forcing" occurs, our cases have found the tying arrangement to be unlawful.

The hospital has provided its patients with a package that includes a range of facilities and services required for a variety of surgical operations. At East Jefferson Hospital the package includes the services of the anesthesiologist. Petitioners argue that the package does not involve a tying arrangement at all—that they are merely providing a functionally integrated package of services.

Unquestionably, the anesthesiological component of the package offered by the hospital could be provided separately and could be selected either by the individual patient or by one of the patient's doctors if the hospital did not insist on including anesthesiological services in the package it offers to its customers. As a matter of actual practice, anesthesiological services are billed separately from the hospital services petitioners provide. There was ample and uncontroverted testimony that patients or surgeons often request specific anesthesiologists to come to a hospital and provide anesthesia, and that the choice of a hospital is particularly frequent in respondent's specialty, obstetric anesthesiology.

Thus, the hospital's requirement that its patients obtain necessary anesthesiological services from Roux combined the purchase of two distinguishable services in a single transaction. As noted above, there is nothing

continued

inherently anticompetitive about packaged sales. Only if patients are forced to purchase Roux's services as a result of the hospital's market power would the arrangement have anticompetitive consequences.

It is safe to assume that every patient undergoing a surgical operation needs the services of an anesthesiologist; at least this record contains no evidence that the hospital "forced" any such services on unwilling patients. The record therefore does not provide a basis for applying the *per se* rule against tying to this arrangement.

In order to prevail in the absence of *per se* liability, respondent has the burden of proving that the Roux contract violated the Sherman Act because it unreasonably restrained competition.

All the record establishes is that the choice of anesthesiologists at East Jefferson has been limited to one of the four doctors who are associated with Roux and therefore have staff privileges. Even if Roux did not have an exclusive contract, the range of alternatives open to the patient would be severely limited by the nature of the transaction and the hospital's unquestioned right to exercise some control over the identity and number of doctors to whom it accords staff privileges.

Petitioner's closed policy may raise questions of medical ethics, and may have inconvenienced some patients who would prefer to have their anesthesia administered by someone other than a member of Roux & Associates, but it does not have the obviously unreasonable impact on purchasers that has characterized the tying arrangements that this Court has branded unlawful.

Reversed.

CASE QUESTIONS

1. What is East Jefferson's share of the medical care market?

2. Do patients ever indicate any choice or knowledge regarding anesthesiologists?

3. Is the arrangement illegal *per se*?

4. Is the arrangement unreasonable?

5. Why was the issue of "force" important?

CONSIDER...   17.9

David Ungar holds a Dunkin' Donuts franchise. The terms of his franchise agreement require him to use only those ingredients furnished by Dunkin' Donuts. He is also required to buy their napkins, cups, and so on with the Dunkin' Donuts trademark on them. Is this an illegal tying arrangement? What if Dunkin' Donuts maintains that it needs these requirements to maintain its quality levels on a nationwide basis? [*Ungar* v. *Dunkin' Donuts of Am., Inc.*, 531 F.2d 1211 (3d Cir. 1976).]

Exclusive Dealing or Requirements Contracts

Under **exclusive dealing** or **requirements contracts**, a buyer agrees to handle only one manufacturer's goods and not to carry any competitors' brands. These contracts also exist when a buyer agrees to purchase all of its requirements from one seller, such as when the sandwich-meat manufacturer agrees to buy meat from only one slaughterhouse.

These types of agreements are treated as tying arrangements because the buyer has, in effect, agreed not to use another's products; but they are treated more leniently. The contracts must cover a substantial dollar amount of the market, and a substantial share of the market must be foreclosed by the agreement. For example, if the sandwich-meat manufacturer is a national manufacturer, the agreement to buy from one slaughterhouse is substantial. However, if the manufacturer is a local one with limited distribution, the agreement will probably not foreclose much of the market from other slaughterhouses.

Price Discrimination

The Robinson-Patman Act prohibits **price discrimination**, which is selling goods at prices that have different ratios to the marginal cost of producing them. If two goods have the same marginal cost and are sold to different people at different prices, there is price discrimination. Four elements are required in a price discrimination case:

1. A seller engaged in commerce
2. Discrimination in price among purchasers
3. Commodities sold that are of like grade or quality
4. A substantial lessening of competition in any line of commerce or a tendency to create a monopoly; or competition is injured, destroyed, or prevented

If all the elements are established, both the buyer and the seller have violated the Robinson-Patman Act.

Price Discrimination among Purchasers

For price discrimination to occur, there must actually be a purchase; Robinson-Patman does not cover leases and consignments. Also, the purchases must be made at about the same time. The discrimination can come in the form of the actual price charged but can also come from indirect charges. For example, offering different credit terms to equally qualified buyers can constitute price discrimination.

Commodities of Like Grade or Quality

For the Robinson-Patman Act to apply, the products sold must be of **like grade or quality**, which means that there are no physical differences in the product. Label differences do not make the products different. For example, the sandwich-meat manufacturer that makes a private label meat cannot discriminate in price for the sale of that meat if the contents are the same as the manufacturer's advertised label meat and only the label is different. However, if the private-label meat has lower-quality meat in it, there can be a price difference because the products are not the same.

Lessening or Injuring Competition

Generally, injury to competition can be demonstrated by showing that there is a substantial price cut in a certain area by a large manufacturer with the effect of injuring or destroying a smaller competitor. Price discrimination is an example of the use of vertical restraints to lessen horizontal competition. Predatory pricing or pricing below cost is an example of conduct that will injure or destroy competition.

Utah Pie Co. v. *Continental Baking Co.* (Case 17.6) involves an issue of competition injury through price discrimination.

CASE 17.6

Utah Pie Co. **v.** *Continental Baking Co.*
386 U.S. 685 (1967)

Pie in the Sky: Free Market Competition and Pricing

FACTS

Utah Pie Company (petitioner) is a Utah corporation that for thirty years has been baking pies in its plant in Salt Lake City and selling them in Utah and surrounding states. It entered the frozen pie business in 1957 and was immediately successful with its new line of frozen dessert pies—apple, cherry, boysenberry, peach, pumpkin, and mince.

Continental Baking Company, Pet Milk, and Carnation (respondents), based in California, sell pies in Utah primarily on a delivered-price basis.

The major competitive weapon in the Utah pie market was price. Between 1958 and 1961, there was a deteriorating price structure for pies in the Utah market. Utah Pie was selling pies for $4.15 per dozen at the

continued

beginning of the period; at the time it filed suit for price discrimination, it was selling the same pies for $2.75 per dozen. Continental's price went from $5.00 per dozen in 1958 to $2.85 at the time suit was filed. Pet's prices went from $4.92 per dozen to $3.46, and Carnation's from $4.82 per dozen to $3.30.

Utah Pie filed suit, charging price discrimination by the respondents based on allegations outlined in the opinion that follows. The district court found for Utah Pie. The court of appeals reversed, and Utah Pie appealed.

JUDICIAL OPINION

WHITE, Justice

We deal first with petitioner's case against the Pet Milk Company. . . . Pet's initial emphasis was on quality, but in the face of competition from regional and local companies and in an expanding market where price proved to be a crucial factor, Pet was forced to take steps to reduce the price of its pies to the ultimate consumer. These developments had consequences in the Salt Lake City market which are the substance of petitioner's case against Pet.

First, Pet successfully concluded an arrangement with Safeway, which is one of the three largest customers for frozen pies in the Salt Lake market, whereby it would sell frozen pies to Safeway under the latter's own "Bel-air" label at a price significantly lower than it was selling its comparable "Pet-Ritz" brand in the same Salt Lake market and elsewhere. . . .

Second, it introduced a 20-ounce economy pie under the "Swiss Miss" label and began selling the new pie in the Salt Lake market in August 1960 at prices ranging from $3.25 to $3.30 for the remainder of the period. This pie was at times sold at a lower price in the Salt Lake City market than it was sold in other markets.

Third, Pet became more competitive with respect to the prices for its "Pet-Ritz" proprietary label. . . . According to the Court of Appeals, in seven of the 44 months Pet's prices in Salt Lake were lower than prices charged in the California markets. This was true although selling in Salt Lake involved a 30- to 35-cent freight cost.

The burden of proving cost justification was on Pet and, in our view, reasonable men could have found that Pet's lower priced "Bel-air" sales to Safeway were not cost justified in their entirety. Pet introduced cost data for 1961 indicating a cost saving on the Safeway business greater than the price advantage extended to that customer. These statistics were not particularized for the Salt Lake market, but assuming that they were adequate to justify the 1961 sales, they related to only 24 percent of the Safeway sales over the relevant period. The evidence concerning the remaining 76 percent was at best incomplete and inferential. It was insuffi-

cient to take the defense of cost justification from the jury, which reasonably could have found a greater incidence of unjustified price discrimination than that allowed by the Court of Appeals' view of the evidence.

The Court of Appeals almost entirely ignored other evidence which provides material support of the jury's conclusion that Pet's behavior satisfied the statutory test regarding competitive injury. This evidence bore on the issue of Pet's predatory intent to injure Utah Pie. As an initial matter, the jury could have concluded that Pet's discriminatory pricing was aimed at Utah Pie; Pet's own management, as early as 1959, identified Utah Pie as an "unfavorable factor," one which "d[u]g holes in our operation" and posed a constant "check" on Pet's performance in the Salt Lake City market. Moreover, Pet candidly admitted that during the period when it was establishing its relationship with Safeway, it sent into Utah Pie's plant an industrial spy to seek information that would be of use to Pet in convincing Safeway that Utah Pie was not worthy of its customers. . . . Finally, Pet does not deny that the evidence showed it suffered substantial losses on its frozen pie sales during the greater part of time involved in this suit, and there was evidence from which the jury could have concluded that the losses Pet sustained in Salt Lake City were greater than those incurred elsewhere. It would not have been an irrational step if the jury concluded that there was a relationship between the price and the losses.

It seems clear to us that the jury heard adequate evidence from which it could have concluded that Pet had engaged in predatory tactics in waging competitive warfare in the Salt Lake City market. Coupled with the incidence of price discrimination attributable to Pet, the evidence as a whole established, rather than negated, the reasonable possibility that Pet's behavior produced a lessening of competition proscribed by the Act.

Petitioner's case against Continental is not complicated. Continental was a substantial factor in the market in 1957. But its sales of frozen 22-ounce dessert pies, sold under the "Morton" brand, amounted to only 1.3 percent of the market in 1958, 2.9 percent in 1959, and 1.8 percent in 1960. Its problems were primarily that of cost and in turn that of price, the controlling factor in the market. In late 1960 it worked out a co-packing arrangement in California by which fruit would be processed directly from the trees into the finished pies without large intermediate packing, storing, and shipping expenses. Having improved its position, it attempted to increase its share of the Salt Lake City market by utilizing a local broker and offering short-term price concessions in varying amounts. Its efforts for seven months were not spectacularly successful. Then in June 1961, it took the steps which are the heart of petitioner's complaint against it. Effective for the last two weeks of June it offered its 22-ounce frozen apple pies in the Utah area at $2.85 per dozen. It was then selling the same pies at substantially higher prices in other markets. The Salt Lake City price was less than its direct cost plus an allocation for overhead.... Utah's response was immediate. It reduced its price on all of its apple pies to $2.75 per dozen.... Continental's total sales of frozen pies increased from 3,350 dozen in 1960 to 18,800 dozen in 1961. Its market share increased from 1.8 percent in 1960 to 8.3 percent in 1961. The Court of Appeals concluded that Continental's conduct had had only minimal effect, that it had not injured or weakened Utah Pies as a competitor, that it had not substantially lessened competition and that there was no reasonable possibility that it would do so in the future.

We again differ with the Court of Appeals. Its opinion that Utah was not damaged as a competitive force apparently rested on the fact that Utah's sales volume continued to climb in 1961 and on the court's own factual conclusion that Utah was not deprived of any pie business which it otherwise might have had. But this retrospective assessment fails to note that Continental's discriminatory below-cost price caused Utah Pie to reduce its price to $2.75.

Even if the impact on Utah Pie as a competitor was negligible, there remain the consequences to others in the market who had to compete not only with Continental's 22-ounce pie at $2.85 but with Utah's even lower price of $2.75 per dozen for both its proprietary and controlled labels.... The evidence was that there were nine other sellers in 1960 who sold 23,473 dozen pies, 12.7 percent of the total market. In 1961 there were eight other sellers who sold less than the year before—18,565 dozen or 8.2 percent of the total—although the total market had expanded from 184,569 dozen to 226,908 dozen. We think there was sufficient evidence from which the jury could find a violation of § 2(a) by Continental.

Section 2(a) does not forbid price competition which will probably injure or lessen competition by eliminating competitors, discouraging entry into the market or enhancing the market shares of the dominant sellers. But Congress has established some ground rules for the game. Sellers may not sell like goods to different purchasers at different prices if the result may be to injure competition to either the sellers' or the buyers' market unless such discriminations are justified as permitted by the Act. In this case there was some evidence of predatory intent with respect to each of these respondents. There was also other evidence upon which the jury could rationally find the requisite injury to competition. The frozen pie market in Salt Lake City was highly competitive. At times Utah Pie was a leader in moving the general level of prices down, and at other times each of the respondents also bore responsibility for the downward pressure on the price structure. We believe that the Act reaches price discrimination that erodes competition as much as it does price discrimination that is intended to have immediate destructive impact. In this case, the evidence shows a drastically declining price structure which the jury could rationally attribute to continued or sporadic price discrimination.

Reversed.

CASE QUESTIONS

1. Describe the competitors in the Utah Pie frozen pie market.

2. Is it significant that the national competitors were selling their pies at different prices in Utah?

3. Does it matter that the size of the pie market (i.e., number of pies sold) increased during the period examined?

CONSIDER...   17.10

A&P Grocery Stores decided to sell its own brand of canned milk (referred to as "private label" milk). A&P asked its longtime supplier, Borden, to submit an offer to produce the private label milk. Bowman Dairy also submitted a bid, which was lower than Borden's. A&P's Chicago buyer then contacted Borden and said, "I have a bid in my pocket. You people are so far out of line it is not even funny. You are not even in the ballpark." The Borden representative asked for more details but was told only that a $50,000 improvement in Borden's bid "would not be a drop in the bucket."

A&P was one of Borden's largest customers in the Chicago area. Furthermore, Borden had just invested more than $5 million in a new dairy facility in Illinois. The loss of the A&P account would result in underutilization of the plant. Borden lowered its bid by more than $400,000. The Federal Trade Commission has charged Borden with price discrimination, but Borden maintains it was simply meeting the competition. Has Borden violated the Robinson-Patman Act? Does it matter that the milk was a private label milk and not its normal trade name Borden milk? Are the ethics of the A&P representative troublesome? [*Great Atlantic & Pacific Tea Co., Inc.* v. *FTC*, 440 U.S. 69 (1979).]

Defenses to Price Discrimination

If there are legitimate cost differences in the manufacture or handling of a product, there cannot be price discrimination. Additional costs of delivery or of adding specifications to a product can increase the price without violating the Robinson-Patman Act. For example, if a sandwich-meat manufacturer produces a special low-fat bologna, the price for that product can be different. If the manufacturer uses different shipping companies for its customers, there again may be a price differential.

Quantity discounts are permitted so long as the seller can show that there are actual cost savings in the sale of increased quantities and not just an assumption that larger sales are more economical. Limiting the number of buyers who qualify for quantity discounts is some proof that the actual cost savings are not present.

Prices for products also can change according to market, inflation, material costs, and other variable factors. The seller must simply establish that a price change was initiated in response to one of these factors.

Another defense to a charge of price discrimination is **meeting the competition**. This defense must establish that a price change was made in a certain market to meet the competition there. Also, the seller must charge the same as its competitors and not a lower price. Finally, the price differences must be limited to an area or individuals. For example, a national firm may have a different price in one state because of more competition within that particular state.

For more about mergers, price fixing, and vertical restraints visit:

http://www.antitrust.org

Vertical Mergers

Vertical mergers are between firms that have a buyer-seller relationship. For example, if a sandwich-meat manufacturer merged with its meat supplier, there would be a vertical merger. In determining whether a vertical merger violates the Clayton Act, the courts determine the relevant geographic and product markets and then determine whether the effect of the merger will be to foreclose or lessen competition.

The Antitrust Modernization Commission

Congress has enacted a law to establish the Antitrust Modernization Commission (AMC). Congress specified four duties of the AMC:

1. To examine whether the need exists to modernize the antitrust laws and to identify and study related issues

2. To solicit views of all parties concerned with the operation of the antitrust laws

3. To evaluate the advisability of proposals and current arrangements with respect to any issues so identified

4. To prepare and to submit to Congress and the president a report within three years from the formation of the AMC

The commissioners for the AMC were all appointed by the end of 2003.

The report must contain detailed findings and conclusions, together with recommendations for legislative or administrative action. The AMC has members of the U.S. House and Senate and other representatives from agencies such as the FTC and the Justice Department; the commission has the authority to hire experts and consultants in the preparation of its reports and recommendations.

Some of the areas the AMC is expected to examine include mergers and acquisitions, penalties, the rule of reason versus the *per se* violations rule, and clarification of enforcement policies. Antitrust law has continued its evolution since the time of a similar commission in 1955 because there are fundamental economic disagreements underlying its principles. For example, the *Microsoft* case and its surrounding technology issues is an example of an area of lively debate among antitrust scholars and those affected by antitrust law and policy.

ANTITRUST ISSUES IN INTERNATIONAL COMPETITION

As the level of international trade has increased, so also has the number of competitors. For example, three domestic manufacturers produce cars in the United States. However, the availability of international trade markets has resulted in the importing of cars from Japan, Great Britain, Germany, Sweden, and Yugoslavia; and international competition changes the market perspective because the relevant market is not the United States, but the world.

As a result of increased levels of international competition, more joint ventures of competitors and large companies that once would have seemed unthinkable under antitrust protections will be permitted. For example, American Telephone and Telegraph (AT&T) has entered into a joint venture agreement with the Economic Ministry of Taiwan to improve that nation's telecommunications systems. General Mills, Inc. was permitted to acquire RJR Nabisco's cold-cereal business in both the United Kingdom and the United States so that it could compete more effectively in the large North American and European markets.

The EU has developed its own antitrust guidelines and has even questioned the merger of two of the largest U.S. accounting firms in their European operations. There is an increasing concern internationally about antitrust issues because there has been significant activity as U.S. companies merge in order to compete effectively in international markets. The Justice Department is very liberal in permitting both joint ventures and mergers in international markets because of the need for U.S. companies to compete on a global basis. As these large mergers are proposed, the EU and other countries are taking a closer look at their anticompetitive effects. In 2001, General Electric was handed one of the few management setbacks legendary CEO Jack Welch has ever experienced. The proposed acquisition of Honeywell International by General Electric was opposed by EU antitrust enforcers. The EU's Merger Task Force recommended that the $41 billion proposed merger not be permitted to go through in its present form.

The U.S. Supreme Court has held that companies from other countries that engage in commerce in the United States will be subject to U.S. antitrust laws. Foreign corporations doing business here are subject to the same rules of competition required of U.S. corporations.

SUMMARY

What restraints of trade are permissible?

- Covenant not to compete—clause in employment or business sale contracts that restricts competition by one of the parties; must be reasonable in scope and time

What antitrust laws exist?

- Sherman Act—first federal antitrust law; prohibits monopolization and horizontal trade restraints such as price fixing, boycotts, and refusals to deal

- Clayton Act—federal antitrust statute that prohibits tying and interlocking directorates; controls mergers
- Federal Trade Commission Act—federal law that allows the FTC to regulate unfair competition
- Robinson-Patman Act—anti–price discrimination federal statute
- Celler-Kefauver Act—regulates asset acquisitions
- Hart-Scott-Rodino Antitrust Improvements Act—antitrust law that broadened Justice Department authority and provided new merger guidelines

What penalties can be imposed for restraints of trade?

- Equitable remedies—nonmonetary remedies such as injunctions
- Treble damages—three times actual damages available in antitrust cases

What are the forms of horizontal trade restraint and defenses?

- Horizontal restraints of trade—anticompetitive behavior among a firm's competitors
- Price fixing—controlling price of goods through agreement, limiting supply, controlling credit
- Group boycotts—agreement among competitors to exclude competition

- Joint ventures—temporary combinations that may restrain trade
- *Per se* violation—violation of antitrust laws that has no defense or justification
- Monopolization—possession of monopoly power in the relevant market by willful acquisition
- Market power—power to control prices or exclude competition
- Relevant market—geographic and product market used to determine market power
- Predatory pricing—pricing below actual cost to monopolize
- *Noerr-Pennington* doctrine—protection of First Amendment activities from antitrust laws

What are the forms of vertical trade restraints and defenses?

- Resale price maintenance—requiring prices be set in vertical distribution
- Exclusive distributorship—limited dealership rights; not an antitrust violation so long as horizontal competition exists
- Tying—requiring buyers to take an additional product in order to purchase the product they wish
- Price discrimination—selling goods across state lines at prices that have different ratios to marginal costs

QUESTIONS AND PROBLEMS

1. Harold Vogel, an experienced gem appraiser, is a member of the American Society of Appraisers. Mr. Vogel's fee for his work is based on a percentage of the value of the appraised item. The society expelled him under the authority of a bylaw that provides: "It is unprofessional and unethical for the appraiser to do work for a fixed percentage of the amount of value." Mr. Vogel brought suit under Section 1 of the Sherman Act, alleging that his expulsion was a boycott and that he no longer had referrals from the society. Mr. Vogel also claims the bylaw is a means of fixing prices. Is he right? [*Harold Vogel* v. *American Society of Appraisers*, 744 F.2d 598 (7th Cir. 1984).]

2. Denny's is a full-service marine dealer located near Peru, Indiana, that sells fishing boats, motors, trailers, and marine accessories in the central Indiana market. Renfro Productions and others are marine dealers in the same market area that compete with Denny's to sell boats to Indiana consumers. CIMDA is a trade association of marine dealers in that area. Renfro and others are producers of two boat shows held annually at the Indiana State Fairgrounds (the "Fairgrounds Shows"). The February Fairgounds Show (the "Spring Show") origi-

nated over thirty years ago. It is one of the top three boat shows in the United States, attracting between 160,000 and 191,000 consumers annually. The October show (the "Fall Show") is smaller and began in 1987.

Denny's participated in the Fall Show in 1988, 1989, and 1990; it participated in the Spring Show in 1989 and 1990. At all of these shows Denny's was very successful, apparently because it encouraged its customers to shop the other dealers and then come to Denny's for a lower price. During and after the 1989 Spring Show, some of the other dealers began to complain about Denny's sales methods. After the 1990 Spring Show, these dealers apparently spent a good part of one CIMDA meeting "vent[ing] their . . . frustration" about Denny's. The complaints escalated. As a result, Renfro informed Denny's that after the 1990 Fall Show (in which Denny's was contractually entitled to participate), it could no longer participate in the Fairgrounds Shows. Is this an antitrust violation? [*Denny's Marina, Inc.* v. *Renfro Productions, Inc.*, 8 F.3d 1217 (7th Cir. 1993).]

3. Professional Real Estate Investors, Inc. (PRE) operated LaMancha Private Club and Villas, a resort in Palm Springs, California. PRE installed videodisk players in the resort's hotel rooms and assembled a library of more than 200 motion pictures for guests to rent for in-room viewing. PRE was working to develop a market for the sale of similar systems to other hotels.

Columbia Pictures Industries, Inc. and seven other motion picture studios held copyrights on the films PRE was renting. Columbia also licensed transmission of copyrighted motion pictures to hotel rooms through a wired cable system called Spectradyne.

Columbia sued PRE for copyright infringement. PRE countersued, claiming Columbia's suit was a sham that cloaked underlying acts of monopolization and restraint of trade and that Columbia was simply tying up PRE in litigation while it expanded its Spectradyne service in hotels.

Under the law, PRE could sell or lease lawfully purchased videodisks under the "first sale" doctrine of the Copyright Act. The only issue that remained was whether in-room viewing was a performance that required PRE to pay royalties.

Is Columbia's activity subject to antitrust regulation or is it protected under the *Noerr-Pennington* doctrine? [*Professional Real Estate Investors, Inc.* v. *Columbia Pictures, Inc.*, 508 U.S. 49 (1993).]

4. Budget Rent-a-Car and Aloha Airlines have developed a "fly-drive" program. Under their agreement, customers of Aloha receive a $7 first-day rental rate for car rentals (the usual rate is $14). Robert's Waikiki U-Drive has brought suit, challenging the agreement as a tying arrangement and unlawful. Is Robert's correct? [*Robert's Waikiki U-Drive* v. *Budget Rent-a-Car*, 732 F.2d 1403 (9th Cir. 1984).]

5. Eastman Kodak Company introduced its new "pocket 110 cameras" to the market in 1972. The cameras used special film that only Kodak manufactured. Also, only Kodak labs had the technology for developing the 110 film. Foremost Color Lab, a film processor, brought suit on the basis that the 110 system creates a monopoly and is unlawful tying. Is Foremost correct? [*Foremost Pro Color* v. *Eastman Kodak Co.*, 703 F.2d 534 (9th Cir. 1984).]

6. Gardner-Denver, the largest manufacturer of ratchet wrenches and their replacement parts in the United States, has a dual pricing system for wrench parts and components. Its blue list had parts that, if purchased in quantities of five or more, were available for substantially less than its white list prices. Has Gardner-Denver engaged in price discrimination with its two price lists? [*D. E. Rogers Assoc., Inc.* v. *Gardner-Denver Co.*, 718 F.2d 1431 (6th Cir. 1983).]

7. Russell Stover is a candy manufacturer that ships its products to 18,000 retailers nationwide. Stover designates resale prices for its dealers but does not request assurances from them that they are honoring the prices. It has, however, refused to sell to those retailers it be-

lieves will sell below the prices suggested. Is there an antitrust violation in this conduct? [*Russell Stover Candies, Inc.* v. *FTC*, 718 F.2d 256 (8th Cir. 1982).]

8. William Inglis & Sons is a family-owned wholesale bakery with production facilities in Stockton, California, that manufactured and distributed bread and rolls in northern California. ITT Continental is one of the nation's largest wholesale bakeries and was a competitor of Inglis in the northern California market. Both Inglis and Continental sold their bread under a private label and an advertised label. Continental's advertised bread was "Wonder" bread, whereas Inglis's advertised bread was "Sunbeam." The private label bread is sold at a lower price than the advertised brand, but the principal difference between the two is the profit. Inglis filed a complaint stating that Continental was selling its private label bread at below-cost prices in a predatory price scheme designed to drive Inglis out of the market. Inglis also says the lower price on private bread earned Continental more grocery-shelf space for its "Wonder" bread. Is such conduct illegal under the Sherman Act? Is predatory pricing a *per se* violation? [*William Inglis* v. *ITT Continental Baking Co.*, 668 F.2d 1014 (9th Cir. 1980).]

9. On August 1, 1957, Procter & Gamble, the nation's leading manufacturer of soaps, detergents, and other high-turnover household products, acquired Clorox Chemical Company, the nation's leading producer of liquid bleach. Purex Corporation, the second leading producer of liquid bleach, brought suit, challenging the acquisition as violative of the Clayton Act. At the time of the acquisition, Clorox held 48.8 percent of sales and Purex held 15.7 percent of sales. Purex says the enormous financial strength, advertising budget, and marketing skills of Procter & Gamble would make it nearly impossible for any bleach manufacturer to compete. What factors are important in determining whether the merger is a valid one? [*Purex Corp.* v. *Procter & Gamble Co.*, 596 F.2d 881 (9th Cir. 1979).]

10. MacDonald Group, Ltd., owned and operated the Fresno Fashion Fair Mall and leased space to Edmond's, a California retail jeweler. The lease contained a covenant that limited MacDonald to one additional jewelry store as a tenant in the mall. The lease was entered into in 1969. In 1978, MacDonald was involved in the construction of an expansion to the mall and began negotiations to include a retail jeweler in the new space. Edmond's objected and brought suit. The covenant provides that only two jewelry stores would be tenants in the Fresno Fashion Fair Mall. The expansion would still be part of the Fresno Fashion Fair Mall and would not have a separate name. Would the covenant apply to the new addition to the mall? [*Edmond's of Fresno* v. *MacDonald Group, Ltd.*, 217 Cal. Rptr. 375 (1985).]

Old, Onerous, and Still on the Books: Are Dusty Consent Decrees Hobbling Corporate America? Strategies for Coping with Regulatory Constraints

11. As anniversaries go, October 12 was an odd one for General Electric Co. It was on that day eighty-three years ago that GE signed an agreement with the government designed to weaken the company's dominance of the lighting industry. Among other measures, the consent decree banned GE from manufacturing private label or generic lighting products and required the company to disclose its ownership of several lighting businesses that had been thought to be independent.

Today, GE and a growing number of other companies constrained by decades-old consent decrees say it's time to remove the shackles. GE is negotiating with the Justice Department's Antitrust Division to lift the order, arguing that its provisions are hindering the company's ability to compete in a global economy. "By lifting this order, we would be able to do exactly what our competitors are doing," says company spokesman John J. Betchkal.

What has suddenly spurred these challenges, after years of little or no activity? Part of the answer, say experts, is that global competition has greatly intensified over the past decade. IBM, for instance, has been hit particularly hard and has been frustrated watching competitors flourish under practices it is barred from using.

Slacking Off

Another factor has been a change in the government's attitude. It used to be almost impossible to persuade regulators and courts to abandon or modify consent decrees. But in July, the Federal Trade Commission announced that its antitrust decrees would lapse after twenty years. The agency also invited companies to seek reviews of old decrees. The average life span of the Justice Department's antitrust orders is now ten years. Experts say regulators finally realize that some decrees can impede competition if left unchecked too long. "The problem with these decrees is that they don't learn with society," says Daniel M. Wall, an antitrust lawyer in San Francisco.

GE, for example, wants to begin offering private label lightbulbs to retailers—a business segment that global competitors such as Philips Lighting and Osram Sylvania, Inc., already have. In addition, the company wants to sell generic products to compete in the lower-priced end of the lighting market. The company won't say how much these endeavors would be worth but is concerned that rivals are profiting from its predicament. The government is weighing GE's request.

Experts estimate that more than 100 of these decades-old decrees are still controlling some corporate behavior. Most antitrust agreements entered into today are not open-ended. For example, the settlement reached recently between the government and Microsoft Corp. is due to expire in just three years.

Release?

Yet, for all the sentiment that has been expressed in favor of updating outmoded enforcement measures, companies are encountering stiff opposition. Critics say it is because even with the passage of time and a more global marketplace, many companies still retain too much control over their industries to be freed from certain restraints. IBM is butting heads with a number of its competitors over a 1956 consent decree that, among other things, forced it to offer computer services separately from its manufacturing and sales business. It also required IBM, which had previously only leased its equipment, to sell outright its computers and equipment to competitors.

Such provisions created what are now multibillion-dollar aftermarkets composed of independent leasing and service businesses and dealers of used IBM computer equipment. The 265 independent lessors alone earn more than $15 billion. These companies argue that such revenues would plummet without the decree. "If you don't regulate IBM, it will put handcuffs on companies like ours to compete effectively. And that will cause consumers to suffer," argues Philip A. Hewes, a senior vice president at ComDisco, Inc., the largest independent computer-leasing company.

Independent service organizations (ISOs) agree, arguing that the court should draw a distinction between IBM's diminished strength in manufacturing and its continued dominance of the computer-service business. "There is a superficial appeal to IBM's argument that we need to reassess things after 40 years," says Ronald S. Katz, a San Francisco lawyer who represents the ISOs. "But IBM could hobble or get rid of its competition" if the decree were to be lifted. IBM, which has said it must be free to match such competitors as Electronic Data Systems, Inc., declines to comment.

Ironic

Thus far, the Justice Department has remained silent on the IBM case, which is pending in federal court. Not so with respect to Kodak, which in May persuaded a court to overturn two consent decrees. Kodak successfully argued that it no longer possessed enough power to control prices or hinder competition. Consequently,

Kodak claimed it should be allowed to sell private label film and to bundle its film and photo finishing businesses. Robert B. Bell, Kodak's antitrust counsel in Washington, says his client would have come out with a number of innovative products if it were not for the decrees from 1920 and 1954.

The government has appealed the Kodak case, arguing that the company still wields too much market control. The appeal, which is expected to be heard in January, is deemed so important that Assistant Attorney General Anne K. Bingaman is expected to make a rare court appearance to argue the case herself. That Bingaman would be battling the case so hard strikes some critics as ironic. "It's really baffling to companies to have the government fight decrees that are 80 years old when current policy allows them to expire in 10 years," says Bell.

Baffling, maybe. But the Kodak decision could affect dozens of other decrees on the books by creating a new legal standard for overturning them. That is a feat in antitrust law that has not been accomplished since 1932—the time of prohibition and the kidnapping of Charles Lindbergh Jr.

Issues

a. Why are the older decrees still in effect?
b. Why do the companies feel the decrees should be lifted?
c. What updates can you find on the companies and their decrees?

Source: Linda Himelstein, "Old, Onerous, and Still on the Books." Reprinted from the November 7, 1994, issue of *Business Week* by special permission, copyright © 1994 by The McGraw-Hill Companies, Inc.

NOTES

1. The roots of antitrust law can be found in the private contracts negotiated even centuries ago when businesses were sold. See the course Web site and the *Instructor's Manual* for more information on the roots of law and commerce.

2. The doctrine is named after the two U.S. Supreme Court cases in which it was developed: *Eastern R.R. President's Conference v. Noerr Motor Freight, Inc.*, 365 U.S. 127 (1961), and *United Mine Workers v. Pennington*, 381 U.S. 657 (1965).

Business and Its Employees

■ This portion of the book covers the rights and duties of employers and employees as they work together to operate a business. What are the regulations and restrictions related to the hiring and firing of employees? How much authority do employees have to make decisions and take actions with respect to their work? How are safety regulations enforced in the workplace? What legal limits exist with respect to work hours? What role do unions play in employee and employer relations? What do federal and state antidiscrimination statutes provide? What are their effects on hiring, firing, promoting, and rewarding?

18

Management of Employee Conduct: Agency

update

For up-to-date legal news and real-world business applications, click on **update** *at http://jennings.westbuslaw.com*

All businesses have a common thread: employees. They need them, rely on them, pay them, and give them authority to perform certain business tasks. This chapter focuses on that delegation of authority and these questions: When does an employee act on behalf of an employer? How much authority does an employee have? What duties and obligations do employees owe employers? When is a business liable for an employee's acts?

How to Fire Someone without Being Sued
1. Do not fire anyone.
2. Fire everyone.
3. Fire everyone in the same division.
4. Fire only those employees with well-documented
and written performance problems.
5. Fire only those employees for whom managers can
articulate a legitimate business justification.
6. Do not violate any internal company procedures
when selecting employees for termination.
7. Offer terminated employees a severance package in exchange
for signing a release not to sue the company.
8. Do not threaten the employee.
9. Give the employee a brief but specific reason
for the termination.
10. Be kind.
FROM CAMERON STRACHER, "HOW TO FIRE SOMEONE WITHOUT BEING SUED"
New York Times Magazine, *April 8, 2001, p. 54.*

Jerome Lange was the manager of a small grocery store that carried Nabisco products. Ronnell Lynch had been hired by Nabisco as a cookie salesman-trainee in October 1968. On March 1, 1969, Mr. Lynch was assigned his own territory, which included Mr. Lange's store.

On May 1, 1969, Mr. Lynch came to Mr. Lange's store to place previously delivered merchandise on the shelves. An argument developed between the two over Mr. Lynch's service to the store. Mr. Lynch became very angry and started swearing. Mr. Lange told him to either stop swearing or leave the store because children were present. Mr. Lynch then became uncontrollably angry and said, "I ought to break your neck." He then went behind the counter and dared Mr. Lange to fight. When Mr. Lange refused, Mr. Lynch viciously assaulted him, after which he threw merchandise around the store and left.

Is Nabisco liable for Mr. Lynch's actions?

© MEL CURTIS/PHOTODISC/GETTY IMAGES

NAMES AND ROLES: AGENCY TERMINOLOGY

A principal-agent relationship is one in which one party acts on behalf of another. A clerk who helps you to the dressing room and takes your payment in a department store is an agent. Barry Bonds has an agent who negotiates his contracts for him. A **power of attorney** is a form of agency relationship in which authority is given another to enter into transactions. A special power of attorney is one limited in time or scope, as when a landowner gives another the authority to close a particular land transaction. A general power of attorney is one in which an individual gives another the rights to manage his financial affairs in everything from handling checking accounts to entering into contracts. The common thread in all of these relationships is that one party acts on behalf of another.

Although some terms are used interchangeably, there are exact labels and definitions for the parties in an agency relationship. This section outlines and defines the terminology used to cover that relationship.

Agency

In an agency relationship, one party agrees to act on behalf of another party according to directions. It is a relationship that exists by common consent—both sides agree to it—and a relationship that is fiduciary in nature—there are duties and responsibilities on both sides. The general term *agency* can be used to refer to many different types of relationships. A real estate agent who is hired to help market your house is an agent of yours; a salesclerk in a department store is an agent for that store; talent agents are agents for many actors at the same time.

FOR THE MANAGER'S DESK

RE: POWERS OF ATTORNEY

Powers of attorney generally authorize one person (the agent or attorney in fact) to act on behalf of another person (the principal); but *these grants can vary in scope and have different purposes. A glossary follows.*

SCOPE

Nondurable or Durable

A nondurable, or conventional, power of attorney expires upon the incapacitation of the principal. A durable power of attorney either takes effect or remains in effect upon incapacitation.

Limited or Special

This variety limits the agent's authority to specific areas or transactions, like a real estate closing.

Springing

A springing power of attorney does not become effective until a certain event occurs—the incapacity of the principal, for example.

PURPOSES

Child Care

Often used in cases of prolonged parental absence or incapacity, for decisions on emergency medical care or school-related matters.

Financial

A very common power of attorney. If durable, it can help avoid costly and protracted judicial conservatorship proceedings when a person becomes incompetent.

Health Care

Allows an agent to make medical decisions for an incapacitated principal. The agent may also enforce the principal's living will, which states his treatment preferences in the event of terminal illness or other conditions.

Source: Laura Pedersen-Pietersen, "When a Friend Needs a Legal Stand-In," *New York Times,* March 15, 1998, p. BU4. Copyright © 1998 by The New York Times. Reprinted by permission.

Principals

In the employer-employee relationship, the employers are referred to as the **principals**. The term *principal* is used because some agents are not truly employees. A literary agent, for example, represents many authors who are the agent's principals, but the principals are not "employers," in the usual sense, of the agent.

Agents

Agents are people hired by a principal to do a task on behalf of the principal. The agent represents the principal in such a way that if the agent negotiates a contract, the principal, but not the agent, is bound by and a party to the contract. A president of a corporation is an agent of the corporation. When the president negotiates a contract, the corporation, not the president, is bound to perform that contract.

All employees are agents of the principal employer, but not all agents are employees. A corporation might hire an architect to design a new office building and obtain bids for the construction of the building. The architect would be an agent for very limited purposes but not an employee of the company.

Employers and Employees: Master-Servant Relationships

A **master-servant relationship** is one in which the principal (master) exercises a great deal of control over the agent (servant).[1] An employer-employee relationship for a production line worker is an example of a master-servant relationship. Among the various factors considered are whether an employee works regular hours, is paid a regular wage, and is subject to complete supervision and control by the employer during work hours. The factors used to determine whether a master-servant relationship exists are as follows:

- Level of supervision of the agent
- Level of control of the agent
- Nature of the agent's work
- Regularity of hours and pay
- Length of employment

Independent Contractors

An **independent contractor** is a person who is hired by another to perform a task but is not controlled directly by the hiring party. For example, a corporation's attorney is an agent of the corporation only for purposes of legal representation and court appearances. The attorney is not a corporate employee, and the corporation has no control over the attorney's office operations. The attorney is an independent contractor. A subcontractor hired to perform partial work on a construction site is also an example of an independent contractor.

Principals have less responsibility for independent contractors than for servants because they have little control over a contractor's conduct. The distinction between master-servant relationships and independent contractor relationships is important because a principal's liability for an agent's actions varies depending on the agent's status as servant or contractor.

Agency Law

Agency law is not statutory; rather, its source is common law. The reflection of common law regarding agency is found in the ***Restatement of Agency***, which is a summary of the majority view of agency law in the United States that is followed by many courts in handling agency cases.

Studying agency law actually involves examining three different components. The first component is the creation of the agency relationship. The second component involves the relationship between principals and agents. The third component examines the relationship of the agents and principals to third parties. In this third component, the areas of contracts *and* torts are covered because principals have both contractual and tort liability for certain acts of their agents.

CREATION OF THE AGENCY RELATIONSHIP

In most cases, determining whether an agency relationship exists is a simple task: A business hires an employee, and that employee is an agent of the business. However, agency relationships can also be created in other ways, and the requirements vary.

Express Authority

An employee who is hired by agreement (oral or written) is an agent and has been given **express authority** to act on behalf of the business. That authority, however, may be limited. A driver employee, for example, may only have the authority to deliver packages; a sales employee may have the authority to represent the company but may be required to obtain another employee's signature to finalize sales contracts. An **express contract** specifies the limitations of an employee/agent's authority.

The Writing

An agency relationship is created by agreement, which need not be in writing, although it is best for both employer and employee if it is. A written contract specifying the agent's authority is required only if the agent will enter into contracts required to be in writing or if a state statute requires an agent's authority to be in writing. For example, many states require that real estate agents' commission contracts be in writing.

Capacity

Because agents will enter into contracts for their principals, the principals must have the **capacity** to contract. *Capacity* here means capacity in the traditional contract sense: age and mental capacity (as covered in Chapter 14).

The contractual capacity of the agent is not an issue in the agency relationship for purposes of the agent's authority to enter into contracts. However, the capacity of the agent to drive, operate equipment, or work with the public is an issue that affects the employer's liability to third parties. Because of this liability, many employers conduct polygraph and psychological tests and drug screening as a precondition to hiring employees. Many firms also have ongoing drug-testing programs to ensure that employees are not reporting for work—or working— under the influence of drugs or alcohol.

One of the most controversial issues in agency law concerns the **unincorporated association**, which is a group that acts as an entity but has no legal existence. Some charitable organizations—churches, for example—have an ongoing existence and have probably built buildings, had fund-raising drives, and entered into many contracts. However, because these organizations are not incorporated and do not have any legal existence, those who sign contracts for these groups are not agents. Moreover, they are liable under contract terms because the organizations are not principals with capacity. For example, suppose that a Little League coach signs a credit contract for the purchase of Little League equipment. The Little League organization is nonprofit and is not incorporated. In the event the league does not raise enough money to pay for the sporting equipment, the signing coach is liable because the league is not a principal with capacity.

The National Conference of Commissioners on Uniform State Laws proposed the *Uniform Unincorporated Nonprofit Association Act* (UUNAA) in 1996, and it has been adopted in ten states. Under the UUNAA, the contract and tort liability of individual members of a nonprofit association would be eliminated if they were acting on behalf of their nonprofit unincorporated association. The UUNAA also gives unincorporated nonprofits the right to bring suits and be sued in their names and to own property in similar fashion.

Implied Authority

An agent under contract not only has the authority given expressly but also has certain **implied authority**. Implied authority is the extension of express authority by custom. For example, a person who is hired as president of a corporation probably does not have his exact duties specified in the contract. However, this president will likely have the same type of authority customarily held by corporate presidents: to sign contracts, to authorize personnel changes, to conduct salary reviews and changes, and to institute operational changes. The law gives the president custom-

---

BUSINESS PLANNING TIP

Before you sign on behalf of an organization, be sure you understand your liability. For example, if you sign a contract with a hotel for a group's meeting, you will have personal liability if your group is not incorporated and if the hotel is not paid. If your group is incorporated, be sure to sign so that the corporation, not you, is personally liable. You can use the following format:

(Your Group Name)

By: (Your Name)

(Your Title)

Here is an example:

Weaving Through the Maze, a nonprofit corporation

By: Marianne M. Jennings

President

ary authority unless the president's contract specifies otherwise. This implied authority can be limited by agreement between the parties if they do not want custom and practice to control their relationship.

Apparent Authority

In many cases an agency relationship arises not by express or implied contracts but because of the way a principal presents himself to third parties. This theory of agency law, called **apparent authority** or **agency by estoppel**, holds a principal liable if the principal makes someone else think he has an agent.

Apparent authority exists by appearance. A third party is led to believe that an agent, although not actually holding express and accompanying implied authority, had the proper authority to deal with the third party. The third party is led to believe that certain promises will be fulfilled. For example, a mobile home dealer who has brochures, note pads, and other materials from a mobile home manufacturer has the appearance of having the authority to sell those homes even if there is no actual authority. *Montoya* v. *Grease Monkey Holding Corp.* (Case 18.1) is a landmark case in agency and corporation laws that deals with issues of apparent authority.

CASE 18.1

Montoya v. *Grease Monkey Holding Corp.*
904 P.2d 468 (Colo. 1995)

A Grease Monkey's Uncle, er, Agent

FACTS

Grease Monkey Holding Corporation is a Utah corporation, and Grease Monkey International is a wholly owned subsidiary of Grease Monkey Holding Company. From 1983 through 1991, Arthur Sensenig was Grease Monkey's President, COO (chief operating officer), and Chairman of the Board. During that time, Mr. Sensenig ran Grease Monkey and had broad authority to act as general officer and agent for Grease Monkey. Mr. Sensenig had authority to raise capital from banks and other lenders. The trial court found that Mr. Sensenig "had implied or had apparent authority to raise capital by borrowing or obtaining loans on behalf of Grease Monkey from private citizens like the . . . [respondents] in this case." Mr. Sensenig did not need Board approval for these loans unless they exceeded $500,000.

Nick and Aver Montoya (respondents) were married for over fifty years. The trial court found Nick Montoya to be a person of "average investor sophistication." Aver Montoya was a factory worker for approximately seventeen years, and she left financial matters primarily to her husband.

Nick Montoya met Mr. Sensenig in the mid-1960s when Mr. Sensenig was a teller at a bank where Mr. Montoya was a customer. During the 1960s and 1970s, Mr. Sensenig gave Mr. Montoya investment advice. Mr.

Montoya was impressed by Mr. Sensenig, who ultimately became vice-president of the bank before leaving. Mr. Montoya also knew Mr. Sensenig through a church connection.

From 1983 through 1991, Mr. Sensenig secured payments from the Montoyas under the guise that the payments were investments in Grease Monkey. Mr. Sensenig secured the payments by representing that, because Grease Monkey was a new company, it did not have its own account, and that as President and Chairman of the Board, Mr. Sensenig used his personal account as the corporate account. In furtherance of his scheme, Mr. Sensenig took Mr. Montoya to the Grease Monkey offices and showed him a promotional slide show presentation used by Grease Monkey to solicit franchise business. However, none of the payments were invested in Grease Monkey, and Grease Monkey did not receive any of the funds. Rather, Mr. Sensenig used the Montoyas' money for his own personal benefit.

Generally, about a week after writing an investment check, the Montoyas received a promissory note as evidence of their investment. When Mr. Sensenig delivered interest payments to the Montoyas, he brought charts showing the growth and success of Grease Monkey. Mailings to the Montoyas concerning

continued

their investments were on Grease Monkey letterhead, and calls regarding the investments were made to Mr. Sensenig at Grease Monkey. Mr. Sensenig gave the Montoyas many Grease Monkey promotional items, such as pens, hats, and sweatshirts.

Dreams turned to dust, and the Montoyas sought to put the monkey on the back of the corporation and filed suit against Grease Monkey, as Mr. Sensenig's employer, for breach of contract, fraud, misrepresentation, breach of duty of good faith and fair dealing, promissory estoppel, extreme and outrageous conduct, and negligent hiring and supervision.

After a trial to the court, the Montoyas prevailed on their fraud and misrepresentation claims, and their other claims were dismissed. The trial court entered judgment against Grease Monkey for the outstanding balance due on the promissory notes. The court of appeals affirmed the trial court's "judgment . . . because, Mr. Sensenig, as its [P]resident, acting within the scope of his apparent authority as an agent of the corporations, engaged in conduct which was customary for an individual employed in Sensenig's position, and was placed in that position by Grease Monkey." Grease Monkey appealed.

JUDICIAL OPINION

ERICKSON, Justice

Section 261 of the Restatement (Second) of Agency provides that "[a] principal who puts a servant or other agent in a position which enables the agent, while apparently acting within his authority, to commit a fraud upon third persons is subject to liability to such third persons for the fraud." The application of section 261 is not limited to principals and agents but extends also to masters and servants.

The scope of employment requirement restricts vicarious liability for tortious conduct to actions that "should be considered as one of the normal risks to be borne by the business in which the servant is employed." Restatement (Second) of Agency § 229 cmt. a (1958). Although the commission of an intentional tort may sometimes be within the scope of employment, the agent's intent in committing the tortious act must be to further the employer's business. However, if an employee commits an intentional tort solely for reasons that do not further his employer's business or cannot be considered a natural incident of employment, the employer cannot be vicariously liable. The scope of employment limitation on vicarious liability partially distinguishes vicarious liability from the tort of negligent hiring.

Section 261 articulates a specific situation where liability will attach to the principal under the apparent authority doctrine.

Under the principal-agent relationship, "[t]he distinguishing characteristic of the agent is that he represents his principal contractually. If properly authorized he makes contracts or other negotiations of a business nature on behalf of his principal and by which his principal is bound."

"Using master-servant principles, [a] servant is one who works physically for another, subject to the control of that other, who is called the master." The statement that the servant is subject to the control of the master does not mean that the master must stand by constantly and observe and supervise the work; it means merely that the relation presupposes a right on the part of the master to have the work performed in such manner as he directs and a correlative duty on the part of the servant to perform in the manner directed, expressly or by implication, by the master.

Under the doctrine of respondeat superior, "a master is liable for the unauthorized torts of his servant if committed while the servant is acting within the scope of his employment." Because "the master's peculiar liability is based on the physical activities of servants, including their batteries, . . . he is liable only if the servant's conduct was in some way caused by an intent to serve his employer's interests and connected with his authorized acts."

A master may also be liable for tortious conduct by a servant, as he would be for the conduct of any agent, whether servant or not. Acts that are apparently authorized or committed within an agent's inherent powers or where the agent's position enables him to commit a tort exemplify the situations where a principal may be liable for the torts of servants and non-servant agents. When the servant or agent uses the apparent authority of the relationship with the master or principal, the Restatement (Second) of Agency also holds principals vicariously liable for the physical torts of agents who are not servants, i.e., if the tort was committed within the scope of the agency. Apparent authority liability is not based upon the rules of respondeat superior, and it is not "essential to find that the agent was motivated by an intent to act for his master's purposes." Actions for misrepresentations and fraud generally fit into the category of torts which do not lie within the scope and principles of respondeat superior. In many of these situations, the agent's position enables him to perpetrate the fraud, and the agent acted for his own purposes. However, "[t]he fact that the agent is acting from purely personal motives is immaterial unless this is known to the other party."

A principal is subject to liability for physical harm to the person or the tangible things of another caused by the negligence of a servant or a non-servant agent:

(a) in the performance of an act which the principal is under a duty to have performed with care; and

(b) in the making of a representation which the agent is authorized or apparently authorized to make or which is within the power of the agent to make for the principal.

Restatement (Second) of Agency § 257 states:

A principal is subject to liability for loss caused to another by the other's reliance upon a tortious representation of a servant or other agent, if the representation is:

(a) authorized;

(b) apparently authorized; or

(c) within the power of the agent to make for the principal.

Comment g states that "[t]he rule stated in this Section applies to physical harm resulting from the misrepresentation, as well as to economic loss."

The application of section 261 to the present case squares with the misrepresentation or fraud analysis of the principal-agent doctrine. Respondeat superior and master-servant principles constitute an aspect of agency law distinct from fraud based on the apparent authority.

In the present case, Grease Monkey did not possess the right to control the physical movements or activities of Sensenig, who was the Chief Operating Officer of Grease Monkey. Sensenig was expected to perform certain tasks for Grease Monkey. Grease Monkey did not monitor Sensenig's physical activities, but was only concerned with the results achieved. "[A] servant sells or gives his time, while a non-servant agent is paid primarily for results rather than for the time which it takes to accomplish them.") Sensenig acted as a non-servant agent for Grease Monkey. Sensenig committed fraud while acting within his apparent authority.

Previously, we recognized that a principal may be held liable for an agent's actions if the agent is acting pursuant to apparent authority, regardless of whether the principal has knowledge of the agent's conduct. Section eight of the Restatement (Second) of Agency provides "[a]pparent authority is the power to affect the legal relations of another person by transactions with third persons, professedly as agent for the other, arising from and in accordance with the other's manifestations to such third persons . . .

Generally, "[a] principal is not bound by the false representations of his agent made without his knowledge, consent, or authority. However, if an agent acts with apparent authority, a principal may be liable even though the agent acts solely for his own purposes. Applying an apparent authority theory, " '[l]iability is based upon the fact that the agent's position facilitates the consummation of the fraud, in that from the point of view of the third person the transaction seems regular on its face and the agent appears to be acting in the

ordinary course of the business confided to him.' " In both state and federal misrepresentation cases, "[c]ourts have commonly imposed liability based on 'apparent authority' . . . particularly when the person making the misrepresentation is an important corporate official."

Section 262 of the Restatement (Second) of Agency clarifies the rationale of the apparent authority doctrine. Section 262 provides "[a] person who otherwise would be liable to another for the misrepresentations of one apparently acting for him is not relieved from liability by the fact that the servant or other agent acts entirely for his own purposes, unless the other has notice of this." . . . "[b]ehind the principal's liability under an apparent authority theory, then, is 'business expediency—the desire that third persons should be given reasonable protection in dealing with agents.' " The rationale behind section 262 is that "[i]t is . . . for the ultimate interest of persons employing agents, as well as for the benefit of the public, that persons dealing with agents should be able to rely upon apparently true statements by agents who are purporting to act and are apparently acting in the interests of the principal."

We conclude that the apparent authority doctrine of section 261 sets forth the appropriate analytical framework for the present case. Section 261 articulates the proper elements of the apparent authority doctrine without conflicting with existing Colorado case law. Next, we consider whether Grease Monkey should be liable for Sensenig's acts under the apparent authority doctrine.

Under section 261, a plaintiff must establish that the servant or other agent was put in a position which enabled the agent to commit fraud, the agent acted within his apparent authority, and the agent committed fraud. First, the trial court found that Sensenig was the highest authority at Grease Monkey. He had authority to raise up to $500,000 without Board approval, and as general officer and agent for Grease Monkey, he had broad authority to act without corporate restrictions. The findings of the trial court support a conclusion that Grease Monkey put Sensenig in a position where he could commit fraud if he had a mind to.

Second, the trial court found that Sensenig acted within his apparent authority when he raised capital from individuals such as respondents. We also note that "[u]nder section 261 and the theory of apparent authority . . . the agent's conduct is seen through the eyes of the third party . . .

Third, the trial court found that Sensenig made false representations to respondents. Sensenig made these representations with the awareness they were

continued

false and with intent to induce respondents to rely on the representations. The representations were material, and respondents reasonably relied on the representations to their detriment. The trial court found for respondents on their claim of fraud and misrepresentation, and we are unwilling to disturb that finding on review.

Grease Monkey contends that the use of section 261 amounts to strict liability for the principal. However, "'few doctrines of the law are more firmly established or more in harmony with accepted notions of social policy than that of the liability of the principal without fault of his own.'" Our decision recognizes the legal principle that "when one of two innocent persons must suffer from the acts of a third, he must suffer who put it

in the power of the wrongdoer to inflict the injury." This policy motivates organizations to see that their agents abide by the law.

Affirmed.

CASE QUESTIONS

1. What did the CEO of the corporation do to a third party?
2. What is the purpose of the apparent authority doctrine?
3. What duties does apparent authority impose on principals?
4. Is Grease Monkey liable to the Montoyas?

C O N S I D E R . . .   **1 8 . 1**

Suppose that a bar owner has employed a bouncer and the bouncer injures someone while removing him from the premises. Is the employer liable for the conduct of the bouncer? [*Byrd* v. *Faber*, 57 Ohio St.3d 56, 565 N.E.2d 584, 587 (1991).]

THINK: The *Grease Monkey* case held that a principal is liable for the acts of an agent that a third party would perceive are within the scope of the authority of the agent.

APPLY: When an agent is hired as a bouncer, battery and assault could be within the agent's apparent scope of authority.

ANSWER: The bar owner is liable for the bouncer's conduct.

C O N S I D E R . . .   **1 8 . 2**

On September 20, 1973, a Beech Model 18 Aircraft carrying singer Jim Croce and his entourage (the group) crashed shortly after takeoff from Natchitoches, Louisiana. All were killed.

At the time of the crash, the plane was being flown by Robert N. Elliott, an employee of Roberts Airways. Roberts had been asked by Mustang Aviation to fly the entourage according to a prepared itinerary. Mustang originally had entered into a contract with Lloyd St. Martin of Variety Artists International, a booking agent for popular singers, to fly the group itself. The agreement was entered into on September 18, 1973. Later that same day, Mustang learned that its aircraft was disabled, so Mustang's director of operations called Roberts and asked it to substitute.

Relatives of Mr. Croce and the others killed in the crash brought suit against Mustang for the crash. What, if any, agency relationships existed in this case? How did they arise? Is Mustang liable for the crash? [*Croce* v. *Bromely Corp.*, 623 F.2d 1084 (5th Cir. 1980).]

B U S I N E S S   S T R A T E G Y   A P P L I C A T I O N

Be sure to do the exercise for this chapter presented on the book's Web site. You can study several scenarios for agency liability and then determine what a company can do to monitor and control the activities of its agents.

Ratification

There are times when an agent without proper authority enters into a contract that the principal later ratifies. **Ratification** occurs when the principal reviews a contract and voluntarily decides that, even though the agent did not have proper authority, the contract will be honored as if the agent had full authority. Once a contract is ratified, it is effective from the time the agent entered into it even though the agent had no authority until after the fact. Ratification is a way for a principal to give an agent authority retroactively.

For example, suppose that an apartment manager does not have the authority to contract for any type of construction work except routine maintenance. Because the fence around the apartment complex is deteriorated, the manager contracts for the construction of a completely new fence at a cost that exceeds by six times any maintenance work he has had done in the past. The contractor begins work on the fence, and the apartment owner drives by, sees the work, and says nothing. By her inaction in allowing the contractor to continue building the fence, the apartment complex owner ratifies the contract.

CONSIDER... 18.3

Benjamin Chavez served as executive director of the National Association for the Advancement of Colored People (NAACP). Mary Stansee, a former employee of the NAACP executive offices, charged Mr. Chavez with sexual harassment, and he settled the claim for $332,400. The NAACP was financially troubled at the time of the settlement, with a deficit of $2.7 million in 1993, and Mr. Chavez did not disclose the settlement to the board until after it was completed. Did Mr. Chavez have implied authority to make the settlement? Did he have apparent authority?

THE PRINCIPAL-AGENT RELATIONSHIP

To this point, the focus has been on the relationship between the agent and the principal on the one hand and third parties on the other. However, it is important to realize that a contractual relationship exists between the agent and the principal, so that each has certain obligations and rights. This section of the chapter covers that relationship.

The Agent's Responsibilities

Principals and agents have a **fiduciary** relationship, which is characterized by loyalty, trust, care, and obedience. An agent in the role of fiduciary must act in the principal's best interests.

Duty of Loyalty: General

An agent is required to act only for the benefit of the principal, and an agent cannot represent both parties in a transaction unless each knows about and consents to the agent's representation of the other. Further, an agent cannot use the information gained or the offers available to or by the principal to profit personally. For example, an agent hired to find a buyer for a new invention cannot interfere with the principal's possible sale by demonstrating his own product. Neither can an agent hired to find a piece of property buy the property and then sell it (secretly, of course) to the principal. *Silva* v. *Bisbee* (Case 18.2) involves an issue of an agent's fiduciary duty in a sale transaction.

CASE 18.2

Silva v. *Bisbee*
628 P.2d 214 (Hawaii 1981)

Did I Forget to Tell You I'm the Buyer as Well as Your Agent?

FACTS

Bernice Bisbee (defendant/appellant) is a real estate broker employed by Midkiff Realty, Inc. In September 1972, she obtained from Richard and Marian Silva (plaintiffs/appellees) an exclusive listing agreement for the sale of their property in Kaleheo, Kauai. The land, which fronted on the Kaumualii highway, consisted of 34,392 square feet and one two-bedroom house and one four-bedroom house. The Silvas told Ms. Bisbee that they wanted $100,000 for the property.

Some time later, Ms. Bisbee obtained an offer for the property from David Larsen. The down payment was set at $35,000, with payments of $2,000 a month at 8 percent a year, but Mr. Larsen backed out before closing. After that, a joint venture of six members formed the Pacific Equity Associates to buy the property. Ms. Bisbee was to manage the joint venture and would receive 10 percent of the profits for her services. One of the joint venture members, Toshio Morikawa, appeared as the buyer at the July 1973 closing of the property sale. Ms. Bisbee did not tell the Silvas of the venture nor of her pecuniary interest in it.

In August 1973, Ms. Bisbee prepared for the venture a financial statement that listed the market value of the Silva property at $149,424. Several times the venture was late making payments, which Ms. Bisbee covered. Mr. Silva and his wife were emotionally distressed about the late payments and told Ms. Bisbee. Eventually, because of defaults on the payments, the Silvas brought suit to cancel the contract and for damages for fraud by Ms. Bisbee, naming Midkiff Realty in the suit as well.

The jury returned a verdict for $29,000 in general damages for the Silvas and $50,000 in punitive damages. Ms. Bisbee and Midkiff appealed.

JUDICIAL OPINION

PADGETT, Judge

Bisbee and Midkiff concede that as brokers under a listing contract, they stood in a fiduciary relationship to the Silvas. It is axiomatic that a fiduciary cannot have a pecuniary interest in the purchase of property from the *cestui que* [beneficiary of the] trust without full disclosure. No such disclosure was made here. Bisbee's conduct in causing the purchase of the property by a joint venture in which she had a pecuniary interest constituted constructive fraud as a matter of law.

As to the issue of emotional distress, the appellants' motion for a directed verdict below was ex-

pressly based on the decision of the Supreme Court of Hawaii in *Rodrigues* v. *State*. Appellants here argue, however, that the emotional distress grew out of the failure to make the payments on time, not out of the fiduciary relationship, and that, therefore, the case is one sounding in contract.

It is well-settled that a party cannot complain on appeal that the motion for a directed verdict should have been granted on a ground not specified.

We read *Rodrigues* to say that given some evidence of emotional distress in the record, the question of whether such distress amounted to serious mental distress which a reasonable man normally constituted could not adequately cope with is one for the jury. Since there was testimony that Bisbee was informed of the fact of emotional upset arising out of the late payments, the test of foreseeability was met.

What we have said disposes of the contention that Midkiff's motion for a new trial was improperly denied. Bisbee was Midkiff's agent and Midkiff is equally liable with her for the damages arising out of her breach of fiduciary duty as well as the damages arising out of the claimed emotional distress.

The last points raised are that the evidence was insufficient to justify the award of punitive damages and that those damages are excessive. There was ample evidence from which the jury could have concluded that what Bisbee did was done willfully, wantonly or maliciously or characterized by some aggravating circumstances. Certainly the jury could have concluded that Bisbee's failure to advise the Silvas that their property was worth more than $100,000 was willful and that Bisbee's failure to advise them of her pecuniary interest in the purchaser was also willful. We cannot say in the circumstances of this case that the award of $50,000 punitive damages shocks the conscience of the court.

Affirmed.

CASE QUESTIONS

1. What did the agent, Ms. Bisbee, fail to disclose?
2. Was Ms. Bisbee representing both sides in a transaction?
3. Can the Silvas recover for their emotional distress?
4. Do you think the jury awarded the difference between the listed value of the property and the actual value as punitive damages?
5. Why is Midkiff also liable?

ETHICAL ISSUES

The Dilemma of Team Doctors: Agents of Players or Agents of Management?

In a 1989 baseball game against the Toronto Blue Jays, Marty Barrett, a second baseman for the Boston Red Sox, "popped" his right knee while running to first base. Mr. Barrett had ruptured his anterior cruciate ligament (ACL). Two days after the game, Dr. Arthur Pappas, the Red Sox team doctor and chair of the University of Massachusetts Medical Center's orthopedic department,

performed surgery and removed most of Mr. Barrett's ACL. Dr. Pappas is also a part owner of the Red Sox and at a press conference described the injury as "torn cartilage" and "a stretched ligament." Do team doctors who are also part owners of the team have a conflict of interest? What if the team needs the player to win and the doctor holds the authority to allow the player to return, but the doctor in him feels the player needs more healing time? Can this conflict ever be resolved or managed?

Duty of Loyalty: Post–Employment

Many companies have their employees sign contracts that include covenants not to compete or covenants not to disclose information about their former employers should they leave their jobs or be terminated from their employment.

The laws on noncompete agreements vary from state to state, with California's being the most protective of employees. California's statute in essence prohibits employers from enforcing agreements that prohibit employees from working in their chosen fields. However, across all states, courts are clear in their positions that there must be an underlying reason for the noncompete agreement such as an employee having had access to the company's proprietary information.

Employees' signatures on these agreements are often questioned, particularly when there is some form of compensation attached to surrender of rights. California has provided protection for employees who refuse to sign noncompete agreements, punishing employers with punitive damages in wrongful termination cases brought by employees terminated following their refusals to sign.

Coady v. *Harpo, Inc.* (Case 18.3) deals with an interesting type of covenant in an employment contract that covers post-employment activities of departed employees.

CASE 18.3

Coady v. *Harpo, Inc.*
719 N.E.2d 244 (Ill. App. 1999)

O! Oprah! Do Tell!

FACTS

Elizabeth Coady (plaintiff) was employed by Harpo, Inc. (defendant), a company owned by Oprah Winfrey, as a senior associate producer for "The Oprah Winfrey Show" from November 1993 until March 1998. Ms. Coady alleged that for some time prior to March 26, 1998, those working at Harpo engaged in conduct so intolerable as to amount to constructive termination. On March 26, 1998, Ms. Coady notified Harpo by letter from her attorney that she resigned effectively immediately.

Ms. Coady, a trained journalist, indicated her intent to write or otherwise report about her experiences as an employee of Harpo. She asserted that she would

write about her experiences as an exercise of her rights of free speech and free press and was not prohibited from doing so by a confidentiality policy, which was entitled "Business Ethics, Objectivity, and Confidentiality Policy," contained in Harpo's September 1996 employee manual.

In a letter dated April 24, 1998, Harpo "reminded" Ms. Coady that she had signed a document entitled "Business Ethics, Objectivity, and Confidentiality Policy" on March 12, 1995, and provided her a copy of the agreement in the letter. The letter further stated that in the March 12, 1995, agreement, Ms. Coady "agreed (among other things) to keep confidential, during her

continued

employment and thereafter, all information about the Company, Ms. Winfrey, her private life, and Harpo's business activities which she acquired during or by virtue of her employment with Harpo." Harpo representatives indicated in the letter their intentions to enforce and ensure compliance with the confidentiality agreement.

Ms. Coady filed suit seeking, among other things, a declaration that the covenant is unenforceable. The trial court dismissed the claim, and Ms. Coady appealed.

JUDICIAL OPINION

GREIMAN, Justice

Both the independent document entitled "Business Ethics, Objectivity, and Confidentiality Policy" (hereinafter the 1995 agreement) and the portion of the employee manual with the same title (hereinafter the 1996 employee manual) include a section entitled "Confidentiality Assurances," which provides in pertinent part as follows:

1. During your employment or business relationship with Harpo, and thereafter, to the fullest extent permitted by law, you are obligated to keep confidential and never disclose, use, misappropriate, or confirm or deny the veracity of, any statement or comment concerning Oprah Winfrey, Harpo (which, as used herein, included all entities related to Harpo, Inc., including Harpo Productions, Inc., Harpo Films, Inc.) or any of her/its Confidential Information. The phrase 'Confidential Information' as used in this policy, includes but is not limited to, any and all information which is not generally known to the public, related to or concerning: (a) Ms. Winfrey and/or her business or private life; (b) the business activities, dealings or interests of Harpo and/or its officers, directors, affiliates, employees or contractors; and/or (c) Harpo's employment practices or policies applicable to its employees and/or contractors.

2. During your employment or business relationship with Harpo, and thereafter, you are obligated to refrain from giving or participating in any interview(s) regarding or related to Ms. Winfrey, Harpo, your employment or business relationship with Harpo and/or amy [sic] matter which concerns, relates to or involves any Confidential Information.

The relevant documents also provide that commitment to the stated policies is required as a condition of employment: "Your commitment to the guidelines set forth in this policy is a condition of your employment or business relationship with Harpo."

In addition, defendant's motion to dismiss attached a copy of plaintiff's acknowledgment of the employee manual, which she signed upon the commencement of her employment at defendant in 1993. The acknowledgment signed by plaintiff states in relevant part:

I acknowledge and understand that I may not use any confidential or proprietary information of HARPO for my own purposes either during or after my employment with HARPO, and I understand that I am prohibited from removing, disclosing or otherwise misappropriating any of HARPO's confidential or proprietary information for any reason.

[P]laintiff asserts that the confidentiality policy is not enforceable, primarily arguing that it is overly broad and not reasonably necessary to protect defendant's legitimate business interests. Defendant, however, contends that the confidentiality agreement is enforceable because it does not violate any public policy, was supported by adequate consideration, was not an adhesion contract and properly protected defendant's legitimate business interests. "A postemployment restrictive covenant will be enforced if its terms are reasonable." To determine the reasonableness of a restrictive covenant, "it is necessary to consider whether enforcement of the covenant will injure the public, whether enforcement will cause undue hardship to the promisor and whether the restraint imposed by the covenant is greater than is necessary to protect the interests of the employer."

The reasonableness of some types of restrictive covenants, such as nonsolicitation agreements, also is evaluated by the time limitation and geographical scope stated in the covenant. However, a confidentiality agreement will not be deemed unenforceable for lack of durational or geographic limitations where trade secrets and confidential information are involved.

Postemployment restrictive covenants typically involve agreements by a past employee not to compete with the business of her former employer, not to solicit clients or customers of her former employer, and not to disseminate trade secrets of her former employer. The covenants in these typical cases are carefully scrutinized because Illinois courts abhor restraints on trade.

Although restraint of trade is a significant concern, "[a]n equally important public policy in Illinois is the freedom to contract." Furthermore, postemployment restrictive covenants "have a social utility in that they protect an employer from the unwarranted erosion of confidential information."

Unlike the traditional line of restrictive covenant cases, the confidentiality agreement at issue in the instant case does not impose any of the typical restrictions commonly adjudicated in restrictive covenant cases. Defendant does not seek to restrain plaintiff's future career. Plaintiff is free to choose her future occupation, the locale in which she may choose to work, and the time when she can commence her new career. Defendant does not object to plaintiff becoming a journalist, competing with defendant in the same venue and in any locale, including Chicago, and in beginning her new venture immediately. The confidentiality agreement does not restrict commerce and does not restrict plaintiff's ability to work in any chosen career field, at any time. Instead, the 1995 confidentiality agreement restricts plaintiff's ability to disseminate confidential information that she obtained or learned while in defendant's employ. Most certainly, plaintiff had no problem with keeping confidences as long as she was a senior associate producer and continued her work with defendant.

Moreover, we find unpersuasive plaintiff's argument that the confidentiality agreement is too broad because it remains effective for all time and with no geographical boundaries. Whether for better or for worse, interest in a celebrity figure and his or her attendant business and personal ventures somehow seems to continue endlessly, even long after death, and often, as in the present case, extends over an international domain.

Under the facts of this case and the terms of the restrictive covenant at issue, we find that the 1995 confidentiality agreement is reasonable and enforceable. Accordingly, we affirm the trial court's order dismissing plaintiff's cause of action as stated in count I of her complaint.

Affirmed.

CASE QUESTIONS

1. What did Ms. Coady agree to when she became a Harpo employee?

2. Does it matter whether it was part of the employee manual or part of a contract?

3. Is there a difference between a confidentiality agreement and a covenant not to compete?

4. Does this restrictive covenant prevent Ms. Coady from working as a journalist?

5. Is the Oprah covenant enforceable?

MAKING ETHICS PERSONAL

The Agents Who "Kiss and Tell"

One publisher has noted that the "kiss and tell" book has become a favorite in the publishing industry. That is, those who have worked for famous people offer to write books disclosing personal and private information about their former employers. Nannies, press secretaries, footmen to royalty, the U.S. Treasury Secretary, chiefs of staff, mistresses, and household employees have all penned books about their former employers.

Most of these authors had not signed agreements with their employers not to make disclosures. Most of these authors also earned six-figure advances for their books, with many earning royalties beyond their advances. Would you write a book about your former employer and disclose private and personal information? Why or why not?

Downsizings in the high-tech industry have brought back the issue of noncompete and confidentiality agreements. When employees were recruited by these upstart firms and lured with stock options, it was difficult for them to imagine a time when the company would need to downsize or would no longer exist. As a result, most of them signed fairly restrictive covenants not to compete.

For example, one dot-com agreed to give its employees stock options if they would sign a noncompete agreement. Amazon.com offered downsized employees an additional ten weeks' pay plus $500 in addition to the normal severance package if they would sign a three-page "separation agreement and general release" in which they promised not to sue Amazon over the layoff or disparage it in any way. Amazon did have all employees sign a confidentiality agreement at the beginning of their employment that it has indicated it will enforce and that is likely to be valid because it is not a restraint on employment and is tied to legitimate business protection interests.

ETHICAL ISSUES

FAO Schwarz filed suit against its former chairman and CEO, John Eyler, because Mr. Eyler left his position at FAO Schwarz and joined Toys "Я" Us in January 2000. The suit was one for breach of contract that alleged specifically that Mr. Eyler violated a clause in his employment agreement that required him to give one year's notice of his departure and also prevents him from working for a competitor for two years after his departure.

Mr. Eyler was hired at FAO Schwarz in 1992 and was paid a $2.4 million bonus in 1999 that the suit describes as a payment made to keep him at the company.

The suit asks for a hearing to determine whether there should be a preliminary injunction against Mr. Eyler to prevent him from going to work for Toys "Я" Us until the merits of the case are decided.

Toys "Я" Us, also named as a defendant in the suit, issued a response denying any wrongdoing and explaining that it would "vigorously defend" against the lawsuit. Toys "Я" Us and FAO Schwarz had been in merger discussions last year, and Toys "Я" Us had signed an agreement that it would not recruit FAO Schwarz employees for two years following the merger discussions if those discussions failed (they did not, in fact, result in a merger).

The suit also alleges that Mr. Eyler took with him trade secrets and that FAO is entitled to protection against their use by Mr. Eyler.

What kinds of trade secrets do you think Mr. Eyler might have? What kinds of covenants not to compete are enforceable? Do you think this covenant should be enforced against Mr. Eyler? Evaluate the ethics of Toys "Я" Us and Mr. Eyler.

Aftermath: FAO Schwarz entered Chapter 11 bankruptcy in 2002.

Source: Dana Canedy, "Schwarz Sues Chief for Move to Toys "Я" Us," *New York Times*, February 18, 2000, pp. C1, C20.

Duty of Obedience

An agent has the duty to obey reasonable instructions from the principal. The agent is not required to do anything criminally wrong or commit torts, of course; but he is required to operate according to the principal's standards and instructions. Failure to do so could mean the agent has gone beyond the authority given and is then personally liable for the conduct.

Duty of Care

Agents have a duty to use as much care and to act as prudently as they would if managing their own affairs. Agents must take the time and effort to perform their principals' assigned tasks. For example, officers of corporations must base their decisions on information, not guesses, and must ensure that their decisions are carried out by employees.

An agent who does not use reasonable care is liable to the principal for any damages resulting from a lack of care. When an agent does not make adequate travel arrangements for a speaker, the agent is liable to the speaker for damages that result from the speaker's nonappearance at an engagement.

For a look at the 100 best companies to work for, visit:
http://www.fortune.com/fortune/bestcompanies

The Principal's Rights and Responsibilities

A principal has the right to expect that an agent will perform within the standards just described. In exchange, the principal has certain obligations. The first obligation is that of compensation, which can take various forms. Some agents work for a fee on a contingency basis. A real estate agent, for example, may have an arrangement in which she receives compensation only if a buyer for the property is found.

There can be a **gratuitous agency**, in which the agent has authority to act for the principal but will not be compensated. For example, some charitable organizations have agents who act in fund-raising capacities, but these agents do not expect compensation. Principals also have an obligation to indemnify agents for expenses the agents incur in carrying out the principal's orders. Corporate officers, for example, are entitled to travel compensation; sales agents are entitled to compensation for ads to sell goods, realty, or services.

LIABILITY OF PRINCIPALS FOR AGENTS' CONDUCT: THE RELATIONSHIP WITH THIRD PARTIES

Contract Liability

Although the types of authority an agent has and the terms of the agency agreement define the authority of the agent, the contract liability of a principal is not determined by either what he intended or by the limitations agreed to privately by the agent and the principal. In other words, third parties have certain contract enforcement rights depending on the nature of the agent's work and the authority given by the principal. The liability of the principal for contracts made by an agent is controlled by the perceptions created for and observed by the third party to the contract. Those perceptions vary, so the liability of the principal varies depending on the way in which the agent does business. For example, an officer of a corporation has the authority to bind the corporation, but what if the officer does not disclose that there is a principal? This section deals with those issues.

The Disclosed Principal

In a situation in which a third party is aware there is a principal involved and also knows who the principal is, the principal is liable to the third party, but the agent is not. This is true whether the agent has express, implied, or apparent authority. If the agent has no authority, however, then the agent, not the principal, is liable. For example, suppose that Paula Abbaduhla is the vice president of Video Television, Inc., and she signs for a line of credit for the corporation at First Bank. So long as she signed the documents "Video Television, Inc., by Paula Abbaduhla, VP," Video would be solely responsible for the line of credit. If, however, she signed that same way but had no authority, she would be liable to Video if it had to honor the agreement. As another example, most title insurers and escrow companies require corporations selling or buying real property to have board authorization in the form of a resolution. If Paula signed to buy land and did not have a resolution, she would have no express authority, and without implied or apparent authority, she would be liable for the land contract. (See Chapter 21 for a more thorough discussion of board resolutions and officers' authority.)

The Partially Disclosed Principal

In this situation, the third party knows that the agent is acting for someone else, but the identity of the principal is not disclosed. For example, an agent might be used to purchase land for development purposes when the developer does not want to be disclosed because disclosure of a major developer's involvement might drive up land prices. In this situation, the third-party seller of the land can hold either the principal or the agent liable on the contract. The agent assumes some risk of personal liability by not disclosing the identity of the principal.

The Undisclosed Principal

In this situation, an agent acts without disclosing either the existence of a principal or the principal's identity. Again, such an arrangement might be undertaken to

EXHIBIT 18.1   Contract Liability of Disclosed Principal

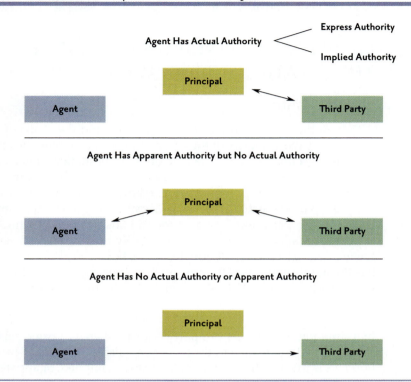

avoid speculation, or it could be intended simply to protect someone's privacy, such as when a famous person purchases a home and does not want any advance disclosure of the purchase or its location. Here, the agent is directly liable to the third party. If the third party discovers the identity of the principal, the third party could hold either the principal or the agent liable. Exhibits 18.1 and 18.2 provide summaries of the liability of agents and principals under the three forms of disclosure of the relationship.

Liability of Principals for Agents' Torts

As for the liability of principals for torts committed by agents, two types of agents must be considered: servants and independent contractors. The amount of liability a principal has for an agent's torts depends first on the status of the agent.

Master–Servant Relationship
As discussed earlier in the chapter, there is a distinction between the liability of a principal for the acts of a servant and for those of an independent contractor. The principal is liable for the torts of the servant—an agent whose work, assignments, and time are controlled by the principal.

Scope of Employment
Employers (principals) are liable for the conduct of employees (agents/servants) while those employees are acting in the **scope of employment**. Scope of employ-

EXHIBIT   18.2 Contract Liability of Undisclosed or Partially Disclosed Principal

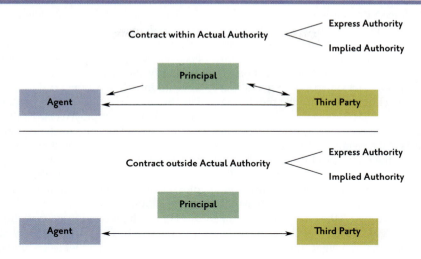

ment means that an employee is doing work for an employer at the time a tort occurs. Suppose a florist delivery driver, while delivering flowers, has an auto accident that is the delivery driver's fault. In addition to the driver's responsibility for the negligence in the accident, the florist is also liable to injured parties under the doctrine of **respondeat superior**.

Scope of employment has been defined broadly by the courts. Negligent torts committed while an employee is driving to a sales call or delivery are clearly within the scope of employment.

An employee who takes the afternoon off is not within the scope of employment, and the principal is not liable if an accident occurs during that time. An employee who uses the lunch hour to shop is not within the scope of employment. When an employee is acting on personal business, the scope of employment ends. *Faverty* v. *McDonald's Restaurants of Oregon, Inc.* (Case 18.4) deals with an issue of when the scope of employment ends, in a timing sense.

CASE 18.4

Faverty v. *McDonald's Restaurants of Oregon, Inc.*
892 P.2d 703 (Ct. App. Or. 1995)

Triple Shift Overtime:
Who Is Liable for the Drive Home Afterward?

FACTS

Matt Theurer was an 18-year-old high school senior with many extracurricular activities, including being a member of the National Guard. Mr. Theurer was employed by a McDonald's restaurant (defendant) in Portland, Oregon, on a part-time basis. While his employer called Mr. Theurer an enthusiastic worker, his friends and family felt that he was doing too much and getting too little sleep.

McDonald's employed many high school students on a part-time basis, and their restaurants closed at 11:00 P.M., with clean-up and other procedures taking up another hour until midnight. McDonald's informal

continued

policy did not permit high school students to work more than one midnight shift per week or allow split shifts. Split shifts forced the students to work in the morning and then evening. McDonald's felt the commuting time between the shifts prevented "people from getting their rest." Despite these policies, high school employees frequently complained about being tired, and at least two of McDonald's employees had accidents while driving home after working the closing shift until midnight.

A few times each year, McDonald's scheduled special cleanup projects at the restaurant that required employees to work after the midnight closing until 5 A.M. Student workers were to be used for cleanup shifts only on weekends or during spring break. However, for one scheduled cleanup project, there were not enough regular employees, and the manager asked for volunteers for a midnight to 5 A.M. cleanup shift. Mr. Theurer volunteered; the manager knew that Mr. Theurer had to drive about twenty minutes to and from work.

During the week of the scheduled special cleanup, Mr. Theurer had worked five nights. One night he worked until midnight, another until 11:30 P.M., two until 9 P.M., and another until 11 P.M. On Monday, April 4, 1988, Mr. Theurer worked his regular shift from 3:30 until 7:30 P.M., followed by a cleanup shift beginning at midnight until 5 A.M. on April 5, and then worked another shift from 5 A.M. until 8:21 A.M. During that shift Mr. Theurer told his manager that he was tired and asked to be excused from his next regular shift. The manager excused him, and Mr. Theurer began his drive home.

Mr. Theurer was driving 45 miles per hour on a two-lane road when he became drowsy or fell asleep, crossed the dividing line into oncoming traffic, crashed into the van of Frederic Faverty (plaintiff), and was killed. Mr. Faverty was seriously injured. Mr. Faverty settled his claims with Mr. Theurer's estate and then filed suit against McDonald's. The jury found for Mr. Faverty, and McDonald's appealed.

JUDICIAL OPINION

LANDAU, Judge

Defendant argues that it was Theurer's employer and, because of that relationship, it was subject to a limited duty to both Theurer and plaintiff, as a matter of law.

According to defendant, there is no evidence that it knew or should have known that Theurer was so exhausted or fatigued that it should have foreseen that working him three shifts in one 24-hour period would create a foreseeable risk of harm to motorists such as plaintiff. Plaintiff argues that defendant failed to preserve that argument and that, in any event, the evidence is sufficient to support the trial court's ruling.

There is evidence that defendant controlled all work assignments. Therefore, defendant knew or had reason to know of the number of hours Theurer had been working. There also is evidence that defendant ordinarily did not use high school students to work after midnight, and when it did, it tried to limit that late shift to once a week. Defendant also had a policy of not working its employees two shifts in one day. According to at least one of the defendant's managers, those policies were adopted and enforced out of concern that employees not become overly tired on the job. In fact, defendant was aware that at least two of its employees had recently had automobile accidents as a result of falling asleep while driving home after working late shifts. There is evidence that, during and after his late-night shift, Theurer was visibly fatigued, and that defendant's managers were on site and saw Theurer throughout that shift. It is undisputed that defendant knew that Theurer was a high school student, and that most of the high school students who worked there drove to work in their own cars. On the basis of that evidence, a reasonable jury could conclude that defendant knew or should have known that working Theurer so many hours would impair his ability to drive home safely.

Defendant and the dissent insist that, because Theurer "volunteered" to work so many hours, the evidence simply is insufficient to establish defendant's negligence, as a matter of law. First of all, in so characterizing the facts, defendant and the dissent put a "spin" on the evidence to which they are not entitled. The evidence, taken in the light most favorable to plaintiff, shows that Theurer did not, out of the blue, volunteer to take three shifts in one 24-hour period. Defendant affirmatively asked him to work those hours. Moreover, the evidence shows that defendant—not its employees—generally controlled all work assignments and that defendant penalized its employees for not working as assigned.

Second, even indulging the assumption that Theurer volunteered for his all-night shift, the evidence still is sufficient to support the jury's verdict. Defendant's managers knew that Theurer already had been scheduled to work more than its own policies permitted. Moreover, they saw him in a visibly fatigued state and continued to work him as scheduled. In that regard, defendant was much like a bartender who served alcoholic beverages to a visibly intoxicated person who then caused an automobile accident that harmed another. No one required the intoxicated person to have the extra drink. He or she asked for the drink and "volunteered" to pay for it. Nevertheless, the courts have held that, because the bartender saw the driver in a visibly intoxicated state, and it is reasonably foreseeable that the customer will drive when he or she leaves, the bartender is liable for the consequences of the automobile accident.

Finally, defendant itself conceded at trial that, if it had allowed Theurer to "volunteer" to work around the clock three full days, the "court can almost say as a matter of law, allowing someone to work that long without any rest or sleep might very well constitute affirmative misconduct by an employer, but [it] may be a matter of degrees. . . ."

Thus, whether Theurer volunteered or not simply is not the point. The point is whether, as plaintiff alleged in his complaint, defendant "was negligent in working Theurer more hours than was reasonable." That is, as defendant said at trial, "a matter of degrees." In other words, it is a matter for the jury to decide, not for the court to resolve as a matter of law.

Defendant, the dissent and the *amici curiae* the National Council of Chain Restaurants and the Defense Research Institute, Inc., implore us to reverse the trial court's judgment on the public policy ground that the result is "patently unreasonable," "shocking," "far-fetched" and "goes beyond the common-sense application of tort law." However, that argument was not made to the trial court, and we will not consider it for the first time on appeal.

Affirmed.

DISSENTING OPINION

EDMUNDS, Judge

The majority holds that a restaurant can be held liable for common law negligence because its adult employee fell asleep while driving home from work, crossed the center line into the oncoming lane of traffic and collided with plaintiff's vehicle. The reason for the restaurant's liability: It accepted the employee's offer to work overtime, and, according to the majority, thereby became responsible for the risk of injury caused by the employee's state of fatigue. That holding is without precedent in the State of Oregon. It makes all employers potentially liable for their employees' off-premises negligence when an employee becomes tired as a result of working. That has never been the law in Oregon nor should it be now.

The majority need have gone no further than defendant's motion for a directed verdict in deciding this case. Defendant is entitled to a directed verdict as a matter of law because of certain uncontroverted facts. First, Theurer was not a minor, but an adult at the time of the accident. He was 18 years old and serving in the National Guard. Defendant did not owe any special responsibility to him because he also attended high school. The fact that he was a student working part time and had over-extended himself physically is of no import to defendant's liability. No rule of negligence requires an employer to inquire into the private lives of its adult employees to determine if, on a given occasion, the employee is not getting enough sleep.

Second, Theurer volunteered to work the clean-up shift. He was not sought out by defendant and "required" to work on April 5, 1988.

Third, Theurer never asked to be relieved from working the shift either before the shift started or during it; nor is there any evidence that defendant refused such a request.

Fourth, Theurer was not on defendant's business premises and was on his own time when he drove home from work that morning. Theurer was not acting on defendant's behalf, nor did defendant have actual control of or the right to control Theurer's driving conduct or where he went after he got off work. Moreover, no omission or affirmative act by defendant prevented Theurer from choosing to have someone pick him up after work, or to take a nap in his car before driving home, or some other preventive measure.

The majority's analysis is wrong because the facts relied on by it are not controlling unless defendant's conduct created an "unreasonable" risk of harm to plaintiff. In the context of this case, the question is whether defendant created an unreasonable risk of harm to every person on the highway that morning when it scheduled Theurer to work. That question must be answered in the light of the uncontroverted facts that Theurer was an adult employee, that defendant did not require him to work the shift, that Theurer assured defendant's manager that he would rest between shifts and that he would be able to handle the shift physically, that Theurer never asked to be relieved from the shift, and that the harm to plaintiff occurred off defendant's work premises as a result of an activity over which defendant had no right of control. By holding defendant responsible for the safety of all persons on the roadway, the majority makes "general foreseeability" the test for determining whether defendant's conduct is deemed "negligent."

In effect, the opinion says to Oregon employers, "Do not schedule your employees in a manner that will cause fatigue, because if you do, you risk liability for negligence in the event that your employee acts in a negligent manner off-premises and after work." That is not the law of this state and it cannot be unreasonable conduct for an employer to accept an offer from an adult employee, made days in advance of the shift, to

continued

work overtime, insofar as the safety of motorists is concerned after the employee gets off work. Because the majority opinion extends the duty of care owed to the general public by employers in the scheduling of their employees' work shifts to beyond any reasonable boundary, I dissent.

CASE QUESTIONS

1. Of what significance is the fact that Mr. Theurer volunteered for the all-night shift?

2. Why would a restaurant association have an interest in the outcome of the case?

3. Did McDonald's violate any Oregon statute?

4. Was Mr. Theurer acting within the scope of employment?

5. Is McDonald's liable to Mr. Faverty?

6. What counterpoints does the dissenting judge make?

Generally, intentional acts not authorized by employers do not result in liability. However, as *Lange* v. *National Biscuit Co.* (Case 18.5) discusses, employers may have concerns and potential liability for intentional acts that occur during work for the employer. This case also provides the answer for the chapter's opening Consider.

CASE 18.5

Lange v. *National Biscuit Co.*
211 N.W.2d 783 (Minn. 1973)

Shelf Space Is My Life: Flipping Out over Oreos

FACTS

Jerome Lange (plaintiff) was the manager of a small grocery store in Minnesota that carried Nabisco (defendant) products. Ronnell Lynch had been hired by Nabisco as a cookie salesman-trainee in October 1968. On March 1, 1969, Mr. Lynch was assigned his own territory, which included Mr. Lange's store.

Between March 1 and May 1, 1969, Nabisco received numerous complaints from grocers about Mr. Lynch being overly aggressive and taking shelf space in the stores reserved for competing cookie companies.

On May 1, 1969, Mr. Lynch came to Mr. Lange's store to place Nabisco merchandise on the shelves. An argument developed between the two over Mr. Lynch's service to the store. Mr. Lynch became very angry and started swearing. Mr. Lange told him to either stop swearing or leave the store because children were present. Mr. Lynch then became uncontrollably angry and said, "I ought to break your neck." He then went behind the counter and dared Mr. Lange to fight. When Mr. Lange refused, Mr. Lynch viciously assaulted him, after which he threw cookies around the store and left.

Mr. Lange filed suit against Nabisco and was awarded damages based on the jury's finding that although the acts of Mr. Lynch were outside the scope of employment, Nabisco was negligent in hiring and retaining him. The judge granted Nabisco's motion for judgment notwithstanding the verdict, and Mr. Lange appealed.

JUDICIAL OPINION

TODD, Justice

There is no dispute with the general principle that in order to impose liability on the employer under the doctrine of *respondeat superior* it is necessary to show that the employee was acting within the scope of his employment. Unfortunately, there is a wide disparity in the case law in the application of the "scope of employment" test to those factual situations involving intentional torts. The majority rule as set out in Annotation, 34 A.L.R.2d 372, 402, includes a twofold test: (a) Whether the assault was motivated by business or personal considerations; or (b) whether the assault was contemplated by the employer or incident to the employment.

Under the present Minnesota rule, liability is imposed where it is shown that the employee's acts were motivated by a desire to further the employer's business. Therefore, a master could only be held liable for an employee's assault in those rare instances where the master actually requested the servant to so perform, or the servant's duties were such that that motivation was implied in law.

The fallacy of this reasoning was that it made a certain mental condition of the servant the test by which to determine whether he was acting about his master's business or not. Moreover, with respect of all intentional acts done by a servant in the supposed furtherance of his master's business, it clothed the master with immunity if the act was right, because it was right, and, if it was wrong, it clothed him with a like immunity, because it was wrong. He thus got the benefit of all his servant's acts done for him, whether right or wrong, and escaped the burden of all intentional acts done for him which were wrong. Under the operation of such a rule, it would always be more safe and profitable for a man to conduct his business vicariously than in his own person. He would escape liability for the consequences of many acts connected with his business springing from the imperfection of human nature, because done by another, for which he would be responsible if done by himself. Meanwhile, the public, obliged to deal or come in contact with his agents, for intentional injuries done by them, might be left wholly without redress. . . . A doctrine so fruitful of mischief could not long stand unshaken in an enlightened system of jurisprudence.

In developing a test for the application of *respondeat superior* when an employee assaults a third person, we believe that the focus should be on the basis of the assault rather than the motivation of the employee. We reject as the basis for imposing liability the arbitrary determination of when, and at what point, the argument and assault leave the sphere of the employer's business and become motivated by personal animosity. Rather, we believe the better approach is to view both the argument and assault as an indistinguishable event for purposes of vicarious liability.

We hold that an employer is liable for an assault by his employee when the source of the attack is related to the duties of the employee and the assault occurs within work-related limits of time and place. The as-sault in this case obviously occurred within work-related limits of time and place, since it took place on authorized premises during working hours. The precipitating cause of the initial argument concerned the employee's conduct of his work. In addition, the employee originally was motivated to become argumentative in furtherance of his employer's business. Consequently, under the facts of this case we hold as a matter of law that the employee was acting within the scope of employment at the time of the aggression and that plaintiff's posttrial motion for judgment notwithstanding the verdict on that ground should have been granted under the rule we herein adopt. To the extent that our former decisions are inconsistent with the rule now adopted, they are overruled.

Plaintiff may recover damages under either the theory of *respondeat superior* or negligence. Having disposed of the matter on the former issue, we need not undertake the questions raised by defendant's asserted negligence in the hiring or retention of the employee.

Reversed and remanded.

CASE QUESTIONS

1. What previous indications did Nabisco have that Mr. Lynch might cause some problems?

2. Was the attack of Mr. Lange within the scope of employment?

3. What test does the court give for determining scope of employment?

4. What is the "motivation test"?

5. Does this court adopt or reject the "motivation test"?

Negligent Hiring and Supervision

A rapidly evolving area of tort liability relates to one part of the discussion in the *Lange* case and is referred to as the tort of negligent hiring and/or supervision of employees. Negligent hiring requires proof that the principal/employer hired an agent/employee whose background made him ill-suited for the position. For example, a school district that does not check the background of a bus driver or teacher for, particularly, past charges or history of child abuse and molestation has committed the tort of negligent hiring. Negligent supervision liability results when an employer has been put on notice that an employee has engaged in behavior that is harmful to others but leaves the employee in his position. An example is a college or university leaving a professor in the classroom after having received complaints regarding his inappropriate conduct in class and with students. If the professor then harms one of his students, the college or university would be liable to the student for the failure to make a timely termination, suspension, or other action to remove the professor from student contact or at least provide appropriate monitoring of the professor with the students. *Doe v. Norwich Roman Catholic Diocesan Corp.* (Case 18.6) involves a sensitive issue that revolves around the question of negligence in hiring and supervision.

CASE 18.6

Doe v. Norwich Roman Catholic Diocesan Corp.
268 F.Supp.2d 139 (Conn. 2003)

Confessing Liability

FACTS

Jane Doe (plaintiff) brought suit against the St. Columba Church and the Norwich Diocese (defendants) alleging that while a parishioner at St. Columba Church, she was sexually assaulted and abused by Patrick Sullivan, a Roman Catholic priest assigned to perform various tasks on behalf of the Diocese and St. Columba. From 1968 through 1969, Sullivan allegedly sexually abused the plaintiff, who was 15 to 16 years old at the time. The alleged sexual abuse occurred at various locations, including the St. Columba rectory.

The Diocese moved to dismiss the complaint.

JUDICIAL OPINION

GOETTEL, District Judge

In order for an employer to be liable for the intentional torts of its employee under *respondeat superior,* the employee must have been acting "in furtherance of the employer's business." Usually, "it is a question of fact as to whether a wilful tort of the servant has occurred within the scope of the servant's employment and was done to further his master's business. . . . But there are occasional cases where a servant's digression from duty is so clear-cut that the disposition of the case becomes a matter of law."

Cases of sexual abuse often represent such a strong deviation from furthering an employer's business. In most cases of alleged sexual abuse by priests, the courts have held that *respondeat superior* is not applicable to hold a church or diocese liable, because such acts by the priests are not in furtherance of the church's business. See *Nutt* v. *Norwich Roman Catholic Diocese,* 921 F.Supp. 66, 71 (D.Conn.1995).

In *Nutt,* former altar boys claimed that a priest had shown them pornographic movies and taken them on trips where he engaged in sexual abuse. The court noted that the Roman Catholic Church expressly forbids its priests from engaging in any sexual activity, so any form of sexually abusive acts would demonstrate abandonment of the church's business; thus, the court granted the defendant church's and diocese's motions for summary judgment on all counts relating to respondeat superior.

Even at the pleading stage, Connecticut courts have dismissed claims of *respondeat superior* in cases of sexual abuse by a priest, because as a matter of law, those acts did not further the interests of the church or diocese. See *Doe* v. *Hartford Diocesan,* 45 Conn.Supp. at 395, 716 A.2d 960. In *Doe* v. *Hartford Diocesan,* a minor, female parishioner alleged that her priest had sexually abused her. The court determined that there was a clear digression from duty and the misconduct was beyond the scope of employment, because the church would neither benefit directly nor indirectly from the priest's actions. Therefore, it granted the pastor's, church's, and diocese's motion to strike the claim of *respondeat superior,* because even if the alleged facts were proven, they were insufficient to constitute actions within the scope of the priest's employment.

Similarly, in this case, Plaintiff has merely made the conclusory statement that "Sullivan was acting within the scope of his duties as a Roman Catholic priest for the Defendant Diocese and/or the Defendant St. Columba Church and within the scope of his employment with the aforementioned Defendants and in furtherance of their business purpose." As a Roman Catholic priest, Sullivan would have abandoned the business of the Church by engaging in sexual conduct with Plaintiff, which is expressly forbidden, so as a matter of law it could not be shown that his actions were in furtherance of Church business.

Plaintiff urges us to deny the motion because *respondeat superior* has been applied in some cases of sexual abuse by priests, but those cases involved very unique circumstances, which are not present here. See *Martinelli* v. *Bridgeport Roman Catholic Diocesan Corp.,* 989 F.Supp. 110, 118 (D.Conn.1997). In *Martinelli,* the plaintiff claimed that a priest attempted to teach the sacraments to him and other teenage boys by using sexual contact. The district court denied summary judgment for the diocese, because there was a genuine dispute as to whether the priest's activities represented a "total departure from the [d]iocese's business."

Unlike *Martinelli,* in this case, Plaintiff has not alleged any facts to indicate that the nature of the alleged sexual acts by the priest somehow furthered the Church's business. The allegations of this case are more similar to those cases where the courts have found that as a matter of law respondeat superior does not apply. Accordingly, we GRANT Defendants' Motions to Dismiss Count Seven without prejudice to Plaintiff's filing an amended complaint alleging sufficient facts to indicate that the alleged misconduct by the priest was conducted in furtherance of Church's and/or Diocese's business.

Plaintiff claims that St. Columba and Diocese were negligent in any of the following ways:

(a) Failing to properly screen, evaluate, or investigate Sullivan's past activities, moral fitness for working with children and teenagers, and fitness for the priesthood prior to his ordination and assignment to the Diocese;

(b) Failing to properly supervise and investigate Sullivan's activities while he was within the jurisdiction of the Diocese and while he was residing at St. Columba's rectory, failing to recognize Sullivan's inappropriate behavior which made him ill-suited for the priesthood or for which he should have been counseled, and failing to recognize warning signs that Sullivan was engaging in sexual abuse with a minor;

(c) Failing to establish guidelines and procedures to prevent injuries to Plaintiff, failing to properly train Sullivan regarding his role as a priest and the boundaries of appropriate behavior and decorum in the rectory, and failing to provide appropriate counseling for priests having difficulties with the constraints of celibacy;

(d) Due to the frequency, duration, and location of the alleged misconduct, Defendants should have known or did know that Sullivan was engaging in sexual abuse with Plaintiff on Church premises.

Defendants argue that the only aspects of this negligence count that should be permitted are the allegations involving negligent disregard of a known danger, and that the rest of the count should be dismissed because (a) the Eighth Count involves entanglement of the Court in religious matters of the Church, violating the First Amendment; ... The First Amendment prohibits Congress from making "any law respecting an establishment of religion or prohibiting the free exercise thereof ... ," U.S. Const. Amend. I, and is applied to the states through the Fourteenth Amendment.

In cases "where resolution of disputes cannot be made without extensive inquiry by civil courts into religious law and polity, the First and Fourteenth Amendments mandate that civil courts shall not disturb the decisions of the highest ecclesiastical tribunal within a [hierarchical] church." "But, [the Supreme] Court never has suggested that those constraints similarly apply outside the context of such intraorganizational disputes." The Connecticut Supreme Court recognized that it is "well-established that state judicial intervention is justified when it can be accomplished by resort[ing] to neutral principles of the law ... that eschew consideration of doctrinal matters such as the ritual and liturgy of worship or the tenets of faith." The Supreme Court has "never held that an individual's religious beliefs excuse him from compliance with an otherwise valid law prohibiting conduct that the State is free to regulate. On the contrary, the record of more than a century of our free exercise jurisprudence contradicts that proposition." In a case of priest sexual misconduct, the Second Circuit held it was permissible under the First Amendment for the jury to have considered church doctrine to determine if a fiduciary duty arose between a parishioner and the diocese. *Martinelli v. Bridgeport Roman Catholic Diocesan Corp.*, 196 F.3d 409, 431 (2d Cir.1999). The court noted that "Martinelli's [parishioner's] claim was brought under Connecticut law, not church law; church law is not ours to assess or to enforce. Martinelli's claim neither relied upon nor sought to enforce the duties of the [d]iocese according to religious beliefs, nor did it require or involve a resolution of whether the [d]iocese's conduct was consistent with them." Id.

" ... [s]ince the Supreme Court has consistently failed to allow the Free Exercise Clause to relieve an individual from obedience to a general law not aimed at the promotion or restriction of religious beliefs, the defendants [church and diocese] cannot appropriately implicate the First Amendment as a defense to their alleged negligent conduct."

Several courts outside this jurisdiction have refused to adjudicate cases regarding negligent supervision of priests by the church for fear that "any inquiry into the policies and practices of the Church Defendants in hiring or supervising their clergy raises ... First Amendment problems of entanglement ... which might involve the Court in making sensitive judgments about the propriety of the Church Defendants' supervision in light of their religious beliefs ... [and][a]ny award of damages would have a chilling effect leading indirectly to state control over the future conduct of affairs of a religious denomination, ..." [T]he District Court of Connecticut in *Nutt*, rejected such an argument, because the First Amendment does not offer blanket immunity for religious institutions, and because an inquiry into the defendants' alleged negligent supervision would not "prejudice or impose upon any of the religious tenets or practices of Catholicism. Rather such a determination would involve an examination of the defendants' possible role in allowing one of its employees to engage in conduct which they, as employers, as well as society in general expressly prohibit."

This Court recognizes the concerns of religious institutions regarding entanglement of the courts in examining their religious practices. This Court does not, will not, and cannot sit as the reviewing authority for religious practices and doctrinal matters. But, as far as negligent supervision and employment are concerned, such inquiries can generally be conducted without any entanglement in the religious doctrines and practices of the church. Here, Plaintiff has broadly alleged negligent hiring and supervision of Sullivan by St. Columba and Diocese. As we construe her claims, they do not involve the entanglement of this Court with the church's

continued

religious practices. However, we would caution the parties to carefully limit the scope of this claim to the secular matters of negligent hiring and supervision. In cases regarding the liability of religious organizations for negligent supervision of their clergy, the courts have held that in order for a duty to have existed, the organizations must have known or should have known that misconduct was occurring. For example, in *Nutt,* the district court denied a church's and diocese's original motion for summary judgment because the facts regarding their knowledge of the priest's alleged misconduct were disputed. The church and diocese then submitted to the court affidavits indicating that church officials had no notice of the sexual misconduct, which were not challenged by the plaintiffs, so the court granted a renewed motion for summary judgment.

In another case, the district court granted summary judgment to a diocese because there was no "evidence that could reasonably give rise to an inference that [the priest's] sexual abuse was the foreseeable result of any action or omission by the [d]iocese."

All of these cases, however, have involved motions for summary judgment, and in those cases, the courts have relied on the many facts demonstrating defendants' knowledge and foreseeability of harm, such as the treatment of priests for sexual abuse, a diocesan "policy of reporting, investigating and dealing with any of its priests alleged to have engaged in any misconduct," records regarding moral character and the ability to relate to children effectively, and affidavits indicating that church officials were notified about sexual abuse.

For example, it might be necessary to explore Defendants' supervision of Sullivan, because if he had been properly supervised that could suggest that Defendants truly lacked knowledge of the alleged abuse. But, if improper supervision occurred, that could indicate that Defendants should have known about the alleged misconduct. If we were to dismiss these claims prematurely, some potentially relevant fact-finding would be precluded.

At this point, all we are concerned with is whether Plaintiff has alleged enough to state a claim. Even though some of the allegations are quite broad, they do provide sufficient information from which knowledge could be inferred, even if it is not explicitly alleged.

Nevertheless, we again caution both parties that just as this Court will not entangle itself in the Church's religious practices or doctrine, it will not examine the specific employment practices of the Church and Diocese unless they clearly indicate that Defendants knew or should have known that Sullivan was likely to engage in sexual misconduct. It is not the place of this Court to determine the fitness of individuals for the priesthood or the internal policies that are maintained to promote the clergy's morality. We are merely concerned with whether Defendants had knowledge or should have known about Sullivan's alleged misconduct.

Diocese argues that even if it and St. Columba had a duty to Plaintiff, they should not be liable, because the "proximate cause of the plaintiff's alleged injuries must necessarily have been the alleged sexual misconduct of . . . Sullivan and not any breach of duty on the part of the Diocese . . . or St. Columba."

In *Nutt,* a church and diocese argued that even if they were found to have a duty to plaintiffs who had been sexually abused by a priest, the church and diocese could not be found liable because the plaintiffs' injuries were proximately caused by the priest, not by negligence of the church or diocese. In that case, there was a disputed issue of fact regarding whether defendant church and diocese knew of the priest's sexual misconduct. Because it was not clear how much the defendants knew about the misconduct, the court held that it could not "determine, as a matter of law, that the defendants' alleged negligence in supervising Doyle was not the proximate cause of the plaintiffs' injuries."

Applying the reasoning of the Restatement, we must conclude, as the court did in *Nutt* that there is a possibility that if Defendants had knowledge regarding Sullivan's misconduct, Defendants could have been a proximate cause of injury to Plaintiff. Therefore, we would need to know what level of knowledge Defendants had about Sullivan's alleged misconduct, because they would only be relieved of liability if Plaintiff's alleged harm was not within the scope of risk created by their conduct.

At this point we simply do not have enough facts regarding Defendants' knowledge of Sullivan's alleged misconduct to make a determination regarding whether Defendants could have proximately caused the harm. A motion to dismiss is often ill-suited for disposing of proximate cause without the benefit of evidence indicating the Defendants' knowledge, and it would be would be premature and inappropriate to dismiss the negligence claim at this stage of the pleadings, even though Plaintiff may have difficulty ultimately proving knowledge, and therefore, proximate cause.

Accordingly, we DENY Defendants' Motion to Dismiss.

CASE QUESTIONS

1. What is the general position of the courts on the liability of churches and dioceses for the sexual misconduct of priests?

2. What must a plaintiff allege to be able to recover from a church or diocese?

3. What must a plaintiff prove to be able to recover from a church or diocese?

4. Is there liability for negligent supervision of priests?

CONSIDER... 18.4

Oklahoma Nursing Homes, Ltd. employed numerous health care professionals at its various nursing homes, including nurse's aides, who assisted occupants of the homes with daily activities such as eating, bathing, and dressing.

Glen Rodebush, a victim of Alzheimer's disease, was a resident of one of the company's homes. His condition caused him to be combative sometimes. Mr. Rodebush's wife, Zelda, arrived one day for a visit and discovered large welts and red marks on his face. Mrs. Rodebush called her husband's doctor, who found that the marks were caused by slaps of the human hand and were six to twelve hours old. Earlier in the day, Mr. Rodebush had been bathed by a male nurse's aide and, during the course of the bath, Mr. Rodebush had become unruly. Following the bath, a supervisor noted that the aide smelled of liquor and saw from his time card that he had arrived thirty minutes late. The nurse's aide confessed that he had "partied all night." The aide had been hired without a background check. Following the incident and Mrs. Rodebush's complaint about the marks, the company discovered that the aide had a felony conviction for violent assault and battery with intent to kill, escape, and carrying a weapon following conviction of a felony.

The company, which had never given the aide training, had been cited by the State Department of Human Services for violations of reporting requirements as well as the failure to take proper steps against employees who report to work while intoxicated.

Mrs. Rodebush has filed suit against the nursing home on behalf of her husband. The nursing home claims it cannot be held liable for the intentional and unauthorized acts of its employees. Who is correct? Should there be recovery? [*Rodebush* v. *Oklahoma Nursing Homes, Ltd.*, 867 P.2d 1241 (Okl.1993).]

The liability of principals for the torts of agents has become a costly part of doing business. Many firms are undertaking various forms of testing to prevent employees who could cause injuries from driving, operating machinery, or otherwise working in situations in which human safety is an issue.

In *Skinner* v. *Railway Labor Executives' Association*, 489 U.S. 602 (1989), the U.S. Supreme Court dealt with the issue of the validity of drug testing in the railroad industry. Under the Federal Railroad Safety Act of 1979, railroads were authorized to administer breath and urine tests to employees who had violated certain safety rules. A union brought suit against the secretary of transportation, alleging that railroad employees' rights to privacy under the Fourth Amendment (see Chapter 9) were intruded upon by the law and the testing. However, the Supreme Court held that the need for safety and the government's responsibility for ensuring railroad safety permitted the testing. Although the court ruled that the tests did violate individual privacy, they were also held to be necessary for the greater interest of public safety, at least in this case, of a governmental employer.

CONSIDER... 18.5

The FAA announced required drug testing by all airlines for the following employees: flight crew members, flight attendants, flight or ground instructors, flight testing personnel, aircraft dispatchers, maintenance personnel, aviation security or screening personnel, and air traffic controllers. The tests required included screening for marijuana, cocaine, opiates, phencyclidine (PCP), and amphetamines.

Is this testing appropriate? Is it an unnecessary invasion of privacy? Should all employees be tested? [*Bluestein* v. *Skinner*, 908 F.2d 451 (9th Cir. 1990).]

Independent Contractors

Principals are not generally liable for the torts of independent contractors, but there are three exceptions to this general no-liability rule. The first exception covers **inherently dangerous activities**, which are those that cannot be made safe. For example, using dynamite to demolish old buildings is an inherently dangerous activity. Without this liability exception, a principal could hire an independent contractor to perform the task and then assume no responsibility for the damages or injuries that might result.

The second exception to the no-liability rule occurs when a principal negligently hires an independent contractor. A landlord who hires a security guard, therefore, must check that guard's background because if a tenant's property is stolen by a guard with a criminal record, the landlord is responsible. Similarly, if a principal hires independent contractors knowing of their past employment history, the principal is liable for the conduct of those independent contractors. A business that hires a collection agency to collect past-due accounts, knowing that agency's reputation for violence, is liable for the agency's torts even though they are independent contractors.

The third exception is the situation in which the principal has provided the specifications for the independent contractor's procedures or process.

TERMINATION OF THE AGENCY RELATIONSHIP

An agency relationship can end in several different ways. First, the parties can have a definite duration for the agency relationship. A listing agreement for the sale of real property usually ends after ninety days. An agency can also end because the agent quits or the principal fires the agent. When the principal dies or is incapacitated, an agency ends automatically because the agent no longer has anyone to contract on behalf of.

Although the agency ends easily when an agent is fired or quits, the authority of the agent does not end so abruptly or easily. An agent can still have **lingering apparent authority** that exists beyond the termination of the agency in relation to third parties who are unaware of the agency termination. For example, if the purchasing agent for a corporation retires after twenty-five years, the agency between the agent and corporation has ended. However, many customers are used to dealing with the agent and may not be aware of the end of the agency. That purchasing agent could still bind the principal corporation even though actual authority has ended. The principal corporation can end lingering apparent authority by giving public or **constructive notice** and private or **actual notice**. Public notice is publication of the resignation. In many trade magazines and business newspapers, there are announcements and personal columns about business associate changes and other personnel news. These are public notices; and, even though not everyone dealing with the agent may see the notice, they are deemed to have been given constructive notice. However, the principal must also give private notice to those firms that have dealt with the agent or have been creditors in the past. This notice is accomplished by a letter sent to each firm or individual who has dealt with the agent. Without this notice, the agent's apparent authority lingers with respect to those third parties who have not received notice.

TERMINATION OF AGENTS UNDER EMPLOYMENT AT WILL

Most employees do not have written contracts that specify the start and duration of their employment. Rather, most employees work at the discretion of their employers, which is to say that they have **employment at will**. Recent cases have placed some restrictions on this employer freedom to hire and fire at will, as courts have been giving employees/agents the benefit of their reliance. Employees have based their protection rights on several theories, including implied contract and public policy. Exhibit 18.3 summarizes the "dos" and "don'ts" of terminating employees.

The Implied Contract

Visit the ACLU Web site for employment issues:
http://www.aclu.org/

Many courts have implied the existence of a contract because of the presence of promises, procedures, and policies in an employee personnel manual. Personnel manuals have been held to constitute, both expressly and impliedly, employee contracts or to become part of the employee contracts when they are given to employees at the outset. One of the factors that determines whether a personnel manual and its terms constitute a contract is the reliance of an employee on its procedures and terms.

Because the employee manual represents a potential contract for the employer, its nature and content should be considered carefully. There are two approaches to employee manuals. One approach is the detailed approach in which all rules, rights, and expectations are carefully established. Another approach is the simple one, in which overall general policies and rights are established with details to be filled in as individual issues arise. *Dillon* v. *Champion Jogbra, Inc.* (Case 18.7) deals with one state's view on the issue of implied contract .

EXHIBIT 18.3 **The Dos and Don'ts of Laying People Off**

DO	DON'T
Conduct regular reviews of employees, using objective, uniform measures of performance.	Don't make oral promises of job security to employees who might later be laid off. **Danger: breach-of-contract suit.**
Give clear, business-related reasons for any dismissal, backed by written documentation when possible.	Don't put pressure on an employee to resign in order to avoid getting fired. **Danger: coercion suit.**
Seek legal waivers from older workers who agree to leave under an early-retirement plan, and make sure they understand the waiver terms in advance.	Don't make derogatory remarks about any dismissed worker, even if asked for a reference by a prospective employer. **Danger: defamation suit.**
Follow any written company guidelines for termination, or be prepared to show in court why they're not binding in any particular instance.	Don't offer a fired employee a face-saving reason for the dismissal that's unrelated to poor performance. **Danger: wrongful-discharge suit.**

Source: "Layoffs Take Careful Planning to Avoid Losing the Suits that Are Apt to Follow," *Wall Street Journal*, November 2, 1990, p. 131 by Arthur S. Hayes. Copyright © 1990 by Dow Jones & Company, Inc. Reprinted by permission of Dow Jones & Company, Inc. via the Copyright Clearance Center.

CASE 18.7

Dillon v. Champion Jogbra, Inc.
819 A.2d 703 (Vt. 2002)

Letting a Champion Employee Go

FACTS

Linda Dillon began working for Jogbra part-time in January 1997. She was hired on as a full-time employee in August 1997 in the position of charge-back analyst. In the summer of 1998, the position of sales administrator was going to become vacant. Ms. Dillon was approached by Jogbra management about applying for the position, which started on July 31. She eventually decided to apply and interviewed for the position. In the course of interviewing, Ms. Dillon recalls that she was told that she would receive "extensive training." More specifically, the human resources manager told her that she would overlap with her predecessor, who would train her during those days. Originally, her predecessor was scheduled to leave August 15. In the course of Ms. Dillon's interview with the vice president of sales, who would be her immediate supervisor, he informed her that her predecessor was actually leaving earlier and would be available for only two days of training before Ms. Dillon started the job. He reassured her, though, that the predecessor would be brought back sometime thereafter for more training. Ms. Dillon also recalls that he told her that "it will take you four to six months to feel comfortable with [the] position" and not to be concerned about it. Ms. Dillon was offered and accepted the position. She spent most of her predecessor's remaining two days with her. Her predecessor then returned in early September for an additional two days of training. Ms. Dillon stated that she felt that, after the supplemental training, she had received sufficient training for the job.

On September 29, Ms. Dillon was called into her supervisor's office. The human resources manager was also present. They informed Ms. Dillon that things were not working out and that she was going to be reassigned to a temporary position, at the same pay and benefit level, that ended in December. She was told that she should apply for other jobs within the company, but if nothing suitable became available, she would be terminated at the end of December. According to Ms. Dillon, her supervisor stated that he had concluded within ten days of her starting that "it wasn't going to work out." Prior to the meeting, Ms. Dillon was never told her job was in jeopardy, nor did Jogbra follow the procedures laid out in its employee manual when terminating her.

Ms. Dillon applied for one job that became available in the ensuing months but was not selected for it. She left Jogbra in December when her temporary position terminated. Ms. Dillon then brought suit against Jogbra for wrongful termination. She asserted claims for breach of contract and promissory estoppel. Jogbra filed a motion for summary judgment, which the trial court granted. Ms. Dillon appealed.

JUDICIAL OPINION

MORSE, Justice

We affirm with respect to Dillon's claim for promissory estoppel, but reverse and remand on her breach of contract claim.

Jogbra has an employee manual that it distributes to all employees at the time of their employment. The first page of the manual states the following in capitalized print:

> The policies and procedures contained in this manual constitute guidelines only. They do not constitute part of an employment contract, nor are they intended to make any commitment to any employee concerning how individual employment action can, should, or will be handled.
>
> Champion Jogbra offers no employment contracts nor does it guarantee any minimum length of employment. Champion Jogbra reserves the right to terminate any employee at any time "at will," with or without cause.

During the period from 1996 to 1997, however, Jogbra developed what it termed a "Corrective Action Procedure." This procedure established a progressive discipline system for employees and different categories of disciplinary infractions. It states that it applies to all employees and will be carried out in "a fair and consistent manner." Much of the language in the section is mandatory in tone.

In approaching this issue, we are mindful at the outset that at-will employment relationships have fallen into disfavor. In the implied contract context, we have noted the motivating policy considerations that inform this trend: when an employer takes steps to give employees the impression of job security and enjoys the attendant benefits that such an atmosphere confers, it should not then be able to disregard its commitments at random. Additionally, it must be remembered when analyzing Dillon's argument that principles of contract law govern such determinations. In fact, we have noted repeatedly that the presumption that employment for an indefinite term is an "at-will" agreement is simply a general rule of contract construction. Additionally, an employer may modify an at-will employment agreement unilaterally. When determining whether an employer has done so, we look to both the employer's written policies and its practices. An employer not only may implicitly bind itself to terminating only for cause through its manual and practices, but may also be bound by a commitment to use only certain procedures in doing so. . . . At least one court has interpreted our case law to hold that the interpretation of employment manuals is always a question for the jury. A closer reading of our case law, however, demonstrates that only when the terms of the manual are ambiguous should the question be submitted to the jury.

When the terms of a manual are ambiguous, however, or send mixed messages regarding an employee's status, the question of whether the presumptive at-will status has been modified is properly left to the jury. This may be the case even if there is a disclaimer stating employment is at-will, as the presence of such a disclaimer is not dispositive in the determination. Furthermore, an employer's practices can provide context for and help inform the determination. The question of whether a written manual is ambiguous is a determination of law that we review *de novo*. In this case, we cannot agree with the trial court that the terms of Jogbra's manual are unambiguous such that, as a matter of law, Dillon's status was not modified, especially considered in light of the conflicting record before the court regarding Jogbra's employment practices.

Notwithstanding the disclaimer contained on the first page of the manual quoted above, the manual goes on to establish in Policy No. 720 an elaborate system governing employee discipline and discharge. It states as its purpose: "To establish Champion Jogbra policy for all employees." It states that actions will be carried out "in a fair and consistent manner." It provides that "[t]he Corrective Action Policy requires management to use training and employee counseling to achieve the desired actions of employees." It establishes three categories of violations of company policy and corresponding actions to be generally taken in each case. It delineates progressive steps to be taken for certain types of cases, including "[u]nsatisfactory quality of work," and time periods governing things such as how long a reprimand is considered "active." All of these terms are inconsistent with the disclaimer at the beginning of the manual, in effect sending mixed messages to employees. Furthermore, these terms appear to be inconsistent with an at-will employment relationship, its classic formulation being that an employer can fire an employee "for good cause or for no cause, or even for bad cause."

With respect to the record before the court on Jogbra's employment practices, Dillon herself was aware

of at least one employee whose termination was carried out pursuant to the terms set forth in the manual. She also testified in her deposition to conversations with the human resources manager, with whom she was friendly, in which the manager had described certain procedures used for firing employees. She stated that the manager had told her that Jogbra could not "just get rid of" people, but instead had to follow procedures. The human resources manager herself testified that, although the progressive discipline system was not generally applied to salaried employees, it was "historically" used for nonsalaried employees. She could only recall two instances in which the portion of the manual providing for documentation of progressive action was not followed, one of which resulted in a legal claim against the company and the other of which involved an employee stealing from the company. In fact, the manual specifically provides that stealing "will normally result in discharge on the first offense." Thus, it is not clear how that discharge deviated from the provisions of the manual.

In conclusion, the manual itself is at the very least ambiguous regarding employees' status, and Jogbra's employment practices appear from the record to be both consistent with the manual and inconsistent with an at-will employment arrangement. Therefore, summary judgment was not proper on Dillon's breach of implied contract claim.

Dillon also argues that the trial court's grant of summary judgment on her claim of promissory estoppel was erroneous. Dillon based her claim on two separate statements: the assurance that she would receive training and the assurance that it would take her four to six months to become comfortable with the sales administrator position.

We have held that, even if an employee otherwise enjoys only at-will employment status, that employee may still be able to establish a claim for wrongful termination under a theory of promissory estoppel if that employee can demonstrate that the termination was in breach of a specific promise made by the employer that the employer should have reasonably expected to induce detrimental reliance on the part of the employee, and that the employee did in fact detrimentally rely on the promise. We agree with the trial court in this case, however, that essential elements of promissory estoppel are absent with regard to both statements.

With respect to Jogbra's promise to Dillon that she would receive training, Dillon specifically conceded that, upon her predecessor's return in September, she had received adequate training to perform the job. In other words, Jogbra had delivered on its promise. Furthermore, even assuming that Jogbra failed to provide

continued

the full extent of promised training, Dillon has failed to explain how, as a matter of law, the promise of training modified her at-will status. In other words, it is not clear from Dillon's brief how the promise of training foreclosed Jogbra from nevertheless terminating her either on an at-will basis or for cause.

In his deposition, Dillon's supervisor expressed the firm opinion that even with training, or corrective action for that matter, Dillon simply did not possess the skills necessary to successfully perform the job of sales administrator. Specifically, he did not think that her time-management, prioritization or computer skills were adequate for the position.

With respect to the assurance that it would take four to six months to become comfortable with the position, the statement cannot reasonably be relied upon as a promise of employment in the sales administrator position for a set period of time. Courts have generally required a promise of a specific and definite nature before holding an employer bound by it.

In sum, the trial court properly granted Jogbra summary judgment on Dillon's promissory estoppel claim. The grant of summary judgment on Linda Dillon's claim for promissory estoppel is affirmed; the grant of summary judgment on her breach of contract claim is reversed and remanded.

DISSENTING OPINION

AMESTOY, Chief Justice, dissenting
We have previously noted that "disciplinary procedures are not inconsistent or in conflict with the at-will doctrine." A policy that expressly leaves the disciplinary sanction to the employer's discretion does not create an enforceable promise to terminate for cause. Moreover, even a statement which expressly or impliedly includes a promise to an employee for specific treatment in specific situations will not bind an employer "if it conspicuously and effectively states that the policy is not intended to be part of the employment relationship." As noted above, the employment manual contained the following statement in capital letters: "THE POLICIES AND PROCEDURES CONTAINED IN THIS MANUAL CONSTITUTE GUIDELINES ONLY. THEY DO NOT CONSTITUTE PART OF AN EMPLOYMENT CONTRACT." If the majority consid-

ers this statement to be insufficient, then it is difficult to imagine the language an employer could use in order to conspicuously state that the policy is not intended to be part of the employment relationship.

I do not believe that the manual at issue in this case can reasonably be construed as ambiguous. The "mixed message" the majority discerns more accurately describes the message conveyed by an opinion which observes that "at-will employment relationships have fallen into disfavor," when recently this Court cautioned against interpretations that "irreconcilably conflict[ ] with the employment at-will doctrine . . . and result[ ] in unreasonable judicial interference into what is a private relationship. The trial court correctly determined that the terms of the employer's manual are unambiguous as a matter of law.

Nor do I agree with the majority's second justification that the record before the court of employer's practices created ambiguity. In support of employee's contention that employer's practices were at odds with an at-will policy, employee cites to her own deposition, wherein she claimed to have known of other employees who received progressive discipline prior to termination. When pressed, however, employee admitted that, of the three employees with whose discharge she was familiar, she could state with certainty that only one received progressive discipline. Moreover, employee stated that she was unfamiliar with the manner in which the other two employees' cases were handled prior to their discharge. While her own experience is relevant, it does not by itself suggest a definitive company wide practice. Hearsay statements about what employee "had heard" is insufficient to raise a genuine issue.

CASE QUESTIONS

1. What is the effect of the disclaimer in the Jogbra employment manual?
2. What is the importance of an ambiguity?
3. Why is there no promissory estoppel claim?
4. What changes the application of the employment-at-will doctrine to Dillon?
5. What is the dissenting justice's concern?

 CONSIDER . . .   **18 . 6**

Joan Leikvold was hired by Valley View Community Hospital in 1972 as its operating room supervisor. In 1978, she became director of nursing. In 1979, she asked to return to her supervisor position. Carl Nusbaum, the director of Valley View, indicated that it was inadvisable for her to go from a managerial position to a subordinate position. In November 1979, Ms. Leikvold was fired.

Valley View's personnel manual provided as follows:

Every effort is made to help an employee to adjust himself to his work. If the employee's work, however, should be considered unsatisfactory during the first three months of employment, the hospital reserves the right to discontinue his services without notice. If an employee is discharged for unsatisfactory service after the three-month probationary period is completed, two weeks notice of such discharge will be given. Gross violations of conduct and hospital rules are grounds for immediate dismissal and will cause an employee to forfeit the usual two weeks notice. On such occasion, the employee will be paid in full only to the time of discharge. No notice or terminal pay is given for the following:

1. *Frequent tardiness*
2. *Sleeping on the job*
3. *Insubordination*
4. *Intoxication*
5. *Malicious gossip*
6. *Excessive garnishments*
7. *Conviction of a felony*
8. *Gambling on hospital premises*
9. *Unexcused absences*
10. *Soliciting tips or other serious misconduct*

The discharged employee who feels himself aggrieved by the terms of the discharge may appeal to Administration and will be granted a hearing.

Ms. Leikvold claims this section limits Valley View's right to discharge a nonprobationary employee to those cases in which the employee's work has been unsatisfactory or in which the employee has committed a gross violation of conduct or hospital rules. Is she correct? [*Leikvold* v. *Valley View Community Hosp.*, 688 P.2d 170 (Ariz. 1984).]

Source: Patrick McDonnell, *Forbes*, November 28, 1988, p. 117. Reprinted with permission of Patrick McDonnell © 1988.

The Public Policy Exception

In a second group of employment-at-will cases, the courts have afforded protection to those employees called *whistle-blowers* who report illegal conduct and to those who refuse to participate in conduct that is illegal or that violates public policy. For example, an employee was found to be wrongfully discharged when fired after supplying information to police who were investigating alleged criminal violations by a coemployee [*Palmateer* v. *International Harvester Co.*, 421 N.E.2d 876 (Ill. 1981)]. Other cases in which courts have found a wrongful discharge involve a refusal by an employee to commit perjury, a refusal by an employee to participate in price fixing, and an employee-reported violation of the Food, Drug, and Cosmetic Act.

In *Gardner* v. *Loomis Armored, Inc.* (Case 18.8), a court deals with the issue of an employer firing an employee who has taken action in an area not directly related to his employment.

Learn more about whistle–blowing:
http://www. whistleblowers.org

CASE 18.8

Gardner v. *Loomis Armored, Inc.*
913 P.2d 377 (Wash. 1996)

Termination for Helping During a Knife Attack

FACTS

Kevin Gardner is a driver with Loomis Armored, Inc., which is a company that supplies armored truck delivery services to banks, businesses, and others requiring secure transport of funds and other valuables. Because of the safety and liability issues surrounding armored truck deliveries, Loomis has adopted a policy for all drivers that their trucks cannot be left unattended. The policy is provided in the employee handbook and the penalty for violation of the rule is as follows:

Violations of this rule will be grounds for termination.

While Mr. Gardner was making a scheduled stop at a bank for a pickup of funds, he noticed a woman being threatened with a knife by an obviously agitated man. Mr. Gardner left his truck unattended as he went to the aid of the woman. The woman was saved and her assailant apprehended, and Mr. Gardner was then fired by Loomis for violating the company policy of not leaving the truck unattended. Mr. Gardner filed suit for wrongful termination in violation of public policy.

JUDICIAL OPINION

DOLLIVER, Justice

The narrow public policy encouraging citizens to rescue persons from life threatening situations clearly evinces [demonstrates] a fundamental societal interest. . . . The value attached to such acts of heroism is plainly demonstrated by the fact that society has waived most criminal and tort penalties stemming from conduct necessarily committed in the course of saving a life. If our society has placed the rescue of a life above constitutional rights and above the criminal code, then such conduct clearly rises above a company's work rule. Loomis' work rule does not provide an overriding justification for firing Gardner when his conduct directly served the public policy encouraging citizens to save persons from serious bodily injury or death.

We find that Gardner's discharge for leaving the truck and saving a woman from an imminent life threatening situation violates the public policy encouraging such heroic conduct. This holding does not create an affirmative legal duty requiring citizens to intervene in dangerous life threatening situations. We simply observe that society values and encourages voluntary rescuers when a life is in danger. Additionally, our adherence to this public policy does nothing to invalidate Loomis' work rule regarding drivers' leaving the trucks. . . . Our holding merely forbids Loomis from firing Gardner when he broke the rule because he saw a woman who faced imminent life threatening harm, and he reasonably believed his intervention was necessary to save her life. Finally, by focusing on the narrow public policy encouraging citizens to save human lives from life threatening situations, we continue to protect employers from frivolous lawsuits.

CASE QUESTIONS

1. Why is this case different from one in which an employee "rescues" a member of the public from fraud in bids or injury from defective products?

2. Did Mr. Gardner do the right thing in leaving his truck unattended? What were his ethical obligations under the circumstances? What would you have done?

3. Does this case create any affirmative legal duty for helping those in danger?

4. Can an employee in Washington be fired for assisting a citizen who is a crime victim?

BUSINESS STRATEGY

The Employee Handbook as a Source of Litigation: Taking Precautionary Steps

The employee handbook continues to be a source of litigation. Every appellate court that has heard a case on the issue of employee handbooks has ruled that an implied contract results from the terms in the employee handbook.

This focus on employee handbooks has been combined with the majority of courts finding the right of an employee to recover for wrongful discharge. Only Florida, Georgia, North Carolina, and Rhode Island do not recognize wrongful employment action rights. Indiana, Louisiana, and Texas have not ruled on the issue of wrongful discharge.

The law on employee handbooks is as follows.

1. The offer of employment is made to the employee by the employer, and included in the terms of the offer are the terms in the employee handbook.

2. Those handbooks include grounds for termination as well as the process that must be followed in order for termination to occur.

3. The employee accepts these terms by beginning employment.

Here is some advice from lawyers on employee handbooks.

1. Avoid using general phrases such as "employees may only be terminated for cause."

© DEANNA ETTINGER/THOMSON LEARNING

2. Avoid phrases such as employment continues so long as the employee "does a satisfactory job."

3. Say what you mean and mean what you say.

4. State that the employee relationship is an at-will relationship and can be ended at any time.

5. Make sure supervisors know the terms and procedures in the handbook and follow them.

6. Don't make reference to long-term employment, uninterrupted employment, continuing employment.

7. Don't make promises to employees in the handbook.

8. Update handbooks and review them periodically.

9. Make sure employees receive copies of changes and modified handbooks.

10. Have employees acknowledge receipt of the handbook.

For more information:

Mark W. Bennett, *Employment Relationship: Law & Practice* (2000).

Pleva v. *Norquist*, 195 F.3d 905 (7th Cir. 1999).

Knight v. *Vernon*, 214 F.3d 544 (4th Cir. 2000).

Demasse v. *ITT Corp.*, 984 P.2d 1138 (Ariz. 1999).

For information on downsizing, visit the American Psychological Association Web site:

http://www.apa.org

There has been a tremendous increase in suits brought by employees for improper discharge. Many companies, in the interest of maintaining fairness and saving expenses, have adopted a peer review policy. **Peer review** is a formal grievance procedure for nonunion employees. Employees who feel that they cannot get an adequate response from their supervisors or by following the lines of authority have the opportunity to present their cases to a panel of fellow employees and managers (three employees, two managers is the general configuration). Panel members listen to the presentation, can ask for more information, vote on the issue, and issue a written opinion with an explanation.

FOR THE MANAGER'S DESK

RE: SEVERANCE PACKAGES AND COVENANTS NOT TO COMPETE

When there are layoffs by a company, departing employees may be given generous severance packages, but those packages carry consideration on both sides. The departing employee may be given months of compensation, assistance with placement, retirement buy-outs and even educational loans or grants. However, the employer/company has its right to benefits on its side of the contract. The employer may ask for the following:

- Covenant not to compete
- Promise not to litigate the layoff
- Promise not to share the terms of the agreement with others
- Promise not to work for a competitor

These types of promises extracted by an employer may or may not be enforceable. There are several factors for the employer and employee to consider as they enter into these agreements.

The first factor is voluntariness. Was the agreement voluntary? The burden here is on the employer because, after all, this is someone who is about to be without a job and his or her compensation for the next few weeks or months is tied to signing this agreement.

Whether an agreement is voluntary could be determined by:

- Whether the employee was subject to time constraint in the decision to sign the agreement
- Whether the employee was permitted to have independent advice

- Whether the employee was already subject to noncompete agreements as part of his or her original employment agreement
- Whether the employee was permitted to consult a lawyer
- Whether the employee had the agreement proposed and was then given the opportunity to take it from the workplace for consideration or review

The second factor is whether the state recognizes noncompete agreements. The geographic tendencies are that noncompete agreements tend to be honored more in states east of the Mississippi. These noncompete agreements are more difficult to enforce in the West. Even in those states that have recognized the clauses as enforceable, there is a burden on the employer to show that the enforcement of the clause does not present an unreasonable hardship for the departing employee. And the concept of "unreasonable hardship" is a nebulous one.

Employers should understand these principles as well as the laws of their state of operation prior to proposing such departure agreements. Having the contract subject to the laws of their state is another important clause to put in the agreement, particularly when your state of operation recognizes the validity of noncompete clauses.

Source: Janet Novak, "Just a piece of paper?" Forbes, May 5, 1997, p. 156. Reprinted by permission of Forbes Magazine ©2004 Forbes Inc.

Review the False Claims Act:
http://www.taf.org

Many companies (including Coors and GTE) are avoiding lawsuits through what seems to be a mutually satisfactory resolution of wrongful termination and other grievance cases. Some employers say this process encourages both managers and employees to make better decisions. The peer review process should be in the employee handbook, should be required prior to court action, and should be widely publicized.

The Antiretaliation Statutes: Protections for Whistle-Blowers

Rather than having employees rely on a case-by-case determination of when they are protected in taking action in the course of employment and when they are not, many states as well as the federal government have passed whistle-blower protections statutes, which prevent employers from firing employees who report violations, note safety concerns, or in some way take action that benefits the public but does not help or reflect well on their employers.

Two generic federal statutes afford protection for federal employees: the Civil Service Reform Act of 1978 and the Whistleblower Protection Act of 1989. The statutes protect federal employees who report wrongdoing and permit them to recover both back pay and their attorney's fees in the event they litigate or protest a

---

BIOGRAPHY

JOHN E. SWANSON: AN ETHICS OFFICER AND A WHISTLE-BLOWER

John Swanson was hired by Dow Corning in 1966 at age 30 as an advertising supervisor. He was promoted to manager of industrial marketing a short time later, and in that position he began to write speeches for the then chairman and CEO of the company, William C. Goggin. When Mr. Goggin retired, his successor, Jack S. Ludington, continued to rely on Mr. Swanson for advice as well as speeches.

Just three years prior to Mr. Swanson's arrival at Dow Corning, the company had introduced its silicone breast implants to the market. From the time the product was released to market, there were complaints about ruptures.

Mr. Ludington and Mr. Swanson, along with three managers, formed a Business Conduct Committee in 1976 and began to draft guidelines for ethical conduct, develop processes for monitoring compliance, and create methods for correction of questionable conduct within the company. Mr. Swanson slowly took on the full task of ethics within Dow Corning and developed the company's code of ethics, called *A Matter of Integrity*. One provision in the code explained a standard for employees to use in deciding whether their conduct is appropriate: "We will act with the idea that everything we do will eventually see the light of day."

By 1990, Mr. Swanson's job primarily involved updating the code, making presentations to employees, and performing conduct reviews.

While Mr. Swanson climbed the corporate ladder, his wife, Colleen, became interested in the company's silicone implants. She received implants in 1974. Her physician warned that the long-term implications could not be known because implants were so new and also indicated that there were side effects in a small number of cases. Mrs. Swanson had the implants put in and almost immediately began to experience headaches. Other symptoms followed with no

medical explanation obtained despite ongoing doctor visits, tests, and evaluations. Fifteen years later, in 1990, Mrs. Swanson's daughter called and explained the story of a California woman who had implants and was experiencing similar difficulties. Mrs. Swanson passed the information along to her husband.

Mr. Swanson took the information about his wife to officers in the company and then recused himself from any further work on the issue. The first lawsuits on the implants had been won in 1984, and Dow Corning continued to battle class action litigation on a national basis. The medical connection has still not been completely established. However, Mrs. Swanson had her implants removed in 1991 and sued Dow Corning in 1992. Mr. Swanson was not a party to the litigation.

When Dow Corning's CEO, Keith McKennon, learned of Mrs. Swanson's suit, he confronted Mr. Swanson: "Look, what does Colleen want out of this? Does she want a zillion dollars? This could be messy. Can't we just talk this out and see if we can get it resolved?" No resolution was reached.

Mrs. Swanson settled her lawsuit in May 1993, and Mr. Swanson retired three months later, in August 1993, on the date he was eligible for retirement. Following a $4.23 billion global settlement on the class action lawsuits, Dow Corning filed for bankruptcy in May 1995.

The Swansons have since cooperated for a book by *Business Week* reporter John Byrne called *Informed Consent*. Mr. Swanson will receive half of the royalties from the book but had no editorial control.

ISSUES

1. Did Mr. Swanson do the right thing?
2. How was his timing?

---

termination for their disclosure of possible violations of the law. Some federal statutes also have specific provisions for certain categories of federal employees. For example, a portion of the Energy Reorganization Act provides protection for employees of nuclear facilities who report violations of federal laws and regulations at nuclear plants. The False Claims Act permits employees of government contractors whose tips and disclosures to federal investigators and agencies result in fines and penalties to collect 25 percent of those fines and penalties. Whistle-blowers who have obtained recovery under the False Claims Act include former GE employees who disclosed time-card fraud on defense contracts and many employees of the health care providers involved in Medicare/Medicaid fraud cases (an employee in one case recovered $17.5 million after a $70 million fine was paid).

Sarbanes-Oxley provides specific protections for whistle-blowers who disclose financial fraud. Section 806 prohibits a publicly traded company from discharging or otherwise discriminating against an employee because the employee: (1) assists in an investigation of prohibited conduct, and the investigation includes both federal and internal or board investigations; or (2) files or participates in a suit or other action for fraud by the company against shareholders. Remedies for whistle-blowers under Sarbanes-Oxley include reinstatement, back pay, and compensatory damages.

All fifty states plus the District of Columbia have antiretaliation whistle-blower protection statutes of some type. About half of the states protect all employees, while the other half provide protection only for government employees. Three states offer monetary rewards for employees who report wrongdoing that results in the collection of fines from a company, as the federal government does. Thirty-two states provide protection for employees who report civil rights violations, and nineteen states provide protections for reporting minimum wage violations. Other areas in which the states provide whistle-blower protection include reporting violations of environmental laws, child welfare laws, and child-care facility health and safety standards.

AGENCY RELATIONSHIPS IN INTERNATIONAL LAW

One of the complexities that has developed in law because of global business organizations is the liability of various subsidiaries, officers, and owners of multinational organizations when the interrelationships and operations may not be clear or even known to them. Perhaps the best example of the pitfalls of global structure is the multinational bank BCCI, a bank that proved elusive as authorities from several countries investigated it for criminal activity. BCCI was a layered, multinational organization with banks in seventy countries, including the United States (First American Bankshares, headed by the late Clark Clifford and Robert Altman). The banks and businesses in the different countries were staffed by residents of those countries, and the full global network of BCCI was not disclosed to these subsidiaries and the individuals operating them. Regulations of operations were limited to the entities located in each of the various nations. Jurisdiction over other operations was limited. The layers of the organization made it difficult for anyone, even those in the subsidiaries, to be certain of the roles and activities of the full organization or of other subsidiaries.

BCCI collapsed and surrendered its U.S. assets to U.S. regulators in settlement of various charges. The late Clark Clifford and Robert Altman were indicted for activities involving BCCI, although they were affiliated with U.S. operations only. Mr. Altman was acquitted of the charges, but Mr. Clifford was determined to be too ill to stand trial.

Following this complex case and the structure of principals and agents to evade the laws of any country, England, the United States, and other countries have been working together to determine who was responsible for the bank's collapse and how such tangled and evasive structures can be avoided in the future. One of the proposals considered is to require filing and full disclosure of all principal-agent and parent-subsidiary relationships in all countries in which a bank conducts business.

SUMMARY

When is an employee acting on behalf of an employer?

- Principal—employer; responsible party
- Agent—party hired to act on another's behalf
- *Restatement of Agency*—common law view of agent-principal relationship
- Unincorporated association—nonlegal entity; no legal existence as natural or fictitious person

How much authority does an employee hold?

- Express authority—written or stated authority
- Implied authority—authority by custom
- Apparent authority—authority by perceptions of third parties
- Lingering apparent authority—authority left with terminated agent because others are not told of termination
- Actual notice—receipt of notice of termination
- Constructive notice—publication of notice of termination
- Ratification—after-the-fact recognition of agent's authority by principal
- Disclosed principal—existence and identity of principal are known
- Partially disclosed principal—existence but not identity of principal is known
- Undisclosed principal—neither existence nor identity of principal is known

- Gratuitous agency—agent works without compensation

When is a business liable for an employee's acts?

- Master-servant relationship—principal-agent relationship in which principal exercises great degree of control
- Independent contractor—principal-agent relationship in which principal exercises little day-to-day control over agent
- Scope of employment—time when agent is doing work for the principal
- Inherently dangerous activities—activities for which, even if performed by independent contractor, principal is liable

What duties and obligations do employees owe employers?

- Fiduciary—one who has utmost duty of trust, care, loyalty, and obedience to another

How is an agency relationship terminated?

- Employment at will—right of employer to terminate noncontract employees at any time
- Protections for employees through express contract (manuals), implied contracts, and public policy
- Whistle-blowers protected by antiretaliation statutes

QUESTIONS AND PROBLEMS

1. Dr. Warren Lesch had a leak in his car's gas tank that had been repaired by Malcolm Weeks, an employee of Walker's Chevron, Inc. in Bel Air, Maryland. The tank was not repaired properly, and Dr. Lesch's home and garage were destroyed when the gas tank exploded. Dr. Lesch and his wife were severely burned as a result.

Walker's Chevron is a "branded" station: It displays only Chevron signs and colors and sells only Chevron gas and oil. The Lesches have sued Mr. Weeks, Walker's Chevron, and Chevron USA. Who is liable for the explosion? [*Chevron USA, Inc.* v. *Lesch*, 570 A.2d 840 (Md. 1990).]

2. On September 29, 1984, Wilton Whitlow was taken to Good Samaritan Hospital's emergency room in Montgomery County, Ohio, because he had suffered a seizure and a blackout. He was examined by Dr. Dennis Aumentado, who prescribed the anti-epileptic medication Dilantin. Mr. Whitlow experienced no further seizures and was monitored as an outpatient at Good Samaritan over the next few weeks.

Mr. Whitlow complained to Dr. Aumentado of warm and dry eyes, and his Dilantin dose was reduced. On October 20, 1984, he was again admitted to the emergency room with symptoms that were eventually determined to be from Stevens-Johnson syndrome, a condition believed to be caused by a variety of medications. Mr. Whitlow sued Dr. Aumentado and Good Samaritan for malpractice and Parke-Davis, the manufacturer of Dilantin, for breach of warranty.

The hospital maintains it is not liable because Dr. Aumentado was an independent contractor. Is the hospital correct? [*Whitlow* v. *Good Samaritan Hosp.*, 536 N.E.2d 659 (Ohio 1987).]

3. On March 29, 1983, Barry Mapp was observed in the J. C. Penney department store in Upper Darby, Pennsylvania, by security personnel, who suspected that he might be a shoplifter. Michael DiDomenico, a security guard employed by J. C. Penney, followed Mr. Mapp when he left the store and proceeded to Gimbels department store. There, Mr. DiDomenico notified Rosemary Federchok, a Gimbels security guard, about his suspicions. Even though his assistance was not requested, Mr. DiDomenico decided to remain to assist in case Ms. Federchok, a short woman of slight build, required help in dealing with Mr. Mapp if he committed an offense in Gimbels. It came as no surprise when Mr. Mapp was observed taking items from the men's department of the store; when he attempted to escape, he was pursued. Although Ms. Federchok was unable to keep up, Mr. DiDomenico continued to pursue Mr. Mapp and ultimately apprehended him in the lower level of the Gimbels parking lot. When Ms. Federchok arrived with Upper Darby police, merchandise that had been taken from Gimbels was recovered. Mr. Mapp, who had been injured when he jumped from one level of the parking lot to another, was taken to the Delaware County Memorial Hospital, where he was treated for a broken ankle.

Mr. Mapp filed suit against Gimbels for injuries sustained while being chased and apprehended by Mr. DiDomenico. He alleged in his complaint that Mr. DiDomenico, while acting as an agent of Gimbels, had chased him, had struck him with a nightstick, and had beaten him with his fists. Gimbels says it is not liable because Mr. DiDomenico was not its agent. Is Gimbels correct? [*Mapp* v. *Gimbels Dep't Store*, 540 A.2d 941 (Pa. 1988).]

4. Nineteen-year-old Lee J. Norris was employed by Burger Chef Systems as an assistant manager of one of its restaurants. On a day when he was in charge and change was needed, Mr. Norris left to get change but also decided to get Kentucky Fried Chicken at a nearby store for his lunch to take back to Burger Chef. The bank where Mr. Norris usually got change is 1.6 miles from Burger Chef, and the Kentucky Fried Chicken outlet is 2.5 miles from Burger Chef. After Mr. Norris left the bank and was on his way to the Kentucky Fried Chicken restaurant, he negligently injured Lee J. Govro in an accident. Is Burger Chef liable for the accident? [*Burger Chef Systems* v. *Govro*, 407 F.2d 921 (8th Cir. 1969).]

5. Dewey Nabors operates a real estate brokerage under the trade name Nabors & Company, which shares an office, telephone, and secretary with Midtown, a real estate management corporation that had hired Robert Keaton to oversee the completion of a shopping center. Mr. Nabors asked Mr. Keaton to order siding, pipes, and flooring for his personal residence and directed him to order these materials in the name of Nabors & Company. Mr. Keaton contracted with Richardson, Inc. for the flooring. Richardson understood that Mr. Keaton was working for Midtown and billed Midtown for Mr. Nabors's materials. Mr. Nabors refused to pay for the materials because he was dissatisfied. Is Midtown liable? What theory is Richardson using? [*Midtown Properties, Inc.* v. *Richardson, Inc.*, 228 S.E.2d 303 (Ga. 1976).]

6. Reverend John Fisher is the pastor of St. James Episcopal Church in Ohio. Catherine Davis served there as parish secretary from 1978 until six months after Reverend Fisher arrived at St. James in January 1988. Reverend Fisher fired her after she went to the bishop of the diocese to complain about sexual harassment by Reverend Fisher. The bishop promised an investigation, which was not conducted because Reverend Fisher denied the allegations. Ms. Davis then brought suit against the Episcopal Diocese. The diocese denied liability, claiming it was not in control of Reverend Fisher's actions because he was an independent contractor. Do you agree? [*Davis* v. *Black*, 591 N.E.2d 11 (Ohio 1991).]

7. Lennen & Newell, Inc. (L&N) is an advertising agency hired by Stokely-Van Camp to do its advertising. L&N contracted for the purchase of ad time from CBS, but no Stokely representative's signature is on the contract. If L&N does not pay for the ad time, is Stokely liable? [*CBS, Inc.* v. *Stokely-Van Camp, Inc.*, 456 F. Supp. 539 (E.D.N.Y. 1977).]

8. John Guz, 49, first hired in 1971, had worked for Bechtel Corporation for twenty-two years. In 1986, he was assigned to BNI, a division specializing in engineering, construction, and environmental remediation that focuses on federal government programs, principally for the Departments of Energy and Defense (BNI-MI). Mr. Guz worked his way up through Bechtel and BNI both, going from administrative assistant, beginning at a salary of $750 per month, to financial reports supervisor, earning $70,000 per year. During his time with Bechtel and BNI, Mr. Guz had been given generally favorable performance evaluations, steady pay increases, and a continuing series of promotions.

During this time, Bechtel maintained Personnel Policy 1101, dated June 1991, on the subject of termination of employment (Policy 1101). Policy 1101 stated that "Bechtel employees have no employment agreements guaranteeing continuous service and may resign at their option or be terminated at the option of Bechtel."

Between 1986 and 1991, BNI-MI's size was reduced from thirteen to six persons, and its costs were reduced from $748,000 in 1986 to $400,000 in 1991. Bechtel eventually eliminated Mr. Guz's division. Mr. Guz was discharged, as were all the employees in the division. Mr. Guz brought suit against Bechtel alleging that he had an "implied-in-fact contract" with Bechtel that prevented the company from terminating him so long as the company was performing well financially.

The trial court granted Bechtel's motion for summary judgment and dismissed the action. In a split decision, the Court of Appeal reversed. Bechtel appealed. Who should prevail on appeal? [*Guz* v. *Bechtel*, 8 P.3d 1089 (Cal. 2000).]

9. Richard Woolley was hired by Hoffman-LaRoche (HL) in October 1969 as an Engineering Section Head in HL's Central Engineering Department at Nutley, New Jersey. There was no written employment contract. Mr. Woolley began work in 1969 and had his first promotion in 1976 and a second promotion to Group Leader for Civil Engineering in 1977. In 1978, he was asked to write a report for his supervisors about piping problems in a building at Nutley.

Mr. Woolley submitted the report a month later, and one month after that he was told that the general manager had lost confidence in him. Mr. Woolley's immediate supervisors asked him to resign, but he refused. A formal letter asking for his resignation followed, and he again refused. He was fired two months after he was asked for his resignation.

Mr. Woolley filed suit based on the express and implied promises in the employment manual, which he had first read in 1969. He maintained that he could not be fired at will and could only be terminated for cause according to the terms of the manual. Is Mr. Woolley correct? [*Woolley* v. *Hoffman-LaRoche, Inc.*, 491 A.2d 1257 (N.J. 1985).]

10. The physician for the Philadelphia Eagles football team examined Don Chuy, a player, and determined that because of a medical condition, Mr. Chuy should not play football. The team's general manager then reported to a sports columnist that Mr. Chuy had a fatal blood disease. A report of the illness appeared in print and was picked up by other sources. Mr. Chuy's personal physician never diagnosed the disease. Mr. Chuy sued the football club for defamation. Is the club liable for the remarks made by the general manager? [*Chuy* v. *Philadelphia Eagles Football Club*, 595 F.2d 1265 (3d Cir. 1979).]

RESEARCH PROBLEM

Public Relations Issues, Strategy, and the Problem Employee

11. Former Indiana University basketball coach Bobby Knight had a long history of violent temper eruptions both on and off the court. Nonetheless, he had been a successful coach for the team, often taking Indiana to the NCAA Final Four competition. The flamboyant coach had been known to confront officials during games, throw chairs during games, and use colorful language continually. A videotape captured the coach lunging for the throat of an Indiana University student and player during a practice session.

Coach Knight initially denied that it happened, and then the videotape was produced. The trustees of Indiana University placed the coach on probation and wrote in a letter to him that any violation of the terms of the probation—including no striking of students, no temper eruptions, no foul language—was grounds for termination.

Many fans and alumni were outraged at the agreement and defended keeping the coach in good standing because he never had any NCAA violations (i.e., he ran a "clean" program) and he saw to it that most of his players also graduated from college in addition to playing basketball or being recruited by professional teams.

Write a memo explaining why the trustees took the action they did. Be sure to include discussion of the principles of agency law, potential liability, and the rights of Coach Knight with regard to his employment contract.

NOTE

1. The terminology of master and servant has its roots in the historical nature of the employment relationship of indentured servants and slaves. For more information, see the course Web site and the Instructor's Manual.

Management of Employee Welfare

The employer-employee relationship has evolved from one of a paternal nature in the 1600s and 1700s to one of a contractual nature.[1] In the earlier period, employers often assumed responsibility for the well-being of their employees, a personal relationship made possible because of the less-complex nature of business at the time. With the Industrial Revolution, however, more employees were needed and the personal relationship factor was lost. The employer-employee relationship became thoroughly contractual.

The result of this contractual relationship was that both parties became interested in maximizing their own economic benefits. Employers wanted the most work for the least amount of money. Employees wanted maximum pay, safe working conditions, and some type of insurance for retirement, unemployment, and disability. Because employers had the upper hand—they controlled the jobs—their bargaining positions were better than those of employees. As a result, workers organized to give themselves more bargaining power, and the federal government passed legislation to assure workers that some of their needs would be met.

This chapter discusses the work and safety standards covered in federal legislation and answers the following questions: What wage and work hour protections exist for employees? Are there restrictions on children's work? What protections exist for safety in the workplace? What happens when an employee is injured in the workplace? Are workers entitled to pensions, and are they regulated? What is the Social Security system, and what benefits does it provide? What rights do unemployed workers have? How are labor unions formed, and what is their relationship with employees?

▶ update ◀

For up-to-date legal news and real-world business applications, click on **update** *at http://jennings.westbuslaw.com*

Tendinitis, DeQuervain's tendinitis, carpal tunnel syndrome,
and tennis elbow: the four most common workplace injuries
following the dot-com bubble

4.7 million: the number of work-related injuries
and illnesses in 1999

5,524: the number of fatal occupational injuries in 2002

609: the number of homicides in the workplace in 2002

83,562: the number of OSHA violations found
in the workplace

OCCUPATIONAL SAFETY AND HEALTH ADMINISTRATION
http://www.osha.gov

Accident rate in the workplace in 1992: 8.3 per 100

Accident rate in the workplace in 2002: 5.4 per 100
U.S. DEPARTMENT OF LABOR

CONSIDER...

Two Whirlpool employees were working the production line when they were asked to walk on the netting beneath the production line in order to retrieve dropped parts. The employees knew walking on the netting was dangerous because it was not designed to hold humans. They refused to walk on the netting and retrieve the parts. They were clocked out and lost their shift hours. They want to know if they can be forced to lose pay for refusing to perform unsafe work. Can you offer them some advice?

© RYAN McVAY/PHOTODISC/GETTY IMAGES

EXHIBIT   19.1   Statutory Scheme for Employee Welfare

STATUTE	DATE	PROVISIONS
Worker's Compensation	1900	Absolute liability of employers for employee injury; no common law tort suits by employees against employers
Social Security Act 42 U.S.C. § 301	1935	FICA contributions; unemployment compensation; retirement benefits
Fair Labor Standards Act 29 U.S.C. § 201	1938	Minimum wages; child labor restrictions; overtime pay
Equal Pay Act 29 U.S.C. § 206	1963	Amendment to FLSA; equal pay for equal work
Occupational Safety and Health Act 29 U.S.C. § 651	1970	Safety in the workplace; employee rights; employer reporting; inspections
Employment Retirement Income Security Act 29 U.S.C. § 441	1974	Disclosure of contributions, investments, loans; employee vesting; employee statements
Family and Medical Leave Act 29 U.S.C. § 2601	1993	Protection of job after family leave (for pregnancy, child care, adult illness, elderly care)

WAGES AND HOURS PROTECTION

Exhibit 19.1 summarizes the series of laws affecting employee rights over the past fifty years, which are discussed in this chapter.

The Fair Labor Standards Act

Review the Fair Labor Standards Act:
http://www.law.cornell.edu/uscode/29/ch8.html

The **Fair Labor Standards Act** (FLSA) is commonly called by workers the "minimum wage law" or the wage and hour law. This act does establish a minimum wage, but it also includes provisions regulating child labor, overtime pay requirements, and equal pay provisions. The FLSA was originally introduced in the Senate by Hugo L. Black when he was a senator from Alabama. His 1937 appointment to the U.S. Supreme Court may have helped it pass the high Court's scrutiny. Having been amended several times, the FLSA is an enabling statute that sets up various administrative agencies to handle the regulations and necessary enforcement.

Coverage of FLSA

The FLSA applies to all businesses that affect interstate commerce. As discussed in Chapter 5, "affecting" interstate commerce is a very broad standard, and even small businesses using mail and phone services are involved in interstate commerce.

FLSA Minimum Wage and Overtime Regulations

Under FLSA, all covered employees must be paid a **minimum wage**. The minimum wage is established by Congress and is increased through legislation. The FLSA also includes an hours protection for covered employees in the form of time-and-one-half pay for hours worked above forty hours per week. Regardless of the pay period for covered employees (monthly, weekly, or biweekly), overtime is com-

ETHICAL ISSUES

Working off the Clock

Wal-Mart continues to face legal difficulties with its employees regarding the issue of working "off the clock." In this practice, employees clock out and then continue to put in hours doing extra assignments. Some employees do so with the hope of gaining favor with supervisors or possibly an advantage in earning a promotion.

While Wal-Mart's handbook specifically prohibits supervisors from asking employees to work off the clock, and Wal-Mart has disciplined and even terminated supervisors and managers who have asked employees to do so, in 2000 Wal-Mart did settle a 69,000-employee class action lawsuit on overtime for $50 million.

Some industry experts say that Wal-Mart's incentive plan contributes to the tendency of store managers to ask employees to work off the clock. Under Wal-Mart's store manager bonus plan, store managers earn a base salary of $52,000. Their bonuses can range from $70,000 to $120,000, but those bonuses are tied to the profits earned in their individual stores. The program creates tremendous incentives for managers to keep costs down. In the retail industry, Wal-Mart's operating expenses are the lowest, at 16.6% of sales. Kmart is at 21%, Target at 22.3%, Sears at 24.9%, and Nordstrom at 30.7%. Operating costs include payroll expenses.

What federal law applies to off-the-clock work? Under what statute would the employees be bringing their suits? What are they entitled to recover?

If the allegations are true, what are the ethics of having employees work off the clock?

Source: Steven Greenhouse, "Suits Say Wal-Mart Forces Workers to Toil Off the Clock," *New York Times,* June 25, 2002, A1, A20. Copyright © 2002 by The New York Times Co. Reprinted with permission.

---

puted on the basis of forty hours per week. For example, if a covered employee worked thirty-eight, forty-two, thirty-five, and forty-seven hours in four consecutive weeks and is paid on a monthly basis, that employee is entitled to nine hours of **overtime pay**.

The definition of covered employees is provided in the FLSA. Some categories of employees are covered for purposes of minimum wage protections but not for overtime pay. For example, professionals, executives, and others who exercise discretion and judgment in their positions may be covered for purposes of minimum wage protections but not for purposes of overtime protections. The reason for this exemption is that these employees, often referred to as "white-collar" workers, possess sufficient training, knowledge, and experience to counter employer unfairness. Certain types of jobs are exempt from overtime protections, such as taxicab drivers, railroad employees, and those in commercial service and domestic service.

One coverage issue that has received extensive attention during the last decade because of the impact of downsizing has been whether employees can be required to work overtime hours. The FLSA simply provides the right to time-and-one-half pay for overtime worked; it does not include limitations on hours (except in child labor regulations for children under the age of 18). There is no statutory right to refuse to work overtime. Union collective bargaining agreements can impose restraints, and many employers seek volunteers for overtime. However, employers should exercise caution with overly tired employees because, as *Faverty v. Mc-Donald's Restaurants of Oregon, Inc.* (Chapter 18, Case 18.4) held, employers may be liable for accidents of such employees even when employees are on their way home.

FLSA and Child Labor Provisions

The child labor provisions of the FLSA were created to keep children in school for at least a minimum number of years. The provisions of the act govern particular ages and restrict the types of employment those age groups can hold.

1. *Eighteen years old and older.* This group is not covered, as this age is the cutoff for the child labor provisions. Anyone 18 or older can work in any type of job for unlimited hours.

2. *Sixteen to seventeen years old.* This age group can work in any "nonhazardous" job for unlimited hours. Hazardous jobs include mining, logging, roofing, and excavation.

3. *Fourteen to fifteen years old.* This group can work only in nonhazardous, non-manufacturing, and nonmining jobs, and only during nonschool hours. Work hours are limited on school days and during school weeks. There are also time-of-day restrictions for work hours.

There are exemptions to the laws; young actors and actresses, for example, are exempt. But even in this field, many states require approval of their contracts and also require that some of the earnings be put in trust for use by the child when the child becomes an adult. Other exemptions apply to work-study programs and farm work. (For information on child labor in international business, see pp. 780–782.)

Enforcement of FLSA

Enforcement of the FLSA requirements may begin in several different ways. Employees can initiate the process by filing a complaint with the U.S. Department of Labor. Upon receipt of the complaint, the department begins an investigation that could lead to a finding of no violation, a violation and a settlement with the employer, or a violation and litigation by the employees for collection of back wages.

In some cases, employers make the laws self-enforcing by requesting interpretations from the Labor Department that are then published in the *Code of Federal Regulations.*

In a final type of case, the Labor Department initiates its own investigation of a firm for possible violations. The department has broad investigatory authority, including the right to ask for records and target particular industries and portions of the law for enforcement. For example, in 1999, the Labor Department focused on the car dealership programs that had high-school-age vocational students working in service departments. While the mechanical work was permissible, using the under-18 students as car jockeys to bring the customers' cars around to them following service was a violation of the age restrictions in the labor laws on certain types of work.

FLSA and Record-Keeping Requirements

Employers subject to the FLSA are required to keep records of hours and wages of their employees. There are no particular formats for these records, but failure to keep them can result in a fine.

Penalties for FLSA Violation

The FLSA carries both civil and criminal penalties. Employees have the right to sue civilly to recover from an employer any wages that were not paid or any overtime compensation that was denied, plus reasonable attorney fees required to bring the action to recover. In addition to the employees' rights, the U.S. Department of Labor's Wage and Hour Division has enforcement power for violations. A willful violation of FLSA carries a maximum $10,000 fine and possible imprisonment of up to six months.

To help employees pursue their rights, the FLSA makes it a violation for any employer to fire an employee for filing an FLSA complaint or for participating in any FLSA proceeding.

Visit the Department of Labor's Wage and Hour Division:
http://www.dol.gov/ esa/whd

Liability for FLSA Violation

Employers, of course, are liable for FLSA violations; but, because most employers are corporations, the question arises as to who in the corporation is liable. The answer is that anyone who actively participates in running the business is liable under the FLSA. Officers of the corporation can be held individually liable for the corporation's violations. The FLSA imposes fines on both corporations and officers involved in managing employees.

The Equal Pay Act of 1963

Review the Equal Pay Act:
http://www.law.cornell.
edu/uscode/29/206.html

The **Equal Pay Act of 1963** is an amendment to the FLSA that makes it illegal to pay different wages based on gender to men and women who are doing substantially the same work. If the jobs involve equal responsibility, training, or skill, men and women must have equal pay. Merit systems and seniority systems instituted in good faith do not violate the Equal Pay Act even though they may result in different pay rates for the same jobs. So long as the disparate pay is based on length of employment or a merit-raise system, the disparity is within the act.

The Equal Pay Act is not an act that requires the application of the doctrine of comparable worth. This doctrine extends the concept of the Equal Pay Act a step further and says men and women should be paid on the same scale, not just for the same jobs but when they are doing different jobs that require equal skill, effort, and responsibility. This issue came to light in 1983 when Louise Peterson, a licensed practical nurse at Western State Hospital in Tacoma, Washington, brought suit when she discovered that her salary of $1,462 per month for her supervision of the daily care of sixty men convicted of sex crimes was $192 less per month than that of the hospital groundskeeper and $700 less per month than men doing similar jobs at Washington's state prisons. Although a trial judge found the pay scales to be discriminatory and ordered the state to reimburse its female employees $838 million in back pay, the ruling was later reversed. Presently, federal standards do not require comparable worth pay scales.

WORKPLACE SAFETY

The Occupational Safety and Health Act

Review the Occupational Safety and Health Act:
http://www.law.cornell.
edu/uscode/29/651.html

Visit OSHA:
http://www.osha.gov

One of the worker welfare concerns of Congress has been safety in the workplace. In the past, the economic concerns of employers often overshadowed their concern for proper safety precautions. To ensure worker safety, Congress passed the **Occupational Safety and Health Act** of 1970. Its application was broad, protecting virtually every employee in the country. It was an enabling statute that created three agencies responsible for worker safety standards: the **Occupational Safety and Health Administration** (OSHA), the Occupational Safety and Health Review Commission (OSHRC), and the National Institute for Occupational Safety and Health (NIOSH). OSHA is the agency responsible for the promulgation and enforcement of workplace safety standards. OSHA's enforcement powers include investigations, record-keeping requirements, and research. The stated purpose of the act is to "assure so far as possible every working man and woman in the nation safe and healthful working conditions and to preserve our human resources."

The Occupational Safety and Health Act gives the secretary of labor responsibility for administration. OSHA is within the Department of Labor, and its function is to develop safety standards and enforce them through inspections, citations, and

Visit the National Institute for Occupational Safety and Health:

http://www.cdc.gov/ niosh/homepage.html

court actions. NIOSH often undertakes studies of workplace safety issues. Issues that have been a focus of NIOSH study have included long-term exposure hazards. While OSHA and OSHRC have focused on the traditional issues of equipment use and protective gear, NIOSH has studied the effects of long-term exposure to chemicals and particles.

OSHA Coverage and Duties

OSHA coverage is broad: Every employer with one or more employees who is in a business affecting commerce is covered by OSHA. Several other federal acts regulate safety for particular industries, including the Coal Mine and Safety Act and the Railway Safety Act.

The basic responsibilities of employers are to know and follow OSHA's rules, inspect for hazards and correct them, inform employees of their rights, keep statutorily mandated records, and post citations given by OSHA.

Search for proposed OSHA rules:

http://www.osha.gov
Click on "laws and regulations."

OSHA Responsibilities

Promulgating Rules and Safety Standards

OSHA is responsible for promulgating rules and regulations for safety standards and procedures. The rules are adopted by the standard administrative process of notice in the *Federal Register*, public input, and final decision (see Chapter 6).

FOR THE MANAGER'S DESK

RE: CURBING WORKPLACE VIOLENCE

Over the past few years, the following workplace shootings have made international news:

- Alfred Eugene Miller—August 5, 1999—killed three of his co-workers with an automatic weapon in Billingly, Alabama
- Bryan Uyesugi—Xerox repairman—November 2, 1999—shot and killed seven of his co-workers during a team meeting

Most employers believe that workers' compensation systems apply to such incidents. However, there are an increasing number of decisions that impose liability on employers to the relatives of deceased employees for their failure to provide adequate security. For example, in a 1994 Texas case, a court imposed liability on an employer who was aware that a man had made threats and who took no extra precautions. In *Vaughn v. Granite City Steel*, 576 N.E.2d 874 (Ill. App. 1991), an employee's family was awarded $415,000 following the employee's shooting death in the employer's parking lot when the jury determined that security was "grossly inadequate." A North Carolina jury awarded $7.9 million to the families of two employees killed by another employee who the employer knew had a history of violence.

The *National Law Journal* offers the following checklist for employers in reducing workplace violence:

1. Issue a policy statement that the company intends to prevent workplace violence.

2. Implement a zero tolerance policy for threats and violent acts.

3. Encourage employees to report threats and violent acts.

4. Take remedial action, including discharge, against those employees who make threats or show violence in the workplace.

5. Protect employees who report acts and threats of violence.

6. Have procedures in place for taking action if customers become violent.

7. Refer employees for assistance and counseling if they exhibit signs of strain or violent tendencies.

8. Do more comprehensive background checks on potential employees.

9. Provide training on recognizing violent tendencies—offer to all employees.

10. Implement some type of survey or anonymous reporting system.

11. Create a team to assess issues of security and violence.

Source: Donald F. Burke, "When Employees Are Vulnerable, Employers Are, Too. Bosses Can Be Liable for Workplace Violence When They Fail to Prevent a Known Threat." Reprinted with permission from the January 17, 2000, edition of the *New York Law Journal*. © 2000 ALM Properties, Inc. All rights reserved. Further duplication without permission is prohibited.

Inspections

OSHA inspections are an enforcement tool. Inspectors can enter the workplace "without delay and at a reasonable time" to inspect. They can check the workplace and the records and can question employees. OSHA's inspection power is limited by numbers, however. Because of OSHA's limited staff, the regulations provide for an order of priority on inspections:

1. Hazards or conditions that could cause death
2. Investigations of fatal accident sites
3. Employee complaints
4. Particularly hazardous industries
5. Random inspections incorporating an emphasis on certain types of industries (roofing, lumbering, meat packing, transportation [car, truck] manufacturing, and longshoring)

Inspection procedures are regulated. An OSHA inspector who appears at a workplace must show identification and ask the employer's permission to conduct an inspection. If the employer allows the inspection, the employer or an agent of the employer can accompany the OSHA inspector. After the inspection, the inspector and employer meet to discuss violations, and the problems are often worked out on the spot and the violations remedied immediately.

Employee Rights, Inspections, and OSHA If an inspection is the result of an employee complaint, the employer cannot take any retaliatory action against that employee. Because of OSHA's limited staff, the agency relies on those in the workplace to bring violations to its attention. If workers fear retaliation, the violations will remain unreported. An employee who is fired, demoted, or discriminated against for registering an OSHA complaint can file a complaint, and the Department of Labor can pursue the employee's rights in federal district court. *Whirlpool Corporation* v. *Marshall* (Case 19.1) is a landmark case on the issue of employer retaliatory conduct and offers the answer to the chapter's opening Consider.

CASE 19.1

Whirlpool Corporation v. *Marshall*
445 U.S. 1 (1980)

You Can't Make Me Do It:
Employee Defiance and Danger

FACTS

Whirlpool is a manufacturer of household appliances. In its plant in Marion, Ohio, Whirlpool uses a system of overhead conveyor belts to send a constant stream of parts to employees on the line throughout the plant. Beneath the conveyor belt is a netting or mesh screen to catch any parts or other objects that might fall from the conveyor belt.

Some items did fall to the mesh screen, located some 20 feet above the plant floor. Maintenance employees had the responsibility for removing the parts and other debris from the screen. They usually stood on the iron frames of the mesh screen, but occasionally they found it necessary to go onto the screen itself. While one maintenance employee was standing on the mesh, it broke, and he fell the 20 feet to his death on the floor below. After this fatal accident, maintenance employees were prohibited from standing on the mesh screen or the iron frames. A mobile platform and long hooks were used to remove objects.

Two maintenance employees, Virgil Deemer and Thomas Cornwell, complained about the screen and its safety problems. When the plant foreman refused to

continued

make corrections, Mr. Deemer and Mr. Cornwell asked for the name of an OSHA inspector, and Mr. Deemer contacted an OSHA official on July 7, 1974.

On July 8, 1974, Mr. Deemer and Mr. Cornwell reported for work and were told to do their maintenance work on the screen in the usual manner. Both refused on safety grounds, so the plant foreman sent them to the personnel office. They were then forced to punch out and were not paid for the six hours left on their shift.

On behalf of Mr. Deemer and Mr. Cornwell, the Secretary of Labor (Marshall) brought suit against Whirlpool for the lost six hours of pay and to have the written reprimands for the incident removed from the files of the employees. The trial court found for Whirlpool, and the Secretary of Labor appealed. The court of appeals found for the secretary, and Whirlpool appealed.

JUDICIAL OPINION

STEWART, Justice

... The Secretary is obviously correct when he acknowledges in his regulation that, "as a general matter, there is no right afforded by the Act which would entitle employees to walk off the job because of potential unsafe conditions at the workplace." By providing for prompt notice to the employer of an inspector's intention to seek an injunction against an imminently dangerous condition, the legislation obviously contemplates that the employer will normally respond by voluntarily and speedily eliminating the danger. And in the few instances where this does not occur, the legislative provisions authorizing prompt judicial action are designed to give employees full protection in most situations from the risk of injury or death resulting from an imminently dangerous condition at the worksite.

As this case illustrates, however, circumstances may sometimes exist in which the employee justifiably believes that the express statutory arrangement does not sufficiently protect him from death or serious injury. Such circumstances will probably not often occur, but such a situation may arise when (1) the employee is ordered by his employer to work under conditions that the employee reasonably believes pose an imminent risk of death or serious bodily injury, and (2) the employee has reason to believe that there is not sufficient time or opportunity either to seek effective redress from his employer or to apprise OSHA of the danger.

Nothing in the Act suggests that those few employees who have to face this dilemma must rely exclusively on the remedies expressly set forth in the Act at the risk of their own safety. But nothing in the Act explicitly provides otherwise. Against this background of legislative silence, the Secretary has exercised his rulemaking power and has determined that, when an employee in good faith finds himself in such a predicament, he may refuse to expose himself to the dangerous condition, without being subjected to "subsequent discrimination" by the employer.

The question before us is whether this interpretative regulation constitutes a permissible gloss on the Act by the Secretary.

The regulation clearly conforms to the fundamental objective of the Act—to prevent occupational deaths and serious injuries. The Act, in its preamble, declares that its purpose and policy is "to assure so far as possible every working man and woman in the Nation safe and healthful working conditions and to preserve our human resources. . . ."

To accomplish this basic purpose, the legislation's remedial orientation is prophylactic in nature. The Act does not wait for an employee to die or become injured. It authorizes the promulgation of health and safety standards and the issuance of citations in the hope that these will act to prevent deaths or injuries from ever occurring. It would seem anomalous to construe an Act so directed and constructed as prohibiting an employee, with no other reasonable alternative, the freedom to withdraw from a workplace environment that he reasonably believes is highly dangerous.

Moreover, the Secretary's regulation can be viewed as an appropriate aid to the full effectuation of the Act's "general duty" clause. That clause provides that "[e]ach employer shall furnish to each of his employees employment and a place of employment which are free from recognized hazards that are causing or are likely to cause death or serious physical harm to his employees." Since OSHA inspectors cannot be present around the clock in every workplace, the Secretary's regulation ensures that employees will in all circumstances enjoy the rights afforded them by the "general duty" clause.

The regulation thus on its face appears to further the overriding purpose of the Act, and rationally to complement its remedial scheme.

[T]he Secretary's regulation must, therefore, be upheld, particularly when it is remembered that safety legislation is to be liberally construed to effectuate the congressional purpose.

CASE QUESTIONS

1. What workplace hazard was at issue?
2. What type of remedy does the secretary of labor (acting on behalf of OSHA) want?
3. Is this remedy provided by statute?
4. Is this remedy provided by regulation?
5. Does the decision allow employees to walk off the job when there is a workplace hazard?

EXHIBIT   19.2   OSHA Penalties

TYPE OF OFFENSE	DESCRIPTION	PENALTY
Willful	Employer aware of danger or a repeat violator	Up to $70,000 (not less than $5,000) and/or six months imprisonment
Serious	Violation is a threat to life or could cause serious injury	$7,000
Nonserious	No threat of serious injury	Up to $7,000
De minimis	Failure to post rights	Up to $7,000 per violation
Failure to correct	Citation not followed	$7,000 per day

OSHA Search Warrant Requirements

Although most businesses voluntarily permit OSHA inspections, employers do have the right to refuse access. In *Marshall v. Barlows, Inc.*, 436 U.S. 307 (1978), the U.S. Supreme Court ruled that OSHA inspectors must obtain warrants if employers refuse access.

OSHA Penalties

There are five types of OSHA violations, each of which carries a different range of penalties. Exhibit 19.2 is a summary of OSHA penalties.

After an inspection, OSHA can issue a citation, which begins the penalty process. Although some employers enter into a consent decree and settle the matter with OSHA, any citation can be challenged by an employer, who must give notice of challenge within fifteen days of receiving the citation. A hearing is then conducted by an administrative law judge (ALJ). The ALJ makes a recommendation to OSHRC, which decides what action to take. Once the OSHRC decision is made, the employer has sixty days to seek review of the decision by a U.S. court of appeals.

State OSHA Programs

Most federal regulatory laws preempt state laws, but state laws addressing occupational safety are not generally preempted, and the states share responsibility for workplace safety with the federal government. Also, state criminal laws may be used to prosecute officers and companies already sanctioned by OSHA.

For a state to assume responsibility for an OSHA program, the agency must be assured that the state plan will be as effective as federal OSHA would be. Also, OSHA is in charge of the Complaints against State Program Administration, which permits those affected and interested in safety to file complaints

BUSINESS PLANNING TIP

Some Don'ts for Drug Testing

- Don't misuse the Drug-Free Workplace program to discipline employees for unrelated problems.

- Don't single out any employee or group of employees for scrutiny under the policy. Be consistent in your actions with all employee groups or classes.

- Don't confront a suspected drug dealer (or user) alone. Always have a witness.

- Don't implement a verbal policy. An effective policy must be written, circulated, and acknowledged in writing by employees in order to have strong legal standing.

- Don't treat employees who test positive differently. All employees who test positive must be treated consistently to maintain the integrity of the program.

- Don't take action against employees based on the results of a drug screen only. Always obtain the results of a gas chromatography/mass spectrometry (GC/MS) confirmation test before taking action.

- Don't offer rehabilitation selectively.

- Don't address drug abuse without including alcohol abuse in the policy.

- Don't implement a policy and program unilaterally if the workforce is represented by a union. The National Labor Relations Act requires that terms and conditions be included in your bargaining agreement, and a drug program falls into that requirement. (Source: OSHA) with OSHA regarding state performance. OSHA can then investigate and, if necessary, eliminate state approval.

Employee Impairment and Testing Issues

One safety problem in the workplace is the presence of impaired coworkers. An employee operating equipment, whether a drill press or a delivery van, while under the influence of drugs or alcohol presents a substantial safety concern for any business. Current estimates are that between 14 and 20 percent of the U.S. workforce is impaired on the job. Employees who use drugs are almost four times more likely to be involved in workplace accidents. Further, the cost in reduced productivity attributable to impaired workers is $100 billion (see For the Manager's Desk, "Re:

FOR THE MANAGER'S DESK

RE: ISSUES IN DRUG TESTING

The percentage of employers who test employees for drugs increased from 22 percent in 1987 to 67 percent in 2001. However, some employees have questioned the accuracy of the drug tests and have filed suit challenging the tests and the resulting terminations. And some employers note that employees can tamper with the test results.

Because of the accusations and confusion, the U.S. Department of Health and Human Services issued its employee drug-testing guidelines. The guidelines dictate certain types of jobs for which employees must always be tested (e.g., pilots, conductors) and also provide procedures for conducting the tests that will then become *prima facie* evidence of accuracy of the test results.[*]

What steps do you think an employer should take to ensure the validity of the drug tests?

Consider the following list developed by the Department of Health and Human Services in conjunction with representatives from unions, employers and others as a means of justifying an employer's need for drug testing employees:[†]

- Administrative losses, e.g., absenteeism, tardiness, overtime pay, sick leave abuse, health insurance claims, disability payments, and costs associated with accidents
- Hidden losses, e.g., diverted supervisory and managerial time, friction among workers, material waste, equipment damage, poor decisions, damage to public image, and costs associated with turnover and premature death
- Losses with legal implications, e.g., Workers' Compensation, drug trafficking on the job, disciplinary actions, grievances, threat to public safety, and worksite security
- Costs of health and mental health care services

Is there a difference between drug tests for new employees and using company-wide ongoing drug testing? Is ongoing drug testing necessary?

The Department of Health and Human Services also lists its ideal components for creating a drug-free workplace.[‡]

What Issues Should Be Covered in a Drug-Free Workplace Policy?

It is beneficial to both the employer and the employees to have a program and policies designed to reduce and eliminate the negative effects of alcohol and drug abuse and provide a safe Workplace. The employer should provide a written policy that

- *Explains why the product or service provided is inconsistent with employee alcohol and drug abuse;*
- *Provides information about the dangers of alcohol and drug abuse;*
- *Spells out what kind of assistance will be provided to substance abusers who voluntarily report their abuse problems or have been identified as a drug or alcohol abuser through other means;*
- *Spells out the roles, rights and responsibilities for employees and supervisors under the program;*
- *Describes the sanctions which will apply for violations of the polices;*
- *Assures personal privacy and dignity in reaching the goal of a Drug-Free Workplace.*
- *In addition, the written policy should include provisions for training supervisors on their role in the program and drug testing, if necessary, on a carefully controlled and monitored basis. If the policy will include testing, it should specify the nature, frequency, and type of testing that will be included. It should also include the identification of the drugs for which employees will be tested.*

Source: Stephanie Armour, "Accused Workers Challenge Drug-Test Results in Court," *USA Today,* July 16, 2001, p. 1B.
[*]You can find the guidelines at http://workplace.samhsa.gov/DrugTesting/MGuidelines.htm.
[†]See http://workplace.samhsa.gov/DrugFreeWP/Benefits.html.
[‡]Drug Tesing Guidelines, Department of Health and Human Services

*Visit Web sites on workplace
and other privacy issues:*
http://www.epic.org
and
http://www.privacyrights.org

Issues in Drug Testing," for a list of the types of costs associated with impaired workers on the job). In 1989, the U.S. Supreme Court issued two decisions—*Skinner* v. *Railway Labor Executives' Association,* 489 U.S. 602 (1989), and *National Treasury Employees Union* v. *Von Raab,* 489 U.S. 656 (1984)—that upheld the right of government employers to conduct drug screening of federal employees without a warrant and without probable cause if those employees were in "safety sensitive" positions. These two particular cases involved railway employees and customs officers, respectively.

In the area of drug and alcohol screening, the interests of employee privacy collide with safety and business issues. Courts at the state and federal levels have adopted a near uniform position of holding safety concerns above employees' right of privacy. Their decisions have upheld the right of employer testing even in the private sector, especially in work situations where safety is a concern.

EMPLOYEE PENSIONS, RETIREMENT, AND SOCIAL SECURITY

One of the concerns of workers is what happens to them when they retire: Will they have an income? Other concerns are whether they will have a source of income in the event of disability, or whether their survivors will have income in the event of their death. Finally, what if no work is available? What income will they have until they find another job? These issues are the social issues of employment law—providing for those who, because of age, disability, or unemployment, are unable to provide for themselves.

Social Security

*Review the Social Security
Act of 1935:*
**http://www.ssa.gov/
history/35act.html**

The **Social Security Act of 1935** was a key component of the massive reforms in federal government during Franklin Roosevelt's presidency.

The idea of the Social Security system was to have those who could work shoulder the social burden of providing for those who could not. Every employer and employee is required to contribute to the Social Security programs under the **Federal Insurance Contributions Act** (FICA). The amount employees contribute is based on their annual wage, but there is a maximum wage amount for contributions. FICA contributions are paid one-half by employers and one-half by employees. Independent contractors pay their own FICA contributions. There are death benefits for spouses and children, as well as disability and retirement benefits.

The benefits paid to retired and disabled people are based on formulas. The amount depends on how long an individual worked and within what salary range. Surviving spouse and children's benefits are likewise tied to work and salary history.

FOR THE MANAGER'S DESK
RE: WHO IS AN EMPLOYEE AND WHO IS AN INDEPENDENT CONTRACTOR?

For purposes of Social Security taxes, unemployment compensation, workers' compensation, and, of course, principal liability, the definition of an employee versus that of independent contractor is critical. Many businesses apply a label of "independent contractor" to agents doing work for them, but the activities of those independent contractors may, in fact, make them employees. Employers should check the status of those who are doing work so that they are paying wage taxes properly and have adequate coverage for liability.

continued

In a 1987 revenue ruling, the Internal Revenue Service (IRS) listed the following twenty factors for determining whether an employer has sufficient control to label an agent an employee (servant) as opposed to an independent contractor.

1. Instructions on worker's performance of duties versus independent work
2. Training by coworkers versus no training required
3. Integration of worker's services into the business
4. Services benefit the business personally as opposed to a group of employers
5. Worker hires, supervises, and pays his own assistants (more likely to be independent contractor)
6. Continuing relationship as opposed to one-time projects
7. Set hours of work as opposed to flexibility
8. Full time required as opposed to working for others
9. Doing work on the employer's premises as opposed to own facilities
10. Order of tasks established by employer
11. Oral or written reports as opposed to independence
12. Payment by hour, week, or month as opposed to payment by project or task
13. Payment of business or travel expenses as opposed to personal payment as part of fee
14. Furnishing tools and materials versus furnishing own supplies
15. Use of and payment for outside facilities
16. Realization of profit or loss by worker
17. Working for more than one firm at a time
18. Making services available to the general public
19. Employer's right to discharge versus employee processes and procedures
20. Worker's right to terminate without consequences such as breach of contract

These twenty complex and burdensome factors were consolidated by the ninth circuit in *Donovan* v. *Sureway Cleaners*, 656 F.2d 1368 (9th Cir. 1981) into six factors:

1. Degree of control over workers
2. Whether the worker has the risk of profit or loss
3. Whether the worker makes an investment
4. Level of skills and training for the work
5. Permanency of worker
6. Integration into economics of the business

One consistent factor not present in any of the evaluation lists is what the employer labels the worker—the label is irrelevant, and courts are consistent in their unwillingness to accept employers' labels of workers.

A new proposal for determining independent contractor status will require a focus on the degree of control as the key factor. The IRS has a new training manual for examiners who determine whether workers are independent contractors or employees. The twenty-point test is simply background information for the ultimate determination under the guidelines, which are designed to look at the overall relationship of the business with the worker.

Private Retirement Plans

For many, Social Security retirement benefits do not provide enough security, and at present there is no assurance that those employed today will be able to collect their Social Security benefits upon retirement. For these reasons, many employees have invested in their own private retirement plans.

Many retirement and pension plans are set up by employers, who enjoy tax benefits from some plans. However, when there were indications that employees' funds in plans were being misused, not invested wisely, and in some cases embezzled, Congress enacted the **Employee Retirement Income Security Act of 1974** (ERISA).

Review the Employee Retirement Income Security Act of 1974:
http://www.law.cornell.edu/uscode/29/ch18.html

Coverage of ERISA
ERISA applies to any employer engaged in or affecting interstate commerce and to any organization (such as a union) representing employees in interstate commerce. ERISA covers any medical, retirement, or deferral-of-income plan.

Requirements of ERISA Plans
Covered employers and organizations must give participants an annual report on the insurance or retirement fund that must include a financial statement and an

For more information on pensions and ERISA, visit:
http://www.pbgc.gov

actuarial statement. The annual report must also list any loans made from the fund, including amounts and to whom they were made. The cost of reporting and fiduciary duties under ERISA have caused many employers to drop pension plans. ERISA does not require employer pension plans—it only regulates those employers that have them.

For more information on what happens to your pension if your company goes bankrupt, go to:
http://www.dol.gov/ebsa/newsroom/fsbankruptcy.html

ERISA Employee Rights

ERISA employees are entitled to receive an annual statement showing both their total benefits in any of the covered plans and the amount that is vested or that is nonforfeitable should they leave their jobs. In addition, ERISA provides minimum vesting requirements or sets standards for when employees will have rights in their retirement, pension, or annuity plans.

Visit the Financial Accounting Standards Board:
http://www.fasb.org

FASB 106, Retirees, and Pensions

In 1995, the Financial Accounting Standards Board (FASB) required companies to reflect as a current expense the costs of benefits for retired employees. This accounting rule will continue to affect earnings as the population ages and benefit costs increase. A new issue that has evolved is the use of earnings on the pension plan as a means of reflecting higher earnings for the company. These earnings must be called out for investors so that they can see what revenues come from operations as opposed to investment of employees' funds.

ETHICAL ISSUES

The pension benefits due to employees under ERISA are substantial expenses for companies. When companies are enduring difficult times, they often employ creative measures to eliminate the pension obligations. For example, the story of Massey-Ferguson and its employees and pension plans is one that took resolution at the U.S. Supreme Court.

Charles Howe and his coworkers were employed by Massey-Ferguson, a wholly owned subsidiary of the parent corporation, Varity Corporation. Massey-Ferguson was not performing well, and Varity developed a plan to place Massey-Ferguson and all other weak subsidiaries into a new subsidiary called Massey Combines. Because of the weakness of the companies to be combined in Massey Combines, the officers and board of Varity understood that Massey Combines might fail. However, their goal was to eliminate the debts of these poorly performing subsidiaries. One of the debts they hoped to eliminate through this restructuring was the medical and pension benefits due to Massey-Ferguson employees, including Mr. Howe.

Varity held employee information sessions when employees became concerned about their futures and the status of their retirement plans. During these meetings, Varity officers gave their assurances that the benefits would be secure if the employees transferred to Massey Combines. Known as the Project Sunshine campaign,

the meetings offered assurances along with a letter saying: "When you accept employment with Massey Combines Corp. . . . benefit programs will remain unchanged." "We are all very optimistic that our new company has a bright future."

The employees were persuaded to become employees of Massey Combines, but Massey Combines was insolvent from the day of its formation. It was placed into receivership, and the employees of Massey Combines, formerly of Massey-Ferguson, lost all of their pension benefits. Varity cut off health benefits for retirees, pointing to language in its official health plan: "The company hereby reserves the right, by action of the board, to amend or terminate the plan or trust at any time." Mr. Howe and others filed suit under ERISA, and the U.S. Supreme Court held, in *Varity Corp.* v. *Howe*, 516 U.S. 489 (1996), that Mr. Howe and the others had the right to bring a private suit against Varity for its breach of its fiduciary duties under ERISA.

Refer to Chapter 2 and list the categories of ethical breaches Varity committed. Was Varity honest with the employees? Did it take unfair advantage of them? Did Varity give a false impression? What ethical test could the officers and board of Varity have employed to avoid the resulting litigation and eventual liability to the employees for their pensions?

Unemployment Compensation

Benefits Provided

State laws provide for the amount of **unemployment compensation** that will be paid. The amount is tied to the average amount earned by an individual during the months preceding employment termination. The benefits are usually paid on a weekly or biweekly basis. Most states also have a minimum and maximum amount that can be collected regardless of average earnings during the base period. Further, benefit payments in most states are limited to twenty-six weeks.

Qualifying for Benefits

Each state has its own standards for payment of benefits. Generally, eligibility requirements demand that an individual be (1) involuntarily terminated from a job, (2) able and available for work, and (3) involved in seeking employment.

The payment of unemployment benefits raises many social issues regarding its effects. For example, many opponents of such benefits maintain that awarding them encourages unemployment. In addition, unemployment compensation has created some conflicts in federal labor legislation. In *Wimberly* v. *Labor and Indus. Relations Comm'n of Missouri* (Case 19.2), the U.S. Supreme Court dealt with the conflicting federal rights for labor, management, and unemployment compensation.

CASE 19.2

Wimberly v. *Labor and Indus. Relations Comm'n of Missouri*
479 U.S. 511 (1987)

Post-Partum Employment

FACTS

After the birth of her child on November 5, 1980, Linda Wimberly (petitioner) was on pregnancy leave from her job at J. C. Penney. Under Penney policy, she could return to work only if a position was available. A position was not available when Mrs. Wimberly tried to return, and she then filed a claim for unemployment benefits with the Missouri Division of Employment Security. She was denied the claim because she had left "work voluntarily without good cause attributable to [her] work or [her] employer," a provision of a Missouri statute.

Mrs. Wimberly filed suit, and the trial court held that the Missouri statute was inconsistent with the Federal Unemployment Tax Act that prohibits denying compensation "solely on the basis of pregnancy or termination of pregnancy." The court of appeals affirmed, but the Missouri Supreme Court reversed. Mrs. Wimberly appealed to the U.S. Supreme Court.

JUDICIAL OPINION

O'CONNOR, Justice

The Federal Unemployment Tax Act (Act), 26 U.S.C. §§ 3301 *et seq.*, enacted originally as Title IX of the So-

cial Security Act in 1935, 49 Stat. 639, envisions a cooperative federal-state program of benefits to unemployed workers. The standard at issue in this case, § 3304(a)(12), mandates that "no person shall be denied compensation under such State law solely on the basis of pregnancy or termination of pregnancy."

Apart from the minimum standards reflected in § 3304(a), the Act leaves to state discretion the rules governing the administration of unemployment compensation programs.

The treatment of pregnancy-related terminations is a matter of considerable disparity among the States. Most States regard leave on account of pregnancy as a voluntary termination for good cause. Some of these States have specific statutory provisions enumerating pregnancy motivated termination as good cause for leaving a job, while others, by judicial or administrative decision, treat pregnancy as encompassed within larger categories of good cause such as illness or compelling personal reasons. A few states, however, like Missouri, have chosen to define "leaving for good cause" narrowly. In these states, all persons who leave their jobs are disqualified from receiving benefits unless they leave for reasons directly attributable to the work or to the employer.

Petitioner does not dispute that the Missouri scheme treats pregnant women the same as all other persons who leave for reasons not causally connected to their work or their employer, including those suffering from other types of temporary disabilities. She contends, however, that § 3304(a)(12) is not simply an antidiscrimination statute, but rather that it mandates preferential treatment for women who leave work because of pregnancy. According to petitioner, § 3304(a)(12) affirmatively requires states to provide unemployment benefits to women who leave work because of pregnancy when they are next available and able to work, regardless of the state's treatment of other similarly situated claimants.

Contrary to petitioner's assertions, the plain import of the language of § 3304(a)(12) is that Congress intended to prohibit states from singling out pregnancy for unfavorable treatment. The text of the statute provides that compensation shall not be denied under state law "solely on the basis of pregnancy." The focus of this language is on the basis of the state's decision, not the claimant's reason for leaving her job. Thus, a state could not decide to deny benefits to pregnant women while at the same time allowing benefits to persons who are in other respects similarly situated: The "sole basis" for such a decision would be on account of pregnancy. On the other hand, if a state adopts a neutral rule that incidentally disqualifies pregnant or formerly pregnant claimants as part of a larger group, the neutral application of that rule cannot readily be characterized as a decision made "solely on the basis of pregnancy."

Even petitioner concedes that § 3304(a)(12) does not prohibit states from denying benefits to pregnant or formerly pregnant women who fail to satisfy neutral eligibility requirements such as ability to work and availability for work. Missouri does not have a "policy" specifically relating to pregnancy: It neutrally disqualifies workers who leave their jobs for reasons unrelated to their employment.

In *Turner* v. *Department of Employment Security*, this Court struck down on due process grounds a Utah statute providing that a woman was disqualified for 12 weeks before the expected date of childbirth and for 6 weeks after childbirth, even if she left work for reasons unrelated to pregnancy. The Senate Report used the provision at issue in *Turner* as representative of the kind of rule that § 3304(a)(12) was intended to prohibit.

> *In a number of states, an individual whose unemployment is related to pregnancy is barred from receiving any unemployment benefits. In 1975 the Supreme Court found a provision of this type in the Utah unemployment compensation statute to be unconstitutional. . . . A number of other states have similar provisions although most appear to involve somewhat shorter periods of disqualification.*

S. Rep. No. 94–1265, at 19, 21, U.S. Code Cong. & Admin. News 1976, pp. 6031, 6015.

In short, petitioner can point to nothing in the Committee Reports, or elsewhere in the statute's legislative history, that evidences congressional intent to mandate preferential treatment for women on account of pregnancy. There is no hint that Congress disapproved of, much less intended to prohibit, a neutral rule such as Missouri's. Indeed, the legislative history shows that Congress was focused only on the issue addressed by the plain language of § 3304(a)(12): prohibiting rules that single out pregnant women or formerly pregnant women for disadvantageous treatment.

Because § 3304(a)(12) does not require states to afford preferential treatment to women on account of pregnancy, the judgment of the Missouri Supreme Court is affirmed.

CASE QUESTIONS

1. Why was Mrs. Wimberly denied unemployment compensation?
2. Was the pregnancy given as a reason?
3. What is the difference between the Utah statute mentioned in the Court's opinion and the Missouri statute?
4. Is the Missouri statute valid?
5. What implications does the decision carry for maternity leaves?

CONSIDER...   **19.1**

Alfred Smith and Galen Black were fired by a private drug rehabilitation center because they ingested peyote for sacramental purposes at a ceremony of the Native American Church, of which both are members. When Mr. Smith and Mr. Black applied for unemployment compensation from the state of Oregon, their requests were denied because they were fired for "misconduct." They challenged the decision as a violation of their religious freedom. Are Mr. Smith and Mr. Black correct? [*Employment Div., Dep't of Human Resources of Oregon* v. *Smith*, 496 U.S. 913 (1990).]

Who Pays for Unemployment Benefits?

Although the idea and mandate for unemployment compensation came from the federal government, the states actually administer their own programs. Employers in each state are taxed based on the number of workers they employ and their wages. Those taxes are collected by the states on a quarterly basis. These funds are deposited with the federal government, which maintains an unemployment insurance program with the funds. Each state has an account in the federal fund on which it can draw. Employers effectively pay the costs of the unemployment compensation system.

WORKERS' COMPENSATION LAWS

For an example of a state workers' compensation law, review the Texas Worker's Compensation Act:

http://www.twcc.state.tx.us

The purpose of **workers' compensation** laws is to provide wage benefits and medical care to victims of work-related injuries. Although each state has its own system of workers' compensation, several general principles remain consistent throughout the states:

1. An employee who is injured in the scope of employment is automatically entitled to certain benefits (a discussion of work-related injuries and the scope of employment follows).

2. Fault is immaterial. Employees' contributory negligence does not lessen their right to compensation. Employers' care and precaution do not lessen their responsibility.

3. Coverage is limited to employees and does not extend to independent contractors.

4. Benefits include partial wages, hospital and medical expenses, and death benefits.

5. In exchange for these benefits, employees, their families, and dependents give up their common-law right to sue an employer for damages.

6. If third parties (e.g., equipment manufacturers) are responsible for an accident, recovery from the third party goes first to the employer for reimbursement.

7. Each state has some administrative agency responsible for administration of workers' compensation.

8. Every employer who is subject to workers' compensation regulation is required to provide some security for liability (such as insurance).

Employee Injuries

As they originated, workers' compensation systems were created to provide benefits for accidental workplace injuries. Over the years, however, the term *accident* has been interpreted broadly. Most injuries are those that result suddenly, such as broken arms, injured backs caused by falls, burns, and lacerations. But workers' compensation has been extended to cover injuries that develop over time. For example, workers involved in lifting heavy objects might eventually develop back problems. Even such medical problems as high blood pressure, heart attacks, and nervous breakdowns have in some cases been classified as work related and compensable.

The standard for recovery under the workers' compensation system is that the injury originate in the workplace, be caused by the workplace, or develop over time in the workplace. Even stress, when shown to be caused or originated by employment, is a compensable injury.

Workers' compensation issues have become more complex, and many of the hearings involve the issue of determining whether a disability originated on the job or would have existed independently of the job. *Gacioch v. Stroh Brewery Co.* (Case 19.3) deals with this type of issue.

CASE 19.3

Gacioch v. *Stroh Brewery Co.*
396 N.W.2d 1 (Mich. 1990)

Free–Beer Lunches, Alcoholism, and Workers' Comp

FACTS

Casimer Gacioch (plaintiff) began working for Stroh Brewery on February 24, 1947. When he began his work for Stroh, he was predisposed to alcoholism, but he had not yet become an uncontrolled alcoholic.

Beer was provided free at the brewery and was available to all employees on the job at "designated relief areas." This availability had been negotiated through a collective bargaining agreement. Employees could drink beer during their breaks and at lunch with no limit on the amount.

Mr. Gacioch did not drink at home during the week but drank three or four bottles of beer on the weekend. At work he drank twelve bottles a day. He was not a test taster; he ran a machine that fed cases of beer to a soaker.

In 1973, Stroh Brewery noticed Mr. Gacioch's drinking problem and required him to sign an agreement stating that he could no longer drink on the job. He continued to drink, and seven months after the first agreement he signed a second agreement not to drink on the job. He again continued to drink, was intoxicated on the job, and could not perform his work. He was fired on August 30, 1974.

From April 1976 until September 1978, Mr. Gacioch worked part-time as a church custodian. He pursued a workers' compensation claim against Stroh, alleging he was disabled because of alcoholism. He was denied recovery and appealed to the Workers' Compensation Appeal Board (WCAB), which found that alcoholism is a disease, that the free-beer policy accelerated the problem, and that Stroh should pay compensation. Stroh appealed.

JUDICIAL OPINION

ARCHER, Justice
This case involves a claim for workers' compensation benefits for the chronic alcoholism suffered by plaintiff. We must determine whether, under the circumstances extant in this case, chronic alcoholism suffered by plaintiff who, during breaks drank beer provided free by Stroh Brewery pursuant to a collectively bargained contract provision negotiated by the union is compensable under the Workers' Disability Compensation Act as a personal injury which arose out of and in the course of plaintiff's employment.

The statute in effect on the last day of plaintiff's employment at Stroh Brewery read:

> *An employee, who receives a personal injury arising out of and in the course of his employment by an employer who is subject to the provisions of this act, at the time of such injury, shall be paid compensation in the manner and to the extent provided in this act, or in case of his death resulting from such injuries the compensation shall be paid to his dependents as defined in this act. Time of injury or date of injury as used in this act in the case of a disease or in the case of an injury not attributable to a single event shall be the last day of work in the employment in which the employee was last subjected to the conditions resulting in disability or death.*
>
> *"Personal injury" shall include a disease or disability which is due to causes and conditions which are characteristic of and peculiar to the business of the employer and which arises out of and in the course of the employment. Ordinary diseases of life to which the public is generally exposed outside of the employment shall not be compensable.*

Defendants contend that alcoholism is not a disease, but, rather, a "social aberration." All three experts testifying in this case, Drs. Smith and Tanay, plaintiff's experts, and Dr. Rauch, defendants' expert, referred to alcoholism as a disease. Dr. Smith described alcoholism as a "lifelong metabolic disease, much like diabetes." Dr. Tanay testified that alcoholism is associated with particular personality disorders which begin during a person's childhood. The WCAB treated plaintiff's chronic alcoholism as a disease. Our review of the professional literature on the subject indicates that various organizations representing health care professionals have officially pronounced alcoholism as a disease. Hence, plaintiff's chronic alcoholism is a disease for purposes of the above statute.

continued

Plaintiff asserts that his chronic alcoholism was an occupational disease. We disagree. A review of the record indicates that the WCAB also did not conclude that plaintiff's alcoholic condition was an occupational disease. The board treated plaintiff's alcoholism as an ordinary disease of life. The proper inquiry in this case, therefore, is whether plaintiff's chronic alcoholism was a disease or disability which was due to causes and conditions which are characteristic of and peculiar to the business of Stroh and which arose out of and in the course of employment. In reaching the question concerning whether chronic alcoholism is a disease which is due to causes and conditions which are characteristic of and peculiar to the business of Stroh and which arose out of and in the course of plaintiff's employment, we must be careful not to equate "circumstance" of employment with "out of and in the course" of employment. If chronic alcoholism can be categorized as an ordinary disease of life to which the public is generally exposed outside of the employment, plaintiff is not entitled to a workers' compensation award. The pertinent question then is whether the board made specific findings as to whether brewery workers are more prone to develop chronic alcoholism than is the general public.

We are unable to discern from the opinion of the board whether it found as fact that brewery workers are more prone to suffer from chronic alcoholism (an ordinary disease of life) than is the general public. We note that none of the experts testifying in this case stated that plaintiff's alcoholism was due to the inherent characteristics and peculiarities of his employment in the brewery industry as a production worker respon-

sible for running a machine. Dr. Smith, for example, testified that "Mr. Gacioch would have most likely become an alcoholic anyway and his drinking outside of work eventually [was] far greater than during work." Dr. Rauch opined that individuals who are predisposed to alcoholism, like plaintiff herein, are likely to become an alcoholic no matter where they work.

We are unable to determine from the opinion of the WCAB whether it understood the applicable legal standard and what facts it specifically relied upon in reaching its conclusion that plaintiff's alcoholism was compensable under the Workers' Disability Compensation Act.

We therefore remand this case to the WCAB for its statement of the law and the specific facts relied upon to support its conclusion.

CASE QUESTIONS

1. What was Stroh's free-beer policy?
2. Who negotiated the policy?
3. Was Mr. Gacioch predisposed to alcoholism?
4. Is alcoholism a disease?
5. Is alcoholism a disease that originated in the workplace in this case?
6. What additional factual information is needed to resolve the case?
7. How do you feel about the free-beer policy? Can you foresee other issues of liability for Stroh beyond workers' compensation?

Fault Is Immaterial

The fact that an injury occurs in the workplace is enough for recovery. Employee negligence, employer precautions, contributory negligence, and assumption of risk are generally not issues in workers' compensation cases.

Employees versus Independent Contractors

Workers' compensation applies to employees but not to independent contractors. Employees are those who are present at the workplace on a regular basis, paid a wage, and supervised. **Independent contractors** are those who work on a job basis, work irregular hours, and are not supervised by the employer. A backhoe operator working daily from 5 A.M. to 1 P.M. for a plumbing company and paid a weekly wage is an employee. A backhoe operator hired and paid on a per-job basis is an independent contractor. A more complete discussion of employee status can be found in Chapter 18 and on p. 751.

Benefits

Workers' benefits can be grouped into three different categories: medical, disability, and death. Medical benefits include typical insurance-covered costs such as hospital costs, physician and nursing fees, therapy fees, and rental costs for equipment needed for recovery.

Disability benefits are payments made to compensate employees for wages lost because of a disability injury. The amount of benefits is based on state statutory figures. Most states base disability benefits on an employee's average monthly wage, and they also specify a maximum amount. State statutes also generally have a list of **scheduled injuries**, which will carry a percentage disability figure. For example, loss of a body part is a typical injury. In Arizona, the disability amount for a lost thumb is 55 percent of the average monthly wage for fifteen months (Ariz. Rev. Stat. § 23–1044). For a lost foot, the amount is 55 percent of the average monthly wage for fifty months. Total disability is also defined by statute. Workers who have total disability are generally entitled to two-thirds of their average monthly salary for the period of the disability. Total disability usually includes the loss of both eyes or both hands or complete paralysis.

Some injuries suffered by workers are not listed in statutes. Those not specifically described in statutes are called **unscheduled injuries**. The amount allowed for unscheduled injuries is discretionary and an area of frequent litigation.

Death benefits are paid to the family of a deceased employee and generally include burial expenses. In addition, survivors who were economically dependent on an employee are also paid benefits. The amount of death benefits is generally some percentage of the average monthly salary; for example, a surviving spouse might be entitled to a 35 percent benefit.

Forfeiture of the Right of Suit

The majority of states require employees to forfeit all other lawsuit rights in exchange for workers' compensation benefits. Employees receive automatic benefits but lose the right to sue their employers for covered incidents. Some states even prohibit employees from suing their coworkers under most conditions. In addition, some states allow family members to sue employers for direct injury to themselves. In those states, a spouse could bring a lawsuit against an employer for loss of consortium (marital companionship).

Third-Party Suits

If an employee is injured by a machine malfunction while on the job, the employee is covered by workers' compensation. However, there is an issue of product liability in the accident. If suit is brought against the machine's manufacturer for product liability, any recovery goes first to the employer to compensate for the cost of the employee's benefits. In other words, third-party recovery is first used to reimburse the employer.

Administrative Agency

Every state has some administrative agency responsible for the administration of claims, hearings, and benefits. In most states, this agency holds hearings for claims, and its decision is appealable in the same manner as any other agency decision.

The procedure for compensation requires employees to file claims with the agency along with medical documentation for the claim. Most claims are paid without contest; but, when there is a challenge to a decision, a hearing with evidence and testimony is held.

Insurance

All states with workers' compensation systems require employers to be financially responsible for benefits under their systems. Employers can show financial responsibility by (1) maintaining an insurance policy, (2) obtaining a policy through the state agency, or (3) offering evidence of sufficient assets and resources to cover potential claims and benefits.

Problems in Workers' Compensation Systems

Increasingly, states and employers are experimenting with reforms to workers' compensation systems. Concerns focus on fraud that stems from incentives in the system. For example, medical benefits in workers' compensation are better than most medical plans. Because nearly all disability payments are tax-free, employees may be living on close to 90 percent of what they lived on (after taxes) before their disability.

Some doubts exist about the legitimacy of many complaints. A janitor moonlighting for HGO, Inc. hurt his little finger while on the job. He collected $16,800 in disability payments over the next three years, even though he was able to continue his regular day job as a police officer.

Suggested reforms have included the elimination of certain claims, as in California, where attempts are being made to eliminate "mental stress" from workers' compensation coverage. Georgia no longer makes lifetime disability payments but instead limits their duration to eight years. Other states have hired more investigators to detect fraud. Companies are also attempting to cut costs by using staff doctors or by returning employees to other jobs that can be done despite an injury.

The nature of work in the United States has changed and continues to change rapidly. The workers' compensation systems were established during the Industrial Revolution, when the injuries sustained were primarily the types of factory and machinery accidents we traditionally associate with workers' compensation claims. However, the majority of jobs in the United States are now in service industries, and the nature of work-related injuries has changed from sudden-accident types to ongoing, progressive problems that are more expensive to treat and correct. For example, the repetitive hand and arm motions of computer keyboard operators can injure word processors, journalists, reservationists, and cashiers. This injury, often called carpal tunnel syndrome, can require expensive surgery and results in many lost work days, if not new job assignments. Such repetitive stress injuries (RSIs) are the basis of pending lawsuits by workers against keyboard and equipment manufacturers.

The office environment itself is presenting new and difficult-to-control health-related problems for workers. Ergonomics is a rapidly growing field that examines the design of work areas and office equipment to minimize such worker injuries as repetitive motion syndromes and back problems. Architects and engineers are working together to design buildings that eliminate the so-called sick-building syndrome, in which poor air quality or the lack of fresh air circulation increases the incidence of illness and causes other symptoms in office workers.

Explore the Americans with Disabilities Act:
http://www.jan.wvu.edu/links/adalinks.htm

A final issue in workers' compensation is the relationship between the state systems and the Americans with Disabilities Act (see Chapter 20), which prohibits discrimination against employees with disabilities and requires accommodation of employer facilities to permit disabled persons to work. Traditionally, when an accident caused disability, an employee collected payment in lieu of being rehired. An issue that arises as the systems of laws interact is whether an employer is required to rehire a disabled employee.

LABOR UNIONS

History and Development of Labor Legislation

When workers first began organized efforts to improve their employment situations, the courts were particularly harsh. In early eighteenth-century England, participants in organized labor were prosecuted for criminal conspiracy, which is the crime of organizing with others for the commission of another crime. The first case in the United States, *Commonwealth* v. *Pullis* (1806), also charged organized laborers with criminal conspiracy that resulted in a criminal conviction for laborers participating in a strike.

Many employers tried to stifle the labor union movement by requiring their employees to sign **yellow-dog contracts**, which prohibited employees from joining unions. With these attempts came the beginning of protective labor legislation.

The Railway Labor Act of 1926

Review the Railway Labor Act:
http://www.law.cornell.edu/uscode/45/151.html

The **Railway Labor Act** was the first federal legislation to address union issues specifically, but its application was limited to labor relations in the railroad industry. However, the act did establish some basic rights for railway employees that would later carry over to general labor statutes. Railway employees were given the right to form and join unions without employer interference. The employees were also given the right to bargain collectively with their employers. The underlying purpose of the act was to promote peaceful labor-management relations. This act was expanded to cover airline employees in 1936 and is still effective today.

The Norris–LaGuardia Act of 1932

Review the Norris–LaGuardia Act:
http://www.law.cornell.edu/uscode/29/101.html

In addressing the problem of courts issuing injunctions to stop union strikes, the **Norris-LaGuardia Act** prohibited the injunction as a remedy in labor disputes and eliminated the common law application of the use of government to control employer-employee relations. Under the act, the government (including the courts) became a neutral force in labor-management disputes.

Violent strikes can still be enjoined, provided there is evidence that there would be or had been violence and that public officers could not control the violence and any resulting damage. A hearing on these issues is required prior to the issuance of an injunction.

The Wagner Act

Review the National Labor Relations Act:
http://www.law.cornell.edu/uscode/29/151.html

Visit the NLRB:
http://www.nlrb.gov

The **Wagner Act**, also known as the **National Labor Relations Act** (NLRA) of 1935, gave employees the right to organize and choose representatives to bargain collectively with their employers. Further, it established the **National Labor Relations Board** (NLRB), which had two functions: to conduct union elections and to investigate and remedy unfair labor practices.

The Taft–Hartley Act: The Labor–Management Relations Act of 1947

Review the Taft–Hartley Act:
http://www.law.cornell.edu/uscode/29/141.html

Over President Truman's veto, Congress passed the **Taft-Hartley Act**, which was a response to the public's concern about too many strikes, secondary boycotts, and the unrestrained power of union officials. The act amended the Wagner Act by applying the principle of unfair labor practices to unions as well as employers. Strikes to force employers to discharge nonunion employees, secondary boycotts, and strikes over work assignments were prohibited as unfair labor practices. Employees were also given the right to remove a union they no longer wanted as their representative. The act also contains provisions that allow the president to invoke a **cooling-off period** of bargaining before a strike that threatens to imperil the public health and safety can begin. This power has been used by presidents in transportation and coal strikes.

The Landrum–Griffin Act: The Labor–Management Reporting and Disclosure Act of 1959

Review the Landrum–Griffin Act:
http://www.law.cornell.edu/uscode/29/ch11.html

As unions grew, evidence of corruption and undemocratic procedures within them came to light. The **Landrum-Griffin Act** was passed to ensure employee protection within union organizations. The act gave union members a bill of rights, required certain procedures for election of officers, prescribed financial reporting requirements for union funds, and established criminal and civil penalties for union misconduct.

Visit the AFL-CIO:
http://www.aflcio.org

Today there are nearly 450 active unions in the United States, from the Screen Actors Guild to the Airline Pilots Association. However, over 75 percent of these unions are affiliated with the AFL-CIO (the American Federation of Labor and Congress of Industrial Organizations), the giant that resulted from the merger of the two original labor unions in 1955. These unions, however, make up only 13.9 percent of today's workforce (a steady figure since 1998), compared to 35 percent in 1955.

Union Organizing Efforts

Employees make the decision as to whether a union will represent them and, if so, which will serve as their representative. This process is called selecting a bargaining representative, and the NLRB has strict procedures for such selection. The NLRB carefully chooses how employees will be grouped together so that they share common interests.

The Collective Bargaining Unit

The first step in union organization is the establishment of a collective bargaining unit. The **collective bargaining unit** is a group of employees recognized by the NLRB as appropriate for exclusive representation of all employees in that group. Collective bargaining units are determined by the NLRB. The standard for a collective bargaining unit is that it must consist of homogeneous employees.

In determining the appropriateness of a collective bargaining unit, the NLRB considers the following factors:

1. The type of union and its history of bargaining—types of employees and types of industries
2. The duties, wages, and skills of the employees
3. How the bargaining unit fits in an employer's structure
4. The wishes of the employees

Some bargaining units consist of entire plants of workers, whereas others are specialized units within a plant, such as the maintenance staff or the line workers in an assembly plant. For some national companies, the bargaining unit is all employees, whereas for other national firms the bargaining unit is one particular plant or store. Defining the bargaining unit is crucial, for it can control whether the union will gain enough votes. A union might not have enough votes in a particular plant, but it could have enough votes if the unit were company-wide; in such cases, the union will want the larger bargaining unit.

CONSIDER... 19.2

Trump Taj Mahal Associates, a limited partnership, operates the Trump Taj Mahal Casino Resort in Atlantic City, New Jersey. The entertainment department at the Taj Mahal Casino includes stage technicians, convention lounge technicians, and entertainment event technicians.

Trump maintains a list of approximately forty on-call or "casual" employees who are called in on an intermittent basis to perform the same technical functions as regular technical employees when there are not enough regular employees to perform the work. Trump maintains this casual list because the casino industry is regulated by the New Jersey Casino Control Commission, which requires employees to be "badged" or licensed. The lists and prequalifications enable Trump to draw from a pool of technicians who have already met certain procedural and technical requirements in order to satisfy short-term labor needs.

During the first eleven months of operation at the Taj Mahal Casino, Trump operated its entertainment department with three full-time stage technicians and five full-time convention lounge technicians, and did not employ any part-time technicians. About March 1, 1991, Trump increased its staff to twenty-eight full-time technicians and ten regular part-time technicians by hiring from the casual list. Trump selected those employees from the casual list who had worked the most hours at the Taj and had the necessary skills for the particular job. A number of casuals who had worked a considerable number of hours in the past remained on the casual list.

The 1990 list of casual employees entitled "entertainment technicians" shows that those employees worked from 30 to 952 hours during that year. The regional director found that during 1990 the casuals worked an average of 379 hours during the year, or approximately 7 hours a week, and during early 1991 the casuals worked an average of 119 hours, or approximately 17 hours a week.

The employees sought to have their collective bargaining unit expanded to include both the full-time technicians and the on-call (i.e., casual) employees.

Is this a proper bargaining unit? [*Trump Taj Mahal Associates Ltd.* v. *International Alliance of Theatrical Stage Employees,* 306 N.L.R.B. No. 57 (1992).]

The Petition, Cards, and Vote

Once the collective bargaining unit is set, the union, employees, or employers can file a petition for exclusive representation of employees within a unit. The petition is filed with the NLRB and must be supported by at least 30 percent of the members of the bargaining unit. The 30 percent support is shown by signed and dated **authorization cards** filled out by employees. These authorization cards must be signed willingly, and the employee must understand the effect of the cards.

Once the cards are filed, an employer has two choices. First, the employer can voluntarily recognize the union. If the union has obtained authorization cards from a majority of the employees, such recognition is wise unless the employer knows of some illegal conduct used to obtain the cards.

If the authorization cards do not amount to a majority of employees in the bargaining unit, the employer can insist on a formal election. In an election, the employees vote for or against the union that petitions for representation and has the right to campaign and distribute literature before an upcoming election. However, employers can prohibit oral campaigning during work hours and can restrict literature distribution both during and, to a degree, before and after work hours. Employer restrictions cannot be imposed so as to limit possibility of the union. The restrictions must be reasonable and serve some purpose, such as controlling litter and requiring employees to do their work during their work hours.

The election is conducted by secret ballot by the NLRB. A simple majority of the employees must vote in favor of the union for certification to occur.

CONSIDER...   19.3

The Republic Aviation Plant in Suffolk County, New York, was holding a union certification election. The plant had adopted, well before any union activity, a rule against soliciting that provided: "Soliciting of any type cannot be permitted in the factory or offices."

An employee who had been reminded of the rule persisted in passing out cards to fellow employees during his lunch hour. Three other employees wore UAW-CIO union buttons to work and were asked to remove them, but they refused. All four employees were discharged. The four filed a complaint with the NLRB on grounds they had been denied the right to distribute information about the union. Did the plant rule violate the employees' right to distribute information? [*Republic* v. *NLRB*, 324 U.S. 793 (1945).]

Certification

Once **certification** of a union has taken place, either because of the employer's consent or a valid election, that union has the exclusive right to represent the employees in all contract negotiations. An employer who refuses to deal with the certified union can be forced to by an injunction obtained by the NLRB.

After a union has been certified, an election for a new union cannot be held for twelve months from the time of certification. If the union signs a collective bargaining agreement, no union certification election can be held until the collective bargaining agreement expires. These limitations on elections and certifications prevent chaos in the workplace that would result from constant changeovers in union representation. Exhibit 19.3 summarizes the steps in the union certification process.

Nonunion Members in the Certified Workplace   Although the NLRA gave unions the right to exist, it also gave workers the right to a choice. Workers are not required to join unions and cannot be coerced into supporting union action. Attempts by a union to force its members to participate in strikes and other union activities are considered unfair labor practices. *Pattern Makers' League of North America, AFL-CIO* v. *NLRB* (Case 19.4) is an interpretation of whether a union coerced employees into participating in a strike.

EXHIBIT   19.3 Union Certification

CASE 19.4

Pattern Makers' League of North America, AFL–CIO v. NLRB
473 U.S. 95 (1985)

You Can't Make Me Strike If I Want to Work

FACTS

The Pattern Makers' League of North America, AFL-CIO, provides in its constitution that union members may not resign during a strike or when a strike is imminent. The league fined ten of its members who, in violation of this provision, resigned during a strike and returned to work. The NLRB held that the union rule violated section 8(b) of the NLRA, which provides: "It shall be an unfair labor practice for a labor organization or its agents—(1) to restrain or coerce (A) employees in the exercise of rights guaranteed herein. . . ."

The union rule (League Law 13) provides: "No resignation or withdrawal from an Association or from the League shall be accepted during a strike or lockout, or at a time when a strike or lockout appears imminent."

The U.S. court of appeals for the Seventh Circuit enforced the board's order. The league appealed.

JUDICIAL OPINION

POWELL, Justice
Section 7 of (the NLRA) grants employees the right to "refrain from any or all (concerted) activities." The general right is implemented by § 8(b)(a)(A). The latter section provides that a union commits an unfair labor practice if it "restrains or coerces employees in the exercise" of their § 7 rights. When employee members of a union refuse to support a strike (whether or not a rule prohibits returning to work during a strike), they are refraining from "concerted activity." Therefore, imposing fines on these employees for returning to work "restrains" the exercise of their § 7 rights. Indeed, if the terms "refrain" and "restrain or coerce" are interpreted literally, fining employees to enforce compliance with any union rule or policy would violate the Act.

Language and reasoning from other opinions of this Court confirm that the Board's construction of § 8(b)(1)(A) is reasonable. In *Scofield* v. *NLRB,* 394 U.S. 423 (1969), the Court upheld a union rule setting a ceiling on the daily wages that members working on an incentive basis could earn. The union members' freedom to resign was critical to the Court's decision that the union rule did not "restrain or coerce" the employees within the meaning of § 8(b)(1)(A).

The decision in *NLRB* v. *Textile Workers,* 409 U.S. 213 (1972) also supports the Board's view that Section 8 prohibits unions from punishing members not free to resign. There, thirty-one employees resigned their union membership and resumed working during a strike. We held that fining these former members "restrained or coerced" them. In reaching this conclusion, we said "the vitality of Section 7 requires that the member be free to refrain in November from the actions he endorsed in May."

League Law 13 curtails (the) freedom to resign from full union membership. Nevertheless, the petitioners (League) contend that League Law 13 does not contravene the policy of voluntary unionism imbedded in the Act. They assert that this provision does not interfere with workers' employment rights because offending members are not discharged, but only fined. We find this argument unpersuasive, for a union has not left a "worker's employment rights inviolate when it exacts (his entire) paycheck in satisfaction of a fine imposed for working." Congress in 1947 (with the Taft-Hartley Act) sought to eliminate completely any requirement that the employee maintain full union membership. Therefore, the Board was justified in concluding that by restricting the right of employees to resign, League Law 13 impairs the policy of voluntary unionism.

Petitioners . . . argue that the proviso to § 8(b)(1)(A) expressly allows unions to place restrictions on the right to resign.

Neither the Board nor this Court has ever interpreted the proviso as allowing unions to make rules restricting the right to resign. Rather, the Court has assumed that "rules with respect to the . . . retention of membership" are those that provide for expulsion of employees from the union. Accordingly, we find no basis for refusing to defer to the Board's conclusion that League Law 13 is not a "rule with respect to the retention of membership" within the meaning of the proviso.

The petitioners next argue that the legislative history of the Taft-Hartley Act shows that Congress made a considered decision not to protect union members' right to resign.

The legislative history does not support this contention. The "right to resign" apparently was included in the original House bill to protect workers unable to resign because of "closed shop" agreements. Union constitutions limiting the right to resign were uncommon in 1947.

The Board has the primary responsibility for applying "the general provisions of the Act to the

continued

complexities of industrial life." Where the Board's construction of the Act is reasonable, it should not be rejected. . . . [T]he Board has consistently construed § 8(b)(1)(A) as prohibiting the imposition of fines on employees who have tendered resignations invalid under a union constitution. Therefore we conclude that the Board's decision here is entitled to our deference.
   Affirmed.

CASE QUESTIONS

1. What union rule is at issue?
2. Does the rule affect union membership?
3. Can the union enforce the rule?
4. What is the purpose of § 8(b)(1)(A)?
5. Does the legislative history support a prohibition of the union rule?

Union Contract Negotiations

Once a union is certified as the employees' representative, one of its major roles is to obtain a contract or **collective bargaining agreement** between employer and employees. This section discusses the roles of the parties in obtaining that agreement.

Good–Faith Bargaining

Visit the U.S. Department of Labor:
http://www.dol.gov

Section 8(d) of the NLRA defines **good-faith bargaining** as a mutual obligation of employer and union to meet at reasonable times, confer in good faith on employment issues, and execute a written agreement reflecting their oral agreement. Both parties must bargain with an open mind and the sincere intent of reaching an agreement.

Whether there has been good-faith bargaining on the part of the parties depends on each situation and on various factors, such as the reasonableness of the position taken, repeated failures to show up at bargaining sessions or to be available for them, and holding steadfast to a predetermined position during the course of bargaining. Most of the cases dealing with the problem of failure to bargain in good faith are the result of employer conduct.

Subject Matter of Good–Faith Bargaining

Two types of subject matters can be discussed during bargaining: (1) mandatory or compulsory subject matter and (2) permissive subject matter. As to the former, the NLRA describes **mandatory bargaining terms** as those dealing with "wages, hours, and other terms and conditions of employment." Obviously, the amount to be paid as wages is included but so also are related issues, such as merit pay, vacations, overtime, work hours, leaves, and pay days. Exhibit 19.4 lists the usual topics covered in a collective bargaining agreement.

One of the issues that has been a subject of good-faith bargaining is the two-tier wage structure. In the past, unions have agreed to two-tier wage structures in order

EXHIBIT   19.4 Usual Topics for a Collective Bargaining Agreement

COLLECTIVE BARGAINING TOPICS		
Recognition of the union	Insurance	Union announcements
Wages	Pension/retirement plans	(bulletin board rights)
Work hours	Employee grievances	Definition of terms
Vacations	Length of agreement/	Leaves of absence
Sick leave	expiration date	Drug testing
Seniority	Incentive plans	

to help financially struggling firms survive. Now, however, many corporations are raising the issue in bargaining in order to control wage increases. For example, in the airline industry, pilots with the greatest seniority work under a wage structure that affords them very high pay levels. But more pilots are available now than before, and some new pilots are willing to enter employment under a different wage and age scale. Although there are many management and labor concerns about a two-tier structure, it appears to be a good-faith bargaining topic that will remain an issue for both groups.

Permissive subject matters, in contrast to compulsory subject matters, would be those the parties are required to negotiate but on which they need not reach an agreement. A strike vote of employees before a strike starts is an example of a permissive subject. Any topic that does not directly concern employer-employee relations is a permissive subject. A refusal to bargain on a permissive subject is not, however, an unfair labor practice; a refusal to bargain on mandatory subject matter *is* an unfair labor practice.

Some subjects are "unbargainable." Employers and employees cannot bargain to give away statutory rights—for example, the procedures for certifying a union. Nor can they bargain about having a **closed shop**, which requires employees to be union members before they can be hired. Such shops are illegal under the Taft-Hartley Act.

CONSIDER... 19.4

Are insurance plans a mandatory, permissive, or nonbargainable topic?

THINK: The law says that the terms and conditions of employment are mandatory collective bargaining topics.

APPLY: Insurance is a term and condition of employment—it determines the level of employee benefits.

ANSWER: Insurance plans are a mandatory topic.

Now determine whether the following subjects are mandatory, permissive, or nonbargainable:
- Maternity leaves
- Plant rules
- Subcontracting procedures
- Strikes
- Layoffs
- Union bookkeeping procedures
- Meal periods

CONSIDER... 19.5

E. I. Du Pont de Nemours & Company is renegotiating its contract with the International Brotherhood of Du Pont Workers. Two issues have arisen during the course of bargaining. The union has asked Du Pont to release a map that was developed as a result of a Du Pont study on its toxic waste locations. The second issue was Du Pont's implementation of its business ethics policy and its application to union members without its being a subject of bargaining. Must the map be released? Is this a mandatory subject? Must the application of the ethics policy be negotiated? [*Du Pont v. International Bhd. of Du Pont Workers*, 301 N.L.R.B. No. 14 (1991).]

Failure to Bargain in Good Faith

Failure to bargain on mandatory subject matter is an **unfair labor practice**, which is conduct prohibited by statute or NLRB decision. If there is a failure to bargain on a mandatory topic, a charge can be brought and the NLRB can proceed with a complaint.

Protected Concerted Activities

The following forms of union activities are protected under the NRLA as being necessary for union members to give each other "mutual aid and protection," as it is expressed in the statute.

Public Advertisements

Ads and handbills that explain the union's issues and position are permitted and can be an effective tool for obtaining boycotts, yet another protected activity in which employees encourage customers not to deal with their employer until the strike is settled.

Picketing

A union currently recognized as a certified collective bargaining agent can engage in **picketing** an employer, but picketing for recognition of a union is not permitted.

The Strike

The **strike** is the best known and most widely used economic weapon of unions. A strike is a work stoppage because employees no longer report to work. As a result of replacement threats and downsizing, strikes in 1995 were at a level one-half of that in 1985.

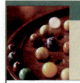

BUSINESS STRATEGY

Unions, Employees, Employers, and E-Mails

The issue of the use of e-mail continues to be problematic for the NLRB, employers, and union organizers. All recognize the efficiency of e-mail contact because, according to the U.S. Census, as of the end of 2003, an estimated 52 percent of all Americans have access to a private computer for viewing private e-mail. Both unions and employers would benefit from such direct contact.

© JIM ARBOGAST/PHOTODISC/GETTY IMAGES

However, clear statements of the law allow employers to control access of union members to employees while they are on the job so that there is no interference with their work or disruption of facilities. If union organizers cannot enter the plant to distribute pamphlets and buttons, they cannot invade the company e-mail and have employees use company time to read their messages.

However, some scholars have proposed a solution to the dilemma of efficient communication and rights under the law.

- Use employees' private e-mail accounts for contact, not their work e-mails. The employer's e-mail system need not be used or taxed as a result.

- If employees reading private e-mails while on the job becomes a problem, employers can issue a generic policy of no private e-mails while at work. This way they will not run into any accusations or issues over singling out unions and union organizers for different treatment.

The Shareholders

In recent years, unions have developed a new economic tool—contacting institutional shareholders and board members to put public pressure on corporate officers to work with unions. These public-attention tactics have been effective.

Unfair Employee Practices

While employees have certain rights protected under Section 8 of the NLRA, they are also prohibited from engaging in activities that are classified as unfair labor practices.

Hot Cargo Agreements

A clause in a collective bargaining agreement in which an employer agrees not to use, handle, or sell certain products or use the services of an unfair employer is a **hot cargo agreement**. In some cases, the agreement prohibits an employer from handling the products of a nonunion company. Because these types of agreements are rarely voluntary, they have been prohibited, with some exceptions for the clothing and construction industries.

The Slowdown

A **slowdown** is an economic tool that interrupts the employer's business but falls short of a stoppage or strike. Slowdowns usually occur when employees refuse to perform work or use certain equipment that is in violation of their collective bargaining agreement with the employer. For example, in early 1999, American Airlines pilots staged a slowdown by calling in sick, known as a sickout. After more than 1,000 flights per day were canceled, a federal court ordered the pilots to halt their slowdown.

ETHICAL ISSUES

There is a new trend among employers to rank employees as part of their annual performance evaluations. For example, Ford Motor Company has 18,000 managers who are grouped into sets of 30 to 50. Of each group, 10 percent must be assigned an "A" grade, 80 percent must be assigned a "B" grade, and 10 percent must be given a "C" grade. Those with the bottom grades are then eased out of the company. Those with a "C" grade cannot be given a pay raise, and those with a "C" grade for two years in a row are demoted or terminated. There are no exceptions made for any of the groups, but Ford did cut back on the "C" requirement to 5% for 2001.

Other companies with grading systems include Sun Microsystems. Employees given a "C" there are given ninety days to improve. If they do not improve, they are given one chance to resign and take a severance package or risk termination.

Cisco Systems has established a goal of getting rid of one of every twenty employees with the focus being on employees given substandard performance evaluations.

GE has a 20–70–10 plan for ranking employees. GE follows a carrot approach in that it rewards the top 20 percent so well that few ever leave the company. GE uses the 10 percent group to terminate employees, and it terminates about 8,000 management and professional employees each year. Jack Welch has noted that these in the 10 percent would end up leaving the company anyway because they are unhappy in not performing, and GE just makes the inevitable decision for them early.

Workers' rights groups call the systems inhumane. Some say that instead of motivating employees to do better, the result is that they are demoralized and do worse or leave the company.

Do these systems violate any laws? Are they a mandatory collective bargaining issue? Are you comfortable with them from the perspective of business ethics?

Source: Del Jones, "More Firms Cut Workers Ranked at the Bottom to Make Way for Talent," *USA Today*, May 30, 2001, pp. 1B, 2B.

Featherbedding

Featherbedding is payment for work not actually performed. It is an unfair labor practice for a union to negotiate an agreement that requires an employer to pay for work that was not actually performed. For example, some bricklayers' unions at one time required payment for a minimum number of bricks even though the work might not have actually involved that many bricks. Other examples include paying workers for tasks completed by someone else. An agreement requiring payment for the task of pressing in a clothing manufacturing firm would be unfair if the clothing was sometimes shipped unpressed.

Secondary Boycotts

The **primary boycott** is a protected economic weapon of unions, but the concept of a **secondary boycott** is a complex and difficult one. Nonetheless, asking a third party not to handle an employer's goods appears to be unfair only if there is coercion involved. Further, the request cannot be one to stop work—it must be simply a request that the third party cease doing business with the employer.

CONSIDER...   19.6

Local 760 of the Teamsters Union called a strike against fruit packers and warehouses doing business in Yakima, Washington. The firms sold their apples to the Safeway chain of retail grocery stores. Local 760 began a consumer boycott against the firms, with union members picketing outside the forty-six Safeway stores in Seattle. The pickets wore placards that read: "To the Consumer: Non-Union Washington State apples are being sold at this store. Please do not purchase such apples. Thank you. Teamsters Local 760, Yakima, Washington."

The pickets distributed handbills outside the stores and to the public generally. A typical handbill read:

DON'T BUY WASHINGTON STATE APPLES

The 1960 Crop of Washington State Apples is being Packed by Non-Union Firms. Included in this non-union operation are twenty-six firms in the Yakima Valley with which there is a labor dispute. These firms are charged with being

UNFAIR

by their employees who, with their union, are on strike and have been *replaced by non-union strikebreaking workers* employed under substandard wage scales and working conditions.
In justice to these striking union workers who are attempting to protect their living standards and their right to engage in good-faith collective bargaining, we request that you

DON'T BUY WASHINGTON STATE APPLES

Teamsters Union Local 760
Yakima, Washington
This is not a strike against any store or market.

Is the action taken by Local 760 an unfair labor practice, or is it a proper secondary boycott? [*NLRB* v. *Fruit Packers*, 377 U.S. 58 (1964).]

Employer Rights

Freedom of Speech

Employers have the right to give information to employees about unions and the results of union organization. The speech of employers cannot be controlled by the NLRB unless the speech is accompanied by some unlawful conduct, such as a threat of physical force or a promise of benefit. For example, an employer who threatens the loss of jobs if employees join the union is not protected by the free speech rule. An employer who tells employees that it will not negotiate with a union is also not protected by the free speech rule. These types of statements are considered unfair labor practices, as is the promise of temporary benefits.

Exhibit 19.5 is a summary of management dos and don'ts when faced with an upcoming union election.

Right-to-Work Laws

Section 14(b) of the Taft-Hartley Act is in some ways a protection for employers as well as for employees. This section outlaws the closed shop, which, as discussed earlier, is a business that requires union membership before an employee can be hired. Based on this section of Taft-Hartley, states can pass **right-to-work laws** that give people the right to work without having to join a union. About half the states have right-to-work statutes.

Right to an Enforceable Collective Bargaining Agreement

Once a union is certified and agrees to the terms of a collective bargaining agreement, an employer has the right to expect that the terms of that agreement will be honored. So long as the employer abides by its terms, the union and other employees cannot stage a strike during the period of its effectiveness. Neither can the agreement be abandoned by employees during this period.

EXHIBIT 19.5 Management Dos and Don'ts in the Unionization Process

DO	DON'T
1. Tell employees about current wages and benefits and how they compare to other firms.	1. Promise employees pay increases or promotions if they vote against the union.
2. Tell employees you will use all legal means to oppose unionization.	2. Threaten employees with termination or discriminate when disciplining employees.
3. Tell employees the disadvantages of having a union (especially cost of dues, assessments, and requirements of membership).	3. Threaten to close down or move the company if a union is voted in.
4. Show employees articles about unions and negative experiences others have had elsewhere.	4. Spy or have someone spy on union meetings.
5. Explain the unionization process to your employees accurately.	5. Make a speech to employees or groups at work within twenty-four hours of the election (before that, it is allowed).
6. Forbid distribution of union literature during work hours in work areas.	6. Ask employees how they plan to vote or if they have signed authorization cards.
7. Enforce in a consistent and fair manner disciplinary policies and rules.	7. Urge local employees to persuade others to vote against the union (such a vote must be initiated solely by the employee).

Source: R. L. Mathis and J. H. Jackson, *Human Resource Management*, 8th ed, p. 533. © 1997. Reprinted with permission of South-Western College Publishing, a division of International Thomson Publishing. Fax 800-730-2215.

BUSINESS STRATEGY

Striking When the Riches Don't Come

In 1982, Gilmore Steel, located in Oregon, was a company suffering losses. Management tried to get concessions from the union for pay reductions, and a year-long strike resulted. Gilmore hired replacement workers and then developed a plan for a management-led buyout. The Employee Share Ownership Plan offered the newly hired employees 100 percent ownership in what would become Oregon Steel. Top management in the firm would own less than 5 percent, and employees as shareholders would receive 20 percent of the company's pre-tax earnings in profit sharing. Management perks and time clocks were eliminated, and shop-floor workers were placed on the same compensation system as the top executives.

© DANNY LEHMAN/CORBIS

The initial years were tough; it looked as if the buyout was a failure. By 1988 the company had gone public. The employees' shares that were once worth only pennies climbed to $38 a share. Oregon Steel's profits per ton are now the best in the industry. It has no debt, and productivity is double the steel industry average. Average pay for workers is $50,000, which is 25 percent above the industry average, and many of the employees are millionaires.

Did the union do the right thing with the strike? Are employees better off without union representation? What if the gamble the employees took had not worked?

Economic Weapons of Employers

Employers have economic weapons that can be used in response to employee economic weapons.

Plant and Business Closings

In response to union certifications and strikes, some employers have opted to close the affected plants. In some cases, employers have abandoned the business altogether. It is clear that these shutdowns and closures are strong economic weapons, and their legality under the federal labor law scheme has some restrictions. In *Textile Workers Union* v. *Darlington Manufacturing Co.*, 380 U.S. 263 (1965), the Supreme Court ruled that employers have the right to terminate their entire business for any reason. Even if the reason for the closing is vindictiveness toward the union, neither the NLRB nor the courts can require an employer to stay in business. However, the closing of part of a business (such as a particular plant or one store) is subject to review as a possible unfair labor practice.

Employers cannot use a temporary closing with a promise of reopening after a union is defeated in an election. Further, employers cannot stage a **runaway shop**, which is when work is transferred to another plant or a new plant is opened to carry the workload of the old plant.

The concern of the NLRB in the closing of one plant is that employees in other plants, fearful that their plants will be closed, will fail to exercise their rights to unionize. For a plant closure to be an unfair labor practice, the evidence must show that the closure was done with the intent of curbing unionization in that and other plants owned by the employer. The "purpose and effect" of the closing must have been foreclosure of union activity.

Review the Worker Adjustment and Retraining Notification Act:
http://www.law.cornell. edu/uscode/29/2101.html

Federal plant-closing legislation is called the **Worker Adjustment and Retraining Notification Act of 1988** (WARN). Under this act, employers with 100 or more workers are required to give workers sixty days' advance notice of plant shutdowns that would affect at least 50 workers and of layoffs that would last more than six months and affect one-third of the workers at the site. There are some exceptions to the sixty-day notice requirement, such as unforeseeable circumstances and seasonal, agricultural, and construction businesses. Penalties for violations include back pay and benefits for employees for each day of violation and up to $500 per day for each day notice was not given.

Some businesses voluntarily provide for the workers at a closed plant by giving them hiring priority at their other plant locations, but unions often argue that the ability to close a plant gives employers too much power at the bargaining table and that employers can coerce communities into giving them special tax treatment or additional services by threatening to close a facility. On the other hand, employers often argue that plant-closing laws unfairly restrict their ability to manage their resources and can force a business to continue operating an unprofitable unit rather than face the costs of closing.

Plant Flight

One result of the increased globalization of business is the increasing availability of lower-cost labor pools outside the United States. When union demands increase business costs beyond what management feels will allow a firm to remain competitive, plants are closed and work is transferred to plants outside the United States. The global marketplace provides management with a bargaining tool that becomes difficult for unions to address. Demands for wage increases, more benefits, and better working conditions are often met with a plant closing in the United States and a plant opening in another country where the labor pool is large and the wages low.

ETHICAL ISSUES

Bleeding from losses of $4.45 billion for 1991, General Motors Corporation (GM) announced on February 24, 1992, that it would close 21 plants over the next few years and named 12 plants it would close in 1992, affecting over 16,300 workers. GM is the nation's largest manufacturer, and the $4.45 billion loss was the largest ever in U.S. corporate history. Robert C. Stempel, GM's then chairman, said the United States was in an unusually deep automotive slump: "The rate of change during the past year was unprecedented. And no one was immune to the extraordinary events which affected our lives and the way in which we do business."*

More than 3,400 workers at GM's North Tarrytown, New York, plant were laid off by 1995. The Tarrytown plant manufactured GM's minivans: the Chevrolet Lumina, the Pontiac Trans Sport, and the Oldsmobile Silhouette. The minivan, originally designed in the United States, was executed by GM with a wide stance and a sloping, futuristic nose. Projections were that 150,000–200,000 of the vans would be sold annually. Instead, sales reached only 100,000 per year, which represented one-half of the Tarrytown plant's capacity. Dealers maintained that the shape of the van was too avant-garde for

significant sales. "It looks like a Dustbuster," noted a GM manager anonymously.† GM executives acknowledged that building one model per plant was a sloppy and expensive way to do business.

Tarrytown United Auto Workers had negotiated with GM in 1987 to get the minivan plant. The union members voted for innovative and cooperative work rules to replace expensive union practices. Also, state and local governments contributed job training funds, gave tax breaks, and began reconstruction of railroad bridges to win the minivan production plant.

When unions (workers) and governments make payments in exchange for promises from a manufacturer to locate a plant in a particular area, should the plant owner have an obligation to continue operations? Did GM just make a business decision to stop losses? Should workers and governments absorb business risks such as a poor-selling minivan?

*Doran P. Levin, "GM Picks 12 Plants to Be Shut as It Reports a Record U.S. Loss," *New York Times,* February 25, 1992, p. A1.
†Doran P. Levin, "Vehicle's Design Doomed Van Plant," *New York Times,* February 26, 1992, p. C4.

The Lockout

A **lockout** is an employer's economic weapon in which the employer refuses to allow employees to work. Lockouts have been recognized by the U.S. Supreme Court as a legitimate measure to help an employer avoid a strike at an economically damaging time. The reason for an employer's lockout must be economic. A lockout to discourage union membership, therefore, is an unfair labor practice.

Conferring Benefits

Employers can use benefits as economic weapons; the only restriction is the timing of those benefits. Offering them too close to an election can be an unfair labor practice. Conferring benefits on a temporary basis to gain an advantage (precluding the union) is also an unfair labor practice.

Bankruptcy

Bankruptcy has become a solution for many business problems, labor problems among them. When strikes extend for long periods of time, the financial well-being of the firms affected can deteriorate, often to the degree that some firms declare bankruptcy. The type of bankruptcy proceedings initiated will determine the fate of labor contracts. In a reorganization, the contracts remain in force. In a straight bankruptcy, the workers stand in line (although with some priority) to collect any wages due and any contributions made to the firm's retirement plan. Bankruptcy can be an escape for a firm, but the bankruptcy laws themselves limit the availability of this economic weapon. The firm must still meet the tests for declaring bankruptcy, so the weapon is not entirely optional.

Exhibit 19.6 provides a summary of labor weapons, rights, and unfair practices.

EXHIBIT   19.6   Union Disputes: Economic Weapons and Rights of Employers and Employees

ECONOMIC WEAPONS	RIGHTS	UNFAIR LABOR PRACTICES
Employer		
1. Business closing Plant closings	1. Freedom of speech	1. Refusal to bargain in good faith
	2. Demand election (30%)	2. Refusal to bargain on a mandatory issue
2. Lockouts		3. Yellow-dog contracts
3. Right to confer benefits (timing)		4. Violation of collective bargaining agreement
		5. Interference with joining union
		6. Timing of benefits
		7. Observation of union activities
		8. Domination of labor union
		9. Discrimination in promotion of union members
		10. Blacklisting
Employee		
1. Strike	1. Freedom of speech	1. Violation of collective bargaining agreement
2. Ads	2. Right to union representation upon investigation	2. Secondary boycotts
3. Picketing		3. Payment for union cards
4. Boycotts	3. Right to join union	4. Coercion or discrimination in union membership
5. Shareholders	4. Right of members to adequate representation	5. Causing an employer to pay excessive wages— featherbedding
	5. Right to union office	6. Hot cargo agreements

BIOGRAPHY

AARON FEUERSTEIN: AN ODD CEO

Methuen, Massachusetts, is a small city not unlike the Bedford Falls of *It's a Wonderful Life.* Over the years, the working-class town on the border of New Hampshire and Massachusetts has come to rely on the good heart of one man. While Aaron Feuerstein may not look much like Jimmy Stewart, he is the protagonist of a Christmas story every bit as warming as the Frank Capra movie—or the Polartec fabric made at his Malden Mills.

On the night of December 11, just as Feuerstein was being thrown a surprise 70th birthday party, a boiler at Malden Mills exploded, setting off a fire that injured 27 people and destroyed three of the factory's century-old buildings. Because Malden Mills employs 2,400 people in an economically depressed area, the news was as devastating as the fire. According to Paul Coorey, the president of Local 311 of the Union of Needletrades, Industrial and Textile Employees, "I was standing there seeing the mill burn with my son, who also works there, and he looked at me and said, 'Dad, we just lost our jobs.' Years of our lives seemed gone."

When Feuerstein arrived to assess the damage to a business his grandfather had started 90 years ago, he kept himself from crying by thinking back to the passage from *King Lear* in which Lear promises not to weep even though his heart would "break into a thousand flaws." "I was telling myself I have to be creative," Feuerstein later told the *New York Times.* "Maybe there's some way to get out of it." Feuerstein, who reads from both his beloved Shakespeare and the Talmud almost every night, has never been one to run away. When many other textile manufacturers in New England fled to the South and to foreign countries, Malden Mills stayed put. When a reliance on fake fur bankrupted the company for a brief period in the early '80s, Feuerstein sought out alternatives.

What brought Malden Mills out of bankruptcy was its research-and-development team, which came up with a revolutionary fabric that was extremely warm, extremely light, quick to dry, and easy to dye. Polartec is also ecologically correct because it is made from recycled plastic bottles. Clothing made with Polartec or a fraternal brand name, Synchilla, is sold by such major outdoor clothiers as L. L. Bean, Patagonia, Eastern Mountain Sports, and Eddie Bauer, and it accounts for half of Malden's $400 million-plus in 1995 sales.

Even though the stock of a rival textile manufacturer in Tennessee, the Dyersburg Corp., rose sharply the day after the fire, L. L. Bean and many of Malden's other customers pledged their support. Another apparel company, Dakotah, sent Feuerstein a $30,000 check. The Bank of Boston sent $50,000, the union $100,000, the Chamber of Commerce in the surrounding Merrimack Valley $150,000. "The money is not for Malden Mills," says Feuerstein. "It is for the Malden Mills employees. It makes me feel wonderful. I have hundreds of letters at home from ordinary people, beautiful letters with dollar bills, $10 bills."

The money was nothing to the workers compared to what Feuerstein gave them three days later. On the night of December 14, more than 1,000 employees gathered at the gym of Central Catholic High School to learn the fate of their jobs. Feuerstein entered the gym from the back, and as he shook the snow off his coat, the murmurs turned to cheers. The factory owner, who had already given out $275 Christmas bonuses and pledged to rebuild, walked to the podium. "I will get right to my announcement," he said. "For the next 30 days—and it might be more—all our employees will be paid their full salaries." What followed, after a moment of awe, was a scene of hugging and cheering that would have trumped the cinematic celebration for *Wonderful Life's* George Bailey.

True to his word, Feuerstein has continued to pay his employees in full, at a cost of some $1.5 million a week and at an average of $12.50 an hour—already one of the highest textile wages in the world. "I really haven't done anything," says Feuerstein. "I don't deserve credit. Corporate America has made it so that when you behave the way I did, it's abnormal."

AFTERMATH: On January 29, 1996, Mr. Feuerstein extended the pay guarantee for another 30 days as he continued the process of rebuilding the plant. He continued the employees' medical benefits for 90 days. Mr. Feuerstein continued the pay guarantee through June 1996, when nearly all employees were back to full-time status. Those employees who were not fully employed were those displaced by the rebuilt factory's new technology. Mr. Feurstein developed on-site retraining and retooling for these employees, and Malden Mills has a near 100% outplacement record for these former employees. By the time the mill was reopened and functioning at 100%, Mr. Feuerstein had paid out about $25 million in wages to his employees during downtime. The grand reopening of the fully rebuilt plant was in September

continued

1997. Polartec and the company performed well for a time, riding on the goodwill of Mr. Feuerstein's actions following the fire. However, Mr. Feuerstein did enjoy his first litigation by employees in 1998 over employment practices. He admitted to being stunned by the suit. Further, he realized the strategic error his company made when it did not patent PolarTec. Competition became quite fierce as others developed and sold the same product.

Near the end of 2001, Malden Mills was teetering near bankruptcy. The union, about to negotiate a new agreement, indicated it would agree to whatever Mr. Feuerstein wanted in order to save the company. By 2002, Malden Mills was in bankruptcy. Feuerstein labored to raise the money to pay off creditors and buy his company back, but he was unable to meet the bankruptcy deadline. Malden Mills emerged from bankruptcy on September 30, 2003, but under management other than Mr. Feuerstein. He still hopes to buy the company back, but the price, originally $93 million, has increased to $120 million. Feuerstein is the president of Malden Mills, serves on its board, and earns a salary of $425,000 per year, but he is no longer in charge and cannot be until the creditors are repaid. In January 2004, members of the U.S. House and Senate were lobbying to convince the Export-Import Bank to loan Mr. Feuerstein the money he needed to buy back his company. The Export-Import Bank, swayed by Mr. Feuerstein's commitment to keep Malden's production in the United States, increased the loan amount from the $20 million it had originally pledged to the $35 million Mr. Feuerstein needed.

By the end of January 2004, Malden Mills had three new strategies: Mr. Feuerstein was selling Polarfleece blankets on QVC, the company would be in partnership in China with Shanghai Mills, and the company announced it would expand its military contracts. Mr. Feuerstein remains as president and chairman of the board.

Issues

1. Why did Mr. Feuerstein choose to continue paying his employees?
2. Do you think Mr. Feuerstein emphasized ethics too much?

Source: Steve Wulf, "The Glow from a Fire," *Time,* January 8, 1996, p. 49. © 1996 Time Inc. Reprinted with permission.

MAKING ETHICS PERSONAL

Take the Money and Run or Take it and Stay?

If you were Mr. Feuerstein, would you have rebuilt the factory or just taken the insurance money and retired?

How do you think he felt when the workers demanded more after what he had done for them?

INTERNATIONAL ISSUES IN LABOR

Today's labor market is considerably different from the market that existed at the time of the enactment of federal labor legislation. Both operations within the United States and operations in other countries are affected by a new international labor force. Domestic operations must be certain that all employees from other countries are documented workers. International operations present numerous ethical and public policy issues in the conditions and operations of plants in other countries with different labor standards.

Immigration Laws

The **Immigration and Naturalization Act** (INA), the **Immigration Reform and Control Act of 1986** (IRCA), and the **Immigration Act of 1990** (8 U.S.C. § 11101 et seq.) are the federal laws that apply to immigrants in the United States and impose requirements on employers in the United States that employ immigrants. The Immigration Act of 1990, or IMMACT 90, increased legal immigration by 35 percent, enabled more family-sponsored immigration, and increased employment-based immigration, while providing a "diversity" program to increase the number of immigrants from countries traditionally underrepresented in the U.S. immigrant mix (e.g., Ireland and some African countries). This program is also known as the "green card visa lottery."

View more statistics on immigration, employment, citizenship, and deportation:
http://www.uscis.gov

In 1996, two federal statutes changed dramatically the issues of immigration, deportation, and penalties for hiring illegal immigrants: the **Illegal Immigration Reform and Immigrant Responsibility Act of 1996** and the **Antiterrorism and Effective Death Penalty Act** (18 U.S.C. § 1). The statutes served to increase the types and numbers of crimes that rendered illegal immigrants deportable from the United States and denied them entry from other countries. The statutes also decreased the defenses to deportation as well as the procedural protections for opposing deportation. In 1984, the U.S. government deported approximately 1,000 aliens in one year. In September 2003 alone, the **U.S. Department of Homeland Security** (DHS) deported 13,462 noncitizens from the United States; 5,598 of these were deemed criminals under the definitions in the statutes. Removals totaled more than 180,000 for 2003, a 22 percent increase. Of this total, more than 71,700 were criminal removals.

With the passage of the **Uniting and Strengthening America by Providing Appropriate Tools Required to Intercept and Obstruct Terrorism Act (USA Patriot Act**; 18 U.S.C. § 1) and the Homeland Security Act of 2002, the nature of immigration enforcement issues changed. These statutory changes created the new DHS, with a head who has cabinet level status. Immigration is now part of this new agency's jurisdiction and responsibilities. The Immigration and Naturalization Service (INS), originally housed within the U.S. Department of Justice, was abolished. INS's responsibilities have been divided into three separate bureaus under the DHS. The law enforcement bureaus of the INS were renamed **Immigration and Customs Enforcement** and **Customs and Border Protection.** The benefits side of INS was renamed U.S. Citizenship and Immigration Services. In addition, the USA Patriot Act toughened security clearances and background checks for nonimmigrant and immigrant admittance into the United States, tightened coordination between immigration-related government agencies, and increased the U.S. government's ability to track foreign nationals in the United States.

Before hiring a new employee, employers must verify that the employee is either a U.S. citizen or is permitted to work in the United States. All non-U.S. citizens must have an I-9 form on file with the employer. Form I-9 provides complete information about noncitizens and requires the employer to verify the information provided through an Alien Registration Card, commonly called a "green card." Verification of U.S. citizenship can be provided by a driver's license from a state in the United States, a Social Security card, or a U.S. passport. If someone with a foreign accent can provide evidence of U.S. citizenship, the employer is not permitted to question further or require additional documentation, for such would be an act of discrimination under the immigration laws.

Because of lobbying from the high-tech industries, Congress passed the **American Competitive and Workforce Investment Act of 1998** in order to increase the number of "highly skilled" workers who could enter the United States and stay for purposes of employment. The number of such highly skilled workers was increased on a sliding scale through the year 2000, and then Congress passed the

FOR THE MANAGER'S DESK

RE: THE PROCESS OF IMMIGRATION IN THE UNITED STATES

Under our double-check admissions system, foreign nationals wishing to enter the United States ordinarily must first obtain an appropriate visa at a U.S. consular post overseas. A visa is not a guarantee of entry to the United States, however. When a foreign national arrives at a port of entry, whether at an airport, seaport, or land border, an immigration inspector makes an independent determination whether the foreign national should be admitted to the United States. This process is known as "inspection." As discussed above, a person is not lawfully admitted to the United States until he/she has been inspected. A person may be physically on U.S. soil, but not be admitted yet. A person undergoing secondary inspection at an airport; a person in a car talking to an immigration inspector at a border crossing post; passengers on a ship in a U.S. harbor waiting to deboard: all these are examples of people physically in the United States who have not yet been inspected and admitted.

All foreign nationals seeking admission into the United States must undergo a security clearance name check against government databases.

The visa application process differs for nonimmigrants and immigrants. Nonimmigrants must prove that they are qualified for the visa category they are seeking. Upon arrival at the port of entry, the nonimmigrant applicant must present a passport and visa, if required, and may be asked questions bearing on eligibility for admission. If admitted, the nonimmigrant normally will be given an arrival-departure record (Form I-94), endorsed to show the visa status and period of admission. Form I-94, usually stapled to a passport page, is to be turned in when leaving the United States. CBP (Customs and Border Patrol) keeps a counterpart as a control.

A nonimmigrant may apply to USCIS to extend his or her stay in the United States or change to another nonimmigrant status. A change of status does not require a new visa if the foreign national will not be leaving the United States. But neither does it eliminate the need for a visa; if the foreign national goes abroad and wishes readmission in the new status, a visa in the new classification is required.

The immigrant admission process is usually more elaborate. Nearly all potential immigrants must be sponsored by a family member who is a U.S. citizen or resident foreign national, or a U.S. employer. The immigrant visa application is usually examined carefully and questions are sometimes put relating to its contents, but ultimately to the issue of admissibility. Admission is recorded in the passport, and the foreign national registration card is processed for later delivery to the foreign national, who becomes a lawful permanent resident when the inspection ends.

Technically, any foreign national who appears inadmissible to the CBP inspector at the port of entry is to be detained for a removal hearing. In practice, an inspector facing a long line will detour a questionable applicant to "secondary" inspection for more intensive interrogation. If the foreign national is not admitted there, the inspector may "defer" inspection to a later time at the local district office. The foreign national is usually paroled into the United States pending the deferred inspection. Alternatively, the inspector may serve the foreign national with a notice of removal hearing for determination of admissibility by an immigration judge.

In some circumstances an immigration inspector may permit a foreign national to withdraw his or her application for admission and return home. In that case, the foreign national's visa is canceled and the issuing consulate is advised of the circumstances. By withdrawing an application for admission a foreign national avoids the legal restrictions placed on those who have undergone removal procedures in the United States.

Source: Yale-Loehr, Stephen. Overview of U.S. Immigration Law. <http://www.twmlaw.com/resources/general20cont.htm> 10/22/2004. Reprinted with permission.

American Competitiveness in the Twenty-First Century Act of 2000 to increase the number of such workers through 2004. Also, under this statute, employers cannot lay off American employees within the ninety days following their submission of an application for entrance and employment of one of these highly skilled workers. Referred to as *H-1B professionals,* their pay scale is also controlled by the act so that their pay is equivalent to what an equally skilled U.S. worker would earn in the same position. This constraint on wages eliminates the incentive for companies to hire all foreign H-1B professionals at much lower salaries.

Working Conditions and International Labor Law

*Review the Labor Manage-
ment Cooperation Act:*
http://www.law.cornell.
edu/uscode/29/171.html

With the passage of GATT and NAFTA, a worldwide market has been emerging. Today's management is also different from the management in power at the time the labor laws were passed. From true adversaries always looking for a way to "win," labor and management have grown to realize the importance of a working relationship that seeks to avoid confrontation and the use of economic weapons. In 1978, Congress passed the **Labor Management Cooperation Act** (29 U.S.C. § 171), which was designed to use the Federal Mediation and Conciliation Service (set up in 1947) to encourage alternative solutions to labor disputes. The act allocated funds for the study of ways to increase communication and encourage the use of collective bargaining as a means for resolving disputes.

Companies today are using more conciliatory methods to balance the economic interests of management and labor. Labor law is moving from the strike to arbitration in advance of disputes.

Solutions to labor issues have been occurring outside the statutory protections and rights given in the massive union legislation of earlier decades. Employees have turned to an individual posture and have sought the protection of individual rights, such as employment at will (see Chapter 18 for a discussion of these individual rights).

BUSINESS STRATEGY APPLICATION

Be sure to do the exercise for this chapter on the book's Web site so that you can study various companies' policies and approaches to employee safety, rights, and relations.

Many employers have reorganized their companies around teams of employees to empower them and use their knowledge and ideas. Motorola and Ford are among team companies that let workers make key decisions. A concern raised by unions is that the mixing of labor and management violates the Wagner Act. For example, teams of workers at Electromation, Inc. in Elkhart, Indiana, determined that a wage hike should be skipped because of heavy losses and instead developed programs for absenteeism.

Foreign competition has made it difficult for unions to organize and for laborers to command more than minimum wage. Mexican laborers earn 70 cents an hour, and Chinese workers 8 cents. During the 1980s, 500,000 of the 1.2 million U.S. manufacturing jobs that were sent abroad were apparel and textile jobs.

*Review the International
Covenant on Economic,
Social, and Cultural Rights:*
http://www.umn.edu/
humanrts/instree/b2esc.htm

The United Nations Commission on Human Rights has developed the International Covenant on Economic, Social, and Cultural Rights. This covenant includes the right to work; join trade unions; enjoy leisure; earn a decent living; and receive education, medical care, and Social Security. Although this international covenant would carry with it the protections outlined in this chapter for U.S. workers, there is no enforcement of the covenant. Its real strength comes through documentation and disclosure of its violation.

*Visit the International Labour
Organization (ILO):*
http://www.ilo.org

One of the most successful organs of the United Nations is the International Labour Organization (ILO). This commission, founded in 1920, continues to work to develop such principles as the right to work, to join trade unions, and to have a safe work environment. Member nations submit reports on their nation's status and compliance with the standards of the ILO agreement.

Some nations have individual legislation for their workers. For example, Germany has its own OSHA-like agency for the administration of worker safety issues. Germany's agency has existed longer than OSHA and tends to experience more self-reporting by employers.

The National Labor Committee (NLC), an activist group, periodically releases information on conditions in foreign factories and the companies utilizing those factories. In 1998, the NLC issued a report that Liz Claiborne, Wal-Mart, Ann Taylor, Esprit, Ralph Lauren, J. C. Penney, and Kmart were using subcontractors in China that use Chinese women (between the ages of 17 and 25) to work sixty to ninety hours per week for as little as 13–23 cents per hour. The Chinese subcontractors do not pay overtime, house the workers in crowded dormitories, feed them a poor diet, and operate unsafe factories.

The Mariana Islands are currently a site of investigation by the Department of Interior for alleged indentured servitude of children as young as 14 in factories there. Wendy Doromal, a human rights activist, issued a report that workers there have tuberculosis and oozing sores. Approximately $820 million worth of clothing items are manufactured each year on the islands, which are a U.S. territory. Labels manufactured there include The Gap, Liz Claiborne, Banana Republic, J. C. Penney, Ralph Lauren, and Brooks Brothers.

U.S. companies' investments in foreign manufacturing in major developing nations like China, Indonesia, and Mexico have tripled in fifteen years to $56 billion, a figure that does not include the subcontracting work. In Hong Kong, Singapore, South Korea, and Taiwan, where plants make apparel, toys, shoes, and wigs, national incomes have risen from 10 percent to 40 percent of American incomes over the past ten years. In Indonesia, since the introduction of U.S. plants and subcontractors, the portion of malnourished children in the country has gone from one-half to one-third.

In a practice that is widely accepted in other countries, children ages 10 to 14 labor in factories for fifty or more hours per week. Their wages enable their families to survive. School is a luxury, and children attend only until they are able to work in a factory. The Gap, Levi Strauss, Esprit, and Leslie Fay have all been listed in social responsibility literature as exploiting their workers.

In the United States, the issue of sweatshops came to the public's attention when it was revealed that talk-show host Kathie Lee Gifford's line of clothing at Wal-Mart had been manufactured in sweatshops in Guatemala and CBS ran a report on conditions in Nike subcontractor factories in Vietnam and Indonesia. The reports on Nike's factories issued by Vietnam Labor Watch included the following: women required to run laps around the factory for wearing nonregulation shoes to work; payment of subminimum wages; physical beatings, including with shoes, by factory supervisors; and employment mostly of women between the ages of 15 and 28. Philip Knight, CEO of Nike, included the following in a letter to shareholders:

Q: Why on earth did Nike pick such a terrible place as Indonesia to have shoes made?
A: Effectively the U.S. State Department asked us to. In 1976, when zero percent of Nike's production was in Taiwan and Korea, Secretary of State Cyrus Vance asked Charles Robinson . . . to start the U.S.-ASIAN Business Council to fill the vacuum left by the withdrawal of the American military from that part of the world. . . . Chuck Robinson accepted the challenge, put together the council and served as Chairman of the U.S. side for three years. Mr. Robinson was a Nike Board member at that time as he is today. . . . "Nike's presence in that part of the world," according to a senior state department official at that time, "is American foreign policy in action."

Nike sent former U.N. Ambassador Andrew Young to its overseas factories in order to issue a report to Mr. Knight, the board, and the shareholders. Mr. Young did tour factories but only with Nike staff and only for a few hours. Mr. Young issued the following findings:

- Factories that produce Nike goods are "clean, organized, adequately ventilated, and well-lit."

- No evidence of a "pattern of widespread or systematic abuse or mistreatment of workers."

- Workers don't know enough about their rights or about Nike's own code of conduct.

- Few factory managers speak the local language, which inhibits workers from lodging complaints or grievances.

- Independent monitoring is needed because factories are controlled by absentee owners and Nike has too few supervisors on site.

On October 18, 1997, there were international protests against Nike in thirteen countries and seventy cities. On October 13, 1997, 6,000 Nike workers went on strike in Indonesia followed by a strike of 1,300 in Vietnam.

On November 8, 1997, an Ernst & Young audit about unsafe conditions in a Nike factory in Vietnam was leaked to the *New York Times* and made front-page news.

Michael Jordan, NBA and Nike's superstar endorser, agreed to tour Nike's factories in July 1998, stating, "the best thing I can do is go to Asia and see for myself. The last thing I want to do is pursue a business with a negative over my head that I don't have an understanding of. If there are issues . . . if it's an issue of slavery or sweatshops, [Nike executives] have to revise the situation."

From June 1997 to January 1998, Nike distributed 100,000 plastic "code of conduct" cards to plant workers. The cards list workers' rights. Nike's performance dropped. Its stock price dropped from a 1996 high of $75.75 per share to a March 1998 low of $43 per share. Retailers canceled orders so that sales decreased 3 percent for 1997. Nike reduced its labor force by 10–15 percent or 2,100–3,100 positions.

Press for Change and Global Exchange, an activist group, made the following demands of Nike in 1998.

1. *Accept independent monitoring by local human rights groups to ensure that Nike's Code of Conduct is respected by its subcontractors.* The GAP has already accepted independent monitoring for its factories in El Salvador, setting an important precedent in the garment industry. If Nike were to accept such monitoring in Indonesia, it would set a similar positive precedent in the shoe industry, making Nike a true leader in its field.

2. *Settle disputes with workers who have been unfairly dismissed for seeking decent wages and work conditions.* There are dozens of Indonesian workers who have been fired for their organizing efforts and thousands who have been cheated out of legally promised wages. Nike must take responsibility for the practices of its subcontractors and should offer to reinstate fired workers and repay unpaid wages.

3. *Improve the wages paid to Indonesian workers.* The minimum wage in Indonesia is $2.26 a day. Subsistence needs are estimated to cost at least $4 a day. While Nike claims to pay double the minimum wage, this claim includes endless hours of overtime. We call on Nike to pay a minimum of $4 a day for an eight-hour day and to end all forced overtime.

The American Apparel Manufacturers Association (AAMA), which counts 70 percent of all U.S. garment makers in its membership, has a database for its members to check labor compliance by contractors. The National Retail Federation has established the following statement of Principles on Supplier Legal Compliance (now signed by 250 retailers).

1. *We are committed to legal compliance and ethical business practices in all of our operations.*

2. *We choose suppliers that we believe share that commitment.*

3. *In our purchase contracts, we require our suppliers to comply with all applicable laws and regulations.*

4. *If it is found that a factory used by a supplier for the production of our merchandise has committed legal violations, we will take appropriate action, which may include canceling the affected purchase contracts, terminating our relationship with the supplier, commencing legal actions against the supplier, or other actions as warranted.*

5. *We support law enforcement and cooperate with law enforcement authorities in the proper execution of their responsibilities.*

6. *We support educational efforts designed to enhance legal compliance on the part of the U.S. apparel manufacturing industry.*

The U.S. Department of Labor has recommended the following to improve the current situation.

1. *All sectors of the apparel industry, including manufacturers, retailers, buying agents and merchandisers, should consider the adoption of a code of conduct.*

2. *All parties should consider whether there would be any additional benefits to adopting more standardized codes of conduct [to eliminate confusion resulting from a proliferation of different codes with varying definitions of child labor].*

3. *U.S. apparel importers should do more to monitor subcontractors and homeworkers [the areas where child labor violations occur].*

4. *U.S. garment importers—particularly retailers—should consider taking a more active and direct role in the monitoring and implementation of their codes of conduct.*

5. *All parties, particularly workers, should be adequately informed about codes of conduct so that the codes can fully serve their purpose.*

By 2000, Nike, still experiencing campus protests for its overseas plant conditions, began to experience economic impact as the students protested their colleges and universities signing licensing agreements with Nike. For example, Nike ended negotiations with the University of Michigan for a six-year, multimillion-dollar licensing agreement because Michigan joined the consortium. Phil Knight withdrew a pledge to make a $30 million donation to the University of Oregon because the university also joined the consortium. Nike continues to support the Fair Labor Association, an organization backed by the White House with about 135 colleges and universities as members, but its membership there has not halted the consortium's activities.[2] As noted in Chapter 5, Nike settled a case related to its free speech rights with regard to this international labor issue.

SUMMARY

What wage and hour protections exist for employees?

- Fair Labor Standards Act—federal law that regulates minimum wage and overtime pay
- Minimum wage—federal hourly rate of pay
- Overtime pay—rate of 1½ times the hourly rate for hours over 40 per week worked
- Equal Pay Act—equal wages for equal work regardless of gender
- Child labor standards—restrictions on hours and types of work for children under the age of 18

What protections exist for safety in the workplace?

- Occupational Safety and Health Act—federal law setting and enforcing workplace safety standards
- Occupational Safety and Health Administration (OSHA)—federal agency responsible for safety in the workplace
- Drug testing—screening of employees for impairment

What happens when a worker is injured in the workplace?

- Workers' compensation—state-by-state system of employer strict liability for injuries of workers on the job; the few exceptions to recovery include self-inflicted injuries

What is the Social Security system, and what benefits does it provide?

- Social Security Act—federal law establishing disability, beneficiary, and retirement benefits
- Federal Insurance Contributions Act (FICA)—statute establishing system for withholding contributions for Social Security benefits

Are workers entitled to pensions, and are they regulated?

- Employment Retirement Income Security Act (ERISA)—federal law regulating employer-sponsored pension plans
- Financial Accounting Standards Board (FASB) 106—accounting disclosure for a company's employee retirement obligations

What rights do unemployed workers have?

- Unemployment compensation—federal program handled by states to provide temporary support for displaced workers
- Workers' compensation—system of no-fault liability for employees injured on the job

How are labor unions formed, and what is their relationship with employees?

- Railway Labor Act—first federal law providing union protections
- Norris-LaGuardia Act—federal law prohibiting injunctions to halt strikes
- National Labor Relations Act (Wagner Act)—federal law authorizing employee unionization
- Labor Management Relations Act (Taft-Hartley Act)—federal law limiting union economic weapons
- Labor-Management Reporting and Disclosure Act (Landrum-Griffin Act)—federal law regulating union membership and organizations
- National Labor Relations Board (NLRB)—federal agency responsible for enforcing labor laws
- Collective bargaining unit—group of employees recognized as exclusive bargaining agent
- Authorization cards—employee-signed support for election
- Certification—recognition of union as exclusive bargaining agent
- Collective bargaining agreement—exclusive rights agreement between employer and employee
- Good-faith bargaining—requirement that parties negotiate terms in earnest
- Unfair labor practice—conduct by labor or management prohibited by statute
- Concerted activities—union-sponsored activities
- Picketing—public appearance of striking union members
- Boycotts—refusal to work for or to buy from or handle products of an employer
- Slowdown—workers report to job but do not operate at full speed
- Right-to-work laws—right to work at a company without being required to join a union
- Worker Adjustment and Retraining Notification Act (WARN)—federal law requiring employers to give sixty days' notice of plant shutdowns
- Lockout—employer closure of plant or business so workers cannot work

What are the laws and procedures related to immigrants and employment?

- Immigration and Naturalization Act (INA)
- Immigration Reform and Control Act of 1986 (IRCA)
- Immigration Act of 1990

- Illegal Immigration Reform and Immigrant Responsibility Act of 1996
- Antiterrorism and Effective Death Penalty Act
- Uniting and Strengthening America by Proving Appropriate Tools Required to Intercept and Obstruct Terrorism Act (USA Patriot Act)

- The Homeland Security Act
- American Competitive and Workforce Investment Act of 1998
- American Competitiveness in the Twenty-First Century Act of 2000

QUESTIONS AND PROBLEMS

1. Ruth Saludes is a Harvard University graduate with a master's degree in linguistics and education. She had worked for several years in various counseling and teaching positions. Feeling "burned out," Ms. Saludes decided she wanted to be a carpenter and left her position at the Free Clinic of Tucson, although she had no skill or experience in construction or carpentry. She filed for unemployment compensation but refused to take counseling jobs and insisted on a carpentry job. Her unemployment was cut off when she refused to take a counseling job. Ms. Saludes brought suit. Is she entitled to compensation? [*Saludes* v. *Department of Employment Security*, 628 P.2d 63 (Ariz. 1981).]

2. H. M. Wilson hired H. J. High as the general contractor for the construction of one of its stores in a shopping center in Tampa, Florida. The shopping center was owned and operated by Edward J. DeBartelo Corporation and had eighty-five tenants. The tenants paid a minimum rent plus a percentage of gross sales for maintenance of the common areas in the shopping center.

H. J. High's workers went on strike, posted themselves at the four entrances to the shopping center, and distributed handbills to customers. The handbills asked customers not to shop at any of the eighty-five stores until their dispute with High was settled. Is this an unlawful secondary boycott? [*Edward J. DeBartelo Corp.* v. *NLRB,* 463 U.S. 147 (1983).]

3. Joe Ortiz was discharged from Magma Copper Co. for absenteeism. He missed the last shift of work before he was fired because he was temporarily in custody following an arrest for a criminal offense. He filed for unemployment but was denied. Mr. Ortiz said he notified Magma that he was missing because of being detained in jail. The unemployment compensation agency says Mr. Ortiz is disqualified for benefits because he was fired for misconduct. Who is right? [*Magma Copper* v. *Department of Employment Security,* 625 P.2d 935 (Ariz. 1981).]

4. Donald Thompson worked as a machine operator for Hughes Aircraft for thirteen years. During that time, the skin on his hands was exposed to Wynn's 331, a coolant oil. In 1978, while working with machines and using Wynn's 331 oil, Mr. Thompson developed an active scaly eruption. He required medical attention but continued to work. The scaly eruption stopped only when Mr. Thompson was off work for medical treatment. He was certified to return to work but only if he avoided contact with Wynn's 331 oil. Hughes refused to rehire him, and Mr. Thompson filed for a permanent unscheduled disability. Does he qualify? [*Hughes Aircraft* v. *Industrial Comm'n,* 606 P.2d 819 (Ariz. 1981).]

5. Janice W. Craig was employed by Drenberg and Associates, an insurance agency. She had approximately fifteen years' experience when she started to work at Drenberg in August 1974 and was initially assigned underwriting duties in the personal and commercial lines of insurance. About the time she started to work, Drenberg began a year of explosive growth. Under normal conditions, an agency with 400,000 accounts could expect to acquire approximately 40,000 new accounts in the period of a year. Drenberg grew from 400,000 to 1,200,000 in just over one year. Craig and the agency's employees worked many overtime hours. Yet, in spite of their best efforts, the agency remained thirty days behind in its accounts.

Mrs. Craig was a conscientious perfectionist. She also took over a part of the commercial desk, handling correspondence, renewals, and changes. She was under constant pressure.

In April 1975, Drenberg purchased another agency, thereby acquiring 500 new accounts and an additional employee. Mrs. Craig was given responsibility for supervising the new employee and merging the books of the two agencies. The additional responsibility and mounting pressure began to affect her. She began to feel frustrated and ineffective. She experienced difficulty relating to her coworkers and on occasions had heated exchanges with customers. On September 25, 1975, she engaged in a particularly emotional telephone conversation with one of the agency's customers, after which she eventually left the office in tears.

In addition to Mrs. Craig's difficulties at the office, she was experiencing domestic disharmony. She and her husband argued frequently concerning his drinking habits. She encountered difficulties in relating to her daughters, and her mother's death caused additional internal pressures. On the evening of September 25, 1975, the Craigs again argued, following which she took an overdose of medication.

The following day she sought help at the Tri-City Mental Hospital and was subsequently admitted to Camelback Hospital, where her condition was diagnosed as neurotic depression, or a mental breakdown.

Mrs. Craig filed a claim with the Industrial Commission wherein she related facts establishing that she was suffering from a disabling mental condition brought on by the gradual buildup of the stress and strain of her employment.

Should Mrs. Craig receive workers' compensation? [*Fireman's Fund Ins. Co.* v. *Industrial Comm'n*, 579 P.2d 555 (Ariz. 1979).]

6. Harry Connelly was an embalmer's helper. When he cut his hand during the preparation of a corpse, germs from the gangrenous corpse got into his cut and caused blood poisoning, and he eventually died. Would Mr. Connelly's survivors be entitled to workers' compensation? [*Connelly* v. *Hunt Furniture*, 147 N.E. 366 (N.Y. 1925).]

7. Beth Israel Hospital had a rule prohibiting solicitation and distribution of literature in all areas of the hospital except the employee locker rooms. The union challenged the rule as unfair because employees could not be approached in the hospital cafeteria or coffee shop. Can an employer restrict literature distribution? Is this rule too restrictive? [*Beth Israel Hosp.* v. *NLRB*, 437 U.S. 483 (1978).]

8. OSHA requires vehicles with an obstructed rear view to be equipped with a reverse signal alarm. Mr. Knight, an independent contractor working for Clarkson Construction, operated a Clarkson dump truck that had no warning signal but had an obstructed rear view. If an injury resulted to a pedestrian when Mr. Knight backed onto the highway, what liability would there be? What could OSHA do? What could the pedestrian do? What effect does Mr. Knight's being an independent contractor have? If Mr. Knight were also injured, could he recover? [*Clarkson Constr. Co.* v. *OSHA*, 531 F.2d 451 (10th Cir. 1980).]

9. Earl Webster was a 39-year-old construction worker in good health. While shoveling sand into a wheelbarrow on a Texas road crew in 97-degree heat, he complained to fellow workers that he was sick. He stopped to have a drink of water, pushed two more wheelbarrows, lost consciousness, and was taken unconscious in the car to the company offices. He died a short time later of heat prostration. Is his spouse entitled to death benefits under workers' compensation? Would it make a difference if the water given to him to drink was bad? [*American General Ins.* v. *Webster*, 118 S.W. 2d 1082 (Tex. 1938).]

10. Suppose an employer decided to spin off a particular plant or part of its business to avoid either unionization or the recognition of a collective bargaining agreement. Would the spin-off work, or is this an unfair labor practice? [*International Union, UAW* v. *NLRB*, 470 F.2d 422 (D.C. 1972).]

RESEARCH PROBLEM

Wages, Hours, and Colorful Jobs

11. Analyze the following questions and research the cited cases to discover the complex issues involved related to the minimum wage, overtime, and covered employees under the FLSA.

Would the following count as part of hours worked?

- Mandatory training time [*Martin* v. *Parker Fire Protection Dist.*, 988 F.2d 1064 (10th Cir. 1993)]
- Firefighters' sleep time while on 24-hour duty [*Alldread* v. *Granada*, 988 F.2d 1425 (5th Cir. 1993)]
- Being on call in case of emergency [*Berry* v. *County of Sonoma*, 30 F.3d 1174 (9th Cir. 1994)]
- Time spent by employees at meat slaughter/processing plant waiting in line at the knife room to get their knives sharpened [*Reich* v. *IBP, Inc.*, 820 F. Supp. 1315 (D.C. Kan. 1993)]

Would the following employees be covered by the minimum wage and overtime protections of FLSA?

- Inmates who are required to work as part of their sentences and perform labor within a state-run correctional facility [*McMaster* v. *Minnesota*, 819 F. Supp. 1429 (D.C. Minn. 1993)]
- Manager of Chick-Fil-A mall restaurant who has a capital investment in the restaurant but must follow corporate standards of operation [*Howell* v. *Chick-Fil-A*, 7 FLW Fed.D. 641 (N.D. Fla. 1993)]
- Migrant farm workers who harvested pickling cucumbers and are paid regardless of employer's profit on sale [*Cavazos* v. *Foster*, 822 F. Supp. 438 (W.D. Mich. 1993)]
- Dancers at an upscale topless nightclub in Dallas who furnish their own costumes but are told when to appear [*Martin* v. *Priba Corp.*, 123 CCH LC 35737 (N.D. Tex. 1992)]
- Formerly homeless alcoholic who is working for the Salvation Army under its rehabilitation program and is residing at the Salvation Army facility [*Williams* v. *Strickland*, 837 F. Supp. 1049 (N.D. Cal. 1994)]

NOTES

1. For more information on the history of employment law, see the course Web site and the Instructor's Manual.

2. Steven Greenhouse, "Anti-Sweatshop Group Invites Input by Apparel Makers," *New York Times*, April 29, 2000, p. A9.

20

Employment Discrimination

▶ update ◀

*For up-to-date legal news and
real-world business applications,
click on* **update** *at
http://jennings.westbuslaw.com*

■ Employment discrimination has been one of the fastest-growing legal issues of the past decade. There has been a dramatic increase in the number of suits for discrimination and reverse discrimination and of cases in matters of unequal pay, sexual harassment, seniority, and maternity leave. Few employers have remained unaffected by the impact of antidiscrimination laws and cases.

This chapter answers the following questions: What laws governing employment discrimination exist? What types of discrimination exist? Are there any defenses to discrimination? What penalties or damages can be imposed for violations?

Nature of Complaint	Number of Complaints
Race	28,526
Sex	24,362
Disabilities	15,377
Age	19,124
National origin	8,450
Religion	2,532
Equal pay	1,167

EEOC 2003 DATA ON EMPLOYMENT DISCRIMINATION CASES

I have a dream that one day this nation will rise up and live out the true
meaning of its creed: "We hold these truths to be self-evident; that all
men are created equal." I have a dream. . . . I have a dream that my
four little children will one day live in a nation where they will not be
judged by the color of their skin but by the content of their character.
I have a dream. . . .

DR. MARTIN LUTHER KING JR.

CONSIDER...

Kimberly Ellerth's supervisor, Ted Slowik, was interviewing her for a promotion. He said that she was not "loose enough," and then reached over and touched her knee. In a conversation between them in which Mr. Slowik told Ms. Ellerth she got the job, he commented that the men in the factories she would be working with "certainly like women with pretty legs." Ms. Ellerth complained to no one but then quit and filed suit for sexual harassment. Can she recover?

© DIGITAL VISION/PHOTODISC/GETTY IMAGES

HISTORY OF EMPLOYMENT DISCRIMINATION LAW

Protections against employment discrimination are strictly statutory. Common law afforded employees no protection against discrimination. Indeed, common law viewed the entire employment relationship as a private contractual matter in which there should be no judicial interference.[1]

Review the Civil Rights Acts of 1866 and 1870:
http://www.law.cornell.edu/uscode/42/1981.html

Notwithstanding the **Civil Rights Acts of 1866 and 1870**, the first effective antidiscrimination employment statute was a long time in coming. The first federal legislation to deal directly with the issue of discrimination was the **Equal Pay Act of 1963** (see Chapter 19 for more details). The statutory right to equality was expanded beyond the issue of pay less than a year later by **Title VII** of the **Civil Rights Act of 1964**. Title VII is the basis for discrimination law and judicial decisions in such matters. Although it has been amended many times, its basic purpose is to prohibit discrimination in employment on the basis of race, color, religion, sex, or national origin.

Explore the Equal Pay Act:
http://www.law.cornell.edu/uscode/29/206.html

Title VII was first amended by the **Equal Employment Opportunity Act of 1972**. This amendment gave the act's enforcer, the **Equal Employment Opportunity Commission** (EEOC), greater powers—for example, the right to file suits in federal district court. In 1975, Title VII was again amended, with the **Pregnancy Discrimination Act**, which defined "sex" discrimination to include discrimination on the basis of pregnancy and childbirth.

Review Title VII of the Civil Rights Act of 1964:
http://www.law.cornell.edu/uscode/42/ch21.html

Laws have also been enacted to protect against discrimination because of age or handicap. Discrimination on the basis of age was prohibited by the **Age Discrimination in Employment Act of 1967** (discussed later in this chapter). Under the **Rehabilitation Act of 1973**, federal contractors are prohibited from discriminating against certain employees in performing their contracts. With the **Americans with**

Disabilities Act, passed in 1990, employers of twenty-five or more employees (progressed to include employers of fifteen or more employees in 1994) are prohibited from discriminating against employees with disabilities and are required to make reasonable accommodations for qualified employees with disabilities. Although the substance of the existing antidiscrimination laws remains, the **Civil Rights Act of 1991** made significant changes in procedural aspects of Title VII litigation. Exhibit 20.1 provides a summary of federal antidiscrimination legislation to date.

In addition to this legislation, several executive orders that apply to administrative agencies (see Chapter 6) have been issued. These orders require federal government contractors to institute, among other things, affirmative action programs in their labor forces.

EXHIBIT   20.1 Employment Discrimination Statutory Scheme

STATUTE	DATE	PROVISIONS
Civil Rights Acts of 1866 and 1870 42 U.S.C. § 1981	1866 1870	Prohibited intentional discrimination based on race, color, national origin, or ethnicity; permit lawsuits
Equal Pay Act 29 U.S.C. § 206	1963	Prohibits paying workers of one sex different wages from the other when the jobs involve substantially similar skill, effort, and responsibility; Wage and Hour Division of Department of Labor enforces; private lawsuits permitted; double damage recovery for up to three years' wages plus attorney fees
Civil Rights Act of 1964 42 U.S.C. § 1981	1964	Outlaws all employment discrimination on the basis of race, color, religion, sex, or national origin; applies to hiring, pay, work conditions, promotions, discipline, and discharge; EEOC enforces; private lawsuits permitted; costs and attorney fees recoverable
Age Discrimination in Employment Act 42 U.S.C. § 6101	1967	Prohibits employment discrimination because of age against employees over 40 and mandatory retirement restrictions; EEOC enforces; private lawsuits permitted; attorney fees and costs recoverable
Equal Employment Opportunity Act 42 U.S.C. § 2000	1972	Expanded enforcement power of EEOC
Rehabilitation Act 29 U.S.C. § 701	1973	Prohibits employment discrimination on the basis of handicaps
Pregnancy Discrimination Act 42 U.S.C. § 2000e	1975	Prohibits discrimination on the basis of pregnancy and childbirth
Americans with Disabilities Act 42 U.S.C. § 12101	1990	Prohibits discrimination against the handicapped
Civil Rights Act of 1991 42 U.S.C. § 1981	1991	Clarifies disparate impact suit requirements; clarifies the meaning of "business necessity" and "job related"; changes some Supreme Court decisions (*Wards Cove*); punitive damage recovery
Glass Ceiling Act 42 U.S.C. § 2000e	1991	Creates commission to study barriers to women entering management and decision-making positions
Family and Medical Leave Act 29 U.S.C. § 2601	1993	Establishes twelve weeks of unpaid leave for medical or family reasons

EMPLOYMENT DISCRIMINATION:
TITLE VII OF THE CIVIL RIGHTS ACT

Title VII of the Civil Rights Act of 1964—also known as the **Fair Employment Practices Act**—as amended in 1991, prohibits discrimination in all areas of employment on the basis of race, color, religion, national origin, and sex (including pregnancy, childbirth, or abortion). Other acts prohibit discrimination based on physical disability or age.

Application of Title VII

Groups Covered

Title VII does not apply to all employers but is limited to the following groups:

1. Employers with at least fifteen workers during each working day in each of twenty or more calendar weeks in the current or preceding year (state anti-discrimination statutes may apply to employers with fewer than fifteen employees)

2. Labor unions that have fifteen members or more or operate a hiring hall that refers workers to covered employers

3. Employment agencies that procure workers for an employer who is covered by the law

4. Any labor union or employment agency, provided it has fifteen or more employees

5. State and local agencies

Noncovered Employers

Certain employers and employment situations are *not* subject to Title VII.

1. Employment of aliens outside the United States is exempt.

2. Religious corporations, associations, educational institutions, or societies are exempt when the employment of individuals of a particular religion is connected with the activities of such corporations, associations, educational institutions, or societies.

3. Congress is exempt from the Civil Rights Act of 1964 (including Title VII).

4. The federal government and corporations owned by the federal government are exempt from Title VII, but the same prohibitions against discrimination appear in other statutes from which they are not exempt.

5. Indian tribes and departments or agencies in the District of Columbia subject to the procedures of the civil service are exempt.

Employment Procedures Covered

Every step in the employment process is covered by Title VII. Hiring, compensation, training programs, promotion, demotion, transfer, fringe benefits, employer rules, working conditions, and dismissals are all covered. In the case of an employment agency, the system for the agency's job referrals is also covered.

THEORIES OF DISCRIMINATION UNDER TITLE VII

There are three basic but not mutually exclusive theories of discrimination under Title VII: **disparate treatment**, **disparate impact**, and **pattern or practice of discrimination**.

Disparate Treatment

The most common form of discrimination at the time Title VII was passed was treating employees of one race or sex differently from employees of another race or sex. This different, or disparate, treatment results in unlawful discrimination when an individual is treated less favorably than other employees because of race, color, religion, national origin, or sex. The U.S. Supreme Court established the elements required to be shown to establish disparate treatment under Title VII in *McDonnell Douglas Corp.* v. *Green*, 411 U.S. 792 (1973). The case involved the rights of a black mechanic who had been laid off during a general workforce reduction and then not rehired. McDonnell claimed Mr. Green was not rehired because of his participation in a lock-in at the plant to protest racial inequality. Mr. Green brought suit for a Title VII violation, and the Supreme Court established the following elements as a *prima facie* case for discrimination.

1. The plaintiff belongs to a racial minority.
2. The plaintiff applied for and was qualified for a job with the employee.
3. The plaintiff, despite job qualifications, was rejected.
4. After the plaintiff's rejection, the job remained open and the employer continued to seek applicants.

It is the employer's burden of proof to show that there was a nondiscriminatory reason for the employment decision. That burden arises when the employee-plaintiff establishes the four elements established in *Green*. *Chescheir* v. *Liberty Mutual Ins. Co.* (Case 20.1) deals with an issue of disparate treatment and proof of discrimination in an employment decision.

CASE 20.1

Chescheir v. *Liberty Mutual Ins. Co.*
713 F.2d 1142 (5th Cir. 1983)

Why Can He Go to Law School but I Can't?
The Case of the Law Student Claims Adjuster

FACTS

Liberty Mutual Insurance Company has a rule prohibiting its adjustors and first-year supervisors from attending law school. This "law school rule" was proposed and implemented on a national basis by Edmund Carr, a vice president and general claims manager, in November 1972.

Joan Chescheir (plaintiff) was hired by Liberty Mutual's Dallas office in March 1973 as a claims adjustor. In January 1975, she voluntarily resigned but in June of that year was hired in Liberty's Houston office as a claims adjustor.

In August 1976, Wyatt Trainer, the claims manager at the Houston office, received an anonymous letter informing him that Ms. Chescheir was attending law school. After consulting with his assistants and superior, Mr. Trainer fired her after she admitted she was attending law school.

Charity O'Connell also worked in the Houston office as a claims adjustor during the same period Ms. Chescheir did. During a coffee break with a new employee, Timothy Schwirtz (also an adjustor), Ms. O'Connell relayed the story of Ms. Chescheir's firing. Mr. Schwirtz then said, "Oh, that's strange, because when I was hired, when Wells [Southwest Division claims manager] interviewed me, he told me that I could go to law school and in fact if I came down to the Houston office, there were law schools in Houston." Ms. O'Connell then went to her supervisor and told him she also was attending law school. She refused to quit law school and was fired.

William McCarthy, Liberty's house counsel in its Houston office, attended law school while working as an adjustor and was retained as house counsel upon his graduation. The trial court found that Mr. McCarthy's supervisors were aware of his contemporaneous law school career. Alvin Dwayne White was employed as an adjustor in Liberty's Fort Worth office and asked for a transfer to Houston so he could attend law school. He was given the transfer and attended law school in Houston. James Ballard worked as an adjustor in Houston, attended law school, and was promoted to supervisor while in law school. Supervisors and employees were aware of his law school attendance, but the law school rule was not enforced against him. In short, none of the male employees known to have been attending law school was fired.

Ms. Chescheir and Ms. O'Connell both filed complaints with the EEOC, were given right of suit letters, and filed suit in federal district court. After a lengthy trial, the court found that Liberty Mutual had violated Title VII. Both women were given back pay. Liberty Mutual appealed.

JUDICIAL OPINION

GOLDBERG, Circuit Judge

Title VII applies . . . not only to the more blatant forms of discrimination, but also to subtler forms, such as discriminatory enforcement of work rules.

The four part test for demonstrating a *prima facie* case for discriminatory discharge due to unequal imposition of discipline [is]:

1. That plaintiff was a member of a protected group;
2. That there was a company policy or practice concerning the activity for which he or she was discharged;
3. That nonminority employees either were given the benefit of a lenient company practice or were not held to compliance with a strict company policy; and
4. That the minority employee was disciplined either without the application of a lenient policy, or in conformity with the strict one.

Of course, if an employer is unaware that a nonminority employee is in violation of company policy, the absence of discipline does not demonstrate a more le-

nient policy. It follows from this that if an employer applies a rule differently to people it believes are differently situated, no discriminatory intent has been shown.

The district court made multitudinous findings of subsidiary facts and concluded in a finding of ultimate fact: "The defendant applied its law school rule differently to male and female employees." The subsidiary facts detail a plethora of individual instances that each tend to suggest discrimination.

It is clear that the plaintiffs are members of a protected group and that there was a company policy or practice concerning the activity for which the plaintiffs were discharged; thus the first two elements of the test are met. It is also clear that minority employees were disciplined without the application of a lenient policy, and in conformity with a strict policy. All women known to violate the law school rule were immediately discharged. Furthermore, even potential violations of the rule by women were investigated promptly. An anonymous letter was sufficient to trigger an investigation of Chescheir, and the fact that Chescheir was attending law school moved the company to interrogate another woman.

The only remaining element of the *prima facie* case is a finding that male employees either were given the benefit of a lenient company practice or were not held to compliance with a strict company policy. This is the element upon which Liberty Mutual focuses its attack. Recasting Liberty Mutual's argument slightly, it claims that other males were strictly disciplined in accord with the law school rule, and that Liberty Mutual never knew that McCarthy, White, and Ballard were attending law school. Thus, claims Liberty Mutual, the third element was not met.

We are not persuaded. First, our review of the record does not disclose any males in the Southwest Division who were discharged because of the law school rule. Second, even were we to accept Liberty Mutual's contention that it did not actually know McCarthy, White, and Ballard were attending law school, we would still affirm the judgment. The operative question is merely whether Liberty Mutual applied a more liberal standard to male employees. The district court found that there were widespread rumors that McCarthy and Ballard were attending law school. Also, the EEOC notified Liberty Mutual that a male adjustor was attending law school (Ballard) and requested an explanation. Key managerial employees, at a minimum, suspected McCarthy was attending law school but preferred not to ask and confirm their suspicions. One male adjustor was told when he was hired that he could attend law school. In contrast to Liberty

continued

Mutual's energetic investigation of women it believed might be attending law school, Liberty Mutual never investigated any of these allegations, suspicions, or rumors about male adjustors. The case of Mr. White is even more dramatic. After he expressed a desire to transfer to Houston in order to attend law school, that transfer was granted and he was never told he could not attend law school.

The preceding facts are more than enough to support the third leg [of the test]. Males at Liberty Mutual were subject to lenient enforcement of the law school rule. The district court's ultimate finding of fact that Liberty Mutual applied its law school rule discriminatorily finds firm support in the record; all four elements of the *prima facie* case are present.

Once Chescheir and O'Connell established a *prima facie* case of discrimination, the burden shifted to Liberty Mutual to present a justification. The district court found that Liberty Mutual offered no justification. Accordingly, the judgment of the district court is affirmed.

CASE QUESTIONS

1. What employer rule is at issue?
2. How were the plaintiffs fired using the rule?
3. Had any male employees ever been fired under the rule?
4. Were there examples of disparate use of the rule?
5. Is there a *prima facie* case?
6. What damages were awarded?

CONSIDER . . .   20.1

White employees at A.J. Gerrard Manufacturing were warned about their excessive absenteeism before they were discharged, but black employees were simply discharged for excessive absenteeism without warning. Is such a policy discriminatory? [*Brown v. A. J. Gerrard Mfg. Co.,* 643 F.2d 273, 25 Fair Empl. Prac. Cas. (BNA) 1089, 25 Empl. Prac.Dec. (CCH) ¶31758 (5th Cir. 1981).]

THINK: The rulings in *Green* and *Chescheir* are that employers cannot treat those who are members of different groups or protected classes (race, gender, religion) using different standards or rules, with the result being that the members of the nonprotected group are hired or retained while those in the protected class are not.

APPLY: A.J. Gerrard did not apply the same standard to all employees. White employees were warned; black employees were not. The result was that white employees were retained, and black employees were not.

ANSWER: The treatment was disparate and constituted discrimination.

Use a similar method to determine your answer to the factual scenario presented in Consider 20.2.

CONSIDER . . .   20.2

When a white employee refused to perform cleanup work that was not within his job description, there were no repercussions. When four black employees refused to perform the same cleanup work for the same reason, they were discharged. Is there discrimination? [*Slack v. Havens,* 522 F.2d 1091 (9th Cir. 1975).]

Disparate Impact

Many employment hiring, promoting, and firing practices are not intentionally discriminatory. In fact, the basis for such decisions may be quite rational. Even so, the effect or impact of many employment standards is to discriminate against particular races or on the basis of sex.

In one case, the Alabama prison system had a minimum height requirement of 5'2" and a minimum weight requirement of 120 pounds for all of its "correctional counselors" (prison guards). The impact of the rule was to exclude many females and very few males [*Dothard* v. *Rawlinson*, 433 U.S. 321 (1977)]. Although the rule had a purpose other than one of discrimination, namely, making sure guards were large enough to perform their jobs, the effect of the rule was to exclude women from the job position.

Disparate impact cases do not require the four steps of proof outlined in the *Green* case. Rather, the proof required in disparate impact cases is a statistical showing of the impact of an employment practice.

The 1991 amendments to the Civil Rights Act require a plaintiff to establish that a practice or practices have a disparate impact on a protected class. The burden then shifts to the employer to show "business necessity" for the practice. The employer must show that the practice is "job related for the position in question and consistent with business necessity." However, disparate impact cases cannot be based on an analysis of only the demographics of the labor market; the proper comparison is between the skilled labor force (as defined by the position in question) and those actually holding the position.

Review the 1991 amendments to the Civil Rights Act:
http://www.law.cornell.edu/uscode/42/1981.html

CONSIDER . . .   2 0 . 3

A federal district court judge certified a class action lawsuit against Wal-Mart for discrimination charges brought by female employees of the worldwide retailer. In *Dukes* v. *Wal-Mart Stores*, 222 F.R.O. 137 (N.D.Cal.2004), the female employees of Wal-Mart allege under Title VII of the 1964 Civil Rights Act, 42 U.S.C. § 2000e *et seq.*, that women employed in Wal-Mart stores (1) are paid less than men in comparable positions, despite having higher performance ratings and greater seniority; and (2) receive fewer promotions to in-store management positions than do men, and those who are promoted must wait longer than their male counterparts to advance.

The court allowed the women to use statistical evidence as a basis for certification as a class. The statistical evidence cited was the approximate percentages of women in specific hourly and salaried management positions as follows:

Salaried Positions
- Store manager—14%
- Comanager (only in larger stores)—23%
- Assistant manager—36%

Hourly Positions
- Management trainee—42%
- Support manager—50%
- Department manager—78%
- Customer service manager—85–90%
- Other hourly positions—70%

The class certification simply means that the women have the right to pursue the case as a group. They are represented by two nonprofit public interest law firms as well as three private law firms. Wal-Mart could take the certification to the Ninth Circuit to challenge it.

What do the women have to prove to establish discrimination? Are the statistics enough? What explanation could Wal-Mart offer for the numbers that would evidence no discrimination on its part?

Pattern or Practice of Discrimination

The "pattern or practice" theory involves discrimination not against one person but, rather, against a group or class of persons (for example, women or African-Americans). Generally, a party bringing suit seeks to show that a particular minority group is underrepresented in an employer's workforce as compared with that group's representation in the population base. Circumstantial evidence and statistics are used to establish a pattern or practice of discrimination. For example, percentages are often compared. An employer's workforce may consist of 6 percent African-Americans, whereas the city's population consists of 30 percent African-Americans.

The standards for establishing a pattern or practice of discrimination are affected by the 1991 amendments to the Civil Rights Act; the burdens of proof are those discussed under disparate impact, with a "reasonable justification" defense for employers. The plaintiff must show causation between the practice of the employer and the disparate impact. For example, in one case that immediately preceded the 1991 amendments, the Seventh Circuit found that a company's low percentage of African-Americans in its workforce was due to its location in a Hispanic neighborhood and not because of its practice of hiring by word of mouth [*EEOC* v. *Chicago Miniature Lamp Works*, 947 F. 2d 292 (7th Cir. 1991)].

In pattern or practice cases, the initial burden of proof of discrimination is upon the plaintiff or the EEOC.

BIOGRAPHY

TEXACO: THE JELLY BEAN DIVERSITY FIASCO

In November 1996, Texaco, Inc. was rocked by the disclosure of tape-recorded conversations among three executives about a racial discrimination suit pending against the company. The suit, seeking $71 million, had been brought by 6 employees, on behalf of 1,500 other employees, who alleged the following forms of discrimination:

I have had KKK printed on my car. I have had my tires slashed and racial slurs written about me on bathroom walls. One co-worker blatantly called me a racial epithet to my face. Throughout my employment, three supervisors in my department openly discussed their view that African-Americans are ignorant and incompetent, and, specifically, that Thurgood Marshall was the most incompetent person they had ever seen.

Sheryl Joseph, formerly a Texaco secretary in Harvey, Louisiana, was given a cake for her birthday, which occurred shortly after she announced that she was pregnant. The cake depicted a black pregnant woman and read, "Happy Birthday, Sheryl. It must have been those watermelon seeds."

The suit also included the following data on Texaco's workforce.

| 1989 | Minorities as a percentage of Texaco's workforce | 15.2% |
| 1994 | Minorities as a percentage of Texaco's workforce | 19.4% |

NUMBER OF YEARS TO PROMOTION, BY JOB CLASSIFICATION

Minority Employees	Job	Other Employees
6.1	Accountant	4.6
6.4	Senior Accountant	5.4
12.5	Analyst	6.3
14.2	Financial Analyst	13.9
15.0	Assistant Accounting Supervisor	9.8

TEXACO MANAGEMENT COMPOSITION

	Senior Managers	
	White	Black
1991	1,887	19
1992	2,001	21
1993	2,000	23
1994	2,029	23

RACIAL COMPOSITION (% OF BLACKS) BY PAY RANGE

Salary	Texaco	Other Oil Companies
$51,000	5.9%	7.2%
$56,900	4.7%	6.5%
$63,000	4.1%	4.7%
$69,900	2.3%	5.1%
$77,600	1.8%	3.2%
$88,100	1.9%	2.3%
$95,600	1.4%	2.6%
$106,100	1.2%	2.3%
$117,600	0.8%	2.3%
$128,800	0.4%	1.8%

(African-Americans make up 12% of the U.S. population.)

Faced with the lawsuit, Texaco's former treasurer, Robert Ulrich, senior assistant treasurer, J. David Keough, and senior coordinator for personnel services, Richard A. Lundwall, met and discussed the suit. A tape transcript follows.

They look through evidence, deciding what to turn over to the plaintiffs.

Lundwall Here, look at this chart. You know, I'm not really quite sure what it means. This chart is not mentioned in the agency, so it's not important that we even have it in there. . . . They would never know it was here.

Keough They'll find it when they look through it.

Lundwall Not if I take it out they won't.

The executives decide to leave out certain pages of a document; they worry that another version will turn up.

Ulrich We're gonna purge the [expletive deleted] out of these books, though. We're not going to have any damn thing that we don't need to be in them—

Lundwall As a matter of fact, I just want to be reminded of what we discussed. You take your data and . . .

Keough You look and make sure it's consistent to what we've given them already for minutes. Two versions with the restricted and that's marked clearly on top—

Ulrich But I don't want to be caught up in a cover-up. I don't want to be my own Watergate.

Lundwall We've been doing pretty much two versions, too. This one here, this is strictly my book, your book . . .

Ulrich Boy, I'll tell you, that one, you would put that and you would have the only copy. Nobody else ought to have copies of that.

Lundwall O.K.?

Ulrich You have that someplace and it doesn't exist.

Lundwall Yeah, O.K.

Ulrich I just don't want anybody to have a copy of that.

Lundwall Good. No problem.

Ulrich You know, there is no point in even keeping the restricted version anymore. All it could do is get us in trouble. That's the way I feel. I would not keep anything.

Lundwall Let me shred this thing and any other restricted version like it.

Ulrich Why do we have to keep the minutes of the meeting anymore?

Lundwall You don't, you don't.

Ulrich We don't?

Lundwall Because we don't, no, we don't because it comes back to haunt us like right now—

The executives discuss the minority employees who brought the suit.

Lundwall They are perpetuating an us/them atmosphere. Last week or last Friday I told . . .

Lundwall Yeah, that's what I said to you, you want to frag grenade? You know, duck, I'm going to throw one. Well, that's what I was alluding to. But the point is not, that's not bad in itself but it does perpetuate us/them. And if you're trying to get away and get to the we . . . you can't do that kind of stuff.

Ulrich [Inaudible.] I agree. This diversity thing. You know how black jelly beans agree. . . .

Lundwall That's funny. All the black jelly beans seem to be glued to the bottom of the bag.

Ulrich You can't have just we and them. You can't just have black jelly beans and other jelly beans. It doesn't work.

Lundwall Yeah. But they're perpetuating the black jelly beans.

Ulrich I'm still having trouble with Hanukkah. Now, we have Kwanza (laughter).

The release of the tape prompted the Reverend Jesse Jackson to call for a nationwide boycott of Texaco. Sales fell 8 percent, Texaco's stock fell 2 percent, and several institutional investors were preparing to sell their stock.

Texaco did have a minority recruiting effort in place and the "jelly bean" remark was tied to a diversity trainer the company had hired.

Within days of the release of the tape, Texaco settled its bias suit for $176.1 million, the largest sum, at that time, ever allowed in a discrimination case. The money allowed a 11 percent pay raise for blacks and other minorities who joined in the lawsuit. Texaco's chairman and CEO at that time, Peter I. Bijur, issued the following statement after agreeing to a settlement:

Texaco is facing a difficult but vital challenge. It's broader than any specific words and larger than any lawsuit. It is one we must and are attacking head-on.

We are a company of 27,000 people worldwide. In any organization of that size, unfortunately, there are bound to be people with unacceptable, biased attitudes toward race, gender and religion.

Our goal, and our responsibility, is to eradicate this kind of thinking wherever and however it is found in our

continued

company. And our challenge is to make Texaco a company of limitless opportunity for all men and women.

We are committed to begin meeting this challenge immediately through programs with concrete goals and measurable timetables.

I've already announced certain specific steps, including a redoubling of efforts within Texaco to focus on the paramount value of respect for the individual and a comprehensive review of our diversity programs at every level of our company.

We also want to broaden economic access to Texaco for minority firms and increase the positive impact our investments can have in the minority community. This includes areas such as hiring and promotion; professional services such as advertising, banking, investment management and legal services; and wholesale and retail station ownership.

To assist us, we are reaching out to leaders of minority and religious organizations and others for ideas and perspectives that will help Texaco succeed in our mission of becoming a model of diversity and workplace equality.

It is essential to this urgent mission that Texaco and African-Americans and other minority community leaders work together to help solve the programs we face as a company—which, after all, echo the problems faced in society as a whole.

Discrimination will be extinguished only if we tackle it together, only if we join in a unified, common effort.

Working together, I believe we can take Texaco into the 21st century as a model of diversity. We can make Texaco a company of limitless opportunity. We can make Texaco a leader in according respect to every man and woman.

Even after the announcement, Texaco stock was down $3 per share, a loss of $800 million total, and the boycott was continued. Texaco's proposed merger with Shell Oil began to unravel as Shell's CEO expressed concern about Texaco's integrity. However, after the settlement, additional information about the case began to emerge.

Holman W. Jenkins, Jr. wrote the following piece for *The Wall Street Journal*:

"Texaco Ransoms Its Image for $176 million," November 26, 1996, p. A21.

Quietly, corporate America is debating whether Texaco's Peter Bijur did the right thing.

Mr. Bijur gets paid to make the hard calls, and with the airwaves aflame over "nigger" and "black jelly beans," Texaco took a battering in the stock and political markets. He had every reason for wanting to put a stop-loss on the media frenzy. "Once the taped conversations were revealed," he says, settling was "reasonable and honorable." So now Texaco is betting $176 million that paying

off minority employees and their lawyers is the quickest way out of the news.

But as the company's own investigation showed, the truly inflammatory comments reported in the media never took place. They were purely a fabrication by opposing lawyers, and trumpeted by a credulous New York Times. *And some digging would have shown this problem cropping up before in the career of Mike Hausfeld, lead attorney for the plaintiffs.*

In an antitrust case years ago, he presented a secret recording that he claimed showed oil executives conspiring to threaten gasoline dealers. But a check by the same expert who handled the Nixon Watergate tapes showed no such thing. Says Larry Sharp, the Washington antitrust lawyer who opposed Mr. Hausfeld: "To put it generously, he gave himself the benefit of the doubt in making the transcript."

But this time the lie has been rewarded, and the broader public, unschooled in legal cynicism, heads home believing Texaco an admitted racist.

The catechism of corporate crisis management says you can't fight the media. Mr. Bijur had to consider that Jesse Jackson was threatening a boycott if Texaco failed to "regret, repent and seek renewal." Mr. Jackson pointedly added that "any attempt to shift to denial would add insult to injury"—a warning against trying to spread some egg to the faces of those who were fooled by the fake transcript.

There may have been wisdom, if not valor, in Mr. Bijur's decision to run up the white flag. But he also evinced symptoms of Stockholm Syndrome, telling CNN that Texaco was just the "tip of the iceberg" of corporate racism. Ducking this fight so ignominiously may yet prove a penny-wise, pound-foolish strategy. The City of Philadelphia has decided to dump its Texaco holdings anyway, partly out of fear of more litigation.

What else could Texaco have done? It could have apologized for any offense, but stuck up for its former treasurer Bob Ulrich, who was wronged by the phony transcript and stripped of his medical benefits by Texaco. And the company could have vowed to fight the lawsuit like the dickens, arguing that Texaco is not the cause of society's racial troubles but has tried to be part of the solution.

Start with the tapes: A fair listening does not necessarily reveal a "racist" conversation by executives at Texaco, but certainly a candid conversation about the problems of race at Texaco. They spoke of "jelly beans" dividing into camps of "us" and "them," an honest representation of life at many companies, not just in the oil patch.

This is what affirmative action, by throwing people together, was supposed to get us past. And it may be no accident that our most quota-ridden newspaper, USA Today, jumped off the bandwagon on the Texaco tapes, noting the ambiguity of whether the "jelly bean" remarks were meant to be hostile or friendly to blacks.

And McPaper kept on asking intelligent questions, like whether the New York Times *had been "used by plaintiffs in the case to promote a faulty but more inflammatory transcript?" ("Not unless the court was used," answered* Times *Business Editor John Geddes, sounding like a lawyer himself.)*

So Mr. Bijur was not facing a uniformly hopeless media torrent. The truth, even a complicated truth, catches up with the headlines eventually.

If companies were set free to assemble the work forces most useful to them, they could sweep away a heap of excuses for recrimination. Whites couldn't feel cheated out of jobs. Blacks wouldn't end up at companies that want them only for window-dressing. And the world could go back to feeling OK about being an interesting place. We might even allow that cultural patterns other than racism may explain why so many rednecks, and so few blacks, become petroleum engineers.

Mr. Bijur may have made the best of a bad deal for his shareholders. Whether it was best for America is a different judgment.

Texaco hired attorney Michael Armstrong to investigate the underlying allegations. Mr. Armstrong agreed with Mr. Jenkins and concluded that the tapes had not been transcribed correctly.

A federal grand jury began an investigation at Texaco to determine whether there had been obstruction of justice in the withholding of documents. Richard Lundwall, the executive who taped the sessions with the other executives, was charged with one count of obstruction of justice. Mr. Lundwall had turned over the tapes of the conversations to lawyers for the plaintiffs in the discrimination suit on October 25, 1996. Lundwall had been terminated. Robert W. Ulrich was indicted in 1997.

The following interview with CEO Bijur appeared in *Business Week:*

"Texaco: Lessons from a Crisis in Progress," *Business Week,* December 2, 1996, p. 44.

Q: *How did your legal strategy change once the news of the tapes was printed?*

A: When I saw [the story], I knew that this lawsuit was pending and moving forward. I made the judgment that we needed to accelerate the settlement process. And those discussions on settlement commenced almost immediately.

Q: *It has been reported that you didn't get the board of directors involved with the settlement talks and other issues. Why not?*

A: You're drawing conclusions that are erroneous. The board was fully involved throughout the entire process. I talked to numerous directors personally.

We had several board and executive committee meetings. The board was fully supportive of our actions.

Q: *Have you met with shareholders?*

A: Yes, of course. I went down to [New York] and met with the Interfaith Center on Corporate Responsibility, which is a group of religious shareholders. I expressed our position on this and listened carefully to their position and got some good counsel and guidance. But I wanted to provide our side of the issue as well. I have met with [New York State Comptroller] Carl McCall and [New York City Comptroller] Alan Hevesi about concerns that they had, and I will continue to meet with other shareholders as I normally do.

Q: *Why do you think the oil industry has such a poor reputation on issues of racial diversity and gender equality? How does Texaco stack up against the others?*

A: The percentage of minorities within Texaco is just about average for the petroleum industry. We have made really significant progress in the last several years in improving the percentage. But there are some very interesting points that need to be examined to place in context what may be going on in this industry. I just read a study that showed that in 1995, there were only nine petroleum engineering minority graduates that came out of all engineering schools in the United States—only nine. That's not an excuse. But it is indicative of why it is difficult for this industry to have a lot of people in the pipeline. Now, of course, that does not apply to accountants, finance people, and anybody else. But we are a very technically oriented industry.

Q: *Have you personally witnessed discrimination at Texaco?*

A: In the nearly 31 years I have been with Texaco, I have never witnessed an incident of racial bias or prejudice. And had I seen it, I would have taken disciplinary action. I've never seen it.

Q: *Is there a widespread culture of insensitivity at Texaco?*

A: I do not think there is a culture of institutional bias within Texaco. I think we've got a great many very good and decent human beings, but that unfortunately we mirror society. There is bigotry in society. There is prejudice and injustice in society. I am sorry to say that, and I am sorry to say that probably does exist within Texaco. I can't do much about society, but I certainly can do something about Texaco.

Q: *Are there other lessons in terms of your style of management?*

A: I don't think I would do anything different the next time than what I did this time.

continued

Q: *How will you make sure the spirit as well as the letter of the policy is followed at Texaco?*

A: We're going to put more and more and more emphasis on it until we get it through everybody's head: Bigotry is not going to be tolerated here.

Mr. Lundwall entered a "not guilty" plea on July 8, 1997. Both Mr. Ulrich and Mr. Lundwall were found not guilty in 1998 and acquitted of all criminal charges. Lawyers argued successfully that the tapes were interrupted over 500 times and were "utterly untrustworthy" and that the executives had not been adequately instructed by their lawyers on document production. J. David Keough sued Texaco for libel (you can read his complaint at http://www.contilaw.com/pleadings/KeoughvTexaco.htm). Texaco moved to dismiss the complaint in 1999, but the judge ordered the trial to go forward on three of the eight causes of action. *Keough v. Texaco Inc.,* 1999 WL 61836 (S.D.N.Y.)

Texaco named Mary Bush, a financial consultant, as its first black female board member and has pledged to continue its drive for diversity and fight against bigotry. As part of its settlement, Texaco agreed to, at a cost of $55 million, assign a task force to police hiring and promotion as well as requiring mentors for black employees and sensitivity training for white employees. The task force's interim report on progress toward the settlement goals revealed the following:

Hiring Asked search firms to identify wider arrays of candidates. Expanded recruiting at historically minority colleges. Gave 50 scholarships and paid internships to minority students seeking engineering or technical degrees.

Diversity Initiatives Conducted two-day diversity training for more than 8,000 of 20,000 U.S. employees. Tied management bonuses to diversity goals. Developing alternative dispute resolution and ombudsman programs.

Purchasing Nearly doubled purchases from minority- or women-owned businesses. Asking suppliers to report their purchases from such companies.

Financial Services Substantially increased banking, investment management and insurance business with minority- and women-owned firms. A group of such firms underwrote a $150 million public financing.

Retailing Added three black independent retailers, eighteen black managers of company-owned service stations, twelve minority or female wholesalers, thirteen minority- or women-owned Xpress Lube outlets and six minority- or women-owned lubricant distributors.

Mr. Bijur's conduct in the "Jelly Bean Fiasco" was heralded by managers and academics worldwide. He was in demand at virtually all large conferences as a guest speaker. However, Texaco did not perform as well as other oil companies during his tenure. For example, Texaco's profits were $2.5 billion, as compared to Chevron's $5.2 billion. Near the end of 2000, the Texaco board agreed to merge the company with Chevron.

Before that merger occurred, Mr. Bijur resigned abruptly from Texaco after being summoned by the Texaco board to a meeting at which the board announced that it had lost confidence in him. There had been a series of issues such as the $2 million remodeling of the corporate suite at New York City's Carlyle Hotel, the use of the company jet, and his romance with a subordinate whom he eventually married in the summer of 2000. Texaco and Mr. Bijur have declined to discuss the issues, but an audit concludes that while there may have been bad judgment in Mr. Bijur's behavior and decisions, there was nothing illegal or even "serious."

Discussion Questions

1. Provide a summary of the players and their concerns.

2. Discuss the ethics of the recording.

3. Why do you think the executives discussed document destruction?

4. What ethical issues surround diversity training and affirmative action?

5. Evaluate Texaco's performance and Mr. Bijur's behavior since the time of the settlement of this case. Consider that Texaco's spending with minority firms was at $528 million, just 2 years into its 5-year $1 billion promise.

Source: Adapted from Marianne M. Jennings, "Texaco: The Jelly Bean Diversity Fiasco," in *Business Ethics: Case Studies and Selected Readings,* 5th ed., forthcoming by Marianne M. Jennings, pp. 102–110. Copyright © 2005. Reprinted with permission of South-Western College Publishing, a division of International Thomson Publishing. Fax 800-730-2215.

SPECIFIC APPLICATIONS OF TITLE VII

The various theories of Title VII discrimination apply to specific types of discrimination. The following sections cover these types of discrimination and Title VII's application to them.

Sex Discrimination

Although Title VII included sex discrimination in its prohibitions, its presence and effects were not as obviously in existence as the more blatant racial discrimination. Many of the initial discrimination suits were brought in response to "protective legislation," which consisted of state statutes that prohibited women from working in certain fields and occupations for safety reasons. The reasons for such prohibitions were that the jobs were too strenuous, too dangerous, or too stressful. Because the effect of the statutes was to keep women from certain higher-paying occupations and men from certain female-dominated jobs, the EEOC issued guidelines providing that employers guilty of discrimination could not use these statutory cloaks. As a result, in *Dothard* v. *Rawlinson*, 433 U.S. 321 (1977), the Supreme Court held that an Alabama Board of Corrections administrative regulation establishing minimum height and weight requirements violated Title VII.

Review the Glass Ceiling Act:
http://www.law.cornell.
edu/uscode/42/2000e.html

A *prima facie* case of sex discrimination by an employer requires proof of the same elements established in the *Green* case. The only difference is that the issue of rejection, firing, or demotion is based on sex rather than race.

Other more subtle hints of discrimination have slowly been eliminated from every area of employment. Even job listings in classified ads cannot carry any sexual preference. For example, an employer cannot advertise for just a "waitress"; the ad must be for a "waiter/waitress." Further, state laws and company policies that prohibit women from working during certain hours if they have school-age children are violations of Title VII.

Sexual Harassment

Sexual harassment has been a very public topic since the Senate confirmation hearings for Justice Clarence Thomas, at which Professor Anita Hill raised allegations of sexual harassment, which is a violation of Title VII of the Civil Rights Act. Company policies on this issue should attempt to make it clear that an environment of harassment is not appropriate for any employee. Companies should also enforce policies uniformly.

Sexual harassment cases take two forms. There are the *quid pro quo* cases, in which an employee is required to submit to sexual advances in order to remain employed, secure a promotion, or obtain a raise. There are also the *atmosphere of harassment* cases, in which the invitations, language, pictures, or suggestions become so pervasive as to create a hostile work environment.

> **BUSINESS PLANNING TIP**
>
> **Office Romances**
>
> New York lawyer Sidney Siller, who defends sexual harassment suits, offers this advice for office etiquette to avoid litigation.
>
> **1.** Leave your office door open during meetings.
>
> **2.** Don't go out to lunch with opposite sex coworkers.
>
> **3.** Don't offer rides home (even in inclement weather).
>
> **4.** Avoid physical contact in the office.
>
> Some companies have adopted a policy of no fraternization among employees.

Employers are held liable for the conduct of employees that amounts to sexual harassment, as *Burlington Industries, Inc.* v. *Ellerth* (Case 20.2), which answers the chapter's opening Consider, illustrates.

CASE 20.2

Burlington Industries, Inc. v. Ellerth
524 U.S. 742 (1998)

The Boorish Supervisor Meets Vicarious Liability

FACTS

Kimberly Ellerth (respondent) worked as a salesperson in one of Burlington's divisions from March 1993 to May 1994. During her employment, she reported to a mid-level manager, Ted Slowik. Ms. Ellerth worked in a two-person office in Chicago and was one of Burlington's 22,000 employees. Mr. Slowik was based in New York but was responsible for Ms. Ellerth's office. The following incidents of boorish and offensive behavior occurred during Ms. Ellerth's employment.

Summer 1993   While on a business trip, Ms. Ellerth accepted Mr. Slowik's invitation to the hotel lounge. Mr. Slowik made remarks about Ms. Ellerth's breasts, told her to "loosen up," and said, "You know, Kim, I could make your life very hard or very easy at Burlington."

March 1994   Ms. Ellerth was being considered for a promotion, and Mr. Slowik expressed concern during the interview that she was not "loose enough." Mr. Slowik then reached out and rubbed her knee.

March 1994   Mr. Slowik called Ms. Ellerth to give her the promotion and said, "You're gonna be out there with men who work in factories, and they certainly like women with pretty butts/legs."

May 1994   Ms. Ellerth called Mr. Slowik for permission to insert a logo into a fabric sample. Mr. Slowik said, "I don't have time for you right now, Kim—unless you want to tell me what you're wearing." Ms. Ellerth ended the call.

May 1994   Ms. Ellerth called again for permission, and Mr. Slowik said, "Are you wearing shorter skirts yet, Kim, because it would make your job a whole heck of a lot easier."

In May 1994, the supervisor in the Chicago office cautioned Ms. Ellerth about returning phone calls. Ms. Ellerth quit and faxed a letter giving reasons for her decision unrelated to the alleged sexual harassment. Three weeks later, however, she sent another letter complaining of Mr. Slowik's behavior.

During her employment at Burlington, Ms. Ellerth did not tell anyone about Mr. Slowik's behavior. She chose not to tell her supervisor in the Chicago office because, "It would be his duty as my supervisor to report any incidents of sexual harassment."

Ms. Ellerth filed suit against Burlington for violation of Title VII in that the sexual harassment forced her constructive discharge.

The District Court found Mr. Slowik's behavior created a hostile work environment but found that Burlington neither knew nor should have known about the conduct. The Court of Appeals reversed, with eight separate opinions imposing vicarious liability on Burlington. Burlington appealed.

JUDICIAL OPINION

KENNEDY, Justice
At the outset, we assume an important proposition yet to be established before a trier of fact. It is a premise assumed as well, in explicit or implicit terms, in the various opinions by the judges of the Court of Appeals. The premise is: a trier of fact could find in Slowik's remarks numerous threats to retaliate against Ellerth if she denied some sexual liberties. The threats, however, were not carried out or fulfilled. Cases based on threats which are carried out are referred to often as quid pro quo cases, as distinct from bothersome attentions or sexual remarks that are sufficiently severe or pervasive to create a hostile work environment. The terms quid pro quo and hostile work environment are helpful, perhaps, in making a rough demarcation between cases in which threats are carried out and those where they are not or are absent altogether, but beyond this are of limited utility.

"Quid pro quo" and "hostile work environment" do not appear in the statutory text. The terms appeared first in the academic literature, see C. MacKinnon, *Sexual Harassment of Working Women* (1979); found their way into decisions of the Courts of Appeals, see, e.g., *Henson v. Dundee*, 682 F.2d 897, 909 (CA11 1982); and were mentioned in this Court's decision in *Meritor Savings Bank, FSB v. Vinson*, 477 U.S. 57 (1986).

Nevertheless, as use of the terms grew in the wake of *Meritor*, they acquired their own significance. The standard of employer responsibility turned on which type of harassment occurred. If the plaintiff established a quid pro quo claim, the Courts of Appeals held, the employer was subject to vicarious liability.

We do not suggest the terms quid pro quo and hostile work environment are irrelevant to Title VII litigation. To the extent they illustrate the distinction between cases involving a threat which is carried out and offensive conduct in general, the terms are relevant when there is a threshold question whether a plaintiff can prove discrimination in violation of Title VII. When a plaintiff proves that a tangible employment action resulted from a refusal to submit to a supervisor's sexual demands, he or she establishes that the employment decision itself constitutes a change in the terms and conditions of employment that is actionable under Title VII. For any sexual harassment preceding the employment decision to be actionable, however, the conduct must be severe or pervasive. Because Ellerth's claim involves only unfulfilled threats, it should be categorized as a hostile work environment claim which requires a showing of severe or pervasive conduct.

We must decide, then, whether an employer has vicarious liability when a supervisor creates a hostile work environment by making explicit threats to alter a subordinate's terms or conditions of employment, based on sex, but does not fulfill the threat. We turn to principles of agency law, for the term "employer" is defined under Title VII to include "agents." In express terms, Congress has directed federal courts to interpret Title VII based on agency principles. Given such an explicit instruction, we conclude a uniform and predictable standard must be established as a matter of federal law. We rely "on the general common law of agency, rather than on the law of any particular State, to give meaning to these terms."

Section 219(1) of the Restatement sets out a central principle of agency law:

A master is subject to liability for the torts of his servants committed while acting in the scope of their employment.

An employer may be liable for both negligent and intentional torts committed by an employee within the scope of his or her employment. Sexual harassment under Title VII presupposes intentional conduct. While early decisions absolved employers of liability for the intentional torts of their employees, the law now imposes liability where the employee's "purpose, however misguided, is wholly or in part to further the master's business."

As Courts of Appeals have recognized, a supervisor acting out of gender-based animus or a desire to fulfill sexual urges may not be actuated by a purpose to serve the employer.

The concept of scope of employment has not always been construed to require a motive to serve the employer.

The general rule is that sexual harassment by a supervisor is not conduct within the scope of employment.

Scope of employment does not define the only basis for employer liability under agency principles. In limited circumstances, agency principles impose liability on employers even where employees commit torts outside the scope of employment.

In a sense, most workplace tortfeasors are aided in accomplishing their tortious objective by the existence of the agency relation: Proximity and regular contact may afford a captive pool of potential victims.

Tangible employment actions are the means by which the supervisor brings the official power of the enterprise to bear on subordinates.

For these reasons, a tangible employment action taken by the supervisor becomes for Title VII purposes the act of the employer. Whatever the exact contours of the aided in the agency relation standard, its requirements will always be met when a supervisor takes a tangible employment action against a subordinate. In that instance, it would be implausible to interpret agency principles to allow an employer to escape liability.

An employer is subject to vicarious liability to a victimized employee for an actionable hostile environment created by a supervisor with immediate (or successively higher) authority over the employee. When no tangible employment action is taken, a defending employer may raise an affirmative defense to liability or damages, subject to proof by a preponderance of the evidence. The defense comprises two necessary elements: (a) that the employer exercised reasonable care to prevent and correct promptly any sexually harassing behavior, and (b) that the plaintiff employee unreasonably failed to take advantage of any preventive or corrective opportunities provided by the employer or to avoid harm otherwise. While proof that an employer had promulgated an anti-harassment policy with complaint procedure is not necessary in every instance as a matter of law, the need for a stated policy suitable to the employment circumstances may appropriately be addressed in any case when litigating the first element of the defense. And while proof that an employee failed to fulfill the corresponding obligation of reasonable care to avoid harm is not limited to showing any unreasonable failure to use any complaint procedure provided by the employer, a demonstration of such failure will normally suffice to satisfy the employer's burden under the second element of the defense. No affirmative defense is available, however, when the supervisor's harassment culminates in a tangible employment action, such as discharge, demotion, or undesirable reassignment.

Affirmed.

continued

DISSENTING OPINION

Justice THOMAS, with whom Justice SCALIA joins, dissenting

The Court today manufactures a rule that employers are vicariously liable if supervisors create a sexually hostile work environment, subject to an affirmative defense that the Court barely attempts to define. This rule applies even if the employer has a policy against sexual harassment, the employee knows about that policy, and the employee never informs anyone in a position of authority about the supervisor's conduct. As a result, employer liability under Title VII is judged by different standards depending upon whether a sexually or racially hostile work environment is alleged. The standard of employer liability should be the same in both instances: An employer should be liable if, and only if, the plaintiff proves that the employer was negligent in permitting the supervisor's conduct to occur.

Sexual harassment is simply not something that employers can wholly prevent without taking extraordinary measures—constant video and audio surveillance, for example—that would revolutionize the workplace in a manner incompatible with a free society. Indeed, such measures could not even detect incidents of harassment such as the comments Slowik allegedly made to respondent in a hotel bar. The most that employers can be charged with, therefore, is a duty to act reasonably under the circumstances.

The Court's holding does guarantee one result: There will be more and more litigation to clarify applicable legal rules in an area in which both practitioners and the courts have long been begging for guidance. It thus truly boggles the mind that the Court can claim that its holding will effect "Congress' intention to promote conciliation rather than litigation in the Title VII context." All in all, today's decision is an ironic result for a case that generated eight separate opinions in the Court of Appeals on a fundamental question, and in which we granted certiorari "to assist in defining the relevant standards of employer liability."

Popular misconceptions notwithstanding, sexual harassment is not a freestanding federal tort, but a form of employment discrimination. As such, it should be treated no differently (and certainly no better) than the other forms of harassment that are illegal under Title VII. I would restore parallel treatment of employer liability for racial and sexual harassment and hold an employer liable for a hostile work environment only if the employer is truly at fault. I therefore respectfully dissent.

CASE QUESTIONS

1. What is vicarious liability?
2. When will an employer be held liable for sexual harassment despite a lack of actual knowledge?
3. What is the liability of a company for harassment of an employee by an immediate supervisor?
4. What defenses exist to vicarious liability?
5. What impact does a tangible employment action have on vicarious liability?
6. What major issues does the dissenting opinion raise?

Handling Harassment Charges

Sexual harassment law demands that executives not only avoid inappropriate words and actions, but also take seriously complaints of harassment by their colleagues, even their superiors. A case in point: Earlier this month CNA Financial Corp. announced the resignation of its top life-insurance executive, Jack Kettler, and his deputy, Robert Teske. Mr. Kettler was accused of making "offensive comments" to two female employees; Mr. Teske, of failing to act on the women's complaints.

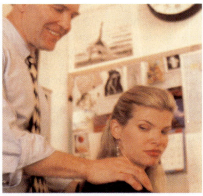
© JACK STAR/PHOTOLINK/GETTY IMAGES

Equal Employment Opportunity Commission guidelines require employers to investigate complaints of sexual harassment "promptly and thoroughly." Based on a review of relevant court cases and on my investigative work for corporate counsel over the past two decades, here are some practical suggestions for minimizing the legal, internal, and public-relations fallout from sexual harassment charges:

Move quickly to begin an investigation. It's tempting to wait until the

dust settles, but companies can help protect themselves from liability by starting an investigation immediately—preferably within 24 hours of a complaint. In the case of *Nash* v. *Electrospace System Inc.*, a federal district judge praised the accused company for wrapping up its investigation quickly. "The investigation and transfer were accomplished within one week of [the plaintiff's] first complaints," the court noted. "Surely this [promptness] reflected a prudent response to an unpleasant situation." An appeals court, upholding the district court's ruling in favor of Electrospace, called the company's response "prompt and sensitive."

Interview potential witnesses, as well as people who may be aware of a pattern of harassment. Such testimony is critical, especially when the alleged harasser denies the charge. And co-workers can provide important corroborating or exculpatory details, such as each individual's demeanor at the time of the alleged act, whether the harasser had the opportunity to commit it and whether there existed a broader pattern of behavior. If the accuser is a young female secretary, for example, an investigator should consider interviewing her young female predecessors.

Carefully regulate the alleged harasser's contact with accusers and potential witnesses. Soon after a female employee of Astra USA filed a sexual harassment complaint against the unit's chief executive, he reportedly called her and asked if she felt her job was "in jeopardy" and if she "felt pressured." Later, the CEO reportedly summoned a female employee to his hotel room, told her he was going to fire another complainant, then directed her to sign an affidavit stating that he had not harassed her. Such overtures are clearly inappropriate, but even routine contact should be minimized or prevented until the situation is resolved. If it's practical, remove both accuser and accused from the workplace, making clear to their colleagues that the separation does not imply any prejudgment but is simply a way to minimize pressure on everyone concerned.

Choose the sequence of interviews carefully. The first investigative step is interviewing the accuser to learn about specific alleged acts, dates, and other details. If the alleged harasser is likely to cooperate with the investigation or admit the harassment, interviewing him next could lead to a quick, informal resolution of the situation. But if the alleged harasser is considered hostile and the accuser says there is a pattern of behavior, it's probably best to interview other witnesses first.

Conduct interviews far from prying eyes. While an investigation is in progress, employee interest in who is under suspicion, who is assisting the investigation, and what they're saying is always intense. Even an interview's duration may be fodder for office gossip. To limit speculation and preserve confidentiality, conduct all interviews in a private area, preferably off site. Ask all employees, whether interviewed or not, to refrain from rumor and speculation, which can only hurt morale, productivity, and the company's public image.

Ask for documents and other hard evidence. In one case I worked on, a series of inappropriate messages in birthday cards from a boss to an employee were an important break in the investigation. Ask the complainant, alleged harasser and witnesses for any documents—notes, hotel receipts, and the like—that might corroborate or refute an accuser's claims. Voice and e-mail messages can also provide concrete evidence that harassment has occurred.

Reveal details about the allegation to interview subjects only when absolutely necessary. A company risks a defamation charge if "raw," unconfirmed information obtained during a sexual harassment investigation leaks.

Investigate thoroughly, but don't let investigations drag on. A major law firm, Baker & McKenzie, challenged the veracity of a secretary who complained about a partner's alleged groping—only to find later that a number of similar complaints had been made against the same partner. In 1994 a jury ordered the firm to pay its former employee several million dollars. In press interviews after the verdict, one juror cited the firm's failure to follow up on the prior complaints. Yet an overlong, overzealous investigation can do as much damage as a perfunctory one. If victims believe that a company's internal resolution process has failed because the investigation drags on, they may go outside the organization to seek satisfaction. That can escalate the seriousness of the situation that could have been resolved had the investigation been completed in a timely manner.

A badly managed sexual harassment investigation can seriously damage an organization—internally, in the courts, and in the public eye. But a prompt, thorough, professional investigation can help preserve, even enhance, the credibility of its leadership, the morale of its workers, and the value of its stock.

Source: James B. Mintz, "Harassment 101: How to Handle Complaints," *Wall Street Journal,* March 31, 1997, p. A14. Reprinted with permission of *The Wall Street Journal* © 1997 Dow Jones & Company, Inc. All rights reserved.

CONSIDER...   **20.4**

Between 1985 and 1990, while attending college, Beth Ann Faragher worked part time and during the summers as an ocean lifeguard for the Parks and Recreation Department of the City of Boca Raton.

Ms. Faragher worked for three immediate supervisors during this period: Bill Terry, David Silverman, and Robert Gordon. Ms. Faragher resigned in June 1990 and brought a Title VII sexual harassment suit against the City in 1992. She alleged a sexually hostile atmosphere because of "uninvited and offensive touching," lewd remarks, and Mr. Silverman's comment, "Date me or clean the toilets for a year."

Ms. Faragher had not complained to higher management, and the lifeguards had no significant contact with higher city officials. Two months before Ms. Faragher's resignation, a former lifeguard, Nancy E. Wanchew, wrote to the City's personnel director complaining about Mr. Terry and Mr. Silverman's harassment of female lifeguards.

Should the City be held liable? Does it matter that Ms. Faragher asked only for nominal damages, attorney's fees, and costs? [*Faragher* v. *City of Boca Raton,* 524 U.S. 775 (1998).]

CONSIDER...   **20.5**

Joseph Oncale worked for Sundowner Offshore Services on a Chevron U.S.A., Inc. oil platform in the Gulf of Mexico. He was employed as part of an eight-man crew. Mr. Oncale complained in his pink slip when he quit that he "left voluntarily due to sexual harassment and verbal abuse." Mr. Oncale said that he was called names suggesting homosexuality and threatened with rape.

Mr. Oncale filed suit under Title VII for sexual harassment. Is recovery for same-sex sexual harassment possible under Title VII? [*Oncale* v. *Sundowner Offshore Services, Inc.* 523 U.S. 75 (1998).]

CONSIDER...   **20.6**

Determine whether the following would constitute sexual harassment (either *quid pro quo* or atmosphere of harassment) under Title VII.
1. A manager who referred to female customers as "bitchy" or "dumb," flirted with an employee's female relatives, and told of spending a weekend at a nudist camp [*Gleason* v. *Mesirow Financial, Inc.,* 118 F. 3d 1134 (7th Cir. 1997)]
2. A manager who told a single, pregnant female employee that he disapproved of premarital sex [*Brill* v. *Lante,* 119 F. 3d 1266 (7th Cir. 1997)]
3. Calendar photographs of women in swimwear posted in a coemployee's workstation [*Guidry* v. *Zale Corp.,* 969 F. Supp. 988 (M.D.La. 1997)]
4. A supervisor who called his wife "ignorant" and women in his department "dumb" and used the term "gals" for all his female employees [*Penry* v. *Federal Home Loan Bank of Topeka,* 970 F.Supp. 833 (D. Kan. 1997)]
5. A supervisor who referred to the architecture of a shopping mall as looking like "two hooters" and a "bra bazaar," while having dinner with an employee on a business trip [*Penry* v. *Federal Home Loan Bank of Topeka,* 970 F. Supp. 833 (D. Kan. 1997)]
6. Two uninvited hugs by a supervisor and notes to employees signed, "Love, Steph" [*Drew* v. *First Sav. of New Hampshire,* 968 F. Supp. 762 (D. N. H. 1997)]

Derogatory, suggestive, and offensive e-mails and electronic bulletin boards on servers sponsored by an employer can be the basis for a hostile environment sexual harassment suit. Employers not only have the responsibility to prohibit employees from posting such materials; they also have a responsibility to supervise such bulletin boards and e-mails to be certain that no atmosphere of harassment results from the contents.

Further, in litigation over such materials, plaintiffs may rely on printed copies of the materials and messages to use in establishing their cases even though the materials may have already been deleted from the company system.

Sex Discrimination and Pensions

Visit the Women's Legal History Biography Project:
http://www.stanford.edu/group/WLHP

Another area of sex discrimination in employment involves the statistical fact that women live longer than men. It costs more for a female employee to have a pension than a male employee because she will likely live longer after retirement. In *City of Los Angeles Department of Water v. Manhart,* 435 U.S. 702 (1978), the Supreme Court held that employers could not require female employees to contribute more to their pension plans than males. The additional contributions for the female employees were required by the employer because the pension planner had statistical evidence that longevity of female employees exceeded that of male employees. If the Supreme Court had sanctioned the disparity in pension plan payments, the higher cost of having female employees could have been cited by employers as the reason for their hiring practices. Insurers and employers are required to treat employees as a group and not to break them down by their age, sex, or other characteristics.

Sex Discrimination and Pregnancy Issues

Review the Pregnancy Discrimination Act:
http://www.eeoc.gov/abouteeoc/35th/thelaw/pregnancy_discrimination-1978.html

The Pregnancy Discrimination Act was added to Title VII in 1974. Prior to this act, women were forced to take maternity leaves at certain times and for certain lengths of time solely because of their pregnancies. Many women who returned to work after their pregnancies discovered that their pay had been cut or that they had been demoted. Even employees' insurance coverage treated pregnancy differently from other medical ailments, and pregnancy was not treated as an illness by most employers in terms of sick leave.

This act, which revolutionized maternity issues in the employment world, prohibits the following specific acts:

1. Forcing a resignation due to pregnancy
2. Demoting or limiting an employee's job upon her return to work
3. Refusing to allow a mother to return to work after pregnancy
4. Providing different sick leave rules for pregnancy and other medical ailments
5. Providing different medical insurance benefits or disability leave for pregnancy and other ailments
6. Refusing to hire or promote on the basis of pregnancy or family plans

The landmark case *International Union* v. *Johnson Controls, Inc.* (Case 20.3) focuses on new issues in sex discrimination.

CASE 20.3

International Union v. *Johnson Controls, Inc.*
499 U.S. 187 (1991)

The Acid Test for Women:
The Right to Choose High-Risk Jobs

FACTS

Johnson Controls, Inc. (respondent) manufactures batteries. In the manufacturing process, the element lead is a primary ingredient. Occupational exposure to lead entails health risks, including the risk of harm to any fetus carried by a female employee.

Before the Civil Rights Act of 1964 became law, Johnson Controls did not employ any woman in a battery-manufacturing job. In June 1977, however, it announced its first official policy concerning its employment of women in jobs with lead exposure risk:

> [P]rotection of the health of the unborn child is the immediate and direct responsibility of the prospective parents. While the medical profession and the company can support them in the exercise of this responsibility, it cannot assume it for them without simultaneously infringing their rights as persons. . . .
>
> Since not all women who can become mothers wish to become mothers (or will become mothers), it would appear to be illegal discrimination to treat all who are capable of pregnancy as though they will become pregnant.

Consistent with that view, Johnson Controls "stopped short of excluding women capable of bearing children from lead exposure" but emphasized that a woman who expected to have a child should not choose a job in which she would have such exposure. The company also required a woman who wished to be considered for employment to sign a statement indicating that she had been advised of the risk of having a child while she was exposed to lead. The statement informed the woman that although there was evidence "that women exposed to lead have a higher rate of abortion," this evidence was "not as clear . . . as the relationship between cigarette smoking and cancer," but that it was, "medically speaking, just good sense not to run that risk if you want children and do not want to expose the unborn child to risk, however small. . . ."

In 1982, Johnson Controls shifted from a policy of warning to a policy of exclusion. Between 1979 and 1983, eight employees became pregnant while maintaining lead levels in excess of 30 micrograms per deciliter of blood. The company responded by announcing a broad exclusion of women from jobs that exposed them to lead:

> [I]t is [Johnson Controls'] policy that women who are pregnant or who are capable of bearing children will not be placed into jobs involving lead exposure or which could expose them to lead through the exercise of job bidding, bumping, transfer or promotion rights.

The policy defined "women . . . capable of bearing children" as "[a]ll women except those whose inability to bear children is medically documented."

Several employees (petitioners) and their unions filed suit alleging that Johnson Controls' fetal protection policy violated Title VII of the Civil Rights Act. Included in the group were:

- Mary Craig—sterilized to avoid losing her job
- Elsie Nason—50-year-old divorcee who lost compensation when transferred out of lead exposure job
- Donald Penney—denied request for leave of absence to lower his lead level before becoming a father

The district court entered summary judgment for Johnson Controls. The court of appeals affirmed, and the employees appealed.

JUDICIAL OPINION

BLACKMUN, Justice

The bias in Johnson Controls' policy is obvious. Fertile men, but not fertile women, are given a choice as to whether they wish to risk their reproductive health for a particular job. Section 703(a) of the Civil Rights Act of 1964, 78 Stat. 255, as amended, 42 U.S.C. § 2000e-2(a), prohibits sex-based classifications in terms and conditions of employment, in hiring and discharging decisions, and in other employment decisions that adversely affect an employee's status. Respondent's fetal-protection policy explicitly discriminates against women on the basis of their sex. The policy excludes women with childbearing capacity from lead-exposed jobs and so creates a facial classification based on gender. Respondent assumes as much in its brief before this Court.

Nevertheless, the Court of Appeals assumed, as did the two appellate courts who already had confronted this issue, that sex specific fetal-protection policies do not involve facial discrimination. These courts analyzed the policies as though they were facially neutral, and had only a discriminatory effect upon the employment opportunities of women. Consequently, the courts looked to see if each employer in question had established that its policy was justified as a business necessity. The business necessity standard is more lenient for the employer than the statutory BFOQ [bona fide occupational qualification] defense. The court assumed that because the asserted reason for the sex-based exclusion (protecting women's unconceived offspring) was ostensibly benign, the policy was not sex-based discrimination. That assumption, however, was incorrect.

First, Johnson Controls' policy classifies on the basis of gender and childbearing capacity, rather than fertility alone. Respondent does not seek to protect the unconceived children of all its employees. Despite evidence in the record about the debilitating effect of lead exposure on the male reproductive system, Johnson Controls is concerned only with the harms that may befall the unborn offspring of its female employees.

Our conclusion is bolstered by the Pregnancy Discrimination Act [PDA] of 1978, 42 U.S.C. § 2000e(k), in which Congress explicitly provided that, for purposes of Title VII, discrimination "on the basis of sex" includes discrimination "because of or on the basis of pregnancy, childbirth, or related medical conditions." "The Pregnancy Discrimination Act has now made clear that, for all Title VII purposes, discrimination based on a woman's pregnancy is, on its face, discrimination because of her sex." In its use of the words "capable of bearing children" in the 1982 policy statement as the criterion for exclusion, Johnson Controls explicitly classifies on the basis of potential for pregnancy. Under the PDA, such a classification must be regarded, for Title VII purposes, in the same light as explicit sex discrimination. Respondent has chosen to treat all its female employees as potentially pregnant; that choice evinces discrimination on the basis of sex.

We concluded above that Johnson Controls' policy is not neutral because it does not apply to the reproductive capacity of the company's male employees in the same way as it applies to that of the females. Moreover, the absence of a malevolent motive does not convert a facially discriminatory policy into a neutral policy with a discriminatory effect. Whether an employment practice involves disparate treatment through explicit facial discrimination does not depend on why the employer discriminates but rather on the explicit terms of the discrimination.

In sum, Johnson Controls' policy "does not pass the simple test of whether the evidence shows 'treatment of a person in a manner which but for that person's sex would be different.'"

We therefore turn to the question whether Johnson Controls' fetal-protection policy is one of those "certain instances" that come within the BFOQ exception.

Johnson Controls argues that its fetal-protection policy falls within the so-called safety exception to the BFOQ. Our cases have stressed that discrimination on the basis of sex because of safety concerns is allowed only in narrow circumstances. In *Dothard* v. *Rawlinson*, 433 U.S. 321 (1977), this Court indicated that the danger to a woman herself does not justify discrimination. We there allowed the employer to hire only male guards in contact areas of maximum-security male penitentiaries only because more was at stake than the "individual woman's decision to weigh and accept the risks of employment." We found sex to be a BFOQ inasmuch as the employment of a female guard would create real risks of safety to others if violence broke out because the guard was a woman. Sex discrimination was tolerated because sex was related to the guard's ability to do the job—maintaining prison security. We also required in *Dothard* a high correlation between sex and ability to perform job functions and refused to allow employers to use sex as a proxy for strength although it might be a fairly accurate one.

Similarly, some courts have approved airlines' layoffs of pregnant flight attendants at different points during the first five months of pregnancy on the ground that the employer's policy was necessary to ensure the safety of passengers.

The unconceived fetuses of Johnson Controls' female employees, however, are neither customers nor third parties whose safety is essential to the business of battery manufacturing. No one can disregard the possibility of injury to future children; the BFOQ, however, is not so broad that it transforms this deep social concern into an essential aspect of battery making.

Our case law makes clear that the safety exception is limited to instances in which sex or pregnancy actually interferes with the employee's ability to perform the job. This approach is consistent with the language of the BFOQ provision itself, for it suggests that permissible distinctions based on sex must relate to ability to perform the duties of the job. Johnson Controls suggests, however, that we expand the exception to allow fetal-protection policies that mandate particular standards for pregnant or fertile women. We decline to do so. Such an expansion contradicts not only the language of the BFOQ and the narrowness of its exception but the plain language and history of the Pregnancy Discrimination Act.

A word about tort liability and the increased cost of fertile women in the workplace is perhaps necessary. One of the dissenting judges in this case expressed concern about an employer's tort liability and concluded that liability for a potential injury to a fetus is a social cost that Title VII does not require a company to ignore. It is correct to say that Title VII does not prevent the employer from having a conscience. The statute, however, does prevent sex-specific fetal-protection policies. These two aspects of Title VII do not conflict.

More than 40 States currently recognize a right to

continued

recover for a prenatal injury based either on negligence or on wrongful death. According to Johnson Controls, however, the company complies with the lead standard developed by OSHA and warns its female employees about the damaging effects of lead. It is worth noting that OSHA gave the problem of lead lengthy consideration and concluded that "there is no basis whatsoever for the claim that women of childbearing age should be excluded from the workplace in order to protect the fetus or the course of pregnancy." Instead, OSHA established a series of mandatory protections which, taken together, "should effectively minimize any risk to the fetus and newborn child." Without negligence, it would be difficult for a court to find liability on the part of the employer. If, under general tort principles, Title VII bans sex-specific fetal-protection policies, the employer fully informs the woman of the risk, and the employer has not acted negligently, the basis for holding an employer liable seems remote at best.

Although the issue is not before us, the concurrence observes that "it is far from clear that compliance with Title VII will preempt state tort liability."

Our holding today that Title VII, as so amended, forbids sex-specific fetal-protection policies is neither remarkable nor unprecedented. Concern for a woman's existing or potential offspring historically has been the excuse for denying women equal employment opportunities.

It is no more appropriate for the courts than it is for individual employers to decide whether a woman's reproductive role is more important to herself and her family than her economic role. Congress has left this choice to the woman as hers to make.

The judgment of the Court of Appeals is reversed and the case is remanded for further proceedings consistent with this opinion.

CASE QUESTIONS

1. Describe Johnson Controls' evolving policy on lead exposure.
2. Describe the plaintiffs who brought suit in the case.
3. Are circumstances given when sex is a BFOQ?
4. What problem is presented by the exclusion of men from the policy?
5. What is the court's position on tort liability of the company with respect to the fetus?

BUSINESS STRATEGY

Dangerous Exposure

The *Johnson Controls* decision has allowed many women to work in jobs that expose them to toxins. The U.S. Supreme Court did acknowledge in its holding that tort liability might result from its decision but that such liability was often used as a guise or cover for gender discrimination. However, fourteen years after the decision, women who were held to be entitled to the high-risk jobs are now suing their employers for the birth defects in their children. For example, IBM has several suits from employees and their children against it for defects allegedly tied to production line toxins. The position of many of the employers is that even if there were evidence linking the toxins to birth defects, the women took the jobs with knowledge about the risk and agreed to that risk. How can employers, legislators, and public policy specialists reconcile antidiscrimination laws and these risks of exposure?

Source: Stephanie Armour, "Workers take employers to court over birth defects," *USA Today,* February 26, 2002, pp. 1A, 2A. For more information, visit http://www.cdc.gov/niosh.

Religious Discrimination

Employers are required to make reasonable efforts to accommodate an employee's religious practices, holidays, and observances. Not all religious or church activities, however, are protected; for example, the observance of a religion's Sabbath is a protected activity, but taking time to prepare for a church bake sale or pageant is an unprotected activity. The 1972 amendments to Title VII defined religion to include "all aspects of religious observance and practice, as well as belief." The accommodation

CONSIDER...   20.7

Lora Ilhardt began working for Sara Lee in April 1988. She was the first female attorney to be hired in Sara Lee's Chicago office. She was given several raises and promoted to director, which gave her the opportunity to participate in the company's bonus plan.

In October 1989, Ms. Ilhardt gave birth to her first child and took a three-month maternity leave. She asked to return, working part time at three days per week. Her request was granted and her salary was adjusted, but she was still given full bonus participation.

Her part-time status caused some inconvenience, but both clients and coworkers gave her high performance reviews.

In July 1991, Ms. Ilhardt began her second maternity leave, and Sara Lee was undergoing a corporate reduction in force. Gordon Newman, Sara Lee's general counsel, decided, if necessary, to eliminate Ms. Ilhardt's position since she worked a part-time position. Mr. Newman told her that if she worked full time, he could better protect her job.

Ms. Ilhardt did not take a full-time job and by April 1993 was in the midst of her third pregnancy. A reduction in force came at the end of April. Mr. Newman offered her an eight-month maternity leave but could not guarantee a job after it was over. Ms. Ilhardt refused, took her maternity leave, and then asked to return. Sara Lee had no openings. Ms. Ilhardt filed a Title VII discrimination claim. Should she recover? [*Ilhardt* v. *Sara Lee Corp.,* 118 F. 3d 1151 (7th Cir. 1997).]

---

of religion thus defined is required unless an employer is able to establish that allowing the employee such an accommodation would result in "undue hardship on the conduct of the employer's business."

In *Trans World Airlines, Inc.* v. *Hardison,* 432 U.S. 63 (1977), the Supreme Court confirmed the clear language of the 1972 act that requires an employer to demonstrate inability to accommodate an employee's religious needs. As a member of a church that worshiped on Saturdays, Larry G. Hardison expressed a desire not to work that day. TWA worked through several alternatives to afford Mr. Hardison the opportunity for Saturdays off, including asking the union to waive a seniority rule that limited substitutes for him and looking for an alternative job that would not require Saturday work. The union would not waive its rule, and no managers were available to take the shift. When Mr. Hardison refused to work on Saturdays, he was dismissed and filed suit, but the Court found for TWA because of its extensive efforts and the constraints that prevented shifting of workers without substantial interference in TWA's operations.

Title VII requires only reasonable accommodation. Employees are not necessarily entitled to the accommodation they desire. For example, in *American Postal Workers Union* v. *Postmaster General,* 781 F.2d 772 (9th Cir. 1986), several postal employees refused to work at a window in the post office where draft registration forms were handled. They asked to be able to direct draft registrants to the windows of employees who did not have religious objections to the draft. The Postal Service transferred the employees to nonwindow jobs, which was supported by the court as a reasonable accommodation.

Further, employees are expected to cooperate with their employers in making an accommodation, such as finding a fellow employee to take a shift. In *TWA* v. *Hardison,* the Court noted, "The statute is not to be construed to require an employer to discriminate against some employees in order for others to observe their Sabbath." In *Buonanno* v. *AT&T Broadband, LLC* (Case 20.4), a federal court faced a new and emotionally charged issue related to accommodation.

CASE 20.4

Buonanno v. AT&T Broadband, LLC
313 F. Supp. 2d 1069 (D.Colo. 2004)

Give It to Me Straight:
Does Title VII Protect My Religious Beliefs?

FACTS

Albert Buonanno (plaintiff) was employed by AT&T from January 10, 1999 to February 1, 2001. Initially he worked as a cable dispatcher, scheduling jobs and dispatching field technicians.

Mr. Buonanno is a Christian who believes that the Bible is divinely inspired. He attempts to live his life in accordance with its literal language. Because the Bible requires that he treat others as he would like to be treated, Mr. Buonanno values and respects all other AT&T employees as individuals. He never has nor would he discriminate against another employee due to differences in belief, behavior, background, or other attributes. However, his religious beliefs prohibit him from approving, endorsing, or esteeming behavior or values that are repudiated by Scripture.

In January 2001, AT&T promoted a new "Employee Handbook" that addressed "How We Work: Employee Guidelines" and "Doing What's Right: Business Integrity & Ethics Policies."

AT&T maintains a "Certification Policy," which provides that "[e]ach AT&T Broadband employee must sign and return the Acknowledgment of Receipt and Certificate of Understanding form indicating that you have received a copy of the handbook and the AT&T Code of Conduct and that you will abide by our employment policies and practices."

AT&T's diversity policy reads as follows:

The company places tremendous value on the fresh, innovative ideas and variety of perspectives that come from a diverse workplace. Diversity is necessary for a competitive business advantage—and the company is competing for customers in an increasingly diverse marketplace. To make diversity work to our advantage, it's our goal to build an environment that:

- *respects and values individual differences*
- *reflects the communities we serve*
- *promotes employee involvement in decision making*
- *encourages innovation and differing perspectives in problem solving*
- *allows our diverse employee population to contribute richly to our growth.*

We want to create a team that is diverse, committed and the most talented in America. To that end, AT&T Broadband has a "zero tolerance" policy toward any type of discrimination, harassment or retaliation in our com-

pany. Each person at AT&T Broadband is charged with the responsibility to fully recognize, respect and value the differences among all of us. This is demonstrated in the way we communicate and interact with our customers, suppliers and each other every day.

Mr. Buonanno questioned the meaning of the third sentence in the second paragraph which reads "Each person at AT&T Broadband is charged with the responsibility to fully recognize, respect and value the differences among all of us." The court refers to this portion of the diversity policy as the Diversity Philosophy. He believed that some behavior and beliefs were deemed sinful by Scripture, and thus that he could not "value," that is, hold in esteem or ascribe worth to, such behavior or beliefs without compromising his own religious beliefs. Mr. Buonanno was fully prepared to comply with the principles underlying the Diversity Philosophy. However, he could not comply with the challenged language insofar as it apparently required him to "value" the particular belief or behavior that was repudiated by Scripture. Accordingly, if the challenged language literally required him to do so, he could not sign the Certificate of Understanding, agreeing to "abide by" such language.

Mr. Buonanno consulted with his pastor, Scott McCall, of the Crow Hill Bible Church for guidance. Mr. Buonanno also discussed his concerns with his supervisor, Mr. Dunn, a practicing Christian. Mr. Dunn did not believe that the challenged language was inconsistent with his personal, religious beliefs as a Christian, but he urged Mr. Buonanno to clarify the issue in a written communication to his AT&T Human Resources Manager, Susan Batliner. Mr. Buonanno slipped a letter under Ms. Batliner's office door with the following included:

I can't comply with the ambiguous statement under "Diversity" on pages six and seven [of the Handbook]. . . . As an AT&T employee I am fully cognizant of the fact that there is diversity among its members. Since being hired on January 10, 1999, I have indiscriminately conducted myself in a professional manner with all people. . . . However, . . . I believe it's wrong for any individual or organization to attempt to persuade me to fully respect and fully value any differences which are contrary to God's word. In order for me to comply with this diversity statement in the company handbook, I would have to deny my faith; this I will not do. It is this reason that prohibits me from signing the certificate of acknowledgment. . . . As an AT&T employee I give you my word that I will continued [sic] to conduct myself in the same professional manner. But I can't allow any group or individual to choose for me what I must respect or place value on.

The letter was accompanied by an unsigned copy of the Certificate.

Ms. Batliner discussed the letter with her superior, Debora Davis, the Vice President of Human Resources for AT&T's Colorado operation. Ms. Davis instructed Ms. Batliner to talk to Mr. Buonanno's supervisor and then with Mr. Buonanno to clarify his concerns. Ms. Batliner was instructed to ask questions, get information, and explain the importance of the diversity policy. Ms. Davis told Ms. Batliner that signing the Certificate was required of all employees, but she did not authorize Ms. Batliner to terminate Mr. Buonanno's employment if he did not sign.

Ms. Batliner then scheduled a morning meeting with Mr. Dunn and Mr. Buonanno. On the way to the meeting, Mr. Dunn informed Mr. Buonanno that signing the Certificate was a requirement for continued employment. He suggested that Mr. Buonanno seek clarification of the challenged language, suggesting that Mr. Buonanno inquire whether the language would require him to value, for example, a "neo-Nazi skinhead's" beliefs.

The meeting among Ms. Batliner, Mr. Buonanno, and Mr. Dunn lasted between 30 and 40 minutes. When Mr. Buonanno attempted to clarify the meaning of the Certificate by asking how it would apply to the beliefs of "neo-Nazi skinheads," Ms. Batliner refused to engage in what she characterized as a "philosophical debate."

Without clarification as to the identified language, Mr. Buonanno explained, he could not sign the Certificate. Ms. Batliner terminated his employment and proceeded to conduct an exit interview. Mr. Buonanno filed suit against AT&T for its failure to accommodate his religious beliefs. Following a bench trial, the court issued its decision.

JUDICIAL OPINION

KRIEGER, District Judge

As is clear from the language of the Diversity Philosophy, as well as the numerous references to "diversity" elsewhere in the Handbook, AT&T maintains an overarching policy of inclusiveness. AT&T defines "diversity" broadly—contemplating all attributes, history, experience, skill, perspective, etc. that make one individual different from another, and considers all of those various characteristics as having potential value to its business development. AT&T believes that its Diversity Philosophy helps it better acquire customers,

understand customer needs, and increase its sales and provide better customer service. For example, Senior Vice President of Human Resources David Brunick testified that in the past, English-speaking employees recognizing the differences between themselves and Spanish- or Russian-speaking employees allowed the company to expand into Spanish- and Russian-speaking markets that were otherwise unavailable.

AT&T maintains that permitting an employee to certify anything other than full agreement with all of the language in the Handbook would destroy the competitive advantage its Diversity Philosophy creates. Doing so would demonstrate to other employees that AT&T's policies were not uniformly applied and enforced.

Five corporate officials testified about the challenged language.

No AT&T representative explored or explained the intended meaning (or any of the various interpretations) of the challenged language to Buonanno. No AT&T employee inquired as to the particulars of Buonanno's concerns, sought to devise ways to accommodate Buonanno's religious beliefs, or reassured him that the challenged language did not require him to surrender his religious beliefs. At all relevant times, Buonanno was presented with a choice of between accepting the language of the Handbook without any additional clarification and signing the Certificate, or losing his employment.

The Plaintiff articulated two distinct theories of religious discrimination in his closing argument: (i) direct religious discrimination; and (ii) failure to accommodate.

. . . [a] claim of direct religious discrimination lies where an employee contends that he received unfavorable treatment "motivated by an animus directed against" his particular religious persuasion. In such circumstances, the Court applies a slightly modified version of the customary shifting-burden test. A plaintiff must come forward with evidence establishing: (i) that he was subjected to some adverse employment action; (ii) that, at the time the employment action was taken, the employee's job performance was satisfactory; and (iii) an inference that the employment actions were taken because of a discriminatory motive based upon the employee's failure to hold or follow his or her employer's religious beliefs. The employer must then present evidence to support a non-discriminatory reason for the adverse action. In rebuttal, the employee must prove pretext, all in accordance with the classic *McDonnell Douglas* analysis.

Here, Buonanno did not establish the third element of the prima facie case, that the actions taken against him were motivated by his failure to follow his

continued

employer's religious beliefs. With the exception of Dunn, nothing in the record establishes that any of his supervisors held particular religious beliefs, much less that their beliefs were in conflict with Buonanno's. Dunn, Buonanno's immediate supervisor, is a Christian. Thus, Buonanno has not proved that he was terminated based on his failure to follow the religious beliefs of his employer. Accordingly, AT&T prevails on this claim.

To establish of a claim of religious discrimination based on a failure to accommodate theory, a plaintiff must prove: (i) he had a bona fide religious belief that conflicts with an employment requirement; (ii) he informed his or her employer of this belief, and (iii) he was fired for failure to comply with the conflicting employment requirement. The burden then shifts to the employer to either conclusively rebut one or more elements of the plaintiff's prima facie case, to show that it offered a reasonable accommodation, or to show that it was unable reasonably to accommodate the employee's religious needs without undue hardship on the conduct of its business.

Where an employer has made no efforts to accommodate the religious beliefs of an employee before taking action against him, the employer may only prevail if it shows that no accommodation could have been made without undue hardship.

The reasonableness of a proposed accommodation is considered in light of all of the facts and circumstances of the case. A proposed accommodation poses an "undue hardship" on the employer if it bears more than a de minimis cost or significant impact on efficiency, or disrupts a bona fide seniority system. *Trans World Airlines, Inc.* v. *Hardison,* 432 U.S. 63, 84, 97 S.Ct. 2264, 53 L.Ed.2d 113 (1977). However, the claimed hardship must be more than merely speculative. An employer's costs of accommodation "must mean present undue hardship, as distinguished from anticipated or multiplied hardship."

Buonanno established that he has a bona fide religious belief that conflicted with an employment policy. As Buonanno stated in his written communication to Batliner, his religion teaches that certain (unidentified) behavior is sinful, yet the challenged language requires him to "value" differences among employees presumably, some of those "differences" might involve conduct proscribed by Buonanno's religion.

It is also evident that Buonanno communicated the existence of such a conflict to AT&T.

AT&T must either show that it offered a reasonable accommodation, or to show that it was unable reasonably to accommodate Buonanno's religious needs without undue hardship on the conduct of its business. AT&T failed to offer any accommodation, thus the sole question is whether it could have accommodated Buo-

nanno's belief without undue hardship. AT&T contends that it could not have carved out an exception to the "Diversity Policy" for Buonanno without diminishing the value of the "policy" as a whole.

As noted earlier, AT&T's Diversity Philosophy reflects a legitimate and laudable business goal. The Court accepts AT&T's contention that allowing employees to strike piecemeal portions of the Handbook or Certification could pose an undue hardship on its business, making uniform application of company policies much more difficult. Nevertheless, had AT&T gathered more information about Buonanno's concerns before terminating his employment, it may have discovered that the perceived conflict between his beliefs and AT&T's policy was not an actual conflict at all, or that if a true conflict existed, it was possible to relieve that conflict with a reasonable accommodation.

Had Batliner, Davis, Brunick, or Wilson ever explained that they understood the challenged language to have a figurative, rather than literal, meaning and listened to his concerns, the issue could have been resolved without any need for accommodation. Accordingly, AT&T has failed to show that it could not have accommodated Buonanno's beliefs without undue hardship.

. . . AT&T could nevertheless have accommodated Buonanno without suffering undue hardship. Although AT&T's Diversity Philosophy confers a business advantage, AT&T did not show that the literal application of the challenged language was necessary to obtain such advantage. For example, Wilson explained the advantages conferred by the "Diversity Policy" by relating an anecdote in which homosexual employees at American Express, sensing a need for estate-planning services in the gay community, proposed the creation of a successful new targeted product. In such example, no employee at American Express was required to ascribe any "value" to the practice of homosexuality in order to capitalize on the opportunity. Rather, American Express officials simply recognized that homosexual employees had a unique perspective on ways to market the company's product. Thus, as Wilson admitted, a minor revision of the challenged language, requiring all employees company-wide to "fully recognize, respect and value that there are differences among all of us" would have "accomplished [AT&T's] goals" as set forth in the Diversity Philosophy, without imposing any apparent hardship on AT&T. Whether such a change is characterized as clarifying AT&T's interpretation of the existing Handbook language or a reasonable accommodation for Buonanno is irrelevant. AT&T violated Title VII by failing to engage in the required dialogue with Buonanno upon notice of his concerns and by failing to clarify the challenged language to reasonably accommodate Buonanno's religious beliefs.

Accordingly, Buonanno is entitled to a damage award as follows: backpay and lost 401(k) matching contributions, plus prejudgment interest totaling $93,370; compensation for emotional distress of $4,000; and front pay in the amount of $48,899, for a total damage award of $146,269.

CASE QUESTIONS

1. What portion of the certificate did Mr. Buonanno feel was inconsistent with his beliefs?
2. What mistake did the AT&T supervisors and executives make in dealing with Mr. Buonanno's objections?
3. What could have been offered as an accommodation?
4. What does Mr. Buonanno get as damages?

Racial Discrimination

When Title VII was first enacted, its clear intent was to prevent discrimination against the minority workforce. After Title VII had been in effect for several years, an unanticipated problem arose: Does Title VII's protection extend to all races? Are white employees entitled to the same protection Title VII affords other races?

In 1976, the Supreme Court provided the answer in *McDonald* v. *Santa Fe Trail Transportation Co.*, 427 U.S. 273 (1976). Here, some black employees had been reinstated after committing the same offense as a group of white employees who were not reinstated. The Court held that Title VII prohibited such racial discrimination.

In *Patterson* v. *McClean Credit Union*, 491 U.S. 164 (1989), the U.S. Supreme Court was faced with reprehensible conduct by an employer in the consideration of a black female for promotion. The Court held that there was no violation of the Civil Rights Act because a promotion was not part of a contract as required to establish race discrimination under Section 1981, a nineteenth-century antidiscrimination statute. The effect of the case was changed by the 1991 Civil Rights Act, which permits victims of racial or ethnic discrimination to recover unrestricted compensatory and punitive damages without regard to the technical issue of whether the terms of employment fit within the Court's narrow construction of a contract.

ANTIDISCRIMINATION LAWS AND AFFIRMATIVE ACTION

Some employers, either voluntarily or through the EEOC, have instituted **affirmative action** programs. Nothing prohibits such programs under Title VII, and the Supreme Court has sanctioned them as methods for remedying all the past years of discrimination. Although Title VII does not mandate such programs, employers may legally institute them.

Affirmative action has been described by some as the tool necessary to put all races and the sexes on an equal footing after years of discrimination. Others, however, have described it as an unfair system that discriminates against whites and males and often reduces the self-esteem of those who benefit from it because of their feelings about being hired or promoted solely because of their race or sex. Others have argued that affirmative action encourages inefficiency because it prevents the most qualified or the most deserving from earning a promotion or being hired in the first instance.

What Is Affirmative Action?

Although Title VII prohibits discrimination against any group, there is well-established judicial and legislative support for the establishment of affirmative action programs. Affirmative action is a remedial step taken to ensure that those who have been victims of discrimination in the past are given the opportunity to work in positions they would have attained had there not been discrimination.

Affirmative action programs are used to improve job opportunities for African-Americans, Hispanics, Native Americans, Asians, women, persons with disabilities, and Vietnam veterans.

Who Is Required to Have Affirmative Action Programs?

Some federal funding laws, such as those for education and state and local governments, mandate affirmative action programs.

Some employers have an obligation to take steps to equalize the representation of minorities and women in their labor forces. This equalization of representation in the labor force is the process of affirmative action. The following types of employers are obligated to undertake affirmative action programs:

1. Employers who, pursuant to consent decree or court order, must implement plans to compensate for past wrongs
2. State and local agencies, colleges, and universities that receive federal funds
3. Government contractors
4. Businesses that work on federal projects (10 percent of their subcontract work must employ minority businesses)

Affirmative action plans cannot simply be **quotas**; a quota program is an unlawful infringement of the rights of a majority group of employees. Rather, affirmative action programs set goals—for example, a certain number of minorities employed by a certain date. If the goal is not met, a business has not violated the law so long as it has made a good-faith effort to recruit and hire minorities. That good-faith effort can be established by a showing of internal and external advertising, monitoring of the program's progress, and changes and improvements in the program's development.

Preparing an Affirmative Action Program

An employer should begin with an equal employment opportunity statement, which says simply that decisions on recruiting, hiring, training, and promotion will be made without regard to race, color, religion, sex, national origin, veteran status, or disability. The statement should be displayed at the place of business, made evident in all recruiting materials, and reaffirmed each year to reestablish commitment to it. The firm should also appoint an affirmative action or equal employment opportunity officer. The role of this employee is to identify problems and propose solutions.

A business should then conduct an initial audit and maintain good records regarding hiring, promoting, and recruiting employees. In such an audit, the employer examines job titles and determines key areas in which women and minorities are underrepresented with respect to their availability in the workforce. A system of goals and timetables should be established for each underrepresented job title. The employer then monitors the data to see whether the goals are met. If the goals are not met, the employer should take further steps, such as more aggressive recruiting.

Affirmative Action Backlash:
The Theory of Reverse Discrimination

Currently, some legislative movements and grassroots referenda mandate the elimination of affirmative action programs. The University of California system eliminated affirmative action programs in 1995, but the programs were reinstated by a court after the elimination was challenged. A state referendum then passed, eliminating racial preferences by any state agency, including its colleges and universities.

In *Adarand Constructors, Inc.* v. *Pena,* 515 U.S. 200 (1995), the U.S. Supreme Court was faced with the issue of affirmative action programs in a case brought by a contractor that challenged the federal government's program granting socially and economically disadvantaged contractors and subcontractors preferences in the awarding of government contracts. The case was remanded for trial after a ruling by the Court that such programs were subject to a standard of review known as strict scrutiny. The Court held that the government's set-aside program offering preferences to minority-owned businesses was a racial classification. To survive the strict scrutiny test, which is derived from the Equal Protection Clause of the U.S. Constitution (see Chapter 5), the federal government must be able to show, when a case goes to trial, that the contractor preferences serve a compelling government interest. *Adarand II,* heard by the U.S. Supreme Court in 2001, was upheld without opinion.[2]

In *Taxman* v. *Board of Education of Piscataway* [91 F.3d 1547 (3d Cir. 1996), *cert.* granted, 521 U.S. 1117 (1997); *cert.* dismissed, 522 U.S. 1010 (1997)], a school district, when facing the need to reduce the size of its teaching staff, decided to retain an African-American schoolteacher, Debra Williams. Sharon Taxman, a white schoolteacher, challenged the decision as discriminatory, and the school board defended on the grounds of its affirmative action program. On appeal, the circuit court held that the decision was unconstitutional because the school board's program was adopted to promote diversity and not to remedy any past wrongs the school district had committed. The U.S. Supreme Court granted *certiorari* to review the case, but the school board agreed to a settlement, paying Ms. Taxman $433,500, of which $308,500 was paid by national civil rights organizations. The civil rights organizations indicated that they agreed to pay the bulk of the settlement because they were fearful that the court might outlaw affirmative action programs. A few years later, the U.S. Supreme Court issued on the same day two landmark decisions on affirmative action in admissions programs: *Gratz* v. *Bollinger* (Case 20.5) and *Grutter* v. *Bollinger* (Case 20.6).

CASE 20.5

Gratz v. *Bollinger*
539 U.S. 244 (2003)

Admit It: Affirmative Action Programs
Are Difficult to Explain

FACTS

Jennifer Gratz and Patrick Hamacher (petitioners), along with other students in a class action suit, were denied admission to the University of Michigan's College of Literature, Science, and the Arts (LSA). Both Ms. Grazt and Mr. Hamacher are Caucasian. Ms. Gratz, who applied for admission for the fall of 1995, was

continued

notified in January of that year that a final decision regarding her admission had been delayed until April. This delay was based on the University's determination that, although Ms. Gratz was "well qualified," she was "less competitive than the students who ha[d] been admitted on first review." Ms. Gratz was notified in April that the LSA was unable to offer her admission. She enrolled in the University of Michigan at Dearborn, from which she graduated in the spring of 1999.

Mr. Hamacher applied for admission to the LSA for the fall of 1997. A final decision as to his application was also postponed because, though his "academic credentials [were] in the qualified range, they [were] not at the level needed for first review admission." Mr. Hamacher's application was subsequently denied in April 1997, and he enrolled at Michigan State University. He has since graduated from Michigan State University.

In October 1997, Ms. Gratz and Mr. Hamacher filed a lawsuit in the U.S. District Court for the Eastern District of Michigan against the University of Michigan, the LSA, James Duderstadt, and Lee Bollinger (administrators at the University of Michigan) for discrimination on the basis of their race.

The University's Office of Undergraduate Admissions (OUA) oversees the LSA admissions process. In order to promote consistency in the review of the large number of applications received, the OUA uses written guidelines for each academic year. OUA considers a number of factors in making admissions decisions, including high school grades, standardized test scores, high school quality, curriculum strength, geography, alumni relationships, and leadership. OUA also considers race. During all periods relevant to this litigation, the University considered African-Americans, Hispanics, and Native Americans to be "underrepresented minorities," and it is undisputed that the University admits "virtually every qualified . . . applicant" from these groups. During 1995 and 1996, OUA counselors evaluated applications according to grade point average combined with what were referred to as the "SCUGA" factors. These factors included the quality of an applicant's high school (S), the strength of an applicant's high school curriculum (C), an applicant's unusual circumstances (U), an applicant's geographical residence (G), and an applicant's alumni relationships (A). After these scores were combined to produce an applicant's "GPA 2" score, the reviewing admissions counselors referenced a set of "Guidelines" tables, which listed GPA 2 ranges on the vertical axis, and American College Test/Scholastic Aptitude Test (ACT/SAT) scores on the horizontal axis. Each table was divided into cells that included one or more courses of action to be taken, including admit, reject, delay for additional information, or postpone for reconsideration.

In both years, applicants with the same GPA 2 scores and ACT/SAT scores were subject to different admissions outcomes based on their racial or ethnic status. For example, as a Caucasian in-state applicant, Ms. Gratz's GPA 2 score and ACT score placed her within a cell calling for a postponed decision on her application. An in-state or out-of-state minority applicant with Ms. Gratz's scores would have fallen within a cell calling for admission.

Under the 1997 procedures, Mr. Hamacher's GPA 2 score and ACT score placed him in a cell on the in-state applicant table calling for postponement of a final admissions decision. An underrepresented minority applicant placed in the same cell would generally have been admitted.

Beginning with the 1998 academic year, the OUA dispensed with the Guidelines tables and the SCUGA point system in favor of a "selection index," on which an applicant could score a maximum of 150 points. This index was divided linearly into ranges generally calling for admissions dispositions as follows: 100–150, admit; 95–99, admit or postpone; 90–94, postpone or admit; 75–89, delay or postpone; and 74 and below, delay or reject.

Each application received points based on high school grade point average, standardized test scores, academic quality of an applicant's high school, strength or weakness of high school curriculum, in-state residency, alumni relationships, personal essay, and personal achievement or leadership. Of particular significance here, under a "miscellaneous" category, an applicant was entitled to 20 points based on his or her membership in an underrepresented racial or ethnic minority group.

In all application years from 1995 to 1998, the guidelines provided that qualified applicants from underrepresented minority groups be admitted as soon as possible in light of the University's belief that such applicants were more likely to enroll if promptly notified of their admission. Also from 1995 through 1998, the University carefully managed its rolling admissions system to permit consideration of certain applications submitted later in the academic year through the use of "protected seats." Specific groups—including athletes, foreign students, ROTC candidates, and underrepresented minorities—were "protected categories" eligible for these seats.

Starting in 1999, however, the University established an Admissions Review Committee (ARC), to provide an additional level of consideration for some applications. Under the new system, counselors may, in their discretion, "flag" an application for the ARC to review after determining that the applicant (1) is academically prepared to succeed at the University, (2) has achieved a minimum selection index score, and (3) possesses a quality or characteristic important to the University's composition of its freshman class, such as high class rank, unique life experiences, challenges, circumstances, interests or talents, socioeconomic disadvantage, and underrepresented race, ethnicity, or geography. After reviewing "flagged" applications, the ARC determines whether to admit, defer, or deny each applicant.

Following complicated proceedings at the district and appellate levels that eventually concluded in a holding in favor of the University, the former students appealed.

JUDICIAL OPINION

REHNQUIST, Chief Justice

As they have throughout the course of this litigation, petitioners contend that the University's consideration of race in its undergraduate admissions decisions violates § 1 of the Equal Protection Clause of the Fourteenth Amendment, Title VI, and 42 U.S.C. § 1981.

From the time petitioners filed their original complaint through their brief on the merits in this Court, they have consistently challenged the University's use of race in undergraduate admissions and its asserted justification of promoting "diversity."

Specifically, they contend that this Court has only sanctioned the use of racial classifications to remedy identified discrimination, a justification on which respondents have never relied. Petitioners further argue that "diversity as a basis for employing racial preferences is simply too open-ended, ill-defined, and indefinite to constitute a compelling interest capable of supporting narrowly-tailored means." But for the reasons set forth today in *Grutter* v. *Bollinger,* ante, at —— - ——, 123 S.Ct., at 2338–2341, 2003 WL 21433492, the Court has rejected these arguments of petitioners. [See Case 20.6.]

Petitioners alternatively argue that even if the University's interest in diversity can constitute a compelling state interest, the District Court erroneously concluded that the University's use of race in its current freshman admissions policy is narrowly tailored to achieve such an interest. Petitioners argue that the guidelines the University began using in 1999 do not "remotely resemble the kind of consideration of race and ethnicity that Justice Powell endorsed in *Regents of Univ. of Cal. v. Bakke,* 438 U.S. 265, 317, 98 S.Ct. 2733, 57 L.Ed.2d 750." Respondents reply that the University's current admissions program is narrowly tailored and avoids the problems of the Medical School of the University of California at Davis program (U.C. Davis) rejected by Justice Powell. They claim that their program "hews closely" to both the admissions program described by Justice Powell as well as the Harvard College admissions program that he endorsed. Specifi-

cally, respondents contend that the LSA's policy provides the individualized consideration that "Justice Powell considered a hallmark of a constitutionally appropriate admissions program."

For the reasons set out below, we do not agree.

It is by now well established that "all racial classifications reviewable under the Equal Protection Clause must be strictly scrutinized." *Adarand Constructors, Inc.* v. *Pena,* 515 U.S. 200, 224, 115 S.Ct. 2097, 132 L.Ed.2d 158 (1995). This "'standard of review . . . is not dependent on the race of those burdened or benefited by a particular classification.'" Thus, "any person, of whatever race, has the right to demand that any governmental actor subject to the Constitution justify any racial classification subjecting that person to unequal treatment under the strictest of judicial scrutiny."

To withstand our strict scrutiny analysis, respondents must demonstrate that the University's use of race in its current admission program employs "narrowly tailored measures that further compelling governmental interests. . . ." Because "[r]acial classifications are simply too pernicious to permit any but the most exact connection between justification and classification," . . . We find that the University's policy, which automatically distributes 20 points, or one-fifth of the points needed to guarantee admission, to every single "underrepresented minority" applicant solely because of race, is not narrowly tailored to achieve the interest in educational diversity that respondents claim justifies their program.

In *Bakke,* Justice Powell reiterated that "[p]referring members of any one group for no reason other than race or ethnic origin is discrimination for its own sake." He then explained, however, that in his view it would be permissible for a university to employ an admissions program in which "race or ethnic background may be deemed a 'plus' in a particular applicant's file." He explained that such a program might allow for "[t]he file of a particular black applicant [to] be examined for his potential contribution to diversity without the factor of race being decisive when compared, for example, with that of an applicant identified as an Italian-American if the latter is thought to exhibit qualities more likely to promote beneficial educational pluralism." Such a system, in Justice Powell's view, would be "flexible enough to consider all pertinent elements of diversity in light of the particular qualifications of each applicant." . . . Justice Powell's opinion in *Bakke* emphasized the importance of considering each particular applicant as an individual, assessing all of the qualities that individual possesses, and in turn, evaluating that individual's ability to contribute to the unique setting of higher education. The admissions program Justice

continued

Powell described, however, did not contemplate that any single characteristic automatically ensured a specific and identifiable contribution to a university's diversity. Instead, under the approach Justice Powell described, each characteristic of a particular applicant was to be considered in assessing the applicant's entire application.

The current LSA policy does not provide such individualized consideration. The LSA's policy automatically distributes 20 points to every single applicant from an "underrepresented minority" group, as defined by the University. The only consideration that accompanies this distribution of points is a factual review of an application to determine whether an individual is a member of one of these minority groups. Moreover, unlike Justice Powell's example, where the race of a "particular black applicant" could be considered without being decisive, the LSA's automatic distribution of 20 points has the effect of making "the factor of race . . . decisive" for virtually every minimally qualified underrepresented minority applicant.

"The Admissions Committee, with only a few places left to fill, might find itself forced to choose between A, the child of a successful black physician in an academic community with promise of superior academic performance, and B, a black who grew up in an inner-city ghetto of semi-literate parents whose academic achievement was lower but who had demonstrated energy and leadership as well as an apparently abiding interest in black power. If a good number of black students much like A but few like B had already been admitted, the Committee might prefer B; and vice versa. If C, a white student with extraordinary artistic talent, were also seeking one of the remaining places, his unique quality might give him an edge over both A and B. Thus, the critical criteria are often individual qualities or experience not dependent upon race but sometimes associated with it."

This example further demonstrates the problematic nature of the LSA's admissions system. Even if student C's "extraordinary artistic talent" rivaled that of Monet or Picasso, the applicant would receive, at-most, five points under the LSA's system. At the same time, every single underrepresented minority applicant, including students A and B, would automatically receive 20 points for submitting an application. Clearly, the LSA's system does not offer applicants the individualized selection process described in Harvard's example. Instead of considering how the differing backgrounds, experiences, and characteristics of students A, B, and C might benefit the University, admissions counselors reviewing LSA applications would simply award both A and B 20 points because their applications indicate that they are African-American, and student C would receive up to 5 points for his "extraordinary talent."

Respondents contend that "[t]he volume of applications and the presentation of applicant information make it impractical for [LSA] to use the . . . admissions system" upheld by the Court today in *Grutter*. But the fact that the implementation of a program capable of providing individualized consideration might present administrative challenges does not render constitutional an otherwise problematic system. Nothing in Justice Powell's opinion in *Bakke* signaled that a university may employ whatever means it desires to achieve the stated goal of diversity without regard to the limits imposed by our strict scrutiny analysis.

We conclude, therefore, that because the University's use of race in its current freshman admissions policy is not narrowly tailored to achieve respondents' asserted compelling interest in diversity, the admissions policy violates the Equal Protection Clause of the Fourteenth Amendment. We further find that the admissions policy also violates Title VI and 42 U.S.C. § 1981. Accordingly, we reverse.

CASE 20.6

Grutter v. *Bollinger*
539 U.S. 306 (2003)

The Law of Admissions
and the Admissions of Law

FACTS

The University of Michigan Law School ranks among the nation's top law schools. It receives more than 3,500 applications each year for a class of around 350 students. Seeking to "admit a group of students who individually and collectively are among the most capable," the Law School looks for individuals with "substantial promise for success in law school" and "a strong likelihood of succeeding in the practice of law and contributing in diverse ways to the well-being of others." More broadly, the Law School seeks "a mix of students with varying backgrounds and experiences who will respect and learn from each other." In 1992, the dean of the Law School charged a faculty committee with crafting a written admissions policy to implement these goals. In particular, the Law School sought to ensure that its efforts to achieve student body diversity complied with this Court's most recent ruling on the use of race in university admissions.

Upon the unanimous adoption of the committee's report by the Law School faculty, it became the Law School's official admissions policy.

The hallmark of that policy is its focus on academic ability coupled with a flexible assessment of applicants' talents, experiences, and potential "to contribute to the learning of those around them." The policy requires admissions officials to evaluate each applicant based on all the information available in the file, including a personal statement, letters of recommendation, and an essay describing the ways in which the applicant will contribute to the life and diversity of the Law School. In reviewing an applicant's file, admissions officials must consider the applicant's undergraduate grade point average (GPA) and Law School Admissions Test (LSAT) score because they are important (if imperfect) predictors of academic success in law school. The policy stresses that "no applicant should be admitted unless we expect that applicant to do well enough to graduate with no serious academic problems."

The policy makes clear, however, that even the highest possible score does not guarantee admission to the Law School. Nor does a low score automatically disqualify an applicant. Rather, the policy requires admissions officials to look beyond grades and test scores to other criteria that are important to the Law School's educational objectives. So-called "'soft' variables" such as "the enthusiasm of recommenders, the quality of the undergraduate institution, the quality of the applicant's essay, and the areas and difficulty of undergraduate course selection" are all brought to bear in assessing an "applicant's likely contributions to the intellectual and social life of the institution."

The policy aspires to "achieve that diversity which has the potential to enrich everyone's education and thus make a law school class stronger than the sum of its parts."

The policy does not restrict the types of diversity contributions eligible for "substantial weight" in the admissions process, but instead recognizes "many possible bases for diversity admissions." The policy does, however, reaffirm the Law School's longstanding commitment to "one particular type of diversity," that is, "racial and ethnic diversity with special reference to the inclusion of students from groups which have been historically discriminated against, like African-Americans, Hispanics and Native Americans, who without this commitment might not be represented in our student body in meaningful numbers." By enrolling a "'critical mass' of [underrepresented] minority stu-

dents," the Law School seeks to "ensur[e] their ability to make unique contributions to the character of the Law School."

The policy does not define diversity "solely in terms of racial and ethnic status." Nor is the policy "insensitive to the competition among all students for admission to the [L]aw [S]chool." Rather, the policy seeks to guide admissions officers in "producing classes both diverse and academically outstanding, classes made up of students who promise to continue the tradition of outstanding contribution by Michigan Graduates to the legal profession."

Barbara Grutter (petitioner) is a white Michigan resident who applied to the Law School in 1996 with a 3.8 GPA and 161 LSAT score. The Law School initially placed her on a waiting list but subsequently rejected her application. In December 1997, Ms. Grutter filed suit in the U.S. District Court for the Eastern District of Michigan against the Law School, the Regents of the University of Michigan, Lee Bollinger (Dean of the Law School from 1987 to 1994), and others. She alleged that respondents discriminated against her on the basis of race in violation of the Fourteenth Amendment; Title VI of the Civil Rights Act of 1964, 78 Stat. 252, 42 U.S.C. § 2000d; and Rev. Stat. § 1977, as amended, 42 U.S.C. § 1981.

She alleged that her application was rejected because the Law School uses race as a "predominant" factor, giving applicants who belong to certain minority groups "a significantly greater chance of admission than students with similar credentials from disfavored racial groups." Ms. Grutter also alleged that the respondents "had no compelling interest to justify their use of race in the admissions process." After a complicated battle in the lower courts that held for the law school and university, Ms. Grutter appealed.

JUDICIAL OPINION

O'CONNOR, Justice

We last addressed the use of race in public higher education over 25 years ago. In the landmark *Bakke* case, we reviewed a racial set-aside program that reserved 16 out of 100 seats in a medical school class for members of certain minority groups. The decision produced six separate opinions, none of which commanded a majority of the Court. Four Justices would have upheld the program against all attack on the ground that the government can use race to "remedy disadvantages cast on minorities by past racial prejudice." Four other Justices avoided the constitutional question altogether and struck down the program on statutory grounds. Justice Powell provided a fifth vote not only for invalidating the set-aside program, but also for reversing the

continued

state court's injunction against any use of race whatsoever. The only holding for the Court in *Bakke* was that a "State has a substantial interest that legitimately may be served by a properly devised admissions program involving the competitive consideration of race and ethnic origin." Thus, we reversed that part of the lower court's judgment that enjoined the university "from any consideration of the race of any applicant."

Since this Court's splintered decision in *Bakke*, Justice Powell's opinion announcing the judgment of the Court has served as the touchstone for constitutional analysis of race-conscious admissions policies. Public and private universities across the Nation have modeled their own admissions programs on Justice Powell's views on permissible race-conscious policies.

In the wake of our fractured decision in *Bakke*, courts have struggled to discern whether Justice Powell's diversity rationale, set forth in part of the opinion joined by no other Justice, is nonetheless binding precedent [f]or the reasons set out below, today we endorse Justice Powell's view that student body diversity is a compelling state interest that can justify the use of race in university admissions.

Because the Fourteenth Amendment "protect[s] persons, not groups," all "governmental action based on race—a group classification long recognized as in most circumstances irrelevant and therefore prohibited—should be subjected to detailed judicial inquiry to ensure that the personal right to equal protection of the laws has not been infringed." *Adarand Constructors, Inc. v. Pena*, 515 U.S. 200, 227, 115 S.Ct. 2097, 132 L.Ed.2d 158 (1995)

We have held that all racial classifications imposed by government "must be analyzed by a reviewing court under strict scrutiny." This means that such classifications are constitutional only if they are narrowly tailored to further compelling governmental interests. "We apply strict scrutiny to all racial classifications to " 'smoke out' illegitimate uses of race by assuring that [government] is pursuing a goal important enough to warrant use of a highly suspect tool." . . .

Although all governmental uses of race are subject to strict scrutiny, not all are invalidated by it. As we have explained, "whenever the government treats any person unequally because of his or her race, that person has suffered an injury that falls squarely within the language and spirit of the Constitution's guarantee of equal protection."

With these principles in mind, we turn to the question whether the Law School's use of race is justified by a compelling state interest. Before this Court, as they have *throughout this litigation, respondents assert only one justification for their use of race in the admissions process: obtaining "the educational benefits that flow from a diverse student body." In other words, the Law School asks us to recognize, in the context of higher education, a compelling state interest in student body diversity.

The Law School's educational judgment that such diversity is essential to its educational mission is one to which we defer. The Law School's assessment that diversity will, in fact, yield educational benefits is substantiated by respondents and their amici. Our scrutiny of the interest asserted by the Law School is no less strict for taking into account complex educational judgments in an area that lies primarily within the expertise of the university. Our holding today is in keeping with our tradition of giving a degree of deference to a university's academic decisions, within constitutionally prescribed limits . . .

We have long recognized that, given the important purpose of public education and the expansive freedoms of speech and thought associated with the university environment, universities occupy a special niche in our constitutional tradition.

As part of its goal of "assembling a class that is both exceptionally academically qualified and broadly diverse," the Law School seeks to "enroll a 'critical mass' of minority students." The Law School's interest is not simply "to assure within its student body some specified percentage of a particular group merely because of its race or ethnic origin." That would amount to outright racial balancing, which is patently unconstitutional. Rather, the Law School's concept of critical mass is defined by reference to the educational benefits that diversity is designed to produce.

These benefits are substantial. As the District Court emphasized, the Law School's admissions policy promotes "cross-racial understanding," helps to break down racial stereotypes, and "enables [students] to better understand persons of different races." These benefits are "important and laudable," because "classroom discussion is livelier, more spirited, and simply more enlightening and interesting" when the students have "the greatest possible variety of backgrounds."

The Law School's claim of a compelling interest is further bolstered by its amici, who point to the educational benefits that flow from student body diversity. In addition to the expert studies and reports entered into evidence at trial, numerous studies show that student body diversity promotes learning outcomes, and "better prepares students for an increasingly diverse workforce and society, and better prepares them as professionals."

These benefits are not theoretical but real, as major American businesses have made clear that the skills needed in today's increasingly global marketplace can only be developed through exposure to widely diverse people, cultures, ideas, and viewpoints. What is more, high-ranking retired officers and civilian leaders of the

United States military assert that, "[b]ased on [their] decades of experience," a "highly qualified, racially diverse officer corps . . . is essential to the military's ability to fulfill its principle mission to provide national security . . .

We have repeatedly acknowledged the overriding importance of preparing students for work and citizenship, describing education as pivotal to "sustaining our political and cultural heritage" with a fundamental role in maintaining the fabric of society. Effective participation by members of all racial and ethnic groups in the civic life of our Nation is essential if the dream of one Nation, indivisible, is to be realized.

Moreover, universities, and in particular, law schools, represent the training ground for a large number of our Nation's leaders. Individuals with law degrees occupy roughly half the state governorships, more than half the seats in the United States Senate, and more than a third of the seats in the United States House of Representatives. The pattern is even more striking when it comes to highly selective law schools. A handful of these schools accounts for 25 of the 100 United States Senators, 74 United States Courts of Appeals judges, and nearly 200 of the more than 600 United States District Court judges. . . .

The Law School does not premise its need for critical mass on "any belief that minority students always (or even consistently) express some characteristic minority viewpoint on any issue." To the contrary, diminishing the force of such stereotypes is both a crucial part of the Law School's mission, and one that it cannot accomplish with only token numbers of minority students. Just as growing up in a particular region or having particular professional experiences is likely to affect an individual's views, so too is one's own, unique experience of being a racial minority in a society, like our own, in which race unfortunately still matters. The Law School has determined, based on its experience and expertise, that a "critical mass" of underrepresented minorities is necessary to further its compelling interest in securing the educational benefits of a diverse student body.

To be narrowly tailored, a race-conscious admissions program cannot use a quota system—it cannot "insulat[e] each category of applicants with certain desired qualifications from competition with all other applicants." Instead, a university may consider race or ethnicity only as a "'plus' in a particular applicant's file," without "insulat[ing] the individual from comparison with all other candidates for the available seats." In other words, an admissions program must be "flexible enough to consider all pertinent elements of diversity in light of the particular qualifications of each applicant, and to place them on the same footing for

consideration, although not necessarily according them the same weight."

We find that the Law School's admissions program bears the hallmarks of a narrowly tailored plan. As Justice Powell made clear in *Bakke,* truly individualized consideration demands that race be used in a flexible, nonmechanical way.

We are satisfied that the Law School's admissions program, like the Harvard plan described by Justice Powell, does not operate as a quota. Properly understood, a "quota" is a program in which a certain fixed number or proportion of opportunities are "reserved exclusively for certain minority groups."

Justice Powell's distinction between the medical school's rigid 16-seat quota and Harvard's flexible use of race as a "plus" factor is instructive. Harvard certainly had minimum goals for minority enrollment, even if it had no specific number firmly in mind.

The Law School's goal of attaining a critical mass of underrepresented minority students does not transform its program into a quota. To the contrary, the Law School's admissions officers testified without contradiction that they never gave race any more or less weight based on the information contained in these reports. Moreover, as Justice KENNEDY concedes, between 1993 and 2000, the number of African-American, Latino, and Native-American students in each class at the Law School varied from 13.5 to 20.1%, a range inconsistent with a quota.

THE CHIEF JUSTICE believes that the Law School's policy conceals an attempt to achieve racial balancing, and cites admissions data to contend that the Law School discriminates among different groups within the critical mass. But, as THE CHIEF JUSTICE concedes, the number of underrepresented minority students who ultimately enroll in the Law School differs substantially from their representation in the applicant pool and varies considerably for each group from year to year.

That a race-conscious admissions program does not operate as a quota does not, by itself, satisfy the requirement of individualized consideration. When using race as a "plus" factor in university admissions, a university's admissions program must remain flexible enough to ensure that each applicant is evaluated as an individual and not in a way that makes an applicant's race or ethnicity the defining feature of his or her application. The importance of this individualized consideration in the context of a race-conscious admissions program is paramount.

Here, the Law School engages in a highly individualized, holistic review of each applicant's file, giving serious consideration to all the ways an applicant

continued

might contribute to a diverse educational environment. The Law School affords this individualized consideration to applicants of all races. There is no policy, either de jure or de facto, of automatic acceptance or rejection based on any single "soft" variable. Unlike the program at issue in *Gratz* v. *Bollinger,* the Law School awards no mechanical, predetermined diversity "bonuses" based on race or ethnicity.

What is more, the Law School actually gives substantial weight to diversity factors besides race. The Law School frequently accepts nonminority applicants with grades and test scores lower than underrepresented minority applicants (and other nonminority applicants) who are rejected. This shows that the Law School seriously weighs many other diversity factors besides race that can make a real and dispositive difference for nonminority applicants as well. By this flexible approach, the Law School sufficiently takes into account, in practice as well as in theory, a wide variety of characteristics besides race and ethnicity that contribute to a diverse student body. Justice KENNEDY speculates that "race is likely outcome determinative for many members of minority groups" who do not fall within the upper range of LSAT scores and grades.

The requirement that all race-conscious admissions programs have a termination point "assure[s] all citizens that the deviation from the norm of equal treatment of all racial and ethnic groups is a temporary matter, a measure taken in the service of the goal of equality itself."

We take the Law School at its word that it would "like nothing better than to find a race-neutral admissions formula" and will terminate its race-conscious admissions program as soon as practicable. It has been 25 years since Justice Powell first approved the use of race to further an interest in student body diversity in the context of public higher education. Since that time, the number of minority applicants with high grades and test scores has indeed increased. We expect that 25 years from now, the use of racial preferences will no longer be necessary to further the interest approved today.

In summary, the Equal Protection Clause does not prohibit the Law School's narrowly tailored use of race in admissions decisions to further a compelling interest in obtaining the educational benefits that flow from a diverse student body. Consequently, petitioner's statutory claims based on Title VI and 42 U.S.C. § 1981 also fail. The judgment of the Court of Appeals for the Sixth Circuit, accordingly, is affirmed.

CASE QUESTIONS

1. Explain the undergraduate admissions process.
2. Explain the Law School admissions process.
3. Which process does the U.S. Supreme Court uphold? Why?
4. What standards could you offer to colleges and universities trying to establish admissions programs that create diversity but do not violate the U.S. Supreme Court's standards for affirmative action programs?

THE DEFENSES TO A TITLE VII CHARGE

Title VII is not a strict liability statute. The act provides some defenses that employers can use to defend against a charge of discrimination.

Bona Fide Occupational Qualification

A **bona fide occupational qualification** (BFOQ) is a job qualification based on sex, religion, or national origin that is necessary for the operation of business. A particular religious belief is a BFOQ for a pastor of a church. Similarly, an actor, to qualify for a role, may need to be a certain sex for purposes of realism and thus sex is a BFOQ for such employment.

The BFOQ exception has been applied narrowly, however. For a discriminatory qualification for employment to fall within the BFOQ exception, the employer must be able to establish that the job qualification is carefully formulated to respond to public safety, privacy, or other public needs; and the formulation of the policy must not be broader than is reasonably necessary to preserve the safety or privacy of individuals involved. For example, a restriction on hiring male employees for work in a nursing home occupied by women is excessive if male employees can work in jobs not involved with the personal care of the residents. Nor is personal preference a justification for a BFOQ; for example, many airlines have argued that there is a customer preference for female as opposed to male flight attendants. But customer preference is not a basis for a BFOQ; it is not a business necessity.

Seniority or Merit Systems

The goals and objectives of Title VII are often inconsistent with labor union rules of operation. Although matters of discrimination and union supervision are both covered by federal law, there are some conflicts between the two statutory schemes. Which controls the other: the remedial effect of Title VII or the long-standing history of seniority and other union rules? Although the exception for seniority and merit systems has always been a part of Title VII, early decisions made Title VII goals superior and invalidated many of the seniority and merit systems.

The following criteria are used to determine whether a seniority or merit system is valid.

1. The system must apply to all employees.
2. Whatever divisions or units used for the system must follow the industry custom or pattern; that is, the divisions cannot be set up so as to discriminate against particular races or groups.
3. The origins of the system cannot lie in racial discrimination.
4. The system must be maintained for seniority and merit purposes and not to perpetuate racial discrimination.

Aptitude and Other Tests

Any employer charged with Title VII discrimination because of employee aptitude testing must be able to show that the tests used are valid. Validity means that the tests are related to successful job performance and that a test does not have the effect of eliminating certain races from the employment market.

An employer can validate a test in any of several different ways. Test scores of applicants can later be compared with the applicants' eventual job performance to validate the test. An employer can also give the test to current employees and use the correlation between their scores and job performance as a means for validating the test. Some tests can be validated by their content. For example, requiring potential police officers to complete a driving course, a physical fitness test, and a marksmanship test is valid because the tests are based on the things police officers actually do.

Misconduct

For many years, an absolute defense to discrimination was employee misconduct. If an employee violated company rules, there was no discrimination case. The defense was so broad that even evidence the employer acquired *after* the termination and charge of discrimination could be used as a defense. In *McKennon* v. *Nashville Banner Publishing Co.* (Case 20.7), the Supreme Court limited this defense.

CASE 20.7

McKennon v. Nashville Banner Publishing Co.
524 U.S. 742 (1995)

Lying Is Not a Defense for Discrimination

FACTS

For 30 years, Christine McKennon (petitioner) worked for Nashville Banner Publishing Company (respondent), but she was terminated as part of a work reduction plan. She was 62 years old at the time of her termination. Ms. McKennon filed suit, alleging her termination was a violation of the Age Discrimination in Employment Act (ADEA).

In preparation of the case, Banner took Ms. McKennon's deposition. She testified that during her final year of employment, she had copied several confidential documents bearing upon the company's financial condition. She had access to these records as secretary to Banner's comptroller. Ms. McKennon took the copies home and showed them to her husband. Her motivation, she averred, was apprehension that she was about to be fired because of her age. When she became concerned about her job, she removed and copied the documents for "insurance" and "protection." A few days after these deposition disclosures, Banner sent Ms. McKennon a letter declaring that removal and copying of the records was in violation of her job responsibilities and advised her (again) that she was terminated. Banner's letter also recited that had it known of Ms. McKennon's misconduct, it would have discharged her at once for that reason.

Nashville Banner conceded its discrimination in district court, which granted summary judgment for Banner on grounds that Ms. McKennon's misconduct was a defense. The court of appeals affirmed, and Ms. McKennon appealed.

JUDICIAL OPINION

KENNEDY, Justice

We shall assume that the sole reason for McKennon's initial discharge was her age, a discharge violative of the ADEA. Our further premise is that the misconduct revealed by the deposition was so grave that McKennon's immediate discharge would have followed its disclosure in any event. We do question the legal conclusion reached by those courts that after-acquired evidence of wrongdoing which would have resulted in discharge bars employees from any relief under the ADEA. That ruling is incorrect.

The ADEA, enacted in 1967 as part of an ongoing congressional effort to eradicate discrimination in the workplace, reflects a societal condemnation of invidious bias in employment decisions. The ADEA is but part of a wider statutory scheme to protect employees in the workplace nationwide.

The ADEA and Title VII share common substantive features and also a common purpose: "the elimination of discrimination in the workplace." Congress designed the remedial measures in these statutes to serve as a "spur or catalyst" to cause employers "to self-examine and to self-evaluate their employment practices and to endeavor to eliminate, so far as possible, the last vestiges" of discrimination. The ADEA, in keeping with these purposes, contains a vital element found in both Title VII and the Fair Labor Standards Act: it grants an injured employee a right of action to obtain the authorized relief.

The objectives of the ADEA are furthered when even a single employee establishes that an employer has discriminated against him or her. The disclosure through litigation of incidents or practices which violate national policies respecting nondiscrimination in the work force is itself important, for the occurrence of violations may disclose patterns of noncompliance resulting from a misappreciation of the Act's operation or entrenched resistance to its commands, either of which can be of industry-wide significance. The efficacy of its enforcement mechanisms becomes one measure of the success of the Act.

As we have said, the case comes to us on the express assumption that an unlawful motive was the sole basis for the firing. McKennon's misconduct was not discovered until after she had been fired. The employer could not have been motivated by knowledge it did not have and it cannot now claim that the employee was fired for the nondiscriminatory reason. Mixed motive cases are inapposite here, except to the important extent they underscore the necessity of determining the employer's motives in ordering the discharge, an essential element in determining whether the employer violated the federal antidiscrimination law. As we have observed, "proving that the same decision would have been justified . . . is not the same as proving that the same decision would have been made."

The ADEA, like Title VII, is not a general regulation of the workplace but a law which prohibits discrimination. The statute does not constrain employers from exercising significant other prerogatives and discretions in the course of the hiring, promoting, and discharging of their employees. In determining appropriate remedial action, the employee's wrongdoing becomes relevant not to punish the employee, or out of concern "for the relative moral worth of the parties," but to take due account of the lawful prerogatives of the employer in the usual course of its business and the corresponding equities that it has arising from the employee's wrong-doing.

The proper boundaries of remedial relief in the general class of cases where, after termination, it is discovered that the employee has engaged in wrongdoing must be addressed by the judicial system in the ordinary course of further decisions, for the factual permutations and the equitable considerations they raise will vary from case to case. We do conclude that here, and as a general rule in cases of this type, neither reinstatement nor front pay is an appropriate remedy. It would be both inequitable and pointless to order the reinstatement of someone the employer would have terminated, and will terminate, in any event and upon lawful grounds.

The object of compensation is to restore the employee to the position he or she would have been in absent the discrimination, but that principle is difficult to apply with precision where there is after-acquired evidence of wrongdoing that would have led to termination on legitimate grounds had the employer known about it.

Where an employer seeks to rely upon after-acquired evidence of wrongdoing, it must first establish that the wrongdoing was of such severity that the employee in fact would have been terminated on those grounds alone if the employer had known of it at the time of the discharge. The concern that employers might as a routine matter undertake extensive discovery into an employee's background or performance on the job to resist claims under the Act is not an insubstantial one, but we think the authority of the courts to award attorney's fees, mandated under the statute, 29 U.S.C. §§ 216(b), 626(b), and in appropriate cases to invoke the provisions of Rule 11 of the Federal Rules of Civil Procedure will deter most abuses.

The judgment is reversed.

CASE QUESTIONS

1. Why is the timing of the misconduct disclosure important?
2. Does Banner deny discriminatory intent?
3. Why are "mixed motive" cases not relevant in this analysis?
4. Is reinstatement a remedy?

ETHICAL ISSUES

Consider the following circumstances and decide whether there has been a violation of Title VII. Consider the ethical implications of the conduct along with the legal.

1. An employee must be dismissed. Two women, one white and the other black, have been with the company for the same amount of time and have the same rate of absenteeism. Their performance evaluations are about the same. Can the black employee be dismissed without violating Title VII?
2. Company B has had a significant problem with absenteeism, tardiness, and failure to follow through on job assignments among the employees who are of a certain race. The personnel director is concerned about company productivity, the costs of training, and the costs of constant turnover. The personnel director is also aware of the constraints of Title VII. The director instructs those staffing the front office to tell members of that particular race who apply for a job that the company is not accepting applications. The director's theory is that his applicant pool will be prescreened and he will not have to make discriminatory hiring decisions. Is the director correct?

ENFORCEMENT OF TITLE VII

Visit the EEOC:
http://www.eeoc.gov

Title VII is an enabling act that created the Equal Employment Opportunity Commission for the purpose of administration and enforcement. The EEOC is a five-member commission whose members are appointed by the president with the approval of the Senate. As with all other federal commissions, no more than three members can belong to the same political party.

The EEOC was given very broad powers under Title VII. In addition to its rule-making and charging powers, the EEOC has very broad investigatory authority, including the authority to subpoena documents and testimony.

Steps in an EEOC Case

The Complaint

An EEOC complaint can be filed by an employee or by the EEOC. An employee has 180 days (in some cases, up to 300 days) from the time of the alleged violation to file a complaint. The EEOC does not have such a statute of limitations.

The complaint is filed with either the EEOC or the state administrative agency set up for employment discrimination issues. For the state agency to continue handling the complaint, it must be an EEOC-approved program. If it is not, the EEOC handles the complaint. The EEOC has special forms that can be filled out by any employee wishing to file such a complaint.

Notification of the Employer

Once a complaint has been filed, the EEOC has ten days to notify the employer of the charges. Employers are prohibited from the time of notification from taking any retaliatory action against the charging employee.

EEOC Action

After the complaint is filed, the EEOC has 180 days from that time to take action in the case before the complaining party can file suit on the matter. During this time, the EEOC can use its investigatory powers to explore the merits of the charges. In the case of *University of Pennsylvania* v. *EEOC,* 493 U.S. 182 (1990), the Supreme Court ruled that the EEOC could have access to all information in an employee's file—even evaluation letters in which evaluators were promised confidentiality. This is also a conciliation period during which the EEOC may try to work out a settlement between the employer and the employee.

The Right-to-Sue Letter

If the EEOC has not settled its complaint within 180 days from the time of its filing, the employee has the right to demand a **right-to-sue letter** from the EEOC, which is a certification that the employee has exhausted his administrative remedies. If a state agency is involved, the time for its settlement of the matter must also expire before the employee can take the matter to court.

The employee has the right to this letter regardless of the EEOC's findings. Even if the EEOC has investigated and determined that there are no merits to the charges, the employee can still pursue the case in court. Under *EEOC* v. *Waffle House,* 534 U.S. 279 (2002), the U.S. Supreme Court held that the EEOC, as an agency, has the right to proceed with its remedies even if the private remedies are dismissed or not available to the affected employee.

Remedies Available under Title VII

Remedies available under Title VII include injunctions, back pay, punitive damages, and attorneys' fees. If a court finds a violation, it may order that corrective or affirmative action be taken to compensate for past wrongs. An injunction usually requires the employer to stop the illegal discrimination and then institute a plan to hire or promote minorities. Back-pay awards are limited to two years under Title VII. Section 706(b) of the act permits successful parties to recover "reasonable attorneys' fees."

An employer cannot take retaliatory action against employees who file charges or who are successful in a suit; Title VII makes such action unlawful.

Title VII originally allowed damages for back pay for all forms of discrimination. Punitive and compensatory damages are now permitted in racial and ethnic discrimination cases. The 1991 amendments extend the recovery of punitive and compensatory damages to cases involving sex, religion, or disability.

OTHER ANTIDISCRIMINATION LAWS

Age Discrimination in Employment Act of 1967

Review the Age Discrimination in Employment Act:
http://www.law.cornell.edu/uscode/29/62l.html

Title VII does not cover the very real problem of age discrimination, which generally involves companies' hiring preference for younger people. To correct this loophole, the Age Discrimination in Employment Act (ADEA) was passed in 1967, and the EEOC was given responsibility for its enforcement. The act covers all employers with twenty or more employees and prohibits age discrimination in the hiring, firing, and compensation of employees. All employment agencies are covered. The act protects workforce members above age 40.

The elements in an age discrimination case are similar to those in other discrimination cases—simply substitute that the terminated employee was replaced with a younger employee. The replacement need not be below the age of 40 [*O'Connor* v. *Consolidated Coin Caterers Corp.,* 517 U.S. 308 (1996)].

CONSIDER...   2 0 . 8

The superiors for a 58-year-old terminated employee commented that the employee had a "1970s management style." Is such a statement evidence of age discrimination? [*Rifakes* v. *Citizen Utilities Co.,* 968 F. Supp. 315 (N.D. Tex. 1997).]

CONSIDER...   2 0 . 9

On October 29, 1982, Preview Subscription Television, Inc., a subsidiary of Time, Inc., hired Thomas Taggart as a print production manager for Preview's magazine guide. Mr. Taggart was 58 years old at the time and had over 30 years of experience in the printing industry. In May 1983, Time notified Mr. Taggart that Preview would be dissolved and that Preview employees would receive special consideration for all Time positions.

Mr. Taggart applied for thirty-two positions in various divisions at Time and its subsidiaries, including *Sports Illustrated, People, Life, Money, HBO,* and *Cinemax Guide.* He was interviewed but never hired. The reason given was that he was "overqualified." Mr. Taggart filed suit, alleging age discrimination. Time responded by saying he performed poorly at interviews, his letters and resumes for jobs contained numerous typographical errors, and he was argumentative with management and counselors.

Time hired less-qualified younger applicants for all the jobs. Has there been age discrimination? [*Taggart* v. *Time, Inc.,* 924 F. 2d 43 (2nd Cir. 1991).]

Equal Pay Act of 1963

The Equal Pay Act of 1963 is an amendment to the Fair Labor Standards Act. (The details of its coverage are outlined in Chapter 19.)

Communicable Diseases in the Workplace

Whether employees can be fired because they may carry a communicable disease has recently become a crucial issue. Court decisions on the treatment of infected employees have varied, but the Supreme Court decision *School Board of Nassau County v. Arline*, 480 U.S. 273 (1987), has been touted as a protectionist measure as a result of its finding that a school board could not discriminate against a teacher because she had tuberculosis (a contagious disease). The Americans with Disabilities Act will provide new issues and remedies with regard to communicable diseases (see below).

Rehabilitation Act of 1973

Review the Rehabilitation Act:
http://www.law.cornell.
edu/uscode/29/701.html

Congress enacted the Rehabilitation Act to prohibit discrimination in employment against handicapped persons by persons and organizations that receive federal contracts or assistance. The Labor Department is responsible for enforcing the act. The Rehabilitation Act laid the groundwork for the Americans with Disabilities Act, but is limited in application to employers who have federal contracts and requires the same reasonable accommodation standards now required under ADA.

Americans with Disabilities Act

Review the Americans with
Disabilities Act:
http://www.usdoj.gov/
crt/ada/adahom1.htm

The intent of the Americans with Disabilities Act (ADA) was to eliminate discrimination against individuals with disabilities. The ADA has been called the "Emancipation Proclamation" for disabled U.S. citizens.

Portions of the ADA apply to employment discrimination issues while other sections ensure that those with disabilities have access to public streets, walkways, buildings, and transportation.

The ADA became effective on July 26, 1992, for employers with twenty-five or more employees and went into effect on July 26, 1994, for employers with fifteen or more employees. The employment provisions apply to private businesses and to state and local government agencies but not to the federal government.

Under the ADA, employers cannot discriminate in hiring, promotion, and selection criteria against a "qualified individual with a disability." "Qualified" means that the individual, with reasonable accommodation, can perform all "essential functions" of the job. Impairments such as gambling, kleptomania, pyromania, illegal drugs, and sexual disorders are excluded from protection.

A disability is defined by the ADA as a physical or mental impairment that substantially limits one or more major life activities such as seeing, hearing, speaking, walking, breathing, learning, or self-care. The ADA also includes as a disability having a record of impairment or having something others regard as a disability. Pursuant to a U.S. Supreme Court case [*Bragdon v. Abbott*, 524 U.S. 624 (1998)], human immunodeficiency virus (HIV) is considered a physical impairment for purposes of the ADA. In that case, a dentist's refusal to treat an HIV-positive patient who needed a cavity filled violated the ADA public accommodation provisions.

Employers must make "reasonable accommodations" for disabled individuals to enable them to perform essential functions. Included in reasonable accommodations are providing employee facilities that are readily accessible to and usable by disabled individuals, job restructuring, allowing part-time or modified work schedules, reassigning disabled individuals to vacant positions, acquiring or modifying equipment, and providing qualified readers or interpreters. Perhaps the accommodation best known to the public is the right golfer Casey Martin won in *PGA Tour, Inc. v. Martin* (CASE 20.8) to use a cart in PGA tournaments because of his circulatory ailment.

CASE 20.8

PGA Tour, Inc. v. Martin
531 U.S. 1049 (2001)

A Stroke of Genius for an ADA in Full Swing

FACTS

Casey Martin (respondent) is a talented golfer. As an amateur, he won 17 Oregon Golf Association junior events before he was 15 and won the state championship as a high school senior. He played on the Stanford University golf team that won the 1994 National Collegiate Athletic Association (NCAA) championship. As a professional, Mr. Martin qualified for the Nike Tour in 1998 and 1999, and based on his 1999 performance, he qualified for the PGA Tour in 2000. In the 1999 season, he entered 24 events, made the cut 13 times, and had 6 top-10 finishes, coming in second twice and third once.

Mr. Martin is also an individual with a disability as defined in the Americans with Disabilities Act of 1990 (ADA). Since birth he has been afflicted with Klippel-Trenaunay-Weber Syndrome, a degenerative circulatory disorder that obstructs the flow of blood from his right leg back to his heart. The disease is progressive; it causes severe pain and has atrophied his right leg. During the latter part of his college career, because of the progress of the disease, Mr. Martin could no longer walk an 18-hole golf course. Walking not only caused him pain, fatigue, and anxiety but also created a significant risk of hemorrhaging, developing blood clots, and fracturing his tibia so badly that an amputation might be required. For these reasons, Stanford made written requests to the Pacific 10 Conference and the NCAA to waive for Mr. Martin their rules requiring players to walk and carry their own clubs. The requests were granted.

The PGA Tour, Inc. (petitioner), a nonprofit entity formed in 1968, sponsors and cosponsors professional golf tournaments conducted on three annual tours. About 200 golfers participate in the PGA Tour; about 170 in the Nike Tour; and about 100 in the Senior PGA Tour. PGA Tour and Nike Tour tournaments typically are four-day events, played on courses leased and operated by the PGA. The entire field usually competes in two 18-hole rounds played on Thursday and Friday; those who survive the cut play on Saturday and Sunday and receive prize money in amounts determined by their aggregate scores for all four rounds. The revenues generated by television, admissions, concessions, and contributions from cosponsors amount to about $300 million a year, much of which is distributed in prize money.

The basic rules of golf apply equally to all players in tour competitions. As one of the petitioner's witnesses explained with reference to "the Masters Tournament, which is golf at its very highest level . . . the key is to have everyone tee off on the first hole under exactly the same conditions and all of them be tested over that 72-hole event under the conditions that exist during those four days of the event." The PGA interpretation of its rules was that Mr. Martin's use of a cart for participation in the four-day, 72-hole event would be an unfair advantage. The PGA would not allow him to use a cart.

The lower court and the court of appeals found that the hard cards (that contain the PGA rule on no carts) violated the ADA and required the PGA to permit Mr. Martin to use a cart pursuant to the act's rules on reasonable accommodation. The PGA appealed.

JUDICIAL OPINION

STEVENS, Justice

This case raises two questions concerning the application of the Americans with Disabilities Act of 1990, to a gifted athlete: first, whether the Act protects access to professional golf tournaments by a qualified entrant with a disability; and second, whether a disabled contestant may be denied the use of a golf cart because it would "fundamentally alter the nature" of the tournaments, § 12182(b)(2)(A)(ii), to allow him to ride when all other contestants must walk.

On the merits, because there was no serious dispute about the fact that permitting Martin to use a golf cart was both a reasonable and a necessary solution to the problem of providing him access to the tournaments, the Court of Appeals regarded the central dispute as whether such permission would "fundamentally alter" the nature of the PGA TOUR or NIKE TOUR.

Title III of the ADA prescribes, as a "[g]eneral rule":

No individual shall be discriminated against on the basis of disability in the full and equal enjoyment of the goods, services, facilities, privileges, advantages, or accommodations of any place of public accommodation by any person who owns, leases (or leases to), or operates a place of public accommodation.

continued

42 U.S.C. § 12182(a).

The phrase "public accommodation" is defined in terms of 12 extensive categories, which the legislative history indicates "should be construed liberally" to afford people with disabilities "equal access" to the wide variety of establishments available to the nondisabled.

It seems apparent, from both the general rule and the comprehensive definition of "public accommodation," that petitioner's golf tours and their qualifying rounds fit comfortably within the coverage of Title III, and Martin within its protection. The events occur on "golf course[s]," a type of place specifically identified by the Act as a public accommodation. In addition, at all relevant times, petitioner "leases" and "operates" golf courses to conduct its Q-School and tours.

According to petitioner, Title III [of the ADA] is concerned with discrimination against "clients and customers" seeking to obtain "goods and services" at places of public accommodation, whereas it is Title I that protects persons who work at such places. As the argument goes, petitioner operates not a "golf course" during its tournaments but a "place of exhibition or entertainment," and a professional golfer such as Martin, like an actor in a theater production, is a provider rather than a consumer of the entertainment that petitioner sells to the public. Martin therefore cannot bring a claim under Title III because he is not one of the "'clients or customers of the covered public accommodation.'" Rather, Martin's claim of discrimination is "job-related" and could only be brought under Title I— but that Title does not apply because he is an independent contractor (as the District Court found) rather than an employee.

We need not decide whether petitioner's construction of the statute is correct, because petitioner's argument falters even on its own terms. In our view, petitioner's tournaments (whether situated at a "golf course" or at a "place of exhibition or entertainment") simultaneously offer at least two "privileges" to the public—that of watching the golf competition and that of competing in it. Although the latter is more difficult and more expensive to obtain than the former, it is nonetheless a privilege that petitioner makes available to members of the general public. In consideration of the entry fee, any golfer with the requisite letters of recommendation acquires the opportunity to qualify for and compete in petitioner's tours. Additionally, any golfer who succeeds in the open qualifying rounds for a tournament may play in the event. That petitioner identifies one set of clients or customers that it serves (spectators at tournaments) does not preclude it from having another set (players in tournaments) against whom it may not discriminate.

Petitioner does not contest that a golf cart is a reasonable modification that is necessary if Martin is to play in its tournaments. Martin's claim thus differs from one that might be asserted by players with less serious afflictions that make walking the course uncomfortable or difficult, but not beyond their capacity. In such cases, an accommodation might be reasonable but not necessary. In this case, however, the narrow dispute is whether allowing Martin to use a golf cart, despite the walking requirement that applies to the PGA TOUR, the NIKE TOUR, and the third stage of the Q-School, is a modification that would "fundamentally alter the nature" of those events.

We are not persuaded that a waiver of the walking rule for Martin would work a fundamental alteration in either sense.

As an initial matter, we observe that the use of carts is not itself inconsistent with the fundamental character of the game of golf. From early on, the essence of the game has been shot-making—using clubs to cause a ball to progress from the teeing ground to a hole some distance away with as few strokes as possible. That essential aspect of the game is still reflected in the very first of the Rules of Golf, which declares: "The Game of Golf consists in playing a ball from the teeing ground into the hole by a stroke or successive strokes in accordance with the rules." Over the years, there have been many changes in the players' equipment, in golf course design, in the Rules of Golf, and in the method of transporting clubs from hole to hole. Originally, so few clubs were used that each player could carry them without a bag. Then came golf bags, caddies, carts that were pulled by hand, and eventually motorized carts that carried players as well as clubs. "Golf carts started appearing with increasing regularity on American golf courses in the 1950's. Today they are everywhere. And they are encouraged. For one thing, they often speed up play, and for another, they are great revenue producers." There is nothing in the Rules of Golf that either forbids the use of carts, or penalizes a player for using a cart. That set of rules, as we have observed, is widely accepted in both the amateur and professional golf world as the rules of the game. The walking rule that is contained in petitioner's hard cards, based on an optional condition buried in an appendix to the Rules of Golf, is not an essential attribute of the game itself.

Even if we accept the factual predicate for petitioner's argument—that the walking rule is "outcome affecting" because fatigue may adversely affect performance—its legal position is fatally flawed. Petitioner's refusal to consider Martin's personal circumstances in deciding whether to accommodate his disability runs counter to the clear language and purpose of the ADA. As previously stated, the ADA was enacted to eliminate discrimination against "individuals" with disabilities, and to that end Title III of the Act requires without exception that any "policies, practices, or procedures" of a public accommodation be reasonably modified for disabled "individuals" as necessary to afford access unless doing so would fundamentally alter what is offered. To comply with this command, an individualized inquiry must be made to determine whether a specific modification for a particular person's disability would be reasonable under the circumstances as well as necessary for that person, and yet at the same time not work a fundamental alteration.

To be sure, the waiver of an essential rule of competition for anyone would fundamentally alter the nature of petitioner's tournaments. As we have demonstrated, however, the walking rule is at best peripheral to the nature of petitioner's athletic events, and thus it might be waived in individual cases without working a fundamental alteration.

The judgment of the Court of Appeals is affirmed.

DISSENTING OPINION

Justices SCALIA and THOMAS
In my view today's opinion exercises a benevolent compassion that the law does not place it within our power to impose. The judgment distorts the text of Title III, the structure of the ADA, and common sense. I respectfully dissent.

The Court holds that a professional sport is a place of public accommodation and that respondent is a "custome[r]" of "competition" when he practices his profession. It finds, that this strange conclusion is compelled by the "literal text" of Title III of the Americans with Disabilities Act of 1990(ADA), 42 U.S.C. § 12101 et seq., by the "expansive purpose" of the ADA, and by the fact that Title II of the Civil Rights Act of 1964, 42 U.S.C. § 2000a(a), has been applied to an amusement park and public golf courses. I disagree.

The ADA has three separate titles: Title I covers employment discrimination, Title II covers discrimination by government entities, and Title III covers discrimination by places of public accommodation. Title II is irrelevant to this case. Title I protects only "employees" of employers who have 15 or more employees, §§ 12112(a), 12111(5)(A). It does not protect independent contractors. Respondent claimed employment discrimination under Title I, but the District Court found him to be an independent contractor rather than an employee.

The provision of Title III at issue here (§ 12182, its principal provision) is a public-accommodation law, and it is the traditional understanding of public-accommodation laws that they provide rights for customers.

The one place where Title III specifically addresses discrimination by places of public accommodation through "contractual" arrangements, it makes clear that discrimination against the other party to the contract is not covered, but only discrimination against "clients or customers of the covered public accommodation that enters into the contractual, licensing or other arrangement." And finally, the regulations promulgated by the Department of Justice reinforce the conclusion that Title III's protections extend only to customers. "The purpose of the ADA's public accommodations requirements," they say, "is to ensure accessibility to the goods offered by a public accommodation." Surely this has nothing to do with employees and independent contractors.

The Court, for its part, pronounces respondent to be a "customer" of the PGA TOUR or of the golf courses on which it is played. That seems to me quite incredible. The PGA TOUR is a professional sporting event, staged for the entertainment of a live and TV audience, the receipts from whom (the TV audience's admission price is paid by advertisers) pay the expenses of the tour, including the cash prizes for the winning golfers. The professional golfers on the tour are no more "enjoying" (the statutory term) the entertainment that the tour provides, or the facilities of the golf courses on which it is held, than professional baseball players "enjoy" the baseball games in which they play or the facilities of Yankee Stadium. To be sure, professional ballplayers participate in the games, and use the ballfields, but no one in his right mind would think that they are customers of the American League or of Yankee Stadium. They are themselves the entertainment that the customers pay to watch.

Respondent did not seek to "exercise" or "recreate" at the PGA TOUR events; he sought to make money (which is why he is called a professional golfer). He was not a customer buying recreation or entertainment; he was a professional athlete selling it.

It is as irrelevant to the PGA TOUR's compliance with the statute whether walking is essential to the game of golf as it is to the shoe store's compliance whether "pairness" is essential to the nature of shoes. If a shoe store wishes to sell shoes only in pairs it may; and if a golf tour (or a golf course) wishes to provide only walk-around golf, it may. The PGA TOUR cannot deny respondent access to that game because of his disability, but it need not provide him a game different (whether in its essentials or in its details) from that offered to everyone else.

Nowhere is it writ that PGA TOUR golf must be classic "essential" golf. Why cannot the PGA TOUR, if it wishes, promote a new game, with distinctive rules (much as the American League promotes a game of baseball in which the pitcher's turn at the plate can be

continued

taken by a "designated hitter")? If members of the public do not like the new rules—if they feel that these rules do not truly test the individual's skill at "real golf" (or the team's skill at "real baseball") they can withdraw their patronage. But the rules are the rules. They are (as in all games) entirely arbitrary, and there is no basis on which anyone—not even the Supreme Court of the United States—can pronounce one or another of them to be "nonessential" if the rulemaker (here the PGA TOUR) deems it to be essential.

If one assumes, however, that the PGA TOUR has some legal obligation to play classic, Platonic golf—and if one assumes the correctness of all the other wrong turns the Court has made to get to this point—then we Justices must confront what is indeed an awesome responsibility. It has been rendered the solemn duty of the Supreme Court of the United States, laid upon it by Congress in pursuance of the Federal Government's power "[t]o regulate Commerce with foreign Nations, and among the several States," U.S. Const., Art. I, § 8, cl. 3, to decide What Is Golf. I am sure that the Framers of the Constitution, aware of the 1457 edict of King James II of Scotland prohibiting golf because it interfered with the practice of archery, fully ex-

pected that sooner or later the paths of golf and government, the law and the links, would once again cross, and that the judges of this august Court would some day have to wrestle with that age-old jurisprudential question, for which their years of study in the law have so well prepared them: Is someone riding around a golf course from shot to shot really a golfer? The answer, we learn, is yes. The Court ultimately concludes, and it will henceforth be the Law of the Land, that walking is not a "fundamental" aspect of golf.

Either out of humility or out of self-respect (one or the other) the Court should decline to answer this incredibly difficult and incredibly silly question.

CASE QUESTIONS

1. Why does Mr. Martin wish an accommodation?
2. Does use of a cart fundamentally alter the game of golf?
3. Is Mr. Martin seeking a public accommodation or an employee accommodation?
4. Do the dissenting justices believe that the court must define the essential elements of the game of golf?

Employers are not required to make accommodations that would result in "undue hardship," as determined by examining four factors:

1. The nature and cost of the accommodation
2. The size, workforce, and resources of the specific facility involved
3. The size, workforce, and resources of the covered entity
4. The nature of the covered entity's entire operation

Preemployment medical examinations are prohibited under the ADA, as are specific questions about a protected individual's disabilities. However, an employer may inquire about the ability of the applicant to perform job-related functions. "Can you carry fifty pounds of mail?" is an appropriate question; "Do you have the use of both arms?" is not.

Employers can refuse employment if an ADA-protected individual cannot perform necessary job functions. Also, employers can refuse to hire individuals who pose a direct threat to the health and safety of others in the workplace (assuming the risk cannot be minimized through accommodation).

The ADA is enforced through the EEOC and carries the same rights and remedies provided under Title VII. Exhibit 20.2 provides a list of items to help employers comply with ADA. Exhibit 20.3 examines proper and improper questions for job interviews under ADA.

Visit the family and work Web site:
http://www. familiesandwork.org

The Family and Medical Leave Act

Passed in 1993, the Family and Medical Leave Act (FMLA) requires companies with fifty or more employees to provide twelve weeks' leave each year for medical or

EXHIBIT 20.2 Compliance Tips for ADA

Minimizing an Employer's ADA Risks

1. Post notices describing the provisions of the ADA in your workplace.

2. Review job requirements to ensure that they bear a direct relationship to the ability to perform the essential functions of the job in question.

3. Identify, in writing, the "essential functions" of a job before advertising for or interviewing potential candidates.

4. Before rejecting an otherwise qualified applicant or terminating an employee on the basis of a disability, first determine that (a) the individual cannot perform the essential duties of the position, or (b) the individual cannot perform the essential duties of the position without imminent and substantial risk of injury to self or others, and (c) the employer cannot reasonably accommodate the disability.

5. Articulate factors, other than an individual's disability, that are the basis of an adverse employment decision. Document your findings and the tangible evidence on which a decision to reject or terminate was based; make notes of accommodations considered.

6. Ask the disabled individual for advice on accommodations. This shows the employer's good faith and a willingness to consider such proposals.

7. Institute programs of benefits and consultation to assist disabled employees in effectively managing health, leave, and other benefits.

8. Check with insurance carrier regarding coverage of disabled employees and attempt (within economic reason) to maintain provided coverage or arrange for separate coverage.

9. Keep disabled individuals in mind when making structural alterations or purchasing office furniture and equipment.

10. Document all adverse employment actions, including reasons for the employment action with respect to disabled employees; focus on the employee's inability to do the job effectively rather than any relation to the employee's disability.

Source: EEOC Enforcement Guidance, http://www.eeoc.gov.

EXHIBIT 20.3 Legal and Illegal Versions of Similar Job Interview Questions

Legal	Illegal
1. Do you have 20/20 corrected vision?	What is your corrected vision?
2. How well can you handle stress?	Does stress ever affect your ability to be productive?
3. Can you perform this function with or without reasonable accommodation?	Would you need reasonable accommodation in this job?
4. How many days were you absent from work last year?	How many days were you sick last year?
5. Are you currently illegally using drugs?	What medications are you currently taking?
6. Do you regularly eat three meals per day?	Do you need to eat a number of small snacks at regular intervals throughout the day in order to maintain your energy level?
7. Do you drink alcohol?	How much alcohol do you drink per week?

Source: EEOC's "Enforcement Guidance on Pre-Employment Disability-Related Inquiries," May 12, 1994.

C O N S I D E R . . .   2 0 . 1 0

Margaret Christian was fired by St. Anthony's Medical Center after she disclosed to them that she had hyper-cholesterolemia (her cholesterol count is 319 milligrams), which would require blood draining and thus an extra day or two off per month. After Ms. Christian was fired, she filed suit, alleging a violation of ADA. St. Anthony's says she was not currently disabled and ADA does not protect all medically afflicted persons. Ms. Christian says the treatment itself is disabling. Who is right? [*Christian* v. *St. Anthony Medical Center, Inc.*, 117 F.3d 1051 (7th Cir. 1997).]

Review the Family and Medical Leave Act:
http://www.law.cornell.edu/uscode/29/2601.html

family reasons, including the birth or adoption of a child or the serious health condition or illness of a spouse, parent, or child. Although pay is not required during the leave, medical benefits of the employee must continue, and the same or an equivalent job must be available for the employee upon return.

FOR THE MANAGER'S DESK

RE: THE FMLA: NO FREE VACATION

Abusing the FMLA

The abuse of the FMLA centers mostly on the way employees and/or their healthcare providers interpret their own or a family member's serious illness. According to the law's regulations, a serious health condition can include an illness that incapacitates the person for more than three days, requires at least one visit to a healthcare professional, and leads to ongoing treatment. Examples of serious health conditions include heart attack, stroke, most types of cancer, back conditions requiring extensive therapy or surgery, pneumonia, emphysema, asthma, severe arthritis, Alzheimer's disease, diabetes, epilepsy, migraines and appendicitis. Examples of nonserious health conditions that are not given FMLA protections, unless complications develop, include: the common cold, flu, earaches, stomachaches, minor ulcers, headaches other than migraines, and routine dental problems. Workers can take leave in as little as one-hour increments and their managers usually lack discretion to deny leave.

In the following examples, the employees attempted to use FMLA protections but were denied by their employers and the legal system.

"Mommy, It Hurts" and Other Ailments

A 4-year-old child's ear infection kept him home from daycare and his mother home from work for four days. The mother took her child to the doctor once and administered antibiotics herself for 10 days. The mother requested four days of job-protected absence but did not receive it. Was she entitled to FMLA protections? No.

The court in *Seidle* v. *Provident Mutual Life Insurance Co.* found that the child was not incapacitated for more than three days. On the fourth day the child had a runny nose. The only reason the child did not return to daycare on the fourth day was that the daycare center has a policy which prohibits attendance by children with runny noses. There was also no evidence of continuing treatment by a healthcare provider as set forth by the act. In this case, the mother administered the medication herself. She never scheduled a follow-up visit with the doctor and did not telephone the doctor to communicate her child's condition.

In another case, an employee was fired for poor work performance, but she claimed that the firing was due to her need to take time off to attend to her ill daughter, who had to stay in bed due to an asthma attack. Is the woman entitled to FMLA protections? No. The court in *Sakelarion* v. *Judge & Dolph, Ltd.*, found that the employee's assertion that her daughter needed to be in bed due to asthma, without any evidence that she was incapable of self-care, was insufficient for FMLA protections.

An employee claimed to have a case of food poisoning with no evidence of inpatient care and no continued treatment by a healthcare provider. Was he entitled to FMLA protections? No. The court claimed in *Oswalt* v. *Sara Lee Corp.* that because the employee's food poisoning did not require inpatient care or continuing medical treatment, it could not be considered a serious health condition.

The Good Word?

The courts have also proved that FMLA requires more than the patient's word. In *Bauer* v. *Dayton-Walther Corp.*, the company had a "no fault" attendance policy whereby employees who missed work time accumulated points of absenteeism. Upon the accumulation of six absenteeism points in six months, the employee could be automatically terminated. In this case, an employee was terminated, but he tried to be reinstated, claiming to have rectal bleeding. He also claimed that he was afraid his condition could eventually become cancerous. The court did not reinstate him because he was never incapacitated for more than three days, he sought medical attention only once, and treatment was never administered. It also claimed that a condition must be looked at for what it is, not what it can or may become.

Employees in other cases have attempted to misapply the FMLA provisions. In one such case, a Chicago bus driver took leave under the FMLA for constipation, while in another case an employee remained out of work for seven weeks because of the removal and subsequent infection of an ingrown toenail.

To avoid abuse of the FMLA at your company, human resources professionals should consider what I call the EEI strategy; establish and/or update the company's FMLA policy, educate and train supervisors about the FMLA, and inform employees about their rights under the FMLA. These are briefly explained below.

Update company-leave policies. Companies must have an FMLA policy that is clear and consistent in delineating and explaining:

- The right of employees to take leave under the FMLA.
- The steps that employees need to take when requesting leave.
- Whether medical certification, including second and third opinions, are required.

- If applicable, the substitution of paid leave for unpaid family and medical leave.
- Whether an employee who fails to return to work after a leave will be required to reimburse the employer for health-insurance premiums covering the leave period.
- Whether an employee on leave is entitled to earn employment benefits.

It is important to remember that a company's policy must give the same or more protections as the federal law.

Educate and train supervisors. Supervisors must be familiar with the company FMLA policy. They also must understand that there are certain practices prohibited under the act, such as interfering with an employee's right to take leave, discharging or discriminating in any way against people who are exercising their rights under the FMLA, or interfering with proceedings concerning the law.

Inform employees. Employees must be informed of their rights and obligations under the FMLA in the company handbook, manual, and/or fact sheets that outline FMLA protections.

Source: "The FMLA: No Free Vacation," *Management Review,* June 1997, p. 43 by Teresa Brady. Copyright © 1997 American Management Association International. Reprinted by permission of American Management Association International via the Copyright Clearance Center.

THE GLOBAL WORKFORCE

Currently 2,000 U.S. companies have 21,000 subsidiary operations in twenty-one countries throughout the world. With the free trade agreements (see Chapter 7), those numbers will increase, as will the sizes of global operations. One of the many employment issues that arise with respect to employees in the subsidiary operations is whether the protections of Title VII apply to workers in these foreign operations. In *EEOC* v. *Arabian American Oil Co.,* 499 U.S. 244 (1991), the U.S. Supreme Court was faced with the issue of whether U.S. companies could engage in employment discrimination against U.S. citizens when they are working in countries outside the United States. The Court held that the companies are governed by the employment laws of the country of operations and not the provisions of U.S. legislation.

Congress responded to the Supreme Court's ruling in *Arabian American Oil* by adding a section to the Civil Rights Act of 1991 addressing the issue of foreign operations. The statutory provision on foreign operations and civil rights protections is neither universal nor automatic. The amendment provides basically that if there is a conflict between U.S. employment discrimination laws and those of a host country, a company should follow the laws of the host country. An example is a law in the

Review the Universal
Declaration of Human Rights:
http://www.un.org/
Overview/rights.html

host country that prohibits the employment of women in management. The company would be required to follow that prohibition for operations located in the host country. If the host country has no laws on employment discrimination, the company is then required to follow all U.S. antidiscrimination laws.

Several multilateral treaties govern the rights of workers. In 1948, the United Nations adopted its Universal Declaration of Human Rights. The declaration supports, among other things, equality of pay and nondiscriminatory employment policies. Also, the Helsinki Final Act of 1973 supports nondiscriminatory employment policies. In 1977, the International Labor Office issued its Tripartite Declaration of Principles Concerning Multinational Enterprises, which supports equal pay and nondiscriminatory payment policies. The EU has adopted all of these treaties and policies for their implementation.

FOR THE MANAGER'S DESK

RE: THE RESPECT OF RANK

Charlene Barshefsky is the U.S. trade representative. She is both an ambassador and a cabinet officer. With the recent vote to open trade with China, Ms. Barshefsky saw the culmination of years of negotiations with the Chinese.

When interviewed by the *New York Times* about her experience as a woman serving as the United States' chief negotiator, she explained that in China and other countries, gender is not as important as rank:

Because my rank is high, my foreign counterparts treat me with the deference one might expect. Rank is much more important than gender, and rank can tend to overcome any potential gender bias. To the extent women are thought to

be, in general, more perceptive about people, more aware of their surroundings, more sensitive to body language, it is a decided advantage to be a woman in a negotiation, particularly in watching. The body always speaks well before the mouth ever opens.

Are other nations ahead of the United States in treating women as equals? Should rank matter more than gender? What other examples can you point to outside the United States where women have achieved high ranks?

Source: Eric Schmitt, "The Negotiator," *New York Times Magazine*, October 1, 2000, p. 21.

SUMMARY

What laws govern employment discrimination?

- Civil Rights Acts of 1866, 1964, 1991—federal statutes prohibiting discrimination in various aspects of life (employment, voting)

- Equal Pay Act—equal pay for the same work regardless of gender

- Equal Employment Opportunity Act—antidiscrimination employment amendment to Civil Rights Act

- Pregnancy Discrimination Act—prohibits refusing to hire, refusing to promote, or firing because of pregnancy

- Age Discrimination in Employment Act (ADEA)—prohibits hiring, firing, promotion, benefits, raises based on age

- Rehabilitation Act of 1973—federal statute prohibiting discrimination on basis of disability by federal agencies and contractors

- Americans with Disabilities Act (ADA)—federal law prohibiting discrimination on basis of disability by certain employees

- Family and Medical Leave Act (FMLA)—federal law providing for twelve weeks of leave for childbirth, adoption, or family illness

What types of discrimination exist?

- Disparate treatment—form of discrimination in which members of different races/sexes are treated differently

- Disparate impact—test or screening device that affects one group more than another

- Pattern or practice of discrimination—theory for establishing discrimination that compares population percentages with workplace percentages

- Sexual harassment—form of discrimination that involves a *quid pro quo* related to sexual favors or an atmosphere of harassment

Are there any defenses to discrimination?

- Bona fide occupational qualification (BFOQ)—job qualification of sex, religion, or national origin that is necessary for the operation of a business, such as religious affiliation for the pastor of a church

- Affirmative action—programs created to remedy past wrongs that permit choices on the basis of race, sex, or national origin

QUESTIONS AND PROBLEMS

1. Patricia Lorance is an hourly wage employee at the Montgomery Works AT&T electronics products plant. She had been employed there since the early 1970s and under union rules accrued seniority through her years of service at the plant. In 1979, the union entered into a new collective bargaining agreement providing that seniority would be determined by department and not on a plant-wide basis. The effect of the change was to put Ms. Lorance at the bottom of the seniority ladder in the testing areas despite her longevity in the plant. When layoffs became necessary, she and the other female testers were laid off because of the new seniority rule. Without the new rule, Ms. Lorance and the other women would not have been victims of the cutbacks. Does the seniority system violate Title VII? [*Lorance* v. *AT&T Technologies, Inc.*, 490 U.S. 900 (1989).]

2. Calvin Rhodes began as a salesman with Dresser Industries in 1955. In 1986, the oil industry experienced a severe economic downturn, and Mr. Rhodes was laid off. His severance report said he was discharged as part of a reduction in force. Within two months, Dresser had hired a 42-year-old replacement. Mr. Rhodes sued for violation of ADEA. Will he win? [*Rhodes* v. *Guiberson Oil Tools* (subsidiary of Dresser), 75 F.3d 989 (5th Cir. 1996).]

3. Vivian Martyszenko was working as a cashier at a Safeway grocery store in Ogallala, Nebraska, when she received a call from the police informing her that her two children might have been molested. Ms. Martyszenko's supervisor gave her two weeks' vacation leave to care for her children.

The psychiatrist's exam of the children was inconclusive, and Ms. Martyszenko was told it would take time for their recovery. She asked for leave under the FMLA, which Safeway denied. She then filed suit, alleging Safeway had violated FMLA. Was the boys' condition a serious health condition covered under FMLA? [*Martyszenko* v. *Safeway, Inc.*, 120 F.3d 120 (8th Cir. 1997).]

4. On August 11, 1980, Shelby Memorial Hospital hired Sylvia Hayes, a certified x-ray technician, to work the 3–11 P.M. shift in the hospital's radiology department. Two months later, she was fired after she informed her supervisor that she was pregnant. The supervisor fired Ms. Hayes because Dr. Cecil Eiland, the hospital's radiology director and director of radiation safety, recommended that Ms. Hayes be removed from all areas using ionizing radiation, and the hospital could not find alternative work for her. After her dismissal, Ms. Hayes filed suit for violation of the Pregnancy Discrimination Act and Title VII. Should she recover? [*Hayes* v. *Shelby Memorial Hosp.*, 726 F.2d 1543 (11th Cir. 1984).]

5. The Masonic nursing home has mostly female occupants and hires fewer male attendants than female ones. Home administrators maintain that the female occupants (for privacy reasons) would not consent to intimate personal care by males and would, in fact, leave the home. A substantial portion of the women at the home are "total care" patients who require assistance in performing virtually all activities, including bathing, dressing, and using toilets, catheters, and bedpans. In a suit brought by a male nurse's aide who was denied employment, who would win? [*Fessel* v. *Masonic Home*, 17 FEP Cases 330 (Del. 1978).]

6. Woolworth Victor Davis applied for a position as a firefighter with the city of Philadelphia in 1977. When he reported for his physical exam, the physician noticed a scar; and Mr. Davis explained that he had used amphetamines in 1972 but had not engaged in drug use since then. He was told he could not be hired because the city would not employ anyone with a drug history. Mr. Davis filed suit under the Rehabilitation Act of 1973. What outcome? Would the ADA protect him? [*Davis* v. *Butcher*, 451 F. Supp. 791 (E.D. Pa. 1978).]

7. Audra Sommers (aka Timothy Cornesh) a self-claimed "female with the anatomical body of a male," was hired by Budget Marketing on April 22, 1980. She was fired on April 24, 1980, because the female workers at Budget refused to allow her in the women's restroom and threatened to quit if she/he were allowed in. Ms. Sommers brought suit for a violation of Title VII alleging discrimination on the basis that she was a transsexual. Does Title VII apply? [*Sommers* v. *Budget Marketing, Inc.,* 667 F.2d 748 (8th Cir. 1982).]

8. Would the following actions constitute sexual harassment?

   a. Making sexual comments or innuendoes; telling sexual jokes or stories
   b. Asking questions about social or sexual life
   c. Telling lies or spreading rumors about a person's personal sex life
   d. Making sexual comments about a person's body
   e. Turning work discussions to sexual topics
   f. Looking a person up and down
   g. Staring repeatedly at someone
   h. Blocking a person's path or hindering them
   i. Giving unwanted gifts of a sexual nature
   j. Invading a person's body space
   k. Making sexual gestures or kissing sounds or offering massages
   l. Displaying sexual posters, cartoons, or handouts

9. American Airlines passed a grooming rule that prohibited a "corn row" hairstyle on all employees. Renee Rogers, a black woman, brought a Title VII suit alleging that the denial of her right to wear the hairstyle intruded upon her rights and discriminated against her. What will be the result? [*Rogers* v. *American Airlines, Inc.,* 527 F. Supp. 229 (S.D.N.Y. 1981).]

10. American Airlines has a policy of not hiring flight officers over the age of 40. The reason for their policy is that it takes ten to fifteen years for a flight officer to become a copilot and then another ten to fifteen years for a copilot to become a captain. Because the FAA requires retirement at age 60, service would be limited. Edward L. Murnane, age 43, was denied employment on the basis of age and filed an age discrimination suit. Is age a BFOQ for the job? [*Murnane* v. *American Airlines, Inc.,* 667 F.2d 98 (D.C. 1981).]

RESEARCH PROBLEM

Kafka Wasn't Kidding

11. Develop a solution for employers to the problems/conflicts raised in the following report.

   You know the sad story: In the early hours of the morning of Mar. 24, 1989 the tanker *Exxon Valdez* hit a reef in Prince William Sound, Alaska, spilling 11 million gallons of crude oil. Exxon paid billions in fines and cleanup costs. Many people still curse Exxon as a despoiler of the environment.

   It is widely believed that the captain of the tanker was drunk. To minimize the chances of another such disaster, Exxon implemented a new policy: While offering employees help in getting treatment for alcohol or drug dependency, the company declared some jobs, were safety is critical—tanker captains, for example— off-limits to anyone who has a history of abuse of alcohol or some other substance.

   Now Exxon is in court again.

   This time the bureaucrats in the U.S. Equal Employment Opportunity Commission are suing the company to protect ships' captains and the like who have had drinking or drug problems.

   No, we are not kidding.

   The feds say Exxon's policy, aimed at minimizing accidents, violates the 1990 Americans with Disabilities Act. The EEOC says that Exxon is discriminating against some 50 employees who have had alcohol or drug problems but have since been rehabilitated.

   Chrys Meador, an EEOC trial attorney, defends her agency's kafkaesque action. "Exxon believes they cannot get a guarantee that somebody who's had a substance abuse problem will never relapse." "Well, we can't give them that guarantee. But the experts we have consulted have said that there are very positive employee assistance programs that actively monitor individuals, and there are telltale signs so that you can detect these things before they become a problem."

   In other words, it's the company's responsibility to know when an ex-drunk is about to slip off the wagon or when a schizophrenic has stopped taking his pills. Only it had better be careful how it monitors these things.

   Meador says the agency is just following what Congress said in the 1990 Disabilities Act. Scary thing is, she's right.

Source: David A. Price, "Kafka Wasn't Kidding," *Forbes,* June 2, 1997. Reprinted by permission of Forbes Magazine © Forbes Inc., 2004.

NOTES

1. See the Web site and the Instructor's Manual for additional background on the history of employment discrimination law.

2. For updates on affirmative action and other issues in employment discrimination law, be sure to visit the course Web site.

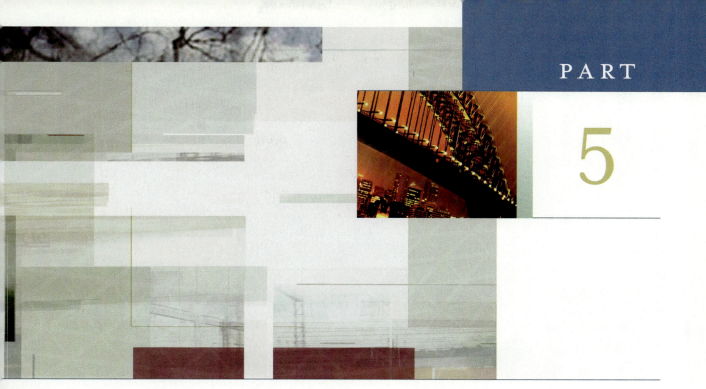

Business Forms and Capitalization

■ This portion of the book covers legal issues in forming and financing a business. The structure of a business determines its owners' rights and liabilities. Different business forms afford varying levels of flexibility for operations. In addition, the type of business structure creates opportunities for both initial financing of the business and its expansion.

Some forms of business financing require compliance with state and federal laws for sales of such business interests as securities and bonds. These laws include disclosure requirements for sales; they also provide remedies for investors and impose liabilities on businesses when disclosures made about the nature of the interest and the business are incomplete or inaccurate.

Some businesses combine or merge in order to compete better in the evolving global economy. State and federal laws afford disclosure and protections for merging businesses and their owners and investors.

21

Forms of Doing Business

▶ **update** ◀

For up-to-date legal news and real-world business applications, click on **update** *at* http://jennings.westbuslaw.com

■ Creating a sole proprietorship is a popular way to do business, but the most popular forms of business organizations and the ones producing the most revenues are those formed by more than one person. Partnerships, limited partnerships, limited liability companies, and corporations are all multi-individual forms of doing business. This chapter answers the following questions: How are various business entities formed? What are the advantages and disadvantages of various entities? What are the rights, responsibilities, and liabilities of the individuals involved?

Each of the forms of doing business is examined by reviewing its formation, sources of funding, the personal liability of owners, tax consequences, management and control, and the ease of transferring interest. Exhibit 21.1 presents an overview of the types of business entities.

> **Please accept my resignation. I don't want to belong to any organization that will accept me as a member.**
> Groucho Marx

> **Although our form is corporate, our attitude is partnership. We do not view the company itself as the ultimate owner of our business assets but instead view the company as a conduit through which our shareholders own the assets.**
> Warren Buffett
> *Chairman, Berkshire Hathaway*

In 1984, General Motors bought 100 percent of Electronic Data Systems' stock, a company founded and chaired by H. Ross Perot, who was also EDS's largest shareholder. Mr. Perot was given a 0.8 percent interest in GM voting stock and was elected to the GM board. Mr. Perot became a thorn in the side of GM's board, saying publicly, "Until you nuke the old GM system, you'll never tap the full potential of your people." GM's board voted to reacquire Perot's interest for $745 million. GM shareholders were outraged. Can the board do this? What rights do shareholders have?

© RYAN McVAY/PHOTODISC/GETTY IMAGES

SOLE PROPRIETORSHIPS

Formation

A **sole proprietorship** is not a true business entity because it consists of only an individual operating a business. According to the U.S. Small Business Association, most small businesses operate as sole proprietorships, with 50 percent operating as home-based businesses. Often, a sole proprietorship is evidenced by the following language: "Homer Lane d/b/a Green Grower's Grocery"; "d/b/a" is an acronym for "doing business as." Because a sole proprietorship comprises but one individual and no separate organization exists, there are no formal requirements for formation. The individual simply begins doing business. In some states, "d/b/a" businesspeople are required to publish and file the fictitious names under which they will be doing business.

Visit the Small Business Association:
http://www.asbaonline.org

Sources of Funding

Most sole proprietorships are small businesses, and initially their business capital needs are small. Their financing usually comes from loans, either direct loans from banks or loans through such government agencies as the Small Business Administration.

Some sole proprietorships are started with financial backing from other people, usually in the form of a personal loan. In such cases, the sole proprietor may have the skills or clients for a successful business but not the funds necessary to begin.

Visit the Small Business Administration:
http://www.sbaonline.sba.gov

EXHIBIT 21.1 Comparison of Forms of Conducting Business

FORM	FORMATION	FUNDING	MANAGEMENT	TRANSFER CONTROL	TAXES	DISSOLUTION	LIABILITY
Sole proprietorship	No formal requirements	Individual provides funds	Individual	No transfer	Individual pays on individual return	Death; voluntary	Individual
Partnership	Articles of partnership	Capital contributions of partners	All partners or delegated to one	Transfer interest but not partner status	Partner takes profits and losses on individual return (flow-through)	Dissolution upon death; withdrawal of partner	Partners are personally liable
Limited partnership	Filing of articles of partnership	Capital contributions of general and limited partners	General partner	More easily transferred	Same as partnership (flow-through)	Death of general partner	General partner is personally liable; limited partners liable to extent of contribution
Corporation	Formal filing of articles of incorporation	Debt (bonds)/equity (shareholders)	Board of directors, officers, and/or executive committee	Shares (with reasonable restrictions) are easily transferred	Corporation pays taxes; shareholders pay taxes on dividends	Dissolved only if limited in duration or shareholders vote to dissolve	No shareholder personal liability unless (1) watered or (2) corporate veil
S corporation* or Subchapter S	Same as above (special IRS filings to create special tax [flow-through] status)	Same as above	Same as above	Restrictions on transfer to comply with S corporation	Shareholders pay taxes on profits; take losses	Same as above	Same as above
C corporation†	Created as normal corporation	Same as corporation	Same as above	No restrictions	Same as above	Same as above	Same as above
Limited liability company (LLC)	Formal filing—articles of organization	Capital contributions of members	All members manage or delegate to one member	No admission without consent of majority	Flow-through treatment	Dissolved upon death, bankruptcy	Same as above (except professional negligence)
Limited liability partnership	Filing of articles of limited liability partnership	Capital contributions of partners	All partners or delegated to one	No admission without consent of majority	Flow-through treatment	Dissolved upon death, bankruptcy	Varies by state but liability for acts of partners is limited in some way

*S corporations are formed under state incorporation laws but structured to obtain flow-through or pass-through status for income and losses under IRS regulations.
†C corporation is again a label for tax purpose.

Liability

Because financing for a sole proprietorship is based on the sole proprietor's credit rating and assets, the proprietor is personally liable for the business loan, and her assets are subject to attachment should there be a default. To get financing, a sole proprietor takes personal financial risk.

Tax Consequences

The positive side of a sole proprietor's unlimited personal liability is the right to claim all tax losses associated with the business. The income of the business is the income of the sole proprietor and is reported on the individual's income tax return. There is no separate filing requirement for the business itself. Moreover, although sole proprietors owe all the taxes, they also get the benefit of all business deductions.

Management and Control

The proprietor is the manager of the business. In many businesses, the sole proprietor is both manager and employee. The proprietor makes all decisions. This form of business operation is truly centralized management.

Transferability of Interest

Because the business in many ways is the owner, the business can be transferred only if the owner allows it. When a sole proprietor's business is transferred, the transfer consists of the property, inventory, and goodwill of the business. The sole proprietor is generally required to sign a noncompetition agreement so that the goodwill paid for is preserved (see Chapters 17 and 18 for more details). In addition, upon the owner's death the heirs or devisees of the owner would inherit the property involved in the business. They could choose to operate the business, but the business usually ends upon the death of the sole proprietor.

PARTNERSHIPS

Review Arizona's Uniform Partnership Act:
http://www.azleg.state.az.us/ArizonaRevisedStatutes.asp?Title=29

Partnerships are governed by some version of the **Uniform Partnership Act** (UPA), which has been adopted in forty-nine states. In 1994, a new final version of the UPA was adopted by the commissioners. Most states have adopted the **Revised Uniform Partnership Act** (RUPA), but some did not repeal the UPA. The UPA defines a partnership as an "association of two or more persons to carry on as co-owners, a business for profit." "Persons" can include corporations, known as "artificial" persons, and natural persons.

Formation

A partnership can be formed voluntarily by direct action of the parties, such as through a partnership agreement or articles of partnership (see Exhibit 21.2 for a list of content for this formation), or its formation can be implied by the ongoing conduct of the parties.

Conduct That Forms: Partnerships by Implication

A partnership can arise even though there is no express agreement and the parties do not call themselves partners. In certain circumstances, courts infer that a partnership exists even if the persons involved say they are not partners.

EXHIBIT   21.2 Information Included in Articles of Partnership

MINIMUM REQUIREMENTS	SUGGESTED PROVISIONS
1. Names of the partners	1. Disability issues
2. Name of the partnership	2. Insurance coverage
3. Nature of the partnership's business	3. Sale of interest
4. The time frame of operation	4. Divorce of one of the partners
5. Amount of each partner's capital contribution	5. Indemnity agreements
6. Managerial powers of partners	6. Noncompetition agreements
7. Rights and duties of partners	7. Leaves of absence
8. Accounting procedures for partnership books and records	
9. Methods for sharing profits and losses	
10. Salaries (if any) of the partners	
11. Causes and methods of dissolution	
12. Distribution of property if the partnership is terminated	

Simply owning property together does not result in a **partnership by implication**. A cousin to apparent authority (see Chapter 18), a partnership by implication arises because the behaviors of the principals lead others to believe there is a partnership. Courts examine a number of factors in determining whether a partnership exists by implication. Section 7 of the RUPA provides that if two or more parties share the profits of a business, it is *prima facie* evidence that a partnership exists. (*Prima facie* evidence means there is a presumption that a partnership exists.) However, the presumption of partnership by profit sharing can be overcome if someone received profits for any of the following reasons:

1. Profits paid to repay debts

2. Profits paid as wages or rent

3. Profits paid to a widow or estate representative

4. Profits paid for the sale of business goodwill

Many shopping center leases, for example, provide for the payment of both a fixed amount of rent and a percentage of net profits. The owners of the shopping center thus profit as the stores do, but they profit as landlords, not as partners with the shopping center businesses.

Byker v. *Mannes* (Case 21.1) addresses the question of whether a partnership is implied by the conduct of two principals.

CASE 21.1

Byker v. *Mannes*
641 N.W.2d 210 (Mich. 2002)*

Dumb and Dumbfounded

FACTS

In 1985, David Byker (plaintiff) was doing accounting work for Tom Mannes (defendant). The two talked about going into business together because they had complementary business skills. Mr. Mannes could locate certain properties because of his real estate back-

ground, and Mr. Byker could raise money for their property purchases. Indeed, the parties stipulated the following as part of the litigation process in this case:

[T]he Plaintiff . . . and Defendant . . . agreed to engage in an ongoing business enterprise, to furnish capital, labor and/or skill to such enterprise, to raise investment funds

and to share equally in the profits, losses and expenses of such enterprise. . . . In order to facilitate investment of limited partners, Byker and Mannes created separate entities wherein they were general partners or shareholders for the purposes of operating each separate entity.

They also stipulated that they had investment interests in five real estate limited partnerships. With regard to these partnerships in which they invested over a nine-year period, they shared equally in the commissions, financing fees, and termination costs. The two also personally guaranteed loans for these investments from several financial institutions.

The business relationship between the parties began to deteriorate after they created Pier 1000 Ltd. in order to own and manage a marina. Shortly after the creation of Pier 1000 Ltd., the marina encountered serious financial difficulties. To address these difficulties, the parties placed their profits from another partnership, the M & B Limited Partnership II, into Pier 1000 Ltd. and borrowed money from several financial institutions.

Eventually, Mr. Mannes refused to make any additional monetary contributions. Mr. Byker, however, continued to make loan payments and incurred accounting fees on behalf of Pier 1000 Ltd., as well as on behalf of other business entities. Mr. Byker also entered into several individual loans for the benefit of Pier 1000 Ltd. These business transactions were performed without Mr. Mannes's knowledge.

The marina was eventually returned to its previous owners in exchange for their assumption of Mr. Byker's and Mr. Mannes's business obligations. At this point, the business ventures between Mr. Byker and Mr. Mannes ceased.

Mr. Byker then approached Mr. Mannes to obtain his share of the payments required as a result of the losses from the various businesses. Mr. Mannes testified that this was the first time he had received notice from Mr. Byker concerning any outstanding payments and that he was "absolutely dumbfounded" by the request for money.

Mr. Byker then filed suit for the payments, saying that the two had entered into a partnership. Mr. Byker maintained that the obligations between him and Mr. Mannes were not limited to their formal business relationships established by the individual partnerships and corporate entities, but that there was a "general" partnership underlying all their business affairs. In response, Mr. Mannes said that he merely invested in separate business ventures with Mr. Byker and that there were no other understandings between them.

Following a bench trial, the court determined that the parties had created a general partnership that included all of the business entities. The Court of Appeals reversed that decision. Mr. Byker appealed.

JUDICIAL OPINION

MARKMAN, Justice

[In the Court of Appeals decision], Judge White dissented. She stated that, although Michigan had not adopted § 202 [of the UPA], the trial court correctly recognized that Michigan's existing definition of partnership was consistent with that provision. Pursuant to Michigan law, "intent of the parties is determinative, whether or not they attached the term 'partnership' to that intent." Thus, in Judge White's view, "[t]here is no necessity that the parties attach the label 'partnership' to their relationship as long as they in fact both mutually agree to assume a relationship that falls within the definition of a partnership." We agree with Judge White's reasoning.

In determining whether a partnership exists, the focus is not on whether individuals subjectively intended to form a partnership, that is, it is unimportant whether the parties would have labeled themselves "partners." Instead, the focus is on whether individuals intended to jointly carry on a business for profit within the meaning of the Michigan Uniform Partnership Act, M.C.L. § 449.1 et seq., regardless of whether they subjectively intended to form a partnership. Accordingly, we reverse the Court of Appeals decision and remand this matter for further consideration.

Whether Michigan partnership law, M.C.L. § 449.6(1), requires a subjective intent to form a partnership or merely an intent to carry on as co-owners a business for profit is a question of law.

In 1917, the Michigan Legislature drafted the Michigan Uniform Partnership Act. 1917 PA 72.[†] In this act, a partnership was defined as "an association of two [2] or more persons to carry on as co-owners a business for profit. . . ." Over the years, the definition has remained essentially constant. At present, partnership is defined as "an association of 2 or more persons, which may consist of husband and wife, to carry on as co-owners a business for profit. . . ." This definition, as well as its predecessors, was modeled after the definition of partnership set forth in the 1914 UPA.

In 1994, however, the UPA definition of partnership was amended by the National Conference of Commissioners. The amended definition stated that "the association of two or more persons to carry on as co-owners a business for profit forms a partnership, whether or not the persons intend to form a partnership." Although the commissioners were apparently satisfied with the existing judicial construction of the definition of partnership, the commissioners added the new language "whether or not the persons intend to form a partnership" in order to "codif[y] the universal judicial

continued

construction of UPA Section 6(1) that a partnership is created by the association of persons whose intent is to carry on as co-owners a business for profit, regardless of their subjective intention to be 'partners.'" Section 202 (Comment 1). The commissioners emphasized that "[n]o substantive change in the law" was intended by the amendment of § 6. Id. To date, Michigan has not adopted the amended definition of partnership.

Although Michigan has not adopted the amended definition of partnership as set forth in § 202 of the Uniform Partnership Act of 1994, we believe nonetheless that M.C.L. § 449.6 is consistent with that amendment.

As already noted, a partnership in Michigan is statutorily defined as "an association of 2 or more persons, which may consist of husband and wife, to carry on as co-owners a business for profit. . . ." That is, if the parties associate themselves to "carry on" as co-owners a business for profit, they will be deemed to have formed a partnership relationship regardless of their subjective intent to form such a legal relationship. The statutory language is devoid of any requirement that the individuals have the subjective intent to create a partnership. Stated more plainly, the statute does not require partners to be aware of their status as "partners" in order to have a legal partnership.

Further, the Court of Appeals emphasis upon subjective intent as being of "prime importance in ascertaining whether a partnership exists," belies the absence in the statute of even a reference to such "intent" as a factor for consideration. Indeed, M.C.L. § 449.7, entitled "Rules for determining existence of a partnership," contains a listing of items to be specifically considered in this process and the subjective intent of the parties is conspicuously absent.

Although the provisions of M.C.L. § 449.6(1) set forth the standard for determining whether a partnership has been formed, we note that the Court of Appeals relied heavily on several of our earlier cases that, in the Court's view, focused this inquiry on whether the parties mutually intended to form a partnership. However, upon further examination of these cases, we respectfully disagree with the Court of Appeals. Rather, we find that, despite language that could potentially lead to such a conclusion, these cases, in fact, contemplated an examination of all the parties' acts and conduct in determining the existence of a partnership.

Pursuant to this common law, individuals would be found to have formed a partnership if they acted as partners, regardless of their subjective intent to form a partnership. Speaking through Justice Cooley, this Court stated the following with regard to the law of partnership:

> If parties intend no partnership the courts should give effect to their intent, unless somebody has been deceived by their acting or assuming to act as partners; and any such case must stand upon its peculiar facts, and upon special equities.
>
> It is nevertheless possible for parties to intend no partnership and yet to form one. If they agree upon an arrangement which is a partnership in fact, it is of no importance that they call it something else, or that they even expressly declare that they are not to be partners. The law must declare what is the legal import of their agreements, and names go for nothing when the substance of the arrangement shows them to be inapplicable.

Thus, one analyzes whether the parties acted as partners, not whether they subjectively intended to create, or not to create, a partnership.

This proposition has been consistently adhered to by this Court, although our decisions on occasion have utilized imprecise language and, therefore, created the possibility for some confusion.

In addition, we note that there are numerous other cases that expressly indicate that the focus of inquiry is on the parties' intent to "carry on as co-owners a business for profit," M.C.L. § 449.6(1), and on whether that intent is manifest in the actual agreement formed.

Accordingly, we believe that our prior case law has, consistent with M.C.L. § 449.6(1), properly examined the requirements of a legal partnership by focusing on whether the parties intentionally acted as co-owners of a business for profit, and not on whether they consciously intended to create the legal relationship of "partnership." We emphasize, however, that any future development of case law regarding partnership in our state must take place in accord with the provisions of the Michigan Partnership Act.

With the language of the statute as our focal point, we conclude that the intent to create a partnership is not required if the acts and conduct of the parties otherwise evidence that the parties carried on as co-owners a business for profit. Thus, we believe that, to the extent that the Court of Appeals regarded the absence of subjective intent to create a partnership as dispositive regarding whether the parties carried on as co-owners a business for profit, it incorrectly interpreted the statutory (and the common) law of partnership in Michigan.

Accordingly, we remand this matter to the Court of Appeals for analysis under the proper test for determining the existence of a partnership under the Michigan Uniform Partnership Act.

CASE QUESTIONS

1. What type of relationship did Mr. Byker and Mr. Mannes have?
2. When did the relationship end? When did the parties believe it ended?

3. What does the court say about the intent of the parties?

4. Is Mr. Mannes liable to Mr. Byker for the payments Mr. Byker made with regard to their investments?

*This case created a bit of a tussle between the Michigan Court of Appeals and its Supreme Court. Following this decision and remand, the

Court of Appeals found that there was no partnership because the parties had to be aware of it to be liable, thus defying the Michigan Supreme Court. On appeal, the Michigan Supreme Court reversed the Court of Appeals, 668 N.W.2d 909 (Mich. 2003), not offering an opinion but explaining it was reversing for the reasons stated in the dissenting opinion at the Court of Appeals on the second round.

†Note how the court traces the history of the law of partnership. Refer to the Web site and the Instructor's Manual for more information on the history of business organizations.

CONSIDER...   **21.1**

Richard Chaiken entered into agreements with both Mr. Strazella and Mr. Spitzer to operate a barbershop. Mr. Chaiken was to provide barber chairs, supplies, and licenses. Mr. Strazella and Mr. Spitzer were to bring their tools, and the agreements included work hours and holidays for them. The Delaware Employment Security Commission determined that Mr. Strazella and Mr. Spitzer are employees, not partners, and seeks to collect unemployment compensation for the two barbers. Mr. Chaiken maintains that they are partners and not employees. Who is correct? [*Chaiken* v. *Employment Security Comm'n*, 274 A.2d 707 (Del. 1971).]

Conduct That Forms: Partnership by Estoppel

There are times when someone can be held to be a partner because he acted like a partner. Some court decisions have held that anyone who helps a new business obtain a loan is holding himself out as a partner. Section 16 of the UPA provides as follows:

> When a person by words spoken or written or by conduct, represents himself, or consents to another representing him to anyone as a partner in an existing partnership or with one or more persons not actual partners, he is liable to any party to whom such representation has been made.

In other words, if the conduct of two or more parties leads others to believe a partnership exists, that partnership may be found to exist legally under the notion of **partnership by estoppel**. Partnerships by estoppel arise when others are led to believe there is a partnership.

Sources of Funding

Funding for a partnership comes from the partners who initially contribute property, cash, or services to the partnership accounts. These contributions are the capital

CONSIDER...   **21.2**

Triangle Chemical Company supplied $671.10 worth of fertilizer and chemicals to France Mathis to produce a cabbage crop. When Mr. Mathis first asked for credit, he was denied. He then told Triangle that he had a new partner, Emory Pope. The company president called Mr. Pope, who said he was backing Mr. Mathis. Mr. Pope had loaned Mr. Mathis money to produce the crop, and Mr. Mathis said Mr. Pope would pay the bills. Mr. Pope said, "We're growing the crop together and I am more or less handling the money." When Mr. Mathis could not pay, Triangle wanted to hold Mr. Pope personally liable. Mr. Pope said his promise to pay another's debt would have to have been in writing. Triangle claimed Mr. Pope was a partner and personally liable. Is he? [*Pope* v. *Triangle Chemical Co.*, 277 S.E.2d 758 (Ga. 1981).]

Visit the American Bar
Association's business
law section:
http://www.abanet.org/
buslaw

of the partnership. Not only are these contributions put at the risk of the business, but so also are each of the partners' personal assets: Partners are personally liable for the full amount of the partnership's obligations.

Partner Liability

Each partner is both a principal and an agent to the other partners and is liable both for the acts of others and to the others for individual acts. If one partner enters into a contract for partnership business supplies, all the partners are liable. Similarly, if one partner has a motor vehicle accident while on a partnership delivery, the individual partner is liable for her own negligence, but because she was in the scope of partnership business, the partners and the partnership are also liable. Under the RUPA, partners are jointly and severally liable for all obligations.

If partnership assets are exhausted, each partner is individually liable. Creditors can satisfy their claims by looking to the assets of the individual partners after the partnership assets are exhausted.

Vrabel v. *Acri* (Case 21.2) deals with an issue of partnership liability.

CASE 21.2

Vrabel v. *Acri*
103 N.E.2d 564 (Ohio 1952)

Shot Down in a Ma & Pa Cafe: Is Ma Liable When Pa Goes to Jail?

FACTS

On February 17, 1947, Stephen Vrabel and a companion went into the Acri Cafe in Youngstown, Ohio, to buy alcoholic drinks. While Mr. Vrabel and his companion were sitting at the bar drinking, Michael Acri, without provocation, drew a .38-caliber gun, shot and killed Mr. Vrabel's companion, and shot and seriously injured Mr. Vrabel. Mr. Acri was convicted of murder and sentenced to a life term in the state prison.

Florence and Michael Acri, as partners, had owned and operated the Acri Cafe since 1933. From the time of his marriage to Mrs. Acri in 1931 until 1946, Mr. Acri had been in and out of hospitals, clinics, and sanitariums for the treatment of mental disorders and nervousness. Although he beat Mrs. Acri when they had marital difficulties, he had not attacked, abused, or mistreated anyone else. The Acris separated in September 1946, and Mrs. Acri sued her husband for divorce soon afterward. Before their separation, Mrs. Acri had operated and managed the cafe primarily only when Mr. Acri was ill. Following the marital separation and until the time he shot Mr. Vrabel, Mr. Acri was in exclusive control of the management of the cafe.

Mr. Vrabel brought suit against Mrs. Acri to recover damages for his injuries on the grounds that, as Mr. Acri's partner, she was liable for his tort. The trial court

ordered her to pay Mr. Vrabel damages of $7,500. Mrs. Acri appealed.

JUDICIAL OPINION

ZIMMERMAN, Judge

The authorities are in agreement that whether a tort is committed by a partner or a joint adventurer, the principles of law governing the situation are the same. So, where a partnership or a joint enterprise is shown to exist, each member of such project acts both as principal and agent of the others as to those things done within the apparent scope of the business of the project and for its benefit.

Section 13 of the Uniform Partnership Act provides: "Where, by any wrongful act or omission of any partner acting in the ordinary course of business of the partnership or with the authority of his copartners, loss or injury is caused to any person, not being a partner in the partnership, or any penalty is incurred, the partnership is liable therefor to the same extent as the partner so acting or omitting to act."

However, it is equally true that where one member of a partnership or joint enterprise commits a wrongful and malicious tort not within the actual or apparent scope of the agency, or the common business of the particular venture, to which the other members have not assented, and which has not been concurred in or ratified by them, they are not liable for the harm thereby caused.

Because at the time of Vrabel's injuries and for a long time prior thereto Florence had been excluded from the Acri Cafe and had no voice or control in its management, and because Florence did not know or have good reason to know that Michael was a dangerous individual prone to assault cafe patrons, the theory of negligence urged by Vrabel is hardly tenable.

We cannot escape the conclusion, therefore, that the above rules, relating to the nonliability of a partner or joint adventurer for wrongful and malicious torts committed by an associate outside the purposes and scope of the business, must be applied in the instant case. The willful and malicious attack by Michael Acri upon Vrabel in the Acri Cafe cannot reasonably be said to have come within the scope of the business of oper-

ating the cafe, so as to have rendered the absent Florence accountable.

Since the liability of a partner for the acts of his associates is founded upon the principles of agency, the statement is in point that an intentional and willful attack committed by an agent or employee, to vent his own spleen or malevolence against the injured person, is a clear departure from his employment and his principal or employer is not responsible therefor.

Judgment reversed.

CASE QUESTIONS

1. What was the nature of the business?
2. What type of injury occurred, and who caused it?
3. Why was Mr. Acri not a defendant?
4. Is Mrs. Acri liable for the injuries?

Tax Consequences in Partnerships

A partnership does not pay taxes. It simply files an informational return. The partners, however, must report their share of partnership income (or losses) and deductions on their individual tax returns and must pay taxes on the reported share.

Management and Control

Partnership Authority

Unless agreed otherwise, each partner has a duty to contribute time to manage the partnership. Each partner has an equal management say, and each has a right to use partnership property for partnership purposes. No one partner controls the property, funds, or management of the firm (unless the partners so agree).

The partners may agree to delegate day-to-day management responsibilities to one or more of the partners. However, the agency rules of express, implied, and apparent authority (see Chapter 18) apply to partnerships. Each partner is an agent of the other partners, and each has express authority given by the UPA and any partnership agreement, implied authority relating to those powers, and apparent authority as is customary in their business. Some management matters are simply a matter of a vote; a majority of the partners makes the decision. The unanimous consent of the partners is required for some decisions, however, such as confessing a judgment (settling a lawsuit), transferring all the partnership's assets, or selling its goodwill. Basically, unusual transactions in which no apparent authority could be claimed require all the partners' approval.

The partners are not entitled to compensation for their management of the partnership's business, unless so specified in the partnership agreement. Under the UPA, a partner who winds up a dissolved partnership's business can be compensated.

Partner Fiduciary Duties

Because each partner is an agent for the partnership and the other partners as well, each owes the partnership and the other partners the same fiduciary duties an agent owes a principal. Partners' obligations as fiduciaries are the same as agents' duties to principals.

CONSIDER...   2 1 . 3

Silvio Giannetti, his daughter, Anne Marie, and her husband, Jerry Prozinsky, were partners in the Giannetti Investment Company (GIC). GIC owned and operated the Brougham Manor Apartments. Mr. Prozinsky signed a contract with Omnicon to give it the right to install the equipment for and promote cable television in the apartment complex. Mr. Giannetti was most disturbed when he learned that Mr. Prozinsky had signed the agreement. He refused to allow Omnicon further access to the complex. The result was that cable service was interrupted, lines could not be repaired, and Omnicon was forced to discontinue all its cable customers in the apartment complex. Omnicon filed suit against GIC for breach of contract. Mr. Giannetti maintains that GIC is not liable because Mr. Prozinsky did not have the authority to sign such a contract. Is Mr. Giannetti correct? [*Omnicon v. Giannetti Investment Company*, 561 N.W.2d 138 (Mich. App. 1997).]

Partnership Property

Partnership property is defined as property contributed to the firm as a capital contribution or property purchased with partnership funds. Partners are co-owners of partnership property in a form of ownership called *tenancy in partnership*. Tenants in partnership have equal rights in the use and possession of the property for partnership purposes. On the death of one of the partners, rights in the property are transferred to the surviving partner or partners. The partnership interest in the property remains, and the property or a share of the property is not transferred to the estate of the deceased partner. The estate of the deceased partner simply receives the value of the partner's interest, not the property.

Partner Interests

Partners' interests in the partnership are different from partnership property. A partner's interest is a personal property interest that belongs to the partner. It can be sold (transferred) or pledged as collateral to a creditor. Creditors (personal) can attach a partner's interests to collect a debt.

There are several effects on the partnership of a transfer of a partner's interest. The transfer does not result in the transferee becoming a new partner because no person can become a partner without the consent of all the existing partners. Further, the transfer does not relieve the transferring partner of personal liability. A transfer of interest will not eliminate individual liability to existing creditors.

Some partnership agreements place restrictions on transfer. For example, there may be a provision that allows the partnership the right to buy out a partner before the partner has the authority to transfer interest.

Transferability of Interests

A partner cannot transfer her partnership status without the unanimous consent of the other partners. However, if that transfer is approved, the departing or outgoing partner and the incoming partner should be aware of their liability. Absent an agreement from creditors, the outgoing partner remains personally liable for all partnership debts up to the time of departure. If the departing partner gives public notice of her disassociation, no further personal liability results from contracts and obligations entered into after departure. The incoming partner is liable for all contracts after the date he comes into the firm. Incoming partners are liable for existing debts only to the extent of their capital contribution.

The *Byker* case also illustrates that partnership liabilities do not end when the partners no longer do business together. The debts remain and must be satisfied, even from partners no longer involved in running the business.

Dissolution and Termination of the Partnership

Dissolution is not necessarily termination. The UPA defines dissolution as one partner's ceasing to be associated with carrying on the business. The RUPA refers to "dissociation" of partners, which may or may not lead to dissolution. When a partner leaves, retires, or dies, the partnership is dissolved, though not terminated. Dissolution is basically a change in the structure of the partnership. Dissolution may have no effect on the business: The partnership may be reorganized and continue business without the partner who is leaving.

Dissolution *can* lead, however, to termination of the partnership. Termination means all business stops, the assets of the firm are liquidated, and the proceeds are distributed to creditors and partners to repay capital contributions and distribute profits (if any). There are several grounds for dissolution.

Dissolution by Agreement

The partnership agreement itself may limit the partnership's time of existence. Once that time expires, the partnership is dissolved. If the agreement does not specify the time or there is no partnership agreement, the partners can (by unanimous consent) agree to dissolve the partnership.

Dissolution by Operation of Law

Another way a partnership is dissolved is by operation of law. This means that certain events require the dissolution of the partnership. When one partner dies, the partnership is automatically dissolved. The business could go on, but the partnership as it once existed ends, and the deceased partner's estate must be paid for her interest. Also, if the partnership or an individual partner becomes bankrupt, the partnership is dissolved by law.

Dissolution by Court Order

For a discussion of the pros and cons of the various business structures, visit:
http://www.sba.gov/library/ pubs/mp-25.pdf

The third method for dissolution of a partnership is by court order. Sometimes partners just cannot work together any longer. In such circumstances, they can petition a court for dissolution in the interest of preserving their investments.

LIMITED PARTNERSHIPS

A **limited partnership** is a partnership with a slight variation in the liability of those involved. There are two types of partners in a limited partnership: at least one **general partner** and one **limited partner**. General partners have the same obligations as partners in general partnerships—full liability and full responsibility for the management of the business. Limited partners have liability limited to the amount of their contribution to the partnership, and they cannot be involved in the management of the firm. General partners run the limited partnership, and the limited partners are the investors.

The Uniform Limited Partnership Act (ULPA) was drafted in 1916. At that time there were very few limited partnerships, and most of them were quite small. The limited partnership, however, has become a favored type of business structure, particularly over the past twenty years. It has been the predominant form of business organization for oil exploration and real estate development because of the tax advantages available through limited partnerships. The attractiveness of limited liability combined with tax advantages has resulted in an increase in the numbers and sizes of limited partnerships.

Because of this increased use, the ULPA proved to be inadequate for governing the creation, structure, and ongoing operations of limited partnerships. In 1976, the National Conference of Commissioners on Uniform State Laws developed the **Revised Uniform Limited Partnership Act** (RULPA). The act was designed to update limited partnership law to address the ways limited partnerships were doing business. The RULPA was revised in 1985 and has been adopted in nearly every state.

Formation

As discussed earlier, a valid general partnership can be created through the conduct of the parties and without a formal partnership agreement. A limited partnership, however, is a statutory creature and requires compliance with certain procedures in order to exist. If these procedures are not followed, it is possible that the limited partners could lose their limited liability protection.

The RULPA requires the following information for filing at the appropriate government agency:

1. Name of the limited partnership (cannot be deceptively similar to another corporation's or partnership's name and must contain the words "limited partnership"; no abbreviations permitted)
2. Address of its principal office
3. Name and address of the statutory agent
4. Business address of the general partner
5. Latest date for dissolution of the partnership

Under the RULPA, the limited partners need not be named in the certificate, nor are they all required to sign the certificate. These changes resulted from recognition of the size of limited partnerships and the tremendous paperwork burden created by the ULPA. If an error is made in formation, the partnership could be deemed a general partnership, and the limited partners could lose the protection of their limited liability. However, under RULPA, limited partners are permitted to file an amendment correcting the problem or withdrawing from the business altogether. A limited partner would still be liable to any third parties for liabilities incurred by the general partnership prior to the time the correction is made.

The certificate of limited partnership is simply public disclosure of the formation and existence of the limited partnership; it does not deal with the many more rights and obligations that the partners may agree on among themselves. Those issues are generally addressed in a much longer document called a **limited partnership agreement** or the **articles of limited partnership**.

Sources of Funding

Capital contributions supply the initial funding for a limited partnership. Both the general and limited partners make contributions upon entering the partnership. Under the RULPA, the contribution can be in the form of cash, property, services already performed, or a promissory note or other obligation to pay money or property. The RULPA requires that limited partners' promises to contribute must be in writing to be enforceable. The limited partners are always personally liable for the difference between what has actually been contributed and the amount promised to be contributed.

Some partners make **advances** or loans to the partnership. The partnership can also borrow money from third parties. However, only the general partner has any personal liability for repayment of the loan to the third party.

Liability

The principal advantage of a limited partnership is the limited personal liability. To ensure personal limited liability, several requirements must be met. First, as already discussed, a certificate of limited partnership must be filed, indicating the limited liability status of the limited partners. Second, there must be at least one general partner. The general partner can be a corporation. Third, the limited partners cannot be involved in the management of the business because such involvement would give the appearance of general partner status. Finally, limited partners cannot use their names in the name of the partnership, which would give the wrong impression to outside parties and create an estoppel type of relationship.

Under the RULPA, a limited partner who participates in the management of the firm in the same way the general partner does is liable only to those persons who are led to believe by the limited partner's conduct that the limited partner is a general partner. The RULPA also provides a list of activities that limited partners can engage in without losing their limited liability status, such as:

1. Being employed by the general partnership as an employee or a contractor
2. Consulting with or advising the general partner
3. Acting as a surety or guarantor for the limited partnership
4. Voting on amendments, dissolution, sale of property, or assumption of debt

If limited partners comply with the rules for limited liability, their liability is limited to the amount of their capital contribution. If they have pledged to pay a certain amount as capital over a period of time, they are liable for the full amount. For example, some real estate syndications that are limited partnerships allow the limited partners to make their investment in installment payments over two to four years. Limited partners in these arrangements are liable for the full amount pledged whenever an obligation to a creditor is not paid.

Tax Consequences

Limited partnerships are taxed the same way as general partnerships. The general and limited partners report the income and losses on their individual returns and pay the appropriate taxes. A limited partnership files an information return but does not itself pay any taxes.

One of the benefits of limited partnership status is the combination of limited liability with direct tax benefits. In this sense, a limited partnership is the best of both worlds. Because of this ideal situation, limited partnership interests are closely scrutinized by the IRS to determine whether they are, in reality, corporations as opposed to true limited partnerships. Some of the factors examined in determining whether an organization is a corporation or a limited partnership are (1) the transferability of the interests, (2) the assets of the general partners, and (3) the net worth of the general partners. From the perspective of the IRS, organization as a limited partnership is no assurance of treatment as such for tax purposes.

For a chart and discussion of tax issues related to the various forms of business structure, visit:

http://www.irs.gov/ businesses/small/article/ 0,,id=98191,00.html

Management and Control

Profits and Distributions

A general partner has absolute authority to decide not only when distributions are made but whether they will be made; for example, the general partner might decide not to distribute funds but to put them back into the business.

Profits and losses are allocated on the basis of capital contributions. Under the RULPA, the agreement for sharing of profits and losses must be in writing.

Partner Authority

The authority of the general partner in a limited partnership is the same as the authority of the partners in a general partnership. These powers can be restricted by agreement. There are, however, some general activities the general partner cannot perform without the consent of the limited partners, including the following:

1. Admitting a new general partner (also requires consent of other general partners)
2. Admitting a new limited partner unless the partnership agreement allows it
3. Extraordinary transactions, such as selling all the partnership assets

Limited partners can monitor the general partner's activity with the same rights provided to partners in general partnerships: the right to inspect the books and records and the right to an accounting.

Transferability of Interests

Although the assignment of limited partnership interests is not prohibited by the RULPA, a limited partnership agreement may provide for significant restraints on assignment. There are two reasons for transfer restrictions on limited partners' interests. First, limited partnership interests may have been sold without registration as exemptions to the federal securities law (see Chapter 22 for more details on securities registrations). If those exempt interests are readily transferable, the exemption could be lost. Second, for the limited partners to enjoy the tax benefits of limited partner status, the ease of transferability is a critical issue. The more easily an interest can be transferred, the more likely the limited partnership will be treated (for tax purposes) as a corporation.

The assignment of a partnership interest does not terminate a limited partnership. The assignee is entitled to receive only the distributions and profits to which the partner is entitled. The assignee does not become a partner without the consent of the other partners. Under the RULPA, a limited partnership can agree that the assigning limited partner will have the authority to make the assignee a limited partner. The effect of the RULPA provision is to simplify transfers and allow limited partners to decide whether they want to transfer their interest or their limited partner status.

Dissolution and Termination of a Limited Partnership

A limited partnership can be dissolved in one of the following ways:

1. Expiration of the time period designated in the agreement or the occurrence of an event causing dissolution, as specified in the agreement
2. Unanimous written consent of all partners
3. Withdrawal of a general partner
4. Court order after application by one of the partners

Upon dissolution, a partnership can continue (assuming a general partner remains); but the partnership can also be terminated after dissolution. If termination occurs, all assets of the partnership are liquidated. The RULPA specifies that the money from the sale of the assets be used to pay partnership obligations in the following order of priority:

1. Creditors (including partners, but not with respect to distributions)
2. Partners and former partners, for distributions owed to them
3. Return of capital contributions
4. Remainder split according to distribution agreement

CORPORATIONS

Corporations have the following characteristics: unlimited duration, free transferability of interest, limited liability for shareholders/owners, continuity, and centralized management. Corporations are legal entities in and of themselves. Because they are treated as persons under the law, they can hold title to property, they can sue or be sued in the corporate name, and they are taxed separately. The latest U.S. economic census figures (from 1997; the 2002 numbers have not been tabulated yet) indicate that there are 1.6 million partnerships in the United States but 3.6 million corporations. Corporations earn nearly 90 percent of all business profits.

Types of Corporations

Each of the diverse types of corporations can be described by one or more adjectives. For example, there are **profit corporations** (those seeking to earn a return for investors) and **nonprofit corporations**. There are **domestic corporations** and **foreign corporations**. A corporation is a domestic corporation in the state in which it is incorporated and a foreign corporation in every other state. Further, corporations organized by government agencies that exist to achieve a social goal are called **government corporations**. **Professional corporations** are corporations organized by physicians, dentists, attorneys, and accountants; they exist by statute in most states. Professional corporation shareholders have no personal liability for any corporate debts, as in any other corporation, except for professional malpractice claims. The **corporate veil** or shield (explained later) will not give individuals personal immunity for professional negligence despite their general liability limitation through incorporation. **Close corporations** are the opposite of **publicly held corporations**; that is, the former are corporations with very few shareholders. Close corporations and publicly held corporations are created in the same way, but most states then have a separate statute governing the operation of close corporations. Close corporation owners are generally given more discretion in their internal operations, and the degree of formality required for publicly held corporations is not required.

BUSINESS PLANNING TIP

Under the Small Business Job Protection Act of 1996, S corporation requirements were modified. An S corporation must meet specific qualifications, including:

- Being a domestic corporation
- Having no more than seventy-five shareholders
- Having as shareholders no persons other than an individual or certain trusts and estates, S corporations, and certain exempt organizations including charitable organizations and qualified retirement trusts
- Having no nonresident aliens as shareholders
- Having no more than one class of stock
- Not being a member of an affiliated group
- Not being a financial institution
- Not being an insurance company
- Not being a corporation to which IRC § 936 (dealing with Puerto Rico and possession tax credits) applies

The **S corporation** (sometimes called subchapter S or sub S corporation) is formed no differently from any other corporation, but it must meet the IRS requirements for an S corporation and must file a special election form with the IRS indicating it wishes to be treated as an S corporation. The benefit of an S corporation is that shareholders' income and losses are treated like those of partners, but the shareholders enjoy the protection of limited liability behind a corporate veil. The income earned and losses incurred by an S corporation are reported on the shareholders' individual returns, but the shareholders' personal assets are protected from creditors of the business. For tax purposes, the S corporation is like a partnership in the sense of the flow-through of profits and losses, and the shareholders avoid the double taxation of having the corporation pay tax on its earnings and their paying tax on the dividends distributed to them.

The term *C corporation* is often used in discussions of corporate formation. This tax term means that the corporation has no pass-through benefits; the corporation pays tax on its income and individuals pay taxes on their dividends (see p. 862).

*Examine Arizona's
Corporation Laws:*
http://www.azleg.state.az.us/
ArizonaRevisedStatutes.asp?
Title=10

The Law of Corporations

The **Model Business Corporation Act** (MBCA), as drafted and revised by the Corporate, Banking and Business Section of the American Bar Association, is the uniform law on corporations. The provisions of the MBCA are quite liberal and give management great latitude in operations. The MBCA tends to follow the principles of corporate law long established in Delaware, a state where many of the country's major companies are incorporated. Delaware boasts a rich body of case law on corporate governance that offers the stability companies want as they incorporate. Despite the ability to draw on the Delaware case law and experience, the MBCA is not adopted as widely as the UPA or the Uniform Commercial Code (UCC). Even those states that have adopted the MBCA have made significant changes in their adopted versions. As a result, each state's law on corporations is quite different. The following sections cover the revised MBCA rules, but each state may have its own variations.

*Examine New York's
Corporation Laws:*
http://www.law.cornell.edu/
ny/statutes/buscorp.htm

Formation

A corporation is a statutory entity. Formal public filing is required to form a corporation. The following procedures for corporate formation are those of the MBCA.

Where to Incorporate

The following factors should be considered when determining in which state to incorporate:

1. The status of the state's corporation laws. (See the discussion about Delaware above; also, some states' laws and judicial decisions are oriented more toward management than to shareholders.)
2. State tax laws.
3. The ability to attract employees to the state.
4. The incentives states offer to attract the business (new freeways, office space, attractive urban renewal).

The Formation Document

All states require **articles of incorporation** to be filed in order to create a corporation. These articles give the structure and basic information about the corporation. Under the MBCA, the articles of incorporation must include the following information:

1. The name of the corporation.
2. The names and addresses of all incorporators. (In addition, each incorporator must sign the articles of incorporation.)
3. The share structure of the corporation: (a) the common and preferred classes, (b) which shares vote, and (c) the rights of shareholders—preemptive rights.
4. The statutory agent (the party who will be served with any lawsuits against the corporation).

Who Is Incorporating

The **incorporators** (required to be listed in the articles of incorporation) are the parties forming the corporation. Under the MBCA, only one incorporator is required, and that person may be a natural person, a corporation, a partnership, a limited partnership, or an association.

Incorporators are personally liable for any contracts entered into or actions taken during the pre-incorporation stage. Until the corporation exists, incorporators are acting as individuals. After incorporation, the corporation could agree to assume liability through a **novation** of the incorporators' acts.

For example, if an incorporator of a lumberyard entered into a contract for the purchase of lumber and the corporate board (after formation) agreed that the contract was a good one, the corporation could ratify it or enter into a novation to assume liability. In novation, the lumberyard agrees to substitute the corporation as the contracting party. In a **ratification**, the corporation assumes primary liability for payment, but the incorporator still remains liable. Incorporators generally are paid for their efforts in shares of the corporation's stock. They may also be the contributors of initial corporate assets and may be paid in shares for their contributions.

Postformation

After the paperwork of incorporating is complete, a corporation must begin its day-to-day operations with an **initial meeting**. At this meeting, the officers of the corporation are elected and **bylaws** are adopted to govern corporate procedures. The bylaws define the authority of each of the officers, prescribe procedures for announcing and conducting meetings (such as quorum numbers and voting numbers), and set the terms of officers and directors and who is eligible to serve in such offices. Articles of incorporation give an overview of a corporate entity; the bylaws constitute the operational rules.

Capital and Sources of Corporate Funds

A corporation has a variety of sources for funds. It may use short-term financing, which consists of loans from banks or credit lines. The problems with short-term financing are higher interest rates and shorter payback periods. The other forms of financing used most frequently by corporations are debt and equity.

Debt Financing: The Bond Market

Long-term debt financing is available to corporations when they issue bonds. Bonds are, in effect, long-term promissory notes from a corporation to the bond buyers. The corporation pays the holders interest on the bonds until the maturity date, which is when the bonds are due or must be paid. The interest is fixed and is a fixed-payment responsibility regardless of the corporation's profitability. The benefits of debt financing include the tax deductibility of interest as an expense. Further, bondholders have the benefit of first rights in corporate assets in the event of insolvency. However, a corporation cannot maintain a sound financial policy or rating with debt financing only.

Equity Financing: Shareholders

Equity financing comes through the sale of stock in a corporation. It provides a means of raising capital up front with the exchange of proportionate corporate ownership and the promise of proportionate profits. Shareholders are given shares of stock in exchange for their money. To avoid personal liability, the shareholders must pay at least par value for their shares and must honor the terms of their subscription agreement (share purchase agreement). A shareholder who has not paid at least par value is said to hold **watered shares** and is liable to creditors for the amount not paid. For example, if a shareholder paid $500 for shares with a par value of $1,000, the shareholder would be personally liable for the $500 difference. Along with those shares of stock come certain promises of future performance from the corporation. The rights of shareholders depend on the type of stock purchased. A discussion of the various types of stock follows.

Common Stock

Common stock is the typical stock in a corporation and is usually the most voluminous in terms of the number of shares. Common stock generally carries voting rights so that common shareholders have a voice in the election of directors, the amendment of articles and bylaws, and other major corporate matters. Common stock generally does not have a fixed dividend rate and does not carry with it any right to have a dividend declared. Thus, common stock dividends depend on both profitability and decisions of the board of directors. If a corporation is dissolved, the common shareholders have a right to a proportionate share of the assets (after creditors and preferred stockholders have been paid).

Preferred Stock

Preferred stock is appropriately named because its owners enjoy preferred status over holders of a corporation's common stock. For example, preferred stockholders have priority in the payment of dividends. Some preferred dividends are even at a fixed rate, and **cumulative preferred stock** guarantees the payment of a dividend so that if a dividend is not paid one year, the holder's right to be paid carries over until funds are available. Preferred shareholders also have priority over common shareholders in the event the corporation is dissolved and the assets distributed.

Liability Issues

Limited liability for shareholders is one of the advantages of corporate organization. However, there are times when individuals—such as shareholders, directors, and officers—can be personally liable for corporate obligations.

Shareholder Liability

Shareholders' personal liability is limited to the amount of their investment in the corporation. The personal assets of shareholders are not subject to the claims of corporate creditors. In some circumstances, however, a shareholder is liable for more than the amount of investment. For example, if a shareholder has not paid for his shares or has paid for them with overvalued property, creditors could turn to the shareholder's personal assets for satisfaction of his debt, but only to the extent of the amount due on the shares.

In other more serious circumstances, shareholders can be held liable for the full amount of corporate debts. A creditor who successfully pierces the corporate veil overcomes the shield of limited liability protecting shareholders from having to accept personal liability for corporate debts. The corporate veil can be pierced for several reasons. One is inadequate capitalization. The owners of a corporation are required to place as much capital at risk in the corporation as is necessary to cover reasonably anticipated expenses of the business. The purpose of this requirement is to ensure that someone does not use the corporation to avoid liability without actually transferring to the corporation some assets for the payment of corporate liabilities.

 CONSIDER...   **2 1 . 4**

Max Rupe was the sole shareholder of Updike Oil Company, a corporation. There was no transfer of shares to Mr. Rupe. No records of any meetings or financial records existed. Updike had $56,328 in liabilities and $100 in capital stock. A creditor is seeking to pierce the corporate veil. Is success likely? [*U.S. National Bank of Omaha* v. *Rupe*, 296 N.W.2d 474 (Neb. 1980).]

Another theory a court can use to pierce the corporate veil is the **alter ego theory**, which means that the owners and managers of the corporation have not treated the corporation as a separate entity but have used the structure more as a personal resource. Personal and corporate assets and debts are mixed, there is no formality with regard to operations and meetings, and there are transfers of property without explanation or authorization.

U.S. v. *Bestfoods* (Case 21.3) deals with an issue of piercing the corporate veil in a situation in which there is CERCLA liability (see Chapter 12).

CASE 21.3

U.S. v. *Bestfoods, Inc.*
524 U.S. 51 (1998)

Lifting the Veil Is Best for Cleanup,
but Not Shareholders

FACTS

In 1957, Ott Chemical Co. manufactured chemicals at its plant near Muskegon, Michigan, and both intentionally and unintentionally dumped hazardous substances in the soil and groundwater near the plant. Ott sold the plant to CPC International, Inc.

In 1965, CPC incorporated a wholly owned subsidiary (Ott II) to buy Ott's assets. Ott II then continued both the chemical production and dumping. Ott II's officers and directors had positions and duties at both CPC and Ott.

In 1972, CPC (now Bestfoods) sold Ott II to Story Chemical, which operated the plant until its bankruptcy in 1977. Aerojet-General Corp. bought the plant from the bankruptcy trustee and manufactured chemicals there until 1986.

In 1989, the EPA filed suit to recover the costs of cleanup on the plant site and named CPC, Aerojet, and the officers of the now defunct Ott and Ott II.

The District Court held both CPC and Aerojet liable. After a divided panel of the Court of Appeals for the Sixth Circuit reversed in part, the court granted rehearing *en banc* and vacated the panel decision. This time, seven judges to six, the court again reversed the District Court in part. Bestfoods appealed (Ott settled prior to the appeal).

continued

JUDICIAL OPINION

SOUTER, Justice

The United States brought this action for the costs of cleaning up industrial waste generated by a chemical plant. The issue before us, under the Comprehensive Environmental Response, Compensation, and Liability Act of 1980 (CERCLA), is whether a parent corporation that actively participated in, and exercised control over, the operations of a subsidiary may, without more, be held liable as an operator of a polluting facility owned or operated by the subsidiary. We answer no, unless the corporate veil may be pierced. But a corporate parent that actively participated in, and exercised control over, the operations of the facility itself may be held directly liable in its own right as an operator of the facility.

The District Court said that operator liability may attach to a parent corporation both directly, when the parent itself operates the facility, and indirectly, when the corporate veil can be pierced under state law. The court explained that, while CERCLA imposes direct liability in situations in which the corporate veil cannot be pierced under traditional concepts of corporate law, "the statute and its legislative history do not suggest that CERCLA rejects entirely the crucial limits to liability that are inherent to corporate law."

Applying that test to the facts of this case, the court found it particularly telling that CPC selected Ott II's board of directors and populated its executive ranks with CPC officials, and that a CPC official, G.R.D. Williams, played a significant role in shaping Ott II's environmental compliance policy.

> [W]here a parent corporation is sought to be held liable as an operator pursuant to 42 U.S.C. § 9607(a)(2) based upon the extent of its control of its subsidiary which owns the facility, the parent will be liable only when the requirements necessary to pierce the corporate veil [under state law] are met. In other words, . . . whether the parent will be liable as an operator depends upon whether the degree to which it controls its subsidiary and the extent and manner of its involvement with the facility, amount to the abuse of the corporate form that will warrant piercing the corporate veil and disregarding the separate corporate entities of the parent and subsidiary.

Applying Michigan veil-piercing law, the Court of Appeals decided that neither CPC nor Aerojet was liable for controlling the actions of its subsidiaries, since the parent and subsidiary corporations maintained separate personalities and the parents did not utilize the subsidiary corporate form to perpetrate fraud or subvert justice.

We granted certiorari to resolve a conflict among the Circuits over the extent to which parent corporations may be held liable under CERCLA for operating facilities ostensibly under the control of their subsidiaries.

It is a general principle of corporate law deeply "ingrained in our economic and legal systems" that a parent corporation (so-called because of control through ownership of another corporation's stock) is not liable for the acts of its subsidiary.

Although this respect for corporate distinctions when the subsidiary is a polluter has been severely criticized in the literature, nothing in CERCLA purports to reject this bedrock principle, and against this venerable common-law backdrop, the congressional silence is audible.

But there is an equally fundamental principle of corporate law, applicable to the parent-subsidiary relationship as well as generally, that the corporate veil may be pierced and the shareholder held liable for the corporation's conduct when, inter alia, the corporate form would otherwise be misused to accomplish certain wrongful purposes, most notably fraud, on the shareholder's behalf.

Nothing in CERCLA purports to rewrite this well-settled rule, either. If a subsidiary that operates, but does not own, a facility is so pervasively controlled by its parent for a sufficiently improper purpose to warrant veil piercing, the parent may be held derivatively liable for the subsidiary's acts as an operator.

The fact that a corporate subsidiary happens to own a polluting facility operated by its parent does nothing, then, to displace the rule that the parent "corporation is [itself] responsible for the wrongs committed by its agents in the course of its business." It is this direct liability that is properly seen as being at issue here.

Under the plain language of the statute, any person who operates a polluting facility is directly liable for the costs of cleaning up the pollution. This is so regardless of whether that person is the facility's owner, the owner's parent corporation or business partner, or even a saboteur who sneaks into the facility at night to discharge its poisons out of malice. If any such act of operating a corporate subsidiary's facility is done on behalf of a parent corporation, the existence of the parent-subsidiary relationship under state corporate law is simply irrelevant to the issue of direct liability.

This much is easy to say: the difficulty comes in defining actions sufficient to constitute direct parental "operation." Here of course we may again rue the uselessness of CERCLA's definition of a facility's "operator" as "any person . . . operating" the facility, which leaves us to do the best we can to give the term its "ordinary or natural meaning."

In a mechanical sense, to "operate" ordinarily means "[t]o control the functioning of; run: operate a sewing machine." And in the organizational sense more obviously intended by CERCLA, the word ordinarily means "[t]o conduct the affairs of; manage: operate a business." So, under CERCLA, an operator is simply someone who directs the workings of, manages, or conducts the affairs of a facility. To sharpen the definition for purposes of CERCLA's concern with environmental contamination, an operator must manage, direct, or conduct operations specifically related to pollution, that is, operations having to do with the leakage or disposal of hazardous waste, or decisions about compliance with environmental regulations.

With this understanding, we are satisfied that the Court of Appeals correctly rejected the District Court's analysis of direct liability. But we also think that the appeals court erred in limiting direct liability under the statute to a parent's sole or joint venture operation, so as to eliminate any possible finding that CPC is liable as an operator on the facts of this case.

In imposing direct liability on these grounds, the District Court failed to recognize that "it is entirely appropriate for directors of a parent corporation to serve as directors of its subsidiary, and that fact alone may not serve to expose the parent corporation to liability for its subsidiary's acts."

This recognition that the corporate personalities remain distinct has its corollary in the "well established principle [of corporate law] that directors and officers holding positions with a parent and its subsidiary can and do 'change hats' to represent the two corporations separately, despite their common ownership."

The Government would have to show that, despite the general presumption to the contrary, the officers and directors were acting in their capacities as CPC officers and directors, and not as Ott II officers and directors, when they committed those acts. The District Court made no such enquiry here, however, disregarding entirely this time-honored common-law rule.

In sum, the District Court's focus on the relationship between parent and subsidiary (rather than parent and facility), combined with its automatic attribution of the actions of dual officers and directors to the corporate parent, erroneously, even if unintentionally, treated CERCLA as though it displaced or fundamentally altered common-law standards of limited liability.

We accordingly agree with the Court of Appeals that a participation-and-control test looking to the parent's supervision over the subsidiary, especially one that assumes that dual officers always act on behalf of the parent, cannot be used to identify operation of a facility resulting in direct parental liability. Nonetheless, a return to the ordinary meaning of the word "operate" in the organizational sense will indicate why we think that the Sixth Circuit stopped short when it confined its examples of direct parental operation to exclusive or joint ventures, and declined to find at least the possibility of direct operation by CPC in this case.

Again norms of corporate behavior (undisturbed by any CERCLA provision) are crucial reference points. The critical question is whether, in degree and detail, actions directed to the facility by an agent of the parent alone are eccentric under accepted norms of parental oversight of a subsidiary's facility.

There is, in fact, some evidence that CPC engaged in just this type and degree of activity at the Muskegon plant. The District Court's opinion speaks of an agent of CPC alone who played a conspicuous part in dealing with the toxic risks emanating from the operation of the plant. G.R.D. Williams worked only for CPC; he was not an employee, officer, or director of Ott, and thus, his actions were of necessity taken only on behalf of CPC. The District Court found that "CPC became directly involved in environmental and regulatory matters through the work of . . . Williams, CPC's governmental and environmental affairs director. Williams . . . became heavily involved in environmental issues at Ott II." He "actively participated in and exerted control over a variety of Ott II environmental matters," and he "issued directives regarding Ott II's responses to regulatory inquiries."

We think that these findings are enough to raise an issue of CPC's operation of the facility through Williams's actions, though we would draw no ultimate conclusion from these findings at this point. Not only would we be deciding in the first instance an issue on which the trial and appellate courts did not focus, but the very fact that the District Court did not see the case as we do suggests that there may be still more to be known about Williams's activities. Prudence thus counsels us to remand, on the theory of direct operation set out here, for reevaluation of Williams's role, and of the role of any other CPC agent who might be said to have had a part in operating the Muskegon facility.

The judgment of the Court of Appeals for the Sixth Circuit is vacated, and the case is remanded.

CASE QUESTIONS

1. Describe the corporate ownership history that surrounds the Muskegon facility.
2. Is there a special CERCLA rule for piercing the corporate veil?
3. What must be shown to hold a parent liable for the actions of the subsidiary?
4. Are joint directors of parent and corporate subsidiaries evidence of a need to pierce the corporate veil?
5. What does the court suggest shows there may be some evidence that the corporate veil can be pierced?

Corporate Tax Consequences

The Double-Taxation Cost of Limited Liability

Although corporations have the benefit of limited liability, they have the detriment of double taxation. This means that not only does the corporation pay taxes on its earnings but also the shareholders must report their dividend income on their separate returns and pay individual taxes on their dividend income. However, these shareholders pay taxes only if the dividends are paid. Unlike partnerships in which the partners pay taxes on earnings whether they are distributed or not, shareholders pay taxes on corporate earnings only when they are distributed to them.

Statutory Solutions to Double Taxation

There are ways to resolve the problem of the cost of double taxation. The S corporation (see p. 856) is one solution.

Corporate Management and Control: Directors and Officers

Election of Directors

A corporation might be owned by a million shareholders, but its operation will be controlled by the hands of a few, the **board of directors**. The shareholders elect these directors, who serve as the corporate policy makers. The directors also have responsibility for management of the corporation. To that end, the directors usually set up an **executive committee** composed of three board members to handle the more routine matters of running the corporation so that board meetings are not required as frequently.

Role of Directors

Directors are the strategic planning and policy makers for the corporation. They are also the outside perspective for the company. They can provide insight on current management practices (see the *Perot* case on p. 865 and the Disney biography on p. 863). They also serve a watchdog role, as with the now mandatory **audit committees** required of all stock exchange companies. Audit committees, made up of independent outside directors and now at least one financial expert under Sarbanes-Oxley who have no contracts or former salary ties with the company, are responsible for assuring that the financial reports the management issues are accurate.

Institutional investors and other groups have been placing increasing pressure on boards for accountability. Some have developed standards for service on boards such as required stock ownership in the company, nominating committees to assure sufficient business background and knowledge, and term limits so that members do not become complacent. Some companies have procedures for the board to evaluate itself and its performance.

One area of director responsibility that receives ongoing attention is that of officers' compensation. Directors not only elect the officers of the corporation; they also decide the salaries for these officers and themselves. The issue of officer compensa-

BUSINESS STRATEGY APPLICATION

Be sure to do the exercise for this chapter on the book's Web site so you can study the corporate governance and board practices of different companies.

BIOGRAPHY

THE MOUSEY DIRECTOR WHO ROARED

Disneyland may be the happiest place on earth, but its boardroom has been a contentious battlefield. Roy E. Disney, nephew of Walt Disney, who began the company in 1923, resigned as chairman of Disney's feature animation division and as vice chairman of the board in December 2003, calling Disney CEO Michael Eisner "rapacious, soulless, and always looking for a quick buck."* Mr. Disney released his resignation letter, which contained seven points of problems, to the media before delivering it to Mr. Eisner under his door in a New York hotel room where Mr. Eisner was staying for business. One week later, Mr. Disney's financial advisor and long-time friend, Stanley P. Gold, also resigned from the board, with a letter of complaints that would take hours for the media to digest and a simple summary that Mr. Eisner was no longer capable of running the company. While Mr. Eisner had been at the helm of Disney for 20 years, "He just ran out of gas," were Mr. Gold's parting words.† Mr. Disney and Mr. Gold were the last two of six directors to depart the board in the period from 2001 to 2003. Other directors who resigned were Reveta F. Bowers, Sidney Poitier, Robert A. M. Stern, and Andrea L. Van de Kamp.

Interestingly, the departures resulted, in most of the cases, from new rules of independence that Disney adopted for its board and that Mr. Eisner used to his advantage. For example, Mr. Gold, Raymond Watson, and Ms. Bowers all had children employed by Disney and were no longer considered independent. Mr. Gold lost his key position as chair of the governance and nominating committee on the board because of his business alliances with Mr. Disney. Mr. Disney was not considered an independent director because of his employment with the company, with the result that his chairmanship was in jeopardy. While both directors were concerned about the company's financial performance and had confronted Mr. Eisner about it, they became virtually powerless to do anything because the new governance proposals demanded independent directors for positions of power, and Mr. Gold and Mr. Disney could not be classified as independent. In a strange twist of events, the very rules of governance and independence they sought to impose on the company in order to achieve more accountability and better performance left them powerless and then, following their resignations, on the outside.

With the departure of these key board members, who were also dissident shareholders, support for Mr. Eisner as CEO began to wane. By February 2004, the California Public Employees' Retirement System (Calpers), Disney's twenty-ninth largest shareholder, announced that it would withhold its support for Mr. Eisner, commenting that, "We have lost complete confidence in Mr. Eisner's strategic vision and leadership in creating shareholder value in the company."‡ At nearly the same time, a large investment advisory firm also recommended to Disney shareholders that they withhold their support of Mr. Eisner. The research report indicated that the Securities Exchange Commission (SEC) had investigated Disney's handling of a takeover bid from Comcast, a cable company. The investigation centered around conflicts of interest among the directors. While the conflicts were disclosed eventually, the SEC was working with Disney to reach a settlement on their later disclosure.

The New York State Common Retirement Fund, the Massachusetts Pension Reserves Investment management board, the Connecticut Pension Fund, the New Jersey Division of Investment, the Virginia Retirement System, and T. Rowe Price's Media & Telecommunications fund then followed and announced that they too could no longer support Mr. Eisner's board position or leadership. Finally, Institutional Shareholder Services objected to Mr. Eisner holding both the position of CEO and chairman of the board, two positions the organization felt should be split between two people.

When Disney's annual shareholder meeting was held on March 3, 2004, 43 percent of the shareholders voted against Mr. Eisner as chairman of the board. Nearly 60 percent of Disney's institutional shareholders voted against Mr. Eisner in the annual meeting. Director George Mitchell, a former U.S. Senator and a Disney board member, became the chairman of the board. Oddly, following the shareholder meeting and board shake-up that ousted Mr. Eisner from the board, the board voted to retain Mr. Eisner as CEO.

Since Mr. Eisner took over in 1984, Disney stock has climbed 2,100 percent, compared with 590 percent for the S&P 500 during that same period. If you had invested $10,000 in 1984 when Mr. Eisner took over, you would have $225,000 today.

continued

The media coverage of the battle and ouster makes it clear that corporate governance and board relationships are most complex and intense. And in the shuffle the question still remains: Is the board serving the shareholders well?

*Ronald Grover, Tom Lowry, and Louis Lavelle, "Keeping the Keys to the Kingdom," *Business Week*, December 15, 2003, p. 46.
†Laura M. Holson and Sharon Waxman, "Criticism of Disney Chief Grows Bolder," *New York Times*, December 8, 2003, pp. C1, C10.
‡Paul Davidson, "Eisner loses support of big investor, advisory firm," *USA Today*, February 26, 2004, p. 1B.

FOR THE MANAGER'S DESK

RE: CEO COMPENSATION

CEO pay figures for the 2004 proxy season (reflecting 2003 payments) are presented below. The following average figures indicate trends in CEO compensation.

	Cash, Salary, and Bonuses	Restricted Stock	Stock Options
2002	$2.6 million	$2.2 million	$5.2 million
2003	$3.0 million	$2.4 million	$3.2 million

The *New York Times* offered a comparison of the compensation packages of Cendant's CEO and that of Costco.

	Operating Income % Change	Market Value % Change
Cendant	36%	–29%
Costco	28%	–18%

	Salary	Bonus	Options
Cendant	$3,125,000	$7,054,000	$19,158,000
Costco	$351,000	$75,000	$2,187,000

The highest paid CEOs are as follows.

Company	CEO	Total Compensation
MBNA	Charles M. Cawley	$46,285,747
Bear Stearns	James E. Cayne	$39,533,712
Occidental Petroleum	Ray R. Irani	$29,470,293
SBC	Edward Whitacre	$28,894,652
Merrill Lynch	E. Stanley O'Neal	$28,097,489
Sprint	Gary D. Forsee	$27,157,374
KB Home	Bruce Karatz	$26,858,373
Altria Group	Louis C. Camilleri	$23,936,679
Cendant	Henry R. Silverman	$22,813,045
Goldman Sachs	Henry M. Paulson, Jr.	$21,400,579
Lehman Brothers	Richard S. Fuld, Jr.	$20,878,386
Lockheed Martin	Vance D. Coffman	$20,260,325

Warren Buffett's total compensation is $308,000.

For More Information

Go to the companies' 10-K forms at http://www.sec.gov; click on EDGAR.
Patrick McGeehanm, "Is C.E.O. Pay Up or Down? Both," *New York Times*, April 4, 2004, Section 3.
Gretchen Morgenson, "Two Packages, Two Different Galaxies," *New York Times*, April 4, 2004, Section 3–1.

tion has received congressional attention with the deductibility of officer compensation limited to $1 million annually and ongoing attention from shareholders in terms of limits on compensation. Shareholders continue to make proposals to limit executive compensation (see Chapter 22 for more information on such proposals) and exercise their rights of director removal if they feel the board is not responsive to their concerns about compensation.

Director Liability

Officers and directors are **fiduciaries** of the corporation, which means they are to act in the best interests of the corporation and not profit at the corporation's expense. They are subject to the **business judgment rule**, a standard of corporate behavior under which it is understood that officers and directors can make mistakes, but they are required to show that their decisions were made after careful study and discussion. In those decisions, they may consult experts, such as attorneys, accountants, and financial analysts; but again, they need to show that these experts were well-chosen and reliable individuals.

Grobow v. *H. Ross Perot* (Case 21.4) deals with the business judgment rule and provides the answer for the chapter's opening Consider.

CASE 21.4

Grobow v. *H. Ross Perot*
539 A.2d 180 (Del. 1988)

Now Looky Here: H. Ross Perot as GM Gadfly

FACTS

In 1984, General Motors Corporation (GM) acquired 100 percent of the stock of Electronic Data Systems (EDS). Under the terms of the merger, H. Ross Perot, founder, chairman, and largest stockholder of EDS, exchanged his EDS stock for GM Class E stock. Mr. Perot became GM's largest shareholder, controlling 0.8 percent of GM voting stock. Mr. Perot was also elected to GM's Board of Directors.

Management differences developed, and Mr. Perot became increasingly vocal in his criticism of GM management. Saying he could no longer be a "company man," Mr. Perot said in public, "Until you nuke the old GM system, you'll never tap the full potential of your people," and "GM cannot become a world-class and cost-competitive company simply by throwing technology and money at its problems."

The Board decided to repurchase Mr. Perot's shares for $745 million if Mr. Perot would: (1) stop criticizing GM management (a penalty for default here was $7.5 million); (2) not purchase GM stock or engage in a proxy battle; and (3) not compete with EDS for three years or recruit EDS executives.

Shareholders of GM (plaintiffs) filed derivative actions for breach of fiduciary duty by the directors for violations of their duties of loyalty and due care. The court of chancery dismissed the case, and the shareholders appealed.

JUDICIAL OPINION

HORSEY, Judge

As previously noted, the business judgment rule is but a presumption that directors making a business decision, not involving self-interest, act on an informed basis, in good faith and in the honest belief that their actions are in the corporations' best interest. Thus, good faith and the absence of self-dealing are threshold requirements for invoking the rule. *Unocal Corp.* v. *Mesa Petroleum Co.*, Del. Supr., 493 A.2d 946 (1985). Assuming the presumptions of director good faith and lack of self-dealing are not rebutted by well-pleaded facts, a shareholder derivative complainant must then allege further facts with particularity which, "taken as true, support a reasonable doubt that the challenged transaction was [in fact] the product of a valid exercise of business judgment."

Plaintiffs must plead particularized facts demonstrating either a financial interest or entrenchment on the part of the GM directors. Plaintiffs plead no facts demonstrating a financial interest on the part of GM's directors. The only averment permitting such an inference is the allegation that all GM's directors are paid for their services as directors. However, such allegations, without more, do not establish any financial interest.

Plaintiffs also do not plead any facts tending to show that the GM directors' positions were actually threatened by Perot, who owned only 0.8 percent of GM's voting stock, nor do plaintiffs allege that the repurchase was motivated and reasonably related to the directors' retention of their positions on the Board. Plaintiffs merely argue that Perot's public criticism of GM management could cause the directors embarrassment sufficient to lead to their removal from office. Such allegations are tenuous at best and are too speculative to raise a reasonable doubt of director disinterest. Speculation on motives for undertaking corporate action are wholly insufficient to establish a case of demand excusal.

Plaintiffs' remaining allegations bearing on the issue of entrenchment are: the rushed nature of the transaction during a period of GM financial difficulty; the giant premium paid; and the criticism (after the fact) of the repurchase by industry analysts and top GM management. Plaintiffs argue that these allegations are sufficient to raise a reasonable doubt of director disinterest. We cannot agree. Not one of the asserted grounds would support a reasonable belief of entrenchment based on director self-interest. The relevance of these averments goes largely to the issue of due care, next discussed. Such allegations are patently insufficient to raise a reasonable doubt as to the ability of the GM Board to act with disinterest. Thus, we find plaintiffs' entrenchment claim to be essentially conclusory and lacking in factual support sufficient to establish excusal based on director interest.

Having concluded that plaintiffs have failed to plead a claim of financial interest or entrenchment sufficient to excuse presuit demand, we examine the complaints as amended to determine whether they raise a reasonable doubt that the directors exercised proper business judgment in the transaction. By proper business judgment we mean both substantive due care (purchase terms), see *Saxe* v. *Brady,* Del. Ch., 40 Del. Ch. 474, 184 A.2d 602, 610 (1962), and procedural due care

continued

(an informed decision), see *Smith* v. *Van Gorkom*, Del. Supr., 488 A.2d 858, 872–73 (1985).

With regard to the nature of the transactions and the terms of repurchase, especially price, plaintiffs allege that the premium paid Perot constituted a *prima facie* waste of GM's assets. Plaintiffs argue that the transaction, on its face, was "so egregious as to be afforded no presumption of business judgment protection." In rejecting this contention, the Vice Chancellor reasoned that, apart from the hush-mail provision, the transaction must be viewed as any other repurchase by a corporation, at a premium over market, of its own stock held by a single dissident shareholder or shareholder group at odds with management, [which] have repeatedly been upheld as valid exercises of business judgment.

The law of Delaware is well established that, in the absence of evidence of fraud or unfairness, a corporation's repurchase of its capital stock at a premium over market from a dissident shareholder is entitled to the protection of the business judgment rule.

We have already determined that plaintiffs have not stated a claim of financial interest or entrenchment as the compelling motive for the repurchase, and it is equally clear that the complaints as amended do not allege a claim of fraud. They allege, at most, a claim of waste based on the assertion that GM's Board paid such a premium for the Perot holdings as to shock the conscience of the ordinary person.

Thus, the issue becomes whether the complaints state a claim of waste of assets, i.e., whether "what the corporation has received is so inadequate in value that no person of ordinary, sound business judgment would deem it worth that which the corporation has paid." By way of reinforcing their claim of waste, plaintiffs seize upon the hush-mail feature of the repurchase as being the motivating reason for the "giant premium" approved by the GM Board. Plaintiffs then argue that buying the silence of a dissident within management constitutes an invalid business purpose. Ergo, plaintiffs argue that a claim of waste of corporate assets evidencing lack of director due care has been well pleaded.

Plaintiffs' complaints as amended fail to plead with particularity any facts supporting a conclusion that the primary or motivating purpose of the Board's payment of a "giant premium" for the Perot holdings was to buy Perot's silence rather than simply to buy him out and remove him from GM's management team. To the contrary, plaintiffs themselves state in their complaints as amended several legitimate business purposes for the GM Board's decision to sever its relationship with Perot: (1) the Board's determination that it would be in GM's best interest to retain control over its wholly-owned subsidiary, EDS; and (2) the decision to rid itself of the principal cause of the growing internal policy dispute over EDS' management and direction.

In addition to regaining control over the management affairs of EDS, GM also secured, through the complex repurchase agreement, significant covenants from Perot, of which the hush-mail provision was but one of many features and multiple considerations of the repurchase. Quite aside from whatever consideration could be attributed to buying Perot's silence, GM's Board received for the $742.8 million paid: all the class E stock and contingent notes of Perot and his fellow EDS directors; Perot's covenant not to compete or hire EDS employees; his promise not to purchase GM stock or engage in proxy contests; Perot's agreement to stay out of and away from GM's and EDS' affairs, plus the liquidated damages provision should Perot breach his no-criticism covenant.

Plaintiffs' effort to quantify the size of the premium paid by GM is flawed, as we have already noted, by their inability to place a dollar value on the various promises made by Perot, particularly his covenant not to compete with EDS or to attempt to hire away EDS employees. Thus, viewing the transaction in its entirety, we must agree with the Court of Chancery that plaintiff's have failed to plead with particularity facts sufficient to create a reasonable doubt that the substantive terms of the repurchase fall within the protection of the business judgment rule.

Finally we turn to the other aspect of director due care, whether plaintiffs have pleaded facts which would support a reasonable belief that the GM Board acted with gross negligence, i.e., that it was uninformed in critical respects in negotiating the terms of the repurchase. On this remaining issue, plaintiffs assert that GM's Board failed to exercise due care and to reach an informed business judgment due to the absence of arms-length negotiations between the Board and Perot and the absence of "appropriate board deliberation."

Approval of a transaction by a majority of independent, disinterested directors almost always bolsters a presumption that the business judgment rule attaches to transactions approved by a board of directors that are later attacked on grounds of lack of due care. In such cases, a heavy burden falls on a plaintiff to avoid presuit demand.

Furthermore, plaintiffs recount that the repurchase proposal was first submitted to a Special Review Committee, consisting (presumably) of three outside directors and thereafter to the full Board. The complaints as amended, however, contain no allegations raising directly or by inference a reasonable doubt either that the Committee served a purposeful role in the review of the repurchase proposal or that the full Board reached an informed decision. On the contrary, it is clear from the record before us that the GM directors had been living with the internal dispute for months and had been considering a buy-out of Perot's interests for a number of weeks.

Apart from whether the Board of Directors may be subject to criticism for the premium paid Perot and his associates for the repurchase of their entire interest in GM, on the present record the repurchase of dissident Perot's interests can only be viewed legally as representing an exercise of business judgment by the General Motors Board with which a court may not interfere.

Affirmed.

CASE QUESTIONS

1. What must the shareholders prove to recover?
2. What is entrenchment?
3. Why is director independence important?
4. What does the court find regarding the payment of a premium to Mr. Perot?
5. How does the business judgment rule apply in the repurchase?
6. Do you think Mr. Perot was disruptive to running the company?

 CONSIDER... **21.5**

William Shlensky was a minority shareholder of Chicago National League Ball Club, Inc. (the Cubs). In 1966, he brought suit against the directors of the Cubs for violation of the business judgment rule because at the time of the suit the Cubs did not play night games at Wrigley Field, their home field. All of the other nineteen teams in the major leagues had some night games with substantially all of their weekday and nonholiday games scheduled under the lights. Between 1961 and 1965, the Cubs had sustained operating losses. Mr. Shlensky filed a derivative suit (a suit on behalf of shareholders) against the Cubs' directors for negligence and mismanagement.

Mr. Shlensky's suit maintained that the Cubs would continue to lose money unless night games were played. The directors' response was that baseball was a "daytime" sport and that holding night games would have a "deteriorating effect upon the surrounding neighborhood."

Why does Mr. Shlensky believe the directors did not use good judgment? Is there a difference between negligence and differing business opinions? Does the business judgment rule allow directors to make mistakes? [*Shlensky* v. *Wrigley,* 237 N.W. 2d 776 (Ill. 1968).]

THINK: Under the principles of liability for directors and the protection of the business judgment rule, a director and board can make mistakes. They can make decisions that ultimately prove to be big mistakes, even in judgment. However, courts do not step in and, with hindsight, second-guess the directors. So long as the directors have given their time, thought, and effort to the decision and obtained independent advice, their judgment is protected from liability to shareholders, even if they are proven completely wrong.

APPLY: While the parties disagree over whether to hold day games or night games, the Cubs organization has articulated its reasons, rightly or wrongly.

ANSWER: The reasons show that the Cubs directors have devoted the time, energy, and thought necessary to make the decision and thus enjoy protection from liability under the business judgment rule.

Officers and directors are also required to follow the **corporate opportunity doctrine,** under which officers and directors may not take an opportunity for themselves that the corporation might be interested in taking. For example, a director of a lumber company who discovers a deal on timberland would be required to present that opportunity to the corporation before she could take it. If the director does not first present the idea to the corporation, a constructive trust is put on the profits the director makes, and the corporation is the beneficiary of that trust. If, however, the director presents the opportunity and the corporation is unable or unwilling to take it, the director may go ahead with the opportunity without the problem of a constructive trust.

C O N S I D E R . . .   **2 1 . 6**

Jerome Van Gorkom, chairman and CEO of Trans Union, Inc., had a proposal from another company for a merger. The proposal was made on September 18 (Thursday), with a decision demanded by September 21 (Sunday). Mr. Van Gorkom called a board meeting and did a twenty-minute presentation on the merger. No consultants or advisors were present. The merger, at a price of $55 per share, was approved within two hours from the time the board meeting began. After the value of their shares dropped dramatically, shareholders brought suit against the directors, claiming that the decision was not shielded by the business judgment rule. Are they correct or are the directors protected by the business judgment rule? [*Smith* v. *Van Gorkom*, 488 A.2d 858 (Del. 1985).]

C O N S I D E R . . .   **2 1 . 7**

Former Governor J. Fife Symington of Arizona was, during the 1980s, a director of Southwest Savings & Loan, a federal thrift headquartered in Phoenix. Mr. Symington was also a developer who constructed two major commercial projects in Phoenix, with Southwest Savings & Loan providing the loans for development. Southwest was a victim of the 1980s downturn and was taken over by the Resolution Trust Corporation (RTC). The RTC brought suit against Mr. Symington, alleging that he took advantage of his board position to obtain the loans. Mr. Symington said he was required to present the projects to the Southwest Board as part of the corporate opportunity doctrine and Southwest took the investment. Who is correct?

Officer Liability

Recent prosecutions have demonstrated an increased effort to hold corporate officers criminally responsible for the acts of the corporation. In environmental law, changes in the law and aggressive prosecutions have brought about convictions of officers, particularly concerning the disposal of hazardous waste. The issues of officer liability are covered in Chapters 9, 12, 18, and 22.

Officers, Boards, and Sarbanes–Oxley

Sarbanes-Oxley, the legislation passed following the collapse of companies such as Enron and WorldCom, has imposed dramatic new requirements on boards and officers of publicly traded companies (see Chapter 9 for more details). These reforms are required above and beyond any statutory requirements imposed by state corporation laws such as the MBCA.

Prohibitions on Loans to Officers   Corporations can no longer make loans to officers and directors. This provision is the result of revelations that companies such as WorldCom, Adelphia, and others had made hundreds of millions of dollars in loans to their CEOs and other executives because they had pledged their shares in the company for their personal investments. When those investments did not perform well, their shares needed to be sold to satisfy the loans. A sell-off of their major holdings would have sent the company's stock into a dive. The result was a vicious circle in which more loans were made in order to prevent the sale of shares, with ever-increasing pressure to keep the share price up in order to satisfy the loans the shares secured. (See "Buoying Bernie.")

Codes of Ethics for Financial Reporting   Companies must now have codes of ethics in place for the financial officers of their companies. While 97 percent of pub-

FOR THE MANAGER'S DESK

RE: BUOYING BERNIE

Bernie Ebbers, the former CEO of WorldCom, was a flamboyant, charming, 6'4" man. When, because of WorldCom's growth and acquisitions, Mr. Ebbers was a billionaire, he went on a personal buying spree. He purchased the largest private ranch in Canada, his native land, as well as dealerships, lumber companies, and a number of other businesses near Mississippi. In order to make these purchases, Mr. Ebbers obtained loans, some of them secured by his WorldCom stock holdings. Mr. Ebbers had a great idea on how to build a phone company, but he was not known for his ability to execute ideas or even handle the day-to-day management tasks of business. As a result, many of his personal investments were in great financial difficulty.

Low on cash, Mr. Ebbers was able to persuade the WorldCom board to extend loans to him, in excess of $415 million, to rescue his failing businesses. The problem with the loans, among many others, was that the stock Mr. Ebbers used to secure them was also the stock he had pledged to his creditors in order to obtain financing for his ventures. The result was that WorldCom directors had taken a subordinated security interest in stock that had already been pledged, placing the company well at the end of the line in terms of creditors. Worse, everyone was acting on the assumption that the value of the WorldCom stock would remain at equal or higher levels.

While the board's loans to Mr. Ebbers put it at risk of losing $415 million, the control of the company was actually at greater risk because Mr. Ebbers had pledged about $1 billion in WorldCom stock in total to his creditors for loans. By 2001, when WorldCom's stock price began to drop, Mr. Ebbers' net worth had slipped to $295 million, $286.6 million of which was WorldCom stock. The board had to continue to make loans to cover margin calls on Mr. Ebbers' loans because otherwise Mr. Ebbers would have had to dump his shares onto the market, thus depressing the price of WorldCom's already depressed shares even further as well as jeopardizing the collateral for the loans. The board had climbed into a bottomless pit. The loans continued from 2000 through 2002. The compensation committee, headed by a longtime friend of Mr. Ebbers, approved the loans, but the issue of the loans was not presented to the full board because legal counsel for WorldCom indicated full board approval was not necessary.

Knowing the pressure the board faced with the loans tied to the WorldCom share price, Scott Sullivan, the CFO, a board member, and secretary to the corporation, and other financial officers within the company began capitalizing ordinary expenses to keep earnings numbers high. During the period from 2000 to 2002, the officers, who have all entered guilty pleas or have charges pending, capitalized $9 billion in ordinary expenses. When the expenses were actually announced and the proper accounting entries made, WorldCom reversed its earnings for those two years and was forced into Chapter 11 bankruptcy. The story of the WorldCom loans to Mr. Ebbers, more so than any of the other failed companies, motivated the prohibition against corporate loans to officers that is now part of Sarbanes-Oxley and federal law.

Sources: Jared Sandberg and Susan Pulliam, "Report by WorldCom Examiner Finds New Fraudulent Activities," *Wall Street Journal,* November 5, 2002, p. A1; Kurt Eichenwald, "Corporate Loans Used Personally, Report Discloses," *New York Times,* November 5, 2002, p. C1.

licly held companies now have codes of ethics, this provision requires specific content about the standards for financial reporting and accounting in the company. These financial officers are also subject to greater federal penalties for certifying false financial statements (see Chapter 9 for more information on their criminal liability).

Role of Legal Counsel for the Company In many of the collapsed companies, two of the questions that arose were "Where were the auditors?" and "Where were the lawyers?"[1] As Congress and the SEC grappled with these questions, they imposed extensive new legal requirements and disclosure obligations on auditors and accountants (see Chapter 22 for those requirements), but they also imposed reporting requirements on legal counsel for corporations. Under the new requirements, lawyers have several progressive steps in their duties and disclosure requirements.[2]

- A lawyer who believes there are material violations must instigate an investigation to determine whether or not such violations have occurred.
- The lawyer must inform the CEO of the investigation.

- The lawyer must report material violations of the law to the CEO.

- If no action is taken, the lawyer must go "up the ladder" and report the material violations to the audit committee or a group of independent board members.

- Companies must create a legal compliance committee with the idea that there is strength in numbers, in that the committee will be told of investigations and findings and can take the matter "up the ladder."

ETHICAL ISSUES

Sitting in the Hot Seat for Officers' Loans

Tyco has experienced financial setbacks following the indictment of its CEO, Dennis Kozlowski (best known for his $6,000 shower curtain and Jimmy Buffet birthday party for his wife), its CFO, Mark Swartz, and its legal counsel, Mark Belnick, on state charges of crimes related to larceny and embezzlement. Some of the charges stemmed from Tyco's Key Employee Corporate Loan Program (the KELP), a program established to encourage officers and some employees to own Tyco shares by offering them loans to pay income taxes due when their ownership of shares granted to them under Tyco's restricted share ownership plan vested. This way, instead of selling some of their shares, the officers could pledge their shares in exchange for cash to pay the taxes on this employee benefit.*

The second loan program was a relocation program established to help employees who had to move from New Hampshire to New York. The idea was to provide low-interest loans for employees who had to relocate from one set of company offices to another in order to lessen the impact on their budgets of the move to a much costlier housing market. One of the requirements of the relocation program was the employee's certification that he or she was indeed moving from New Hampshire to New York, or, in some cases, to Boca Raton, another site for company offices.

Mr. Belnick has maintained that he was entitled to the loans from the relocation program because he had such authorization in writing from Mr. Kozlowski. Mr. Belnick had been a partner in a New York City law firm and had done work for Tyco when he was hired as general counsel for the company. He would still be working in New York City if he hadn't accepted the position with Tyco. However, he received a relocation loan for a difference of 25 miles between his home in Connecticut and Tyco's New York offices, despite the fact that he had never lived in New Hampshire as the relocation program required. Mr. Belnick used the $4 million he borrowed under the program to buy and renovate an apartment in New York City. He later borrowed another $10 million to construct a home in Park City, Utah, because he was moving his family there and planned to divide his time between the two locations and the exten-

sive international travel his job required. Mr. Belnick got Mr. Kozlowski's approval for both loans, but he didn't do the corporate paperwork for relocation.

Mr. Swartz availed himself of $85 million in KELP loans. However, he used only $13 million for payment of taxes and spent the remaining $72 million for personal investments, business ventures, real estate holdings, and trusts. Mr. Swartz used more than $32 million of interest-free relocation loans, and, according to SEC documents, used almost $9 million of those relocation loans for purposes not authorized under the program, including purchasing a yacht and investing in real estate.

The issue of board approval on the loans remains a question, but compensation committee minutes from February 21, 2002, show that the committee was given a list of loans to officers and also approved Mr. Belnick's new compensation package. There was no public disclosure of these developments or the committee's review. In grand jury testimony, Patricia Prue, the Tyco employee in charge of administration of the two loan programs, indicated that board member Joshua Berman pressured her in June 2002 to change the minutes from that February compensation committee meeting. Mr. Berman denies the allegation. However, Ms. Prue did send a memo on June 7, 2002, to John Fort (a Tyco board member), Mr. Swartz, and the board's governance committee with the following included: "As a result of the fact that I was recently pressured by Josh Berman to engage in conduct which I regarded as dishonest—and which I have refused to do—I will decline to have any personal contact with him in the future. In addition, I ask that Josh not go to my staff with any requests for information or directions." Both sides acknowledge that Ms. Prue sent the memo.

Do you think Ms. Prue did the right thing? Should she have done more to stop the loans? Is it a crime if the board authorized the loans and all the paperwork is in place? Did Ms. Prue facilitate abuse of the loan programs? Should she have notified someone? Should she have resigned? What would you have done if you had been in her position?

*This information was obtained from the SEC's press release issued when it filed suit against Mark Swartz, Dennis Kozlowski, and Mark Belnick for the return of the loan amounts. See *http://www.sec.gov;* click on litigation releases.

Because of concerns and objections from the American Bar Association, the SEC did not adopt the so-called noisy withdrawal rule, a process that would have required a lawyer who has found a material violation that the company will not remedy to resign from the company and report the violation to the SEC.

Board Membership   Under rules promulgated under Sarbanes-Oxley direction, boards must consist of a majority of members who are independent. *Independent* is defined as someone who has not been an officer, employee, or manager of the company during any of the past three years; who is not related to anyone who works for

---

BUSINESS STRATEGY

Governing Corporate Governance

In addition to incorporating the statutory requirements under Sarbanes-Oxley, many companies are adopting new policies and procedures for corporate governance. Some of those changes, policies, and processes are mentioned here as possible strategies for effective governance.

© DIGITAL VISION/GETTY IMAGES

- Some companies have created the position of a corporate ombudsperson who will create the audit and ethics committees in their boards and will watch for officer share trading.
- Some companies have had the majority of their board resign.
- WorldCom paid Richard Breeden to prepare a 149-page report on "Restoring Trust" and will implement all of his recommended changes. The changes are part of the articles of incorporation and now cannot be changed without shareholder approval.
- Tyco is required to submit annual reports on its board and corporate governance processes.
- At WorldCom, an executive's salary and compensation package cannot exceed $1.5 million without shareholder approval.
- Some companies have agreed to fund university research into effective corporate governance.

Companies are also working to change their board policies and processes beyond the requirements under Sarbanes-Oxley. One company highlighted in the *Wall Street Journal* for its changes is E*Trade, a company that carried a black eye when in 2001 it revealed that its CEO had an $80 million pay package despite significant problems with the company's performance and a plunging share price. The share price had dropped from over $60 per share to less than $5 per share when the pay package for then-CEO Christos Cotsakos was announced. (He did return $20 million of the package.)

The following changes have taken place at the E*Trade board.

- Board meetings are now two days in length (they were four hours or less).
- All directors must have a three-hour orientation session before beginning their service. (Tyco also now requires this training.)
- The CFO was terminated in June when a financial restatement was necessary.
- All pay packages have been revamped and bonuses for executives are limited to three times their annual salaries.
- The $14,000 per month concierge service for employees has ended.
- As leases expire, the company has moved into less expensive office spaces.
- The board members who allowed the compensation package of $80 million have resigned and been replaced.
- The board has open access to all E*Trade executives.

Ironically, Mr. Cotsakos just received his Ph.D. from the University of London in corporate governance. His degree was paid for by E*Trade.

Sources: Susanne Craig, "How One Firm Uses Strict Governance to Fix Its Troubles," *Wall Street Journal,* August 21, 2003, pp. A1, A6; Edward Iwata, "Prosecutors slap new rules on companies," *USA Today,* March 22, 2004, p. 1B.

MAKING ETHICS PERSONAL

Perks of the Job

A feature in *Forbes* magazine on corporate governance found, by perusing the SEC filings of publicly traded companies, that the following behaviors for the companies were not unusual.

Activity	Percentage of Companies
Purchasing or selling insiders' products or services	47%
Making loans to executives	39%
Allowing directors to sell legal or banking services to the company	35%
Buying, selling, lending to, or investing in companies that insiders own	21%
Hiring relatives	14%
Creating consulting arrangements with directors	11%
Leasing, selling, or buying airplanes to or from insiders	10%
Borrowing from insiders or insiders' companies	6%

Compare this list with the requirements under Sarbanes-Oxley and also the ethical issues of conflicts of interest. Which of these activities are risky? Which ones should the companies discontinue?

Source: Elizabeth Macdonald, "Crony Capitalism," *Forbes,* June 21, 2004, p. 140.

ETHICAL ISSUES

Many companies have outside directors on their boards who are also paid as consultants to the company. For example, Dr. Henry A. Kissinger, the former secretary of state, was a member of the American Express Board for a number of years. Dr. Kissinger received a $64,000 annual retainer, a $30,000 pension, free life insurance, and the right to have the company make a $500,000 charitable gift at the time of his death as part of his director compensation. He also received $350,000 a year in consulting fees from the company. W. R. Grace & Co. had five outside directors who also earned $1.5 million in consulting fees from the company.

Shareholder advocacy groups have proposed resolutions to reduce director compensation because such high payments mean they may not represent the interests of the shareholders.

The National Association of Corporate Directors has condemned the consultant-director dual role as a conflict of interest.

The American Express Board voted to halt the practice as a "bad idea" that "just confuses roles." Do you agree? Are there conflicts when directors also work for the corporation in exchange for large fees? Why do you think the SEC refuses to count these directors as independent directors?

the company; who is not under any type of consulting or remuneration arrangement with the company; and who is not a principal or owner of a company that does business with the board or the company. The chair of the audit committee must be an independent director, and at least one member of the audit committee must meet standards for certification as a financial expert.

Corporate Management and Control: Shareholders

Shareholder Rights: Annual Meetings

Shareholders have the opportunity to express their views at the annual meeting by electing directors who represent their interests. Annual meetings also give shareholders the opportunity to vote on critical corporate issues. Under the MBCA, the failure to hold an annual meeting does not result in dissolution or revocation of corporate status.

Shareholder Rights: Voting

At annual and special meetings, voting share shareholders have the right to vote. Shareholders may vote their own shares or delegate their votes in a variety of ways.

The Proxy   The most common method of delegating voting authority is the **proxy**, with which shareholders can transfer their right to vote to someone else. This type of vote assignment is temporary. Under the MBCA, a proxy is good only for eleven months, which allows a shareholder to decide to give a different proxy before the next annual meeting. Many shareholder groups solicit proxies to obtain control. Those solicitations are subject to the federal securities laws, and certain disclosures are required (see Chapter 22).

Pooling Agreements   Another method of grouping shareholder votes is the **pooling agreement**. This is a contract among shareholders to vote their shares a certain way or for a certain director. One of the problems with pooling agreements is enforceability: If the agreements are breached, it is really too late to do anything about the breach because the corporation will take the action authorized by the votes or a particular director will take a seat.

Voting Trust   One last form of shareholder cooperation is the **voting trust**. In this form of group voting, shareholders actually turn their shares over to a trustee and are then issued a trust certificate. The shareholders still have the right to dividends and could sell or pledge the certificate. However, the shares remain in the hands of the trustee, and the trustee votes those shares according to the terms of the trust agreement. The shareholders get their shares back only when the trust ends. Most states have specific requirements for the voting trust: A copy must be filed with the corporate offices, and some states have a maximum duration (such as ten years) for such trusts.

Shareholder Rights in Combinations

Because shareholders' interests are involved, corporations are not free to combine at will or to merge or consolidate without shareholder input. All states have procedures for obtaining shareholder approval for business combinations.

The Procedure   For all mergers, consolidations, and sales of assets (other than in the ordinary course of business), there must be shareholder approval. Further, that approval must be obtained in a manner prescribed by the MBCA.

- *Board resolution.* The process of obtaining shareholder approval begins with the board of directors. They must adopt and approve a resolution favoring the merger, consolidation, or asset sale.
- *Notice to shareholders.* Once the resolution is adopted, it must be sent to the shareholders along with a notice of a meeting for the purpose of taking action on the resolution. A notice is sent to all shareholders regardless of whether they are entitled to vote under the corporation's articles.
- *Shareholder approval.* The shareholders must then vote to approve the resolution at the announced meeting. In the cases of mergers and consolidations, all shareholders are entitled to vote whether they own voting or nonvoting shares because their interests are affected by the results. The number of votes needed to approve a merger under the MBCA is a majority. However, the articles of incorporation or the bylaws may require more, known as a super majority.

Shareholder approval is not required for a short-form merger, which is one between a subsidiary and a parent that owns at least 90 percent of the stock of the subsidiary. In the absence of these narrow requirements, the long-form merger provisions of resolution and voting must be followed.

Shareholder Rights: The Dissenting Shareholder

Not all shareholders vote in favor of a merger or a consolidation. Under the MBCA and most state statutes, these **dissenting shareholders** are entitled to their appraisal rights. **Appraisal rights** allow shareholders to demand the value of their shares. Under the MBCA, a dissenting shareholder must file a written objection to the merger or consolidation before the meeting to vote on either is held.

If the merger or consolidation is approved, the corporation must notify dissenting shareholders and offer them the fair value of the shares. Fair value is determined as of the *day before* the action is taken on the merger or consolidation because the action taken will affect the value of the shares. If the dissenting shareholders do not believe the corporation's offer is fair, they can bring suit against the corporation for establishing fair value. However, if the value the corporation offered is found to be fair and the dissenting shareholders' rejection arbitrary, they will be required to pay the corporation's costs of the lawsuit.

Shareholders also enjoy some protections during merger activity that are offered under federal securities laws in terms of notice and disclosure (see Chapter 22).

Some corporations have experienced a **freeze-out**, which is a merger undertaken to get rid of the minority shareholders in a corporation. Although these minority shareholders have their dissenting rights, it is expensive to pursue a court action for a determination of fair value. The majority shareholders are thus able to buy out, at a low price, the minority shareholders, who are left without a remedy and usually with a loss. For this reason, many courts now impose on majority stockholders a fiduciary duty to the minority stockholders and will prevent a merger without a business purpose from freezing out minority shareholders. Courts, and some state laws (corporate constituency statutes), also require a showing that a merger or consolidation is fair to the minority shareholders. These general terms of "business purpose" and "fairness" are defined on a case-by-case basis.

Shareholder Rights: Inspection of Books and Records

The MBCA gives shareholders the absolute right to examine shareholder lists. For other records (minutes, accounting), shareholders must give notice of their request. In addition to this mechanical requirement, some courts also require a **proper purpose**, which means a shareholder has a legitimate interest in reviewing corporate progress, financial status, and fiduciary responsibilities. Improper purposes are those related to use of corporate records to advance the shareholders' moral, religious, or political ideas.

Shareholder Rights: Transfer of Shares

Stock shares can have **transfer restrictions**, which are valid so long as the following requirements are met.

1. The restrictions must be necessary. Valid circumstances include family-owned corporations, employee-owned corporations, and corporations that need restrictions to comply with SEC registration exemptions (see Chapter 22).
2. The restrictions must be reasonable. Requiring that the shares first be offered to the board before they can be sold is reasonable; requiring that the shares be

offered to all the other shareholders first may be unreasonable if there are more than five to ten shareholders.

3. The restrictions and/or their existence must be conspicuously noted on the stock shares.

The Dissolution of a Corporation

A corporation can continue indefinitely unless its articles of incorporation limit its duration. Long before perpetuity, however, a corporation can be dissolved voluntarily or involuntarily.

Voluntary Dissolution

Voluntary dissolution occurs when the shareholders agree to dissolve the corporation. This type of dissolution occurs in smaller corporations when the shareholders no longer get along, the business does not do well, or one of the shareholders is ill or dies.

A voluntary dissolution begins with a resolution by the board of directors, which is then put before the shareholders at a special meeting called for that purpose. Under the MBCA, all shareholders (voting and nonvoting alike) vote on the issue of dissolution because all of them will be affected by it. Once the shareholders pass the resolution (a majority or two-thirds vote in most states), the assets of the corporation are liquidated, and debts and shareholders are paid in the order of their priorities. Each state also has filing and publication requirements for dissolution.

Involuntary Dissolution

An involuntary dissolution is forced by some state agency, usually the state-level attorney's office. A dissolution can be forced because of fraud or failure to follow state law regarding reporting requirements for corporations.

LIMITED LIABILITY COMPANIES

Examine a state comparison chart, among other materials, for limited liability laws:
http://www.llcweb.com

The **limited liability company** (LLC), first created in 1997, is relatively new to the United States and available in forty-eight states and the District of Columbia. The LLC has actually been in existence for many years in Europe (known as a GMBH) and South America (*limitada*). The LLC is more of an aggregate form of business organization than an entity such as a corporation. Owners of an LLC are called members. An LLC provides limited liability (members lose only up to their capital contributions) and flow-through tax treatment like a partnership in that there is tax only at the member's level of income and not at the business level. An LLC is not a corporation or a partnership. It can be taxed as a partnership, with limited liability for all its owners, unlike a limited partnership, and all personal owners can participate in management without risking liability.

Review "An Introduction to New Jersey's Limited Liability Company Act," by Lisa M. Fontoura:
http://www.cfg-lawfirm. com/articles/llc.html

It has been said that the LLC combines the best of all of the business structures: limited liability for the owners, flexibility in management in that all the owners can participate in management, and flow-through of the income directly to personal profits and losses and resulting tax liability. However, this ideal creation, in order to enjoy the flow-through characteristics necessary for the tax break, must be distinguished from a corporation. The result is that LLCs are limited in duration, with most statutes allowing them to run for periods of thirty to forty years. The point at which LLCs dissolve by statutory limitations has not yet arrived because LLCs did not exist until 1977. However, when those dissolutions come, the restructuring and recreation should create interesting issues among and between the owners of the LLCs.

Formation

An LLC is formed through the filing of a document called the **articles of organization** that is filed with a centralized state agency. The name of the business formed must contain either "limited liability company," "L.L.C.," or "LLC."

Sources of Funding

Members of an LLC make capital contributions in much the same way as partners make capital contributions.

Liability

Members of an LLC have limited liability; the most they can lose is their capital contributions. Debts belong to the LLC, and creditors' rights lie with the LLC's assets, not the personal assets of the members. However, many states require that the nature of the business organization appear on the business cards and stationery of the company so that members of the public are not misled about the nature of the business as well as the nature of the limited liability of the owners.

CONSIDER...   2 1 . 8

Larry Clark and David Lanham formed a limited liability company in Colorado called Preferred Income Investors, LLC (PII). All of the necessary paperwork for the creation of an LLC had been filed with the secretary of state, as required by Colorado statute.

Mr. Clark negotiated with a Westec representative about doing construction work for PII on a Taco Cabana restaurant the LLC was building. Mr. Clark gave the Westec rep his card, which had PII's name above Mr. Clark's name. Westec drew up a contract that was never signed by anyone from PII. However, Mr. Clark gave oral authorization for the work, and Westec completed it. PII did not have the assets to pay the bill for the work, and Westec sued to hold Mr. Clark liable for the contract. Mr. Clark said that as an owner of a limited liability company, he had no personal liability. Westec says it was never made aware that PII was an LLC and that it should be given that information in advance. Is Mr. Clark personally liable? [*Water, Waste, & Land, Inc., dba Westec* v. *Lanham*, 995 P.2d 997 (Colo. 1998).]

FOR THE MANAGER'S DESK

RE: ENRON AND ITS LLCS AND LLPS

Part of Enron's collapse was due to its reliance on extensive creation of LLCs and LLPs across which it could spread its debt without carrying that debt on its balance sheet. At the time of Enron's massive creation of LLCs and LLPs, the GAAP and FASB standards for disclosure of a company's transactions with related entities (FASB 125), or those entities in which the company holds an interest, applied only when the company owns at least 50 percent of the related entity. If a company owned 49 percent or less of an entity, any debt obligations the related entity carried did not have to be carried as debt on the company's balance sheet. Consolidation was not required until the company owned 50% or more of its subsidiaries and other business ventures.

Enron began creating off-the-book entities in 1997. By the time of Enron's collapse in 2001, it had created 3,000 special purpose entities (SPEs), with 881 of them located in the Cayman Islands. Their offshore status was designed to eliminate the need for the entities and other business ventures to pay U.S. federal income tax.*

A shareholder class action lawsuit filed in November 2001 includes the following descriptions of Enron's practices:

> One of Andrew Fastow's "innovative" accounting techniques was to create entities (trusts) to which Enron would issue millions of dollars in mandatory convertible debentures or depreciated assets. The trust would then use the assets as collateral to receive billions of dollars in financing for Enron projects, including Broadband. Although Enron Corp. officially owned less than fifty percent of these entities, Enron controlled them. Defendants, improperly, did not consolidate these entities into Enron's disclosed financials; rather, Defendants hid the true nature of all of these transactions from the public. This meant Enron was engaged in business deals, risky hedging, self-dealing transactions that were never disclosed to the SEC.[†]

The names of these off-the-books LLCs and LLPs provide insight into the nature of Enron's business, its culture, and the hubris that engulfed its senior management. Some were named after *Jurassic Park* creatures, some were named after *Star Wars* creatures and characters, and one name was a thumb of the nose to the accounting rule (FASB 125) being capitalized upon to hide the company's true financial picture: Hawaii 125–0.

To satisfy FASB 125, the SPEs were required to have at least 3 percent equity ownership by outsiders. As time went by, the definition of "outsiders" became flexible the more the labyrinthine web of Enron finances grew. For example, Andrew Fastow, Enron's CFO, proposed using his wife's family as the outside investors. When the accounting firm Arthur Andersen nixed the idea, Mr. Fastow used Michael Kopper, a mid-level manager whose interest in the outside LLCs and LLPs did not have to be disclosed on securities documents.

The basic theme of the SPEs and all other Enron partnerships was as follows.

- Enron created a partnership (an SPE).
- Enron recruited an outside owner to invest the 3 percent required in order to comply with the FASB 125 rule.
- The SPE purchased Enron assets (the riskier ones such as broadband width, shares in subsidiaries in high-tech fields), but the sale was simply for an IOU from the SPE.
- Enron was able to show a profit on its books for the sale.
- The debt (IOU) of the SPE was not carried on Enron's books.
- If the value of the sold asset fell, the SPE couldn't pay the IOU.
- Enron would then issue its stock to the SPE.
- The SPE sold the shares of stock to raise cash.

The entire scenario depended on Enron's share price remaining high. If the share price fell, as it did beginning in the summer of 2001, all of the SPEs had no assets and no value. Although Enron told analysts its SPEs were nonrecourse, Enron often was the guarantor for SPE's IOUs—it was the only way to recruit the outside investors.

Mr. Fastow was the principal in many of the partnerships and LLCs and netted more than his Enron salary by serving as the broker for the various deals between the SPEs and Enron. The relationships were actually far more complex, with resulting liability exposure for Enron. In many of the SPEs, Enron advanced the funds for the outside parties to invest in the SPEs, or the money used to finance transactions with the SPEs was borrowed from syndicates of lenders who accepted Enron stock as the security for their loans. Although Enron often served as the guarantor for loans to the SPEs, there was no disclosure in Enron's financial statements about its potential exposure as a guarantor, one of the factors that did cause some discussion between company executives and Andersen auditors. All of these transactions depended on Enron being able to maintain its share price, a price that was tied directly to the volatility of prices in the energy market.

It seems that most board members understood the SPEs' overall effect. Notes from Enron's corporate secretary at a meeting of one of Enron's board committees reads, "Does not transfer economic risk, but transfers P&L volatility." ("P&L" is profit and loss.)

Evaluate the director's comment and the board's oversight.

AFTERMATH: Enron had created a Byzantine empire of financial layers that were impenetrable by investors until the company's collapse, when all documents were made public. The documents dribbled out over a period of months as Enron finally came to grips with the fact that it could not pay the debts it had created via the SPEs. By November 2001, Enron had been downgraded to "junk" grade.[‡] Enron's former chairman, Kenneth Lay, left the company shortly after the collapse. Mr. Lay waived any rights to his parachute, reportedly worth $60 million, and also agreed to repay a $2 million loan from the company.

Mr. Fastow entered a guilty plea and will be serving a ten-year sentence (see Chapter 9). Mr. Lay was indicted in July 2004. The company's current CEO, Jeffrey Skilling, has also been indicted, and his trial is pending. Others associated with the LLCs and LLPs have been indicted; some have entered guilty pleas and some have trials pending.

---

*"The Enron Scandal by the Numbers," *USA Today,* January 22, 2002, p. 3B.
†Complaint, shareholder class action, November 5, 2001, N.D. California. (In possession of author via shareholder.)
‡Ibid.

Tax Consequences

The LLC enjoys the so-called flow-through treatment: The LLC does not pay taxes; income and losses are passed through to the members to be reported on their individual returns. LLC agreements must be drafted carefully to enjoy flow-through status.

Management and Control

Members of an LLC adopt an operating agreement that specifies the voting rights, withdrawal rights and issues, responsibilities of members, and how the LLC is to be managed. The members can agree to manage collectively, delegate authority to one member, or hire an outsider to manage the business.

Transferability of Interest

A member's LLC interest is personal property and is transferable. However, the transferee does not become a member without approval by the majority of members. Members do not hold title to LLC property; the LLC owns the property, and each member has an interest in the LLC that reflects the property's value. Further, the owners of the LLC should structure their LLC and its operation in order to address their tax status issues.

Dissolution and Termination

Most LLC statutes provide that the LLC dissolves upon the withdrawal, death, or expulsion of a member. Some states permit judicial dissolution, and all states permit voluntary dissolution upon unanimous (usually written) consent of the owners.

LLC agreements can dictate terms, timing, and results of dissolution, as well as the rights of withdrawing partners.

LIMITED LIABILITY PARTNERSHIPS

A **limited liability partnership** (LLP) is a partnership with unique statutory protection for all its members.

Formation

Not all states have LLP statutes, but those that do have strict formal requirements for the creation of an LLP. The failure to comply with these requirements results in a general partnership with full personal liability for all the partners. The general requirements for LLP registration are filing (1) the name of the LLP (which must include LLP or Reg LLP); (2) the name of the registered agent; (3) the address; (4) the number of partners; and (5) a description of the business.

Sources of Funding

As in partnerships and limited partnerships, LLP partners make capital contributions.

Liability

In most of the states with LLP statutes, partners are shielded from liability for the negligence, wrongful acts, or misconduct of their partners. Other states provide more extensive protection, such as limited liability even for debts entered into by other partners. In order to attain this liability limitation, some states require, upon registration, evidence of adequate liability insurance. In some states, professional negligence by partners is not covered by the shield from liability.

Tax Consequences

All LLP income is a flow-through or pass-through to partners.

Management and Control

Partners can manage without risking personal liability exposure because the LLP is identified as such and registered with the state.

Transferability

For tax and security regulation reasons, the transferability must be restricted and is generally governed by the same principles of transfer for limited partnerships.

Dissolution and Termination

Causes similar to those for the dissolution of limited partnerships and notification to the state are required.

INTERNATIONAL ISSUES IN BUSINESS STRUCTURE

Global trade has resulted in global business structures, with many companies discovering the benefits of **joint ventures**. A joint venture is a partnership of existing businesses for a limited time or a limited purpose. The existing businesses are then partners for that limited transaction or line of business. The Justice Department has relaxed antitrust merger rules to permit joint ventures so that U.S. firms can compete more effectively internationally. For example, Mobil and Exxon are involved in a joint oil exploration venture in the West Siberian Basin in Russia. The joint venture allows the combination of their experience and financing so that Russian negotiators can be persuaded to contract for the exploration rights.

In an attempt to break into the Japanese toy market, Toys "Я" Us, Inc. entered into a joint venture with McDonald's Co., Ltd., a Japanese toy company with 20 percent of the market. Nestlé and Coca-Cola have formed a joint venture to market ready-to-drink coffees and teas; Nestlé's expertise is in dry goods (instant coffee) and Coca-Cola is a beverage company, so each plans to take advantage of the other's established reputation.

Business structures vary in other countries. In Germany, for example, a public company has both a board of directors and a shareholder advisory committee, which elects the board of directors. It is quite likely, however, that the shareholder advisory committee is composed of shareholders that are large institutional investors (such as banks) or representatives from labor unions.

SUMMARY

What are the various forms of business organization?

- Sole proprietorship—individual ownership and operation of a business
- Partnership—voluntary association of two or more persons as co-owners in a business for profit
- Corporation—an entity formed by statute that has the rights of a legal person along with limited liability for its shareholder owners
- Limited liability company—newer form of business organization in which liability is limited except for conduct that is illegal
- Limited liability partnership—newest form of business organization, in which partners' liability is limited

How is a partnership formed and operated?

- Uniform Partnership Act (UPA)—law on partnerships adopted in forty-nine states
- Revised Uniform Partnership Act (RUPA)—update of partnership law
- Partnership by implication—creation of a partnership by parties' conduct
- Partnership by estoppel—partnership that arises by perception of third parties of its existence
- Dissolution—when partner ceases to be associated with the partnership
- Limited partnership—partnership with two types of partners: general and limited
- General partner—full and personal liability partner
- Limited partner—partner whose personal liability is limited to capital contributions
- Uniform Limited Partnership Act (ULPA)—uniform law adopted in nearly every state
- Revised Uniform Limited Partnership Act (RULPA)—update of limited partnership law
- Advances—partners' loans to partnership

How is a corporation formed and operated?

- Corporation—business organization that is a separate entity with limited liability and full transferability
- Domestic corporation—a corporation is domestic in the state in which its incorporation is filed

- Foreign corporation—category or label for corporation in all states except in state in which it is incorporated
- Professional corporation—entity with limited liability except for malpractice/negligence by its owners
- S corporation—IRS category of corporation with flow-through characteristics
- Model Business Corporation Act (MBCA)—uniform law adopted in approximately one-third of the states
- Articles of incorporation—document filed to organize a corporation
- Common stock—generally most voluminous type of corporate shares and usually allows shareholders to vote
- Preferred stock—ownership interest with priority over common stock
- Corporate veil—liability shield for corporate owners
- Watered shares—failure to pay par value for shares
- Business judgment rule—standard of liability for directors
- Corporate opportunity doctrine—fiduciary responsibility of directors with respect to investments
- Board of directors—policy-setting body of corporations
- Proxy—right to vote for another
- Pooling agreement—shareholder contract to vote a certain way
- Voting trust—separation of legal and equitable title in shares to ensure voting of shares in one way
- Dissenting shareholder—shareholder who objects to merger
- Appraisal rights—value of shares immediately before merger that is paid to dissenting shareholder

How is a limited liability company formed?

- Articles of organization
- Flow-through of income

How is a limited liability partnership formed?

- Register with state
- Flow-through of income
- May need proof of liability insurance

QUESTIONS AND PROBLEMS

1. Gailey, Inc., incorporated in 1980, removed asbestos and mechanical insulation on contract jobs that required union labor. Richard Gailey had been the president, controlling shareholder, and director of Gailey, Inc. from its inception.

Universal Labs, Inc. was incorporated by Mr. Gailey in March 1984 to analyze asbestos samples and air samples and to perform general laboratory work. Mr. Gailey was the sole shareholder of Universal Labs.

As president and director of Gailey, Inc., Mr. Gailey directed Gailey to pay certain debts of Universal Labs. Subsequent to that, $14,500 was provided by Gailey, Inc. to Universal Labs to pay for the latter's start-up expenses and costs.

Gailey, Inc. filed a voluntary petition pursuant to Chapter 11 of the Bankruptcy Code on January 28, 1985. The case was converted to a Chapter 7 proceeding on September 30, 1985.

The trustee in bankruptcy filed suit alleging that Mr. Gailey usurped a corporate business opportunity belonging to Gailey, Inc. when he incorporated Universal Labs. Is the trustee correct? [*In re Gailey, Inc.,* 119 B.R. 504 (Bankr. W.D. Pa. 1990).]

2. Until his death in 1980, Cody Morton, husband of Dormilee Morton, operated a construction business from his home in Salem, Missouri. Upon Mr. Morton's intestate death, Mrs. Morton succeeded to her husband's ownership interest in the business, including ownership of supplies, material, and construction equipment. Steve Morton, their son, took over the operation and management of the construction company with Mrs. Morton contributing the capital assets of business, which consisted of the construction equipment.

From time to time, Mrs. Morton signed bank notes and supporting documents granting security interests in the equipment, designating the borrower as "Dormilee Morton and Steven Morton d/b/a Morton Construction Company." In addition, she also provided funds for the operation of the business. The telephone for the business was situated in Mrs. Morton's home, where she also received the business's mail.

Between 1980 and 1984, Morton Construction Company employed laborers and other persons to construct commercial and residential buildings and was required to withhold federal income and Federal Insurance Contributions Act (FICA) taxes from wages paid to its employees. For the taxable quarters between 1980 and 1984, quarterly federal tax returns and an annual federal unemployment tax return for Morton Construction Company were filed with the IRS in the names of Dormilee Morton and Steven D. Morton, partners, by Steven D. Morton.

As a result of business conditions and difficulties, Morton Construction Company failed to make the required deposits of federal withholding and FICA taxes or otherwise pay the amounts of these taxes to the United States.

The IRS imposed assessments against Dormilee Morton, Steven Morton, and Morton Construction for $44,460.52. Tax liens were filed.

Mrs. Morton asserts that she should not be liable for taxes as she was not a general partner in the business but, at most, a limited partner. In support of this contention, she cites Steven Morton's notation on the appropriate tax forms that Morton Construction Company was a limited partnership and he was the general partner.

Is Mrs. Morton correct? Is she a limited partner? Is she personally liable for the wage taxes? [*United States* v. *Morton,* 682 F. Supp. 999 (E.D. Mo. 1988).]

3. Aztec Enterprises, Inc., was incorporated in Washington with a capital contribution of $500. Aztec's incorporator and sole stockholder was H. B. Hunting. Aztec operated a gravel-hauling business and was plagued with persistent working capital problems. Carl Olson, a frequent source of loans for Aztec, eventually acquired the firm. Mr. Olson, who had no corporate minutes or tax returns, personally paid Aztec's lease fees but did not pay when he had Aztec deliver gravel to his personal construction sites. Mr. Olson never had stock certificates issued to him. Despite annual gross sales of over $800,000, Aztec was unable to pay its debts. Truckweld Equipment Company, a creditor of Aztec, brought suit to pierce the corporate veil and recover its debt from Mr. Olson. Can it pierce the corporate veil? [*Truckweld Equipment Co.* v. *Olson,* 618 P.2d 1017 (Wash. 1980).]

4. The SEC has charged HealthSouth with inflating its earnings by $1.4 billion over a three-year period, with total inflated earnings of $2.5 billion over a decade. The case is the first one brought under the new provisions of Sarbanes-Oxley for financial fraud.

In a federal district court hearing in Alabama in which former CEO Richard Scrushy is asking for the release of $70 million in his funds in order to pay legal fees and living expenses, the following information emerged.
- Two of the company's CFOs and its current CFO have been indicted for fraud.
- CFO William Owen recorded his conversations with Mr. Scrushy at the request of the FBI.
- Mr. Scrushy said on tape to Mr. Owen, "We just need to get those numbers where we want them yo be. You're my guy. You've got the technology and the know-how."

- Mr. Scrushy has sold $175 million in HealthSouth shares since the accounting fraud began.
- Mr. Scrushy's bookkeeper for his personal companies committed suicide in September 2002. His new bookkeeper, Mary Schabacker, indicated that all of Mr. Scrushy's five corporations owe debts to each other, and there is never any intention to repay them.
- HealthSouth stock has been delisted from the NYSE. It was listed at $15 per share one year ago and is worth pennies today.
- Mr. Owen's wife told him that if he kept signing "phony financial statements" that he might go to jail.
- Mr. Scrushy maintains that he knew nothing about the accounting fraud and that Mr. Owens did it all.
- The acting chairman of the HealthSouth board said, "We [directors] really don't know a lot about what has been occuring at the company."
- For seven years, one director was paid a consulting contract of $250,000 per year.
- One director purchased a $395,000 resort property as a partner with Mr. Scrushy.
- One director secured a $5.6 million contract to install glass at a hospital HealthSouth was constructing.
- MedCenterDirect.com had as investors HealthSouth, Mr. Scrushy's private investment company, six of HealthSouth's directors, and the wife of one of the HealthSouth directors.
- HealthSouth directed business to MedCenterDirect.com, almost $174 million last year.
- The audit committee and compensation committee were joint committees made up of the same directors.
- HealthSouth invested $2 million in the Acacia Venture Partners, a venture capital fund founded and run by C. Sage Givens, a director of HealthSouth. When a shareholder questioned her independence as a result, HealthSouth defended her board position.
- Ernst & Young served as HealthSouth's auditor. It earned $1.2 million for financial statement audits and $2.5 million for other services.

Discuss the legal issues that each of these revelations raises. Be sure to cover the changes that Sarbanes-Oxley would impose. Also, refer back to Chapter 9 and determine whether criminal charges could be brought.

For More Information

Anne Berryman, "Ex-Official of HealthSouth Refuses to Answer Questions," *New York Times*, April 12, 2003, p. C2.

Greg Farrell, "Scrushy 'was set up,'" says lawyer," *USA Today*, April 15, 2003, p. 3B.

Greg Farrell, "Tape of ex-HealthSouth CEO Revealed," *USA Today*, April 11, 2003, p. 1B.

JoAnn S. Lublin and Ann Carrns, "Directors Had Lucrative Links At HealthSouth," *Wall Street Journal*, April 11, 2003, pp. B1, B3.

Carrick Mollenkamp, "HealthSouth's Security Chief Calls U.S. Witness 'Distraught,'" *Wall Street Journal*, April 16, 2003, p. A6.

Carrick Mollenkamp and Chad Terhune, "Scrushy Lawyers Dispute U.S. Case," *Wall Street Journal*, April 15, 2003, p. A6.

"Ousted Chief of HealthSouth Resists Questions on His Assets," *New York Times*, April 10, 2003, p. C4.

"Secret Recording Is Played at a HealthSouth Hearing," *New York Times*, April 11, 2003, p. C2.

Jonathan Weil, "Did Ernst Miss Key Fraud Risks At HealthSouth?" *Wall Street Journal*, April 10, 2003, pp. C1, C3.

5. Allan Jones sold a ski shop franchise to Edward Hamilton. Although Mr. Jones did not contribute equity to the business or share in the profits, he did give Mr. Hamilton advice and share his experience to help him get started. Most of Mr. Hamilton's capital came in the form of a loan from Union Bank. When Mr. Hamilton failed to pay, Union Bank sued Mr. Jones for payment under the theory that Mr. Jones was a partner by implication or estoppel. Was he? [*Union Bank* v. *Jones*, 411 A.2d 1338 (Vt. 1980).]

6. Heritage Hills (a land development firm) was organized on July 2, 1975, as a limited partnership, but the partnership agreement was never properly filed. Heritage Hills went bankrupt, and the bankruptcy trustee has sought to recover the debts owed by the partnership from the limited partners. Can he? [*Heritage Hills* v. *Zion's First Nat'l Bank*, 601 F.2d 1023 (9th Cir. 1979).]

7. In June 1985, Carolyn Boose sought the dental services of Dr. George Blakeslee, who proposed to fill two cavities in her teeth. As part of the procedure, he administered nitrous oxide to Ms. Boose. She was rendered semiconscious by the drug and while in this state Dr. Blakeslee lifted her shirt and fondled one of her breasts. He was subsequently charged with, and pled guilty to, the crime of indecent liberties.

Prior to the incident in question, Dr. Blakeslee had incorporated his dental practice as a professional services corporation. He was the corporation's sole shareholder, officer, and director. The corporation thereafter executed an employment agreement with Dr. Blakeslee, who signed the agreement both as an employee of the corporation and as its president.

At the time of the incident in question, Dr. Blakeslee and the corporation were together covered by an insurance policy with Standard Fire Insurance Company that provided general and professional liability coverage. The general liability portion of the policy provided coverage for bodily injury or property damage caused by an "occurrence" arising out of the use of the insured premises. The insurance contract defined "occurrence" as "an accident, including continuous or repeated exposure to conditions, which results in bodily injury or property damage *neither expected or intended by the insured."*

The professional liability portion of the policy limited coverage to damages for "injury . . . arising out of the rendering of or failure to render, during the policy period, professional services by the individual insured, or by any person for whom acts or omissions such insured is legally responsible. . . ."

In November 1985, Ms. Boose commenced an action against Dr. Blakeslee and the professional services corporation for the damages she allegedly sustained as a result of his conduct. Standard subsequently commenced a declaratory judgment action against Ms. Boose and Dr. Blakeslee in order to obtain a declaration of its rights and duties in connection with the lawsuit by Ms. Boose against Dr. Blakeslee and the corporation. All parties moved for summary judgment. The trial court granted judgment to Standard, concluding that it had no duty to defend or indemnify the insured (that is, Dr. Blakeslee and the corporation) against Ms. Boose's claim. Should the corporate veil be pierced to hold Dr. Blakeslee liable? [*Standard Fire Insurance Co.* v. *Blakeslee,* 771 P.2d 1172 (Wash. 1989).]

8. Master Chemical Company of Boston, Massachusetts, manufactured chemicals used primarily in the shoe industry. In 1982, when Master discovered that its underground storage tank filled with toluene was leaking, the two-thousand-gallon tank was emptied. In 1984, Master sold its plant, and the tank was removed.

Goldberg-Zoino & Associates, Inc. (GZA) was hired to do the cleanup, and it hired MacDonald & Watson to do the excavation, transportation, and disposal of the toluene-contaminated soil in the area where the tank had been.

MacDonald & Watson had a permit for liquid waste disposal but none for solid waste disposal. MacDonald & Watson transported nine 25-yard dump-truck loads and one 20-yard load of toluene-contaminated soil to the disposal lot. The Justice Department brought criminal actions against MacDonald & Watson and three of its officers, including Eugene K. D'Allesandro, its president.

Can Mr. D'Allesandro be convicted? [*United States* v. *MacDonald & Watson Waste Oil Co.,* 933 F.2d 35 (1st Cir. 1991).]

9. Johnson & Johnson, Procter & Gamble, and Eastman Kodak have joined together to form a joint venture in order to develop security tags for their products in drug and grocery stores. Shoplifting thefts of drug store items are estimated to be $16 billion per year. The manufacturers point to Pampers, Tylenol, and Preparation H as the most frequently stolen items from stores.

The companies will jointly fund the development of security tags designed to set off alarms at store doors, much as the tags on clothing do today.

What is the liability of the companies as joint venturers on this project?

10. A. W. Ham Jr. served on the board of directors for Golden Nugget, Inc., a Nevada corporation. In 1969, while Mr. Ham was a director and legal counsel for Golden Nugget, he obtained a leasehold interest with an option to purchase in the California Club. The California Club is at 101 Fremont Street, Las Vegas, Nevada, and is located next to a series of properties on which Golden Nugget operates its casinos. Mr. Ham leased the property from his former wife. Golden Nugget was looking for property to expand and had, in fact, been expanding onto other lots in the area. Was there a breach of a corporate opportunity? What if Mr. Ham offers to lease the property to Golden Nugget? [*Ham* v. *Golden Nugget, Inc.,* 589 P.2d 173 (Nev. 1979).]

> ### RESEARCH PROBLEM
>
> **Recovery from Corporate Misdeeds**
>
> **11.** In the Ethical Issues feature on p. 872, the issue of conflicts of interest on the boards of American Express and W. R. Grace was raised. Go to these companies' Web sites (http://www.americanexpress.com and http://www.grace.com, respectively) and evaluate how well these firms have performed over the past five years. Be sure to look at their boards of directors and their policies. After studying these companies and their boards, develop a set of guidelines for selecting board members for a company.

NOTES

1. The questions were actually a resurrection of questions asked by Judge Stanley Sporkin when he was dealing with all of the fraud cases from the savings and loan collapses in the early 1990s. [*Lincoln Savings & Loan Ass'n* v. *Wall,* 743 F. Supp. 901, at 920 (D.D.C. 1990).]

2. The final rules can be found at 17 C.F.R. § 205 (2003).

Securities Law

update

For up-to-date legal news and real-world business applications, click on **update** *at http://jennings.westbuslaw.com*

One of the methods for raising the capital needed for a corporation or partnership is to sell interests in them. Corporations sell shares, and partnerships sell limited partnership interests. Investors provide the capital these businesses need to operate. They give the businesses their money to work with and in return are given an interest in the business. The investors' hope is that the business will give them a profit on their investment (dividends on stock and interest income on bonds and other forms of securities) and that the value of their investment will grow as the business in which they have invested increases in value. The investment arrangement in theory is mutually beneficial. However, because people are so eager to have their money grow and because businesses need money, the interests of business and investors are so often at odds that there seems to be an inherent conflict of interest in the investment relationship. Because of this conflict, there are laws regulating investments at both state and federal levels. These laws, called securities laws, govern everything from the sale of securities to soliciting proxies from owners of securities. This chapter answers these questions: Why do we have securities laws, and what is their history? What requirements affect primary offerings of securities? How do securities laws regulate the secondary market? How do those laws protect shareholders in share and company acquisitions?

October. This is one of the peculiarly dangerous months to speculate stocks in. The others are July, January, September, April, November, May, March, June, December, August and February.

Mark Twain
Pudd'nhead Wilson

Wall Street has only two emotions: fear and greed.

Bill McGowan
CEO of MCI

Total Enforcement Actions by the SEC

YEAR	TOTAL ENFORCEMENT ACTIONS INITIATED
1990	300
1995	490
2000	500
2001	490
2002	600
2003	680

The SEC's annual reports
(http://www.sec.gov; *figures rounded for enforcement actions*)

CONSIDER...

James Herman O'Hagan was a partner in the law firm of Dorsey & Whitney in Minneapolis, Minnesota. In July 1988, Grand Metropolitan PLC, a company based in London, retained Dorsey & Whitney as local counsel to represent it regarding a potential tender offer for common stock of Pillsbury Company.

Mr. O'Hagan did not work on the Grand Met matter, but on August 18, 1988, he began purchasing call options for Pillsbury stock. Each option gave him the right to purchase 100 shares of Pillsbury stock. By the end of September, Mr. O'Hagan owned more than 2,500 Pillsbury options. Also in September, Mr. O'Hagan purchased 5,000 shares of Pillsbury stock at $39 per share.

Grand Met announced its tender offer in October, and Pillsbury stock rose to $60 per share. Mr. O'Hagan sold his call options and made a profit of $4.3 million.

The SEC indicted Mr. O'Hagan on fifty-seven counts of illegal trading on inside information. He says he did nothing wrong. Who is right?

© DIGITAL VISION/GETTY IMAGES

HISTORY OF SECURITIES LAW

Although most people think of the market crash of 1929 as the beginning of securities regulation, regulation actually began nearly twenty years earlier at the state level. In 1911, Kansas passed the first securities law, which regulated the initial sale of securities to members of the public. Some states followed the lead of Kansas, but until 1929 the field of securities was relatively free of regulation.[1]

There was at that time a great deal of speculation in stocks. Investors traded "on margin," which means they borrowed money to invest in stock and when the stock went up in value, they sold it, paid off the loan, and still made money. On a Friday in 1929, however, stock prices dropped on all the exchanges and continued to drop. Investors defaulted on the margin loans, lenders foreclosed on their properties, and the entire country was thrown into a depression.

Review the Securities Act of 1933 and the Securities Exchange Act of 1934:
http://www.law.uc.edu/CCL

Because of the 1929 market crash, Congress perceived a problem with the investment market. As a result, the **Securities Act of 1933** and the **Securities Exchange Act of 1934** were passed, the former to regulate initial sales of stock by businesses and the latter to regulate the secondary trading of stock on the markets. These statutes and their accompanying regulations still govern the sale of securities today.

PRIMARY OFFERING REGULATION: THE 1933 SECURITIES ACT

A **primary offering**—an offering by an issuer, which could be its first, known as an initial public offering (IPO)—is a sale of securities by the business itself. The 1933 act regulates these initial sales of securities.

What Is a Security?

The 1933 act applies only to the sale of **securities**. The language of the act itself is very broad in the definition of "securities" and approximately twenty items are considered securities, including notes; stock; bonds; debentures; warrants; subscriptions; voting-trust certificates; rights to oil, gas, and minerals; and limited partnership interests. Every investment contract that gives the owner evidence of indebtedness or business participation is a security.

In interpreting the application of the 1933 act, the courts have been very liberal. The landmark case on the definition of a security is *SEC v. W. J. Howey Co.*, 328 U.S. 293 (1946). In holding that the sale of interests in Florida citrus groves constituted the sale of securities, the U.S. Supreme Court defined a security as "a contract, transaction, or scheme whereby a person invests his money in a common enterprise and is led to expect profits solely from the efforts of a promoter or a third party." With this even broader definition than the actual 1933 act language, known as the *Howey* **test**, courts have been reluctant to impose restrictions on the definition of a security. In recent years, the only type of arrangement the U.S. Supreme Court has excluded from this definition is an employer pension plan in which employees are not required to make contributions. The exclusion of these plans from securities laws is probably based on the fact that employees are afforded other statutory protections (see Chapter 19 and the discussion of the Employment Retirement Income Security Act).

CONSIDER...   **22.1**

Determine whether general partnership interests would be considered securities for purposes of the 1933 Securities Act.

THINK: The *Howey* definition is that securities are investments in a common enterprise with profits to come from the efforts of others.

APPLY: While partnerships are investments in a common enterprise, we learned in Chapter 21 that each partner is required to contribute work and effort to the partnership. General partners, unless otherwise specified, are not paid salaries for their work and effort in making the partnership work. Because of this obligation to work and the full liability exposure, the results from investing in a partnership do not come primarily from the efforts of others but through the partnership itself.

ANSWER: A general partnership interest is not a security for purposes of the 1933 act.

Now determine whether the following are securities under the 1933 Securities Act.
- Limited partnership interests
- Limited liability company interests
- Limited liability partnership interests
- Oil and gas leases
- Limited partnership in an oil field
- An interest in a real estate investment trust
- Options to buy tickets for the World Series if your team makes it to that point

Regulating Primary Offerings: Registration

Visit the Securities and Exchange Commission:
http://www.sec.gov

The **Securities and Exchange Commission** (SEC) is the administrative agency responsible for regulating the sale of securities under both the 1933 and 1934 acts. The SEC is subject to all of the administrative rules covered in Chapter 6, for it is an administrative agency created in an enabling act of Congress, the 1934 Securities Exchange Act. The SEC can issue injunctions, institute criminal proceedings, enter into consent decrees, handle enforcement, and promulgate rules.

View the structure of the SEC:
http://www.sec.gov/
divisions.shtml

The rules promulgated by the SEC provide the requirements for the registration of securities, financial reporting, and stock exchange operations. The SEC has a complete staff of lawyers, accountants, financial analysts, and other experts to assist in both the review of informational filings and the enforcement of the securities laws.

Regulating Primary Offerings: Exemptions

Unless an **exemption** applies, anyone selling securities must complete certain filing requirements before the securities can be sold legally. There are two types of exemptions: exempt securities and exempt transactions. These exemptions work only for the 1933 act.

Exempt Securities

Certain investments, called **exempt securities**, have been excluded specifically from coverage of the 1933 act. The following is a list of some of the exemptions:

1. Securities (bonds, etc.) issued by federal, state, county, or municipal governments for public purposes

2. Commercial paper (includes notes, checks, and drafts with a maturity date under nine months)

3. Banks, savings and loans, and religious and charitable organizations

4. Insurance policies

5. Annuities

6. Securities of common carriers (those regulated by the Interstate Commerce Commission)

7. Stock dividends and stock splits

8. Charitable bonds

Exempt Transactions

Exempt transactions are more complicated than exempt securities; more details are required to comply with the exempt transaction standards. The following subsections discuss these transaction exemptions, which are summarized in Exhibit 22.1.

The Intrastate Offering Exemption

This exemption exists because the Commerce Clause prohibits the federal government from regulating purely intrastate matters (see Chapter 5 for a full discussion of Commerce Clause issues). To qualify for the intrastate exemption, the investors (offerees) and issuer must all be residents of the same state. (If there is one out-of-state offeree, the exemption will not apply.) Further, the issuer must meet the following requirements:

1. Eighty percent of its assets must be located in the state.

2. Eighty percent of its income must be earned from operations within the state.

3. Eighty percent of the proceeds from the sale must be used on operations within the state.

Under the SEC's Rule 147, there are restrictions on the transfer of exempt intrastate offerings, including a nine-month transfer restriction to state residents only.

Small–Offering Exemption: Regulation A

Examine registration form S–1:
http://www.sec.gov/about/forms/secforms.htm

Although it is not a true exemption, **Regulation A** is a shortcut method of registration. The lengthy, complicated processes of full registration are simplified in that only a short-form registration statement is filed. Regulation A applies to issues of $5 million or less during any twelve-month period.

The SEC groups or "integrates" registration. Three registrations of $2 million each would not qualify for this exemption if issued within one twelve-month period. They would qualify, however, if issued over three years.

Small–Offering Exemption: Regulation D

Review Regulations A and D:
http://www.law.uc.edu/CCL/33ActRls/index.html

Regulation D is the product of the SEC's evaluation of the impact of its rules on the ability of small businesses to raise capital. It was designed to simplify and clarify existing exemptions, expand the availability of exemptions, and achieve uniformity between state and federal exemptions.

Regulation D creates a three-tiered exemption structure that consists of Rules 504, 505, and 506, which permits sales without registration. Sellers are, however, required to file a Form D informational statement about the sale. Rule 501 of Regulation D lists the definitions of various terms used in the three exemptions. For example, an **accredited investor** is any investor who at the time of the sale falls into any of the following categories:

EXHIBIT 22.1 1933 Securities Act Transaction Exemptions

NAME	SIZE LIMITATION	GENERAL SOLICITATION	OFFEREE/ BUYER LIMITATION	RESALE LIMITATION	DISCLOSURE	PUBLIC OFFERING	SEC FILING	TIME
Intrastate exemption, 15 U.S.C. §77(c)(a)(11)	No	No	Buyers must be residents of state of incorporation; triple 80% requirements	Yes, stock transfer restrictions Rule 147— 9 months	No	Yes, in state	No	No restriction
Small-offering or small-issues exemption, 15 U.S.C. §77D, Regulation A	$5,000,000	Yes	Short-form registration required (offering circular)	No	Offering circular	Yes	Short-form	12-month period
Rule 504 Regulation D	$1,000,000* or less (in 12-month period)	Yes	None, unlimited accredited and nonaccredited alike	Yes	No†	Yes	Notice of offering within 15 days of first sale	12-month period
Rule 505, Regulation D	Up to $5,000,000	No	No more than 35, excluding accredited investors	Yes—2 years†	Yes, to non-accredited†	No	Notice of offering (15 days)	12-month period
Rule 506, Regulation D	No	No	Unlimited accredited and 35 nonaccredited investors; (nonaccredited must be sophisticated)	Yes, stock restrictions	Yes, to non-accredited†	No	Notice of offering (15 days)	12-month period
Rule 144 (Private placement)								

*In certain circumstances. $2,000,000 if blue sky registration (504). Up to $7,500,000 if blue sky registration (505).
†Must verify purchaser is buying for himself must have restrictions on shares.

1. Any bank
2. Any private business development company
3. Any director, executive officer, or general partner of the issuer
4. Any person who purchases at least $150,000 of the securities being offered
5. Natural persons whose net worth is greater than $1 million
6. Any natural person who had an individual income in excess of $200,000 in each of the two most recent years or joint income with that person's spouse in excess of $300,000 in each of those years and has a reasonable expectation of reaching the same income level in the current year

Rule 502 places a number of limitations on the means an issuer can use in offering securities. In order to qualify for these exemptions, securities cannot be sold through general advertising or through seminars initiated through advertising. Further, all of the securities sold must be subject to restrictions to prevent the immediate rollover of the securities involved in these exempt transactions.

The three tiers of Regulation D exemptions are as follows.

- The **Rule 504** exemption applies to offerings of $1 million or less (within any twelve-month period). Sales of stock to directors, officers, and employees are not counted in the $1 million limitation. Recent changes permit the use of the Rule 504 exemption in offerings of up to $2 million, provided the offering is registered under a state **blue sky law**.

- The **Rule 505** exemption covers sales of up to $5 million, provided there are no more than thirty-five nonaccredited investors. Again, with state registration, it is possible to take a Rule 505 exemption up to $7.5 million. Issuers qualifying under this exemption cannot engage in public advertising. Also, if the issue is sold to both accredited and nonaccredited investors, the issuer must give all buyers a prospectus.

- The **Rule 506** exemption has no dollar limitation, but the number and type of investors are limited. There can be any number of accredited investors, but the number of nonaccredited investors is limited to thirty-five, and these investors must be sophisticated (capable of evaluating the offering and its risk). Under a Rule 506 exemption, there must be restrictions on the resale of the shares.

Corporate Reorganizations

If a firm is issuing new shares of stock under a Chapter 11 bankruptcy reorganization supervised by a bankruptcy court, registration is not necessary, provided there is court approval for the issue.

What Must Be Filed: Documents and Information for Registration

For information on filing electronically, see:
http://www.abanet.org/buslaw/efss/home.html

If none of the exemptions applies, the offeror of the securities must go through the registration process. The offeror (issuer) must file a **registration statement (S-1)** and sample **prospectus** with the SEC. A prospectus here means the formal document the SEC requires all shareholders to have. However, for purposes of disclosure and misrepresentation issues, a prospectus is any ad or written materials the offeror provides or places.

There is a filing fee based on the aggregate offering price of the sale. The SEC has twenty days to act on the filing, after which the registration statement automatically becomes effective. The SEC, however, always acts within that time period in some fashion. It need not actually approve or disapprove the offering within that time limit so long as a **comment letter** or **deficiency letter** is issued. A new registration, for a first-time offeror, generally takes about six months to get through the SEC. In 2000, a highpoint for the market in terms of both IPOs and securities issuances, the SEC reviewed 3,970 proposed stock offerings, of which 1,350 were IPOs. In 2003, the SEC reviewed only 370 IPOs, an additional 180 stock offerings, and 30 exempt offerings.

The SEC's guide in reviewing the registration materials is the **full-disclosure standard**. The SEC does not pass on the merits of the offering or the soundness of the investment; rather, it simply requires that certain information be supplied. The following information is required in the registration statement:

1. A description of what is being offered, why it is offered, how the securities will fit into the business's existing capital structure, and how the proceeds will be used

2. An audited financial statement

3. A list of corporate assets

4. The nature of the issuer's business

5. A list of those in management and their shares of ownership in the firm

6. Other relevant and material information, such as pending lawsuits

The SEC does not verify the accuracy of the information, only that it is on file.

Before the registration statement is filed, the issuer is very much restricted in what can be done to sell the securities. And even after the registration is filed but is not yet effective, the issuer is restricted.

However, the issuer can run a **tombstone ad**, as shown in Exhibit 22.2, which simply announces that securities will be sold and who will have information—but clearly indicates that the ad is not an offer. Also, before the registration statement becomes effective, the issuer can send out a **red herring prospectus**, which has printed in red at the top that the registration is not yet effective. These red herrings are a way to get out information while waiting for SEC approval.

During this interval between filing and the effective date, there can be no sales and no general advertising. Activity is limited until the date the registration gets SEC approval and becomes effective. Exhibit 22.3 is a diagram of federal securities registration and exemptions.

The SEC permits firms to complete *shelf registrations*. Under this process, a firm completes all the registration requirements and is then free to issue the securities any time within a two-year period, generally when market conditions are most favorable. The company's quarterly and annual filings serve to update the shelf registration. This means of filing was permitted to help corporations raise capital.

Violations of the 1933 Act

Section 11 Violations

Section 11 of the 1933 act imposes civil and criminal liability on those who do not comply with the act's requirements regarding the submission of a registration statement. Section 11 is used when full disclosure has not been made in the registration statement or if any of the information in that registration statement is false. Section 11 is a statutory fraud section that applies to security registrations.

EXHIBIT 22.2 Sample of a Tombstone Ad

This announcement is neither an offer to sell nor a solicitation of offers to buy any of these securities. The offering is made only by the Prospectus, copies of which may be obtained in any State or jurisdiction in which this announcement is circulated only from such of the underwriters as may legally offer these securities in such State.

NEW ISSUE

January 22, 1999

$50,000,000

<allaire>

2,500,000 Shares
Common Stock

NASDAQ Symbol: "ALLR"

Price $20 Per Share

Prior to the offering there had been no public market for these securities. Allaire Corporation develops, markets and supports application development and server software for a wide range of Web development, from building static Web pages to developing high volume, interactive Web applications.

CREDIT SUISSE | FIRST BOSTON

Credit Suisse First Boston

Dain Rauscher Wessels
a division of Dain Rauscher Incorporated
NationsBanc Montgomery Securities LLC

Hambrecht & Quist

Invemed Associates, Inc.

Needham & Company, Inc.

Charles Schwab & Co., Inc.

Tucker Anthony
Incorporated
C.E. Unterberg, Towbin

Wedbush Morgan Securities

What Is Required for a Violation?

For an investor to recover civilly under Section 11, the following elements must be proved.

1. The investor purchased a security that was required to have a registration statement.

2. The registration statement contained a material misstatement or omission.

3. The investor need not show reliance unless the purchase was made over a year after the effective date.

4. The investor experienced a loss.

EXHIBIT 22.3 Federal Securities Registration and Exemptions

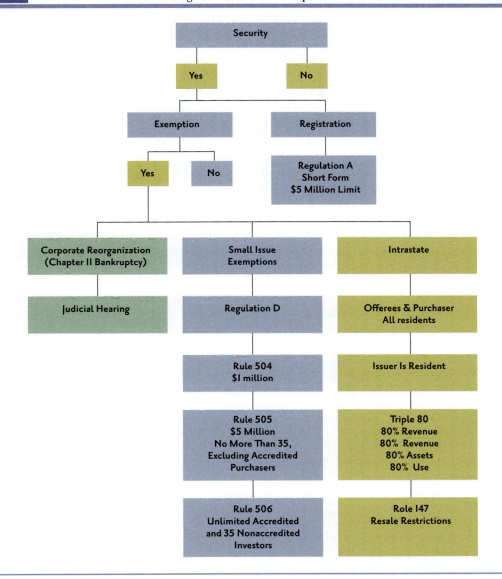

Who Is Liable?

Liability under Section 11 attaches to all individuals who signed the registration statement—each director and officer of the issuing corporation and every account- ant, engineer, appraiser, attorney, geologist, or other expert whose input was used in the preparation of the statement. Underwriters are also included as potential de- fendants. Experts (such as accountants, engineers, appraisers, lawyers) are liable only for the information they provided. Directors and officers are jointly and sever- ally liable under Section 11.

Defenses for Section 11 Violations

Several defenses are available to defendants. Proof of these defenses is the burden of the defendants.

1. *Immateriality.* Because proving that a **material misstatement** or omission was made is part of the investor's case, proving that the statement or omission was immaterial is a valid defense. The standards for what is or is not material are basically the same standards used in contract misrepresentation cases.

2. *Investor knowledge.* If the investor knew of the misstatement or omission and purchased the stock anyway, there is no Section 11 liability. Section 11 defendants can offer proof of knowledge of the investor to establish a defense.

3. *Due diligence.* The **due diligence** defense is one that allows defendants (non-issuers) to show that they were acting reasonably in preparing and signing the registration statement. The experts are required to show that they acted within the standards of their profession in preparing their portions of the registration statement. Officers and directors are required to show that they had no reason to suspect or had no knowledge of an omission or misstatement.

Due Diligence and Sarbanes–Oxley

Sarbanes-Oxley imposed new requirements on auditors as experts for certification of financial reports that are to be part of both securities offerings under the 1933 act and annual financial reports under the 1934 act. One of the concerns reflected in Sarbanes-Oxley's provisions was that auditors were not exercising sufficient discretion and independence in conducting audits of their clients. Sarbanes-Oxley takes several steps to increase the auditor's independence while conducting audits of company financial records.

Public Company Accounting Oversight Board   The first section of Sarbanes-Oxley creates a new Public Company Accounting Oversight Board (PCAOB, often referred to as Peek-a-Boo) that will be responsible for promoting high professional standards among auditors. PCAOB, which will consist of five presidential appointees, will not be a governmental body but rather a nonprofit organization with its own budgeting and staffing authority. No more than two members of PCAOB can be CPAs, and members operate on a full-time basis. PCAOB will have the following responsibilities:

- Developing a registration system for public accounting firms that prepare audit reports for companies that issue securities
- Establishing rules to ensure audit quality, ethics, and auditor independence
- Conducting inspections of public accounting firms to determine their compliance with Sarbanes-Oxley requirements
- Investigating violations and imposing disciplinary sanctions where necessary for members of the profession
- Encouraging the highest professional standards among public accounting firms and auditors

Registration with PCAOB   Any public accounting firm that conducts audits for companies that issue securities must register with PCAOB. That registration will require the accounting firm to disclose all the companies for which it has done audits and the fees it was paid, and for both its audit of the company as well as its nonaudit fees commonly referred to as "consulting services," from that company.

The registration also requires the accounting firm to disclose any sanctions and pending civil or criminal proceedings against it along with its policies and procedures for quality control in audits.

PCAOB will then approve accounting firms for continued work in the audit of securities issuers. That approval or denial must be made within forty-five days following the accounting firm's filing of its annual registration statement.

Auditor Independence   In many of the companies that experienced financial collapse prior to Sarbanes-Oxley, there was a clear pattern of a lack of independence by the auditors issuing the certified financial statements. In other words, the auditors had conflicts that may have tainted their independent judgment on accounting issues with the company or even on whether the company was a viable entity. For example, many of the audit firms received substantial fees for management consulting services they performed for the companies for which they were providing certified statements. For example, Arthur Andersen received $21 million annually for its audit work with Enron but $29 million for its consulting services. The desire to maintain the consulting contract created a conflict with the accounting firm's ability to make honest calls and decisions on its audit work.

To help eliminate conflicts of interest, Sarbanes-Oxley now prohibits certain activities by audit firms for their audit clients. The specific section of Sarbanes-Oxley prohibits:

1. Bookkeeping or other services related to the accounting records or financial statements of the audit client

2. Financial information systems design and implementation

3. Appraisal or valuation services, fairness opinions, or contribution-in-kind reports

4. Actuarial services

5. Internal audit outsourcing services

6. Management functions or human resources

7. Broker or dealer, investment adviser, or investment banking services

8. Legal services and expert services unrelated to the audit

9. Any other service that PCAOB determines, by regulation, is impermissible

All nonaudit services to be conducted by the auditor for its audit client (except those listed above as expressly prohibited) require prior approval by PCAOB.

In addition, to ensure that audit partners do not become entrenched, Sarbanes-Oxley requires audit firms to change audit partners at least once every five years. The specific statutory section provides:

> *It shall be unlawful for a registered public accounting firm to provide audit services to an issuer if the lead (or coordinating) audit partner (having primary responsibility for the audit), or the audit partner responsible for reviewing the audit, has performed audit services for that issuer in each of the 5 previous fiscal years of that issuer.*

The rotation of the audit partner in charge of a company account brings a new perspective to the issues in the financial systems and reports and also helps eliminate the bias of close, personal relationships that develop over long-standing working relationships.

Sarbanes-Oxley also requires accounting firms to set up internal systems for developing and monitoring professional ethics and for discussing ethical issues that arise while auditing clients.

Escott v. *BarChris Constr. Corp.* (Case 22.1) is the leading case on Section 11 liability. It involves a variety of defendants, including an accounting firm and audit partners, and discusses the defense of due diligence.

CASE 22.1

Escott v. BarChris Constr. Corp.
283 F. Supp. 643 (S.D.N.Y. 1958)

Bowling for Fraud: Right Up Our Alley

FACTS

BarChris was a bowling alley company established in 1946. The bowling industry grew rapidly when automatic pin resetters went on the market in the mid-1950s. BarChris began a program of rapid expansion and in 1960 was responsible for the construction of over 3 percent of all bowling alleys in the United States. BarChris used two methods of financing the construction of these alleys, both of which substantially drained the company's cash flow.

In 1959 BarChris sold approximately one-half million shares of common stock. By 1960, its cash flow picture was still troublesome, and it sold debentures. The debenture issue was registered with the SEC, approved, and sold. In spite of the cash boost from the sale, BarChris was still experiencing financial difficulties and declared bankruptcy in October 1962. The debenture holders were not paid their interest; BarChris defaulted.

The purchasers of the BarChris debentures brought suit under Section 11 of the 1933 act. They claimed that the registration statement filed by BarChris contained false information and failed to disclose certain material information. Their suit, which centered around the audited financial statements prepared by a CPA firm, claimed that the statements were inaccurate and full of omissions. The following chart summarizes the problems with the financial statements submitted with the registration statements.

1. *1960 Earnings*

   (a) *Sales*

Per prospectus	$9,165,320
Correct figure	8,511,420
Overstatement	$ 653,900

   (b) *Net Operating Income*

Per prospectus	$1,742,801
Correct figure	1,496,196
Overstatement	$ 246,605

   (c) *Earnings per Share*

Per prospectus	$ .75
Correct figure	.65
Overstatement	$ .10

2. *1960 Balance Sheet*

   Current Assets

Per prospectus	$4,524,021
Correct figure	3,914,332
Overstatement	$ 609,689

3. *Contingent Liabilities as of December 31, 1960, on Alternative Method of Financing*

Per prospectus	$ 750,000
Correct figure	1,125,795
Understatement	$ 375,795
Capitol Lanes should have been shown as a direct liability	$ 325,000

4. *Contingent Liabilities as of April 30, 1961*

Per prospectus	$ 825,000
Correct figure	1,443,853
Understatement	$ 618,853
Capitol Lanes should have been shown as a direct liability	$ 314,166

5. *Earnings Figures for Quarter Ending March 31, 1961*

   (a) *Sales*

Per prospectus	$2,138,455
Correct figure	1,618,645
Overstatement	$ 519,810

   (b) *Gross Profit*

Per prospectus	$ 483,121
Correct figure	252,366
Overstatement	$ 230,755

6. *Backlog as of March 31, 1961*

Per prospectus	$6,905,000
Correct figure	2,415,000
Overstatement	$4,490,000

7. *Failure to Disclose Officers' Loans Outstanding and Unpaid on May 16, 1961* $386,615

8. *Failure to Disclose Use of Proceeds in Manner Not Revealed in Prospectus: Approx.* $1,160,000

9. *Failure to Disclose Customers' Delinquencies in May 1961 and BarChris's Potential Liability with Respect Thereto: Over* $1,350,000

10. *Failure to Disclose the Fact that BarChris Was Already Engaged and Was About to Be More Heavily Engaged in the Operation of Bowling Alleys*

The federal district court reviewed all of the exhibits and statements included in the prospectus and dealt with each defendant individually in issuing its decisions. The defendants consisted of those officers and directors who signed the registration statement, the underwriters of the debenture offering, the auditors (Peat, Marwick, Mitchell & Co.), and BarChris's attorneys and directors.

JUDICIAL OPINION

McLEAN, District Judge

Russo. Russo was, to all intents and purposes, the chief executive officer of BarChris. He was a member of the executive committee. He was familiar with all aspects of the business. He was personally in charge of dealings with the factors. He acted on BarChris's behalf in making the financing agreement with Talcott and he handled the negotiations with Talcott in the spring of 1961. He talked with customers about their delinquencies.

Russo prepared the list of jobs which went into the backlog figure. He knew the status of those jobs.

It was Russo who arranged for the temporary increase in BarChris's cash in banks on December 31, 1960, a transaction which borders on the fraudulent. He was thoroughly aware of BarChris's stringent financial condition in May 1961. He had personally advanced large sums to BarChris of which $175,000 remained unpaid as of May 16.

In short, Russo knew all the relevant facts. He could not have believed that there were no untrue statements or material omissions in the prospectus. Russo has no due diligence defenses.

Vitolo and Pugliese. They were the founders of the business who stuck with it to the end. Vitolo was president and Pugliese was vice president. Despite their titles, their field of responsibility in the administration of BarChris's affairs during the period in question seems to have been less all-embracing than Russo's. Pugliese in particular appears to have limited his activities to supervising the actual construction work. Vitolo and Pugliese are each men of limited education. It is not hard to believe that for them the prospectus was difficult reading, if indeed they read it at all.

But whether it was or not is irrelevant. The liability of a director who signs a registration statement does not depend upon whether or not he read it or, if he did, whether or not he understood what he was reading.

And in any case, Vitolo and Pugliese were not as naive as they claim to be. They were members of BarChris's executive committee. At meetings of that committee BarChris's affairs were discussed at length. They must have known what was going on. Certainly they knew of the inadequacy of cash in 1961. They knew of their own large advances to the company which remained unpaid. They knew that they had agreed not to deposit their checks until the financing proceeds were received. They knew and intended that part of the proceeds were to be used to pay their own loans.

All in all, the position of Vitolo and Pugliese is not significantly different, for present purposes, from Russo's. They could not have believed that the registration statement was wholly true and that no material facts had been omitted. And in any case, there is nothing to show that they made any investigation of anything which they may not have known about or understood. They have not proved their due diligence defenses.

Kircher. Kircher was treasurer of BarChris and its chief financial officer. He is a certified public accountant and an intelligent man. He was thoroughly familiar with BarChris's financial affairs. He knew the terms of BarChris's agreements with Talcott. He knew of the customers' delinquency problems. He participated actively with Russo in May 1961 in the successful effort to hold Talcott off until the financing proceeds came in. He knew how the financing proceeds were to be applied and he saw to it that they were so applied. He arranged the officers' loans and he knew all the facts concerning them.

Moreover, as a member of the executive committee, Kircher was kept informed as to those branches of the business of which he did not have direct charge. He knew about the operation of alleys, present and prospective. In brief, Kircher knew all the relevant facts.

Knowing the facts, Kircher had reason to believe that the expertised portion of the prospectus, i.e., the 1960 figures, was in part incorrect. He could not shut his eyes to the facts and rely on Peat, Marwick for that portion.

As to the rest of the prospectus, knowing the facts, he did not have a reasonable ground to believe it to be true. On the contrary, he must have known that in part it was untrue. Under these circumstances, he was not entitled to sit back and place the blame on the lawyers for not advising him about it. Kircher has not proved his due diligence defenses.

Trilling. Trilling's position is somewhat different from Kircher's. He was BarChris's controller. He signed the registration statement in that capacity, although he was not a director.

Trilling entered BarChris's employ in October 1960. He was Kircher's subordinate. When Kircher asked him for information, he furnished it. On at least one occasion he got it wrong.

Trilling may well have been unaware of several of the inaccuracies in the prospectus. But he must have known of some of them. As a financial officer, he was familiar with BarChris's finances and with its books of account. He knew that part of the cash on deposit on December 31, 1960, had been procured temporarily by Russo for window dressing purposes. He should have

continued

known, although perhaps through carelessness he did not know at the time, that BarChris's contingent liability was greater than the prospectus stated. In the light of these facts, I cannot find that Trilling believed the entire prospectus to be true.

But even if he did, he still did not establish his due diligence defenses. He did not prove that as to the parts of the prospectus expertised by Peat, Marwick he had no reasonable ground to believe that it was untrue. He also failed to prove, as to the parts of the prospectus not expertised by Peat, Marwick, that he made a reasonable investigation which afforded him a reasonable ground to believe that it was true. As far as appears, he made no investigation. As a signer, he could not avoid responsibility by leaving it up to others to make it accurate. Trilling did not sustain the burden of proving his due diligence defenses.

Birnbaum. Birnbaum was a young lawyer, admitted to the bar in 1957, who, after brief periods of employment by two different law firms and an equally brief period of practicing in his own firm, was employed by BarChris as house counsel and assistant secretary in October 1960. Unfortunately for him, he became secretary and director of BarChris on April 17, 1961, after the first version of the registration statement had been filed with the Securities and Exchange Commission. He signed the later amendments, thereby becoming responsible for the accuracy of the prospectus in its final form.

It seems probable that Birnbaum did not know of many of the inaccuracies in the prospectus. He must, however, have appreciated some of them. In any case, he made no investigation and relied on the others to get it right. Unlike Trilling, he was entitled to rely upon Peat, Marwick for the 1960 figures, for as far as appears, he had no personal knowledge of the company's books of account or financial transactions. As a lawyer, he should have known his obligations under the statute. He should have known that he was required to make a reasonable investigation of the truth of all the statements in the unexpertised portion of the document which he signed. Having failed to make such an investigation, he did not have reasonable ground to believe that all these statements were true. Birnbaum has not established his due diligence defenses except as to the audited 1960 exhibits.

Auslander. Auslander was an "outside" director, i.e., one who was not an officer of BarChris. He was chairman of the board of Valley Stream National Bank in Valley Stream, Long Island. In February 1961 Vitolo asked him to become a director of BarChris. As an inducement, Vitolo said that when BarChris received the proceeds of a forthcoming issue of securities, it would deposit $1 million in Auslander's bank.

Auslander was elected a director on April 17, 1961. The registration statement in its original form had al-

ready been filed, of course without his signature. On May 10, 1961, he signed a signature page for the first amendment to the registration statement which was filed on May 11, 1961. This was a separate sheet without any document attached. Auslander did not know that it was a signature page for a registration statement. He vaguely understood that it was something "for the SEC."

Auslander attended a meeting of BarChris's directors on May 15, 1961. At that meeting he, along with the other directors, signed the signature sheet for the second amendment which constituted the registration statement in its final form. Again, this was only a separate sheet without any document attached.

Auslander never saw a copy of the registration statement in its final form. It is true that Auslander became a director on the eve of the financing. He had little opportunity to familiarize himself with the company's affairs.

Section 11 imposes liability in the first instance upon a director, no matter how new he is.

Peat, Marwick. Peat, Marwick's work was in general charge of a member of the firm, Cummings, and more immediately in charge of Peat, Marwick's manager, Logan. Most of the actual work was performed by a senior accountant, Berardi, who had junior assistants, one of whom was Kennedy.

Berardi was then about thirty years old. He was not yet a CPA. He had had no previous experience with the bowling industry. This was his first job as a senior accountant. He could hardly have been given a more difficult assignment.

After obtaining a little background information on BarChris by talking to Logan and reviewing Peat, Marwick's work papers on its 1959 audit, Berardi examined the results of test checks of BarChris's accounting procedures which one of the junior accountants had made, and he prepared an "internal control questionnaire" and an "audit program." Thereafter, for a few days subsequent to December 30, 1960, he inspected BarChris's inventories and examined certain alley construction. Finally, on January 13, 1961, he began his auditing work which he carried on substantially continuously until it was completed on February 24, 1961. Toward the close of the work, Logan reviewed it and made various comments and suggestions to Berardi.

It is unnecessary to recount everything that Berardi did in the course of the audit. We are concerned only with the evidence relating to what Berardi did or did not do with respect to those items found to have been incorrectly reported in the 1960 figures in the prospectus.

Accountants should not be held to a standard higher than that recognized in their profession. I do not do so here. Berardi's review did not come up to that standard. He did not take some of the steps which Peat,

Marwick's written program prescribed. He did not spend an adequate amount of time on a task of this magnitude. Most important of all, he was too easily satisfied with glib answers to his inquiries.

This is not to say that he should have made a complete audit. But there were enough danger signals in the materials which he did examine to require some further investigation on his part. Generally accepted accounting standards required such further investigation under these circumstances. It is not always sufficient merely to ask questions.

CASE QUESTIONS

1. How much time transpired between the sale of the debentures and BarChris's bankruptcy?
2. Did BarChris disclose the amount of delinquent debts?
3. Who was sued under Section 11?
4. Were all of the misstatements or omissions material?
5. Who was held liable?

Penalties for Violations of Section 11

Violations of Section 11 carry maximum penalties of $10,000 and/or five years imprisonment. In addition, the SEC has the authority to bring suit seeking an injunction to stop sales based on false or omitted information in the registration statement. Purchasers harmed by the false or omitted statements have a right of civil suit in federal district court for recovery of their losses and other damages.

The nature of the levels of damages and the certainty of recovery of awards led to large numbers of sizable class action suits under Section 11. In 1995, Congress passed, over a presidential veto, the Private Securities Litigation Reform Act of 1995, which is the first major change to the 1933 Securities Act since its enactment.

This detailed act contains provisions that limit attorneys' fees to a reasonable percentage of the amount recovered or the agreed-upon settlement amount. The problem of "professional plaintiffs" was also addressed through a section that prevents a plaintiff from being named in more than five class action securities lawsuits in a three-year period.

Despite the intent of this 1995 statute, by 1998, additional congressional hearings established that although the federal restrictions on class actions were effective, class actions had simply shifted to state courts. In late 1998, Congress passed the Securities Litigation Uniform Standards Act to establish uniform requirements for bringing class actions in all courts (state or federal).

One final portion of the 1995 reform of the act is the so-called safe-harbor protection. With certain precautions and qualifications, companies can now make forward-looking predictions for company performance in materials given to investors without the automatic liability that resulted formerly if future events were even addressed.

Sarbanes-Oxley lengthened the statute of limitations under the 1933 act. The time for bringing a suit was changed from one year from the time of the discovery of a material misstatement in the registration statement and a maximum of three years from the time of the offering by the underwriters to two years from the time of discovery and a maximum of five years from the time of the offering.

Section 12 Violations

Section 12 carries the same criminal penalties as Section 11 and covers the following offenses.

1. Selling securities without registration and without an exemption.
2. Selling securities before the effective date of the registration statement.
3. Selling securities using false information in the prospectus. (In this case, "prospectus" includes not only the formal document but all ads, circulars, and so on used in the sale of securities.)

The SEC also has injunctive remedies here, and buyers also have the right of civil suit. The same defenses as those for Section 11 apply to Section 12.

THE SECURITIES EXCHANGE ACT OF 1934

The **Securities Exchange Act of 1934** regulates securities and their issuers once they are on the market. Securities sales, brokers, dealers, and exchanges are all regulated under the 1934 act. In addition, the act requires public disclosure of financial information for certain corporations. In effect, the 1934 act is responsible for the regulation of the securities marketplace. The SEC accomplishes its goal of regulating undesirable market practices in several ways, which are discussed in the following sections.

Securities Registration

Under the 1934 act, all securities traded on a national stock exchange must be registered. In addition, any issuer with over $10 million in assets and 500 or more shareholders must register its equity stock (not bonds) under the 1934 act if those shares are traded in interstate commerce. This registration is in addition to all the filing requirements for issuing discussed under the 1933 act.

Periodic Filing

Search the SEC's EDGAR (Electronic Data Gathering, Analysis, and Retrieval) database for corporate 10-Q, 10-K, and 8-K filings:
http://www.sec.gov/edgar.shtml

In addition to the one-time registration required under the 1934 act, those same companies (national stock exchange companies or those with 500 or more shareholders and $10 million in assets) must comply with the periodic reporting requirements imposed by the SEC. Each quarter, these firms must file a **10-Q form**, which is basically a quarterly financial report. An annual report, the **10-K form**, must be filed by the company at the end of its fiscal year. Any unusual events—bankruptcies, spin-offs, takeovers, and other changes in company control—must be reported on the **8-K form**.

Certifications of the Periodic Filings under Sarbanes–Oxley
Sarbanes-Oxley chose direct and personal accountability as one tool for improving the accuracy of periodic reports from publicly traded companies. Under Sarbanes-Oxley's provisions, both the CEO and the CFO must provide written certification of the 10-Q and 10-K reports issued by their companies. When the CEO and CFO certify a periodic report, they are, by statute, stating the following.

- They have reviewed the report.
- Based on their knowledge, the report contains no untrue statements, has no omissions of fact, and includes nothing misleading.
- Based on their knowledge, the financial statements included with the periodic reports fairly present all material aspects of the company's financial performance.
- They are responsible for establishing, maintaining, and certifying internal controls for the financial operations and reporting of the company.

If information in these reports contains a "knowing" misrepresentation, the penalty is up to a $1 million fine and/or ten years imprisonment. If there is a willful misrepresentation in the reports, the penalty is up to $5 million and/or twenty years [18 U.S.C. §1350(c)].

These new requirements have resulted in SEC recommendations in order to ensure that the officers can certify the reports. For example, the SEC recommends that each company establish a disclosure committee to evaluate whether the requirement of fair and material disclosure is met with the financial statements to be certified and then released. A committee structure may help others raise issues and encourage discussion and dissent, something not readily present in companies such as Enron and WorldCom.

These new certification requirements were passed to curb the tendency of companies, especially during the dot-com bubble, to rely on pro forma financial statements. These statements were not developed according to GAAP principles and did not, for the most part, provide a full and accurate picture of the company's true financial picture. If a company wishes to present non-GAAP financial reports, it may do so under the law, but the non-GAAP measures must be presented with GAAP measures so that investors and shareholders can compare, with some degree of reliance, the numbers offered.

If a CEO or CFO certifies financial statements in violation of these provisions, the penalties are $1 million and/or ten years imprisonment.

The Antifraud Provision

Review the rules promulgated under the Securities Exchange Act of 1934:
http://www.law.uc.edu/ CCL/34ActRls/index.html

In addition to regulating the reporting of information, the 1934 act regulates the propriety of sales in the marketplace. **Section 10(b)** and **Rule 10b-5** are the antifraud provisions of the 1934 act. These sections are statutory versions of common law fraud. If the idea of the free market is to work, all buyers and sellers must have access to the same information. To withhold information is to commit fraud and is a violation of Section 10(b). The language of Rule 10b-5 follows:

> *It shall be unlawful for any person, directly or indirectly, by use of any means or instrumentality of interstate commerce, or of the mails, or of any facility of any national securities exchange,*
> > *(1) to employ any device, scheme, or artifice to defraud,*
> > *(2) to make any untrue statement of a material fact or to omit to state a material fact necessary in order to make the statement made, in the light of the circumstances under which they were made, not misleading, or*
> > *(3) to engage in any act, practice, or course of business which operates or would operate as a fraud or deceit upon any person, in connection with the purchase or sale of any security.*

Application of Section 10(b)

Of all the provisions of the 1934 act, Section 10(b) has the broadest application. It applies to all sales of securities: exempt, stock-exchange-listed, over-the-counter, public, private, small, and large. The only prerequisite for 10(b) application is that interstate commerce be involved in the sales transaction. As Chapter 5 indicates, it is not difficult to find an interstate commerce connection; for example, if the mails or phones were used in the transaction, 10(b) applies. The practical effect is that 10(b) applies to all sales of securities.

Proof of Section 10(b) Violation

The language of 10(b) does not really specify what constitutes an offense of misrepresentation. Determination of 10(b) violations has been left to the SEC and the courts, which have shown that violations of 10(b) can take a variety of forms. In its simplest form, a 10(b) violation occurs when a seller has information not generally available to the public and sells his shares without disclosing that information to the buyer. For example, a seller who knows of a pending merger (something that

*For information on material
information disclosures,
visit the SEC site:*
http://www.sec.gov

causes a jump in share price), when the rest of the investing public does not, and sells his shares to an unwitting buyer without disclosure of the pending merger commits a 10(b) violation. If an owner of shares gives a buyer false or misleading information, the owner-seller is liable under 10(b). Market manipulations in which brokers buy and sell stock in wash or cover sales in an effort to create the appearance of activity are also covered under 10(b). Churning, in which shares are sold for the sake of commissions or the appearance of activity, and "pump and dump" (see below) are examples of 10(b) violations in this category. Finally, if a corporation releases false information about dividends, company growth, or earnings, purchasers and sellers of the corporate stock would have a 10(b) action against corporate management and directors.

One of the most famous 10(b) cases is *SEC* v. *Texas Gulf Sulphur Co.*, 401 F.2d 833 (2d Cir. 1968). In that case, Texas Gulf Sulphur was involved in test-drilling operations in Canada. Early tests indicated that the company would make a substantial strike. Press releases did not indicate the richness of the strike. Corporate officers, geologists, and relatives bought stock before the richness of the find was finally disclosed, and the price of the stock soared. The court found that the overly pessimistic press release was misleading under 10(b) and held the purchasers liable. Sarbanes-Oxley's reforms focused on this form of 10(b) violations because the release of financial reports that contain manipulated results constitutes a 10(b) violation. These overly optimistic financial reports result in manipulation of the market price and, as a result, the market.

Coverage of Section 10(b)

Anyone who has access to information not readily available to the public is covered under 10(b). Officers, directors, and large shareholders are included in this group. However, 10(b) also applies to people who get information from these corporate **insiders**. These people are called **tippees**. For example, relatives of officers and directors would be considered tippees if they were given nonpublic information.

Who is covered under Section 10(b) has been a critical question during the past few years. The Supreme Court has made a distinction between true insiders and those who misappropriate information. *United States* v. *O'Hagan* (Case 22.2) is the most recent U.S. Supreme Court ruling on 10(b) and misappropriation. The case answers the chapter's opening Consider.

CASE 22.2

United States v. *O'Hagan*
521 U.S. 657 (1997)

Pillsbury Dough Boy:
The Lawyer/Insider Who Cashed In

FACTS

James Herman O'Hagan (respondent) was a partner in the law firm of Dorsey & Whitney in Minneapolis, Minnesota. In July 1988, Grand Metropolitan PLC (Grand Met), a company based in London, retained Dorsey & Whitney as local counsel to represent it regarding a potential tender offer for common stock of Pillsbury Company (based in Minneapolis).

Mr. O'Hagan did no work on the Grand Met matter, but on August 18, 1988, he began purchasing call options for Pillsbury stock. Each option gave him the right to purchase 100 shares of Pillsbury stock. By the end of September, Mr. O'Hagan owned more than 2,500 Pillsbury options. Also in September, Mr. O'Hagan purchased 5,000 shares of Pillsbury stock at $39 per share.

Grand Met announced its tender offer in October,

and Pillsbury stock rose to $60 per share. Mr. O'Hagan sold his call options and made a profit of $4.3 million.

The SEC indicted Mr. O'Hagan on 57 counts of illegal trading on inside information, including mail fraud, securities fraud, fraudulent trading, and money laundering. The SEC alleged that Mr. O'Hagan used his profits from the Pillsbury options to conceal his previous embezzlement and conversion of his clients' trust funds. Mr. O'Hagan was convicted by a jury on all 57 counts and sentenced to 41 months in prison. A divided Court of Appeals reversed the conviction, and the SEC appealed.

JUDICIAL OPINION

GINSBURG, Justice

We hold, in accord with several other Courts of Appeals, that criminal liability under § 10(b) may be predicated on the misappropriation theory.

Under the "traditional" or "classical theory" of insider trading liability, § 10(b) and Rule 10b-5 are violated when a corporate insider trades in the securities of his corporation on the basis of material, nonpublic information. Trading on such information qualifies as a "deceptive device" under § 10(b), we have affirmed, because "a relationship of trust and confidence [exists] between the shareholders of a corporation and those insiders who have obtained confidential information by reason of their position with that corporation." *Chiarella* v. *United States,* 445 U.S. 222, 228 (1980). That relationship, we recognized, "gives rise to a duty to disclose [or to abstain from trading] because of the 'necessity of preventing a corporate insider from . . . tak[ing] unfair advantage of . . . uninformed . . . stockholders.'" The classical theory applies not only to officers, directors, and other permanent insiders of a corporation, but also to attorneys, accountants, consultants, and others who temporarily become fiduciaries of a corporation. See *Dirks* v. *SEC,* 463 U.S. 646, 655, n. 14 (1983).

The "misappropriation theory" holds that a person commits fraud "in connection with" a securities transaction, and thereby violates § 10(b) and Rule 10b-5, when he misappropriates confidential information for securities trading purposes, in breach of a duty owed to the source of the information. Under this theory, a fiduciary's undisclosed, self-serving use of a principal's information to purchase or sell securities, in breach of a duty of loyalty and confidentiality, defrauds the principal of the exclusive use of that information. In lieu of premising liability on a fiduciary relationship between company insider and purchaser or seller of the company's stock, the misappropriation theory premises liability on a fiduciary-turned-trader's deception of those who entrusted him with access to confidential information.

The two theories are complementary, each addressing efforts to capitalize on nonpublic information through the purchase or sale of securities. The classical theory targets a corporate insider's breach of duty to shareholders with whom the insider transacts; the misappropriation theory outlaws trading on the basis of nonpublic information by a corporate "outsider" in breach of a duty owed not to a trading party, but to the source of the information. The misappropriation theory is thus designed to "protec[t] the integrity of the securities markets against abuses by 'outsiders' to a corporation who have access to confidential information that will affect th[e] corporation's security price when revealed, but who owe no fiduciary or other duty to that corporation's shareholders."

We agree with the Government that misappropriation, as just defined, satisfies § 10(b)'s requirement that chargeable conduct involve a "deceptive device or contrivance" used "in connection with" the purchase or sale of securities. We observe, first, that misappropriators, as the Government describes them, deal in deception. A fiduciary who "[pretends] loyalty to the principal while secretly converting the principal's information for personal gain" "dupes" or defrauds the principal.

Deception through nondisclosure is central to the theory of liability for which the Government seeks recognition.

Here, by contrast, Rule 10b-5's promulgation has not been challenged; we consider only the Government's charge that O'Hagan's alleged fraudulent conduct falls within the prohibitions of the rule and § 10(b). In this context, we acknowledge simply that, in defending the Government's interpretation of the rule and statute in this Court, the Government's lawyers have pressed a solid point too far, something lawyers, occasionally even judges, are wont to do.

The misappropriation theory comports with § 10(b)'s language, which requires deception "in connection with the purchase or sale of any security," not deception of an identifiable purchaser or seller. The theory is also well-tuned to an animating purpose of the Exchange Act: to insure honest securities markets and thereby promote investor confidence. Although informational disparity is inevitable in the securities markets, investors likely would hesitate to venture their capital in a market where trading based on misappropriated nonpublic information is unchecked by law. An investor's informational disadvantage vis-a-vis a misappropriator with material, nonpublic information stems from contrivance, not luck; it is a disadvantage that cannot be overcome with research or skill.

In sum, considering the inhibiting impact on market participation of trading on misappropriated

continued

information, and the congressional purposes underlying § 10(b), it makes scant sense to hold a lawyer like O'Hagan a § 10(b) violator if he works for a law firm representing the target of a tender offer, but not if he works for a law firm representing the bidder. The text of the statute requires no such result. The misappropriation at issue here was properly made the subject of a § 10(b) charge because it meets the statuary requirement that there be "deceptive" conduct "in connection with" securities transactions.

In sum, the misappropriation theory, as we have examined and explained it in this opinion, is both consistent with the statute and with our precedent. Vital to our decision that criminal liability may be sustained under the misappropriation theory, we emphasize, are two sturdy safeguards Congress has provided regarding scienter. To establish a criminal violation of Rule 10b-5, the Government must prove that a person "willfully" violated the provision. Furthermore, a defendant may not be imprisoned for violating Rule 10b-5 if he proves that he had no knowledge of the rule. O'Hagan's charge that the misappropriation theory is too indefinite to permit the imposition of criminal liability thus fails not only because the theory is limited to those

who breach a recognized duty. In addition, the statute's "requirement of the presence of culpable intent as a necessary element of the offense does much to destroy any force in the argument that application of the [statute]" in circumstances such as O'Hagan's is unjust.

The Eighth Circuit erred in holding that the misappropriation theory is inconsistent with § 10(b). The Court of Appeals may address on remand O'Hagan's other challenges to his convictions under § 10(b) and Rule 10b-5.

Reversed.

CASE QUESTIONS

1. What did Mr. O'Hagan do with information obtained through his employment?

2. What does the court say the misappropriation theory is?

3. Did Mr. O'Hagan make money from nonpublic information?

4. Could others have done research and obtained the same information?

5. Will Mr. O'Hagan's conviction stand?

ETHICAL ISSUES

Dan Dorfman is a former *Wall Street Journal* reporter and respected commentator on the financial markets. He was a commentator for CNBC and has written commentaries for *USA Today* and *Money*.

During late 1995 and early 1996, financial press reports revealed that Mr. Dorfman was a good friend of Douglas A. Kass, the chief of research and institutional trading at J. W. Charles Securities of Boca Raton, Florida. Mr. Dorfman has been a speaker at J. W. Charles's top-producer weekends. He was not paid a fee, but his hotel room and travel expenses for himself and his girlfriend

were paid by J. W. Charles. Mr. Dorfman recommended several of J. W. Charles's securities in 1994, securities that performed poorly.

CNBC investigated the relationship of the friends and concluded that Mr. Dorfman had done nothing wrong, and the network supported him and the integrity of his reporting.

Assume that Mr. Dorfman has done nothing illegal. Do you see any ethical breaches in his conduct? Did Mr. Dorfman create suspicions, even if they were unjustified?

MAKING ETHICS PERSONAL

Pss't . . . Want to Make a Bundle?
What's Ethical in Insider Trading?

Suppose you hear something that you think will make a stock move. When is it legal to take advantage of the information? The law on insider trading is confusing, even to the experts. See how well you know the subject.

1. The woman you live with, vice president of a large company, wants to take you out to celebrate. She's not supposed to tell anybody, but she lets you know

that her company just landed a big government contract. Can you call your broker before the deal is announced?

__Yes   __No   __Law unclear

2. You're in the theater lobby at intermission. You overhear a conversation between two men you know are top executives of a big company. "Our stock should

really jump when we announce those earnings tomorrow," says one. Can you buy call options now?

__Yes __No __Law unclear

3. A small textile company calls you in as a marketing consultant. Its president shows you samples of a new fabric that sheds dirt and never wears out. You're bowled over—but too busy to take on the account. Can you buy stock in the company?

__Yes __No __Law unclear

4. You're a personnel executive at Mammoth Oil. You learn that the company has just hit a gusher. Can you buy before the news becomes public?

__Yes __No __Law unclear

5. Your broker has an uncanny knack for picking takeover targets. Either he's very smart—or he's getting inside information. He just called to recommend Maximove, an obscure over-the-counter company. Should you buy?

__Yes __No __Law unclear

6. You own stock in the company you work for, and you've been selling twenty-five shares each month to make payments on your Ferrari. You learn that the next quarterly report will show a huge, unexpected loss. Can you make your regular sale before the bad news hits?

__Yes __No __Law unclear

7. You are a scientist at a research institute. Tomorrow you are going on television to release a study showing that a major fast-food chain's hamburgers cause baldness—and a Wall Street reaction is likely. Can you sell the chain's stock short now?

__Yes __No __Law unclear

Here are the "correct" responses, compiled with the help of securities experts at Kirkpatrick & Lockhart and Gibson, Dunn & Crutcher:

1. **No.** A person who gets a tip from an insider can't trade if he knows the insider revealed the news improperly and if the insider gets some benefit from

passing the tip. The SEC says that when there is a "private personal relationship," there is enough of a "personal benefit" to make the trade illegal.

2. **Yes.** The men probably didn't intend to give you the information, and they didn't get anything themselves for doing so. There is no securities fraud under these conditions.

3. **Law unclear.** There is no violation of the law unless there is some obligation to keep information confidential. A court might, however, say that the company president had a reasonable expectation that you would keep the discussion under your hat.

4. **No.** All employees are covered by the insider-trading rules. You can't take advantage of shareholders by trading because of significant information you pick up at work.

5. **Yes.** He and his source may be breaking the law. But as long as you don't know that—or don't have reason to know—you are safe.

6. **Law unclear.** This is a murky area, but some experts say it is illegal only if you make a trade motivated by inside information. The SEC would be likely to argue that simply trading while in possession of the information is enough to make the trade illegal.

7. **Law unclear.** It is not illegal simply to trade on information that will move markets. But prosecutors and the SEC have successfully alleged that someone who "misappropriates" his employer's information can be guilty of securities fraud.

If you answered all the questions correctly, you should be giving lectures on the subject. A score of three to six means you're as knowledgeable as most judges. Suppose you did worse. You clearly aren't inhibited by legal theory—and you may have piled up enough trading profits to mount a top-notch defense.

Source: "Pss't . . . Want to Make a Bundle?" Reprinted from April 29, 1985 issue of *Business Week* by special permission, copyright © 2002 by The McGraw-Hill Companies, Inc.

When Disclosure Must Be Made

Once information becomes public knowledge, insiders and tippees are free to buy and sell the shares affected. However, the time of "public knowledge" is not always easy to determine. In *SEC* v. *Texas Gulf Sulphur*, 401 F.2d 833 (2d Cir. 1968), some of the insiders and tippees waited to buy Texas Gulf Sulphur stock until after a press conference announcement had been made regarding a major mineral find. However, the information released at the press conference had not yet made its way out of the press conference room; there was not enough dissemination for it to be public knowledge. Those who bought by phone immediately following the announcement were found to be in violation of 10(b).

In 2000, the SEC promulgated a new rule that requires companies to release publicly any information they disclose to institutional investors and analysts. Known as the **"fair-disclosure rule" (Regulation FD),** material information about the company must be made available to everyone at the same time.

The rule was controversial during its promulgation—more than 6,000 investors sent in comments on the proposed rule and wrote in favor of the fair-disclosure standard. Many companies were already in compliance with the rule, citing the Internet and its ease of communication. For example, many companies broadcast their conference calls to analysts at CCBN.com so that any investor can participate.

The application and enforcement of Section 10(b) have become two of the most significant issues affecting Wall Street. The complicated scenarios of insider trading are addressed in the Making Ethics Personal quiz from *Business Week* on pp. 904–905.

What Must Be Disclosed

Any material item must be disclosed. To determine whether an item is material, the question to be answered is, "Is this the type of information that would affect the buying or selling decision?" Examples of items that have been held to be material are:

1. Pending takeovers
2. Drops in quarterly earnings
3. Pending declaration of a large dividend
4. Possible lawsuit on product line

One of the trends that has emerged in stock trading is the practice of "pump and dump." This practice uses the rapid communication of the Internet to disperse information about a company so that the market price is affected. Those who have pumped the stock then sell, or dump, their shares when their efforts on the Internet have caused a sufficient jump in the price.

For example, Mark S. Jakob was dealing in call options in Emulex stock in mid-August. His prediction that Emulex stock would take a dive was wrong, and the stock in fact increased in value. He had a loss of $100,000. In order to cover his losses, the 23-year-old sent an e-mail press release to an Internet wire service. The fake press release indicated that the CEO of Emulex would resign due to the fact that earnings had been overstated. The news release was then distributed to various Web sites. The overall loss to shareholders in reaction to the negative news was $2.5 billion as the share price plummeted. However, Mr. Jakob made $240,000 on his trades in the stock.

Mr. Jakob was arrested for securities fraud and wire fraud.[2]

*Visit the SEC Web site
for the actual wording
of the new rule:*
http://www.sec.gov/rules/
final/33-7881.htm

Visit conference call Web sites:
http://www.bestcalls.com
http://www.on24.com

*The following Web sites
highlight some of the issues
of the Internet as a source of
information about companies:*
http://www.ifilmpro.com
http://www.vault.com
http://www.greedy
associates.com

BUSINESS PLANNING TIP

Annual reports and 10-Ks have become a critical part of disclosure for companies. Most companies disclose all environmental cleanup sites and note that it is impossible to predict future cleanup locations or costs. This disclosure is nearly universal for firms.

CONSIDER...   22.2

In August 1994, Mervyn Cooper, a psychotherapist, was providing marriage counseling to a Lockheed executive. The executive had been assigned to conduct the due diligence (review of the accuracy of the books and records) of Martin Marietta, a company with which Lockheed was going to merge.

At his August 22, 1994, session with Mr. Cooper, the executive revealed to him the pending, but nonpublic, merger. Following his session with the executive, Mr. Cooper contacted a friend, Kenneth Rottenberg, and told him about the pending merger. They agreed that Mr. Rottenberg would open a brokerage account so they could buy Lockheed call options and common stocks and then share in the profits.

When Mr. Rottenberg went to some brokerage offices to set up an account, he was warned by a broker about the risks of call options. Mr. Rottenberg told the broker that Lockheed would announce a major business combination shortly and that he would not lose his money.

Did Mr. Rottenberg and Mr. Cooper violate Section 10(b)? What about the broker? [*SEC v. Mervyn Cooper and Kenneth E. Rottenberg*, No. 95–8535 (C.D. Cal. 1995).]

FOR THE MANAGER'S DESK

RE: DISCLOSING IN PLAIN ENGLISH

Corporations are renewing their commitment to plain English in communicating with their shareholders. The SEC is in the process of developing plain English rules for financial products sold by insurers. Plain English reduces sentence size and eliminates technical terms. For example, Texaco's 1996 annual report contained the following:

The increase in sales volumes included the impact of Texaco's aggressive strategy of marketing purchased crude oil, effectively utilizing the company's expansive trading and distribution network. Crude oil sales also reflected an increase in crude oil and NGL production volumes during 1996.

The similar disclosure in 1998 was as follows:

Our sales revenues decreased in 1998 due to historically low commodity prices throughout our global markets. Crude oil, natural gas and refined product prices were all lower. Partly offsetting lower sales revenue due to declining prices were higher volumes.

In 1997, CEO Peter Bijur's first sentence in the annual report contained 51 words. In 1998, with the mark of true plain English apparent, the first sentence has 15 words.

The federal government has been under an executive order to rewrite, by the end of 2002, all documents the public sees. Labels for over-the-counter drugs are to be rewritten in plain English by the end of 2005.

The benefits companies and agencies cite of plain English is less cost because employees require less training in complex forms and procedures. Customers are happier because they understand the information, and the costs of handling customer complaints and questions drop significantly because the volume is reduced dramatically.

The drawbacks include concerns from lawyers about substituting words that do not have a rich body of precedent behind them and possibly changing the true meaning of phrases, words, and disclosures.

The handbooks for plain English are:

- William Strunk and E. B. White, *The Elements of Style*
- *The Complete Essays of Montaigne*
- Edward R. Tufte, *The Visual Display of Quantitative Information*

Simplify and Firehouse Communications are two companies offering services in changing reports for companies into plain English.

Source: David Leonhardt, "In Language You Can Understand," *New York Times*, December 8, 1999, pp. C1, C16.

The issue of earnings reports has been a significant one over the past ten years as the SEC has investigated hundreds of cases of accounting fraud involving companies that "cooked the books." Since the collapse of Enron in 2001, followed by other companies such as WorldCom, Adelphia, and HealthSouth, Congress passed Sarbanes-Oxley and required massive reforms in corporate governance, auditing, financial statement reporting, and the penalties for violations of Section 10(b). The issue of forthrightness in financial reports has become the focal point of SEC activity, government prosecution, legislative reform, and ethics and compliance programs in corporations. The issues surrounding forthrightness in financial reporting do not always amount to fraud but to questions of interpretation and classification of accounting revenues and expenses. The SEC continues to work to draw the line between "earnings management" and misrepresentation of the true financial picture of a company. For example, America Online entered into a consent decree with the SEC, agreeing to pay a $3.5 million fine for overstatement of its earnings in 1995 and 1996. Although AOL did not admit any wrongdoing, the SEC questioned

AOL's booking of advertising expenses in future years. The general accounting rule is that advertising can be booked as an expense and only rarely capitalized over time unless the company can prove that it has determined an accurate formula showing that current advertising costs will bring in future revenues. AOL, using its model that the SEC disputed, was able to avoid booking as expenses over $385 million in advertising costs when it was struggling to survive during the 1995 and 1996 period. Its reported earnings would have been very different had it not capitalized the advertising costs.

However, there are disagreements about these kinds of expenses; AOL clearly has demonstrated that its enormous advertising expenses during that time have resulted in increased customers and earnings, with its share price in 2000 being thirty-eight times what it was during the 1995–1996 period.

Another change Sarbanes-Oxley made was to require companies to have a specific code of ethics for their financial officers. The purpose of this requirement was to encourage those involved in developing the financial reports for the company to be attuned to the ethical issues in their decision-making processes about financial reports. Under the changes in the law, the code of ethics for financial officers must emphasize the following:

1. Honest and ethical conduct, including the ethical handling of actual or apparent conflicts of interest between personal and professional relationships
2. Full, fair, accurate, timely, and understandable disclosure in the periodic reports required to be filed by the issuer
3. Compliance with applicable governmental rules and regulations

While investigating the Enron case, regulators discovered that the company had waived its own code of ethics in order to allow CFO Andrew Fastow to serve as a principal for off-the-book entities that were doing business with Enron (see Chapter 21). As a result, Sarbanes-Oxley requires that companies file immediately an 8-K form that discloses any waiver of its code of ethics for a financial reporting officer. Generally in the past, 8-Ks have been filed by the end of the month in which an event occurred. Sarbanes-Oxley demands more timely disclosures—most of the changes require the 8-K form to be filed within one day.

Sarbanes-Oxley continues to emphasize the importance of **blackout periods**, or those times when companies place absolute prohibitions on trading by company employees. Most companies now have policies that also require employees to clear any stock transactions with legal counsel prior to engaging in those transactions. Such programs are important for showing compliance and, if wrongdoing does occur, for reducing fines and penalties under the corporate sentencing guidelines (see Chapter 9).

Standing to Sue under Section 10(b)

To be able to recover under Section 10(b), a party suing must have standing. **Standing** in these cases has been defined by the U.S. Supreme Court as the actual sale or purchase of stock in reliance upon the information or lack of information given. For example, persons who would have purchased stock had they known the truth could not recover for damages under 10(b). Likewise, they cannot recover damages because they would have sold their stock had they known the truth. There must be an actual sale or purchase for a plaintiff to satisfy the standing requirements of 10(b). In *Blue Chip Stamp* v. *Manor Drug Store*, 421 U.S. 723 (1975), the U.S. Supreme

Court held that a pessimistic statement of income and potential was not a 10(b) violation because a potentially interested buyer who did not buy because of the pessimism did not have actual damages and, hence, no standing.

The U.S. Supreme Court has held that shareholders cannot immediately bring suit under 10(b) against their brokers if their brokerage contracts contain an arbitration provision. Standing now requires an exhaustion of arbitration methods [*Shearson/American Express, Inc.* v. *McMahon,* 482 U.S. 220 (1987)].

The Requirement of Scienter under Section 10(b)

A conviction under 10(b) cannot be based on negligence—that is, the failure to discover financial information. Because 10(b) is a criminal statute, there must be some intent to defraud or knowledge of wrongdoing, or **scienter,** on the part of the violator. Convictions are only for knowing the financial information but failing to disclose it.

In *Ernst & Ernst* v. *Hochfelder,* 425 U.S. 185 (1978), the Supreme Court held that an accounting firm that had negligently performed an audit of a business based on a fraud could not be held liable under 10(b) because, although the accounting firm made a mistake, it had no intent to defraud.

CONSIDER...   22.3

In the month preceding the drop in the NASDAQ in 2000, many insiders at dot-com companies sold their stock and avoided the losses a 17 percent drop in NASDAQ had caused.* Insider sales of stocks on the NASDAQ typically average $1 billion to $3 billion per month, but the average jumped to $12 billion per month from November 1999 to February 2000. Some analysts noted that the sell-offs by insiders may have prompted the drop in the market. Examples of the trading include the following.

- Drugstore.com founder Jed Smith sold 150,000 of his 950,000 shares at a price of $23 per share. The price now is $9.88.
- MicroStrategy CEO Michael Saylor sold $80 million in his company's shares. The price of MicroStrategy shares dropped 62 percent within a few weeks of his sales.
- Beyond.com ex-CEO Mark Breier sold 80,000 shares of his company for $440,000 after he quit as CEO.
- Former surgeon general C. Everett Koop sold $3 million in shares of his drkoop.com site at about $9 per share in February. The spokesperson for drkoop.com indicated the insiders there were "diversifying their portfolios."

Could these transactions be labeled as insider trading? What would you need to know about them to determine whether these stockholders were trading on inside information? Under the Sarbanes-Oxley changes, sales of shares by officers now require immediate reporting on 8-K forms. The previous standard of reporting by the close of the month in which the transactions occur has been changed to a one-day period (as with the waiver of the code of ethics mentioned earlier).

*Del Jones, "Net Execs Sold Stock before Big Drop," *USA Today,* April 6, 2000, p. B1.

Penalties for Section 10(b) Violations

Review the Insider Trading and Securities Fraud Enforcement Act of 1988:
http://www.law.uc.edu/ CCL/34Act/sec2IA.html

While the **Insider Trading and Securities Fraud Enforcement Act of 1988**, an amendment to the 1934 act, increased substantially the penalties for violations of Section 10(b), the Sarbanes-Oxley changes have more than doubled the penalties of those earlier reforms. Violations of 10(b) carry prison terms of up to twenty-five years plus penalties. Corporate financial officers also face the penalties noted above with regard to certification of financial statements. In addition, officers who earn bonuses and other compensation based on false financial information will be required to return those funds to the company. Further, the bankruptcy code was amended to prohibit the discharge of these debts in bankruptcy so that repayment becomes a lifetime obligation. In addition to these criminal penalties, the SEC is authorized to bring civil actions against the companies and its officers and collect civil penalties for financial reporting violations, insider trading, and other activities related to 10(b) violations.

To increase the likelihood of corporate employees coming forward with information on fraudulent financial reporting, the SEC can pay bounties of up to 10 percent of the amount recovered to informants who report violations. Under Sarbanes-Oxley there are protections for company whistle-blowers who report violations to the SEC. These protections are similar to those provided in many antiretaliation statutes at the federal and state levels and provide the employees with a shield against termination for reporting violations. Officers and legal counsel are also protected under this provision. In 2003, the American Bar Association (ABA) even amended its Model Code of Ethics to allow lawyers, without being considered in violation of their duty of client confidentiality, to report the conduct of clients who are using the lawyer's advice to commit a fraud. As noted in Chapter 21, lawyers are also required to report conduct of company officers "up the ladder"

FOR THE MANAGER'S DESK

Re: Audit Fees in the Post-Sarbanes-Oxley Era

Because of new requirements under Sarbanes-Oxley, audit fees at publicly traded companies have increased substantially. A recent study shows the following among Standard & Poor's 500 index (S&P 500).

- The average increase in audit fees for the S&P 500 is 27%.
- The average increase for the S&P midcaps is 35%.
- The average increase for the S&P smallcaps is 28%.

A number of explanations account for the increases in fees. One is that more services are now counted as audit services, such as the work by auditors on company pension plans. Those were once listed as "other fees," and now they are counted as audit fees. But most companies and auditors explain the increase as being the result of extra time spent trying to ensure that the company is in compliance with Sarbanes-Oxley.

The companies that have experienced the greatest increase in audit fees are those that had Arthur Andersen as their auditors. For example, Bristol-Myers Squibb's audit fees doubled after it terminated Andersen and hired Ernst & Young. Newmont, a gold-mining company, not only had its audit fees quadruple when it hired PriceWaterhouseCoopers following its termination of Andersen but also had to restate its earnings going back to 1999.

What are accountants' liabilities under federal securities laws?

Source: Matt Krantz, "Audit fees swell after scandals, new law," *USA Today*, May 6, 2003. Reprinted with permission. See also http://www.foleygardner.com for a copy of the study on costs of audits after Sarbanes-Oxley.

in the corporation to the board and audit committee, and the ABA changed its Model Code of Ethics to allow such reporting.

Insider Trading and Short-Swing Profits

In addition to the application of Section 10(b) and Rule 10b-5 to trading on inside information, the 1934 act also has a form of a strict liability statute for insider trading. Officers, directors, and 10 percent or more shareholders have greater access to inside information. They are involved in setting a corporation's policy and directions in dividend decisions, in product decisions, and in expansion decisions. They will always have access to information that is not yet available to the public. **Section 16** of the 1934 act is a *per se* liability section designed to deal with stock trading by corporate insiders, who are defined as officers, directors, and 10 percent shareholders of those companies required to be registered under the 1934 act.

Under 16(a), officers, directors, and 10 percent shareholders (10 percent of any class of stock) are required to file reports declaring their holdings. In addition, they must file updated reports after any change in ownership (purchase, sale, or transfer). While previously the requirement was that they report such changes within twenty days, Sarbanes-Oxley now mandates reporting changes within one day.

Under 16(b), officers, directors, and 10 percent shareholders are required to give to the corporation any **short-swing profits**—that is, profits earned on the sale and purchase or purchase and sale of stock during any six-month period. For example, suppose Director Cadigan of a New York Stock Exchange company engaged in the following transactions:

April 11, 2001—Ms. Cadigan buys 200 shares of her corporation's stock at $50 each.

April 30, 2001—Ms. Cadigan sells 200 shares at $30 each.

May 15, 2001—Ms. Cadigan buys 200 shares at $20 each.

The SEC will match the highest sale with the lowest purchase. Ms. Cadigan has a profit of $10 per share even though she has a net loss. This profit must be returned to the corporation. It is irrelevant whether the officer, director, or 10 percent shareholder actually used inside information: The presumption under 16(b) for short-swing trades is that the officer, director, or 10 percent shareholder had access to inside information.

These rules also apply to stock options. However, the issue of stock options and compensation has become a sensitive one following their role in the collapse of so many companies. To minimize or eliminate the incentives for making the financial picture brighter for purposes of increasing the value of stock options, some companies, such as GE and Coca-Cola, have changed their compensation plans to eliminate options and offer employees special classes of stock that have predetermined values or that are awarded only after a period of years following the release of earnings. These types of changes are the voluntary ones that have accompanied the massive Sarbanes-Oxley reforms on financial reporting.

Exhibit 22.4 provides a summary of the Sarbanes-Oxley changes covered in this chapter as well as the rest of the book. Go to http://www.sec.gov for a complete copy of the legislation.

EXHIBIT   22.4 The Massive Reforms of Sarbanes-Oxley

NEW RULE/LAW	CHAPTER REFERENCE
1. SEC certification of financial statements—"untrue statement of a material fact."	Chapter 22
2. SEC certification of financial statements—"no covered report omitted to state a material fact necessary to make the statements in the covered report, in light of the circumstances under which they were made, not misleading as of the end of the period covered by such report."	Chapter 22
3. SEC certification of financial statements—officer signatures.	Chapter 22
4. Sarbanes-Oxley Section 203—audit partner rotation. Companies must rotate audit partners once every 5 years.	Chapters 21 and 22
5. Sarbanes-Oxley Section 204—auditor reports to audit committees.	Chapter 21
6. Sarbanes-Oxley Section 206—conflicts of interest. There are strict prohibitions on consulting activities beyond financial statement certification. Exceptions require board approval.	Chapter 21
7. Sarbanes-Oxley Section 301—public company audit committees. Members cannot be employed by the company or have family members employed at the company. Members cannot be hired as consultants, and there are restrictions on their business with the company.	Chapters 2 and 21
8. Sarbanes-Oxley Section 407—audit committee must have at least one "financial expert" as defined by the SEC.	Chapter 21
9. Sarbanes-Oxley Section 304—forfeiture of certain bonuses and profits. If the company must restate a financial statement, the officers responsible lose their bonuses for any twelve-month period surrounding the original financial statement and must return any profits realized on sales of stock.	Chapters 21 and 22
10. Sarbanes-Oxley Section 306—insider trades during pension fund blackout periods. During this blackout period officers and directors cannot trade any stock or interests acquired through company affiliation.	Chapter 22
11. Sarbanes-Oxley Section 307—rules of professional responsibility for attorneys. Attorneys must report financial fraud or misdeeds to CEO or chief counsel, and if they fail to act, attorneys must report such to the audit committee. If the audit committee is not independent with regard to the issue, the attorney must report the issue to another committee or the board itself.	Chapters 21 and 22

NEW RULE/LAW	CHAPTER REFERENCE
12. Sarbanes-Oxley Section 402—enhanced conflict of interest provisions. Section 403—disclosures of transactions involving management and principal stockholders.	Chapter 21
13. Sarbanes-Oxley Section 406—code of ethics for senior financial officers. Officers must certify along with financials that the company has a code of ethics.	Chapter 22
14. Sarbanes-Oxley Section 806—protection for employees of publicly traded companies who provide evidence of fraud. This section amends the Federal Whistleblower Protection Act to provide coverage for employees who report financial fraud internally or to federal agencies.	Chapters 17, 18, and 22
15. Penalties. The penalty for securities fraud has increased to 25 years. The White-Collar Crime Penalty Enhancement Act of 2002, enacted as part of the Sarbanes-Oxley bill, increases penalties for mail and wire fraud from 5 to 20 years. Violations of ERISA now carry greater penalties, with $5,000 fines for individuals increased to $100,000; 1 year imprisonment increased to 10 years; and company fines of $100,000 increased to $500,000. New provisions for certification of financial reporting impose penalties of $1 million and/or 10 years; for willful violations, $5 million and 20 years. The Corporate Fraud Accountability Act of 2002, also part of Sarbanes-Oxley, imposes penalties for the concealment or destruction of documents related to the financial reports of a company (20 years). Penalties under the Securities Exchange Act of 1934 are increased: $1 million and/or 10 years is increased to $5 million and/or 20 years, and company penalties are increased from $2.5 million to $25 million.	Chapters 9 and 22
16. Debts from financial fraud cannot be discharged in bankruptcy.	Chapter 22

Regulating Voting Information

There was once a time when shareholders could give their proxies to the company just by endorsing the backs of their dividend checks; proxies then were obtained easily and without much disclosure. The 1934 act changed the way proxies were solicited. With the same philosophy used for registration, the SEC required full disclosure to be the goal of all **proxy solicitations**. To achieve that goal, the SEC now requires prior filing and adequate representation of shareholder interests.

The Proxy Statement

Under Section 14 of the 1934 act, all companies required to register under the act must file their proxy materials with the SEC at least ten days before those materials are to be sent. Proxy materials include the proxy statement and all other solicitation materials that will be sent to shareholders. The proxy statement required by the SEC must contain the following details:

1. Who is soliciting the proxy
2. How the materials will be sent
3. Who is paying for the costs of soliciting
4. How much has been spent to date on the solicitation
5. How much is expected to be spent on the solicitation
6. Why the proxy is being solicited—annual meeting elections, special meeting on a merger, and so on

Exhibit 22.5 shows a sample proxy.

EXHIBIT 22.5 Sample Proxy

P   **ARIZONA PUBLIC SERVICE COMPANY**   PROXY CARD
P.O. Box 53999
Phoenix, Arizona 85072-3999

R   **THIS PROXY IS SOLICITED ON BEHALF OF THE BOARD OF DIRECTORS FOR THE ANNUAL MEETING ON MAY 21, 1996.**

O   The undersigned hereby appoints O. Mark DeMichele and Nancy C. Loftin, and each of them, proxies for the undersigned, each with full power of substitution, to attend the annual meeting of shareholders of Arizona Public Service Company to be held May 21, 1996, at 10:00a.m., Phoenix time, and at any adjournment thereof, and to vote as specified in this Proxy all the shares of stock of the company which the undersigned would be entitled to vote if personally present.

X

   Voting with respect to the election of directors and the proposals may be indicated on the reverse of this card. Nominees for director are: O. Mark Demichele, Martha O. Hesse, Marianne Moody Jennings, Robert G. Matlock, Jaron B. Norberg, John R. Norton III, William J. Post, Donald M. Riley,

Y   Henry B. Sargent, Wilma W. Schwada, Richard Snell, Dianne C. Walker, Ben F. Williams Jr., and Thomas G. Woods, Jr.

Your vote is important! Please sign, date, and mail promptly in the enclosed postage-paid envelope.

This proxy, when properly executed, will be voted in the manner directed herein. If no direction is made, it will be voted FOR the election of directors and FOR the proposals.

The board of Directors recommends a vote FOR the election of directors.	The board of Directors recommends a vote FOR the proposal to amend Article Sixth of the Company's Articles of Incorporation.	The board of Directors recommends a vote FOR the proposal to amend Article Fifth of the Company's Articles of Incorporation.
1. Election of Directors (see other side)	2. Proposal to amend Article Sixth of the Company's Articles of Incorporation.	3. Proposal to amend article Fifth of the Company's Articles of Incorporation.
FOR* WITHHELD ☐ ☐ *For all nominees, except withhold vote for the following: _____	FOR AGAINST ABSTAIN ☐ ☐ ☐	FOR AGAINST ABSTAIN ☐ ☐ ☐

4.   In their discretion, the proxies are to vote upon such other business as may properly come before the meeting.

_____   _____
Signature   date

_____   _____
Signature   date
Please sign as your name(s) appear to the left. Joint owners should both sign. Fiduciaries, attorneys, corporate officers, etc., should state their capacities.

Source: Reprinted with permission of the Arizona Public Service Company.

ETHICAL ISSUES

Iroquois Brands, Ltd., is a food company that imports French foie gras, a pâté made from the enlarged livers of force-fed geese. There is a French practice in raising the geese of funneling corn down the geese's throats and gagging them with rubber bands to keep them from regurgitating. A shareholder wishes to include in the proxy materials a proposal that the company study this method of force-feeding as an unethical business practice (cruelty to animals). Should the proposal be included? Does Section 14 require that it be included? [*Lovenheim v. Iroquois Brands, Ltd.*, 618 F. Supp. 554 (D.C. 1985).]

BUSINESS STRATEGY APPLICATION

Be sure to do the exercise for this chapter on the book's Web site, where you will have a chance to see actual company proxy materials, types of disclosures, and shareholder proposals.

Visit the Web site of the national corporate secretaries' organization:

http://www.ascs.org

Also, visit the Web site of one of the country's most active institutional shareholders:

http://www.calpers-governance.org

Shareholder Proposals

Because the purpose of Section 14 is full disclosure, the representation of views other than those of corporate management is important in proxy solicitations. Shareholders can submit proposals to be included in proxy solicitation materials. If the company does not oppose what is being proposed, the proposition is included as part of the proxy materials. If management is opposed, the proposing shareholder has the right of a 200-word statement on the proposal in the materials. These proposals are not permitted along with their 200-word statements unless they propose conduct that is legal and related to business operations, as opposed to social, moral, religious, and political views. During the Vietnam era, many shareholders wanted to include proposals in proxy materials for companies that were war suppliers. Their proposals centered around the political opposition to the war and not the business practices of the company.

CONSIDER...   22.4

A shareholder for Cracker Barrel Cheese has submitted for SEC approval a proposal that would require the company not to discriminate against employees who are homosexuals. Should the SEC allow the proposal?

Remedies for Violations of Section 14

If proxies are solicited without following the Section 14 guidelines, the proxies are invalid. They must then be resolicited, and if the meeting has been held in which the invalid proxies were used, the action taken at the meeting can be set aside.

Shareholder Rights in Takeovers, Mergers, and Consolidations

Definitions

Mergers A **merger** is a combination of two or more corporations, after which only one corporation continues to exist. If Hubbard Company and Inez Corporation decide to merge, then the newly merged corporation must be either Hubbard Company or Inez Corporation. One of the corporations ceases to exist, and the two continue under one name. If Hubbard and Inez decide to merge into Inez Corporation, then Inez will own all of Hubbard's assets and will assume all of Hubbard's liabilities. There are three types of mergers: horizontal, vertical, and conglomerate.

Consolidations   In a **consolidation**, two or more companies combine into one new company and none of the old companies continues to exist. Instead of Hubbard Company and Inez Corporation becoming Inez Corporation, under a consolidation Hubbard and Inez become Jasmine Corporation. Each company involved in the consolidation gives all its rights and liabilities to the new company, which holds all assets of the consolidating companies and assumes all their liabilities.

Tender Offers   A **tender offer** is not a business combination; it is a method for achieving a business combination. An offer that is publicly advertised to shareholders for the purchase of their stock is a tender offer. The offering price for the stock is usually higher than the market price of the shares, which makes the tender offer attractive to the shareholders. Oracle made a tender offer for People Soft in 2004.

Originally the tender offer was used as a means for a corporation to reacquire its shares. However, it has become a tool of business combinations of every sort, sometimes friendly and sometimes hostile.

Takeovers   **Takeovers** are accomplished through the use of tender offers and can be either friendly or hostile. A **friendly takeover** is one the management of a firm favors, whereas a **hostile takeover** is one the management of a firm opposes. Restrictions on the use of tender offers and procedures for accomplishing a takeover are discussed later in the chapter.

Acquisitions   The acquisition of another firm's assets is either a means of expanding or a way to eliminate a creditor; **asset acquisition**, however, is different from the other business combinations. Because the corporate structure does not change, shareholder approval is not required for an asset acquisition. However, asset acquisitions are subject to the constraints of the Clayton Act.

1934 Act Regulation of Takeovers

In all of these business combinations (except asset acquisitions), someone is buying enough stock to own a company. That much buying and selling has long had the attention of the SEC. The Williams amendment to the Securities Exchange Act of 1934 regulates these offers to buy stock or tender offers, and the **Williams Act** was passed in 1968 to apply to all offers to buy more than 5 percent of a corporation's securities.

Filing Requirements under the Williams Act   Any offeror subject to the Williams Act is required to file a tender offer statement with both the SEC and the target company. The offeror must also send or publish for shareholders of the target company all the information and details about the offer. If the target company is opposing the takeover (that is, if it is hostile), the target must also file its materials with the SEC.

A registration statement for a tender offer must include the name of the offeror, its source of funding for the offer, its plans for the company if its attempted takeover is successful, and the number of shares now owned.

Shareholders have seven days after a tender offer to withdraw their shares. This seven-day period is to prevent shareholders from being forced into a "now-or-never" transaction. The actual purchase of the shares cannot take place until at least fifteen days after the tender offer began. If the offeror changes the tender offer terms, shareholders must be notified; and if a better price is offered, all shareholders must be given ten days to tender their shares at that price (even those who have already tendered their shares at the lower price).

BUSINESS STRATEGY

Making a Pass at the Pepsi Shareholders

Steve Hindi is an animal rights activist who owns $5,000 in Pepsi stock. He discovered that Pepsi advertises in bull rings in Spain and Mexico, and he has attended annual shareholder meetings and put forward shareholder proposals to have the company halt the practice.

His proposal did not pass, but he did not give up easily and started a Web site (http://www.pepsibloodbath.com)

© IAN TYLER/ISTOCKPHOTO

to increase pressure on the company.

Pepsi has withdrawn from bullfighting ads in Mexico but continues with them in Spain. Mr. Hindi continues his quest. Should the proposal have been approved? Does Mr. Hindi run any risk with his Web site activism?

Source: Constance L. Hays, "A PepsiCo Shareholder Meeting and a Very Unhappy Shareholder," *New York Times,* April 22, 2000, pp. B1, B4.

Williams Act Penalties for Violations The Williams amendments provide for both civil and criminal penalties for violations of the act's procedures. The penalties are based on the same type of language used for 10(b) violations. Criminal and civil penalties are imposed for "fraudulent, deceptive or manipulative" practices used in making a tender offer. There are also penalties for omissions or misstatements of material facts in the tender offer materials.

Proposed Changes As the number of takeover bids has increased, concern over the adequacy of regulation has also increased. Both Congress and the SEC have proposed changes to tighten regulation of tender offers. For example, some proposals would require the tender offeror to disclose its financial situation and plans for the acquired company.

Special Protections for the Hostile Takeover In a noncontested takeover, the target company (within ten days after the date the tender offer commenced) must declare to its shareholders one of the following:

1. That it recommends acceptance or rejection of the offer
2. That it has no opinion and remains neutral
3. That it is unable to take a position

The target company must also justify its position.

In those cases in which the target company does not want to be taken over, both the target company and the offeror develop strategies for stopping the other. Some of the tactics used by a target company to fight takeovers are:

1. Persuading shareholders that the tender offer is not in their best interests
2. Filing legal suits or complaints on the grounds that the takeover violates provisions of the antitrust laws
3. Matching the buyout with a target company offer
4. Soliciting a "white knight" merger or a merger from a friendly party

State Laws Affecting Tender Offers

For an example of a state law governing takeovers, review:
**http://www.in.gov/
legislative/ic/code**

Today over forty states have passed laws regarding takeovers. Initially these laws were Williams Act provisions at the state level. However, upon review of these types of statutes, the U.S. Supreme Court held that they were a violation of the Supremacy Clause (see Chapter 5) in that Congress had preempted the field by establishing a full regulatory scheme for takeovers under the Williams Act [*Edgar* v. *MITE Corp.*, 457 U.S. 624 (1982)]. Following the *MITE* case, the states have developed a new type of antitakeover statute that permits shareholders to have some say in whether a corporation should be taken over. This new breed of state law focuses on corporate governance and not securities regulation, and hence it avoids the preemption issues raised by the earlier statutes. However, these statutes are still subject to judicial review.

ETHICAL ISSUES

Joseph Horne Company, a department store in Pennsylvania, entered into an agreement to have Dillard's (a national retail chain) take it over. Dillard's performed its due diligence—the process of getting internal access to computers and records to verify financial statements. During due diligence, Dillard's assumed responsibility for ordering and shipping merchandise. Employees in Horne's management were told that they would no longer have jobs, and nearly 500 employees left Horne. Horne's Christmas merchandise was delayed and was often wrong, and the merger fell through. Horne says that Dillard's went too far. Dillard's says that due diligence is part of a takeover, that Horne's financial statements were inaccurate, and that Horne could have stopped the ordering and shipping at any time. One of the officers at Horne's bank says a Dillard's official told him that Dillard's would just wait until the company was in Chapter 11 bankruptcy and pick it up cheaply. Evaluate the ethics of both parties.

The Future for State Antitakeover Statutes

Review Wisconsin's takeover statute (Chapter 180, Business Corporations):
**http://www.legis.state.
wis.us/rsb/stats.html**

State antitakeover statutes are often classified into three generations. The first generation was the Illinois statute invalidated in *MITE* as preempted by the Williams Act. The second-generation statute is the Indiana statute upheld as valid in *CTS Corp.* v. *Dynamics Corp. of Am.*, 481 U.S. 69 (1987), as part of corporate governance regulation. There is now a third generation of antitakeover statutes, in which bidders are required to wait three years before taking over a company unless the board of the target company agrees to such a takeover. These statutes were enacted after the *CTS* decision and further extend the control of shareholders and the entrenchment of existing management. The effect is to make a takeover very unattractive because of the delay. Wisconsin's three-year, third-generation statute was upheld by the Seventh Circuit Court of Appeals in *Amanda Acquisition Corp.* v. *Universal Foods Corp.*, 877 F.2d 496 (7th Cir. 1989), and the U.S. Supreme Court denied *certiorari* for the review, giving an implicit validation to these more restrictive state statutes. The Court noted in its review of the Wisconsin statute:

> *If our views of the wisdom of state law mattered, Wisconsin's takeover statute would not survive. Like our colleagues who decided* MITE *and* CTS, *we believe that antitakeover legislation injures shareholders. . . . Skepticism about the wisdom of a state's law does not lead to the conclusion that the law is beyond the state's power. We have not been elected custodians of investors' wealth. States need not treat investors' welfare as their summum bonum. Perhaps they choose to protect managers' welfare instead. . . . Unless a federal statute or the Constitution bars the way, Wisconsin's choice must be respected.*

Since the time of the Wisconsin statute's passage and its declared judicial validity, other states have passed even more protective legislation for companies within their state borders. These statutes, for example, permit corporations to prevent 100 percent acquisition of their stock unless the takeover is done over a three-year period. Other statutes permit corporations to dilute the interest of an offeror by issuing new shares to existing shareholders once a takeover begins.

Proxy Regulations and Tender Offers

Once some shares are acquired, a firm poised for a takeover wages a proxy battle, which means it solicits proxies in order to be able to command the number of votes needed to gain control of the board. Even though these proxy solicitations originate outside the company, the proxy statement and solicitation materials must be filed with the SEC.

Failure to file these materials makes the proxies invalid, and any action taken at a meeting using the proxies can be set aside. Mergers voted on with invalid proxies can be "unwound." Either the SEC or shareholders are entitled to bring an action to prevent the use or undo the use of invalid proxies. If a shareholder successfully brings an action seeking a remedy for a violation of the SEC proxy solicitation rules outlined in Section 14, the offeror must fully reimburse the shareholder for all costs of the court action.

Proxies obtained by using misleading information or by not disclosing material information are also invalid. Again, either the SEC or individual shareholders can bring suit to stop the use of these proxies or to set aside action taken with them.

Proxy contests are expensive. Who pays for their costs? If management wins, they can be reimbursed for reasonable costs. However, some courts limit this reimbursement right to battles waged over corporate policy and not over personality conflicts. If the new group wins, they can vote to reimburse for reasonable expenses, but many states require shareholders to ratify such reimbursement.

THE FOREIGN CORRUPT PRACTICES ACT

In the early 1970s, the nation, Congress, and other officials learned that U.S. companies doing business in other countries were bribing foreign officials for various reasons. Furthermore, these bribes were not disclosed anywhere and in fact were secret payments concealed by internal accounting procedures. As a result, the **Foreign Corrupt Practices Act** (FCPA) was passed in 1977 as an amendment to the 1934 Securities Exchange Act. (See Chapter 7 for more details.) The FCPA is part of the 1934 act and it carries the same penalties for officers and others who authorized or performed the conduct in violation of this antibribery statute.

STATE SECURITIES LAWS

Today all states have their own securities laws. In addition to federal laws, all issuers are required to follow state **blue sky laws** in all states in which their securities are sold. There are two types of state securities laws for registration purposes: those that follow the SEC standards for full disclosure and those that follow a merit review standard. Under SEC standards, a filing is required, and so long as all the required information is there, the offering will be approved for public sale. Under a **merit review** standard, the regulatory agency responsible for securities enforcement can actually examine a filed offering for its merits as to adequate capitalization, excessive stock ownership by the promoters, and penny-stock problems. These agencies apply a general standard that the offering must be "fair, just, and equitable." This general standard gives them great latitude in deciding which issues will be approved.

EXHIBIT 22.6 State and Federal Securities Law

1933 ACT	1934 ACT	BLUE SKY
S1—Registration statement Financial information Officers/directors Prospectus 20-day effective date, deficiency letter	*Application* 500 or more shareholders with $5 million or more in assets or listed on national exchange Sec. 10b—insider trading/fraud	Separate financial certification penalties under Sarbanes-Oxley State securities registration Merit vs. disclosure standards Federally exempt securities may still need to register at state level
Section 11—Filing false registration statement Liability: Anyone named in prospectus or offering expert materials for it Material, false statement; privity not required unless longer than one year Defenses; due diligence; buyer's knowledge	*10K* Annual reports *10Q* Quarterly report *Foreign Corrupt Practices Act* Financial reports Internal controls Applies to 1933 and 1934 act registrants	
Section 12—Failure to file; selling before effective date; False prospectus Materials; false statement; privity required Defenses; due diligence; buyer's knowledge	*Section 14* Proxy registration Compensation disclosure *Section 16A* Officers, directors, 10% shareholders Sales registration	
Penalties $100,000 and/or five years (criminal/civil suit)	*Section 16B* Short-swing profit Tender offer regulations (Williams Act) *Penalties* Penalties plus up to 25 years	

Many companies do not register their offerings in states where there is merit review. They sell in the other states to avoid the problems of being denied registration.

As on the federal level, all states have their own exemptions from registration. Most SEC exemptions also work at the state level, the only requirement being that the issuer file a notice of sale with the state agency.

In addition to regulating securities offerings, these state agencies also control the licensing of brokers and agents of securities within the state. The licensing process consists of an application and a background check conducted by the agency to identify possible criminal problems.

Exhibit 22.6 provides a summary of securities regulation under state and federal law.

INTERNATIONAL ISSUES IN SECURITIES LAWS

The following policy statement from the State Department summarizes the nature of international capital markets today: "The United States Government is committed to an international system which provides for a high degree of freedom in the movement of trade and investment flows." There is free flow of money across borders, and although the United States does restrict foreign investments in atomic energy, air transport, hydroelectric power, and fishing, there is much international investment in U.S. projects.

The United States has ten stock exchanges; Germany, eight; France, seven; and Switzerland, seven. The United Kingdom, Japan, Canada, the Netherlands, Belgium, Luxembourg, Norway, Kuwait, Australia, and many other countries have at least one stock exchange each.

A directive from the European Union has developed uniform requirements for disclosure in primary offering. Often called a "listing of particulars" instead of a "prospectus," uniform information is given to shareholders prior to their purchases. One difficulty that must be resolved is that accounting practices outside the United States are not uniform. Often these practices create different financial pictures for investors.

Insider trading has been prosecuted vigorously in the United States for the past thirty years. European enforcement has been limited. For example, in 1988, the French government began investigating suspicious trades in Societe Generale SA stock. Most financial experts agree that insider trading in Europe is pervasive. There are few convictions and very light, if any, sentences and fines.[3] From 1995 to 2000, in the stock markets of Britain, Germany, France, Italy, and Switzerland, there were only nineteen criminal convictions. The total for just Manhattan in the United States for the same time period was forty-six convictions. Britain had only three convictions in that time, and France had none. Britain has the largest financial market in Europe.

In addition to the lack of convictions, there is little regulatory structure for investigation and prosecution. The following chart compares the size of securities regulatory agencies in various countries.

The United States is the only country with proxy disclosure requirements. Although Japan regulates solicitations, Germany requires only advance notice of meetings.

COUNTRY	STAFF	LISTED COMPANIES	COMPANIES/ STAFF
Denmark	20	242	12
U.K.	200	2,399	12
Luxembourg	5	53	11
Ireland	10	78	8
Switzerland	30	232	8
Germany	130	741	6
Sweden	50	258	5
Netherlands	43	214	5
Finland	27	129	5
Greece	65	246	4
France	219	784	4
Austria	30	96	3
Spain	92	481	3
Belgium	80	156	2
Portugal	112	135	1
Italy	403	239	1
Europe	1,616	6,483	5
U.S.	2,807	6,850	2

Source: Data is from the Organization for Economic Cooperation & Development (OECD).

SUMMARY

What requirements affect primary offerings?

- Primary offering—sale of securities by the business in which interests are offered
- Security—investment in a common enterprise with profits to come from efforts of others

Why do we have securities laws, and what is their history?

- Securities Act of 1933—federal law regulating initial sales of securities
- Securities Act of 1934—federal law regulating securities and companies in the secondary market

How do securities laws regulate the secondary market?

- 10-Q—periodic reporting forms required of 1934 act companies
- Certification of financial reports by CEO and CFO
- 10-K—periodic reporting forms required of 1934 act companies
- 8-K—periodic reporting forms required of 1934 act companies
- Section 10(b)—antifraud provision of Securities Exchange Act
- Rule 10b-5—SEC regulation on antifraud provision of Securities Exchange Act
- Insider—person with access to nonpublic information about a company
- Tippee—person who gains nonpublic information from an insider
- Fair Disclosure Rule—SEC regulation on disclosure to analysts
- Insider Trading and Securities Fraud Enforcement Act of 1988—federal law increasing penalties for insider trading violations
- Section 16—portion of 1934 act regulating short-swing profits by officers, directors, or 10 percent shareholders
- Short-swing profits—gain on sale and purchase or purchase and sale of securities within a six-month period
- Proxy solicitations—formal paperwork requesting authority to vote on behalf of another
- Blue sky laws—state securities registration regulations
- Merit review—regulation of merits of an offering as opposed to disclosure

How do securities laws protect shareholders in share and company acquisitions?

- Mergers, consolidations, tender offers, and asset acquisitions are regulated
- Williams Act regulates tender offers
- States have antitakeover statutes
- *Howey* test—Supreme Court definition of security
- SEC—federal agency responsible for enforcing federal securities laws
- Exemption—security not required to be registered
- Exempt transaction—offering not required to be registered
- Regulation D—small offering exemption rules
- Accredited investor—investor who meets threshold standards for assets and income
- Rules 504, 505, 506—portion of Regulation D affording exemptions for variously structured offerings
- Registration statement—disclosure statement filed by the offeror with the SEC
- Prospectus—formal document explaining offering or any ad or written materials describing offering
- Comment letter—request by SEC for more information
- Deficiency letter—request by SEC for more information
- Full-disclosure standard—review for information, not a review on the merits
- Tombstone ad—ad announcing offering that can be run prior to effective date of registration statement
- Red herring prospectus—redlined prospectus that can be given to potential purchasers prior to effective date of registration statement
- Shelf registrations—SEC approval process that allows approval and then waiting period for market conditions
- Material misstatement—false information that would affect the decision to buy or sell
- Section 11—portion of 1933 act that provides for liability for false statements or omissions in registration statements
- Due diligence—defense of good faith and full effort to Section 11 charges
- Section 12—portion of 1933 act that provides for liability for selling without registration or exemption before effective date or with a false prospectus

QUESTIONS AND PROBLEMS

1. The Farmer's Cooperative of Arkansas (Co-Op) was an agricultural cooperative that had approximately 23,000 members. In order to raise money to support its general business operations, the Co-Op sold promissory notes payable on demand by the holder. The notes were uncollateralized and uninsured and paid a variable rate of interest that was adjusted to make it higher than the rate paid by local financial institutions. The notes were offered to members and nonmembers and were marketed as an "investment program." Advertisements for the notes, which appeared in the Co-Op newsletter, read in part: "YOUR CO-OP has more than $11,000,000 in assets to stand behind your investments. The Investment is not Federal [sic] insured but it is . . . Safe."

Despite the assurance, the Co-Op filed for bankruptcy in 1984. At the time of the bankruptcy filing, over 1,600 people held notes worth a total of $10 million.

After the bankruptcy filing, a class of note holders filed suit against Arthur Young & Co., alleging that Young had failed to follow generally accepted accounting principles in its audit, specifically with respect to the valuation of the Co-Op's major asset, a gasahol plant. The note holders claimed that if Young had properly treated the plant in its audited financials, they would not have purchased the notes. The petitioners were awarded $6.1 million in damages by the federal district court. Are the notes securities? [*Reves* v. *Ernst & Young*, 494 U.S. 56 (1990).]

2. Time, Inc. acquired all stock of Warner Communications, Inc. at $70 per share in 1989. Time, which became Time Warner, Inc., was saddled with over $10 billion in debt as a result of the purchase.

The company embarked on a highly publicized campaign to find an international "strategic partner" who would infuse billions of dollars of capital into the company and who would help the company realize its dream of becoming a dominant worldwide entertainment conglomerate. Ultimately, Time Warner formed only two strategic partnerships, each on a much smaller scale than had been hoped. Faced with a multibillion-dollar balloon payment on the debt, the company was forced to seek an alternative method of raising capital—a new stock offering that substantially diluted the rights of the existing shareholders. The company first proposed a variable price offering on June 6, 1991. This proposal was rejected by the SEC, but it approved a second proposal announced on July 12, 1991. Announcement of the two offering proposals caused a substantial decline in the price of Time Warner stock. From June 5 to June 12, the share price fell from $117 to $94. By July 12, the price had fallen to $89.75.

A group of shareholders that purchased Time Warner stock between December 12, 1990, and June 7,

1991, brought suit under Section 10(b) alleging that Time Warner made materially misleading statements and misrepresented the status of its strategic partnership discussions.

Did Time Warner violate Section 10(b)? [*Time Warner, Inc.* v. *Ross*, 9 F.3d 259 (3d Cir. 1993).]

3. Marshall Field & Co., a Delaware corporation with its principal office in Chicago, has operated retail department stores since 1852 and is the eighth largest department store chain in the United States, with thirty-one stores. Carter Hawley Hale (CHH), a California corporation that owned Neiman-Marcus, attempted several times to merge or take over Field's. During this time, Field's also received merger offers from Federated Department Stores and Dayton-Hudson. Still another retailer—Gamble-Skogmo—offered to acquire a 20 percent block of Field's stock to prevent a takeover. Field's turned down all offers. CHH finally offered a last-effort deal that Field's refused. CHH then began an unfriendly takeover.

In its information to shareholders, Field's suggested that independence was best, growth would continue, and stock prices would increase. These statements were doubtful, but shareholders rejected the takeover offer. CHH withdrew, and Field's stock declined dramatically. A Field's shareholder has sued for misrepresentation. Can he win? [*Panter* v. *Marshall Field & Co.*, 646 F.2d 271 (7th Cir. 1981).]

4. On March 24, 1977, Anschutz Corporation purchased from Kay Corporation a 50 percent interest in Metal Traders, Inc. (MTI). MTI trades in metal ores and concentrates, and it operates a Bolivian antimony mine. In its financial statement, Kay showed that MTI had just declared a $2 million cash dividend. It did not disclose that, to declare the dividend, it had to use a substantial portion of an unsecured line of credit, making it unlikely that MTI could continue its operations. When MTI went bankrupt, Anschutz filed suit under Section 11 of the 1933 act. Will Anschutz win? [*Anschutz Corp.* v. *Kay Corp.*, 507 F. Supp. 72 (S.D.N.Y. 1981).]

5. Beginning in March 1981, R. Foster Winans was a *Wall Street Journal* reporter and one of the writers of the "Heard on the Street" column (the "Heard" column), a widely read and influential column in the *Journal*. David Carpenter worked as a news clerk at the *Journal* from December 1981 through May 1983. Kenneth Felis, who was a stockbroker at the brokerage house of Kidder Peabody, had been brought to that firm by another Kidder Peabody stockbroker, Peter Brant, Mr. Felis's longtime friend who later became the government's key witness in this case.

Since February 2, 1981, it was the practice of Dow Jones, the parent company of the *Wall Street Journal,* to distribute to all new employees "The Insider Story," a forty-page manual with seven pages devoted to the company's conflicts-of-interest policy. Mr. Winans and Mr. Carpenter knew that company policy deemed all news material gleaned by an employee during the course of employment to be company property and that company policy required employees to treat nonpublic information learned on the job as confidential.

Notwithstanding company policy, Mr. Winans participated in a scheme with Mr. Brant and later Mr. Felis and Mr. Carpenter in which he agreed to provide the two stockbrokers (Mr. Brant and Mr. Felis) with securities-related information that was scheduled to appear in "Heard" columns; based on this advance information, the two brokers would buy or sell the subject securities. Mr. Carpenter, who was involved in a private, personal, nonbusiness relationship with Mr. Winans, served primarily as a messenger for the conspirators. Trading accounts were established in the names of Kenneth Felis, David Carpenter, R. Foster Winans, Peter Brant, David Clark, Western Hemisphere, and Stephen Spratt. During 1983 and early 1984, these defendants made prepublication trades on the basis of their advance knowledge of approximately twenty-seven *Wall Street Journal* "Heard" columns, although not all of those columns were written by Mr. Winans. Generally, he would inform Mr. Brant of an article's subject the day before its scheduled publication, usually by calls from a pay phone and often using a fictitious name. The net profits from the scheme approached $690,000. Was this scheme a 10(b) violation? [*United States* v. *Carpenter,* 791 F.2d 1024 (2d Cir. 1986); *affirmed, Carpenter* v. *United States,* 484 U.S. 19 (1987).]

6. Raymond Dirks was an officer in a Wall Street brokerage house. He was told by Ronald Secrist, a former officer of the Equity Funding of America Company, that Equity Funding had significantly overstated its assets by writing phony insurance policies. Mr. Secrist urged Mr. Dirks to investigate and expose the fraudulent practices. Mr. Dirks checked with Equity Funding management and received denials from them, but he received affirmations from employees.

Mr. Dirks discussed the issue with clients, and they "dumped" nearly $6 million in Equity Funding stock, but Mr. Dirks and his firm did not trade the stock. The price of the stock fell from $26 to $15 during Mr. Dirks's investigation. He contacted the *Wall Street Journal* bureau chief about the problem, but the bureau chief declined to get involved.

The SEC charged Mr. Dirks with violations of 10b-5 for his assistance to his clients. Did he violate 10b-5? [*Dirks* v. *SEC,* 463 U.S. 646 (1983).]

7. Vincent Chiarella was employed as a printer in a financial printing firm that handled the printing for takeover bids. Although the firm names were left out of the financial materials and inserted at the last moment, Mr. Chiarella was able to deduce who was being taken over and by whom from other information in the reports being printed. Using this information, Mr. Chiarella was able to dabble in the stock market over a fourteen-month period for a net gain of $30,000. After an SEC investigation, he signed a consent decree that required him to return all of his profits to the sellers he purchased from during that fourteen-month period. He was then indicted for violation of 10(b) of the 1934 act and the SEC's Rule 10b-5. Did Mr. Chiarella violate 10b-5? [*Chiarella* v. *United States,* 445 U.S. 222 (1980).]

8. The president's letter in Rockwood Computer Corporation's annual report stated that most of its inventory consisted of its old computer series. The letter suggested that its new series would cost more money for all users. However, the letter did not disclose, although evidence had indicated, that the new system might be less expensive for those who needed greater performance and capacity. Walter Beissinger (who sold his shares based on the information) brought suit under 10(b). Rockwood claims the statements were based on opinions of sales and were not statements of fact. Who should win? [*Beissinger* v. *Rockwood Computer Corp.,* 529 F. Supp. 770 (E.D. Pa. 1981).]

9. William H. Sullivan Jr. gained control of the New England Patriots Football Club (Patriots) by forming a separate corporation (New Patriots) and merging it with the old one. Plaintiffs are a class of stockholders who voted to accept New Patriots' offer of $15 a share for their common stock in the Patriots' corporation. They now claim that they were induced to accept this offer by a misleading proxy statement drafted under the direction of Mr. Sullivan, who owned a controlling share in the voting stock of the Patriots at the time of the merger. The proxy statement, plaintiffs claim, contained various misrepresentations designed to paint a gloomy picture of the financial position and prospects of the Patriots, so that the shareholders undervalued their stock. They seek to rescind the merger or to receive a higher price per share for the stock they sold. Does the court have the authority to rescind under Section 14? [*Pavlidis* v. *New England Patriots Football Club,* 737 F.2d 1227 (1st Cir. 1984).]

10. The National Bank of Yugoslavia placed $71 million with Drexel Burnham Lambert, Inc. for short-term investment just months before Drexel's bankruptcy. In effect, the bank made a time deposit. Would the bank be able to proceed under a theory of securities laws violations? Would these time deposits be considered securities? [*National Bank of Yugoslavia* v. *Drexel Burnham Lambert, Inc.,* 768 F.Supp. 1010 (S.D.N.Y 1991).]

RESEARCH PROBLEM

More Than a Book Offering

11. Simon & Simon, Inc. (SSI) is a Fortune 500 company primarily involved in publishing magazines and fiction and nonfiction popular press. Like other publishing firms, SSI has been interested in expansion through the acquisition of publishing firms or companies with a multimedia focus. Its shares are listed on the New York Stock Exchange.

SSI has been approached by University Press (UP), a small but successful publishing house with a focus on academic and research-oriented books that would like to sell its assets (physical as well as titles [copyrights]) to SSI. UP is a national company that markets largely through direct mailings and whose stock is sold on the over-the-counter market. SSI has its own bookstores in malls, downtown city centers, and a few strip malls. It releases approximately thirty major fiction titles (excluding its romance novel line) and twenty major nonfiction titles each year. Other releases include children's books, cookbooks, "how to" books, coffee table (art) books, and several college and test-preparation guides. These types of releases total 100 per year. UP releases twenty-five new books each year, but it is in the unique position of having some of its titles continue selling long after the usual six-month hard-cover life of popular press books.

UP's board authorized its CEO to approach SSI. SSI's board heard the proposal for the first time yesterday. SSI's CEO told them, "We should act quickly. The price is right." Another board member asked, "Aren't there some legal issues here? Can we act this quickly?"

Prepare a memorandum for the SSI board and also for the UP board outlining all the legal issues, including corporate, antitrust, and securities issues.

NOTES

1. For more on the history of securities law, see the Web site and the Instructor's Manual.

2. Alex Berenson, "Man Charged in Stock Fraud Based on Fake News," *New York Times,* September 1, 2000, pp. C1, C2.

3. Anita Raghavan, Silvia Ascarelli, and David Woodruff, "Insider Trading in Europe Is Virtually Risk-Free," *Wall Street Journal,* August 17, 2000, p. C1.

The United States Constitution

We the People of the United States, in Order to form a more perfect Union, establish Justice, insure domestic Tranquility, provide for the common defence, promote the general Welfare, and secure the Blessings of Liberty to ourselves and our Posterity, do ordain and establish this Constitution for the United States of America.

Article I

Section I

All legislative Powers herein granted shall be vested in a Congress of the United States, which shall consist of a Senate and House of Representatives.

Section 2

The House of Representatives shall be composed of Members chosen every second Year by the People of the several States, and the Electors in each State shall have the Qualifications requisite for Electors of the most numerous Branch of the State Legislature.

No Person shall be a Representative who shall not have attained to the Age of twenty five Years, and been seven Years a Citizen of the United States, and who shall not, when elected, be an Inhabitant of that State in which he shall be chosen.

Representatives and direct Taxes shall be apportioned among the several States which may be included within this Union, according to their respective Numbers, which shall be determined by adding to the whole Number of free Persons, including those bound to Service for a Term of Years, and excluding Indians not taxed, three fifths of all other Persons. The actual Enumeration shall be made within three Years after the first Meeting of the Congress of the United States, and within every subsequent Term of ten Years, in which Manner as they shall by Law direct. The Number of Representatives shall not exceed one for every thirty Thousand, but each State shall have at Least one Representative; and until such enumeration shall be made, the State of New Hampshire shall be en-

titled to choose three, Massachusetts eight, Rhode Island and Providence Plantations one, Connecticut five, New York six, New Jersey four, Pennsylvania eight, Delaware one, Maryland six, Virginia ten, North Carolina five, South Carolina five, and Georgia three.

When vacancies happen in the Representation from any State, the Executive Authority thereof shall issue Writs of Election to fill such Vacancies.

The House of Representatives shall chuse their Speaker and other Officers; and shall have the sole Power of Impeachment.

Section 3

The Senate of the United States shall be composed of two Senators from each State, chosen by the Legislature thereof, for six Years; and each Senator shall have one Vote.

Immediately after they shall be assembled in Consequence of the first Election, they shall be divided as equally as may be into three Classes. The Seats of the Senators of the first Class shall be vacated at the Expiration of the second Year, of the second Class at the Expiration of the fourth Year, and of the third Class at the Expiration of the sixth Year, so that one third may be chosen every second Year; and if Vacancies happen by Resignation, or otherwise, during the Recess of the Legislature of any State, the Executive thereof may make temporary Appointments until the next Meeting of the Legislature, which shall then fill such Vacancies.

No Person shall be a Senator who shall not have attained to the Age of thirty Years, and been nine Years a Citizen of the United States, and who shall not, when elected, be an Inhabitant of that State for which he shall be chosen.

The Vice President of the United States shall be President of the Senate, but shall have no Vote, unless they be equally divided.

The Senate shall chuse their other Officers, and also a President pro tempore, in the Absence of the Vice President, or when he shall exercise the Office of President of the United States.

The Senate shall have the sole Power to try all Impeachments. When sitting for that Purpose, they shall be on Oath or Affirmation. When the President of the United States is tried the Chief Justice shall preside: And no Person shall be convicted without the Concurrence of two thirds of the Members present.

Judgment in Cases of Impeachment shall not extend further than to removal from Office, and disqualification to hold and enjoy any Office of honor, Trust or Profit under the United States: but the Party convicted shall nevertheless be liable and subject to Indictment, Trial, Judgment and Punishment, according to Law.

Section 4

The Times, Places and Manner of holding Elections for Senators and Representatives, shall be prescribed in each State by the Legislature thereof; but the Congress may at any time by Law make or alter such Regulations, except as to the Places of chusing Senators.

The Congress shall assemble at Least once in every Year, and such Meeting shall be on the first Monday in December, unless they shall by Law appoint a different Day.

Section 5

Each House shall be the Judge of the Elections, Returns and Qualifications of its own Members, and a Majority of each shall constitute a Quorum to do Business; but a smaller Number may adjourn from day to day, and may be authorized to compel the Attendance of absent Members, in such Manner, and under such Penalties as each House may provide.

Each House may determine the Rules in its Proceedings, punish its Members for disorderly Behaviour, and, with the Concurrence of two thirds, expel a Member.

Each House shall keep a Journal of its Proceedings, and from time to time publish the same, excepting such Parts as may in their Judgment require Secrecy; and the Yeas and Nays of the Members of either House on any question shall, at the Desire of one fifth of those Present, be entered on the Journal.

Neither House, during the Session of Congress, shall, without the Consent of the other, adjourn for more than three days, nor to any other Place than that in which the two Houses shall be sitting.

Section 6

The Senators and Representatives shall receive a Compensation for their Services, to be ascertained by Law, and paid out of the Treasury of the United States. They shall in all Cases, except Treason, Felony and Breach of the Peace, be privileged from Arrest during their Attendance at the Session of their respective Houses, and in going to and returning from the same; and for any Speech or Debate in either House, they shall not be questioned in any other Place.

No Senator or Representative shall, during the Time for which he was elected, be appointed to any civil Office under the Authority of the United States, which shall have been created, or the Emoluments whereof shall have been encreased during such time; and no Person holding any Office under the United States, shall be a Member of either House during his Continuance in Office.

Section 7

All Bills for raising Revenue shall originate in the House of Representatives; but the Senate may propose or concur with amendments as on other Bills.

Every Bill which shall have passed the House of Representatives and the Senate, shall, before it become a Law, be presented to the President of the United States; If he approve he shall sign it, but if not he shall return it, with his Objections to that House in which it shall have originated, who shall enter the Objections at large on their Journal, and proceed to reconsider it. If after such Reconsideration two thirds of that House shall agree to pass the Bill, it shall be sent, together with the Objections, to the other House, by which it shall like wise be reconsidered, and if approved by two thirds of that House, it shall become a Law. But in all such Cases the Votes of both Houses shall be determined by Yeas and Nays, and the names of the Persons voting for and against the Bill shall be entered on the Journal of each House respectively. If any Bill shall not be returned by the President within ten Days (Sundays excepted) after it shall have been presented to him, the Same shall be a Law, in like Manner as if he had signed it, unless the Congress by their Adjournment prevent its Return, in which Case it shall not be a Law.

Every Order, Resolution, or Vote to which the Concurrence of the Senate and House of Representatives may be necessary (except on a question of Adjournment) shall be presented to the President of the United States; and before the Same shall take Effect, shall be approved by him, or being disapproved by him, shall be repassed by two thirds of the Senate and House of Representatives, according to the Rules and Limitations prescribed in the Case of a Bill.

Section 8

The Congress shall have Power To lay and collect Taxes, Duties, Imposts and Excises, to pay the Debts and provide for the common Defense and general Welfare of the United States; but all Duties, Imposts and Excises shall be uniform throughout the United States;

To borrow Money on the credit of the United States;

To regulate Commerce with foreign Nations, and among the several States, and with the Indian Tribes;

To establish an uniform Rule of Naturalization, and uniform Laws on the subject of Bankruptcies throughout the United States;

To coin Money, regulate the Value thereof, and of foreign Coin, and fix the Standard of Weights and Measures;

To provide for the Punishment of counterfeiting the Securities and current Coin of the United States;

To establish Post Offices and post Roads;

To promote the Progress of Science and useful Arts, by securing for limited Times to Authors and Inventors the exclusive Right to their respective Writings and Discoveries;

To constitute Tribunals inferior to the supreme Court;

To define and punish Piracies and Felonies committed on the high Seas, and Offenses against the Law of Nations;

To declare War, grant Letters of Marque and Reprisal, and make Rules concerning Captures on Land and Water;

To raise and support Armies, but no Appropriation of Money to that Use shall be for a longer Term than two Years;

To provide and maintain a Navy;

To make Rules for the Government and Regulation of the land and naval Forces;

To provide for calling forth the Militia to execute the Laws of the Union, suppress Insurrections and repel Invasions;

To provide for organizing, arming, and disciplining, the Militia, and for governing such Part of them as may be employed in the Service of the United States, reserving to the States respectively, the Appointment of the Officers, and the Authority of training the Militia according to the discipline prescribed by Congress;

To exercise exclusive Legislation in all Cases whatsoever, over such District (not exceeding ten Miles square) as may, by Cession of particular States, and the Acceptance of Congress, become the Seat of the Government of the United States, and to exercise like Authority over all Places purchased by the Consent of the Legislature of the State in which the Same shall be, for the Erection of Forts, Magazines, Arsenals, dock-Yards, and other needful Buildings;—And

To make all Laws which shall be necessary and proper for carrying into Execution the foregoing Powers, and all other Powers vested by this Constitution in the Government of the United States, or in any Department or Officer thereof.

Section 9

The Migration or Importation of such Persons as any of the States now existing shall think proper to admit, shall not be prohibited by the Congress prior to the Year one thousand eight hundred and eight, but a Tax or duty may be imposed on such Importation, not exceeding ten dollars for each Person.

The Privilege of the Writ of Habeas Corpus shall not be suspended, unless when in Cases of Rebellion or Invasion the public Safety may require it.

No Bill of Attainder or ex post facto Law shall be passed.

No Capitation, or other direct, Tax shall be laid, unless in Proportion to the Census or Enumeration herein before directed to be taken.

No Tax or Duty shall be laid on Articles exported from any State.

No Preference shall be given to any Regulation of Commerce or Revenue to the Ports of one State over those of another; nor shall Vessels bound to, or from, one State, be obliged to enter, clear or pay Duties in another.

No Money shall be drawn from the Treasury, but in Consequence of Appropriations made by Law; and a regular Statement and Account of the Receipts and Expenditures of all public Money shall be published from time to time.

No Title of Nobility shall be granted by the United States: And no Person holding any Office of

Profit or Trust under them, shall, without the Consent of the Congress, accept of any present, Emolument, Office, or Title, of any kind whatever, from any King, Prince or foreign State.

Section 10

No State shall enter into any Treaty, Alliance, or Confederation; grant Letters of Marque and Reprisal; coin Money; emit Bills of Credit; make any Thing but gold and silver Coin a Tender in Payment of Debts; pass any Bill of Attainder, ex post facto Law or law impairing the Obligation of Contracts, or grant any Title of Nobility.

No State shall, without the Consent of the Congress, lay any Imposts or Duties on Imports or Exports, except what may be absolutely necessary for executing its inspection Laws: and the net Produce of all Duties and Imposts, laid by any State on Imports or Exports, shall be for the Use of the Treasury of the United States; and all such Laws shall be subject to the Revision and Control of the Congress.

No State shall, without the Consent of Congress, lay any Duty on Tonnage, keep Troops, or Ships of War in time of Peace, enter into any Agreement or Compact with another State, or with a foreign Power, or engage in War, unless actually invaded, or in such imminent Danger as will not admit of delay.

Article II

Section I

The executive Power shall be vested in a President of the United States of America. He shall hold his Office during the Term of four Years, and, together with the Vice President, chosen for the same Term, be elected, as follows:

Each State shall appoint, in such Manner as the Legislature thereof may direct, a Number of Electors, equal to the whole Number of Senators and Representatives to which the State may be entitled in the Congress: but no Senator or Representative, or Person holding an Office of Trust or Profit under the United States, shall be appointed an Elector.

The Electors shall meet in their respective States, and vote by Ballot for two Persons, of whom one at least shall not be an Inhabitant of the same State with themselves. And they shall make a List of all the Persons voted for, and of the Number of Votes for each; which List they shall sign and cer-

tify, and transmit sealed to the Seat of the Government of the United States, directed to the President of the Senate. The President of the Senate shall, in the Presence of the Senate and House of Representatives, open all the Certificates, and the Votes shall then be counted. The Person having the greatest Number of Votes shall be the President, if such Number be a Majority of the whole Number of Electors appointed; and if there be more than one who have such Majority, and have an equal Number of Votes, then the House of Representatives shall immediately chuse by Ballot one of them for President; and if no Person have a Majority, then from the five highest on the List the said House shall in like Manner chuse the President. But in chusing the President, the Votes shall be taken by States, the Representation from each State having one Vote; a quorum for this Purpose shall consist of a Member or Members from two thirds of the States, and a Majority of all the States shall be necessary to a Choice. In every Case, after the Choice of the President, the Person having the greatest Number of Votes of the Electors shall be the Vice President. But if there should remain two or more who have equal Votes, the Senate shall chuse from them by Ballot the Vice President.

The Congress may determine the Time of chusing the Electors, and the Day on which they shall give their Votes; which Day shall be the same throughout the United States.

No Person except a natural born Citizen, or a Citizen of the United States, at the time of the Adoption of this Constitution, shall be eligible to the Office of President; neither shall any Person be eligible to that Office who shall not have attained to the Age of thirty-five Years, and been fourteen years a Resident within the United States.

In Case of the Removal of the President from Office, or of his Death, Resignation, or Inability to discharge the Powers and Duties of the said Office, the Same shall devolve on the Vice President, and the Congress may by Law provide for the Case of Removal, Death, Resignation, or Inability, both of the President and Vice President, declaring what Officer shall then act as President, and such Officer shall act accordingly, until the Disability be removed, or a President shall be elected.

The President shall, at stated Times, receive for his Services, a Compensation, which shall neither be increased nor diminished during the Period for which he shall have been elected, and he shall not receive within that Period any other Emolument from the United States, or any of them.

Before he enter on the Execution of his Office, he shall take the following Oath or Affirmation:— "I do solemnly swear (or affirm) that I will faithfully execute the Office of President of the United States, and will to the best of my Ability, preserve, protect, and defend the Constitution of the United States."

Section 2

The President shall be Commander in Chief of the Army and Navy of the United States, and of the Militia of the several States, when called into the actual Service of the United States; he may require the Opinion, in writing, of the principal Officer in each of the executive Departments, upon any Subject relating to the Duties of their respective Offices, and he shall have Power to grant Reprieves and Pardons for Offenses against the United States, except in Cases of Impeachment.

He shall have Power, by and with the Advice and Consent of the Senate, to make Treaties, provided two thirds of the Senators present concur; and he shall nominate, and by and with the Advice and Consent of the Senate, shall appoint Ambassadors, other public Ministers and Consuls, Judges of the supreme Court, and all other Officers of the United States, whose Appointments are not herein otherwise provided for, and which shall be established by Law: but the Congress may by Law vest the Appointment of such inferior Officers, as they think proper, in the President alone, in the Courts of Law, or in the Heads of Departments.

The President shall have Power to fill up all Vacancies that may happen during the Recess of the Senate, by granting Commissions which shall expire at the End of their next Session.

Section 3

He shall from time to time give to the Congress Information of the State of the Union, and recommend to their Consideration such Measures as he shall judge necessary and expedient; he may, on extraordinary Occasions, convene both Houses, or either of them, and in Case of Disagreement between them, with Respect to the Time of Adjournment, he may adjourn them to such Time as he shall think proper; he shall receive Ambassadors and other public Ministers; he shall take Care that the Laws be faithfully executed, and shall Commission all the Officers of the United States.

Section 4

The President, Vice President and all Civil Officers of the United States, shall be removed from Office on Impeachment for, and Conviction of, Treason, Bribery, or other high Crimes and Misdemeanors.

Article III

Section 1

The judicial Power of the United States, shall be vested in one supreme Court, and in such inferior Courts as the Congress may from time to time ordain and establish. The Judges, both of the supreme and inferior Courts, shall hold their Offices during good Behaviour, and shall, at stated Times, receive for their Services, a Compensation, which shall not be diminished during their Continuance in Office.

Section 2

The judicial Power shall extend to all Cases, in Law and Equity, arising under this Constitution, the Laws of the United States, and Treaties made, or which shall be made, under their Authority;—to all Cases affecting Ambassadors, other public Ministers and Consuls;—to all Cases of admiralty and maritime Jurisdiction;—to Controversies to which the United States shall be a Party;—to Controversies between two or more States;—between a State and Citizens of another State;—between Citizens of different States,—between Citizens of the same State claiming Lands under Grants of different States, and between a State, or the Citizens thereof, and foreign States, Citizens or Subjects.

In all Cases affecting Ambassadors, other public Ministers and Consuls, and those in which a State shall be Party, the Supreme Court shall have original Jurisdiction. In all the other Cases before mentioned, the supreme Court shall have appellate Jurisdiction, both as to Law and Fact, with such Exceptions, and under such Regulations as the Congress shall make.

The Trial of all Crimes, except in Cases of Impeachment, shall be by Jury; and such Trial shall be held in the State where the said Crimes shall have been committed; but when not committed within any State, the Trial shall be at such Place or Places as the Congress may by Law have directed.

Section 3

Treason against the United States, shall consist only in levying War against them, or in adhering to their Enemies, giving them Aid and Comfort. No Person shall be convicted of Treason unless on the Testimony of two Witnesses to the same overt Act, or on Confession in open Court.

The Congress shall have Power to declare the Punishment of Treason, but no Attainder of Treason shall work Corruption of Blood, or Forfeiture except during the Life of the Person attainted.

Article IV

Section 1

Full Faith and Credit shall be given in each State to the public Arts, Records, and judicial Proceedings of every other State. And the Congress may by general Laws prescribe the Manner in which such Acts, Records and Proceedings shall be proved, and the Effect thereof.

Section 2

The Citizens of each State shall be entitled to all Privileges and Immunities of Citizens in the several States.

A Person charged in any State with Treason, Felony, or other Crime, who shall flee from Justice, and be found in another State, shall on Demand of the executive Authority of the State from which he fled, be delivered up, to be removed to the State having Jurisdiction of the Crime.

No Person held to Service or Labour in one State, under the Laws thereof, escaping into another, shall, in Consequence of any Law or Regulation therein, be discharged from such Service or Labour, but shall be delivered up on Claim of the Party to whom such Service or Labour may be due.

Section 3

New States may be admitted by the Congress into this Union; but no new State shall be formed or erected within the Jurisdiction of any other State; nor any State be formed by the Junction of two or more States, or Parts of States, without the Consent of the Legislatures of the States concerned as well as of the Congress.

The Congress shall have Power to dispose of and make all needful Rules and Regulations respecting the Territory or other Property belonging to the United States; and nothing in this Constitution shall be so construed as to Prejudice any Claims of the United States, or of any particular State.

Section 4

The United States shall guarantee to every State in this Union a Republican Form of Government, and shall protect each of them against Invasion; and on Application of the Legislature, or of the Executive (when the Legislature cannot be convened) against domestic Violence.

Article V

The Congress, whenever two thirds of both Houses shall deem it necessary, shall propose Amendments to this Constitution, or, on the Application of the Legislatures of two thirds of the several States, shall call a Convention for proposing Amendments, which, in either Case, shall be valid to all Intents and Purposes, as Part of this Constitution, when ratified by the Legislatures of three fourths of the several States, or by Conventions in three fourths thereof, as the one or the other Mode of Ratification may be proposed by the Congress; Provided that no Amendment which may be made prior to the Year One thousand eight hundred and eight shall in any Manner affect the first and fourth Clauses in the Ninth Section of the first Article; and that no State, without its Consent, shall be deprived of its equal Suffrage in the Senate.

Article VI

All Debts contracted and Engagements entered into, before the Adoption of this Constitution, shall be as valid against the United States under this Constitution, as under the Confederation.

This Constitution, and the Laws of the United States which shall be made in Pursuance thereof; and all Treaties made, or which shall be made, under the Authority of the United States, shall be the supreme Law of the Land; and the judges in every State shall be bound thereby, any Thing in the Constitution or Laws of any State to the Contrary notwithstanding.

The Senators and Representatives before mentioned, and the Members of the several State Legislatures, and all executive and judicial Officers, both of the United States and of the several States, shall be bound by Oath or Affirmation, to support this Constitution; but no religious Test shall ever be required as a Qualification to any Office or public Trust under the United States.

Article VII

The Ratification of the Conventions of nine States, shall be sufficient for the Establishment of this Constitution between the States so ratifying the Same.

Amendment I (1791)

Congress shall make no law respecting an establishment of religion, or prohibiting the free exercise thereof; or abridging the freedom of speech, or of the press; or the right of the people peaceably to assemble, and to petition the Government for a redress of grievances.

Amendment II (1791)

A well regulated Militia, being necessary to the security of a free State, the right of the people to keep and bear Arms, shall not be infringed.

Amendment III (1791)

No Soldier shall, in time of peace be quartered in any house, without the consent of the Owner, nor in time of war, but in a manner to be prescribed by law.

Amendment IV (1791)

The right of the people to be secure in their persons, houses, papers, and effects, against unreasonable searches and seizures, shall not be violated, and no Warrants shall issue, but upon probable cause, supported by Oath or affirmation, and particularly describing the place to be searched, and the persons or things to be seized.

Amendment V (1791)

No person shall be held to answer for a capital or otherwise infamous crime, unless on a presentment or indictment of a Grand Jury, except in cases arising in the land or naval forces, or in the Militia, when in actual service in time of War or public danger; nor shall any person be subject for the same offense to be twice put in jeopardy of life or limb; nor shall be compelled in any criminal case to be a witness against himself, nor be deprived of life, liberty, or property, without due process of law; nor shall private property be taken for public use, with out just compensation.

Amendment VI (1791)

In all criminal prosecutions, the accused shall enjoy the right to a speedy and public trial, by an impartial jury of the State and district wherein the crime shall have been committed, which district shall have been previously ascertained by law, and to be informed of the nature and cause of the accusation; to be confronted with the witnesses against him; to have compulsory process for obtaining Witnesses in his favor, and to have the Assistance of Counsel for his defense.

Amendment VII (1791)

In Suits at common law, where the value in controversy shall exceed twenty dollars, the right of trial by jury shall be preserved, and no fact tried by a jury, shall be otherwise reexamined in any Court of the United States, than according to the rules of the common law.

Amendment VIII (1791)

Excessive bail shall not be required nor excessive fines imposed, nor cruel and unusual punishments inflicted.

Amendment IX (1791)

The enumeration in the Constitution, of certain rights, shall not be construed to deny or disparage others retained by the people.

Amendment X (1791)

The powers not delegated to the United States by the Constitution, nor prohibited by it to the States, are reserved to the States respectively, or to the people.

Amendment XI (1798)

The Judicial power of the United States shall not be construed to extend to any suit in law or equity, commenced or prosecuted against one of the United States by Citizens of another State, or by Citizens or Subjects of any Foreign State.

Amendment XII (1804)

The Electors shall meet in their respective states and vote by ballot for President and Vice President, one of whom, at least, shall not be an inhabitant of the same state with themselves; they shall name in their ballots the person voted for as President, and in distinct ballots the person voted for as Vice-President, and they shall make distinct lists of all persons voted for as President, and of all persons voted for as Vice-President, and of the number of votes for each, which lists they shall sign and certify, and transmit sealed to the seat of the government of the United States, directed to the President of the Senate;—The President of the Senate shall, in the presence of the Senate and House of Representatives, open all the certificates and the votes shall then be counted;—The person having the greatest number of votes for President, shall be the President, if such number be a majority of the whole number of Electors appointed; and if no person have such majority, then from the persons having the highest numbers not exceeding three on the list of those voted for as President, the House of Representatives shall choose immediately, by ballot, the President. But in choosing the President, the votes shall be taken by states, the representation from each state having one vote; a quorum for this purpose shall consist of a member or members from two-thirds of the states, and a majority of all the states shall be necessary to a choice. And if the House of Representatives shall not choose a President whenever the right of choice shall devolve upon them, before the fourth day of March next following, then the Vice-President shall act as President, as in the case of the death or other constitutional disability of the President—The person having the greatest number of votes as Vice-President, shall be the Vice-President, if such number be a majority of the whole number of Electors appointed, and if no person have a majority, then from the two highest numbers on the list, the Senate shall choose the Vice-President; a quorum for the purpose shall consist of two-thirds of the whole numbers of Senators, and a majority of the whole number shall be necessary to a choice. But no person constitutionally ineligible to the office of President shall be eligible to that of Vice President of the United States.

Amendment XIII (1865)

Section 1

Neither slavery nor involuntary servitude, except as a punishment for crime whereof the party shall have been duly convicted, shall exist within the United States, or any place subject to their jurisdiction.

Section 2

Congress shall have power to enforce this article by appropriate legislation.

Amendment XIV (1868)

Section 1

All persons born or naturalized in the United States and subject to the jurisdiction thereof, are citizens of the United States and of the State wherein they reside. No State shall make or enforce any law which shall abridge the privileges or immunities of citizens of the United States; nor shall any State deprive any person of life, liberty, or property, without due process of law; nor deny to any person within its jurisdiction the equal protection of the laws.

Section 2

Representatives shall be apportioned among the several States according to their respective numbers, counting the whole number of persons in each State, excluding Indians not taxed. But when the right to vote at any election for the choice of electors for President and Vice President of the United States, Representatives in Congress, the Executive and Judicial officers of a State, or the members of the Legislature thereof, is denied to any of the male inhabitants of such State, being twenty-one years of age, and citizens of the United States, or in any way abridged, except for participation in rebellion, or other crime, the basis of representation therein shall be reduced in the proportion which the number of such male citizens shall bear to the whole number of male citizens twenty-one years of age in such State.

Section 3

No person shall be a Senator or Representative in Congress, or elector of President and Vice President, or hold any office, civil or military, under the United States, or under any State, who, having previously taken an oath, as a member of Congress, or as an officer of the United States, or as a member of any State legislature, or as an executive or judicial officer of any State, to support the Constitution of the United States, shall have engaged in insurrection or rebellion against the same, or given aid or comfort to the enemies thereof. But Congress may by a vote of two-thirds of each House, remove such disability.

Section 4

The validity of the public debt of the United States, authorized by law, including debts incurred for payment of pensions and bounties for services in suppressing insurrection or rebellion, shall not be questioned. But neither the United States nor any State shall assume or pay any debt or obligation incurred in aid of insurrection or rebellion against the United States, or any claim for the loss or emancipation of any slave; but all such debts, obligations and claims shall be held illegal and void.

Section 5
The Congress shall have power to enforce, by appropriate legislation, the provisions of this article.

Amendment XV (1870)

Section 1
The right of citizens of the United States to vote shall not be denied or abridged by the United States or by any State on account of race, color, or previous condition of servitude.

Section 2
The Congress shall have power to enforce this article by appropriate legislation.

Amendment XVI (1913)

The Congress shall have power to lay and collect taxes on incomes, from whatever source derived, without apportionment among the several States, and without regard to any census or enumeration.

Amendment XVII (1913)

The Senate of the United States shall be composed of two Senators from each State, elected by the people thereof, for six years; and each Senator shall have one vote. The electors in each State shall have the qualifications requisite for electors of the most numerous branch of the State legislatures.

When vacancies happen in the representation of any State in the Senate, the executive authority of such State shall issue writs of election to fill such vacancies: *Provided,* That the legislature of any State may empower the executive thereof to make temporary appointments until the people fill the vacancies by election as the legislature may direct.

This amendment shall not be so construed as to affect the election or term of any Senator chosen before it becomes valid as part of the Constitution.

Amendment XVIII (1919)

Section 1
After one year from the ratification of this article the manufacture, sale, or transportation of intoxicating liquors within, the importation thereof into, or the exportation thereof from the United States and all territory subject to the jurisdiction thereof for beverage purposes is hereby prohibited.

Section 2
The Congress and the several States shall have concurrent power to enforce this article by appropriate legislation.

Section 3
This article shall be inoperative unless it shall have been ratified as an amendment to the Constitution by the legislatures of the several States, as provided in the Constitution, within seven years from the date of the submission hereof to the States by the Congress.

Amendment XIX (1920)

The right of citizens of the United States to vote shall not be denied or abridged by the United States or by any State on account of sex.

Congress shall have power to enforce this article by appropriate legislation.

Amendment XX (1933)

Section 1
The terms of the President and Vice President shall end at noon on the 20th day of January, and the terms of Senators and Representatives at noon on the 3d day of January, of the years in which such terms would have ended if this article had not been ratified; and the terms of their successors shall then begin.

Section 2
The Congress shall assemble at least once in every year, and such meeting shall begin at noon on the 3d day of January, unless they shall by law appoint a different day.

Section 3
If, at the time fixed for the beginning of the term of the President, the President elect shall have died, the Vice President elect shall become President. If a President shall not have been chosen before the time fixed for the beginning of his term, or if the President elect shall have failed to qualify, then the Vice President elect shall act as President until a President shall have qualified; and the Congress may by law provide for the case wherein neither a President elect nor a Vice President elect shall have

qualified, declaring who shall then act as President, or the manner in which one who is to act shall be selected, and such person shall act accordingly until a President or Vice President shall have qualified.

Section 4

The Congress may by law provide for the case of the death of any of the persons from whom the House of Representatives may choose a President whenever the right of choice shall have devolved upon them, and for the case of the death of any of the persons from whom the Senate may choose a Vice President whenever the right of choice shall have devolved upon them.

Section 5

Sections 1 and 2 shall take effect on the 15th day of October following the ratification of this article.

Section 6

This article shall be inoperative unless it shall have been ratified as an amendment to the Constitution by the legislatures of three fourths of the several States within seven years from the date of its submission.

Amendment XXI (1933)

Section 1

The eighteenth article of amendment to the Constitution of the United States is hereby repealed.

Section 2

The transportation or importation into any State, Territory, or possession of the United States for delivery or use therein of intoxicating liquors, in violation of the laws thereof, is hereby prohibited.

Section 3

This article shall be inoperative unless it shall have been ratified as an amendment to the Constitution by conventions in the several States, as provided in the Constitution, within seven years from the date of the submission hereof to the States by the Congress.

Amendment XXII (1951)

Section 1

No person shall be elected to the office of the President more than twice, and no person, who has held the office of President, or acted as President, for more than two years of a term to which some other person was elected President shall be elected to the Office of the President more than once. But this Article shall not apply to any person holding the office of President when this Article was proposed by the Congress, and shall not prevent any person who may be holding the office of President, or acting as President, during the term within which this Article becomes operative from holding the Office of President or acting as President during the remainder of such term.

Section 2

This article shall be inoperative unless it shall have been ratified as an amendment to the Constitution by the legislatures of three fourths of the several States within seven years from the date of its submission to the States by the Congress.

Amendment XXIII (1961)

Section 1

The District constituting the seat of Government of the United States shall appoint in such manner as the Congress may direct:

A number of electors of President and Vice President equal to the whole number of Senators and Representatives in Congress to which the District would be entitled if it were a State, but in no event more than the least populous State; they shall be in addition to those appointed by the States, but they shall be considered, for the purposes of the election of President and Vice President, to be electors appointed by a State; and they shall meet in the District and perform such duties as provided by the twelfth article of amendment.

Section 2

The Congress shall have power to enforce this article by appropriate legislation.

Amendment XXIV (1964)

Section 1

The right of citizens of the United States to vote in any primary or other election for President or Vice President, for electors for President or Vice President, or for Senator or Representative in Congress, shall not be denied or abridged by the United States or any State by reason of failure to pay any poll tax or other tax.

Section 2

The Congress shall have power to enforce this article by appropriate legislation.

Amendment XXV (1967)

Section 1

In case of the removal of the President from office or of his death or resignation, the Vice President shall become President.

Section 2

Whenever there is a vacancy in the office of the Vice President, the President shall nominate a Vice President who shall take office upon confirmation by a majority vote of both Houses of Congress.

Section 3

Whenever the President transmits to the President pro tempore of the Senate and the Speaker of the House of Representatives his written declaration that he is unable to discharge the powers and duties of his office, and until he transmits to them a written declaration to the contrary, such powers and duties shall be discharged by the Vice President as Acting President.

Section 4

Whenever the Vice President and a majority of either the principal officers of the executive departments or of such other body as Congress may by law provide, transmit to the President pro tempore of the Senate and the Speaker of the House of Representatives their written declaration that the President is unable to discharge the powers and duties of his office, the Vice President shall immediately assume the powers and duties of the office as Acting President.

Thereafter, when the President transmits to the President pro tempore of the Senate and the Speaker of the House of Representatives his written declaration that no inability exists, he shall resume the powers and duties of his Office unless the Vice President and a majority of either the principal officers of the executive department or of such other body as Congress may by law provide, transmit within four days to the President pro tempore of the Senate and the Speaker of the House of Representatives their written declaration that the President is unable to discharge the powers and duties of his office. Thereupon Congress shall decide the issue, assembling within forty-eight hours for that purpose if not in session. If the Congress, within twenty-one days after receipt of the latter written declaration, or, if Congress is not in session, within twenty-one days after Congress is required to assemble, determines by two-thirds vote of both Houses that the President is unable to discharge the powers and duties of his office, the Vice President shall continue to discharge the same as Acting President; otherwise, the President shall resume the powers and duties of his office.

Amendment XXVI (1971)

Section 1

The right of citizens of the United States, who are eighteen years of age or older, to vote shall not be denied or abridged by the United States or by any State on account of age.

Section 2

The Congress shall have power to enforce this article by appropriate legislation.

Amendment XXVII (1992)

No law varying the compensation for services of the Senators and Representatives shall take effect until an election of representatives shall have intervened.

The Freedom of Information Act (FOIA) (Excerpts)

Section 552. Public Information; Agency Rules, Opinions, Orders, Records, and Proceedings (the Freedom of Information Act)

(a) Each agency shall make available to the public information as follows:

(1) Each agency shall separately state and currently publish in the Federal Register for the guidance of the public—

(A) descriptions of its central and field organization and the established places at which, the employees (and in the case of a uniformed service, the members) from whom, and the methods whereby, the public may obtain information, make submittals or requests, or obtain decisions;

(B) statements of the general course and method by which its functions are channeled and determined, including the nature and requirements of all formal and informal procedures available;

(C) rules of procedure, descriptions of forms available or the places at which forms may be obtained, and instructions as to the scope and contents of all papers, reports, or examinations;

(D) substantive rules of general applicability adopted as authorized by law, and statements of general policy or interpretations of general applicability formulated and adopted by the agency; and

(E) each amendment, revision, or repeal of the foregoing.

Section 552b. Open Meetings ("Sunshine Law")

(a) For purposes of this section—

(1) the term "agency" means any agency, as defined in section 552 (e) of this title, headed by a collegial body composed of two or more individual members, a majority of whom are appointed to such position by the President with the advice and consent of the Senate, and any subdivision thereof authorized to act on behalf of the agency;

(2) the term "meeting" means the deliberations of at least the number of individual agency members required to take action on behalf of the agency where such deliberations determine or result in the joint conduct or disposition of official agency business, but does not include deliberations required or permitted by subsection (d) or (e); and

(3) the term "member" means an individual who belongs to a collegial body heading an agency.

(b) Members shall not jointly conduct or dispose of agency business other than in accordance with this section.

Section 553. Rule Making

(c) After notice required by this section, the agency shall give interested persons an opportunity to participate in the rule making through submission of written data, views, or arguments with or without opportunity for oral presentation. After consideration of the relevant matter presented, the agency shall incorporate in the rules adopted a concise general statement of their basis and purpose. When rules are required by statute to be made on the record after opportunity for an agency hearing, sections 556 and 557 of this title apply instead of this subsection.

(d) The required publication or service of a substantive rule shall be made not less than 30 days before its effective date, except—

(1) a substantive rule which grants or recognizes an exemption or relieves a restriction;

(2) interpretive rules and statements of policy; or

(3) as otherwise provided by the agency for good cause found and published with the rule.

(e) Each agency shall give an interested person the right to petition for the issuance, amendment, or repeal of a rule.

Section 603. Initial Regulatory Flexibility Analysis

(a) Whenever an agency is required by section 553 of this title, or any other law, to publish general notice of proposed rulemaking for any proposed rule, the agency shall prepare and make available for public comment an initial regulatory flexibility analysis. Such analysis shall describe the impact of the proposed rule on small entities. The initial regulatory flexibility analysis or a summary shall be published in the Federal Register at the time of the publication of general notice of proposed rulemaking for the rule. The agency shall transmit a copy of the initial regulatory flexibility analysis to the Chief Counsel for Advocacy of the Small Business Administration.

(b) Each initial regulatory flexibility analysis required under this section shall contain—

(1) a description of the reasons why action by the agency is being considered;

(2) a succinct statement of the objectives of, and legal basis for, the proposed rule;

(3) a description of and, where feasible, an estimate of the number of small entities to which the proposed rule will apply;

(4) a description of the projected reporting, recordkeeping and other compliance requirements of the proposed rule, including an estimate of the classes of small entities which will be subject to the requirement and the type of professional skills necessary for preparation of the report or record;

(5) an identification, to the extent practicable, of all relevant Federal rules which may duplicate, overlap or conflict with the proposed rule.

(c) Each initial regulatory flexibility analysis shall also contain a description of any significant alternatives to the proposed rule which accomplish the stated objectives of applicable statutes and which minimize any significant economic impact of the proposed rule on small entities. Consistent with the stated objectives of applicable statutes, the analysis shall discuss significant alternatives such as—

(1) the establishment of differing compliance or reporting requirements or timetables that take into account the resources available to small entities;

(2) the clarification, consolidation, or simplification of compliance and reporting requirements under the rule for such small entities;

(3) the use of performance rather than design standards; and

(4) the exemption from coverage of the rule, or any part thereof, for such small entities.

Title VII of the Civil Rights Act (Employment Provisions) (Excerpts)

Section 703. Unlawful Employment Practices

Employer Practices

(a) It shall be an unlawful employment practice for an employer—

(1) to fail or refuse to hire or to discharge any individual, or otherwise to discriminate against any individual with respect to his compensation, terms, conditions, or privileges of employment, because of such individual's race, color, religion, sex, or national origin; or

(2) to limit, segregate, or classify his employees or applicants for employment in any way which would deprive or tend to deprive any individual of employment opportunities or otherwise adversely affect his status as an employee, because of such individual's race, color, religion, sex, or national origin.

Employment Agency Practices

(b) It shall be an unlawful employment practice for an employment agency to fail or refuse to refer for employment, or otherwise to discriminate against, any individual because of his race, color, religion, sex, or national origin, or to classify or refer for employment any individual on the basis of his race, color, religion, sex, or national origin.

Labor Organization Practices

(c) It shall be an unlawful employment practice for a labor organization—

(1) to exclude or to expel from its membership, or otherwise to discriminate against, any individual because of his race, color, religion, sex, or national origin;

(2) to limit, segregate, or classify its membership or applicants for membership, or to classify or

fail or refuse to refer to employment any individual, in any way which would deprive or tend to deprive any individual of employment opportunities, or would limit such employment opportunities or otherwise adversely affect his status as an employee or as an applicant for employment, because of such individual's race, color, religion, sex, or national origin; or

(3) to cause or attempt to cause an employer to discriminate against an individual in violation of this section.

Training Programs

(d) It shall be an unlawful employment practice for any employer, labor organization, or joint labor-management committee, controlling apprenticeship or other training or retraining, including on-the-job training programs to discriminate against any individual because of his race, color, religion, sex, or national origin in admission to, or employment in, any program established to provide apprenticeship or other training.

Businesses or Enterprises with Personnel Qualified on Basis of Religion, Sex, or National Origin; Educational Institutions with Personnel of Particular Religion

(e) Notwithstanding any other provision of this subchapter, (1) it shall not be an unlawful employment practice for an employer to hire and employ employees, for an employment agency to classify or refer for employment any individual, for a labor organization to classify its membership or to classify or refer for employment any individual, or for an employer, labor organization, or joint labor-management committee controlling apprenticeship or other training or retraining programs to admit or employ any individual in any such program, on the basis of his religion, sex, or national origin in those certain instances where religion, sex, or national origin is a bona fide occupational qualification reasonably necessary to the normal operation of that particular business or enterprise, and (2) it shall not be an unlawful employment practice for a school, college, university, or other educational institution or institution of learning to hire and employ employees of a particular religion if such school, college, university, or other educational institution or institution of learning is, in whole or in substantial part, owned, supported, controlled, or managed by a particular religion or by a particular religious corporation, association, or society, or if the curriculum of such school, college, university, or other educational institution or institution of learning is directed toward the propagation of a particular religion.

Seniority or Merit System; Quantity or Quality of Production, Ability Tests; Compensation Based on Sex and Authorized by Minimum Wage Provisions

(h) Notwithstanding any other provisions of this subchapter, it shall not be an unlawful employment practice for an employer to apply different standards of compensation, or different terms, conditions, or privileges of employment pursuant to a bona fide seniority or merit system, or a system which measures earnings by quantity or quality of production or to employees who work in different locations, provided that such differences are not the result of an intention to discriminate because of race, color, religion, sex, or national origin, nor shall it be an unlawful employment practice for an employer to give and to act upon the results of any professionally developed ability test provided that such test, its administration or action upon the results is not designed, intended or used to discriminate because of race, color, religion, sex, or national origin. It shall not be an unlawful employment practice under this subchapter for any employer to differentiate upon the basis of sex in determining the amount of the wages or compensation paid or to be paid to employees of such employer if such differentiation is authorized by the provisions of section 206(d) of Title 29.

Section 704. Other Unlawful Employment Practices

Discrimination for Making Charges, Testifying, Assisting, or Participating in Enforcement Proceedings

(a) It shall be an unlawful employment practice for an employer to discriminate against any of his employees or applicants for employment, for an employment agency, or joint labor-management committee controlling apprenticeship or other training or retraining, including on-the-job training programs to discriminate against any individual, or for a labor organization to discriminate against any member thereof or applicant for membership, because he has opposed any practice, made an unlawful employment practice by this subchapter, or because he has made a charge, testified, assisted, or participated in any manner in an investigation, proceeding, or hearing under this subchapter.

Printing or Publication of Notices or Advertisements Indicating Prohibited Preference, Limitation, Specification, or Discrimination; Occupational Qualification Exception

(b) It shall be an unlawful employment practice for an employer, labor organization, employment agency, or joint labor-management committee controlling apprenticeship or other training or retraining, including on-the-job training programs, to print or publish or cause to be printed or published any notice or advertisement relating to employment by such an employer or membership in or any classification or referral for employment by such a labor organization, or relating to any classification or referral for employment by such an employment agency, or relating to admission to, or employment in, any program established to provide apprenticeship or other training by such a joint labor-management committee, indicating any preference, limitation, specification, or discrimination, based on race, color, religion, sex, or national origin, except that such a notice or advertisement may indicate a preference, limitation, specification, or discrimination based on religion, sex, or national origin when religion, sex, or national origin is a bona fide occupational qualification for employment.

The Civil Rights Act (Excerpts)

§ 1981. Equal rights under the law

(a) All persons within the jurisdiction of the United States shall have the same right in every State and Territory to make and enforce contracts, to sue, be parties, give evidence, and to the full and equal benefit of all laws and proceedings for the security of persons and property as is enjoyed by white citizens, and shall be subject to like punishment, pains, penalties, taxes, licenses, and exactions of every kind, and to no other.

(b) For purposes of this section, the term "make and enforce contracts" includes the making, performance, modification, and termination of contracts, and the enjoyment of all benefits, privileges, terms, and conditions of the contractual relationship.

(c) The rights protected by this section are protected against impairment by nongovernmental discrimination and impairment under color of State law.

§ 1981a. Damages in cases of intentional discrimination in employment

(a) Right of recovery. (1) Civil rights. In an action brought by a complaining party under section 706 or 717 of the Civil Rights Act of 1964 (42 U.S.C. § 2000e-5 [or 2000e-16]) against a respondent who engaged in unlawful intentional discrimination (not an employment practice that is unlawful because of its disparate impact) prohibited under section 703, 704, or 717 of the Act (42 U.S.C. § 2000e-2 or 2000e-3 [or 2000e-16]), and provided that the complaining party cannot recover under section 1977 of the Revised Statutes (42 U.S.C. § 1981), the complaining party may recover compensatory and punitive damages as allowed in subsection (b), in addition to any relief authorized by section 706(g) of the Civil Rights Act of 1964 [42 USCS § 2000e-5(g)], from the respondent.

The Americans with Disabilities Act (Excerpts)

Title I—Employment

Sec. 101. Definitions.

As used in this title: . . .

(8) Qualified individual with a disability.—The term "qualified individual with a disability" means an individual with a disability who, with or without reasonable accommodation, can perform the essential functions of the employment position that such individual holds or desires. For the purposes of this title, consideration shall be given to the employer's judgment as to what functions of a job are essential, and if an employer has prepared a written description before advertising or interviewing applicants for the job, this description shall be considered evidence of the essential functions of the job.

(9) Reasonable accommodation.—The term "reasonable accommodation" may include—

(A) making existing facilities used by employees readily accessible to and usable by individuals with disabilities; and

(B) job restructuring, part-time or modified work schedules, reassignment to a vacant position, acquisition or modification of equipment or devices, appropriate adjustment or modifications of examinations, training materials or policies, the provision of qualified readers or interpreters, and other similar accommodations for individuals with disabilities.

(10) Undue Hardship.—

(A) In general.—The term "undue hardship" means an action requiring significant difficulty or expense, when considered in light of the factors set forth in subparagraph (B).

(B) Factors to be considered.—In determining whether an accommodation would impose an undue hardship on a covered entity, factors to be considered include—

(i) the nature and cost of accommodation needed under this Act;

(ii) the overall financial resources of the facility or facilities involved in the provision of the reasonable accommodation; the number of persons employed at such facility; the effect on expenses and resources, or the impact otherwise of such accommodation upon the operation of the facility;

(iii) the overall financial resources of the covered entity; the overall size of the business of a covered entity with respect to the number of its employees; the number, type, and location of its facilities; and

(iv) the type of operation or operations of the covered entity, including the composition, structure, and functions of the workforce of such entity; the geographic separateness, administrative, or fiscal relationship of the facility or facilities in question to the covered entity.

Sec. 102. Discrimination.

(a) General Rule.—No covered entity shall discriminate against a qualified individual with a disability because of the disability of such individual in regard to job application procedures, the hiring, advancement, or discharge of employees, employee compensation, job training, and other terms, conditions, and privileges of employment.

(b) Construction.—As used in subsection (a), the term "discriminate" includes—

(1) limiting, segregating, or classifying a job applicant or employee in a way that adversely affects the opportunities or status of such applicant or employee because of the disability of such applicant or employee;

(2) participating in a contractual or other arrangement or relationship that has the effect of subjecting a covered entity's qualified applicant or employee with a disability to the discrimination prohibited by this title (such relationship includes a relationship with an employment or referral agency, labor union, an organization providing fringe benefits to an employee of the covered entity, or an organization providing training and apprenticeship programs);

(3) utilizing standards, criteria, or methods of administration—

(A) that have the effect of discrimination on the basis of disability; or

(B) that perpetuate the discrimination of others who are subject to common administrative control;

(4) excluding or otherwise denying equal jobs or benefits to a qualified individual because of the known disability of an individual with whom the qualified individual is known to have a relationship or association;

(5) (A) not making reasonable accommodations to the known physical or mental limitations of an otherwise qualified individual with a disability who is an applicant or employee, unless such covered entity can demonstrate that the accommodation would impose an undue hardship on the operation of the business of such covered entity; or

(B) denying employment opportunities to a job applicant or employee who is an otherwise qualified individual with a disability, if such denial is based on the need of such covered entity to make reasonable accommodation to the physical or mental impairments of the employee or applicant;

(6) using qualification standards, employment tests or other selection criteria that screen out or tend to screen out an individual with a disability or a class of individuals with disabilities unless the standard, test or other selection criteria, as used by the covered entity, is shown to be job-related for the position in question and is consistent with business necessity; and

(7) failing to select and administer tests concerning employment in the most effective manner to ensure that, when such test is administered to a job applicant or employee who has a disability that impairs sensory, manual, or speaking skills, such test results accurately reflect the skills, aptitude, or whatever other factor of such applicant or employee that such test purports to measure, rather than reflecting the impaired sensory, manual, or speaking skills of such employee or applicant (except where such skills are the factors that the test purports to measure). . . .

Sec. 104. Illegal Use of Drugs and Alcohol. . . .

(b) Rules of Construction.—Nothing in subsection (a) shall be construed to exclude as a qualified individual with a disability an individual who—

(1) has successfully completed a supervised drug rehabilitation program and is no longer engaging in the illegal use of drugs, or has otherwise been rehabilitated successfully and is no longer engaging in such use;

(2) is participating in a supervised rehabilitation program and is no longer engaging in such use; or

(3) is erroneously regarded as engaging in such use, but is not engaging in such use; except that it shall not be a violation of this Act for a covered entity to adopt or administer reasonable policies or procedures, including but not limited to drug testing, designed to ensure that an individual described in paragraph (1) or (2) is no longer engaging in the illegal use of drugs. . . .

The Family and Medical Leave Act (Excerpts)

29 U.S.C. § 2601 et seq. § 2601.
Findings and purposes

(a) Findings

Congress finds that—

(1) the number of single-parent households and two-parent households in which the single parent or both parents work is increasing significantly;

(2) it is important for the development of children and the family unit that fathers and mothers be able to participate in early childrearing and the care of family members who have serious health conditions;

(3) the lack of employment policies to accommodate working parents can force individuals to choose between job security and parenting;

(4) there is inadequate job security for employees who have serious health conditions that prevent them from working for temporary periods;

(5) due to the nature of the roles of men and women in our society, the primary responsibility for family caretaking often falls on women, and such responsibility affects the working lives of women more than it affects the working lives of men; and

(6) employment standards that apply to one gender only have serious potential for encouraging employers to discriminate against employees and applicants for employment who are of that gender.

(b) Purposes

It is the purpose of this Act—

(1) to balance the demands of the workplace with the needs of families, to promote the stability and economic security of families, and to promote national interests in preserving family integrity;

(2) to entitle employees to take reasonable leave for medical reasons, for the birth or adoption of a child, and for the care of a child, spouse, or parent who has a serious health condition;

(3) to accomplish the purposes described in paragraphs (1) and (2) in a manner that accommodates the legitimate interests of employers;

(4) to accomplish the purposes described in paragraphs (1) and (2) in a manner that, consistent with the Equal Protection Clause of the Fourteenth Amendment, minimizes the potential for employment discrimination on the basis of sex by ensuring generally that leave is available for eligible medical reasons (including maternity-related disability) and for compelling family reasons, on a gender-neutral basis; and

(5) to promote the goal of equal employment opportunity for women and men, pursuant to such clause.

§ 2611. Definitions

(2) Eligible employee

(A) In general

The term "eligible employee" means an employee who has been employed—

(i) for at least 12 months by the employer with respect to whom leave is requested under section 2612 of this title; and

(ii) for at least 1,250 hours of service with such employer during the previous 12-month period.

(B) Exclusions

The term "eligible employee" does not include—

(i) any Federal officer or employee covered under subchapter V of chapter 63 of Title 5; or

(ii) any employee of an employer who is employed at a worksite at which such employer employs less than 50 employees if the total number of employees employed by that employer within 75 miles of that worksite is less than 50.

§ 2612. Leave requirement

(a) In general

(1) Entitlement to leave

Subject to section 2613 of this title, an eligible employee shall be entitled to a total of 12 workweeks of leave during any 12-month period for one or more of the following:

(A) Because of the birth of a son or daughter of the employee and in order to care for such son or daughter.

(B) Because of the placement of a son or daughter with the employee for adoption or foster care.

(C) In order to care for the spouse, or a son, daughter, or parent, of the employee, if such spouse, son, daughter, or parent has a serious health condition.

(D) Because of a serious health condition that makes the employee unable to perform the functions of the position of such employee.

(2) Expiration of entitlement

The entitlement to leave under subparagraphs (A) and (B) of paragraph (1) for a birth or placement of a son or daughter shall expire at the end of the 12-month period beginning on the date of such birth or placement.

(b) Leave taken intermittently or on a reduced leave schedule

(1) In general

Leave under subparagraph (A) or (B) of subsection (a)(1) of this section shall not be taken by an employee intermittently or on a reduced leave schedule unless the employee and the employer of the employee agree otherwise. Subject to paragraph (2), subsection (e)(2) of this section, and section 2613(b)(5) of this title, leave under subparagraph (C) or (D) of subsection (a)(1) of this section may be taken intermittently or on a reduced leave schedule when medically necessary. The taking of leave intermittently or on a reduced leave schedule pursuant to this paragraph shall not result in a reduction in the total amount of leave to which the employee is entitled under subsection (a) of this section beyond the amount of leave actually taken.

(2) Alternative position

If an employee requests intermittent leave, or leave on a reduced leave schedule, under subparagraph (C) or (D) of subsection (a)(1) of this section, that is foreseeable based on planned medical treatment, the employer may require such employee to transfer temporarily to an available alternative position offered by the employer for which the employee is qualified and that—

(A) has equivalent pay and benefits; and

(B) better accommodates recurring periods of leave than the regular employment position of the employee.

(c) Unpaid leave permitted

Except as provided in subsection (d) of this section, leave granted under subsection (a) of this section may consist of unpaid leave. Where an employee is otherwise exempt under regulations issued by the Secretary pursuant to section 2613(a)(1) of this title, the compliance of an employer with this subchapter by providing unpaid leave shall not affect the exempt status of the employee under such section.

(d) Relationship to paid leave

(1) Unpaid leave

If an employer provides paid leave for fewer than 12 workweeks, the additional weeks of leave necessary to attain the 12 workweeks of leave required under this subchapter may be provided without compensation.

(2) Substitution of paid leave

(A) In general

An eligible employee may elect, or an employer may require the employee, to substitute any of the accrued paid vacation leave, personal leave, or family leave of the employee for leave provided under subparagraph (A), (B), or (C) of subsection (a)(1) of this section for any part of the 12-week period of such leave under such subsection.

(B) Serious health condition

An eligible employee may elect, or an employer may require the employee, to substitute any of the accrued paid vacation leave, personal leave, or medical or sick leave of the employee for leave provided under subparagraph (C) or (D) of subsection (a)(1) of this section for any part of the 12-week period of such leave under such subsection, except that nothing in this subchapter shall require an employer to provide paid sick leave or paid medical leave in any situation in which such employer would not normally provide any such paid leave.

§ 2614. Employment and benefits protection

(a) Restoration to position

(1) In general

Except as provided in subsection (b) of this section, any eligible employee who takes leave under section 2612 of this title for the intended purpose of the leave shall be entitled, on return from such leave—

(A) to be restored by the employer to the position of employment held by the employee when the leave commenced; or

(B) to be restored to an equivalent position with equivalent employment benefits, pay, and other terms and conditions of employment.

(2) Loss of benefits
The taking of leave under section 2612 of this title shall not result in the loss of any employment benefit accrued prior to the date on which the leave commenced.

(3) Limitations
Nothing to this section shall be construed to entitle any restored employee to—

(A) the accrual of any seniority or employment benefits during any period of leave; or

(B) any right, benefit, or position of employment other than any right, benefit, or position to which the employee would have been entitled had the employee not taken the leave.

§ 2617. Enforcement

(a) Civil action by employees
(1) Liability
Any employer who violates section 2615 of this title shall be liable to any eligible employee affected—

(A) for damages equal to—

(i) the amount of—

(I) any wages, salary, employment benefits, or other compensation denied or lost to such employee by reason of the violation; or

(II) in a case in which wages, salary, employment benefits, or other compensation have not been denied or lost to the employee, any actual monetary losses sustained by the employee as a direct result of the violation, such as the cost of providing care, up to a sum equal to 12 weeks of wages or salary for the employee;

(ii) the interest on the amount described in clause (I) calculated at the prevailing rate; and

(iii) an additional amount as liquidated damages equal to the sum of the amount described in clause (I) and the interest described in clause (ii), except that if an employer who has violated section 2615 of this title proves to the satisfaction of the court that the act or omission which violated section 2615 of this title was in good faith and that the employer had reasonable grounds for believing that the act or omission was not a violation of section 2615 of this title, such court may, in the discretion of the court, reduce the amount of the liability to the amount and interest determined under clauses (i) and (ii), respectively; and

(B) for such equitable relief as may be appropriate, including employment reinstatement, and promotion.

The Uniform Commercial Code (Excerpts)*

ARTICLE I GENERAL PROVISIONS
Part I Short Title, Construction, Application and Subject Matter of the Act

[Note: As marked, there are sections of both the Revised UCC and the old UCC. The old UCC sections for the revised sections that have had accompanying controversy are included because as states adopt these revisions, they may opt for variations.]

Section 1—203. Obligation of Good Faith
Every contract or duty within this Act imposes an obligation of good faith in its performance or enforcement.

Section 1—303. Course Of Performance, Course Of Dealing, And Usage Of Trade (Revised UCC) (formerly Section 2—208)

(a) A "course of performance" is a sequence of conduct between the parties to a particular transaction that exists if:

(1) the agreement of the parties with respect to the transaction involves repeated occasions for performance by a party; and

(2) the other party, with knowledge of the nature of the performance and opportunity for objection to it, accepts the performance or acquiesces in it without objection.

(b) A "course of dealing" is a sequence of conduct concerning previous transactions between the parties to a particular transaction that is fairly to be regarded as establishing a common basis of understanding for interpreting their expressions and other conduct.

(c) A "usage of trade" is any practice or method of dealing having such regularity of observance in a place, vocation, or trade as to justify an expectation that it will be observed with respect to the transaction in question. The existence and scope of such a usage must be proved as facts. If it is established that such a usage is embodied in a trade code or similar record, the interpretation of the record is a question of law.

(d) A course of performance or course of dealing between the parties or usage of trade in the vocation or trade in which they are engaged or of which they are or should be aware is relevant in ascertaining the meaning of the parties' agreement, may give particular meaning to specific terms of the agreement, and may supplement or qualify the terms of the agreement. A usage of trade applicable in the place in which part of the performance under the agreement is to occur may be so utilized as to that part of the performance.

(e) Except as otherwise provided in subsection (f), the express terms of an agreement and any applicable course of performance, course of dealing, or usage of trade must be construed whenever reasonable as consistent with each other. If such a construction is unreasonable:

(1) express terms prevail over course of performance, course of dealing, and usage of trade;

(2) course of performance prevails over course of dealing and usage of trade; and

(3) course of dealing prevails over usage of trade.

(f) Subject to Section 2–209, a course of performance is relevant to show a waiver or modification of any term inconsistent with the course of performance.

(g) Evidence of a relevant usage of trade offered by one party is not admissible unless that party has given the other party notice that the court finds sufficient to prevent unfair surprise to the other party.

Section 1—206. Statute of Frauds for Kinds of Personal Property Not Otherwise Covered
(1) Except in the cases described in subsection (2) of this section a contract for the sale of personal property is not enforceable by way of action or defense beyond five thousand dollars in amount or value of remedy unless there is some writing which indi-

cates that a contract for sale has been made between the parties at a defined or stated price, reasonably identifies the subject matter, and is signed by the party against whom enforcement is sought or by his authorized agent.

(2) Subsection (1) of this section does not apply to contracts for the sale of goods (Section 2—201) nor of securities (Section 8—319) nor to security agreements (Section 9—203).

ARTICLE II SALES
Part 1 Short Title, General Construction and Subject Matter

SECTION 2–102. SCOPE (revised UCC)

(1) Unless the context otherwise requires, and subject to Section 2–108, this article applies to transactions in goods. This Article does not apply to any transaction which although in the form of an unconditional contract to sell or present sale is intended to operate only as a security transaction.

(2) Except as provided in subsection (4), in the case of a transaction involving both goods and non-goods, a court may resolve a dispute by the application of this article to the entire transaction, by the application of other law to the entire transaction, or by the application of this article to part of the transaction and other law to part of the transaction. In making the determination as to the law applicable to the transaction, the court shall take into consideration the nature of the transaction and of the dispute.

(3) This article does not apply to transactions that do not involve goods.

(4) A transaction in a product consisting of computer information and goods that are solely the medium containing the computer information is not a transaction in goods, but a court is not precluded from applying provisions in this article to a dispute concerning whether the goods conform to the contract.

(5) Nothing in this article alters, creates, or diminishes rights in intellectual property.

SECTION 2–103. DEFINITIONS AND INDEX OF DEFINITIONS (revised UCC)

(1) In this article unless the context otherwise requires

(a) "Buyer" means a person that buys or contracts to buy goods.

(b) "Computer information" means information in electronic form which is obtained from or through the use of a computer or which is in a form capable of being processed by a computer.

(c) "Conspicuous", with reference to a term, means so written, displayed, or presented that a reasonable person against which it is to operate ought to have noticed it. A term in an electronic record intended to evoke a response by an electronic agent is conspicuous if it is presented in a form that would enable a reasonably configured electronic agent to take it into account or react to it without review of the record by an individual. Whether a term is "conspicuous" or not is a decision for the court. Conspicuous terms include the following:

(i) for a person:

(A) a heading in capitals equal to or greater in size than the surrounding text, or in contrasting type, font, or color to the surrounding text of the same or lesser size;

(B) language in the body of a record or display in larger type than the surrounding text, or in contrasting type, font, or color to the surrounding text of the same size, or set off from surrounding text of the same size by symbols or other marks that call attention to the language; and

(ii) for a person or an electronic agent, a term that is so placed in a record or display that the person or electronic agent cannot proceed without taking action with respect to the particular term.

(d) "Consumer" means an individual who buys or contracts to buy goods that, at the time of contracting, are intended by the individual to be used primarily for personal, family, or household purposes.

SECTION 2–104. DEFINITIONS: "MERCHANT"; "BETWEEN MERCHANTS"; "FINANCING AGENCY" (Revised UCC)

(1) "Merchant" means a person ~~who~~ that deals in goods of the kind or otherwise is held out by occupation as having knowledge or skill peculiar to the practices or goods involved in the transaction or to which the knowledge or skill may be attributed by the person's employment of an agent or broker or other intermediary that is held out by occupation as having ~~such~~ the knowledge or skill.

Part 2 Form, Formation and Readjustment of Contract

SECTION 2–201. FORMAL REQUIREMENTS; STATUTE OF FRAUDS (Revised UCC)

(1) A contract for the sale of goods for the price of $5,000 or more is not enforceable by way of action or defense unless there is some record sufficient to indicate that a contract for sale has been made

between the parties and signed by the party against which enforcement is sought or by ~~his~~ the party's authorized agent or broker. A record is not insufficient because it omits or incorrectly states a term agreed upon but the contract is not enforceable under this subsection beyond the quantity of goods shown in the record.

(2) Between merchants if within a reasonable time a record in confirmation of the contract and sufficient against the sender is received and the party receiving it has reason to know its contents, it satisfies the requirements of subsection (1) against the recipient unless notice of objection to its contents is given in a record within 10 days after it is received.

(3) A contract which does not satisfy the requirements of subsection (1) but which is valid in other respects is enforceable

(a) if the goods are to be specially manufactured for the buyer and are not suitable for sale to others in the ordinary course of the seller's business and the seller, before notice of repudiation is received and under circumstances which reasonably indicate that the goods are for the buyer, has made either a substantial beginning of their manufacture or commitments for their procurement; or

(b) if the party against which enforcement is sought admits in ~~his~~ the party's pleading, or in the party's testimony or otherwise ~~in court~~ under oath that a contract for sale was made, but the contract is not enforceable under this paragraph beyond the quantity of goods admitted; or

(c) with respect to goods for which payment has been made and accepted or which have been received and accepted (Sec. 2–606).

(4) A contract that is enforceable under this section is not rendered unenforceable merely because it is not capable of being performed within one year or any other applicable period after its making.

SECTION 2–202. FINAL EXPRESSION IN A RECORD PAROL OR EXTRINSIC EVIDENCE (revised UCC)

(1) Terms with respect to which the confirmatory records of the parties agree or which are otherwise set forth in a record intended by the parties as a final expression of their agreement with respect to such terms as are included therein may not be contradicted by evidence of any prior agreement or of a contemporaneous oral agreement but may be supplemented by evidence of:

(a) course of performance, course of dealing or usage of trade (Section 1–303); and

(b) consistent additional terms unless the court finds the record to have been intended also as a complete and exclusive statement of the terms of the agreement.

(2) Terms in a record may be explained by evidence of course of performance, course of dealing, or usage of trade without a preliminary determination by the court that the language used is ambiguous.

SECTION 2–204. FORMATION IN GENERAL (Revised UCC)

(1) A contract for sale of goods may be made in any manner sufficient to show agreement, including offer and acceptance, conduct by both parties which recognizes the existence of such a contract, the interaction of electronic agents, or the interaction of an electronic agent and an individual.

(2) An agreement sufficient to constitute a contract for sale may be found even though the moment of its making is undetermined.

(3) Even though one or more terms are left open a contract for sale does not fail for indefiniteness if the parties have intended to make a contract and there is a reasonably certain basis for giving an appropriate remedy.

(4) Except as otherwise provided in Sections 2–211 through 2–213, the following rules apply:

(a) A contract may be formed by the interaction of electronic agents of the parties, even if no individual was aware of or reviewed the electronic agents' actions or the resulting terms and agreements.

(b) A contract may be formed by the interaction of an electronic agent and an individual acting on the individual's own behalf or for another person. A contract is formed if the individual takes actions that the individual is free to refuse to take or makes a statement that the individual has reason to know will:

(i) cause the electronic agent to complete the transaction or performance; or

(ii) indicate acceptance of an offer, regardless of other expressions or actions by the individual to which the electronic agent cannot react.

SECTION 2–205. FIRM OFFERS (Revised UCC)

An offer by a merchant to buy or sell goods in a signed record which by its terms gives assurance that it will be held open is not revocable, for lack of consideration, during the time stated or if no time is stated for a reasonable time, but in no event may such period of irrevocability exceed three months;

but any such term of assurance <u>in a form record</u> supplied by the offeree must be separately signed by the offeror.

SECTION 2–206. OFFER AND ACCEPTANCE IN FORMATION OF CONTRACT *(Revised UCC)*

(1) Unless otherwise unambiguously indicated by the language or circumstances

(a) an offer to make a contract shall be construed as inviting acceptance in any manner and by any medium reasonable in the circumstances;

(b) an order or other offer to buy goods for prompt or current shipment shall be construed as inviting acceptance either by a prompt promise to ship or by the prompt or current shipment of conforming or non-conforming goods, but <u>the</u> shipment of non-conforming goods does not constitute an acceptance if the seller seasonably notifies the buyer that the shipment is offered only as an accommodation to the buyer.

(2) Where the beginning of a requested performance is a reasonable mode of acceptance an offeror <u>that</u> is not notified of acceptance within a reasonable time may treat the offer as having lapsed before acceptance.

<u>(3) A definite and seasonable expression of acceptance in a record operates as an acceptance even if it contains terms additional to or different from the offer.</u>

Section 2–207. Additional Terms in Acceptance or Confirmation *(Old UCC)*

(1) A definite and seasonable expression of acceptance or a written confirmation which is sent within a reasonable time operates as an acceptance even though it states terms additional to or different from those offered or agreed upon, unless acceptance is expressly made conditional on assent to the additional or different terms.

(2) The additional terms are to be construed as proposals for addition to the contract. Between merchants such terms become part of the contract unless:

(a) the offer expressly limits acceptance to the terms of the offer;

(b) they materially alter it; or

(c) notification of objection to them has already been given or is given within a reasonable time after notice of them is received.

(3) Conduct by both parties which recognizes the existence of a contract is sufficient to establish a contract for sale although the writings of the par-

ties do not otherwise establish a contract. In such case the terms of the particular contract consist of those terms on which the writings of the parties agree, together with any supplementary terms incorporated under any other provisions of this Act.

SECTION 2–207. TERMS OF CONTRACT; EFFECT OF CONFIRMATION *(Revised UCC)*

<u>If (i) conduct by both parties recognizes the existence of a contract although their records do not otherwise establish a contract, (ii) a contract is formed by an offer and acceptance, or (iii) a contract formed in any manner is confirmed by a record that contains terms additional to or different from those in the contract being confirmed, the terms of the contract, subject to Section 2–202, are:</u>

<u>(a) terms that appear in the records of both parties;</u>

<u>(b) terms, whether in a record or not, to which both parties agree; and</u>

<u>(c) terms supplied or incorporated under any provision of this Act.</u>

Section 2–208. Course of Performance or Practical Construction *(Now Article 1, Section 303 under Revised UCC)*

SECTION 2–211. LEGAL RECOGNITION OF ELECTRONIC CONTRACTS, RECORDS AND SIGNATURES *(Revised UCC)* *(Completely new section)*

<u>(1) A record or signature may not be denied legal effect or enforceability solely because it is in electronic form.</u>

<u>(2) A contract may not be denied legal effect or enforceability solely because an electronic record was used in its formation.</u>

<u>(3) This article does not require a record or signature to be created, generated, sent, communicated, received, stored, or otherwise processed by electronic means or in electronic form.</u>

<u>(4) A contract formed by the interaction of an individual and an electronic agent under Section 2–204(4)(b) does not include terms provided by the individual if the individual had reason to know that the agent could not react to the terms as provided.</u>

SECTION 2–213. ELECTRONIC COMMUNICATION *(Revised UCC)* *(Completely new section)*

<u>(1) If the receipt of an electronic communication has a legal effect, it has that effect even though no individual is aware of its receipt.</u>

(2) Receipt of an electronic acknowledgment of an electronic communication establishes that the communication was received but, in itself, does not establish that the content sent corresponds to the content received.

Part 3 General Obligation and Construction of Contract

SECTION 2–302. UNCONSCIONABLE CONTRACT OR TERM (revised UCC)

(1) If the court as a matter of law finds the contract or any term of the contract to have been unconscionable at the time it was made the court may refuse to enforce the contract, or it may enforce the remainder of the contract without the unconscionable term, or it may so limit the application of any unconscionable term as to avoid any unconscionable result.

(2) When it is claimed or appears to the court that the contract or any ~~clause~~ term thereof may be unconscionable the parties shall be afforded a reasonable opportunity to present evidence as to its commercial setting, purpose and effect to aid the court in making the determination.

SECTION 2–312. WARRANTY OF TITLE AND AGAINST INFRINGEMENT; BUYER'S OBLIGATION AGAINST INFRINGEMENT (revised UCC)

(1) Subject to subsection (2) there is in a contract for sale a warranty by the seller that

(a) the title conveyed shall be good and its transfer rightful and shall not, because of any colorable claim to or interest in the goods, unreasonably expose the buyer to litigation; and

(b) the goods shall be delivered free from any security interest or other lien or encumbrance of which the buyer at the time of contracting has no knowledge.

(2) Unless otherwise agreed a seller that is a merchant regularly dealing in goods of the kind warrants that the goods shall be delivered free of the rightful claim of any third person by way of infringement or the like but a buyer that furnishes specifications to the seller must hold the seller harmless against any such claim that arises out of compliance with the specifications.

(3) A warranty under this section may be disclaimed or modified only by specific language or by circumstances that give the buyer reason to know

that the seller does not claim title, that the seller is purporting to sell only the right or title as the seller or a third person may have, or that the seller is selling subject to any claims of infringement or the like.

SECTION 2–313. EXPRESS WARRANTIES BY AFFIRMATION, PROMISE, DESCRIPTION, SAMPLE; REMEDIAL PROMISE (Revised UCC)

(1) In this section, "immediate buyer" means a buyer that enters into a contract with the seller.

(2) Express warranties by the seller to the immediate buyer are created as follows:

(a) Any affirmation of fact or promise made by the seller which relates to the goods and becomes part of the basis of the bargain creates an express warranty that the goods shall conform to the affirmation or promise.

(b) Any description of the goods which is made part of the basis of the bargain creates an express warranty that the goods shall conform to the description.

(c) Any sample or model which is made part of the basis of the bargain creates an express warranty that the whole of the goods shall conform to the sample or model.

(3) It is not necessary to the creation of an express warranty that the seller use formal words such as "warrant" or "guarantee" or that the seller have a specific intention to make a warranty, but an affirmation merely of the value of the goods or a statement purporting to be merely the seller's opinion or commendation of the goods does not create a warranty.

(4) Any remedial promise made by the seller to the immediate buyer creates an obligation that the promise will be performed upon the happening of the specified event.

SECTION 2–313A. OBLIGATION TO REMOTE PURCHASER CREATED BY RECORD PACKAGED WITH OR ACCOMPANYING GOODS (Revised UCC)

(1) This section applies only to new goods and goods sold or leased as new goods in a transaction of purchase in the normal chain of distribution. In this section:

(a) "Immediate buyer" means a buyer that enters into a contract with the seller.

(b) "Remote purchaser" means a person that buys or leases goods from an immediate buyer or other person in the normal chain of distribution

SECTION 2–314. IMPLIED WARRANTY: MERCHANTABILITY; USAGE OF TRADE (Revised UCC)

(1) Unless excluded or modified (Section 2–316), a warranty that the goods shall be merchantable is implied in a contract for their sale if the seller is a merchant with respect to goods of that kind. Under this section the serving for value of food or drink to be consumed either on the premises or elsewhere is a sale.

(2) Goods to be merchantable must be at least such as

(a) pass without objection in the trade under the contract description; and

(b) in the case of fungible goods, are of fair average quality within the description; and

(c) are fit for the ordinary purposes for which ~~such~~ goods of that description are used; and

(d) run, within the variations permitted by the agreement, of even kind, quality and quantity within each unit and among all units involved; and

(e) are adequately contained, packaged, and labeled as the agreement may require; and

(f) conform to the promise or affirmations of fact made on the container or label if any.

(3) Unless excluded or modified (Section 2–316) other implied warranties may arise from course of dealing or usage of trade.

Section 2–315. Implied Warranty: Fitness for Particular Purpose (Old and Revised UCC)

Where the seller at the time of contracting has reason to know any particular purpose for which the goods are required and that the buyer is relying on the seller's skill or judgment to select or furnish suitable goods, there is unless excluded or modified under the next section an implied warranty that the goods shall be fit for such purpose.

SECTION 2–316. EXCLUSION OR MODIFICATION OF WARRANTIES (Revised UCC)

(1) Words or conduct relevant to the creation of an express warranty and words or conduct tending to negate or limit warranty shall be construed wherever reasonable as consistent with each other; but subject to the provisions of this Article on parol or extrinsic evidence (Section 2–202) negation or limitation is inoperative to the extent that such construction is unreasonable.

(2) Subject to subsection (3), to exclude or modify the implied warranty of merchantability or any part of it in a consumer contract the language must be in a record, be conspicuous and state "The seller undertakes no responsibility for the quality of the goods except as otherwise provided in this contract," and in any other contract the language must mention merchantability and in case of a record must be conspicuous,—Subject to subsection (3), to exclude or modify the implied warranty of fitness the exclusion must be in a record and be conspicuous. Language to exclude all implied warranties of fitness in a consumer contract must state "The seller assumes no responsibility that the goods will be fit for any particular purpose for which you may be buying these goods, except as otherwise provided in the contract," and in any other contract the language is sufficient if it states, for example, that "There are no warranties which extend beyond the description on the face hereof." Language that satisfies the requirements of this subsection for the exclusion and modification of a warranty in a consumer contract also satisfies the requirements for any other contract.

(3) Notwithstanding subsection (2):

(a) unless the circumstances indicate otherwise, all implied warranties are excluded by expressions like "as is", "with all faults" or other language which in common understanding calls the buyer's attention to the exclusion of warranties ~~and,~~ makes plain that there is no implied warranty, and in a consumer contract evidenced by a record is set forth conspicuously in the record; and

(b) when the buyer before entering into the contract has examined the goods or the sample or model as fully as ~~he~~ desired or has refused to examine the goods after a demand by the seller there is no implied warranty with regard to defects which an examination ought in the circumstances to have revealed to ~~him~~ the buyer; and

(c) an implied warranty can also be excluded or modified by course of dealing or course of performance or usage of trade.

(4) Remedies for breach of warranty can be limited in accordance with the provisions of this article on liquidation or limitation of damages and on contractual modification of remedy (Sections 2–718 and 2–719).

SECTION 2–318. THIRD PARTY BENEFICIARIES OF WARRANTIES EXPRESS OR IMPLIED (Revised UCC)

(1) In this section:

(a) "Immediate buyer" means a buyer that enters into a contract with the seller.

(b) "Remote purchaser" means a person that buys or leases goods from an immediate buyer or other person in the normal chain of distribution.

Alternative A *to subsection (2)*

(2) A seller's warranty whether express or implied to an immediate buyer, a seller's remedial promise to an immediate buyer, or a seller's obligation to a remote purchaser under Section 2–313A or 2–313B extends to any natural person who is in the family or household of the immediate buyer or the remote purchaser or who is a guest in the home of either if it is reasonable to expect that the person may use, consume or be affected by the goods and who is injured in person by breach of the warranty, remedial promise or obligation. A seller may not exclude or limit the operation of this section.

Alternative B *to subsection (2)*

(2) A seller's warranty whether express or implied to an immediate buyer, a seller's remedial promise to an immediate buyer, or a seller's obligation to a remote purchaser under Section 2–313A or 2–313B extends to any natural person who may reasonably be expected to use, consume or be affected by the goods and who is injured in person by breach of the warranty, remedial promise or obligation. A seller may not exclude or limit the operation of this section.

Alternative C *to subsection (2)*

(2) A seller's warranty whether express or implied to an immediate buyer, a seller's remedial promise to an immediate buyer, or a seller's obligation to a remote purchaser under Section 2–313A or 2–313B extends to any person that may reasonably be expected to use, consume or be affected by the goods and that is injured by breach of the warranty, remedial promise or obligation. A seller may not exclude or limit the operation of this section with respect to injury to the person of an individual to whom the warranty, remedial promise or obligation extends.

Section 2—318. *Third Party Beneficiaries of Warranties Express or Implied (Old UCC)*

Note: If this Act is introduced in the Congress of the United States this section should be omitted. (States to select one alternative.)

Alternative A

A seller's warranty whether express or implied extends to any natural person who is in the family or household of his buyer or who is a guest in his home if it is reasonable to expect that such person may use, consume or be affected by the goods and who is injured in person by breach of the warranty. A seller may not exclude or limit the operation of this section.

Alternative B

A seller's warranty whether express or implied extends to any natural person who may reasonably be expected to use, consume or be affected by the goods and who is injured in person by breach of the warranty. A seller may not exclude or limit the operation of this section.

Alternative C

A seller's warranty whether express or implied extends to any person who may reasonably be expected to use, consume or be affected by the goods and who is injured by breach of the warranty. A seller may not exclude or limit the operation of this section with respect to injury to the person of an individual to whom the warranty extends. As amended 1966.

SECTION 2–615. *EXCUSE BY FAILURE OF PRESUPPOSED CONDITIONS (revised UCC)*

Except so far as a seller may have assumed a greater obligation and subject to the preceding section on substituted performance:

(a) Delay in performance or non-performance in whole or in part by a seller that complies with paragraphs (b) and (c) is not a breach of the seller's duty under a contract for sale if performance as agreed has been made impracticable by the occurrence of a contingency the non-occurrence of which was a basic assumption on which the contract was made or by compliance in good faith with any applicable foreign or domestic governmental regulation or order whether or not it later proves to be invalid.

(b) Where the causes mentioned in paragraph (a) affect only a part of the seller's capacity to perform, the seller must allocate production and deliveries among his its customers but may at its option include regular customers not then under contract as well as its own requirements for further manufacture. The seller may so allocate in any manner which is fair and reasonable.

(c) The seller must notify the buyer seasonably that there will be delay or non-delivery and, when allocation is required under paragraph (b), of the estimated quota thus made available for the buyer.

The Securities Act of 1933 and the Securities Exchange Act of 1934 (Excerpts)

Securities Act of 1933

Civil Liabilities on Account of False Registration Statement

SECTION 11. (a) In case any part of the registration statement, when such part became effective, contained an untrue statement of a material fact or omitted to state a material fact required to be stated therein or necessary to make the statements therein not misleading, any person acquiring such security (unless it is proved that at the time of such acquisition he knew of such untruth or omission) may, either at law or in equity, in any court of competent jurisdiction, sue—

(1) every person who signed the registration statement;

(2) every person who was a director of (or person performing similar functions) or partner in, the issuer at the time of the filing of the part of the registration statement with respect to which his liability is asserted;

(3) every person who, with his consent, is named in the registration statement as being or about to become a director, person performing similar functions, or partner;

(4) every accountant, engineer, or appraiser, or any person whose profession gives authority to a statement made by him, who has with his consent been named as having prepared or certified any part of the registration statement, or as having prepared or certified any report or valuation which is used in connection with the registration statement, with respect to the statement in such registration statement, report, or valuation, which purports to have been prepared or certified by him;

(5) every underwriter with respect to such security.

If such person acquired the security after the issuer has made generally available to its security holders an earning statement covering a period of at least twelve months beginning after the effective date of the registration statement, then the right of recovery under this subsection shall be conditioned on proof that such person acquired the security relying upon such untrue statement in the registration statement or relying upon the registration statement and not knowing of such omission, but such reliance may be established without proof of the reading of the registration statement by such person.

(b) Notwithstanding the provisions of subsection (a) no person, other than the issuer, shall be liable as provided therein who shall sustain the burden of proof—

(1) that before the effective date of the part of the registration statement with respect to which his liability is asserted (A) he had resigned from or had taken such steps as are permitted by law to resign from, or ceased or refused to act in, every office, capacity, or relationship in which he was described in the registration statement as acting or agreeing to act, and (B) he had advised the Commission and the issuer in writing that he had taken such action and that he would not be responsible for such part of the registration statement; or

(2) that if such part of the registration statement became effective without his knowledge, upon becoming aware of such fact he forthwith acted and advised the Commission, in accordance with paragraph (1), and, in addition, gave reasonable public notice that such part of the registration statement had become effective without his knowledge; or

(3) that (A) as regards any part of the registration statement not purporting to be made on the authority of an expert, and not purporting to be a copy of or extract from a report or valuation of an expert, and not purporting to be made on the authority of a public or official document or statement, he had, after reasonable investigation, reasonable ground to believe and did believe, at the

time such part of the registration statement became effective, that the statements therein were true and that there was no omission to state a material fact required to be stated therein or necessary to make the statements therein not misleading; and (B) as regards any part of the registration statement purporting to be made upon his authority as an expert or purporting to be a copy of or extract from a report or valuation of himself as an expert, (i) he had, after reasonable investigation, reasonable ground to believe and did believe, at the time such part of the registration statement became effective, that the statements therein were true and that there was no omission to state a material fact required to be stated therein or necessary to make the statements therein not misleading, or (ii) such part of the registration statement did not fairly represent his statement as an expert or was not a fair copy of or extract from his report or valuation as an expert; and (C) as regards any part of the registration statement purporting to be made on the authority of an expert (other than himself) or purporting to be a copy of or extract from a report or valuation of an expert (other than himself), he had no reasonable ground to believe and did not believe, at the time such part of the registration statement became effective, that the statements therein were untrue or that there was an omission to state a material fact required to be stated therein or necessary to make the statements therein not misleading, or that such part of the registration statement did not fairly represent the statement of the expert or was not a fair copy of or extract from the report or valuation of the expert; and (D) as regards any part of the registration statement purporting to be a statement made by an official person or purporting to be a copy of or extract from a public official document, he had no reasonable ground to believe and did not believe, at the time such part of the registration statement became effective, that the statements therein were untrue, or that there was an omission to state a material fact required to be stated therein or necessary to make the statements therein not misleading, or that such part of the registration statement did not fairly represent the statement made by the official person or was not a fair copy of or extract from the public official document.

(c) In determining, for the purpose of paragraph (3) of subsection (b) of this section, what constitutes reasonable investigation and reasonable ground for belief, the standard of reasonableness shall be that required of a prudent man in the management of his own property.

Civil Liabilities Arising in Connection with Prospectuses and Communications

SECTION 12. Any person who—(1) offers or sells a security in violation of section 5, or

(2) offers or sells a security (whether or not exempted by the provisions of section 3, other than paragraph (2) of subsection (a) thereof), by the use of any means or instruments of transportation or communication in interstate commerce or of the mails, by means of a prospectus or oral communication, which includes an untrue statement of a material fact or omits to state a material fact necessary in order to make the statements, in the light of the circumstances under which they were made, not misleading (the purchaser not knowing of such untruth or omission), and who shall not sustain the burden of proof that he did not know, and in the exercise of reasonable care could not have known, of such untruth or omission, shall be liable to the person purchasing such security from him, who may sue either at law or in equity in any court of competent jurisdiction, to recover the consideration paid for such security with interest thereon, less the amount of any income received thereon, upon the tender of such security, or for damages if he no longer owns the security.

Penalties

SECTION 24. Any person who willfully violates any of the provisions of this title, or the rules and regulations promulgated by the Commission under authority thereof, or any person who willfully, in a registration statement filed under this title, makes any untrue statement of a material fact or omits to state any material fact required to be stated therein or necessary to make the statements therein not misleading, shall upon conviction be fined not more than $10,000 or imprisoned not more than five years, or both.

Securities Exchange Act of 1934

Regulation of the Use of Manipulative and Deceptive Devices

SECTION 10. It shall be unlawful for any person, directly or indirectly, by the use of any means or instrumentality of interstate commerce or of the mails, or of any facility of any national securities exchange—

(a) To effect a short sale, or to use or employ any stop-loss order in connection with the purchase or sale, of any security registered on a national securities exchange, in contravention of such rules and regulations as the Commission may prescribe as necessary or appropriate in the public interest or for the protection of investors.

(b) To use or employ, in connection with the purchase or sale of any security registered on a national securities exchange or any security not so registered, any manipulative or deceptive device or contrivance in contravention of such rules and regulations as the Commission may prescribe as necessary or appropriate in the public interest or for the protection of investors.

Proxies

SECTION 14. (a) It shall be unlawful for any person, by the use of the mails or by any means or instrumentality of interstate commerce or of any facility of a national securities exchange or otherwise, in contravention of such rules and regulations as the Commission may prescribe as necessary or appropriate in the public interest or for the protection of investors, to solicit or to permit the use of his name to solicit any proxy or consent or authorization in respect of any security (other than an exempted security) registered pursuant to section 12 of 78(*l*) this title.

Directors, Officers, and Principal Stockholders

SEC. 16. DIRECTORS, OFFICERS, AND PRINCIPAL STOCKHOLDERS.

" (a) DISCLOSURES REQUIRED.—

"(1) DIRECTORS, OFFICERS, AND PRINCIPAL STOCKHOLDERS REQUIRED TO FILE.— Every person who is directly or indirectly the beneficial owner of more than 10% of any class of any equity security (other than an exempted security) which is registered pursuant to section 12, or who is a director or an officer of the issuer of such security, shall file the statements required by this subsection with the Commission (and, if such security is registered on a national securities exchange, also with the exchange).

"(2) TIME OF FILING.—The statements required by this subsection shall be filed—

"(A) at the time of the registration of such security on a national securities exchange or by the effective date of a registration statement filed pursuant to section 12(g);

"(B) within 10 days after he or she becomes such beneficial owner, director, or officer;

Liability for Misleading Statements

SECTION 18. (a) Any person who shall make or cause to be made any statement in any application, report, or document filed pursuant to this title or any rule or regulation thereunder or any undertaking contained in a registration statement as provided in subsection (d) of section 15 of this title, which statement was at the time and in the light of the circumstances under which it was made false or misleading with respect to any material fact, shall be liable to any person (not knowing that such statement was false or misleading) who, in reliance upon such statement, shall have purchased or sold a security at a price which was affected by such statement, for damages caused by such reliance, unless the person sued shall prove that he acted in good faith and had no knowledge that such statement was false or misleading. A person seeking to enforce such liability may sue at law or in equity in any court of competent jurisdiction. In any such suit the court may, in its discretion, require an undertaking for the payment of the costs of such suit, and assess reasonable costs, including reasonable attorneys' fees, against either party litigant.

(b) Every person who becomes liable to make payment under this section may recover contribution as in cases of contract from any person who, if joined in the original suit, would have been liable to make the same payment.

(c) No action shall be maintained to enforce any liability created under this section unless brought within three years after the discovery of the facts constituting the cause of action and within five years after such cause of action accrued.

The Copyright Act (as Amended) (Excerpts)

Section 102. Subject matter of copyright: In general

(a) Copyright protection subsists, in accordance with this title, in original works of authorship fixed in any tangible medium of expression, now known or later developed, from which they can be perceived, reproduced, or otherwise communicated, either directly or with the aid of a machine or device. Works of authorship include the following categories:

(1) literary works;

(2) musical works, including any accompanying words;

(3) dramatic works, including any accompanying music;

(4) pantomimes and choreographic works;

(5) pictorial, graphic, and sculptural works;

(6) motion pictures and other audiovisual works;

(7) sound recordings; and

(8) architectural works.

(b) In no case does copyright protection for an original work of authorship extend to any idea, procedure, process, system, method of operation, concept, principle, or discovery, regardless of the form in which it is described, explained, illustrated, or embodied in such work.

Section 106. Exclusive rights in copyrighted works

Subject to sections 107 through 120, the owner of copyright under this title has the exclusive rights to do and to authorize any of the following:

(1) to reproduce the copyrighted work in copies or phonorecords;

(2) to prepare derivative works based upon the copyrighted work;

(3) to distribute copies or phonorecords of the copyrighted work to the public by sale or other transfer of ownership, or by rental, lease, or lending;

(4) in the case of literary, musical, dramatic, and choreographic works, pantomimes, and motion pictures and other audiovisual works, to perform the copyrighted work publicly; and

(5) in the case of literary, musical, dramatic, and choreographic works, pantomimes, and pictorial, graphic, or sculptural works, including the individual images of a motion picture or other audiovisual work, to display the copyrighted work publicly.

Section 107. Limitations on exclusive rights: Fair use

Notwithstanding the provisions of sections 106 and 106A, the fair use of a copyrighted work, including such use by reproduction in copies or phonorecords or by any other means specified by that section, for purposes such as criticism, comment, news reporting, teaching (including multiple copies for classroom use), scholarship, or research, is not an infringement of copyright. In determining whether the use made of a work in any particular case is a fair use the factors to be considered shall include—

(1) the purpose and character of the use, including whether such use is of a commercial nature or is for nonprofit educational purposes;

(2) the nature of the copyrighted work;

(3) the amount and substantiality of the portion used in relation to the copyrighted work as a whole; and

(4) the effect of the use upon the potential market for or value of the copyrighted work.

Section 406. Copyright registration in general

(a) Registration Permissive.—At any time during the subsistence of copyright in any published or unpublished work, the owner of copyright or of any exclusive right in the work may obtain registration of the copyright claim by delivering to the Copyright Office the deposit specified by this section, together with the application and fee specified by sections 409 and 708. Such registration is not a condition of copyright protection.

Section 591. Infringement of copyright

(a) Anyone who violates any of the exclusive rights of the copyright owner as provided by sections 106 through 118 or of the author as provided in section 106A(a), or who imports copies or phonorecords into the United States in violation of section 602, is an infringer of the copyright or right of the author, as the case may be. For purposes of this chapter (other than section 506), any reference to copyright shall be deemed to include the rights conferred by section 106(a). As used in this subsection the term "anyone" includes any State, any instrumentality of a State, and any officer or employee of a State or instrumentality of a State acting in his or her official capacity. Any State, and any such instrumentality, officer, or employee, shall be subject to the provisions of this title in the same manner and to the same extent as any nongovernmental entity.

(b) The legal or beneficial owner of an exclusive right under a copyright is entitled, subject to the requirements of section 411, to institute an action for any infringement of that particular right committed while he or she is the owner of it. The court may require such owner to serve written notice of the action with a copy of the complaint upon any person shown, by the records of the Copyright Office or otherwise, to have or claim an interest in the copyright, and shall require that such notice be served upon any person whose interest is likely to be affected by a decision in the case. The court may require the joinder, and shall permit the intervention, of any person having or claiming an interest in the copyright.

Remedies for Infringement: Damages and Profits

Section 504.

(a) In General. Except as otherwise provided by this title, an infringer of copyright is liable for either—

1. the copyright owner's actual damages and any additional profits of the infringer, as provided by subsection (b); or

2. statutory damages, as provided by subsection (c).

(b) Actual Damages and Profits.—The copyright owner is entitled to recover the actual damages suffered by him or her as a result of the infringement, and any profits of the infringer that are attributable to the infringement and are not taken into account in computing the actual damages. In establishing the infringer's profits, the copyright owner is required to present proof only of the infringer's gross revenue, and the infringer is required to prove his or her deductible expenses and the elements of profit attributable to factors other than the copyrighted work.

(c) Statutory Damages—(1) Except as provided by clause (2) of this subsection, the copyright owner may elect, at any time before final judgment is rendered, to recover, instead of actual damages and profits, an award of statutory damages for all infringements involved in the action, with respect to any one work, for which any one infringer is liable individually, or for which any two or more infringers are liable jointly and severally, in a sum of not less than $500 or more than $20,000 as the court considers just. For the purposes of this subsection, all the parts of a compilation or derivative work constitute one work.

(2) In a case where the copyright owner sustains the burden of proving, and the court finds, that infringement was committed willfully, the court in its discretion may increase the award of statutory damages to a sum of not more than $100,000. In a case where the infringer sustains the burden of proving, and the court finds, that such infringer was not aware and had no reason to believe that his or her acts constituted an infringement of copyright, the court in its discretion may reduce the award of statutory damages to a sum of not less than $200. The court shall remit statutory damages in any case where an infringer believed and had reasonable grounds for believing that his or her use of the copyrighted work was a fair use under section 107, if the infringer was: (i) an employee or agent of a nonprofit educational institution, library, or archives acting within the scope of his or her employment who, or such institution, library, or archives itself, which infringed by reproducing the work in copies or phonorecords; or (ii) a public broadcasting entity which or a person who, as a regular part of the nonprofit activities of a public broadcasting entity (as defined in subsection (g) of section 118) infringed by performing a published nondramatic literary work or by reproducing a transmission program embodying a performance of such a work.

Section 506. Criminal offenses

(a) Criminal infringement—Any person who infringes a copyright willfully and for purposes of commercial advantage or private financial gain shall be punished as provided in section 2319 of title 18.

The Foreign Corrupt Practices Act (Excerpts)

15 U.S.C. § 78dd-1

§ 78dd-1. Prohibited foreign trade practices by issuers

(a) Prohibition

It shall be unlawful for any issuer which has a class of securities registered pursuant to section 78l of this title or which is required to file reports under section 78o(d) of this title, or for any officer, director, employee, or agent of such issuer or any stockholder thereof acting on behalf of such issuer, to make use of the mails or any means or instrumentality of interstate commerce corruptly in furtherance of an offer, payment, promise to pay, or authorization of the payment of any money, or offer, gift, promise to give, or authorization of the giving of anything of value to—

(1) any foreign official for purposes of—

(A)(i) influencing any act or decision of such foreign official in his official capacity, (ii) inducing such foreign official to do or omit to do any act in violation of the lawful duty of such official, or (iii) securing any improper advantage; or

(B) inducing such foreign official to use his influence with a foreign government or instrumentality thereof to affect or influence any act or decision of such government or instrumentality, in order to assist such issuer in obtaining or retaining business for or with, or directing business to, any person;

(2) any foreign political party or official thereof or any candidate for foreign political office for purposes of—

(A)(i) influencing any act or decision of such party, official, or candidate in its or his official capacity, (ii) inducing such party, official, or candidate to do or omit to do an act in violation of the lawful duty of such party, official, or candidate, or (iii) securing any improper advantage; or

(B) inducing such party, official, or candidate to use its or his influence with a foreign government or instrumentality thereof to affect or influence any act or decision of such government or instrumentality. in order to assist such issuer in obtaining or retaining business for or with, or directing business to, any person; or

(3) any person, while knowing that all or a portion of such money or thing of value will be offered, given, or promised, directly or indirectly, to any foreign official, to any foreign political party or official thereof, or to any candidate for foreign political office, for purposes of—

(A)(i) influencing any act or decision of such foreign official, political party, party official, or candidate in his or its official capacity, (ii) inducing such foreign official, political party, party official, or candidate to do or omit to do any act in violation of the lawful duty of such foreign official, political party, party official, or candidate, or (iii) securing any improper advantage; or

(B) inducing such foreign official, political party, party official, or candidate to use his or its influence with a foreign government or instrumentality thereof to affect or influence any act or decision of such government or instrumentality, in order to assist such issuer in obtaining or retaining business for or with, or directing business to, any person.

(b) Exception for routine governmental action

Subsections (a) and (g) of this section shall not apply to any facilitating or expediting payment to a foreign official, political party, or party official the purpose of which is to expedite or to secure the performance of a routine governmental action by a foreign official, political party, or party official.

(c) Affirmative defenses

It shall be an affirmative defense to actions under subsection (a) or (g) of this section that—

(1) the payment, gift, offer, or promise of anything of value that was made, was lawful under the written laws and regulations of the foreign official's, political party's, party official's, or candidate's country; or

(2) the payment, gift, offer, or promise of anything of value that was made, was a reasonable and bona fide expenditure, such as travel and lodging expenses, incurred by or on behalf of a foreign official, party, party official, or candidate and was directly related to—

(A) the promotion, demonstration, or explanation of products or services; or

(B) the execution or performance of a contract with a foreign government or agency thereof.

15 U.S.C. §78-dd-2

(g) Penalties

(1)(A) Any domestic concern that is not a natural person and that violates subsection (a) or (i) of this section shall be fined not more than $2,000,000.

(B) Any domestic concern that is not a natural person and that violates subsection (a) or (i) of this section shall be subject to a civil penalty of not more than $10,000 imposed in an action brought by the Attorney General.

(2)(A) Any natural person that is an officer, director, employee, or agent of a domestic concern, or stockholder acting on behalf of such domestic concern, who willfully violates subsection (a) or (i) of this section shall be fined not more than $100,000 or imprisoned not more than 5 years, or both.

(B) Any natural person that is an officer, director, employee, or agent of a domestic concern, or stockholder acting on behalf of such domestic concern, who violates subsection (a) or (i) of this section shall be subject to a civil penalty of not more than $10,000 imposed in an action brought by the Attorney General.

(3) Whenever a fine is imposed under paragraph (2) upon any officer, director, employee, agent, or stockholder of a domestic concern, such fine may not be paid, directly or indirectly, by such domestic concern.

(h) Definitions

For purposes of this section:

(1) The term "domestic concern" means—

(A) any individual who is a citizen, national, or resident of the United States; and

(B) any corporation, partnership, association, joint-stock company, business trust, unincorporated organization, or sole proprietorship which has its principal place of business in the United States, or which is organized under the laws of a State of the United States or a territory, possession, or commonwealth of the United States.

(2)(A) The term "foreign official" means any officer or employee of a foreign government or any department, agency, or instrumentality thereof, or of a public international organization, or any person acting in an official capacity for or on behalf of any such government or department, agency, or instrumentality, or for or on behalf of any such public international organization.

(B) For purposes of subparagraph (A), the term "public international organization" means—

(i) an organization that is designated by Executive order pursuant to section 1 of the International Organizations Immunities Act (22 U.S.C. 288); or

(ii) any other international organization that is designated by the President by Executive order for the purposes of this section, effective as of the date of publication of such order in the Federal Register.

(3)(A) A person's state of mind is "knowing" with respect to conduct, a circumstance, or a result if—

(i) such person is aware that such person is engaging in such conduct, that such circumstance exists, or that such result is substantially certain to occur; or

(ii) such person has a firm belief that such circumstance exists or that such result is substantially certain to occur.

(B) When knowledge of the existence of a particular circumstance is required for an offense, such knowledge is established if a person is aware of a high probability of the existence of such circumstance, unless the person actually believes that such circumstance does not exist.

(4)(A) The term "routine governmental action" means only an action which is ordinarily and commonly performed by a foreign official in—

(i) obtaining permits, licenses, or other official documents to qualify a person to do business in a foreign country;

(ii) processing governmental papers, such as visas and work orders;

(iii) providing police protection, mail pick-up and delivery, or scheduling inspections associated with contract performance or inspections related to transit of goods across country;

(iv) providing phone service, power and water supply, loading and unloading cargo, or protecting perishable products or commodities from deterioration; or

(v) actions of a similar nature.

(B) The term "routine governmental action" does not include any decision by a foreign official whether, or on what terms, to award new business to or to continue business with a particular party, or any action taken by a foreign official involved in the decision-making process to encourage a decision to award new business to or continue business with a particular party.

(5) The term "interstate commerce" means trade, commerce, transportation, or communication among the several States, or between any foreign country and any State or between any State and any place or ship outside thereof, and such term includes the intrastate use of—

(A) a telephone or other interstate means of communication, or

(B) any other interstate instrumentality.

(i) Alternative jurisdiction

(1) It shall also be unlawful for any United States person to corruptly do any act outside the United States in furtherance of an offer, payment, promise to pay, or authorization of the payment of any money, or offer, gift, promise to give, or authorization of the giving of anything of value to any of the persons or entities set forth in paragraphs (1), (2), and (3) of subsection (a), for the purposes set forth therein, irrespective of whether such United States person makes use of the mails or any means or instrumentality of interstate commerce in furtherance of such offer, gift, payment, promise, or authorization.

(2) As used in this subsection, the term "United States person" means a national of the United States (as defined in section 101 of the Immigration and Nationality Act (8 U.S.C. 1101)) or any corporation, partnership, association, joint-stock company, business trust, unincorporated organization, or sole proprietorship organized under the laws of the United States or any State, territory, possession, or commonwealth of the United States, or any political subdivision thereof.";

Sarbanes–Oxley Key Provisions

SEC. 201. SERVICES OUTSIDE THE SCOPE OF PRACTICE OF AUDITORS

(a) PROHIBITED ACTIVITIES.—Section 10A of the Securities Exchange Act of 1934 (15 U.S.C. 78j-1) is amended by adding at the end the following:

"(g) PROHIBITED ACTIVITIES.—Except as provided in subsection (h), it shall be unlawful for a registered public accounting firm (and any associated person of that firm, to the extent determined appropriate by the Commission) that performs for any issuer any audit required by this title or the rules of the Commission under this title or, beginning 180 days after the date of commencement of the operations of the Public Company Accounting Oversight Board established under section 101 of the Sarbanes-Oxley Act of 2002 (in this section referred to as the 'Board'), the rules of the Board, to provide to that issuer, contemporaneously with the audit, any non-audit service, including—

"(1) bookkeeping or other services related to the accounting records or financial statements of the audit client;

"(2) financial information systems design and implementation;

*496

"(3) appraisal or valuation services, fairness opinions, or contribution-in-kind reports;

"(4) actuarial services;

"(5) internal audit outsourcing services;

"(6) management functions or human resources;

"(7) broker or dealer, investment adviser, or investment banking services;

"(8) legal services and expert services unrelated to the audit; and

"(9) any other service that the Board determines, by regulation, is impermissible.

"(h) PREAPPROVAL REQUIRED FOR NON-AUDIT SERVICES.—A registered public accounting firm may engage in any non-audit service, including tax services, that is not described in any of paragraphs (1) through (9) of subsection (g) for an audit client, only if the activity is approved in advance by the audit committee of the issuer, in accordance with subsection (i)."

SEC. 203. AUDIT PARTNER ROTATION

Section 10A of the Securities Exchange Act of 1934 (15 U.S.C. 78j-1), as amended by this Act, is amended by adding at the end the following:

"(j) AUDIT PARTNER ROTATION.—It shall be unlawful for a registered public accounting firm to provide audit services to an issuer if the lead (or coordinating) audit partner (having primary responsibility for the audit), or the audit partner responsible for reviewing the audit, has performed audit services for that issuer in each of the 5 previous fiscal years of that issuer."

SEC. 302. CORPORATE RESPONSIBILITY FOR FINANCIAL REPORTS

(a) REGULATIONS REQUIRED.—The Commission shall, by rule, require, for each company filing periodic reports under section 13(a) or 15(d) of the Securities Exchange Act of 1934 (15 U.S.C. 78m, 78o(d)), that the principal executive officer or officers and the principal financial officer or officers, or persons performing similar functions, certify in each annual or quarterly report filed or submitted under either such section of such Act that—

(1) the signing officer has reviewed the report;

(2) based on the officer's knowledge, the report does not contain any untrue statement of a material fact or omit to state a material fact necessary in order to make the statements made, in light of the circumstances under which such statements were made, not misleading;

(3) based on such officer's knowledge, the financial statements, and other financial information included in the report, fairly present in all material respects the financial condition and results of operations of the issuer as of, and for, the periods presented in the report;

(4) the signing officers—

(A) are responsible for establishing and maintaining internal controls;

(B) have designed such internal controls to ensure that material information relating to the issuer and its consolidated subsidiaries is made known to such officers by others within those entities, particularly during the period in which the periodic reports are being prepared;

(C) have evaluated the effectiveness of the issuer's internal controls as of a date within 90 days prior to the report; and

(D) have presented in the report their conclusions about the effectiveness of their internal controls based on their evaluation as of that date;

(5) the signing officers have disclosed to the issuer's auditors and the audit committee of the board of directors (or persons fulfilling the equivalent function)—

(A) all significant deficiencies in the design or operation of internal controls which could adversely affect the issuer's ability to record, process, summarize, and report financial data and have identified for the issuer's auditors any material weaknesses in internal controls; and

(B) any fraud, whether or not material, that involves management or other employees who have a significant role in the issuer's internal controls; and

(6) the signing officers have indicated in the report whether or not there were significant changes in internal controls or in other factors that could significantly affect internal controls subsequent to the date of their evaluation, including any corrective actions with regard to significant deficiencies and material weaknesses.

SEC. 304. FORFEITURE OF CERTAIN BONUSES AND PROFITS

(a) ADDITIONAL COMPENSATION PRIOR TO NONCOMPLIANCE WITH COMMISSION FINANCIAL REPORTING REQUIREMENTS.—If an issuer is required to prepare an accounting restatement due to the material noncompliance of the issuer, as a result of misconduct, with any financial reporting requirement under the securities laws, the chief executive officer and chief financial officer of the issuer shall reimburse the issuer for—

(1) any bonus or other incentive-based or equity-based compensation received by that person from the issuer during the 12-month period following the first public issuance or filing with the Commission (whichever first occurs) of the financial document embodying such financial reporting requirement; and

(2) any profits realized from the sale of securities of the issuer during that 12-month period.

SEC. 406. CODE OF ETHICS FOR SENIOR FINANCIAL OFFICERS

(a) CODE OF ETHICS DISCLOSURE.—The Commission shall issue rules to require each issuer, together with periodic reports required pursuant to section 13(a) or 15(d) of the Securities Exchange Act of 1934, to disclose whether or not, and if not, the reason therefor, such issuer has adopted a code of ethics for senior financial officers, applicable to its principal financial officer and comptroller or principal accounting officer, or persons performing similar functions.

SEC. 802. CRIMINAL PENALTIES FOR ALTERING DOCUMENTS

(a) IN GENERAL.—Chapter 73 of title 18, United States Code, is amended by adding at the end the following:

§ 1519. Destruction, alteration, or falsification of records in Federal investigations and bankruptcy

Whoever knowingly alters, destroys, mutilates, conceals, covers up, falsifies, or makes a false entry in any record, document, or tangible object with the intent to impede, obstruct, or influence the investigation or proper administration of any matter within the jurisdiction of any department or agency of the United States or any case filed under title 11, or in relation to or contemplation of any such matter or case, shall be fined under this title, imprisoned not more than 20 years, or both.

§ 1520. Destruction of corporate audit records

(a)(1) Any accountant who conducts an audit of an issuer of securities to which section 10A(a) of the Securities Exchange Act of 1934 (15 U.S.C. 78j- 1(a)) applies, shall maintain all audit or review workpapers for a period of 5 years from the end of the fiscal period in which the audit or review was concluded.

(2) The Securities and Exchange Commission shall promulgate, within 180 days, after adequate notice and an opportunity for comment, such rules and regulations, as are reasonably necessary, relating to the retention of relevant records such as workpapers, documents that form the basis of an audit or review, memoranda, correspondence, communications, other documents, and records (including electronic records) which are created, sent, or received in connection with an audit or review and contain conclusions, opinions, analyses, or financial data relating to such an audit or review, which is

conducted by any accountant who conducts an audit of an issuer of securities to which section 10A(a) of the Securities Exchange Act of 1934 (15 U.S.C. 78j-1(a)) applies. The Commission may, from time to time, amend or supplement the rules and regulations that it is required to promulgate under this section, after adequate notice and an opportunity for comment, in order to ensure that such rules and regulations adequately comport with the purposes of this section.

(b) Whoever knowingly and willfully violates subsection (a)(1), or any rule or regulation promulgated by the Securities and Exchange Commission under subsection (a)(2), shall be fined under this title, imprisoned not more than 10 years, or both.

SEC. 906. CORPORATE RESPONSIBILITY FOR FINANCIAL REPORTS

(a) IN GENERAL.—Chapter 63 of title 18, United States Code, is amended by inserting after section 1349, as created by this Act, the following:

"§ 1350. Failure of corporate officers to certify financial reports

(a) CERTIFICATION OF PERIODIC FINAN-CIAL REPORTS.—Each periodic report containing financial statements filed by an issuer with the Securities Exchange Commission pursuant to section 13(a) or 15(d) of the Securities Exchange Act of 1934 (15 U.S.C. 78m(a) or 78o(d)) shall be accompanied by a written statement by the chief executive officer and chief financial officer (or equivalent thereof) of the issuer.

(b) CONTENT.—The statement required under subsection (a) shall certify that the periodic report containing the financial statements fully complies with the requirements of section 13(a) or 15(d) of the Securities Exchange Act pf 1934 (15 U.S.C. 78m or 78o(d)) and that information contained in the pe-riodic report fairly presents, in all material respects, the financial condition and results of operations of the issuer.

(c) CRIMINAL PENALTIES.—Whoever—

"(1) certifies any statement as set forth in subsections (a) and (b) of this section knowing that the periodic report accompanying the statement does not comport with all the requirements set forth in this section shall be fined not more than $1,000,000 or imprisoned not more than 10 years, or both; or

(2) willfully certifies any statement as set forth in subsections (a) and (b) of this section knowing that the periodic report accompanying the statement does not comport with all the re-quirements set forth in this section shall be fined not more than $5,000,000, or imprisoned not more than 20 years, or both.

SEC. 1102. TAMPERING WITH A RECORD OR OTHERWISE IMPEDING AN OFFICIAL PROCEEDING

Section 1512 of title 18, United States Code, is amended—

(1) by redesignating subsections (c) through (i) as subsections (d) through (j), respectively; and

(2) by inserting after subsection (b) the following new subsection:

(c) Whoever corruptly—

(1) alters, destroys, mutilates, or conceals a record, document, or other object, or attempts to do so, with the intent to impair the object's integrity or availabilityfor use in an official proceeding; or

(2) otherwise obstructs, influences, or impedes any official proceeding, or attempts to do so, shall be fined under this title or imprisoned not more than 20 years, or both."

The Federal Trade Commission Act (Excerpts)

Section 5. Unfair Methods of Competition Unlawful; Prevention by Commission— Declaration of Unlawfulness; Power to Prohibit Unfair Practices

(a) (1) Unfair methods of competition in or affecting commerce, and unfair or deceptive acts or practices in or affecting commerce, are declared unlawful.

Penalty for Violation of Order; Injunctions and Other Appropriate Equitable Relief

(1) Any person, partnership, or corporation who violates an order of the Commission after it has become final, and while such order is in effect, shall forfeit and pay to the United States a civil penalty of not more than $10,000 for each violation, which shall accrue to the United States and may be recovered in a civil action brought by the Attorney General of the United States. Each separate violation of such an order shall be a separate offense, except that in the case of a violation through continuing failure to obey or neglect to obey a final order of the Commission, each day of continuance of such failure or neglect shall be deemed a separate offense. In such actions, the United States district courts are empowered to grant mandatory injunctions and such other and further equitable relief as they deem appropriate in the enforcement of such final orders of the Commission.

Section 7. Acquisition by One Corporation of Stock of Another

No corporation engaged in commerce shall acquire, directly or indirectly, the whole or any part of the stock; or other share capital and no corporation subject to the jurisdiction of the Federal Trade Commission shall acquire the whole or any part of the assets of another corporation in any section of the country, the effect of such acquisition may be substantially to lessen competition, or to tend to create a monopoly.

No corporation shall acquire, directly or indirectly, the whole or any part of the stock or other share capital and no corporation subject to the jurisdiction of the Federal Trade Commission shall acquire the whole or any part of the assets of one or more corporations engaged in commerce, where in any line of commerce in any section of the country, the effect of such acquisition, of such stocks or assets, or of the use of such stock by the voting or granting of proxies or otherwise, may be substantially to lessen competition, or to tend to create a monopoly.

The Clayton Act (Excerpts)

Section 8. Interlocking Directorates and Officers

No private banker or director, officer, or employee of any member bank of the Federal Reserve System or any branch thereof shall be at the same time a director, officer, or employee of any other bank, banking association, savings bank, or trust company organized under the National Bank Act or organized under the laws of any State or of the District of Columbia, or any branch thereof, except that the Board of Governors of the Federal Reserve System may by regulation permit such service as a director, officer, or employee of not more than one other such institution or branch thereof; . . .

The Sherman Act (Excerpts)

Section 1. Trusts, etc., in Restraint of Trade Illegal; Penalty

Every contract, combination in the form of trust or otherwise, or conspiracy, in restraint of trade or commerce among the several States, or with foreign nations, is declared to be illegal. Every person who shall make any contract or engage in any combination or conspiracy hereby declared to be illegal shall be deemed guilty of a felony, and, on conviction thereof, shall be punished by fine not exceeding one million dollars if a corporation, or, if any other person, one hundred thousand dollars or by imprisonment not exceeding three years, or by both said punishments, in the discretion of the court.

Section 2. Monopolization; Penalty

Every person who shall monopolize, or attempt to monopolize, or combine or conspire with any other person or persons, to monopolize any part of the trade or commerce among the several States, or with foreign nations, shall be deemed guilty of a felony, and, on conviction thereof, shall be punished by fine not exceeding $10,000,000 if a corporation, or, if any other person, $350,000 or by imprisonment not exceeding three years, or by both said punishments, in the discretion of the court.

The Robinson–Patman Act (Excerpts)

Section 2. Discrimination in Price, Services, or Facilities—Price; Selection of Customers

(a) It shall be unlawful for any person engaged in commerce, in the course of such commerce, either directly or indirectly, to discriminate in price between different purchasers of commodities of like grade and quality, where either or any of the purchases involved in such discrimination are in commerce, where such commodities are sold for use, consumption, or resale within the United States or any Territory thereof or the District of Columbia or any insular possession or other place under the jurisdiction of the United States, and where the effect of such discrimination may be substantially to lessen competition or tend to create a monopoly in any line of commerce, or to injure, destroy, or prevent competition with any person who either grants or knowingly receives the benefit of such discrimination, or with customers of either of them; Provided, That nothing herein contained shall prevent differentials which make only due allowance for differences in the cost of manufacture, sale, or delivery resulting from the differing methods or quantities in which such commodities are to such purchasers sold or delivered: Provided, however, That the Federal Trade Commission may, after due investigation and hearing to all interested parties, fix and establish quantity limits, and revise the same as it finds necessary, as to particular commodities or classes of commodities, where it finds that available purchasers in greater quantities are so few as to render differentials on account thereof unjustly discriminatory or promotive of monopoly in any line of commerce; and the foregoing shall then not be construed to permit differentials based on differences in quantities greater than those so fixed and established: And provided further, That nothing herein contained shall prevent persons engaged in selling goods, wares, or merchandise in commerce from selecting their own customers in bona fide transactions and not in restraint of trade: And provided further, That nothing herein contained shall prevent price changes from time to time where in response to changing conditions affecting the market for or the marketability of the goods concerned, such as but not limited to actual or imminent deterioration of perishable goods, obsolescence of seasonal goods, distress sales under court process, or sales in good faith in discontinuance of business in the goods concerned.

Section 3. Discrimination in Rebates, Discounts, or Advertising Service Charges; Underselling in Particular Localities; Penalties

It shall be unlawful for any person engaged in commerce, in the course of such commerce, to be a party to, or assist in, any transaction of sale, or contract to sell, which discriminates to his knowledge against competitors of the purchaser, in that, any discount, rebate, allowance, or advertising service charge is granted to the purchaser over and above any discount, rebate, allowance, or advertising service charge available at the time of such transaction to said competitors in respect of a sale of goods of like grade, quality, and quantity; to sell, or contract to sell, goods in any part of the United States at prices lower than those exacted by said person elsewhere in the United States for the purpose of destroying competition, or eliminating a competitor in such part of the United States; or, to sell, or contract to sell, goods at unreasonably low prices for the purpose of destroying competition or eliminating a competitor.

Any person violating any of the provisions of this section shall, upon conviction thereof, be fined not more than $5,000 or imprisoned not more than one year, or both.

The Fair Labor Standards Act (Excerpts)

Unfair Labor Practices

Section 8

(a) It shall be an unfair labor practice for an employer—

(1) to interfere with, restrain, or coerce employees in the exercise of the rights guaranteed in section 7;

(2) to dominate or interfere with the formation or administration of any labor organization or contribute financial or other support to it: *Provided,* That subject to rules and regulations made and published by the Board pursuant to section 6, an employer shall not be prohibited from permitting employees to confer with him during work hours without loss of time or pay;

(3) by discrimination in regard to hire or tenure of employment of any term or condition of employment to encourage or discourage membership in any labor organization:

(4) to discharge or otherwise discriminate against an employee because he has filed charges or given testimony under this Act;

(5) to refuse to bargain collectively with the representatives of his employees, subject to the provisions of section 9(a).

(b) It shall be an unfair labor practice for a labor organization or its agents—

(1) to restrain or coerce (A) employees in the exercise of the rights guaranteed in section 7: *Provided,* That this paragraph shall not impair the right of a labor organization to prescribe its own rules with respect to the acquisition or retention of membership therein; or (B) an employer in the selection of his representatives for the purpose of collective bargaining or the adjustment of grievances;

(2) to cause or attempt to cause an employer to discriminate against an employee in violation of subsection (a) (3) or to discriminate against an employee with respect to whom membership in such organization has been denied or terminated on some ground other than his failure to tender the periodic dues and the initiation fees uniformly required as a condition of acquiring or retaining membership;

(3) to refuse to bargain collectively with an employer, provided it is the representative of his employees subject to the provisions of section 9(a);

(4) (i) to engage in, or to induce or encourage any individual employed by any person engaged in commerce or in an industry affecting commerce to engage in, a strike or a refusal in the course of his employment to use, manufacture, process, transport, or otherwise handle or work on any goods, articles, materials, or commodities or to perform any services; or (ii) to threaten, coerce, or restrain any person engaged in commerce or in an industry affecting commerce, . . .

(5) to require of employees covered by an agreement authorized under subsection (a) (3) the payment, as a condition precedent to becoming a member of such organization, of a fee in an amount which the Board finds excessive or discriminatory under all the circumstances. In making such a finding, the Board shall consider, among other relevant factors, the practices and customs of labor organizations in the particular industry, and the wages currently paid to the employees affected;

(6) to cause or attempt to cause an employer to pay or deliver or agree to pay or deliver money or other thing of value, in the nature of an exaction, for services which are not performed or not to be performed; and

(7) to picket or cause to be picketed, or threaten to picket or cause to be picketed, any employer where an object thereof is forcing or requiring an employer to recognize or bargain with a labor organization as the representative of his employees, or forcing or requiring the employees of an employer to accept or select such labor organization as their collective bargaining representative, unless such labor organization is currently certified as the representative of such employees.

Glossary

A

absolute privilege A defense to defamation; a protection given to legislators and courtroom participants for statements made relating to the proceedings; encourages people to come forward and speak without fear of liability.

acceptance Offeree's positive response to offeror's proposed contract.

accord and satisfaction An agreement (accord) to pay a certain amount, the payment of which constitutes full payment (satisfaction) of that debt.

accredited investor For purposes of Regulation D, an investor with certain financial stability who is not counted in the number of purchaser limitations for Rules 505 and 506.

acid rain Environmental phenomenon caused when acid from coal smoke enters the atmosphere and then appears in precipitation in large areas, sometimes quite far from the coal-burning area.

act of state doctrine In international law, a theory that each country's governmental actions are autonomous and not subject to judicial review by the courts in other countries.

actual notice Private or individual notice sent directly to affected parties; this type of notice is effective only if the party actually receives it, as compared to constructive notice, for which publication is sufficient.

actus reus Latin term for the criminal act or conduct required for proof of a crime.

administrative agency Governmental unit created by the legislative body for the purposes of administering and enforcing the laws.

administrative law judge (ALJ) Special category of judicial official who presides over agency enforcement hearings.

Administrative Procedures Act (APA) Basic federal law governing the creation, operation, and reporting of federal administrative agencies.

advances In partnerships, loans by the partners to the partnership; makes the partner a creditor of the partnership.

adverse possession Acquisition of land title through use for the required statutory period.

affirm Action taken by an appellate court on an appealed case; the effect is that the court upholds the lower court's decision.

affirmative action Label given to employment processes and programs designed to help underrepresented groups obtain jobs and promotions.

Age Discrimination in Employment Act of 1967 (ADEA) Federal law that prohibits job discrimination on the basis of age; prohibits the consideration of age in an employment decision.

agency by estoppel Theory for creation of an agency relationship that holds the principal liable because the principal has allowed the agent to represent him as his principal.

agent One who acts on behalf of and at the direction of another.

Air Pollution Control Act (1955) The first federal legislation to deal with air pollution.

Air Quality Act (1967) Federal law that designated HEW to oversee state plans for controlling pollution.

air rights Ownership rights of a surface owner to the air above the land surface.

alter ego theory Theory used for disregarding the corporate protection of limited liability for shareholders; results when individuals treat the corporation's properties and accounts as their own and fail to follow corporate formalities.

alternative dispute resolution (ADR) Means other than litigation used to resolve disputes and claims; includes arbitration, mediation, and negotiated settlements.

American Competitive and Workforce Investment Act of 1998 Federal law that permits greater numbers of immigrants who are highly skilled.

American Competitiveness in the Twenty-First Century Act of 2000 Federal law that extended additional quotas for highly skilled immigrants.

Americans with Disabilities Act (ADA) A 1991 federal law that prohibits discrimination in the workplace against persons with disabilities and requires employers to make reasonable accommodations for employees with disabilities who are otherwise qualified to perform a job.

annual percentage rate (APR) A financing term representing the annual debt cost and a required disclosure under Regulation Z.

answer Pleading filed by the defendant in a lawsuit; contains the defendant's version of the basis of the suit, counterclaims, and denials.

Antiterrorism and Effective Death Penalty Act One of several post 9/11/2001 federal statutes passed to increase grounds for deportation and penalties for criminal conduct for terrorist activities.

apparent authority Authority of an agent to act on behalf of a principal that results from the appearance of the agent's authority to third parties.

appellant The name on appeal for the party who appeals a lower court's decision.

appellate Adjective that describes courts and processes above the trial level; management of the appeals after trial court procedures.

appellate brief Lawyer's summation of issues of law and/or error for appellate court to consider.

appellate court A court of appeals or a court of review; a court whose function is to review the decision and actions of a trial court; does not hear witnesses; only reviews the transcript and studies the arguments and briefs of the parties.

appellee The name on appeal for the party who won a lower court's decision—that is, the party who does not appeal the lower court decision.

appraisal rights Rights of dissenting shareholders after a merger or takeover to be paid the value of their shares before the takeover or merger.

appropriation In international law, the taking of private property by a government; also known as expropriation; in torts, use of the name, likeness, or image of another for commercial purposes.

arbitrary and capricious Standard for challenging administrative agency rules; used to show decisions or rules were not based on sufficient facts.

arbitration Alternative form of dispute resolution in which parties submit evidence to a third party who is a member of the American Arbitration Association and who makes a decision after listening to the case.

arraignment Hearing in criminal procedure held after an indictment or information is returned; trial date is set and plea is entered.

articles of incorporation Organizational papers of a corporation; list the company's structure, capitalization, board structure, and so on.

articles of limited partnership Contract governing the rights and relations of limited partners.

articles of partnership Organizational papers of a partnership; often called the partnership agreement; list rights of partners, profit/loss arrangements, and so on.

Asbestos Hazard Emergency Response Act (AHERA) Federal environmental legislation that requires removal of asbestos from public schools and other facilities where exposure is particularly dangerous (where young children are present).

asset acquisition Form of takeover in which another firm buys all the assets of a firm and gains control through control of the firm's property.

Asset Conservation, Lender Liability, and Deposit Insurance Protection Act of 1996 Federal law that clarified the liability of lenders for CERCLA violations and

clean-up upon their foreclosure and repossession of debtor's property.

assignment In contract law, the transfer of the benefits under a contract to a third party; the third party has a right to benefits but is subject to any contract defenses.

assumption of risk Defense in negligence cases that prevents an injured party from recovering if it can be established that the injured party realized the risk and engaged in the conduct anyway.

attorney-client privilege Protection of client's disclosures to her attorney; attorney cannot disclose information client offers (with some exceptions, such as the client telling the attorney he is going to commit a crime); the confession of a crime already committed cannot be disclosed by the lawyer.

audit committee Committee of the board responsible for oversight of company financial statements.

authorization cards Cards signed by employees and required to establish the 30 percent support necessary to hold an election for a union as exclusive bargaining agent for the collective bargaining unit.

B

bailee Party who has temporary possession of the property of another.

bailment Temporary transfer of possession of personal property.

bailor Party who owns property and surrenders possession.

bait and switch Term given to advertising technique in which a low-price product is advertised and then the customer is told that the product is unavailable or is talked into a higher-priced product; prohibited by the FTC.

bankruptcy Federal process of obtaining relief from debts in exchange for the surrender of most assets.

bargain and sale deed A special warranty deed.

bargained-for exchange The mutual exchange of detriment as the consideration element in a contract.

basis of the bargain Information the buyer relies on in making the decision to make a purchase.

battle of the forms Term used to describe the problem of merchants using their purchase orders and invoices with conflicting terms as their contractual understanding; problem is remedied by § 2–207 of the UCC.

Berne Convention Implementation Act of 1988 Federal law that changed U.S. copyright law to comply with international agreement at Berne Convention.

best available treatment (BAT) In environmental law, the most advanced and effective technology for preventing pollution; a higher standard than the best conventional treatment.

best conventional treatment (BCT) Requirement imposed by EPA on point source pollution that requires firms to use the best existing treatments for water pollution.

bilateral contract Contract in which both parties make promises to perform.

bilateral treaty In international law, a treaty between two nations.

bill of lading Receipt for goods issued by a carrier; used as a means of transferring title in exchange for payment or a draw on a line of credit.

Bill of Rights Portion of the U.S. Constitution that consists of the first ten amendments and includes such rights as freedom of speech, right to privacy, the protections afforded in criminal procedures under the Fourth Amendment search and seizure, and the Fifth Amendment protections against self-incrimination.

bill of sale Informal document or contract that serves to prove and transfer title to tangible personal property.

binding arbitration Arbitration from which there is no judicial appeal.

blacklisting Tactic used by employers to prevent employees involved with unions from getting work elsewhere; an exchange of employees' names to prevent unionism.

blackout period Period during which employees of a company cannot trade the company's stock because of pending events or announcements that will affect the company's performance and/or share price.

blue sky laws State laws regulating the sale of securities.

board of directors Policy-setting governing group of a corporation.

bona fide occupational qualification (BFOQ) A justification for discrimination on the basis of sex if it can be established that gender is a requirement for a job; also applies to discrimination on the basis of religion, national origin, and so on.

brief Document prepared by lawyers on the appeal of a case to provide the appellate court with a summary of the case and the issues involved.

bubble concept Tactic employed by the EPA in determining levels of air pollution that determines appropriate levels of release by assuming that all the pollution in an area comes from one source.

burden of proof The responsibility of the party for proving the facts needed to recover in a lawsuit.

business ethics *See* **ethics.**

business judgment rule Duty of care imposed upon members of corporate boards that requires adequate review of issues and information, devotion of adequate time to deliberations, and hiring of outside consultants as necessary for making decisions; the standard does not require foolproof judgment, only reasonable care in making the judgment.

business-to-business (B2B) transactions Direct contracts between manufacturers and customers; no middle-man transactions between producers and retailers; also refers to the practice of intertwining customer operational records with those of the supplier for direct communication and ordering.

"but for" test In negligence, the standard used for determining whether the defendant's negligence caused the plaintiff's injury; "but for" the fact that the defendant was negligent, the plaintiff would not have been injured.

bylaws Operating rules of a corporation and its board; usually describe the officers and their roles and authority, along with meeting procedures and notices.

C

capacity Legal term for the ability to enter legally into a contract; for example, age capacity (minors do not have capacity).

causation In negligence, an element that requires the plaintiff to show that the defendant's lack of care caused the plaintiff's injury.

caveat emptor Latin term for "Let the buyer beware"; summarizes an attitude that once prevailed in contract law of a lack of protection for a buyer of defective goods.

celebrity endorsements Public figures advertising products on the basis of their personal use.

Celler-Kefauver Act Act that amended Section 7 of the Clayton Act and closed the loophole of merger through asset acquisition by regulating asset acquisitions.

certification Process of authorizing a union to represent exclusively a group of workers.

certiorari Latin term meaning "to become informed." A court agrees to hear a case when it grants *certiorari*.

charge Complaint to the NLRB brought by a private party.

charitable subscription A promise to make payment to a charitable organization; a pledge; it is enforceable even though the charity gives nothing in exchange.

chattel mortgage Lien on personal property.

checks and balances Term describing our tripartite system of government, in which each branch has some check mechanism to control abuses of powers by the other branches.

Child Pornography Prevention Act Federal law that prohibited the transmission of child pornography over the Internet; struck down as unconstitutional infringement of right to free speech.

citation Name given to abbreviated description of a court case or statute; for example, 355 F. Supp. 291.

cite *See* **citation.**

civil law Laws affecting the private rights of individuals.

Civil Rights Act of 1964 Cornerstone of the antidiscrimination statutes; the original statute passed to prevent discrimination in housing, education, and employment.

Civil Rights Acts of 1866 and 1870 Initial acts of Congress to help curb discrimination in employment; little was done with them once passed.

Civil Rights Act of 1991 Amendments to original civil rights laws that changed damages, burden of proof, and claims standards for private suits for discrimination.

class action suit In civil law, a suit by a group of plaintiffs with the same claims; generally used in antitrust and securities lawsuits.

Clayton Act One of the major antitrust laws; governs the control of business through mergers, acquisitions, and interlocking directorates.

Clean Air Act The first effective anti-air-pollution act and the cornerstone of air pollution legislation.

Clean Air Act Amendments of 1990 First major changes to federal environmental laws on air pollution since 1977; impose additional requirements on industrial emissions controls, auto emissions, and other types of chemical emissions that affect the ozone layer.

Clean Water Act The first effective anti-water-pollution act and the cornerstone of water pollution legislation.

close corporation A type of corporation created by statute that allows limited liability with direct tax benefits.

closed-end transaction Term used in Regulation Z to describe credit transactions with definite times for and amounts of repayment that are not ongoing; for example, retail installment contracts.

closed shop A place of employment restricting hirees to union members only.

closing argument The summary attorneys give to the jury before it deliberates and after all the evidence has been presented.

code of ethics A set of rules adopted by a company to establish acceptable behavior standards for its employees.

Code of Federal Regulations (C.F.R.) Series of volumes carrying the enactments of all federal agencies.

collateral Property subject to a lien, security interest, or chattel mortgage.

collective bargaining agreement Contract between management and labor represented by one union for a collective bargaining unit.

collective bargaining unit NLRB term for a group of employees represented by one bargaining agent and agreement; can be a plant, a national group, or a subpart of a plant.

comment letter SEC response to registration filing; requires additional information or clarification on proposed offering.

Commerce Clause Provision in the U.S. Constitution controlling the regulation of intrastate, interstate, and foreign commerce and delineating authority for such regulation.

commercial impracticability Contract defense for nonperformance under the UCC that excuses a party when performance has become impossible or will involve much more than what was anticipated in the contract negotiations.

commercial speech The speech of business in the form of advertising, political endorsements, or comments on social issues.

common law Originally, the law of England made uniform after William the Conqueror; today, the nonstatutory law and the law found in judicial precedent.

common stock Type of shares in a corporation; the voting shares of the corporation and generally the bulk of ownership.

community-right-to-know substance Under federal environmental laws, a toxin used by a business or an operation that must be publicly disclosed; EPA filing is required.

comparative negligence In negligence, a defense that allocates responsibility for an accident between the plaintiff and defendant when both were negligent and determines liability accordingly.

compensatory damages Damages to put nonbreaching party in the same position he would have been in had the breach not occurred.

complaint The first pleading in a lawsuit; the document that outlines the plaintiff's allegations against the defendant and specifies the remedies sought; with respect to federal agencies, can also be a formal change of rules or statutory violations by a company or individual.

Comprehensive Environmental Response, Compensation, and Liability Act (CERCLA) Federal law that authorized federal funds to clean up hazardous waste disposal.

computer crime Theft, espionage, and other illegal activities accomplished through the use of a computer.

Computer Software Copyright Act of 1980 Provides copyright protection for software.

concerted activities Organized economic weapons of union.

concurrent jurisidiction Authority of more than one court to hear a case.

condition precedent In contracts, an event or action that must take place before a contract is required to be performed; for example, qualifying for financing is a condition precedent for a lender's performance on a mortgage loan.

conditions Events that must occur before contract performance is due.

conditions concurrent (conditions contemporaneous) In contracts, the conditions that must occur simultaneously for contract performance to be required; for example, in an escrow closing in real property, an agent collects title, insurance, funds, and other documents and sees that all the exchanges under the contract occur at the same time; the parties perform their part of the agreement at the same time.

confidential relationship A relationship of trust and reliance; necessary to establish the defense to undue influence.

confiscation In international law, the taking of private property by a government.

conglomerate merger A merger between two firms in different lines of business.

congressional enabling act Legislation that creates a new agency for enforcement of legislation or assigns enforcement of a new law to an existing agency; establishes the authority of the agency and scope of enforcement responsibilities.

consent decree For administrative agencies, a type of plea bargain; a settlement document for an administrative agency's charges.

consequential damages Damages resulting from a contract breach, such as penalties or lost profits.

consideration In contracts, what each party gives to the other as part of the contract performance.

consolidation A form of merger in which two firms unite and become known by a new name.

constitution Document that contains the basic rights in a society and the structure of its government; cannot be changed without the approval of the society's members.

constructive notice Notice given in a public place or published notice, as opposed to actual notice.

Consumer Credit Protection Act Act that provides disclosure requirements for lenders and protections for debtors; more commonly referred to as the Truth in Lending Act.

consumer debt Debt entered into for the purpose of purchasing goods or services for personal or household use.

Consumer Leasing Act Act that provides for disclosure protection for consumers who are leasing goods.

Consumer Product Safety Commission Federal agency that establishes safety standards for consumer goods.

contentious jurisdiction Consensual jurisdiction of a court that is consented to when the parties have a dispute; for example, UN courts.

contract Binding agreement between two parties for the exchange of goods, real estate, or services.

contract defense Situation, term, or event that makes an otherwise valid contract invalid.

contract interference Tort involving a third party's actions resulting in a valid contract being lost or invalidated; an unfair method of competition.

contributory negligence Negligence defense that results when the injured party acted in a negligent way and contributed to her own injuries.

Convention on Combating Bribery of Foreign Public Officials in International Business Transactions Treaty agreed to by OECD nations by which all agreed to make bribery of public officials a criminal act so as to curb corruption in business.

conventional pollutant EPA classification of water pollutant that must be treated prior to its release into waterways.

cooling-off period Under the Taft-Hartley Act, a provision that can be invoked by the president to require laborers threatening to strike in an industry that affects the health and safety of the nation to continue to work during a negotiation period.

copyright Under federal law, a right given to protect the exclusive use of books, music, and other creative works.

corporate opportunity doctrine A business proposition or investment opportunity that a corporation would have an interest in pursuing; precludes directors from taking a profit opportunity when the corporation would have an interest.

corporate political speech *See* **political speech.**

corporate veil The personal liability shield; the corporate protection that entitles shareholders, directors, and officers to limited liability; can be pierced for improper conduct of business or fraud.

corporation Business entity created by statute that provides limited liability for its owners.

corrective advertising Potential FTC remedy required when ads run by a firm have been deceptive; requires company to run ads explaining previous ads or run a new statement in future ads.

Council on Environmental Quality (CEQ) Agency under the executive branch created in 1966 to formulate environmental policy and make recommendations for legislation.

counterclaim Pleading in a lawsuit in which the defendant makes allegations against the plaintiff in response to the plaintiff's complaint.

counteroffer Response by offeree to offer or when offeree changes terms of offer.

county courts Lesser trial courts that hear smaller disputes and misdemeanor cases; like justice of the peace courts in many states.

course of dealing Pattern of a relationship between two parties who have contracted previously.

Court of Justice of European Communities The court of dispute settlement for the nations of the European Community.

courts of chancery Courts that were once separate and administered equitable remedies; now chancery courts are not separate; most courts have the authority to order legal or equitable remedies.

covenants not to compete Promises to protect employers and buyers from loss of goodwill through employee or seller competition.

crime A wrong against society that carries penalties of imprisonment and/or fines.

criminal fraud A crime in which the victim is defrauded by an intentional act of the perpetrator.

criminal law As opposed to civil law, the law on wrongs against society.

cross-elasticity Economic term describing the willingness of customers to substitute various goods; for example, waxed paper for plastic wrap.

cross-examination Questioning by opposing parties of a witness in court; that is, defendant cross-examines plaintiff's witnesses and plaintiff cross-examines defendant's witnesses.

cumulative preferred stock Type of ownership in a corporation that gives the stock owners preference in the distribution of dividends and also guarantees earnings each year; in the event those earnings are not paid, they are carried over or accumulate until they can be paid.

customer and territorial restrictions Manufacturer's restrictions on retail sales locations and customers.

cyber law Collection of laws from various sources that apply to transactions, use and abuse of Internet, and e-mail communications.

cybersquatting Process of registering sites and domain names that are deceptively or confusingly similar to existing names, trade names, and trademarks.

D

deed Transfers title to real property.

deed of trust Alternative form of creditor security in land purchases.

defamation Tort of making untrue statements about another that cause damage to his reputation or character.

default Judgment entered when the defendant fails to file an answer in a lawsuit.

defendant The party who is alleged to have committed a wrong in a civil lawsuit; the charged party in a criminal prosecution.

deficiency letter *See* **comment letter**.

del credere **agency** Agent who sells principal's goods to a buyer on credit and agrees to pay the principal if the buyer does not pay for the goods.

delegation Transfer of obligations under a contract; generally accompanied by assignment of benefits.

de minimis Latin term meaning small or minimal.

de novo Latin term for starting over or anew; a trial *de novo* is a special form of appeal of a trial decision that allows the case to be retried in a different forum.

deposition Form of discovery in which witnesses or parties can be questioned under oath in recorded testimony outside the courtroom.

derivative Type of investment that derives its earnings from a contractual agreement based on other obligations.

derivative suit Lawsuit brought on behalf of another through the other's rights; for example, a shareholder suing to enforce corporation's rights.

dicta In a judicial opinion, the explanation for the decision; not the actual rule of law but the reasoning for the ruling.

Digital Millennium Copyright Act (DMCA) 1998 amendment to federal copyright laws that includes use of computer technology to copy music and other copyrighted materials as infringement.

digital signature Authorization for a contract provided via electronic means.

direct examination Term that describes a party's questioning of her own witness.

directed verdict Verdict entered by judge upon motion of a party after the presentation of either side's case; can be entered if the plaintiff has not met his burden of proof or if the defendant fails to rebut the plaintiff's case.

disclaimer A provision in a contract that eliminates liability such as a warranty disclaimer or a disclaimer of tort liability.

discovery Process occurring before a trial that involves each side's investigation of the case, the evidence, and the witnesses; consists of depositions, interrogatories, requests for admissions and productions, and so on.

disparagement Form of unfair competition in which a business, its trademark, or its name is maligned; business defamation.

disparate impact Theory for establishing discrimination; involves using statistical analysis to demonstrate that a particular practice or an employer's hiring practices have a greater impact on protected classes.

disparate treatment In discrimination law, the application of different rules or standards to people of different races, genders, or national origins.

dissenting opinion In an appellate court's review of a case, an opinion written by a judge who disagrees with the decision of the majority of the court.

dissenting shareholder Shareholder who has objected to a merger or consolidation and votes against it; is entitled to receive the value of her shares before the merger or consolidation.

dissolution In partnerships, occurs when one partner ceases to be associated with the business; in corporations, the termination of the corporate existence.

diversity of citizenship A term referring to a requirement for federal court jurisdiction that plaintiff and defendant must be citizens of different states.

documents of title Formal legal document that serves to prove and transfer title to tangible personal property.

domain registration Public filing for ownership of the name for a Web site.

domestic corporation A term used to describe a corporation in the state in which it is incorporated.

double jeopardy In criminal law, a constitutional prohibition against being tried twice for the same crime.

due diligence Under the Securities Act of 1933, a defense for filing a false registration statement that requires proof that the individuals involved did all they could to uncover the truth and could not have discovered the false statements despite their due diligence.

due process Constitutional protection ensuring notice and a fair trial or hearing in all judicial proceedings.

duress In contract law, a defense that permits nonperformance of a contract if the party can show that physical or mental force was used to obtain the agreement to enter into the contract.

E

early neutral evaluation A third party's assessment of the issues and likely resolution of a dispute prior to any significant judicial process.

easement Right or privilege in the land of another.

EEOC complaint Complaint against an employer filed by either an employee or the EEOC; initiates an investigation by the EEOC.

effluent guidelines In environmental law, the standards for release of nonnatural substances into natural waters.

8-K form A filing required by the SEC under the 1934 Securities Act; an 8-K is filed by a registered company within ten days of a significant or material event affecting the company (e.g., a dividend being suspended).

Electronic Communications Privacy Act of 1986 (ECPA) Federal statute that prohibits the interception of and/or eavesdropping on live conversations; designed to prevent listening device use on phone conversations, the act has reemerged with the Internet to be used against those who intercept or "eavesdrop" on e-mail.

electronic digital interchange (EDI) Precursor to the Internet and B2B transactions that permitted direct ordering and replenishment between manufacturers and their customers.

Electronic Signatures in Global and National Commerce Act (E-sign) A federal law that recognizes digital signatures as authentic for purposes of contract formation; E-sign puts electronic signatures on equal footing with paper contracts.

elements The requirements for proof of a crime.

embezzlement Name for the crime of an employee stealing funds, property, or services from his employer.

eminent domain In constitutional law, the taking of private property by a government entity for a public purpose, with compensation paid to the owner.

emissions offset policy EPA procedure for approval of new facilities in nonattainment areas.

employment at will Doctrine that gives the employer the right to fire an employee at any time with or without cause; the doctrine and its protection for employers have been eroded by judicial decisions over recent years.

Employment Retirement Income Security Act of 1974 (ERISA) Congressional act establishing requirements for disclosure and other procedures with relation to employees' retirement plans.

enabling act Act of a legislative body establishing an administrative agency and providing it with guidelines and authority for the enforcement of the law.

en banc French term for the full bench; refers to an appellate hearing in which the full court, as opposed to a panel of three judges, hears a case on review.

Endangered Species Act (ESA) Federal environmental law that requires federal agencies to disclose the impact of proposed projects on species listed as protected under the act.

enlightened self-interest Theory of corporate social responsibility under which managers believe that by serving society they best serve their shareholders.

environmental impact statement (EIS) Report required to be filed when a federal agency is taking action that will affect land, water, or air; an analysis of the effect of a project on the environment.

Environmental Protection Agency (EPA) The main federal agency responsible for the enforcement of all the federal environmental laws.

Equal Credit Opportunity Act (ECOA) Federal law that prohibits discrimination on the basis of race, sex, national origin, marital status, or ethnicity in the decision to extend credit.

Equal Employment Opportunity Act of 1972 Congressional act that established the EEOC and provided strong enforcement powers for Title VII provisions.

Equal Employment Opportunity Commission (EEOC) Federal agency responsible for the enforcement of Title VII and other federal antidiscrimination laws.

Equal Pay Act of 1963 Act prohibiting wage discrimination on the basis of age, race, sex, ethnicity, and so on.

equal protection Constitutional right of all citizens to be treated in the same manner and afforded the same rights under law regardless of sex, race, color, or national origin.

equitable remedy A remedy other than money damages, such as specific performance, injunction, and so on.

equity That portion of the law that originated to afford remedies when money damages were not appropriate; currently, remedies of law and equity have merged and courts can award either or both.

estoppel Doctrine of reliance; prevents parties from backing out of an obligation they have created; for example, a partner by estoppel has allowed others to use her name in connection with a partnership and is estopped from denying liability to third parties who have relied on that representation.

ethics Moral behavior constraints.

European Court of Human Rights A noncommercial court dealing with disputes over the treatment of a country's citizens.

exclusionary conduct Monopolistic behavior that attempts to prevent market entry and exclude competition.

exclusive dealing Antitrust term for contract arrangements in which the seller sells to only one buyer in an area.

exclusive distributorship *See* **sole outlet**.

exclusive jurisdiction Authority granted to only one court for particular types of cases.

exculpatory clause Clause that attempts to hold a party harmless in the event of damage or injury to another's property.

executed contracts Contracts in which performance has been completed.

executive branch That portion of the federal government that consists of the president and the administrative agencies; often referred to as the enforcement branch.

executive committee A working board of directors' committee that usually includes company officers and makes day-to-day decisions between regular board meetings; manages ongoing operations.

executive order Law of the executive branch; sets policies for administrative workers and contracts.

executory contracts Contracts that have been entered into but not yet performed.

exempt securities Securities not required to be registered with the SEC under the 1933 Securities Act.

exempt transactions Under the 1933 Securities Act, sales of securities not required to be registered, such as shares issued under a Chapter 11 bankruptcy court reorganization.

exemptions Under the Securities Act of 1933, the securities and transactions that need not be registered with the SEC.

exhausting administrative remedies Requirement that all procedures internal to an administrative body be exhausted before an individual pursues a remedy in court.

ex parte **contacts** Latin term for contacts with a judicial figure or hearing officer outside the presence of the opposing side.

express authority In agency law, the authority given either in writing or orally to the agent for his conduct.

express contract Contract agreed to orally or in writing.

express warranty Expressed promise by seller as to the quality, abilities, or performance of a product.

expropriation The taking of private property by a government for government use, also known as appropriation.

F

failing-company doctrine Under the Clayton Act, a justification for a generally illegal merger on the basis that the firm being merged is in financial difficulty and would not survive alone.

Fair Credit Billing Act Federal law governing credit card bills and requiring monthly statements, disclosure of dispute rights, and so on.

Fair Credit and Charge Card Disclosure Act of 1988 Amendment to the Truth in Lending Act that requires disclosure of terms in credit card solicitations.

Fair Credit Reporting Act (FCRA) Federal law governing the disclosure of credit information to consumers and the content of those credit reports.

Fair Debt Collections Practices Act (FDCPA) Federal law controlling the methods debt collectors may use in collecting consumer debts and also requiring disclosures to consumers when the debt collection process begins.

Fair Employment Practices Act The Civil Rights Act of 1964.

Fair Labor Standards Act (FLSA) Federal law on minimum wages, maximum hours, overtime, and compensatory time.

fair trade contracts Agreements requiring retailers not to sell products below a certain price; permitted in some states.

fair use One of the exceptions to copyright protection; permits limited use of copyright material; for example, an excerpt from a poem.

false imprisonment The intentional tort of retaining someone against that person's will.

Family and Medical Leave Act (FMLA) Federal law that permits unpaid leave up to twelve weeks with a job guarantee upon return; allowed for birth or adoption of child or illness of parent, spouse, or child.

featherbedding Union unfair labor practice of requiring payment for work not actually performed; for example, requiring payment for a minimum number of bricks even though the job does not involve that many bricks.

federal circuits Geographic groupings of the federal district courts for purposes of appellate jurisdiction.

Federal Consumer Product Warranty Law of 1975 The Magnuson-Moss Act; governs the definitions of limited and full warranties; requires disclosure of warranty terms.

federal district court The trial court of the federal system.

Federal Environmental Pesticide Control Act Federal law that requires registration of all pesticides with the EPA.

federal implementation plan (FIP) Under the Clean Air Act Amendments of 1990, requirements established by the EPA (in the absence of state action) regarding the control of emissions by plants and autos.

Federal Insurance Contributions Act (FICA) Federal law that requires the joint contribution by employers and employees of the funds used for the Social Security system.

Federal Privacy Act Federal law that prohibits exchange of information about individuals among agencies without request and notification, unless for law enforcement purposes.

Federal Register A daily federal publication that reports the day-to-day actions of administrative agencies.

Federal Register Act Federal law that establishes all the publications and reporting mechanisms for federal administrative law, such as the *Federal Register* and the *Code of Federal Regulations*.

Federal Register System Part of the federal government responsible for the publication of government notices and rules.

Federal Reporter Series of volumes reporting the decisions of the U.S. Court of Appeals.

Federal Supplement Series of volumes reporting the decisions of the federal district courts.

Federal Trade Commission (FTC) Federal agency responsible for regulation of unfair and deceptive trade practices, including deceptive advertisements.

Federal Trade Commission Act Federal law establishing the FTC and its regulatory role.

Federal Trademark Dilution Act Federal law that permits litigation to halt the use of a trademark that results in the loss of unique appeal for its owner.

Federal Water Pollution Control Act of 1972 Federal law that set goals of swimmable and fishable waters by 1983 and zero pollution discharge by 1985.

Federal Water Pollution Control Administration (FWPCA) Separate federal agency established to monitor water quality standards.

fee simple Highest degree of land ownership; full rights of mortgage and transferability.

fiduciary Position of trust and confidence.

Fifth Amendment Portion of the Bill of Rights of the U.S. Constitution providing protection against self-incrimination and ensuring due process.

finance charges For credit cards, the interest paid each month on outstanding balances.

financing statement Publicly filed document reflecting security interest.

First Amendment Portion of the Bill of Rights of the U.S. Constitution providing protection for freedom of speech and religious freedom.

fixtures Property that was once personal in nature that is affixed real property and becomes a part of it.

FOIA request Request to a government agency for information retained in that agency's files.

force majeure Clause in a contract that excuses performance in the event of war, embargo, or other generally unforeseeable event.

foreclosure Process of creditor acquiring mortgaged land for resale.

foreign corporation A corporation in any state except the state in which it is incorporated.

Foreign Corrupt Practices Act (FCPA) Federal law prohibiting bribes in foreign countries and requiring the maintenance of internal controls on accounting for firms registered under the Securities Exchange Act of 1934.

formal rulemaking Process for developing rules in an administrative agency; involves hearings and public comment period.

Fourteenth Amendment Provision of the U.S. Constitution that provides for equal protection and due process.

Fourth Amendment Part of the Bill of Rights of the U.S. Constitution that provides protection and assurance of privacy; the search and seizure amendment.

fraud Term for deception or intentional misrepresentation in contract negotiation.

Freedom of Information Act (FOIA) Federal law that permits access to information held by federal administrative agencies.

freeze-out Merger undertaken with the objective of eliminating minority shareholders.

friendly takeover A takeover of one firm by another firm when the target firm solicits or agrees to the takeover.

frolic or detour In agency law, set of rules used to determine when an agent is in the scope of employment; a frolic is a major deviation from duty and eliminates the principal's liability; a detour is a slight deviation such as lunch for a salesperson who makes calls all day.

FTC Improvements Act of 1980 Federal act that provided change in the role of the FTC and placed some limitations on its authority after the FTC's attempt to regulate children's television advertising.

full-disclosure standard SEC standard for registration; materiality disclosure requirements; not a merit standard.

G

garnishment Judicial process of taking funds or wages for satisfaction of a judgment.

GATT Multilateral trade treaty to which the U.S. is a signatory.

general partner Partner in a general or limited partnership whose personal assets are subject to partnership creditors in the event of nonpayment of partnership debts.

general warranty deed Deed that transfers title with highest guarantees of title.

geographic market Relevant geographic location for a firm's market; used as a basis for determining monopoly power and market share.

good-faith bargaining Mutual obligation of employer and union to meet at reasonable times, confer in good faith on employment issues, and execute a written agreement.

government corporation Corporation created by a government agency to achieve a social goal.

Government in the Sunshine Act Federal law that requires advance notice and open meetings of agency heads.

grand jury Special group of jurors established as a review board for potential criminal prosecutions; generally established for a year to eighteen months.

gratuitous agency Agency relationship in which the agent has the authority to act for the principal but will not be compensated.

gray market Market in which trade name goods are sold through unauthorized dealers or without authorization from the owner of the trade name.

group bids Takeover offer by more than one offeror acting in concert.

group boycotts A practice, prohibited by federal antitrust laws, in which several firms agree not to sell or buy from one or several other firms.

H

Hart-Scott-Rodino Antitrust Improvements Act Act passed in 1976 that gave the Justice Department greater investigative authority in antitrust violations and established premerger notification requirements.

Hazardous Substance Response Trust Fund Fund set up by CERCLA for waste site cleanup that is funded by the responsible company.

hearing examiner *or* **hearing officer** Quasi-judicial figure for agency hearings.

hearsay Testimony about the statements of another; often inadmissible evidence in a trial.

Home Equity Loan Consumer Protection Act of 1988 Amendment to the Truth in Lending Act that requires disclosures in home equity loan documents, including the possibility of foreclosure, and allows three-day rescission period for home equity loans.

home solicitation sales Sales originated in the home of the buyer.

Homeland Security Act of 2002 Federal law that created the Department of Homeland Security and added additional funds and processes for security and antiterrorism tools.

horizontal merger A merger between two competitors.

horizontal restraint of trade Anticompetitive activity among competitors; for example, price fixing among competitors.

hostile takeover A takeover not solicited or approved by the target's management.

hot cargo agreements Union economic weapon in which others agree not to handle the products of the struck employer.

Howey test U.S. Supreme Court definition of a security; investment in a common enterprise with profits to come from the efforts of others.

hung jury Term used to describe a jury unable to come to a verdict.

hybrid rulemaking Process by which agency promulgates rules with some hearings but relies mostly on public comments.

I

Illegal Immigration Reform and Immigrant Responsibility Act of 1996 Federal statute that increased employer responsibility for use of illegal immigrants in their workforces.

Immigration Act of 1990 Federal law that requires an I-9 form for every employee who is an immigrant.

Immigration and Naturalization Act (INA) Original federal act governing employer obligations on employing immigrants.

Immigration Reform and Control Act of 1986 (IRCA) Federal law imposing additional requirements on employers for lawful employment of immigrants.

implied authority Authority of an agent that exists because of business custom in the principal's operation and in industry.

implied contract A contract that arises from circumstances and is not expressed by the parties.

implied warranty of fitness for a particular purpose Warranty given by seller to buyer that promises goods will meet the buyer's specified needs.

implied warranty of merchantability Under the Uniform Commercial Code, Article 2, Sales, a warranty that the goods are of average quality; given in every sale of goods by a merchant.

implied-in-fact contract A contract deemed to exist because of the way the parties have interacted (e.g., accepting treatment at a doctor's office).

implied-in-law contract *See* **quasi-contract**.

impossibility Contract defense that excuses performance when there is no objective way to complete the contract.

in personam jurisdiction Jurisdiction over the person; type of jurisdiction court must have to require a party to appear before it.

in rem jurisdiction Jurisdiction over the thing; a method whereby a court obtains jurisdiction by having property or money located within its geographic jurisdiction.

inadequate capitalization In corporation law, the lack of sufficient funds to cover the anticipated debts and obligations of a corporation.

incidental damages Damages suffered by the nonbreaching party to a contract as a result of the breach; for example, late performance fees on a buyer's contract because the seller failed to deliver on time.

incorporators Individuals who sign the incorporation papers for a newly formed corporation.

independent contractor Person who works for another but is not controlled in her day-to-day conduct.

indictment Formal criminal charges issued by the grand jury.

infant A minor; a person below the age of majority, in most states below the age of 18.

informal rulemaking Process by which an agency promulgates rules without formal public hearings.

information Formal criminal charges issued by a judge after a preliminary hearing.

infringement The use of a copyright, patent, trademark, or trade name without permission.

inherence Theory of corporate social responsibility under which managers serve shareholders only.

inherently dangerous activities In agency law, those activities that carry a high risk and for which the party hiring an independent contractor cannot disclaim liability; for example, dynamiting a building to demolish it.

initial appearance In criminal procedure, the first appearance of the accused before a judicial figure; must take place shortly after arrest.

initial meeting First meeting of a corporation's organizers after the state provides certification that the corporation exists.

initial public offering (IPO) The first public offering of securities by a corporation.

injunction Equitable remedy in which courts order or enjoin a particular activity.

insider A corporate officer or director or other executive with access to corporate information not available to the public.

Insider Trading and Securities Fraud Enforcement Act of 1988 Act increasing the Securities Exchange Act of 1934 penalties for insider trading.

instructions Explanation of the law applicable in a case given to the jury at the end of the evidence and arguments.

intangible property Intellectual property, such as patents and copyrights.

intentional infliction of emotional distress Intentional tort in which the defendant engages in outrageous conduct that is psychologically damaging to the plaintiff.

intentional torts Civil wrongs against individuals that are committed with a requisite state of mind and intent to harm; includes defamation, false imprisonment, battery, assault, and intentional infliction of emotional distress.

Inter-American Court of Human Rights In international law, the court for resolution of noncommercial issues or the violation of human rights by a particular nation in North or South America.

interbrand competition Competition among like products; for example, competition between Pepsi and Coke.

interlocking directorates In antitrust law, the presence of the same directors on the boards of various companies that occupy positions in the same chain of distribution or are competitors; the concern is the concentration of power.

International Chamber of Commerce (ICC) Voluntary body with uniform rules on commerce and contracts.

International Court of Justice (ICJ) Voluntary court in the international system of law; nonbinding decisions.

Internet Corporation for Assigned Names and Numbers (ICANN) Organization that registers domain names for purposes of protection of those names as intellectual property.

interrogatories Method of discovery in which parties send written questions to each other, with responses required to be given under oath.

intervenors Interested parties who are permitted to participate in agency hearings even though they are not parties to the case.

intrabrand competition Competition among products made by the same manufacturer; for example, competition between Coke and Diet Coke.

invisible hand Theory of corporate social responsibility under which managers believe they serve society but do so in the best way by being accountable to shareholders.

J

joint venture A partnership for one activity or business venture.

judge Elected or appointed government official responsible for supervising trials, hearing appeals, and ruling on motions.

judgment The final decision of a court; formal entry of the decision or verdict.

judgment NOV Judgment *non obstante veredicto;* a judgment notwithstanding the verdict; a judgment issued by the judge after the jury has rendered a verdict; a trial court's reversal of a jury's decision on the grounds that the verdict was against the weight of the evidence.

judgment on the pleadings A dismissal of a suit by a court for the failure of the plaintiff to state a case in the complaint.

judicial branch The one (of three) branches of the federal government that consists of all levels of federal courts.

judicial review Review by appellate court of decisions and actions of a lower court to determine whether reversible errors in procedure or law were made.

junk bond Method for financing takeovers in which buyers have as their security the assets of the target firm; such security is only as good as the takeover is successful.

jurisdiction The concept of authority of a court to settle disputes.

jurisprudence The philosophy of law.

jury instructions Explanation to the jury of the law applicable in the case.

just compensation Principle in eminent domain that requires the government entity taking private property to pay the owner a fair amount.

justice of the peace courts Lower courts generally handling traffic citations and other lesser civil matters.

K

knock-off goods Goods manufactured by someone other than the trademark or trade name holder without authorization and not according to the standards of the owner.

L

Labor Management Cooperation Act Federal law providing funding for the study of alternative solutions to labor disputes.

Labor-Management Relations Act The Taft-Hartley Act; governs management conduct in its relationships with unions.

Landrum-Griffin Act Labor-Management Reporting and Disclosure Act; legislation passed to regulate unions and their governance.

Lanham Act Federal law dealing with trademark and trade name protection.

lawyer Licensed professional who serves as a representative for another in private negotiations and in judicial and other types of legal proceedings.

Lawyer's Edition Private publisher's series of volumes reporting U.S. Supreme Court decisions; contains summaries of the cases and the briefs of counsel.

lease Temporary possession and use of real property, or right of use and possession of personal property.

legal remedy In common law, a legal remedy consisted of money damages versus equitable remedies of injunctions and specific performance; different courts afforded different remedies in common law England, but the distinction has disappeared today, and all courts have authority to award legal and equitable remedies.

legislative branch One of the three branches of government; at the federal level, consists of the Congress (the Senate and the House of Representatives) and is the branch responsible for making laws.

letter of credit Generally used in international transactions; an assurance by a bank of the seller's right to draw on a line of credit established for the buyer.

libel Written defamation; defamation in a newspaper or magazine or, in some states, on television.

license Right of access; generally oral; personal right that is not transferrable.

lien An interest in property used to secure repayment of a debt; entitles creditor to foreclosure rights in the event the debt is not repaid; creditor's right in property to secure debt.

life estate Right to use and occupy property for life.

life tenant Party who holds the right to use, possession of property for the period of his or her life.

like grade or quality Under Robinson-Patman Act, this means that there are no differences in the physical product.

limited jurisdiction Specialty courts that have only limited authority over certain types of cases with distinct subject matter; probate courts have limited jurisdiction over probate matters only.

limited liability company (LLC) A business entity with limited liability but management participation permitted by all; statutory creature.

limited liability partnership (LLP) Partnership in which *all* partners have limited liability; statutory creature with strict formation requirements.

limited partner Partner in a limited partnership who has no personal liability and can only lose his investment in the partnership; must be formed according to statutory requirements; cannot use name in partnership name and cannot participate in the firm's management.

limited partnership Type of partnership in which some partners have unlimited liability (general partners) and other partners have only their investments at risk in the business (limited partners); must follow statutory procedures to properly create a limited partnership.

limited partnership agreement Contract governing the rights and relations of limited partners.

line of commerce Area of business; determination used by the Justice Department in evaluating mergers.

lingering apparent authority Type of authority an agent has when the principal fails to announce that the agent is no longer associated with her.

liquidated damages Damages agreed to in advance and provided for in the contract; usually appropriate when it is difficult to know how much the damages will be.

lockout Economic weapon of employer in which employees are not permitted to work; shop is closed down to avoid a strike.

long arm statutes Statutes in each state that allow the state courts to bring in defendants from outside the state so long as they have some "minimum contact" with the state.

M

Madrid Agreement Concerning the International Registration of Trademarks In international law, 1891 multilateral treaty for protection of trademarks that permits registration and protection through a centralized registrar in Geneva.

mailbox rule Timing rule in contract acceptances that provides that acceptance is effective upon mailing if properly done.

mandatory bargaining terms In collective bargaining, the terms both sides are required to discuss, such as wages, hours, and so on.

market power The ability of a firm to control prices and product demand.

master-servant relationship Type of agency relationship in which the principal directly controls the agent; for example, principal controls hours and supervises work directly.

material fact (or material misstatement**)** A statement of fact that would influence an individual's decision to buy or sell.

maximum achievable control technology (MACT) Under the 1990 Clean Air Act, the standard required for factories in controlling air emissions; replaced the old, less-stringent standard of best available technology (BAT).

mediation Alternative dispute resolution mechanism in which a third party is brought in to find a common ground between two disputing parties.

meeting the competition Defense to price discrimination that allows the defense of price reduction when competition in the area dictates that price.

mens rea Mental intent or state of mind necessary for the commission of a crime.

merchant's confirmation memoranda Memos between merchants, signed by one of them, that will satisfy the statute of frauds requirements and create an enforceable contract against both parties.

merchant's firm offer Under § 2–205 of the UCC, an offer required to be held open if made in writing by a merchant, even though no consideration is given.

merger Process of combining firms so that one firm becomes a part of the other and only one firm's name is retained.

merit review Process at the state level of reviewing securities registrations for their merit, as opposed to the federal review for full disclosure.

mineral rights Ownership rights to materials beneath the land surface.

minimum contacts Standard used for determining *in personam* jurisdiction over residents outside the state of the court of litigation; nonresident defendants must have some contact with the state to justify a court taking jurisdiction.

minimum wage Part of the FLSA that requires all employees to be paid a minimum wage.

minitrial Alternative dispute resolution method in which the officers of two firms in a dispute listen to the key evidence in a case to see if a settlement can be determined.

minor An infant; an individual under the age of majority; generally someone under the age of 18.

Miranda **warnings** Statement required to be given to individuals when taken into custody to alert them to their right to remain silent, the fact that statements can be used against them, their right to an attorney, and the right to an appointed attorney if they cannot afford one.

misappropriation Intentional tort of using someone's name, likeness, voice, or image without permission.

misrepresentation In contract formation, misstatements of materials facts.

misuse In product liability, a defense based on the plaintiff's failure to follow instructions or use of a product for improper purposes.

Model Business Corporation Act (MBCA) Uniform law on corporations.

modify An option for an appellate court in its review of a lower court case; an action that is something less than reversing a decision but something more than simply affirming it; for example, an appellate court could agree with the verdict but modify the judgment amount or the remedy.

monopolizing Controlling a product or geographic market.

monopoly power The ability to control prices and exclude competition.

moral relativism Ethical theory holding that there is no absolute right and wrong and that right and wrong vary according to circumstances, often referred to as "situational ethics."

moral standards Ethical standards, as opposed to legal standards.

mortgage Lien on real property.

motion A party's request to the court for action.

motion for judgment on the pleadings A motion made to dismiss a suit for failure by the plaintiff to establish a cause of action in the pleadings.

motion for summary judgment A motion made for final disposition of a case in which there is no dispute of facts and only a dispute of law and its application.

motion to dismiss A motion made after the presentation of the plaintiff's case or the defendant's case for failure to establish a *prima facie* case (in the case of the plaintiff) or failure to rebut the presumption (in the case of the defendant).

multilateral treaty A treaty agreed to by several nations.

N

National Environmental Policy Act (NEPA) The federal legislation on environmental impact statements.

National Labor Relations Act (Wagner Act 1935) (NLRA) First universal federal legislation that gave employees the right to organize and choose representatives for collective bargaining.

National Labor Relations Board (NLRB) Federal agency charged with supervising union elections and handling unfair labor practice complaints.

National Pollution Discharge Elimination System (NPDES) A system established by the EPA that requires those who discharge pollutants to obtain a permit, the granting of which is based on limits and pretreatments.

nationalization The taking of private property by a government for governmental use.

natural law Law or principles of behavior that exist without being written; supreme laws that cannot be circumvented.

necessaries With regard to minors, items for which minors can be held responsible.

negligence Tort of accidental wrong committed by oversight or failure to take precautions or corrective action.

nexus Connection; a term used in constitutional analysis of the authority to tax; there must be a sufficient connection between the business and the taxing state.

NLRB National Labor Relations Board.

Noerr-Pennington **doctrine** An exception to the antitrust laws that allows business to lobby against competitors before legislative and administrative bodies, even though the effect may be anticompetitive.

Noise Control Act of 1972 Federal statute controlling noise levels and requiring product labels.

nolo contendere A "no contest" plea; the charges are neither denied nor admitted.

nonattainment area In federal air pollution regulation, an area unable to meet federal clean air goals and guidelines.

nonbinding arbitration Arbitration in which the decision is not final, that is, the parties can still take the matter to court.

nonconventional pollutant EPA classification of pollutant that requires the highest level of treatment prior to release into waterways.

nonprofit corporations Those corporations performing a function that covers cost but does not provide a return on investment.

Norris-LaGuardia Act The anti-injunction act; one of the first federal labor acts passed to prevent courts from issuing injunctions to stop labor strikes except in dangerous or emergency situations.

novation Process of reworking a contract to substitute parties or terms, so that the old contract is abandoned and the new contract becomes the only valid contract.

nuisance Civil wrong of creating a situation (noise, dust, smell) that interferes with others' ability to enjoy the use of their properties.

O

Occupational Safety and Health Act Worker safety statute passed by Congress in 1970 that established OSHA and directs the development of safety standards in the workplace as well as systems for record keeping and compliance.

Occupational Safety and Health Administration (OSHA) Federal agency responsible for the enforcement of federal health and safety standards in business and industry.

offer Indication of present intent to contract; the first step in making a contract.

offeree In contract negotiations, the person to whom the offer is made.

offeror In contract negotiations, the person who makes the offer.

Oil Pollution Act (OPA) Federal law providing penalties for oil spills and authorizing federal cleanup when private companies' cleanup efforts fail; also authorizes federal government to collect for costs of cleanup when firm or firms responsible for the spill fail to do so.

omnibus hearing In criminal procedure, a hearing held before the trial to determine the admissibility of evidence.

open-end credit transaction Under Regulation Z, credit transactions without a definite beginning and ending balance; for example, credit cards.

open meeting law Law (at either state or federal level) requiring that notice be given of meetings of agency heads and that they be open to the public.

opening statement In a trial, each side's overview of the case and the evidence that will be presented.

opposition proceedings In non-U.S. countries, the patent process that allows third parties to appear and object to a patent application.

option A contract for time on an offer; an agreement to hold an offer open for a period of time in exchange for consideration.

oral argument Upon appeal of a case, the attorneys' presentation of their points on appeal to the panel of appellate judges.

ordinances Laws at the city, town, or country level.

ordinary and reasonably prudent person In negligence, standard used for determining the level of care required in any given situation.

Organization for Economic Cooperation and Development (OECD) International organization of countries committed to developing trade, initially through the elimination of corruption.

original jurisdiction Jurisdiction of trial courts; jurisdiction of courts where a case begins.

overtime pay Pay rate required for work beyond the maximum forty-hour work week.

P

palming off Unfair trade practice of passing off mock goods as the goods of another.

Pan American Convention A 1929 treaty offering trademark protection to member countries.

parol evidence Extrinsic evidence regarding a contract.

partnership Voluntary association of two or more persons, co-owners in a business for profit.

partnership by estoppel *See* **estoppel**.

partnership by implication A partnership that exists because of the conduct of the parties rather than by agreement.

party autonomy The right of parties to determine privately their choice of law.

patent Government license or protection for a process, product, or service.

pattern or practice of discrimination In employment discrimination, a theory for establishing discrimination based on a pattern of dealing with minorities, women, and certain ethnic groups.

peer review Method of dispute resolution in which peers of the party making a claim decide on its merits; for example, employee peer review of claims against the employer.

per curiam A judicial opinion of the full court with no judge or justice claiming authorship.

peremptory challenge Right to strike jurors with or without cause; lawyer's discretionary tool in selecting a jury; number of peremptory challenges is usually limited.

perfection Process of attaining priority position over other secured creditors.

periodic tenancy Lease that runs from period to period, such as month to month.

per se "On its face"; "without further proof."

petition Often the first document in a case.

petitioner Party filing a petition; or in the case of an appeal, the party filing the appeal of a lower court decision.

picketing Economic weapon of labor unions; right to demonstrate in front of employer's place of business to display grievances publicly.

plain view exception Under the Fourth Amendment, an exception to the warrant requirement that applies when what is seen is in the "plain view" of the law enforcement official.

plaintiff Party filing suit, who is alleging a wrong committed by the defendant.

plea bargain A negotiated settlement of a criminal case prior to trial.

pleadings The complaint, answer, and counterclaim filed in a lawsuit.

point and click The process of using the Internet and a computer to form a contract—pointing to a box that indicates affirmation and clicking the mouse.

point sources In environmental law, direct discharges of effluents.

police power Constitutional term describing the authority given to the states to regulate the health, safety, and welfare of their citizens.

political speech Term given to speech of businesses related to political candidates or issues; given First Amendment protection.

pooling agreement Agreement among shareholders to vote their stock a certain way.

positive law Codified law; law created and enforced by governmental entities.

power of attorney A lay term for granting another the right to act on your behalf; a general power of attorney grants full contractual and financial authority; a special power of attorney is one that is limited by function or time.

precautionary principle A principle used to guide regulations in the area of the environment and product liability; the principle mandates regulation as a prevention measure even when data are not clear as to whether harm results from product or practice (in environmental context).

precedent Prior judicial decisions; the law as it exists; *see also* **stare decisis**.

predatory pricing Discount pricing below cost for a short period of time in an attempt to drive new competition out of the market.

preemption Constitutional term from the Supremacy Clause, which provides that the federal government preempts state law where such preemption was intended or where the federal regulation is so pervasive that it prevents state regulation.

preferred stock Nonvoting shares of a corporation entitling its holders to dividend preference above the common shareholders.

Pregnancy Discrimination Act Federal law prohibiting discrimination in hiring or promotion decisions on the basis of pregnancy or plans for pregnancy.

preliminary hearing In criminal procedure, the hearing in which the prosecution establishes there is sufficient evidence to bind the defendant over for trial.

pretrial conference Meeting among lawyers and court to narrow issues, stipulate to evidence, and determine method of jury selection.

prevention of significant deterioration (PSD) areas Clean air areas given special protection by the EPA regarding the maintenance of air quality.

price discrimination Charging a different price for different customers on a basis other than different marginal costs.

price fixing Agreement among horizontal competitors to charge a uniform price.

prima facie **case** A case establishing all the necessary elements; without rebuttal evidence from the defendant, entitles the plaintiff to a verdict.

primary boycott Boycott by an employee or union against the employer.

primary offering In securities, the initial offering of the security for sale.

principal The employer or master in the principal-agent relationship.

private law The law of contracts and the intrabusiness laws such as personnel rules.

Private Securities Litigation Reform Act of 1995 Federal law passed with the goal of reducing litigation against companies in the form of class action suits by shareholders.

privity Direct contractual relationship.

probable cause Sufficient cause or grounds for the issuance of a search warrant.

probate courts Specialized courts set up to handle the probate of wills and estates and, generally, issues of guardianships and conservatorships.

pro bono Represented without fee, as when a lawyer agrees to represent a client without compensation for the representation.

procedural due process Constitutional protection that gives litigants in civil cases and defendants in criminal cases the right to notice in all steps in the process and the right of participation.

procedural laws Laws that provide the means for enforcing rights.

process servers Individuals licensed by a state to deliver summonses and subpoenas to individuals.

product liability Generic term used to describe the various contract and tort theories for holding parties liable for defective products.

product market Relevant product market for a firm; used as a basis for determining monopoly power.

professional corporation A statutory entity that permits professionals such as lawyers and doctors to incorporate and enjoy limited personal liability on all debts except for those arising from malpractice.

profit corporations Those corporations seeking to earn a return for their investors.

promissory estoppel A promise that causes another to act in reliance upon it; if the reliance is substantial, the promise is enforceable.

promulgation The process of passing administrative agency rules.

proper purpose A shareholder's legitimate interest in accessing a corporation's books and records.

prospectus A formal document describing the nature of securities and the company offering them; an ad or other description of securities.

proxy Right (given in written form) to vote another's shares.

proxy solicitation The process of seeking voting rights from shareholders.

public comment period In administrative rulemaking, the period during which any member of the public can comment on the rule, its content, and potential efficacy.

public law Law passed by some governmental agency.

publicly held corporation A corporation owned by shareholders outside the officers and employees of the firm.

puffing Offering opinion about the quality of goods and products; not a basis for misrepresentation; not a material statement of fact.

pump and dump Practice of buying a stock, touting it to many who then buy it, and then selling the stock at an inflated price; not a new practice, but it is easier and faster over the Internet.

Q

qualified privilege A defense to defamation available to the media that permits retraction and no liability so long as the information is not printed or given with malice or with reckless disregard for whether it is true.

quasi-contract A theory used to prevent unjust enrichment when no contract is formed; the court acts as if a contract had been formed and awards damages accordingly.

quitclaim deed Transfer of title with no warranties.

quotas Affirmative action plans that dictate a specific number of minority or female applicants be accepted for jobs, graduate school, and so on. Outlawed by U.S. Supreme Court; can only have affirmative action goals, not specific quotas.

R

Railway Labor Act The first federal labor legislation that controlled strikes by transportation employees.

ratification A principal's recognition of a contract entered into by an unauthorized agent.

record Expanded form of documentation that qualifies as a "writing" for purposes of contracts under the UCC.

recording Public filing of land documents.

red herring prospectus A prospectus issued in advance of the effective date of a securities registration statement; permissible to release these before the registration statement is effective so long as a disclaimer that it is not an offer to sell securities is noted in red on the prospectus.

redirect examination Plaintiff's questioning of his own witness after defendant's cross-examination is complete; or vice versa when defendant's witness is involved.

regional reporter Series of volumes reporting the appeals and supreme court decisions of state courts; grouped by geographic region; for example, Pacific Reporter for the western states.

registration statement Requirement under the 1933 Securities Act ; a filing with the SEC that discloses all the necessary information about a securities offering and the offeror.

Regulation A Short form offering regulation under 1933 Securities Act.

Regulation D A regulation of the SEC governing the small offering exemptions under the 1933 Securities Act.

Regulation Z The Federal Reserve Board's regulation for the Truth in Lending Act; specifies disclosure requirements and offers examples of required forms.

Regulatory Flexibility Act Reform act for federal agency rules promulgation; requires publication of proposed rules in trade magazines so that industries and individuals affected can properly respond during the public comment period.

Rehabilitation Act of 1973 Federal law prohibiting discrimination by federal contractors on the basis of a handicapping condition.

relevant market Term used to describe the market studied to determine whether a particular seller has a monopoly.

reliance In misrepresentation, the element that establishes that the buyer placed some importance on the statement.

remainderman Interest in a third party following the death of the life tenant in a life estate.

remand Term used to describe the action an appellate court takes when a case is sent down to a lower court for a retrial or other proceeding on the basis of the appellate court decision.

rent-a-judge Means of alternative dispute resolution in which the parties hire a former judge and a private hearing room and have the judge determine liability.

repatriation Reaffiliating as a citizen of a country after having renounced that citizenship through expatriation.

request for admissions Discovery tool in which one side asks the other to admit certain facts as proven in a case.

request for production Discovery tool in which one side asks the other side to produce documents relevant to the case.

requirements contract Contract in which the buyer agrees to buy all requirements for her business from one seller.

resale price maintenance Practice of manufacturer attempting to control the price at which a product is sold at retail level.

rescission Process of rescinding a contract.

Resource Conservation and Recovery Act of 1976 (RCRA) Federal law governing the transportation of hazardous materials; requires a permit for such transportation; also encourages environmental cleanup.

Resource Recovery Act Federal law that gave aid to state and local governments with recycling programs.

respondeat superior "Let the master answer"; doctrine holds principal responsible for torts of agent in scope of employment.

respondent On appeal of a case, the party who is not appealing; in a petition for a divorce, the party against whom the petition is filed.

restatement A summary of existing common law on a particular topic; for example, *Restatement of Contracts.*

Restatement of Agency A summary of the majority view of the states of the law of agency followed by courts in resolving agency issues and disputes.

Restatement (Second) of Contracts General summary of the nature of common law contracts in the United States.

Restatement § 402A Portion of the *Restatement of Torts* that deals with product liability.

reverse Action of an appellate court in changing the decision of a lower court because a reversible error has been made.

reversible error Mistake made in lower court proceedings that is ruled as improper by an appellate court and that requires a reversal of the case and possible retrial.

Revised Uniform Limited Partnership Act (RULPA) New version of the Uniform Limited Partnership Act that includes changes in the rights of limited partners and distributions on liquidation.

Revised Uniform Partnership Act (RUPA) Newest uniform revision of law on limited partnerships.

revocation In contract law, the retraction by the offeror of an outstanding offer.

RICO Racketeer Influenced and Corrupt Organizations Act; federal statute regulating enterprises involved in gambling and other businesses that tend to attract organized crime figures.

right-to-sue letter Letter issued by the EEOC to a complainant after all necessary administrative steps have been taken in the case; permits the complainant to pursue court action.

right-to-work laws State laws providing employees with the right to work even though they are not union members.

Rivers and Harbors Act of 1899 A federal law revitalized during the 1960s and 1970s (prior to the enactment of specific federal legislation controlling emissions) to control water pollution.

Robinson-Patman Act Federal law that prohibits price discrimination.

rule of reason Standard for evaluation of antitrust activity that allows the court to consider various factors and does not require an automatic finding of a violation of antitrust laws.

Rule 10b-5 SEC antifraud rule.

Rules 504, 505, and 506 *See* Regulation D; the rules governing small offering exemptions under the 1933 Securities Act .

runaway shop Employer economic weapon in which work is transferred to another plant to avoid the impact of a strike.

S

Safe Drinking Water Act Federal law passed in 1986 that sets standards for drinking water systems and requires states to enforce them.

scheduled injuries Under workers' compensation systems, listed injury for which certain payments are to be made to the injured worker.

scienter Mental intent; under 10(b) of the Securities Exchange Act of 1934, a requirement of intent to defraud as opposed to a standard of negligence.

scope of employment Phrase used to describe the liability limits of the principal for the agent; an act must be committed within this scope for the imposition of liability on the principal.

search warrant Judicially authorized document allowing the search of individuals' or businesses' premises.

secondary boycott Union economic weapon in which others are asked not to deal with the struck employer.

Section 10(b) Antifraud provision of the Securities Exchange Act of 1934.

Section 16 Section of the Securities Exchange Act of 1934 that regulates sales and purchases of shares by directors, officers, and 10 percent shareholders.

securities Investments in a common enterprise with profits to come largely from the efforts of others.

Securities Act of 1933 The federal law governing the initial issuance and sale of securities to the public.

Securities and Exchange Commission (SEC) Federal agency responsible for enforcement of federal securities laws.

Securities Exchange Act of 1934 The federal law governing secondary sales of securities, the markets, and the firms dealing with securities.

security agreement Contract that creates a security interest.

security interest Lien in personal property; created under Article IX of the UCC.

self-incrimination Protection provided under the Fifth Amendment of not being required to be a witness against oneself.

separation of powers Principle of U.S. Constitution that divides authority for various governmental functions among the three branches of government.

sexual harassment Unlawful suggestions, contact, or other advances in the workplace; prohibited under federal law.

shelf registration Process of obtaining advance registration of securities offering and then waiting, or putting it on the shelf, until the market is at its best rates for issuance; can be valid for up to two years with regular filings such as the 10-K.

Sherman Act Original federal antitrust law; prohibits monopolization and horizontal trade restraints, such as price-fixing and boycotts.

shopkeeper's privilege A defense to the tort of false imprisonment for storeowners; allows reasonable detention of shoppers upon reasonable suspicion of shoplifting.

short-swing profits Profits made by corporate insiders during a period of less than six months between purchase and sale.

Sixth Amendment Amendment to U.S. Constitution that guarantees the right to a jury trial in criminal cases.

slander Tort of oral defamation.

slander of title Slander of business.

slowdown Economic weapon that interrupts the employer's business but falls short of a stoppage or strike.

small claims court Specialized court designed to allow the hearing of claims of limited monetary amounts without the complexities of litigation and without attorneys.

small-company doctrine Exemption from merger prohibitions that permits two smaller firms to merge in order to compete better against other, larger firms in the market.

social responsibility Theory of corporate social responsibility under which managers serve society by being accountable to society, not shareholders.

Social Security Act of 1935 Federal legislation that provides for the benefits of Social Security and the payment mechanisms through FICA deductions.

sole outlet Manufacturer's only designated seller in a particular area.

sole proprietorship Method of business ownership; one person owns business, receives all profits, and is personally liable for all debts.

Solid Waste Disposal Act Federal law that provided money to state and local governments for research in solid waste disposal.

Sonny Bono Copyright Term Extension Act (CTEA) Federal law that amends copyright law to extend period of protection for copyrighted works.

sovereign immunity Doctrine that provides that courts in one country are that country's law and cannot be reversed by decisions of courts in other countries; for example, a U.S. court cannot reverse a finding of not guilty by a court in Germany.

special warranty deed Deed that offers title protection only for grantor's period of ownership.

specific performance Equitable remedy in which party asks for performance of the contract as damages.

standing Right to bring suit; party who has experienced damages.

stare decisis Latin term for "Let the decision stand"; the doctrine of following or distinguishing case precedent.

state codes State laws passed by legislatures.

state implementation plans (SIPs) State plans for attaining federal air quality standards.

statute of frauds Generic term referring to statutes requiring certain contracts to be in writing.

statute of limitations Generic term referring to various state statutes controlling the time periods in which suits must be brought by plaintiffs; time varies according to the nature of the suit; for example, contract statutes of limitations are generally four years.

statutory law Law codified and written; passed by some governmental entity.

stipulated means In contracts, a method of acceptance specified or stipulated in the offer; if followed by the offeree, the mailbox rule applies for the timing of the acceptance.

stock restrictions Restrictions on the transfer of stock in a corporation; must be noted on the shares to be valid.

strict liability Degree of liability for conduct; an absolute standard of liability.

strict tort liability Standard established under the *Restatement of Torts* that holds product manufacturers and sellers liable for injuries resulting from their products regardless of whether they knew of the danger that caused the injury.

strike Economic weapon of employees; refusal to work for a given period of time.

Subchapter S corporation or S corporation A form of corporation for tax purposes that permits the direct flow-through of income and losses to the shareholders.

subject matter jurisdiction The right of a court to hear disputes involving certain areas of law and/or amounts.

subliminal persuasion A method of advertising using subtle and undetected means to persuade consumers to make purchases.

submarket In antitrust law, a segment of a market examined for purposes of determining either the impact on competition of a merger or the market strength of a competitor (e.g., tennis court shoes as a submarket of the tennis shoe market).

substantial evidence test Basis for challenging the actions of an administrative agency on the grounds that the rule promulgated was not based on enough evidence.

substantial performance Contract defense for performing a contract slightly differently from what was agreed upon; justification for substitute but equal performance; generally applicable in construction contracts.

substantive due process Constitutional protection that requires laws to apply equally to all and not to deny property or rights without prior notice.

substantive laws Laws that give rights and responsibilities to individuals.

summary judgment Method for terminating a case at the trial court level when there are no issues of fact and only a decision on the application of law needs to be made.

summary jury trial A private method of alternative dispute resolution in which the parties present a summary of their evidence to a private jury and then agree to abide by their decision or settle, depending on what the jury concludes; held privately and can often save the cost of going to court for a real trial.

summons Court document issued to the defendant in a lawsuit that explains the requirement of filing an answer and the time period in which it must be done.

sunset law Law that places an ending date on an administrative agency; if not renewed, an agency terminates at sunset on a particular date; the sun sets on the agency.

Superfund Federal fund used to clean up toxic waste disposal areas.

Superfund Amendment and Reauthorization Act Federal legislation extending CERCLA's authority and the liability of property owners and waste handlers for the cleanup of polluted lands.

superior skill, foresight, and industry Defense to monopolization based on "building a better mousetrap" and customers flocking to your door.

Supremacy Clause Constitutional provision allowing federal laws to preempt state laws where Congress intended or where the regulation is pervasive.

Supreme Court Reporter Series of volumes reporting the decisions of the U.S. Supreme Court.

Surface Mining and Reclamation Act of 1977 Federal law that requires restoration of surface coal mining land.

T

Taft-Hartley Act Labor Management Relations Act; federal law governing management in union relations.

takeover Process of one firm taking over another firm.

tangible property Form of personal property that includes goods, but not intellectual property such as stocks, bonds, patents, trademarks, and copyright.

target firm The firm to be taken over in a takeover.

tender offer Offer to more than 10 percent of the shareholders of a firm for the purchase of their shares; generally part of a takeover effort.

10-K form Annual report filed with the SEC; required of all 1934 Act firms.

10-Q form Quarterly report filed with the SEC; required of all 1934 Act firms.

theft Crime of taking property away from another permanently.

three-day cooling-off period Under Regulation Z, the period a buyer has to change his mind about a transaction initiated in the home.

tippee Party who is privy to inside information about a corporation or its securities and uses the information to trade securities profitably.

title insurance Insurance purchased for buyer's benefit; insures the land title from recorded defects.

Title VII Portion of the Civil Rights Act of 1964 prohibiting employment discrimination.

tombstone ad Ad run in newspapers announcing an upcoming securities offering; permissible after the registration statement is filed but not yet effective; must indicate it is not an offer for sale.

tort Private intentional or negligent wrong against an individual.

tortious interference with contracts Conduct by one party that results in another's breaching her contract with a third person (applies also to corporations).

toxic pollutant EPA classification of pollutant that requires the highest level of treatment prior to release.

Toxic Substances Control Act (TOSCA) Federal statute governing the control of the release of toxic substances into the environment.

trade dress The look, color, and decorative design of a business.

trade fixtures Personal property used in a trade or business that is attached to real property but is considered personal property.

trade libel Libel of a business.

trade name Name of a firm or product; entitled to federal protection for exclusive use.

trade restraints Obstacles to free and open competition.

trade secret A protected method for doing business or an item crucial to a business's success (such as a customer list).

trademark The symbol of a firm; entitled to federal protection for exclusive use.

traffic court Lesser trial court, in which traffic cases and violations of other city ordinances are tried.

transfer restrictions Limitations on the resale of shares of a corporation.

treaty In international law, an agreement between two or more nations.

treble damages In antitrust law and securities law, a civil remedy that permits successful claimants to recover three times the amount of their actual damages.

trial Process in a court of presenting evidence for a determination of guilt, innocence, or liability.

trial court First stop in the judicial system when a suit is filed; the court where the case is presented and witnesses testify.

trial *de novo* Latin for "trial again" or "trial anew."

trusteeship National union's action of taking control of a local union's treasury (through a trustee) and suspending all democratic union processes.

Truth in Lending Act (TILA) The Consumer Credit Protection Act; affords disclosure protection for consumer debt.

tying Anticompetitive behavior requiring the purchase of another product in order to get the product actually needed.

U

ultra vires Action taken beyond the scope of authority; with federal agencies, action taken that is beyond the congressional authority given in the enabling statute.

unauthorized appropriation The use of someone's name, likeness, or voice without permission for commercial advantage.

unconscionable Term used to describe contracts that are grossly unfair to one side in the contract; a defense to an otherwise valid contract.

underwriter In securities transactions, the brokerage house offering the shares in a company to the public.

undue influence Contract defense based on one party taking advantage of a relationship of trust and confidence.

unemployment compensation Funds paid to individuals who are without a job while they attempt to find new employment; a federal program administered by the states.

unenforceable contract A contract that cannot be enforced because of a procedural error.

unfair labor practice An economic weapon used by an employer or employee that is prohibited under the federal labor laws.

Uniform Commercial Code (UCC) Uniform law adopted in forty-nine states governing sales contracts for goods, commercial paper, security interests, documents of title, and securities transfers.

Uniform Computer Information Transactions Act (UCITA) Uniform law that governs sales of software, databases, and other products used on computers.

Uniform Domain Name Dispute Resolution Policy (UDRP) Policy of ICANN that provides the means, timing, and rules for resolving disputes over domain names.

Uniform Electronic Transactions Act (UETA) Uniform law for states that provides the rule for formation of electronic contracts.

uniform laws Series of laws drafted by groups of businesspeople, law professors, and lawyers; adopted and codified by states to help attain a more uniform commercial environment for transactions.

Uniform Partnership Act (UPA) Uniform law adopted in 49 states governing the creation, operation, and termination of general partnerships.

Uniform Unincorporated Nonprofit Association Act (UUNAA) Uniform law that governs liability and other issues related to nonprofit organizations.

unilateral contract Contract in which one party promises to perform in exchange for the performance of the other party.

unincorporated association A group of individuals that acts as an entity but has no legal existence.

union shop A plant or business controlled by a union.

United Nations Convention on Contracts for the International Sale of Goods (CISG) U.N. version of Article II on sales of goods for international transactions.

United States Code (U.S.C.) Statutory volumes of congressional enactments.

United States Reports Official U.S. government reporter for Supreme Court decisions.

Uniting and Strengthening America by Proving Appropriate Tools Required to Intercept and Obstruct Terrorism Act (USA Patriot Act) Federal law that permits expanded warrant and investigation techniques for federal agencies as well as the sharing of information about suspected terrorists; also imposes control on large cash transactions for banks, real property, and vehicles.

universal treaty A treaty accepted and recognized by all countries; for example, the Warsaw Convention on an travel.

unscheduled injuries Workplace injuries without specific award amounts covered in the workers' compensation statutes.

UPA Uniform Partnership Act.

U.S. Constitution The cornerstone of the federal government's structure and the basis of private citizens' rights and protections.

U.S. Court of Appeals The appellate court of the federal system; hears appeals from lower federal courts.

U.S. Government Manual Book published by the U.S. government that includes descriptions and organizational charts for all federal agencies.

U.S. Supreme Court The highest appellate court in the federal system and also the highest appellate court for state appeals.

usury Charging interest above the statutory maximum.

V

venue Geographic location of a trial.

verdict The outcome or decision in a trial.

vertical merger Merger between a manufacturer and a retailer; a merger between two companies in the chain of vertical distribution.

vertical trade restraint Trade restraints among firms in the distribution system.

void contract In contracts, a contract that neither side is required to perform; for example, an illegal contract is void.

voidable contract In contracts, a contract one side can choose not to perform; for example, a minor can choose not to perform his contract.

voir dire Process of questioning jurors to screen for bias and determine whether a lawyer wishes to exercise her peremptory challenge.

voting trust Arrangement among shareholders to gain uniform voting and some power by signing over voting rights on shares to a trustee; shareholders still get dividends, but trustee votes the shares; must be in writing and recorded with the corporation.

W

Wagner Act National Labor Relations Act; federal law governing the rights of unions and establishing the NLRB.

warrant Court document authorizing an arrest or a search.

warranty A promise of performance or guarantee of quality on a good or service.

warranty deed Highest level of title protection in real property transfer; greatest number of warranties.

warranty of merchantability Warranty given in all sales by merchants that provides that goods are of average quality, are packaged properly, and will perform normally.

Warsaw Convention Agreement among various nations on the liability of air carriers for injuries, accidents, loss of luggage, and so on; an international agreement.

Water Pollution Control Act of 1948 First federal law directed at water pollution; authorized the surgeon general to study the problem.

Water Quality Act (1965) First federal law to set water quality standards.

watered shares Shares for which par value was not paid; shareholder is liable for the difference between what was paid and the par value per share.

Wheeler-Lea Act Amendment to the FTC Act that permits prosecution under Section 5 if a consumer is injured, even though there is no injury to a competitor.

whistle-blowing Act of an employee of a company disclosing to a regulatory agency or the press any violations of laws by his or her employer.

white-collar crime Crimes committed in business administration and/or professional capacity; the so-called paperwork crimes.

Williams Act Federal law governing the tender offer process.

work product An attorney's thoughts, research, and strategy in a case; nondiscoverable.

Worker Adjustment and Retraining Notification Act of 1988 (WARN) Federal plant-closing law requiring advance notice of plant closures and layoffs.

workers' compensation State system of providing for payment for workers injured on the job to avoid having liability suits by employees against employers.

working requirements Non-U.S. countries' patent requirement that the process or product be placed on the market within a certain time after the patent is granted, or the patent protection is lost.

writ of certiorari Order of the U.S. Supreme Court for hearing a case; *see* **certiorari**.

Y

yellow-dog contract Agreement by employee with employer whereby employee will not join a union.

Z

zero-based budgeting Process of agency budgeting in which the budget starts with a figure of zero rather than at the level of the previous year's budget; effect is to require an agency to justify its functions and expenditures for each budget period.

Table of Cases

Table of Products, People, and Companies

Index